Moše ben Baruḵ Almosnino

Regimiento de la vida
Tratado de los suenyos

(SALONIKA, 1564)

Medieval and Renaissance Texts and Studies

Volume 255

Moše ben Baruk Almosnino

Regimiento de la vida
Tratado de los suenyos
(SALONIKA, 1564)

by

John M. Zemke

Arizona Center for Medieval and Renaissance Studies
Tempe, Arizona
2004

*Generous grants from the
Program for Cultural Cooperation between
Spain's Ministry of Culture and the United States Universities
and from the University of Missouri
have assisted with meeting the publication costs of this volume.*

© Copyright 2004
Arizona Board of Regents for Arizona State University

Library of Congress Cataloging-in-Publication Data
Almosnino, Moses ben Baruch, ca. 1515–ca. 1580.
    [Hanhagat ha-hayim]
    Regimiento de la vida ; Tratado de los suenyos : (Salonika, 1564) / Moshe ben Baruch Almosnino ; [edited] by John M. Zemke.
    p. cm. — (Medieval and Renaissance texts and studies ; v. 255)
    Text in Ladino with introd. in Hebrew and English translation; commentary in English.
    Includes bibliographical references and index.
    ISBN 0-86698-298-1 (alk. paper)
    1. Aristotle — Ethics. 2. Ethics, Jewish. 3. Rabbinical literature — History and criticism. I. Title: Moshe ben Baruch Almosnino. II. Zemke, John. III. Almosnino, Moses ben Baruch, ca. 1515–ca. 1580. Tratado de los suenyos. IV. Title: Tratado de los suenyos. V. Title. VI. Medieval & Renaissance Texts & Studies (Series) ; v. 255.

B491.E7A46 2003
296.3'6—dc21
                                                                         2003040341

This book is made to last.
It is set in Footlight,
smythe-sewn and printed on acid-free paper
to library specifications.

Printed in the United States of America

For Deborah and Rachel

Contents

List of Plates	ix
Acknowledgments	xi
Abbreviations and Symbols	xiii

INTRODUCTION

R. Moše ben Baruk Almosnino	2
The Present Edition	11
Transliteration	13
Language	15
Regimiento de la vida (RV)	16
Tratado de los suenyos (TS)	30
Conclusion	32
Appendices	
Contents of the *Regimiento de la vida* and *Tratado de los suenyos*	35
Chronology	38
Complete Works	42

EDITION

1.	*RV* Introduction	47
2.	*RV* Prologue	87
3.	*RV* Part One	92

Contents

4.	*RV* Part Two	169
5.	*RV* Part Three	288
6.	*TS*	379
7.	Spanish–Hebrew Glossary	436
8.	Errata	452

Biblical, Talmudic, and Midrashic Passages
- Biblical Passages ... 455
- Rabbinic Passages ... 461
- Talmud ... 462
- Commentary ... 464
- Midrashim ... 464
- Other ... 465

Glossary ... 467

Bibliography ... 479

Index ... 503

List of Plates

All plates are from MS. Bodleian Library Oppenheimer 4.º 969.
The four plates are found following page xv.

Plate 1: Fol. 1a, page one of *Regimiento de la vida.*

Plate 2: Fol. 138b, last page of *Regimiento de la vida.*

Plate 3: Fol. 139a, page one of *Tratado de los suenyos.*

Plate 4: Fol. 162b, final page of *Tratado de los suenyos.*

Acknowledgments

To thank properly everyone who took a hand in bringing this project to fruition is not possible. Nevertheless, I recognize and deeply appreciate those who encouraged it toward completion. First I thank Deborah and Rachel for their support and patience. Generous grants in support of this edition were received from the Research Board and the Research Council of the University of Missouri. Among the friends and colleagues who supported the project are Ross Silberberg, his memory is for a blessing, and Mrs. Yaffa Tauber and Mr. Israel Tauber, who were helpful at an early stage of the translation of the Hebrew introduction.

Invaluable contributions of support and encouragement were given me by Professor Samuel G. Armistead, University of California, Davis; Professor Ora Schwarzwald Rodrigue, Bar-Ilan University; Professor Hava Tirosh-Samuelson, Arizona State University; Professor Henry Sullivan, Tulane University; Professor Alan D. Deyermond, Queen Mary and Westfield College, University of London; Professor John Miles Foley, University of Missouri; and Dean Richard Schwartz of the School of Arts & Science, University of Missouri. The staff of the Interlibrary Loan Office of Ellis Library, University of Missouri, cheerfully located and obtained many recondite items. Signal help was received from Dr. Richard Judd, Hebrew Specialist Librarian, Department of Oriental Books, The Bodleian Library, which granted permission to publish Opp. 4° .969. Dr. Paskov and the archivists of the General Department on Archives, Council of Ministers, Sofia, graciously helped with my work in the Bulgarian State Collection of Hebraica. Finally, I owe a debt of sincere gratitude to Dr. Leslie S. B. MacCoull for careful reading and splendid scholarship; her erudition enlightens many of these pages.

Dr. Robert E. Bjork, Director and General Editor, William F. Gentrup, Assistant Director, Karen Lemiski, Production Manager, and Laura Gross, Associate Editor of Medieval and Renaissance Texts and Studies expertly

ACKNOWLEDGMENTS

turned my manuscript into this book. Their combined efforts have prevented many errors; those remaining are mine alone.

John Zemke
December 2001
Jerusalem

Abbreviations and Symbols

1. EDITORIAL MARKS

( )	editorial suppression or reference
< >	expansion of abbreviation or unpointed Hebrew item
[ ]	editorial addition or clarification
// //	correction noted in 1564 edition
{ }	encloses editorial remark, folio

Bk.	Book
chap.	chapter
fol.	folio
Heb.	Hebrew
Jerus.	Jerusalem
n.	note
Rev.	Review or Revised

2. BIBLICAL BOOKS

Gen.	Genesis
Exod.	Exodus
Lev.	Leviticus
Num.	Numbers
Deut.	Deuteronomy
Josh.	Joshua
Judg.	Judges
Sam.	Samuel
Chron.	Chronicles
Ps.	Psalm
Prov.	Proverbs

ABBREVIATIONS AND SYMBOLS

Eccles.	Ecclesiastes
Song of Sol.	Song of Solomon
Isa.	Isaiah
Jer.	Jeremiah
Lam.	Lamentations
Dan.	Daniel
Mal.	Malachi
MN	*More Nevukim*
NE	*Nicomachean Ethics*
R.	Rabbi, Rabbah
Rambam	R. Moses ben Maimon
Ramban	R. Moses ben Naḥman
Rashi	R. Shlomo ben Yiṣhak
RV	*Regimiento de la vida*
Targ.	Targum
TS	*Tratado de los suenyos*

3. SOURCES AND AUTHORITIES

BHi	*Bulletin Hispanique*
CAG	*Commentaria in Aristotelem Graeca*
CSIC	Consejo Superior de Investigaciones Científicas
DCECH	*Diccionario crítico etimológico castellano hispánico*
EJ	*Encyclopaedia Judaica*
HR	*Hispanic Review*
JE	*Jewish Encyclopaedia*
JPSA	The Jewish Publication Society of America
JQR	*Jewish Quarterly Review*
PLPLS	*Proceedings of the Leeds Philosophical and Literary Society*
REJ	*Revue des Études Juives*
RFH	*Revista de Filología Española*
RPh	*Romance Philology*

Hebräischen Übersetzungen	Moritz Steinschneider. *Die Hebräischen Übersetzungen des Mittelalters.* Graz: Nachdruck der Akademischen Druck, 1893, repr. 1956.

ABBREVIATIONS AND SYMBOLS

Neubauer-   Arthur Neubauer and Arthur E. Cowley. *Catalogue of the He-*
Catalogue   *brew Manuscripts in the Bodleian Library. Compiled by Adolf*
                     Neubauer and Arthur E. Cowley, 2 vols. Oxford: Clarendon
                     Press, 1886–1906, rev. ed. Oxford–New York: Oxford University Press, 1994.

ספר הנהגת החיים

אשר חבר החכם השלם הכולל כמוהר"ר משה אלמושנינו נר"ו

לדרישת ינוק וחכים להקיס בונה צדקת הנסגתו בן לקותו לעיהו בלכתתו אותו
לנחותו הדרך ילך בה לאור באור החיים ה' צמתים : ועץ הדעת בכל הארץ מודעת
בעו ונתעצמות התעלומו' החכמתו המדינית בתוך גן עדניו : כשלחן ערוך לפניו :

חסד אלוו לחבריו ספר לחד קטן בכמות ורב האיכות בלהי אריכות : חסד
הבר המחבר עצמו לדרישת הסר המאוסר הסדון דון יוסף נשיא ירום
ונשא על מעלהו ורוממתו : יסדותו בסדרי קדם מעלות ומדות החלונות ושומות
בכתב אמת וסאר חלומו בני אדם בטוב טעם ודעת הבודקים מנכס וסבת קנינתם
וצדקתם עומדת לעד : וידיעת כבתרונות הכנוונת בחקירלת יקרות וביחור כהובים
רבים הנגלים אליהס ומדברי רז"ל : הזל נטל אמרתו בפיד נזרתו : ובקופס ביתור
סעלות הזרות מפוזרות ביניהם : ומסנותו בלוימה בטה שחבר עוד בהתחלתם מפתק"ן
מפוהקוה בסניהם : מעשה ידיו בורך בהוראה שבילהיס :
למען ירון כל הדוו הקודס בגס :

ליברו אינטיטולאדו ריגימיינטו דילה וידה

בודיינדוסי גרדלדידה מינטו ניאמנד איסמפאל בייון לוינטורלדוס
קונסוקיבטו פור איל פלחונידימו תכפו כמהר"ר משה אלמושנינו כלרו אה
ריקירימיינטו דיסו אינטיטו קירד : לי סובדינו אינול קוחל שי קונטייני קונטנטו
קונביייני פלדר ביין אנדאר טודה לה גונדאלה דילה וידה אומחנה סין אירול
קונפדינדויינדו אינגיל טודה לה פילוסופייה מורחל מוי קוטיוזה מינטו אי
שיגרשיחה דיפוקים דיאל סיר דילום שוחינים אי די שום קאושאם בודרד
ביקיניש קחסיוטנינס לי סונלטנידהם וידדלהידאם קי טחכבין קונפוטיס חה חיל
עניימיינטו דינה וידה : קונפוחיסטו פור חיל מיספי לקבור אה דייריימיינטו
אייל מוי אילוסטרי שיניור איל שיניור דון יוסף נשיא קי איל דין קונסידרי הו
אלומיינטו סו סרומסירו איסמעלו
לחמן :

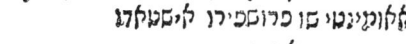

נדפס בעייון רב בבית צעיר המחזקים יוסף בן לא"ח החכם השלם מוהר"ל
יצחק בן לרב החסיד מנוהר"ל יוסף בן יעבץ כדוהס זלה"ה והיתה התחלתו בחדש
אלול השבד לעזרך ה' ברחמיו יזכנו להדפיס ספרים אחרים קדבקך אין קץ :

Plate 1: Fol. 1a, page one of *Regimiento de la vida*.

הלק ג ׃ פרק יג

פרופ̇יאה מינטי ליאיי דיל אומברי   או לס פארטי קי קונסיסטי אין לה ויאה לס
בירטוקסיאון דיל אינטינדימיינטו טיאוריקו אין שאביר לאס קוסאס דיוינאס סיגון
ליאוטאר פרופיאה פינטי לו דיל דיין   פור לו קואל דיב̇ו סיקנישיתאנדו לם
פרימירס פארטידס קי ליא בואינס די לה̇וס קומו קי דינוסי וס ה̇י לה̇נה פלרטידס די לו
קי אין אובנ̇יקטו די ה̇יויאל אים אין נוסותרום   אי פואת̇די סיר קי טו̇ה קומו קי
דינוס קי לי דיל ביין די אס ווס קי אים לס פרנידה פאלרטוידס קי טיניתוס דינו קי
אים לסוירקק די לו קי סי טומה די באנו די דאון די ביין   אי סיקנישיקאנדו לס
סיגונדה פאלטידה קי אים דיבאנודי דאוי די וירד̇אד דיבו מי לי נו ליב̇יאים אים כי
או   פואת̇די סיר קי נואיםו דיינסימו ריי דוד סו פאדרי קינסי סיקנישיקאה
לו מיםנו אין דיחיר קי סאלון אין ליי ד ה̇   םו וולונטאד אי אין סו ליאה
אסטנו וכהולתו כו פאבלאלרס די דיהה לי דיונב̇י אי סים.   קי קאיילי דיוי אנהלה פאלרטידס קי אים
סו לי די אין אומברי ביין אונטורלסדון קי איריבה דינו אה מינאסטיר ב̇אבלאלפ̇
פ̇אניאליא די דיהה אי די נונבי פאדרה אקוסטומברואר אה האזיר איל ביין
אין פורו לאוטו :   קונגלו קואל קונקלויין רונ̇אדו אם
בוה̇ינו אלטיםינו בינייול טב̇סונגה   די קונטינו אין
ונלונטאד דינו איסיר דיאיל קאמינו דילם ביין
אינסטוידלהנסה פ̇אדה אלקאנסאר אה נוח̇ף
די לס סופרימה דיליטסיאון קי אין
איל סיגיר טחל קאמינו
קונסיסטי טונייננדו ביין
אנה מימוריאה
איסטי
דוינסימו אינב̇ינפלו קי טי לי פרוםופתיסו איל קואל טו סיס מן לוטיל פלפ̇אם
סיגני איל ביאטיסימו קאמינו די איסטה וידע טינייננדו פור איספינו לו קי אין איםםטם
פדלטאדו טנגו איםפריסו איל כוד סו פיאד̇אד קי מיודיר קולריאה אינגליניםם מי כי
דיסקאנסין אין קונטיניטאמיינטו פלדס פונדיגלו ביין איסיטקטונאד אמן :

פין דיל רגימיינטו די לה̇וידה

תם

 אקי קומינסה איל טראטאדו די לוש שואינוש

 תמרמה

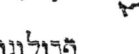 פרולוגו דיל אאוטור

מי אילושטרי שינור   די איקוריינדו מוצֿאס וזיס פור לה מימוריאה מונגוס
כי דלאדום קי אין פריסינסיאה די וואישה מירסיד
שי פרלטיקַ[ל]רון אינטרי טיינפו קי יו גוזי דיטו דיוינט
קונוירבֿאסיאון אינטרי אילייום שי מי אקורדו אל פריסינטי   לוניר מי דינו און שבת
איסטאנדו אין ביל ו'ידיר קי דישיאבה אין נרגאברי מאינרד אוּמיר קוסֿ בוּאינ אינגל
קאטוביר לום שוֿאינייום אנסי אינגלֿה ליסיינסיאה דיליוֿיום אינגזוּם קאלוסאם אי שיר
שטאביסיגו די טרים דוֿבאם קי לסיראום דילויום שיינפרי טובו :

לה פרימירה שאביר קומו שי אוייאה די אינטינדיר   לוקי אלגונום שטאביאוש
דיזין קי שיגון שון לאש קונפליסיאונים די לוש אומברים אשי שון שואינום
די"דינטים   קי פואינטש לה קונליסיאון איש שיגון לה קונפושיסיאוןאן   מאטיריאל
בֿור שיר קָאלידָד קי שי ריזולטה די קאלידדים קונטרארים שינון שון דיפינסיאון
אי לה אימגינסיאוון פור אינטריסאיסיאוון די לוש קנאל פאריסי שיר לוש שואֿנייום איש
וירטוד אינגל אניאמה אי נו מאטיריאה   קומו כאזי שוםכונסוֿוצמאם דישוֿדרינטים שינון לה
דישודינסיאה דילה בֿאל קונסֿוזיסיאון מאטיריאל :   לה   שינונדה איקי
מאש דישואיבה שאביר מירה שי אוייאה די אינגלה אלגונה דאחזן   נאטונראל קי
שאטושפיסים פדרה ביין אינטיידיר קומו שיקוצ'יקַאן לאם פורמאם   קי פאליסֿי
קונטוניר לה אימצֿובעאנטסיאון קונאם קי אן די ויניר אין פישיטה שיירם קומו אינגל
שואיניין שי שיקניסיקה שינון נואֿ שום שאבֿיאום קי לה טורסיר קי
שיבי לה קאות קי שוֿאיניאל איל אומברי קורחא די מוגֿבו טיינפו   איל וידֿאדאם קי
איבטחאנדו דיספאירטו נו לי וייני אלה מימוריא   אי בֿונטם קוניסטו קי דיסיאב׳ה אין
איסטרימו אוֿייד ביין אישפוניר איל טיאסט שוברי לוש שואינייום קי יוסף שולטאבה לא
שונייאדוש   אי שאב׳יר שי שופונדרה דליר אינצלויים אלגונה דאחזן נאטוראל אלגוניגֿי דו
שיר קומו פאריסי שי שיפונדיאה אינצלוֹאיניאה"שה דיוינק   יוֹ   שינ'יור דישיאנדו מוצֿו די
דאבֿטסֿ'נאל לה שי וואישה מירסיד לאון קי אין   אקיל איסטאנטי מיפֿאריס אֿון
לוֿיר דינו   אין לונביריסדאל אלגוניאש דאחזנים מונסֿ'שיניטו שואליונסיבור פאריסיאומי נוקֿ
וואישה מירסיד דילי טודו בואמישבֿנו הֿאלֿ"אנדומי אל פריסיניטי אינגל טיונסט קי
ליאימוס לוש שואינייום קי יוסף מנסו מונייאבא אי סוֿלטאבו   אי פינגטו קוניסטא אבייגֿוגֿ
שונייאדו אינגל מיסמו טייננו און שוֿאינייו מונבו אימי קונטיננט אמי וטלדס לאס
שיר'קוֿנסטאנציאם קי שי ריקיידן פדראן שיר שו שיקניב'יצֿאבייֿאן וורדֿאדירה אשירקה
איל קריבמייֿנטו אי מאנוימיננטו דיל פרוספירו אי פילוסין איסטֿדו די נֿואישה מירסיד
איל קואל די"לאטטאלדרי אל צֿין די מודו פור איסטיענדו בונו קון שו שיקניציבֿאסייאון קי
אינגל ניטתמנו בוא'איניי   בוסקאנדו דאחֿן נאטוראל פאדרה שיר איל אישיקוֿ
די לוֿ שיקנישיקאדו בֿיירטו מי פארייטיאן דיסברעין טיאוטה מאטיריאה

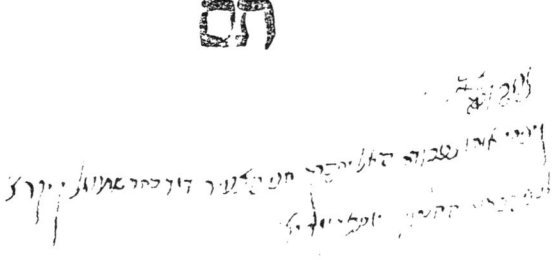

Plate 4: Fol. 162b, final page of *Tratado de los suenyos*.

Introduction

Moše ben Baruk Almosnino's *Regimiento de la vida* (= *RV*) and *Tratado de los suenyos* (= *TS*) (1564) comprise a unique historical record of the ethical and intellectual outlook of sixteenth-century Sephardim in the Ottoman Empire. Facsimile editions of *RV* have appeared,[1] but no modern edition or transcription has been available until now. The present edition contains the following parts: (1) an introduction to the work; (2) an English translation of the original Hebrew introduction; (3) a Latin-letter transcription of the Rashi-character Spanish text; and, finally, (4) notes, bibliography, and indices.

In his introduction to *Meᶜam Loᶜez* (1730), Jacob ben Meir Kulli laments the general decline in study and knowledge of Hebrew among his contemporaries and mentions certain writings in Judeo-Spanish, notably, Joseph Karo's *Šulḥan Aruk*, Bahya Ibn Paquda's *Ḥovot ha-Levavot,* and Moše Almosnino's *Regimiento de la vida*. Kulli observes that study of such titles was problematic owing to difficulties grounded as much in language change as in scarcity of time for study:

> I en tiempo pasado obo un sabyo ke deklaró el *Šulḥan ᶜaruk* en ladino [...].
> I lo mezmo izieron en el libro ke se lyama *Ḥôbôt ha-lᵉbābôt;* pero ni kon akelyo obo remedyo bastante por muĉas *sibbôt* (*causas*), si *mēḥămát* (*por motivo*) ke el lo eskribyó a su modo kon modos de ablas espanyolas, ke para la ŷente de estas partes de Turkía, i Anadol i Arabistán son muy karas i seradas, i ansí los más de la ŷente están sin meldar ninguna lisyón. *Û-bi-fᵉrāṭ* (*y especialmente*) el libro ke izo el *Rab Rabbi Mōšeʰ Almoxnino, z.l* ke se lyama *Režimiento de la vida,* ke es un libro muy luzyo, pero sus ablas son muy seradas. I tambien el solotreo de ditos senyores es de otra

---

[1] For facsimile editions, see those issued by Gregg International Publishers (Farnborough, 1971) and Charles Reich (New York, 1992) (see Bibliography).

Introduction

manera, ke aun ke sierto es ke lo sulyo es lo dereĉo i bedradero, pero siendo la ŷente de estas partes no lo entienden, no puede aprobeĉarse de él. I tambien ke es menester saber estudyar para entender lo ke kižo dezir, siendo kižo akortar con dar a-entender munĉa sensya kon pokas palabras, i no es remedyo para el *hāmon hā-ʿām* (*vulgo*) ke no tienen modo de emplear el día para entender una koza, siendo en kual ker paso ke kerán meldar se detadran kuándo para entender los bierbos ke no están uzados en elyos, kuándo por el solotreo, kuándo para entender la *hăbānā ʰ* de las ablas, ke siendo son muy kortas, keren munĉo estudyadas.²

MOŠE BEN BARUK ALMOSNINO

Almosnino's biography and bibliography have been outlined by Eliakim Carmoly (*La famille Almosnino,* 1850), Heinrich Graetz ("Moses Almosnino," 1864), Moritz Steinschneider (*Die hebraeischen Übersetzungen des Mittelalters,* 1893), Abraham Danon ("La communauté juive de Salonique au XVIᵉ siècle," 1900), Isaac Emmanuel (*Israélites de Salonique,* 1936), Isaac Molho ("Rabbi Moshe Almosnino," 1942; "Un humaniste sefardí," 1964, "Rabbi Moshe Almosnino," 1967), M. N. Zobel ("History of R. Moses Almosnino," 1942), Naftali Ben-Menahem ("Studies on R. M. Almosnino," 1946), Charles Abeles ("Moses Almosnino," 1957), and Meir Zvi Bnaya ("Moses Almosnino," 1988; *Moše Almosnino,* 1996).³ Hava Tirosh-Samuelson ("Jewish Philosophy," 1997; "Post-Expulsion Philosophic Literature," 1997) has described

---

² D. Gonzalo Maeso and P. Pascual Recuero, *Meʿam Loʿez* (Madrid, 1964), 47–48. The following and subsequent translations are mine. "And in past days, one scholar interpreted the *Shulḥan Aruk* in Ladino [...] And others did so for *Hovot ha-Levavot,* but even that was not sufficient help, among other reasons, because he wrote in his own Spanish style and people in this part of Turkey, Anatolia, and Arabistan find it difficult to understand. Thus, most people read no lesson at all. R. Moše Almosnino's *Regimiento de la vida* is a very enlightening book, but its words are difficult. And those scholars' writing is different. Although theirs is the true and correct one, here people do not understand it and cannot take full advantage of it. Also, it is necessary to know how to study in order to understand their intention — since they tried to be brief, and give much knowledge in a few words. Everyday people can't spend all day studying. Should they want to study, they have nothing to help them understand unfamiliar words or the writing or the words' intention. Because the words are few they require much study."

³ For a thorough review of M. Z. Bnaya, *Moše Almosnino* (Tel Aviv, 1996), see H. Tirosh-Samuelson in *JQR* 89 (1998): 250–52.

INTRODUCTION

Almosnino's philosophy and importance in the history of the reception of Aristotle's *Ethics* among Jews. Almosnino's own writings, together with those of his contemporaries, provide most of what is known about him. Nevertheless, his biographers' accounts disagree on many details including the year of his birth, his brothers and sisters, the dates of composition and publication of his writings, his rabbinical appointments, and his travels. The accounts coincide, however, in the portrayal of an extraordinary figure in Salonikan communal life, a man who advanced the Jewish community's interests during a crucial period of its history.[4]

Rabbi, scholar, and preacher, Almosnino was born in 1518[5] in Salonika to an aristocratic family that had been exiled from Huesca in 1492; he died ca. 1581, and the place of his burial is unknown.[6] His life spanned the "Golden Age of Ottoman

---

[4] H. Tirosh-Samuelson qualifies him as the pre-eminent philosopher and communal leader of his day ("Jewish Philosophy on the Eve of Modernity," in *History of Jewish Philosophers*, ed. D. H. Frank and D. Leaman [London, 1997], 531). The number of studies of Salonikan Jewry is impressive. Among those consulted in the preparation of this introduction are the following: Amarillo, "Talmud Torah of Salonica"; Benbassa and Rodrigue, *Juifs des balkans* and *Jews of the Balkans;* Bnaya, "Moses Almosnino" and *Moše Almosnino;* Danon, "Communauté juive de Salonique"; Emmanuel, *Industrie des tissus* and *Israélites de l'Empire Ottoman;* Epstein, *Ottoman Jewish Communities;* Franco, *Israélites de l'Empire Ottoman;* Goodblatt, *Samuel de Medina;* Grunebaum-Ballin, *Joseph Naci;* Hacker, "Intellectual Activity" and "Superbe et désespoir"; Landau, *Jews in Ottoman Egypt;* Levy, *Sephardim in the Ottoman Empire;* Lowry, "Ottoman Selanik"; Molho, "Procurer of Independence," "Rabbi Moses Almosnino," "Humaniste Sefardi" and "Rabbi Moshe Almosnino"; Molho and Amarillo, "Communal Regulations"; Nehama, *Israélites de Salonique;* Roth, *House of Nasi;* Shaw, *Jews of the Ottoman Empire;* Shmuelevitz, *Jews of the Ottoman Empire;* Starr, *Romania;* Vakalopoulos, *Thessaloniki;* Weiker, *Jews of Turkey;* and Zobel, "R. Moses Almosnino."

[5] Emmanuel reports the birth occurred in January (*Israélites de Salonique,* 176, n. 38); Abeles ("Moses Almosnino," 26) and Bnaya (*Moše Almosnino,* 11) concur in 1518 as the date of birth. Franco, following Kayserling, cites the year 1510 (*Israélites de l'Empire Ottoman,* 77), as does Shaw (*Jews of the Ottoman Empire*). Carmoly, following Rosanes, calculates 1523 as the date of birth; *EJ* consigns ca. 1515.

[6] Shmuelevitz, among others, notes that after the Turkish conquest of Constantinople in 1453, over forty Jewish communities were moved there from Asia Minor to populate the city (*Jews of the Ottoman Empire,* 12). For a detailed study of Salonika's demography before 1492, see Lowry ("Ottoman Selanik"). The Jewish *mahalle* (quarter) was located in the lowlying area east of the docks: "it was in the southcentral area of Selanik that the 3,143 households of Jewish refugees were settled in the early sixteenth century" (Lowry, "Ottoman Selanik," 269). The influx between 1492 and 1519 of those immigrants "drastically altered the demographic profile of the

INTRODUCTION

Jewry."[7] His father, Baruk Almosnino, was born in Salonika and prospered there, a wealthy man active in communal affairs and a leader of the Catalan synagogue.[8] The family were the legal proprietors of the synagogue and, after its destruction in the fire of 1545, the elder Almosnino underwrote its reconstruction, donating the land and money.[9] Mošeʼs mother (her name is unknown) was a Conimbriel [Cocumbriel], an aristocratic Aragonese family related to the Almosninos that received Baruk upon his arrival in Salonika. She bore three sons, Japhet, Moše, and Isaac, and a daughter whose name is unknown (Bnaya, *Moše Almosnino*, 15).[10]

Almosninoʼs mother and elder brother took charge of the boyʼs early education. Carmoly suggests Moše studied in Constantinople and learned Arabic and Turkish (*Famille Almosnino*, 11). Abeles reports that Almosnino was instructed in rabbinic subjects by R. Moše de Boton,[11] and presumably by his father and his uncle Samuel, rabbis of the Catalan congregation and yeshiva. The curriculum would have included "Scriptures, Talmud and commentaries, the Turim (codes) of Jacob Asher, philology and grammar" (Abeles, "Moses Almosnino," 26–27). R. Daniel ben Perahiah Hacohen was in charge of astronomy and mathematics, and R. Aharon Afia oversaw Almosninoʼs studies in philosophy and medicine (Abeles, "Moses Almosnino," 26–27).[12]

---

city [. . .] 53% of its residents were Jews from Western Europe" (Lowry, "Ottoman Selanik," 292).

[7] The phrase is Shawʼs (*Jews of the Ottoman Empire*).

[8] Emmanuel confirms this (*Israélites de Salonique*, 176).

[9] *EJ* 2:668. Goodblatt, relying on Rosanes, adds the details of a donation of land and money for the synagogue (*Jews of the Ottoman Empire*, 16 n. 52). Shaw lays out how the Catalan synagogue split in 1510 into Old and New Catalan synagogues which were later reconciled by R. Samuel de Medina in 1540. After the fire of 1545, Baruk Almosninoʼs prestige held the community together until his death, when it divided again (*Jews of the Ottoman Empire*, 52).

[10] Emmanuel identifies the elder brother as Absalom (*Israélites de Salonique*, 176 n. 40). *EJ* mentions Japhet, but not Isaac, while Abeles cites sermon four of Almosninoʼs collection of sermons, *Meammes Koah* (32) in support of the elder brotherʼs name being Absalom ("Moses Almosnino," 44 n. 6), but that sermon identifies him as Japhet. The seventh sermon of *Meammes Koah* also states plainly that Almosnino preached the same sermon the seventh day following his elder brother Japhetʼs demise (55). Shaw mentions an Absalom Almozlinos who was a member of a cultural group active in Salonika contemporary with Moše (*Jews of the Ottoman Empire*, 87).

[11] See *Meammes Koah*, sermon ten (86).

[12] For a fine introduction to Almosnino with a translation of one of his sermons, see M. Saperstein (*Jewish Preaching*). Tirosh-Samuelson ("Jewish Philosophy" and "Post-Expulsion Philosophic Literature") provides the best understanding of Almosninoʼs philosophy, its innovations, and its place in the Jewish reception of Aristotelian philosophy. Abelesʼ unpublished dissertation, a useful introduction to Moše Almosninoʼs thought, cites *Meammes Koah*, sermon ten

INTRODUCTION

Bnaya, recognizing that there is no certainty as to who Mošeʼs teachers were, suggests the likelihood that the boy studied with R. Joseph Taitazak, albeit Almosninoʼs name does not figure on lists of Taitazakʼs students (*Moše Almosnino*, 18).

Mošeʼs father died in 1563; his elder brother Japhet died in 1568 (*Moše Almosnino*, 17). The funeral oration Moše wrote after his motherʼs death in Salonika in 1570 (*Famille Almosnino*, 28) declares his abiding reverence for her and lauds her "faith, piety, and self denial."[13]

His sister married into the Garçon family, and it was her son, Moše, who would be the destinatory of *RV*. Moše Almosnino himself married a daughter of R. Joshua Safarti, Simḥa, and she bore two sons, Baruk and Shimon, and a daughter, whose name is unknown. Simḥa died in 1554.[14]

Almosnino was among the signatories to a rabbinic reform of the Salonikan wool trade (1565),[15] an economic mainstay of the community, and several times an emissary to the court of Süleiman (the Magnificent) I.[16] He held rabbinic posts in

---

(86) which Almosnino gave at de Botonʼs funeral. Emmanuel concurs in both assertions (*Israélites de Salonique*, 176). Bnaya states that Almosnino studied with R. Aharon Afia (*Moše Almosnino*, 19), which is confirmed by Tirosh-Samuelson ("Post-Expulsion Philosophic Literature," 230).

[13] See *Meammeṣ Koaḥ*, sermon eleven (97) cited by Abeles in his translation ("Moses Almosnino," 28).

[14] See Bnaya, *Moše Almosnino*, 17–18. He refers to Simḥa as Almosninoʼs "first" wife but I do not find any mention of a second wife (17); regarding Almosninoʼs children see especially 18 n. 27.

[15] For an outline of the orderʼs content, see Emmanuel (*Industrie des tissus*, 27). For community documents in which Almosnino had a hand, see Molho and Amarillo ("Communal Regulations") and Danon ("Communauté juive de Salonique"); the latter specifies Almosninoʼs role as author, copyist, or signatory (99). The wool trade is studied in depth by Emmanuel (*Industrie des tissus*), and its importance is emphasized in Goodblattʼs analysis of R. Samuel de Medinaʼs responsa (*Samuel de Medina*, 56–58), which provide a vivid portrayal of life in Salonika. Epsteinʼs splendid study of trade networks notes that tax-farming, customs, docks, and salt warehouses were important areas of Jewish commercial success in the Ottoman Empire (*Ottoman Jewish Communities*, 65). He articulates the position that the Sephardim "introduced cloth weaving after the pattern of the Spanish wool industry and brought with them munitions making and other technological skills from the West" (102). His fascinating account of the vital role Jews had in commerce, shipping, wharfage, and warehousing in the Empire notes that Salonika was a "stronghold of Jewish merchants, weavers, and dyers" (90).

[16] One of ten emissaries sent to the Sultan at Constantinople, Almosnino pleaded the communityʼs appeal to retain historic privileges and rights in the face of extreme local pressures that abrogated them; the embassy endured nearly two years (1566–1567) before its successful

INTRODUCTION

several synagogues: the Catalan in 1551; the following year the Calabrese, *Neve Šalom;* and, after December 1559, *Leviath Ḥen,* established, apparently in contradiction to the wider community's wishes, by Doña Gracia Mendes and her son the Duke of Naxos, Don Joseph Nasi, for the purpose of absorbing the waves of Portuguese *conversos* who swelled mid-sixteenth-century Salonikan Jewry.[17]

---

outcome. The economic and social motives for the embassy are discusssed by Goodblatt (*Samuel de Medina,* 123–25) and Molho ("Procurer of Independence"). Shmuelevitz's general discussion of the forms and administration of taxation mentions the specific instance: "[A] heavy tax [was] imposed on the Jewish community in Salonica by Sultan Süleyman as a result, according to the Hebrew sources, of an intervention by non-Jewish citizens in Salonica. The community sent a delegation to the Sultan's Court in 1562 to try to cancel this tax or at least to obtain concessions. The delegation, helped by the court's Jews, met the Sultan five times, but to no avail. On the contrary, he imposed an additional annual sum of 50,000 *akçe.* Only in 1567, after Sultan Selim II's accession to the throne, did the delegation manage to achieve its goal — the abolition of the special tax, but in return for (an) undertaking to pay in advance 600,000 *akçe* for six years" (*Jews of the Ottoman Empire,* 126). Weiker identifies the recision of the longstanding privileges as part of a broader trend brought on by weaker central government controls and concomitant increase in local power: "In 1567, for example, the privileges granted to Jews were questioned by local officials in several places and were reconfirmed only through the intercession of Moise Almosnino and a sizable payment to the Grand Vizier" (*Jews of Turkey,* 37). Almosnino submitted his report on the negotiations to the community assembled in the Talmud Torah (Goodblatt, *Samuel de Medina,* 21). For a study of this sermon, see: Shaul Regev, "R. Moses Almosnino's Charter of Liberty (*Musellimik*) Sermon: Philosophical or Historical Source," in *Ladinar,* ed. J. Dishon and S. Refael (Tel Aviv: Institute for Study of the Jews of Salonika, 1998), 139–55. Almosnino's detailed account is given in *Crónica de los Reyes Otomanos* (1567). A partial and mutilated edition of this work appeared in 1638 in Madrid under the title *Extremos y grandezas de Constantinopla.* Students of the Ottoman Empire regard Almosnino's history as a uniquely important firsthand account of Constantinople. The manuscript and the language have been studied by Hassan and Romeu, "Apuntes sobre la lengua"; Pascual Recuero, "Aproximación"; and Romeu Ferré, "Diferencias y paralelismos." For an edition of the only manuscript extant, study, and bibliography, see Romeu Ferré, ed., *Moisés Almosnino: Crónica.*

[17] The synagogue was later known as *Kahal Kadosh Yahya;* the circumstances surrounding its foundation are discussed by Abeles, "Moses Almosnino," 33–50; Bnaya, "Moses Almosnino" and "*Moše Almosnino,* 32–36; Emmanuel, *Israélites de Salonique,* 177, 216–18; Goodblatt, *Samuel de Medina,* 117; Nehama, *Israélites de Salonique,* 3:92–95; and Roth, *House of Nasi,* 1:128–31. A communal ruling of 1525 forbade the creation of a new community or synagogue (Abeles, 34). The endless intracommunal contentiousness so complicated the rabbis' ability to enforce ritual and financial matters that they threatened anyone who formed a new synagogue

Introduction

Abeles' sympathetic study of Almosnino portrays his communal role thus: " 'What other Salonikan rabbis could not accomplish, Almosnino succeeded in doing' by the employment of patience and tact, firmness and mercy."[18] The testimonial is confirmed by Goodblatt's summary: "Almosnino greatly distinguished himself in the service of his community. One of his major objectives was to establish peace among the various congregations and to bring order and unity into the community" (*Samuel de Medina,* 17).[19]

The body of Almosnino's writings exemplifies the interests of a scholar expert in traditional Jewish learning as well as in science and philosophy.[20] His renowned rhetorical gifts earned him the sobriquet "the Orator."[21] As rabbi, his congregation

---

with excommunication; Salonika in mid-century could count twenty-six Jewish communities (Shaw, *Jews of the Ottoman Empire,* 53). Under the Salonika system of self-rule the different communities were represented in a municipal Jewish council (Epstein, *Ottoman Jewish Communities,* 72).

[18] The internal quote's provenance is unclear, although Abeles refers to Rosanes ("Moses Almosnino," 34 n. 45).

[19] That contentiousness and abuse of power and position characterized much of intra-communal relations in Salonika, and elsewhere, as well as the intercommunal relations among Jews, Muslims, and Christians, is made clear by Emmanuel, *Israélites de Salonique,* 151–55; Nehama, *Israélites de Salonique,* 3:125ff.; Epstein, *Ottoman Jewish Communities,* 45–46, 72–74, 86; and Shmuelevitz's lucid reading of Jewish life in the Ottoman Empire as reflected in the responsa: "Nevertheless, rifts and traditional enmities [between congregational units] continued to prevail during the sixteenth century, and these sometimes caused tragic results when Ottoman authorities were asked to intervene or were used by one side against the other [. . .] the region of origin loyalty sometimes superseded geographical proximity so that widely dispersed congregations sharing a point of origin might cooperate with one another against some other group" (*Jews of the Ottoman Empire,* 13–14). Shaw aptly summarizes the situation: "All the Sephardic synagogues of Salonica were divided by discord during the sixteenth century" (*Jews of the Ottoman Empire,* 52). The abuse of official powers reached a zenith in the person of one Baruch, who exploited his office as kahya (i.e., kethüda, the steward or fiscal administrator of a community and its agent before the central government [Weiker, *Jews of Turkey,* 65; Epstein, *Ottoman Jewish Communities,* 292]) of Salonika "to tyrannize the Jewish community and to enrich himself by exploiting his ties to local officials" (Weiker, *Jews of Turkey,* 74 n. 76). One of the kethüda's responsibilities was "to protect Jews against the depredations of officials and from other communities" (Epstein, *Ottoman Jewish Communities,* 64).

[20] For a precise characterization of Almosnino's philosophy, see Tirosh-Samuelson, "Jewish Philosophy" and "Post-Expulsion Philosophic Literature."

[21] Emmanuel highlights the gift with a citation from Saadia Longo's elegy for Almosnino

INTRODUCTION

would have relied upon him for guidance through the mundane disputes, problems, and dilemmas, large and small, common to the human experience.[22] His regard for the community's welfare is evidenced in the contract he made with Leviath Ḥen at the time of its founding.[23] His patron and protector, Joseph Nasi, was among the wealthiest and most powerful men in the Ottoman Empire of Selim II,[24] and the ultimately successful conclusion of Almosnino's negotiations in Constantinople on behalf of the Salonikan community attests to Nasi's influence there, as well as to Almosnino's political acumen.[25]

Joseph Hacker's engaging study of Jewish intellectual life in the Ottoman Empire elucidates several unusual and crucial circumstances specific to the Salonika of Almosnino's day. The concentration in a single community of scores of scholars in the fields of Jewish law, thought, science, and medicine fomented cutthroat competition ("Intellectual Activity," 96–97), intellectual ferment and public awareness of spiritual

---

(*Israélites de Salonique,* 178). Carmoly too emphasizes Almosnino's oratorical power; he preached in the Italian, Aragonese, German, Pouille, Catalan, Castilian, and Sicilian synagogues, among others (*Famille Almosnino,* 15–16).

[22] A vivid portrait of rabbinic and communal life is found in the writings of Almosnino's contemporary Samuel de Medina; see Goodblatt, *Samuel de Medina,* 66–70. Shmuelevitz's cogent summary of the rabbis' role is pertinent: "The rabbis were deeply involved in the daily life not only of their community, but also in that of the whole population, especially in matters concerning their community relations with the non-Jewish communities and the Ottoman authorities. After all they were, to a large extent, the sole authority within their community with power to solve problems of daily life, because Jewish daily life was based on the regulations of the *halakhah* and on traditional customs which became binding over the years" (*Jews of the Ottoman Empire,* 7).

[23] Among several conditions his agreement stipulated: all members were to attend services Monday, Thursday, and Sabbath; any dispute not resolved in two days would be decided by arbitration; the poor would defer to the wealthy, and the wealthy would provide for the poor. See Roth, *House of Nasi,* 1:129; Abeles cites *Meammeṣ Koaḥ,* 177 ("Moses Almosnino," 35).

[24] For splendid summaries of his career, see Weiker, *Jews of Turkey,* 33, 76, 77; and Epstein, *Ottoman Jewish Communities,* 89–96. For longer studies of Joseph Nasi, see Roth, *House of Nasi;* Grunebaum-Ballin, *Joseph Naci;* and Baron, *History of the Jews,* 18:84–103. Carmoly cites no source for the statement that Joseph Nasi endowed Almosnino with a considerable pension (*Famille Almosnino,* 12).

[25] Shaw places the ultimate success of the embassy squarely with Joseph Hamon (*Jews of the Ottoman Empire,* 87). Compare Roth's vastly different interpretation, perhaps owing to the influence of Almosnino's recounting of his travails and the oneiric herald of triumph at Adrianople in late 1567 in the *Crónicas Otomanas* (*House of Nasi,* 2:165–69).

INTRODUCTION

affairs (102), an active Hebrew printing press[26] supported by the wealthiest class — some of whom bought books so as not to appear illiterate or indifferent to spiritual matters, the collecting of books and manuscripts in private and public libraries (104–6), wide support for public houses of study, and, finally, philosophical and scientific endeavors of an encyclopedic if unoriginal nature (109).[27] Hacker underscores the fact that the like-minded scholars who wrote commentaries on the books of al-Ghazzali and Aristotle, and translated scientific, philosophical, geographical, and astronomical writings, worked as members "of knowledge-seeking circles, [that] carried on [their work] with the encouragement of *haverim* (sages) and to their benefit."[28]

Almosnino wrote numerous Hebrew responsa, sermons, and biblical commentaries, and declared in *RV*'s prologue a preference for writing in Hebrew rather than Spanish. Only three Spanish titles are extant: the so-called *Crónicas Otomanas* (1567), a travelogue and description of life in Constantinople based on his sojourn there between 1565 and 1567 on behalf of the Salonikan community; and *RV*, a summa of ethics and moral philosophy, and *TS*.[29]

His Hebrew responsa, biblical commentaries, and sermons were cited by his contemporaries, and are still cited today.[30] A polymath, he produced writings on ethics, logic, philosophy, history, and astronomy (he translated a Latin version of Aristotle's

---

[26] Among patrons of printing, Weiker mentions Joseph Nasi and the press his widow installed in the Belvedere palace, and also notes: "The first printing press in Salonika was that of Don Yehuda Gedalia in 1510 with type brought from Portugal" (*Jews of Turkey*, 97). In the second half of the sixteenth century the Yaabeṣ brothers relocated to Constantinople and there produced many rabbinical and philosophical titles (98). For a fuller account of Jewish printing in Salonika, see Mehlman, "History of Printing"; for Constantinople, see Yaary, *Hebrew Printing*.

[27] For a more detailed explanation of the import of this copious production see Tirosh-Samuelson, who notes that philosophy and science were "hallmarks of Judeo-Hispanic culture" ("Post-Expulsion Philosophic Literature," 228).

[28] Hacker, "Intellectual Activity," 119. This superb article on Jewish intellectual and philosophical activities during the seventeenth and eighteenth centuries in the Ottoman Empire characterizes the kind of philosophical work that engaged a part of Almosnino's attention: "In the writings of R. Moshe Almosnino, [...], and others, the philosophic ideas, opinions and currents are what determine the character of the work, as well as its content [...] This trend [...] was based on the concept well enunciated by Maimonides: "Accept the truth from whoever speaks it" (125).

[29] These two last titles figure among the early Spanish titles printed in the Balkans.

[30] Almosnino consulted R. Samuel de Medina on matters of ritual law (Goodblatt, *Samuel de Medina*, 26).

9

INTRODUCTION

Problems into Hebrew[31]) that embody an impressive breadth of knowledge.[32] Among his titles are the following: *Meammeṣ Koah* (1588), a collection of twenty-eight sermons and speeches for solemn occasions; *Yede Moše* (1572), a commentary on the Five Scrolls; *Pirke Moše* (1563), a commentary on *Pirke Avot*; *Tefillah le-Moše* (1563), a commentary on the Pentateuch and the prayer book; *Migdal ʿOz* (1569), a study of Al-Ghazzali's *Maqasid al-falasifa*;[33] *Tikkun Soferim* (undated); *Beth Elohim ve-Šaʿar ha-Šamayyim* (1546), a translation of and commentary on Georg von Puerbach's *Theorica Nova Planetarum* and Sacrobosco's *Sphere*;[34] *Tosafot Beur ʿal Divrei ha-Raba*, a supercommentary on Abraham Ibn Ezra's Bible commentary; *Pne Moše*, a commentary on Aristotle's *Ethics*;[35] and his first work, a preface to Abraham Shalom's defense of Maimonides, *Neve Šalom*. The number and character of Almosnino's titles bear out both Joseph Nehama's apposite characterization of him as "un véritable homme de la Renaissance, ouvert à tous les courants de la pensée" (*Israélites de Salonique*, 3:8) and Hava Tirosh-Samuelson's judgment that Almosnino was "by far the most outstanding philosopher of his generation" ("Post-Expulsion Philosophic Literature," 536).

---

[31] Tirosh-Samuelson confirms Almosnino's mastery of Latin (Review of Bnaya, *Moše Almosnino*, 251, and "Post-Expulsion Philosophic Literature," 223) and Greek ("Post-Expulsion Philosophic Literature," 239).

[32] The best introduction to his thought is that of Tirosh-Samuelson, "Jewish Philosophy" and "Post-Expulsion Philosophic Literature."

[33] Cantera Burgos' description of a manuscript copy in the library of the Real Academia de Historia, Madrid, excerpts and translates fols. 2v and 170v ("Manuscritos hebreos," 4–9). Compare Hacker's somewhat different understanding of Almosnino's words there ("Intellectual Activity," 119).

[34] These commentaries were on the most important sources of late medieval cosmography and astronomy. Almosnino's commentary includes a geography of the world including a seven-page description of America. Hacker provides insight into the work's genesis with a quotation of R. Aharon Afia's notation on the title page, "This is *Sefer Ha-Ashpira* with one of the comprehensive commentaries," and another of R. Solomon Le-Bet Ha-Levi made on his copy of it: "Collected by the scholarly physician, R. Aaron Afia, and written down directly from him by the exalted scholar, R. Moses Almosnino, who may have, while writing, added a few original remarks of his own" ("Intellectual Activity," 118 n. 50).

[35] Tirosh-Samuelson qualifies this as "the most important philosophical text to be produced in the Ottoman Empire" ("Jewish Philosophy," 536).

Introduction

THE PRESENT EDITION

The *editio princeps* of *RV*, printed in Rashi characters by Yosef Yaabeṣ in Salonika (August, 1564 [Elul, 5324]), was bound with *TS*.[36] *RV* occupies fols. 1–138a, *TS* fols. 138b–167a, each folio side contains a heading and 36 or 37 lines of text. The present edition is a transcription of MS. Bodleian Library Opp[enheimer] 4.º 969. My own examination of exemplars at the Bulgarian National Archives, at the New York Public Library, and at the College of Physicians of Philadelphia, confirms that Salonika 1564 is the only Hebrew-character edition of *RV*; some bibliographers mention a 1604 Venice edition, but I have found no evidence to substantiate that phantom.[37] The editors of the Amsterdam 1729 Latin-letter edition excised, rewrote, and otherwise modernized sections of *RV*, rendering it an unreliable witness to Salonika 1564.[38]

---

[36] Almosnino frequently mentions in *TS* ideas discussed previously in *RV*; seemingly, Joseph Nasi requested a condensed version of *RV*: "el reğimyento dela vida [...] ke al prezente tengo repasado 'i abreveyado algo maś por mandado de vu'eśa mersed" (the *Regimen of life* [...] which, by your order, I have now reviewed and further abbreviated) (fol. 139b).

[37] The existence of the copy in the Bulgarian State Collection of Hebraica was reported by Brad Sabin Hill ("Bulgarian State Collection"), and kindly brought to my attention by Richard Judd, Hebrew Specialist Librarian of the Bodleian Library. Although Wolf and Fürst attest to a Venice 1604 edition, no modern authority confirms it. Mr. Judd observed in private correspondence that the 1604 date is probably a misreading of 1564. The Bodleian copy lacks the Hebrew–Spanish glossary extant in the copies of the Bulgarian, New York, and Philadelphia copies, and errata preserved in the first two.

[38] The 1729 title page discloses the content: "Libro de mucha erudicion, y doctrina. En el qual como en ún Cristalino espejo podrá el hombre corregir sus yerros, y enmendár sus vicios, encaminandose en la virtud, haziendose en esta vida momentanea merecedor de alcançar la Gloria Eterna" ("A book of much learning and doctrine. In it, as in a crystalline mirror, a man may correct his errors, emend his vices, place himself on the path of virtue, and make himself meritorious in this momentary life for the achievement of Eternal Glory"). The Lusophone editors' labors were recognized in the *aprovação* conferred on their work by David Israel Athias, Hakam of the Portuguese Amsterdam community between 1728 and 1753, and Isaac Ḥayyim Abendana de Brito, Hakam of the community and head of the Talmudic academy ʿEṣ Ḥayyim: "Semuel Mendes de Sola; Yosseph Sipruth de Gabay; e Yeudáh Piza para dár á estampa obra de tanto util, e beneficio para o publico, contribuindo, com seus doctos genios, pulindo o linguaje com os proprios termos, para facilitar a inteligencia da doctrina, que athé o prezente hera muy deficil a alguns, tanto pellos caracteres como pello linguaje" (fol. 4b) ("[the persons named are given approval to] print a book of such utility and benefit to the public, contributing with their own

INTRODUCTION

The author's introduction (fols. 1a–12b) is redacted in *melisa* style Hebrew, a highly allusive and metaphorical register; it is followed by a key to the contents of the parts and chapters and a list of biblical verses quoted in *RV*. Marginalia throughout are in Hebrew. Marginal calls are terse, a summary of the exposition, the statement of a biblical verse or Talmudic sentence, or the identification of an authority. The last page of Opp[enheimer] 4.° 969 preserves a three-line handwritten note in Hebrew stating that the book was purchased by David, the son of Samuel ben Yakar, for his son Joseph Yakar, possibly as a memorial after the son's death.[39] The body of the work (fols. 12–138b) is written in a literary register of Spanish, in some respects not dissimilar to contemporary peninsular prose. Lamentably, the unpointed Rashi characters leave the exact vocalization of Almosnino's language doubtful, particularly for unstressed vowels. It is probable that unstressed vowels were neutralized, $e \sim i$, $o \sim u$, as in the *Pentateuco de Constantinopla* (1547) and myriad other medieval and Renaissance Spanish writings. The fact that the Spanish of the biblical verses differs from the expository portions in lexicon, syntax, and morphology suggests that the author may have quoted a medieval *romanceamiento* of the Bible. The literal translations of *Razal* sentences (Midrashic and Talmudic sages and later commentators) similarly embody archaizing or unidiomatic and artificial lexicon and syntax. A glossary of Hebrew equivalents for five hundred and fifteen Spanish scientific and philosophical terms, and a list of errata, close out the volume (fols. 163–168). The glossed Spanish items, printed *Merouba* (with vocalization indicated by the traditional Hebrew points), offer the only clear evidence for the vocalization of Almosnino's Spanish.[40]

---

learning the proper words, and polishing the language, facilitating understanding of the doctrine, which until now was difficult for some whether because of the the script or the language"). Beyond justifying the editors' labors, the statement suggests the considerable linguistic distance separating the eighteenth-century Amsterdam community from Almosnino's sixteenth-century language, incidentally confirming Kulli's description of the Eastern Sephardim. Both statements are evidence of linguistic change over the century and a half that separates those communities from the time Almosnino composed *RV*. The Amsterdam edition refashions the style and character of *RV*, if not its substance, intercalates and excises materials, and offers an impersonal narrative voice in place of the familiar tone of the *editio princeps*.

[39] It is not altogether clear if one should read Wakar or Yakar. The note is undated and may signal the book was purchased after Joseph's death and donated to the community as a memorial.

[40] For a partial edition of the glossary, see A. W. Wainman, "An Analysis of the Judeo-Spanish Glossary in *El regimiento de la vida* by M. Almosnino (Salonica, 1564), in *Actes du premier Congrès international des études balkaniques et sud-est européennes* (Sofia, 1967–1977), 6:175–79.

INTRODUCTION

Almosnino gives *RV* and *TS* explicit closure, and each one identifies its own specific destinatory. Such indications of each book's autonomy, however, should not obscure the intrinsic affinity linking their subject matters. *RV*'s general introduction and key index summarize the contents of *TS*, which in turn reveals a marked reliance on issues and principles enunciated and resolved in *RV*. The title page of *RV* situates *TS* within its context:

'I śegirśe'a depu'eś de[ ]'el 'otro muy śublimado tratado śobre la 'esensy'a 'i śer deloś śu'enyoś 'i de śuś kauśaś 'i śiknifikasyoneś 'i śolturaś verdaderaś ke tanbyen konpeten 'a 'el re ğimyento dela vida : konpu'eśto por 'el meśmo 'aktor 'a rekerimyento del muy 'ilu śtre śenyor 'el śenyor don Yosef Naśi' ke 'el Dyo konśerve 'i a'umente śu prośpero 'eśtado. (fol. 1a)[41]

This statement justifies the inclusion of *TS* with *RV* because the essence and being, causes and meanings, and true interpretation of dreams clearly pertain to the regimen of living.

TRANSLITERATION

The transliteration scheme here adopted alters slightly the standard system. In *RV*, ט (Tet) and ק (Kof) occur far more often than ת (Taf) and כ (Kaf). For ease of legibility, it has been deemed preferable to transcribe ט as t, ק as k, ת as ṭ, and כ as ḳ. The scheme is given below:

Consonants

א	'Alef	'	ו	Vav	v
ב	Bet	b	ז	Zayin	z
ג	Gimel	g	ח	Het	h
ג	+ diacritic	ğ	ט	Tet	t
ד	Dalet	d	י	Yod	y
ה	He	h	ך, כ	Kaf	ḳ

---

[41] "And following it there is a sublime treatise on the essence and existence of dreams, their causes, significance, and true interpretations which also pertain to the regimen of life. It was composed by the same author at the request of the illustrious lord, the prince Yosef ha-Nasi, may God protect and increase his prosperity."

INTRODUCTION

ל	Lamed	l	ץ, צ	Ṣade	ṣ	
ם, מ	Mem	m	ק	Kof	k	
ן, נ	Nun	n	ר	Reš	r	
ס	Samek	s	ש	Śin, (Šin)	ś, (š)	
ע	ʿAyin	ʿ	ש	+ diacritic	š	
ף, פ	Pe	p	ת	Tav	t	
ף, פ	+ diacritic	f+ f				

Vowels

Short			Long	
ַ pataḥ	a		ָ qameṣ	ā
ֶ seghôl	ε		ֵ serê	e
ִ ḥirek	i		ֵי	ê
ֻ quibbûṣ	u		ִי ḥirek	î
ָ qameṣ-ḥatuf	o		וּ šûrek	û
			וֹ ḥolem	ô
			ׂ	o

The colon is the sole punctuation mark found in the *editio princeps*. The English translation of the Hebrew introduction inserts other punctuation: commas, periods, semicolons, quotation marks, and so on; no such punctuation is introduced into the transliterated Spanish text. The following conventions are observed for the English translation: braces { } indicate a page beginning or end or an editorial remark; parentheses ( ) enclose source references not provided in the original; and brackets [ ] enclose a Hebrew word or explanatory material. The same holds for the transliterated Spanish except that parentheses enclose an editorial suppression, brackets an editorial addition, angular brackets < > mark an expanded abbreviation, and references are provided in footnotes. Throughout the English translation the line number of the original Hebrew text is indicated. The inconvenience of reading continuous unbroken text necessitated introducing paragraphs into the English translation and the Spanish transliteration. The paragraph breaks correspond to words set in uppercase in the original.

INTRODUCTION

LANGUAGE

As mentioned, determining the precise character of a vowel, particularly in atonic position, is problematic owing to inconsistent use of *matres lectionis* in *RV*. The neutralization of high front and back vowels (*i~e, u~o*) in sixteenth-century Spanish and in modern Judeo-Spanish compounds the difficulty. An initial objective for this project was to construct an accurate phonetic description of Almosnino's written language on the basis of letter-pattern representations of sounds. After close examination of the text, however, it seems plain enough that neither the author, typesetter, nor reader required a consistent spelling system in order to read with ease, *pace* Pascual Recuero (*Ortografía del Ladino*), and the search for such a system is a chimera, an illusion of fixity. Except for those wordforms found in the Spanish-Hebrew glossary, the vocalization of this edition, therefore, is necessarily approximate.[42] It is plausible to suppose that unpointed *aljamía* was read in the same fashion as unpointed Hebrew: a reader recognizes a known wordform. In this respect, the 515 pointed items constitute the only unambiguous evidence for the vocalic system of Almosnino's language. Although some of it is contradictory, in the main its testimony is respected here. Owing to the *matres lectionis,* and the combination of י (Yod) with ל (Lamed) to represent palatal /λ/, it has been convenient to distinguish semi-consonant and semi-vowel /j/ from vocalic /i/ or /e/ in the transcription.

What is not certifiable for the vowel system may, conversely, be assured for the consonant system: the transcription represents the exact Hebrew letter employed. Some readers may find the method entails an intial, albeit short-lived, visual inconvenience. For greater ease of reading, the transcription regularizes the diacritic distinguishing /p/ from /f/, /s/ from /ʃ/, and /g/ from /ʧ/, /ʤ/, /ʒ/ by suppression of the diacritic where it was provided.[43]

---

[42] In the glossary, where šᵉwā'îm appear under contiguous consonants in a word, the second one is transcribed. It is not to be considered a mobile šᵉwā. Although šᵉwā is not represented in the Spanish text, it is provided by the editor for Hebrew words.

[43] The sole exception to blanket suppression are occurrences of an otiose diacritic which is marked for deletion. A digitized transcription made in the course of preparing this edition retains the diacritic where it was printed and supplies one where it was not printed.

INTRODUCTION

REGIMIENTO DE LA VIDA (RV)

The avuncular duty to educate a nephew, typical of many cultures, is present in the author's addressing of *RV* (*Ha-Nᶜhagat ha-Ḥayyim*) to his nephew (and namesake) Mošé Garçon.[44] An epistle instructing Garçon in correct comportment in daily activities, the treatise expounds on topics ranging from the prosaic — sleeping, eating, walking, sitting — to the sublime: speculation, true happiness, and prophecy. It is a map guiding its reader on a sure path through the physical, ethical, intellectual, and spiritual perils a mid-sixteenth-century Jewish youth would encounter in Salonika or elsewhere.[45]

RV reveals itself to be a narrative profoundly concerned with the individual's knowledge of proper order and method, and Almosnino's task is to persuade the reader that understanding and enacting each behavior in an ideal manner propagates the experience of true happiness and consequent purposefulness.[46] The title page succinctly illustrates this point:

> LIBRO 'ENTITULADO REĞIMYENTO DELA VIDA
> pudyendośe verdader'a mente lyyamar 'eśpeğo de śabyoś 'i byen aventuradoś konpu'eśto por 'el famozisimo śabyo kabod morenu ha-Rab Rabbi Mošeh Almośnino n"rv 'a rekerimyento deśu 'intimo kerido 'i śobrino 'enel kual śe kontyene kuanto konbyene para poder byen 'andar toda la ğornada dela vida 'umana śin 'erar konprendyendo 'enel toda la filosofi'a moral muy kopyoza mente. (fol. 1a)[47]

---

[44] One of Almosnino's remarks, "tu tyerna 'edad" ("your tender years") (fol. 20b), implies that Garçon is still rather young.

[45] The Hanhagot genre generally makes use of halakha and ethics to instruct the individual in the minutest details of daily behavior: see *EJ* 6:922–32. In this strict sense, *RV* diverges from that genre in avoidance of minutiae, but coincides with its aspiration to inculcate doctrine for vouchsafing the individual's well-being. Tirosh-Samuelson judges the signal contribution of Ottoman intellectuals (whom she characterizes as "obsessed with the pursuit of spiritual perfection") to be in the field of moral philosophy ("Jewish Philosophy," 535).

[46] Tirosh-Samuelson argues that late fifteenth-century Jewish philosophy placed emphasis on "the final aim of human life [that] consists of the beatific vision of God in the world to come, namely, in the infinite bliss of personal immortality" ("Post-Expulsion Philosophic Literature," 234) brought about by the virtuous man purifying himself of iniquity by subordinating the body to reason by means of will ("Jewish Philosophy," 538).

[47] "A book entitled the *Regimen of Life,* which may truly be called a mirror for the wise and

Introduction

Almosnino divides *RV* into three interrelated sections treating physical health, the ethical virtues, and the intellectual virtues.[48] He states his objective at the outset: to place the means for performing virtuous actions at the reader's disposal; actions which are, in turn, subordinate to the most perfect virtue, the pure service of God:

'el fin verdadero dela kreasy'on del 'ombre por re śpekto del kual todoś loś 'otroś fineś śon 'eś la 'obra dela virtud 'i todo ś loś 'otroś fineś śon kamino para 'elyya 'i para la ma ś perfekta ke 'eś 'el puro śerbisy'o del Dyyo glory'ozo : 'I 'A 'opiny'on de nu'e śoś śabyoś 'eśte 'eś 'el fin dela kreasy'on del mundo glozando 'el primer bokablo dela śagrada 'eśkritura dizyendo por 'el prin-

---

felicitous, composed by the famous scholar, our honorable teacher R. Moše Almosnino at the request of his intimate beloved nephew, which contains everything necessary for completing successfully and without error the journey of human life. All moral philosophy is copiously included therein."

[48] The wise men of the Amsterdam community who approved the 1729 edition gave a wonderfully clear summary of *RV*'s content: "achamos ser huma obra de muyta importancia digna a seu Sapientissimo Authór, que com muyta razaõ [sic], e propriedade o intitulou Regimento da vida; por quanto (se) para [se] andár bem regido com prudencia, e virtude os que se podem chamár vivos nesta materiál vida, seguros de merecerem a espiritual, devem andár muy solicitos em tres principais pontos, a sabér, na Ethica, aplicandose ás couzas que-os constituam perfeitos; na Economica, procurando a boa educação, na Pulitica, em advertir o bom governo para com a republica; com cuidado repartiu o referido Authòr os assumptos de seus scientes discursos e salutiferos documentos em tres partes, mostrando em huma, com muyta erudicaõ [sic], e claros exemplos, as regras para conseguir a perfeiçaõ [sic] na Ethica de sua pessoa; advertindo com exactitude na outra aboa economia, com verdadeiras instremçoins [sic] para encaminhar os moços nas sendas da virtude; e na ultima manifestando os meyos dos direitos legais, alegando as particularidades do amor em que estriba a pulitica Divina, para concervaçam da republica" (fol. 4b). ("We find it is a work of great importance, worthy of its learned author who titled it *Regimen of Living*. Therefore, in order to govern themselves with prudence and virtue, and be certain of meriting spiritual life, those who may be called alive in this material life should be careful in three principal matters. In Ethics, applying themselves to those things that will make them perfect. In Economy, searching out good education. In Politics, understanding good government for the republic. The mentioned author distributed carefully the topics of his learned discourse and salutiferous documents in three parts. In one he teaches with erudition and clear examples the rules for attaining perfection of one's ethical person. In another he advises with exactitude on good economy with true instructions that direct youth towards the paths of virtue. In the last he manifests the median in legal justice, detailing the particulars of love on which the Divine politic rests, for the preservation of the republic.")

INTRODUCTION

sipy'o kre'o 'el Dyyo 'i set- ke 'e ś komo ke diğeśe por la ley ke śe lyyama prinsipy'o 'i por lo ś ğudyoś tanbyen ke śe ly[a]man prinsipy'o keryendo śinifikar ke śi śe halyyan la ley 'i 'el ğudyo kontiga mente ğuntoś ke 'eneśto konsiśte la perfeksy'on 'umana 'e śtonseś śon 'elyoś 'el fin dela kreasy'on del mundo 'i por 'e śto lo kre'o. (fols. 13b–14a)[49]

Each of the sections prescribes behaviors and activities belonging to a stage in the physical, intellectual, and spiritual development of a human being. They correlate, in turn, with what Almosnino calls the "three worlds" or "times of the soul." For the organization of its content the treatise relies on prior ethical, medical, philosophical, and religious authorities, particularly Aristotle's *Ethics,* Ibn Sina *Canon,* and Maimonides' *Laws of Character Traits, Eight Chapters,* and *Guide,* and al-Ghazzali. The conceptual and material legacy of those authorities is readily apparent in *RV*. The mosaic of voices and citations elicits what Herbert Davidson describes as "stylistically a medley of biblical, rabbinic and philosophical phraseology" (*Abraham Shalom,* 3–4). An amalgam of quotes, *exempla,* problems, and principles, biblical and rabbinic texts, theoretical medicine, classical and later philosophers, allegorical tales, and astronomical works,[50] *RV* represents the author's certainty that the universe is ordered and orderly. In such a universe it is incumbent upon the individual to realize fully the human potential for perceiving and experiencing the business of living in its just measure. Almosnino's theory of political life establishes how proper principles of social conduct and self-knowledge bring about a clear understanding of society's

---

[49] "The true end of man's creation, for which purpose all other ends exist, is virtuous action; all other ends are paths leading to virtuous action and the most perfect is the pure service of glorious God. And in the opinion of our sages this is the purpose of the creation of the world: glossing the first word of the Holy Scriptures reading "In the beginning God created" etc.; that is, as if it said for the Law that is called beginning and for the Jews, too, who are called beginning, meaning that as the Law and the Jews are found together, in this consists human perfection. Thus they are the purpose of the creation of the world, and for that reason He created it."

[50] Abeles notes among Almosnino's non-Jewish sources the following: Bias, Lycurgus, Socrates, Hippocrates, Dionysius, Plato, Demosthenes, Diogenes, Euclid, Epicurus, Plutarch, Epictetus, Porphyry, Themistius, Cicero, Seneca, Ibn Sina, al-Ghazzali, and Ibn Rushd. Jewish writers include Maimonides, R. Sholomo Yizahi, R. Abraham Ibn Ezra, R. Isaac Bedersi, R. Abraham Ibn Daud, R. Solomon Ibn Adret, R. Levi ben Gerson ("Moses Almosnino," 52). Tirosh-Samuelson lists a diverse cast of commentators alluded to in *Pne Mośe:* "Eustratius of Nicea, Albertus Magnus, Thomas Aquinas, Geraldus Odonis, John Buridan, Walter Burley, and Lefèvre d'Étaples" ("Jewish Philosophy," 536).

Introduction

requirements and benefits, and recognition of the human being's ultimate purpose.[51] Such knowledge dispels the confusing distortion of human purpose fantasized by the unethical who are unaware of a code of moral behavior. For Almosnino this is properly a matter for speculation, for philosophical inquiry into ultimate causes.[52]

As was mentioned, *RV* contains a lengthy Hebrew introduction, a brief Spanish prologue, and three main parts or treatises, each corresponding to a "time of the soul." Part One prescribes the appropriate behavior for young men to follow in order to live correctly and "to place their soul in life." Almosnino discusses at length ten everyday activities: eating and drinking, sleeping and waking, lying down and rising up, sitting and walking, speaking and silence. This section also defines the three worlds, or "times of the soul": the terrestrial, the celestial, and the world of the resurrection. It concludes with a sophisticated deliberation intended to resolve two enduring, yet merely apparent, paradoxes: first, why are the wicked long-lived but the righteous perish prematurely; and, second, why does all past time seem better than the present?

Almosnino's choice prompts a question: why those ten activities and not some others? What unifies them? A possible response lies in connecting the term *regimiento* from the book's title with the *regimen* of the medieval medical treatises.

Following ancient Greek sources, medieval medical doctrine distinguished between theoretical and practical spheres. Theoretical medicine was subdivided into three areas: the *res naturales,* i.e., the body's constituents, such as elements, humors, faculties, and spirits; the *res non naturales,* those items which have an effect on bodily health, such as air, food and drink, and exercise; and the *res contra naturam,* the diseases, their causes and consequences. The tripartite structure of theoretical medicine repeated itself in practical medicine, which in turn consisted of three areas: regimen, drugs, and surgery (Olson, *Literature as Recreation,* 40). The authoritative medical treatises of Almosnino's period, e.g., Ibn Sina's *Canon,* Hunain Ibn Isḥaq's *Isagoge,* and Maimonides' *Regimen of Health,* follow this sequence of subject matters.

---

[51] Tirosh-Samuelson characterizes the dynamic thus: "The revealed Torah is not only the most perfect law, the observance of which assures perfection of body and soul, but a sacred medium through which the human self and the divine self can encounter each other" ("Post-Expulsion Philosophic Literature," 245).

[52] A precise summary is offered by Tirosh-Samuelson: "Almosnino's analysis of the interplay of will and the intellect is that human happiness requires the perfection of both" [. . .] because love is "the perfection of the will and therefore the perfection of practical reason. The love of God thus belongs to the realm of praxis (*maʿseh*) rather than theoria (*ʿiyyun*)" ("Post-Expulsion Philosophic Literature," 249).

INTRODUCTION

Regimen, practical medicine's first category, concerns itself with the correct use of the *res non naturales* as set out by theoretical medicine. Regimen embodies a convenient thematic and narrative structure which Almosnino utilizes for his exposition. In medicine, a regimen of the non-naturals governs the individual's use of air, food and drink, motion and rest, sleep and waking, repletion and evacuation, and the accidents of the soul, in accordance with the individual's basic physical constitution.[53] For Almosnino, the *res non naturales* are amenable to elaboration as ethical doctrine, and it is in this sense that he explains them, substituting and altering the sequence in which some items are considered. Ethics and moral philosophy take precedence over medicine. For example, in discussing the causes underlying sleeping and waking, activities which figure prominently in *RV*, occasionally as metaphors for innocence and recognition, Almosnino incorporates the first non-natural, air, into a digression on meteorological phenomena, rain, snow, sleet, lightning, and so on.

Other examples of Almosnino's modified treatment of the non-naturals arise in the exposition on sleeping and waking. Here, the paired activities of lying down and rising up, absent from the medical regimen, are intercalated into the discussion and connect sleeping and waking with movement and rest, the next pair of non-naturals prescribed in the standard medical regimen. Similarly, Almosnino substitutes an inquiry into the properties, advantages, and disadvantages of speech and silence for the medical regimen's topic of evacuation and repletion. Examination of each non-natural and prescription for its practice rest upon reasoned ethical, moral, and religious arguments. In a valuable study of literature as recreation, Glending Olson observes: "The ethical implications of the regimens become more explicit in the hands of someone writing not as a physician but as a wise and learned counselor" (*Literature as Recreation*, 52–53). The voice of a "wise and learned counselor" shifts the regimen's focus from the somatic so as to include the ethical and moral.

The second part of *RV* opens with a review of the philosophical arguments surrounding free will. Here Almosnino argues that free will is a necessary fact of the Creation,[54] and on this basis examines the significance and practice of the ten moral

---

[53] G. Olson, *Literature as Recreation in the Later Middle Ages* (Ithaca, NY: Cornell University Press, 1982), 42. Whether Almosnino considered the doctrine developed in his explication of the non-naturals as immanent or superimposed is beyond the scope of the present discussion.

[54] Tirosh-Samuelson's penetrating analysis of Almosnino's philosophy reveals that he considered human action to be the expression of a hierarchical relationship between the intellect and the will ("Jewish Philosophy," 539–40).

INTRODUCTION

virtues described in Aristotle's *Ethics:* courage, temperance, liberality, magnificence, magnanimity, humility, patience, affability, truthfulness, and friendliness. Following the model outlined in the *Ethics* (Books III.6–V.9), the middle section investigates the last component of the *res non naturales,* "the accidents of the soul," human emotions. Although medieval medical regimens are not uniform with regard to the physician's legitimate role in treatment of the accidents of the soul, Almosnino appears to follow Maimonides' view expressed in the *Regimen of Health* that treatment of the passions and the role they play in the individual's general welfare pertains to practical philosophy: "Indeed, just as the philosophers have composed books in the various sciences, so have they composed many books about the rectification of morals and the discipline of the psyche so that it acquires a virtuous nature, until nothing comes from it but good actions" (*"Regimen of Health,"* trans. Bar-Sela et al., 25). Almosnino's subordination of medical questions to the ethical, moral, or religious issues they imply for "the discipline of the psyche" is founded on then-current medical thought. In this sense, the middle section of *RV* takes a category from the medical regimen, "the accidents of the soul," for its thematic and narrative framework; medicine seems to interest Almosnino only in so far as one's general health regulates the ability to apprehend and comprehend. Of paramount importance is recognition of the individual's free will, from which flows control of the emotions. Assimilation of the moral virtues in practice promotes the individual's apprehension of the ultimate goal of well-being and true happiness.[55]

Part Three is given over to analysis of the two remaining moral virtues, justice and friendship, and a brief review of the five intellectual virtues: intelligence, science, wisdom, prudence, and art. The topics presented depart from the medical regimen, but closely follow Aristotle's *Ethics*. A parable about a king and his three sons, followed by Almosnino's interpretation of it, closes *RV*.

A case can be made that Part One's narrative framework derives from the practical medical regimen's sequence of topics (relying on the *Ethics*).[56] Part Two derives from the second area of theoretical medicine, the *res non naturales,* and from Aristotle's *Ethics*. Part Three, correlated with the third "time of the soul," lacks a clear link with practical medicine's regimen, but, like Part Two, follows Aristotle.

---

[55] For a detailed analysis of the dynamic, see Tirosh-Samuelson, "Post-Expulsion Philosophic Literature," 240–49.

[56] Abeles observes that Part One of *RV* is derived mainly from Maimonides' *Hilkot Deʿot* ("Moses Almosnino," 29).

INTRODUCTION

RV glosses the *Nicomachean Ethics*,[57] but departs from Aristotle at a juncture Joseph Dan defines as a constant of Hebrew ethics: "[The] insistence on presenting ethical ideas as directly resulting from the correct interpretation of biblical verses and talmudic and midrashic sayings" (*Jewish Mysticism and Jewish Ethics*, 10). Almosnino did not advance a new theological concept: Maimonides had long since reconciled rabbinic thought with a general ethical system based on Aristotle (*Eight Chapters*); rather, *RV* reflects the continued vitality of that achievement.[58]

Almosnino's prescription for resolving the human predicament is derivative,[59] yet it is accumulative and amplificatory: a synthesis of methods and models for attaining true happiness worked out by the prophets and sages, by ancient philosophers — Aristotle, Plato, Seneca, Cicero, Macrobius, and Boethius — and rabbis and later

---

[57] Abeles concludes that *RV* is patterned in plan but not content after Aristotle's ethical system: "In discussing the virtue fortitude, Scriptures, rabbinical references and Euclid serve his [Almosnino's] purposes best in the development of the subject, and Aristotle's thesis plays but a small supporting role" ("Moses Almosnino," 54). Nevertheless, a comparison of *RV* and Aristotle's pertinent writings reveals many places where Almosnino literally follows Aristotle. Tirosh-Samuelson's concise summation merits citation: "The pursuit of perfection required a theoretical framework. It was provided by Aristotle's *Nicomachean Ethics* as interpreted by Maimonides [...] the first to fuse Aristotle's theory of happiness (*eudamonia*) with the rabbinical ideal of human perfection and his view dominated all subsequent reflections in moral philosophy" ("Jewish Philosophy," 535).

[58] Joseph Gorfinkle characterized Maimonides' achievement as "the most remarkable instance in medieval ethical literature of the harmonious welding of Jewish religious belief and tradition with Greek Philosophy" ("*Eight Chapters*," 5). Almosnino's first work was an introduction to Abraham Shalom's defense of Maimonides, *Neve Šalom*, wherein Shalom argues that although scriptural and talmudic studies are more important than philosophy, philosophy is permitted in order better to understand Scripture (Abeles, "Moses Almosnino," 27). Herbert Davidson's exhaustive and illuminating study of *Neve Šalom* does not identify Almosnino as editor or author of the introduction to it. Davidson describes the book's objectives as apologetic, homiletic, and philosophic (*Abraham Shalom*, 3). He leaves no doubt concerning its tenor: "Shalom's declared motto was that 'Moses Maimonides is true and his teaching (*torah*) is true'." He stresses that Maimonides' importance cannot be overestimated: "When we consider the fact that most of the philosophical conceptions with which Shalom operates derive either directly or indirectly from Maimonides, we are provided a gauge of the striking dominance which Maimonides continued to exercise among Jews up to the end of the Middle Ages" (v). The same reliance on Maimonides' thought is typical of Almosnino's *RV*.

[59] Tirosh-Samuelson qualifies it thus: "a moral philosophy that eclectically fused Aristotelian, Platonic, Stoic, and rabbinic ideals" ("Jewish Philosophy," 536).

INTRODUCTION

philosophers — Rav Saadia Gaon, Rabbi Solomon Ibn Gabirol, Baḥya Ibn Paquda, and Maimonides.[60] Almosnino derives his definition of true happiness from Aristotle:

> [T]he Good of man is the active exercise of his soul's faculties in conformity with excellence or virtue, or if there be several human excellences or virtues, in conformity with the best and most perfect among them. Moreover this activity must occupy a complete lifetime [...] one day or a brief period of happiness does not make a man supremely blessed and happy. (*NE* I.vii.15–16 [1098a 17–21])

Almosnino addresses this ancient motif with a quintessential medieval Jewish method: Let us work to understand the written and oral Torah, for in them are blessed doctrine and true speculation, and knowledge of them is the ultimate degree of true happiness.[61] But direct knowledge of them entails an epistemological complication. The order of divine knowledge manifest in the Law so differs from human knowledge that an unbridgeable void precludes direct human comprehension of the divine. To ameliorate the hindering difference one may have recourse to philosophy, the human sciences.

Almosnino's apology for his curriculum[62] is made within a definition of

---

[60] Joseph Dan's summary of the historical development of ethics in Jewish thought notes: "In fact, if we follow general definitions of the meaning of ethics, there is no doubt that the enormous edifice of Jewish law, constructed by scores of generations of scholars interpreting and reinterpreting their sources and creating a vast system of detailed instructions concerning every facet of a human's behavior toward his God and toward his fellow men, on the principles of justice, fairness, and respect for the rights of the individual, as well as in conformity with God's demands from man, is a clear example of a comprehensive system of ethical behavior" (*Jewish Mysticism and Jewish Ethics*, 4). Dan notes that the development of medieval Jewish ethics can be traced in four key philosophical ethical treatises: Saadia Gaon, *Emunot ve-De'ot* (The Book of Beliefs and Ideas), tenth century; Baḥya Ibn Paquda, *Ḥovot ha-Levavot* (The Duties of the Heart), eleventh century; Moses Maimonides, *Shemonah Perakim* (Eight Chapters), eleventh century; and Solomon Ibn Gabirol, *Tikkun Midot ha-Nefesh* (The Correction of the Soul's Inclinations), twelfth century.

[61] Tirosh-Samuelson argues that for Almosnino the love of God lies not in the perfection of the theoretical intellect but in the perfection of the will ("Post-Expulsion Philosophic Literature," 251). On how such perfection is achieved, see 245.

[62] The order of study R. Solomon Le-Bet Ha-Levi prescribed in *Lev Avot* compares advantageously with his contemporary Almosnino's program: "First a person should begin to learn Torah in order to achieve perfection in behavior [...]. After this he should learn logic in order to

Introduction

speculation and true happiness:

'Eś manifyeśto ke 'el medyo verdadero 'i maś konvenible para alkansar 'el 'ultimo fin dela filisidad 'e ś 'entender byen nu'eśa śantiśima ley 'i palabraś de nu'eśoś śaby'oś ke 'enelya 'i 'en śuś maravilyozoś diğoś 'eśta konklu'ida toda la dotrina beatiśima 'i 'eśpikulasy'on verdader'a ke 'e ś 'el śumo grado dela byen aventuransa maś komo śe'a la klaridad de nu'eśa devinisima ley muy 'eśtremada 'i nu'eśo 'in ğeny'o muy flako para poderla 'entender 'e ś nesesary'o buśkar 'otroś medyoś ke maś fasil mente śe pu'edan ko[n]prender para venir a'el verdadero konosimyento de 'elyya no değando ğamaś de trabağar 'en 'elyya kon toda la vehemensy'a 'i dili ğensy'a posible 'i syendo aśi te baśtara byen 'eśte mi reğimyento ke riğendote por 'el 'i ponyendo laś myenteś 'enla śegunda 'i tersera partida de 'el fasil mente podra ś 'ente[n]der 'el libro delaś 'etikaś ke larga mente tengo glozado 'el kual aplike 'a muğa sensy'a de nu'eśa ley śanta 'onde śe deklaran muğoś ś[ek]retoś de nu'eśo Talmud porke 'enloś diğoś dela ley 'i de nu'eśoś śaby'oś 'a meneśter 'una fu'erte 'e śpikulasy'on 'i grave konosimyento 'enla ś sensyaś 'umanaś para ver kuanto śin konparasyon la devina ley lyeba vantağe. (fol. 19b)[63]

Confidence in the practical utility of philosophy is reiterated towards the treatise's conclusion:

---

avoid mistakes and misinterpreting omens and analogies ... After this he should learn physics to be able to comprehend metaphysics [...]. Afterwards he should devote himself to providing the necessities of his life, and lastly, he must return to study Torah so as to understand it with all its secrets and so as to observe its commandments with their true intent" (Hacker, "Intellectual Activity," 124 n. 62).

[63] "It is manifest that the true and best means for achieving the ultimate end of happiness is understanding truly our Holy Law and our sages' words. In it, and in their wondrous sayings, is included all holy doctrine and true speculation, which is the supreme degree of true happiness. But because the clarity of our Divine Law is so intense, and our intellect so weak, it is necessary to search for other more easily comprehended means for arriving at a true knowledge of the Law, never ceasing from occupying yourself in it with all possible passion and diligence. And thus my regimen will be sufficient for you. Govern yourself by its precepts; give due attention to the second and third parts and you will easily understand the [*Nicomachean*] *Ethics* which I glossed extensively and applied scientifically to our Holy Law. In my gloss many secrets of our Talmud are revealed. For in the sayings of the Law and of our sages speculation and human sciences are required in order to see how incomparable is the advantage of the Divine Law."

INTRODUCTION

ŚOLO 'eś mi 'intensy'on dezirte aki 'en breve 'el 'e śtilo ke deveś lyevar 'en deprender la sensy'a por śuś prinsipy'oś śola mente lo ke te baśtara para 'entender laś palabraś de nu'eśoś śaby'oś 'en nu'eśo Ṭalmud 'i 'en 'otro ś lugareś ke no değaron sensy'a ni śabiduri'a ke no 'eśpekularon 'i komo vengan śuś palabraś muy seradaś ke no kiğeron dezir maś ke laś śiknifikasy'oneś de laś kozaś porke para loś śaby'oś akelyyo abaśta por tanto 'eś meneśter le'er 'en alguna manera por lo ś libroś deloś f[i]losofoś ke alargaron 'enla sensy'a para poder byen konprender la 'intensy'on de nu'e śoś śaby'oś : 'I porke la vida 'eś muy breve 'i la śabiduri'a muy larga 'i la ś 'okupasy'oneś muğaś 'eś razon de buśkar 'el ma ś breve kamino ke konbyene 'enel le'er 'eśtaś sensyaś para diśtribu'ir 'el ma ś del tyenpo 'i 'el meğor 'en nu'eśa śantisima ley. (fols. 132a–132b)[64]

Almosnino's preferred rhetorical technique follows a simple, ingenious pattern.[65] Upon a full or partial quotation of a biblical verse,[66] rabbinic sentence, or philosophical dictum there follows an interpretation of various subdivisions of that quotation, and then a corroborative proof-text that authenticates a complete accord between received truth and philosophical speculation; philosophy is seen to be the handmaiden of truth. Almosnino's tenets are verified through a synchretic syllogistic method that combines rabbinic tradition with dialectic and ethics, especially the Aristotelian median applied to appetite, conduct, and judgment. The rhetorical strategy of citing biblical verses as premise or proof reinforces the treatise's ideological authority and moral purpose.

Almosnino doubtless had knowledge of some portion of Aristotle's writings: when

---

[64] "My intention is only to instruct you in brief on how you should study science by its principles. Only what is necessary for understanding the words of our sages in the Talmud and in other places; for there is no science or wisdom on which they did not speculate. And because their words may be hard to understand, for they tried to say nothing more than the meanings of the words, because for sages that is enough, it is necessary to read the books of the philosophers who examined science at length in order to understand well our sages' meaning. And because life is short, and wisdom is great, and the tasks are many, it is right to search the best, shortest path for reading these sciences so that the best and most of one's time is taken up with our Holy Law."

[65] Saperstein (*Jewish Preaching*) elucidates on this innovative rhetorical procedure, already noted by Abeles ("Moses Almosnino").

[66] Several hundred biblical verses quoted and glossed in the corpus are copied in a prefatory list.

INTRODUCTION

articulating the principle of the median[67] his words echo Maimonides in his treatise *Laws Concerning Character Traits* (*Hilkot De῾ot*): "The right way is the mean in every single one of man's character traits [...] the wise men of old commanded that a man continuously appraise his character traits and evaluate them and direct them in the middle way so that he becomes perfect" (*Laws Concerning Character Traits,* in *Ethical Writings,* 29). The Aristotelian median is both benchmark and technique for emending character flaws. As for curing the diseases of the soul, Almosnino again follows Maimonides' formulation: "Good deeds are such as are equibalanced, maintaining the mean between two equally bad extremes, the *too much* and the *too little*" ("Eight Chapters," ed. Gorfinkle, 54).[68] In all circumstances, recourse to the median sifts correct from incorrect interpretation and signals a right course of action. So too the median is an explicit statement of the prophets' and sages' esoteric wisdom: adherence to it elucidates the proper thoughts and actions that draw the soul closer to true happiness. Almosnino's ideal human being, the virtuous man, is a sage who speculates on the Intelligibles and the Creator, i.e., the pursuit of true happiness.[69]

Consistent with rabbinic thought, free will and predestination are settled matters in Almosnino's study, i.e., everything is foreseen, but choice is given.[70] His exposition amplifies its sources' treatment of the ethical virtues: courage, temperance, liberality, magnificence, magnanimity, humility, patience, affability, truthfulness, friendship, and justice. Aristotelian virtue is a median between two extremes, deficit and surfeit, and a habit in the soul. Almosnino's virtue is, additionally, preceded by and anchored in the Holy Scriptures. The conceptual frameworks are complementary: Aristotelian virtue, comprehensible by the human intellect, points to the prepotent Law, the full import of which is incomprehensible but may be more fully grasped by the human intellect through the agency of philosophy.

Illuminated by divine light, the sages and prophets enjoyed superlative knowledge of all disciplines and a nonpareil linguistic economy. Their discourse lacks superfluity; the characteristic redundancy of everyday conversation is absent. So complete was their grasp of the essential truths in all fields of knowledge that, unlike

---

[67] His prologue emphasizes that the content of the book is useful for attaining true happiness by means of a general rule, the median, a moderation of the appetites.

[68] "Chapter IV deals with the cure of the diseases of the soul. In agreement with Aristotle, Maimonides declares that actions are good when they follow a medium course between two extremes which are both bad" (Gorfinkle, introduction to *"Eight Chapters,"* 14).

[69] For a full description of the "virtuous man," see Tirosh-Samuelson, "Jewish Philosophy," 538, 542.

[70] On the central role of free will in Almosnino's moral philosophy, see Tirosh-Samuelson, "Jewish Philosophy," 539–40, and "Post-Expulsion Philosophic Literature," 246–49.

Introduction

Almosnino's reader, they required no secondary explication. From this standpoint, philosophy is read in order to comprehend accurately the sages' and prophets' meaning; its justification is as an interpretive tool for insight into, and acquisition of, a truer understanding of the Law (see the previous quotation of *RV,* fols. 132a–132b).

The crux of the matter, then, is that theoretical knowledge is useful only to the extent that its potentiality is realized in an actuality. The knowledge that virtue is a habit in the soul is significant: the possession of a virtue is its exercise. The soul imbued with ethical virtue promotes physical well-being and moderates the appetites (the accidents of the soul) until perfect self-control (*sophrosyne*) is achieved.[71] Self-control is correlate with intellectual refinement, that is, the speculative virtues prerequisite for a more perfect understanding of the Law.

The practical counterparts of the intellectual virtues include intelligence (a knowledge of first principles), science (a knowledge of dialectics), and wisdom (distinguishing truth), which is actualized as prudence (working to a good end) or as art (the more perfect making of an article). Learned through a curriculum of study — the *trivium* and *quadrivium* — the intellectual virtues are propaedeutic for Almosnino's advanced course: more perfect comprehension of the Law. Just as philosophical enquiry promotes fuller understanding of the intention in the Law, such an appreciation, in turn, is requisite for the paramount objective, loving God and placing the soul in true happiness in speculation on Him:

> 'el verdadero konosimyento prosede de la 'eśpikulasy'on 'enla ko śa ke śe kyere por tanto 'eś viśto ke 'el 'amor ke prosede de la 'e śpikulasy'on 'eś 'el 'amor verdadero ke vyene por vi'a dere ğa 'i linyya rek(ś)[t]a [. . .] ŚOLO kiğe dezir 'en todo lo diğo ke 'el verdadero 'i po śtrero fin 'umano 'i byen verdadero 'eś 'el amar al Dyyo 'i kontenplar 'enel 'i glorifikar śe konla tal kontenplasy'on ke 'eśto todo śe śige de la verdader'a 'eśpikulasy'on komo tenemoś diğo. (fols. 125b–126a)[72]

---

[71] For a detailed review of the body/soul dynamic, see Tirosh-Samuelson, "Jewish Philosophy," 538, 542.

[72] "True knowledge proceeds from speculation about the thing that is loved. Therefore, it is seen that the love which proceeds from speculation is true love that comes via a direct and straight line [. . .] In everything said, I tried only to say that the true and final human end, and the true good, is to love God, contemplate Him, and glorify oneself in that contemplation. That is what follows from true speculation, as we have said."

INTRODUCTION

How is Aristotelian philosophy connected with prophecy?[73] Maimonides answers (in *"Eight Chapters"*) that ethical and moral defects prevent the individual from drawing near to God:

> The Rabbis said that Moses, our teacher, saw God from behind a single, clear, that is transparent, partition. As they express it, "He looked through a translucent *specularia*" (Yebamot 49b). *Specularia* is the name of a mirror made of some transparent body like crystal or glass [...] Let me now explain the above statement. In accordance with what we have made clear in Chapter II, virtues are either intellectual or moral. Similarly, vices are intellectual [...] or moral [...] Each of these defects is a partition separating man from God. (*"Eight Chapters,"* trans. Gorfinkle, 79–80)

That perfection of moral and intellectual virtues is a *sine qua non* for prophecy is made plain in Joseph Gorfinkle's delineation of what is to be derived from Maimonides' discussion:

> In Chapter VII, Maimonides discusses the *partitions* or *walls* (Meḥiṣot) which separate man from God, and also describes what prophecy is. As explained in Chapter II, there are intellectual and moral virtues, and their opposite vices. These vices, which are termed *partitions,* prevent man from beholding God. As many vices, intellectual or moral, a man has, by so many *partitions* is he separated from God. The prophets "looked upon" God from behind the least number of *partitions*. The fewer they were, the higher was the rank of the prophet [...] Moses was the only prophet in whom all moral and intellectual virtues were combined. The only *partition* or *wall* between him and God was his physical body, from which the spirit of man cannot divorce itself on earth. This *partition* the rabbis call *specularia,* a transparent wall, through which Moses gazed upon the highest truth, but not as one does with human eyes. (Gorfinkle, introduction to *"Eight Chapters,"* 16–17)

---

[73] Tirosh-Samuelson's response is a succinct and authoritative summation: "With Maimonides, the Jewish rationalists interpreted Mosaic prophecy as the highest form of philosophical knowledge ever attained by a human being, and therefore, regarded the Torah as an esoteric philosophical text" ("Jewish Philosophy," 505).

INTRODUCTION

Speculation, which discerns and vouchsafes true doctrine, is served by metaphysics. Almosnino's curriculum — al-Ghazzali, Maimonides, and Abraham Ibn Ezra — presents metaphysics as a tool for learning the summa, theology. Again, the final ultimate purpose is speculation and more perfect understanding of divine matters in the Law:

> I para loke konbyene para la 'ultima śenśy'a ke 'es la metafizika loke 'entre nos'otros 'es kur śado le'er 'es la de 'Abu ḥamid 'Algazel la kual si tu kiğeres le'er halyyaras ke kon las nota śy'ones ke yo tengo 'eskrito al deredor del libro bastara byen para 'entender loke konbyene 'entender de palabras de nu'esos saby'os trava ğando de pu'es de todo 'esto 'enel famozisimo libro ke hizo 'el senyor Rabbenu Mošeh ke lyyamo 'el Moreh kon perkurar de 'entender byen 'el senyyor Rabi 'Ab[r]aham Ibn ᶜEzra' 'en todos sus libros ke a'un ke akorto muğo 'enla habla alarga muğo 'enla 'inten śy'on siknifikando 'en breves terminos loke 'otros 'en muy largos no lo abastan 'a deklarar atanto ke soy de 'opiny'on ke le'idos byen 'i byen 'entendidos los tratados destos dos senyyores 'en kuanto 'eskribyeron no 'es menester mas le'er para loke toka 'a nu'esa te'olo ği'a fin de todo saber para 'entender las kozas devinas ke vyenen 'en nu'esa santi śima ley ke 'es 'el fin 'ultimo de nu'esa 'espikula śy'on para la perfekśy'on de la anima 'i 'entendimyento te'oriko. (fol. 133a)[74]

True happiness, which is the love of God and the final ultimate human purpose, depends upon the perfection of the theoretical and practical virtues:

---

[74] "Regarding the last science, metaphysics, the usual course of study among us is to read Abuḥamid Algazel. If you want to read it, you will find that with the marginal notes I have made there it is sufficient for understanding what it is proper to understand of our sages' words. Finally, [there is] the famous book our teacher Moše [Maimonides] wrote, the *Moreh*. And by trying to understand well all the books of R. Abraham Ibn Ezra, for though he condensed much he increased insight greatly, saying in brief what others could not say at length. So much so, that I am of the opinion that reading and understanding properly these two authors' treatises there is no reason to read anything else regarding our theology, the purpose of all knowledge, for understanding the divine things discussed in our Holy Law, which is the ultimate end of our speculation, for the perfection of the soul and theoretical intellect." Tirosh-Samuelson summarizes Maimonides' view: "The figurative language of the Torah expresses the truths of Aristotelian physics and metaphysics and the laws of the Torah establish the most perfect social order in which the philosophic elite can attain and reach the ultimate end of human life, knowledge of God" ("Jewish Philosophy," 505).

Introduction

'i 'e śta byen visto ke 'el kamino verdadero para alyegar al fin 'ultimo 'i śumo grado dela byen aventuransa 'eś la perfeksy'on del 'entendimyento te'oriko 'i pratiko ke del depende 'el 'amor del Dyyo ke 'e ś 'el 'ultimo fin verdadero komo tenemoś diğo. (fol. 134b)[75]

TRATADO DE LOS SUENYOS (TS)

The *Tratado de los suenyos* (*Iggeret ha-Ḥalomot*) studies the dream and its connection with prophecy.[76] Writing for the Duke of Naxos, Almosnino endeavors to answer three questions his patron had raised: (1) Are man's dreams in accordance with his complexion (i.e., character)?; (2) Is there a natural explanation for how dream forms (images) signify future events?; and, finally, a two-part question (3) What causes a person to dream of things long since forgotten, and can natural reasons account for Joseph's dream interpretations?

In part a restatement of Aristotle's analysis of sleep and dreams (in the *Parva Naturalia*), and in part a summary of Maimonides' study of the essential link between dreams and prophecy (*Guide,* Book Three), Almosnino's work analyzes Joseph's prophetic dreams and interpretations of the dreams of the chief butler, the chief

---

[75] "And it is plain to see that the true path for coming to the final supreme degree of true happinesss is the perfection of the theoretical and practical intellect. For on it depends the love of God which is the true ultimate end, as we have said." The point is made clear by Tirosh-Samuelson: "Philosophy became the handmaiden of popular hermeneutics. The philosopher's task was to apply his human wisdom (culled from the study of philosophy) to interpret suprarational, supranatural divine revelation" ("Post-Expulsion Philosophic Literature," 235).

[76] An unpublished English translation in typescript was made by Leon Klmaleh, "Dreams ... by Rabbi Moses ben Baruch Almosnino" (Philadelphia, 1934). For an earlier dreambook in Salonika, see Annelies Kuyt, "A 'Traumdeutung' Before the *Traumdeutung:* Shlomo Almolis' *Pitron Ḥalomot,*" *Frankfurter Judaistische Beiträge* 23 (1996): 55–73. On dreams in ancient and medieval writings, see Bodeham, "Nature of the Dream"; Gnuse, "Dream Reports" and *Dreams and Dream Reports;* Goldberg, "The Dream Report"; Oberhelman, "Interpretation of Prescriptive Dreams," "Galen," "The Diagnostic Dream," and "Dreams in Graeco-Roman Medicine"; Palley, *Ambiguous Mirror;* and Peden, "Macrobius." For ancient systems of dream classification, see Kessels, "Ancient Systems," and Oberhelman, ed., *Oneirocriticon.* Both Von Grunebaum and Caillois, *The Dream,* and to a lesser extent Oberhelman, "Dreams in Graeco-Roman Medicine," bring together a comprehensive general treatment of the dream.

INTRODUCTION

baker, and Pharaoh.[77] He argues that the foundation of Joseph's interpretations is a complete knowledge of the natural sciences. The discussion catalogues the hallmarks that distinguish true dreams from false ones: a true dream occurs in the early morning, it is doubled, the dreamer is aware that the experience is a dream, and the dream is its own interpretation. Having satisfied Nasi's three questions, Almosnino recounts and interprets his own dream about the Duke, the Duke's brother Samuel, and their mother, Doña Gracia.[78] Endowed with all the traits of true dreams, it portends Joseph Nasi's continued triumphs, the family's continued good fortune, and their ceaseless support of the community. The dream, Almosnino confides, prompted him to speculate on the causes, classes, and interpretations of dreams.

The reason why *RV* and *TS* were bound together may have been programmatic, the essential connection among ethics, dreams, and prophecy outlined above, or merely economic. *RV* and *TS* do identify separate destinatories and both books are replete with authorial asides to the respective destinatory: the nephew is admonished for his quick temper and fondness for sleeping, while the patron's generosity and intellectual curiosity are praised, and the many pleasant conversations at Belvedere on Shabbat afternoons are recalled. The nephew is now chided, now encouraged, and reminded of books his uncle had read with him in the past, or would lend him in the future. A second group of asides is made to a general reader, whoever may read the book, especially youths and young men. As the title page declares, Almosnino considered *RV* to be an *espejo* (Lat. *speculum*), a summa of the whole of moral philosophy.[79]

The well-established connection linking dreams with prophecy, e.g., Maimonides' *Guide,* may account for Almosnino's treatment of *TS* as a separate work included under the same cover with *RV.* The treatises' subject matters separate along an ambiguous line between consciousness and unconsciousness: this division underscores their complementariness. The familiar theory of perception, sense-imagination-reason-intellect, that underlies Almosnino's analysis of how a waking dream differs

---

[77] An analogy between the generation of the Exodus from Egypt and that of Almosnino's day emerges towards the treatise's conclusion (fol. 162a).

[78] The dream scenario is a Succoth celebration in the Bet Midrash that Joseph Nasi built in Belvedere.

[79] R. Bradley reviews the various connotations of *speculum* as a title word: "Backgrounds of the Title *Speculum* in Medieval Literature," *Speculum* 29 (1954): 101–15. See also H. Grabes, *The Mutable Glass* (Cambridge: Cambridge University Press, 1973, repr. 1982).

INTRODUCTION

from a sleeping dream suggest an imprecise frontier between consciousness and unconsciousness; Aristotle describes the operation and perception of the dream as analogous with those of waking experience. For Almosnino, the waking dream differs from the sleeping dream in the greater activity of the exterior senses, the degree and extent to which the imagination is occupied with external stimuli during the waking dream. Individual character and intelligence also play crucial roles in the dream theory, and Almosnino thus reviews different types of personalities. The central point is that *RV* examines and discusses materials that pertain to waking volitional activities, while *TS* concerns itself with experiences acquired through the unconscious, usually in sleep, extraordinarily while awake.

Even a self-evident opposition such as waking/sleeping acquires transcendence when brought into a belief system that conceives of its defining establishment myth as historical experience inflected by prophecy, a dream or a vision, and its interpretation. Almosnino doubtless subscribed to Maimonides' declaration: "Prophecy is given either in a vision or in a dream, as we have said so many times" (*Guide*, trans. Friedlander, 240). Abraham Shalom observed that prophecy aids man in areas where no scientific premise buttresses the prophet's knowledge. Knowledge acquired through prophecy is "... knowledge lying outside the scope of the human intellect, and containing (a) religious dogmas, (b) a code of ethics, and (c) predictions of the future" (Davidson, *Abraham Shalom*, 99). Here, then, is a ground for understanding *TS* as a logical extension of the material treated in *RV*. *RV* imparts knowledge about the physical, moral, and social dimensions of the individual's experience and addresses behaviors over which the individual is presumed to exercise conscious control. Almosnino's discussion of everyday activities consistently draws out their moral and spiritual implications. *TS* rationalizes the unconscious, uncontrolled experience of the dream world, a dimension of human experience wherein prophecy may occur. He describes and analyzes three classes of dream, and endeavors to show how Joseph's dream interpretations relied on a complete knowledge of the "natural sciences." The treatment corresponds with Almosnino's view of the interrelation between philosophy and prophecy mentioned above (notes 73 and 76).

CONCLUSION

At several points in the narrative of *RV* Almosnino laments the heavy community responsibilities and demands weighing on him; moreover he states that he is proofreading another work, *Pne Mose,* and has little time for his own studies. Throughout its length and breadth, *RV* quotes authorities abundantly; the author refers to his own

INTRODUCTION

commentaries and glosses, and even to those he previously read with Mośe Garçon.[80] The asides and allusions set an important rhetorical tone, and are complemented by invitations to read further in related works. Taken together, they pose a question about Almosnino's motives for undertaking a project that required him to compile, translate, and integrate a substantial quantity of medical, ethical, and theological writings and assemble them into treatises when, as he repeatedly notes, he is laboring under a great press of time.[81]

From an examination of the quotations from Ibn Sina's *Canon,* Aristotle's *Ethics, Rhetoric, Problems, Meteorologica,* and *Parva Naturalia,* and Maimonides' *Laws Concerning Character Traits,* the *"Eight Chapters,"* and the *Guide,* Almosnino's close reliance on sources, not solely for content but often for the very wording of a phrase, emerges clearly. The complaints concerning the heavy demands on him are doubtless a *captatio benevolentiae,* but the fact does not necessarily invalidate their accuracy. Why not simply assign his nephew the *auctoritates* on which he drew? That Garçon would eventually read them is plausible enough. Did Almosnino's avuncular obligation compel his composition of *RV,* or did a more general obligation to share his learning with his community motivate it? As rabbi of *Leviat Ḥen,* founded by Doña Gracia Mendes specifically for the Portuguese community in Salonika,[82] a course of studies as laid out in *RV* would present basic religious tenets and a popularization of

---

[80] A reference to the uncle reading to his nephew is made here: "algo maś te deklare 'enla 'eśpozisy'on del diǧo kapitulo del Bederśi 'i a'un 'e śto note kiǧera 'eśkrivir ke no 'eś de mi kondisy'on tratar muǧo deśtaś tan śutileś materyyaś fu'era deśu lugar pero hizelo porke vide kuando te le'i akel kapitulo dubdabaś 'en algunaś kozaś ke por no śaber 'el 'oriǧin de adonde manavan me paresy'o ke kedavaś algo śuśpenso" (fol. 51a): "I further interpreted this in my notes on the same chapter of Bederśi. And although I didn't want to mention it here, since such subtleties shouldn't be discussed out of context, I did so because when I read the chapter to you I noticed you had some doubts, because you do not know the origin of those thoughts, and it seemed to me you were baffled."

[81] Almosnino states that he was writing *RV* while proofreading *Pne Mośe.* Is *RV* derived from *Pne Mośe,* or is it a vernacular translation of *Pne Mośe?* Many of the author's asides, in that they refer to books in Hebrew the uncle and nephew read together, suggest not. Although it is possible that Almosnino translated those books for Garçon, a young man of his situation would have known Hebrew, indeed the uncle notes that his nephew could read Maimonides (*RV,* fol. 30a). More plausibly, *RV* is intended for the returned Portuguese *converso* community, separated by a one-generation hiatus from Jewish thought, as a bridge to their heritage.

[82] Regarding *Leviat Ḥen,* see Roth, *House of Nasi,* 128–31; Abeles, "Moses Almosnino," 33–36; and, finally, Bnaya, "Moses Almosnino" and *Mośe Almosnino,* 32–36.

contemporary Jewish philosophy to a generation estranged from its heritage while exiled in Portugal. In this regard, Joseph Dan stresses a fundamental issue in Jewish ethics: "... the emphasis on explanation and inducement, rather than the simple statement of the action that should be performed" (*Jewish Mysticism and Jewish Ethics,* 5). That was Almosnino's responsibility as the teacher of his nephew and of the youth within the sphere of his influence. Nehama's succinct assessment points up the immense efficiency of Almosnino's treatise: "C'est un livre qui a été le vade-mecum de bien des générations. Almosnino y étudie les bons et les mauvais caractères, la finalité de l'existence, le problème de la responsabilité morale et du déterminisme psychologique, les règles de la bienséance et les conditions pour bien conserver sa santé" (*Israélites de Salonique,* 3:13).

In conclusion, it is reasonable to presume that Almosnino intended *RV* to serve as a primer. An introduction to the rudiments of health, ethics, philosophical inquiry, textual interpretation, and religious belief, *RV* would provide its youthful reader a grounding in the moral and ethical virtues necessary for a successful life, and stimulate intellectual curiosity for speculation. If in its historical milieu *RV* was a primer, the constant and complex interplay among Scriptures, Talmud, Greek philosophy, medicine, and natural science constitute a relatively more advanced text today, one that invites reflection on the Renaissance cosmology of a Salonikan Jewish philosopher.

Introduction

APPENDIX I:
CONTENTS Of *REGIMIENTO DE LA VIDA*
AND *TRATADO DE LOS SUENYOS*

A listing of the chapter headings from both treatises allows for a rapid overview of the general and specific issues addressed, as well as an appreciation of the graduated and interdependent relationship between the concepts therein framed.

The Regimen of Living

Prologue and Universal Key to the Treatise

Prologue to his nephew

Part 1: For the young to keep company with the good

Chap. 1. Three species of good: spiritual, physical, external.
Chap. 2. Resolution of the question: why does good come to the evil and evil to the good?
Chap. 3. Knowledge of the sciences, the pathway to virtue.
Chap. 4. The regimen for eating.
Chap. 5. The regimen for drinking before and after eating.
Chap. 6. The causes of sleeping and its definition; the origins of rain and snow, comets, winds and storms, etc.
Chap. 7. The essence and being of sleep; the regimen for sleeping and waking.
Chap. 8. The regimen for lying down and rising up to perfect the soul and preserve the body.
Chap. 9. The regimen for sitting and walking in the company of parents, teachers, and elders.
Chap. 10. The regimen for speaking and not speaking.
Chap. 11. Examples of the same subject: praise of brevity and condemnation of prolixity.
Chap. 12. Choosing good and rejecting evil. The three worlds: terrestrial, celestial, and that of the resurrection of the dead, called "days" by the sages.
Chap. 13. Resolution of the question: why are the wicked long-lived and the good short-lived?
Chap. 14. Why does the past seem better than the present?

INTRODUCTION

Part 2: Free will and the twelve moral virtues

Chap. 1. The regimen for guiding oneself to what is good; concerning free will.
Chap. 2. Free will or predestination: an explanation of divine influence on human beings.
Chap. 3. The twelve moral virtues: their essence and being, their extremes and vices.
Chap. 4. The first virtue: courage; its three species.
Chap. 5. Five properties that should accompany each of the twelve virtues.
Chap. 6. The second virtue: temperance.
Chap. 7. The third virtue: liberality.
Chap. 8. The extremes and vices of liberality.
Chap. 9. The fourth virtue: magnificence; its essence, extremes, and properties.
Chap. 10. The fifth virtue: magnanimity; its fifty properties, and a proof that it includes all virtues.
Chap. 11. Fifteen of magnanimity's fifty properties described.
Chap. 12. The remaining thirty-five properties described.
Chap. 13. The sixth virtue: humility and its extremes.
Chap. 14. The seventh virtue: patience and its two extremes.
Chap. 15. The choleric (irascible) and the choleric's complexion.
Chap. 16. More on patience.
Chap. 17. The eighth virtue: affability.
Chap. 18. The ninth virtue: truthfulness.
Chap. 19. The different species of truthfulness and the resolution of two questions.
Chap. 20. The tenth virtue: friendliness.

Part 3: The eleventh and twelfth moral virtues and the intellectual virtues

Chap. 1. The eleventh virtue: justice and its particularities according to Cicero and Aristotle.
Chap. 2. How justice is a median like the other virtues.
Chap. 3. The median of legal justice and its extremes.
Chap. 4. The twelfth virtue: friendship, its four causes and examples of them.
Chap. 5. Different kinds of friendship: of virtue, of pleasure, of utility.
Chap. 6. Three distinctions: love for good, for utility, and for profit.
Chap. 7. Three reasons for losing friendship.
Chap. 8. What is best in degree, goodness, and perfection: to be loved or to

Introduction

          love? The common people think it is to be loved; the truth is it is to love.
- Chap. 9.   How to love.
- Chap. 10. An explanation of the being and essence of the five intellectual virtues.
- Chap. 11. The same question.
- Chap. 12. The sciences, their number, and how to learn them.
- Chap. 13. Three kinds of men according to the kinds of friendship.

The Treatise on Dreams

Author's prologue: Three questions put to him by Joseph Nasi

1. Are a man's dreams in accordance with his complexion (i.e., character)?
2. Is there a natural explanation for dream forms (images) that signify what will come to pass?
3. What causes men to dream of things long since forgotten, and is there a natural reason that explains Joseph's interpretation of dreams?

Errata

Spanish-Hebrew Glossary

INTRODUCTION

APPENDIX II:
CHRONOLOGY [83]

1518   January. M. Almosnino [= M.A.] born in Salonika. His father is Baruk Almosnino; his mother, given name unknown, is a Conimbriel [Cocumbriel] of a family related to the Almosninos. The two families continue to intermarry in subsequent years. The three sons of Baruk are Japhet, Moše, and Isaac (Emmanuel, *Israélites de Salonique,* 176 n. 39; *EJ* mentions Japhet only). A sister marries into the Garçon family, and her son, Moše Garçon, is the destinatory of *RV;* he and his brother Isaac correct the 1588 edition of *Meammeṣ Koaḥ.* M.A.'s mother and elder brother Japhet take charge of his early education. He studies Talmud with R. Moše de Boton, and, it is conjectured, sciences and philosophy with the physicians Peraḥia Hacohen and Aharon Afia (Emmanuel, *Israélites de Salonique,* 176).

1536   Establishment of Portuguese Inquisition provokes massive emigration of *conversos* to Salonika.

1537   Süleyman the Magnificent grants a charter of privileges to Salonikan Jews.

1538   M.A. composes *Ha-Kᶜdemah le-Sefer Neve Šalom* (Constantinople: Eleazar Soncino, 5298). Emmanuel claims that M.A. also edited this book (*Israélites de Salonique,* 177). Carmoly suggests that M.A. studied in Constantinople (*Famille Almosnino,* 11).

1543   Fire in Salonika.

1545   4 Av. Great fire and plague. The fire destroyed eight thousand homes, twenty synagogues, and many private libraries. Several hundred Jews lost their lives, and the communities were impoverished (Goodblatt, *Samuel de Medina,* 22). The acts of the privileges granted by Süleyman to the Salonika Jews are lost in the fire. Baruk Almosnino rebuilds the Catalan synagogue after its destruction in the 1545 fire.

1546   M.A. composes *Tefillah le-Moše* and *Pirke Moše* in Pelestria during plague (Emmanuel, *Israélites de Salonique,* 179). Emmanuel cites *Tefillah le-Moše* (fol. 75b) for his claim that *Pirke Moše* was written for a certain Isaac, who resided elsewhere than Salonika and who was writing a treatise on medicine.

---

[83] Dates and titles follow N. Ben-Menahem, "The Bibliography of R. M. Almosnino" [Hebrew], *Otsar Yehude Sefarad* 5 (1962): 126–28, except where otherwise noted.

INTRODUCTION

M.A. also composes *Beth Elohim ve-Šaʿar ha-Šamayyim*. Emmanuel states that Almosnino used Solomon Avigdor's Hebrew translation of Puerbach's *Theorica Nova Planetarum*, and that R. Aharon Afia helped M.A. to translate Sacrobosco's *Sphere* from Latin into Hebrew (*Israélites de Salonique*, 181–82). Emmanuel dates the completion of *Beth Elohim* to 11 January, 1548 (*Famille Almosnino*, 182). Carmoly dates the translation to 1553 (12). The colophon of the Lawrence J. Schoenberg codex of *Beth Elohim ve-Šaʿar ha-Šamayyim* (University of Pennsylvania) indicates the first text was copied in Salonika for Pereṣ ben Yehuda Minṣ Ashkenazi by Hayyim Luzio in 1551 and the second was written by M.A. in 1546 and copied by Hayyim Luzio.

Salonika community is now required to send a tribute of 7,800 rams per annum to the Porte (Bnaya, *Moše Almosnino*).

1548	Great plague, 7,000 Jews died (Goodblatt, *Samuel de Medina*, 22). 11 January: M.A. finishes *Beth Elohim*.
1551	M.A. becomes rabbi of Catalan synagogue.
1552	Plague year. 22 January, signatory of rabbinic documents. Month of Adar, M.A. delivers his first sermon.
1553	M.A. becomes rabbi of *Neve Šalom* (Calabrese) synagogue.
1554	Plague year. 4 March, M.A.'s wife, Simḥa, dies (Emmanuel, *Israélites de Salonique*, 184). Carmoly places her death after 1572, which he cites as the date of M.A.'s death (*Famille Almosnino*, 16). For the epitaph on her headstone, see Carmoly (*Famille Almosnino*, 17); Emmanuel avers the elegy was catalogued by Neubauer-Cowley, *Catalogue* (no. 2000, p. 167b) at the Bodleian Library (*Israélites de Salonique*, 184 n. 60). Don Joseph Nasi and Doña Gracia visit Salonika. Joseph marries his cousin Reyna.
1556	27 January: M.A. completes *Pne Moše* (Emmanuel, *Israélites de Salonique*, 180).
1558	*Pne Moše*. Steinschneider indicates it was printed by Simon Almosnino in 1584 (*Hebräische Übersetzungen*, 215), but Emmanuel claims it was never printed. Graetz cites a 1558 manuscript (as does Ben-Menahem, "Bibliography"), but observes that M.A. already quoted from it in a 1552 sermon ("Moses Almosnino," 31 n. 14). Finally, Carmoly claims it was composed between 1546 and 1553 in Pelestria (*Famille Almosnino*, 12), and cites a manuscript version at the Bodleian (19).
1559	In December Doña Gracia establishes *Leviat Ḥen* synagogue for Portuguese Marranos. M.A. becomes rabbi of *Leviat Ḥen* (later renamed *Kahal Kadoš Yaḥia*). He serves as one of a delegation to Constantinople (Emmanuel, *Israélites de Salonique*, 211). M.A. frequents Belvedere.
1561	Plague year.

INTRODUCTION

1562   M.A. writes *Regimiento de la vida* (*Ha-N^ehagat ha-Hayyim*). Graetz cites *Pirke Mose* (fol. 27a) for the date of composition ("Moses Almosnino," 32 n. 16). M.A. mentions in the introduction that while writing *RV* he was also proofreading *Pne Mose*. Carmoly claims that M.A. was living at the time in Langaza, a village near Salonika, and that *Pirke Mose* was written there (*Famille Almosnino*, 12).

1563   M.A.'s father dies. Carmoly cites the date as 30 Kislev 5323 (25 December 1562) (*Famille Almosnino*, 10 n. 1).

Pirke Mose and *Tefillah le-Mose* are printed in Salonika by Yosef Yaabeṣ (5323). Emmanuel notes similarities with *RV* (*Israélites de Salonique*, 179). Graetz cites 1546 as the date of composition of *Tefillah le-Mose* ("Moses Almosnino," 31 n. 15); Emmanuel claims it was written in Pelestria (*Israélites de Salonique*, 179).

1564   Plague. Four of M.A.'s commentaries on the Five Scrolls are written in Levadi (Emmanuel, *Israélites de Salonique*, 179 n. 44). *RV* and *TS* are printed in Salonika by Yosef Yaabeṣ (5324). Carmoly claims both were written in Langaza (*Famille Almosnino*, 12).

1565   M.A. serves as one of the delegates to Constantinople to procure confirmation of the 1537 privileges and tax exemptions. Carmoly states that M.A. was chosen to lead the deputation owing to his scholarly reputation (*Famille Almosnino*, 13).

1566   3 February. M.A. travels to Constantinople by way of Brusa and Kara Hissar with R. Yaakov ben Naḥmias and R. Moše Baruk. The former dies in Brusa; the latter perishes en route to Constantinople. Gravely ill, M.A. forms a ten-person negotiating committee. In May, before the Salonika entourage arrives in Constantinople, Süleyman leaves at the head of a Hungarian campaign. M.A. is resident at Belvedere 5 September: Süleyman's death leads to the succession of Selim II.

1567   Plague. 24 April: M.A. completes *Extremos y grandezas de Constantinopla* (Emmanuel, *Israélites de Salonique*, 182). M.A. follows the court to Adrianople.

1568   Plague. 25 January: the seventh attempt at negotiation is successful. The Salonika community's payment of 300,000 *aspris* commutes all extraordinary taxes (15 February), and the ram tax of 1546 is rescinded. The Salonika community is now considered a *müsellimlik,* which Roth describes as "a self-governing political entity, independent of the city in which it was situated" (*House of Nasi*, 2:168). There is disagreement among historians as to what the Salonika community paid for and why.

28 (26?) February: M.A.'s sermon in the Talmud Torah recounts the entourage's travails in Constantinople. Among the twelve persons instrumental to its success, M.A. counts Joseph Nasi first and foremost (Carmoly, *Famille Almosnino*, 14).

23 March: In order to raise funds to pay the *müsellimlik* tax, the Council of

INTRODUCTION

Synagogues accords a ten-year tax on all Jewish merchandise embarking or disembarking from the port of Salonika, including previously exempted items (Emmanuel, *Israélites de Salonique,* 212–16).

1569. *Migdal Oz.* Emmanuel cites a manuscript, MS Parma R. 1218, and claims it was composed before 19 January 1556 for a *marrano,* Isaac, who had come to Salonika (*Israélites de Salonique,* 180). Emmanuel erroneously considered it lost. Doña Gracia and her son Samuel Nasi die.

1570 M.A. begins a commentary on the Song of Solomon (Emmanuel, *Israélites de Salonique,* 179 n. 44).

11 August: M.A.'s mother dies (Carmoly, 10).

18 August (5 Elul 5330): M.A. delivers elegy for his mother (Carmoly, *Famille Almosnino,* 10 n. 3).

1572 Plague. *Yede Mośe* is printed in Salonika by Yosef Yaabeṣ (5332). Carmoly reports another edition at Venice by Daniel Zaneti in 1597 (*Famille Almosnino,* 18). Emmanuel confirms both editions (*Israélites de Salonique,* 178 n. 43). Carmoly claims that M.A. traveled to Constantinople on behalf of the Salonika community (for unknown reasons), and died there (16).

1573 Earthquake in Salonika. M.A. travels to Constantinople (Emmanuel, *Israélites de Salonique,* 184).

1579 M.A. travels to Constantinople (Goodblatt [*Samuel de Medina,* 17] cites Emmanuel who located the journey in 1573)?

2 August: Joseph Nasi dies.

2 October: Samuel de Medina refers to M.A. as deceased (Emmanuel, *Israélites de Salonique,* 84 n. 63).

1588 *Meammeṣ Koaḥ,* a collection of twenty-eight sermons, is printed in Venice by Jean de Gara.

Emmanuel notes that it was edited by M.A.'s sons and corrected by his nephews Isaac and Mośe Garçon (*Israélites de Salonique,* 179). Carmoly reports the prologue and epilogue by Simon Almosnino (*Famille Almosnino,* 19).

1638 *Extremos y grandezas de Constantinopla* is printed in Madrid.

1729 A Latin-letter edition of *Regimiento de la vida* is printed by Semuel Mendes de Sola, Joseph Siprut Gabay, and Jeudah Piza in Amsterdam (5489).

1734 A Latin-letter edition of *Tratado de los suenyos* is printed in Amsterdam by Semuel Mendes de Sola and Abraham Mendez Chumazero (5494) under the title *Transformaciones de Morpheo.*

INTRODUCTION

APPENDIX III:
COMPLETE WORKS

n.d.   Rešit Da'at. Salonika: n.p.
n.d.   Tikkun Soferim. Livorno: Yaakov Nunes Weis, 1789.
n.d.   Tešuvot.
n.d.   Tosafot Beur al Divrei ha-Raba (Abraham Ibn Ezra).

Manuscripts

1546.   Beth Elohim.
1546.   Beth Elohim ve-Ša'ar ha-Šamayyim.
1551.   Ša'ar ha-Šamayyim.
1558.   Pne Moše.
1567.   Crónica de los reyes otomanos.
1569.   Migdal Oz.
1574.   Tefillah le-Moše.
1582.   Piruš al Piruš ha-Torah le-Rashi.
1582.   Tosafot le-Piruš ha-Rabbi Abraham Ibn' Ezra le-Torah.
15th cent. Derašot.
1630.   Mebo' be-Astrologiah be-Sefaradit.
16th cent.–17th cent.   Kibuṣ Ša'alot ve-Tešuvot ve-Pesuqim me-Ḥokme ha-Mizraḥit.
17th cent. Tikkun soferim.
n.d.   Ḥibbur betaḵonah.

Lost Works

Before 1563.   Iggeret ha-Nefeš (cited in Pirke Moše, fol. 37b).
Before 1563.   Iggeret Teḥiyat ha-Metim (cited in Pirke Moše, fol. 37a).
n.d.   Deruše ha-Našim (cited in Meammeṣ Koaḥ, fol. 134a) given to Doña Gracia in Adrianople.
1568.   Al Binyan ha-Ḥalirut ("Muslimlik") le-Yehudei Saloniki, concerning the events of 1565 through 1568 (cited in Meammeṣ Koaḥ, fol. 5b).
Before 1564.   Piruš al Sefer ha-Š'maa ha-Taba'i (cited in Ha-N'hagat ha-Ḥayyim, fol. 133a).
Before 1572.   Piruš al Tehilim (cited in Yede Moše, fol. 92a).
Before 1563.   Piruš al Mišle (cited in Tefillah le-Moše, fol. 17a).
Before 1563.   Piruš al Iyob (cited in Tefillah le-Moše, fol. 28a).

INTRODUCTION

Before 1563. *Torat Moše* (cited in introduction of *Pirke Moše,* and *Tefillah le-Moše,* fol. 11b).

Carmoly reports that certain decisions of M.A. are to be found in the responsa of Samuel de Medina and Samuel Kelai (*Famille Almosnino,* 19). Emmanuel cites commentaries on different passages of Talmud, Rashi, and Rabbenu Nissim mentioned by M.A.'s sons in *Meammeṣ Koaḥ* (*Israélites de Salonique,* 179). Ben-Menahem confirms the existence of a commentary on Rashi in manuscript. Emmanuel cites a third Spanish title, a letter on the Resurrection, which must be *Iggeret Teḥiyat ha-Metim,* composed before 19 January 1556 at the request of a Marrano named Isaac. Emmanuel reports that it is mentioned in *Meammeṣ Koaḥ,* sermon 28 (*Israélites de Salonique,* 180). Bnaya confirms the Spanish letter but cites sermon 27 (fol. 214a) as his source for knowledge of it ("Moses Almosnino," 98).

Emmanuel observes that M.A. wrote poetry, specifically an epitaph for Simḥa now at the Bodleian (Neubauer-Cowley, *Catalogue,* no. 2000 [p.167b]), and a *Tehina* for Yom Kippur (*Israélites de Salonique,* 184). Carmoly (*Famille Almosnino,* 17) mentions the same epitaph among a collection of poems subscribed by Jacob Ibn Naḥmias that he discussed in *Revue Orientale* 1 (1848), which latter I have not seen. Finally, Davidson mentions three lost volumes of responsa from M.A. (*Abraham Shalom*).

Moše ben Baruḵ Almosnino

Regimiento de la vida
Tratado de los suenyos

(SALONIKA, 1564)

{{RMK: Oppenheimer 4°.969.}
⟨fol. 1a⟩

SEFER HA-NᵉHAGAT HA-ḤAYYIM

{RMK: Hebrew text lines 1–12.}

1.1: Book of the Regimen of Living

ll.2–5: Written by the wise, perfect, and comprehensive, our honored master and teacher, R. Moše Almosnino, may God preserve him, at the request of the young and wise, to establish a dwelling of righteous conduct for his nephew, the son of his sister and companion, because of his love for him, to show him the way he will go (Prov. 22.6), to be lighted by the light of the eternal life : And the tree of wisdom will be known throughout the earth and the great strength and essence and secrets of political wisdom [ethics] in the midst of His paradise : As a table set before him (Ps. 23.5) :

ll.6–12: And accompanying it after is another book, of small quantity but high quality, without prolixity composed by the author at the request of the blessed minister don Yosef Nasi who is exalted above all : "Its foundation is on the holy mountains", (Ps. 87.1) the existence and essence of dreams recorded in true writing [prophetic biblical dreams], and the remaining [ordinary] dreams of human beings, in [them] wisdom, and the knowledge of the righteous learned from them. And the cause of their existence and their righteousness endures forever : And to know the correct interpretations by valuable investigations and explain many writings accompanying them [the interpretations and investigations] and the sentences [*midrashim*] of Razal [our Sages of blessed memory] : "His words shall distill as the dew" [alters Deut. 32.2, "his" for "my"]. "His polishing was as of a sapphire" (Lam. 4:7). And at the end, the foreign words scattered throughout are explained. And his study is completed by what he wrote at the beginning, the indices for both [*RV* and *TS*]. His handiwork was blessed by the teaching of their ways. So that every diligent reader will quickly run through them.

Book of the Regimen of Living ⟨fol. 1a–1b⟩

ll.13–25:

LIBRO 'ENTITULADO REĞIMYENTO DELA VIDA

pudyendośe verdader'a mente lyyamar 'eśpeğo de śabyoś 'i byen aventuradoś konpu'eśto por 'el famoziśimo śabyo k⟨abod⟩ m⟨orenu⟩ ha-Rab Rabbi {RMK: our honored Master and Teacher.} Mošeh Almośnino n"rv {RMK: May God preserve him.} 'a rekerimyento deśu 'intimo kerido 'i śobrino 'enel kual śe kontyene kuanto konbyene para poder byen 'andar toda la ğornada dela vida 'umana śin 'erar konprendyendo 'enel toda la filosofi'a moral muy kopyoza mente

'I śegirśe'a depu'eś de[ ]'el 'otro muy śublimado tratado śobre la 'esensy'a 'i śer deloś śu'enyoś 'i de śuś kauśaś 'i śiknifikasyoneś 'i śolturaś verdaderaś ke tanbyen konpeten 'a 'el reğimyento dela vida : konpu'eśto por 'el meśmo 'aktor 'a rekerimyento del muy 'iluśtre śenyor 'el śenyor don Yosef Naśi' ke 'el Dyo konśerve 'i a'umente śu prośpero 'eśtado am⟨e⟩n :

{RMK: Hebrew text.}

ll.26–28: It was printed with great care in the printing house of the young man Yosef, son of his revered father, the perfectly wise, our honored master and teacher, R. Yiṣḥak, the son of the righteous rabbi, our honored master and teacher, R. Yosef Yaabeṣ, the Preacher, of blessed memory. And it was begun in the month of Elul 5324 from God's Creation [1564 C.E.], may God in His mercy make us worthy to print many other books without end.}

⟨fol. 1b⟩
{HAKᵉDEMAH [INTRODUCTION]

1.1: Said Moše, the son of his revered father, the most exalted and eminent, our honoured rabbi Baruk Almosnino, God and God of our fathers,

1.2: There was upon me a righteous right hand, the rock of my heart and my portion. As a precious son to me who dwells in my tent.

ll.3–8: And in my palace he will feel neither sorrow nor pain, "A wise son makes his father happy" (Prov. 15.20). The son of my sister and companion, "the walls of my heart" (Jer. 4.19), "even my spirit in me I have sought" (Isa. 26.9), may God preserve him, by enquiry and searching, persistently asking me to write straight to true happiness, and because the difficult times frighten me, the heavy obligation of proofreading my long book *Pne Moše* [Face of Moses], and my heart's desire, to study sublime Talmud, I cannot daily [attend] to it. Friends seek my advice, and, moreover, [ask me] to leave my duties, to observe and do the counsel of his [the nephew's] common sense, bound by thick ropes of love of the good [which justifies] what is lacking in my ability :

BOOK OF THE REGIMEN OF LIVING ‹FOL. 1B›

ll.8–11: I removed my coat, the coat of my everyday troubles and obligations, and I responded to his request and his seeking and his wish, knowing that his soul is fastened with love of beauty and intelligence, which is pleasing in the eyes of God and human beings on the face of the earth. "But come what may, I will run" (2 Sam. 18.23) and show him with my pen what is found in my understanding in my hour and season.

ll.11–14: Concerning this, he entreats me, and brings me out from my protected place, my shield and my strength, and my fortress [variation on Ps. 18.2, 144.2], he is strengthened from my strength. My words will be in a foreign language: to study and to teach the work of study on the board of his heart "engraved on the Law of Moses" [variation on Jer. 17.1] "the inheritance of the congregation of praise of Jacob" [variation on Deut. 33.4] "And the rugged shall be made level" (Isa. 40.4) by understanding the intention of the words included "in your sacks" (Gen. 43.23); phrases spoken "by the gate of Bath-rabbim" (Song of Sol. 7.5), and in the courtyards of kings, "and all their encampments" (Num. 31.10), and "the words of the wise, and their dark sayings" (Prov. 1.6).

ll.15–17: And in the eyes of Moše the deed [writing in Spanish] is bad, but there is no comfort in resting from the work [of] God, [to do so would be] contemptible and despised, "everything that was of no account and feeble" (Isa. 15.9), for as strong as death is the love (Song of Sol. 8.6) for my first master [Hebrew], the holy language accustomed to pass my lips.

ll.17–19: Clearly, plainly, written conversations, "the love of thine espousals" (Jer. 2.2), the inward words [?], "And let my name be named in them, and the name of my fathers" (Gen. 48.16). And when I saw him knock with longing at my door, his soul strong [and] in training to seek words of strength, and "this thing that He hath spoken" (Isa. 38.7), I did, "I inclined my heart to perform" (Ps. 119.112) for him, this short book, nothing is lacking from it

ll.20–23: about strength, essence, "the secrets of wisdom" (Job 11.6), and knowledge, and piety, according to his yearning. My heart intends to make suitable in the eyes of all that is fitting, "that I may walk before God" (Ps. 56.14), "[His] compassions fail not" (Lam. 3:33), "And shall make his footsteps a way" (Ps. 85.14). And for the sake of what is good for him and everyone his age,

ll.23–27: at the end of this book is a table explaining all the foreign words scattered in it so that the reader may understand them. Also, I saw and placed it in my heart to open this study with a key to the interpreters' conversations, and the interpretations I mention, biblical phrases, and sentences of Razal: "My speech shall distil as the dew" (Deut. 32.2). And I put in them the secret foundation, the basic meaning, in signed

BOOK OF THE REGIMEN OF LIVING ⟨FOL. 1B–2A⟩

[hewn] judgments, to find words of strength, "Every man with his own standard, according to the ensigns" (Num. 2.2).

l.28: I divided the whole book into three parts.

ll.29–32: In Part One, I explained a short straightforward method of proper conduct for youths and young men to guide them on the way that puts their soul in life (Ps. 66.9), to behave fittingly in ten important matters, in study and in practice : surely [they are] : eating and drinking, sleeping and waking, lying down and getting up, walking and sitting, speaking and silence :

ll.33–34: In accord [with] Moše [Rambam], a careful explanation of proper conduct, unprecedented. In them, the words are set in valuable investigations, and they are "lights in the firmament" (Gen. 1.14), the Divine name is introduced in them, "For they are life unto those who find them" (Prov. 4.22).

ll.35–37: In Part Two, I give an explicit and extensive explanation of the existence and essence of ten ethical virtues, universal in the human species for their benefit and welfare, to keep back their souls "from the pit" (Job 33.18), and diminish the diverse vices that link them to matter : they are courage, temperance, liberality, magnificence and magnanimity, and humility}

⟨fol. 2a⟩
{B
HAKʿDEMAH

ll.1–3: and patience, and affability : and courtesy, and truthfulness : and the suitable conduct for achieving them is explained with new investigations and ancient beliefs, the worm of truth and justice is well trained :

ll.4–7: In Part Three, two great virtues which subsume all of the ethical virtues are explained, surely [they are] justice and friendship. Also, five intellectual virtues are explained and they are: science [*daʿat*, first principles], and wisdom [*hokmah*, dialectics], and reason [*sekel*, intelligence; the Beʾur glosses it as 'inteligencia'], and prudence [*tebunah*], and art [*ha-malʾakah*] : by explaining precious and agreeable matters to the finders of knowledge.

l.8: The First Part will be divided into fourteen chapters, excluding the introduction.

ll.9–11: In the introduction, the benefit of conduct for the good in so far as it is good, which everyone desires, is explained with a careful proof, especially for youth and young men in the years of their youth, to settle them on a method for becoming accustomed to good acts

Book of the Regimen of Living ‹fol. 2a›

ll.11–15: that bring them to the intellectual virtues by telling a proverb befitting the true meaning [and] explaining the saying, "Most children take after their mothers", etc. (Exod. R. 7.5), and the sentence, "He who [wishes] to take a wife should inquire about [the character of] her brothers", etc. (Bava Batra 110a, Rashi Exod. 6.23), and Midrash Bereshit, "For the sake of the Torah which is called 'The beginning of His way' (Prov. 8.22)", etc. (Rashi Gen. 1.1), and the saying: "Let a man always sell all he has and marry the daughter of a scholar", etc. (Pesaḥim 49ab).

ll.16–20: In Chapter One, the great benefits to be drawn by young men from the company of those who honor and esteem perfect men, and men who draw near to God in everything they turn to, will be explained. And in it the famous doubt concerning why good things touch the wicked in this world and misery and chastisements touch the righteous (Seneca, *On Providence* I.1; Ralbag Job 4.26); the essential, ancient, and noted complaint voiced unanimously by the prophets and the sages, will be completely refuted

ll.20–22: by explaining the valuable judgments of the wise Seneca, and of Alexander the Macedonian, and other scholars of ethics, with fitting proverbs, corresponding in every way, that annul the aforementioned doubt. And the sentence [*mishnah*], "Who is worthy of honor? He who respects his fellow-men", etc. (Avot 4.1) is explained.

ll.23–25: Chapter Two discusses what remains of the aforementioned doubt, if good and bad things come because of Providence, and even more so if they come because of the constellations, it does not confirm the doubt, but it is annulled by the principle written in the previous chapter :

ll.25–30: And it discusses explicitly into how many different species and categories good and bad are divided, and for which of them the aforementioned doubt is necessary. And it mentions wonderful proverbs and valuable sentences spoken between honored scholars of ethics that are very helpful for understanding the meaning of this lesson: And the midrash on the verse: "The Lord trieth the righteous (Ps. 11.5) this pot [allusion to Jer. 18.4–6]", etc. {RMK: Ps. 11 treats the issue of God punishing the wicked.}; and a Razal saying: "the death of the righteous [is conducive to procuring] atonement", etc. (Moed Katan 28a); and the sentence of Raba [one of the Tanaaim] in Moed Katan "[Length of] life, children and sustenance depend not on merit", etc. (Moed Katan 28a) are discussed at length.

ll.31–35: Chapter Three explains the allegory [*mashal*] that Rambam, of blessed memory, mentions in *MN*, part three, chapter 51 {RMK: How the Perfect Worship God; those with their backs turned towards the king's palace, etc., and those who enter the palace and can stand before the king.} regarding those who possess truth and the level of those who attain to unity with God [so] that its meaning is established properly, and the complaint the Ḥasidim level against him, that he put the Talmudim [Tanaaim and Amoraim] on a lower level than the philosophers [Beth Yosef 'Oraḥ Ḥayyim, siman 181], Heaven forbid. And there is another good counsel for youth and young men, to show them a method for putting their soul in eternal life through the moral instruction of the ancients, to train them in good actions. And the teaching of Razal, "Happy is he who comes hither with his learning in his hand" (Pesaḥim 50a, Moed Katan 28a, Ketubot 76b, Bava Batra 10b) will be explained.}

⟨fol. 2b⟩
{HAKᶜDEMAH

ll.1–4: Chapter Four discusses a careful proof [of] the proper conduct for all men, and especially for youth and young men, regarding food, with all the conditions necessary for the perfection of the soul and the health of the body, and makes clear Rambam's meaning in *Ha-Yad* [*Mishneh Torah*] in the chapter on the regimens of health, and explains clearly Ibn Sina's meaning in the *Canon* about this. And the saying, "If three have eaten at a table", etc. (Avot 3.4) will be explained.

ll.5–9: Chapter Five discusses at length the proper conduct for drinking water and wine during and after a meal, and the benefit actualized from it for the perfection of the soul and the health of the body for all men, and especially for youth and young men, by explaining Ibn Sina's meaning in the *Canon,* in the specific chapter on the regimen of water and wine, etc. And a Razal saying, "Always [it is better that] a man urinate before a hundred than drink in front of one", etc. (*Otsar Hamidrashim,* Amud 27, p. 56), and the sentence, "[There is] no invitation in water", etc. (Rashi Moed Katan 6b) are explained.

ll.10–16: Chapter Six discusses a careful proof of the essence of sleep, and the cause of its existence. And it also makes clear the cause of the formation of rain, dew, snow, ice, hail, lightning, thunder, comet, and an owner of a tail [a comet], and the cause of winds and earthquakes will be explained : And the existence and essence of each one is explained correctly according to Aristotle's opinion. And it discusses the meanings and sayings he wrote in *Meteorologica,* and *On Sleeping and Waking, On Sense and Sensible Objects* : and *On the Soul* : and *Physics,* a proof proper for a true understanding of his interpretation of them :

ll.17–20: Chapter Seven discusses further the essence of sleep, expressly the causes that compel sleep and the proper conduct regarding sleep and waking for the soul's benefit and for the body's health: And it discusses the manner of the perception of ideas by the external senses, from which the imagination conceives the imagined forms by means of the common faculty :

BOOK OF THE REGIMEN OF LIVING ‹FOL. 2B›

ll.20–27: And the manner of unity of the intellect [*sekel, intellectus*] and the intellectual [*maskil, ens intelligens*] and the intelligible [*muskal, idea*] is made clear by explaining the sayings of RAV the teacher [Rambam], of blessed memory, who discussed this at length and in detail in Part One, chapter 68 of his worthy book {RMK: *MN* Pt.1 chap. 68 On the Terms : *Intellectus,* the *Intelligens* and the *Intelligible*} and what he wrote concerning the regimen of health : And Aristotle's reasoning on this in *On Sleep and Waking* : and *On Sense and Sensible Objects,* and *Nicomachean Ethics* : And the statement of Abukrat [Hippocrates] in Part Two of the *Aphorisms* : And Galyeno's [Galen's] statement in Part Two of the *Introduction to Knowledge* [*Ars Parva?*], and Ibn Sina's statement in Book One, and the sentence of Abuḥamid [al-Ghazzali] on the divineness in all the mentioned studies, all of which are very valuable sentences : And in it [chap. seven] a Razal saying on the verse: "[And skillful in knowledge and discerning in thought,] and such as had ability to stand [in the king's palace]", etc. (Daniel 1.4), "they restrained themselves from (levity, conversation, and) sleep", etc. (Sanhedrin 93b), and the saying: "Sleep is one-sixtieth part of death" (Berakot 57b) will be explained :

ll.28–34: Chapter Eight makes clear the proper conduct concerning lying down and rising up during the day and at night for everyone, for the soul's perfection and the body's health, especially for youth and young men, the benefit of proper conduct for their studies. And a careful proof concerning the manner and order of lying down at night according to the opinion of the physicians is made clear. And a difficulty is explained, Rambam's, of blessed memory, meaning in *Mishneh Torah* concerning the regimen of health, where it seems he differs with the physicians, all his opinion in that same chapter will be understood [i.e. he will reconcile Rambam's position with that of the physicians] by understanding Ibn Sina's meaning in the third *ofan* (Bk. I, *ofan* [thesis, saying] 3, doctrine 2, chap. 7) concerning the regimen of health, explicitly, a right description [shows] that their opinions on this are all in accord : And a Razal saying (Sukkah 52a, Sanhedrin 99b, Rashi Shevu'oth 3b) on the verse: "Woe unto them that draw iniquity with cords of vanity", etc. (Isa. 5.18) will be explained.

ll.35–37: Chapter Nine points out the proper conduct for every perfect man, especially for youth and young men, to guide them on the right way all men [are to] choose for themselves regarding sitting and walking, resting and rising, with proverbs befitting the intention. And a careful proof about}

BOOK OF THE REGIMEN OF LIVING ‹FOL. 3A›

‹fol. 3a›
{G
HAKᶜDEMAH
ll.1–5: the proper conduct for youth and young men in the company of older and more important men. And the conduct of a son with his father and with his rabbi in their walking and sitting, and at the time of prayer, and when entering the bathhouse (Rambam *Hilkot Talmud Torah,* chap. 5, Halakah 6 and Rashi Talmud Berakot 41b), in accordance with the Razal's opinion in all respects : And it explains a Razal saying: "Idleness leads to dullness [idiocy]", etc. (Ketubot 59b), and their saying: "The old scholars, the older they grow, the more clear-minded they become in their judgments", etc. (Kinim 25a, Shabbat 152a), and they say: "The ignorant old men, the older they become, the more unbalanced they become in their judgments", etc. (Kinim 25a, Shabbat 152a).

ll.6–8: Chapter Ten explains the proper conduct for perfect men, and especially youth and young men who have begun the study of speaking and keeping silent, and the proper time for speaking and the proper [time] for being silent, according to the place,

ll.8–15: and according to the quality of the matter, with other necessary conditions for behaving as necessary in each one. And the dignity of truth and the absurdity of the lie are discovered and shown in wonderful proverbs and correct arguments useful for uprightness, keeping oneself away from deceit and lying. And it discusses wise Socrates' saying, in the story of what happened to him in Athens when they chastised him with whips, from which it will seen that punishment meted out justly is more painful than one meted out unjustly; this is a valuable investigation having reasons for both. And it makes clear a Razal saying: "The seal of God is the truth", etc. (Sanhedrin 94b), and the saying: "There is no hero like the pure [without sin] and no weak [one] like the sinner", etc. [source ?].

ll.16–18: Chapter Eleven addresses at length the conduct of speaking and silence according to the place, time, and subject to be discussed. It mentions excellent proverbs and valuable stories in accord with this [subject] in every respect,

ll.18–21: things that happened among ancient scholars and sages about the matter of speech and silence, that will be very helpful placed as a sign directly before them [youth and young men]. And it mentions the excellence of brevity in writing and speaking, especially for the perfect [ones] from whose mouth and writing is recognized a definition of their perfection and virtue.

ll.22–24: Chapter Twelve further explains the proper conduct for youth and young men in choosing good and hating evil by a related valuable parable concerning a perfect man who dies young, teaching them to put their soul in eternal life : And it will also become clear that existence is infinite.

ll.25–30: It is divided into three parts and different times. The first existence is this world until the day of death. And the second is the next world, which is the world of the souls, until the resurrection. And the third is the time of the resurrection until infinity. And every one of them is called [a] day, as will be explained from the Torah and the Prophets with a related proof. And these sayings are explained: a Razal saying: "In the future world there is no eating nor drinking [nor propagation nor business nor jealousy nor hatred nor competition,] but the righteous sit", etc. (Berakot 17a); and the midrash: "The Lord knoweth the days of them that are without blemish" (Ps. 37.18), "As they are whole [unblemished] {RMK: both honest and complete.} so are their years whole", etc. (Gen. R. 58.1).

ll.30–33: Chapter Thirteen refutes the famous and controversial doubt among scholars, why is the perfect man stricken with woe in half his days, before his natural end arrives, but the wicked have long days upon the earth? And a careful proof is discussed concerning

ll.33–37: how at whatever time a perfect man dies, he dies old and full in years according to the proportion of his achievement, that his achievement is the necessary reckoning of his years, not the time *per se*. And the wicked, even if he lives a thousand years, dies twice before his time, brief in years, far from his achievement. And it discusses how the first existence mentioned in the previous chapter, life in this world, is divided into three different parts. And a Razal saying (Ḥagigah 5a, Rashi Gen. 28) on the verse: "He putteth no trust in His holy ones" (Job 15.15)}

‹fol. 3b›
{HAKᶜDEMAH
ll.1–2: "R. Yoḥannan when he came to the [following] verse, wept", etc. (Ḥagigah 5a), and the interpretation (Shabbat 30b) of the verse: "So I commended mirth", etc. (Eccles. 8.15) — because it has been stated, "Every eating and drinking in Kohelet is eating and drinking of Torah", etc. (Rashi Eccles. 8.15) — will be discussed with a careful proof.

ll.3–11: Chapter Fourteen explains an important related question and a valuable investigation into good reason, rational knowledge, and natural science: The natural cause for why it seems to everyone that the past is better than the present, even though the past was worse than the present. And it is pointed out that this [misapprehension] is not true, only temporal goods and physical pleasures [seemed better in the past] because they are material and [subjects of] the external senses, but not for intellectual matters. And from this will be explained the reason why as a man grows day to day he lacks happiness, and why he will be happier in spring than in any other season of the year : and why on a clear day than on a cloudy one, and why during the day more than at night, by explaining other valuable details according to Nature : And a Razal saying: "The eye and the heart are two agents of sin", etc. (Num. R. 10.2) will be explained.

1.12: The Second Part Will Be Divided Into Twenty Chapters.

ll.13–20: Chapter One discusses a careful proof for the second position in a man's life, the position of walking in the Torah of Ha-Shem [God], after they [men] are perfect in all the details explained in the previous part [Part One] and desire the good in so far as it is good *per se* {RMK: they desire what is good by reason of its goodness}, and then they themselves will be gladdened in their completeness and perfection: "But as for such as turn aside unto their crooked ways" (Ps. 125.5) "Their perverseness will chastise them" [akin with Shabbat 88b], "But envy is the rotteness of the bones" (Prov. 14.30) : And three false opinions found among unbelievers and sceptics concerning choice and free will are discussed : The first sect believes human actions follow [are determined by] the constellation at the time of birth, and man has no free will to do something not necessitated by the constellation.

ll.21–22: The second sect believes His knowledge, may He be blessed, is compelling and binding, and it follows logically that there is no possibility that human action [is] other than what He, may He be blessed, knows, and this is the famous and ancient doubt concerning His knowledge, may He be blessed :

ll.23–28: And the third is the sect of the Lutherans which came into existence in our time. They believe that a man is compelled in his actions because the object and the perception of the concrete drive the perceiver to those actions, just like irrational animals : And a careful proof dispels the doubt concerning His knowledge, may He be blessed, and will be explained with an extensive explanation, with an awesome and wonderful simile in which the doubt is annulled in its principle in accordance with the opinion of Rav the teacher [Rambam], of blessed memory, properly explaining his reasoning in part three, chapter nineteen of his book, about which many were confused.

ll.28–31: Chapter Two makes clear everything necessary for refuting the first opinion: "And every tongue that shall rise against thee in judgment thou shalt condemn" (Isa. 54.17) them from their beginning to their end according to writers and books : And the way the Divine Emanation is emanated upon human intellect will be explained with a wonderful analogy, corresponding in all respects, that compares the emanation and the object of emanation with the light of the sun

BOOK OF THE REGIMEN OF LIVING ‹FOL. 3B–4A›

ll.31–36: and the sense of sight : And it discusses a profound study on divinity: how does the Prime Mover, may His Name be blessed, participate in human actions, as He is the first cause of motion [logically first]. And regarding evil transitory actions, how His existence, may He be blessed, will be conceived [represented to the mind], and their [evil actions] principal cause and actualization [is] man, Heaven forbid that He do wickedness or it result from Him: And this is a very valuable investigation and it will be explained extensively so that no difficulty remains : And it is made clear how sinners are divided into three different species}

‹fol. 4a›
{D
{HAK^eDEMAH
ll.1–3: but the good and perfect are one species always : And a Razal saying: "If a man comes to purify himself support is given to him" (Avodah Zarah 55a, Menaḥoth 29b); and the saying: "but if he comes to defile himself", etc. (Avodah Zarah 55a, Menaḥoth 29b); and the saying: "[Everyone] who makes use of the 'light' of the Torah the 'light' of the Torah will revive", etc. (Ketubot 111b) are explained.

ll.4–7: Chapter Three discusses the true reason why the ethical virtues were divided into twelve, following Aristotle's system in *NE*, and why they were no less and no more, expressly, their existence, essence, and universality : And it explains the existence and essence of deficit and surfeit for each one [virtue] with a general method. And the ancient speculations about it [their number] are mentioned : "according to their number, after the ordinance" (Num. 29.18);

l.8: because some [philosophers] divided them into three and not more. And some said that all of them are subsumed in one : Also, it will

ll.9–11: explain how it is necessary to divide them into twelve, following Aristotle's system, according to the divisions of the sensible faculties, which correct them in all their particulars according to the appetitive faculty and the irascible faculty : And virtue is clearly defined, it is a habit [positive property], or attribute resting in the median :

ll.12–16: Chapter Four describes a careful demonstration of courage, which is principal among the moral virtues. And it will be explained how it is divided into three different species (*NE* III.vi.1–viii.9). The first class Razal defined as: "the one who subdues his [evil] impulse", etc. (Avot 4.1, Tamid 32a). The second class is the [one who is] patient in hard trials and sufferings, and the one who faces dangers in the necessary place, and it includes one who suffers without complaint.

ll.16–19: The third is what the public calls a hero, physical heroism, a material body that prevails when a man fights with another, one who rises up against the enemy and defeats him : And in the three of them it is necessary that the perfect median be chosen in accord with the virtue, in all of its conditions, generalities, and particulars.

ll.20–23: And it will be explained how for a perfect man, especially a king who is happy with his army, it is not necessary to risk danger because many people depend upon him : And it discusses the greatness of the virtue of the one who died sanctifying His Name : And explains the midrash: "Who is the one who is great? The one who subdues his passion", etc. (Avoth 4.1, Tamid 32a), and the saying on the verse: "What man is there that is fearful and faint-hearted", etc. (Exod. 20.8), "The one who is afraid of the Mitzvot", etc. (Misudat David Prov. 13.13). And the saying: "When R. Akiba was taken out for execution [...] and while they combed his flesh with iron combs", etc. (Berakot 61b) is discussed at length :

ll.24–26: Chapter Five points out the greatness of courage, and the manner of its proper conduct, all the particularities of its species will be completely explained : And it also discusses the praiseworthy virtue of fitting advice regarding all actions, and especially heroic actions :

ll.26–31: And it points out which action or actions are not subject to counsel [on which no advice can be given]. And it explains five nonessential properties [conditions] that necessarily are found in every action according to the virtue and, explicitly, twelve conditions found in every matter about which counsel can be taken, by making clear the manner by which advice is taken on all matters, in general and in particular : And it considers at length Hillel the elder's saying: "that he was coming from a journey, and he heard a great cry in the city" (Berakot 60a) : And the saying: "that just as one says a blessing for good hap, so he should say one for evil hap", etc. (Berakoth 48b) :

ll.32–35: Chapter Six explains temperance with its two extremes, which are surfeit and deficit, and the proper conduct regarding it. And it will also be made clear that although temperance concerns pleasure and sorrow, it applies particularly to pleasure : And it annuls the opinion of an ancient philosopher who thought that since pleasure

ll.35–37: awakens naturally in man, no error or sin occurs in what a man sinned, because nature is ordered by a Separate Intellect [SEKEL NIVDAL, God] in which no error is imaginable : And [these are] considered the specific objects of each of the five senses, an extensive proof that}

BOOK OF THE REGIMEN OF LIVING ‹FOL. 4B›

‹fol. 4b›
{HAK⁽DEMAH
ll.1–10: temperance pertains to them : And the existence of five generic objects regarding each of the five senses is properly explained, all in accord with Aristotle's opinion in *On Sense and Sensibility,* and in the second [book] of *On the Soul,* explicitly, his intention in what he said: "The sense of touch is a disgrace for us", etc. (*MN* II.36, II.40, III.8, III. 49) {RMK: Maimonides' rendition of *NE* III.x.11 on profligacy}. And it is pointed out that temperance does not pertain to only two senses from the aspect of their essence, touch and taste, but to three others [sight, hearing, and smell] [as well], [although] the praiseworthy virtue of temperance is not in them from the aspect of their essence, but only from the standpoint of their being considered with the two mentioned [touch and taste]. And it is a very wonderful study that explains the matter of the perception of the objects of the senses with a popular saying from Seneca and other sages that agrees with this intention. And it makes clear a Razal saying: "A man will not be familiar with his wife like a cock", etc. (*Hilkot De⁽ot,* chap. 5, halakah 4); and the saying: "There is a small organ in man which satisfies him in his hunger but makes him hunger when satisfied", etc. (Sanhedrin 107a); and they say: "[A man] will not look at her colorful clothes", etc. [source ?]; and they say: "It is allowed to taste the food on [a] fast day" (Berakot 14a) :

ll.11–13: Chapter Seven discusses liberality, which pertains to giving and receiving, and explains the proper conduct in all its conditions : And sixteen nonessential properties necessarily found in liberality are explained at length:

ll.13–17: And on the validity of six assertions it will be explained how liberality, although it concerns giving and receiving, pertains especially to giving, in accord with Aristotle's opinion in book four of *NE,* explicitly his words there and in the third and fifth books, expressly the second and the third nonessential properties. And stories and proverbs from ancient scholars, and the sayings of Seneca and Diogenes in accord with the aforementioned meaning are considered :

ll.18–20: And the [Ra]zal saying on the verse: "And walk in His ways", etc. (Deut. 28.9); "[In] What He [God] is gracious also you", etc. (Ramban Deut. 11.1); and a Razal saying on the verse: "And Jacob was left alone"(Gen. 32.25) which teaches "He remained behind for the sake of some small jars", etc. (Hullin 91a). And the saying: "to the righteous their money is dearer than their body" (Hullin 91a, Rashi Num. 24.16 ?); and the saying: "From Heaven a thing may be given but once; it is never taken away again" [akin with Hullin 25a] will be explained.

ll.21–22: Chapter eight discusses the nonessential properties of liberality's two extremes, ll.22–25: prodigality and meanness, in accord with Aristotle's opinion in

BOOK OF THE REGIMEN OF LIVING ‹FOL. 4B–5A›

the fourth [book] of *NE* (IV.i), explaining his words properly, and the description of the virtue and its extremes [vices] is completed. And a careful demonstration is made that the vice of meanness is worse and more disgraceful than the vice of prodigality, it is more difficult to remove and repair, by explaining the wise Diogenes' wonderful sayings concerning this.

ll.26–32: And it explains the many divisions of meanness, and censures them in detail : And it makes clear that for one who is perfect in liberality, it is necessary to be careful to act liberally for the principle of the good in so far as it is good, and not for the purpose of honor, or to become famous like great [men], [for] that is disgraceful : And a Razal saying about the daughter of Nakdimon ben Gurion with all that happened to her with Raban Yoḥanan ben Zakay, etc. (Ketubot 66b) will be explained, and [Razal] say: "A proverb current in Jerusalem: 'The salt of money is diminution'" (Ketubot 66b) {RMK: "The salt, the means of preservation, of wealth is its diminution" (Jastrow, *Dictionary,* 788)}

ll.30–31: And they say: "In accordance with the camel is the burden", etc. (Ketubot 67a, Sota 13b, Gen. R. 19.1);

l.32: and the saying: "There is to you a man that his money is more dear to him than his soul", etc. (Berakot 61b) {RMK: [. . .] "you loved your wealth (of cattle) more than your souls" (Midrash Tanḥuma Matt. 7, quoted in Jastrow, *Dictionary,* 794)}.

ll.33–37: Chapter Nine explains carefully the existence and the essence of magnificence, and the existence of its two extremes, and the proper conduct regarding it. And its nonessential properties and those of its two extremes are made clear : And the matters that are proper to this virtue, and the difference between this virtue and liberality, since both pertain to giving and receiving there is no division, except that magnificence applies to great matters and giving more than does}

‹fol. 5a›
{H
MAFTEḤOT

ll.1–3: liberality. And it will be mentioned that this virtue's deficit is less bad than the extreme of deficit in liberality. And it makes clear the definition of this virtue in all its details, parts, and extremes in general and specifically :

ll.3–11: Chapter Ten discusses magnanimity and its two extremes, surfeit and deficit. And it explains with a careful and extensive proof how this great virtue includes all of the other ethical virtues, and it concerns great men, and ministers, and important matters, by explaining correctly its definition and the matters which are and are not proper to it, and the difference between it and magnificence, being that

BOOK OF THE REGIMEN OF LIVING ‹FOL. 5A›

both pertain to important matters. And it makes clear ten nonessential properties from those mentioned previously that are found in this great virtue. And a Razal saying: "When Moses was born the whole house was full of light", etc. (Sota 12a); and [Razal] say: "Whoever sacrificed his life on the strict laws", etc. (Tanḥuma Shemot 12?); and the saying: "Those who are insulted but do not insult, hear themselves reviled without answering" (Shabbat 88b) {RMK: Connected in the same paragraph with the verse: "But they who love Him are as the sun when he goeth forth in his might" (Judges 5.31)} will be explained. And the prayer: "Moses was pleased with the gift bestowed on him", etc. (Shabbat 10b).

ll.12–13: Chapter Eleven will explain an extensive proof of fifteen of the aforementioned nonessential properties found in magnanimity and also found in Moses, Our Rabbi, may he rest in peace,

ll.13–17: in complete perfection by explaining Aristotle's saying in *NE*, Bk. IV, in what he mentions about Queen Thetis who asked Jupiter for kindness [charity] because for him she did many manners [and] species of work, etc. (*NE* IV.iii.15–16). And a Razal saying: "Prophecy does not rest except upon the wise, the mighty [heroic], and the rich", etc. (Shabbat 92a, also Rambam *Yesode Ha-Torah* 7a and Miṣudat David, 2 Kings 3.15); and their saying on the verse: " 'which Thou broke' (Exod 34.1) Thou hast done well to break", etc. (Bava Batra 14b, Menaḥot 99b) will be explained.

ll.18–24: Chapter Twelve describes the twenty-five remaining nonessential properties, in them the exact description of this great virtue, its existence, essence, and proper conduct in it, in all of its particularities and generalities and details will be completed, explicitly a definition of truthfulness, [in which] the mouth and the heart are at one: what is in the soul accords with what is outside of the soul. And it discusses how the word "honor" is derived from heaviness, because it is necessary for the honorable to be heavy [deliberate] in his movements. And a Razal saying on the verse: " 'And could not speak peaceably unto him' (Gen. 37.4) from the tribes' disgrace we studied their praise" (Rashi Gen. 37.4). And they [Razal] say that the Psalm, "Who shall sojourn in Thy tabernacle" (Ps. 15.1), was said about Moses our Teacher, may he rest in peace (Makkot 24a) [which] are explained :

ll.25–28: Chapter Thirteen discusses carefully and succinctly humility, which is related to magnanimity as liberality is to magnificence in the giving of money; explicitly, it points out the two extremes, surfeit and deficit, and the proper conduct in humility to avoid them.

ll.29–33: Chapter Fourteen deals carefully with patience, which Razal call modesty, expressly its two extremes. And it explains which of the two extremes is more disgraceful and worse, [for] it is necessary to avoid an extreme, explicitly, the sayings

BOOK OF THE REGIMEN OF LIVING ⟨FOL. 5A–5B⟩

of Rambam, of blessed memory, in his commentary on *Pirke Avot*, "Be exceedingly humble of spirit", etc. (Avot 4.4), which apparently differs with Aristotle's opinion. And it mentions two wonderful nonessential properties which are necessarily found in the patient [man]. And it points out

ll.34–37: in accordance with this the sayings of the ancient scholars {RMK: the sayings agree with the idea of the two nonessential properties necessarily found in the patient man.}, and the wise Seneca's opinion will be refuted in arguments and method, necessary, sound, and good, against his position, that anger is unnecessary from any standpoint or at any time. And it discusses the saying of R. Levitas, of Yavneh, who said in Avot: "Be exceedingly lowly of spirit", etc. (Avot 4.4); and the saying: "The one who comes under the influence of anger comes under the influence of mistaken judgment", etc. (Rashi Num. 31.21)}

⟨fol. 5b⟩
{MAFTEHOT

ll.1–9: Chapter Fifteen points out the varieties of anger found in human beings in accordance with the varieties of their temperament, according to their dominant humor, and mentions proverbs that agree in all aspects with this study, and deeds that passed between ancient scholars that agree with its intention. From all of them the greatness of the praiseworthy virtue of patience will be discovered and shown: And humility is "Comely as Jerusalem" [Song of Sol. 6.4] : And a Razal saying on the verse: "Because I feared the great multitude", etc. (Job 31.34); "When Job heard that the Chaldeans put three chiefs he moved to war", etc. (Targ. Job 10.17) it will be explained carefully: And the saying: "He who in his anger tears his garment or breaks his vessels, let him be in your sight like an idolator", etc. (Shabbat 105b) : And the saying: "Wherever you find [in the Scriptures] the power of the Holy One, blessed be He, you also find his gentleness mentioned" (Megillah 41a); and the saying: "Every man in whom is haughtiness of spirit is fit to be hewn down like an Asherah" (Sota 5a); and the saying: "Every man in whom is haughtiness of spirit, his dust will not be disturbed [for the Resurrection]" (Sota 5a).

ll.10–12: Chapter Sixteen carefully discusses mercy according to what is necessarily included in justice, as will be mentioned in Part Three of this book :

ll.13–22 And it explains how mercy differs from patience, despite the appearance of being included in patience : And it explains who is the more praiseworthy in perfect patience: whether the red [choleric] or the white [phlegmatic]: And assertions and reasons for both sides are considered, and the famous question is answered clearly: Who is more praiseworthy, the completely righteous man or the repentant? : And my

Book of the Regimen of Living ‹fol. 5b›

own valuable investigation {RMK: Almosnino's sole refererence to himself in this introduction}, into whether the repentant sinner, of whom Razal said: "The one who subdues" (Avot 4.1), is the more worthy, political philosophers mention him, or the perfectly righteous man {RMK: Rambam states there is a general agreement among philosophers that it is the virtuous man who is better ["*Eight Chapters,*" chap. 6]} is carefully discussed and demonstrated : And true assertions and proofs are considered that a repentant sinner is also a thoroughly righteous man by necessity, [for] after he repents he does not suppress : By the explanation of a difficulty in the words of Rambam, of blessed memory, in chapter six of the *Eight Chapters,* introduction to Avot, and in chapter seven of the Laws of Repentance, where it appears he contradicts himself in those two places. And it is a valuable and ordered study explained with a careful proof in accordance with the truth in all respects : And it explains a Razal saying, "R. Abbahu said: In the place where penitents stand even the wholly righteous cannot stand", etc. (Berakot 34b).

ll.22–24: And another very deep saying of the same R. Abbahu: "From the beginning of the world's creation the Holy One, blessed be He, foresaw the deeds of the righteous and the deeds of the wicked", etc. (Gen. R. 2.5).

ll.24–29: Chapter Seventeen discusses affability and courtesy necessary with interlocutors, and expressly the two extremes : And it mentions how and in what affability differs from friendship [love] : And explains four nonessential properties that are necessary for one who is affable in alliance with friends [loved ones]; he is chosen by his fellows because of his speech [wittiness], and it is a great virtue and it is a great necessity in alliances between friends [loved ones] :

ll.30–35: Chapter Eighteen makes clear a proof for the praiseworthiness of truthfulness, that it is proper and much required for human beings in their alliances, speech, deeds, and negotiations : And it explains how it concerns speech especially, also thoughts and deeds; truth and justice pertain to all three. And carefully explains this virtue's two extremes, explicitly defining the median between them necessary for discerning it :

ll.35–37: And this discussion mentions valuable and beneficial investigations : And makes clear how the extreme of surfeit is divided into three different species : And the extreme of deficit [is divided] into two species, and both [surfeit and deficit] are equally bad, differing only in more and less : And it discusses with a proper and correct explanation of how hypocrisy shows}

Book of the Regimen of Living ‹fol. 6a›

‹fol. 6a›
{V
MAFTEHOT
l.1: that what is not in them [the two extremes] is, in truth, one of the species of the extremes of truthfulness :

ll.2–10: Chapter Nineteen makes clear a proper and complete description for discerning truthfulness, explicitly two valuable studies that consider at length the ancient scholars' intentions. The first, to know if this virtue pertains to the ethical virtues and is to be included under the perfection of the practical intellect : or if it belongs to the intellectual virtues and is the object of the theoretical intellect; there are reasons for both [positions], as will be made clear with a long explanation. The second [is] if it is necessary to alter, or lie, or deal falsely at any time for any cause. For about this also there are reasons for both [positions] : Expressly, the first study will discuss into how many different categories and different species truth is apportioned; it is divided into five different species. And the second study discusses into how many different categories and species the falsehood and the lie are divided;

ll.10–11: they are divided into twelve different species; to comprehend their truth [to gain a profound understanding] properly so that a man will guard himself from them :

ll.12–16: And in it are explained a Razal saying: "One may modify a statement in the interests of peace" (Yevamot 65b); and the saying: "This one declares forbidden what the others allow" (Ḥagigah 3b); "These and these are the words of the living EloKim [God]", etc. (Eruvin 13b, Gittin 6b); and Razal sayings: "How does one dance before the bride? Beth Shammai say: 'The bride as she is' ", etc. "And Beth Hillel say: 'Beautiful and graceful bride' ", etc. (Ketubot 16b–17a); and a Razal study [midrash] on the verse: "And the sea returned to its strength when the morning appeared" (Exod. 14.27) {RMK: The midrash may be Gen. R. 5.5, on miracles generally, which names Hananiah, Mishael, and Azariah, mentioned below; Almosnino does not repeat Razal's interpretation}, an extensive and very subtle explanation, and the saying: "the condition the Holy One, blessed be He, made with it at its creation", etc. (Exod. R. 21.6)

ll.17–18: Chapter Twenty discusses at length [how] affability is necessary, and how to conduct oneself properly, discussing properly its two extremes, surfeit and deficit.

ll.19–22 And the manner for finding the median between them [extremes], which is the chosen [way] as [in] the other ethical virtues, by explaining two nonessential properties found regarding this virtue : And a Razal saying: "When the Rabbis became

BOOK OF THE REGIMEN OF LIVING ‹FOL. 6A–6B›

exhausted from studying they were accustomed to engage in entertaining conversation" (Shabbat 30b, see Maimonides, "*Eight Chapters,*" 72 n. 4); and the saying: "Even the ordinary talk of scholars needs studying" (Avoda Zarah 19b); and the study: "Laughter and lightheadedness", etc. (Berakot 31a, Shabbat 30b, Pesaḥim 117a) :

1.23: The Third Part will be divided into thirteen chapters.

ll.24–28: Chapter One discusses, in a general way, justice according to Aristotle's definition in chapter five of *NE,* expressly, to which actions justice pertains on the material level [natural laws]. And it explains the wise Cicero's division of all actions regarding which there may be justice: three divisions, according to the division, laws necessary for man to do them and live by them, [that is] laws necessary

ll.29–33: according to nature, natural laws : And laws according to political custom [ethics] : and laws according to religious [legal] laws : And, explicitly, how many other minute divisions are subsumed under each of three divisions mentioned. And it also discusses Aristotle's division of the actions subject to justice, and he too said there are three divisions: religious [legal] justice : And distributive : And corrective (*NE* V.) : And all are explained carefully and properly with all their divisions :

ll.34–35: Chapter (Three) [Two] discusses at length a second matter that it is necessary to consider concerning justice: the form of its proportion, and how to discern the median between its two extremes,}

‹fol. 6b›
{MAFTEHOT
ll.1–10: which is a difficult concept : And regarding this, an understanding of Aristotle's intention in the fifth book of *NE* will be discussed: the significance of this great virtue's two extremes seems not to be what we assume. Aristotle's reasoning is confirmed as being in accordance with our postulates, a true and correct affirmation : And the meaning and general intention of Rambam, may his memory be a blessing, regarding the tenets of the Commandments will be explained : And it discusses a valuable related study about the beatings mentioned in the Torah — we distinguish the one who harms from the one who is harmed — and on the issue of beating we do not compare them : And why it is not an eye for an eye [in] substance, but the value of an eye, by explaining Rambam's meaning in Part Three of the *MN,* chapter 41, that by correct natural and theological arguments monetary equivalence is necessary : And it will discuss a Razal saying: "Every judge who judges a true judgment according to its truth even for a single hour, the Writ gives him credit as though he had become a partner to the Holy One, blessed be He", etc. (Shabbat 10a) : And the saying: "An

BOOK OF THE REGIMEN OF LIVING ⟨FOL. 6B⟩

eye for an eye (Exod. 21.24, Lev. 24.20) 'Eye for eye' means pecuniary compensation", etc. (Bava Kamma 84a). And the saying: "ALL DEPENDS ON THE STATUS OF THE OFFENDER AND THE OFFENDED", etc. (Ketubot 40a, Bava Kamma 83b, Bava Kamma 86a).

ll.11–12: Chapter Three will discuss carefully a demonstration of how to take the median in religious justice. In explaining this, it discusses at length
ll.12–22: the matter of the quality of piety, a great virtue involved in religious justice and joined to it, pointing out how to estimate rightly its median according to truth, and its two extremes, explicitly, without difficulty : And it discusses a Razal saying said in many places: "Not because the judgment is this but because the hour needs this" (Yevamot 90b, Sanhedrin 46a); and the saying: " 'According to the law that they shall teach thee' (Deut. 17.11) [Thou shalt not turn aside from] the sentence which they shall declare unto thee to the right hand nor to the left : [...] even if they shall tell you that the right hand is left", etc. (Song of Sol. R. I.2.2); And the saying: "All judgment is judgment for truth", etc. (Shabbat 10a, Megillah 15b, Sanhedrin 7a, Tanhuma Parshat Shoftim, Siman 8); and they say: "It is permitted to desecrate Shabbat (Yoma 83a) for an invalid [sick person] whose life is endangered", etc. (Shabbat 61a), and the saying, it is right "the thing is done even by prominent Jews", etc. (Yoma 84b, Rambam *Hilkot Shabbat* chap. 2, halakah 3; akin to Ramban Gen. 28.12, where it names 'angels' not 'prominent Jews'); and the saying: "Whoever appoints an unworthy judge is as though he plants an Asherah", etc. (Avoda Zarah 52a); And the saying: "For she hath cast down many wounded", etc. (Prov. 7.26) refer to the disciple who [gives decisions though he] has not reached the age of ordination", etc. (Avoda Zarah 19b); and the saying: "What is a foolish pietist like? — e.g., a woman is drowning in the river", etc. (Sotah 21b); And the saying: "Moses, may he rest in peace, devoted his life [...] to the laws" (Exod. R. 30.4, Tanhuma Parshat Bishlah chap. 10) :

ll.23–29: Chapter Four discusses at length how friendship [love], the greatest [of the virtues], has four causes, and satisfactory reasons for why it is necessary for a political philosopher to speak about friendship as of the other ethical virtues. And the four [causes] will be discussed at length with wonderful proverbs and stories that occurred in ancient days between friends, in accordance with the intention. And a Razal saying: "Or company or death", etc. (Ta'anit 23a); and the saying: "They are making parables in Jerusalem, 'Salt and money are lacking' ", etc. (Ketubot 66b); and the saying: "We found a verse which includes all of the Torah, 'Love your neighbor as yourself' ", etc. (Lev. 19.18, Rashi Lev. 19.18 cites Siphra, Jerusalem Talmud Nedarim IX.3); and the saying: "And a man found him, this was Gabriel", etc. (Rashi Gen. 37.15) are mentioned.

BOOK OF THE REGIMEN OF LIVING ‹FOL. 6B–7A›

ll.33–35: Chapter Five explains satisfactorily how friendship will be divided into three species, [namely] friendship of virtue, friendship of pleasure, and friendship of utility, and discusses a valuable related study investigated in ancient days: to know if friendship [love] exists because of similarity or contrariety, there being reasons for both positions. And a general method for defining friendship and distinguishing the three mentioned species one from another is discussed in the course of examining valuable investigations into the existence and essence of all of friendship's species and particulars.

ll.35–36: And it will make clear how the first species, friendship of virtue, subsumes the other two species by discussing many sayings}

‹fol. 7a›
{Z
MAFṬEHOṬ
ll.1–2: of the ancient philosophers in valuable proverbs : And a Razal saying: "The desire of the rain is for nought but the earth" (Gen. R. 20.7) is mentioned.

ll.3–9: Chapter Six comments on three essential differences between friendship of virtue and the other two species : And it describes six nonessential properties found in the friendship of virtue, and with them friendship is discovered and shown in its completeness, and nothing [in them] changes, telling valuable proverbs and stories from the ancient scholars that accord in all respects with the aforementioned study : And the sentence : "All love which depends on sensual attraction", etc. (Avot 5.19), "Which love was dependent on sensual attraction", etc. (Avot 5.19), "And which depended on nothing selfish", etc. (Avot 5.19) will be explained. And a Razal study which interpreted "All the songs are holiness and the Song of Songs is the most holy" (Rashi Song of Sol. 1.1, Tanḥuma Parashat Teṣaveh, Siman 5).

ll.10–14: Chapter Seven considers three assertions from which it seems that friendship of virtue changes, but all three assertions are wholly refuted by sound and good proofs from the ancient philosophers' sayings, proofs that show it [friendship] does not change in any respect : And it will become clear that a man may not have even one friend of this species :

ll.14–18: this is established by three correct arguments taken from ancient books : And the distinction between friendship of virtue and the two other species is discussed : it makes clear that it [friendship of virtue] has greater similarity with the friendship of pleasure than with friendship of utility : And it mentions a fourth species of friendship [love] which is the friendship [love] between father and son : and master and servant : and husband and wife : and others like them which differ one from the

BOOK OF THE REGIMEN OF LIVING ‹FOL. 7A–7B›

other, all of this is explained at great length in this chapter :

ll.19–26: Chapter Eight discusses a related valuable inquiry carried out by the ancient scholars to know who is more praiseworthy in the virtue of love, the lover being the active [giver of] love, or the beloved one receiving love, and it will be demonstrated by necessary and straightforward [proofs] how the one who loves is more praiseworthy, although the masses praise more the beloved by unreliable analysis : And it will become clear that as friendship of virtue does not change between friends, the inverse characterizes the two other species which quickly arise and are quickly destroyed, mentioning new and ancient proverbs, stories, and tales from the ancient books in accordance with this :

ll.26–35: And it will also comment on the three categories of species of friendship being similar in all respects with three species of possible political regimes, the regime of a monarch or prince whose decree the people can change in no part [monarchy], or the regime of authority [held] between many leaders [republic], or the regime of one man chosen by the majority of the people, [one] who leads them out and brings them in [democracy]. And it will explain properly Aristotle's seemingly contradictory statements concerning the love of father and son, in one place it appears the father's love for the son is greater than the son's love for the father, but in the other places the opposite, by comprehending the ancient philosophers' many sayings on this. And a Razal saying: "The scattering of the wicked benefits themselves and the world", etc. (Sanhedrin 71b); "The assembling of the wicked injures themselves", etc. (Sanhedrin 71b); and they say: "The assembly of the righteous benefits themselves and the world", etc. (Sanhedrin 71b); and the saying: "The wicked are full of regrets" [akin with Jer. 5.27, Ps. 32.10, Prov. 10.24, Job 15.20]; and the saying: "Is it not a matter of course? Even a weaver in his own house must be commander" (Megillah 12b) will be explained.

ll.36–37: Chapter Nine discusses at length what is necessary for a man to act in accordance with the friendship of virtue, to know how to conduct himself properly with his friend. And it mentions}

‹fol. 7b›
{MAFTEHOT
ll.1–10: and inspects regarding this exceedingly valuable virtue proverbs and tales and stories from the ancients : And discusses a careful demonstration of how, and according to what, one will love a friend so that his friend [may] love him, because their hearts are like mirrors [Prov. 27.19], by discussing Ibn Sina's meaning at the beginning of the *Canon,* on the definition of the elements : And it will make clear a very

Book of the Regimen of Living ‹fol. 7b›

deep study about the love of the Name, blessed be He, and how that love is the ultimate human purpose : And it increases and grows as one increases in attainment of divine matters : And it will explain an understanding of the intention of Rambam, of blessed memory, in his study of this, explaining a difficulty in his language in the last chapter of his honorable book (*MN* Pt. 3 chap. 54, On True Wisdom), and in chapter 51 from the last part mentioned (*MN* Pt. 3 chap. 51, How the Perfect Worship God), where it seems speculation is a premise, [there he] places speculation as the ultimate final purpose [*summum bonum*]. And it will explain truly that Rav Ibn Hasdai did not come to the end of understanding the meaning of Rav [Rambam], of blessed memory, about this, that the opinion of Rav, of blessed memory, is also that love [of God] is the ultimate final purpose, as was said : And it discusses a Razal saying: "When they took out R. Akiba to execution and they flayed his flesh with iron combs", etc. (Berakot 61b);

ll.10–14: and they say: "A Bath Kol went forth and proclaimed: Happy art thou, R. Akiba, that thy soul has departed with the word *ehad*", etc. (Berakot 61b); and the saying: " 'With all thy soul': even if He takes away thy soul", etc. (Berakot 61b); and a Razal saying at the end of Rashi's commentary on Kiddushin about the controversy between R. Akiba and R. Tarfon, "Is study greater, or practice?", etc. (Kiddushin 40b, Song of Sol. R. 2.5) : And explaining the language of Rashi, of blessed memory, on the aforementioned saying (Rashi Kiddushin 40b) and the saying: "Anyone whose fear of sin precedes his wisdom" (Avot 3.11).

ll.15–22: Chapter Ten will discuss in a general way the existence and essence [of] the five intellectual virtues, and the reason they are five and not fewer or more, according to the difference [among] objects of the intellect's two parts, the speculative and the practical : And it points out that the ethical virtues exist because of [man's] will, according to what man directs [makes straight] to the deed : And the intellectual virtues exist because of the intellect, according to the study of universal existence, and this is the speculative [intellect] : Explicitly, the meaning of Rambam, of blessed memory, in Part One, chapter two of his honorable book {RMK: *MN* on : "and ye shall be as God." (Gen. 3.5)} : And it will explain a Razal saying: "And God said to Moses", etc. (Exod. 3.6) "Thou wishest to know My name. Well I am called according to my work [. . .] When I am judging created beings I am called 'God' ", etc. (Exod. R. 3.6, Tanhuma Parsha Shemot, page 20) :

ll.23–30: Chapter Eleven will discuss each of the five intellectual virtues in their details by their definitions so that their existence and their essence will be made known properly, and the difference between them : And it will discuss a very valuable study, that the causes of things are made known in the intellect more than their

BOOK OF THE REGIMEN OF LIVING ‹FOL. 7B–8A›

effects, because the causes make known the effects : Explicitly, the meaning of Rambam, of blessed memory, in Part One, chapter one of his honorable book {RMK: *MN* Pt. 1 chap. 1 On the Homonymity of *Ṣelem*.} : And it explains a very deep study from the books of the philosophers, how a thing possible *per se* is also necessary owing to its causes, etc. (Cf. Aristotle, *Metaphysics,* V.v (1015a20–1015b16), V.xii (1019a15–1020a7); trans. Tredennick, 1:222–27, 248–55). And it will become more clear the commonality between understanding [*tevunah*] and temperance [*histapkut*] and it discusses the study [*mishnah*]: "If there is no counsel there is no understanding" (akin to Prov. 21.30, Berakot 19b, etc.) :

ll.30–32: Chapter Twelve explains the different external [secular] sciences in accordance with the system of the ancients and moderns, their particulars and, "their number, after the ordinance" (Num. 29.18), [as] the divisions possible
ll.32–37: change according to the subject discussed. It explains the correct reason why the Prophets and Razal name the Torah with diverse names, in truth, according to the different wisdoms the Torah includes together in one : And it discusses at length the necessary order for studying secular sciences, logic, mathematics, natural sciences, and theology : And the necessary books for studying each one, [as] in our time "Life is short, and the art is long" (First Hippocratic Aphorism, similar to Avot 2.20). And it will explain a Razal saying:}

‹fol. 8a›
{H
MAFTEHOT
ll.1–2: "These are the wicked who in their lifetime are called dead" (Berakot 18b); And the story of Rav Yehoshua Ben-Levi who was walking on the road and a man walking on the road found him : And they say he went from there and found "a little boy sitting at a crossroad", etc. (Eruvin 53b, Lam. R. I.1.19) {RMK: The story of the long and short road to the city exemplifies the wisdom of the children of Jerusalem.} with a very extensive explanation :

ll.3–12: Chapter Thirteen will discuss carefully the varieties of men in human life, in their dealings and endeavors in this world, because among them are those whose whole tendency and endeavors are in friendship of utility : and those who seek [friendship of] pleasure, and those for whom, and they are the chosen portion, all their deliverance and all their desire and longing is for the good in so far as it is good : And in the conclusion of the chapter, which is the conclusion of the book, is placed and transmitted a very wonderful allegory [*mashal*] I found in a book of the modern philosophers. And I added to it what is necessary so that it accord with our intention

Book of the Regimen of Living ⟨fol. 8a⟩

in all respects by reducing the superfluous, which is not useful. In it the aforementioned three categories of species of human beings are apportioned and portrayed. And it is a highly useful allegory for discerning the virtue of praising the love of the good in so far as is good, "to those who take hold of it" (Prov. 3.18) to show them the path that places their souls in eternal life by the light of the King's countenance. And with it all of the book is completed. Blessed is the Lord eternally, amen, amen.

1.13: TORAH

1.14: "Visiting the iniquity of the fathers upon the children unto the third and fourth generation", etc. (Exod. 20.5 and 34.7) — Bk. 1, chap. 2.

1.15: "Show me now Thy ways, that I may know", etc. (Exod. 33.13) — Bk. 1, chap. 2.

1.16: "Thou shalt rise up before the hoary head, and honour the face of the old man", etc. (Lev. 19.32) — Bk. 1, chap. 3.

1.17: "And the mixed multitude that was among them fell a lusting", etc. (Num. 11.4) — Bk. 1, chap. 4.

1.18: "It is not good that the man should be alone; I will make him a help meet", etc. (Gen. 2.18) — Bk. 1, chap. 8.

1.19: "This day the LORD thy God commandeth thee to do these statutes", etc. (Deut. 26.16) — Bk. 1, chap. (11) [12].

1.20: "Every man shall give as he is able, according to the blessing of the LORD thy God which He hath given thee", etc. (Deut. 16.17) — Bk. 2, chap. 7.

1.21: "Thou shalt surely give him, and thy heart shall not be grieved when thou givest unto him", etc. (Deut. 15.10) — Bk. 2, chap. 7.

1.22: "And when she saw him that he was a goodly child, she hid him", etc. (Exod. 2.2) — Bk. 2, chap. 10.

1.23: "Hearken now unto my voice, I will give thee counsel, and God be with thee", etc. (Exod. 18.19) — Bk. 2, chap. 10.

1.24: "And he saw an Egyptian smiting a Hebrew, one of his brethren", etc. (Exod. 2.11) — Bk. 2, chap. 10.

1.25: "And Moses chose able men out of all Israel", etc. (Exod. 18.25) — Bk. 2, chap. 11.

1.26: "Moreover the man Moses was very great", etc. (Exod. 11.3) — Bk. 2, chap. 12.

1.27: "And Moses made haste, and bowed his head toward the earth, and worshipped. And he said", etc. (Exod. 34.8–9) — Bk. 2, chap. 12.

1.28: "And he said unto him that did the wrong : 'Wherefore smitest thou thy fellow?' ", etc. (Exod. 2.13) — Bk. 2, chap. 12.

1.29: "Remember what Amalek did unto thee", etc. (Deut. 25.17), "Thou shalt blot out", etc. (Deut. 25.19) — Bk. 2, chap. 14.

Book of the Regimen of Living ⟨fol. 8a–8b⟩

l.30: "And Miriam and Aaron spoke", etc. (Num. 12.1), "Now the man Moses was very meek", etc. (Num. 12.3) — Bk. 2, chap. 14.

l.31: " 'It is not in me; God will give Pharaoh an answer of peace' ", etc. (Gen. 41.16) — Bk. 2, chap. 18.

l.32: "Honour thy father and thy mother, that", etc. (Exod. 20.12), "Thou shall not covet", etc. (Exod. 20.14) — Bk. 3, chap. 1.

l.33: "Ye shall not respect persons in judgment; ye shall hear the small and the great alike", etc. (Deut. 1.17) — Bk. 3, chap. 2.

l.34: "If there arise a matter too hard for thee in judgment", etc. (Deut. 17.8), "And thou shall come unto the priests", etc. (Deut. 17.9), "According to the law", etc. (Deut. 17.11) — Bk. 3, chap. 3.

l.35: "Every raven after its kind", etc. (Lev. 11.15) — Bk. 3, chap. 4; "But thou shalt love thy neighbour as thyself", etc. (Lev. 19.18) — Bk. 3, chap. 5.}

⟨fol. 8b⟩

{MAFTEḤOT

1.1: "And a certain man found him, and, behold, he was wandering in the field. And the man asked him", etc. (Gen. 37.15) — Bk. 3, chap. 5.

1.2: "Shall I hide from Abraham that which I am doing", etc. (Gen. 18.17) — Bk. 3, chap.5.

1.3: "Honour thy father and thy mother, that thy days may be long", etc. (Exod. 20.12) — Bk. 3, chap. 8.

1.4: "HEAR, O ISRAEL : THE LORD OUR GOD, THE LORD IS ONE", etc. (Deut. 6.4), "And thou shalt love the LORD thy God", etc. (Deut. 6.5) — Bk. 3, chap. 9.

1.5: "And God created man in His own image, in the image of God", etc. (Gen. 1.27) — Bk. 3, chap. 11.

1.6: "And He hath filled him with the spirit of God", etc. (Exod. 35.31), "And to devise skilful works", etc. (Exod. 35.32) — Bk. 3, chap. 11.

1.7: "For they are a nation void of counsel, And there is no understanding in them", etc. (Deut. 34.28) — Bk. 3, ch 11.

1.8: "And God saw the earth, and, behold, it was corrupt", etc. (Gen. 6.12) — Bk. 3, chap. 11.

1.9: "For dust thou art, and unto dust shall thou return", etc. (Gen. 3.19), "See, I have set before thee this day", etc. (Deut. 30.15) — Bk. 3, chap. 13.

    1.10: PSALMS

1.11: "Thou makest me to know the path of life; In thy presence is fulness of joy", etc. (Ps. 16.11) — Introduction.

Book of the Regimen of Living ‹fol. 8b›

1.12: "When the wicked spring up as the grass", etc. (Ps. 92.8), "Deliver my soul from the wicked, by thy sword", etc. (Ps. 17.13) — Bk. 1, chap. 1.

1.13: "And meditate on Thee in the night-watches", etc. (Ps. 63.7), "At midnight I will rise to give thanks unto Thee", etc. (Ps. 119.62) — Bk. 1, chap. 1.

1.14: "He that speaketh falsehood shall not be established before mine eyes", etc. (Ps. 101.7) — Bk. 1, chap. 10.

1.15: "Many are the sorrows of the wicked; But he that trusteth in the LORD, mercy", etc. (Ps. 32.10) — Bk. 2, chap. 1.

1.16: "Grant thee according to thine own heart, And fulfil all thy counsel", etc. (Ps. 20.5) — Bk. 2, chap. 8.

1.17: "A Psalm [of David. LORD,] who shall sojourn in Thy tabernacles? Who shall dwell", etc. (Ps. 15.1) — Bk. 2, chap. 12.

1.18: "The righteous shall rejoice when he seeth the vengeance", etc. (Ps. 58.11) — Bk. 2, chap. 15.

1.19: "HAPPY IS the man that hath not walked in the counsel of the wicked", etc. (Ps. 1.1), "But [his delight is] in the law of the LORD", etc. (Ps. 1.2) — Bk. 2, chap. 18.

1.20: "Guide me in Thy truth", etc. (Ps. 25.5) — Bk. 2, chap. 19.

1.21: "For the LORD is righteous, He loveth righteousness; The upright shall behold his face", etc. (Ps. 1.7) — Bk. 3, chap. 1.

1.22: "He that walketh uprightly, and worketh righteousness", etc. (Ps. 15.2), "That hath no slander upon his tongue", etc. (Ps. 15.3), "The mouth of the righteous uttereth wisdom", etc. (Ps. 37.30) — Bk. 3, chap. 1.

1.23: "The law of his God is in his heart", etc. (Ps. 37.31) — Bk. 3, chap. 2.

1.24: "Also unto Thee, O Lord, belongeth mercy; For Thou renderest to every man according to his work", etc. (Ps. 62.13) — Bk. 3, chap. 3.

1.25: "It is time for the LORD to work; They have made void Thy law", etc. (Ps. 119.126), "Many are the sorrows of the wicked", etc. (Ps. 32.10) — Bk. 3, chap. 8.

1.26: "HAPPY IS the man that hath not walked in the counsel of the wicked", etc. (Ps. 1.1), "But [his delight is] in the law of the LORD", etc. (Ps.1.2) — Bk. 3, chap. 8 and chap. 13.

 1.27: PROVERBS

1.28: "The righteous eateth to the satisfying of his desire", etc. (Prov. 13.25) — Bk. 1, chap. 1.

1.29: "Give not sleep to thine eyes", etc. (Prov. 6.4), "Yet a little sleep", etc. (Prov. 6.10), "How long wilt thou sleep, O sluggard?", etc. (Prov. 6.9) — Bk. 1, chap. 7.

1.30: "For three things the earth doth quake", etc. (Prov. 30.21), "For a servant", etc. (Prov. 30.22), "For an odious woman", etc. (Prov. 30.23) — Bk. 1, chap. 8.

1.31: "A man hath joy in the answer of his mouth; And a word in due season", etc. (Prov. 15.23) — Bk. 1, chap. 11.
1.32: "In all thy ways acknowledge Him, And He will direct thy paths", etc. (Prov. 3.6) — Bk. 1, chap. 12.
1.33: "Length of days is in her right hand; In her left hand are riches and honor", etc. (Prov. 3.16), "The refining pot is for silver", etc. (Prov. 17.3, 27.21) — Bk. 2, chap. 11.
1.34: "The dissembler in heart shall have his fill from his own ways", etc. (Prov. 14.14), "Let another man praise thee, and not thine own mouth", etc. (Prov. 27.2) — Bk. 2, chap. 12.
1.35: "The wicked earneth deceitful wages", etc. (Prov. 11.18) — Bk. 2, chap. 18.
1.36: "The king that faithfully judgeth the poor", etc. (Prov. 29.14) — Bk. 2, chap. 19.
1.37: "All the brethren of the poor do hate him", etc. (Prov. 19. 7), "A friend loveth at all times", etc. (Prov. 17.17) — Bk. 3, chap. 1.}

⟨fol. 9a⟩
{T
MAFTEHOT
1.1: "Better is open rebuke Than love that is hidden", etc. (Prov. 27.5) — Bk. 3, chap. 5.
1.2: "My son, if thy heart be wise, My heart will be glad, even mine", etc. (Prov. 23.15) — Bk. 3, chap. 8.
1.3: "As in water face answereth to face, So the heart of man", etc. (Prov. 27.19) — Bk. 3, chap. 9.
1.4: "In all thy ways acknowledge Him, And He will direct", etc. (Prov. 3.6), "For I give you good doctrine", etc. (Prov. 4.2) — Bk. 3, chap. 13.
   1.5: JOB
1.6: ["And that] man was wholehearted and upright, and one that feared God", etc. (Job 1.1) — Bk. 1, chap. 2.
1.7: "Behold, He putteth no trust in His servants", etc. (Job 4.18) — Bk. 1, chap. 12.
1.8: "And though thy beginning was small, Yet thy end should [greatly] increase", etc. (Job 8.7) — Bk. 2, chap. 17.
1.9: "Now when Job's three friends heard", etc. (Job 2.11), "they came every one from his own place", etc. (Job 2.11) — Bk. 3, chap. 4.
1.10: "Naked came I out of my mother's womb", etc. (Job 1.21) — Bk. 3, chap. 13.
   1.10: DANIEL
1.11: "Youths in whom was no blemish", etc. (Dan. 1.4), and such as had the ability to stand in the [king's] palace", etc. (Dan. 1.4) — Bk. 1, chap. 7.

BOOK OF THE REGIMEN OF LIVING ⟨FOL. 9A⟩

l.12: ISAIAH

l.13: "Woe unto them that draw iniquity with cords of vanity", etc. (Isa. 5.18) — Bk 1, chap. 8.

l.14: "Thine own wickedness shall correct thee, And thy backslidings shall reprove thee :", etc. (Jer. 2.19) — Bk. 2, chap. 1.

l.15: "Why sayest thou, O Jacob, And speakest", etc. (Isa. 40.27), "Hast thou not known? hast thou not heard", etc. (Isa. 40.28) — Bk. 2, chap. 1.

l.16: "Say ye of the righteous, that it shall be well with him; [For they shall eat] the fruit of their doings", etc. (Isa. 3.10), "Woe unto the wicked! It shall be ill with him", etc. (Isa. 3.11) — Bk. 3, chap. 8.

l.17: "Thine own wickedness shall correct thee, And thy backslidings", etc. (Jer. 2.19), "All we like sheep did go astray", etc. (Isa. 53.6) — Bk. 3, chap. 8.

l.18: JEREMIAH

l.19: "Man's way is not his own", etc. (Jer. 10.23) — Bk. 2, chap. 2.

l.20: "But the LORD God is the true God", etc. (Jer. 10.10) — Bk. 2, chap. 19.

l.21: THE TWELVE PROPHETS

l.22: "Before the great and terrible day of the LORD come", etc. (Joel 3.4, Mal. 3.23), "After two days will He revive us, On the third day", etc. (Hos. 6.2) — Bk. 1, chap. 12.

l.23: SONG OF SOLOMON

l.24: "THE SONG of songs which is Solomon's", etc. (Song of Sol. 1.1) — Bk. 3, chap. 6.

l.24: ECCLESIASTES

l.25: "A good name is better than precious oil", etc. (Eccles. 7.1), "Be not overmuch wicked", etc. (Eccles. 7.17) — Bk. 1, chap. 12.

l.26: "Rejoice, O young man, in thy youth", etc. (Eccles. 11.9), "So I commended mirth", etc. (Eccles. 8.15) — Bk. 1, chap. 13.

l.27: "A good name is better than precious oil", etc. (Eccles. 7.1), "Say not thou: 'How was it that the former days' ", etc. (Eccles. 7.10) — Bk. 1, chap. 13.

l.28: "There is a grievous evil which I have seen under the sun", etc. (Eccles. 5.12) — Bk. 2, chap. 7.

l.29: "And this also is a grievous evil, that in all the points as he came", etc. (Eccles. 5.15) — Bk. 2, chap. 18.

l.30: "Vexation is better than laughter; For by the sadness of the countenance", etc. (Eccles. 7.3) — Bk. 2, chap. 14.

l.31: "Be not hasty in thy spirit to be angry", etc. (Eccles. 7.9) — Bk. 2, chap. 15.

1.32: "A time to weep, and a time to laugh"[1], etc. (Eccles. 3.4), "A time to mourn, and a time to dance", etc. (Eccles. 3.4) — Bk. (2) [3], chap. 2
1.33: "Riches kept by the owner thereof", etc. (Eccles. 5.12) — Bk. 3, chap. 4.
   1.34: RUTH
1.35: " 'Entreat me not to leave thee, and to return from following after thee' ", etc. (Ruth 1.16), "for whither thou goest, I will go", etc. (Ruth 1.16) — Bk. 3, chap. 6.
1.36: "Where thou diest, will I die, and there will I be buried", etc. (Ruth 1.17), "the LORD do so to me and more also", etc. (Ruth 1.17) — Bk. 3, chap. 6.}

⟨fol. 9b⟩
{MAFTEḤOT
   1.1: LAMENTATIONS
1.2: "The joy of our heart is ceased", etc. (Lam. 5.15), "Woe unto us!", etc. (Lam. 5.16) — Bk. 1, chap. 12.
1.3: "Out of the mouth of the Most High proceedeth not evil and good?", etc. (Lam. 3.38), "Wherefore doth a living man complain", etc. (Lam. 3.39) — Bk 2, chap. 2.
   1.4: SCROLL OF ESTHER
1.5: "In the third year of his reign, he made a feast", etc. (Esther 1.3), "when he showed the riches", etc. (Esther 1.4) — Bk. 2, chap. 9.
1.6: "Then the king made a great feast unto [all his princes and his servants,] even Esther's feast", etc. (Esther 2.18) — Bk. 2, chap. 9.
1.7: "And he sent and fetched his friends", etc. (Esther 5.10) — Bk. 3, chap. 4.
1.8: "[The king] commanded Vashti the queen to be brought before him", etc. (Esther 1.17) — Bk. 3, chap. 8.
   1.9: FIRST PROPHETS
1.10: "What man is there that is fearful and faint-hearted?", etc. (Deut. 20.8) — Bk. 2, chap. 4.
1.11: " 'O my son Absalom, my son' ", etc. (2 Sam. 19.1), "would that I had died for thee", etc. (2 Sam. 19.1) — Bk. 2, chap. 4.
1.12: "Now therefore, I pray you, swear unto me by the LORD", etc. (Josh. 2.12), "And the men said unto her:", etc. (Jos. 2.14), "But Rahab the harlot", etc. (Josh. 6.25) — Bk. 2, chap. 11.
1.13: "And Absalom spoke unto Amnon" (2 Sam. 13. 22) — Bk. 2, chap. 12.
1.14: "But Saul and the people spared Agag", etc. (1 Sam. 15.19), "Wherefore then

---

[1] The text cites these two hemistichs in inverse order.

didst thou not hearken to the voice of the LORD", etc. (1 Sam. 15.19) — Bk. 2, chap. 14.

l.15: "In their lives, even in their death they were not divided", etc. (2 Sam. 1.23) — Bk. 3, chap. 6.

l.16: " 'Fear not; for the hand of (Absalom) [Saul my father] shall not find thee' ", etc. (1 Sam. 23.17), "and thou shalt be king over Israel", etc. (1 Sam. 23.17) — Bk. 3, chap. 7.

l.17: "Then spoke the woman whose the living child was", etc. (1 Kings 3.26), " 'Oh, my lord, give her the living child' ", etc. (1 Kings 3.26) — Bk. 3, chap. 7.

l.18: The Keys to the Regimen of Living are completed

ll.19–20: And these are the Keys of the Conversations viz. what was mentioned in the Treatise of Dreams, by strength and powers and mysteries of wisdom.

ll.21: Note that it is divided into prologue and epilogue and three classes in the middle [of the treatise] and each class into its different species :

ll.22–25: The first class are the simple, untrue, and uncertain dreams and is divided into three species : The first species are the dreams caused by a dominant humor in the human body or from the aspect of a temporary quality of perceptible great heat or cold that compels untrue dreams according to the dominant quality, as was said :

ll.26–32: The second species are the uncertain dreams formed and created from the aspect of great [deep] thoughts in the dreamer that occur in the imagination during sleep and the dreamer dreams according to the thoughts that absorbed him while awake : The third species are the uncertain dreams by reason of the dreamer's weakness of soul [simpleness]. The dreamer's intellect rebels against the imagination [but fails] to counteract its delusion and destroy the imagined forms it [the imagination] combines "according to their number after the manner" (Num. 29.18). The second class are the simple and certain dreams and is divided into two species. The first species are the dreams of the wise and the perfect in their knowledge who have power, strength, and common sense [capable of] counteracting the imagination, to break "the cheek-teeth" (Ps. 58.7) of its delusions :}

⟨fol. 10a⟩
{Y
MAFTEHOT

ll.1–2: The second species are the majority of the dreams of the masses who are not deep thinkers but they have the power to counteract the imagination with common sense because of their experience :

BOOK OF THE REGIMEN OF LIVING ⟨FOL. 10A⟩

ll.3–8: The third class are the certain and true dreams that are divinely inspired or divine emanation accompanies them and it too is divided into two different species : The first species are the dreams that are seen by people who are unworthy in themselves to receive [such dreams], an abundant emanation influences them: "And the good will of Him that dwelt in the bush" (Deut. 33.16) {RMK: They dream such because God gave them the gift to dream true dreams for the benefit of Israel not because they deserve it.} and inspiration for the benefit of the nation of Israel, or for the benefit of an especially perfect [individual], as was the dream of Pharaoh, Abimelech, Laban the Arami, and others like them : The second species are the true prophetic dreams in all aspects that occur to all prophets worthy in themselves to achieve that degree in His absolute will :

ll.9–11: The prologue explains a careful proof for the reality and essence of sleep and dream, their causes [are described] properly and [it] discusses further what we explained in the Regimen of Living, Bk. one, chap. seven, concerning the way intellectual perception [apprehension] is through the imagination by means of the senses; ll.12–19 with an explanation of Rambam's reasoning in Part One, chapter 68 {RMK: *MN* Pt. 1 chap. 68 On the Terms: the *Intellectus,* the *Intelligens,* and the Intelligible "the principle of the philosophers that God is the *intellectus,* the *ens intelligens,* and the *ens intelligibile.*"} on [the] question [of the] intellect [*sekel, intellectus*], intellectual [*maskil, ens intelligens*], and the intelligible [*muskal, idea*], and the linking of them together [their unity] : And it will be made clear how the soul is one and is the cause of the intellect [*hamaskelet*] and the perceiver senses [*hamergeshet*] and the imagination [*vehamedamah*], etc. in accordance with what Rambam, of blessed memory, explained in chapter one of the eight chapters that preface his commentary on tractate Avot : And it discusses another true premise for why Razal attributed in many places the part for the whole with the number sixty, more than any other number, in accordance with the opinion of the theologians regarding this number, explicitly a Razal saying: "Sleep is one-sixtieth part of death", etc. (Berakot 57b), a true and correct explanation. And it discusses another matter, the issue of the essence of the demons and the cause of their being shown to men in the day and in the night and how they are imaginary visions due to the imagination in accordance with the opinion of Rambam, of blessed memory :

l.19: Class One

ll.20–24: Concerning the first species of the first class the natural reason is explained for how the uncertain dreams exist by reason of the prevalent humor in the sleeping body, or by reason of [a] temporary external quality of heat or cold, etc., and how the dreams will be related to that quality in accordance with Razi's [Abu Bakr al-

Razi's] exposition in the second part of the *Almanṣur* [*Manṣuri*], and it will also discuss the reason for the destruction [decay] of the imagination, or other rational faculties from the aspect of injuries to

ll.24–33: the bones of the brain [cranium?], such as abscesses and similar maladies from deleterious injuries. And it also explains clearly the true reason for why it happens that one who is between sleeping and waking dreams in most cases about things that are [actually] happening, but thinks it is a dream, and upon awakening [perceives] it was definitely as he dreamed. And it also discusses the reality and essence of the disease called *incubus* in accordance with the opinion of Ibn Sina in book three of the *Canon* from the first, *ofan* [thesis, saying] five, chap. three, and the reason it afflicts during sleep and the dreamer dreams that a human form or some other figure is standing upon him and he feels a great weight [upon him] until sometimes, when the cause is strong, he dreams [they] are strangling him, and the masses call this disease *pezadilyya* [Sp. "nightmare"] and it discusses how the disease occurs most often in nursing children close to the time of birth because there is an excess of moisture in them, and they are too weak to melt [dry ?] the continuous vapors; for this reason the moisture strangles [the dreamer], and this is what the old women call *brusas* [Sp. "witches"] in a foreign language :

ll.33–34: Regarding the second species of the first class a careful proof is discussed about how uncertain dreams are compelled [into existence] in accordance with natural reason by reason of increased thoughts while asleep

ll.35–37 and how they [the dreams] occur in sleep by reason of the interweaving of the thoughts with the imagination. And it also explains that in many men uncertain dreams most often logically follow words spoken while awake, even if the words do not pass into thought, and the dreamer is not the originator of the thoughts, because the impression the words make}

⟨fol. 10b⟩
{MAFTEHOT
ll.1–5: on the imagination while [the dreamer] is awake, explicitly, the words of Solomon, may he rest in peace, in Kohelet in two verses, a valid proof, certainly it is the sentence: "Be not rash with thy mouth, and let not thy heart be hasty to utter a word before God", etc. "For a dream cometh through a multitude of business", etc. (Eccles. 5.1–2). And it discusses the verse: "Behold, this dreamer cometh", etc. (Gen. 37.19) "And we shall see what will become of his dreams", etc. (Gen. 37.20), and the verse: "Come now therefore, and let us slay him and cast him into one of the pits", etc. (Gen. 37.20) : and discusses the saying of Isaiah the prophet, may he rest in peace, when

BOOK OF THE REGIMEN OF LIVING ‹FOL. 10B›

he says: "And it shall be as when an hungry man dreameth and behold he eateth", etc. (Isa. 29.8).

ll.6–10: In the third species of this class a proper proof is discussed of how uncertain dreams logically follow according to nature in the simple [people of weak intellect] incapable of counteracting the imagination and destroying the false forms and delusions consequent upon them, because the imagination then runs in vigorous crushing to compose compounds from everything it retains in itself from the imagined forms it received through the external senses, as was mentioned in the prologue :

l.11: The Second Class

ll.12–14: The first species from the second class discusses how the dreams of the perfect and the wise who are complete in their knowledge, thoughts, and virtues, in good health, when no humor or external quality dominates, are certain because they [the wise] possess complete knowledge and integrity of reason to infer the truth of things in accordance with the aspect of their causes.

ll.15–21: The second species from the second class discusses how it follows logically that certain dreams occur in people from among the masses who do not study science [thus] few of whom are wise : And it explains how for those people, and they are the majority, certain dreams come from the aspect of what their intellect inferred and judged from experience, what they saw in something that happened, and from that they judge the future according to habit and custom, the majority of such dreams will be true : And it mentions a careful proof of the Razal saying: "Every dream just before morning is fulfilled" (Berakot 55b), explicitly, the correct natural cause for it. ll.21–22 And it discusses a Razal saying: "The dream is one-sixtieth of prophecy", etc. (Berakot 57b) :

ll.23: And it explains that it is possible that the two species of this second class are true according to nature for one of two reasons :

ll.24–32: The first, and it is the more natural, is from the aspect of the dreamer's intuition [inference] concerning the causes of things, that he judges from the effects what is logically necessary and is in accordance with them most often : And the explanation discusses a careful proof of how and why a man cannot apprehend intellectual things [ideas] and the separate abstract intellects [intelligences] as they are in themselves from [imagined] material form : And it also makes clear a Razal saying: "Twenty-four dream diviners were in Jerusalem", etc. (Berakot 55b) and explains the Razal saying: "The one who dreams that the beams of his house are broken, his wife will bear a male" (Gen. R. 89.8 and Lam. R. I.1.18) and explains the natural cause for it : And it also discusses the argument that all the dream interpretations mentioned in the Talmud, in the portion *Ha-Ro'eh,* and in many other places, are alike in each dream as it appears in it [the dream]

ll.32–36: without considering the other conditions it is necessary to consider, which are the time of the dream, the place, the dreamer, and other matters pertaining to the interpreter's decision, etc. And it also mentions a proper proof for the manner of the dream interpreters' conjecture [hypothesis] in Talmudic days about all of the conditions required for the diviner's interpretation to be true : And a proper explanation according to nature for why the dreams of the wise and the clever are true}

‹fol. 11a›
{Y'
MAFTEHOT
ll.1–7: according to the degree of their wisdom and their knowledge : And it also mentions the natural causes for what Betalmius [Ptolemy] stated in the book *One Hundred Sentences* [*Centiloquium*], that one who knows the time of conception can know the time of birth and vice versa : And in this wise, according to nature, it discusses why many dreams of ordinary people who have not studied science [wisdom] are true provided they possess a strong intellect and are certain [steady] in their knowledge [moral disposition, character], etc. And it discusses a valid and proper proof for all of the verses pertaining to Joseph's interpretation [of the dreams] of the chief of the butlers and the chief of the bakers, explicitly, the natural causes that from their own aspect [in and of themselves] [the reasons] those dreams were formed in this way, their true interpretation being in both of them according to natural causes
ll.7–8: mentioned in explaining properly the difficulty in the writings :

ll.9–14: The second cause, certainly it is according to the opinion of those who place the active intellect in our intellect and outside externally under the concavity of the lunar sphere [the sublunar realm of Nature], and they are Ibn Sina and Abuhamid al-Ghazzal, and after them the great Rav Rambam, of blessed memory, and after him, all the honest who say that while asleep the dreamer's soul is attached to the active intellect, since it [the soul] is resting from the activities of the external senses, and unites with it [the active intellect] until they are one, and in this way [the soul] conceives and understands the causes of all things in their generality from their beginning to their end, and from them [knowing the reasons of the things generally] it [the soul] judges and weighs the truth of the temporary particulars into which they are transposed {RMK: The soul has knowledge of causes generally and can interpret particulars as to the future.}

ll.15–21: And it mentions a very wonderful analogy [*mashal*] in all respects in accordance with the attachment of the dreamer's soul to the active intellect, as the author of the vanishing view [*Perspectiva*] demonstrated, when two mirrors are placed one opposite the other so that an image reflected in one is reflected in the other with all of the reflected forms. And this is seen thus in the sense of one who experiences it, when the dreamer's soul is joined with the active intellect, it is joined with the universal forms that always exist there, and by means of them the dreamer judges carefully the correctness of the future particulars created from them [the universal forms], as was mentioned : And it also explains the solution of a second difficult doubt awakened in us concerning this, why is it a man remembers in a dream things long forgotten that are not remembered when awake, a reasoned proof according to nature :

1.22: The Third Class

ll.23–30: The first species of the third class discusses a proper proof concerning how divine inspiration [influence] comes upon people who are not themselves prepared or worthy, and it is an influence from Him, may He be blessed, for a cause among the causes known to Him, to do His Will by means of the dreamer, explicitly, the language of Rambam, Part Two chapter 41 {RMK: *MN* Pt. 2 chap. 41 "What is meant by Vision."} and it makes clear that the differences between the two species of this third class stand on their true essences, explicitly, the language of Rambam, of blessed memory, in Part Three, chapter eighteen {RMK: *MN* Pt. 3 chap. 18, "Every individual member of mankind enjoys the influence of Divine Providence in proportion to his intellectual perfection."} and it further discusses in detail the dream in which God appeared to Abimelech (Gen. 20.6), and to Laban the Aramean (Gen. 31.24), explaining all the verses written about them, a valid proof, and the cause for Pharaoh's inspiration (Gen. 41.17–23), being that he was completely wicked and unworthy himself, as was said :

ll.31–34: And it discusses a suitable proof for the hypothesis that Rambam, of blessed memory, postulated in many places in his book on the essence, subject, and law of the wonders that His Name Will Be Blessed brings from nature, and R. Abraham Ibn Ezra of blessed memory explained it in many places in his Bible commentary : And it also makes clear the difference between the simple certain dream and the divinely inspired dream.

ll.34–37: And it also resolves a famous difficulty, [namely] why Pharaoh's dream interpreters and wise men did not know and understand Joseph's interpretation, it being a clear matter [through the intellect]; the interpretation accords in all aspects with the dream. And it discusses a Razal saying about the interpreters' interpretation for Pharaoh: "Thou wilt beget seven daughters and wilt bury seven daughters", etc. (Gen. R. 89.6, Rashi Gen. 41.8)}

BOOK OF THE REGIMEN OF LIVING ‹FOL. 11B›

‹fol. 11b›
{MAFTEḤOT
ll.1–10: And another difficulty concerning the chief butler is also examined. Why did he not remember Joseph at the outset of the matter when his heart saw Pharaoh was telling his dream and seeking an interpretation : but only at the end after he saw that they [the Egyptian diviners] had no interpretation for Pharaoh? : And in connection with it a significant difficulty is explained, [namely] how did the chief butler know that Joseph would interpret the dream, since all the Egyptian wise men and Pharaoh's diviners failed to interpret it correctly? It cannot be said that the chief butler decided a universal from a particular. Why believe that because Joseph interpreted [correctly] the chief butler's dream, so Joseph would interpret all dreams? Perhaps if the chief butler had told his dream to Pharaoh's diviners, they too would have interpreted it correctly. And why place himself in danger by mentioning his sins for doubtful benefit, and perhaps it would bring Joseph great harm? Joseph did not ask him to mention to Pharaoh that he, Joseph, was a dream interpreter and place him in the danger of a test, but only that he remember him for good. And all these difficulties are settled correctly by understanding the intention of all the writings in detail with a valid proof :

ll.10–19: And it discusses a Razal saying on the verse: "But there was none that could interpret them unto Pharaoh", etc. (Gen. 41.8); "There were many diviners but not for Pharaoh", etc. (Gen. R. 89.6) and explains all the writings from the beginning of the portion *Mikkeṣ:* "And it came to pass" (Gen. 41.1), until: "There is none so discreet and wise as thou", etc. (Gen. 41.39) with a valid proof : And it explains a Razal saying: "And behold he stood over the river" (Gen. 41.1) R. Yoḥanan said: "The wicked stand over their gods", etc. (Gen. R. 89.4). And explicitly the verses, for me a great difficulty is resolved, how in telling the interpretation did Joseph say: "Let Pharaoh do this and let him appoint overseers", etc. (Gen. 41.34). It seems, in fact, that he gave advice in an unethical way to the king. And the solution of another difficult problem, a different disputed matter. Why did Pharaoh suddenly believe everything Joseph said to him, instead of waiting to see if Joseph's words were credible or not? If two of the seven lean [years] came, Pharaoh could then make the necessary arrangements. Instead, he ordered straight away that Joseph's advice be carried out completely. And what Pharaoh understood in this, and what sign reached him that Joseph was more true than the Egyptian diviners, will be settled completely in a fine and acceptable manner :

ll.20–31: Concerning the second species of the third class, [the chapter] explains that the existence and essence of the prophetic dream is the divine inspiration that comes upon the prophet, His Complete Will, after the necessary preparation

BOOK OF THE REGIMEN OF LIVING ‹FOL. 11B–12A›

according to the conditions Razal explained. And the differences between them [prophetic dreams] and the simple certain dreams [the first species] of the third class are made clear with proper explanation, explicitly, a Razal saying: "Prophecy does not rest except upon the wise, the mighty [heroic], and the rich", etc. (Shabbat 92a). And the sayings of Rambam, of blessed memory, in many places in *MN,* Part Two, chapter 36 {RMK: *MN* Pt. 2 chap. 36, "On the mental, physical and moral properties of the prophets."} and in Part Two, chapter forty-five {RMK: *MN* Pt. 2 chap. 45, "The various classes of prophets."} and in his Prologue to the book, explicitly, the verse: "He is trusted in all my house, with him do I speak mouth to mouth", etc. (Num. 12.7–8) are explained generally in order to understand properly the true essence and definition of prophecy suitable for understanding this last species. Two very valuable Razal sayings will be explained from the Midrash, Numbers Rabbah on the portion: "And Balak saw" (Num. 22.2), a valid and true explanation [of both sayings], each in accord with the other. The first saying: "R. Isaac said: Before the Tabernacle was set up prophecy was current among the heathen nations of the world; after the Tabernacle was erected it departed from them", etc. (Lev. R. 1.12);

ll.32–33: The second saying: "What is the difference between the prophets of Israel and those of other nations? R. Ḥama b. R. Ḥanina and R. Issachar of Kefar Mandi said that", etc. (Gen. R. 52.5) in the explanation some of the many difficulties surrounding this issue are resolved :

ll.34–36: The epilogue of the Treatise interprets a dream of the simple species that I dreamed about the great and virtuous minister, his majesty Don Joseph Nasi. The dream was interpreted when it was doubled at dawn, both are proofs coming in the dream and showing that the matter is certain [and]}

‹fol. 12a›
{YB
MAFTEḤOT
ll.1–5: from God and that He is hurrying to do it, explicitly, the correct natural causes for its true interpretation. And it is a certain dream according to all the causes and signs we mentioned concerning the second of the three classes mentioned. And it explains a Razal sentence: "Every dream just before morning is fulfilled immediately" (Gen. R. 89.5), explicitly, the natural cause, which is sufficient cause, and it makes clear Razal's intention concerning that sentence :

ll.5–9: And it explains properly the natural causes for why, when a dream is doubled to the dreamer, this indicates that it is true and arranged by God (Berakot 55b), explicitly, the verse: "And for that the dream was doubled unto Pharaoh twice", etc.

Book of the Regimen of Living ‹fol. 12a›

(Gen. 41.32) : And it also explains the natural cause for why when the dream is interpreted in the dream itself; this shows that the interpretation is true (Berakot 55b), in the judgment of the common sense by right and proper reason to understand Razal's intention concerning this very valuable teaching :

ll.9–12: And, explicitly, Aristotle's meaning about this in *On Sleep and Waking* [where] he said the dreamer who dreams the dream a second time, and dreams that he is dreaming, the dream is not from the imagination, [but] rather it is a judgment of the intellect. And it is stimulated by the intellect itself in such a way that there is no doubt concerning it :

ll.12–16: The epilogue of the whole book explains how it is necessary that this dream and its true and certain interpretation in all its details will be in accordance in every respect with the dreams Joseph dreamed and told his brothers. And it explains the verses in *Vayyeshev* (Gen. 37.1) about this, all of them, with good argument and knowledge of the essential natural cause of their truth, and this is the matter which the soul of the mentioned blessed minister yearned for and longed to know :

PROLOGO 'I LYYABE 'ONIBERSAL DEL 'AUTOR

TRATADO 'ordenado 'a rekerimyento demi 'intimo kerido 'i śobrino maś ke hiğo 'enel 'amor : vyendo 'enel 'una bu'ena diśpozisy'on 'i natural abilidad devina mente 'otorgada para todo genero de virtud 'i verdader'a 'eśpikulasyon 'enel kual śe kontyene 'una regla 'onibersal 'en toda la ğornada dela vida 'umana para 'enderesar a'el byen verdadero 'i 'ultimo fin titulo del kual 'eś : REĞIMYENTO DELA VIDA reparteśe 'en treś parteś 'i kada parte de 'elyaś 'en kapituloś śegun śe 'ofreśe para meğor poder konprender la 'intensyon de kada koza ke 'enel śe trata : dela primera delyyaś ke 'eś 'el prinsipyo dela ğornada la kual śe reparte 'en katorze kapituloś śe konprende 'una regla general asaś 'util para loś ke 'el difisil kamino dela byen aventuransa kyeren śegir : 'eśpasifikando la 'orden ke śe deve de tener para moderar 'el 'apetito śensual 'i propy'a mente 'en loś mosoś 'en dyeś kozaś konvyene 'a śaber 'enel komer : 'i 'enel bever : 'enel dormir : 'enel velar : 'enel eğar : 'enel alevantar : 'enel andar : 'enel aśentar : 'enel hablar : 'enel kalyyar : laś kualeś śon regladaś 'i 'ordenadaś komo konbyenen 'i traen śuprema 'utilidad aśi 'a 'el ku'erpo komo ala anima
    DELA śegunda partida la kual śe reparte 'en vente kapituloś śe}

‹fol. 12b›
{HAKᵉDEMAH [INTRODUCTION]
komprende la deśkrisyon de[ ]dyez vertudeś moraleś konforme ala 'intensyon del filosofo 'enel tersero 'i kuarto dela 'etika ke śon la fortaleza la templansa la liberalidad la maknifisensya la manyanimidad la modeśty'a la manśedumbre la afabilidad la korteśi'a la verdad :
    DELA tersera partida la kual śe reparte 'en treze kapituloś śe konprende la deśkrisyon de doś vertudeś moraleś maś 'oniverśaleś ke laś primeraś ke śon la ğuśtisy'a 'i la amiśtad konforme ala 'intensyon del meśmo filosofo 'enel kinto 'i 'oktavo 'i nono dela 'etika 'i de sinko vertudeś 'intelektualeś śegun 'el filosofo 'enel śeśto dela meśma 'etika 'i śon la sensya la śapyensya 'el 'entendimyento la prudensya 'i la

BOOK OF THE REGIMEN OF LIVING ‹FOL. 12B–13A›

arte 'en la meśma partida śe deklara la regla ke śe deve tener 'enel le'er de laś sensyyaś komo konvyene para śer maś probeğośo 'a 'el leente konforme ala brevedad dela vida 'i 'okupasyon kontinu'a ke śe rekyere 'en nu'eśa śantisima ley :
   'EŚ tratado muy 'util para 'enderesar a'el kamino dela 'ultima filisidad ke śoy syerto 'el ke 'eśta 'orden sigyere śin 'erar 'eneśta ğornada de nu'eśa vida prezente śera a'uto 'i śofisyente para ke trabağando 'en nu'eśtra śakra 'eśkritura alkanse 'a 'entender 'i 'obrar kuanto al 'umano 'inğeny'o 'eś 'otorgado alkansar konlo kual śe glorifikara 'enla glory'a perdurable para śyenpre :

PROLOGO PARTIKULAR AŚU ŚOBRINO

MAŚ ke hiğo natural 'enel 'amor 'i deśe'o de tu prośperidad yṣv" [May God protect and preserve him] demandaśteme 'una regla ğeneral de reğimyento 'enloś kośtumbreś ke por veześ te tengo amoneśtado 'enel modo del bib(+)ir konforme ala dereğa razon para 'enderesar a'el kamino dela virtud paresyendote digna de 'enkomendar ala memory'a yo viśta tu bu'ena konsiderasy'on la kual 'en kerer 'obrar vertudeś 'i 'enla verdader'a 'eśpekulasy'on konśiśte lo konsedo porke 'eśpero verdader'a mente ke aś de śubir 'enla kumbre dela filisidad 'i kon 'eśto bibiraś 'en kontino plazer śin meśkla de pasyon alguna komunikando kon loś ke 'el 'eśtreğo 'i dulse kamino dela virtud śigen donde laś animaś gozan de 'in'istimable deleytasyon :
   POREL kual rogaba nu'eśtro prinsipe 'i devino rey David 'enśuś śalmoś dizyendo haśme śaber śendero de vidaś fartura de alegriaś 'a tu kara hermozuraś 'en tu dereğa 'i set-[1] 'el kual 'a mi ver kizo śentir ke todo 'el kamino ke falta de 'enderesar al hito del byen verdadero no merese lyyamarśe kamino de vida porke la ke propy'a mente vida śe pu'ede lyyamar 'eś la de 'el bu'eno 'i por 'eśto rogaba al Dyyo glory'ozo 'el bu'en rey ke 'enelyya lo 'enkaminaśe 'i de}

‹fol. 13a›
{YG
kamino aśenyala laś propyedadeś 'i probeğoś de la tal vida dizyendo ke ayy 'en 'elyya hartura de alegriaś 'i set- keryendo śinifikar ke 'el ke śige loś byeneś korporaleś nunka śe harta dela alegri'a delyoś porke kuanto maś loś 'enyade tanto maś a'umenta la kobdisya śenpre konelyoś 'i komo ninguno ğamaś pyenśa aber alyegado al fin delyoś ğamaś śe kumple śu alegri'a 'i fin de śu deśe'o : anteś śyenpre 'eśta 'en kontino

---

[1] Ps. 16.11.

Book of the Regimen of Living ‹fol. 13a–13b›

mobimyento de manera ke nunka 'eś maś de 'una alegri'a 'i nunka harta lo kual 'el ke śige la vida verdader'a tyene al kontraryo ke 'en kual kyera 'obra de virtud 'i kual kyera forma 'intelektual ke 'el 'entendimyento konprende resibe 'una alegri'a muy farta komo kyen alyega al fin delyya 'i por 'eśto diğo fartura de alegriaś 'i set- ke śon laś alegriaś muğaś 'i kada 'una porśi 'i śer fartaś śin miśty'on alguna de 'apetito 'i konkluye kon 'otra propyedad śinifikando śer 'el tal byen perp(+)etu'o kuando 'eś 'influ'ido dela dereğa del Dyyo 'i śu ayuda 'i 'eśto kiğo dezir hermozuraś 'en tu dereğa 'i se- :

'I por ke la dotrina tanto maś śe konfirma kuanto maś 'eś produzida de kyen kon meğor animo 'i verdader'a veluntad de 'efektuar 'el fruto delyya la asebta tengo por byen konseder tu lisita demanda pu'eś kon tan bu'en perpozito 'i 'efikas veluntad la demandaś pu'eśto ke aś byen viśto mi kontinu'a 'okupasyon 'enel 'eśtudy'o de diversaś le'esy'oneś de ninguna delaś kualeś me pu'edo 'eśkuzar faltandome tyenpo a'un para lo nesesaryo ami preśona :

'I A'UN ke maś fasil me fu'era 'eśkrivirte 'en nu'eśtra śantisima 'i fakundisima lengu'a por śer ami maś familyyar no me kyero 'eśkuzar del trabağo de 'eśkribir 'en romanse komo me ru'egaś lo haga pu'eś por nu'eśtroś pekadoś śon todaś nu'eśtraś platikaś 'en lengu'a ağena 'a(l)noś 'i tanbyen ganaraś de kamino 'entender algunoś terminoś ke 'entendyendoloś abyendo de platikar kon algunoś 'ombreś śaby'oś no pratikoś 'en nu'eśtra śantisima lengu'a śete śegira grande probeğo :

'EŚ verdad ke śeme haze algo difisil por averme de( )mandado koza ke por muğo ke alarge 'enelya devo śer kondenado de muy korto 'a todo me ofreśko paresyendome śer obligado 'a ley de 'uma(d)nidad 'a reśponder 'i note defraudar del grande probeğo ke deśta mi 'eśkritura śe te deve śegir por la konformidad ke deti ami la razon natural mośtra aver por la komunikasyon de śemeğansa do diğeron nu'eśtroś śaby'oś ke loś maś deloś hiğoś śemeğan aloś ermanoś dela madre 'i set-[2] 'i la razon natural 'eśta viśta delo diğo ke komo loś ermanoś laś maś delaś veześ śon śemeğanteś alyende dela 'igualdad de śuś konplisy'oneś 'i konpozisy'on por śer dotrinadoś de 'una meśma madre 'i la madre dotrina al hiğo konforme aśuś kośtumbreś alyende de śer śemeğanteś tanbyen 'enla konplisy'on de aki śe śige}

‹fol. 13b›
{kelaś kośtumbreś del hiğo śean śemeğanteś alaś del 'ermano deśu madre
'I POR 'eśta meśma kabza noś akabida tanbyen ke 'el ke kaza deve primero

---

[2] Exod. R. 7.5.

Book of the Regimen of Living ‹fol. 13b›

de[ ]mirar muğo 'enloś ermanoś dela muğer ke toma por 'el fin deloś fiğoś ke konelyya 'eśpera de aver[3] de manera ke por la natural śemeğanśa ke de ti ami deve aver 'eś razon ke tu kyeraś imitar miś kośtumbreś 'i yo perkuro inponerte enelyaś kon kunplida veluntad 'i vehemente deze'o 'eśpesyal porke śoy syerto por parte dela d[i]ğa komunikasy'on te śera maś fasil resibir la dotrina deloś kośtumbreś ke yo śigo 'i fu'erte 'esortasy'on para retenerloś no komo de ti'o śino komo de padre 'i maeśtro ke śegun 'eśkriby'o Briśon filosofo antigo[4] 'i 'otroś muğoś konbyene dotrinar loś mośos 'enśuś prinsipyos ke 'eśtonseś 'eśtan ağenoś de kośtumbreś por lo kual fasil mente śe śometan al bu'en reğimyento 'i śe akośtumbren dende śu ninyeś alaś 'obraś de virtud porke kreśyendo 'i 'eğersitandośe enelyaś ğamaś śe hartara de śegirlaś 'i 'ira de di'a 'en di'a 'en kontino a'umento de virtud haśta lyegar al śumo grado de 'eksel[e]nsy'a kuando alyegare ala 'edad del perfekto ğu'izyo 'i konosimyento dela virtud 'i byen verdadero 'i śe aśabentara para ke śyenpre 'enyyada 'enel fruto syendo śyenpre gobernado 'i mantenido dela dereğa razon :

'I POR 'el kontrary'o śi deśkuidaren de 'el 'enel prinsipy'o deśu kryasy'on 'i śe rindyeren alaś pasy'oneś del 'apetito konkupisible 'i irasible śera muy difisil śakarlo delyaś porke akaese 'enloś mośos komo 'enloś arboleś 'enel prinsipy'o deśu ğenerasyon kuando lu'ego fu'eron plantadoś 'i no śe 'enderesaron ke vinyendo deśpu'eś 'en a'umento śu tortura nunka maś śe pu'eden 'enderesar anteś kuanto maś lo kyeren 'enderesar maś śe danyan de modo ke anteś kebran ke doblen 'i de aki nase loke la 'eśperensy'a noś mu'eśtra ke loś maś deloś 'ombreś mal 'ensenyadoś kargadoś de visy'oś śon taleś por no aver śido dotrinadoś 'enel tyenpo de śuś mosedadeś 'i poreśto vemoś muğoś visy'ozoś ke śobre konoser desi meśmoś tener laś maś feaś kulpaś ke 'eś posible 'i konoser la 'ekselensy'a delaś vertudeś kontraryaś a'elyyaś nośe pu'eden kontener ke no peken 'i śigan śuś akośtumbradoś yeroś atanto ke muğoś d[e]lyoś śobre puğando la vergu'ensa dela ğente 'o 'el temor dela pena keryendośe apartar deśu mal kośtumbre 'en publiko no pu'eden deśar de tornar a'el 'en śekreto 'i todo 'eśto leś vyene(n) por la korup(')sy'on del 'apetito 'enel tyenpo dela mosedad por 'el mal 'enbezo 'enelyya 'i 'enla ninyeś :

'I LAŚ maś veześ akaese 'eśto por falta dela madre 'enel regalo del hiğo 'i deśkuido del padre 'enśu dotrina ke deven de advertir ke 'el fin verdadero dela kreasy'on del 'ombre por}

---

[3] Bava Batra 110a, Rashi Exod. 6.23.
[4] Bryson, 4th-c. B.C.E. philosopher: see *Oxford Classical Dictionary,* 3rd ed., 264.

Book of the Regimen of Living ‹fol. 14a›

‹fol. 14a›

{YD PEREK RI'ŚON [CHAPTER ONE]

reśpekto del kual todoś loś 'otroś fineś śon 'eś la 'obra dela virtud 'i todoś loś 'otroś fineś śon kamino para 'elyya 'i para la maś perfekta ke 'eś 'el puro śerbisy'o del Dyyo glory'ozo :

'I 'A 'opiny'on de nu'eśoś śabyoś 'eśte 'eś 'el fin dela kreasy'on del mundo glozando 'el primer bokablo dela śagrada 'eśkritura dizyendo por 'el prinsipy'o kre'o 'el Dyyo 'i set-[5] ke 'eś komo ke diğeśe por la ley ke śe lyyama prinsipy'o 'i por loś ğudyoś tanbyen ke śe ly[a]man prinsipy'o keryendo śinifikar ke śi śe halyyan la ley 'i 'el ğudyo kontiga mente ğuntoś ke 'eneśto konsiśte la perfeksy'on 'umana 'eśtonseś śon 'elyoś 'el fin dela kreasy'on del mundo 'i por 'eśto lo kre'o :

'I PU'EŚ 'eśte 'eś 'el fin prinsipal 'eś razon ke buśke 'el 'ombre 'el kamino por 'onde meğor śe 'efektu'e 'eśte fin ke 'eś perkurar de aber la muğer virtu'oza 'eśperando aber de śer taleś loś 'iğoś ke delyoś prosedyeren ke 'eś 'el śupremo fin :

POR lo kual akonseğaron nu'eśtroś śantiśimoś śaby'oś por muğaś veześ 'i 'en muğoś lugareś ke deve 'el 'ombre vender kuanto tyene por tomar hiğa de 'ombre śaby'o por muğer[6] porke syendo hiğa de tal varon śera kryada 'en toda virtud de adonde śe 'eśpera salir muy hermozo 'i śabrozo fruto 'i 'eśto tanto deśu natural konserbando śyenpre la bondad dela raiz komo por la bu'ena dotrina 'enbebida dende la ninyeś ke la meśma razon 'eś 'enel 'eleğir 'el yerno para la hiğa :

'I PU'EŚ 'el Dyyo por śu grande merse[d] te kizo dotar de[ ]bu'en padre no menor tela hizo 'en te probe'er de tal madre kuyaś vertudeś por atodoś śeren notoryaś 'i yo śośpeğo 'en dezilyaś kalyyo no pu'ede mankar de śer produzido 'el fruto 'en toda perfeksy'on 'i aśi śe'a amen

---

[5] Gen. 1.1.
[6] Pesaḥim 49ab.

KOMYENSA 'EL LIBRO

KAPITULO PRIMERO

'UNA koza 'onibersal ke aloś mosoś konbyene muǧo atentar 'enel prins[i]py'o dela ǧornada de śu bu'en 'andar te kyero anteś de todo dezir porke 'eś muǧo meneśter ke śeaś 'enelyya advertido 'i 'eś ke pu'eś śaliśte de laś alaś de tu madre perkureś de akonpanyyarte kon bu'enoś 'i virtu'ozoś fuyendo 'a r[y]enda śu'elta komo de 'enemigoś de loś maloś visy'ozoś porke no śolo 'eś meneśter ke no śe kebre 'el hilo del bu'en reǧimyento de la ninyeś śino ke kontinu'a mente śiga śu beatisimo kamino fasta ke konla perfekta kontinuasyon lyege al verdadero konosimyento del byen}

‹fol. 14b›
{'i mal 'i no sese hata ke śe haga fišo 'i firme 'el bu'en abito śin reselo de korupsyyon alguna ke no abaśtan todoś loś bu'enoś kośtumbreś dela ninyeź para reśiśtir aloś tempeśtu'ośoś vyentoś deloś apetitoś 'enla flor dela mansebi'a śino śige 'a( )śi byen hata atemarśe de '[e]fektuar 'el fruto konloś firmeś abitoś : 'i śi de 'otro modo lo hizyereś perderaś kuanto de tu madre aś tom[a]do 'i de mi aś deprendido :

DELO diǧo nasyo 'el probervyyo antigu'o ke śe śu'ele dezir no kon kyen naseś śino kon kyen paśeś[7] ke 'en aber meneśter dezir no kon kyen naseś denota de śer kon kyen nase nesesary'o por lo kual fu'e meneśter amoneśtar ke no abaśta akelyya konpanyi'a del nasimyento śer bu'ena śi la ke depu'eś delyya susede no la konfirma porke para koronperlo akośtum[b]rado dende ninyeś 'un śolo visy'o 'o konpanyi'a de 'un śolo visy'ozo abaśta maś para konfirmar 'el byen kontra loś apetitoś muy muǧo 'a meneśter trabaǧar haśta venir 'en grado de pose'er 'el abito firme para 'obrar byen ke depu'eś del kontino kośtumbre 'i konf[i]rmaśyon dela virtud deśpu'eś de araygado

---

[7] The Marqués de Santillana included this proverb in his *Refranes que dizen las viejas tras el fuego* (ed. U. Cronan, "Refranes," *Revue Hispanique* 25 [1911]: 134–219; 166, no. 490).

Book of the Regimen of Living ⟨fol. 14b–15a⟩

'enla mosedad 'el arbol deloś abitoś plantado 'enla ninyeś kresidaś laś ramaś dela virtud ke de 'elyo śon produzidas no abaśtan todoś loś vyentoś deloś apetitoś 'i deleyteś korporaleś 'a 'inpedirlo ke no nuzen deśu fruto ke 'eś 'el śumo byen 'i 'obra virtu'oza porke alyi śe halya 'una fasilidad kon kunplida veluntad para byen 'obrar śin reziśtensy'a de triśteza ke deśta 'obra apartar lo pu'eda por lo kual todo akel ke 'el Dyyo amo tanto ke kon 'eśta fasilidad le ayudo 'a alyegar 'a 'el śumo grado de filisidad no śe pu'ede del dezir ke padeśka de 'obra alguna dela fortuna 'i 'eśte tal bibe vida beata

'I KON 'eśto śe śa(t)ś[t]ifaze akelyya grande dubda ke anśi aloś śaby'oś antigoś de nu'eśtra ley komo aloś modernoś 'i anśi meśmo 'a akelyoś ke kon śolo 'el lumbre de la naturaleza 'eśpekularon śe hizo difisil ǧuśgar la kual menoś śantoś 'i profetaś mobyeron 'i aberiguaron 'i 'eś porke vyenen byeneś aloś maloś 'i maleś aloś bu'enoś[8] 'enla kual algunoś k[i]ǧeron dezir kela dubda no 'eś dubda por parte de śer 'el śuǧebto ke reśibe 'el mal 'i 'el byen 'ignoto 'a noś por kuanto no podemoś śaber kyen 'eś verdader'a mente malo 'o kyen 'eś bu'eno porke 'el byen 'i 'el mal no konśiśten tanto 'enla 'obra por śi meśma komo 'enlaś kondiśy'oneś 'i 'elik(')syon de 'elya komo adelante deklararemoś aśerka delaś vertudeś moraleś konforme aloke tengo byen largo 'eśkrito 'enel komento dela 'etika[9] 'en 'el nobeno 'i 'enel deśimo de adonde[10] 'eśta 'ibidente ke la perfekśyon dela 'obra konśiśte 'enla veluntad kon ke śe 'obra kon todaś laś kondiśy'oneś pu'eśtaś 'en muǧoś teśtoś 'enel terśero 'i kinto dela diǧa 'etika[11] ke para 'eśto śe rekyeren 'i komo śolo 'el Dyyo 'eś 'el śavedor delaś 'intrinsikaś veluntadeś}

⟨fol. 15a⟩
{TV
'i 'eliksyoneś 'el śolo 'eś 'el konośedor de 'el bu'eno 'i del malo :
ALYENDE de 'eśto śo yo de 'opiny'on konforme ala de muǧoś antigoś ke por parte del byen 'o mal ke akaeśe al śuǧebto la dubda no 'eś dubda ke byen 'eśpekulando nunka al bu'eno vyene mal ni al malo byen

---

[8] Job 21.7–21. *Avot* responds to the paradox thus: "R. Yannai said, It is beyond our power to explain either the prosperity of the wicked or the afflictions of the righteous" (4.19 [some editions 4.15]); see also Ralbag Job 4:26. Seneca examines the same question at length in *On Providence* II.1 (ed. and trans. J. W. Basore [Cambridge, MA, 1928], 1:7).

[9] He refers to *Pne Mośe*, his commentary on Aristotle's *Ethics*; see fol. 1b above.

[10] Aristotle, *NE* IX.viii.6 (1168b 35–1169a 3), X.ix.11 (1180a 15–18).

[11] Aristotle, *NE* III.1 (1109b 30–1111b 3), III.v (1113b 4–1115a 6), V.viii (1135a 16–1136a 9).

Book of the Regimen of Living ⟨fol. 15a–15b⟩

PARA lo kual 'eś meneśter śaber ke loś byeneś śon repartidoś 'en treś 'eśpesyaś 'i modoś diferenteś porke primero śon loś byeneś verdaderoś 'eśpritualeś lyamadoś byeneś dela alma loś kualeś śon de 'el 'entendimyento 'eśpekulatibo 'o te'oriko ke 'eśpekula laś kozaś 'onibersaleś śakando deloś 'endibidu'oś 'intensy'oneś ǧenerikaś 'i 'eśpisifikaś konsidrando laś kozaś 'en kuanto śon parteś del mundo 'i anśi meśmo la 'obra de 'el 'entendimyento hazedor 'i pratiko konlo kual śe konsideran laś kozaś para 'obrarlaś 'i konel ǧuśgamoś śi laś devemoś hazer 'i śon laś kozaś 'enke kabe 'el konśeǧo komo śe ve'e del tersero 'i seśto dela 'etika anśi meśmo la 'eliksy'on 'i determinasyyon dela veluntad ke susede al konśeǧo 'eśte 'eś primero modo de 'eśpesy'a 'i todoś 'eśtoś byeneś śon del 'ombre 'en kuanto 'ombre porke 'a todo 'ombre 'i 'a ninguno 'otro konpeten :

ŚEGUNDO śon loś byeneś korporaleś halyyadoś 'enel 'ombre propya mente 'en kuanto animal 'i śon loś del ku'erpo komo la hermozura la fu'ersa 'i laś kozaś aneǧaś a'elyaś komo ver 'i 'o'ir 'i 'otroś śemeǧanteś

TERSERO modo śe reparte 'en doś 'eśpeśyaś 'i todaś doś komunikan 'en śer byeneś 'eśtrinsikoś dela primera śon loś byeneś ke lyyamamoś dela fortuna 'i vyenen loś maś por parte dela kośtelasy'on 'o akazo komo rikeza 'i hiǧoś 'i set-

DELA śegunda 'eś la 'onra ke 'eś 'eśtrinsika 'i prosede de parte de 'el 'ombre kela da anśi meśmo diremoś aver treś 'eśpesyaś de maleś kontraryoś a'eśtoś byeneś loś kualeś de aki śon śabidoś kon 'eśto digo śer viśto ke 'en ninguno deśtoś byeneś 'eśta la dubda porke śi deloś byeneś dela p(i)rimera 'eśpesy'a hablamoś 'eś viśto ke 'el bu'eno 'eś 'el leǧitimo pose'edor deloś diǧoś byeneś 'i kon muǧo dereǧo loś pośe'e 'i ninguno 'otro loś pu'ede tener 'i 'el malo 'eś ala kontra anteś 'eś la dubda porke vyenen loś 'otroś maleś aloś ke tyenen 'eśtoś byeneś dela prim[e]ra 'eśpesy'a 'i porke vyenen byeneś de 'otra 'eśpesy'a aloś ke tyenen loś maleś deśta :

PU'EŚ 'enla śegunda 'eśpesy'a tanbyen no tyene lugar la dubda porke loś taleś byeneś korporaleś komo śon la hermozura la konplisy'on 'i set- proseden del prinsipy'o de śu nasimyento anteś ke bu'enoś 'i maloś kon verdad śe pu'edan}

⟨fol. 15b⟩
{lyyamar por lo kual 'eś byen viśto no poder kaber la dubda 'en alguna manera 'en 'eśtoś taleś byeneś :

REŚTA lu'ego ke la dubda no 'eś śino 'enloś byeneś de la tersera 'eśpesy'a 'i 'eś la keśty'on porke aloś virtu'ozoś akaesen maleś loś kualeś śon 'infortuny'oś 'i deś'onraś deśdiǧaś 'i 'otraś taleś loś kualeś śuś kontrary'oś ke śon byeneś vyenen aloś maloś :

'I kuanto al modo śegundo deśtoś byeneś ke 'eś la 'onra ke 'eś byen 'eśtrinsiko dado de 'el 'ombre al 'ombre dezimoś ke no pu'ede śer la dubda porke la 'onra 'eś śenyyal dela virtud śegun kiǧo Aristotel 'i 'otroś muǧoś por lo kual 'el bu'eno dara la

Book of the Regimen of Living ‹fol. 15b›

'onra devida al bu'eno 'i śi 'el ke la merese no la resibe 'o 'el ke la resibe no la merese ke lo primero akaese kuando 'el 'ombre ke la deve de dar 'eś malo 'i 'el ke la 'a de resibir bu'eno 'i lo śegundo syendo todoś doś maloś : porke 'el bu'eno dereğo ğu'ez de la bondad śyenpre 'onrara al meresedor de 'elyya 'i nunka a'el ke no la merese 'en kual kyera deśtoś doś kauzoś keda la dubda śaśtifeğa porke śi 'el resebidor no 'eś tal ke mereśka śer 'onrado no kabe 'enel la dubda porke no lo pu'ede śenyalar por bu'eno śino 'el ke no lo 'eś pu'eś śi 'el ke śe la da 'eś malo 'eśta tal no 'eś 'onra śino deś'onra 'i mal śe deve lyyamar 'i śi 'el ke merese la 'onra no śela dan 'eśto no pu'ede śer śino de 'el malo del kual no śer 'onrado 'eś grande 'onra 'i śenyal de virtud lo kual 'eś manifyeśto del diğo de akel grande moral 'Epiteto ke dize no pyerde 'el bu'eno porke 'el malo lo pribe dela 'onra debida porke a'un ke lo 'onraśe no kedari'a poreso maś 'onrado de lo ke 'el porśi 'era[12]

'I 'EŚTO 'eś loke loś benerableś padreś śaby'oś de nu'eśtra śanta dotrina kizyeron dezir 'enla difinsy'on de 'el 'onrado dizyendo ke 'eś 'el ke 'onra laś kryaturaś[13] keryendo śinifikar ke 'el ke 'onrado śe pu'ede lyyamar 'eś akel por 'el kual śegura mente śe pu'ede dezir ke 'onra laś kryaturaś kyero dezir ke kuando laś 'onra kedan 'onradaś ke 'eśte tal 'onrador tanbyen 'el keda 'onrado de akelyaś ke 'el 'onro : por ke 'elyaś mośtran akel tal 'onrador śer 'el bu'eno 'i digno de 'onrar 'a 'otro pu'eś śe 'onraron kon 'el : 'i 'el ke penśando 'onrarlaś no śolo no laś 'onra maś anteś laś deś'onra por śu poka a'utoridad 'eśte tal no śe lyyamara 'onrado pu'eś no śe 'onran konel de manera ke 'enla 'onra no tyene 'entrada nu'eśtra dubda :

KEDA noś de aberiguar la dubda 'enla primera parte de loś byeneś 'eśtrinsikoś ke por fortuna 'o ventura vyenen 'i 'a 'eśto digo ke 'eśtoś taleś no śon byeneś ni maleś por śi}

---

[12] Although no exact parallel has come to my attention, the sense resembles Epictetus' remarks in the *Enchiridion:* "20. Bear in mind that it is not the man who reviles or strikes you that insults you, but it is your judgement that these men are insulting you" (*Manual,* ed. and trans. W. A. Oldfather [London, 1926], 2:499). Similarly: "24. For, if lack of honour is an evil, you cannot be evil through the instrumentality of some other person, any more than you can be in shame" (2:501); cf. no. 42 (2:527). Seneca expresses the same idea to Serenus citing Cato's example: "no wise man can receive either injury or insult" (*De Constantia Sapientis* 2, trans. Basore, 1:51).

[13] Avot 4.1.

Book of the Regimen of Living ‹fol. 16a›

‹fol. 16a›
{YV
meśmoś śalvo por parte de akel ke loś pośe'e : konforme al diğo del po'eta ke dize no aver ningun byen ni mal por parte dela fortuna śi no ke todoś pro śede(')n de parte de 'el 'ombre propy'o[14] : keryendo 'eneśto dezir ke loś byeneś fortu'itoś no śon byeneś ni maleś 'enśi //[śalvo]// śegun 'enla reputasy'on 'i 'eśtima ke loś 'ombreś loś tyenen 'i śegun ke kada 'uno leś diśtribuye 'i 'uza delyoś ke aveześ muğoś maleś proseden dela końtelasy'on 'i vyenen dela fortuna no pensando aloś kualeś komun mente lyyaman maleś 'i loś bu'enoś śe sirben de 'elyyoś por byen mośtrandośe magnyanimoś 'enla toleransy'a de 'elyyoś vensyendo kon 'elyya ala ventura de modo ke a'umentan śu propyo byen 'onesto kon 'elyyoś :

'I POR konśigyente vyenen byeneś aloś maloś de loś kualeś 'uzan mal diśtribuyendoloś 'en kozaś torpeś 'i vileś deś'oneśtaś akresentando kon 'elyyaś śu maldad de manera ke 'eśtoś taleś byeneś 'enloś maloś no śe pu'eden dezir byeneś pu'eś śon 'eśturmentoś para deśtru'ir loś byeneś de la alma ni loś maleś 'enloś bu'enoś śe pu'eden dezir maleś pu'eś kon 'elyyoś śe adk[y]eren loś byeneś propy'oś ke śon loś de 'el alma :

KE ANŚI komo 'en laś ğoyyaś de 'oro 'i plata laś perlaś 'i pyedraś presy'ozaś no konśiśte 'el presy'o por parte del valor de 'elyyaś por śi ke muy poka nesesidad de 'elyyaś ayy para la vida 'umana 'i 'otraś muğo maś meğoreś kozaś 'i maś 'utileś śon 'eśtimadaś 'en menoś ke debyeran śer 'eśtimadaś kon maś razon śalvo por parte de loś 'ombreś ke kyeren 'i śon konformeś 'a tenerlaś 'en presy'o 'i 'eśtima anśi todoś loś 'otroś byeneś no śon maś ke śegun loś 'ombreś loś 'eśtiman 'i śe sirben de 'elyyoś para byen 'o para mal 'i anśi hazen delyoś byeneś 'i maleś 'i pu'eś loś bu'enoś virtu'ozoś 'i byen aventuradoś śon kontentoś 'i alegreś kon kuanto dela ventura prosede 'i la debina probidensy'a 'ordena 'i kon 'eśto biben lyenoś de 'eśpritual plazer 'i glory'ozoś 'en deleyte no śe pu'ede dezir ke 'en modo alguno tengan mal porke la delektasy'on 'en la 'obra demu'eśtra śuma bondad 'enel bu'eno 'i 'el malo śyenpre tyene triśteza 'i komo kyera ke śyenpre 'el deleyte 'eśta pegado kon 'el virtu'[o]zo śin mudansa alguna 'eś śenyyal verdadero de 'eśtar kontino 'en kontino byen 'i por konśigyente 'el malo 'en kontino mal :

---

[14] Cf. Ovid, *Tristia* V.5.47. Cf. Seneca, *On the Fickleness of Fortune:* "For men make a mistake, my dear Lucilius, if they hold that anything good, or evil either, is bestowed upon us by Fortune; it is simply the raw material of Goods and Ills that she gives to us — the sources of things which, in our keeping, will develop into good or ill" (*Ep. Mor.* 98.2, ed. and trans. R. M. Gummere [London, 1925], 3:119).

Book of the Regimen of Living ‹fol. 16a–16b›

'I DE aki nasy'o akel śingular diğo de Aleğandre Magno ke dezi'a por śi śer śeguro dela probeza ke de śemeğante śaby'o 'i 'iluśtre [CW. prinsipe]}

‹fol. 16b›
{prinsipe komo 'el nośe deve kre'er ke śoberby'a mente pensaśe no poder venir 'en pobreza por kauzo ninguno fortu'ito vyendo por 'eśperensy'a ke kuanto maś altoś 'eśtan loś prinsipeś tanto menoś śeguroś śon dela kaida[15] pero kizo dezir ke abyendo lyegado al grado dela virtud ke al bu'eno konbyene no podi'a la fortuna fazerle triśte ni venirle dany'o ke mal śe pudyeśe dezir ke todo śeri'a para 'el puro byen pu'eś śe avi'a de śerbir delyo 'a fin de byen 'i 'oneśto de manera ke a'un ke la adversa fortuna lo derokaśe dela kumbre de śu prośperidad 'i pośesy'on de byeneś fortu'itoś no podi'a koneśto derokarlo dela altura dela virtud 'i bondad adonde 'elyya no lo avi'a pu'eśto ni podi'a poner porke akel afamado 'i śaby'o rey śe preśyava maś śin konparasyon de śer filosofo ke prinsipe 'eśtimandośe maś por śu preśona ke por la dignidad real :

LO KUAL śe mu'eśtra por laś palabraś ke dišo śobre Dy'oğeneś al kual konśuś mayoraleś fu'e 'a viğitar 'en la kuba 'enke moraba 'i 'engrandeśyendo laś repu'eśtaś ke Dy'oğeneś komo filosofo 'i menośpresyador del mundo le daba dišo śino fu'er[a] Aleśandre fu'era Dy'oğeneś[16] palabraś de varon prudente 'i bu'eno diśiplo de tan śabyo maeśtro komo 'era Aristot[e]leś ke 'eś byen de notar ke no dišo śino fu'era rey fu'era Dy'oğeneś por ke kišo dezir ke śino fu'era partiśipante 'enla filosofi'a anśi natural komo moral a'un ke fu'era rey deśeara śer Dy'oğeneś por śer 'enśuś 'oğoś 'el byen dela śensy'a 'i virtud śin konparaśyon mayor ke 'el 'eśtado real maś pu'eś 'era filosofo 'i rey keri'a anteś śerlo ke śer filosofo śolo komo Dy'oğeneś 'era komo śi dišera maś 'eś rey 'i filosofo ke filosofo śolo 'i maś filosofo śolo ke rey śin śer filosofo anteponyendo la śensy'a al reynado ke 'eś la mayor dignidad 'umana por lo kual afirmaba śin reselo śer śeguro ke 'eś 'eśtar śin kuidado dela pobreza por la kual 'entendi'a todoś loś maleś dela fortuna por śer deśpreśyador delyya 'i set- kuanto maś ke 'eśtoś byeneś 'eśtrinsikoś no śon byeneś ke pereteneśkan ala 'eśensy'a del byen aventurado para ke śe pu'eda dezir ke por la a'uzensy'a 'i prezensy'a delyoś le vengan 'a 'el maleś 'o byeneś ke no śon maś ke para lo ke konśiśte de 'el 'a 'otroś :

KOMO dezi'a Śeneka ke loś maleś fortu'itoś ke vyenen aloś bu'enoś śon komo laś nubeś ke 'inpiden la klaridad del śol[17] komo muğaś veześ akaese ke 'eśtando 'el śol

---

[15] Unidentified source.

[16] Diogenes Laertius, *Philosophers,* VI. 32 (ed. and trans. R. D. Hicks [Cambridge, MA, 1966], 2:35; Plutarch, *Alexander,* XIV (*Lives,* ed. and trans. B. Perrin [London, 1919], 7:259).

[17] This seems to be Seneca, *Ep. Mor.* 80.6, trans. Gummere, 2:217.

'enel vigor de śu klaridad śe ponen algunaś nubeś delante del 'i 'a akelyoś 'a kyen alunbraba 'inpiden ke no alunbre 'i anśi komo laś diǧaś nubeś nada diminu'en dela klaridad del śol 'enśi meśma ni le hazen danyo alguno maś todo danyo ke delyyaś vyene lo padeśen akelyoś ke de śu klaridad gozaban anśi la perdida ['i] privasyon deloś byeneś 'eśtrinsikoś no diminuyen la glory'a de 'el virtu'ozo de manera ke 'el virtu'ozo 'a kyen loś [CW. byeneś]}

⟨fol. 17a⟩
{YZ PEREK ŠENIY [CHAPTER TWO]
byeneś tenporaleś faltan no deǧa de śer felise para śi meśmo a'un ke para 'otroś no lo śe'a komo 'el śol nublado 'i 'iklipsado ke no deǧa de śer lusidisimo a'un ke aninguno kom(y)[u]nike śu luz 'i aśi meśmo 'el malo no deǧa de śer malo a'un ke loś 'eśturmentoś para 'uzar la maldad le falten komo śon loś byeneś tenporaleś 'i fortu'itoś :

KAPITULO ŚEGUNDO

ŚI śobre lo diǧo keraś a'un dubdar ke pu'eśto ke 'otorgeś ke loś byeneś 'enel malo no śon byeneś ni loś maleś 'enel bu'eno śon maleś toda vi'a no deǧan loś bu'enoś de śer 'inpedidoś deśu byen hazer 'i loś maloś muǧo maś deśpedidoś para 'obrar konforme 'a śu malisy'a de adonde parese ke fu'era meǧor tener 'el bu'eno loś 'eśturmentoś para 'eǧersitar śu bondad 'i 'el malo kareser de 'elyoś ke deśte modo 'el byen de 'el bu'eno fu'era meǧor śyendo komunikado 'a 'otroś 'i 'el mal de 'el malo menor śyendo śu dany'o 'inpedido 'i de doś maleś 'el menor keda byen śegun 'el proberby'o deloś vyeǧos ke dizen de doś maleś 'el menor śe'a de 'eskoǧer[18] :
'A 'eśto te digo ke a'un ke al prezente baśtava byen lo diǧo 'a śaśtifazer ala dubda 'en 'oniversal ke 'eś aver byen viśto ke ni aloś bu'enoś vyenen maleś ni aloś maloś byeneś aś de śaver ke muǧaś veześ 'el bu'eno śe mu'eśtra meǧor 'i da meǧor 'enǧenplo deśi 'eśtando 'enloś maleś fortu'itoś mośtrandośe animozo 'en śufrirloś ke no 'enloś byeneś 'i por 'eśta kabza le suseden loś diǧoś maleś :
'I PORKE no kyero ke 'en taleś kozaś kedeś perpleśo ke śeri'a grande 'eśkandalo te dire algunaś razoneś 'ibidenteś 'eneśta pośtrera dubda ke muǧoś de loś antigoś 'i modernoś 'eśkribyeron perśuponyendo ke loś taleś byeneś 'o maleś śean 'ordenadoś por parte dela probidensyy'a 'i dirlo'e breve mente para ke meǧor lo pu'edaś konprehender :

---

[18] Compare the *refrán*, "De dos males, el menor" (Luis Martínez Kleiser, *Refranero general, ideológico español* [Madrid: Real Academia Española, 1953], p. 438 [no. 38,220]).

Book of the Regimen of Living ‹fol. 17a–17b›

'EN kuanto ala primera partida dela dubda ke 'eś porke vyenen maleś aloś bu'enoś aś de śaver keloś bu'enoś śon 'en diversoś gradoś 'i modoś de bondad de maś 'a menoś ke ayy algunoś ke śyendo algo bu'enoś afiguran 'i 'imağinan śer 'elyoś propyoś kabza deśu prośperidad aloś kualeś śuseden adversidadeś para tirarloś de akelyya 'erada 'imağinasy'on 'i deśto śele śige 'a 'elyoś byen 'i a'umento de virtud 'i 'el Dyyo 'eś kon 'eśtoś komo 'el bu'en padre 'o mediko ke da la medisina aśu 'enfermo a'un kele du'ela :

AYY 'OTROŚ muğo meğoreś keloś primeroś loś kualeś a'un ke śon syertoś proseder todoś 'eśtoś byeneś dela prima kabza por pura probidensyya devina 'i nunka 'el kontrary'o 'imağinan 'eśtando prośperoś reselan la kaida 'i temen śer 'eśprimentadoś porke no śaben komo śabran sufrir la adversidad}

‹fol. 17b›

{'i 'a 'eśtoś taleś 'eśprimenta la probidensy'a devina por śu 'utilidad de 'elyoś meśmoś para ke konośkan kuan fiśoś 'eśtan 'enla bondad por 'amor de 'el Dyyo 'i de śi meśmoś 'i ganan 'el abito dela pasensy'a 'enla fortuna śin[y]eśtra 'i śe afinan 'enla bondad para ke de 'el deprendan 'otroś 'a śufrir :

KONFORME aloke diğo Plutarko ke loś bu'enoś śon komo laś yerbaś 'odoriferaś ke kuanto maś mağadaś maś trasyende śu 'olor[19] 'i deśte modo fu'e 'Iyob kabalyero 'inbensible konforme alo ke yo anpla mente tengo probado por todo śu libro[20] no aver yerado 'en kuanto diğo śuśtentando 'el teśtigo ke 'el Dyyo de 'el dyyo ke 'era varon temyente al Dyyo kunplido 'i rekto 'i set-[21] 'eś 'el Dyyo koneśtoś komo 'el prudente kapitan ke pone loś fu'erteś kavalyeroś 'i de fu'erśaś avantağadaś 'enel maś rezy'o dela batalyya para ke a'un ke 'eśkapen feridoś śean 'enğenplo de 'onra 'i 'eśpeğo aloś 'otroś kavalyeros :

AYY tersero modo 'i 'eś de bu'enoś 'en śumo grado de bondad 'i 'eroyyka virtud loś kualeś śyenpre konsidran komo de la kabza primera no pu'ede proseder mal maś anteś delyya prosede toda perfeksy'on 'i byen 'i koneśte firme konosimyento biven 'en kontino kontentamyento tanto kon 'el byen de fortuna komo konel mal śin fazer 'en

---

[19] This seems to closely parallel Plutarch's characterization of old men in government: "just as they say the iris, when it has grown old and has blown off its fetid and foul smell, acquires a more fragrant odour, so no opinion of old men is turbulent, but they are all weighty and composed" (*Moralia,* trans. Fowler, 10:119).

[20] He makes reference to his commentary on Job, *Piruš al Iyob;* see Ben-Menahem, "Bibliography," 284.

[21] Job 1.8.

BOOK OF THE REGIMEN OF LIVING ⟨FOL. 17B–18A⟩

'elyoś mudansa de modo alguno maś anteś dan por todo al Dyyo glory'ozo muğoś lo'oreś aśi por 'el mal komo por 'el byen :
'I 'a 'eśtoś taleś vyenen loś maleś por reśpektoś diverśoś ke algunoś padesen por parte dela partikular probidensy'a para darleś maś premyo por 'el meresimyento de śufrir akelyya tribulasyon 'i adversidad 'i de 'eśte modo fu'e ami ver 'Abraham nu'eśtro śanto patryarka 'enla tribulasy'on de akel abto 'ero'iko de kerer śakrifikar śu hiğo[22] : por 'obedeser al precebto devino por ke 'el Dyyo glory'ozo 'i verdadero ğu'eś 'eśprimenta loś taleś por puro 'amor para ke kon ğuśta razon por 'el abto meritory'o 'en ke loś 'eśprimenta alkansen śeguroś 'el premy'o de śu śervisy'o śabyendo 'el Dyyo 'i konsidrando de 'elyoś 'eśtar firmeś 'enla bondad al modo ke dizen nu'eśoś śaby'oś del 'olyero ke haze 'eśperensya 'enlaś 'olyyaś maś kozidaś 'i śanaś ke 'eś syerto ke no śean de ronper 'i set-[23] 'eś aśi 'el Dyyo kon 'eśtoś komo padre 'o komo bu'en gobernador dela republika ke tyene 'un śudito śuyo 'enselente varon 'i depu'eś de averle heğo muğaś mersedeś por notifikar śu bondad 'a todoś lo kual 'eś 'ignota por aver bivido 'en paś le demanda hazer abtoś difisilimoś 'a ke loś 'otroś sibdadanoś no podrian lyegar para ke 'en toda virtud śe mu'eśtre byen śu perfeksy'on :
'I 'a algunoś vyenen loś taleś maleś no por śi meśmoś śino por 'el pu'eblo 'i republika 'entre loś}

⟨fol. 18a⟩
{YH
kualeś biven para ke konśu tribulasyon 'i mu'erte 'el Dyyo perdone 'a todoś konforme alo ke dizen nu'eśtroś śaby'oś ke la mu'erte deloś ğuśtoś perdona 'i set-[24] 'i 'eśto 'eś manifyeśto śer puro byen para 'el bu'eno ke parese la probidensy'a 'obrar 'enel konforme aloke 'el meśmo hari'a por śalvar 'una republika 'el Dyyo 'eś aki komo 'onibersal ğu'ez 'i 'un prinsipe dereğo 'el kual todo śu pu'eblo 'o 'una sibdad yero 'i 'el moderando la ğuśtisy'a 'i toda vi'a no deśando de hazerla le deśtruye la mayor fortaleza por ke kon 'eśte dany'o keden todoś perdonadoś 'i śe reku'erden dela mersed ke śu prinsipe kon 'elyoś fizo :
'I 'A algunoś śe leś śigen maleś por parte deloś padreś ke la probidensya devina

---

[22] Gen. 22.1–18.
[23] Unidentified midrash on Ps. 11.5. A similar sentence is attributed to Plato in *El libro de los buenos proverbios:* "Los vasos del ollero pruebanlos por los suenos que fasen quando los fieren por saber quales son sanos e quales son quebrados" (ed. H. Knust, *Mittheilungen aus dem Eskurial*, Bibliothek des Litterarischen Vereins in Stuttgart [Tübingen: Litterarischer Verein, 1879]: 209).
[24] Moed Katan 28a.

Book of the Regimen of Living ⟨fol. 18a–18b⟩

'eśekuta 'el mal deloś padreś 'enloś hiǧoś²⁵ ke śon parte de 'el padre aśi komo 'eśekuto 'el Dyyo la pena 'enloś susesoreś de ᶜEli por 'el pekado de śuś padreś 'i set-²⁶ 'i la razon 'eneśto 'eś śekreto perfundo śiknifikado por 'el śenyor Rabbenu Mošeh 'en repu'eśta de 'una demanda ke le demandaron por ke dizen depender 'el byen ke susede al hiǧo dela bondad de 'el padre 'i set-²⁷ no 'eś aki lugar para alargar maś 'enelyo poderloaś ver 'en loke yo tengo notado 'enel komento desimo de 'el tersero dela 'etika²⁸ donde tengo byen deklarado śuś palabraś ayy 'otra kauśa 'i muy verdader'a ami ver la kual 'eś ke śabyendo puntual mente la probidensy'a devina la konplisy'on 'i konpozisy'on de loś taleś bu'enoś leś da loś byeneś de fortuna konforme aloke konbyene para alkansar 'el poś́trer fin 'o byen aventuransa 'i porke algunoś kon abundansy'a deloś taleś byeneś alkansan meǧor 'eśte fin 'i 'a 'otroś leś 'eś kauza ke lo 'inpide da 'a kada kual konforme aśu konplisy'on para adkerir 'el tal fin de manera ke al kele śobra 'eś komo konbyene 'i kuando falta lo meśmo 'i koneśto pyenso 'entenderśe akel diǧo de nu'eśtroś śaby'oś ke dizen ke loś hiǧoś la vida 'i loś mantenimyentoś no dependen dela bondad śalvo dela kośtelasy'on²⁹ 'i traen 'enśenplo de doś famozisimoś śaby'oś 'igualeś 'en virtud 'i bondad 'en 'eśte prośtero modo 'i 'el 'uno 'era prośpero 'en todaś treś kozaś 'i 'el 'otro falto 'en todaś 'elyyaś 'i se-³⁰ ke lo ke kyere dezir 'a mi ǧu'izyo 'en dezir ke no dependen 'eśtoś treś byeneś de la bondad komo ke dišeśe ke por parte dela bondad śon syertoś 'i no śuśpensoś 'i dekolgadoś dar 'a kada 'uno loke le konbyene 'i kuando śe śigen por parte dela kostelasyyon no śon muy syertoś ke muy faśil mente por muǧaś kauśaś śe 'inpiden :

'I traen preba deśtoś doś śenyoreś de 'un meśmo grado de bondad ke lyegaron al śumo byen por medy'oś diversoś de rikeza 'i pobreza ke 'eś śenyyal śer produzidoś 'enelyoś por pura probidensy'a devina ke da}

⟨fol. 18b⟩
{'a kada kual loke konbyene para alkansar akel grado de bondad 'i virtud 'i śi faltara 'el prośpero de śu prośperidad 'i 'el 'otro de śu adversidad no alkansaran tanbyen 'el propy'o fin 'umano 'eś viśto lu'ego por kua[n]taś kauzaś pu'eden proseder 'eśtoś ke lyamamoś maleś 'a loś bu'enoś 'i śyenpre por śu byen :

---

²⁵ Exod. 20.5 and 34.7.
²⁶ 1 Sam. 4.11.
²⁷ Berakot 7a, Sanhedrin 27b, Makkot 24a.
²⁸ He refers to *Pne Moše*. The Aristotle passage seems to be *NE* III.xii.5–8 (1119b 1–16).
²⁹ Moed Katan 28a.
³⁰ Moed Katan 28a.

BOOK OF THE REGIMEN OF LIVING ‹FOL. 18B›

'I kuanto 'a loś byeneś ke vyenen aloś maloś 'eś muy maś fasil reśponder ke pu'ede śer por muğaś kauśaś 'i ke muy verdaderaś konbyene 'a śaber para vedarloś de 'otro mal mayor ke faltando akel tal byen farian de manera ke leś prosede por pura mersed devina 'i 'a veześ para ke por 'enteresisyon de akelyoś byeneś śe arepyentan de 'el mal 'i vengan al byen ke 'eśto 'eś loke 'el Dyyo kyere deloś maloś komo dezi'a 'el profeta ke no 'envelunto 'en mu'erte del malo 'i set-[31] 'i kuando śon 'eśtremadoś 'en 'el mal leś vyene 'el tal byen para atemarloś 'i konfundirloś por ke no danyen 'a 'otroś pu'eś 'elyoś no tyenen remedy'o komo śe dize 'enel śalmo de Šabbaṭ 'en floreser maloś komo la yerba 'i set-[32] 'i alaś veześ para poder hazer konelyoś mal 'a 'otroś ke lo meresen de manera ke śean verdugo dela probidensy'a komo dezi'a 'el rey David 'eśkapa mi alma de 'el malo tu 'eśpada[33] śiknifikando śer 'el malo 'eśpada dela devina probidenśy'a komo tenemoś diğo 'i 'a veześ leś da 'eśtoś byeneś para ke reśten aśuś hiğoś porke ve'e la devina probidensya ke an deśer bu'enoś 'i 'otraś muğaś kauzaś alyende de 'eśtaś ke śe pu'eden dezir konforme 'a nu'eśtra śantisima ley ke no ayy ninguno tan bu'eno ke no haga algun pekado ni ninguno tan malo ke no śe'a partiçipante 'en algun byen 'i kyere śaśtifazer 'el Dyyo 'eneśte mundo 'i pagar aloś 'unoś 'i aloś 'otroś lo poko 'i değar lo maś para 'el venidero mundo dela verdad todo kuanto tenemoś diğo śe 'entyende preśuponyendo ke '[e]śtoś taleś maleś 'o byen[e]ś prosedan dela probidensy'a devina abśuluta mente lo kual yo p[y]enso ke partiçipe 'en 'elyo la kośtelasy'on 'i koneśto 'eś maś viśta la asulusy'on dela dubda ke komo śe'a verdad ke de 'el Dyyo no prosede mal śino śolo privasy'on de 'el byen 'el kual konśiśte 'en 'enkubrir śuś faseś de 'el malo[34] : śile susede byen por parte dela kośtelasy'on no noś devemoś keğar dela probidensy'a devina ke muğa kabza 'a de aver para ke por parte dela probidensy'a śe prive 'el byen a'un deloś maloś śino fu'ere por fin de 'un gran byen ke delyyo śe rezulte 'i por 'eśta kabza me paresy'o ami śyenpre mayor la dubda 'en venir maleś aloś bu'enoś ke byeneś aloś maloś a'un ke 'a 'opiny'on de muğoś śaby'oś 'eś al kontrary'o tengo byen diśkutido 'eśto 'enla deklarasy'on dela demanda de Mošeh Rabbenu 'a 'el Dyyo kuando diğo haśme śaber agora tuś kareraś 'i set-[35] ke ami ver fu'e śu 'inte[n]sy'on 'ensu demanda śaber la asulusy'on de 'eśta dubda : 'i muğo maś dubdo 'enloś maleś ke vyenen aloś bu'enoś ke 'enloś byeneś ke vyenen}

---

[31] Ezek. 18.32.
[32] Ps. 92.8.
[33] Ps. 17.13.
[34] Cf. Ps. 11.7.
[35] Exod. 33.13.

Book of the Regimen of Living ‹fol. 19a›

‹fol. 19a›
{YT
aloś maloś komo veraś muy larga mente deklar(d)a[d]o 'en[e]l komento primero de 'el primero dela 'etika[36] de adonde veraś ke no śe pu'ede byen konsidrar la kabza de loś maleś ke vyenen 'a loś bu'enoś śino 'eś por 'el premy'o 'eśpritual ke 'eśperamoś 'enla vida advenidera ke no kontraśta 'el Dyyo la kośtelasy'on ke 'obliga mal 'a loś bu'enoś vyendo ke no leś 'ofende muǧo 'i leś keda 'el premy'o de 'el byen por 'entero guardado para la vida 'eterna śino 'eś 'en 'ombreś muǧo 'eśtremadoś 'enla bondad komo nu'eśoś padreś antigoś ke 'enloś taleś tenemoś verdader'a notisy'a kontraśtar 'el Dyyo la kośtelas[y]'on para loke a'el[y]oś konveni'a kontra 'eśtoś maleś 'i 'eśto 'en kauzoś ke avi'a de 'elyo nesesidad grande komo śe mu'eśtra por diǧoś de nu'eśoś śaby'oś de manera ke no keda la dubda por ninguna vi'a poderśe formar komo tenemoś verifikado :

'I 'EN todo lo diǧo no fu'e mi 'intensy'on maś al prezente ke dart[e] 'a 'entender kuanto 'el ke śige 'el kamino dela virtud ['i] kośtumbra 'a 'eśersitarśe deśde ǧiko 'enel byen 'obrar 'i puro śaver b[ive] alegre 'i kontento toda śu vida 'i kuando vyene 'en kresimyento '[i] konosimyento verdadero fasil mente haze laś 'obraś de virtud kon kontina alegri'a śin śentir ningun modo de triśteza de kuanto la kośtelasy'on 'o fado 'en 'el 'obra loke 'eś al kontrary'o 'enel visy'ozo 'ignorante ke toda śu vida 'eś mizeryya śin deleyte kunplido 'i todo 'eśto vyene śegun śe kośtumbra deśde 'el tyenpo deśu ninyeś 'i mosedad ke tanto kuanto 'eś 'el trabaǧo del maeśtro 'en abezar al diśiplo 'en śu mosedad 'a 'obrar 'i śegir 'el kamino dela virtud 'i verdader'a 'eśpikulasy'on tanta 'eś la alegri'a de[ ]'el diśiplo kuando vyene 'en 'entero konosimyento de 'el byen ke pose'e :

'I para 'eśto te traere ala memory'a 'el 'enǧenplo keśe tomo de Likurgo ke algunaś veześ te diǧe 'el kual tomo doś perikoś 'enla 'ora ke nasyeron de 'un meśmo padre 'i madre hermozisimoś 'el 'uno 'enbezo 'a lanber platoś 'enla kozina 'el 'otro 'a kasar lyebreś 'en 'el kanpo de modo ke 'el 'uno śe fizo valyente kasador 'el 'otro 'un flako golozo 'un di'a de fyeśta ke 'eśtaban todoś śuś kavalyeroś 'ensu palasy'o 'en prezensy'a de todoś mando poner 'una 'olyya de vyanda 'i mando śoltar 'una lyebre 'a viśta de loś doś peroś 'el kasador rem[e]ty'o ala lyebre 'el golozo ala 'olyya[37] fu'e notable 'eśperensy'a konke 'el śagasisimo rey mośtro valer maś la kryansa deśde ǧiko

---

[36] The Aristotle passage would be NE I.x (1100a 10–1101a 21).

[37] Unidentified source. I have not found this anecdote in Plutarch's account of Lycurgus (*Lives*, 1:204–303). It is neither in Valerius Maximus nor in Aelian. The tale appears to depend on Lycurgus' fame as reformer and lawgiver in Sparta.

Book of the Regimen of Living ‹fol. 19a–19b›

ke 'el nasimyento de padreś ğenerozoś 'i kuanto 'obra 'enloś animaleś rasy'onaleś kuanto maś 'enel 'ombre kapas de razon ke por maloś kośtumbreś vemoś kada di'a muğoś nasidoś ğene(n)roza mente perder 'el sezo 'otroś de vil kaśta por 'el bu'en kośtumbre ganarlo por aki veraś kuanto deven loś mosoś dende śu mosedad akostumbrarśe 'a abrasar la virtud 'i loar muğo al}

‹fol. 19b›
{PEREK Š^eLIŠIY [CHAPTER THREE]
Dyyo śi tyene ventura de halyar kyen loś 'inponga 'enelya 'i pu'eś 'el Dyyo me hizo grasy'a de apareğar 'enti tan bu'ena diśpoziśy'on para poder 'efektuar mi grande deze'o de tu perfeksy'on no falteś 'en loś medyoś ke por 'enteresisyon de 'elyyoś śe alkansa :

KAPITULO TERSERO

'EŚ manifyeśto ke 'el medyo verdadero 'i maś konvenible para alkansar 'el 'ultimo fin dela filisidad 'eś 'entender byen nu'eśa śantiśima ley 'i palabraś de nu'eśoś śaby'oś ke 'enelya 'i 'en śuś maravilyozoś diğoś 'eśta konklu'ida toda la dotrina beatiśima 'i 'eśpikulasy'on verdader'a ke 'eś 'el śumo grado dela byen aventuransa maś komo śe'a la klaridad de nu'eśa devinisima ley muy 'eśtremada 'i nu'eśo 'inğeny'o muy flako para poderla 'entender 'eś nesesary'o buśkar 'otroś medyoś ke maś fasil mente śe pu'edan ko[n]prender para venir a'el verdadero konosimyento de 'elyya no değando ğamaś de trabağar 'en 'elyya kon toda la vehemensy'a 'i diliğensy'a posible 'i syendo aśi te baśtara byen 'eśte mi reğimyento ke riğendote por 'el 'i ponyendo laś myenteś 'enla śegunda 'i tersera partida de 'el fasil mente podraś 'ente[n]der 'el libro delaś 'etikaś ke larga mente tengo glozado 'el kual aplike 'a muğa sensy'a de nu'eśa ley śanta 'onde śe deklaran muğoś ś[ek]retoś de nu'eśo Talmud porke 'enloś diğoś dela ley 'i de nu'eśoś śaby'oś 'a meneśter 'una fu'erte 'eśpikulasy'on 'i grave konosimyento 'enlaś sensyaś 'umanaś para ver kuanto śin konparasyon la devina ley lyeba vantağe :

'I KIŚA 'eśto kyeren nu'eśoś śaby'oś 'en dezir byen aventurado 'el ke aka vyene 'i trae śu Talmud 'enśu mano 'i set-[38] komo śi diśeśen ke lyebe konśigo loke deprendyere de nu'eśa le'y 'i nu'eśo Talmud byen śabido ke lyebarlo 'enśu mano 'eś tenerlo byen śabido 'i 'ente[n]dido :

'I 'eśta pyenso śe'a la 'intensy'on del śenyor Rabbenu Mośeh 'enla tersera parte

---

[38] Pesaḥim 50a.

BOOK OF THE REGIMEN OF LIVING ‹FOL. 19B-20A›

de śu libro k[a]pitulo n'- [51] do pone 'un 'enšenplo de loś ke pośe'en la glory'a 'enla korte devina 'i 'el grado de kada kual 'i deloś ke śon privadoś delya porke śaber todaś laś sensyaś kuantaś śon no śabyendo 'el 'oriğin de adonde manan ke 'eś nu'eśtra śantiśima le'ey no 'eś śaber : 'i śabyendo nu'eśtra ley perfekta mente 'entendyendo loś devinoś diğoś de nu'eśoś śaby'oś 'en diversas parteś 'eśpesyal 'en nu'eśo Talmud komo śe deven 'entender 'eś 'el śumo grado de perfeksy'on : 'i dize ke 'eś 'enšenplo 'a 'un rey ke 'eśta 'ensu palasy'o 'i śu ğente repartida por muğoś lugareś algunoś dyentro 'enla sib(')dad donde 'el rey abita 'i algunoś fu'era de 'elyya 'i deloś ke 'eśtan 'enla meśma sibdad algunoś}

‹fol. 20a›
{K
tyenen laś 'eśpaldaś al palasy'o del rey 'i la kara 'a la parte kontrary'a 'i 'otroś tyenen la kara hazy[a] 'el palasy'o 'i no lyegan 'a ve[r] 'el muro dela kaza 'i algunoś lyegan ala kaza 'i andan al deredor de 'elyya buśkando śu pu'erta 'i algunoś ayy ke 'entran 'enla kaza por la primera pu'erta pero a'un no 'entran 'enla propy'a kamara adonde 'eśta śu preśona de 'el rey 'i ayy algunoś ke 'entran 'enla propy'a kamara 'i 'eśtan kon 'el rey 'en 'una meśma 'eśtansy'a 'i deśpu'eś ke lyegan 'a 'eśte grado kon śu bu'ena abilidad 'i diliğensyya 'a veześ lyegan 'a hablar kon 'el rey 'i set-[39] 'eśta 'eś la śuma de śu devinisimo 'ešenplo 'i kuando va 'a 'enğenplifikar 'i konferir kon 'el 'eğenplifikado 'enel deśpu'eś de deklarar la śiknifikasyon de laś treś 'i kuatro partidaś de 'el 'enšenplo dize ke la kinta partida ke śon loś ke andan 'a 'el deredor dela kaza śon loś ke le'en 'el Talmud por ke 'eśtoś taleś kre'en loś artikuloś dela ley śin ninguna 'eśpikulasy'on 'enelyoś 'i anśi guardan loś preśebtoś devinoś 'i la śeśta partida dize ke śon loś ke 'eśpekulan loś artikuloś dela ley 'i la śeptima ke śon loś ke 'entran 'enla propy'a kamara dize ke śon loś ke alkansan kuanto 'eś posible alkansar dela verdad 'en laś kozaś devinaś 'i probar loke 'eś posible probar 'i kre'er loke śe deve kre'er a'un ke śe'a 'inpośible probarśe 'i set- 'eśta 'eś la suśtansy'a de loke kizo 'eśte śenyor śentir 'en 'eśte śu 'enšenplo delo kual muğoś śe marabilyyaron paresyendoleś ke 'el śenyor Rabbenu Mošeh puzyeśe 'a loś ke buśkan al Dyyo por vi'a natural filosofika mente 'en mayor grado ke loś śaby'oś 'enel Talmud 'i ami ver loś ke 'eśto dišeron yeraron 'en doś kozaś :

LA primera penśar ke loś śaby'oś ke 'el lyyama śaby'oś 'enlaś kozaś devinaś śean metafizikoś fu'era dela te'oloği'a de nu'eśtra śantisima ley :

LA 'otra penśar ke akelyoś śaby'oś te'ologoś ke 'el nombra śean deśtintoś deloś

---

[39] Maimonides, *Guide of the Perplexed,* trans. S. Pines (Chicago, 1963), 618.

BOOK OF THE REGIMEN OF LIVING ‹FOL. 20A–20B›

Talmudiśtaś loke yo no pyenśo ke tal kre'a anteś kreo ke todoś loś ke 'el 'enǧenplifika dela tersera partida de 'el 'enǧenplo adelante śon todoś loś alumbradoś dela verdader'a luz de nu'eśtra śantisima ley diferenteś śinon maś 'i menoś komo 'eś byen viśto 'a kyen byen 'eśpekulare 'en śuś palabraś 'i dize kela kuarta partida 'eś 'el grado de 'el deleyte deloś ke le'en śolo 'en 'el Ṭalmud śin śaber alguna razon aloś artikul(y)[o]ś 'i presebtoś devinoś 'i dize ke 'el ke śube deśpu'eś de byen le'ido 'el Ṭalmud 'a 'otro mayor grado de śaber ke 'eś 'eśpekular 'enlaś kozaś ke śe deve 'eśpekular 'eśte tal 'entra dela pu'erta 'a dyentro 'i kuando maś 'eśpekulare 'enlaś kozaś devinaś 'i alkansara laś verdaderaś demośtrasy'oneś 'enlo ke 'eś posible demośtrarśe 'eśte tal 'entrara 'enla primera kamara 'i set- de manera}

‹fol. 20b›
{ke 'el pośtrero grado preśupone todo loke śele antisipa de 'el tersero para adelante 'i alyende deśto śe pu'ede dezir ke truśo konparasy'on a'el modo ke tyene 'enel 'eśpekular 'i no a'el grado dela glory'a ke delyyo alkansan : de kual kyer modo deloś ke śe'a me parese śer śaśtifeǧa la admirasy'on 'a kyen kizyere byen mirar 'enelyo 'i śana mente ǧuśgar 'i rekoǧerśe'a delo diǧo kuanta 'utilidad śe śige de kerer 'enviśtigar laś kozaś de nu'eśtra te'oloǧi'a para la devina kontenplasy'on de 'elyyaś komo maś largo tengo 'eśte paso deklarado 'enel prologo de nu'eśo komento ala 'etika :

AG[O]RA al prezente no hare maś ke darte algunaś reglaś komuneś konformeś 'a tu tyerna 'edad 'en la primera partida de 'eśte mi tratado para ke medyante la grasy'a devina konelyaś lyegeś ala kumbre dela virtud ke pertendemoś 'i byen perfekto 'el kual por la śegunda 'i tersera partida śe konprehendera akordandośeme de akel gran diǧo de 'el devino Platon 'a 'opiny'on de algunoś diśiplo de nu'eśtro profeta Yirmᶜyahu[40] donde dize ke deven koś(n)tumbrar loś mosoś dende ǧikoś 'a deleytarśe kon loke konbyene 'i set- la kual a'utorida(r)[d] de 'el alyega Aristoteleś 'enel śegundo dela 'etika[41] 'i tubo muǧa razon pu'eś 'eś byen viśto ke de 'el tyenpo de la mosedad depende 'el byen de toda la vida śigyente :

'I 'eśta fu'e śegun algunoś la 'intensyon de nu'eśtra śantisima ley 'en dezir anteś de śenetud te alevantaraś 'i afermoziguaraś kara de vyeǧo 'i se[t]-[42] : tomando 'el bokabl(y)[o] de ante por antisipasy'on tenporal komo 'en 'otraś parteś ś[e]meǧanteś śe toma kyere dezir ke anteś ke lyege 'el 'ombre al tyenpo dela śenektud śe'a de

---

[40] The legend that Plato was a student of the prophet Jeremiah occurs in Augustine, *De Doctrina Christiana* II.28.43 (ed. J. Martin, CCSL 32 [Turnhout, 1962], 63).
[41] *NE* II.iii.2 (1140b 11–13).
[42] Lev. 19.32.

Book of the Regimen of Living ‹fol. 20b–21a›

alevant[a]r 'a adkerir la perfeksy'on ke 'eś śyendo moso para ke afermozigü'e śu kara al tyenpo dela veǧeś ke śi dende ninyeś no lo haze kedara defektu'ozo de todo :

'I 'a 'eśta meśma 'intensy'on nu'eśo devinisimo śaby'o Š^elomoh 'en śuś probyerby'oś habla śyenpre kon loś mosoś 'i lyyama al oyente hiǧo ke denota 'eśkribir para 'el ke no 'eś a'un 'en 'edad de śer padre 'i śinifika ke aprobeǧara akelyya dotrina 'a 'el ke dende ǧiko la resibyere 'i 'enelyya platikare :

POR tanto 'eśkuǧa aplazible mente mi doktrina 'i akośta byen la 'oreǧa⁴³ 'a lo ke te diśere pu'eś todo 'eś 'enderesado para tu byen 'i prośperidad 'i para ke meǧor pu'edaś konprehender 'el kamino dela vida śegun dereǧa razon śin yerar reparti 'eśte tratado 'en treś parteś ke a'un ke 'en la verdad 'eśta primera 'eśte konprehendida 'enla śegunda ke todo śe konpreh[e]nde de baśo de laś vertudeś moraleś

TODA vi'a 'eś byen deklarar primero laś kozaś 'enke konbyene tener partikular mente muǧa 'orden 'eśpesyal mente loś mosoś de tyerna 'edad 'enlaś kualeś 'el yero śe halyya muǧo 'i fasil [CW. mente]}

‹fol. 21a›
{Ḳ' PEREK R^eBI^cIY [CHAPTER FOUR]
mente 'i 'eś muy vituperable 'i la advertensy'a 'enel 'orden enelyaś diśpone 'el moso 'en grande manera para todo ǧenero de bondad : ke 'uzando de 'elyyaś byen śe alkansa 'el byen prośtero ke śe konprehende 'enla śegunda partida :

'I 'en todo lo diǧo no podraś 'en manera alguna yerar śi 'en 'el 'eśpeǧo de 'eśta mi dotrina te kizyereś 'a menudo mirar ke ati aprobeǧaraś 'i ami haraś kontente 'i alegre ke no kyero mayor premy'o deloke te 'enśenyyare ke śer byen 'enpleado mi trabaǧo :

KAPITUL[O] KUARTO

kuanto 'enla primera koza de laś dyeś ke 'eś 'el komer 'a de mirar 'el moso kuando komera 'a 'oraś devidaś⁴⁴ deputadaś para tal a'uto ke komyendo 'en konpanyya de 'otroś no śe'a 'el 'el primero ke 'enpese śalvo śi kome kon 'otroś menoreś ke 'el pero an deśer taleś ke no deśautorizen śu perśona ke komyendo kon mayoreś no 'eś lisito 'enpesar 'el 'i kon 'igualeś bu'eno 'eś dar la 'onra 'a śu konpanye(v)ro :

TAN BYEN 'a de komer komo deve konvyene 'a śaber repozado śin 'eǧar 'el 'oǧo

---

⁴³ Prov. 5.1.

⁴⁴ The *fe de errata* specifies a superfluous correction here, *devidaś* for a phantom *devididaś*.

ala komida aśi meśmo śe deve de akavidar deno meter la mano fu'era de 'el lugar ke 'eśta śerka de 'el ke muǧoś por no śer 'eneśto byen atentadoś tyenden la mano al deredor de[ ]todo 'el plato 'a laś parteś aǧenaś adonde leś parese 'eśtar 'el meǧor bokado koza ami ver 'enoǧoza 'en 'eśtremo 'i digna de todo repudy'o 'i 'eś '[i]vidente śenyal de poka kryansa 'i menoś vergu'ensa la kual 'eś loke maś deve reśplandeśer 'enloś mosoś 'i loke noś aśegura la 'eśperansa 'enel futuro porke śegun 'eśkriby'o 'el diǧo filosofo Briśon[45] 'el maś 'edony'o para fasil resebir la doktrina 'i difisil para tirarśe de 'elyya 'eś 'el moso vergonsozo por lo kual śe deven de guardar no hagan kośaś ke mu'eśtre 'en 'elyaś poka vergu'ensa 'i apartarśe de 'elyaś de todo punto porke koronpen la regla natural de 'el bu'en kośtumbre :

'I deven de kośtumbrar loś mosoś d(v)[e] no tener 'intensyon maś kc a'un śolo manǧar 'enel meśmo paśto porke la vary'edad de loś manǧareś danyya 'el 'eśtomago 'i śe konturban loś 'eśpritoś 'i śe 'engru'esa 'el 'inǧeny'o 'i 'inpide 'el 'entendimyento :

ǦUNTO kon 'eśto no deven loś mosoś śer presurozoś 'enel propy'o komer maś anteś algo vagarozoś kuando no 'eś la 'intensy'on de ganar 'el tyenpo ke 'en komer de vagar śe gaśta por ke parese śer akelyya prisa de 'el demazyado deze'o ke śobre puǧa 'enel por hartar śu 'apetito de no poder reǧiśtir[46] kontra 'el 'en modo alguno lo kual 'eś muy deś'oneśto 'i digno de ado'eśto :

'I 'eś nesesary'o ke atenten loś mosoś no śean loś pośtreroś ke levanten mano dela komida}

‹fol. 21b›
{porke denota 'elke tal kośtumbra śer 'el maś golozo ke loś ke konel komen 'i 'eś koza muy deśagradable 'i deśplazible mayor mente aloś mosoś :

'I ǧunto kon 'eśto deven de guardarśe deno alebantar loś 'oǧoś 'a mirar la kara de loś ke komen kon 'elyoś 'enla meza 'enla 'ora de 'el komer mayor mente śi śon eśtranǧeroś porke 'eś afrentarloś 'en grande manera 'i śon kabza ke śe[ ]ret[i]r'en de 'el komer maś de loke konbyene 'i kon 'eśto tanbyen śe hazen desvergonsadoś ke 'eś muy taǧado 'enloś mosoś komo tenemoś diǧo :

MAŚ deven amoneśtar aloś mosoś ke de kual kyera ke fu'eren rekeridoś kele den parte de loke komen no le deśen de dar anteś deven perkurar de akośtumbrarśe 'a dar porke de 'eśto śeleś śige 'inkonparable 'ut(v)[i]lidad para hazerśe fiśoś 'i 'inmobileś 'en 'el abito dela templansa 'i refrenar 'el 'apetito 'a śer kontinente 'i liberal 'i śobre todo 'eś 'eśto prinsipy'o de byen kerer 'i byen fazer ke śon a'utoś de amiśtad :

---

[45] The phrase is unclear. The aforementioned philosopher is Plato, not Bryson.
[46] Another superfluous correction in the errata, *reǧiśtir* for *repiśtir*.

Book of the Regimen of Living ⟨fol. 21b–22a⟩

'I konbyene al moso ke no kyera demaziaś 'enla komida anteś śe kontente konlo manko ke pudyere 'i de akelyo ke komyere no śe farte anteś se levante 'un poko fambryento dela meza ke a'un ke lu'ego al prezente no le pareska verśe farto de a'i 'a poko le paresera 'eśtar muy farto 'i a'un muğaś veześ aver komido demazyado ke deśpu'eś ke sesa la 'obra de 'el komer 'i atemado la virtud atraktiba de hazer śu 'operasy'on haze la retintiba la śuya miniśtrando ala diğiśtiba 'i 'en sesando la 'obra dela atraktiba sesa la hambre de adonde dišo Abisena 'enel libro primero [ʾo]f(i)[a]n tersera doktrina śegunda kapitulo śebtimo de 'el reğimyento de loke śe kome 'i beve 'i konvyene ke no śe 'inğa de 'el mantenimyento faśta ke no kede lugar deś'okupado maś anteś konbyene ke alebante la mano kedando algun 'apetito ke akelyo ke reśta de hambre sesa de a'i 'a poko 'i se[t]-[47] 'i 'enel primer kapitu⟨lo⟩ da muy bu'ena regla para konservar la śanidad ke no haze tanto 'a nu'eśo perpozito ke no 'eś aki nu'eśtra 'intensy'on maś ke dar reğimyento de byen bivir 'i 'oneśto 'i no de sanidad ke loś libroś 'eśtan lyenoś de 'elyyo 'i śeri'a meneśter alargar śolo 'eś byen tener 'a memory'a loke dize de kuanto śe deve apartar de komidaś gru'esaś 'i dulseś porke alyende de loś 'inkonbenyenteś ke 'el alyi trae śon syerto kozaś propinkaś 'a danyar 'el 'entendimyento 'i de todo punto le 'inpedir komo śe mu'eśtra por laś palabraś de 'el śenyor Rabbenu Mośeh 'enel r[e]ğimyento dela śanidad 'enel prinsipy'o deśu prinsipal libro 'i mayor tratado[48] :

DE manera ke 'eś byen ke konsidren loś manseboś partikular mente ke anśi komo no 'eś la 'intensy'on 'enlaś medisinaś komo śon purgaś 'i 'otraś taleś kozaś ke śean delektableś al guśto śalbo 'utileś para la}

⟨fol. 22a⟩
{KB
śalud aśi an de tener por śertisimo ke no 'eś la 'intensy'on 'enloś mantenim[y]entoś la delektasy'on deśu guśto śino śolo la śuśtentasy'on de 'el ku'erpo por medyo de 'elyoś 'i anśi komo 'enlaś diğaś medisinaś lo demazyado de loke konbyene para la

---

[47] *Canon*, Bk. I, Ofan 3, doctrine 2, chap. 7; see Ibn Sina, *Treatise on the "Canon of Medicine"* (London, 1930), 395.

[48] The first chapter of *Fi Tadbir al-Siḥah* (*The Regimen of Health*), written for Saladin's son, King al-Afdal, treats overeating; see Maimonides, *"Regimen of Health,"* trans. A. Bar-Sela et al. (Philadelphia, 1964), 16–20. However, Almosnino subsequently remarks that he is referring to *Regimiento de sanidad*— identified in the margin as *Ha-Nᶜhagat ha-Briyuah*— placed at the beginning of Maimonides' principal and most important work, which in this instance would be *Mishneh Torah*, so the work referred to is *Hilkot Deᶜot (Laws on Character Traits)*, chapter four.

Book of the Regimen of Living ‹fol. 22a–22b›

śanidad danyya 'i todo 'ombre huye de tomar maś de loke 'eś m[e]neśter anteś algo menoś anśi śe deve guardar 'enla komida para konservar la śalud de 'el ku'erpo 'i perfeksy'on de 'el 'ente[n]dimyento :
'EL 'eśtudyyante 'a de atentar maś 'i 'eś ke kośtumbre 'a ke śe'a la komida dela noğe menoś kela de 'el di'a para ke 'eśte apareğado para 'el 'eśtudy'o dela noğe 'en kuanto bivyere 'i śyenpre 'a de śer reglado 'en komer manğareś de bu'ena diğeśty'on konformeś kuanto pudyere 'a śu konplisy'on 'iśu fakultad 'i 'enla śena śe avezara maś de fazer 'eśto para ke pu'eda meğor 'entender loke 'eśtudyare 'eśtando menoś 'inpedido 'el ku'erpo ke 'eś verdadero 'eśturmento dela anima :
'EN konkuluzy'on diğo 'a serka de 'eśto 'el gran rey Šᵉlomoh ğuśto kome 'a fartura deśu alma 'i vyentre de maloś falta 'i set-[49] keryendo śiknifikar ke loś bu'enoś no komen maś deloke konbyene para śuśtentasy'on del ku'erpo ke 'eś la kantidad ke farta 'el anima por parte de 'el 'entendimyento 'i loś maloś por kuanto la hartura 'enelyoś no 'eś ğuśgada por parte de 'el 'entendimyento śalvo por parte de 'el 'apetito karesen śyenpre de 'el fin ke por muğo ke koman nunka hartan śu deze'o de komer 'i por meğor dezir śyenpre loś parese śer śu vyentre ğiko 'i flako para resebir 'el manğar ke 'el keri'a ke lyebaśe por muy grande ke 'el tal vyentre śe'a konforme 'a algunaś danyyadaś 'opiny'oneś ke apeteśen 'el 'apetito 'i aman śu deleyte koza ami ver muy torpe 'en 'oğoś de kyen kon dereğa razon lo kyere konsidrar ke buśkar 'el 'ombre apetitoś para ke tenga gana de komer 'eś muy vituperado kuando no 'eś 'a fin de śanidad 'o por deśkaymyento de 'el ape(p+)[t]ito 'i virtud ke delyyo ś(+)e pu'ede śegir alguna 'enfermedad pero kuando 'eś para ke śolo 'el 'apetito deśe'e 'i śe deleyte 'eśta tal lyamo yo 'enfermedad ke 'a meneśter śer byen kurada kon muy bu'ena dy'eta 'i 'eś muy vitupery'ada 'en nu'eśa śantisima ley dizyendo 'i 'el apanyy[a]dizo ke 'entre 'el dezeaban deze'o 'i set-[50] komo śi diğeśe dezeaban dezear ke 'eś 'el 'eśtremo de 'el ap[e]tito danyyado 'i kontra natura dezear loke tyene paresyendole ke śyenpre le falta
'I para konfirmasy'on dela bu'ena 'intensy'on 'en todo lo diğo 'i śer feğo todo 'a śervisy'o del Dyyo 'i fin de bondad konbyene ke deśpu'eś de komer śe'a la prinsipal fruta de śobre meza platikar 'en kozaś de nu'eśtra śantisima ley 'i śuś primoreś para amośtrar la referensya deloś 'ombreś aloś animaleś 'enlaś 'obraś korporaleś ke kon 'elyoś komunikamoś :}

‹fol. 22b›
{PEREK ḤAMIŠIY [CHAPTER FIVE]
POR lo kual ğuśgaron ğuśta mente nu'eśtroś śaby'oś dizyendo ke komyendo treś

---

[49] Prov. 13.25.
[50] Num. 11.4.

BOOK OF THE REGIMEN OF LIVING ‹FOL. 22B›

'en 'una meza 'i no dizyendo śobre 'elyya palabraś de ley 'eś komo śi komyeśen śakrifisy'oś de mu'er(v)toś 'i set-[51] 'enpero treś ke komen 'en 'una meza 'i dizen śobre 'elyya palabr[a]ś de ley 'eś komo śi komyeśen dela meza de 'el Dyyo 'i set-[52] ke a'un ke 'a 'opiny'on de algunoś kon dezir la bendisy'on ke al Dyyo bendezimoś śobre meza baśta para no dezirśe ke 'eś komo śi komyeśen śakrifisy'oś de mu'ertoś 'i set- toda vi'a 'eś muğa razon ke avyendo 'enla meza kyen śepa dezir palabr[a]ś de ley ke laś diga 'i kual kyera kelo 'oyere śi virtu'ozo fu'ere le śera maś deleytozo kela komida 'i 'eśto noś abaśta kuanto 'a 'el bu'en kośtumbre ke śe'a de tener 'en 'el komer ke lo maś 'eś maś de medisina ke de nu'eśo tr[a]tado

KAPITULO KINTO

KUANTO ala śegunda ke 'eś 'el beber lo primero 'i prinsipal śe deve vedar 'el vino 'a 'el moso faśta ke ayya kaśado porke 'eś 'enloś mosoś komo anyyadir fu'ego 'a fu'ego komo kyere Abisena 'enla tersera de 'el primero kapitulo de 'el reğimyento dela agu'a 'i 'el vino[53] ke 'inky'etando l(y)[o]ś 'eśpritoś kita muğo la abilidad para la sensy'a anśi moral komo natural porke 'el animo 'umano kon trankilidad 'i repozo śe haze śaby'o komo śe dize 'enel śeteno deloś fizikoś[54]

VERDAD 'eś ke loś ninyoś de 'un anyo 'i a'un de menoś hata śinko halye por larga 'eśperensy'a śingular medisina para prezervar dela 'epilensy'a 'una śopa moğada 'en vino la kual 'eśfu'ersa 'i klarifika 'el me'olyyo komo kyere Abisena 'enla primera de 'el tersero 'enel kapitulo dela 'epilensya 'i Gordony'o[55] lo konfirma pero de 'eśta 'edad adelante hata 'el tyenpo diğo konśeğare 'a 'el mansebo śe guarde de 'el komo de pesonyya 'i de akonpanyarśe konloś kelo beben :

'I kual kyer bebi(r)[d]a ke bebyere 'eś byen atente no beba maś de loke konbyene 'i lo ke bebyere śe'a deśpu'eś de komer śegun regla de medisina 'i no lu'ego deśpu'eś

---

[51] Avot 3.3.
[52] Avot 3.3.
[53] Ibn Sina, "*Canon of Medicine*," trans. Gruner, 412 (no. 810).
[54] See Aristotle, *Physics,* VII.3 (245b 3–248a 9), trans. Wicksteed and Cornford, 2:207–63. It appears to refer to the statement: "For the condition of understanding or knowing results from the soul coming to a state of stillness out of the turbulence natural to it" (*Physics,* VII.3 (245b 3–248a 9), trans. Wicksteed and Cornford, 2:239).
[55] For a study of the life and medical writings of Bernard de Gordon (Gordonio), see L. Demaitre, *Doctor Bernard de Gordon* (Toronto, 1980). For the Seville 1495 edition of Gordonio's *Libro de medicina,* see J. Cull and B. Dutton, eds., *Un manual básico de medicina medieval* (Madison, WI, 1991).

BOOK OF THE REGIMEN OF LIVING ‹FOL. 22B–23A›

dela komida śalbo 'una 'ora 'o doś deśpu'eś porke 'el muğo bever 'enla komida 'i lu'ego deśpu'eś de aver komido 'eś malo para 'el ku'erpo de donde rezulta grande danyo al alma ke konronpyendośe 'el kilo 'i[ ]relağando 'el 'eśtomago haze muy malaś dolensyaś śegun muğaś kabzaś 'efisyenteś ke enelyaś 'i 'en śu maldad alargaron loś medikoś 'i Abisena 'enel śetabo kapitulo de 'el reğimyento de 'el agu'a 'i vino[56] alargo byen 'en dar la kabza 'en 'eśto 'i 'enel kapitulo anteś de 'eśte 'enel kual def[y]ende 'el 'entendimyento porke bebyendo muğo 'entre la komida 'i lu'ego akabando de komer a'un ke śe'a agu'a faze pasar la komida de 'el 'eśtomago 'endiğiśta por 'el apr[e]suramyento deśu pasar 'i agraby'a 'el ku'erpo :}

‹fol. 23a›
{KG
'i lo 'eśfri'a 'eśpesyal śi 'eś 'invyerno laś kualeś 'obraś todaś 'elyaś 'i kada 'una porśi 'eś kabza baśtante 'a fazer 'el ku'erpo perezozo 'i mal diśpu'eśto para poder śervir 'a laś 'obraś de 'el 'entendimyento por kuyya 'indiśpozisy'on falta 'enloke deve de 'obrar śuś 'obraś :

'EŚ verdad ke śe'a de konsidrar 'eneśto la diversidad de laś konplisy'oneś ke ya podri'a śer la konplisy'on tan kolerika ke kon śufrir la śed baśtan 'a traer 'una terible 'enfermedad 'i 'otra tan flematika ke de 'una śola bebida 'enfermaśe 'i śobre todo śe'a de konsidrar 'el kośtumbre de 'el 'ombre 'enlaś taleś kozaś pero toda vi'a śyenpre la regla 'eś verdader'a 'enloś maś :

'I aśi muğo de mirar ke kuanto maś 'el 'ombre 'en 'eśpesyal 'el 'eśtudyante pudyere śufrir la śed la śufra por loś danyoś ke śe śigen de 'el bever ke la śed śufryendola śe diminuye porke la natureza va rezolbyendo materyya ke haze la śed komo lo 'eśkriby'o Abisena 'enel meśmo kapitulo de 'el reğimyento de 'el agu'a 'i de 'el vino 'i set[57]-

'I śobre todo 'eś meneśter guardarśe loś mośoś ke no bevan 'en 'el tyenpo de 'el 'eśtudy'o por laś meśmaś kabzaś ke syerto konturba muğo 'el śentido 'engrosando loś 'umoreś 'i relašando 'el 'eśtomago 'i śin konservasy'on de śanidad 'eś duro 'obrar laś kozaś de 'el alma :

'I loke te maś defyendo aserka de 'el bever ke 'en miś 'oğoś 'eś muy vitup[e]ryado 'eś ke 'en ninguna manera te pongaś 'a bever 'en prezensy'a de alguno ke fu'ere mayor ke ti fu'era de 'el tyenpo dela komida porke me parese 'eśto tan abominable 'i 'eśtrany'o ke śi no fu'eśe por 'el komun 'uzo ke ayy 'enla ğente de komer 'i bever publika mente 'ozari'a dezir ke fu'eśe tan vitup[e]ryado 'i 'eśtranyyado verlo hazer komo ver hazer 'un akto de luğury'a publika mente 'o 'otro tan beśtyal ke 'a ğuśta

---

[56] This seems to be a reference to Ibn Sina, "*Canon of Medicine,*" trans. Gruner, 410 (no. 801).
[57] Ibn Sina, "*Canon of Medicine,*" trans. Gruner, 408–13 (nos. 797–814).

BOOK OF THE REGIMEN OF LIVING ‹FOL. 23A–23B›

razon poka diferensy'a va de 'uno 'a 'otro :
 PERO ya kela 'uzansa komun 'a prevalesido tanto ke fizo abito para ke śe 'uze 'eśte a'uto tan publiko 'i la kabza de 'elyyo ami ver 'eś ke 'eneśto śe deśkuidaron loś ke tal 'uzo śigyeron dela virtud 'ino perkuraron śalbo konplazer 'a loś śentidoś 'eś( )tery'oreś ke śon 'el ver 'o'ir guśtar 'oler tokar 'i a'eśtoś ğuśgando todo por parte dela śensualidad śin dar 'entrada alguna 'a la dereğa razon :
 'EŚ bu'eno keśe konsidren doś kozaś 'i śe konserben 'en 'eśtoś por parte dela dereğa razon laś kualeś śon lisitaś ami ğu'izy'o la primera ke ningun pekenyo de 'edad delante de ningun grande koma ni 'ensu konp[a]nyi'a 'i tanto śe'a 'eśto ap[a]rtado 'i deśakośtumbrado kuanto la diśtansy'a de dignidad de 'el 'uno al 'otro 'ubyere de manera ke kuando 'un muy bağo delante de 'un grande śenyor 'eśtubyere no 'eś lisito komer 'en prezensy'a de 'el ni kon 'el 'i 'eśto reśpekto 'eś de}

‹fol. 23b›
{'el 'eśklabo kon 'el śenyor 'i de 'el disiplo kon 'el maeśtro 'i de 'el padre kon 'el hiğo śalvo kuando 'el menor fu'ere mandado de 'el mayor de adonde vyene la regla komun 'enloś prinsipeś 'i grandeś śenyoreś ke a'un ke no tyenen por 'inkonvenyente komer 'elyoś 'en prezensy'a de todoś no konsyenten komer śuś miniśtroś 'en śu prezensy'a anteś leś 'eś muy defendido 'el tal komer śino fu'ere 'a algunoś prinsipaleś alguna veś 'ordenado 'i mandado por 'el propy'o prinsipe 'i śenyor por kererleś 'onrar 'en alguna fyeśta 'o regoziğo para śu pasa tyenpo 'i 'ensitasy'on de śu 'apetito 'i def[y]endenlo 'a fin de 'inponer loś 'enel modo ke 'en komer kon 'otroś dizen tener para ke tengan 'el 'apetito śubdito ala razon 'eneśte a'uto de komer 'enlo kual śi kon preśona de a'utoridad no kośtunbraśen hazer lo aśi kiśa por dotrina śola nunka alkansarian 'el abito de 'el :
 'I 'eś la śegunda ke ninguno beba 'en prezensyya de 'otro mayor ke 'el fu'era de 'el tyenpo dela komida 'eśpesyal mente 'eśto guarden loś mosoś por la kabza ke tenemoś diğa ke denota poka verg(+)u'ensa 'i menoś reziśtensy'a kontra 'el sensual deze'o laś kualeś kozaś traen 'en 'eśte kazo aloś mosoś 'a grande deśtenplansa digna de todo vitupery'o 'i 'eśto 'eś tan fe'o ke nu'eśtroś śaby'oś probe'edoreś de 'el kamino verdadero dela virtud apartando loś 'inkonvenyenteś ke 'eneśtoś kazoś śe rekyere apartar diśeron 'eneśto ke maś lisito 'eś verter 'el 'ombre śuś aguaś por śu nesedad 'en prezensy'a de syento ke beber 'en prezensy'a de 'uno[58] palabraś dignaś de śer 'eśkritaś 'enel sezo para perpetu'a memory'a[59] ke enelyaś śe konprehende kuanto 'en 'eśta matery'a śe pu'ede dezir ke la 'intensy'on no fu'e dezir ke 'el verter laś aguaś publika

---

[58] *Otsar Hamidrashim* Amud 27 p. 56.
[59] Cf. Prov. 3.3, 7.3.

BOOK OF THE REGIMEN OF LIVING ‹FOL. 23B–24A›

mente 'en prezensy'a de muǧoś śe'a 'oneśta koza ni śe deba hazer śalbo darnoś 'a 'entender por bu'enoś terminoś ke śobre śer komun 'i notory'o 'a todoś 'el vitupery'o de 'eśte a'uto 'en publiko 'i ke todo 'ombre sibdadano komo ruśtiko śe akabida muǧo 'enel maś vituperable ke 'el 'eś 'el beber 'en publiko por śer 'el virtud maś nesesary'o pu'eś ya 'entro 'i 'el ke menoś śe deve de detener por śuperflu'idad 'eśpilida dela natureza 'a fin de byen delo kual śe nota kuan deś'oneśto 'eś '[e]l beber 'en presensy'a de 'otroś mayoreś :

'E kiśto kargar 'eneśto algo la mano porke ve'o śer 'un 'eror poko 'o nada atentado 'enloś mosoś de 'eśte tyenpo por lo kual no te deveś deśkuidar de 'el ni te deve pareser de poka śustansy'a ni[ ]dar lugar ke śe faga abito por ke deśpu'eś kuando konosyereś kuan grande yero 'eś 'i te arepintyereś de azerlo akostumbrado no te śera fasil tirarlo de ti 'i a'u[n]ke te pareśka ǧiko visy'o śi por ventura 'en prezensy'a de śaby'oś 'i virtu'ozoś lo 'uzareś śeraś notado de 'inkośtante ke 'eś 'oriǧin}

‹fol. 24a›
{KD PEREK ŠIŠIY [CHAPTER SIX]
de todoś loś visy'ośoś 'i para ke te pu'edaś veśtir de akelyoś rikoś hermozoś 'i 'oneśtoś abitoś dela virtud kon 'ekselensy'a de 'el śaber 'i 'eśpikulasy'on 'eś m[e]neśter ke primero te deśnudeś de loś fe'oś panyyaleś de loś visy'oś kyero dezir anśi de loś 'eśtremoś ke śon pekadoś komo delaś visy'ozaś diśpozis(v)yoneś ke traen a'elyoś porke konronpen 'el ku'erpo 'i 'el alma privando al 'ombre de 'el byen verdadero 'i prośtero fin :

'I 'enlo de maś ke konbyene tener 'orden 'enel bever śe deklara por la 'orden ke porpuzimoś 'enel modo de 'el komer ke tanbyen 'enel bever śe deve fu'ir al apreśuram[y]ento 'i perkurar de bever medyana kantidad por 'el meśmo 'orden de 'el komer : śolo 'en[e]śto 'eś razon de advertir ke kuando 'ubyere nesesidad de bever agu'a 'enla komida por 'el kośtum[b]re komun 'o 'en konpanyya deśuś 'igualeś no porfi'e konloś ke 'eśtan 'ensu prezensy'a ke bevan paresyendole 'uzar kortezi'a 'en hazerleś bever primero ke komo śe'a 'el bever muǧo 'i 'eśpesyal agu'a koza ke ninguna 'utilidad trae al ku'erpo ni ala alma maś anteś muǧo danyo komo avemoś prevado no 'eś byen ke śe kometa kon 'elyya :

POR lo kual determinaron nu'eśtroś śaby'oś 'eśpekulando todoś 'eśtoś 'inkonvenyenteś ke no śe deve 'onrar 'en 'el agu'a[60] ke por 'eśto śe deve 'entender porke komo śe'a 'el agu'a 'un śimple alimento de pokito 'i kazi ningun mantenimyento no 'eś lisito kometer anadi kon 'elyya śino fu'eśe kuando 'el kometido manifyeśta kererla ke 'eśtonseś 'eś byen 'uzar de kortezi'a :

---

[60] Rashi Moed Katan 6b.

Book of the Regimen of Living ‹fol. 24a–24b›

KAPITULO SEŚTO

'EN la tersera 'i kuarta koza ke 'eś 'el dormir 'i 'el velar a'un ke no śe'a tanto al perpozito kyero deklarar algo de loke aserka de 'el śu'enyyo 'i dela viǧilyya konśiśte para ke meǧor pu'edaś konoser loś grandisimoś probeǧoś ke ayy 'enla viǧilyya 'i ǧunto kon 'eśto loś ke śe śigen de 'el śu'enyo śyendo komo konvyene porke por 'elyoś veaś kuanto poko deve 'el 'ombre tomar para śi 'el śu'enyo 'i 'uzar de 'el śolo lo nesesary'o para la śuśtentasy'on dela vida 'i no demazyado 'i tanbyen porke śabidaś laś kauzaś śe pu'ede meǧor 'obrar 'en 'el 'efekto 'i maś fasil mente poner 'enel regla śegun dereǧa razon :

'I pu'eśto ke para 'eśto 'ubyera meneśter byen alargar no deśare de dezir 'en muy brebeś palabraś la 'onibersalidad de 'elyyo pu'eś no ayy para maś 'oportunidad ni 'el tyenpo lo padese :

'I lo primero 'eś byen ke śepaś ke koza 'eś śu'enyyo ke 'eś lo ke komun mente lyamamoś dormir 'i ke 'eś viǧilyya ake komun mente lyamamoś velar 'o 'eśpertamyento por lo kual aś de notar ke śu'enyyo 'eś}

‹fol. 24b›
{atamento de 'el śentido komun 'el kual atado priva loś śentidoś de fu'era de śu 'obrar de modo ke śu'enyo 'eś privasy'on de 'el śentido 'i tanbyen de 'el mobimyento voluntary'o de donde konśta ke 'el śu'enyo 'i la viǧilyya śon pasyoneś propyaś de 'el animal 'en kuanto animal kyero dezir śegun ke 'eś śensible konvyene śaber konvenyente para śentir 'i 'el śentir 'eś manifyeśto no śer atribu'ido al ku'erpo śolo ni śolo 'a 'el alma śalbo 'a todoś ǧunta mente porke ni la alma śe pu'ede dezir śentir śin ku'erpo ni 'el ku'erpo śin alma komo la difinsy'on de 'el animal noś 'ensenyya dizyendo animal 'eś śuśtansy'a animada śensible[61] lu'ego 'el śu'enyo 'o la viǧilyya al ku'erpo 'i ala alma ǧuntoś 'eś propy'o ke no ayy animal ke no du'erma 'o 'eśte deśpyerto de adonde nase ke 'a ninguna śuśtansyya animada ni ala animada 'insensible toka dormir 'o velar 'i la śensible nunka 'eśta śin dormir 'i velar a'un ke 'entre laś 'eśpesyaś de 'eśta śuśtansy'a ke śon loś animaleś ayy muǧaś diferensyaś 'en 'el modo 'i 'enel tyenpo 'i kantidad de 'el śu'enyo 'i dela viǧilyya :

'I para deklararte komo śe haze 'el śu'enyo por laś kozaś maś śabidaś ati porke me parese śer nesesary'o lo śepaś para śaberte byen reǧir 'enel telo kyero deklarar por konp[a]rasy'on de akelyyo 'enke te tengo byen 'inpu'eśto 'enla deklarasy'on de 'el kapitulo nono de 'el Bederśi ke 'eś 'el modo dela ǧenerasy'on de la lyubyya 'i laś 'otraś 'enprinsy'oneś ke 'enel alto śe hazen anśi de agu'a komo de ayyre 'i de fu'ego komo

---

[61] Aristotle, *De Anima* II.ii (413b 1–3).

Book of the Regimen of Living ‹fol. 24b–25a›

śon loś tru'enoś relanpagoś rayoś kometaś 'i set-[62]
'ONDE te kize śaver ke deloś rayoś de 'el śol[63] ke aka 'enla tyera 'i 'enel agu'a komo śaetaś 'eğa śe 'elevantan doś diferenteś modoś de alyentoś 'o humoś 'o komo meğor loś pudyeremoś lyyamar 'el kual 'el ke dela tyera śale alevantado de 'el kalor deloś rayoś śolareś 'eś kalyente 'i śeko 'en reśpekto dela tyera porke loś rayoś de 'el śol 'eśkalyentan 'i reśekan 'i 'obrando 'enla tyera śeka 'i fri'a deśhazen laś parteś maś delgadaś laś kualeś 'eśkalyentan fazyendoleś perder śu fryaldad 'i la śekedad a'umentan 'i 'a 'eśto lyyaman propyya mente 'eś'elasy'on 'i 'eś komo 'el humo ke śube de 'el fu'ego ke kema lenyya śeka :

LA śegunda manera de 'el alyento 'eś 'el ke śube dela agu'a porke hiryendo 'el śol kon śuś śaetaś 'eśkalyentando 'i delgazando la agu'a le haze 'evaporar laś parteś śutileś laś kualeś perdyeron śu fryaldad 'i no śu 'omidad porke reğiśte muğo maś 'i 'eśte halyento śe lyyama vapor śemeğaśe 'a 'el fumo ke śube de la 'olyya kuando 'eśta kozyendo al fu'ego 'i 'eśtoś doś 'inperfektoś miśtoś śon la matery'a de laś (m) mete'oroliğikaś 'enprisy'oneś 'i a'un de 'otraś 'enla tyera aveześ kada 'uno porśi aveześ anboś de doś ğunta mente [CW. 'i la kabza]}

‹fol. 25a›
{ḲH

'I la kabza 'efisyente primera śon loś rayoś de 'el śol 'i para ke meğor 'eśto pu'edaś 'entender aś de śaber ke 'el vapor por parte de śu libyandad syendo ku'erpo medyo anśi 'enla kalidad komo 'enel modo de śu śuśtansy'a 'entre agu'a 'i ayyre śube haśta la medya reğy'on de 'el ayre la kual 'eś fri'a 'i 'omida porke komo alyi te deklare 'el ayyre por śer muy pasible 'eś repartido 'en treś reğy'oneś bağa alta medya

LA bağa 'eś dende la tyera faśta do śe akaba la refleksy'on de loś rayoś reperkutidoś de 'elya 'i 'eśta 'eś kalyente 'i 'omida a'uta para la vida 'i konservasy'on de todoś loś miśtoś ke 'enla tyera abitan

LA alta 'enpesa de donde 'el ayyre 'eśta kontigo konel fu'ego 'i śe k(y)[o]ntinu'a para abağo hata 'onde la virtud 'i fu'ersa de 'el fu'ego akabo de 'eśkalyentar 'i diśekar 'el ayyre 'eśta parte 'eś kalyente 'i śeka dende 'el kavo de 'eśta alta faśta 'el kabo de la bağa loke keda 'en medyo 'eś la reğy'on de 'el ayyre fri'a 'i 'omida privatiba mente por falta de 'el kalor de 'el fu'ego ke kema la alta 'i de loś rayoś de 'el śol ke 'eś-

---

[62] Jedaiah ben Abraham Bedersi (Ha-Penini) (1270–1340). It is unclear to which of Bedersi's titles, or his own, Almosnino refers. For a description of Bedersi's writings and bibliography, see *EJ* 9:1308–10; further description and bibliography is found in *JE* 2:625–26.

[63] For this passage cf. Aristotle, *Meteorologica,* I.ix (346b 16–36), trans. Lee, 68.71.

BOOK OF THE REGIMEN OF LIVING ‹FOL. 25A–25B›

kalyentan 'enla bağa 'i 'eś fri'a pozitiba mente 'en reśpekto de laś 'otraś 'i tanbyen por 'el modo ke diremoś de laś kualeś treś reğy'oneś akel 'interpete dela naturaleza Aristotel hablo śofisyente mente 'enel prinsipy'o de 'el libro metaoroś[64] 'i koneśto 'eś byen viśto komo akel vapor ke śube de aka kalyente 'i 'omido ke lyega ala fri'a reğy'on śe 'eśfri'a 'i śe 'engru'esa 'i 'eśpesa porke 'eś agu'a 'en potensy'a 'i bu'elveśe 'a śuś primeraś kalidadeś ke no difyeren 'en 'eśpesy'a de 'el agu'a dela meśma manera ke 'el humo ke śale dela 'olyya ke 'eśta herbyendo al fu'ego lyegando al kobertero ke 'eśta fri'o śe 'engru'eśa 'i bu'elbe 'a fazerśe agu'a komo primero :

'I por ke 'eśte vapor adelgazado de la kalyentura de 'el fu'ego 'eś maś a'uto para resebir kual kyera kalidad 'i rodeado 'el diğo kalor śu kontraryy'o śe 'esfri'a 'i 'engru'esa maś komo kuando keremoś ke 'el agu'a śe 'eśfri'e muğo la kalyentamoś primero porke śe adelgaze 'i la ponemoś 'en lugar no muy kalyente 'i śe bu'elbe maś fri'a ke deanteś 'i lyyaman loś naturaleś 'eśto antipariśtaześ ke kyere dezir pośtura de 'el kontrary'o al deredor 'o rode'o de śu kontrary'o anśi 'el vapor adelgazado de loś rayoś de 'el śol lyegando ala medya reğy'on de 'el ayyre fri'a rodeado de la alta 'i bağa kalyenteś rekoğendośe 'enśi meśmo śe 'eśfri'a 'i 'engrosado śe haze nube 'i final mente śe deśfaze 'en agu'a 'eśta 'eś la lyyuby'a 'i 'eśte vapor de pu'eś de ğunto 'i 'engrosado muğaś veześ śe deśparze 'i deśparzido śe eśvaneśe 'i 'eśto 'eś loke śe lyyama nebla : la lyyubya de ke hablamoś 'eś de diversoś modoś aveześ muğa 'i menuda :}

‹fol. 25b›

{'a veześ muğa 'i gru'esa : 'otraś poka 'i gru'esa 'eśta 'eś laś maś veześ 'enel 'eśti'o 'enel kual la medy'a reğy'on de 'el ayyre 'eś maś fri'a 'i konprehendida 'en muğo menoś 'eśpasy'o por la reberberasy'on de 'el śol śer mayor porke 'eśta maś 'enpinado 'i loś vaporeś śon pokoś porke 'eśtonseś 'el śol reśu'elve muğo 'i 'enlaś noğeś por la mayor parte ayy muğa lyyubya 'i menuda por la medya reğy'on no 'eśtar tan fri'a para 'engrosar 'i deśfazer la nube komo de di'a 'i śe diminuye la kabza de antipariśtaześ 'i ayy muğoś vaporeś alevantadoś deloś rayoś de 'el śol 'enel di'a loś kualeś de noğe śe[ ]no pu'eden rezolber :

TANBYEN 'eś konparado ala lyyubyya la deśtilasy'on de laś yerbaś porke 'el kalor ke 'eśta de bağo de 'elyyaś ke tanto monta de bağo komo 'en śima para benifik[a]r la konparasy'on alevanta 'unoś vaporeś dela meśma śuśtansy'a de laś yerbaś l(a)[o]ś kualeś lyegando al alto de la alkitara 'eśfryadoś 'i 'engrośadoś de 'el plomo kaen abağo feğoś agu'a 'i 'a 'eśta fryal[d]ad de 'el plomo ayudan muğaś veześ loś 'eśtiladoreś kon panyoś moğadoś pu'eśtoś de fu'era para ke ayya mayor fu'ersa para 'eśfryar 'i 'eśpesar

---

[64] A variant title for Aristotle's *Meteorologica*.

Book of the Regimen of Living ⟨fol. 25b–26a⟩

'el vapor alevantado de 'el 'igne'o kalor 'eśta ko[n]parasy'on de la 'eśtilasy'on 'eś muy śemeğante 'enel mikrokozmo ke 'eś 'el 'ombre al sudor ke śe 'eśta 'eśtilando 'i fasil mente śe pu'ede aplikar viśto komo śe haze 'el sudor lo kual yo deklare 'enla 'entrepetasy'on ke yo tengo heğo de loś problemaś de Aristotel de latin 'en nu'eśa lengu'a śanta⁶⁵ 'enla śegunda partikula de diğoś problemaś⁶⁶ 'i nu'eśtra konparasy'on primera 'eś muy propya ala lyyubyya la kual 'enel mundo grande śe haze komo 'el śu'enyo 'enel ğiko śegun ke 'eśkriby'o 'el filosofo 'enel libro de 'el śu'eny'o 'i dela viğilansy'a⁶⁷ komo lu'ego te dire 'enpero porke 'eśta materya de loś metaoroś⁶⁸ 'eś muy 'util 'i guśtoza no me pezara br(y)eve mente 'eneśte lugar pu'eś toka 'eneśta materya lo maś fasil ke pud[y]ere 'enśenyarte komo śe hazen algunaś 'otraś 'enprınsy'oneś :

ŚABRAŚ ke de 'eśte meśmo vapor śe faze 'el rosi'o kuando 'ubyere poka kalor de di'a kele levante syendo la fryaldad dela noğe tan byen tenplada ke 'engru'esa 'eśte vapor 'enel lugar donde śe haze la lyubya 'el kual vapor śi anteś ke śe bu'elba 'en agu'a ke 'eś 'el rosi'o śe konğelare komo akonteśe 'enel tyenpo muğo fri'o bu'elveśe 'en 'elada komo akaeśe 'enlaś manyanaś de 'invyerno mayor mente śoplando 'el vyento dela parte de 'el norte de manera ke la kabza primera 'efisyente 'eś 'el śol 'i 'entyendo por śol todaś laś 'eśtrelyyaś 'i laś planetaś pu'eś todoś toman de 'el śegundary'a de 'el rosi'o 'eś la poka fryaldad de 'el ayyre 'i la del yelo la muğa fryaldad la dela lyyuby'a medyana 'entre}

⟨fol. 26a⟩
{KV
'eśtaś doś la materyal 'el vapor diferente de muğo 'a poko la final la konfirmasy'on del 'oniberso para śi krearen 'i manteneren loś 'endividu'oś
LA nyebe śe haze kuando la nube śe konğela anteś ke śe deśhaga 'en agu'a de modo ke kuando 'el vapor konvertido 'en nube śe 'eśfri'o tanto ke śe kuağo śe hizo nyebe la kual 'eś muğo maś fri'a kela lyubya 'i tyene algo de kalyente kela adelgaza porke śino no śe podri'a la nube alevantar faśta 'el lugar donde śe konğelaśe ke 'eś la reğy'on medyya 'i nota ke rosi'o yelo lyyubya nyebe 'eś todo kazi 'uno kuanto aśu materya 'i kabza 'efisyente 'i 'el modo de la ğenerasy'on śino ke refyere de maś 'a

---

[65] This statement suggests that Almosnino knew Latin.
[66] Aristotle, *Problems* II, trans. Hett, 1:46–73.
[67] Aristotle, *Parva Naturalia* 3 (*On Sleep and Waking*), iii (456a 30–458a 34), trans. Hett, 335–43.
[68] Aristotle, *Meteorologica* I.iv (342a 1–36), ix–x (346b 25–347a 35).

BOOK OF THE REGIMEN OF LIVING ‹FOL. 26A–26B›

menoś la lyubya 'i rosi'o no difyeren 'en maś ke 'en śer la lyubya heǧa de maś vaporeś koliǧidoś 'en maś tyenpo 'i 'el rosi'o deloś vaporeś koliǧid[o]ś 'en 'un di'a śola mente 'el yelo 'i la nyebe difyere 'eneśto ke 'el yelo ake loś latinoś lyyaman glaśyaś 'eś vapor konǧelado la nyebe nube konǧelada :
　'EL pedriśko śe haze kuando por parte del demazyado kalor dela baša reǧy'on de 'el ayyre la medya 'eśta friǧidisima de modo ke derityendo la nube 'en 'unaś gotaś gru'eśaś ake lyaman labroteraś anteś ke laś konvyerta 'en agu'a laś kuaǧa 'i 'eśta 'eś la maś fri'a 'enprinsy'on de todaś ke śe faze 'en fin de 'el 'eśti'o 'i komyenso de a'utono 'enke 'el śol alevanta hartoś vaporeś 'i por la fu'erte antipariśt(e)[a]ześ por la kabza diǧa śe konǧelan 'i śi 'enla parte alta dela medyya reǧy'on kaen redondoś 'i maś ǧikoś 'eś porke śe gaśtan 'enel kamino 'i 'a 'eśtaś 'enprinsy'oneś ayudan muǧo laś ka'[u]zaś śeleśteś komo śon konǧunsy'oneś de planetaś 'i (t)[s]et- ke no 'eś de nu'eśo perpozito averlo de deklarar :
　'I kuando la 'eśelasy'on ke 'eś 'el bafo dela tyera kalyente 'i śeko fu'ego 'en potensy'a por śer maś libyano ke 'el vapor śube faśta la alta reǧy'on de 'el ayyre ǧunto konel fu'eg(+)o adonde fasilima mente śe 'enflama komo vemoś ke 'el humo śe 'enflama de preśto porke la flama 'eś ardor de 'un 'eśprito 'o bafo śeko difyeren 'eśtaś 'enflamasy'oneś ke 'a veześ śe hazen komo 'unaś 'eśtrelyaś fiśeś kon 'una kola 'i 'eśtaś śe lyyaman kometaś 'otraś komo 'unaś ke arden diferenteś 'en muǧedumbre 'i pokedad śityo 'i figura komo 'enel primero de loś metabroś trae Aristotel[69] :
　'EL tru'eno 'i 'el relanpago śe 'enǧendran kuando ambaś adoś 'eǧalasyoneś anśi la aki'a 'omida komo la tere'a śeka alevantadaś 'a 'una ǧuntaś śe hazen nube 'i la śeka maś ariva alevantada śe 'eśpesa por la fryaldad de 'el lugar 'i maś delaś parteś de fu'era 'enla medya reǧy'on 'i la 'omida 'eǧalasy'on 'enserada de dyentro keryendo śalir por loś ladoś de la nube 'eśpesa 'enkontrandośe kon vehemensy'a 'enelyoś haze śonidoś diversoś śegun la diversidad dela konkaba nube}

‹fol. 26b›
{'i vary'edad 'entre raro 'i 'eśpeso porke 'el śonido śe kabza de 'el 'enku'entro de doś ku'erpoś duroś 'i abaśta ke 'uno śe'a duro śegun ke de 'el śegundo de 'el alma 'enel propy'o kapitulo konśta[70] 'i 'eś śemeǧante 'el ke śe haze kuando keman algunoś paloś śekoś por kabzo de 'el 'eśprito dyentro 'enserado ke perkura śalir[71] 'i komo śe haze 'el

---

[69] The foregoing discussion follows Aristotle, *Meteorologica* I.vii (344a 5–345a 10), trans. Lee, 48–57.
[70] Aristotle, *De Anima* (419b 9–25), trans. Hett, 111.
[71] Aristotle, *Meteorologica* II.ix (369a 25–30), trans. Lee, 225.

BOOK OF THE REGIMEN OF LIVING ‹FOL. 26B›

tremor dela tyera por kabza dela 'eğalasy'on 'enserada dyentro śutilada de loś rayoś del śol ke śalyendo ronpe la tyera komo 'eś diğo 'enel śegundo de loś metabroś[72] :
'I porke de 'el fu'erte mobimyento śe 'enğendra kalor komo 'enel śegundo de 'el syelo trae Aristotel[73] 'i la 'eśprensy'a mu'eśtra komo muğaś veześ akaese 'ensenderśe 'eśta 'eğalasy'on lyyamaśe 'eśte tal reśplandor relanpago 'i śe haze laś maś veześ primero ke 'el tru'eno porke deśpu'eś de 'enflamada 'i feğa rara por no śe dar penetrasy'on de dimensy'oneś ronpe la nube para śalir 'o alomenoś 'enel meśmo 'iśtante ke śe 'enflama ronpe 'enpero primero la vemoś ke 'oyamoś 'el tru'eno komo 'enloś navi'oś vemoś loś remoś alevantadoś de 'el agu'a 'i bu'elben 'a herir la śegunda veś primero ke 'oyamoś 'el śonido ke fizyeron kuando la primera veś batyeron 'enel agu'a porke la viśta śe haze śupito 'i 'el 'o'ir 'en tyenpo komo 'enel libro de 'el sentido 'i la koza śentida[74] śe deklara 'i 'enla 'onzena partikula de loś prob(y)lemaś 'eśta probado[75] :
ŚI 'eśta 'eğ(e)[a]lasy'on 'enflamada 'eś 'eğada kon 'inpetu 'i fu'ersa de la nube ke reğiśty'o lyamaśe rayo 'el kual muğaś veześ 'eś 'un 'eśprito 'o bafo muğo delgado ke śe lyyama rayo klaro ke no kema maś 'enflama 'i 'enlaś kozaś duraś 'enke topa deśhaze ke śi da 'en 'un animal deśhaze loś gu'eśoś değando 'el ku'erpo śano porke no śe detyene pasando por 'el ku'erpo raro tanto tyenpo ke pu'eda 'obrar kema la moneda de metal śin hazer ku'enta de la bolsa de ku'ero la 'espada de duro fyero śin tokar la vayna melya[76] :
AYY 'otra 'eśpesy'a de rayo ke śe lyyama rayo fumante 'i ardyente 'el kual kema kuanto halyya 'i 'eśte 'eś maś 'eśpeso 'i 'eś duro ake komun mente lyyaman pyedra de koriśko[77] 'enpero śi la 'eğ'elasy'on ke dyentro 'enla nube 'eś(+)ta fu'ere 'eśpesa la kual keryendo śubir aśima kon 'inpetu fu'ere 'eğa(r)[d]a abaśo śin ronper nube ni 'enflamarśe fara 'un vyento tenpeśtu'ozo 'en grego lyyamado 'enifi'a[78] 'i noś lo lyya-

---

[72] Aristotle, *Meteorologica* II.viii (365b 21–28), trans. Lee, 205.

[73] Aristotle, *De Caelo* II.vii (289a 20–22), trans. W. K. C. Guthrie (London, 1939), 179.

[74] *On Sense and Sensible Objects,* see the translation by Hett, 215–83, esp. vi (446b 3–9), 265–67.

[75] Aristotle, *Problems* XI. 6, 49, 58, trans. Hett, 1:255–57, 287, 291–93.

[76] The reference seems to be Aristotle, *On Marvellous Things Heard,* 48, trans. Hett, 255–57 (833b 25–32).

[77] *Corisco* "relámpago" (*DCECH*).

[78] I have not identified this term, nor do Kahane and Tietze record anything analogous; perhaps a typographical error obscures the Greek συννεφία, "cloudy weather".

BOOK OF THE REGIMEN OF LIVING ‹FOL. 26B–27A›

mamoś tenpeśtal 'i 'eś 'un mal vyento tenpeśt(y)[u]'ozo forśozo barağozo de( )śpu'eś de 'el kual śe śigen grandeś lyyubyyaś deśheğaś laś parteś 'omidaś dela nube 'i kuando 'eśte tal vyento aśi 'eś 'eğado kae dando bu'eltaś al deredor por kabza ke no 'eś pura 'eğalasy'on maś anteś trae konśigo meśkla de parteś vaporozaś 'omidaś 'i 'eś muy temerozo aloś naveganteś}

‹fol. 27a›
{KZ PEREK Š^eBI^cIY [CHAPTER SEVEN]
'i anda al deredor 'i apanya kuanto falyya 'i 'enla mar haze komo 'una ku'eba adonde ahonda loś navi'oś lyyamaśe komun mente 'eśta ku'eba 'enla mar 'i 'eśte apanyyamyento ke parese barer laś kalyeś rodo molino[79] 'i 'el te[n]peśty'ozo vyento śe lyyama śy'on del kual habla Aristo- 'enel tersero de loś metaoroś[80] 'i 'eśto ab[a]śta por agora ke 'a muğo ke de nu'eśtro kamino ap[a]rtadoś noś metimoś 'enel ağeno ke no fu'e aki la 'intensy'on maś ke hazerte śaver de kamino 'en breve 'eśtaś kozaś ke kada di'a vemoś 'i pokoś śaven laś kauśaś naturaleś de ke śe hazen porke no kedeś falto enelyaś pu'eś noś vino 'a perpozito :

KAPITULO ŚEBTIMO

BOLVYENDO al prepozito digo ke anśi komo 'el vapor mobido del śol śube ala medyya rey'on del ayyre 'i alyi 'engrosado desyende abaśo anśi del kilo 'enel 'eśtomago 'el kual 'a'i 'eśta para aver de hazer śangre pośtrero mantenimyento 'enloś ke[ ]śangre tyenen śuben vaporeś faśta 'el śelebro 'i a'i 'eśfryadoś 'i 'eśpesadoś hazen refluğo al korason 'el kual 'eś prinsipy'o del śentimyento 'i 'eśte 'eśfryado 'i 'inpedido śe anublan todoś loś śentidoś kuantoś 'el animal ke du'erme tyene 'i 'eśto 'eś śu'enyyo 'enel kual 'el kalor natural 'eś komo 'el śeleśte del[ ]mundo mayyor 'el 'eśtomago 'o[ ]kilo 'i mantenimyento 'inperfekto donde śe levantan loś vaporeś 'eś komo 'el agu'a śuś vaporeś komo loś dela agu'a 'el śelebro komo la medya rey'on del ayyre 'el re'uma ke desyende 'i 'eśfri'a templando 'el kalor del korason komo haze la lyubyya ala tyera 'i 'eśte modo de hazerśe 'el śu'enyyo 'eś śegun 'el mayor de loś filosofoś Aristotel 'enel propyyo libro del śu'enyo[81] 'i loś medikoś difyeren del nyegando 'el korason śer prinsipyyo del śentir 'i mober maś anteś 'eśte śenyyori'o atribu'en al śelebro 'i dizen ke loś vaporeś ke hata 'el śelebro śuben alyi 'eśpesadoś 'i 'engravesidoś desyenden por

---

[79] Corominas does not record the term (*DCECH*).
[80] Aristotle, *Meteorologica* III.i (370b 3–371b 17), trans. Lee, 233–41.
[81] Aristotle, *Parva Naturalia* 3 (*On Sleep and Waking*), trans. Hett, 319–45.

BOOK OF THE REGIMEN OF LIVING ‹FOL. 27A–27B›

loś nyerboś 'eśturmentoś del śentir 'i mober kuyya 'oriğin 'eś del me'olyyo 'i anśi priban 'el śentimyento 'i mob(y)imyento ke de aki nase ke deśpu'eś de komer vyene 'el śu'enyyo komo 'enpesan śubir loś humoś 'i mayor mente śi la komida 'eś 'omida gru'esa ke loś vaporeś śon muy gru'esoś 'i a'utoś 'a 'opilar muğo 'i 'inpedir no vengan loś 'eśpritoś śensitiboś aloś myenbroś

'I no 'a de śer la komida tanta ke afog(+)e 'el kalor ke no pu'eda levantar loś vaporeś komo faze 'el poko fu'ego 'en muğa lenyya 'i verde por 'eśo laś kozaś muğo friaś komo 'opyo 'i mandragora 'i set-[82] hazen śu'enyo porke miniśtran materya a'uta para 'el 'inpedimyento 'enel śu'enyo rekerido}

‹fol. 27b›
{laś kozaś kalyenteś 'i 'omidaś alebantando laś vaporeś śon śofisyente kabza hazedora del śu'enyyo komo 'eś 'el vino 'i set- 'i de loke diśe 'eśta viśta la kabza 'efiśyente del śu'enyyo :

KE 'eś la primarya 'el kalor natural ke alebanta loś vaporeś del kilo śegundary'a la fryaldad del śelebro ke loś 'engru'eśa la materyyal primary'a 'el kilo śegundary'a loś vapor[e]ś la formal 'eś 'el 'eśpesamyento 'i graveda(r)[d] konla kual 'inpiden la venida deloś 'eśpritoś aloś myenbroś śensibleś 'i motiboś : la final noś keda por dezir : 'i 'eś para ke śe haga meğor la diğeśty'on anśi primera komo śegunda 'i tersera de ke hablan loś mediko larga mente 'i heğaś byen 'eśtaś diğeśty'oneś pu'eda 'el 'omb(y)re meğor viğilar : kyero dezir ke śyenta 'i śe mu'eba meğor : 'i 'eśpekule : ke 'eśte 'eś śu fin anśi ke 'el viğilar 'eś 'el fin del śu'enyo :

'OTRA kabza final kumutat(')iba 'eś 'eśfryar 'el korason : para lo kual nota ke 'el mantenimyento 'enloś animaleś 'a de śer muğo m[e]ğor kozido : ke 'enlaś plantaś : 'i por 'eśo śe koze treś veześ 'enel 'eśtomago : 'enel figado : 'enlaś venaś : 'i komo kyera ke 'el animal śe afatiga 'en moverśe 'i kanśa 'en ś(+)entir śe rezolven muğo śuś 'eś(+)prit[o]ś 'enla viğilyya por la kual śe 'inpide muğo la diğeśty'on probeyo por tanto la natureza ke retenidoś loś 'eśpritoś 'i rekonsentradoś 'a laś parteś 'intiry'oreś ayudan muğo ala diğeśty'on 'el śenyal deśto 'eś ke akabada la diğeśty'on śe deraman por 'el ku'erpo 'i deśpyerta 'el animal 'i deśpu'eś de 'eśpyerto pu'ede byen śentir 'i moberśe no śintyendo trabağo 'enel diğerir 'i 'eśtando deśpedido del kansansy'o ke 'en śentir 'i moberśe anteś del śu'enyo teni'a 'i 'el 'ombre 'eśta galyyardo para poder meğor 'eśpekular komo por 'eśperensy'a vemoś aproběğar maś 'una 'ora de 'eśtudy'o de manyyana akabando loś 'eśpritoś de dar śu parte al ku'erpo ke treś al prinsipy'o dela noğe 'i de loke tenemoś diğo śe mu'eśtra kela noğe 'eś maś a'uta para 'el dormir

---

[82] Aristotle, *On Sleep and Waking* III (456b 29–31), trans. Hett, 337.

Book of the Regimen of Living ‹fol. 27b–28a›

ke 'el di'a por śer fri'a 'i 'omida : 'i 'el 'invyerno maś ke 'el 'eśti'o 'i a'utono porke 'el 'in[v]yerno 'eś tyenpo fri'o 'i 'omido 'i 'el verano kalyente 'i 'omido 'i 'el 'eśti'o kalyente 'i śeko : 'el a'utono fri'o 'i śeko : 'i la 'omidad 'eś muy a'uta para 'el śu'enyo : la śekedad 'ina'uta : 'i loś 'ombreś 'omidoś mašime del śelebro komo śanginoś 'i flematikoś śon dormily'oneś maś keloś śekoś kolerikoś 'i malenkolikoś 'i loś ninyyoś muy muğo maś ke loś 'ombreś :
 'I deśpu'eś del 'ešerśisy'o kuando no 'eś muğo 'i fu'erte ke 'el tal rezolbe 'i dibilita la natureza ke no pu'eda 'obrar vyene lu'ego 'el śu'enyyo para remedyar 'el danyyo 'i por 'eso le lyamaron deśkanso 'i pu'eś 'el śu'enyyo 'eś feğo para poder velar meğor}

‹fol. 28a›
{KḤ
no śe deve tomar maś ke lo ke la n[a]tureza rekyere : ke śera 'obrar kontra ś(y)[u] veluntad 'i śegirśean grandeś danyyoś anśi 'eśpritualeś komo temporaleś
 'I por kuanto te diše ke todo animal du'erme para ke pu'eda velar meğor 'eśtando apareğado para meğor śentir 'a meneśter alargar algo para darte a'entender komo 'enel 'ombre śe śige 'el 'entendimyento de loś śentidoś korporaleś 'i komo tyene neseśidad del 'ešerśisy'o de todoś loś śentidoś 'eśtiry'oreś a'un ke śeme haze al prezente muy difisil porke śon kozaś ke rekyeren aver muğo le'ido 'i muğo 'eśpekulado para poder laś 'entender pero toda vi'a porke no kedeś de todo falto ke śeri'a grande mengu'a te dire la konkluzy'on muy brebe 'i śi kiğereś śaberlo por śuś kabzaś 'i prinsipy'oś byen por 'eśtenso mira loke tengo 'e[ś]krito 'enmiś notasy'oneś śobre laś p[a]labraś de 'Abuḥamid 'Algazel 'ensu metafizika disy'on tersyya[83] 'i la konkuluzyon delyyo 'eś śegun 'el filosofo 'enel libro de śenso śenśato[84] 'eśkriby'o 'i śegun laś palabraś de 'Algazel 'enel diğo lugar ke la koza korporal 'i natural tyene d- [4] maneraś de śer dif[e]renteś 'el 'uno de 'el (f)[']otro 'i 'uno maś 'enselente ke 'otro :
 'EL primer śer dela koza 'i 'el maś korporal 'eś śu śer 'enśi konśerbado por śuś treś dimensy'oneś anteś de śer 'obğekto del śentido korporal 'eśtiry'or śolo 'el 'enśi 'i porśi :

---

[83] Al-Ghazzali, *Intenciones de los filósofos,* trans. M. Alonso (Barcelona, 1963). Abu Ḥamid Muḥammad al-Ghazzali's *Maqasid al-falasifa* (The Meanings of the Philosophers) was a standard medieval textbook of logic, metaphysics and physics. For an overview of al-Ghazzali's writings, see *Encylopaedia of Islam,* 2d ed., 2:1038b–1041b. Almosnino refers to his own commentary on al-Ghazzali, *Migdal Oz.*

[84] Aristotle, *Parva Naturalia* I (*On Sense and Sensible Objects*), trans. Hett, 215–83.

BOOK OF THE REGIMEN OF LIVING ‹FOL. 28A–28B›

ŠEGUNDO šer dela koza 'eš ya dešpu'eš de reprezentada al šentido ke la forma dela propya koza še 'inprime 'enla višta 'i še dize 'eštar la propyya koza 'enel propy'o 'oğo 'en grado maš 'ekselente de loke 'elyya por ši tyene ke 'eš 'el primer šer komo t[e]nemoš diğo primero porke 'ešte šegundo 'eš maš delgado 'i menoš korporal ke 'el primero :

'eš 'el tersero šer dela koza de maš 'ekšelensyya ke 'eštoš doš diğoš 'el kual 'eš la forma de la koza traida ala ke komun mente lyyamamoš 'imağinasy'on 'i fantazi'a[85] propyya mente por 'entresisy'on del šentido komun ke šyendo traida la forma al šentido komun por medyo deloš šentidoš 'eštiry'oreš dešpu'eš ke 'el 'obğekto 'eš 'okulto la 'imağinasy'on 'o fantazi'a konserba 'i guarda la tal forma dela mešma manera ke '[e]l šentido komun la resiby'o deloš šentidoš 'eštiry'oreš kyero dezir šin šer šeparadaš laš formaš dela materyya :

'EL kuarto šer 'i de mayor 'ekšelensyya linpy'o de todo modo de korpulensyya 'eš la forma šuštansyyal de la koza ke resibe 'el 'entendimyento de la fantazi'a apartando la forma de la materyya donde še torna 'el 'entendimyento 'i 'el 'enten(y)der 'i 'el 'entendido 'una mešma koza 'eš kuando 'el 'entendimyento 'umano 'ešta 'en a'uto puro ke anteš ['en] de 'eštar 'en a'uto šon treš kozaš šeparadaš ke 'eš 'el 'entendido}

‹fol. 28b›
{poršì anteš kelo 'entyenda 'i 'el 'entendimyento tanbyen por ši 'i 'el 'entender manka mankando 'el ayuntamyento de loš doš por lo kual 'enel Dyyo glory'ozo ke šyenpre 'entyende 'en puro a'uto 'ino še afigura 'enel potensyya alguna 'eš de kontino 'el 'entendimyento 'i 'el 'ent[e]nder 'i 'entendido todo 'una mešma koza komo dek(')l[a]ro 'ešto 'el šenyyor Rabbenu Mošeh 'enel kapitulo sh- [68] de la primera partikula del Moreh[86] la kual konešto diğo 'entenderaš 'i ši a'un konešto algo dubdareš yo telo hare byen 'entender 'en šu lugar ši 'el Dyyo me dyere vida ğunto kon 'otroš šekretoš maš

POR agora te abašta š(+)aver lo ke 'a nu'eštro perpozito haze 'i 'eš ke 'eštoš d-[4] modoš de šer dela koza 'el 'uno 'eš la kabza del 'otro ke 'el šer dela koza 'enši 'eš kabza de alkansar 'el šentido : 'i alkansarla 'el šentido 'eš kabza de konserbarla 'i guardarla la fantazi'a 'i la forma de la fantazi'a 'o 'imağinasy'on 'eš kabza 'i medyyo para ke 'el 'entendimyento tome la forma šuštansyyal apartada ke 'eš 'oniversal 'intelektual de todo modo de materyya ağena šin korpulensyya 'i falasyya de asidenteš de manera ke tyene 'el 'e[n]tendimyento nesesidad del šentir deloš šentidoš 'eštiry'oreš hašta hazer la koza 'una konel 'entendimyento por la vi'a diğa por tanto konvyene

---

[85] Cf. Aristotle, *De Anima* III.3, trans. Hett, 157–63.
[86] Maimonides, *Guide of the Perplexed,* trans. Pines, 167 (*MN,* Pt. 1, chap. 68).

Book of the Regimen of Living ‹fol. 28b–29a›

śervirśe delyyoś komo konvyene para loke śe rekyere para la 'eśpikulasy'on ke 'eś 'el verdadero fin 'umano 'el kual 'eś la 'obra del 'entendimyento te'oriko 'i amar al Dyyo ke 'eś 'obra dela veluntad por medy'o del 'entendimyento pratiko ke no me pongo aki 'a disirnir 'entre 'eśtaś doś partidaś 'en kual de 'elyaś konśiśte 'el byen 'i 'ultimo fin ke 'eś diferensy'a 'entre doktisimoś śenyoreś 'i famoziśimoś : 'i yo tengo muğo alargado 'enelyo 'enel śeśto 'i deśimo dela 'etika[87] 'i 'eśkrito śofiśyenteś razoneś para ambaś laś parteś 'i 'enla tersera partida deśte tratado hablare 'enelyo maś largo konel ayuda del Dyyo bendito al preśente baśta byen śaber ke de kual kyera manera ke śe'a parese śer byen rekerir 'el tyenpo dela viğilya para 'eśerśitar laś 'obraś del 'entendimyento por lo kual 'eś razon keloś mosoś śean kośtumbradoś deśde śu mosedad 'a dormir poko 'i 'a tomar no maś delo nesesaryo para śuśtentar la śanidad 'i deśkansar loś śentidoś de śuś fatigadaś operasy'oneś ke 'eś grandisima 'utilidad para poderśe meğor 'eğerśitar 'enel tyenpo dela viğilyya 'i poreso 'ordenaron nu'eśtroś śaby'oś dezir bendisy'on 'i dar lo'or al Dyyo glory'ozo al tyenpo del dormir 'i del deśpertar[88] por śer amboś konvenyenteś ala śuśtentasy'on de la vida 'umana 'i muy komodoś al ku'erpo 'i 'a 'el alma 'i syendo kual kyera de loś doś maś de loke konvyene haze muğo danyyo al ku'erpo 'i al 'entendimyento komo 'enla śegunda deloś aforiśmoś 'eśkriby'o 'Ipokreteś[89] [CW. 'i 'eś]}

‹fol. 29a›
{KT
'i 'eśpisifiko Abisena 'enla śegunda del primero śuma primera doktrina śegunda kapitulo yg- [13] do dize kuando fu'ere la viğilyya 'en multitud maś de loke konvyene konronpe la konplisy'on del śelebro 'en 'eśpesy'a de śekedad 'i[ ]śi muda deśu natural konplisy'on konturba 'el 'entendimyento 'i rekema loś 'umoreś 'i 'enğendra dolensyyaś agudaś 'i set-[90] :
'I 'el śu'enyo demazyado de loke konvyene 'enğendra al kontrary'o deśto 'i propyya mente 'enğendra grande pezadumbre 'enel śelebro pereza negliğensy'a 'enlaś vertudeś del alma 'i ala fin kabza dolensyaś friaś de manera ke tubyeron grandisimo fundamyento nu'eśtroś śaby'oś 'en 'ordenar 'enloś b- [2] tyenpoś lo'or 'i bendisy'on

---

[87] Almosnino refers to *Pne Moše*.

[88] Berakot 21a.

[89] Almosnino accurately summarizes the *Aphorisms*, Section II, no. 3: "Both sleep and wakefulness are bad if they exceed their due proportion" (Hippocrates, *Medical Works*, trans. J. Chadwick and W. N. Mann [Oxford, 1950], 151).

[90] Ibn Sina, "*Canon of Medicine*," trans. Gruner, 210–12 and 417–19.

BOOK OF THE REGIMEN OF LIVING ‹FOL. 29A–29B›

al Dyyo pu'eś tanto danyyo śe śige faltando alguno delyyoś deloke konvyene 'i aśi meśmo śi śe haze komo no konvyene 'i kuando no konvyene 'i set-
'I pu'eś śon tantoś loś 'inkonbenyenteś 'en śer demazyado kual kyera deloś doś 'eś razon meter 'orden 'i limite 'enelyyoś por lo kual algunoś modernoś hizyeron 'una razonable repartisy'on donde diǧeron ke 'el tyenpo del di'a natural ke 'eś k'd [24] 'oraś śe debe repartir 'un tersy'o delyyaś ke śon ḥ- [8] 'oraś 'enel 'eśtudy'o 'i 'eśpikulasy'on 'i 'el 'otro tersyyo 'en byen 'obrar 'i 'uzar todaś laś kozaś konvenyenteś al ku'erpo komo komer 'i beber buśkarlo 'i ganarlo 'i 'otraś śemeǧanteś kozaś 'i 'otro tersy'o ke 'eś terminado 'enlaś ḥ- [8] 'oraś pośtreraś 'en dormir 'okuparon 'i syerto 'eś byen konsidrada repartisy'on 'i 'el ke maś anyadyere 'enel primero tersy'o ke 'eś dela 'eśpikulasy'on śakando deloś 'otroś doś kon tal ke no śe'a tanto ke danye 'eśte tal śera de mayor 'ekśelensy'a fu'e muy konforme 'eśta repartisy'on aloke 'eśkriby'o 'el śenyyor Rabbenu Mošeh 'enel reǧim[y]ento de śanidad 'ensu prinsip(y)al tratado do dize 'el di'a 'i la noǧe śon ḵd- [24] 'oraś baśtele 'al 'ombre dormir 'el tersyyo de 'elyyaś ke śon ḥ- [8] 'oraś 'i set-[91]

'I loke maś śe deve aserka deśto advertir 'eś perkurar de no dormir de di'a 'i huyya 'el moso de akośtumbrarśe a'elyyo de modo ke por ningun ku'ento lo haga ke 'eś muǧo danyyozo para 'el ku'erpo 'i para la alma komo tenemoś diǧo 'i 'el ke guardare 'el 'orden 'enel komer 'i bever komo tenemoś diǧo ke koma de di'a poko por laś kabzaś śuzo diǧaś poder( )śe'a guardar del di'urno dormir ke śi muǧo komyere śegun laś kabzaś del dormir ke 'eśkrito avemoś no podra reǧiśtir al śu'enyo 'i śegirśele'a grandisimo danyo por 'el deś'orden de amboś tanbyen 'eś razon de akavidarśe muǧo loś mosoś ke no du'erman 'en prezensyya de 'otroś mayyoreś ke 'elyyoś ke 'eśto 'eś maś vituperyado ke 'el komer ni bever 'en prezensyya de 'otro mayor porke 'enel komer pu'edeśe hazer komedido 'i reglado pu'eś śe śirbe de śuś śentidoś todoś pero 'enel dormir alyende de śer a'uto beśtyal por parte ke 'enel komunikamoś kon loś brutoś}

‹fol. 29b›
{komo 'enel komer tyene maś mal ke komo kyera ke śe'a privasy'on de loś śentidoś no 'eśta 'en mano del ke du'erme deśpu'eś ke du'erme śer moderado 'enel por lo kual anteś ke 'el 'ombre 'enpeśe 'a dormir śe deve retraer 'en lugar ke no śe'a viśto de 'otro mayor ke 'el ke deśpu'eś de dormido no 'eśta 'ensu mano guardarśe de hazer deśplazible śemblante 'a kual kyera kelo vyere :
'I no kale dezir kuan deś'onеśto 'eś kuando 'eśta 'en prezensyya de 'otroś 'en

---

[91] Maimonides, *Character Traits,* ed. Weiss and Butterworth, 36 (*Hilḵot De'ot,* chap. 4, halaḵah 4).

Book of the Regimen of Living ⟨fol. 29b⟩

konversasy'on 'o ala meza 'o 'eśtudyyando 'o hazyendo kual kyera 'otro a'uto 'i śe du'erme 'en prezensyya de kyen konel 'eśta konversando 'o 'en kual kyer lugar deloś diğoś ke denota muy mala 'enklinasy'on 'i deśtenplansa 'i poder poko reğiśtir 'a laś pasy'oneś 'i tener 'en poko loś aśiśtenteś ke 'eś grandisima tağa de deśkortezi'a mayor mente 'enloś manseboś :

'I poreśta kabza fu'eron tan loadoś akelyyoś devinisimoś manseboś Dany'el Ḥanany(')a[h] Miša'el 'i ᶜAzaryah ke tanto 'en 'ekselensyy'a puğaron śin falta alguna averśe halyyado 'enelyyoś loke 'el rey Nᵉbuḳadn'eṣṣar demando ke fu'eśen ninyoś tambyen kryadoś ke no tubyeśen makula alguna 'i se[t]-[92] 'i por fin de todo ke tubyeśen fu'ersa para 'eśtar 'enel palasy'o del rey[93]

'I konsidrando nu'eśtroś śaby'oś la 'ekselensy'a dela kryansa 'en loś mosoś reśplande(r)śer moderando 'el 'apetito 'i reğiśtyendo a'eśta 'umana flakeza del dormir 'i anśi del retener la riza 'i 'otraś pasy'oneś śem[e]ğanteś adonde no konvyene ke 'eś 'en prezensy'a de 'otroś mayoreś ke 'elyyoś 'eśp[e]syal 'en prezensy'a de prinsipeś 'i grandeś śenyyoreś ke 'eś koza muy vituperable komo aberiguado tenemoś tubyeron lugar de glozar ke loke ku'enta la devina 'eśtorya ke demandaba 'el rey mośoś ke tubyeśen poder para 'eśtar 'enel p[a]lasyyo 'i set- keri'a dezir ke śe pudyeśen retener de dormir 'i de re'ir[94] 'i de 'otroś meneśtereś 'umanoś 'i no fu'eśen vensidoś del faśtidy'o delyoś anteś konśtanteś 'en śufrir laś moleśtyaś delante la real mağeśtad delante la kual kontinu'a mente 'eśtaban 'eśtoś 'ekselenteś manseboś lyenoś de toda śanta doktrina 'i 'eroyka virtud : de manera ke śe nota delo diğo kuanto konvyene aloś mosoś kośtumbrarśe 'a dormir poko 'eśpesyal mente 'eśtando 'en konversasy'on de 'otroś 'i no kale dezir śyendo mayoreś ke 'el 'o 'enel tyenpo ke 'eś 'el dormir maś delo nesesary'o para śuśtentasy'on 'i konservasy'on dela śalud porke tanto kuanto du'ermen loś 'om(r)breś tanto dešan de śer byen aventuradoś śi 'enla viğilyya lo śon porke durmyendo no 'obrando ni pudyendo 'obrar laś 'obraś de virtud ni del 'entendimyento no śe pu'eden lyyamar byen aventuradoś śegun la 'opiny'on 'i grande a'utoridad del filosofo 'enel primero dela 'etika 'onde dize ke loś ke du'ermen no śe pu'eden lyyamar byen aventuradoś ni mal aventuradoś[95] 'ino śola mente 'eśto maś a'un lyyamarśe biboś : 'eś 'impropyya mente diğo kela vida keśe bibe durmyendo no 'eś 'entera vida :}

---

[92] Dan 1.4.
[93] Dan 1.4.
[94] Sanhedrin 93b.
[95] Aristotle, *NE* I.xiii12 (1102b 5–8); trans. Rackham, 65.

BOOK OF THE REGIMEN OF LIVING ‹FOL. 30A›

‹fol. 30a›
{de adonde tubyeron grandisima razon nu'eśtroś śaby'oś 'en dezir ke 'el dormir śe'a śesenta parteś dela mu'erte[96] denotando 'i śignifikando no śer 'entera vida pu'eś no śe 'eśerśita 'enelyya 'el 'entendimyento konforme alo kual diğo 'el famozo trovador Ğorğe Manrike mundo pu'eś ke noś mataś fu'era la vida ke diśte toda vida 'i set-[97] : śignifikando ke a'un 'el brebe tyenpo ke bibimoś no 'eś todo 'el 'entera vida pu'eś 'una grande parte śenoś va 'en dormir 'i 'otroś śemeğantes a'utoś 'enloś kualeś konloś brutoś animaleś //komuni[k]amoś// ğunto kon 'otroś ke deśtru'en 'el 'entendimyento : privandolo deśu natural 'eśerśisy'o 'el tyenpo de loś kualeś nośe deve lyyamar //vid[a](d)// ni lo[ ]'eś 'ent[e]ra mente :

'I alyende de todoś loś 'inkonvenyenteś diğoś 'enel dormir deś'ordenado ayy muğoś maś ke danyyan 'el ku'erpo 'i 'el alma por kuanto relağa 'el ku'erpo 'i 'e[n]-gru'esa 'el 'inğeny'o 'i śofoga 'el korason 'i finalmente 'el demazyado [dormir] kabza 'innumberableś danyyoś parte de loś kualeś tenemoś śenyyalado 'i lo de maś de laś partikularidadeś ke śe deven atentar aserka del dormir para la konserbasy'on de la śanidad deśo de dezir komo ya tengo diğo ke no 'eśk(y)rivo śino śolo loke deve 'uzar 'el 'ombre 'en todaś 'eśtaś kozaś śegun dereğa razon de virtud 'i no śegun konvyene para konserv(v)ar la śanidad ke 'eśto maś konbyene amedikoś ke 'a filosofoś moraleś 'eśpesyal ke 'eneśto todoś loś medikoś hab(')l[a]n larg(+)o 'i 'el śenyyor Rabbenu Mośeh deklara muy 'eśpisifikada mente lo kual podraś tu ya le'er 'i byen 'entender śolo 'eśto te amoneśto ke te deśakośtumbreś 'i te değeś de dormir de di'a 'i no śe'a de 'un golpe śalvo diminuyendolo por śu grado poko apoko porke dešarlo de 'un golpe 'el ke 'eś akośtumbrado le haze danyyo manifyeśto 'i deśta manera dan regla loś mediko ś para tirarśe 'el 'ombre del tal 'uzo śegun 'eśkriby'o Abisena 'en[e]l kapitulo t- [9] de la tersera del primero doktrina p(+)rimera porke śi kontinuaś 'el kośtumbre ke haśta agora tubiśte kuando kiğereś kitarte delyyo por 'el danyyo ke adelante śentiraś no śeraś poder(y)[o]zo para lo hazer 'i forsado 'uzaraś del śu'enyyo 'indevida mente porke dormir de di'a 'eś malo 'i dormir fu'era del kośtumbre tanbyen malo porke 'el dormir akośtumbrado 'eś loado komo śe ve'e por 'el śegundo de loś pornośtikoś :

'EŚ BYEN tener amemorya akelyyoś probyerby'oś 'enke nu'eśtro rey Ś^clomoh tan deś(')enganyada mente komo padre 'a hiğo amoneśta por muğaś veześ dizyendo no deś śu'enyyo atuś 'oğoś adormesimyento atuś parpadoś 'i set-[98] : dize maś poko de

---

[96] Berakot 57b.

[97] An exact citation of the first verses of Manrique's *Poesía 50*. See G. Caravaggi, ed., *Jorge Manrique. Poesía* (Madrid, 1984), 132.

[98] Prov. 6.4.

BOOK OF THE REGIMEN OF LIVING ‹FOL. 30A–30B›

śu'enyyoś poko de adormesimyento 'i sete-[99] : 'i maś no ameś śu'enyyo de kuanto no 'enpobresaś abre tuś 'oğoś 'i set-[100] : ke todo 'eśto denota la 'ekselensyya de la viğilyya 'iloś torpeś danyoś ke konśigo trae 'el}

‹fol. 30b›
{PEREK Š°MINIY [CHAPTER EIGHT]
deśtemplado dormir fazyendo 'el 'ombre muy negliğente para todo ğenero de byen konforme aloke 'en konkluzy'on dišo hata kuando negliğente ğazeraś[101] 'i la doktrina deloś kualeś probyerboś śi tomareś nunka yeraraś :

KAPITULO 'OKTABO

LA regla de la kinta 'i seśta koza delaś diğaś ke śon 'el 'eğar 'i levantar śe deklara 'i rekupila delo diğo 'enlo pasado ke śyendo 'el dormir tan danyyozo kuando 'eś maś de loke konvyene śyendo laś noğeś grandeś komo 'eś 'eneśte nu'eśtro klima 'i partikular mente 'en 'eśta nu'eśtra śibdad Śaloniki lyyamada deloś antigoś Teśalonika adonde śe alevanta 'el polo śobre 'el 'orizonte kazi m-' [41] gradoś ke byen kalkulado 'el tyenpo del di'a 'o de la noğe mayor alyega 'a y-d [14] 'oraś 'i y-' [11] dozaboś ke śon n-h [55] minutoś de 'ora kontando s- [60] por 'ora al modo 'eśtroloğiko ke 'eś kuando 'el śol 'entra 'enel primero de kanser 'i 'enel primero de kaprikorno komo tengo byen kalkulado 'i venifikado lo maś puntual mente ke pude 'enel libro ke Kaz(")a d(")el D(")yyo tengo 'entitulado ke 'eś 'una śofisyente gloza del teśto dela 'Eśpera[102] la kual 'eśpero 'enel Dyyo de preśto le'erte por ke 'eś muy deleytoza 'i 'util para 'entender muğaś kozaś deloś śekretoś delaś rebolusyy'oneś del śol 'i dela luna ke para nu'eśtraś fyeśtaś 'i 'orden de meześ 'i nasimyento dela luna konğunsy'oneś 'i 'opuzisyoneś konvyene 'i 'eś sensy'a ke nu'eśtroś muğo loaron 'i tengo tanbyen 'eśkrito śobre 'el

---

[99] Prov. 6.10.
[100] Prov. 20.13.
[101] Prov. 6.9.
[102] The title of his Hebrew commentary *Beth Elohim* on Sacrobosco's *Sphere*. Concerning the former, see Ben-Menahem ("R. M. Almosnino," 279–80) and A. Márcova, "El *Tratado del Astrolabio* de Mośé Almosnino en un manuscrito de Leningrado," *Sefarad* 51 (1991): 437–46. The latter is studied by Thorndike, *The Sphere of Sacrobosco and its Commentators* (Chicago, 1949).

BOOK OF THE REGIMEN OF LIVING ‹FOL. 30B–31A›

testo de la Te'orika de los planetas ke hizo Porbağy'o[103] ala kual 'eśkritura lyyame Pu'erta del syelo[104] keme parese ke leendo 'eśtoś doś tratadoś śegun 'enelyyoś tengo alargado baśta para 'entender kual kyer koza ke 'a 'eśta sensyya de la eśtroloği'a tokare :
'I tornando 'a nu'eśtro perpozito digo ke pu'eś aki 'eneśta nu'eśtra sibdad lyega la noğe mayor kazi akinze 'oraś 'i śin loś krepuśkuloś śeran kazi yg- [13] 'o yb- [12] 'oraś 'i medyya no 'eś razon ke te halye 'el di'a 'enel leğo ke la doktrina de la manyana poko anteś ke amaneśka 'eś la maś 'util komo diğimoś porke 'eś 'el prinsipy'o de la viğilyya kuando akaban de repozar loś śentidoś korporaleś de travağo deśu 'eśerśisyyo pasado 'i kedan ky'etoś śin modo alguno de kansansy'o 'i loś vaporeś ke al śelebro śuben del 'eśtomago 'eśtan ya rezolbidoś 'i purifikadoś 'i tyene 'ombre menoś 'inpedimyento delaś kozaś 'eśtiry'oreś ke no śyente bulisy'o alguno ke le śe'a 'ob(v)śtakulo toda la ğente repoza 'i ninguna koza ayy kele danye por[ ]tanto deveś de trabağar 'en grande manera por kontinuar 'a velar algo de madrugada ke yo te 'ofreśko komo maeśtro dela 'eśperensy'a ke te valga maś ke kuanto todo 'el di'a trabağareś 'i 'uzandolo deśde agora śete fara}

‹fol. 31a›
{L'
tan fasil adelante ke a'un ke kyeraś delyyo apartarte no podraś 'i floreśeraś 'en 'ekśelensyya de śaber 'i 'eśtudy'o :
'I a'un ke pareśka 'eśto algo kontra regla de medisina ke todoś loś ke 'en reğimyento de śanidad 'eśkrivyeron dizen ke deve 'el 'ombre dormir de manyana faśta 'el di'a 'i anśi 'eśkriby'o 'el śenyyor Rabbenu Mośeh 'enel lugar diğo[105] donde dize ke la kantidad del tyenpo de dormir śon ḥ- [8] 'oraś 'i set-[106] dize 'i śean 'enla fin de la noğe para ke ayya dende ke 'enpeśa adormir faśta ke śalga 'el śol ḥ- [8] 'oraś komo fu'eśe

---

[103] See O. Pedersen, "*The Theoricum planetarium* Literature in the Middle Ages," *Classica et Medievalia* 23 (1962): 225–32.

[104] The title of his commentary on George Puerbach's *Theorica Nova Planetarum, Šaᶜar ha-Šamayyim*. For a description of the latter see Ben-Menahem, "R. M. Almosnino," 279–80, and Márcova, "El *Tratado del Astrolabio.*"

[105] Maimonides, *Character Traits,* ed. Weiss and Butterworth, 36 (*Hilkot Deᶜot,* chap. 4, halakah 4).

[106] Maimonides, *Character Traits,* ed. Weiss and Butterworth, 36–37 (*Hilkot Deᶜot,* chap. 4, halakah 5).

BOOK OF THE REGIMEN OF LIVING ‹FOL. 31A›

la 'intensy'on del śenyor Rabbenu Mošeh 'enel diğo libro[107] dar reğimyento de śanidad del ku'erpo konforme 'a regla de medisina no 'esedy'o de lo ke konvyene para śuśtentar la śanidad pero komo aki no 'eś nu'eśtra prinsipal 'intensy'on śalbo buśkar 'el meğor kamino 'i maś śeguro para 'efektuar 'el byen verdadero buśkamoś 'el menor 'inkonvenyente 'i lo tenemoś por byen 'en reśpekto del 'inkonvenyente mayor ke 'eś la privasy'on del 'eśtudy'o 'enel tal tyenpo ke ami ver 'eś śin remedy'o de reśtabrasy'on loke 'el 'inkonvenyente de la śanidad fasil mente śe 'ebita konel kostumbre 'el kual śegunda natureza śe haze :

POR 'onde me parese ke por ningun ku'ento lo deveś dešar de hazer por loś byeneś ke delyyo śe śigen konforme al diğo de nu'eśtro devinisimo rey David ke dize 'en śu P[e]śalteryyo por laś madrugadaś hablare kontigo 'i set-[108] keryendo śignifikar ke tenye[n]do memory'a delaś kozaś devinaś 'en śu kama por la manyyana de madrugada deve hablar 'enelyyaś 'i por 'eśta meśma kabza dezi'a amedy'a noğe me alevantare aloarte 'i set-[109] : mośtrando la 'ekśelensyya del 'eśtudy'o de medya noğe ariba por laś kabzaś diğaś :

'I 'enel 'eğarte deveś tanbyen de advertir 'a no 'eğarte lu'ego deśp[u]'eś de komer porke atrae 'eśto muğoś danyyoś al ku'erpo śegun todoś loś ke hablaron 'en reğimyento de śanidad an '[e]śkrito 'i ningun pobreğo akare'a ala alma anteś muğo danyyo porke hinğe 'el 'eśtomago de maloś 'umoreś ke danyan 'el śel[e]bro 'i le mudan de śu komplisy'on 'i koneśto śe konturba 'el 'entendimyento por tanto deve kual kyera 'eneśto muğo mirar ke a'un ke no śe'a tanto komo dizen loś medikoś no śe'a tan poko ke śe'a 'el danyyo manifyeśto kelo manko 'eś razon ke śe'a 'una 'ora deśpu'eś de la komida 'i loś medikoś diğeron 'eneśto 'un bu'en 'orden 'el kual 'eśkriby'o Abisena 'en la tersera del primero dok(v)tr[i]na śegunda kapitulo z- [7] del reğimyento de la śanidad dizyendo ke loaba Rufuś mediko 'iluśtre 'el paśear deśpu'eś de la komida 'i set-[110] : 'i syerto 'eś 'una bu'ena 'orden 'i todoś śe deven kośt[u]mbrar 'enelya ke deśpu'eś ke 'a ya paśeado śobre la komida medyana mente hata medya 'ora algo maś no le śera tan danyyozo 'el dormir :}

---

[107] Maimonides, *Character Traits*, ed. Weiss and Butterworth, 36 (*Hilkot De^cot*, chap. 4, halakah 4).

[108] Ps. 63.7.

[109] Ps. 119.62.

[110] Almosnino is recalling the statement: "Rufus says, 'Walking after a meal is grateful to me, for it gives a good preparation for the evening meal' " (Ibn Sina, "*Canon of Medicine*," trans. Gruner, 396, no. 765). This is Rufus of Ephesus (1st c. C.E.; see *Oxford Classical Dictionary*, 3rd ed., 1337).

BOOK OF THE REGIMEN OF LIVING ‹FOL. 31B›

‹fol. 31b›
{ 'I deśpu'eś de 'eğado deve 'enpesar adormir 'un poko śobre 'el lado dereğo 'i deśpu'eś boltarśe śobre 'el 'eśkyerdo haśta serka medyya noğe deśpu'eś bolver śobre 'el dereğo faśta fin del śu'enyo 'i 'eśte tal 'orden pu'ede tener 'el 'ombre a'un ke du'erma ke 'eğandośe kon tal perpozito śe reku'erda medyyo durmyendo 'a hazerlo 'i kośtumbrandośe 'a 'elyyo la meśma natureza lo mobera 'a hazelyyo 'eśtando durmyendo por la regla diğa ke 'eś la ke 'eśkriby'o Abisena[111] konforme 'a 'opiny'on de todoś loś antigoś medikoś 'i a'un ke 'el śenyyor Rabbenu Mośeh 'enel diğo kapitulo deśu 'oniversal 'i afamado libro dize ke deve de 'enpesar adormir śobre la parte 'eśkyerda 'i boltar deśpu'eś śobre la dereğa[112] no śe deve de kre'er del syendo tan grande mediko komo parese por śuś aforiśmoś[113] 'i 'otroś muğoś tratadoś ke 'eśkriby'o ke kontra diśeśe 'enloke tan 'ividenteś razoneś ayy para ke 'enel prinsipy'o no śe deve akośtar 'el 'ombre śobre 'el lado 'eśkyerdo śegun 'eśkribyeron muğoś komentadoreś de Abisena : por donde paresyendome ke no 'eś posible 'eśtar 'erado de 'eśkyerdo 'a dereğo porke śi 'onde dize 'eśkyerdo 'ubyeśe de dezir dereğo 'i adonde dize dereğo avi'a de dezir 'eśkyerdo a'un le faltari'a 'otra partida por dezir la kual 'eś ke por pośtrero śe'a de bolber al lado dereğo śegun 'el 'orden de loś medikoś komo avemoś diğo kuanto maś ke laś palabraś no śufren tal yero porke dize ke śobre 'el dereğo śe'a 'el fin de la noğe 'i śi 'onde dize dereğo 'ubyeśe de dezir 'eśkyerdo śeri'a kontra 'opiny'on de todoś ke śon konformeś ake śe'a al fin de la noğe śobre 'el lado dereğo 'i set- tengo por syerto ke 'el śenyyor Rabbenu Mośeh deśo de 'eśkribir 'el 'orden del dormir ke 'eś śobre 'el lado dereğo por śer poka kantidad komo parese por laś palabraś de Abisena 'i 'eśkriby'o loś doś prośteroś ke 'eś 'el prinsipal 'orden 'i lo ke maś konvyene 'i notaśe por śuś meśmaś palabraś śer 'eśta la 'intensy'on 'en repartir toda la noğe 'eneśtaś b" [2] donde dize no du'erma 'el 'ombre śobre kara ni śobre la 'eśpalda śalbo śobre 'el lado 'enel prinsipy'o de la noğe śobre 'el 'eśkyerdo 'i 'enel fin śobre 'el dereğo 'i set-[114] : por donde parese ke kiğo repartir la noğe 'enel prinsipy'o del dormir p[o]rke no fu'e śu 'intensy'on 'enel diğo lugar dar 'orden tan partikular komo 'enla medisina konvyene :

---

[111] Ibn Sina twice states the rule that one begin sleeping on the right and change to the left ("*Canon of Medicine*," trans. Gruner, 397, no. 765 and 419, and no. 819).

[112] Maimonides, *Character Traits,* ed. Weiss and Butterworth, 36–37 (*Hilkot De'ot,* chap. 4, halakah 5).

[113] For an English translation of the *Aphorisms,* see Maimonides, *The "Medical Aphorisms,"* ed. and trans. F. Rosner and S. Munter (New York, 1970–1971).

[114] Maimonides, *Character Traits,* ed. Weiss and Butterworth, 36–37 (*Hilkot De'ot,* chap. 4, halakah 5).

Book of the Regimen of Living ⟨fol. 31b–32a⟩

'I alyende dešto še pu'ede dezir ke komo kyera ke 'el šenyor Rabbenu Mošeh 'eškrive 'enel mešmo kapitulo ke 'el 'ombre no deve 'enpesar adormir fašta pasadaš ǧ- [3] 'o d- [4] 'oraš dešpu'eš de komer[115] kon 'ešto no tubo nesesidad de dezir ke 'enpesase(n) adormir šobre la dereǧa pu'eš la diǧešty'on primera para ke še haze 'ešte boltar 'eš kazi heǧa por lo kual no 'eš menešter 'eškalyentar 'el higado ke 'ešta 'en la dereǧa [CW. de]}

⟨fol. 32a⟩
{LB
de manera ke 'eǧandoše še pu'ede 'eǧar šobre la parte 'eškyerda pu'eš de todoš 'inkonvenyenteš 'eš fu'era de reselo 'eǧandoše treš 'oraš 'o d- [4] dešpu'eš de komer pero porke 'ešte 'orden poko še guarda prinsipal 'en 'invyerno ke 'el 'eštudyyo de prima noǧe 'eš nesesary'o še'a ante de komer 'eš byen šegir 'el 'orden ke 'eškribyeron loš medikoš komo 'eš diǧo :

'I 'enlo de maš no 'eš nesesary'o 'enešto maš dezi[r]te šolo ke perkureš tener byen 'enla memoryya todo akel kapitulo del šenyor Rabbenu Mošeh 'en reǧimyento dela šanidad 'enel tratado šegundo dela primera parte del libro 'i te riǧaš porel de adonde še konprende kuanto kuantoš medikoš 'eškribyeron 'en reǧimyento de šanidad :

'EŠTO šolo 'eš byen deloš akavidar padreš 'i madreš aloš hiǧoš ke no koštumbren dormir 'en kamaš muy blandaš ni ke 'ešten muy kalyenteš 'en 'invyerno 'i fri'oš 'en verano maš anteš 'eš byen ke še abezen 'a šufrir fri'o 'en 'invyerno 'i kalor 'en verano komo še ku'enta 'enla vida de Dy'oǧeneš ke še abrasaba kon laš friaš 'eštatuaš 'en 'invyerno 'iše 'eǧava 'e( )nla kalyente arena 'en medy'o del 'ešti'o para koštumbrarše ašufrir šin pasy'on kuando por kazo fortu'ito[ ]lo 'ubyeše[ ]de šufrir forsado[116] :

'I alyende dešto konvyene al moso ke 'a de šer dišpu'ešto para resebir todo ǧenero de doktrina ke še'a de karne 'ešpesa mašiša 'i šolida no ešponǧoza la kual haze 'el leǧo blando ke kyen tal tyene la karne 'eš de bašo rudo 'i flako 'inǧeny'o 'indišpu'ešto para resebir todo ǧenero de doktrina de 'ešpikulasy'on :

'I por 'ešta mešma kabza konvyene ke noše konsyenta aloš mošoš fazer koša ke konvenga ke noše konsyenta 'a muǧereš maš ke a'ombreš komo diversidad de veštidoš de koloreš difer[e]nteš 'i peynar muǧo loš kavelyyoš 'i 'otroš a'[u]toš šemeǧanteš 'i šobre todo no traer konšigo kozaš 'odoriferaš 'o šean por natura 'o por artifisy'o

---

[115] Maimonides, *Character Traits,* ed. Weiss and Butterworth, 36–37 *(Hilkot Deʿot,* chap. 4, halakah 5).

[116] Diogenes the Cynic. See Diogenes Laertius, *Philosophers* VI.23 trans. R. D. Hicks (Cambridge, MA, 1966), 2:25–27.

BOOK OF THE REGIMEN OF LIVING ‹FOL. 32A–32B›

porke śon laś maś delyyaś defendidaś por nu'eśtroś śaby'oś[117] 'i tanto śon feaś 'enloś 'ombreś kuanto byen pareśkan 'enlaś muğereś a'un ke no muy 'oneśtaś ke a'un 'enelyyaś denotan grande baśeğa de 'inğeny'o poka doktrina 'i grande negliğensyya 'enla virtud pu'eś tanto presyan la parte materyyal 'i 'eś pura śenyyal de konponer la materyya katiba 'i dešar la alma śu śenyora deśkonpu'eśta kede aki vyene 'a 'otro 'eśtremo pe'or ke 'eś fin de la maldad :

KONFORME 'a 'eśto konprehendyendo todaś 'eśtaś 'eśpesyaś de maleś dišo nu'eśtro prudentis[i]mo rey Š^{c}lomoh 'enśuś proberbyyoś por fin de todo de bağo de treś 'eśtremesy'o la tyera 'i set-[118] de bašo de 'eśklabo ke 'enreyna 'i del vil ke śe farta de pan de bašo de aboresida ke fu'ere amaridada 'i 'eśklaba ke 'erede aśu}

‹fol. 32b›
{śenyyora 'i set-[119] keryendo śignifikar ke treś kozaś śon abominableś 'i fu'era de todo śufrimyento ke deve la tyera 'eśtremeser por 'elyaś :

LA primera 'eś kuando 'el 'apetito 'irasible ke 'eś 'el 'eśklabo del 'intelekto[120] kyere reynar 'i deś'obedeśer huyendo 'el yugo dela dereğa razon 'i no śe deša refrenar para ke modere śuś pasyoneś śegun virtud

'I 'eś pe'or ke 'eśto kuando 'el 'apetito konkupisible śe harta del pan deloś apetitoś korporaleś śyendo vil :

'I 'eś la tersyya kuando la materyya śyendo aboresida dela forma por no fazer loke deve perkura 'el 'entendimyento de darle loke 'elyya kyere ke 'eś darle maś lugar para ke śe 'enśenyore'e śobre 'el alma

'I 'eś la kuarta 'inśufrible de todo punto ke 'eś kuando la materyya 'eśklaba 'ereda al alma śu śenyora 'i la alma śige ala materyya ke 'eś 'el 'eśtremo dela maldad 'i korupsy'on del byen 'umano de manera ke śe nota de aki ke konponer la parte materyal ke 'eś 'el ku'erpo kuando no 'eś komo konvyene trae a'otro mayor mal por tanto śe deve defender todo modo de 'apetito korporal ke śe rekyere por parte dela materyya ke de poko vyene 'a muğo :

KONFORME al diğo de nu'eśtro porfeta Y^{c}ša^{c}yahu guay śon trayenteś 'el delito kon ku'erdaś de vanidad 'i komo ku'erdaś dela kareta 'el pekado 'i set-[121] : 'i dišeron nu'eśtroś śaby'oś śobre 'eśto ke 'eś la 'intensy'on deśtaś palabraś 'el modo de hazerśe

---

[117] For a set of similar prohibitions, see Maimonides, *Character Traits,* ed. Weiss and Butterworth, 44 (*Hilkot De^{c}ot,* chap. 4, halakot 8 and 9).
[118] Prov. 30.21.
[119] Prov. 30.22–23.
[120] Aristotle, *De Anima* III.x (433a 10–433b 12), trans. Hett, 186–89.
[121] Isa. 5.18.

BOOK OF THE REGIMEN OF LIVING ‹FOL. 32B–33A›

'el pekado de poko 'a poko donde dišeron ke 'el 'apetito parese 'enel prinsipy'o 'un hilo de aranyya[122] 'i 'eśto 'eś loke lyyamo 'el profeta ku'erdaś de nada deśpu'eś vaśe 'engrosando komo laś ku'erdaś grandeś ke tiran laś karetaś de manera ke 'el 'ombre 'en 'eśpesyal śi 'eś moso śe deve akavidar 'en grande manera 'i loś padreś 'i maeśtroś no deven 'en 'otro maś atentar ke 'en śakarleś kual kyera modo de 'apetito korporal ke a'un ke pareska ǧiko dandole lugar śe va hazyendo grande 'i deśpu'eś de muy gru'eso no śe pu'ede ronper de 'el modo dela ku'erda 'i 'eś devinisimo 'enǧenp(+)lo digno deśu 'eśkrito kela materyya guarda kon la forma la meśma porpo[r]sy'on ke guarda 'el marido konla muǧer ke anśi komo la muǧer no fu'e dada del Dyyo benedito al 'ombre maś ke para ayudarle[123] aśu bu'en perpozito para śer reǧida del[124] 'i no 'el delyya anśi la materya 'a meneśter śegir 'a 'el 'entendimyento 'en kuanto 'el 'ordenare : reǧire 'i mandare para 'el fin del byen del meśmo 'entendimyento :

'I 'eśto 'eś loke diǧo 'el Dyyo no 'eś byen 'eśtar 'el 'ombre śolo hazerle'e ayuda kontra 'el 'i set-[125] 'i diǧeron nu'eśtroś śaby'oś ke śe deve 'entender 'eśte diǧo repartido 'en doś śentensyaś diferenteś śegun tyenpoś diferenteś ke kuando fu'ere 'el bu'eno śera ayuda 'i kuando 'el kontrary'o śera kontra [CW. 'el]}

‹fol. 33a›
{LG PEREK TˁŠIYˁIY [CHAPTER NINE]
'el[126] śemeǧante ala konformidad dela materyya 'i forma komo tenemoś diǧo

'I ŚI 'eśto larga mente kiǧereś ver pu'edeś byen ver loke 'enel tersero dela 'etika[127] tengo 'eśkrito ke śi aki 'ubyeśe 'en 'eśto de alargar śeri'a maś ke kuanto 'en todo 'el reśto pu'edo 'eśkrivir śolo te kize hazer śaber kuanto te deveś vedar delaś kozaś kete paresen no śer nada al prezente 'i deśpu'eś śe śige delyyaś tanto mal keno śe pu'ede 'evitar por tanto deveś perkurar de afeytar 'el alma konloś afeyteś dela virtud 'i devina 'eśpikulas[y]on ke 'eśto 'eś loke da perfekto plazer

'I deveś maś atentar 'enel 'eǧarte kuando fu'ere 'en konpanyya de 'otro ke no śe'a 'en konpanyi'a de mayor ke tu porke parese muy deś'oneśto 'i kuando ayy nesesidad delyyo ke śeaś muy atentado 'enel śityyo detu ku'erpo de manera ke no śe'a moleśto ni 'enoǧozo alke kon tigo durmyere ke todo 'eśto 'i muǧo maś podraś hazer 'eǧandote

---

[122] Sukkah 52a, Gen. R. 22.6.
[123] Gen. 2.18.
[124] Gen. 3.16.
[125] Gen. 2.18.
[126] Gen. R. 17.2.
[127] Aristotle, *NE* III.v (1113b 14–1115a 5).

BOOK OF THE REGIMEN OF LIVING ‹FOL. 33A–33B›

kon perpozito 'i 'inte[n]sy'on de hazerlo ke 'inprimyendośe byen 'enla 'im[a]ǧinasyyon no yeraraś a'un ke du['e]rmaś 'i 'enesto no kyero darte razon natural por hu'ir prolišidad śolo deveś atender 'enel tyenpo kete lebantareś dela kama ke no te alevanteś śupito ke te 'eśpyertaś ke śe pu'eden śegir delyyo muǧoś 'inkonvenyenteś śalbo ke 'eśteś ky'eto 'un pokito deśpu'eś de deśpyerto 'i deśpu'eś te alevantaraś poko apoko ke 'enesto 'i 'en todoś loś 'otroś movimyentoś korporaleś 'eś muy bu'ena 'i muy konvenible la gravedad :

KAPITULO NONO

LOKE konbyene śaber para la śetima 'i 'oktaba ke 'eś 'el 'andar 'i 'el aśentar[ ]'eś lo primero ke deven advertir loś mosoś ke no śean muǧo kaminadoreś kyero dezir ke laś maś pokaś veześ ke posible 'eś śalir de kaza śalgan 'i la veś ke śalyeren śe'a kon nesesidad publika 'i fin manifyeśto porke no śean taǧadoś de 'osy'ozoś ke 'eś la koza maś vituperable 'enloś mosoś ke posible 'eś 'i kon muǧa razon porke la 'osy'ozidad 'eś madre de[ ]todoś loś visy'oś[128] 'i kual kyera prudente ke vyere 'a 'un moso 'osy'ozo śentensyyara kon dereǧa razon śer 'el tal moso kargado de visy'oś ke 'el 'osy'o 'enloś grandeś korompe la virtud kuanto maś 'enloś mosoś ke fasil mente śon lebadoś 'a loś visy'oś 'i kual kyer koza a'un ke flaka abaśta 'a deśtru'irloś delaś 'obraś de virtud

'I alyende deśto 'eś grandisima perdida al 'en[ten]dimyento ke 'el tyempo maś konvenivle para floreśer 'i śubir 'enla kumbre dela filisidad aya de diśtribu'ir 'en kozaś vanaglory'ozaś ke ni al ku'erpo ni al alma 'utilidad ninguna trae}

‹fol. 33b›
{ PU'EŚ kuando 'eśpertare 'el moso del primer śu'enyyo de śu mosedad a'el tyenpo dela veǧeś kuando yya loś visy'oś no halyyan poder para śer pu'eśtoś 'en a'uto 'eśtiry'or kuando ya śon deśteradoś por la flakeza dela materyya 'i śe halyyare falto de todo loke 'imaǧinaba pośe'er deśprove'ido dela provizy'on ke para 'el fin deśta ǧornada de nu'eśtra breve vida le 'eś nesesary'o privado del byen ke para rekuperarlo 'eś menester 'enpeśar la ǧornada de prinsipy'o apartado dela gloryya ke para śyenpre ǧamaś 'a 'elyya śe podra alyegar kargado de arepentimyento śin remedy'o por la śegedad del tyenpo ke pudyera remedyyar lyeno de 'enoǧoś 'i tribulasy'oneś por la falta delo paśado 'i pasy'on delo prezente 'i temor delo futuro kual śe halyyara 'el triśte vyeǧo 'inorante pezado de diaś 'i libyyano de sezo deramando lagrimaś por loke

---

[128] Compare the *refrán*, "La ociosidad es madre de todos los vicios" (Martínez Kleiser, *Refranero*, 532 [no. 46,459]).

BOOK OF THE REGIMEN OF LIVING ‹FOL. 33B–34A›

'el konśuś meśmaś manoś 'i mala 'enklin[a]sy'on 'a kabzado keğandośe de śi meśmo śin ninguna medisina para śu 'inkurable mal 'i deśpu'eś de kitadaś de śuś 'oğoś laś katarataś dela 'inoransy'a no le aprobeğa 'el ver ke le falta 'enloś 'inśturmentoś la virtud ke śe rekyere para alk[a]nsar 'el fin verdadero ke konsiśte 'enla verdader'a 'eśpikulasy'on :

DE adonde dišeron nu'eśtroś śaby'oś kon fortisima razon ke loś vyeğos 'i prudenteś kuanto maś 'enveğeśen tanto maś śe a'umenta 'enelyoś 'el śaber 'i loś vyeğos 'ignoranteś kuanto maś śe 'enveğeśen śe konturba 'enelyoś 'el 'entendimyento[129] 'i la razon 'eneśto 'eś 'ividente : ke komo kyera ke loś śabyoś dende 'el tyenpo dela mosedad śe 'eśerśitaron 'enla sensy'a 'i alkansaron 'a pośe'er la 'enel tyenpo ke loś 'inśturmentoś śentidoś 'i potensyaś korporaleś 'eśtaban 'en śu fu'ersa 'i vigor 'ensu pura p[e]rfeksy'on para alkansar 'el śaber kuanto maś fu'eren a'un ke vayan diminuyendo loś śentidoś 'i vertudeś korporaleś 'el 'entender śe a'umenta 'enla perfeksy'on dela 'obra delaś firmeś propyaś 'i verdaderaś vertudeś dela alma ke ya tyene resebidaś dela fantazi'a komo tenemoś diğo aserka del 'orden del dormir 'enel kapitulo śetabo 'i no tyene tanta nesesidad deloś śentidoś 'eśtiry'oreś 'enpero 'el pobre 'i triśte vyeğo śi 'enel tyenpo dela mosedad no śe aprobeğo de loś śentidoś korporaleś para ke por śu 'entresisy'on śe perfeksy'onaśe 'enel 'entender por averśe değado venśer deloś traydoreś visy'oś 'en 'el tyenpo kele falta 'el poder para 'eśerśitarloś por la flakeza de la matery'a ke kabza faltar 'el 'apetito por faltar loś medy'oś para tal fin no pudyendo perfe[k]sy'onarśe 'el 'entender kuanto maś fu'ere maś śe 'ira konturba(')ndo por parte de la korup(y)sy'on 'i konturbasy'on de la matery'a : [CW. akaesele]}

‹fol. 34a›
{LD
akaesele al ruśtiko pekador del vyeğo deśprobe'ido deśu probizy'on para śu 'infortuno vyağe lo ke akaese ala nave ke 'enel grande mar śe 'engolfa deśprobe'ida de loke le'eś nesesary'o para reğiśtir al 'inpetu del tenpeśt(y)[u]'ozo vyento ke 'eśta tal deśpu'eś dela grande višasy'on navegando kon tan grande tenpeśtad rotaś laś velaś dela 'eśperansa derokado 'el maśtil dela fy'uzyya ke konel navegando 'o byen 'o mal algo la hazian mober perdido por pośtre 'el timon para 'enderesar al kamino dereğo todoś loś 'ignoranteś marineroś kansadoś deśanimado 'el piloto śin śaber ado bolverśe ni poder a'un kelo śepa vyendo deśbaratadoś todoś loś medy'oś ke para śu vyağe tanto meneśter avi'a

---

[129] Kinim 25a, Shabbat 152a.

Book of the Regimen of Living ⟨fol. 34a⟩

KE tal śe falyyara la deśaventurada nave rodeada de vyentoś kontrary'oś ke por todaś parteś la kon(')b[a]ten no pudyendo kon ninguno navegar ningun remed[y]'o 'eśpera

DE la meśma manera akaese al triśte vyeğo 'ensu deśbaratada veğeś perdido 'i korupto 'el 'entendimyento gobernador deśta artifisy'oza kongregasy'on de[ ] 'inśturmentoś 'i 'enśarś(')yaś dela nabe de nu'eśtro ku'erpo de kyen 'el 'eś patron 'i piloto 'engolfandośe 'enel brabo mar deloś visy'oś konkiśtado deloś kontraryoś vyentoś del 'apetito konkupisible 'i 'irasible loś kualeś de kontino le afatigan 'i araśtan de 'una parte 'a 'otra kon śuś teribleś 'ondaś vinyendo ya ala veğeś kuando loś 'inśturmentoś korporaleś śon tan flakoś ke no pu'eden korer kon loś vyentoś deloś apetitoś śusedyendole por pośtre 'el vyento del dezc'o dela kontenplasy'on no pudyendo ya konel navegar por śer kebradaś laś velaś deloś śentidoś kon loś kualeś śe 'eğersita 'el 'entendimyento halyyandośe 'entre 'eśtoś doś apetitoś tan kontrary'oś 'el 'uno porśu natural de kerer śaber lo kual todoś dezean 'el 'otro por 'el kośtumbre kede tanto tyenpo 'enlaś 'entranyyaś śe araygo aplikado 'a śegir loś korporaleś deleyt(v)[e]ś ke 'inpiden 'el śaber faltando abilidad para kual kyera de loś doś ningun remedy'o maś syerto 'eśpera kela deś'eśperada mu'erte[130] ke konelyya śe perdona la mayor parte de śuś pekadoś[131] 'i śi anteś ke mu'era no 'eśta tan korupta la veluntad ke pu'eda 'enderesar al śervisy'o del Dyyo 'i arepentirśe de todo lo pasado 'eś byen remedyyado śin falta 'i porke 'eśto todo[ ]no 'eś materyya ke haze tanto anu'eśo perpozito pongo śilensy'o kon 'eśperansa de alumbrarte 'enelyyo 'en 'otro lugar maś konvenyente śolo te kize hazer śaber 'en todo lo diğo ke todo 'el mal ke vyene aloś 'ignoranteś vyeğoś leś vyene de śer 'osy'ozoś 'enel tyenpo de la mosedad :

POR lo kual konvyene aloś mosoś komo tenemoś diğo ke no śean 'osy'oz[o]ś ni muy andanteś maś anteś konvyene ke no śe aparten del lug(+)ar de śu 'eśtudy'o de bağo laś alaś de śuś maeśtroś śi no fu'ere kon śobrada nesesidad [CW. 'i]}

---

[130] Compare Aristotle, *De Anima* (413a 8–9), trans. Hett, 73 and 89 on the soul being to the body as the sailor is to the ship; similarly a fragment assigned doubtfully to Menander: "If so be one has a fine body and a poor soul he has a fine boat and a poor pilot" (535). A related nautical simile appears in several sixteenth-century Turkish poems cited by Kahane and Tietze: "If you go aweather, you cannot get out; if you go alee, there is a whirlpool; / Whichever way you sail, this ship, your body, will be stranded" (*Lingua Franca,* 352). For a study of this passage, see J. Zemke, "El alma : el cuerpo :: el piloto : la nave (*De anima* 413a 8). *El regimiento de la vida* de Moše ben Baruk Almosnino," in *Proceedings of the European Association of Jewish Studies Congress* (Leiden, 1999), 2: 694–701.

[131] Moed Katan 28a.

BOOK OF THE REGIMEN OF LIVING ‹FOL. 34B›

‹fol. 34b›
{PEREK ᶜAŚIYRIY [CHAPTER TEN]
'i 'ordenado por 'elyyoś 'o por śuś padreś 'i 'eneśto deven loś padreś 'i loś maeśtroś muǧo advertir ke no loś '[o]kupen 'en negosy'oś ke delyyoś śe pu'eda prezumir śer 'osy'ozoś por ningun ku'ento :
'I 'enel tyenpo ke fu'ere lisito śu 'andar kuando porśi śoloś fu'eren konvyene ke atenten 'en grande manera 'enel modo del 'andar ke 'en 'el[ ]medyo konśiśte la virtud anśi komo 'en todaś laś vertudeś komo adelante 'enla śegunda partida deśte tratado deklararemoś 'i la razon aśerka deśto 'eś porke 'el 'andar muǧo de prisa denota poka gravedad 'i kazi ramo de lokura 'i 'el 'andar muǧo de vagar denota negliǧensyya 'i torpeza de śentido 'i 'eś śenyyal de muǧa 'osy'ozidad 'i gana de deśtru'ir 'el tyenpo presyado 'en kozaś ke ninguna 'utilidad traen :
'I kuando fu'eren 'en konpanyya del padre 'o del maeśtro deven atentar 'enel 'andar de manera ke vayya de kontino ala parte 'eśkyerda 'i 'un poko atraś de modo ke mośtren la avantaǧe ke 'el mayor le tyene 'i 'eneśto śe deve partikular mente atentar kuando van 'en kompanyi'a de 'ombreś śaby'oś porke 'elyyoś atyentan 'enelyo 'i alke ve'en ke no 'uza tal reverensy'a tyenen por prezuntu'ozo 'i deśvergonsado 'i 'eś 'eśto tan fe'o 'i vituperado ke nu'eśtroś śaby'oś defyenden ke a'un 'enel tyenpo de dezir la 'orasy'on no pu'eda 'el diśiplo 'eśtar delantre 'el ma[e]ś(y)tro ni de traś ni a'el lado ǧunto konel śalbo algo deśvyado 'i 'eś la kabza de d[e]fender keno 'eśte a'el lado porke denota 'igualarśe konel[132] 'i aśi lo deklara nu'eśtro komentador dela Śanta Ley 'i Talmud Rabbenu Šᵉlomoh[133] 'i kon 'eśto 'eśta viśto kuan muǧo maś fe'o śe'a 'eśtar delante defyendeśe 'eśtar detraś porke kuando atemare 'el maeśtro la 'orasy'on 'i 'ubyere de bolver loś g- [3] pasoś atraś komo 'eś la ley nole 'inpida ke venirle 'inpedimyento por parte deśu diśiplo 'eś vituperyyado : de manera ke por aki śe tomara doktrina para kuando andaren por la kalye 'o pararen 'en kual kyer lugar ke 'en todo tyenpo 'a de[ ]guardar akatar 'i konserbar la venerasy'on 'i devida 'obed[y]ensyya aśu padre 'i al maeśtro partikular[ ]mente 'i 'a kual kyer mayor ke 'el maś 'o menoś śegun la diferensya de kada kual porśu grado :
'I por 'eśta meśma kabza defendyeron nu'eśtroś śaby'oś al hiǧo 'i al diśiplo 'en-

---

[132] This seems to be a reference to *Hilkot Talmud Torah*, perek 5, halakah 6.

[133] Solomon ben Isaac (Troyes 1045–1105) was the leading commentator on the Bible and Talmud. A meticulous grammarian who founded an important school ca. 1070, his authoritative biblical commentary was the first known Hebrew work to be printed (1475); see *EJ* 13:1558–65.

BOOK OF THE REGIMEN OF LIVING ‹FOL. 34B–35A›

trar 'enel banyo konel padre 'o konel maestro[134] ke demu'estra śer diśuluto 'i deśvergonsado 'eśtar deśnudo 'en prezensyya de śu padre 'i deśu maeśtro tenyendo
'eneśto 'otro mayor reśpekto ke no defendyendose śeri'a kabzo de alǧun ramo de menośpresy'o del maeśtro 'en 'oǧoś del diśiplo 'o del padre 'en 'oǧoś del hiǧo lo kual 'eś
defezo}

‹fol. 35a›
{LH
para loke konbyene ala dotrina 'i 'obraś de virtud ke vyendo 'el moso śu padre 'o śu
maeśtro deśnudo ǧunto konel lo menośpreśyyari'a 'en grande manera 'i perderi'a 'el
devido akatamyento 'i śolita reverensyya por śer lyebadoś faśil mente ala 'imaǧinasy'on del menośpresy'o ke alyi 'imaǧinan de donde kedo 'el bu'en kośtumbre ke loś
prinsipeś 'i grandeś śenyyoreś no 'eśten 'en prezensyya deloś śuyyoś deśkubyertoś 'o
deśnudoś 'o de kual kyera 'otro modo de deśa'utorizamyento porke komo kyera ke loś
maś deloś 'ombreś śon levadoś 'i vensidoś laś maś delaś veześ dela 'imaǧinasy'on
vyendo loś deśautorizadoś kedaleś por parte dela fantazi'a 'en menośpresy'o 'en tanto
grado ke 'eś syerto ke kośtu(')[m]brandolo muǧo no śeran 'eśtimadoś maś anteś me-
nośpresyyadoś
KONFORME a'un komun 'i vulgar proberbyo śakado deloś Ǧureś Konśultoś
hablando del 'ofisy'o del pretor 'o ǧu'ez ke dize la muǧa konversasy'on 'eś ramo de
menośpresy'o[135] ke śe deve de 'entender por la konversasy'on kuando 'eś kon
deśa'utorizam[y]ento deśu preśona 'i no toda konversasy'on śalbo deloś viśy'ozoś 'i
'inperfektoś ke 'eś grandisimo yero dezir ke śe'a diǧo komun 'en todo ǧenero de
'ombreś :
PORKE 'enla konversasy'on deloś bu'enoś 'i virtu'ozoś śe konprehende la benivolensy'a 'i la benefisensya 'ila konkordy'a 'i 'unidad ke śon todaś 'obraś dela amiśtad
de donde depende 'el byen 'umano 'i gloryya perpe(k)tu'a komo tengo byen deklarado
'enel 'oǧabo 'i nono dela 'etika[136] 'i 'enla śegunda partida deśte tratado aserka dela
amiśtad śe deklara
PERO komo 'eśta tal konversasy'on muy pokaś veześ śe halyya ke loś bu'enoś 'i
'eśkoǧidoś śon pokoś 'en todo tyenpo konvyene al 'ombre perkurar de no deśa'u-

---

[134] *Hilkot Talmud Torah,* perek 5, halakah 6.
[135] Compare the *refrán:* "La mucha conversación acarrea menosprecio" (Martínez Kleiser, *Refranero,* 149 [no. 13,486]).
[136] He refers to *Pne Moše.* The original passages are Aristotle, *NE* VIII and IX, esp. VIII.v.4–5 (1157b 25–1158a 1), IX.ix.10 (1170b 6–19).

Book of the Regimen of Living ‹fol. 35a–35b›

torizar śu preśona 'en prezensyya de ninguno 'eśpesyyal 'en prezensyya de kyen 'eś nesesary'o kele tenga akatamyento 'ile guarde reverensyya 'i śobre todo de kyen 'a de resebir del doktrina de manera ke 'el hiǧo 'i 'el padre 'el diśiplo 'i 'el maeśtro deven guardar 'el 'orden dela revye[re]nsy'a 'i venerasy'on por la regla diǧa :

'I śi fu'eren maś de doś ke kaminaren an de tener reśpekto ake 'el mayor vaya 'en medyyo 'i 'el ke 'eś śegundo ala dereǧa del 'i 'el minimo aśu 'eśkyerda :

'I 'enel 'andar deśvyado de kyen konel anda 'a de diferir de maś 'a menoś śegun la diferensyy'a dela a'utoridad del mayor kon kyen śe akonpanyan :

'I loś meśmoś reśpektoś deven guardar 'enel asentar ke kuando 'el moso śe asentare aserka deśu padre 'o deśu maeśtro śe asyente 'en lugar maś baǧo aśu lado 'eśkyerdo}

‹fol. 35b›
{'i śi por ventura 'eśtubyere 'en lugar donde no ayya modo ni komodidad para aśentarśe aśu 'eśkyerda 'i śe'a forsado śentarśe aśu dereǧa komo śi fu'eśe la kabesera del lugar ala 'eśkyerda del diśiplo 'eśtonseś 'eś la 'onra donde 'eś la kabesera 'i nośe mira ke lado śe'a 'i de kual kyer modo ke śe'a no deve 'eśtar 'el diśiplo ni 'el hiǧo muy ǧunto delyyoś śalbo algo afaśtado de manera ke kede 'entre 'el diśiplo 'i 'el maeśtro 'o 'entre 'el hiǧo 'i 'el padre algun lugar vazi'o 'i del meśmo modo deve 'uzar 'enel asyento konel ke 'eś mayor ke 'el śegun la a'utoridad delaś preśonaś 'i 'el grado de diferensyya ke de 'el 'a 'elyyoś 'ubyere ke 'eś muy byen 'i muǧa razon de atentar

ŚOBRE todo deven advertir loś mosoś de no śe śentar 'enel lugar donde śe śu'ele asentar 'el padre 'o maeśtro a'un ke śe'a 'enśuś a'uzensyaś amoneśtando aserka deśto ke 'eś muy vedado por nu'eśtra śantisima ley ke no deve 'el hiǧo asentarśe 'enel lugar del padre ni kontra dezir śuś p[a]labraś[137] kuando no 'ofende ala ley 'o ala verdad ke 'entonseś le deve tirar de 'elyyo por bu'enoś terminoś kuanto pudyere :

'I alyende de śer todo 'eśto pro'ibido por nu'eśtra Śanta Ley 'eś vituperado muǧo 'en laś leyś 'umanaś ke denota 'eśtremo de deśavergonsamyento 'i prezunsy'on vana de kererśe konelyyoś 'igualar 'i 'ignoransyya de konoser la vantaǧa alomenoś por la 'edad 'i 'inśuluble 'obligasy'on ke akada 'uno delyyoś debe ke 'el 'uno le dyyo 'el śe'er del ku'erpo 'i 'el 'otro 'el śer dela alma de 'el meśmo modo deven atentar de no asentarśe 'en lugareś apropyadoś a'otroś mayyoreś ke 'elyyoś śalbo 'en lugar de śuś 'igualeś 'o maś baśoś ke 'elyoś 'i deven tambyen advertir loś mosoś kuando 'eśtan 'en prezensyya de 'otroś mayores ke 'elyyoś 'i no kale dezir 'en prezensy'a de śuś maeśtroś 'o padreś 'o muy grandeś śenyyoreś ke no 'eśkupan ni bośeśen ni 'eśtornuden ni

---

[137] Rashi Lev. 19.32.

BOOK OF THE REGIMEN OF LIVING ‹FOL. 35B–36A›

'eśkaren ni monden loś dyenteś ni laben laś manoś kara 'o boka ni 'otra koza śemeǧante ke śon todoś a'utoś muy faśtidy'ozoś 'i deśagradableś ala viśta 'i muy vituperableś 'enloś mosoś 'en prezensyya de mayoreś ke 'elyyoś porke alyende del diśguśto ke lyeban loś ke śimileś a'utoś leś ve'en fazer śon taǧadoś de 'enkontin[en]teś deśavergonsadoś 'i deśtempladoś pu'eś no baśtan reǧiśtir 'el 'apetito 'en tan poka koza komo akelyya śyendo tan vituperable

'I ǧunto koneśto deven atentar kuando 'eśtan aśentadoś 'en preśensyya de 'otroś deno doblar 'una pyerna śobre 'otra ke 'eś koza muy beśtyyal 'i abominable 'en todoś loś 'ombreś kuanto maś 'enloś mosoś ke denota 'en kual kyera ke tal haze muy poka vergu'ensa 'i muǧa śoberbyya 'i menośpresy'o de loś 'ombreś por lo kual śe deven muǧo kitar de 'elyyo :}

‹fol. 36a›
{LV PEREK ᶜAŚIYRIY [CHAPTER TEN]

KAPITULO DESIMO

'ENLOKE toka ala nobena 'i desima koza ke 'eś 'el 'orden ke śe deve tener 'enel hab[l]ar 'i 'enel kalyyar kalyyare muǧo porke por muǧo ke diga śera poko para loke konvyene dezir 'i maś porke 'eś muǧo loke loś antigoś 'i modernoś 'eśkribyeron lo kual halyyaraś deramado por muǧaś parteś 'onde kyera ke leereś 'i alyende de 'eśto 'eśpero algo maś alargar 'enelyyo aserka de la nona virtud de laś vertudeś moraleś 'enla śegunda partida deśte tratado ke 'eś la virtud lyyamada verdad 'o verasidad aserka del moral śolo te dire al prezente algunaś 'oniversalidadeś ke por 'elyyaś deśpu'eś kon bu'ena 'eśtimatiba konprehenderaś todaś laś partikularidadeś ke konvyene śaber porke averlaś de 'eśpiśifikar śeri'a 'una muy 'infortuna proliśidad :

'I 'en kuanto toka al hablar te amoneśto 'una śola koza śobre todaś kuantaś ayy 'i 'eś ke por ningun ku'ento ya maś ningun modo de mentira ni falsedad de tu boka śalga porke todo 'ombre ke 'eśte 'uzo tyene devi'a ami ǧu'iz[y]'o śer deśterado dela republika porke 'eś muy kontaǧy'oza peśte delaś animaś 'i fyero veneno ala vida delyyaś 'i muǧo maś 'enloś mosoś ke no tyenen konsidrasy'on para śaber kuanto mal depende dela mentira 'i falsedad 'i heǧo 'el mentir 'enelyoś naturaleza śegunda porel kośtumbre dende pekenyyoś nunka ya maś śe pu'eden delyyo kitar ni apartar 'un momento por 'ende 'el ke 'en tal manera śe kri'a 'i tan vituperable 'i abominable visy'o tyene nunka ya maś śe terna 'eśperansa del para byen ninguno porke 'eś aboresido 'en 'oǧoś del Dyyo 'i de la ǧente :

KONFORME al diǧo de nu'eśtro devinisimo rey David donde diǧo de mente de 'el

Book of the Regimen of Living ⟨fol. 36a–36b⟩

Dyyo glory'ozo hablan falsedadeś no se konporna delante miś 'oǧoś 'i set-[138] kual kyera ke śemeǧansa de 'entendimyento 'i solombra de prudensyya tubyere vera 'i konsidrara kuan malino 'i koruto visy'o 'eś 'el mentir ke por todaś laś le'eyś fu'e defendido :
POR ley devina komo 'eś manifyeśto por nu'eśtra śagrada 'eśkritura komo aśerka dela verdad muy 'eśpiśifikada mente deklararemoś

POR ley de[ ]natureza kyen atentare byen 'enloś ninyyoś ke 'enpesan 'a hablar vera ke no śaben mentir anteś todoś śon 'enklinadoś ala verdad por lo kual akaese muǧaś veześ ke śyendo demandadoś śi[ ]an feǧo kual kyer koza ke śaben ke 'otorgandola an de śer kaśtigadoś no dešan de dezir la verdad porke la natureza loś 'enklina 'a 'elyya 'i kuando maś kresen 'i śon demandadoś de śemeǧanteś demandaś kalyyan śin reśponder byen ni mal ke por 'el myedo dela pena kalyyan la verdad 'i por śer 'enklinadoś}

⟨fol. 36b⟩
{natural mente ala verdad no la nyegan hata ke vyenen 'en mayor kresimyento ke por loke dela konversasy'on de 'otroś mayoreś ke 'elyyoś maeśtroś del 'ofisyo deprenden vyenen 'a mentir 'a negar 'i 'inventar falśiaś ke vyene por korupsy'on del 'entendimyento ke syerto śi 'el ninyo kresyese 'en lugar donde no lo 'inpuzyeśen 'enel modo de mentir 'el deśuyo śyenpre diri'a la verdad ke tyene tanta fu'ersa la verdad deśu natural ke a'un 'el maś malo vilyyano ke śe halyya śe muda 'enel kolor 'i tenbla 'enel hablar kuando habla la mentira 'i nunka nyega la verdad del todo delante de kyen śabe kela nyega śalbo śi 'eś tan pesimo ke tenga perdido 'el śaber deloś komuneś prinśipy'oś ake loś gregoś lyyaman śenderiziś 'el kual monśtro por maravilyya śe halyya

'Eś d[e]fendido tan byen por ley 'umana 'i 'eśto 'eś maś manifyeśto ke mintyendo 'uno 'a 'otro no śe pu'ede śośtener la republika ni pu'eden loś 'ombreś konserbar ni tratar 'unoś kon 'otroś 'i no tengo yo dubda alguna ke śe śuśtentari'a 'una republika śyendo todoś mudoś meǧor ke śyendo mentirozoś porke śyendo mudoś keda lugar para kaer 'enla verdad delaś kozaś pero kon dezir lo kontrary'o dela verdad 'eś 'inpośible ya maś por la mentira śaber la 'intensy'on verdader'a del[ ]ke habla kon 'eśta diabolika 'invensy'on ke haze deśvaryar 'el 'entendimyento trae 'en kontinu'a preplešidad 'el penśamyento tetubeando 'a diversaś parteś 'i konronpe la ǧuśtisy'a konla kual śe śuśtenta 'el mundo por lo kual por pura ǧuśtisyya 'ozari'a dezir śer meresedor de mu'erte kru'el 'el mentirozo porke kebranta laś le'eyś konronpe la natureza 'enderesada por 'entiliǧ[e]nsyya ke nunka yera deśtru'e 'el 'entendimyento ke para fin de alkansar la verdad fu'e dado al 'ombre 'en konkuluzy'on depyerde 'el fin del śer

---

[138] Ps. 101.7.

BOOK OF THE REGIMEN OF LIVING ‹FOL. 36B–37A›

'umano ke la verdad tyene grande komunikasy'on konla natureza porke 'enelyya no pu'ede aver mentira konel 'entendimyento kuyyo fin 'eś alkansar la verdad 'i śyenpre la anda 'envistigando 'i delyya śe mantyene 'i kon śu 'olor śe śuśtenta porke la le'ey verdad 'eś lyyamada de boka de todoś loś porfetaś de todoś loś śantoś de todoś loś śaby'oś kon muğa razon

TANT[O] 'enkliminaron nu'eśtroś śaby'oś 'el 'ekśelente 'eśtremo de la verdad 'i śublime korona deśu devinidad ke diğeron ke 'el śelyyo del Dyyo g(v)l[o]ry'ozo 'eś la verdad[139] śignif[i]kando ke anśi komo 'enel 'eśtan todaś kozaś ke 'enel mundo śon falyyaraś kunplidaś 'en 'una maś 'enlevada manera de loke 'elyyaś 'en śi meśmaś śon aśi laś kozaś ke 'enel mundo śon falyyadaś kunplidaś 'en la verdad ko[n]prehende todo 'el 'oniverśo konel kual śe śośtyene govyerna 'i mantyene no kyeraś śaber maś vitupery'o de la mentira 'i lo'or de la verdad śino ke la mentira 'elyya porśi śe konro[n]pe ke tyene [CW. grandisima]}

‹fol. 37a›
{LH {RMK: LH=35 but count 37a.}
grandisima śemeğansa konel malo ke 'el meśmo śera la pena komo maś adelante te deklarare kuyo kontrary'o tyene la verdad ke śemeğa al[ ]bu'eno 'i ala śuma bondad 'i por meğor dezir 'eś 'elyya meśma 'i 'eś tal kual 'eś la perfeksy'on del śentro konla śirkunferensyya kela verdad 'eś 'el śentro del byen 'i todaś laś linyaś delaś 'obraś dela virtud 'o formaś 'intelektualeś ke de 'elyya ala śirkunferensyya dela prudensyya 'o 'entendimyento śalen 'o 'a 'elyyoś van śon 'igualeś laś kozaś malaś 'i 'indevidaś śon muğaś 'i varyableś tanto kuanto śon loś puntoś ke 'eseden del śent(y)ro 'i 'el punto dela verdad 'eś 'uno firme para śyenpre ya maś 'i kon 'elyya śon todaś laś kozaś firmeś 'i faltando śon porśi konronpidaś porke 'el śer 'i la verdad 'eś 'una meśma koza komo tenemoś diğo :

TANTO kuanto 'el ke habla verdad 'eś loado 'i agradable 'ensu konversasy'on tanto 'el mentirozo 'eś deśplazible 'i deśagradable atodoś 'i a'un kuando dize verdad no 'eś kre'ido ke tal merese kyen tal haze ke 'el meśmo śe de śu pena :

KU'ENTAŚE de Sokrateś śeleberimo filosofo venerable preśeptor del grande Platon ke śyendo kondenado deloś tiranoś atiny'enśiś kontra ğuśtisyya lebandolo abever la mortal peśonyya konke 'en akel tyenpo matavan aloś mal heğoreś kon publiko pregon śu muğer gritando de traś del agra mente śe keğaba dizyendo ke śin kulpa daban pena kapital aśu marido lo kual komo Sokrateś 'oyeśe śe bolto a'elyya reprehendyendola grave mente dizyendo ke no 'era 'el 'el 'ombre ke ğuśta mente 'i

---

[139] Sanhedrin 94b.

Book of the Regimen of Living ‹fol. 37a–37b›

kon razon avi'a de śer kondenado ke no avi'a 'el de negar la verdad śi 'ubyera heǧo akel delito[140] 'i ami ver pu'eśto ke komun mente maś parese śentir la ǧente 'el dolor de la pena kuando 'eś śin razon pyenso ke maś lo syenten kuando 'eś kon verdad a'un ke maś lo manif[y]eśtan kuando 'eś śin ǧuśtisya por śu 'eśklamasy'on tener algun kolor 'i no śer vituperable lo ke kuando 'eś kon razon 'ibidente faltale razon para keǧarśe a'un ke 'el dolor śe'a mayor por śer 'entonseś 'el dolor por doś kozaś 'una 'el dolor de aver heǧo 'el malefisy'o meresedor del dolor 'i 'otra 'el triśte śentimyento de la pena tan vergonsoza ke padese loke kuando śin razon 'eś ǧuśtisyado 'el gozo de śer libre del yero 'eś konsolasy'on de la pena 'i koneśto teni'a razon 'el gran pasy'ente Sokrateś de no śentir 'i menośpresyyar 'el grabe dolor de la pena konla gloryya 'i pura delektasy'on de la verdad 'i ǧuśtisyya ke teni'a 'i kon razon reprehendyyo 'a Śantipe śu muǧer}

‹fol. 37b›
{RMK: 35b but count 37b} {PEREK ᶜAŚIYRIY
pu'eś de notaba poderśe prezumir 'enel kulpa digna de mu'erte
    AKU'ERDAŚEME aver 'o'ido 'o le'ido 'una notable 'eśtudyya de 'un vyeǧo abundado de byeneś de fortuna aśi hazyenda komo hiǧoś 'i afermoziguado kon toda virtud final mente byen aventurado kuanto 'ombre 'ensu tyenpo śe halyyaśe 'el kual vinyendo 'enel konosimyento del fin de śuś diaś fizo todoś śuś hiǧoś 'i 'erederoś bibir kon 'eśperansa ke teni'a 'una rikisima 'i presy'oza ǧoya de 'ineśtimable valor ke deśarleś la kual śin konparasy'on 'esedi'a 'a toda śu rikeza plata 'i 'oro 'i 'otraś ǧoyyaś ke 'el teni'a 'i aśi meśmo atodaś śuś 'eredadeś 'i no śolo laś śuyyaś si no kuantaś halyyar śe pudyeśen 'i para maś hazerloś bibir kon maś deze'o nunka leś deśkubry'o 'el śekreto deśu 'intensy'on 'en akelyyaś palabraś faśta ke śerkandośe 'el fin de śuś diaś para loś perśuadir 'el prudente vyeǧo 'a hazer kon vehemensyya lo kel dezeaba hizyeśen deśpu'eś deśu mu'erte para śu byen delyoś lyegado 'el di'a kele paresy'o aver de partirśe deśta tranśitoryya fraǧil 'i trabaǧoza vida prezente para akelyya futura permanente 'i deleytable para loś bu'enoś aǧunto todoś śuś hiǧoś 'i ǧuntoś leś diǧo hiǧoś yo komo 'eśprimentado maeśtro de muǧo tyenpo 'enel 'eśkabrozo kamino deśta vida 'enel kual koryendo 'i lyegado al fin dela 'infortuna ǧornada voś dire 'unaś palabraś laś kualeś por fin todoś demi kon muǧa 'intensy'on 'o'yreyś 'i dareyś kredito komo apalabraś de padre 'i tan ansyano komo veś keśo yo loke yo maś presye 'eneśte mundo todo 'el tyenpo ke 'enel bibi 'i loke de kontino me hizo 'eśtar alegre 'i kontente

---

[140] For the kernel of this incident, see Diogenes Laertius, *Philosophers* II. 34, trans. Hicks, 1:165.

Book of the Regimen of Living ⟨fol. 37b–38a⟩

śin temer 'el peligro dela śinyeśtra fortuna fu'e la verdad 'eśta 'oś dešo por verdader'a rikeza por 'eredad mi'a 'eśta 'eś mi hazyenda 'eśta 'eś akelyya perla delante la kual todoś loś avereś śon vileś 'i de poko valor 'eśta 'eś la presy'oza ǧoyya ke ata aki 'oś tengo 'ofresido de dar 'eś la ke trae 'un puro deleyte al ku'erpo 'i al alma 'i haze la republika 'iniśponyable 'eśta haze floreśer al 'ombre 'enla śublimada virtud 'i lo alsa haśta la kumbre dela filisidad 'i lo śośtyene 'enperpetu'o kontentamyento 'i gloryya permanente 'eśta 'eś la ke adkyere konserba 'i konfirma la perfekta amiśtad 'entre loś 'unanimeś amigoś toda konkordyya 'i 'unidad perkura 'enel mundo koneśta alkansaremoś todoś loś byeneś kuantoś kon toda śoliśitud 'i diliǧensyya dineroś 'i avereś mundanoś nunka podremoś alkansar śi perkurardeś de tenerla muy guardada 'i presyyada muy linpyya śegundo śu grande meresimyento śere'eyś kabza de bibir byen aventuradoś 'i yo kon 'eśperansa ke anśi lo hare'eyś mu'ero kont[e]nto 'i śatiśfeǧo dezeando vu'eśtra porśperidad 'i byen verdadero ke koneśta ǧoyya alkansare'eyś 'i koneśto 'el 'onrado vyeǧo}

⟨fol. 38a⟩
{LḤ
dyyo fin aśuś '[e]leganteś 'i dulseś palabraś 'i akavando de hablar śe akabo śu vida[141] 'i 'en verdad tubo fortisima razon 'el prudentisimo vyeǧo komo 'ombre śirkunśpekto 'i byen atentado 'enel kamino de la virtud para venir al śumo byen deśta śanta virtud nase 'el proberby'o ke dize no ayy maś fu'erte muro kela alma ke śabe no aver 'erado[142] 'i koneśta defensa śufry'o la mu'[e]rte Sokrateś śaby'o 'enla ley de natureza śabyendo la verdad deśi meśmo ke 'era śin kulpa komo avemoś diǧo koneśto reǧiśtyeron 'a todoś loś maleś todoś loś fu'erteś kabalyeroś de nu'eśa ley ke por 'elyya śufryeron martiry'o 'i no ayy mayor mal 'i ke maś deroke [a] 'el kelo tyene ke śentirśe 'uno kulpado 'enśi meśmo ke 'eśte tal anda komo mar tenpeśt(y)[u]'ozo akuzado kontinu'a mente del teśtigo ke 'ensu alma tyene ke nunka sesa delo atormentar aśi ke no ayy pe'or mal ke mentir 'i mayor byen ke dezir la verdad perśuponyendo 'el 'ombre de no mentir ni nyegar la verdad por ningun ku'ento ningun malefisy'o hara porke konsidrando kuando lo kiǧere hazer ke syendo delyyo peśkerido 'a de dezir la verdad no nyegando ni 'enkubryendo koza deloke hizo 'eś manifeśto ke 'eśte tal no

---

[141] Stith Thompson, *Motif-Index of Folk Literature* (Bloomington, IN, 1955–1958), J154, *Wise words of dying father;* P236.2, *Supposed chest of gold induces children to care for aged father;* H631.5, *What is strongest? Truth.*

[142] Unidentified source. Diogenes Laertius cites among Epicurus' *Maxims* no. 17: "The just man enjoys the greatest peace of mind, while the unjust is full of the utmost disquietude" (*Philosophers,* X.144.17, trans. Hicks, 2:669).

Book of the Regimen of Living ‹fol. 38a–38b›

lo hara porke afigurando 'enel tyenpo ke lo komete ke lo 'a de manifeśtar syendo preguntado detenerśe'a de hazerlo por no paśar la vergu'ensa de la kondenasy'on de śu meśma boka delante loś akuzadoreś de manera ke hablar verdad 'eś kabza muy porpinka para 'uzar todo ǧenero de virtud :

KAPITULO 'ONZENO

PORKE para byen 'obrar śegun verdad 'i guardarśe de śu kontrary'o 'eś nesesary'o konoser byen todo modo de mentira 'i falsedad 'i para 'eśto 'eśpisif[i]kar śeri'a menester alargar muǧo kedara la rezolusy'on de 'elyo para la śegunda partikula del tratado aserka de la verdad 'i pu'eś śoy forsado hablar alya 'enelyyo śuperflu'o parese traerlo aki ke porel veraś 'en konkluzy'on todaś laś diferenteś 'eśpesyaś de mentiraś 'i laś konsidrasy'oneś de verdad 'i 'en kuantaś maneraś śe deve 'entender anśi meśmo kedara para alyya pu'eś 'eś delaś vertudeś moraleś loke konvyene hablar aserka dela kortezi'a afabilidad 'urbanidad 'i amiśtad komun 'entre loś 'ombreś 'o komo meǧor parese lyyamarle 'i de loś danyoś ke śe śigen del muǧo hablar 'i del kalyyar kuando no konvyene aśi meśmo hablaremoś dela konversasy'on 'i grasyya 'enel hablar 'o dezir donayyreś kuando konvyene keloś gregoś lyyaman 'e'otrapeli'a[143] ke śon todaś 'eśtaś treś vertudeś moraleś aserka dela habla 'enla 'umana konversasy'on 'i komunikasy'on komo konvyene :

'I agora aśerka del hablar 'i kalyyar te digo ke 'enkomendeś ala memoryya //['un]// 'ekselente 'enǧe[n]plo ke 'un doktisimo 'ombre [CW. puzo]}

‹fol. 38b›
{PEREK 'AḤAD ᶜAŚAR [CHAPTER ELEVEN]
puzo aśerka del hablar 'i 'eś ke deve kual kyer 'ombre hazer ku'enta ke la palabra 'eś 'una medisin(y)al konfisy'on 'ordenada por 'un muy afamado mediko para 'un pasyente ke 'eśta 'enel artikulo dela mu'erte 'i ama 'en 'eśtremo la vida 'i 'el mediko aviza 'a 'eśte pasyente ke 'a menester advertir 'i parar byen menteś kon toda la diliǧensy'a posible ke tome 'eśta tal konfisy'on a'un syerto punto deputado para tomar la tal medisina amoneśtandole 'a pena de mu'erte 'i hazyendole śaber ke śi ante‹ś› 'o deśpu'eś la toma le śera puro arśeniko 'i peśtifero veneno dela kual śin ninguna redensy'on amarga mente fenesera śuś triśteś diaś[144] śyendo 'eśto anśi śe deve byen konsidrar kon kuanta śolisitud 'i diliǧensy'a śe diśporna 'el atribulado pasyente 'a

---

[143] Almosnino's definition harkens to the sense of the term in modern Greek "humorous, pleasant talk" rather than the negative sense "frivolous talk, chatter".

[144] Unidentified source.

BOOK OF THE REGIMEN OF LIVING ‹FOL. 38B–39A›

konpasar 'el tyenpo 'enke lo deve de tomar por no varyar punto pu'eś tanto para śu presyyada śanidad 'inporta 'i atal pena 'eśta kondenado śi 'un punto śe deśvyaśe :
    BYEN anśi dela meśma manera deve atentar todo 'ombre 'eśpesyyal 'el moso ke 'eś maś dolyente del 'apetito 'i alomenoś maś diśpu'eśto para del 'enfermar de śakar la p[a]labra deśu boka 'enel momento konvenible puntu(n)al mente no primero ni prośtero 'i 'eśto 'a de kontenplar kon toda diliğensyya pośible 'i kon todo śu 'inğeny'o kon todaś śuś fu'ersaś śegun dereğa razon ke tanto kuanto aproveğa 'i 'eś loado 'ensu tyenpo 'el hablar tanto danyya 'i 'eś vituperado fu'era deśu tyenpo digo fu'era de śu perpozito
    'I 'eśto 'eś loke kiğo śinifikar nu'eśtro rey Š^elomoh 'en śuś proverby'oś alegri'a al varon kon reśponśo de śu boka 'i palabra 'ensu 'ora kuanto bu'ena[145] keryendo dezir kela palabra 'enel 'ombre śyendo aśu tyenpo alyende del 'eśtremado 'i 'ultimo byen ke delyya śe rezulta resibe 'el dezidor śuprema delektasy'on 'i 'inmensa alegri'a 'i de aki śe śige por konśekensya de kontrary'oś ke fu'era deśu punto 'i 'ora 'eś kontra todo lo diğo :
    DIŠO maś akel śaby'o 'enel 'enğenplo diğo ke aśi komo 'el 'ombre memerozo dela mu'erte 'i deze'ozo dela vida 'eśtando dubdozo del punto 'ordenado por 'el mediko śośpeğando aver ya pasado para hu'ir dela mu'erte por 'el danyyo de akelyya medisina la kual śe śige no la tomando aśu 'ora 'el meğor 'i maś śeguro remedy'o ke tyene 'eś 'eğar la tal medisina 'en lugar do nunka ya maś pu'eda pareser porke śu remedy'o 'eś 'en 'un śolo punto 'i 'el danyyo 'en muğoś anśi deve 'el 'ombre hazer de loke p[y]ensa hablar 'ensu tyempo no śyendo syerto deśer 'oportuna mente hablado
    FINAL mente śe nota maś deśte śingular 'enğemplo ke 'eś maś 'el p[e]ligro del hablar ke 'el danyyo del kalyyar 'i ke śin konparasy'on 'a de śer maś 'el tyenpo del kalyyar ke 'el de hablar pu'eś}

‹fol. 39a›
{LZ {RMK: 37a but count 39a.}
'el hablar no 'eś maś ke 'en 'un śolo punto 'i perpozito :
    KONFORME a'eśto diğo 'un letrado śavy'o 'el kual 'eśtando 'en konpanyya de 'otroś grandeś varoneś ayu(')ntadoś 'a platikar 'en kozaś de varya le'esy'on kalyyava hablando loś 'otroś 'uno kon 'otro atentaron loś konpanyeroś 'enel grave śilensyo a'elyyoś 'enoğozo ke por muğo 'eśpasy'o de tyempo moleśtado loś 'oi'a no sesando todoś de prośegir 'ensu platika le demandaron diğeśe la kabza deśu kalyyar 'el 'en breveś p[a]labraś reśpondy'o kela 'utilidad de śu 'oreğa 'era para śu alma 'i la 'utili-

---

[145] Prov. 15.23.

BOOK OF THE REGIMEN OF LIVING ‹FOL. 39A–39B›

dad deśu lengu'a para loś 'oyenteś[146] keryendo dezir ke maś probeǧo śe śegi'a 'en 'o'ir loke 'otroś hablaban deprendyendo loke por ventura no śavi'a ke no 'en hablar porke hablando 'el no podri'a dešar de šer śu habla de 'uno de doś modoś 'o ke fu'eśe bu'ena 'o mala 'i śi fu'eśe mala muǧo meǧor 'era deǧarla de dezir ke la privasy'on del mal 'en todaś laś kośaś 'eś deputado por puro byen 'i śi fu'eśe bu'ena 'i proveǧoza la mayor parte del proveǧo delyya śe śegi'a aloś ke lo 'o'ian por la meśma kabza[147]

FU'E reśpu'eśta korta grabe 'enla kual 'onro muǧo loś aśiśtenteś konpanyeroś guardando tanbyen 'el dekoro deśuś letraś de manera ke kiǧo śinifikar 'i amoneśtar 'eśte prudentisimo letrado kuan probeǧozo 'eś ael 'ombre 'i no kale dezir aloś manseboś 'el 'o'ir 'i 'eśtar atentoś 'en kual kyer ayuntamyento de śaby'oś para rekoǧer la śuabe 'i śabroza fruta del śaber ke deśuś 'elokenteś 'i śabyaś palabraś 'en kual kyer koza ke pratiken śyenpre śe koǧe :

POR lo kual śe ku'enta de 'otro śavy'o ke leendo 'el alto dezir de 'eśte de ke avemoś hablado anyyady'o maś ke 'el hablar śe reparte 'en kuatro 'eśpesyyaś 'i maneraś diferenteś[148] :

LA primera 'eś delaś kozaś ke de dezirlaś śe 'eśpera algun probeǧo 'indevida mente 'i traen konśigo grandisimo dany'o 'i 'eśkandalo por pośtre laś maś delaś veześ komo 'eś komun mente la liǧonǧa : 'i 'el traer nu'ebaś de 'una parte 'a 'otra 'en konkluzy'on tener 'ofisy'o de malśin 'i traydor ke deśtoś taleś śe konfian algunaś śekretaś p[a]labraś 'inǧury'ozaś 'i perǧudisyaleś 'a alguno 'elyyoś meśmoś śelaś van 'a deśkubrir ke laś maś delaś veześ 'el ke laś resibe fu'elga de 'o'ir laś 'i śaberlaś 'i 'eśte tal dezidor de taleś nu'ebaś 'eśta 'a grandisimo peligro porke vinyendo 'a śaberlo akel kele deśkubry'o 'el tal śekreto konfyando del le pu'ede kośtar la vida dandole por 'elyyo mu'erte deśaśtrada 'o 'otro dany'o konforme aśu posiblidad 'o alomenoś reśta}

‹fol. 39b›
{{RMK: 37b but count 39b.}}
'entre 'elyyoś 'enemiśiśimo 'ody'o mortal reynado śyenpre kon 'el 'apetito de kru'el vengansa rezervado para śe 'eśekutar avyendo 'oportunidad :

---

[146] For congeners, see Knust, *Mittheilungen aus dem Eskurial*, 151 n. e and 376 n. e. Compare Solomon Ibn Gabirol, *Selección de perlas,* no. 352: "Cierto árabe en una reunión escuchó pacientemente, y al preguntarle: Cuál es tu rango en la aristocracia árabe?, les contestó: Hermanos, las cualidades auditivas son puramente personales, pero las de la lengua alcanzan a los demás" (ed. D. Gonzalo Maeso [Barcelona, 1977], 103).

[147] Unidentified source.

[148] Ibn Gabirol describes these four classes of speech in nearly identical terms: see *Selección de perlas,* ed. Gonzalo Maeso, 104.

BOOK OF THE REGIMEN OF LIVING ‹FOL. 39B–40A›

POR lo kual fu'e 'en grande manera 'infamado por todaś le'eyś 'el levador 'i traydor de nu'ebaś 'i śuś 'oyenteś por loś 'eśkandaloś 'i danyoś manifyeśtoś ke delyyo śe śige :

ŚEGUNDA 'eśpesyya 'eś de alguna delaś kualeś ningun probeǧo śe 'eśpera anteś śe teme 'i veriśimil mente śe śośpeǧa śeg(+)irśe delyyaś danyyoś 'i perdidaś de 'onraś komo śon komun mente laś ke por reproǧe 'i deś'onra śe dizen 'enlaś maś de laś brigaś 'i peleaś donde śe dizen p[a]labraś 'inǧury'ozaś 'unoś 'a 'otroś de lo kual ningun proveǧo śe 'eśpera maś anteś muǧo danyyo alo menoś 'enoǧo 'i temor kon reselo dela vengansa 'i 'infamyya por kabza delaś 'inǧuryaś diǧaś

TERSERA partida 'eś ke ni śe 'eśpera delyyaś proveǧo alguno ni menoś śe resela de venir danyyo laś maś de laś veześ komo śon laś maś delaś p[a]labraś deloś ke fu'elgan platikar 'enlaś kozaś pasadaś śin 'ofensa de ninguno anśi prezente komo a'uzente ke propyya mente fu'elgan loś vyeǧos kon 'elyaś ke śe deleytan maś de reduzir ala memoryya lo pasado hazyendolo prezente ke kon loke pośe'en prezente por śu prezenśyyal flakeza 'i de 'eśta manera śon laś hablaś 'inventadaś para pasa tyenpo 'o para byen dezir para pyerde tyenpo ke aśi lo pyerde 'el ke 'enelyyaś śe 'okupa apartandośe dela kontemplasy'on del verdadero byen 'i deśu 'eśpikulasy'on delaś kualeś fablaś ninguna 'utilidad śe śige maś anteś byen atentado lu'ego traen kon śigo śu danyyo pago de kontado ke 'eś gaśtar 'el tyempo tan presyado 'en fablaś vanaś por lo kual todo 'ombre śe deve delyyaś apartar 'en grande manera 'i 'en 'eśpesyyal loś mosoś ke 'el kośtum[b]re deśto loś haze 'osy'ozoś 'i reveldeś 'a resebir 'el śuabe yugo dela devina 'eśpikulasy'on 'i felise doktrina :

TODAŚ 'eśtaś treś 'eśpesyaś 'i modoś de hablar śon reprobadoś de maś 'a menoś ke 'el primero 'eś de 'ombreś maloś preversoś aśtutoś 'enel mal 'el śegundo de 'enkontinenteś 'inpasyenteś de 'ira 'el tersero de 'osy'ozoś 'i pozilanimeś[149]

LA kuarta 'eliǧible 'eś 'el hablar delaś kozaś ke [de] dezirlaś śe 'eśpera śuprema 'utilidad 'i ningun danyyo śe resela 'i deśta 'eśpesyya 'eś propyyo 'el hablar 'i platikar 'enla le'ey 'i kozaś de śensyya ke traen grande deleytasy'on 'enel prezente 'i muǧo probeǧo 'enel futuro 'i deśtaś śe śigen todaś laś 'otraś hablaś ke para śuśtentasy'on dela republika śon diriǧidaś

'I 'eśte kuarto modo //'uza// todo śavy'o 'i bu'eno kon hervor vehemente 'i 'insasyable deze'o 'inśesante}

‹fol. 40a›
{M
DE manera ke denota todo 'eśto śer muy apropyyado al 'enǧe[n]plado akel devino

---

[149] Cf. Aristotle, *NE*, VII.i.1 (1145a 15–19).

BOOK OF THE REGIMEN OF LIVING ‹FOL. 40A›

'enǧe[n]plo ke diǧimoś[150] ke syerto deve śer la palabra 'eśmerada anteś ke dela boka śalga porke 'eś verdader'a 'imaǧen retrato 'i 'eśtanpa delaś notisyaś 'i konsebtoś del alma 'i deve śer verdader'a la 'enbaǧada del 'entendimyento denusyada por la lengu'a 'i 'otroś 'inśturmentoś dadoś de natureza para 'eśte fin loś kualeś śon 'el nunśyyo 'orador del alma 'en todaś śuś kozaś 'i 'eś manifyeśto ke kuanto menoś śe habla menoś śe manifyeśta la falta śila ayy 'i menoś śe pu'ede yerar

ŚOBRE todo deve 'el 'ombre akabidarśe no śer proliǧo 'enloke kyere dezir 'eśpesyyal 'enloś mosoś ke porśu poka a'utoridad no śon muǧo 'o'idoś faśta 'el kabo deloke kyeren dezir a'un ke brebe mente lo digan kuanto maś kuando fu'eren proliǧoś ke 'a todoś śeran 'inportunoś por lo kual konvyene perkuren deno dezir 'en muǧoś terminoś loke 'en pokoś pu'eden konprehender porke la proliǧidad 'eś muy 'inpor(n)tuna deśagradable 'i deśgrasyyada śin śabor ninguno 'i śobre todo keda menoś 'entendida la 'intensyon laś maś delaś veześ 'i a'un pyenso ke śe'a 'el maś alto 'i 'eśelente grado 'enel hablar śaber dezir la 'intensy'on 'enel maś brebe 'eśtilo ke posible 'eś śin alargar 'en muǧoś preanbuloś 'i rode'oś ke 'en vano śe dize la koza 'en muǧaś palabraś kuando 'en pokaś śe pu'ede konprehender porke 'enlaś maś delaś nasy'oneś fu'e la proliǧidad muǧo deśabrida 'i 'eśpesyyal 'entre śaby'oś ke tyenen 'el tyenpo śegun la diśtribu'isy'on 'en muǧa 'eśtima

KU'ENTAŚE de 'uno tan poko 'elokente komo śaby'o ke vino delan(')te Aristot[e]leś 'a demandarle 'una demanda 'i fu'e tan lu'engo 'ensu 'orasy'on ke dyyo lugar 'a ke 'el diǧo filosofo śe diśtrayeśe de 'o'irlo 'okupandośe 'en la akośtumbrada kontenplasyyon 'enke 'eśtaba śin 'o'ir palabra de kuantaś 'el 'inportuno 'orador diśo 'i deśke 'el 'orador akabo de hablar śu proliśo śermon demandole perdon por loke avi'a alargado a'el kual reśpondy'o Aristotel maś perdoname tu ami ke nada de kuanto diǧiśte te 'e 'entendido porke tuś proliǧaś p[a]labraś no dyeron lugar 'a deǧar konprehender la 'intensy'on delyyaś 'i hizyeron me 'okupaśe 'en 'otra kontenplasy'on[151] 'i 'eśto diśo por reprehenderlo deśu 'inportunidad 'i proliśo razonar para 'enmendarśe 'otra veś :

AŚI meśmo śe ku'enta deloś Atinyenśeś 'oradoreś ke penśando śer 'elokenteś 'enbyaron 'una proliśa letra aloś Lasedemonyyoś muy kortoś de razon 'en todaś śuś platikaś ala kual letra reśpondyeron dizyendo ke kuando alyegaron al fin delyya śeleś 'olvido 'el prinsipy'o 'i komo 'el fin śin 'el prinsipy'o śe'a 'in( )'entiliǧible no pudyeron konprehender la final 'intensy'on 'i konkuluzy'on dela karta k[e]leś perdonaśen śi non reśpondian}

---

[150] Cf. Knust, *Mittheilungen aus dem Eskurial,* 151 n. e and 376 n. e and Solomon Ibn Gabirol, *Selección de perlas,* ed. Gonzalo Maeso, 103.

[151] Diogenes Laertius, *Philosophers,* V. 20, trans. Hicks, 1:463.

BOOK OF THE REGIMEN OF LIVING ‹FOL. 40B›

‹fol. 40b›
{PEREK Š^eNEYM ^cAŚAR [CHAPTER TWELVE]
'a śu 'enbašada porke no śabian ke 'era todo 'eśto dišeron keryendoloś tağar de prolišoś al modo ke 'uzo 'el filosofo[152] :
'UNA delaś bu'enaś kozaś ke 'eneśta nasyon deloś turkoś 'entre loś kualeś bivimoś ve'o 'eś la brevedad del hablar 'i 'eśkribir la kual pyenso śe'a maś 'enelyoś ke 'en ninguna 'otra nasy'on 'eśpesyyal 'enloś le'idoś delyoś porke śe presyan muğo dela lengu'a arabika ke de nu'eśtra śanta lengu'a tyene grande parte ke śegun 'opinyon de nu'eśtroś śaby'oś 'eś la meśma śanta lengu'a korupta 'i adulteryada 'en algunaś parteś 'i por 'eśto tyene tanta 'ekselensy'a 'enla brevedad 'enla kual nu'eśtra śantisima lengu'a 'eś avantağada śobre todaś[153] anśi 'enla brevedad deloś bokabuloś komo 'enl(h)[aś] fraześ 'i modo de hablar konprehendyendo 'i manifeśtando la 'intensyon del hablador 'en tan kortaś palabraś la kual 'enel doble delyyaś parese śer 'inpośible ninguna 'otra lengu'a poder deklarar :

KAPITULO DOZENO

ŚOBRE lo diğo todo ariba no tengo maś ke dezir śalbo ke nunka śe aparte de tu memory'a guardar la palabra para donde konvyene digo para 'el perpozito 'el tyenpo 'i lugar ke konvyene por 'el 'orden ke maś larga mente 'enla 'oğaba 'i nobena virtud deklararemoś ke para loke te konvyene śaber al prezente hata venir al grado de perfekta konversasy'on 'entre 'ombreś prudenteś baśta byen lo diğo śi[ ]de kontino lo tubyereś 'eśkrito 'i 'eśtanpado 'enla memoryya ke śoy syerto ke mirandote muğaś veześ 'enel 'eśpeğo deśtaś miś dotrinaś tu floreśeraś 'enla virtud hata lyegar aproduzir 'el fruto dela d[e]lleytable 'i 'ekśelente śabiduri'a 'i devina kontenplasy'on 'i todoś ternan por byen de 'enbezarte vyendote a'uto para resebir la verdader'a dotrina ayuntada atoda śy'entifika 'eśpikulasy'on 'i ten presupu'eśto para ti ke hazyendo loke

---

[152] Plutarch's *Moralia:* "When the ambassadors of the Samians spoke at great length, the Spartans said to them, 'We have forgotten the first part, and the later part we did not understand because we forgot the first'" (cf. trans. Flower, 3:395).

[153] Almosnino's expression of the superiority of Hebrew over all other languages echoes a concept developed by medieval Jewish grammarians and writers in response to the Islamic doctrine of *i^cjāz al-qur'ān,* the inimitability of the Qur'ān, the quintessence of literary elegance. Hebrew grammarian-poets answered with the supernatural origin of Hebrew and biblical literature: Hebrew was the flawless, divinely-ordained language, essentially superior to all others; Arabic was a mere derivative.

BOOK OF THE REGIMEN OF LIVING ‹FOL. 40B–41A›

por 'eśta mi regla konprehendraś śeraś 'enbidyado de todoś tuś 'enemigoś ke 'eś la mayor pena ke leś pu'edeś dar ke dela 'enbidyya detu prośperidad śe karkoman śuś gü'eśoś no halyyando 'en ti maś ke tağar ke śi mobyereś 'eśte akatamyento no podraś ya maś yerar

'I ŚI por ventura te kontentareś konke algunoś amigoś tuyoś finğidoś lo'en laś 'obraś ke hizyereś no śyendo taleś 'elyyoś haran komo maloś 'in( )ğuśtoś 'i tu te falyyaraś burlado por lo kual te avizo ke no kyeraś meğor 'enmendador de tu vida ke tu propy'o 'enemigo ke del poko mal hara muğo de manera ke kuando no halyyare ke dezir kalyyando 'eśtaraś śeguro porke 'eś verdadero śenyyal de tu bondad kon 'eśperansa de pośe'er la byen aventuran(t)sa fin de todo 'umano byen 'eneśte mundo 'i 'enel 'otro :}

‹fol. 41a›

{M'

'I 'eneśto śe pu'ede tomar 'enğenplo delaś muğereś prudenteś ke śe afeytan kon 'eśpeğoś de alhinde[154] ke reprezentan laś makulaś mayoreś deloke śon de manera ke mośtrandośe 'eneśtoś 'eśpeğoś śer kitadaś laś makulaś śe deve tener por muy syerto śer anśi 'el kontrary'o akaese alaś ke śe afeytan 'en 'eśpeğo de vidro ke laś grandeś makulaś reprezentan ğikaś de manera ke kontentandośe la śimple hembra kon loke 'el 'eśpeğo mintyendo le reprezenta manifyeśta śu makula no kurandośe dela ğikita manğa 'i kazi 'invizible ke 'el 'enganyyozo 'eśpeğo le mośtro :

DELA meśma manera akaese al 'ombre kon śuś finğidoś amigoś 'i verdaderoś liğunğeroś verdader'a mente keremoś hablar ke śon komo 'el falśo 'eśpeğo ke la grande manğa mu'eśtra ğika 'i la ğika haze '(v)[i]nvizible loś 'enemigoś manifyeśtoś śon komo 'el 'eśpeğo ke la ğika manğa 'engrandeśe 'i por muy ğika ke śe'a no śabe '(v)[e]nkubrirla de manera ke 'el ke 'eś deśkreto 'a de perkurar de alinpyar śuś makulaś 'i remedyar śuś maleś śegun ke 'el 'ody'ozo 'enemigo le pone hata ke 'a dišo del 'enemigo 'eśte śin manğa no t(y)enyendo lugar de dezir del mal ni a'un formarlo 'i śi aeśta śutil śemeğansa atyentaś veraś kuanto maś malo 'i fe'o 'eś 'el liğunğero amigo ke 'el klaro 'enemigo :

PARA lo kual te 'ordene 'eśta primera partida del reğimyento dela vida ke me demandaśte komo 'eśpeğo dela verdad para loke 'eś nesesary'o atu prezente 'edad ke mirandote byen 'enel no tyeneś nesesidad de maś dotrina para śer libre de toda śośpeğa de 'infamyya 'o de visy'o kon 'el kual 'orden śeraś diśpu'eśto para byen pro-

---

[154] *Alhinde* "acero." *DCECH* amply documents the term and describes this kind of mirror: "espejo de acero cóncavo que sirve para quemar objetos o para aumentarlos" (1:174).

Book of the Regimen of Living ⟨fol. 41a–41b⟩

śeder 'en 'el kamino dela byen aventuransa 'i 'el fin 'umano ke 'en byen 'obrar 'i 'eśpekular konśiśte hata la fin dela ǧornada de nu'eśtra breve 'i atribulada vida :
  KE '[e]ś la primera ǧornada de treś ke śe konsidran 'enlaś almaś deloś byen aventuradoś deśde ke aka śon produzidaś 'a 'infinito konforme al teśto de nu'eśtra śantisima ley 'i diǧoś de nu'eśtroś devinoś porfetaś 'i gravisimoś śaby'oś donde śinifikaron śer la primera ǧornada 'eśta vida prezente dende ke nase 'el 'ombre haśta ke mu'era por 'el kual tyenpo diśo nu'eśtra sagrada 'eśkritura 'el di'a 'eśte tu Dyyo te 'enk[o]myenda por haze⟨r⟩ atodoś loś fu'eroś 'i set[e]r-[155] 'i diǧo maś 'enkomendonoś 'el Dyyo por fazer atodoś loś fu'eroś 'eśtoś para byen 'a noś todoś loś diaś para abiviguarno⟨ś⟩ komo 'el di'a 'eśte 'i set[e]r-[156] keryendo dezir ke noś mando nu'eśtro Dyyo glory'ozo hazer loś devinoś preśeptoś para alkansar por śu 'enteresisy'on 'el 'ultimo 'i śumo byen 'en todoś loś diaś ke kyere dezir 'en todoś loś treś para ke śeamoś 'enloś 'otroś doś biboś 'i permanenteś anśi komo 'eneśte 'eśto 'eś loke kiǧo dezir 'en dezir para abiviguarnoś komo 'el di'a 'eśte 'i por[ ]'eśta primera ǧornada fu'e loke diśo nu'eśo devino rey Šᵉlomoh meǧor 'eś fama ke azeyte bu'eno 'i 'el di'a dela mu'erte ke 'el di'a del nasimyento[157]}

⟨fol. 41b⟩
{ke 'eśta primera ǧornada 'enpyeśa deśde 'el punto del nasimyento haśta 'el punto dela mu'erte
  LA śegunda 'enpyeśa dende 'el punto dela mu'erte hata 'el punto dela resureksy'on ke 'eś la vida delaś almaś 'eśtando apartadaś deśuś ku'erpoś lu'ego deśpu'eś dela mu'erte :
  'I komo la glory'a del byen deśta primera ǧornada 'enel fin d[e]lyya śe kanta ke 'eś 'el tyenpo de morir ke 'el Dyyo no konfi'a 'enśuś śantoś 'en[e]śta vida prezente hata ke vyenen 'enel fin deśta ǧornada komo diǧo 'Iyob hek 'en śuś śantoś no konfi'a 'i set-[158] diǧo nu'eśtro śaby'o Šᵉlomoh ke anśi komo 'eś meǧor la bu'ena fama por parte de la bondad de laś bu'en[a]ś 'obraś ke la haze bolar maś ke 'el bu'en azeyte śubir para ariba aśi 'eś meǧor 'el di'a de la mu'erte a'el meśmo ke la tal fama tyene adkerida ke 'el di'a deśu nasimyento porke 'enel di'a de la mu'[e]rte 'eś ya syerto śer pose'edor del byen verdadero 'i 'enel di'a del nasimyento 'eśta 'en muǧa dubda deloke śera 'i hizo la konparasy'on 'enel azeyte porke aśi komo 'el azeyte śube para ariba aśi

---

[155] Deut. 26.16.
[156] Deut. 6.24.
[157] Eccles. 7.1.
[158] Job 4.18.

BOOK OF THE REGIMEN OF LIVING ‹FOL. 41B–42A›

la fama kaminando krese 'i 'eś komo śi diśeśe ke śyendo la fama bu'ena meǧor ke 'el azeyte 'eśtonseś 'eś meǧor 'el di'a ke mu'eren ke 'el di'a ke nasen ke 'eś 'enel bu'eno ke 'enloś maloś 'eś 'el kontrary'o ke maś vale 'el di'a del nasimyento ke a'un no tyene heǧo ni mal ni byen ke 'el di'a ke mu'ere ke 'eś heǧo ya 'el mal :

'EŚ la tersera ǧornada dende ke resurǧen loś mu'ertoś 'a 'infinito ke tanbyen 'eś lyamada di'a por 'el kual d[i]ǧo 'el porfeta ante de venir 'el di'a del Dyyo 'el grande 'i 'el terible[159] 'el kual fu'e lyyamado 'en boka de nu'eś(ś)oś śaby'oś 'el di'a del ǧu'izyyo 'i por 'eśtoś treś diaś diśo 'el porfeta Hośea^c abiviguarnoś'a de doś diaś 'i 'enel di'a 'el ters[e]ro noś alebantara 'i biviremoś delante del 'i set-[160] k[e]ryendo śiknifikar ke 'en loś doś diaś primeroś ke 'eś 'eśta vida prez[e]nte 'ila vida delaś almaś 'eśtando apartad[a]ś deloś ku'erpoś lu'ego deśpu'eś dela mu'erte tyenen neseśidad laś almaś dela ayuda del Dyyo 'i deśu graśyya para 'enkaminarlaś al byen 'i glorya verdader'a ke śin śu graśyya 'i ayuda ninguna koza pu'eden alkansar

'ENEŚTA primera ǧornada 'eś manifyeśto ke nunka 'otro lyyaman 'i rekyeren del Dyyo loś porfetaś loś śantoś byen aventuradoś śalbo k[e]leś ayude 'i 'enkamine para lyegar al śumo byen por lo kual no 'a meneśter relatar ke la 'eśkritura 'eś lyena deśto

PU'EŚ 'enla vida delaś almaś klara mente dizen nu'eśtroś śaby'oś ke 'eśtan alyya laś almaś de loś ǧuśtoś 'i virtu'ozoś 'i ke tyenen śuś koronaś 'en śuś kabeśaś 'i ke śe aprobeǧan de la klarida(r)[d] 'i 'influ'enśyya de la graśyya devina[161] ke 'en dezir tyenen śuś}

‹fol. 42a›
{MB
koronaś 'enśuś kabeśaś kiǧeron śiknifikar ke laś koronaś de laś bu'enaś 'obraś 'i devina 'eśpikulaśy'on ke de aki lyebaron śon laś ke alyya tyene 'enśuś kabeśaś 'i diǧeron ke kon todo 'eśto śe aprobeǧan de la devina 'influ'enśyya 'i set- :

'ENPERO 'enel di'a tersero ke 'eś deśpu'eś de la reśureśy'on śeran tan perfektoś loś ke śe levantaren ke porśi biviran 'i 'eśto 'eś loke 'el porfeta kizo śiknifikar dizyendo 'i 'enel di'a tersero noś abiviguara 'i biviremoś 'enśu perzenśyya 'i set-[162] :

YO AKI 'eneśte mi tratado 'i reǧimyento de vida no dire maś de loke konbyene hazer 'en 'eśta primera ǧornada ke 'eś la prinśipal de donde depende 'el byen verdadero para laś 'otraś doś 'i 'eś la ke konvyene tener 'en 'elya la regla śegun dereǧa

---

[159] Malachi 3.23.
[160] Hosea 6.2.
[161] Berakot 17a. Cf. Wisdom of Solomon 4.2; Ben Sira [Ecclesiasticus] 45.14.
[162] Hosea 6.2.

BOOK OF THE REGIMEN OF LIVING ‹FOL. 42A–42B›

razon para no 'erar ke 'el ke 'eśta primera ǧornada kaminare śin danyo fasil mente pasara ala śegunda 'i tersera 'i śi deśpu'eś kiǧereś śaver loke susede deśpu'eś dela mu'erte 'enlaś diǧaś doś ǧornadaś ke prośeden 'en 'infinito porke la tersera ke 'enpyeśa del prinsipy'o dela reśuresy'on no tyene termino final 'enke śe akabe poderloaś byen ver por 'una letra ke śobre 'eśto 'enby'e a'una preśona nota anoś dela kual fu'e demandado mi pareser 'eneśta parte ke 'eś lo ke akaese alaś almaś dende ke del ku'erpo śe apartan 'en 'infinito al kual reśpondi muy por 'eśtenśo a'un ke breve śi keraś yo tela 'eśkrivire deśpu'eś deśte tratado ke śe te śera agradable[163] :

AGORA no konvyene hablar maś deloke haze para 'eśta primera ǧornada la kual te hago śaber ke śu longura 'o brevedad no 'eśta 'enla multitud deloś diaś ke śe pasan śalbo 'en lyegar maś 'o menoś ala pośesy'on del byen verdadero de manera ke 'el ke bivyendo muǧoś anyoś no alkansa 'el byen 'i mu'ere śin averlo pose'ido mu'ere mansebo 'i 'el ke 'en pokoś diaś alkansa todo loke aśu natural konplisy'on diśpośisy'on 'i abilidad de 'inǧenyyo 'eś posible alkansar avyendo 'en poka 'edad todo 'eśto alkansado 'i heǧo todo loke 'eś obligado 'i aśu natureza devido mu'ere 'eśte tal vyeǧo 'i no mansebo pu'eś ku[n]pl[i]da mente lyego al fin dela ǧornada konforme 'a akelyya śingular konśidrasy'on de Śeneka ke dize ke 'el ke lyega 'a fin de śu fado mu'ere vyeǧo[164] 'el 'entento del kual pyenśo śe'a lo diǧo ke aśi byen komo akaese 'en doś 'o treś ke andaśen 'a 'un ś[y]erto lugar diśtante por 'una ǧornada partyendo todoś doś de manyana 'i 'uno koryendo kon toda la diliǧensyya posible lyegaśe alyya amedyyo di'a 'o anteś 'i 'otro ala noǧe 'i 'el 'otro no pudyeśe 'en toda akelyya ǧornada lyegar a'el lugar maś anteś de lyegar lo tomaśe la noǧe 'en medyo del 'eśkabrozo kamino śe dira aver maś andado 'el ke primero lyego a'un ke lyego maś preśto

DE la meśma manera akaese 'enla vida 'umana ke 'el ke alyega al fin}

‹fol. 42b›
del byen verdadero ke 'eś 'el fin deśta ǧornada mu'ere vyeǧo 'i kuanto maś preśto kon mayor velośidad kamina 'enel byen tanto śe deve dezir aver meǧor kaminado 'i muǧo maś ke 'otro ke deśpu'eś lyego por kuanto 'en 'igual tyenpo paso maś kamino ke śon laś 'obraś medyaś para 'el fin 'i 'en menoś tyenpo kamino 'igual 'eśpasy'o pu'eś lyego maś preśto al fin adon(v)de loś ke lyegan alkansan la korona deśu paśado trabaǧo :

'I akel ake śobre vyene 'enel kamino la 'eśkura noǧe de la mu'erte a'un ke kan-

---

[163] He refers to *Iggeret Tehiyat ha-Metim,* his now lost work on the resurrection of the dead.

[164] I do not find an exact parallel in Seneca's discussion of death in *Natural Questions* VI.i.8–9 (trans. Corcoran, 2:131–33). It seems to be rather Seneca, *De Brevitate Vitae* II.1, trans. Basore, 2:319–21.

BOOK OF THE REGIMEN OF LIVING ‹FOL. 42B›

sado kamino¹⁶⁵ todo 'el di'a mu'ere anteś de tyenpo pu'eś no lyego al fin del 'eśpasy'o ke 'enla ǧornada 'era tenido 'andar aśi ke muryendo de syen anyyoś 'i a'un de mil le falta tyenpo para loke 'era obligado hazer 'i 'el tyenpo ke bibyo kamino muy poko :
   KONFORME alo kual dišo nu'eśtro re'ey Šᵉlomoh no 'enmaleśkaś muǧo 'ino śeaś 'inorante porke kyereś morir anteś detu 'ora 'i set-¹⁶⁶ keryendo śiknif[i]kar ke syendo 'el 'ombre malo ke no śolo śiknifika apar(')tamyento de la perfeksy'on del 'entendimyento pratiko maś a'un ke tyene abito del kontrary'o 'i śyendo 'inorante ke 'eś la 'inperfeksy'on del 'entendimyento te'oriko vyene 'a morir 'el 'o[m]bre anteś deśu tyenpo a'un ke biba syen mil anyyoś pu'eś kauzo ke le faltaśe tyenpo para alkansar 'el fin para 'el kual fu'e kreado komo tenemoś diǧo kontra lo ke akaese aloś bu'enoś 'i perfektoś ke 'en todo tyenpo ke śe parten de 'eśta vida prezente parten 'ensu tyenpo pu'eś lyegan al fin 'i set- ke la vida no 'eś maś ke 'un medyo para alyegar al byen verdadero 'i kuanto menoś śe detubo kual kyera kaminante 'enel kamino medyanero para legar al fin tan(')to maś loado deve śer 'ensu kaminar 'i por 'eso diǧo porke kyereś morir anteś de tu 'ora¹⁶⁷ no por la kantidad de loś diaś ke muǧoś maloś 'i 'inoranteś vemoś morir kargadoś de diaś śalbo por la falta de 'elyyoś para alkansar 'el fin verdadero ke no lo alkansando ninguno delyyoś śe pu'ede dezir ke śe'a lyeno 'o kunplido de diaś komo por loś bu'enoś śe dize :
   POR 'eśta meśma kabza diǧeron nu'eśtroś śaby'oś śobre 'el diǧo de nu'eśtro śantisimo re'ey David ke śabyen 'el Dyyo loś diaś deloś preniśmoś 'i set-¹⁶⁸ ke komo 'elyyoś śon preniśmoś aśi śuś diaś śon 'en(t)[ǧ]idoś 'i set-¹⁶⁹ palabraś muy dignaś de 'eśkulp(+)irśe 'enel sezo de kada 'ombre 'i resitarśe kada di'a 'i di'a para 'eterna memory'a 'enkuanto 'el mundo turare ke no śe pu'ede kre'er ke todoś loś perfektoś biban vida lu'enga lyena perfekta 'i kunplida 'en kantidad deloś anyyoś konforme aśuś perfeksy'oneś porke halyyamoś muǧoś porfetaś śantoś i perfektoś bibir muy pokoś diaś 'i halyyamoś akelyyo ke ku'enta nu'eśtro Ṭalmud de doś śingularisimoś śenyoreś perfektoś 'en 'eśtremo de bondad 'igual mente amboś doś ke 'el 'uno bibyo muǧoś diaś 'i 'el 'otro pokoś aśi meśmo śi aśentamoś [CW. laś]}

---

¹⁶⁵ Cf. Ben Sira [Ecclesiasticus] 41.1.
¹⁶⁶ Eccles. 7.17.
¹⁶⁷ Eccles. 7.17.
¹⁶⁸ Ps. 37.18.
¹⁶⁹ Gen. R. 58.1.

BOOK OF THE REGIMEN OF LIVING ‹FOL. 43A›

‹fol. 43a›
{MG PEREK ŠᵉLOŠAH ᶜAŚAR [CHAPTER THIRTEEN]
laś vidaś de nu'eśtroś śantoś patryarkaś no muryeron todoś de 'una meśma 'edad avyendo todoś lyegado al 'eśtremo 'i śumo grado dela bondad por donde 'eś forsado keloke diǧeron nu'eśtroś śaby'oś ke loś diaś deloś perfektoś śon 'enteroś 'i kunplidoś[170] nośe 'entyenda por la kantidad deloś diaś śer maś 'o menoś śalbo por aver lyegado todoś 'o tarde 'o tenprano al fin dela ǧornada pu'eś lyegaron al fin dela bondad ke 'a 'elyyoś 'era posible hazyendo 'enelyyo todo śu dever para lo alkansar 'i 'eśto kiǧeron śiknifikar 'en dezir ke aśi komo 'elyyoś śon kumplidoś aśi śe kunplyeron śuś diaś[171] 'i todoś loś bu'enoś ke ala pozada 'i fin del d(v)[e]zeado repozo lyegan no difyeren 'uno de 'otro śalbo ke 'unoś lyegan maś preśto porke śe apreśuraron maś 'a 'andar 'i 'otroś tardan por śer algo maś vagarozoś algunoś lyegan 'enel prinsip[y]'o dela ǧornada algunoś 'enel medyo algunoś 'enel kabo por la diversidad de śuś diśp(+)ozisy'oneś 'i 'en fin todoś lyegan tarde 'o temprano 'i lyegando 'a kual kyera 'ora ke śe'a ateman śu kurso por no aver nesesidad de maś kaminar :

KAPITULO Y–G [13]

VYENDO la probidensyya devina ke 'eś lyegado 'el bu'eno al fin de kuanto pu'ede alkansar 'en kual kyer tyenpo ke śe'a no lo deǧa maś aka 'i lu'ego le traśpone 'enla gloryya 'eterna porke 'el 'eśtar maś aka deśpu'eś de alkansado loke 'eś posible a'el alkansar 'eśta maś kon temor de perdida ke kon 'eśperansa de ganansyya :
KONFORME a'eśto mobyo 'un śavy'o 'ekselente 'en nu'eśtro śanto Ṭalmud 'una dubda śobre akel diǧo ke diśo 'Iyob ke 'en śuś śantoś no konfi'a 'i se-[172] dize ke 'eśte śavy'o kuando śele akordaba de akeśto lyyoraba dubdando 'i dizyendo ke śi 'el Dyyo no konfi'a 'en śuś śantoś 'eneśte mundo de kyen pu'ede konfyar hata ke 'un di'a kaminando por 'un kamino vido 'un 'ombre ke koǧi'a higoś deǧaba loś maduroś 'i tomaba loś duroś diǧole no valen maś loś maduroś reśpondy'o 'el diǧo 'ombre keloś koǧi'a para lyebarloś por 'el kamino 'i por tanto deǧaba loś maduroś ke no śe pu'eden śośtener 'i guardar 'enpero loś duroś śe pu'eden guardar 'entonseś kedo śatiśfeǧo akeśte śenyyor deśu dubda[173] :
'I a'un ke parese por la śuperfisy'a de 'eśtaś palabraś ke 'el kamino śe'a 'enǧenplo

---

[170] Gen. R. 58.1.
[171] Gen. R. 58.1.
[172] Job 4.18.
[173] Ḥagigah 5a.

Book of the Regimen of Living ‹fol. 43a–43b›

ala partida del 'ombre de akeśta vida prezente ala advenidera por lo kual da lugar 'a dubdar ke pareska probar lo kontrary'o deveśe 'entender ke 'eśto no 'eś 'enǧenplo ke śe'a konforme por todaś śuś parteś śalbo ke ku'enta komo śele śatiśfizo la dubda por 'un partikular a'uto ke vido 'en akel 'ombre ke koǧi'a loś higoś [CW. 'i 'eś]}

‹fol. 43b›
{'i 'eś ke akel śenyyor śe marabilyyaba deloś manseboś syendo śantoś porke morian mosoś ke de razon 'el Dyyo loś avi'a de deǧar aka ke 'era syerto delyyoś ke 'obrarian byen 'i loś maloś devi'a lyebar porke 'obran mal la kual dubda le fu'e abśuluta vyendo la 'intensy'on 'i repu'eśta de akel ke koǧi'a loś higoś ke pu'eś no keri'a tomar loś maduroś por reselo ke no śe koronpyeśen porke 'eśtaban maś diśpu'eśtoś para 'elyyo pu'eś ya avian //alkansa(n)do// la perfekśy'on deśu madurasy'on porla meśma kabza kita 'el Dyyo loś śantoś 'iloś treśpone 'i treśpasa deśta vida prezente ala advenidera a'un ke śean manseboś pu'eś an lyegado al fin deśu perfeksy'on 'i 'eśtan de a'i por delante maś 'a riśko de perder ke ganar 'i koneśto kedo byen śatiśfeǧo de manera ke noto dela kabza de deǧar akel tal 'ombre loś higoś maduroś śer akelyya meśma kabza śofisyente para la mu'erte deloś manseboś lyegadoś al grado dela perfeksy'on ke 'eś posible aelyyoś lyegar 'eneśta vida prezente :

'I ǧunto konlo diǧo 'eś maś de śaver ke anśi komo todoś loś śavy'oś reparten la vida 'umana śegun konsidrasy'on de loś anyyoś ke komun mente biven 'en treś partidaś a'umento 'eśtado diklinasy'on 'i 'enla meśma manera śe deve konsidrar 'enel kamino de 'eśta ǧornada para loke konvyene al 'ombre 'en kuanto 'ombre haśta lyegar al fin del byen adkerido ke 'eś prinsipy'o 'i medyyo 'i fin 'enlaś kualeś no śe afigura diklinasy'on kuando śe kamina komo konvyene maś anteś kontino a'umento 'i 'en todaś treś 'eśtansyaś 'eś nesesary'o tener 'el temor del Dyyo komo hito a'el kual 'endereśen todaś laś 'obraś ke 'eśte śolo akatamyento 'eś kabza 'efikaś para nunka 'erar maś anteś kontino 'enderesar al hito dela byen aventuransa 'i 'ultimo byen komo 'el śaby'o re'ey nu'eśtro diǧo 'en todoś tuś kaminoś konośelo 'i 'el ad[e]reśara tuś śenderoś 'i set-[174] keryendo śiknifikar ke tenyendo akatamyento 'a 'el Dyyo komo hito 'en todaś laś kozaś ke 'el 'ombre 'obra ke śean afin de byen 'i śu śervisy'o 'eśte tal akatamyento 'endereśa 'a 'el byen 'i 'eśto kyere dezir 'i 'el 'endereśara konvyene aśaver 'el konosimyento diǧo 'el meśmo 'endereśara 'a 'el kamino dela verdad komo 'el hito 'enloś ke tiran laś śaetaś ke 'el diśponerśe 'en kerer 'endereśar al hito 'eś kabza de dar 'enel 'i tenyendo 'eśte akatamyento 'en toda 'eśta ǧornada no 'eś pośible 'erar :

---

[174] Prov. 3.6.

Book of the Regimen of Living ‹fol. 43b–44a›

'I 'EŚ la primera 'eśtansyya 'en 'el tyenpo de la ninyeś myentraś 'eśta 'el moso soto 'el 'enbezo 'i kryansa deśu madre 'i 'eneśte no 'eś men[e]śter hablar pu'eś al Dyyo grasyaś te halye muy byen kryado 'i byen doktrinado del tyenpo dela ninyeś ke 'eś la primera 'eśtansyya 'i parte del kamino deśta ğornada dela kaduka vida 'i}

‹fol. 44a›
{MD
muğo diśpu'eśto para kaminar maś adelante ala śegunda 'eśtansyya ke 'eś 'el tyenpo dela mosedad deśpu'eś ke 'el moso śale de bağo de laś alaś 'i doktrina dela madre 'i 'el padre 'i śe śomete atoda 'enmyenda 'i kore(p)[k]sy'on 'i kaśtigo del maeśtro ala kual te 'enpeśe 'a 'enkaminar por la vi'a diğa śegun 'el 'orden 'i r[e]ğimyento relatado ke propyya mente konbyene para 'el tyenpo dela mosedad ke 'eś śegunda 'eśtansyya dela deleytoza ğorn[a]da komensurada konel devinisimo byen ke 'enel fin delyya konśiśte 'i paresyendote todo byen keryendo 'uzar kon toda d[i]liğensyya 'i vehemensyya posible me rogaśte telo dyeśe por 'eśkrito para ke meğor lo pudyeśeś konprehender 'i kon todaś tuś fu'ersas abrasar 'i pu'eś konsedi tu demanda vyendo tu bu'en deze'o para todo byen haś[ta] ke tengaś todo lo diğo 'en memoryya 'uzando loś preśeptoś dadoś por 'eśta vi'a ke 'eśkritoś 'eśtan śegiraś fasil mente 'el difisil kamino de la virtud hata lyegar al fin de la ğornada ke 'eś la tersera 'eśtansyya 'i ultima de la vida 'umana 'eneśte mundo la kual konśiśte 'en 'uzar laś 'obraś de virtud moraleś 'i 'intelektualeś 'i guardar loś preśep(+)toś del kamino de nu'eśtra śantisima ley ke aś 'enpeśado ya 'a 'andar por 'elyya :

'I 'en konkluzy'on 'eneśta pośtrera 'eśtansy'a konśiśte 'el 'ultimo byen de la kual tratare 'enla śegunda 'i tersera partida lo maś breve ke śer podra śin nada faltar deloke konvyene śaber para kaminar 'eśte kamino de la korta vida śin yerar ke te hara para śyenpre byen aventurado :

PU'EŚ tenemoś aberiguado 'i de śi 'eśta probado ke kada kual alk[a]nsa del byen verdadero kuanto śegun śu diśpośisy'on 'eś kapaś para alkansar 'i resebir konforme aśu komplisy'on 'i diśpośisy'on śegun ke śe apareğa 'enel tyenpo de la ninyeś 'i mosedad : konvyene poner toda diliğensyya posible 'eneśta prezente 'edad tuyya para hazerte 'enelya diśpu'eśto 'a resebir todo modo de 'eśpikulasy'on loke śi algo varyaśeś 'eneśte tyenpo detu prezente 'edad śeri'a mal 'inkurable komo ya 'en algunaś parteś delo ke tenemoś diğo te tengo amoneśtado 'ila razon d[e]lyyo 'eś muy viśta porke 'el yero ğiko kresyendo de kada veś maś śe haze śin konparasyyon grande 'enel fin ke anśi komo akaese al kaminante ke yerando 'el kamino 'enel prinsipy'o dela ğornada kuanto maś kamina maś śe aparta del kamino dereğo 'i tanto maś difisil le'eś bolber a'el porke 'a meneśter bolver atraś kuanto tyene kaminado aśi śi por śu mala ventura 'i pura deśdiğa 'elke yera de ğu'izy'o 'ino śyente śu yero hata tener kaminado lo maś

Book of the Regimen of Living ‹fol. 44a–44b›

dela ğornada detal manera ke loke keda delyya no baśta a'un para tornar al prinsipy'o 'eś śu mal śin remedy'o śu pasy'on śin konsu'elo 'i śu keğa de baldeś}

‹fol. 44b›
{kerelyyandośe de śi meśmo herido de 'un kru'el aśote śordo kele hyere laś 'entranyaś ro'ido de guzanoś[175] konke śu konsensyya kruda akuzadora deśi meśma komo trasa[176] le karkome loś higadoś pasando śuś triśteś anyoś 'en kontina tribulasy'on no diśtante de la pena 'infernal hata śobre venir kuando no śe kata la triśte noğe 'i 'eśkura ke lyegando tan deśprobe'ido 'en medyo del kamino tan peligrozo muy pokita koza abaśta para derokarlo 'i treśpasarlo deśta korupta vida śuyya 'en 'otra pe'or 'i todo 'eśto kabza śu 'inoransyya 'i 'inadvertensyya 'enel prinśipy'o 'en no atentar byen śu kamino śegun konvyene 'enla mosedad por 'el modo perśupu'eśto 'en laś doś 'eśtansyaś deśta beatisima ğornada

'I nota byen la konparasy'on del kaminante kuando yera 'enel kamino ke tyene muy konforme śemeğansa 'el ke yera 'a 'el kamino de nu'eśtra vida porke śin dubda 'el ke yera 'el kamino dela virtud 'enel prinsipy'o deśu ninyeś śi por deśdiğa perśebera 'ensu mosedad toda ke 'eś la mayor parte del kamino por milagre śe 'eśpera del la 'enmyenda porke 'eś nesesary'o deśnudarse del abito malo ke 'a tomado 'i 'enpesar 'el kamino de nu'ebo dende 'el tyenpo deśu ninyeś koza kazi 'inposible

POR todo lo diğo veraś kuanto deveś abrir loś 'oğoś del 'entendimyento aloś danyyoś torpeś 'i abśurdoś 'i maleś 'inkurableś ke śe śigen de yerar 'i perśeverar 'en'el prezente tyenpo de tu mosedad 'i loś 'oneśtoś proveğoś 'i 'eśtremadoś byeneś 'ekśelenteś aśi para 'el ku'erpo komo para 'el alma ke śe śigen del 'uzo dela dereğa razon konforme aloke tenemoś 'eśkrito 'i aloke 'eśkriviremoś 'enla śegunda partikula ke 'eś la prinsipal 'intensy'on deśte tratado 'i la ke verdader'a mente 'enkamina śin yerar al 'ultimo byen śin falta ninguna 'a kyen por 'elyya ś(+)e kiğere reğir

'I koneśto konkuluyyo la primera partida deśte mi tratado traendote ala memoryya anteś ke 'entre 'enla śegunda 'un śublime diğo del 'Eklizyaśteś donde 'el grande re'ey śumo śavy'o kiğo śiknifikar todo lo diğo 'en muy breveś palabraś dignaś de 'eterna memory'a 'enloś manseboś ke 'a 'elyyoś 'endereso śu habla dizyendo alegrate moso kon tu ninyeś 'i aboniguarte'a tu korason 'enloś diaś de tuś mosedadeś 'i anda 'enloś kaminoś de tu korason 'i 'enla viśta de tuś 'oğoś 'i śave ke śobre todoś 'eśtoś te traera 'el Dyyo 'enel ğu'izy'o 'i set-[177] 'i a'un ke por la śuprefisy'a śola deśtaś

---

[175] Cf. Berakot 18b, Shabbat 152a.
[176] Cf. Is. 51.8.
[177] Eccles. 11.9.

BOOK OF THE REGIMEN OF LIVING ‹FOL. 44B–45A›

śantisimaś palabraś śe nota kuanto 'el mansebo śe deve alegrar konlaś kozaś 'enke konśiśte la verdader'a 'i śolida alegri'a ke 'eś 'el byen verdadero dela meśma alegri'a ke 'el propy'o lo'a 'enel meśmo libro do dize 'i lo'e yyo la alegri'a ke no ayy byen al 'ombre de bašo del śol ke śalbo komer 'i bever 'i alegrarśe [CW. 'i 'elyyo lo]}

‹fol. 45a›
{MH ḤELEK '–PEREK YD [PART ONE CHAPTER FOURTEEN]
'i 'elyyo lo akonpanyyara 'ensu trabaǧo loś diaś de śu vida kele dyyo 'el Dyyo de baǧo del śol 'i set-[178] palabraś muy konformeś anu'eśtra 'intensy'on akyen la verdader'a gloza delyyaś aśep(+)tar kiǧere :

LA kual deklararon nu'eśtroś śaby'oś dizyendo ke toda komida 'i bebida mentada 'eneśte libro no[ ]'eś komida 'i bebida devida al ku'erpo para śu śuśtentasy'on śalbo 'eś komida 'i bebida 'inkorporyya de nu'eśtra Śanta Ley para śuśtentasy'on del alma[179] 'i dizen ke deśta a'utoridad ke alyegada tenemoś śe preba para loś 'otroś lugareś 'i pu'eś 'eśta 'eś 'el fundamyento 'i baziś delaś 'otraś forśado 'eś 'entenderśe 'eneśta forma ke lo'a la alegri'a 'i no la ke konśiśte 'enel byen tranzitory'o śuǧekta aloś śeleśteś śalbo la alegri'a del byen verdadero ke no 'eśta debaǧo delyyoś de manera ke deklara 'el ǧenero konśu diferenśyya : komo śi diǧeśe lo'o yo la alegri'a 'i no toda alegri'a śalbo la keno 'eś del byen ke 'eśta de baǧo del syelo ke śe śiknifika por 'el śol ke 'eś luminary'o mayor[180] śalbo la alegri'a ke 'eś byen ke no 'eśta de baǧo la kośtelasy'on la kual konśiśte 'enel komer deviniśima komida śeleśte de nu'eśtra śantisima ley ke 'eś śiknifikaśy'on aloś perśep(+)toś ke 'enelyya ayy 'i beber del śuabe likor 'i 'ekśelente bebida dela devina 'eśpikulasy'on kontenida 'enla misma ley 'i 'eśto 'eś loke diǧo śalbo por komer 'i beber 'i alegrarśe 'i set-[181] ke 'eśta 'eś la verdader'a alegri'a 'i dize ke 'eśta 'eś la ke akonpanyya al 'ombre 'eneśta vida haśta 'el fin dela ǧornada śin nunka del śe apartar 'en todoś diaś kuantoś kyera ke 'el Dyyo lo deša bibir de baǧo del śol ke 'eś 'eneśte mundo

'I por 'eśta verdader'a gloza deśta grande a'utoridad tubyeron fortisima razon nu'eśtroś śaby'oś de probar daki para loś 'otroś lugareś pu'eś aki 'eś forsado śe ayya de 'entender por la komida 'i bebida del alma 'ino del ku'erpo komo tenemoś diǧo ke 'enelyya konśiśte la glory'a verdader'a :

'I por 'eśta 'eśpesy'a de alegri'a pareśe ke diǧeśe 'el rey Š^{e}lomoh amoneśtando al

---

[178] Eccles. 8.15.
[179] Rashi Eccles. 8.15.
[180] Gen. 1.16.
[181] Eccles. 8.15.

Book of the Regimen of Living ‹fol. 45a–45b›

moso ke śe alegraśe 'enelyya ke 'eśta 'eś la ke abona 'el korason 'enel tyenpo dela mosedad 'i dizele ğunto koneśto ke nole veda de 'andar 'enloke 'el korason 'i la viśta rekyere pero ke śe'a kon tal kondisy'on ke śepa de puro śaber 'i tenga kontino 'en memory'a ke de todo loke vyere 'i diğere 'a de dar ku'enta al tyenpo del ğu'izy'o ke konsidrando 'eśto nunka verna 'a yerar de manera ke tanbyen por loke parese 'a prima viśta por laś muğo 'elebadaś palabraś da regla komun aloś manseboś akonśeğandoloś loke konvyene para 'enderesar a'el kamino dela byen aventuransa ke tenyendo 'en memory'a la ku'enta ke an de dar delaś kozaś ke aka 'obraren delante kyen leś 'a de dar 'el premyyo 'i pena 'enel di'a del ğu'izy'o śera kabza de 'enkaminar al byen verdadero 'i apartarśe del mal :}

‹fol. 45b›
{   KAPITULO KATORZE

ALYENDE de todo lo diğo pyenśo ke kizo maś śiknifikar nu'eśtro monarka aśi de loś re'eyś komo deloś śavy'oś 'eneśtaś perfundaś palabraś la kabza de 'una rezya keśty'on ke muğoś śaby'oś anśi antigoś komo modernoś 'ensu 'eśpikulasy'on tubo śuśpensoś 'i 'eś porke komun mente 'el tyenpo pasado parese meğor ke 'el prezente śi 'eś aśi komo parese 'o śi 'eś 'en todaś kozaś 'igual 'el vulgar diğo 'el 'oriğin de donde mana 'eśto 'eś akel diğo ke 'el meśmo śavy'o rey nu'eśtro 'eśkriby'o 'enel propy'o libro aśerka deśta materyya do dize no digaś ke fu'e ke loś diaś primeroś 'eran meğoreś ke 'eśtoś ke no de parte de śensyya demandaśte 'i set-[182] 'i syerto kual kyera dubdara aprimera viśta 'eneśtaś palabraś porke kabza dize keno deve demandar 'el 'ombre 'eśta tal demanda ke parese śer muy liśito demandar 'ombre la kabza porke loś diaś pasadoś paresen meğor ke loś prezenteś a'un ke 'el kontrary'o śe'a verifikado ke muğoś tyenpoś prezenteś konsidradoś por todaś laś parteś śon meğoreś ke muğoś pasadoś ke 'eśtan a'un 'en memoryya deloś 'ombreś 'i kon todo 'eśo parese meğor lo pasado ke 'el prezente por 'onde 'eśpekular 'en śaver la kabza de tal pareser parese tener muğa parte de razon pu'eś komo defendyyo ke no śe demandaśe tal demanda :

'I ya kele paresyyo la demanda 'indevida devyera deś'eğarla kon fasil 'i klara repu'eśta komo śe śu'ele reśponder aloś ke taleś demandaś porponen 'i no dezir ke no demanda por parte de sensyya ke 'eśto no baśta para śaśtifasy'on ala dubda ni kontentamyento del dubdozo demandador ke śi no le paresyese rezyya razon no demandari'a por donde para todo 'eśto remedyar parese ke kiğo śentir ke 'el tyenpo pasado no parese meğor ke 'el prezente śalbo aserka de laś deleytasy'oneś korporaleś

---

[182] Eccles. 7.10.

Book of the Regimen of Living ‹fol. 45b–46a›

'i kozaś ke śe deleyta 'el 'ombre 'enelyyaś komun mente por parte dela śenśualidad pero 'enlaś kozaś dela deleytasy'on del 'entendimyento ke 'eś la memory'a de kozaś del śaver 'i pura 'eśpikulasy'on laś maś delaś veześ le parese al śavy'o śegundo dereǧa razon meǧor lo prezente ke lo pasado porke kuanto maś va maś prosede 'en kontino a'umento floreśyendo 'enla gloryya 'i 'ekśelensyya del śaver de manera ke de kontino lo pasado 'eś pe'or 'i anśi le parese 'enla memory'a konparando konel prezente deke al prezente śu 'entendimyento śe mantyene śi no fu'ere 'en algunoś 'ignoranteś ke 'en prinsipy'o 'enviśtigaron algo 'i deśpu'eś deǧandolo śe 'olvidan poko apoko delo poko ke śavian ke deśtoś taleś nośe haze kabzo pu'eś 'enpeśaron akonośer 'el byen 'ilo deǧaron por tanto dišo ke no de sensyya demandaśte 'i set-[183] [CW. pu'eś]}

‹fol. 46a›
{M(H)[V] {RMK: count 46a.}
pu'eś syendo verdad ke nunka parese 'el tyenpo pasado meǧor ke 'el prezente śalvo aserka laś deleytasy'oneś korporaleś 'eś byen śaber la kabza porke maś 'en 'uno ke 'en 'otro para ke por laś kabzaś 'entendamoś byen 'el 'efekto 'i laś palabraś del śaby'o :

'I la kabza maś śofisyente ke 'eneśto śe pu'ede dezir śegun razon natural 'eś porke 'el 'ombre kuanto maś kamina 'i 'entra 'enloś diaś tanto śe va apartando de śu prinsipy'o 'i alyegando ala korupsy'on 'i dende 'el di'a ke naśe 'enpesa 'a faltar śu natural kalor 'i 'omido radikal 'eśfryandośe 'i śekandośe de kontino śin seśar por lo kual kada di'a 'i a'un kada 'ora 'i kada momento dende ke naśe śe va malenkonizando ata ke lyege al punto dela mu'erte lyyamada deloś medikoś natural fin 'enlo kual lyega ala fryaldad 'i śekedad 'inkopusible konla vida konforme aloke ya aki tenemoś alyegado de nu'eśtro prinsipe Šᵉlomoh do dize ke maś vale fama ke azeyte bu'eno 'i 'el di'a dela mu'erte ke 'el di'a del nasimyento[184] ke śe pu'ede 'entender 'en śegunda 'intensy'on ke 'eś hazernoś śaber ke 'el di'a dela mu'erte 'enpyesa dende 'el punto ke 'enpyesa 'el di'a del nasimyento 'i set-[185] : para afirmar la śuma bondad 'i śuma deleytasy'on dela fama por parte del 'entendimyento ke tyene diǧo ke śobre puǧa atodaś laś kozaś loke 'eś kontrary'o 'enlaś delektasy'oneś korporaleś por 'enpeśar la k[o]rupsy'on delyaś deśde 'el di'a del nasimyento 'i set-

'I komo śe'a koneśto manifyeśto ke no 'eś 'el 'oǧekto deloś śentidoś korporaleś maś del[e]ktable de kuanto la veluntad 'intrinśika 'eśta alegre porśi 'i kontenta 'i no tanto por parte del meśmo 'oǧekto ke śi 'un 'ombre 'eśta muy triśte 'enśi por kual

---

[183] Eccles. 7.10.
[184] Eccles. 7.1.
[185] Eccles. 7.1.

Book of the Regimen of Living ‹fol. 46a–46b›

kyera koza ke śe'a no le hara 'eśtar alegre 'el 'oğekto aplazible komo la muzika 'o kual kyer 'otro ğenero de deleytasy'on maś anteś diri'a yo le a'umenta la triśteza konforme alo kual pyenso ke śe'a akel diğo del porfeta 'enśuś lamentasy'oneś baldośe 'el gozo de nu'eśtro korason treśtornośe por lemuny'o nu'eśtraś kantablinaś 'i set-[186] ke kyere dezir 'enel punto ke śe kito la alegri'a 'i gozo 'intrinsiko del korason 'el meśmo kantar śe noś traśmudo 'en lemuny'o 'i triśteza ke kuanta deleytasy'on noś daba 'o'ir kantar 'en tyenpo de plazer 'i kontentamyento tanto triśteza noś trae 'el meśmo kantar 'en tyenpo dela pasy'on por donde śe ğuśgara verdader'a mente ke maś deleytable śera al 'ombre kuando la vel[u]ntad 'eśte śatiśfeğa kon 'intrinsiko kontentamyento a'un ke 'el 'oğekto 'i kozaś 'eśtrinsikaś śean laś maś aplazibleś ke pośible fu'ere ke kuando fu'ere 'en kontrary'o porke śin dubda maś plazer terna 'un pobre 'ombre 'o ruśtiko labrador śyendo libre 'i kontento 'en śu 'eśtreğa kazilyya : komyendo pan 'i sebolya durmyendo 'enla nuda tyera [CW. 'i śobre]}

‹fol. 46b›
{'i śobre 'una poka de yerba 'o ğunko veśtido de śayal ke veśtido de purpura 'eśtando prezo 'enloś altoś palasy'oś doradoś komyendo realeś manğareś durmyendo 'en rikoś leğoś 'i presy'ozaś almohadaś ke 'eśte labrador śi prezo śe halyyase kon 'eśte aparato real 'eśtando triśte por śu prizy'on nada le śera delektable anteś śele 'enyadera śu triśteza akordandośele del tyenpo deśu libertad lo meśmo diremoś atodo prinsipe 'i śenyyor de alto 'eśtado ke keri'a 'eśtar libre 'i śano morando 'en 'una kavanyya paśtoril 'o 'en 'una ğośa de ganado fazyendo a'uśt[e]ra vida anteś ke 'enfermo 'o prezo 'en śoberby'oś palasy'oś

PU'EŚ śyendo todo 'eśto verdad manifyeśta 'eś viśta la razon de pareser 'el tyenpo pasado de kontino muğo meğor ke 'el prezente ke komo kyera ke kuanto maś bive 'el 'ombre maś malenkoliko śe faze komo provamoś por la primera porpośisy'on 'i kuanto maś malenkoliko fu'ere tanto menoś deleytozaś le śon laś kozaś 'eśtrinsikaś komo probamoś por la śegunda por tanto le parese de kontino 'el tyenpo pasado meğor 'i maś delektozo ke 'el prezente por śer ke 'enel pasado 'era menoś malenkoliko 'i maś śerka deśu prinsipy'o 'i maś alegre porke la malenkoni'a kabza triśteza komo 'eś manifyeśto de donde vyene ke loś vyeğoś ke 'śon ya muğo malenkonikoś kon ninguna koza 'o kon muy pokaś śe alegran :

'I por 'eśta meśma kabza no 'eśta 'el 'ombre tan alegre la noğe komo 'el di'a ke natural mente por la 'eśkuridad dela noğe 'i rekonśentrasy'on de loś 'eśpritoś 'eśta 'el 'ombre malenkolizado maś ke 'el di'a 'i anśi meśmo 'enel di'a 'eśkuro ke 'eś śemeğante 'a noğe maś ke 'enel klaro 'i 'en 'invyerno 'i a'utono maś ke 'en verano 'i 'eśti'o porke

---

[186] Lam. 5.15.

Book of the Regimen of Living ‹fol. 46b–47a›

'enel 'invyerno śon loś diaś nublozoś muy śemeğanteś 'a noğe 'i 'el 'otony'o 'eś fri'o 'i śeko malenkoniko a'un ke loś tyenpoś muy poko 'inprimen 'enloś 'ombreś 'en reśpekto deloke hazen 'enprinsy'on 'enloś 'otroś animaleś

'I la memory'a del byen pasado 'eś por fu'ersa ke de deleyte ke toda koza 'enla kual kuando 'el 'ombre śe halyya resibe delektasy'on tanbyen la memory'a delyya le'eś aplazible 'i delektoza 'o a'un por ventura maś ke 'en 'el tyenpo ke śe pose'e 'i la razon 'eś ke 'enel tyenpo ke śe toma la posesy'on no śe pu'ede gozar de todo ğunto 'en 'un meśmo punto loke deśpu'eś de pasado reprezenta la memory'a la glory'a de todo ğunta mente hazyendo del pasado prezente

POR 'eśta meśma kabza parese delektoza la memory'a del tyenpo pasado maś ke kuando 'el 'ombre 'eśtaba 'enel meśmo tyenpo 'enel kual kiśa śintycra algun travağo ke ayy 'enel hazer dela 'obra 'enla kual 'esta la delektasy'on

'I daki 'eś byen viśto ke 'enlaś kozaś del 'entendimyento tanto kuanto la materyya śe[ ]va aflakando 'i apartando deśu}

‹fol. 47a›
{MZ
prinsipy'o tanto 'el 'entendimyento 'uza maś perfekta mente śu 'obra haśta ke de tal manera falta la materyya kon śuś korporaleś potensyaś ke no pu'eda 'en modo alguno śervir al 'entendimyento kuyo 'eśturmento 'eś por donde 'el tyenpo prezente aserka dela delektasy'on 'eśpritual parese de kontino meğor kel pasado porke 'el meśmo 'entendimyento 'eśta deśi meśmo por parte deśu perfeksy'on maś kontento ke 'enel pasado komo tenemoś diğo 'i koneśto 'eś viśto loke nu'eśtro śapy'entisimo rey Š[c]lomoh diğo ke no deve dezir 'el 'ombre 'oniversal mente ke 'el tyenpo pasado śe'a meğor ke 'el prez[e]nte porke 'eśta tal demanda kyen la 'oyere śi deśkreto fu'ere ğuśgara kon ğuśto ğu'izy'o ke no demanda 'eśte 'en kozaś de sensya 'i 'eśto podra śer ke kiğeśe dezir 'en dezir keno de sensya demandaśte 'i set-[187] keryendo dezir tal demanda no demandeś porke kyen te 'oyere ğuśgara ke demandaś aserka delaś delektasy'oneś korporaleś 'i no aśerka de kozaś de śensyya por donde śeraś ğuśgado 'inorante :

PERO byen 'eśpekulando kizo maś ke 'eśto śiknifikar 'i 'eś ke kuando 'uno demandaśe la kabza porke aśerka delaś delektasy'oneś korporaleś parese 'el tyempo pasado meğor ke 'el prezente śeri'a lisita demanda pero dezir determinada mente porke 'el tyenpo pasado 'en 'oniversal 'eś meğor ke 'el prezente 'eś 'iny'ota pregunta porke proś[u]pone 'una falsedad ke 'eś śer meğor 'el tyenpo pasado 'el kual no 'eś śino śolo parese śer yeraśe 'enel modo del demandar 'en doś maneraś la primera ke no 'eś 'el tyempo pasado meğor śalbo parese meğor por la kabza diğa śegunda ke a'un ke

---

[187] Eccles. 7.10.

BOOK OF THE REGIMEN OF LIVING ‹FOL. 47A–47B›

fu'eśe aśi verdad 'enloś korporaleś delekteś no śe dira 'en konkluzy'on ke 'eś meğor pu'eś aserka de laś 'eśpritualeś 'i delaś kozaś śy'entifikaś ke 'eś lo prinsipal 'eś meğor 'el tyempo prezente 'i 'eśto 'eś loke kiğo dezir 'enlaś 'enlevadaś palabraś ke alyegamoś ke 'el ke 'oniversal mente diğere ke 'el tyempo pasado 'era meğor ke 'el prezente no lo dize śabyya mente pu'eś ke aserka de kozaś de sensya 'eś 'el kontrary'o ke 'el tyempo prezente 'eś meğor kel pasado pu'eś ke 'enel śe halyya maś śaber 'i 'eś komo śi diğeśe no digaś determinada mente porke 'el tyempo pasado 'eś meğor ke 'el prezente 'i set- pu'eś 'en 'oniverśal 'eś deśkonvenyente la demanda porke 'enla sensya ke 'eś lo prinsipal tyene falasyya :

DE manera ke śe nota de todo lo diğo ke 'el ke śaby'o 'i prudente fu'ere 'i śigyere 'el kamino dela byen aventuransa śe alegrara kontinu'a mente konla memoryya del tyempo pasado paresyendole meğor 'el prezente 'i 'el kontrary'o 'eś kuando parese 'el tyenpo pasado meğor : 'i kon todo lo diğo me parese ke śe 'entendera '[e]l primer diğo 'el kual parese difikultozo ke 'ubyera de dezir alegrate moso kon tu mosedad 'o ninyyo kon tu ninyeś}

‹fol. 47b›
{pero kizo amoneśtar al moso dizyendole ke 'en śu mosedad śigyeśe 'en tal manera 'el kamino dela virtud ke kuando truśere ala memory'a 'el tyenpo dela ninyeś ke 'era falto dela tal virtud no śolo no le śe'a moleśto por parte dela delektasy'on korporal dela kual syendo ninyyo avi'a gozado maś anteś le kavze pura alegri'a por parte dela delektasy'on del 'entendimyento konsidrando la falta delo pasado 'i 'el kunplimyento de perfeksy'on 'enel konforme aśuś 'edadeś por 'el 'orden diğo ke 'uzando delyyoś komo konvyene pu'ede śin reselo 'el moso 'andar 'enloke śu korason le 'enderesare por 'el kamino dela verdad śin yerar :

'I koneśto le konsede al moso ke fu'ere tan bu'eno ke 'enel tyempo deśu mosedad śe alegra konla memory'a del tyenpo deśu ninyeś ke de nota śegir 'en gran manera 'el kamino dela virtud deleytasy'on 'i gloryya del 'entendimyento ke 'eśte tal ande 'en loś kaminoś deśu korason 'i viśta de śuś 'oğoś[188] ke śigyendo 'el 'ekśelente kamino dela razon no pu'ede porelyyoś yerar pu'eś 'eśtan abituadoś 'a 'enkaminar al 'ultimo byen verdadero 'i da la kabza porke le dize ke śiga loś kaminoś deśu korason 'i viśta de śuś 'oğoś[189] dandole 'a 'entender ke 'eśtoś doś 'eśturmentoś śon la kabza aśi para 'el byen komo para 'el mal porke medyante la viśta prinsipal mente vyene la forma 'inkorpore'a 'intelektual komo avemoś deklarado aśerka dela deśkrisy'on 'i regla del dormir :

---

[188] Eccles. 11.9.
[189] Eccles. 11.9.

BOOK OF THE REGIMEN OF LIVING ⟨FOL. 47B–48A⟩

'I konosyendo 'el 'entendimyento la verdad lu'ego la 'envelunta 'i manda komo primero mobidor al korason ke śe mu'eba 'a 'elyya 'el kual komo primer mobile[190] 'i mobidor śegundo mu'ebe todoś loś myenbroś 'i armoni'a 'umana 'a śegir la tal koza bu'ena ǧuśgada del 'entendimyento 'i del meśmo modo 'eś 'enla kabza mala para hu'ir delyya de manera kela viśta mośtro 'a 'el 'entendimyento la koza meǧor ke ningun 'otro śentido por śer maś a'uto miniśtro del 'entendimyento 'i 'el korason fu'e 'el 'eśektor śuyo diliǧentisimo :

'I 'eśto 'eś loke kiǧeron nu'eśtroś śaby'oś śentir 'en dezir kel korason 'i loś 'oǧoś śon doś koredoreś del pekado 'i se-[191] por tanto proteśta nu'eśtro śapy'entisimo rey 'enel fin de śuś palabraś dizyendo 'i śabe ke śobre todoś 'eśtoś te'a detraer 'el Dyyo 'enel ǧu'izy'o[192] keryendo dezir ke tanto para 'el byen komo para 'el mal todo 'el ǧu'izy'o ke śe'a de ǧuzgar 'enel 'ombre por 'el kual śe'a asu'elto 'i kondenado 'a de śer śegun abra 'obrado por medyyo 'i 'enteresisy'on deśtoś doś ke śignifikando todaś laś 'obraś partikulareś delyoś diǧo ke śobre todoś 'eśtoś te traera 'el Dyyo 'enel ǧu'izy'o 'i se-[193]

'I koneśto do fin 'a 'eśta primera partida deśte tratado 'el kual 'eś 'el 'orden dela śegunda 'eśtansy'a deśta peligroza ǧornada [CW. dela]}

⟨fol. 48a⟩
{MḤ {RMK: anthropomorphic bird figures, or flowers, bracket the last lines of Part One and the first lines of Part Two.}
dela breve vida 'enderesada al byen verdadero delektabilisima filisidad 'i glory'a perpetu'a amoneśtandote ke tengaś śyenpre fiśo 'en tu memory'a laś śantisimaś palabraś de nu'eśtro devino rey Šᵉlomoh konsidrando ke śobre todaś laś 'obraś partikulareś 'a de dar 'el 'ombre ku'enta 'i razon delante kyen todo loke 'a noś 'eś pasado 'el futuro konel prezente 'a 'el 'eśta 'en kontina prezensy'a :

'I śobre todo tengaś 'el temor del Dyyo 'i 'amor śoberano delante loś 'oǧoś de tu 'entendimyento[194] para ke śobre todaś laś kozaś lo ameś komo 'a kreador 'i konserbador delyyaś de modo ke 'a 'el komo 'a hito 'endereśeś todaś tuś 'obraś aśu śanto śervisy'o 'i koneśto biviraś byen aven(in)turado 'i glory'ozo :

FIN DELA PRIMERA PARTIDA DEL REǦIMYENTO

---

[190] An allusion to Aristotle, *De Anima* III.ix (432b 31) and/or *Physics* VIII.v (258b, 256b).
[191] Num. R. 10.2.
[192] Eccles. 12.14.
[193] Eccles. 12.14.
[194] Cf. Ps. 36.1.

PARTIDA ŚEGUNDA

KAPITULO PRIMERO

DEŚPU'EŚ de ya kaminada la śegunda 'eśtansyya del kamino de nu'eśtra vida śin yerar ni 'eseder dela regla 'i reğimyento preśupu'eśto śyendo ya abituado 'a kontraśtar 'el 'apetito por la doktrina śuzo diğa śete hara maś fasil la tersera 'i 'ultima deśte beatisimo kamino hata 'el fin dela ğornada para aśomar ala śublime pozada dela filisidad 'i hartura del byen verdadero 'onde haze śu abitasy'on la śapyensyya adonde 'eś 'el refriğery'o 'i repozo para laś almaś kansadaś del trabağo del kamino pasado kontraryando giryando konel 'apetito konkupisible 'i '

'I porke 'eśta 'ultima 'eśtansyya ke keda hata 'el fin deśta tan peligroza ğornada śepaś śin 'erar anśi byen komo lo de hata aki te kyero dar 'una regla komun konvenyente a'elyya 'i konforme alo p[a]sado 'enel 'orden keloś śaby'oś filosofos moraleś dyeron para moderar 'el śenśual 'apetito deklarandote muy brebe mente doze vertudeś moraleś 'i śuś visy'ozoś 'eśtremoś para ke del mal te śepaś guardar 'i śegir 'el kamino dela virtud 'i konoseraś 'el grande probeğo ke trae atu preśona}

‹fol. 48b›
{ḤELEK B- PEREK '- [PART TWO CHAPTER ONE]
para ke bivaś tuś diaś 'enla śuma delektasy'on dela 'oneśtidad 'i vida perfekta tanto kuanto 'eś al kontrary'o 'enel malo ke śige 'el kamino 'individo andando komo syego 'en kontino 'eror 'i trabağo deśu triśte alma meśklado konel 'enganyozo korporal delekte 'enpeśando 'a resebir 'el kaśtigo de śu lokura :

'I 'eśto kizo śentir 'el śanto profeta // (Y^eśa^cyahu) [Yirm^eyahu] // dizyendo kontra 'el malo kaśtigarte'a tu mal 'i tuś rebely'oś te kaśtigaran 'i śave 'i ve'e ke malo 'i amargo tu değar 'a ‹Adonay› 'i set-[1] keryendo dezir ke 'el dolor 'i pasy'on ke 'el malo

---

[1] Jer. 2.19.

Book of the Regimen of Living ⟨fol. 48b⟩

tyene 'entreśi hazyendo 'el mal komo diğo nu'eśtro devino śalmiśta muğaś doloreś 'a 'el malo 'i set-[2] syendo taleś doloreś kabzadoś del mal śe halyya ke 'el meśmo mal kaśtiga 'i da pena 'a 'el malo de modo ke 'el meśmo śera la pena deśtruyendośe 'i konronpyendośe perśeverando 'enśuś 'inormeś 'eroreś 'i no śe 'enmendando delyyoś de manera ke de śegir 'el 'indibido kamino śe śigen al malo doś 'inkonvenyenteś muy manifyeśta mente maloś 'uno 'obrar de kontino 'el meśmo mal alo kual śyempre porśu 'inpotensyya 'eśta diśpu'eśto 'i 'eśte 'eś 'el prinsipal 'i 'otro la amargura 'i dolor anešo 'a 'el mal 'i ke śyenpre komo śolombra lo śige 'i 'eśto 'eś loke kiğo śignifikar 'el śanto profeta doblando 'i dizyendo 'i śabe 'i ve'e ke malo 'i amargo 'i set-[3] keryendo dezir ke aserka del mal para konoserlo 'eś nesesary'o śaber ke vyene por parte de tinyebla 'i śegedad del 'entendimyento ke 'eś la 'ignoransyya de mala afiksyyon la kual śe haze krasa 'i supina konronpyendo 'i a'un privando todo bu'en ğu'izy'o ke 'eś 'el don mayor ke 'el alto śenyyor dyo al 'ombre para lo aber de śervir por lo kual diğo 'i śabe 'i set-[4] ke 'eś koza ke depende del 'entendimyento pratiko por razon de byen 'o mal 'i aserka del dolor 'i triśteza ke śele śige de 'obrar 'el mal komo tenemoś diğo ke 'eś koza śensible 'i viśta al 'oğo ke no kabe debašo de razon de śaber diğo 'i ve'e 'i set-[5] :

'I konprendyendo 'i 'eśpisifikando loś doś maleś 'i 'inkonvenyenteś diğoś dišo ke malo 'i amargo 'eś tu dešar 'a H⟨a-Šem⟩ 'i set- keryendo dezir lo diğo ke alyende de 'obrar 'el mal 'eś amargo por 'el dolor 'i triśteza ke del śe śige 'i konkluyo todo ğenero de malisyya kuanto śe pu'ede figurar 'en dezir 'entu değar al Dyyo 'i set- 'i no mi temor ati 'i set-[6] śiknifikando ke todo 'obrar mal 'eś no temer del Dyo 'i todo değar de hazer byen 'eś değar al Dyyo 'ino amarlo ke 'eśtaś doś kozaś konprenden todo ğenero de malisyya 'i diferenteś 'eśpesyaś de torpeś visy'oś ANŚI komo konel temor 'i 'amor del Dyyo glory'ozo śe konfirma todo 'el byen verdadero 'i fin 'umano komo larga mente tengo 'eśkrito śilo kyereś ver 'enel nobeno dela 'etika komento 'oktabo kon graviśimaś a'utoridadeś de nu'eśtra śantisima ley 'i de nu'eśtroś devinoś profetaś[7] a'un ke 'enśi 'eś 'ividente alke tyene klaridad konke ver lo pu'eda ke no tyene 'el 'ombre del śer 'i śuma bondad}

---

[2] Ps. 32.10.
[3] Jer. 2.19.
[4] Jer. 2.19.
[5] Jer. 2.19.
[6] Jer. 2.19.
[7] He refers to *Pne Moše*. The Aristotle passage would be *NE* IX.v.9–10 (1166b 20–29).

Book of the Regimen of Living ‹fol. 49a–49b›

‹fol. 49a›
{MT
maś de kuanto partisipa konel Dyyo 'en śu devino 'amor ke 'eś 'el fin 'i 'ultimo byen de todaś kozaś digo 'ultimo 'enel adkerir a'un ke primero 'enla dignidad : 'i 'el mober 'i atraer todaś laś kozaś 'entre medyaś para śi 'eneśto no 'eś meneśter maś dezir ke 'elyyo porśi śe manifyeśta :
'I anteś ke 'entre ala deśkripsy'on 'i 'orden delaś vertudeś 'en partikular te kyero hazer śaber 'una koza śola ke konvyene śer śabida para 'entender loke adelante kyero dezir porke no kayaś 'enel yero ke algunoś 'ignoranteś por deśkulparśe 'enel mal kiğeron dezir 'i 'eś ke algunoś kon 'eronea 'i nefanda 'opiny'on prezumyeron por parte dela śenśualidad de śuśtentar ke todo 'ombre fu'eśe forsado 'en todaś śuś 'obraś porke loś bu'enoś por parte de 'un devino 'enflušu dende ke nasyeron 'eran bu'enoś 'i komo 'eśte 'enflušu 'i lumbre devino falta 'enloś maloś por parte del fado 'o deśu natural konplisy'on falta delyoś 'el 'obrar byen aśi ke śegun 'eśto 'el 'ombre nase felise 'o 'infelise 'i set- :
ŚEGUNDA śekta 'ubo ke śe kiğeron śalbar kon 'un śofiśtiko argumento para koroborar śu flakeza 'i 'eś ke pu'eś 'el Dyyo śabe lo futuro śin dubda alguna lu'ego loke śabe 'eś forsado aver de śer śino fu'eśe posible aśi para śer komo para no śer pu'ede akaeser ke loke 'el Dyyo śabe no śe'a de manera ke koneśta tan aparente razon paresyendole śalvar 'el śaber del Dyyo kon negar la libertad 'umana dada dela 'infinita bondad 'i devino śaber negaron la alta probidensy'a devina la śuma ğuśtisy'a 'en dar pena 'i glory'a akyen la merese 'i 'el meśmo śaber ke tanto leś paresy'o ke afirmaban tanbyen negaron ke 'eś 'inposible aver 'infinito śaber adonde no 'ubyere 'infinita bondad 'i 'infinita probidensy'a para dar 'a kada 'uno śegun śu merito :
'UBO 'otra tersera 'opinyyon la kual agora 'en algunoś modernoś ğentileś floreśe ke kyeren no aver libertad de 'eliksy'on 'enel 'ombre 'en 'obra alguna ke haga porke afirman todaś laś veluntadeś 'umanaś śer mobidaś de nesesidad del 'obğekto aśi komo laś deloś brutoś animaleś para preva deśto trušeron algunaś aparenteś razoneś delaś kualeś 'opiny'oneś 'el Dyo por śu śanta merse[d] 'i pyadad noś libre :
'ENEŚTAŚ doś pośtreraś 'opiny'oneś no hablare porke śeri'a meneśter muğo alargar para fartarśe la veluntad 'enelyyo śolo te digo ke śepaś ke kuanto diğ[e]ron 'i pensaron fu'e yero manifyeśto 'i no kale dezir kuan manifyeśta la verdad 'eś aloś alumbradoś dela luz devina de nu'eśtra śantisima ley [CW. maś]}

‹fol. 49b›
{maś a'un aloś antigoś filosofoś 'i modernoś alumbradoś konla śentelyya del lumbre dela naturaleza dada del Dyyo fu'e muy konosido :
'I kuando keraś śaber laś verdaderaś razoneś por 'eśtenso por donde loś reprobamoś konputando kuanto diğeron te le'ere loke 'enel komento tersero del tersero de

BOOK OF THE REGIMEN OF LIVING ‹FOL. 49B›

la 'etika[8] tengo 'eśkrito 'onde 'eśta byen viśta la deśtru'isy'on de laś doś 'ultimaś 'opiny'oneś 'i deśbaratadoś śuś simyentoś 'i prinsipy'oś por laś meśmaś razoneś konke laś pensaron afirmar 'i 'enel meśmo lugar tengo tambyen deklarado la śegunda 'opiny'on konforme aloke algunoś letradoś 'i moraleś filosofoś 'enelyyo 'eśkribyeron loś kualeś tokaron byen 'eneśta materyya ǧunto konlaś muy śantaś 'i dignaś palabraś del śenyy(y)or Rabbenu Mošeh 'enel kapitulo y-t [19] dela tersera partikula del Moreh ke pu'eśto ke algunoś śenyyoreś kiǧeron dezir ke 'el śenyyor Rabbenu Mošeh deǧo la dubda 'indiśiza 'en dezir no śabemoś 'el modo de śu śaber del Dyyo[9] pyenso yo ke 'eneśtaś palabraś reśpondyyo 'i konprehendyyo kuanto 'eneśte kazo śe podi'a reśponder 'i 'eś lo meśmo ke 'el śanto profeta Y^eša^cyahu reśpondyyo aniǧilando la dubda 'en muy kortaś p[a]lab(')raś diǧaś por la boka devina do dize porke diześ Ya^cakob 'i fablaś Yiśra'el 'enkubryyośe mi karera de ‹Adonay› 'i de mi Dyyo mi ǧu'izy'o pasara śi no śupiśte śino 'o'iśte Dyyo del mundo ‹Adonay› 'i set-[10] primera mente śe keša kontra kual kyera de nu'eśtra nasyyon higoś de nu'eśtro śanto patryarka Ya^cakob komo 'a de kaver tan grande yero ke dubde tal dubda 'i pone 'el 'orden dela dubda por la razon kontraryya dizyendo ke no pu'ede dešar de śer 'una de doś kozaś 'o ke no śabe 'el Dyyo loś feǧoś deloś 'ombreś 'o śilo śabe 'uza śin ǧuśtisyya ponyendo loś maloś por loś maleś ke hazen pu'eś 'eś forsado hazerloś 'i 'eśto 'eś loke dize amoneśtandoleś kontra tan torpe razon porke diześ Ya^cakob 'i se-[11] 'enkubryyośe mi karera de ‹Adonay›[12] 'i de mi Dyyo mi ǧu'izyyo pasara[13] ke 'en nu'eśtra śantisima lengu'a la konǧunsy'on 'i śe pone por 'o 'i klara mente śe mu'eśtra 'eśto 'enla śanta ley do dize 'i firyen aśu padre 'i aśu madre 'i se-[14] ke 'eś komo śi diǧeśe 'o aśu madre 'i anśi 'en 'otroś luga(l)[r]eś dela ley 'i deśpu'eś ke 'a moneśtado por admiratiba 'enterogasyyon la dubda no para śaverla śino para deklarar la akyen no la śabe kon toda 'efikasyya reśponde loke 'el śenyyor Rabbenu Mošeh dize dizyendo śino śupiśte śi no 'o'iśte[15] konkluyendo ke no ayy fin aśu śaver 'infinito 'inkonprehensible 'a todo 'entendimyento kreado aśi 'umano komo anǧeliko 'i todo kuanto 'imaǧinar śe pu'ede śino aśi meśmo para koneśto poder argu'ir al kontradezidor ke śi śupyeśemoś 'o alkansaśemoś śaber veriamoś 'i alkansariamoś 'ividente

---

[8] He refers to *Pne Moše*. The Aristotle passage would be *NE* III.v.23 (1157a 4–7).
[9] Maimonides, *Guide*, trans. Pines, 483 (*MN*, Pt. 3 chap. 20).
[10] Isa. 40.27–28.
[11] Isa. 40.27.
[12] Isa. 40.27.
[13] Isa. 40.27.
[14] Exod. 21.15.
[15] Isa. 40.28.

mente śin aver 'en noś flakeza para dubdar śer verdad ke śobre śer śabedor de todo lo venidero 'eterna mente śyendo abeterno a'el todo prezente keda la posiblidad 'enla koza śin}

‹fol. 50a›
{N
ke por manera ninguna falte de śer loke 'el śabe 'i 'el kontrary'o nunka śera a'un ke śe'a posible aver de śer 'i śi byen abryereś loś 'oğoś de 'el 'entendimyento 'i parareś muy byen myenteś 'en todaś 'eśtaś brebeś palabraś ke diğe halyy[a]raś de todo abśuluta la dubda
'I para ke algo maś lo 'entyendaś a'un ke 'en 'otraś parteś lo tengo byen aklarado te dire la konkluzy'on dela aśulusy'on 'en breve 'i 'eś ke anśi komo śi 'un 'ombre 'eśtubyeśe hazyendo 'un a'uto 'en prezensyya de 'otro kual kyera ke śe'a ke 'eśte mirando komo 'el 'otro haze śu a'uto no śe dira ke akel ke 'eśta mirando por śu mirar haze śer akel a'uto forsada mente porke 'eś byen viśto ke mirarlo 'uno 'eśtando 'obrando 'otro no le fu'ersa 'a ke śe'a 'o ke deśe de śer akel tal a'uto heğo kon toda la libertad posible ke la viśta del ke lo ve'e no 'inpide 'enel 'i 'eśto 'eś anśi manifyeśto 'i no ayy nesesidad de probarlo aśi meśmo nośe pu'ede dezir ke değe de śer akel tal a'uto 'enla 'ora ke 'eś 'i delante la viśta de kyen lo ve'e śe reprezenta por ningun ku'ento ke śeri'a śer 'i no śer 'en 'un meśmo punto de manera ke toda futura posiblidad śe haze nesesidad prezente por śupuzisy'(y)[o]n 'enla 'ora keśe haze komo 'eś viśto por Aristotel 'enśu Peri'ermin(y)aś[16] :
FIGURANDO 'enel meśmo modo 'enel śaber del Dyyo glory'ozo śe ve'e manifyeśta mente la asulusy'on dela dubda 'i 'eś ke komo 'el Dyyo benedito porśi meśmo ve'e todaś laś kozaś paśadaś 'i prezenteś 'i futuraś komo todoś loś śaby'oś 'eśkribyeron ke 'enel no śe afigura pasado ni venidero śino 'un prezente 'eterno 'i muy 'elebado 'i ağeno de nu'eśtro fuğitibo prezente konpu'eśto de pasado 'i futuro 'el kual śe lyyama 'inśtante de 'eternidad[17] no deśtinto del meśmo Dyyo lu'ego anśi komo nu'eśtra viśta 'enel prezente no fu'ersa 'el a'uto 'eśtando mirando komo lo haze śu a'[u]tor anteś keda 'enśu posibilidad 'i nada kita del vigor poder 'i libertad ke 'el a'utor tyene para lo hazer aśi no maś ni menoś vyendo 'el Dyyo 'el a'uto 'umano anteś ke śe haga 'el kual ve'e por 'el śer śuma kabza de todaś laś kozaś 'i todoś loś medyoś por 'onde 'el 'obrador 'a de 'obrar le śon manifyeśtoś ninguna nesesidad pone 'enel 'obrador 'i nada kita deśu poder 'i libertad 'i anśi komo loke akel 'ombre ke diğimoś ve'e a'el 'otro 'obrar akelyyo 'eś loke śe 'obra 'i 'eśta hazyendo no lo kontrary'o aśi

---

[16] Aristotle, *Peri Hermeneias* (On Interpretation), chap. 9.
[17] Cf. Boethius, *Consolation of Philosophy* V pr. 6.

Book of the Regimen of Living ⟨fol. 50a–50b⟩

loke 'el Dyyo ve'e akelyyo 'eś loke śe hara porke la mente dev[i]na lo ve'e 'i non śe 'obrara lo kontrary'o 'i kuanto a'eśto no difyere 'el ver delo venidero 'enel Dyyo bendito del ver 'enel prezente de kual kyera 'ombre :}

⟨fol. 50b⟩
{   PERO atyenta 'i abre byen loś 'oǧoś del sezo ke 'en doś kozaś difyeren muy muǧo la primera ke 'el Dyyo deś(+)u abśuluto poder pu'ede 'inpedir 'eśte a'uto ke 'el 'otro nolo haga 'i mudarle 'el perpozito para 'otra koza loke 'un 'ombre no hara 'a 'otro la śegunda ke 'el 'ombre ke 'eśta 'obrando vyendole 'el 'otro a'un ke 'obre libre mente 'i pu'eda śesar dela 'obra ke haze pu'eś 'obra 'en tyempo loke ya paso 'enla 'obra lo kual lyamamoś prezente porke toda 'obra prezente 'eś kompu'eśta de pasado 'i futuro 'eś 'inposible no śer porke ya 'eś forsado por śu posisy'on 'ino pu'ede no śer kuando ya 'eś 'enpero loke 'el Dyyo ve'e porke a'un no 'eś ni a'un tyene śuś kabzaś 'enla naturaleza delaś kozaś a'un ke śyenpre 'eśten 'enla mente devina pu'ede no śer 'i 'eśta posiblidad nunka verna 'en a'uto porke no pu'ede venir śin śuś kabzaś laś kualeś a'un ke 'eśten 'enel 'umano poder nunka konkuriran a'eśte 'efekto porke 'eśte 'umano poder 'a de poner toda śu libertad 'en kerer 'el kontrary'o alo kual no halyyara 'inpedimyento ke aśi lo 'eśta vyendo 'el Dyyo

'I loke anoś 'eś 'okulto 'i de todo punto 'enkubyerto 'eś śaber komo 'el futuro 'eś 'a 'el Dyyo bendito prezente 'eternal mente ke no lo podemoś kontenplar ni afigurar komo 'el Dyyo no śe pu'eda dezir 'eśtar 'en tyenpo por śer noś aǧentes finitoś 'obradoreś 'en tyenpo 'i 'eś 'okulto 'a noś 'i aloś profetaś 'i anǧeleś śegun maś 'o menoś partisipan del alto śaber del Dyyo porke ninguno perfekta mente lo pu'ede kontenplar 'i śolo 'el kreador de todoś 'eś deśto śabedor ke śi noś śupyesemoś 'el modo de śu śaber 'o komo lo venidero 'eś 'en puro a'uto prezente 'enśu śaber veriamoś 'i alkansariamoś 'ividente mente ke dela meśma manera ke akaese anoś 'enloke vemoś p(+)rezente anoś aśi 'eś 'ensu śaber 'en loke anoś 'eś venidero del modo ke diǧimoś pero komo śu śaber 'iśu 'eśensyya 'eś todo 'uno 'en pura 'unidad anśi komo śu 'eśensyya 'eś 'okulta 'a noś ke no abaśta nu'eśtro flako 'inǧeny'o por ninguna vi'a poder lo alkansar dela meśma manera 'eś 'okulto śu śaber śolo śavemoś syerto ke komo śu śer 'eś śyempre 'infinito 'inmutable aǧeno de tyenpo komo śenyyor 'i kreador del aśi 'eś śu śaber purisimo 'independente no komo 'el nu'eśtro 'el kual depende del śer dela koza 'i 'eś forsado dela fu'ersa del śer dela meśma koza 'i muǧaś veześ śabemoś koza ke no keriamoś ke fu'eśe aśi 'i 'eśta materyya deloś futuroś kontinǧenteś deklare 'enel kapitulo ḳ-z- [27] del Bederśi[18] hablando de 'eśte śaber del Dyyo

---

[18] This may be a reference to Bedersi's *Beḥinat Olam* (*Examination of the World*). However, it may equally pertain to one of his several commentaries on the intellect: see *EJ* 9:1309. Abeles suggests it refers to *Sefer ha-Pardes*.

BOOK OF THE REGIMEN OF LIVING ‹FOL. 50B–51A›

glory'ozo pero śaber komo lo śabe kyero dezir komo lo venidero 'a noś a'el 'eś prezente : [CW. 'eśto]}

‹fol. 51a›
{N' ḤELEK B- PEREK B- [PART TWO CHAPTER TWO]
'eśto no podemoś śaber por nu'eśtro śaber śer muy diferente del śuyo ke a'un ke 'en reśpekto de nu'(v)[e]śtro śaber 'inposible śer lo futuro prezente 'en śu śaber no 'inplika kontradisy'on por no 'eśtar de bağo del tyenpo 'i 'eśto 'eś loke kiğo śentir 'el śenyyor Rabbenu Mošeh dizyendo ke 'eś diferente śu śaber 'infinito del nu'eśtro komo la diferensyya del syelo ala tyera[19] ke ninguna porprosy'on guardan 'i puzo 'eśta konparasy'on a'un ke śe'a 'en kozaś finitaś por no halyyar kozaś 'enke pu'eda kaber 'eśta deśemeğansa del śaber del Dyyo al nu'eśtro kon mayor śemeğansa de verdad ke 'enel syelo 'i tyera donde todoś nu'eśtroś śantoś doktoreś toman śuś konp[a]raśy'oneś del Dyyo 'a noś 'i a'un ke maś loğika mente tengo diśkutida 'eśta materyya 'enel diğo komento dela 'etika[20] ponyendo maś por 'eśtenśo la dubda 'iśu śulusy'on śin ke ningun 'ombre ya maś tenga razon de dubdar viśto 'a 'oğoś de kual kyera ke 'enel 'eśpeğo dela verdad kera mirar todo fundado śobre laś meśmaś palabraś del śenyyor Rabbenu Mošeh para 'el prezente baśta byen lo diğo parando byen myenteś 'enelyyo ğunto kon loke algo maś te deklare 'enla 'eśpozisy'on del diğo kapitulo del Bederśi 'i a'un 'eśto note kiğera 'eśkrivir ke no 'eś de mi kondisy'on tratar muğo deśtaś tan śutileś materyyaś fu'era deśu lugar pero hizelo porke vide kuando te le'i akel kapitulo dubdabaś 'en algunaś kozaś ke por no śaber 'el 'oriğin de adonde manavan me paresy'o ke kedavaś algo śuśpenso delo kual muğo temi no te kedaśe algun 'eror 'enel 'entendimyento 'i 'el poko 'eror 'en taleś kozaś 'eś komo 'el kaer de muy alto 'i aśi komo 'el ke kamina por 'una ku'erda 'o viga ke 'eśtando muy alto anda muğo atento reselando 'en grande manera la kaida del meśmo modo śe deve atentar 'i reselar 'eneśtaś materyaś fundadaś ke tratan del Dyyo para ke nada śe hable temeraryya mente 'i de todo loke kedareś dubdozo 'i poko śatiśfeğo dimelo śin reselo ke yo fartare tu śed śino baśtare lo diğo ke 'en todo tengo 'eśkrito 'en muğaś 'i diversas parteś muğo por 'eśtenso :

---

[19] Maimonides, *Guide,* trans. Pines, 483 (*MN,* Pt. 3, chap. 20) (cf. Isa. 55.9).
[20] This is a reference to *Pne Moše.*

BOOK OF THE REGIMEN OF LIVING ‹FOL. 51A–51B›

KAPITULO ŚEGUNDO

'I loke konvyene śaber para deśtru'isy'on dela primera 'opiny'on te dire 'en brebe para lo kual aś de ad(y)vertir primero ke la ayuda 'o 'influ'ens[y']a devina 'enloś 'ombreś 'eś 'una grasya ke loś antigoś te'ologoś lyamaron luz devina 'influ'ida dela prima kauśa[21] 'enel 'entendimyento 'umano 'i algunoś kiğeron dezir śer 'influ'ida de 'una 'entiliğensyya ke ponen de bağo 'el konkabo dela 'eśfera dela luna ke fu'e 'opiny'on de Abisena 'i śigela 'el śenyyor Rabbenu Mošeh[22] la kual yo no kre'o ni p[y]enso aver nesesidad de(') kr[e]'erśe ke todaś laś kauzaś por laś kualeś śe fundaron śer forsado averśe de poner me pareśe aver śalvado 'ensu lugar [CW. komo]}

‹fol. 51b›
{komo kyera ke śe'a 'eśte modo de luz konel 'entendimyento 'umano 'enğenplifikaron algunoś modernoś ala luz del śol konla viśta 'umana komo deklaramoś śobre 'el tersyyo de la 'etika[23] ke anśi komo loś rayoś del śol klarifikan 'el ayyre ke 'eś 'el medyo por donde śu 'obğekto śe reprezenta ala viśta 'umana aśi 'eś akelyya devina luz 'i klaridad ke 'eśklareśe 'el 'entendimyento por 'entersisyyon de la kual pu'eda byen 'entender laś kozaś 'obğektaś śi śe diśponyere 'a 'elyyo 'i anśi komo deśpu'eś de klaro 'el ayyre 'eśta 'en pura libertad del 'ombre kerer ver 'el 'obğekto 'o serar loś 'oğoś 'i apartarśe 'i no lo ver aśi 'eśta 'en mano del 'ombre değar de 'entender 'el byen 'i dešar de śegirlo śino śe diśpone a'elyyo pero keryendo 'el 'ombre śegirlo por luz 'i klaridad del 'entendimyento 'influ'ida de la kabza primera nunka falta porke 'eśta luz nunka manka ni ğamaś mankara para aprobeğ(r)ar 'a kuantoś delyya aprobeğar śe kiğeren aśi komo por parte de la diśposisyyon del ayyre ke 'eśtando 'el śol śobre la tyera 'en ningun tyempo falta la perfeksy'on para la viśta 'i 'eśto 'eś loke nu'eśtroś śaby'oś kiğeron śiknifikar dizyendo ke 'el ke vyene 'a śer perfekto 'i linpy'o[24] le ayudan 'i set-[25] keryendo dezir ke no faltandole 'eśta klaridad 'eś grande ayuda para la viśta 'intelektual 'i konforme 'a 'eśto dizen ke śi kyere śer malo le dešan abyertaś laś pu'ertaś deśu libertad[26] p[o]r la vi'a ke 'enğenp(+)lifikamoś :

---

[21] Cf. Aristotle, *Metaphysics,* XII.vii.9 (1072b 29–31).
[22] Cf. Maimonides, *Guide* II.30, trans. Pines, 352.
[23] A reference to *Pne Moše*, the Aristotle reference would be *NE* III.iii.4 (1112a 25–26).
[24] Cf. Ps. 24.4.
[25] Avodah Zarah 55a, Menaḥot 29b.
[26] Avodah Zarah 55a, Menaḥot 29b.

Book of the Regimen of Living ⟨fol. 51b–52a⟩

DE manera ke akaese 'enel byen 'i mal dela forma ke diremoś konforme al śentido del ve'er komo tenemoś diğo 'i 'eś ke kuando 'el 'ombre 'obra 'el byen 'eś 'el prinsipy'o del por parte dela luz devina aśi komo lo primero ke śe rekyere para 'el ver 'eś la klaridad del medyo traśparente śin la kual nośe pu'ede reprezentar 'el 'obğeto 'enla viśta a'un ke 'el śentido del ver śe'a 'el maś perfekto ke śer pudyere 'i deśpu'eś de produzido 'el byen por medyyo dela luz prosede de a'i por delante por parte del 'ombre meśmo abyendo śyenpre klaridad ke mu'eśtre 'el byen aśi komo 'el ver depende del śentido ke ve'e deśpu'eś dela klarifikasy'on 'i a'uta diśposisy'on del ayyre la kual nunka 'a de faltar para reprezentar 'el 'obğekto 'enel śentido 'i kuando 'obra 'el mal prosede 'el prinsipy'o 'i 'el fin todo del 'ombre meśmo ke no falta nada por parte dela luz 'i 'influ'ensy'a devina aśi komo kuando 'el 'ombre syera loś 'oğoś 'i śe aparta 'i no kyere ver 'el 'obğekto 'eśtando 'el ayyre muy klaro ke 'en tal kazo 'el prinsipy'o de dešar de ver 'i 'el fin ke 'eś perseverar 'enla 'eśkuridad todo prosede del meśmo 'ombre śin partisipar 'enelyyo koza 'eśt[e]ry'or porke 'eśta luz devina 'eś dada 'a todo 'ombre :}

⟨fol. 52a⟩
{NB
tanta kuanta abaśta para byen bivir a'un ke 'a 'otroś 'i 'eśto śe ve'e klaro porke no ayy 'ombre ke no tenga 'eśta luz [la] kual nunka pyerde śino śi deśu libre veluntad śe katiba tanto deloś pekadoś ke no śele reku'erde aver a'i Dyyo 'i keda heğo abominable 'i perdido porśi meśmo de todo punto śin redensy'on
'I a'un ke loś 'ombreś tengan diversoś planetaś 'enśuś nasimyentoś 'i diversaś konpli(n)śy'oneś por parte dela kabza 'infiry'or todoś śon dotadoś deśta śantisima 'i 'inmakulada luz devina medyo para todo byen konla kual śino syeran loś 'oğoś veran loś altoś koloreś de toda bondad 'i ninguno deśu natureza 'eś diśpu'eśto para mal por parte del hado 'o dela konplisy'on pu'eś tyene 'eśta luz kuanto maś ke ni 'el hado ni konplisy'on fu'ersa aninguno 'a hazer koza diśforme ala dereğa razon komo śi kiğereś klaro por razon metafizika te prebare kuando kiğereś lo kual aki dešo por hu'ir proliğidad
'I bolbyendo al perpozito digo keśe konsidra 'enel byen 'i mal b- [2] terminoś 'uno 'inisyatibo 'otro final 'i aśi 'enloś byeneś komo 'enloś maleś 'eś la kabza del fin delyyoś digo de 'obrar 'el byen 'o 'el mal 'el meśmo 'ombre pero 'enloś byeneś 'eś 'el 'ombre medyante la luz devina ke lo akonpanyya de manera ke 'en todaś śuś 'obraś tyene al Dyyo por konpanyero 'i 'enloś maleś 'eśta luz 'i grasyya del Dyyo 'eś por de maś ke 'el a'utor del mal no goza delyya ke 'el malo 'eś la pura kabza de śu maldad 'i no 'otro alguno 'i 'el bu'eno kabza deśu byen a'un ke śyenpre konel konkure la devina luz kelo 'enderesa medyante 'el Dyyo ke 'eś kabza prinsipal para la 'obra bu'ena komo la luz ke haze ke 'el kolor 'en potensyya śe'a kolor 'en a'uto komo śe

BOOK OF THE REGIMEN OF LIVING ‹FOL. 52A–52B›

dize 'en śegundo de anima 'i 'eś prinsipal 'enel hazer 'el kolor 'i no la viśta[27] :
A'UN ke de prinsipy'o śyenpre 'el Dyyo ayya konkurido kon 'el bu'eno 'a hazer 'el byen 'i śe'a prinsipal 'enelyyo no poreso kareśe 'el bu'eno de mer[i]to diśponyendośe 'a resebir la klaridad 'i luz dada del Dyyo konla kual 'obra kuyo kontrary'o haze 'el malo por lo kual 'eś meresedor de grandisima pena :
'I konforme alaś kozaś diğaś 'eś loke kiğo śentir nu'eśtro profeta Yirmᵉyahu dizyendo 'enśuś lamentasy'oneś 'elokentisima mente guardara śu śeveredad de hablar de boka del alto no śalen loś maleś ni 'el byen deke śe keğa 'ombre bivo varon śobre śuś pekadoś 'i set-[28] 'i 'eś de dubdar aki komo dize de boka del alto no śale 'i setabyendo 'el meśmo profeta diğo no 'eś del 'ombre śu kamino ni del varon ke ande 'i 'enderese śuś pasoś 'i set-[29] śino ke diremoś ke no 'eśta 'en mano del 'ombre śolo śu kamino ke śin lo ayudar 'el Dyyo no dara paso kela kabza primera ke 'eś 'el Dyyo bendito 'a todaś laś 'obraś konkure konloś}

‹fol. 52b›
{'obradoreś 'i tambyen no 'eś 'el Dyyo śolo 'el ke haze laś kozaś a'un ke 'el śolo laś pu'eda hazer 'i 'eśto 'eś loke diśo la lamentasy'on de boka del alto 'i set-[30]
'I no te 'enganyeś 'enke diśe ke 'el Dyyo konkure kon todoś loś 'obradoreś paresyendote ke konkure kon 'el malo 'a hazer mal ke 'eś verdad ke konkure ala 'obra 'enśi meśma ke no 'eś mala ni bu'ena kela diśformidad dela dereğa razon ke 'eś la maldad de mano del pekador vino 'i no del Dyyo bendito 'i dize no śalen loś maleś 'en prolar 'i 'el byen 'en śingular komo 'eneśto dizen muğoś 'i muy byen porke loś maleś śon muğoś 'i 'el byen 'uno porke 'el byen 'eś hito 'i loś maleś todo loke del śe deśvi'a komo la verdad 'una 'i la mentira de modoś 'infinitoś 'enpero podremoś dezir konforme alo diğo ke por kuanto loś maleś 'unoś hazen loś pekadoreś loś kualeś a'un ke tenga[n] la luz devina śe apartan delyya no keryendo konelyya ver la kolor del byen :
'OTROŚ no śolo śe apartan maś a'un syeran loś 'oğ[o]ś :
'I 'eśtoś śon loś maloś ke 'elke śe aparto tenyendo loś 'oğoś abyertoś no 'eś tanto 'inabil para ver komo 'el ke syera loś 'oğoś ke parese aboreser muğo la luz
'OTROŚ terseroś aboresyeron tanto la luz ke segaron por[ ]no la ver 'i śon loś keśu maldad bolbyyo beśtyaleś 'i 'eśtoś treś modoś śon reduzidoś 'a doś 'unoś ke

---

[27] Aristotle, *De Anima* II.vii (418a 26–419a 25), trans. Hett, 103–9.
[28] Lam. 3.38–39.
[29] Jer. 10.23.
[30] Lam. 3.38.

Book of the Regimen of Living ‹fol. 52b–53a›

pekan tenyendo luz ke 'eś 'eśte visy'o 'umano 'otroś pekan porke ya perdyeron la luz 'el byen nunka śe haze śino de 'un modo kyero dezir medyante la luz devina a'un ke tenga todoś treś gradoś dize lu'ego nu'eśtro profeta ke de 'el Dyyo no śalen loś maleś 'i set-[31] : konbyene śaber aśi loś maleś ke 'obra 'el ke tyene luz devina 'i delyya nośe aprobeğa komo loś ke haze 'el kela perdyyo ni 'el byen ke 'obra 'el bu'eno 'el kual śyenpre 'eś 'uno 'i śyenpre 'eś medyante la luz devina 'i 'entyende ke nolo haze 'el śolo komo diğe adelgazando maś 'el diğo del profeta konlo ke tenemoś diğo śiknifika maś ke todo byen 'i mal tyene prinsipy'o 'i fin 'el prinsipy'o 'eś 'el primer mobimyento para 'obrar produzido de la veluntad 'el fin 'eś 'el śegir la tal 'obra por lo kual kada kual delyyoś 'eś doś pu'eś abyendo 'eśta luz devina komo tenemoś diğo 'el ke 'obrare 'el byen halyyaśe ke 'el prinsipy'o del 'eś produzido del Dyyo por 'eśta luz 'i 'influ'ensyya 'i 'el śegirla 'eś de parte del 'ombre 'i 'el mal prinsipy'o 'i fin todo prosede del meśmo 'ombre ke 'el lo kom[y]ensa 'en tirarśe 'o serar loś 'oğoś ala tal luz 'i 'el lo akaba 'en śegir 'el mal 'i por 'eśto dize ke del Dyyo no śale 'el 'un byen ke 'eś 'el fin 'i 'el śegirlo a'un ke śale del 'el prinsipy'o ni loś maleś ke śon doś śiknifikando 'el prinsipy'o 'i 'el fin ke ninguno śale del śalvo del meśmo 'ombre komo tenemoś diğo dize maś deke śe keśa 'el 'ombre bibo 'i [CW. set-]}

‹fol. 53a›
{NG
set-[32] komo ke diğeśe por śer 'el 'ombre bibo śe keğa ke por śer bibo tyene poder para 'obrar ke kitarlo 'el Dyyo ke no 'obre 'eś kitarlo de śer 'ombre 'i śer bibo 'i dize varon śobre śuś pekadoś[33] ke nombre de varon denota libertad 'i poder komo śi diğeśe libre 'i poderozo para no pekar kuando peka 'i a'un ke hablo 'en byen 'i mal no śalyyo kon la repu'eśta śalvo aloś maloś ke 'eśtoś śon loś ke śe keğan śin sesar anśi del byen ke 'el Dyyo da aloś bu'enoś komo del mal ke da aloś maloś :

TENEMOŚ delo diğo ke ğuśta mente śon apremyadoś loś bu'enoś 'i apenadoś loś maloś 'i syendo 'eśto aśi ke 'el 'ombre śe'a libre 'en todaś śuś 'obraś kontra laś treś 'opiny'oneś 'eronyaś ke diğimoś deve 'el 'ombre perkurar para alkansar loś medyoś konke pu'eda 'obrar hata lyegar al fin 'ultimo del byen 'umano pu'eś śabe śer libre 'i 'eśta 'en śu mano poderlo alkansar :

---

[31] Lam. 3.38.
[32] Lam. 3.39.
[33] Lam. 3.39.

BOOK OF THE REGIMEN OF LIVING ‹FOL. 53A–53B›

PARA lo kual fu'e mi 'intensy'on 'enesta segunda partida dar 'orden komo konbyene para moderar las pasy'ones del 'apetito para 'enklinarlo al ğu'(v)[i]zy'o dela dereğa razon 'a fin de virtud ke despu'es ke ayas konprehendido loke konsiste aserka dela probizy'on del kamino dela virtud 'i moderasy'on del 'apetito subiras fasil mente 'enel monte donde 'es la morada dela filisidad[34] medyante la guardyya de los presep(+)tos del Dyyo kon trabağar 'ensu santisima le'ey ke 'este 'es 'el byen verdadero 'i fin prostero 'i primero al kual todos sean de mober ke 'elyya 'es ami ver la verdader'a luz 'i 'influ'ensyya ke tenemos diğo dada del Dyyo por senyyalada mersed asu pu'eblo[35] para lo 'ilustrar mas la kual 'ilustra nu'estro 'entendimyento tanto kuanto 'el 'ombre delyya se kyere aprobeğar konforme aloke nu'estros saby'os diğeron ke todo 'el ke se sirbe kon la luz de la ley la mesma luz dela ley lo abivigu'a 'i set-[36] palabras muy santas 'enlas kuales siknifikaron kuanto aserka desta materyya tenemos diğo ke 'en dezir kyen se sirbe dela luz dela ley siknifikaron la libertad de kyen kyera ke delya se kyere serbir ke se pu'ede serbir 'i siknifika ke no solo tyene la libertad mas ke a'un la mesma ley le da la vida 'eterna permanente 'i perdurable ke 'es la ke verdader'a mente vida se pu'ede lyyamar 'i siknifikaron mas 'en 'entitularla kon titulo de luz ke 'esta 'es la luz devina 'influ'ida 'enel 'umano 'entendimyento 'i set- 'i a'un ke 'estas vertudes ke yo aki te kyero deklarar para moderar las pasy'ones del 'apetito 'estan muy mas perfekta mente 'en nu'estra santisima ley kyero telas deklarar por 'el 'orden ke Aristotel las deklaro 'en 'el libro dela 'etika[37] por ke meğor las pu'edes konprehender konla memory'a destinta mente :}

‹fol. 53b›
{ḤELEK B P‹EREK› G [PART TWO CHAPTER THREE]

KAPITULO TERSERO

AŚ de saber ke las vertudes morales son doze segun Aristotel las kuales fu'eron para moderar las pasy'ones del 'apetito sensitibo kese divide 'en 'apetito konkupisible 'i 'irasible[38] 'i porke las 'obras podian ser eradas 'i vituperyyadas por parte de 'uno destos dos 'endereso la dereğa razon las 'obras dela virtud konprehendyentes loke konvyene 'en todas las 'obras 'umanas

PORKE 'el 'apetito 'irasible pu'ede ser aserka del byen 'o aserka de 'el mal 'i

---

[34] Cf. Ezek. 20.40 et alibi.
[35] Cf. Ps. 136.
[36] Ketubot 111b.
[37] Cf. Aristotle, *NE* III.xi.8 (1119a 12–21).
[38] Aristotle, *De Anima* III.x (433a 32–433b 13).

Book of the Regimen of Living ‹fol. 53b–54a›

syendo aśerka del mal pu'ede śer ke śe'a aśerka del preśente 'o futuro 'i aśerka de 'eśto 'eś la fortaleza kontra 'el mal ke 'eś la primera virtud delaś doze 'i pu'ede śer aśerka del pasado 'i aśerka del 'eś la manśedumbre ke 'eś la setima 'i konprende kon śi la pasensy'a

'I syendo aśerka del byen śi 'eś grande 'eś la manyanimidad ke 'eś la kinta 'i śi no 'eś grande tanto 'eś la modeśty'a ke 'eś la moderada kobdisy'a ke 'eś la seśta :

'EL 'apetito konkupisible pu'ede śer aśerka del 'util 'o del de[le]yta(p)[b]le syendo aserka del 'util pu'ede śer aśerka del dar 'i resebir ke 'eś aśerka 'el gaśtar medyana mente 'i aśerka deśto 'eś la liberalidad ke 'eś la tersera virtud delaś doze diğaś 'i syendo aśerka de grandeś deśpezaś 'eś la maknifisensy'a ke 'eś la kuarta 'i śi 'eś aśerka de dar 'i tomar lo devido 'eś la ğuśtisy'a ke 'eś la 'onzena 'i syendo aśerka del deleytable pu'ede śer 'enla deleytasy'on ke śe deleyta 'el 'ombre śolo 'i aśerka deśto 'eś la tenplansa ke 'eś la śegunda virtud 'i pu'ede śer aśerka dela deleytasy'on ke 'el 'ombre resibe konversando kon 'otroś 'en 'onibersal 'i anśi 'eś la afabilidad ke 'eś la 'oğaba virtud 'ila kortezi'a ke 'eś bu'ena konversasy'on 'i 'eś la desima kon 'eśtaś doś śe akonpanyya la verdad ke modera loś diğoś 'i heğoś 'umanoś 'i 'eś la nobena :

REŚTA para 'el numero delaś doze la amiśtad ke fu'e 'ordenada para śublimar la 'eselensy'a de todaś laś vertudeś komo maś partikular mente deklararemoś 'en kada 'una delyyaś muy 'eśpisifikada mente :

'OTROŚ reparten 'eśtaś vertudeś moraleś 'en treś no maś alaś kualeś anyaden la prudensy'a virtud 'intelektual gobernadora de todaś laś moraleś 'i dizen no aver maś de kuatro vertudeś laś kualeś lyyaman kardinaleś komo śi diğeśen kiśy'oś śobre loś kualeś bu'elta la pu'erta de toda la vida 'umana la}

‹fol. 54a›

{ND
primera 'eś fortaleza para moderar 'el 'apetito 'irasible la śegunda modera 'el 'apetito konkupisible aśerka delaś deleytasy'oneś 'i 'eś la templansa la tersera modera 'el 'apetito konkupisible 'enel dar 'i tomar 'i 'eś la ğuśtisyya :

'I a'un ke 'eśta divizy'on śigan loś maś por śer 'ekśelente toda vi'a la nu'eśtra aristotelika parese meğor para hazer memory'a deśmembrando maś la virtud por śuś parteś 'i 'eś maś ś[y]'[e]ntifika komo 'enel libro śegundo dela 'etika[39] 'eśkribe :

NO FALTA kyen ponga 'una śola virtud 'i a'elyya atr(')[i]buye todaś laś 'otraś 'i no 'eś muy ağeno del sezo porke 'eśtan tan 'ermandadaś ke parese pekar 'en todaś 'el ke peka 'en 'una 'i 'obrar todaś 'el ke 'obra 'una de aki vyene ke 'el kabalyero akual kyer malo lyyama kobard(v)[e] ke 'eś propy'o visy'o kontra la fortaleza porke de toda

---

[39] Aristotle, *NE* II.v.4–6 (106a 3–14), II.vi.15–20 (1107a 1–26).

BOOK OF THE REGIMEN OF LIVING ‹FOL. 54A–54B›

virtud haze fortaleza 'el kortezano atodo malo lyyama vilyyano 'o deśkorteś porke le parese toda virtud śer kortezi'a 'i todo visy'o deśkortezi'a 'i set- tambyen falyyaraś ke 'eśtoś nombreś delaś vertudeś aki pu'eśtoś śe konfunden aserka deloś a'utoreś 'i śe ponen 'unoś por 'otroś por la grande a(y)finidad ke 'entre 'elyyoś ayy 'i le'endo fasil mente śabraś deke virtud hablan śenyyalandote śu 'esensyya a'un ke 'enel nombre vari'en yo aki śegire la 'orden śegun Aristo‹tel›

'I anteś ke 'entremoś 'enla deklarasy'on delyaś 'eś neśesaryo hazerte śaber ke la virtud konśiśte 'enel medyo 'en reśpekto de la 'obra 'el kual medyo 'eś 'eśtremo grado dela bondad aśi ke toda virtud 'en kuanto 'eś bondad 'eś 'eśtremo 'i 'en kuanto śe refyere alaś 'obraś 'eś abito ke 'eśta 'en medyo de doś 'eśtremoś 'i loś 'eśtremoś śon deśvyadoś deśte medyo 'o por puǧa 'o por falta 'i śon visy'ozoś 'i 'en kuanto śon visy'oś 'i maleś tan śola mente no śon 'entre[ ]si kontrary'oś maś todoś doś śe kontraryan al medyo śegun maś 'i menoś 'i śegun śon 'eśtremoś de deś'igualdad ke denotan puǧa 'o falta diśtanteś del medyo śon 'entre śi kontrary'oś 'i kontrary'oś al medyo 'i maś 'entreśi ke al medyo komo 'en kada virtud 'i virtud podremoś ver

'I agora te deklarare 'eśto 'en 'un notable 'enǧenplo 'enla fortaleza ke 'eś medyo 'entre doś 'eśtremoś ke śon 'ozadi'a 'i temor berbi grasyya 'el ke komete loś 'enemigoś śegun konvyene por loke konvyene kuando komo konvyene 'i set- 'eś fu'erte 'i 'el ke 'eśto haze diśforme 'a algunaś śerk(y)[o]nśtansyyaś 'eś 'ozado 'i śu visy'o śe dize de nu'ebo ('o) 'ozadi'a 'el ke kon todaś 'eśtaś kondis(v)[y]'oneś no 'uza kometer śe lyyama temido kobarde 'i śu visy'o myedo temor kobardi'a de manera ke fortaleza 'eś 'un abito}

‹fol. 54b›
{bu'eno 'entre doś abitoś maloś 'uno por[ ]puǧa ke 'eś la 'ozadi'a 'i 'otro por falta ke 'eś 'el temor loś kualeś 'entre śi śon kontrary'oś porke kometer kuando no konvyene ke 'eś 'obra de 'ozado ko[n]traryya muǧo ano kometer kuando konvyene ke 'eś de temido 'ilo kontraryya maś ke ala fortaleza ke 'eś kometer kuando konvyene porke 'el 'eśtremo mayor 'eś maś diśtante del menor ke del medyo 'i por kuanto 'eśte medyo keśe konsidra 'enla virtud 'eś la konformidad ala dereǧa razon ke 'eś fazer la 'obra por loke konvyene akyen konvyene śegun konvyene 'i set- :

NOTARAŚ ke 'eśtar la virtud 'en medyyo no 'eś 'otra koza ke śer śu 'obra konforme 'a dereǧa razon pezada 'i 'igualada konel fy'el de śu balansa ke 'eś la prudensyya de manera ke diversaś 'obraś śeran virtu'ozaś śegun diversaś śerkośtansyyaś komo 'enel 'enǧenplo pu'eśto 'ir kometer loś 'enemigoś 'en 'un tyenpo sera virtud 'en 'otro 'ozadi'a 'i śera muǧo meǧor retirarśe 'i apartarśe delyyoś tanbyen la meśma 'obra 'a 'uno śera virtud 'a 'otro visy'o porke 'uno la peza konel fy'el dela dereǧa razon 'otro 'enla falsa balansa del 'eronyo ǧu'izyo komo kometer loś 'enemigoś aloś sibdadanoś de loś kualeś śon viśadoś porśi librar delyyoś 'i matar 'el tirano 'eśtru'idor

BOOK OF THE REGIMEN OF LIVING ‹FOL. 54B–55A›

dela sibdad 'eś abito de fortaleza 'ir matar loś 'enemigoś por robarleś śuś hazyendaś 'i por kobdisyya del premyyo ke leś dan por matar loś komo hazen loś vileś śoldadoś ke śe alkilan kon kyen leś da maś śu'eldo vendyendo por dinero śuś vidaś 'i laś ağenaś 'i matar 'uno 'el tirano no por defensa dela republika śino por rey[n]ar 'i tiranizar 'el no śolo no 'eś a'uto bu'eno 'o 'indiferente śino muy malo anśi ke la 'obra 'enśi 'eś 'indiferente 'a mal 'o 'a byen 'i toda 'obra 'eśeptaś algunaś pokaś ke śon malaś komo dize Aristotel 'enel śegundo dela 'etika⁴⁰ ke konelyyaś nombrandośe 'eśta lu'ego la maldad komo adultery'o 'omisidy'o 'i set- pu'ede 'eśtar 'en medyyo 'i śer virtud 'i diferir del medyo :

'I 'eśto 'eś muğo de notar por śer prinsipy'o 'oniversal 'i muy a'uto para 'entender la alta virtud dela prudensyya madre de todaś kuantaś śon 'i muğaś kozaś paśo 'eneśta materyya por no alargar ke 'enla 'eśpośisy'on dela 'etika 'eśtan (d) deklaradaś 'i para ke meğor konprehendaś 'eśtaś doze vertudeś 'i veaś śer medyo kada 'una 'entre doś 'eśtremoś śusinta mente telo deklarare 'en kada 'una 'en 'oniversal 'i konforme 'a Aristotel 'enel śegundo dela 'etika⁴¹ 'i kuanto baśta para la fortaleza ya avemoś diğo :

LA śegunda 'eś la templansa medyo 'entre la puğa ke 'eś la deśtemplansa 'i la falta ke śe lyyama 'insensibilidad virtud moderadora 'i maś aserka delaś deleytasyyoneś ke aserka delaś triśtezaś}

‹fol. 55a›
{NH
porke maś 'enklinadoś śon loś 'ombreś aśegir 'el deleyte ke 'a hu'ir la triśteza 'i propya mente 'eś 'eśta virtud aserka delaś deleytasy'oneś deloś maś materyaleś śentidoś ke śon 'el takto 'i 'el guśto 'i maś aserka del takto 'eneśtoś śe toma propya mente la kontenensya 'i 'enkontinensya de ke Aristotel fablo 'enel śetimo dela 'etika⁴² :

LA tersera virtud 'eś la liberalidad medyo 'enel 'eśpender 'o dar śuś dineroś 'o kozaś ke kon dinero śe 'eśtiman kuyo 'eśtremo porpuğa 'eś prodegalidad ke 'uza deśta dadiba maś deloke konvyene 'i 'el 'eśtremo por falta 'eś abariza kela 'uza menoś

LA kuarta 'eś la manifisensyya tambyen aserka delaś deśpezaś 'i 'eś diferente dela liberalidad 'enke la manifisensyya śolo 'eś aserka laś deśpezaś para fazer kozaś grandeś 'i 'en 'ombreś grandeś puğanteś 'en dignidad 'i 'en rikeza komo mu'eśtra śu

---

[40] Aristotle, *NE* II.vi.18 (1107a 10–19).
[41] Aristotle, *NE* II.vi.15 (1107a 1–4).
[42] Aristotle, *NE* VII.i–x (1145a 15–1152a 36).

Book of the Regimen of Living ⟨fol. 55a–55b⟩

nombre 'i la liberalidad 'enlaś ǧikaś 'o medyanaś la puǧa śe lyyama 'enǧimyento ke 'eś 'uzar 'eśtoś demazyadoś gaśtoś 'inkonvenyente mente la falta 'eś pokedad 'eśkaseza ke 'eś diminu'isy'on de lo ke konvyene 'eneśte grande 'i magnifiko gaśto :

LA kinta 'eś la manyanimidad 'o animozidad 'i grandeza de animo de koro 'i hermozura de todaś laś 'otraś vertudeś virtud de prinsipeś 'i grandeś śenyyoreś medyo konel kual aśep(+)tan laś grandeś dignidadeś akelyyoś akyen konvyene kuando komo 'o porke konvyene 'i se- 'el 'eśtremo p(+)uǧante śe lyyama 'inśa[sya]bilidad ke 'eś 'un 'apetito kanino 'o buliśmo aserka dela 'onra grande 'i 'eś śoberbyya la falta 'eś pozilanimidad ke 'eś no kurar delaś dignidadeś 'i kareser del 'apetito delyyaś akel akyen para laś mereser no falta śino 'eśte 'apetito

LA śeśta 'eś la modeśty'a 'i modera 'el 'apetito aserka de laś 'onraś pekenyyaś 'o medyanaś guarda konla mag[n]yanimidad akelyya proprosy'on ke la liberalidad konla manifisensy'a la puǧa 'eś ambisy'on visyo konel kual śe dezean laś 'onraś 'i ponpaś deśkonvenyente mente diśforme ala dereǧa razon 'i set- la falta śe lyyama regmisy'on flosedad pereza apokamyento ke 'eś faltar de lo ke konvyene 'enel deze'o 'i aśeptasy'on de laś 'onraś 'i set- :

LA śetima 'eś la mansedumbre medyo 'entre la 'irakundy'a ke 'eś la puǧa 'i privasy'on 'o karensyya de 'ira ke 'eś la falta por kuanto la falta no tyene nombre 'enel grego ni 'enel latin ke 'el propy'o nombre de la falta 'eś mansedumbre kuyo visy'o por puǧa 'eś muǧo mayor ke 'el ke 'eś por falta 'i por tanto le dyeron 'el nombre de la falta :

'I nota ke a'un ke la virtud 'eśte 'en medyo komo kyera ke 'el medyo śe'a la konformidad de la dereǧa razon no śon loś visy'oś 'igual mente}

⟨fol. 55b⟩
{HELEK B P⟨EREK⟩ D- [PART TWO CHAPTER FOUR]
apartadoś deśte medyo 'i 'igualeś 'en maldad 'entreśi porke 'uno 'eś maś diśforme de la dereǧa razon ke 'otro komo 'eneśta śantisima virtud de la kual nu'eśtro grande maeśtro 'i leǧeślator fu'e loado del Dyyo[43] la 'irakundyya 'eś mayor visy'o kela karensyya de 'ira 'i 'en kada virtud notaremoś 'eśta diversidad 'enśuś 'eśtremoś

LA oǧaba 'eś la afabilidad gravedad amiśtad 'i set- medyo 'entre la adulasy'on liǧonǧa 'o ǧokareri'a por puǧa 'i kontensy'on por falta konsiśte aserka de la habla 'i konversasy'on komo konvyene 'enlaś 'umanaś komunikasy'oneś ke 'eś la 'intensy'on 'enelyya fazerśe amigable 'i aplazible atodoś de modo ke la podemoś lyyamar kortezi'a 'enla habla 'o komun amiśtad 'i por śuś propyedadeś śe vera loke dif[y]ere dela

---

[43] Num. 12.3.

Book of the Regimen of Living ‹fol. 55b–56a›

amiśtad del 'oğabo 'i nobeno de la 'etika 'i 'enke konvyene la puğa konśiśte 'en kerer agradar atodoś komo no konvyene no maś ke por no '[e]noğar aninguno 'i no por kabza de 'interes[ ][']i la falta 'eś śer brigozo barağozo komo veremoś

LA nobena 'eś la verdad medyo 'ent(y)re la arogansya 'i prezunsy'on 'i la deśimulasy'on tambyen aserka de la konversasyon 'umana la kual deklararemoś muğo partikular mente maś de loke 'emoś heğo 'enla primera partida deklarando maś komo 'eś medyo 'i śuś 'eśtremoś 'ila 'ipokrezi'a 'o śimulasy'on konpu'eśta de deśimulasy'on 'i arogansyya visy'o pesimo

LA desima ke 'eś la konversasy'on grasyya 'o kortezi'a ke 'unoś a'eśta 'otroś ala afabilidad lyyaman kortezi'a 'i 'en grego 'eś diğa 'e'otrapeli'a tambyen 'eś aserka de laś konversasy'oneś medyo 'entre la ğokareri'a ke 'eś puğa 'i loś gregoś lyyaman bomolokiya 'i 'entre la vilyani'a por falta konforme al 'orden de loś 'otroś 'eśtremoś ke deśpu'eś maś por 'eśtenso deklararemoś 'eś medyo ke guarda 'el dekoro 'enla konversasy'on partikular de laś alegriaś ke para deskanso de la vida 'umana 'i refriğery'o de loś trabağoś śon nesesaryaś :

LA 'undesima 'eś la ğuśtisya partikular 'una de laś kuatro kardinaleś 'eś medyo konel kual 'el ke la tyene da akada 'uno lo ke konvyene 'i toma para śi loke konvyene śuś 'eśtremoś śon maś 'i menoś ke toma kada 'uno para śi maś del byen 'i menoś del mal 'i da a'otro maś del mal 'i menoś del byen 'i 'eśto śe lyama śin ğuśtisyya 'i aki śe konprehenden loś 'eśtremoś ke śon maś 'i menoś 'i por kuanto la ğuśtisya śe dize 'en doś modoś konvyene śaber 'oniverśal ke 'eś konśerbasyon dela ley ke pretende 'a 'el byen komun 'i partikular la partikular śe reparte 'en diśtribu'itiba 'i kumutatiba 'el medyo 'en kada 'una deśtaś śe toma diverśa mente

LA dozena 'eś la amiśtad medyo 'entre 'el regalo por puğa 'i 'enemiśtad 'odyo aboresimyento por falta dela kual}

‹fol. 56a›
{NV
hablaremoś algo maś largo ke 'enlaś 'otraś pu'eś Aristotel le dediko 'el 'oktabo 'i nono dela 'etika[44] ke 'enelyya ami ver 'eśta la byen aventuransa 'i fin verdadero :

'EŚTA 'eś la deśkrisy'on delaś vertudeś 'en ğeneral para no maś de (k) konprehenderlaś fasil mente 'enla memoryya pero komo kyera ke para 'obrar śegun virtud perfekta mente ke 'eś nu'eśtra prinsipal 'intensy'on konvyene śaber maś por 'eśtenso laś partikularidadeś delyyaś 'i de śuś 'eśtremoś laś deklararemoś 'una por 'una lo maś breve ke posibil śera śin faltar todo loke 'eś meneśter 'en todo tanbyen diremoś de 'unaś doś pasy'oneś ke konśiśten 'en medyo por lo kual śon muy śeme-

---

[44] Aristotle, *NE* VIII and IX cover the topic of friendship.

BOOK OF THE REGIMEN OF LIVING ‹FOL. 56A–56B›

ğanteś 'a vertudeś a'un ke no lo śean por śer medyoś śon loadoś 'i śuś 'eśtremoś vituperyadoś 'una delyyaś śe dize zelo 'o nemeziś 'en grego ke 'eś holgar konel byen ke tyene loś bu'enoś 'i pezarleś konśu mal 'i pezarleś konel byen de loś maloś holgando konśu mal komo 'i kuando konvyene kuyoś 'eśtremoś śon malebolensy'a ke 'eś holgar konel mal de todoś 'i 'enbidy'a ke 'eś aber pezar de todo bye(y)n anboś de doś 'eśtremoś śon komo puğa 'i komo falta śino śi keremoś lyyamar la malebolensy'a puğa la 'enbidy'a falta la 'otra vergu'ensa 'i 'eś temor de hazer mal 'o dolor del mal ke hizo 'eś medyo 'entre deśvergu'ensamyento ke 'eś no śe[ ]doler delyo 'i korimyento 'i 'eśtupor ke 'eś 'una visy'oza vergu'ensa kuando no konvyene 'i set- :

KAPITULO KUARTO

'I 'en kuanto la primera ke 'eś la fortaleza 'eś de śaber ke śe divide 'en treś maneraś 'i 'eśpesyaś diferenteś 'i por meğor dezir śe toma 'en treś modoś ke śon 'en modo largo 'i 'eśtreğo 'i maś 'eśtreğo :

LA primera 'i 'a 'opiny'on de nu'eśtroś śaby'oś la maś prinsipal 'i ke propyya mente śe lyyama fortaleza 'eś la konserbasy'on de todaś laś vertudeś 'i loś abitoś ke 'eśtando 'el 'ombre fiśo 'i firme 'enlaś 'onraś de virtud 'en tal manera ke tenga 'el 'apetito śobalternado 'i śubdito al 'entendimyento kontraśtandolo 'i vensyendolo 'eśte tal śe lyyamara fu'erte śegun 'eśte primer modo 'i śegun 'eśta manera de fortaleza śe dize konprender 'eśta todaś laś vertudeś :

'I 'eśta 'eśpesy'a de fortaleza loaron nu'eśtroś śaby'oś 'i diśeron kual 'eś 'el fu'erte 'el ke vense śu 'apetito 'i set-[45] ke 'eś razon de ponderar 'el termino kual [CW. ke no]}

‹fol. 56b›
{ke no dize ke koza 'eś 'el fu'erte ke eśtonśeś reśpondyera porśu difinsy'on 'o deśkrisy'on maś diğo kual 'eś keryendo śiknifikar ke śobre dividirśe 'en treś 'eśpesyaś diferenteś 'i modoś diversoś demanda kual 'eś 'el ke maś propyya mente śe pu'ede lyyamar fu'erte 'i reśponde dizyendo ke 'eś 'el ke vense 'el 'apetito 'i lo tyene śubdito ala razon ke 'eśte śe pu'ede dezir maś fu'erte ke 'el ke vense la batalyya 'i toma la sibdad porke no ayy maś fu'erte pele'a ke 'entre razon 'i 'apetito repugnanteś 'en 'un meśmo 'ombre 'i 'eś maś fu'erte 'el ke aśi meśmo vense ke 'el ke vense a'el 'eśtiry'or 'enemigo :

'EL śegundo modo 'eś la ke loś filosofoś moraleś maś propy'a mente lyamaron fortaleza ke 'eś aserka deloś peligroś 'en śufrir loś maleś 'i 'eśperarloś 'i 'eśta forta-

---

[45] Avot 4.1, Tamid 32a.

Book of the Regimen of Living ‹fol. 56b–57a›

leza 'eś tomada maś partikular mente 'i 'eś la ke defendyyo Tulyo dizyendo ke 'eś 'eśperar loś peligroś 'i śufrir kon pasensyya loś trabağoś 'en kantidad determinada[46] :
LA tersera 'eś la ke maś komun mente lyyaman fortaleza dela kual habla 'el filosofo 'enel tersero dela 'etika[47] ke 'eś aserka deloś peligroś mortaleś delaś batalyyaś 'enlaś giraś 'i 'eğersisy'oś militareś adonde 'el 'ombre śe pone ala mu'erte por defensa deśu republika kuando 'i komo konvyene 'i set- 'i deśta 'eśpesy'a de fortaleza 'eśkribyeron todoś loś koronistaś 'i 'eśtoryadoreś 'en lo'or de loś ke 'enelyya śe 'eğerśitaron komo śe de nota por laś devinisimaś koronikaś 'i analeś de nu'eśtro rey David 'i deloś antigoś reyś 'i prinsipeś ke anteś del fu'eron 'i deśpu'eś susedyeron 'i deśta śu'erte de fortaleza śon fu'erteś loś martireś 'i a'un loś maś fu'erteś de todoś śon 'elyyoś ke śufryeron la mu'erte por śervisy'o del Dyo 'i śuśtentasy'on de śu fe 'i ley śantisima para 'ośervansyya deloś devinoś perśep(+)toś 'eśkoğendo morir 'enelyyaś kon mil ğeneroś de tormentoś anteś ke bibir 'en mil deleyteś śin 'elyyoś :

LOKE aki konbyene 'eś śola mente śaber komo todaś laś treś 'eśpesyaś de fortaleza diğaś 'o todaś 'eśtaś fortalezaś tomadaś 'en diversoś modoś śon 'ordenadaś por la dereğa razon 'i tyene grande komunikasy'on 'una kon 'otra ke todaś 'elyyaś kon kuantaś partikularidadeś 'otraś 'ene[l]yy(l)aś śe konprehenden an de śer reğidaś por la prudensy'a kon ğu'izy'o de dereğa razon para ke śe'a la tal fortaleza donde konvyene komo 'i kuando 'i kuanto 'i set- ke 'eneśto konśiśte śu 'ekśelente bondad 'i śublime grado de virtud 'i todo 'elke 'eśtaś śerkośtansyaś no guarda no pu'ede śer bu'eno anteś 'a veześ puğa 'a veześ falta 'i 'eś syerto ke adonde śe halyya 'una 'eśpesyya 'o modo de loś treś diğoś kon todaś laś śerkonśtansyaś ke konvyene para śer virtu'ozo 'i reğido por la prudensyya heğo kon dereğa razon śe halyyan laś 'otraś doś [CW. 'i]}

‹fol. 57a›
{NZ
'i faltando 'una faltan todaś de adonde tubyeron nu'eśtroś śaby'oś fortesisima razon hazyendo muy bu'ena konsekensyya śobre akel diğo ke śe dezi'a aloś ke śalian ala gira deloś reyś de Yiśra'el kyen 'eś 'el varon temerozo 'i tyerno de korason ande 'i bu'elbaśe aśu kaza 'i set-[48] : de donde diğeron ke lo ke kyere dezir temerozo no śe'a de 'entender por 'el temor del peligro dela gira śalvo temerozo de śuś pekadoś[49] porke

---

[46] Cicero, *De Inventione* II.163.
[47] Aristotle, *NE* III.6–9 (1115a 7–1117b 20).
[48] Deut. 20.8.
[49] Miṣudat David Prov. 13.13.

BOOK OF THE REGIMEN OF LIVING ‹FOL. 57A–57B›

'el temerozo deloś peligroś dela gira 'eśta 'eś preśo 'enel termino de tyerno d[e] korason de manera ke keda 'el termino de temerozo śuperflu'o por 'el kual tubyeron lugar de glozarlo ke fu'eśe diğo por 'el temor ke ayy 'enla pele'a del 'apetito 'i śenśualidad konla razon[50] ke 'eś karensy'a dela primera fortaleza 'i syendo syerto 'i manifyeśto ke faltando 'una faltan todaś fazen loś tornar por kual kyera delyyaś ke faltaśe śyendo śyertoś faltarian todaś 'i prinsipal mente 'eśto 'eś muy noto faltando la primera ke 'eś 'eśta virtud tan grande 'i de tanta 'ekselensyya 'eśpesyyal 'eśta tersera manera ke konelyya 'eśtan todaś laś vertudeś moraleś por śer 'una delaś kuatro vertudeś kardinaleś 'i maś kontyene muğaś 'i muy notableś vertudeś komo parteś

'I 'eś de śaber aserka deśto ke no deve 'el perfekto 'i virtu'ozo buśkar 'okazy'on para 'obrar śegun 'el śumo grado deśu 'ekśelensyya 'eneśta virtud ke 'eś aserka delaś triśtezaś 'i danyoś ke lean feğo ke śeri'a de malebolo brigozo vendikatibo deśear 'el tal kabzo anteś lo deve 'ebitar 'en kuanto pudyere śi 'el tal kabzo le suśede 'i vyene 'eśpontanyya mente ala mano 'i de śuyo ke no lo pu'ede 'eśkuzar 'entonśeś hara 'el a'uto de fortaleza komo konvyene haśta venir 'el a'uto 'eroyko dando 'i resibyendo la mu'erte konforme al ğu'izy'o de la dereğa razon porke komo kyera ke 'eś aserka deloś peligroś dela mu'erte no deve ninguno buśkar la mu'erte maś anteś fu'irla por todaś laś viaś pośibleś 'i 'eśperarla 'i no temerla kuando śusede kabzo adonde konvyene komo konvyene 'i set- ni menoś 'a de perkurar de dar la mu'erte 'a 'otro śin grandisima 'okazy'on pezandole muğo aver kyen le ayya feğo koza digna de mu'erte 'i para 'eśto tomaremoś por 'enğenplo laś giraś heğaś por loś prinsipeś 'i fu'erteś varoneś 'en Yiśra'el para śalvar śuś tyeraś 'i śu ğente por mandado del Dyyo 'obrando aśu śanto śervisy'o 'i por 'eśta meśma kabza 'un rey valyente 'ombre deve guardar muğo śu vida porke ayy delyya muğa nesesidad para śalbasy'on de la republika 'onde konvyene 'i kuantoś maś dependen deśu konservasy'on tanto deve 'el maś śegun dereğa razon de guarda(d)r la 'ino 'entregarśe aloś peligroś śino fu'ere 'en lugar a'onde muğo konvyene}

‹fol. 57b›
{komo konvyene 'i kuanto konvyene kon todaś laś 'otraś śerkonśtansyaś 'i eneśto veraś kuanto grande 'ekśelente 'eś la fortaleza ke 'eśtimando 'el fu'erte śu vida tanto la aventura 'i pyerde śi perder śe pu'ede dezir tomando 'en presy'o delyya la śalud deśu pu'eblo :
KONFORME alo kual śiknifiko nu'eśtro fortisimo rey David kuando le fu'e dada la nu'eba dela deśaśtrada mu'erte de Abśalom śu hiğo do ku'enta la 'eśkritura ke lyyorando 'i andando diğo hiğo mi'o Abśalom mi hiğo mi hiğo Abśalom kyen dyeśe

---

[50] Sotah 44a.

Book of the Regimen of Living ⟨fol. 57b–58a⟩

me morir yo 'entu lugar Abšalom mi hiǧo mi hiǧo 'i set-[51] ke 'eś razon de śentir ke nesesidad avi'a de dezir me morir yo ke dizyendo me morir pareśe bastar 'o diǧera kyen dyeśe morir yo 'i set- pero dezir me morir 'i śobre 'eśto dezir yo parese algo śignifikar 'enel doble por lo kual pyenso śe'a 'eśta la 'intensy'on ke syendo tanto 'el 'amor natural paterno ke puǧaba 'a algun 'odyo śilo teni'a 'en vida lo 'entitulaba tantaś veześ 'en titulo de hiǧo keryendo dezir ke por parte de śer śu hiǧo śenti'a tanto śu mu'erte alyende de loke kyeren nu'eśtroś śaby'oś 'eśpesyyal loś m^{e}kublim[52] ke śupyeron loś śekretoś verdaderoś de nu'eśtra śagrada 'eśkritura ke dizen lo nombro syete veześ 'en titulo de hiǧo por 'otro reśpekto maś hondo ke no śon kozaś ke śe pu'edan manifeśtar śalbo 'a kyen 'a le'ido algo de śuś śekretoś pero śolo por loke al literal śentido del teśto parese pyenso ke kizo śignifikar 'el 'eśtremado 'amor natural 'i paterno kele teni'a por lo kual dezi'a ke śi morir 'el 'ensu lugar no 'ofendyeśe maś ke aśi 'ino ala republika tubyera por byen mor(v)[i]r 'el por salbar aśu hiǧo 'i poreso diǧo me morir yo keryendo dezir kyen dyeśe ami morir 'entu lugar kon tal kondisy'on ke padesyeśe 'el mal dela mu'erte śolo yo 'i no tokase ala republika 'i poreso doblo dizyendo me morir yo 'i set- de donde śe nota kuanto deve 'el bu'eno 'i 'eśpesyyal mente 'el fu'erte guardar śu vida kuando deśu byen 'el byen de 'otroś depende komo tenemoś diǧo ke no deve 'entregarśe aloś peligroś śalbo kuando muǧo konvyene por śalvar la republika 'o śu familyya 'i muǧo maś por 'onra de la ley 'i śuśtentasy'on delyya 'i śantifikasy'on del 'ombre del Dyyo glory'ozo ke 'entonśeś bibe la anima 'i muryendo 'el ku'erpo alkansa glory'a 'eterna 'i perdurable :

'I deśta meśma manera 'eś 'el morir 'i padeser 'i deǧarśe 'entregar 'enloś peligroś por no kometer 'un pekado krimen deloś treś ke nu'eśtroś śaby'oś(vś) diǧeron ke śe deve 'el 'ombre deǧar matar 'ino hazerloś loś kualeś śon 'idolatre matar fornikar kon muǧer 'indevida 'i vedada por nu'eśtra śantisima le'ey a'un ke śe'a muy 'okulta mente 'i kual kyera 'otro pekado guarda la regla de 'eśtoś treś syendo feǧ[o]}

⟨fol. 58a⟩
{N Ḥ
'en publiko ke śyendo anśi śon konformeś nu'eśtroś śaby'oś a'una ke śe deve 'el 'ombre deǧar matar anteś ke hazer pekado alguno publika mente porke śyendo 'en publiko 'eś tanto malo 'o pe'or ke kada kual de loś treś diǧoś 'en śekreto porke hazyendole hazer 'un pekadilyyo kual kyera ke śe'a publika mente 'eś 'eśbiblar 'el

---

[51] 2 Sam. 19.1.
[52] The Kabbalists.

Book of the Regimen of Living ⟨fol. 58a–58b⟩

nombre del Dyyo glory'ozo 'i śufryendo 'el dolor dela mu'erte por[ ]no pasalyyo 'eś śantifikar śu nombre śanto de manera ke 'eśperar la mu'erte 'en śemeğanteś kazoś 'i resebirla kon muğa pasensyya 'i kon delektasy'on la kual śyenpre akonpanyya loś a'utoś bu'enoś 'eś la verdader'a fortaleza ke 'el ke goza deśta preklara 'i 'ermoza virtud 'ofresyendośe kazo para 'elyyo 'el tal 'eś 'el ke verdader'a mente śe pu'ede lyyamar byen aventurado pose'edor dela devina glory'a ke no pu'ede śer śin ke śe'a perfekto 'en 'eśtremo de 'ekśele[n]syya 'en todaś vertudeś

KOMO śe de nota de akel a'uto 'eroyko de Rabbi ᶜAkiba' ke ku'entan nu'eśtroś śaby'oś ke kuando lo śakaron amatar le peynaban la karne kon peyneś de hyero 'i komo fu'eśe tyenpo de meldar la Šᵉmaᶜ teni'a 'el 'ekśelente 'eroyko śenyyor 'intensy'on kon toda debosy'on de resib[i]r śobre śi 'el yugo del reyno śupery'or kon toda la kontenplasy'on posible śin konturbarśe 'el animo por laś pasy'oneś korporaleś de loś tormentoś dizen ke le demandaron śuś diśiploś vyendo lo ya 'enel 'ultimo artikulo de la mu'erte śin konturbarśe ni 'inpedirśe 'el 'entendimyento ni la veluntad deśu alta kontenplasy'on 'i ardyente 'amor del Dyyo 'i le diśeron maeśtro nu'eśtro haśta aki alo kual 'el devino varon Rabbi ᶜAkiba' śabya mente reśpondyo toda mi vida 'eśtube triśte śobre loke nu'eśtra le'e dize amaraś atu Dyo kon toda tu alma 'i set-[53] ke kyere dezir a'un ke te kiten 'el alma 'i agora keme vyene ami mano no lo afirmare[54] 'eśta 'eś la konkluśyon de l(k)[a]ś palabraś de nu'eśtroś śabyoś aserka deśte beatiśimo a'uto de Rabbi ᶜAkiba' laś kualeś śon tan śantaś 'i de tanta śuśtansya ke konprehenden todaś laś kondisyoneś deloś śemeğanteś a'utoś 'eroykoś 'enśalsadoś 'enel śublime grado 'i 'i(n)[k]śelensya deśta nobliśima virtud 'i por konśigyente de todaś laś 'otraś ğuntaś konelya konel śervisyo del Dyo gloryośo

'I devese notar aserka deśte tan noble a'uto keloś diśiploś ke parese śe marabilyyaban de komo podi'a turar 'enel tormento no śe marabilyyaban dela konśtansyya del venerable maeśtro ni 'el Dyyo tal kyera ke no śe deve de kre'er de 'elyyoś śyendo kryadoś de śenyyor tan śingular 'i 'uniko 'ensu tyenpo 'i 'elyyoś por śi tan famozoś 'en śensyya 'i virtud pero 'eśpantabanśe komo 'era posible ke padesyendo faśta lyegar al 'eśtremo del tormento korporal nada śe konturbaśe 'el 'entendimyento [CW. ni[ ]śe]}

⟨fol. 58b⟩
{ni[ ]śe varyaśe punto de śu kontemplasyon deklarando 'eśto maś por śer materya muy ardu'a digo ke a'un ke parese no poder 'eśtar 'en 'un meśmo tyempo 'en 'un meśmo śuğekto doś paśyyoneś kontraryaś komo 'eś tener 'uno alegri'a 'i triśteza 'en

---

[53] Deut. 6.5.
[54] Berakot 61b.

BOOK OF THE REGIMEN OF LIVING ‹FOL. 58B›

'un meśmo 'iśtante komo parese tener 'eśte śantiśimo śenyor por parte del tormento korporal dolor 'i triśteza grande 'i por parte dela devina 'eśpikulasyon śuma delektasyon 'i alegri'a 'eś meneśter 'eneśto deśting(+)ir porke 'el filosofo 'enel tersero dela 'etika⁵⁵ dize 'eneśta forma maś parese verdader'a mente ke ayya aserka de la fortaleza por śu fin delektasyon 'enpero por laś kozas ke le arodean śe deśle'e komo akaese lo meśmo 'enel luğar kel fin deloś luğadoreś ayy konel 'una delektasyon ke porel alkansan korona 'i 'onor 'enpero kuando śon heridoś śe du'elen porke śon de karne ke 'en todo trabağo 'i lazeryya ayy triśtezaś 'i 'eśt(o)[a]ś śon muğaś 'en la delektasy'on poka 'i por 'eśto nośe parese la tal delektasy'on 'i la 'intensy'on deśtaś palabraś 'eś manifyeśta 'i 'eś ke 'el fu'erte kuando padese laś feridaś konsidrando śer virtud śufrelaś 'i 'eśtandośe 'entriśtesyendo delaś taleś feridaś śe alegra konla konsidrasy'on 'i kontemplasy'on del fin deśeado ke 'eś 'obrar la virtud aśi komo akaese aloś pasyenteś laś lyyagaś 'o apośtemaś ke śe laś abren por fin de śu śalud 'i 'eśtandośelaś abryendo 'o 'eśtandolaś kabturezando no değan de dolerśe komo śensibleś 'i 'enel propyo tyenpo de dolor śe alegran konla 'eśperansa de la śalud 'i 'enśenplifiko 'el filosofo la delektasy'on del fu'erte 'enel padeser śegun virtud ala glory'a de loś luğadoreś⁵⁶ loś kualeś antigu'a mente 'iban 'a luğar al monte 'Olimpo ke 'eś 'un monte muy alto 'i pyenso ke śe'a 'eśte ke parese de nu'eśtra sibdad ala parte del ś"ol śerka del kaśtilyyo ke śe[llyama Plata mona 'el kual agora lyyam[a]n loś gregoś 'Olimbo 'i por la lonğitud 'i latitud ke loś kośmoğrafoś 'eśkrivyeron del parese śer 'eśte syerto porke 'el monte 'olimpo 'eśkriven tener kuarenta 'i nu'ebe gradoś 'i sinku'enta minutoś de lonğitud 'i trenta 'i nu'ebe gradoś 'i tantoś minutoś de latitud kazi 'igual ala lonğitud 'i latitud de Śaloniki komo halyyaraś 'enla kośmografi'a ke tengo yo 'eśkrita 'enla kam[a]ra kuarta de la kaza śegunda del tratado de la 'Eśpera⁵⁷ śakado de 'un moderno kośmografo 'i muy verdadero por donde tengo por syerto śer 'eśte 'el monte 'Olimpo dizen ke 'el ke vensi'a la luğa 'enel le ponian 'una korona 'enla kabesa 'i śenyal de bitory'a para perpetu'a memorya 'i 'onor de śu vensimyento 'i anśi komo akelyyoś luğadoreś fortisimoś : firyendośe 'uno 'a 'otro 'el ke le paresi'a 'ir de vensida 'i tener meğori'a śobre 'el 'otro 'i vense la luğa a'un ke no podi'a değar de dolerśe 'i}

---

⁵⁵ Aristotle, *NE* III.ix.3–4 (1117b 1–15).
⁵⁶ Aristotle, *NE* III.ix.3 (1117b 1–7).
⁵⁷ M. A. makes reference to his commentary on Sacrobosco's *Sphere*.

BOOK OF THE REGIMEN OF LIVING ‹FOL. 59A›

‹fol. 59a›
{NT
'entriśteserśe por laś heridaś ke le dolian śe alegraba afigurando 'el premyo 'i 'onor ke del vensimyento resibi'a dela meśma manera 'el ke śe 'entrega aloś peligroś 'i padeśe delyyoś al meśmo tyenpo del padeser śe alegra konsidrando 'el fin de 'obrar kon dereğa razon 'el kual 'obrando alkansa 'i a'un ke alegri'a 'i triśteza śean doś kontrary'oś byen pu'eden 'eśtar 'en 'un meśmo śuğekto 'en 'un meśmo tyempo no 'eśtando ninguno de loś kontrary'oś 'en 'eśtremo anśi komo śe halyan 'en kual kyera konpu'eśto kalidadeś kontraryaś fryaldad 'i kalor 'omidad 'i śekedad ke komo ninguna deśtaś kalidadeś 'eśte(n) 'en śumo pu'ede 'eśtar meśklada konśu kontrary'a anteś 'eś forsado śegun la komun 'opiny'on ke no 'eśtando 'una 'enel śumo grado 'eśte meśklada konśu kontrary'o 'en tanto grado kuanto le falta para lyegar al śumo pero 'eś byen viśto ke 'eśtando 'una delyyaś 'en 'eśtremo 'ultimo grado no pu'ede śufrir ni konpadeśer śu kontrary'o porke 'eśte konpadeśer reponya ala dif[i]n(i)sy'on de loś kontrary'oś porke 'uno konronpe a'el 'otro komo śe ve'e por la 'eśperensyya 'i nunka śe byyo miśto ni 'eś posible halyyarśe 'en grado 'intenśo de doś kalidadeś kontraryaś 'i anśi meśmo ke pu'edan śer doś 'obraś kontraryaś hazerśe 'intenśa mente 'en 'un meśmo śuğekto komo 'eśkalye(')ntarśe 'i 'eśfryarśe 'o 'entriśteserśe 'i alegrarśe fu'erte mente de manera ke śyendo la alegri'a 'en 'eśtremo no pu'ede 'eśtar konelyya triśteza 'en manera ninguna aśi komo 'eś la g(v)l[o]ry'a del anima deśpu'eś de ap[a]rtada de la materyy'a 'i anśi komo 'eś la delektasy'on de laś 'entiliğensyaś ke 'eśtan de kontino 'enśu śuma alegri'a por śer formaś 'en a'uto puro ke no śe afigura 'enelyyaś falta alguna komo tengo byen deklarado 'enel tersero de loś fizikoś[58] komento tersy'o konforme al 'inğeny'oziśimo komentador Temiśti'o[59] adonde aserka

---

[58] This refers to his *Piruš al Sefer ha-Š^e maa ha-Tabai*, a commentary on Aristotle's *Physics;* see Ben-Menahem, "R. M. Almosnino," 283–84. The Aristotle passage is *Physics* III.iv (203a 32–203b 13): "hoc autem est unum, quem ille vocat intellectum. Intellectus autem a principio quodam operatur congnoscens; quare necesse est simul aliquando omnia esse et incipere aliquando moveri": *Physica: Translatio Vetus,* ed. F. Bossier and J. Brams, Aristoteles Latinus VII.1.2 (Leiden–New York: Brill, 1990), 111–12. Aegidius Romanus, *Commentaria in octo libros phisicorum* [sic] *Aristotelis* (Venice, 1502, repr. Frankfurt, 1968), 58. This part of Porphyry *In Arist. Phys.* has not survived: cf. *Porphyrii Philosophi Fragmenta,* ed. A. Smith (Stuttgart–Leipzig: Teubner, 1993), 156. It seems not to be Themistius' *In De Anima* but rather his *In Arist. Phys.*, ed. H. Schenkl, CAG 5.2 (Berlin: Reimer, 1900), 81.

[59] Themistius (fl. 400 C.E.) oversaw a philosophical school at Constantinople and wrote paraphrases of Aristotle's *Posterior Analytics* and *On the Soul;* the latter was translated into Arabic by Ishaq Ibn Hunayn (d. ca. A.D. 910), and later into Latin by William of Moerbeke (ca. 1215–ca.

BOOK OF THE REGIMEN OF LIVING ⟨FOL. 59A–59B⟩

dešto deklare largo śu 'opiny'on 'i la de Porfiryo[60] 'i 'Eğidyyo Romano[61] :
'I por 'el kontrary'o kuando la trišteza fu'ere 'en 'estremo no podra aver konelyya meśkla de delektasy'on alguna 'i dešto śe marabilyyaban loś diśiploś de Rabbi ᶜAkiba' ke lyegando al 'estremo de la tristeza 'i dolor korporal vinyendo al punto de la mu'erte ke 'eś korupsy'on de todo 'el ku'erpo komo kedaba lugar para kontemplar ke no podi'a śer śin aver alguna delektasy'on por parte de la konsidrasy'on del fin 'i 'ešto 'eś loke kiğeron dezir 'en dezir maestro hašta aki 'i set-[62] ke la verdader'a 'intensy'on de śu admirasy'on 'era komo 'era posible ke hata 'el punto de la mu'erte ke 'eś 'estremo de tristeza 'en todoś loś 'ombreś 'ubyeśe a'un mišty'on de alegri'a [CW. komo]}

⟨fol. 59b⟩
{HELEK B- PEREK H- [PART TWO CHAPTER FIVE]
komo śe mostraba por la kontemplasy'on alo kual 'el reśpondyendo muy fizika mente konforme aśu 'eroyka virtud no śin grande devinidad dandoleś 'a 'entender kela trišteza 'enel no 'era 'en 'estremo 'ultimo pu'eś 'el propy'o punto de la mu'erte 'era 'el ke dezeaba ke 'el Dyyo le truğeśe ala mano para 'obrar tan alta 'i šublimada virtud ke 'el porśi no 'era lisito aberla de buśkar 'i ke agora kele veni'a komo śe abi'a de değar de delektar konelyya aśi komo kon kual kyera 'otra 'obra de virtud 'ila šuma delektasy'on 'ešpritual kuanto 'en 'ombre śe pudo dezir halyyada 'en Rabbi ᶜAkiba' le diminu'i'a muğo la trišteza del ku'erpo ke al śanto 'ešprito śuğekto 'eštaba komo loś ke 'eštando 'en fu'erte 'imağinasy'on no ve'en loke tyene delante loś 'oğoś 'era lu'ego koza 'eštupenda aver 'en 'un ku'erpo tan 'enfermo delaś feridaś alma tan śana por lo kual fu'e loado 'en grande manera por 'una selik[e]h boz ke śalyo 'i dišo byen

---

1286): for the Latin version, see G. Verbeke, ed. *Thémistius: Commentaire sur le traité de l'âme d'Aristote, traduction de Guillaume de Moerbeke* (Louvain, 1957); E. Grant, *A Source Book in Medieval Science* (Cambridge, MA, 1974), 36, 41 lists other medieval translations. For a note regarding Themistius' contribution to cosmological thought, see D. Lindberg, ed., *Science in the Middle Ages* (Chicago, 1978), 274. For an introduction to Themistius, an English translation of his paraphrases of *On the Soul*, and full bibliography, see now R. B. Todd, trans., *Themistius: On Aristotle's "On the Soul"* (Ithaca, 1996).

[60] Almosnino may be recalling Porphyry's statement in the *Isagoge:* "Nothing then arises from not-being, nor will contradictories exist at the same time in the same thing" (*Isagoge,* trans. S. W. Warren [Toronto, 1975], 46).

[61] Giles of Rome, Archbishop of Bourges (ca. 1243–1316).

[62] Berakot 61b.

BOOK OF THE REGIMEN OF LIVING ‹FOL. 59B–60A›

aventurado 'ereś tu Rabbi ͨAkiba' ke śalyo tu alma konla 'unidad 'i set-[63] keryendo dezir ke 'era asaś byen aventurado pu'eś ke lyego al punto de la mu'erte donde konśiśte 'el 'eśtremo de la triśteza 'i nośe perturbo 'el 'entendimyento ni śe aparto de śu kontemplasy'on ni śe pribo deśu delektasy'on konsidrando la 'ekśelensyya del fin glory'ozo 'eśte tal śenyyor 'uzo kon śuma perfeksy'on la virtud de la fortaleza komo konvyene kuanto 'i komo konvyene :

KAPITULO KINTO

DE loke tenemoś deklarado 'eneśta 'eśpesyya 'eś byen viśto komo 'a de 'uzar 'el 'ombre 'en kual kyera de laś 'otraś doś 'eśpesyaś komo konvyene ala dereğa razon 'i aś de śaber maś para loke konśiśte 'eneśta virtud 'i 'en todaś laś 'otraś 'oniversal mente ke śinko propy'[e]dadeś deven 'eśtar konğuntaś 'i koliği(')daś kon kada virtud ke śin 'elyaś 'inpropyya mente śe lyyamara virtud :

LA primera 'eś ke 'el ke 'obrare kon virtud 'eś nesesary'o ke konośka 'i śepa la 'obra 'ino la 'obre 'ignorandola

LA śegunda ke la 'obra ke 'obrare la 'obre kon pura 'eliksy'on komo deklaramoś larga mente 'enel śegundo tersero kinto de la 'etika[64] :

LA tersera ke kual kyera ke 'obrare la 'obre afin de byen ğuśgado por la dereğa razon

LA kuarta ke śe'a la 'obra produzida de 'un abito fiśo ['i] firme 'i //'inm(y)[u]table// komo śe deklarara akyen mirare loke 'enla kondisy'on de lo(r)[s]' abitoś 'enel śegundo de la 'etika[65] tengo muy larga mente 'eśkrito :

LA kinta śe'a 'obrada kon pura delektasy'on 'i kunplida alegri'a ke 'eśto 'eś śenyal de la konfirmasy'on del abito 'i konośim[y]ento de la virtud :}

‹fol. 60a›
{S
'i tambyen 'eś śenyal de bu'ena 'eliksy'on 'i ke la 'obra no fu'e vy'ole(g)[n]ta mente heğa 'o kon temor laś kualeś kozaś 'inpiden la bondad de la 'obra 'i kual kyer 'obra de la kual faltare alguna deśtaś śinko p(v)ropyedadeś nośe pu'ede dezir śer 'obra de virtud 'i por 'eśta meśma kabza probo 'el filosofo no śer la fortaleza ninguna delaś śinko ke 'el nombro 'enel tersero de la 'etika[66] ke śon loś ke śe ponen 'i 'entregan aloś

---

[63] Berakot 61b.
[64] Aristotle, *NE* II.vi.15 (1107a 1–3), III.ii (1111b 5–1112A 18), cf. V.viii.8 (113b 25–26).
[65] Aristotle, *NE* II.v.5–6 (1106a 8–14).
[66] Aristotle, *NE* III.viii (1116a 16–1117a 29).

Book of the Regimen of Living ‹fol. 60a–60b›

peligroś por 'uno de śinko reśpektoś 'o por la 'onra ke 'eś la primera 'eśpesy'a 'o por śer 'eśp(i)r[i]mentado 'enla arte militar ke 'eś la śegunda 'o por la 'ira ke 'eś la tersera 'o por la 'eśperansa de venser ke 'en kada 'una deśtaś falta alguna de 'eśtaś śinko propyedadeś 'eśpesyyal mente la tersera ke falta 'en todaś śinko 'eśpesyaś ke 'eś la prinsipal propyedad por śer por parte dela mayor 'i prinsipal delaś kabzaś dela 'obra ke 'eś la final ke la fortaleza no 'a de śer śalbo por fin virtu'ozo 'i 'oneśto ke 'eś por la virtud 'enśi 'i śervisy'o del Dyyo 'i no por algun reśpekto 'i daki 'eś viśto ke 'el ke vensyere 'el 'apetito 'i śe 'entregare aloś peligroś 'i śufryere loś maleś komo konvyene kuanto 'i kuando konvyene kon todaś laś 'otraś śerkośtansyaś 'ordenadaś kon dereğa razon 'eśte tal śe lyyamara fu'erte 'i śi faltare 'i temyere 'onde konvyene śer fu'erte 'i tener animo 'eśforsado 'eśte tal 'eś temerozo 'i 'inkure 'enel visy'o kontrary'o śegun falta a'eśta nu'eśtra virtud 'i śi 'obrare 'entregandośe denodada 'i temerarya mente aloś peligroś maś deloke konvyene 'o por loke no konvyene 'i set- 'eśte tal 'eś visy'ozo por puğa deśte tan loado medyyo de virtud :

'I a'un ke maś larga mente śe pudyera 'eneśto poner la mano komo lo prinsipal konke 'eśta virtud śe '[e]sekuta 'i ke muğo 'enelyya aprobeğa ke 'eś 'el śaber dela arte militar 'en noś falta por nu'eśtroś pekadoś haśta ke 'el Dyyo kyera baśta lo diğo para guardarśe kual kyera de loś visy'oś diğoś 'i de śuś partikularidadeś ke por hu'ir proliğidad değo de 'eśpisifikar śolo te kyero hazer śaber ke nu'eśtroś śaby'oś loaron todoś loś treś modoś diferenteś de fortaleza ke kada 'una delyaś tubyeron por virtud śingularisima de la primera 'i prośtera de laś treś 'eś byen viśto komo tenemoś diğo ke la primera 'eś akelyya por la kual diğeron nu'eśtroś śaby'oś śer meğor ke venser la batalyya 'i prender la sibdad 'i set-[67] 'i 'eśto podri'a śer fu'eśe diğo tambyen por la tersera la kual prinsipal mente toka al ke resibe la mu'erte por 'el 'onor de la ley 'i 'el nombre del Dyyo glory'ozo 'i alyende deśto probamoś por 'el 'eroyko heğo de Rabbi ^cAkiba' la 'eksel[e]nsyya deśta prośtera 'eśpesy'a agora no keda ke dezir śalbo del modo śegundo 'el kual maś larga mente śe deklara aserka de la virtud de la mansedumbre ke 'eś śufrir loś maleś [CW. 'i]}

‹fol. 60b›
{'i tribulasy'oneś kon plazer no śintyendo 'el dolor delyyoś por 'el fin del byen ke śe śige de śufrir pasyente mente kon toda konśtansya komo alyya maś larga mente śe deklara :

KONFORME al śupremo grado de dignidad deśta śegunda 'eśpesy'a ku'entan nu'eśtroś śaby'oś ke akaesy'o 'en 'un famoziśimo 'i 'uni(n)ko 'enla tal virtud 'i por tal manifyeśto lyyamado Hillel ke anda[n]do 'un di'a por 'un kamino 'oyo boześ de 'eś-

---

[67] Avot 4.1, Tamid 32a.

Book of the Regimen of Living ⟨fol. 60b–61a⟩

klamasy'on 'enla sibdad 'i dišo konfyado śoy ke no 'eś 'eśto 'en mi kaza[68] śobre 'el dišo la 'eśkritura de 'o'ida mala no temera 'i set-[69] palabraś dignaś de muğa 'eśpikulasy'on porke no śe'a de kre'er de tan śingular śenyyor ke 'ubyeśe de pensar ke 'el mal porel kual 'era 'el grito no pudyeśe śer 'en śu kaza ke anteś nunka vemoś 'otro śalbo 'en kaza deloś bu'enoś maleś 'i 'en kaza de loś maloś byeneś komo ya aserka deśto avemoś hablado 'i kuando śe tubyera 'eśte beatisimo śenyyor por tan bu'eno ke kreera no poderle venir maleś por parte de la fortuna no devyera dezilyyo ni loarśe delyyo por 'ende pyenśo ke śe'a la verdader'a 'intensy'on 'otro de loke parese 'i 'eś ke 'eśte pasyentisimo śenyyor 'era tan akośtumbrado 'a śufrir tanto loś 'infortunoś ke de kontino padesi'a ke por la kontinuasy'on de laś pasy'oneś 'i 'el abito prudensyal para 'el śufrimyento no abi'a ya 'en toda śu kaza kyen śe śupyeśe keğar ni kyen gritaśe por mal ke le vinyeśe 'i 'eśo 'eś loke kizyeron śignifikar nu'eśtroś śaby'oś dizyendo ke 'eśte śenyyor komo 'oyo la boz del gritador 'i 'eśklamador 'enla sibdad dišo ke 'era syerto 'i śeguro no śer akelyya 'eśklamasy'on 'en śu kaza porke a'un ke 'el mal fu'eśe 'ensu kaza śabi'a syerto no śer 'enelyya la 'eśklamasy'on 'i grita por 'el tal mal porke śabi'a kuan abituadoś 'eśtaban todoś 'ensu kaza 'a padeser kon pasensy'a loś maleś de la śinyeśtra fortuna de manera ke no aśeguraba no śer 'el mal 'ensu kaza śalbo la 'eśklamasy'on konforme a'eśto dize ke śobre 'el dišo la 'eśkritura por diğo de nu'eśtro devinisimo śalmiśta de 'o'ida mala no temera 'i set-[70] ke no dize 'o'ida mala no 'o'yra śalbo de 'o'ida mala no temera k[e]ryendo śiknifikar ke a'un ke la 'oya no temera delyya 'i la kabza 'eś porke śu korason 'eśta konfyado 'enel Dyyo[71] ke 'eś abituado 'enla virtud de la mansedumbre konośyendo ke todo lo ke prośede del Dyyo 'eś afin de byen de manera ke no śolo 'el bu'eno 'i virtu'ozo no syente dolor del mal 'i śe amu'eśtra fu'erte kontra 'el 'apetito maś a'un lo v(y)ense 'en tal manera ke da lo'oreś al Dyyo por 'el mal kon tan śinsera veluntad 'i linpyyo animo komo por 'el byen :

'I 'eśto pyenso ke śe'a lo ke kiğeron nu'eśtroś śaby'oś śignifikar 'en dezir ke anśi komo an de bendezir śobre 'el byen anśi an de bendezir śobre mal[72] ke no 'eś la 'intensy'on dezir [CW. tan]}

⟨fol. 61a⟩
{S'
tan śola mente ke an de bendezir ke para 'eśto baśtara ke dišera bendeziran tambyen śobre 'el mal pero kiğeron śignifikar ke del meśmo modo ke bendize 'el 'ombre al Dyo

---

[68] Berakot 60a.
[69] Ps. 112.7.
[70] Ps. 112.7.
[71] Cf. Prov. 3.5 et alibi.
[72] Berakot 48b.

BOOK OF THE REGIMEN OF LIVING ‹FOL. 61A›

śobre 'el byen kele vyene kon 'entero kontentamyento del meśmo modo kon akel propy'o kontentamyento lo'a de bendezir śobre 'el mal 'i set-[73] para ke perfekta mente mu'eśtre śu fortaleza kontra loś trabağoś 'i tribulasy'oneś ke 'eś la śegunda manera komo tenemoś diğo por 'onde 'eś byen viśto śer todaś laś treś 'eśpesyaś 'o modoś diversoś de fortaleza loadaś muğo 'i muy muğo de nu'eśtroś śaby'oś 'i tenidaś por 'elebadisimaś vertudeś 'eśpesyyal la tersera ke parese konśiśtir 'enelyya 'el 'eroyko grado deśta virtud komo tenemoś deklarado lo kual baśta byen para la deśkripsy'on deśta virtud :

'I porke todo abto de fortaleza 'i aśi todo a'uto de kual kyer 'otra virtud ke no śe haze kon 'eliksy'on no 'eś virtu'ozo śegun la propy'edad śegunda ke avemoś prośupu'eśto 'i 'a toda 'el[i]ksy'on 'eś nesesary'o ke śe antisipe 'el konśeğo ke 'enveluntar 'en 'una koza śin tener 'enelyya konśeğo no 'eś 'eliksy'on me parese śera byen tokar algo 'enel modo ke śe deve tener aserka del konśeğo 'enla 'obra ke 'eś meneśter muğo porke 'eś 'el gobernador devino de toda virtud del kual algo maś śe dira dandome 'el Dyo vida kuando hablare de la prudensyya por tanto agora breve mente dire algunaś kozaś neśesaryaś al prezente 'enel konśeğo lo primero ke śe deve de śaber 'eś ke 'el 'oğekto śobre 'el[ ]kual śe deve de tomar konśeğo 'a de tener 'onze kondisy'oneś ke faltando kual kyera delyaś no konśiśte enelyaś konśeğo

'EŚ la primera ke no śe'a delaś kozaś forsadaś 'i permanenteś komo śi loś syeloś turaran 'en 'eterno '(i)[o] śi[ ]an de pereser 'o anśi meśmo śi 'el dyametro 'eś 'inkomenśurable konla kośta ke 'eś 'el lado del kuadro konbyene śaber śi ayy 'entre 'elyyoś porpo[r]sy'on halyyada de 'un numero 'a 'otro 'o śino ke 'enel desimo de 'E'uklideś[74] 'eśta demośtrado no la aver 'en ninguna deśtaś kozaś kabe konśeğo ke la verdad 'o mentira de taleś keśty'oneś 'eśta probada 'enla śensyya ake perteneśe tratar delyyo por loś prinsipy'oś de la tal śensyya ağeno de todo punto del konśeğo :

LA śegunda ke no śe'a de kozaś naturaleś ke no kabe tomar konśeğo śi lyyobera 'o no lyyobera 'o śila pyedra deśendera para bağo 'o śi 'el fu'ego śubira para śima 'i set- 'i a'un ke alaś veześ śe toma konśeğo śi lyyobyendo śe hara tal koza no 'eś 'el konśeğo śobre la lyyuby'a śi śera 'o no śino śobre la koza śi śe deve hazer śi lyyobyere 'i set- :

LA tersera ke no śe'a de laś kozaś 'enlaś kualeś ninguna dubda tenemoś ke la śabemoś syerto anśi komo 'el ke tyene abito de 'eśkrivir no toma konśeğo 'enel hazer de laś letraś śi śe hazen anśi 'o anśi 'i anśi 'enlaś kozaś ś[e]meğanteś :}

---

[73] Berakot 48b.
[74] Euclid, *Elements*, X.9, trans. T. L. Heath (New York, 1956), 28–31.

BOOK OF THE REGIMEN OF LIVING ‹FOL. 61B›

‹fol. 61b›
{ LA kuarta no 'eś 'el konśeğo aserka delaś kozaś aśidentaleś porke enelyaś no kabe konśeğo komo laś kozaś ke vyenen por fortuna komo halyyar 'un tezoro 'a diğa paśando por 'un lugar 'onde no 'eś de prezumir 'eśtubyeśe 'el tal tezoro 'i andando por a'i 'a hazer 'otra koza ke 'en tal kazo 'eś viśto no kaber konśeğo porke no śabe ningun 'ombre komo 'i kuando 'a de śer la tal koza :

LA kinta no ayy konśeğo śobre ko(v)[z]aś ke no 'a de 'obrar 'el ke śe akonśeğa śobre 'elyyaś ke loś de 'una sibdad no konśultaran komo loś de 'otra sibdad śe abran 'enśuś negosy'oś ke śerkando 'un 'ekśersito aKośtantinopoli no konśultaran loś de Śaloniki la manera ke ternan loś de Kośtantinopoli 'ensu defensa no abyendośe de 'obrar por 'el tal konśeğo ke 'el konśeğo 'eś para porel śi 'obrar 'o porśi 'o por 'otro :

LA seśta 'a de śer 'el konśeğo 'en koza ke pu'ede śer 'obrada por 'umana veluntad ke 'eś aserka delaś kozaś ke 'eśta 'en nu'eśtro poder 'obrarlaś por parte del 'entendimyento 'i set- :

LA setima 'a de śer ke śe'a koza ke ayya algun 'eśpasy'o de tyenpo para 'obrarla porke 'enlaś kozaś śupitaś no śe pu'ede tomar konśeğo ni śe pu'ede dezir la tal 'obra konśilyable ni 'eliğible a'un ke śe'a veluntary'a ke todo 'eliğible 'eś vel[un]tary'o 'i no todo veluntary'o 'eliğible :

LA 'oktaba 'a de śer koza ke śu'ele śer laś maś delaś veześ porke aśerka delaś kozaś ke suseden pokaś veześ no kabe konśeğo ke ninguno demandara konśeğo śi deśara de 'ir 'a algun lugar por myedo ke kayyga 'una teğa 'i lede 'enla kabeśa ke 'eś koza ke pokaś veześ akaese verda(r)[d] 'eś ke śi fu'ere tyempo de vyento rezy'o śera byen tomar konśeğo 'en tal kazo por śer ke 'en tal tyempo akaese muğaś veześ :

LA nona 'a de śer ke śe'a koza 'enke 'el 'ombre 'eśte dubdozo 'i ayya razon de dubda śi śera 'o no śera porke 'en laś kozaś ke no ayy dubda aver de śer no kabe 'enelyyaś konśeğo komo 'enla mu'erte 'i 'otraś śemeğanteś kozaś :

LA desima ke śe'a delaś kozaś ke no śe pu'eden ğuśgar por śentido korporal ke śobre laś kozaś ke ğuśga kual kyera de loś śentidoś no kabe konśeğo ke no tomaremoś konśeğo śi 'el pan 'eśta byen kozido 'o no pu'eś 'eś koza ke depende de la viśta 'i anśi 'enlaś śemeğanteś kozaś :

LA 'undesima ke śe'a aserka de loś medyoś ke 'enderesan para 'el fin 'i no aserka del mismo fin ke no śe'a de tomar konśeğo śi 'el tal fin śe deve de alkansar 'o no ke 'eneśo no kabe konśeğo śalbo kuando fu'eśe 'un fin por reśpekto de 'otro fin 'ultimo de todoś ke 'eśtonśeś śeri'a 'eśte fin medyo para 'el 'otro pośtrero 'i prośupu'eśto 'i śe tomari'a konśeğo śi 'eśte 'eś konvenible para 'el 'otro 'o no [CW. de]}

Book of the Regimen of Living ⟨fol. 62a⟩

⟨fol. 62a⟩
{SB
DE todaś 'eśtaś kondisy'oneś śe konprehendera 'el modo ke śe deve tener 'en tomar 'el konśeǧo 'en todaś laś kozaś 'i 'eś por 'eśta vi'a ke primero 'a de prośuponer 'el ke śe kyere akonśeǧar 'el fin deloke 'envelunta 'i tener 'intensy'on a'el deśpu'eś śe'a de akonśeǧar 'enel modo deloś medy'oś para alkansar 'el tal fin ke 'envelunta śegun laś doś kondisy'oneś ke 'ultima mente avemoś perśupu'eśto deśpu'eś 'a de 'eśpekular 'enel tal medyyo 'i ver śilo pu'ede halyyar halyyado 'enel 'entendimyento 'i fantazi'a 'a de konsidrar śi akel medyo abaśta para alkansar 'el tal fin ke tyene 'intensy'on 'o śi 'eś konvenyente para 'elyyo 'i śe ve'e ke 'el medyo no 'eś konvenyente 'o 'inśofisyente lo deve deś'eǧar 'i śi 'util para alkansar 'el fin lo deve alyegar aśi 'i deve mirar śi ayy 'o 'eś posible aver 'otro medyo para akel fin maś baśtante 'i konvenivle śilo halyyare develo de asep(+)tar 'i deǧar 'el primero deśpu'eś ke ayya halyyado 'el medyyo maś apropyado 'i maś konvenyente de todoś deve ver śi tyene poder para hazerlo komo śi 'ubyere meneśter para 'elyyo moneda 'en kantidad ke 'el no pu'eda śuplir lo deve dešar 'i śi fu'ere posible poder 'el śuplir loke konvyene deve de kontenplar śi le 'eś fasil 'eśta posiblidad 'o śile 'eś grave 'i śile 'eś grave deve de kontrapezar śu 'utilidad kon śu difikultad 'i dureza 'i śila 'utilidad ke del rezulta 'eś tanta 'i tal ke alibyana la gravedad 'eśtonseś lo deve śegir 'i śi 'eś maś 'el trabaǧo 'i pezadumbre del medyo ke śu 'utilidad para 'el fin lo deve deǧar deśpu'eś ke ve'a ke 'el probeǧo de 'el fin 'eś maś ke 'el trabaǧo 'enel medyo deve muy byen mirar śi 'el 'obrar 'el tal medyo danya muǧo aloś byeneś 'eśtiry'oreś ke śon 'inśturmentoś para 'el byen verdadero aśi meśmo śi danyan ala śalud del ku'erpo aśi meśmo śi danyan ala 'oneśtidad ala virtud ala konsensy'a ala bondad 'i set- śobre todo deve atentar 'en grande manera ke no danye a'otro por aprobeǧar aśi meśmo 'i konformando todaś 'eśtaś partikularidadeś para alkansar 'el fin deśeado śera 'el konśeǧo 'en toda perfeksy'on ke 'entonśeś ǧuśǧa la prudensyya kon dereǧa razon por parte del 'entendimyen(d)[t]o platiko śer bu'eno akel tal medyo 'i lu'ego lo 'eśkoǧe porke loke 'eś prośtero 'enel konśeǧo 'eś primero 'enla 'elik(')sy'on :

KONFORME aloke 'el devinisimo rey David dišo dara ati komo tu korason 'i todo tu konśeǧo kunplira 'i set-[75] 'en dezir todo tu konśeǧo 'i set- śiknifiko tener 'el konśeǧo muǧaś parteś 'i kiǧo maś dezir ke kuando da al 'ombre loke 'envelunta 'enel korason ke 'eś al tyempo dela 'eliksy'on 'i tyene k(y)[u]mplido todaś laś parteś del konśeǧo 'i set- 'i para ke meǧor pu'edaś 'entender 'eśto para 'uzar delyyo 'onde [CW. konbyene]}

---

[75] Ps. 20.5.

BOOK OF THE REGIMEN OF LIVING ‹FOL. 62B›

‹fol. 62b›
{ḤELEK B- PEREK V [PART TWO CHAPTER SIX]
konvyene por śer 'util te lo kyero deklarar por 'enǧenplo komo śi por kabzo vinyeśe 'un 'eśpirmentado mediko 'i pratiko 'enla medisina 'a kurar 'un pasyente porśupone primero 'el fin deśu 'intensy'on ke 'eś la śanidad 'i 'eśto prośupu'eśto anda buśkando loś medyoś para 'efektuar 'el tal fin deśpu'eś 'eśpekula kual śera 'el meǧor 'i ve'e ke 'a meneśter 'evakuar halyyado 'eśte medyo konśidera ke la 'evakuasy'on pu'ede śer por purga 'o por śangri'a 'i miradoś todoś loś 'inkonvenyenteś konforme aloke konbyene al 'umor pekante ǧuśga ke 'eś maś konvenyente la śangri'a komo śila (')
'enfermedad fu'eśe 'una śinoka⁷⁶ 'i konśidera ke konla śangri'a 'eś maś fasil alkansar 'el fin ke 'eś la śanidad 'ike 'eś maś 'util para la śalud ke por 'elya śe alkansa ke danyoza por 'el partikular danyyo ke delyya pu'ede porśeder deśpu'eś 'eśpekula 'el lugar donde la deve dar śi 'enla medya 'o 'enla śefalyya 'o 'enla śafena 'i set- anśi meśmo 'enla kantidad de la śangre ke deve śakar 'i 'enke di'a 'o ake 'ora de manera ke anda diśkuryendo por todaś laś partikularidadeś ke śon maś konvenibleś para alkansar 'el fin prośupu'eśto 'i deśpu'eś de todo byen kontemplado ǧuśga śer konv[en]yente la śangri'a heǧa 'en tal lugar 'i atal tyempo 'i 'en tanta kantidad 'i set- 'i 'en fin de todo 'el ǧu'izy'o del konśeǧo 'eśkoǧe la 'obra 'i la haze de manera ke 'eś 'el fin del konśeǧo prinsipy'o de la 'eliksy'on komo tenemoś diǧo 'i 'eśto me parese ke baśta para lo ke konvyene śaber 'enel konśeǧo śi byen 'eśpekulareś 'en todaś 'eśtaś kondisy'oneś ke avemoś 'eśkrito a'un ke 'a śido muǧo 'en brebe 'i śi maś por 'eśtenso keraś śaber 'otraś muǧaś partikularidadeś ke konvyene śaber aserka del konśeǧo te le'ere lo ke largo tengo 'eśkrito 'enel tersero de la 'etika⁷⁷ :

KAPITULO SEŚTO

'EN kuanto ala śegunda virtud ke 'eś la templansa aś de śaber kela templansa 'eś aserka delaś delektasy'oneś kyero dezir ke śe lyyama templansa delektarśe 'el 'ombre komo konvyene 'enlaś kozaś ke konvyene delektarśe 'enelyyaś kuanto 'i kuando konvyene 'i set- ǧuśgando por la prudensyya kon dereǧa razon 'i aśi meśmo 'entriśteśerśe komo konvyene kuanto 'i kuando 'i 'enke konbyene 'i set- 'i maś 'eś aserka delaś delektasy'oneś ke aserka de laś triśtezaś 'i doloreś porke natural mente śon loś 'ombreś maś 'enklinadoś 'a śegir 'el delekte ke 'a fu'ir 'el dolor por lo kual ayy maś nesesidad de perkurar maś moderar 'el 'apetito aserka delaś delektasy'oneś ke aserka

---

⁷⁶ Synochus is a prolonged fever; see Maimonides, "*The Medical Aphorisms*," ed. and trans. Rosner and Munter, 1:221.

⁷⁷ The reference is to *Pne Moše,* and alluding to Aristotle, *NE* III.ii (1111b 5–1112a 18).

delaś triśtezaś 'i aś maś de śaber ke antigu'a mente 'ubo 'una śekta de filosofos ke kreeron ke no śe avi'a de tomar medyo 'enlaś delektasy'oneś maś anteś kuanto maś śe del[e]ktaśe 'el 'ombre maś}

⟨fol. 63a⟩
{SG
parte teni'a de la perfeksy'on[78] 'i fundaronśe 'en 'una razon por 'una porpozisy'on de todoś verifikada la kual 'eś ke la naturaleza 'eś reğida 'ordenada por 'entiliğensyya ke no śe afigura 'enelyya yero 'en ninguna manera komo śe deklara 'enel d(y)[o]zeno dela metafizika[79] 'i kon 'eśto diğeron ke pu'eś la delektasy'on 'eś 'ordenada 'i mobida dela naturaleza 'i la naturaleza 'eś 'ordenada por la 'entiliğensyya ke nunka yera de donde śe śige ke 'en kual kyera modo ke 'el 'ombre śe mu'eba ala delektasy'on 'eś byen

'I 'eśta razon no konvenśe ke śe'a toda delektasy'on bu'ena 'enel 'ombre porke la delektasy'on ke konśta śer natural 'enel 'ombre śegun ke 'eś 'ombre no 'eś la delektasy'on 'enlaś kozaś korporaleś ke la tal 'eś 'enel 'ombre śegun ke 'eś animal 'i no śegun ke 'eś 'ombre ke la natural delektasy'on 'enel śegun 'eś lo ke 'eś 'eś la delektasyyon ke por parte de śer rasy'onal śele śige la kual konśiśte 'enla 'eśpikulasy'on 'i bye(y)n[e] de la virtud 'i aserka deśta delektasy'on no 'eś la templansa śalbo aserka de la 'otra ke 'eś 'enel 'ombre śegun 'eś animal por la kual konbyene ke śe'a reğida 'i 'ordenada kon dereğa razon komo kuanto 'i kuando konvyene kon todaś laś 'otraś śerkonśtansyaś 'i kondisy'oneś ke konvyenen para ke śirba ala 'obra 'enla kual śe halye la delektasy'on del 'ombre śegun 'eś 'ombre ke no hara 'enelyya yero :

'I para ke meğor pu'edaś konprehender aserka de ke del[e]ktaśy'oneś 'eś la templansa a'un ke para 'eśto 'era meneśter byen alargar aś de śaber ke laś kozaś korporaleś aserka de laś kualeś śe dize delektasy'on 'i triśteza śon śegun 'el śentimyento de loś śinko śentidoś 'eśtiry'oreś 'i kada kual delyyoś tyene śu 'obğekto apropyado komo deklaro 'el filosofo 'enel libro del śentido 'i śensible[80] 'onde dize ke 'el 'obğekto de la viśta 'eś 'el kolor 'i 'a 'opiny'on de algunoś 'el kolor ğunto konla luz 'el 'obğekto del 'o'ir 'eś la boś 'i 'el del śentido del 'oler 'eś 'un vapor śutil ke śe rezu'elbe 'i rezolbyendośe śale koza ke da 'el 'olor hata 'el śentido ke lo resibe a'el

---

[78] Apparently this refers to the Epicureans.

[79] Unidentified source. Possibly he makes reference to *Metaphysics* XII.vii.9 (1072b 29–31) (trans. Tredennick, 2:151) or XII.x.10 (1075b 18–19) (2:173).

[80] Aristotle, *Parva Naturalia* 2 (*On Sense and Sensible Objects*), 3–5 (439a 6–445b 2), trans. Hett, 229–61.

BOOK OF THE REGIMEN OF LIVING ‹FOL. 63A–63B›

kual no halyyaron nombre propyo 'el 'obğekto del guśto 'eś 'el śabor 'i prinsipal
mente loś 'eśtremoś śaboreś dulse 'i amargo 'el 'obğekto del takto śon laś kalidadeś
primeraś tambyen 'enel śegundo de anima[81] śe deklaro afu'era 'eśtoś propyyoś
'obğektoś de kada śentido aver śinko 'obğektoś komuneś atodoś śentidoś loś kualeś
śon la ku'enta la grandeza la figura 'el mobimyento 'i sosyego 'i muğaś kozaś notableś
hablo 'eneśto 'el filosofo de tal modo ke dišeron aver 'eneśta parte venśido aśi meśmo
laś kualeś no hazen anu'eśtro perpozito śolo konvyene rekoleğir de lo diğo lo ke para
aki 'eś ke loś treś śentidoś ke śon ver 'o'ir 'oler no konśiśte 'enelyyoś tenplansa ni
deśtemplansa kuando 'el śentir delyoś no 'eś diriğido al delekte de alguno deloś 'otroś
doś śentidoś ke śon guśto 'i takto śino śolo al delekte delyoś meśmoś kyero dezir ke
kuando}

‹fol. 63b›
{'el 'ombre śe kyere delektar 'enel ver por śolo ver 'una bu'ena kolor ke 'eś delektarśe
'el śentido 'ensu 'obğekto śimpleś mente no ayy 'eneśto deśtemplansa 'i śi kiğere ver
'el 'ombre muğoś koloreś delektandośe 'enelyoś no śe lyyamara deśtenplansa ni śe
ku'enta 'entre loś visy'oś ver maś deloke konbyene 'i set- dela meśma manera 'enel
'o'ir kuando no 'eś maś ke por 'el 'o'ir 'enśi meśmo 'i por 'el śemeğ(y)ante 'enel 'oler
ke a'un ke 'en todoś 'eśtoś g- [3] ayya maś 'i menoś nośe dize 'enelyyoś templansa ni
deśtemplansa por no śeren tan beśtyaleś komo loś 'otroś doś anteś menoś materyaleś
'i mayoreś śervidoreś del 'entendimyento komo probaron loś naturaleś 'ila 'eśpery'ensyya lo mu'eśtra 'enpero kuando śe delektare 'el 'ombre de ver por 'otro fin
alyende del meśmo ver digo fin 'i delektasy'on konpetente al guśto 'o takto komo śiśe
delektar de ver 'una muğer por reśpekto de[ ]lušuryar 'eneśte tal ver ayy deśtemplansa por lo kual fu'e defendido por nu'eśtroś śaby'oś 'en grande manera[82] 'i śolo
dyeron lugar ke pudyeśe ver 'el śoltero laś śolteraś kuando fu'ere komo konbyene 'i
por loke konbyene ke 'eś para fin de kazar konelyyaś para perpetuarśe 'en śu (')
'eśpesy'a eśtonśeś 'eś koza liśita lo meśmo 'eś aserka del 'o'ir keśi śe delektare konla
muzika porke la tal muzika lo mu'eba 'a a'uto de luğury'a 'o 'a 'otro a'uto deśtemplado 'eneśto 'obra deśtemplada mente por lo kual defendyeron tambyen nu'eśtroś
śaby'oś 'o'ir la boz dela muğer ke mu'ebe 'a a'ukto de deśtemplansa 'i deśta meśma
manera 'eś ('yś) 'en 'el 'oler ke śyendo por 'otro reśpekto deś'oneśto fu'era del 'oler
'enśi komo 'eś delektarśe 'el 'ombre de 'oler loś veśtidoś 'olorozoś delaś muğereś ke
ponen para mober maś aloś 'ombreś akererlaś 'i ayuntarśe konelyyaś lo kual fu'e
tambyen defendido por nu'eśtroś śaby'oś de modo ke 'eneśto 'i 'en 'otroś śemeğanteś

---

[81] Aristotle, *De Anima* II.vi (418a 15–26), trans. Hett, 103.
[82] Prov. 6.25.

Book of the Regimen of Living ‹fol. 63b–64a›

kauzoś śe deve kada 'uno moderar 'i templarśe 'enelyyoś komo konvyene kuanto kuando 'i adonde konvyene 'i set- :
 'I porke algo maś syentaś loke aserka deśto te tengo diǧo te dire la kabza verdader'a 'enelyyo 'i 'eś ke śentir 'el 'ombre śegun 'eśtoś treś śentidoś por 'elyyoś 'enśi śin 'otro ningun reśpekto 'o por śervisy'o del 'entendimyento 'eśto 'eś śegun 'eś 'ombre 'i no śegun 'eś animal 'i 'enlaś delektasy'oneś ke 'el 'ombre śegun ke 'eś 'ombre śe delekta no konśiśte templansa ni destemplansa komo avemoś diǧo 'empero kuando 'eś la delektasy'on deśtoś treś por 'otro reśpekto afin de delektasy'on deloś 'otroś doś śentidoś 'entonseś śe delekta 'enelyyoś śegun animal 'i no śegun rasyonal porke loś brutoś animaleś no śe delektan 'enloś treś śentidoś diǧoś ke śon ver 'o'ir 'oler por 'elyyoś 'enśi 'o para aver de 'entender śalbo por 'amor del delekte}

‹fol. 64a›
{SD
de loś 'otroś doś ke śon guśtar 'i palpar 'enǧenplo 'el pero no śe delekta kon 'el 'olor dela lyebre por la śuabidad del 'olor 'enśi maś de(k)lektaśe por parte del guśto 'el kual 'imaǧina aver 'enla lyebre por 'el 'olor ke 'enelyya konprehendy'o de manera ke no śe delektan loś brutoś konel 'olor śalbo por loke por 'el 'olor konprehenden dela meśma manera śe alegra 'el le'on 'oyendo la boz del bu'ey 'o de 'otro kual kyer animal delektable aśu guśto no por la melodi'a dela boz 'enśi śalbo por loke kon la boz ayy kele parese 'i konprehende por la boz 'eśtar śerka del śebo delektable aśu guśto para poderlo komer anśi meśmo kuando śe alegra 'el propy'o le'on de ver 'el syerbo 'o kual kyer 'otra preśa nośe delekta de ver por 'el meśmo ver śalbo por loke del ver śe śige aśi ke asidental mente śe alegra konel ver 'i set- 'i a'un ke śe 'eśkribe de algunoś animaleś ke parese delektarśe 'en algunoś de loś treś śentidoś diǧoś por 'el meśmo śentido 'enśi komo śe ve'e de algunoś paǧaroś ke śe lyegan aloś kasadoreś 'oyendo śu boz 'i ǧiflo delektable aśu 'oreǧa aśi meśmo śe dize del kavalyyo ke śe del[e]kta de 'o'ir muzika por lo kual 'en 'oyendola relinǧa de plazer aśi meśmo śe 'eśkribe del pavon ke śe delekta 'en ver koloreś de śuś plumaś 'eneśto śon todoś loś ke 'eśkribyeron de animaleś[83] konformeś ke 'eśtoś animaleś śe delektan 'enlaś taleś kozaś por reśpekto ke loś mu'eben 'i deśpyertan a'el koyto de manera ke 'eś viśto 'ividente mente ke ninguno de loś animaleś brutoś śe delekta 'en algunoś deśtoś treś śentidoś por 'elyyoś 'enśi komo ten[e]moś diǧo por lo kual kuando 'el 'ombre śe delekta 'enelyyoś por la vi'a ke loś brutoś animaleś śe delektan eśtonśeś śe dira 'enelyyoś templansa 'i deśtemplansa śegun laś śerkonśtansyaś komo tenemoś diǧo 'enloś 'otroś

---

[83] This may be in reference to Aristotle, *De Anima* II.iii (414a 29–414b 19) or to *Physiologus*.

BOOK OF THE REGIMEN OF LIVING ⟨FOL. 64A–64B⟩

doś śentidoś ke śon 'el guśto 'i 'el takto śe dize propy'a mente la templansa 'i la deśtem[p]lansa 'enla 'obra delyoś por śi meśmoś porke loś animaleś brutoś śe delektan 'eneśtoś śentidoś por 'elyoś 'enśi komo 'eś magnifyeśto 'i deśtoś doś maś propyya mente śe dize la templansa śegun 'el takto ke śegun 'el guśto porke 'el takto 'eś akel 'enel kual śe delektan maś loś animaleś 'i 'eś maś korporal kyero dezir maś konğunto ala matery'a ke todoś loś 'otroś del kual primero śe śirbe 'el ninyyo 'en nasyendo 'i 'eś 'el pośtrero ke pyerde 'el 'ombre al tyenpo de śu feneśer por śer maś konğunto ala matery'a komo tenemoś diğo śyendo śu 'organo de tenplansa tere'a fri'o 'i śeko menoś 'eśpritual 'i maś gru'eso ke todoś 'i no śe afigura animal śentir śin 'el takto 'i guśto porke 'el guśto 'eś 'un takto komo śe dize 'enel śegundo de anima[84] 'i afiguraśe śin ve'er 'o'ir 'oler 'i a'un pu'ede bivir śin 'elyoś de donde śe nota śer 'eśtoś doś konvyene 'a śaber guśto 'i takto loś maś konğuntoś ala}

⟨fol. 64b⟩
{matery'a 'i delyoś doś maś 'el takto porke 'enel guśto por 'el 'enśi poka deśtemplansa pu'ede aver porke 'el guśto no ğuśga śalbo deloś śaboreś del dulse del amargo del 'estiptiko 'i set- 'enpero 'el takto ğuśga muğaś maś kalidadeś komo kalyente fri'o 'omido śeko duro mu'elye libyano pezado raro 'eśpeso 'i set- ke 'eśta 'eś la diferensyya deśtoś doś śentidoś komo 'eś magnifyeśto 'i komo 'el guśto deloś śaboreś no śe'a maś ke 'enla boka hata la raiz dela lengu'a komo 'eś manifyeśto poka deśtenplansa pu'ede aver 'enel guśto porśi ke 'el guśtar 'eś maś 'ofisy'o de kozineroś ke de 'otra alguna śu'erte de 'ombreś por lo kual dyeron lisensyy'a nu'eśtroś śaby'oś de guśtar vyanda 'enel di'a del ayuno hata 'una syerta kantidad[85] paresyendoleś komo 'eś verdad no aver 'enelyyo deśtemplansa de manera keno śon loś 'ombreś ni śe dizen deśtempladoś śalbo aserka del komer 'i del bever 'i del ko'yto por lo kual deve atentar kual kyera de templar 'el 'apetito maś aserka deśte śentido ke aserka deloś 'otroś ke por 'eśto diğo 'el filosofo 'el śentido del takto 'eś vitupery'o anoś 'i set-[86] 'i deve ad-

---

[84] Aristotle, *De Anima,* trans. Hett, 119–121.
[85] Berakot 14a.
[86] The phrase is Maimonides' rendition of Aristotle, *NE* III.x.11 concerning profligacy (Pt. 2, chaps. 36 and 40; Pt. 3, chaps. 8 and 49 [*Guide,* trans. Pines, 369–73; 381–85; 430–36; 601–13]): "Hence the sense to which Profligacy is related is the most universal of the senses: and there appears to be good ground for the disrepute in which it is held, because it belongs to us not as human beings but as animals" (1118b). Almosnino may have wished to condense Aristotle's discussion of how and why excess destroys life (*De Anima* III.xiii [435b 18–19]): "Hence excess in tangible qualities destroys not only the sense organ, but also the animal, because touch is the one sense which the animal must possess" (trans. Hett, 203). I do not find a similarly turned phrase in either *De Anima* or *Sense and Sensible Objects.*

BOOK OF THE REGIMEN OF LIVING ‹FOL. 64B–65A›

vertir 'el bu'eno 'i virtu'ozo ke no śe sirva del maś de lo ke konvyene komo 'i kuando konvyene 'i set- ke 'enesto konśiśte propy'a mente la templansa 'i por tanto akavidaron nu'eśtros śaby'oś aserka del abto venere'o ke no śe'a 'el 'ombre akośtumbrado 'a ayuntarśe kon śu muğer komo 'el galyo[87] ke śe 'eśkrive del śer 'el maś lušuryozo de loś animaleś :

'I a'eśta 'intensy'on śegun 'opiny'on del śenyor Rabbenu Mośeh fu'e defendido 'en nu'eśtra śantisima ley loś ağuntamyentoś konlaś muğereś śerkanaś komo madre 'i hiğa 'i 'ermana 'i set-[88] porke śi 'eśtaś no fu'eran defendidaś por la muğa konversasy'on 'i ayuntamyento kontino śe dyeran muğo al ko'yto 'i fu'era difisilisimo moderarśe 'enel lo kual fu'era grande beśtyalidad 'i braba deśtemplansa 'i 'eśta parese śer verdader'a 'intensy'on 'enla probidensy'a devina alyende de aver 'enesto 'otraś muğaś verdaderaś razoneś 'i śekretoś fundadoś 'inefableś 'enla kabza de defenderśe loś taleś ayuntamyentoś alomenoś notaśe deśta śola razon kuan vituperable 'eś la lušury'a kontina 'i kuan grande pekado 'i yero manifyeśto 'eś 'uzar delyya maś de lo ke konvyene 'i kuanto maś kon kyen 'eś defendido por nu'eśtra śantisima ley alyende de śer abominable por ley de nature(y)za de 'umanidad 'i por toda razon kontado 'entre loś a'utoś beśt[y]aleś por nefandoś 'i 'eś tan vituperable deśtemplansa la lušury'a maś de lo ke konvyene 'i komo no kon[v]yene ke ninguno komete tal visy'o ke no śe arepyenta de averlo feğo por dende śi kual kyera 'imağinaśe 'enel prinsipy'o 'el arepentimyento ke śuśede al fin no abri'a [CW. delinkente]}

‹fol. 65a›
{SH
delinkente 'en tan vituperable visy'o
LE'EŚE de Demośteleś 'el maś 'elegante 'orador[89] ke 'ubo 'entre loś gregoś aver rekerido para 'un deś'oneśto a'uto de lušury'a akel famozo mośtro 'enel a'uto venereo La( )'iś meritriśe ke fu'e 'ensu tyenpo la kual le demando 'una gran śuma de dinero 'el 'eğando mano ala bolsa para śakarlo konsidrando '[e]l fin de tan 'inorme a'uto śe

---

[87] *Hilkot De'ot*, chap. 5, halakah 4.

[88] Lev. 18.6–18 describes the prohibited marriages. Maimonides devotes much of *MN*, Pt. 3, chap. 49 to explaining the reasons for the prohibitions (*Guide*, trans. Pines, 606–8).

[89] That is, Demosthenes. Plutarch mentions the courtesan Lais (*Lives*, trans. Perrin, 13:262; 4:114) in his *Life of Demosthenes* but not the witticism (7:3–79). Aulus Gellius recounts the anecdote in *Noctes Atticae*, Bk. 1, chap. 8: "Said Demosthenes to the courtesan Laïs, 'I decline to buy repentance at the cost of 10,000 drachmas' " (trans. J. C. Rolfe [London, 1927–28], 1:44).

Book of the Regimen of Living ⟨fol. 65a–65b⟩

de tubo 'i diğo no konpro tan karo 'el arepentir palabra por syerto digna de notar ke kizo śignifikar ke de śemeğanteś a'utoś lo maś syerto ke tenemoś 'eś 'el arepentimyento 'i 'eś pura 'ignoransy'a komprar 'el mal por dineroś 'i deśte visy'o śe deven akabidar muğo maś loś manseboś 'i deven de perkurar de apartarśe no śolo del propy'o visy'o maś a'un de laś kozaś ke pu'eden mober 'el 'apetito a'el porke śi al tal visy'o dan 'entrada 'o toman lisensy'a de śegirlo por muy poko ke śe'a śon derokadoś 'i deśtru'idoś śin ningun remedy'o por śer 'eśte tal a'uto por parte deśte śentido maś śenśual 'i maś konğunto ala matery'a ke ningun 'otro de loś 'otroś śentidoś 'enel kual por parte de la matery'a ayy muğa mayor delektasy'on ke 'en ninguno de loś 'otroś 'i 'eś muy difisil de apartarśe 'el ku'erpo de 'el deśpu'eś ke lo 'enpyeśa a'eśerśitar porke śon todoś loś viśy'oś 'i apetitoś korporaleś de tal kalidad 'i maś propyya mente 'eśte partikular 'enke hablamoś de kual kyera ke lo 'uza kontinu'a mente maś śe a'umenta 'el 'apetito de 'uzarlo 'i kuanto maś śe aparta del tanto śe diminu'e konforme alo kual dišeron nu'eśtroś śaby'oś 'en muy breveś palabraś ke 'un myembro pekenyyo ayy 'enel 'ombre ke kyen lo harta 'eśta hambryento 'i kyen lo 'enfambreśe 'eśta harto 'i śet-[90] 'i la 'intensy'on 'eś manifyeśta 'i la razon 'ividente ke 'el kośtumbre haze 'el abito tanto para 'el mal komo para 'el byen 'i śegun 'el abito śalen laś 'obraś kumplidaś kontina mente komo 'eś śabido :

 'I tubyeron por tan vituperable 'eśte deśtemplado viśy'o kon grandisima razon ke a'un kon śu muğer propyya defendyeron muğaś kozaś ke mu'eben la veluntad aśemeğante a'uto beśtyal kuando no konvyene por lo kual defendyeron al 'ombre keno 'entraśe śupito 'ensu meśma kaza 'i no kale dezir 'en kaza deśu kompanyero porke no halye la muğer deśnuda ke śeri'a kabza de moberle 'a lušury'a deś'oneśta śyendo atyenpo keno konvyene por donde defendyeron keno miraśe 'el 'ombre loś veśtidoś dela muğer ke konośe a'un ke 'eśten 'en kaza del šaśtre 'o de 'otro kual kyera śin 'eśtar la diğa muğer prezente por ke por parte de śaber ke śon akelyoś śuś veśtidoś vyene apensar afinkada mente 'enelyya 'i 'eśte tal penśamyento 'i fe'a //kontenplasy'on lo fazen deśtenplado 'y śon tantoś loś maleś 'eneśto//}

⟨fol. 65b⟩
{ke śon śin ku'ento lo kual porśede de la grande 'enklinasy'on ke 'el 'ombre tyene a[']el maś ke aninguno 'otro a'uto 'umano por la grande nesesidad ke 'en la natureza 'ubo de la perpetuasy'on de la 'eśpesy'a konservada konla ğenerasy'on del 'endivido 'i śon tan 'ividenteś loś maleś 'i 'inkonvenye[n]teś ke del śe śigen al ku'erpo 'i ala alma ke no 'eś meneśter hablar 'enelyyo ke ninguna razon de byen tyene kuando 'eś maś de lo ke konbyene para śuśtentasy'on del mundo perpetuando la 'eśpesy'a :

---

[90] Sanhedrin 104a.

BOOK OF THE REGIMEN OF LIVING ‹FOL. 65B–66A›

DE la meśma manera 'eś tambyen la deśtemplansa aserka del komer 'i beber maś de lo ke konvyene 'en tyempo ke no konvyene 'o 'en konpany'a de kyen no konbyene ke 'eś koza ke śe deve muğo atentar de adonde depende muğo la konśervasy'on 'o korupsy'on de la 'onra tan delikada 'i fasil de konro[n]per tanto kuanto difisil de ganar de manera ke śe konkluye de todo lo diğo ke aserka de laś 'obraś del śentido del guśto 'i takto 'i maś propyya mente aserka del takto śe konsidra la templansa 'i la deśtemplansa lo kual 'eś 'uzar de todaś laś partikularidadeś aserka deśto ke śon 'infinitaś komo konvyene 'i kuando 'i kuanto konvyene 'i set- kon todaś laś 'otraś śerkośtansyaś 'i lo ke śe deśvi'a deśtaś śerkośtansyaś 'eś lo ke verdader'a mente śe lyyama deśtemplansa :

PERO aś de notar aserka de loś 'eśtremoś deśta virtud ke 'el 'eśtremo del 'ekśeśo ake lyyamamoś deśtemplansa propyya mente 'eś muy muğo pe'or ke 'el 'eśtremo por falta 'i 'eś 'inkurable visy'o porke komo tenemoś diğo 'el 'ombre 'eś maś 'enklinado aśegir la del[e]ktasy'on ke ahu'ir la triśteza 'i kuando akośtare al 'eśtremo de la puğa delektandośe maś de loke konbyene śera muy difisil kitarśe delyyo : 'i kuando akośtare al 'eśtremo de la falta adelektarśe menoś de lo ke konbyene śera muy fasil traerlo al medyo kuanto maś ke muy pokoś 'inkuren 'eneśte visy'o por lo kual 'el ke 'eneśta virtud dubdare del medyo akośteśe ala falta para meğor poder venir al medyo śegun la ariśtotelika doktrina dada 'enel fin del śegundo dela 'etika[91] 'i 'eneśta śe deve atentar maś ke 'en ninguna de laś 'otraś vertudeś alyende de śer 'eśta 'una de laś kardinaleś 'i śegunda 'en dignidad 'o alomenoś tersera 'entre laś vertudeś laś kualeś śon śimyento del byen 'umano 'en todaś laś operasy'oneś komo avemoś diğo 'i al fin maś deklararemoś

'EŚ nesesary'o maś partikular mente atentar 'i 'andar śobre 'el avizo 'eneśta virtud 'en grande manera porke maś veześ 'i maś fasil mente akaeśe 'erar 'eneśta ke 'enlaś 'otraś ke a'un ke la virtud dela fortaleza parese śer de grado maś alto 'en dignidad ke 'eśta por śer maś difisil 'i aserka de maś difisil ke 'eś aserka de śufrir la mu'erte 'i 'oponerśe aśuś peligroś 'i la templansa 'eś śolo 'enla a'vśtenensy'a delaś delektasy'oneś por 'onde parese śer la fortaleza maś 'ekśelente virtud :}

‹fol. 66a›
{SV

POR śer la templansa 'en kozaś akośtumbradaś 'enlaś kualeś 'el 'ombre 'eś maś kontino 'a yerar 'eś 'eśta virtud grandisima 'i de grande 'ekśelensy'a 'i muy nota 'i

---

[91] Aristotle, *NE* II.ix.8–9 (1109b 19–27).

BOOK OF THE REGIMEN OF LIVING ‹FOL. 66A›

konosida atoda preśona 'i por laś meśmaś kabzaś 'i razoneś toda preśona 'a de atentar muğo 'i no deśkuidarśe 'enelyya 'i 'enśuś partikularidadeś ke śon 'infinitaś laś kualeś kedaran ala bu'ena 'eśtimatiba del lektor para 'uzar delyyaś śegun la dereğa razon kon bu'en ğu'izy'o prudensyal komo kuanto 'i kuando 'i 'enke konbyene 'i set- 'i nota ke tyene 'eśta virtud muğaś parteś 'i 'eśpesyaś komo templansa 'enel ko'yto 'enel komer 'enel bever 'i kada 'una tyene śu nombre 'eśpesyal 'i śuś visy'oś aśi meśmo tyene partikulareś nombreś notoś al vulgo 'i por tanto loś dešo de dezir śolo de 'una koza te kyero akavidar 'i 'eś ke kuanto menoś pudyereś falyyarte 'en komidaś de fyeśtaś 'o banketeś 'o de kual kyer 'otra śu'erte lo hagaś 'i te 'eśkuześ delyyo kon toda la diliğensy'a posible porke laś maś delaś veześ pyerde 'el 'ombre 'enloś taleś lugareś śu a'utoridad 'i haze aloś ke konel komen atreberśe a'el 'o alomenoś 'eś[ ]koza de fazerśe familyar 'a muğoś koza ke Śeneka defendy'o 'en grande manera kon fortisima razon[92] 'i alyende dešto 'el muğo akośtumbrarlo haze a[']el 'ombre deśtemplado 'i kuando fu'ereś forsado de 'ir perkura de śer grabe 'enloś taleś lugareś 'i konbiteś kuanto posible fu'ere 'i no te mu'eśtreś triśte konla śeveredad porke kabzaraś moleśty'a aloś aśiśtenteś 'i śi śusedyere koza de re'ir komo laś maś veześ akaese śe'a tu rizo śin 'eśkarny'o śin 'eśkandalo 'i deśa'utorizam[y]ento 'i tu boz śin grito porke 'el rizo 'eś digno de reprehensy'on śi 'eś demazyado śi 'eś a'eğado komo rizo de ninyyo 'o de muğer ke laś maś veześ 'eś maś de loke konvyene ni śeaś śoberby'o ni malino ni di[gaś] kozaś ke 'ofendan a'otro kual kyera porke 'eśtoś taleś hazen al 'ombre 'odyozo 'i 'en konkluzy'on kuanto te pudyereś apartar del lugar 'i delaś kozaś 'enke ayy śośpeğa de a'uto de deśtenplansa tanto śeraś maś kontente 'i partisiparaś maś 'enel grado dela filisidad 'i byen verdadero konloś bu'enoś 'en śuma delektasy'on:

KAPITULO ŚETENO

'EN kuanto lo ke konvyene śaber para la deśkripsy'on dela tersera virtud ke 'eś la liberalidad śe'a de notar lo primero ke 'eś virtud aserka del dar 'i tomar 'el dinero 'o śu vali'a komo kuanto 'i donde konvyene 'i a'un ke pareśka śer aserka de doś kontrary'oś ke 'eś 'el dar 'i 'el resebir komo kyera ke la virtud no konśiśte 'enel dar kyero dezir 'enla 'obra 'eśtiry'or śalbo 'enel modo del dar 'i del resebir śegun laś kondisyy'oneś dela virtud ğuśgadaś por la dereğa razon [CW. ke 'eś]}

---

[92] Cf. Seneca, *De Clementia* I.xi.2 (trans. Basore, 1:391), II.iii.1 (435); *Ep. Mor.* 14.15 (trans. Gummere, 1:93), 88.29 (2:367).

Book of the Regimen of Living ‹fol. 66b›

‹fol. 66b›

{HELEK B PEREK Z [PART TWO CHAPTER SEVEN]

ke 'eś 'un a'uto 'enla alma del kual śalen todaś laś 'obraś del dar 'i del resebir komo konvyene deśta manera no 'eś aserka de doś kontrary'oś maś anteś 'eś aserka de 'una śola koza ke 'eś la konvenensy'a dela 'obra konla dereğa razon komo tenemoś diğo ke kuando fu'ere 'el dar 'i 'el tomar komo konbyene kuanto 'i kuando konvyene śera virtud 'i śi falta 'o śobra 'eś visy'o 'i porke 'eśta virtud haze muğo para la perfeksy'on dela konversasy'on 'umana para kaptar komun benivolensy'a 'eśpesyal mente 'enel tyempo prezente ke loś 'eśtremoś 'o deśtruyen al 'ombre pekando por puğa 'o lo hazen del todo deśkonversable pekando por falta te dire laś propyedadeś delyya 'i de śuś 'eśtremoś por 'eśtenśo ke por 'elyyaś śe manifeśtara 'el 'entero konosimyento de lo ke konbyene śaber aserka deśta virtud 'i byen 'eśpekulado śe falyyan 'enelyya diziśeyś propyedadeś :

LA primera (y) 'eś ke a'un ke la liberalidad śe'a aśi 'enel resebir komo 'enel dar porke 'un grande śenyyor resibyendo prezente 'i don de 'un śumenoś ke 'el śe pu'ede dezir ke akel śenyyor 'uza de liberalidad 'en kerer resebir 'el tal prezente 'i haze mersed alke śelo da 'en konśentirlo de manera ke 'el kelo da śe pu'ede dezir ke resibe 'i 'el kelo resibe ke da de adonde ğuśgaron nu'eśtroś śaby'oś kon ğuśta razon ke śi 'una muğer dyeśe 'un anilyo 'o kual kyera 'otra vali'a de moneda 'a 'un 'ombre 'i resibyendo akel tal 'ombre 'el anilyyo dela muğer diğeśe ke fu'eśe apropyyada a'el kon loke resibi'a delyya keda akelyya muğer atada a'el śi akel tal 'ombre 'eś kalefikado 'i tenido 'en grande 'eśtima porke konla 'utilidad ke 'elyya resibe 'enke 'el konśinty'o tomar śu prezente 'eś komo ke 'el le dyeśe konla kual 'utilidad la apropyya aśi por leğ[i]tima muğer atandola konlaś palabraś ke nu'eśtroś śaby'oś 'ordenaron kon todo 'eśto maś konśiśte la liberalidad 'enel dar ke 'enel resebir ke 'enel dar śemeğa 'el dador ala kabza prima 'imitandola muğo porke de kontino da 'i nunka resibe konforme aloke dizen nu'eśtroś śaby'oś ke del syelo dan 'i no resiben[93] 'i tanto kuanto 'esede 'en perfeksy'on 'el ağente aśu pasyente 'en kual kyera 'obra 'umana tanto 'esede 'el ke da 'a 'el ke resibe porke la liberalidad aserka del dar 'eś dar donde konbyene 'i komo konvyene 'i set-[94] 'i aserka del resebir aśi meśmo 'eś 'el resebir de kyen konvyene 'i değar de resebir de kyen no konvyene tomar ke todo 'eś pa(r)[d]eser 'o değar de padeser lo ke aserka del dar 'eś todo 'obrar 'i śi alguno 'eś loado muğo por no resebir donde konb[y]ene 'i deś'eğar avereś demazyadoś 'ofresidoś de tiranoś 'i lisita mente no 'eś tanto por la liberalidad komo por magnyanimidad 'i ğuśtisy'a por lo kual 'eś viśto ke la propy'a liberalidad 'eś grande konpanyera de la ğuśtisy'a 'i de

---

[93] This seems to be a reference to Ḥullin 25a.
[94] This seems to be a reference to Ḥullin 60a.

todaś laś 'otraś vertudeś komo 'ermana fy'el por lo kual 'eś tanbyen viśto ke la propyya liberalidad 'eś aserka del dar}

⟨fol. 67a⟩
{SZ
'I 'eśta 'eś la primera propyedad de la liberalidad komo ve(d)[r]ifiko 'el filosofo por śeyś razoneś fortisimaś 'enel kuarto dela 'etika[95] 'enel teśto śegundo 'i por 'eśta meśma kabza 'en nu'eśtra śantisima ley 'i por boka de nu'eśtroś śantoś porfetaś no śe aplika 'eśta noblisima virtud śalbo 'enel dar porke tenemoś por maśima imitar 'en todaś laś kozaś de nu'eśtraś 'obraś alaś devinaś de nu'eśtro Dyyo glory'ozo kuanto pudyeremoś komo noś amoneśta la meśma 'eśkritura dizyendo andaraś 'enśuś kaminoś[96] 'i glozaron nu'eśtroś śaby'oś ke kyere dezir ke 'imitemoś aśuś 'obraś ke aśi komo 'eś pyadozo 'i klemente śe'a 'el 'ombre pyadozo 'i set-[97] 'i 'eśto pyenśo śe'a la 'intensy'on de lo ke dize nu'eśtra śantisima ley aserka de la diśtribu'isy'on ke konbyene para selebrar laś fyeśtaś de nu'eśtraś paśkuaś do konkluye 'en todaś dizyendo kada 'uno komo dadiba de śu mano komo bendisy'on de H⟨a-Šem⟩ tu Dyyo ke dyyo ati[98] keryendo śignifikar ami ver ke todo 'ombre deve perkurar de 'uzar liberalidad 'i ke śe'a propyya mente aserka del dar 'i no aserka del resebir 'i maś ke śe'a komo konvyene 'i 'eśto kiğo konprender dizyendo komo dadiba de śu mano 'i set-[99] primero ke śe'a konforme aśu posiblidad ke 'eś śer dado 'i 'ordenado kon dereğa razon śegundo ke śe'a dadiba 'i no resibimyento 'i da la razon por donde deve śer 'enel dar //maś ke// 'enel tomar ke 'eś la ke tenemoś diğo por imitar ala kabza prima ke kontino da 'i nunka resibe 'i 'eśto 'eś lo ke kizo dezir dizyendo komo bendisy'on de H⟨a-Šem⟩ tu Dyyo ke dyyo ati[100] ke kyere dezir ke dando tu 'i no resibyendo 'imitaś la bendisyon 'i 'obra del Dyyo ke 'el Dyyo ati de kontino [da] 'i nunka resibyo

LA śegunda propyedad 'eś la komun 'en todaś laś vertudeś ke 'eś byen 'eśpisifikarśe 'en kada 'una la kual 'eś śer la 'obra afin del byen 'i dela virtud 'i no por algun reśpekto 'otro ke śi 'el 'ombre da por fin de alkansar fama 'i por śer loado 'o porke śe'a tenido por liberal 'o kual kyer 'otro fin śemeğante 'eśte tal no śe pu'ede lyyamar liberal pu'eś no lo haze por fin dela propyya liberalidad dela meśma manera

---

[95] Aristotle, *NE* IV.1 (1119b 21–1122a 18).
[96] Deut. 28.9.
[97] Ramban Deut. 11.1.
[98] Deut. 16.17.
[99] Deut. 16.17.
[100] Deut. 16.17.

BOOK OF THE REGIMEN OF LIVING ‹FOL. 67A–67B›

śi por ǧuśtisy'a 'eś obligado de dar 'a 'otro de śu hazyenda 'i bolver lo devido pu'eśto ke 'eneśto haze śegun la virtud dela ǧuśtisy'a no por 'eśo śe lyyamara liberal porke 'el ke 'obrare śegun la virtud dela liberalidad 'a de śer por fin dela propyya virtud komo tenemoś diǧo :
    'I nota ke toda 'obra virtu'oza śe denomina por parte del fin 'i a'un ke 'en 'una meśma 'obra konkuran muǧaś vertudeś akelyya tal 'obra 'eś nombrada del fin ke śe haze komo noś 'enśenyyo Aristotel 'enel kinto dela 'etika[101] 'enǧenplo śi 'uno da dineroś komo konvyene para reśgatar katiboś ke 'eś dinero por ǧuśtisy'a śe lyyama ǧuśto 'i no deša de śer liberal porke da kom[o] konvyene śu dinero 'i por loke konvyene 'i set-}

‹fol. 67b›
{maś la propyya liberalidad 'eś 'enlaś donasy'oneś 'i no 'enlaś dadibaś devidaś a'un ke tambyen enelyaś ayya liberalidad 'i aśi 'un 'eśperdisyado gaśtador ke no ama 'el dinero 'i no lo deśpende śi no por deśpender de loś kualeś muy pokoś śe halyyan a'un ke yo 'e viśto algunoś 'eśte tal 'eś puro prodigo 'i 'el ke deśpende śuś dineroś 'en komidaś deś'ordenadaś 'i 'en dar 'a muǧereś por luǧuryar konelyyaś 'eśte 'eś deśtemplado 'i no deǧa de śer prodig(+)o
    LA tersera ke 'eś tambyen komun 'en todaś laś vertudeś 'eś lo ke prinsipal mente śe deve advertir 'enel 'obrar de la virtud 'i 'eś ke śe'a la 'obra 'ordenada kon dereǧa razon por parte de la prudensy'a kon todaś laś śerkonśtansyaś ke śon laś syete deklaradaś 'enel tersero de la 'etika[102] 'i tirando 'el fin ke 'eś 'el prinsipal ke diǧimoś 'enla śegunda propyedad kedan seyś ke śon la preśona ke konvyene dar akyen konbyene komo konvyene loke konvyene ke 'eś la koza ke konbyene darśe 'elyya 'enśi 'i la kantidad delyya kuando adonde kuyoś 'enǧenploś por klaroś deǧamoś 'i 'el ke 'eneśto kizyere ver 'ekśelenteś dotrinaś le'a 'el libro de loś benefisy'oś de Śeneka[103] del kual yo tengo ś[a]kadaś muǧaś a'utoridadeś :
    LA kuarta 'eś ke la 'obra de la liberalidad śe'a kon alegri'a 'i delektasy'on porke la delektasy'on 'i alegri'a 'enlaś 'obraś śegun virtud 'eś verdader'a śenyal de śer firmeś loś abitoś 'enel alma del virtu'ozo 'i śer laś 'obraś produzidaś de 'entera veluntad 'i a'un ke 'eśto 'eś tambyen konǧunto 'a todaś laś vertudeś 'eneśta virtud partikular mente śe deve muǧo atentar porke a[']el 'ombre muǧaś veześ le suseden kozaś 'enke gaśtar konbyene grande śuma de moneda reśpektuado kon lo ke tyene lo kual kuando konbyene akyen tyene 'el abito de la liberalidad muy firme śera

---

[101] Aristotle, *NE* V.v.10–16 (1133a 20–1133b 29).
[102] Aristotle, *NE* III.iii (1112a 19–1113a 14).
[103] For a translation of *De Beneficiis,* see Seneca, *Moral Essays,* trans. Basore, vol. 3.

Book of the Regimen of Living ‹fol. 67b–68a›

'enoǧozo 'i triśte dandole dolor 'i syendo deśta manera no śera liberalidad pu'eś le 'eś 'enoǧozo 'i no lo haze kon kunp(+)lida veluntad 'i delekte por tanto śe deve kavidar kual kyera ke dyere ke lo de kon kunplida veluntad 'i 'entero kontentamyento śin meśkla de triśteza alguna por lo kual diǧo nu'eśtra śagra 'eśkritura aserka del dar a'el deze'ozo 'i meśkino dar daraś a'el 'ino śe 'enmaleśka tu korason 'entu dar a'el ke por la koza 'eśta te bendezira H‹a-Šem› tu Dyo 'i set-[104] keryendo dezir ke 'el premyo ke 'el Dyyo da por 'eśta virtud lo da por śola la veluntad konke śeda por lo kual akabida ke kuando la dadiba 'ubyere nesesidad de śer 'en kantidad komo de nota 'el doble 'en dezir dar daraś 'i set- ke kon todo 'eśto no śele 'enmaleśka 'el korason ni śele danye la veluntad 'enla 'obra del dar amoneśtandole ke por śola 'eśta koza ke 'eś la veluntad da 'el Dyyo la bendisy'on a'el 'ombre 'en śalary'o de[ ]śemeǧante virtud 'i la razon 'eśta byen viśta ke śi 'el 'ombre śe 'entriśteśe kon loke da parese amar maś 'el dinero ke da ke la 'obra bu'ena ke haze 'en darl[o]}

‹fol. 68a›
{SH
     LA kinta 'eś aserka del resebir la kual 'eś ke a[']el liberal no konbyene ke resiba de kyen no konbyene resebir 'en lugar 'i tyenpo deśkonvenyente 'i set- porke 'el ke resibe de kyen no konbyene demu'eśtra kerer maś lo ke resibe ke la 'obra de la virtud ke konśiśte 'en no resebir de kyen no konbyene resebir komo t[e]nemoś diǧo 'i demu'eśtra maś no konoser kuan mizerable 'eś 'el resebir komo śe'a propy'o del liberal no 'eśtimar 'el dinero 'en reśpekto de la 'obra virtu'oza :
     LA śeśta 'eś no śer akośtumbrado 'a demandar demandaś de 'otroś porke komo śe'a la liberalidad propyya mente 'enel dar komo tenemoś diǧo śi śe kośtumbraśe 'a resebir le śeri'a difisil 'el dar lo ke akośtumbrandośe de kontino 'a dar śele hara por 'el muǧo kośtumbre 'el resebir difisil 'i 'uzara delaś 'obraś de liberalidad komo konbyene dereǧero por la dereǧa razon 'i set- :
     LA śebtima 'eś ke 'el liberal resiba de adonde konbyene resebir porke śi 'el dyere de kontino 'i no resibyere aforarśe'a śu hazyenda de manera ke no kede para 'el ni para 'otro por donde dando pyerde 'el poder de dar por lo kual konbyene resebir de 'unoś 'i dar a'otroś komo konvyene de kyen 'i akyen konbyene 'i set- :
     por 'efektuar 'eśta klarisima virtud komo śe ku'enta de Dy'oǧeneś ke no tenyendo ke dar tomaba de 'unoś 'i daba a'otroś porke 'eneśto hazi'a aloś ke le daban

---

[104] Deut. 15.10.

Book of the Regimen of Living ⟨fol. 68a–68b⟩

liberaleś 'i tanbyen aśi meśmo 'en asebtarlo[105] 'E( )paminondaś no poseendo hazyenda konforme aśu kalidad tomo de 'un amigo riko kantidad de moneda para dar a'otro pobre[106] 'uzando kon todoś liberalisima mente pero 'eś meneśter muğo advertir ke 'el ke resibe no resiba de todoś śalbo deloś maś lyegadoś a'el deśuś meneśteroś 'i de śuś hiğoś 'o de śuś paryenteś 'i a'un deśtoś no 'eś razon kelo resiba afin del dinero 'enśi śalbo afin de śuplir śu nesesidad 'i kuando la nesesidad fu'ere muğa 'i no fu'ere śokorido deloś śuyoś 'i no tubyere paryenteś 'i loś 'eśtranyyoś no lo śokoren śin demandarlo 'el 'eśtonseś 'eś lisito demandarlo por 'el maś 'oneśto modo ke pośible fu'ere komo śe ku'enta de Śokrateś[107] ke tenyendo nesesidad de 'una kapa diğo 'en prezensy'a de muğoś nobleś ke śi tubyera panyo 'ubyera heğo 'una kapa 'i śupito ke fu'e 'o'ido de loś ke 'ensu prezensyya 'eśtaban probe'eron lo todoś de panyyo de manera ke a[']el propyo punto ke lo diğo śuplyeron śu falta todoś loś ke aśu notisy'a śu diğo lyego loś kualeś kon todo 'eśto Seneka reprehende dizyendo[108] ke tarde lo dyyo kual kyera ke dyo 'el panyo aŚokrateś por kuanto 'eśperaron ke 'el deśkubryeśe śu mengu'a 'en publiko 'i no fu'e śokorido anteś ke 'el lo 'ubyeśe de śignifikar 'i kual kyera ke lo dyo śe lo 'ubyera de dar anteś ke 'el fu'era forsado ademandarlo 'i konprarlo pidyendolo :

LA 'oğaba propyedad 'eś ke perkure de probe'er 'ensu hazyenda para [CW. konserbarla]}

⟨fol. 68b⟩

{konserbarla 'i multiplikarla ke no śe le pyerda porke guardar la hazyenda 'i 'eśkatimar 'enelyya komo konbyene śyendo la 'intensy'on para diśtribu'irla komo konbyene 'i adonde 'i kuando konbyene 'eś puro a'uto de liberalidad pu'eś la guarda para dar byen 'i konforme al ğu'izyyo prudensyal konforme alo kual diśeron nu'eśtroś śaby'oś 'en nu'eśtro śanto patryarka Ya°akob ke bolbyyo apasar 'el ri'o por 'unoś atu'endoś pekenyoś de poka śuśtansy'a[109] ke śele abian 'olbidado hazyendo 'en akel meśmo vyağe 'un tan grande prezente aśu 'ermano °Eśau komo parese por nu'eśtra

---

[105] Unidentified source. Diogenes Laertius recounts two instances of Diogenes' possessing another's cloak without returning it or bestowing it on a third party (*Philosophers,* trans. Hicks, 2:63–65 and 67).

[106] Unidentified source. Plutarch recalls that Epaminondas received money from Pelopidas (*Lives,* trans. Perrin, 2:213) and consoled his hereditary poverty in philosophy (5:347).

[107] Cf. Aelian *VH* 1.16, and Plato, *Phaedo* 58a–c.

[108] Seneca, *De Beneficiis* VII.24, trans. Basore, 3:511.

[109] Ḥullin 91a.

BOOK OF THE REGIMEN OF LIVING ‹FOL. 68B–69A›

śakra 'eśkritura[110] ke śer 'en tanta abundansa de nota śu primo grado de liberalidad 'i komun mente dizen nu'eśtroś śaby'oś ke loś ǧuśtoś 'eśkatiman śobre śuś hazyendaś[111] porke 'el fin 'eś bu'eno 'i śanto ke 'eś para diśtribu'irla 'onde kuando 'i komo konbyene 'i set- :

LA nona 'eś ke 'el liberal deve atender 'i advertir 'en gran manera akyen da 'o akyen deve dar ke no deve dar 'a todoś ni 'en todo tyenpo ke le fu'ere d[e]mandad(a)[o] porke deśta manera no le kedara para dar 'enel tyenpo ke konbyene ni akyen konbyene :

LA desima 'eś ke 'enel lugar 'onde konbyene kede viśto 'i ǧuśgado por la dereǧa razon de larga mente 'i śupla la nesesidad del ke resibe de manera ke mire maś por śuplir la nesesidad del ke resibe ke la falta ke 'enel haze loke le da

LA 'onzena 'eś ke pu'eśto kazo ke 'el liberal deve de atentar ala nesesidad de lo ke resibe maś de lo ke a'el le keda 'eś razon ke lo ke 'el dyere lo[ ]de konvenible aśu posiblidad porke la liberalidad no konśiśte 'enel muǧo dar śalbo 'enel abito 'i 'enel modo de dar komo kuando 'i kuanto konvyene 'i set- 'i deśta manera podra śer maś liberal kyen poko tyene tenyendo 'el abito perfekto ke 'el muy riko 'i poko abituado 'enla virtud de la liberalidad a'un ke[ ]de maś kantidad ke 'el ke poko tyene pu'eś ke 'en reśpekto de lo ke le keda al riko 'eś poko lo ke da 'i 'el pobre 'en reśpekto de lo ke tyene da muǧo

LA do(n)zena ke loś liberaleś kuando 'eredan la hazyenda ke pose'en 'o ke śela dan 'o ke śela 'enprezentan la diśtribu'en maś larga mente deloke la gaśtan loś ke por śu trabaǧo 'i sudor la ganaron 'i para 'eśto dyeron loś antigoś doś razoneś 'ividenteś 'una de 'elyaś 'eś ke loś 'ombreś ke no adkiryeron 'elyoś la hazyenda no śaben konsidrar la falta de 'elyya ni la pasy'on 'i fatiga ke śe paśa 'en ganarla komo no afiguran 'eśto diśtribu'enla śin reselo del tal trabaǧo no konosyendolo lo kual 'el ke gano 'i trabaǧo 'en adkerirla konsidrando la falta de 'elyya 'i kuan trab[a]ǧoza 'i 'infortuna 'eś la pobreza deśprobe'ida komo 'ombreś 'eśprimentadoś ke konośen la falta del dinero perkuran konśervarlo kuanto pu'eden la śegunda razon 'i maś syerta 'eś ke loke alkansa 'el 'ombre por}

‹fol. 69a›
{ST
śu trabaǧo lo ama maś por śer 'obra deśuś manoś aśi komo 'el padre ama maś aśu hiǧo ke 'a 'otro 'eśtranyyo ahiǧado śuyo porke 'eś natural kual kyer 'obrador amar aśu 'obra :

---

[110] Gen. 32.13–20, 33.9–11.
[111] Hullin 91a.

Book of the Regimen of Living ‹fol. 69a–69b›

AŚI komo akaeśe 'enloś trobadoreś ke aman 'un verso ke 'elyyoś hazen maś ke kuantaś 'obraś antigaś vyeron śuś 'oğoś śyendo śin ningun reśpekto meğoreś ke laś śuyaś 'i kyerenlaś muğo maś por śer 'obraś deśuś manoś 'i dela meśma manera akaese 'en todoś loś artifiśeś 'i 'ofisyaleś 'enlaś 'obraś de śuś 'ofisy'os śyendo afisy'onadoś a'elyyaś maś ke alaś ağenaś porla diğa kabza

POR la kual kabza 'eś tambyen 'el ke 'ereda la hazyenda deśtru'idor delyya maś larga mente ke 'el ke diśtribuye la ke 'el meśmo alkanso por śu tr[a]bağo 'i la kyere maś 'i la preśyya maś 'i por tanto la guarda maś 'i 'eś 'eśto tanbyen viśto ke laś maś veześ loś hiğoś de loś 'ombreś rikoś ke leś keda muğa hazyenda deloś padreś śon tan gaśtadoreś 'i diśtribuyen 'en tanta kantidad la hazyenda ke vyenen akoronper la virtud hata hazerśe prodigoś 'i dar maś de lo ke konbyene kuando 'i komo no konbyene 'i pyerden 'i deśtruyen 'en poko tyempo lo ke 'en muğo loś padreś adkiryeron konśu kontino trabağo 'i aś de śaber ke laś maś de laś veześ ke 'eśto akaese 'eś kuando loś padreś śon 'eśkaśisimoś komo noś mu'eśtra la 'eśpery'ensy'a 'i avemoś viśto muğoś 'en nu'eśtroś diaś ke de loś padreś 'eśkasoś 'i muy rikoś śusedyeron hiğoś prodigoś 'i vinyeron 'a śer pobreś 'i diri'a yo śer la kabza akaeśer 'eśto maś 'eneśtoś ke 'en 'otroś konforme alaś razoneś ke tenemoś diğo porke loś padreś 'eśkasoś komo śon poko konfyadoś deśu hazyenda no fian ni a'un de śuś propyoś hiğoś 'i komo loś taleś hiğoś no an komunikado 'enla hazyenda de loś padreś 'en śu vida maś anteś an bivido kon 'eśtremado dese'o de 'elyya kuando ya leś vyene ala mano komo koza ağena 'i apetitozoś 'i dese'ozoś de la diśtribu'isy'on delyya gaśtan larga mente la tal hazyenda 'en gaśtoś 'eśtra'ordinary'oś śin 'orden alguno 'i 'eś lo meśmo ke nu'eśtro devinisimo rey Š^{e}lomoh diğo ayy mal adoloryado vide debağo del śol rikeza guardada 'a śuś du'enyyoś para śu mal 'i perdy'ośe akelyya rikeza 'en kazo malo 'i 'enğendro hiğo 'i no 'en śu mano nada komo śalyo del vyentre de śu madre deśnudo tornara 'a 'andar 'i set-[112] ke kyere dezir ke ayy 'un gran mal aserka de laś kozaś ke 'eśtan de bağo de la kośtelasy'on 'el kual 'eś ke kuando 'el riko guarda la rikeza 'i no la değa pośe'er aśu hiğo 'o aśu 'eredero faśta ke śe'a 'el tal hiğo patron de la tal rikeza ke 'eś deśpu'eś del mu'erto kuando 'eś 'en tal forma lyegando la tal hazyenda 'en poder de śu 'eredero 'eś para śu mal del tal 'eredero 'i patron porke 'eś toda perdida por la razon ke tenemoś diğo 'i śi por kazo vyene akel 'eredero 'a tener hiğo no le keda koza ninguna}

‹fol. 69b›
{de manera ke komo śalyo 'el prodigo del vyentre de śu madre deśnudo deśtoś byeneś de fortuna aśi bu'elbe 'a 'andar komo vino a'el meśmo mundo advenidero 'i dize ke

---

[112] Eccles. 5.12–14.

Book of the Regimen of Living ⟨fol. 69b⟩

śi kon diśtribu'ir la hazyenda lyebaśe kon śigo algun byen de virtud śeri'a todo byen 'enpleado pero 'eś 'el mal adoloryado ke ni la hazyenda le keda ni 'el byen dela virtud diśtribuyendola 'en kazo malo komo no konbyene de manera ke no lyebo nada 'ensu mano deśu trabağo komo lyeban loś virtu'ozoś 'i 'eśto 'eś loke kiğo dezir 'en dezir 'i nada no tomara 'enśu trabağo ke lyebe 'enśu mano 'i set-[113]

'I podri'a śer 'en śegunda 'intensy'on ke kiğeśe dezir ke syendo la rikeza guardada para śu du'enyyo ke no goza ninguno delyya ni la diśtribuye 'entonśeś 'eś para śu mal porke kuando le vyene alguna fortuna no halyya ningun amigo ke le śokora 'i pyerde śu hazyenda toda 'en kazo malo 'i kuando no la pyerda 'el guardandola kon toda diliğensyya posible vyene a'enğendrar 'un hiğo 'el kual hiğo deśnudo tornara śin nada de kuanto śu padre gano 'i set- de kual kyer modo ke śe'a manifyeśto nu'eśtro rey komo 'eś natural suśeder hiğoś prodigoś aloś padreś abaryentoś komo tenemoś diğo :

POR lo kual d(y)[o]mi konśeğo a[']el ke deśkreto fu'ere śyendo riko 'i tenyend(n)o hiğo alyegado a'edad para śaber diśtribu'ir 'i tratar la hazyenda deve de 'uzar de 'un bu'en primor 'i śegura kabtela la kual 'eś ke haga al hiğo participante 'ensu hazyenda 'en vida śuyya para ke lo pu'eda 'enśenyyar 'i 'enkaminar 'a diśtribu'ir komo konvyene 'onde 'i kuando konvyene 'i set- por ke syendo aśi ya kuando muryere 'el padre pośe'era 'el hiğo akelyya hazyenda ke le kedara komo śuyya komo ke 'el propyyo la 'ubyeś(v)[e] ganado por śu trabağo 'i amarlaa komo koza śuyya 'i no la diśtribuyyra 'onde no konvyene :

[LA] trezena 'eś ke 'el liberal no pu'ede muğo 'enrikeśer porke komo kyera ke 'eśta virtud 'eś maś propyya aserka del dar ke del reśebir komo tenemoś diğo 'i 'el liberal no 'a de adkerir 'el dinero por 'el dinero 'enśi śi no por diśtribu'irlo 'onde konbyene 'i set- 'eś viśto ke ponyendo maś diliğensy'a 'en deśpender ke 'en adkerir la hazyenda nunka faltando 'enel dar mirando maś la neseśidad de akel akyen da ke la falta ke a'el le faze no pu'ede muğo 'enrikeśer por śu trabağo por lo kual 'eś razon ke perkure 'el liberal de dar konforme aśu pośiblidad la kantidad ke konbye(y)ne 'i resiba de kyen komo kuanto 'i kuando konbyene 'i set-

LA katorzena 'eś ke kuando 'el liberal da 'o diśtribuye kantidad de hazyenda 'en lugar ke le parese ke konbyene kon dereğa razon 'i deśpu'eś halyya aver lo dado 'onde no konbyene śe 'entriśteśe 'i aśi haze natural mente todo virtu'ozo porke del virtu'ozo 'eś propyo alegrarśe konla 'obra perfekta 'i 'entriśteśerśe konla 'inperfekta a'un ke śe'a heğa por}

---

[113] Eccles. 5.14.

BOOK OF THE REGIMEN OF LIVING ‹FOL. 70A›

‹fol. 70a›
{ᶜ
'invensible 'ignoransy'a porke 'enesto konśiśte la 'ignoransya ke del a'uto feğo por 'elyya śe 'entriśtesa 'el 'obrador por śer diśforme alo ke 'el kiğera hazer a'un ke 'enel tal akto śepa no śer kulpado śegun ke 'enel tersero de la 'etika[114] largo śe 'eśkribe deklarando la diferensyya 'entre hazer por 'ignoransy'a 'i hazer 'inorante mente 'i tanbyen porke śe du'ele de lo ke 'a dado 'en mal lugar ke resela le falta para darlo 'onde konbyene ke śeri'a komo kitarlo de donde konbyene 'i lo dyeśe adonde no konbyene 'i set[-] por lo kual a'un ke hizo la tal 'obra śegun dereğa razon prudente mente kuanto 'el alkansaba reśibe 'enoğo 'i pasy'on deśpu'eś ke ve'e aver śido komo no konbyene 'i komo 'el no kiğera :

LA kinzena 'eś ke 'el liberal natural mente komunika śu hazyenda konśu prośimo komo ke fu'eśe konpanyero 'i participante 'enelyya la kabza deśto 'eś porke le parese no śer la hazyenda apropyada a'el kela pose'e pu'eś 'el byen delyya 'eś 'en diśtribu'irla 'onde konbyene 'i set- de aki vyene ke 'el liberal muğaś veześ padese algunoś maleś por deśpresyar la hazyenda ke laś maś delaś veześ haze aloś kele deben maloś pagadoreś por tener del konsebido ke despresy'a la moneda dela meśma manera śile śuśeden kazoś deśaśtrado‹ś› fortu'ito‹ś› no tyene konke śalvarśe porśu poka probidensy‹a› 'ensu hazyenda komo tenemoś diğo :

LA desima seśta 'eś ke 'el ke verdader'a mente 'eś liberal śegun dereğa razon resibe mayyor paśy'on 'i triśteza kuando değa de dar 'onde konbyene ke kuando da a'onde no konvyene a'un ke kual kyera deloś doś le śe'a moleśto ke komo la lib[e]ralidad 'eś maś propyya mente aserka del dar śyente maś 'enoğo 'en değar de dar 'onde konvyene ke kuando da 'onde no konbyene porke deśo de hazer la propyya 'obra de virtud ke konśiśte 'enel dar a'un ke Śimonideś fu'e kontra 'eśta 'opiny'on[115] 'i byen 'eśpekulado ayy razoneś para 'una parte 'i para 'otra byen atentado śe deve de afirmar śer verdad komo tenemoś diğo 'i anśi lo tengo yo probado 'enel kuarto de la 'etika[116] muy larga mente 'i reśpondido alaś razoneś por la parte kontrary'a deśtaś dizi seyś propyeda(r)[d]eś 'o kondisy'oneś kual kyera konprehendera la 'ekśelensy'a deśta beatisima virtud 'i 'el modo del reğimyento ke 'enelyya śe deve tener 'enel dar 'i 'enel tomar komo konbyene kuanto 'i kuando konbyene śegun 'el ğu'izy'o de la dereğa razon :

---

[114] Aristotle, *NE* III.i.13–19 (1110b 19–1111a 21).
[115] Cf. Aristotle, *NE* I.x.ii (1100b 23–24).
[116] The reference is to *Pne Mośe;* the Aristotle passage would be *NE* IV.i.27 (1121a 7–8).

BOOK OF THE REGIMEN OF LIVING ‹FOL. 70A–70B›

KAPITULO 'OKTABO

PORKE maś śe pu'eda 'ebitar 'el yero 'eneśta virtud diremoś tambyen a[l]gunaś propyedadeś de śuś 'eśtremoś 'i visy'oś porke 'uno de 'elyyoś ke 'eś la falta floreśe muǧo 'enel tyenpo prezente}

‹fol. 70b›
{HELEK B- PEREK Ḥ [PART TWO CHAPTER EIGHT]
por averśe 'eǧado muǧoś ala kobdisya del dinero por lo kual 'eś razon alargar algo maś 'enel vituperyyo del por 'ebitarlo kuanto posible fu'ere de la veluntad del ke 'eśte mi tratado le'ere ke 'eś pe'or ke 'el mal dela puǧa komo 'eśkriby'o 'el filosofo 'enel kuarto dela 'etika[117] teśto kinto 'ı lo prımero[118] ke śe'a de śaber 'eneśtoś 'eśtremoś 'eś ke la prodegalidad 'i la 'iliberalidad 'o abariza śon aserka del dar 'o del resebir komo la meśma liberalidad 'i śon de tal manera ke 'el 'iliberal falta 'enel dar 'i śobra 'enel resebir ke kuanto le dan resibe śino 'eś kuando resela ke resibyendo śera forsado 'a dar maś deloke resibe 'i 'el prodigo 'eś kontrary'o ke puǧa 'enel dar maś delo ke konvyene 'onde no konvyene 'i komo no konvyene 'i falta 'enel resebir donde kuanto komo kuando konvyene 'i set-
ǦUNTO kon 'eśto 'eś de śaber ke 'el prodigo no pu'ede multiplikar 'ensu hazyenda ke komo kyera ke 'el da maś deloke konvyene 'i anśi akyen konvyene komo akyen [no] konvyene 'eś forsado konsumirśe 'en muy poko 'eśpasy'o de tyenpo śu hazyenda 'i 'eśta 'eśpesy'a de prodigo śimpleś 'i abśoluta mente ke no tyene 'otro reśpekto alguno 'enel dar maś ke 'el dar 'enśi 'eś muǧo meǧor 'o para meǧor dezir muǧo menoś malo ke 'el 'iliberal por śer fasil 'a resebir 'enmyenda por 'una de doś kabzaś la primera alyegandośe ala veǧes ke loś vyeǧos natural mente śe hazen 'eśkarsoś kuanto maś 'entran 'enloś diaś 'i 'eś la razon porke an 'eśprimentado 'el trabaǧo dela falta dela moneda 'i tambyen komo śe van hazyendo maś malenkonikoś no aman muǧo 'el dar ni 'el diśtribu'ir la hazyenda ke porśede de kontentamyento 'i alegri'a 'enśi meśmoś 'i maś porke śe syenten 'inabileś p(r)a[r]a ganarla :
'EŚ la śegunda por donde śe pu'ede perder deloś prodigoś 'el tal visy'o kayendo 'en probeza lo kual 'eś forsado por falta dela matery'a del dar an de dešar de śer prodigoś por lo kual la 'iliberalidad 'eś muy difisil porke śyenpre 'eśta 'en falta 'i kyere 'eśtar :
AYY 'otra kabza mayor por lo kual parese no śer tan malo 'el prodigo komo 'el 'iliberal 'i ke śe'a maś fasil de resebir la 'enmyenda 'i 'eś ke 'el prodigo tyene grande

---

[117] Aristotle, *NE* IV.1.39–43 (1121b 22–1122a 14).
[118] Cf. Aristotle, *NE* I.v.2 (1095b 15–20).

BOOK OF THE REGIMEN OF LIVING ‹FOL. 70B–71A›

śemeğansa konel liberal pu'eś amboś śon aserka del dar 'i no ayy 'entre 'elyyoś 'otra diferensy'a śalbo ke 'el liberal da komo konvyene 'i 'el prodigo no 'enpero 'el 'iliberal 'en ninguna manera śemeğa 'a 'el liberal maś anteś śon 'opozitoś 'en kontrar[y]edad ke 'el liberal 'eś aserka del dar 'i no resebir 'i 'el 'iliberal aserka del resebir 'i no dar 'i 'el prodigo komo diğimoś 'eś tambyen aserka del dar 'ino resebir komo 'el liberal śalbo ke falta 'enlaś śerkonśtansyyaś konsumyendo la hazyenda 'onde no konvyene 'i set- [CW. 'i por]}

‹fol. 71a›
{ʿ)
'i por 'eśta kabza tenyendo maś śemeğansa konla virtud kela 'iliberalidad 'eś viśto no śer tan difisil de alyegar al medyo 'i śer menor mal ke kyen menoś reśta del byen śe deve tener por menor mal :

ĞUNTO kon 'eśto ayy 'otra kabza natural para śer la 'iliberalidad 'inkurable ke 'eś por śer loś maś 'ombreś 'enklinadoś natural mente 'a resebir maś ke al dar de manera ke maś fasil mente śe traera dela prodegalidad al medyo ke dela 'iliberalidad al meśmo medyo ke 'enel konśiśte la virtud :

PERO 'el prodigo tyene 'un grande mal 'i 'eś ke 'el meśmo kon śuś 'obraś konśume śu 'obra ke keryendo dar 'a todoś 'eś kabza de venir 'a no poder dar 'a ninguno lo kual śe śiknifika porel 'Ekliśyaśteś donde dize nu'eśtro śapy'entisimo rey Šᵉlomoh aserka del prodigo 'i tanbyen 'eśt(o)[e] mal adoloryado todo 'eśku'entra ke no anśi anda 'i aventağe a'el ke trabağe al ayyre 'i set-[119] keryendo dezir ke tanbyen 'eśte mal 'eś muy 'eśtremado 'i adoloryado 'enel prodigo 'el kual 'eś ke 'eśku'entra 'onde vyene ke 'eś 'el dar aśi kon akelyyo meśmo va perdyendo 'el meśmo fin de manera ke śe halya trabağar 'enel vyento ke loke pyensan hazer deśhazen komo tenemoś diğo ke 'eśto 'eś trabağar 'enel ayyre :

AKU'ERDAŚEME aver viśto 'enla vida de Dy'oğeneś śiniko ke śyendo akośtumbrado de pedir 'una pekenyya limośna kuando le veni'a nesesidad para 'elyya alyegarśe a'un prodigo 'i konosyendolo por tal (k)[']i k[e]ryendolo reprehender deśu visy'o komo 'era śu kośtumbre le demando 'una gru'eśa moneda de limośna 'i syendo demandado del tal prodigo la kauza de demandarle 'a 'el maś ke 'a todoś loś 'otroś śoli'a demandar reśpondyyo 'el grasy'ozo filosofo kele demandaba muğo porke no 'eśperaba de demandarle muğaś veześ keryendo le amoneśtar ke 'el meśmo dar[ ]ke 'el deśeaba śe 'iba apurando 'i deperdyendo 'i set-[120] :

---

[119] Eccles. 5.15.

[120] Unidentified source. Diogenes Laertius mentions Diogenes' begging: "He once begged alms of a statue, and when asked why he did so, replied, 'To get practice in being refused.' In

Book of the Regimen of Living ‹fol. 71a–71b›

'I tyenen maś mal loś prodigoś ke aveześ 'enrikeśen 'algunoś ke fu'era byen ke fu'eran byen pobreś 'i a'un pauperimoś 'i değan de dar akyen la dereğa razon ğuśga ke dyeśen 'i śobre todo tyenen 'un grande mal ke dan dineroś 'a liğunğeroś loś kualeś no liğunğean por 'otro reśpekto ke por resebir de 'elyyoś de manera ke hazen loś ke leś dan mal aśi meśmoś 'en 'eśperdisyar śu hazyenda ke 'eś 'enśturmento para 'obraś virtu'ozaś 'i aloś 'otroś ke dandoleś loś aguzean ake 'uz'[e]n śu 'inorme 'ofisy'o de truhaneś 'i śobre todoś 'eśtoś maleś ke tyene[n] 'eś maś malo 'el 'otro visy'o 'eśtremo ke 'eś la falta aserka deśta virtud porke 'eś maś 'inkurable komo tenemoś diğo 'i śobre todo ke loke kabza la medisina 'enel prodigo a'umenta la 'enfermedad 'enel 'iliberal porke la veğeś la pobreza 'i laś dolensyaś 'i 'otraś nesesidadeś kela flakeza 'umana trae ke kuran la prodegalidad haze ala avariza maś fu'erte kon reselo de venir amaś [CW. nesesidad]}

‹fol. 71b›
{ḤELEK B PEREK (Z)[Ḥ] {RMK: read eight}
'I 'eś maś de śaber ke ayy doś 'eśpesyaś de 'iliberaleś 'i abaryentoś ke komun mente lyyamamoś 'eśkasoś 'unoś ke śobran 'enel resebir 'i 'otroś ke faltan 'enel dar 'i loś de la śegunda 'eśpesy'a śe dividen 'en 'otraś treś partidaś de abaryentoś 'unoś maś ke 'otroś 'i ğunta mente todoś 'elyyoś no kyeren dar ni kyeren resebir 'i dizen loś maś delyoś ke no kyeren dar porke reselan de venir 'a nesesidad 'i pedir 'i no pudyenḏośe valer an de venir 'a '(b)o[b]rar kozaś 'indevidaś 'i 'inğuśtaś por falta de la moneda para śuplir śuś nesesidadeś de manera ke perkuran de dar razon aśu maldad dizyendo ke lo hazen prudente mente por razon de byen por no venir a'obrar mal 'i ğuśtefikan śu razon kon no kerer resebir nada de ninguno deśandolo de resebir reselando śer 'obligadoś 'a pag[a]r maś de lo ke resibyeren 'i la primera 'eśpesyya ke śon loś ke śobran 'enel resebir śon loś ke komun mente resiben de kual kyera ke leś de 'a tu'erto 'o 'a dereğo komo śon loś maś deloś 'ozureroś kontra toda ley ke śufren repudyyoś 'i vergu'ensaś por hazer hazyenda 'i hazen 'indevidaś kozaś por poka ganansy'a 'i alfin alfin fenesen loś maś delyyoś 'i śuś hazyendaś kon 'infamy'a 'i leś suseden kozaś deśaśtradaś por parte de la probidensy'a devina donde pagan todo ğunto komo avemoś viśto muğoś 'en nu'eśtroś diaś :
AYY 'otra śu'erte deśtoś ke śon loś prinsipeś 'i grandeś śenyyoreś tiranoś ke kyeren 'uzurpar laś hazyendaś de śuś śubditoś :

---

asking alms — as he did at first by reason of his poverty — he used this form: 'If you have already given to anyone else, give to me also; if not, begin with me' " (*Philosophers,* trans. Hicks, 51). Cf. Aelian, *VH* III.29, IV.27 (trans. Wilson, 163, 211).

BOOK OF THE REGIMEN OF LIVING ‹FOL. 71B-72A›

'I ayy 'otroś ke śe ponen 'a muǧoś 'infinitoś peligroś 'i laś maś de laś veześ ponen 'en riśko la vida tan presy'oza por kobdisy'a de la vil hazyenda 'i 'eśtoś śon loś ke nu'eśtroś śaby'oś diśeron por 'elyyoś ke ayy 'ombre ke kyere maś śu moneda ke ś(y)[u] propyya preśona 'i set-[121] 'en konkluzy'on todoś loś ke 'eneśte pesimo visy'o śe '[e]śerśitan vyenen a'uzar kozaś muy vileś 'i abominableś 'i śon menoś presyadoś de todaś laś ǧenteś 'i al fin 'elyyoś meśmoś kabzan śu fin 'i śe koronpen 'i deśtru'en 'en kazoś fe'oś ke por śu avariza le śobre vyenen de manera ke 'eś muǧo maś digno de bitupery'o 'el 'iliberal 'i abaryento ke 'el prodigo śyendo śimpleś komo tenemoś diǧo 'i pu'eśto ke y(')[o] pudyera maś alargar aserka deśta famozisima virtud 'i de śuś 'infameś 'eśtremoś baśta byen lo diǧo para la deśkripsy'on 'i konosimyento delyya 'i de śuś 'eśtremoś 'en ǧeneral amoneśta[n]do akual kyera ke 'eśta 'eśkritura ve'a ke no śiga 'el visy'o ke al prez[e]nte tyenpo floreśe deśta tan noble virtud 'el kual 'eś la 'iliberalidad 'o abariza ke ve'o ke por nu'eśtroś pekadoś ninguno da konforme 'a lo ke tyene maś de kontino falta 'i kuando lo da fazelo 'a fin de śer afamado loado 'i 'onrado por 'elyo ke 'a 'eśte fin lo hazen loś maś por 'el grande deśe'o ke tyenen de manifeśtar la dadiba ke da[n]}

‹fol. 72a›
{ᶜB ḤELEK B PEREK (Z) [H] {RMK: read eight}
'i 'eś manifyeśto ke de kual kyer deśtoś doś modoś ke śe'a 'eś muy mal heǧo 'i muy vituperable por ke 'el muy riko a'un ke muy muǧo dyeśe 'en reśpekto deloke le keda 'i debi'a dar 'eś poko śegun la dereǧa razon 'eś 'iliberal aśi meśmo a'un ke de kuanto konbyene 'en reśpekto deloke tyene śilo da por fin de fama 'o 'onra no 'eś liberal komo konśta dela propyedad śegunda 'i ve'eśe muǧaś vezes por 'eśperensyya keloś muy rikoś ke 'inkuren 'en kual kyer deśtoś doś vyenen por fin aperder kuanto tyenen porke la probidenśy'a devina ke no konśyente koza 'indevida leś kabza tal fin para kaśtigar a'elyyoś 'i ke śe'a para 'otroś 'enǧenplo vyendo 'eneśtoś 'el kaśtigo :

'I 'en tal kazo devian loś 'ombreś tener śyenpre 'enla memory'a loke ku'entan nu'eśtroś śabyoś 'en nu'eśtro Ṭalmud śobre 'una hiǧa de 'un rikisimo 'i famozisimo śenyor lyyamado por nombre Nakdimon hiǧo de Goryon la kual dizen ke an(')daba Rabban Yoḥanan ben Zakkay kon śuś diśiploś 'i śalyendo de Yᵉrušalayim vido 'una du'enyya ke andaba koǧendo loś granoś de la sebada dyentro del 'eśtyerkol de loś kavalyyoś de loś arabigoś kuando 'elyya lo vido kubryośe kon śuś kavelyyoś 'i parośe delante del 'i diǧole Rabbi gobyername diǧole 'el hiǧa mi'a la moneda de la kaza de

---

[121] Berakot 61b. See also Tanḥuma Matot 7: "You loved your wealth more than your souls."

Book of the Regimen of Living ‹fol. 72a–72b›

tu p(+)adre ke śe hizo reśpondyyo 'elyya 'i diǧo Rabbi no sabeś 'el 'enǧenplo ke 'enǧenplan 'en Yᵉrušalayim do dizen ke la śal de la moneda 'eś 'el faltar delyya 'i diśtribu'irla 'i alguno dizen la śal de la moneda ke la konserba 'eś 'el hazer mersedeś konelyy(y)a 'i set[-] 'i dišole maś aku'erdaśte kuando firmaśte 'en mi kᵉṭubbah 'i bolby'ośe akel śaby'o śenyor aśuś diśiploś atemando 'elyya de dezir 'eśto 'i diǧoleś aku'erdame kuando firme 'enla kᵉṭubbah¹²² deśta ke 'eśkribi'a 'enelyya ke truǧo de kaza deśu padre 'un ku'ento de dukadoś de 'oro afu'era lo deśu śu'egro la 'ora lyyoro 'el meśmo Rabban Yoḥanan 'i diǧo byenabenturadoś śon Yiśra'el ke kuando hazen la veluntad del Dyo no ayy nasy'on ni linaǧe ke pudiśte śobre 'elyyoś 'i 'enel tyenpo ke no hazen la veluntad del Dyyo śon 'entregadoś 'en poder dela maś baǧa nasy'on de todaś laś nasy'oneś 'i no śolo 'ensu poder śalbo 'en poder de śuś animaleś kual vino 'eśta desdiǧadisima du'enyya¹²³ 'eśta 'eś la 'intensy'on del kauzo ke akaesyyo a'esta du'enyya kon akel 'ero'iko śenyyor lo kual kontandolo nu'eśtro Ṭalmud arguye komo Nakdimon ben Goryon no hazi'a sᵉdakah¹²⁴ 'i no diśtribu'i'a śu hazyenda pu'eś 'el kontrary'o śe ku'enta del ke dizen ke kada veś ke śali'a deśu kaza ala kaza deśu 'eśtudy'o 'onde le'i'a kon śuś diśiploś todo 'el lugar śobre ke pizaba 'eśpandian de bašo del panyyoś de śeda 'i paśando 'el loś doblaban loś pobreś 'i loś tomaban para śi para lo kual reśponde nu'eśtro Ṭalmud doś repu'eśtaś 'una delyyaś 'eś kelo ke hazi'a 'i daba a'un ke 'era muǧo hazialo por śu 'onra 'i no por fin de virtud śegunda 'eś ke no hazi'a tanto kuanto 'era razon ke hizyera}

‹fol. 72b›
{ḤELEK B PEREK T [PART TWO CHAPTER NINE]
reśpektuando ala grande multitud de hazyenda ke teni'a¹²⁵ para a'utoridad delo kual traen 'un proberbyyo antigo 'en nu'eśtro Ṭalmud ke dize ke 'eśto 'eś loke loś 'ombreś komun mente dizen ke aśegun 'eś 'el gamelyyo ante 'eś la karga¹²⁶ todaś 'eśtaś śon palabraś śantisimaś dignaś de perpetu'a memory'a de adonde 'eś viśta la probidensyya devina kontra loś ke no 'obran 'a fin de virtud 'o faltan deloke konbyene konforme aloke 'enelyya tenemoś diǧo

---

[122] "Marriage contract".
[123] Ketubot 66b.
[124] "Act of philanthropy" or "pious deed".
[125] Ketubot 66b–67a.
[126] Ketubot 67a, Sota 13b, Gen. R. 19.1.

BOOK OF THE REGIMEN OF LIVING ‹FOL. 72B–73A›

KAPITULO NONO

ǦUNTO konesto diremos loke konbyene saber para la kuarta virtud ke 'es la manifisensyya kon sus dos vituperables 'estremos 'i 'enloke konsiste la tal virtud kon algunas propyedades para por 'elyyas venir asu verdader'a deskrip(')sy'on 'i de sus 'estremos 'ilo primero ke se deve de notar 'es ke 'esta virtud 'es aserka dela distribu'isyyon dela hazyenda komo la liberalidad ke no difyere mas ke 'en solo ser la liberalidad aserka de 'otros gastos no grandes komo tenemos diǧo a'un ke algunos diǧeron abastar 'esto p(+)ara las destingir 'en 'espesya 'enpero lo primero parese mas syerto 'i segun 'esta konsiderasy'on se dira ke kual kyera ke fu'ere liberal se lyyamara magnifiko a'un ke no pu'ede hazer abto de magnifisensy'a konforme 'a akel gran diǧo de Seneka ke diǧo todas las vertudes ser posibles 'a todos 'ombres salyendo del vyentre de su madre[127] a'un ke se'a desnudo de todos los byenes 'est[e]ry'ores porke komo 'uno tyene 'el ǧu'izy'o prudensyal konke ǧusga aver de dar kuando komo kuanto 'i akyen konbyene 'i set- 'en ǧeneral lu'ego ǧusga aver de dar grandes dadibas akyen konbyene 'i set- ke no se destinge 'un ǧu'izy'o de 'otro 'i koneste ǧu'izy'o a'una se haze 'el abito 'intiry'or dela veluntad ke 'es la virtud a'un ke falta la 'obra 'estiry'or :

'ES la puǧa aserka 'esta virtud no tanto 'en hazer despezas demazyadas komo 'en hazer las tales despezas a[']el keno konbyene adonde 'o kuando 'o komo no konbyene 'i set- 'i ansi 'es la despeza muy grande konparada serkonstansy'onada kondisy'onada del modo ke se haze :

'I 'es la falta hazer menos deloke konvyene para ser perfekto akto de magnifisensy'a de donde nase kela falta aserka desta virtud no 'es tan vituperable komo la falta aserka dela lib[e]ralidad 'i 'esto todo 'es magnifyesto 'i no ayy nesesidad de preba porke no trae 'utilidad alguna para loke aki konvyene saber solo loke aki 'es menester s(+)on algunas propyedades de 'esta klarisima virtud konla kual se 'onr[a]n los prinsipes 'i grandes senyyores dignos de fama 'i sera para por 'elyyos venir meǧor 'a 'el kabo del konosimyento delyya 'ide sus 'estremos :

'I as de saber ke}

‹fol. 73a›

{ᶜG

'es la primera kazi k[o]nprehen[d]ida delo diǧo 'i 'es ke dela despeza grande se konose la grandeza de la koza 'enke se haze la tal despeza por ser komo tenemos diǧo porporsy'onada ala 'obra 'i la 'obra 'a 'elyya

---

[127] This may be a reference to Seneca, *Ep. Mor.* 124.8, trans. Gummere, 3:439–41.

'I śon la śegunda 'i tersera laś komuneś 'a todaś laś vertudeś ke 'eś lo primero śer heǧa la 'obra 'a bu'en fin śegun dereǧa razon śegundo ke śe'a feǧa kon alegri'a 'i delektasy'on :
'I 'eś la kuarta propya al magnifiko ke kuando hizyere alguna deśpeza grande por mano de alguno no atente 'en demandarle ku'enta del gaśto porke hazyendo 'eśto no śera 'eśta tal 'obra de magnifisensy'a maś anteś grandisima pokedad porke kuando konvyene atentar komo prudente 'eś 'enel tyenpo de 'eleǧir 'a akel por kuyya mano haze la tal deśpeza ke śe'a digno ke śe konfi'e del akelyyo 'i muǧo maś pero deśpu'eś ke[ ]'a konfyado del no deve atentar maś 'enloke gaśtare ni pedirle ku'enta ke de nota śośpeǧa ke loke 'el meśmo 'eliǧyo 'eś mal 'eliǧido 'i maś amu'eśtra tener alguna triśteza 'en pensar ke loke gaśto 'eś demazyado :
'EŚ la kinta komun 'en todaś laś vertudeś la kual 'eś atentar 'en todaś laś śerkonśtansyaś dela 'obra ke śe'a 'eliǧible 'i delektable 'i set- 'i de aki 'eś viśto la śeśta ke 'eś śer 'el magnifiko liberal porke śyendo la magnifisensy'a aserka del dar komo 'el liberal reǧido por la dereǧa razon 'i no avyendo alguna 'otra diferensy'a 'entre 'elyoś maś ke śer la manifisensy'a aserka de kozaś grandeś komo tenemoś diǧo 'eś byen viśto ke 'en todo ǧenero de dar dara 'onde konvyene śegun konvyene kuando 'i kuanto konvyene 'i set- :
'EŚ la śetima 'una syerta deśtinsy'on dela 'obra dela magnifisensy'a ala 'obra dela liberalidad la kual 'eś ke 'el magnifiko kon deśpeza 'igual ala deśpeza del liberal hara 'un akto mayor porke śon diferenteś 'en la posesy'on 'i 'enel poder 'obrar 'i poder dar kantidad mayor 'i tanbyen śon deśtintaś por parte dela koza de ke śe 'a de hazer la 'obra 'i tanbyen por parte dela meśma 'obra ke śon loś treś terminoś ke tenemoś ya nombradoś 'i 'eśpisifikadoś :
'I deśpu'eś de śabidaś 'eśtaś propyedadeś 'eś nesesaryyo śaber aserka de ke kozaś śe dize śer 'el a'uto dela magnifisensy'a para lo kual 'eś meneśter śaber ke aserka de treś ǧeneroś de kozaś diferenteś konśiśte
'EŚ 'el primero aserka de kozaś śagr(d)adaś komo fraguar kazaś grandeś para 'orar 'i 'eśku'elaś ǧeneraleś 'i pagar loś 'eśtudyanteś 'i maeśtroś dela tal 'universidad aśi meśmo 'en śakrifisy'oś kuando 'el Dyyo kyera porśu gran me(ś)[r]sed 'i pyadad 'i 'infinita mizerikordy'a 'i deśte ǧenero fu'eron loś prinsipaleś a'utoś ke nu'eśtroś}

‹fol. 73b›
{no menoś poderozoś ke reliǧyozoś 'i klementeś reyś a[n]t(g)i[g](n)oś fizyeron :
'I 'eś 'el śegundo aserka deloś probeǧoś ke śe hazen ala republika 'i benefisyyos ǧeneraleś 'a toda la komunidad 'i no śolo 'a todo 'el pu'eblo prezente śi no aloś venideroś 'i a'un 'a todaś las nasy'oneś ke deśtoś taleś benefisy'oś algun tyenpo 'uzaren komo hazer '(y)[o]śp(r)italeś pu'enteś 'i fu'enteś 'i 'otraś komuneś 'obraś de mag-

Book of the Regimen of Living ‹fol. 73b›

nifisensy'a 'i aśi meśmo konbiteś komuneś atoda la 'universidad komo fu'e 'el śelebratisimo Pesaḥ de Yo'šiyahu[128] 'i 'otroś deśte ǧenero :
'EŚ 'el tersero aserka de laś kozaś ke konśiśten 'enel 'ombre de śi aśi meśmo komo śon loś konbiteś grandeś 'enlaś bodaś 'a 'ombreś partikulareś anśi meśmo 'el konbidar 'a 'un śenyyor 'o agazaǧar gu'eśpedeś grandeś śenyyoreś 'i prinsipeś altoś 'i mandar muǧoś prezenteś grandeś 'i kontinoś 'a 'ombreś grandeś 'o poderozoś 'i set- 'i deśte ǧenero de magnifisensy'a 'eś la ke ku'enta nu'eśtra śakra 'eśkritura del śanto patryarka 'Abraham[129] 'i deśte meśmo ǧenero 'eś tambyen 'el grande gaśto ke hazen loś magnifikoś 'en fraguar kazaś grandeś śumptu'ozaś para śuś moradaś ke todo 'eśto 'eś demośtrasy'on de grandeza de animo 'i alto grado deśta 'ekselente virtud :
'I para 'eśtaś kozaś 'eśpesyal para laś doś primeraś no todoś loś 'ombreś śon abtoś a'un ke śean muy rikoś śino śon muy adornadoś de nobleza dignidad 'i 'eśtima 'en la republika kon alto linaǧe ke akonpanye 'eśta śoberana virtud por ke no śe asyenta la a'utoridad de tan alta virtud 'en baǧo a'utor ke no śera 'edonyyo konvenyente 'un riko merkader 'a fraguar 'una kaza śanta a'un ke tenga dineroś para la hazer porke no 'eś aśuǧekto a'uto para śi kalefikar kon la grande 'obra deśta grande virtud 'i diminu'e al hiǧo 'el hazedor śalbo śyendo 'eśte de tan alto 'inǧenyyo 'i ǧu'izy'o aǧuntado kon alta proǧene'a 'i antigu'a 'oriǧin de antepasadoś kon ke luśtrando la 'eśkurida(r)[d] del 'ofisy'o reluza 'enel la 'ekśelensy'a de laś vertudeś 'i 'en konkluzy'on 'el magnifiko para ke śe diga ke 'uza 'obra de magn[i]fisensy'a 'a de śer grande 'en virtud 'i 'inǧenyyo 'i 'a de śer aserka de deśpezaś grandeś 'i 'en kozaś grandeś :
'I de aki 'eś viśta la deśkripsy'on del viśy'o 'en la puǧa deśta virtud ke 'eś 'el ke haze grandeś deśpezaś 'en kozaś pekenyaś no kapaześ de la tal deśpeza 'i 'indignaś muy muǧo delyya por ke śon kozaś 'en laś kualeś 'eśtoś grandeś gaśtoś no aprobeǧan śegun dereǧa razon śi śe 'enplean mal de modo ke kompran koza vil por alto presyyo ke 'eś koza baǧa por grande deśpeza la kual roba ala alta 'obra ke konelyya pudyera hazer 'i muǧaś veześ no gaśta konforme aśu posibilidad śino muǧo maś deśtruyendo aśi meśmo kon demazyadoś gaśtoś 'en kozaś demazyadaś ni gaśta por fin de virtud lo kual todo le prosede por no śer [CW. śu]}

---

[128] Cf. 2 Kings 23.21–23.
[129] Cf. Gen. 18.5, 21.8.

⟨fol. 74a⟩
{ᶜD
śu 'obra 'endereśada śegun dereğa razon :
    'I del meśmo modo śe halyyan 'enel visy'o 'opozito ke 'eś la falta 'eśtoś meśmoś 'inkonvenyenteś 'i lo primero 'eś ke da de kontino menoś de lo ke konbyene komo tenemoś diğo 'i kuando algunaś veześ akaeśe aver de haze(d)[r] deśpeza 'en algun grande konbite 'o 'otro kual kyer abito de magnifisensyya ke 'eś forsado de hazerlo por algun grande reśpekto atenta muğo por 'eśkuzar la deśpeza 'en kozaś ke lo ke 'eśkuza 'eś muy poko 'i la falta ke haze 'en akel(v)[y]yo poko ke değa de gaśtar 'eś muğo komo śi hizyeśe 'un konbite donde śe gaśtaśe muğa kantidad de hazyenda 'i paresyendole ke la śalsa 'o 'otra koza śemeğante śe pu'ede 'eśkuzar la deśa de merkar lo kual haze 'enla meza muğa falta 'o 'otraś kozaś śemeğanteś ke por śu 'eśkaśeza deśa de hazer :
    'I 'el segundo 'eś ke kual kyera koza ke gaśta ya ke ve'e ke 'eś forsado de averśe de gaśtar 'i ke no śe pu'ede 'eśkuzar delyyo lo haze kon muğa negliğensy'a 'i 'eś muy tardi'o de hazer 'el gaśto por la moleśty'a ke le da 'el śer forśado de aver de gaśtar :
    'I 'el tersero 'eś ke todoś śuś penśamyentoś śon kuando haze 'el tal a'uto komo 'a de 'eśkuzar la deśpeza 'enel por kuantaś viaś la pu'ede 'eśkuzar :
    'EL kuarto 'eś keśe 'entriśteśe de kontino kon loke gaśta komo śi propyya mente lo perdyeśe
    'I 'eś 'el kinto ke por poko ke gaśte śyenpre le parese ke diśtribuye maś de loke konbyene por donde ğuśga de kontino 'el magnifiko por visy'ozo 'enel 'eśtremo de la puğa de la magnifiśensy'a :
    KON 'eśto me parese ke 'eśta byen viśta la deśkripsy'on deśtoś 'eśtremoś ke abaśta para loke konbyene śaber aserka de 'eśta virtud 'ekśelente por śer kazi śabida por 'el 'orden de la liberalidad komo tenemoś diğo ke no difyeren maś ke śer 'eśta aserka de kozaś grandeś 'i la liberalidad no 'i por 'eśta meśma kabza ağuntaron 'eśta virtud ala liberalidad por la konformidad de laś doś komo 'eś diğo de manera ke kual kyera fasil mente podra konprehender la deśkripsy'on de la 'una por la 'otra 'en todaś laś partikularidadeś ke susedyeren :
    TODA vi'a notaremoś ke a'un ke 'eśta virtud śe'a la meśma kon la liberalidad por kuanto difyere no maś śino śegun maś 'o menoś śe rekyere mayor ğu'izy'o prudensyal para 'uzar 'el a'uto deśta śanta virtud ke para 'uzar 'el a'uto de la liberalidad porke 'eś maś difisil ğuśgar komo kuando 'i donde śe gaśtara 'una śuma de hazyenda ke ğuśgar adonde śe gaśtara 'una medyana 'i por 'eśo 'el magnifiko śe aśemeğa muğo al ś[a]by'o porke komo 'el śaby'o varon 'eś akel ke śabe laś kozaś difisileś 'i 'ignotaś 'a 'otroś grandeś}

BOOK OF THE REGIMEN OF LIVING ‹FOL. 74B›

‹fol. 74b›
{HELEK B- PEREK Y- [PART TWO CHAPTER TEN]
'enśi meśmaś para śer 'eśpekuladaś aśi 'el magnifiko śabe komo śe hara 'obraś grandeś 'i difisileś de hazer 'i de 'entender komo śe haran 'i porke 'i para ke śe deven hazer 'i de aki vyene ke fasil mente śe yera 'eneśta virtud maś ke 'enla liberalidad 'i 'eśto por falta del ğu'izy'o śer 'enelyya difisil

AŚI ke fasil mente 'uno kaera 'enla puğa 'o 'enla falta deśta virtud alo menoś 'en śaber 'obrar 'el a'uto 'eśtiry'or de adonde pribatiba mente no śera magnifiko 'i 'eśte tal śera menoś visy'ozo ke 'el avarento 'o 'el prodigo 'enpero 'el ke tubyere 'un abito kontrary'o 'a 'eśta bu'ena virtud ke no kyera hazer pudyendo 'una 'obra devina 'i komun ala republika 'i set- 'eśte tal 'eś muğo maś visy'ozo ke no 'el avarento por śer kontrary'o 'a mayor virtud 'i aśi diremoś de la puğa 'en reśpekto del prodigo 'i 'eśto śe ve'e maś ponyendo la magnifisensy'a 'i liberalidad deśtintaś 'en 'eśpesyya

MAŚ 'eś de notar ke 'en alguna deśpeza a'un ke 'enśi no śe'a grande śyendo 'enpero grande 'en reśpekto de la koza 'en ke śe gaśta pu'ede śer magnifika komo prezentar 'un ğugete a'un ninyo 'enlo kual a'un ke no śe gaśte muğo śe pu'ede gaśtar manifika mente konforme ala koza ke 'eś 'un ğugete prinsipal mente 'enla heğura śe pu'ede ver la manifisen(y)sy'a de manera ke syendo de materya presy'oza 'i de muğa 'eśtima la 'obra śobre puğe ala matery'a 'i 'eśto baśta para 'eśta loada virtud :

KAPITULO DESIMO

'I aserka de la grande virtud de la magnyanimidad kinta 'enel numero de laś vertudeś moraleś śegun ke delyya trato Aristotel[130] a'un ke śeri'a meneśter muy muğo alargar para śaber por 'eśtenśo laś partikularidadeś 'en ke konśiśte diremoś lo ke konbyene śaber 'en muy brebe 'eśtilo por ke 'el tyenpo no lo padeśe ni mi 'okupasy'on kontinu'a da a'elyyo lugar por lo kual levaremoś 'eneśta 'el 'orden ke avemoś lyebado aserka de todaś laś 'otraś deklarando śuś propyedadeś ke śon śinku'enta delyyaś 'enla propyya virtud 'i delyyaś 'enel virtu'ozo de nominado magnyanimo del nombre de magnyanimidad

'I anteś ke venga 'a deklarar laś diğaś propyedadeś te kyero hazer 'entender la verdader'a difinsyy'on 'o deśkripsy'on del (m) magnyanimo 'i aserka de ke koza 'eś para lo kual aś de śaber ke 'el magnyanimo 'eś aserka de 'onraś grandeś 'i por 'eśo

---

[130] Aristotle, *NE* IV.iii (1123a 35–1125a 36).

Book of the Regimen of Living ‹fol. 74b–75a›

śe ağunto 'eśta virtud ala virtud de la magnifisensy'a por śeren ambaś aserka de kozaś grandeś
'I la diferensyya 'entre laś doś 'eś manif[y]eśta ke la magnifisensy'a 'eś aserka de la diśtribu'is(v)[y]'on de la hazyenda 'i 'eśta virtud}

‹fol. 75a›
{ᶜH
propyya mente 'eś aserka de laś 'obraś grandeś la magnifisensy'a modera 'el 'apetito konkupisible 'enlaś grandeś deśpezaś 'i 'eśta modera 'el 'irasible 'enlaś 'onraś grandeś 'i la virtud ke deśpu'eś deśta deklararemoś ke 'eś la modeśtyya 'eś aserka de laś 'obraś medyanaś 'i pekenyyaś 'i komuneś 'a todo 'ombre de manera ke la modeśtyya tyene tal porprosy'on kon la magnyanimidad komo la liberalidad kon la magnifisensya 'i la deskripsy'on 'o difinisy'on del magnyanimo 'eś ke śe[ ]ponga 'a kozaś grandeś 'i śe'a digno delyyaś 'i meresedor de alkansarlaś ke śi por ventura tubyere la primera kondisy'on (") konbyene 'a śaber ke śe 'opone 'en kozaś grandeś 'i no fu'ere abto para 'elyyaś 'o pensare śer śofisyente para 'elyaś no lo śe[e](g)[n]do 'eśte tal śe pu'ede maś lyyam[a]r loko ke 'otra koza 'i śi tubyere la śegunda ke 'eś digno de ponerśe 'a kozaś g(n)[r]andeś a'uto abil 'i konbenyente para 'elyyaś 'i no śe 'opone a'elyyaś 'eś(ś)[t]e tal peka por la falta 'i śe lyyama pozilanimo 'o de poko animo porke śolo la falta de śu //(mi)[a]nimo// 'i pokedad lo haze deśkonvenyente para la tal 'onra 'i deśdora kon 'eśto 'i 'eśkureśe todo śu merito de manera ke 'el manyanimo 'eś 'el ke śe 'opone 'a kozaś grandeś 'i propyya mente aserka de laś 'onraś grandeś śyendo digno 'i konvenyente para 'elyyo por ke no konśiśte śu abilidad 'i meresimyento 'en tenerśe 'el por tal ni menoś 'en ponerśe 'en kozaś grandeś por ke no konśiśte la virtud 'en la 'obra 'eśtiry'or komo tenemoś muğaś veześ diğo śalbo 'en śer 'el abito 'en la alma
'I 'a de śer 'el virtu'ozo 'eneśta virtud kunplido de todaś laś 'otraś vertudeś ke por parte delyaś 'eś digno de ponerśe akozaś grandeś dignaś de 'onra grande ğunto konlaś 'otraś propyedadeś ke 'a de tener komo deklararemoś 'i śyendo 'enlaś vertudeś abituado śe mu'ebe 'a ponerśe 'en kozaś grandeś 'i śe aśyentan 'enel laś propyedadeś dela magnyanimidad 'i aśepta laś 'onraś grandeś kuando konbyene komo konbyene 'i śegun konvyene :
'INO hazyendo la 'obra aserka deśta virtud kon todaś laś kondisy'oneś ke konbyene hazerśe kon dereğa razon no pu'ede değar de 'erar por puğa 'o por falta ke śi śe puzyere 'a kozaś grandeś maś deloke a'el konbyene 'o 'en tyenpo ke no konbyene śera visy'ozo 'enel 'eśtremo dela puğa deśta virtud ke śe pu'ede lyyamar no fartura 'o śin fartura 'o śin 'enğimyento komo pozo śin hondo 'o śako roto ke nunka śe 'enğe ke aśi 'eś 'el ke puğa 'eneśta virtud ke nunka śe harta ni śe 'enğe de 'onra :

Book of the Regimen of Living ⟨fol. 75a–75b⟩

'I 'el ke falta de 'oponerśe akozaś 'onrozaś ke ğuśga la dereğa razon ke śe pongan 'a 'elyaś 'i laś aśepten 'eśtoś taleś pekan 'enel 'eśtremo de falta 'i śe lyyama pośilanim(e)[o] komo t[e]nemoś diğo 'i 'eś 'eśta virtud la maś 'elevada ke todaś laś 'otraś vertudeś porke 'el ke 'eśta virtud tubyere perśupone śer perfekto}

⟨fol. 75b⟩
{'en todaś laś 'otraś 'i 'eś aserka del mayor deloś byeneś 'eśtiry'oreś ke 'eś la 'onra la kual damoś al Dyyo glory'ozo por śer 'el mayor deloś byeneś por lo kual deve kual kyera perkurar de hazer kozaś konlaś kualeś śe'a a'uto para pose'er 'eśta virtud ke 'eneśto 'imitara 'a nu'eśtro śanto porfeta Mošeh Rabbenu 'enel kual perfekta mente halyyamoś laś kondisy'oneś 'i propyedadeś ke para magnyanimo śe rekyeren ke śon śinku'enta komo tenemoś diğo :

'I 'eś la primera ke 'el manyanimo de nesesidad 'a de śer bu'eno para śer meresedor dela 'onra porke śer digno delyya no śe pu'ede afigurar śin śer virtu'ozo 'eśta propyedad 'en toda perfeksy'on śe halyya 'en nu'eśtro deviniśimo porfeta Mošeh Rabbenu ke deśde śu nasimyento fu'e 'entitulado 'en titulo de bu'eno komo śe manifyeśta do dize 'i vido a'el ke bu'eno 'el 'i 'eśkondyyolo 'i set-[131] de donde tubyeron lugar nu'eśtroś śaby'oś de glozar ke kuando nasy'o śe 'inğo la kaza toda de luz ke 'eś lyyamada byen komo 'eś diğo 'i vido 'el Dyyo ala luz ke bu'ena 'i set-[132] keryendo śignifikar ke nasyyo konel la luz ke śiknifika 'una bu'ena diśpośisy'on para todo ğenero de byen 'i set- :

'EŚ la śegunda ke 'el magnyanimo 'o animozo 'a de 'obrar la 'obra de virtud 'en mayor grado de virtud //(')[k]e// kual kyera 'otro virtu'ozo 'en 'otra virtud hazyendo la tal 'obra kon 'eśtremada alegri'a 'i kunplido kontentamyento kon todaś laś śerkonśtanśyaś 'ordenadaś kon dereğa razon lo kual śe halyyo tanbyen 'enel diğo porfeta ke todaś śuś 'obraś 'eran 'eroykaś kon 'eśtrema alegri'a komo 'eś viśto por diverśaś parteś de nu'eśtra śantisima ley

'EŚ la tersera ke 'el magnyanimo no deve menośpresyar ningun konśeğo maś anteś deve 'eśkuğar 'a todoś 'i śi 'el konśeğo fu'ere śofisyente śe deve mober por 'el a'un ke śe'a de kyen kyera ke fu'ere 'i 'eśto meśmo halyyamoś 'en nu'eśtro śanto porfeta kuando śu śu'egro Yitro le dyyo konśeğo konbenyente dizyendole agora 'oye 'en mi boś akonśeğarte'e 'i śe'a 'el Dyyo kontigo 'i set-[133] ke 'eś la 'intensy'on ami ver

---

[131] Exod. 2.2.
[132] Exod. R. 1.20; cf. Gen. 1.4.
[133] Exod. 18.19.

BOOK OF THE REGIMEN OF LIVING ‹FOL. 75B–76A›

kele keri'a dezir ke śu konśeǧo śeri'a de tal manera ke no perdyeśe porel la kontenplasy'on 'i 'eśpikulasy'on 'enlaś kozaś devinaś maś anteś la a'umentari'a 'i 'eśto kizo dezir dizyendo 'i śera 'el Dyyo kontigo 'i set-[134] 'i vyendo 'el beatisimo porfeta la 'ekśelensyya del konśeǧo komo magnyanimo lo konsedy'o 'i lo 'efektu'o kon śu grande ǧu'izy'o prudensyal : 'EŚ la kuarta ke 'el magnyanimo deve atentar ke haga todaś śuś kozaś kon ǧuśtisy'a ke por ningun modo 'en ningun tyenpo venga 'a hazer kozaś 'indevidaś ni 'inǧuśtaś ni śe'a akuzado delyyaś ni a'un por śośpeǧa 'i 'eśto śe falyyo tanto 'en nu'eśtro devinisimo profeta ke śegun nu'eśtroś śaby'oś kyeren 'entrego śu alma por la ǧuśtisyya[135] 'i anśi śe}

‹fol. 76a›
{ᶜV
mośtro 'enel deśde śu mansebi'a komo ku'enta 'en nu'eśtra śanta 'eśkritura ke vinyendo 'en kresimyento syendo de 'edad de vente anyyoś śegun 'opiny'on de algunoś śalyyo aśuś ermanoś 'i vido 'un varon aǧipsy'o ke feri'a varon ǧudy'o de śuś ermanoś 'i set-[136] donde ku'enta ke kondeno al malo 'i ǧuśtefiko al bu'eno 'i librolo dela meśma manera ku'enta ke śalyyo 'el śegundo di'a donde vido doś ǧudyyoś baraǧando 'i set-[137] 'i fizo lo meśmo komo magnyanimo :

'EŚ la kinta ke 'el magnyanimo no śe deve alegrar ni delektar 'en 'eśtremo 'en aver alkansado kozaś grandeś aserka dela 'onra 'o 'eśtado grande śalbo medyana mente porke komo śe'a verifikado ke 'el magnyanimo 'a de śer meresedor porśi de todo ǧenero de 'onra grande no śe deve muǧo de alegrar konelyya pu'eś delyya 'eś meresedor por lo kual śe deve delektar medyana mente komo kyen alkansa loke merese konvenyente a'el 'i komo nu'eśtro śantisimo porfeta alkansase akel śupremo grado de 'onor ke fu'eśe porśu dignidad 'i grasyya devina meresedor ke śe dyeśe la ley por śu mano avyendo konosido nu'eśtroś śaby'oś kuan perfekto fu'e 'eneśta virtud 'ordenaron 'en nu'eśtra 'orasy'on 'enel Šabbat ke diǧesemoś alegrarśe'a Mošeh konla dadiba deśu parte 'i set-[138] ke 'en no dezir maś ke alegrarśe 'i set- śignifikaron śer la alegri'a komo konvyene 'i no demazyada ke kuando nu'eśtroś śaby'oś kyeren dezir kual kyer koza śer 'en muǧa kantidad lo dizen klaro :

'EŚ la śeśta ke 'el magnyanimo deve resebir la 'onra ke le dyeren a'un ke no śe'a grande kuando deǧare de śer grande por la poka posiblidad de dador 'i deveśe kon-

---

[134] Exod. 18.19.
[135] This seems to be a reference to Tanḥuma Shemot 12.
[136] Exod. 2.11.
[137] Exod. 2.13.
[138] Shabbat 10b.

BOOK OF THE REGIMEN OF LIVING ⟨FOL. 76A–76B⟩

tentar a'un ke 'el mereśka maś pu'eś śabe ke no 'eś por śu falta ni pokedad śalbo por la poka posiblidad del dador ke no tyene koza mayor ke darle komo tenemoś diğo :

'EŚ la śetena ke śi le akaesyere por ventura śer 'onrado por byeneś de fortuna 'o de 'ombreś bašoś 'o por kozaś pekenyyaś ke 'el 'a( )yya heğo deve de aboreser la tal 'onra :

'EŚ la 'oğaba ke 'el magnyanimo kuando le 'eś feğo algun deś'onor śi deś'onor śe pu'ede dezir por kual kyer kabza no le[ ]'eś moleśto ni 'enoğozo aśi komo 'el muğo 'onor no lo altera ni le da demazyada delektasy'on komo tenemoś diğo 'i la kabza deśto 'eś porke ningun agraby'o ni deś'onra śe le pu'ede hazer al magnyanimo ke deś'onra verdader'a mente śe pu'eda dezir ni 'eś ğuśta mente heğa 'i pu'eś 'el 'eś bu'eno 'i virtu'ozo komo tenemoś diğo no pu'ede hazer koza 'inğuśta por la kual mereśka la tal deś'onra :

'EŚ la nobena ke no śe deve alterar ni śoberbearśe konla muğa rikeza ni 'otroś byeneś de fortuna 'eśtiry'oreś a'un ke śe'a 'en abundansa ni menoś śe deve alegrar muğo kon 'elyyoś pu'eś no konśiśte 'enelyyoś śu byen 'i ('i) glory'a śalvo medyana mente 'i set- [CW. 'eś]}

⟨fol. 76b⟩
{ 'EŚ la dezena ke 'enlaś adverśaś fortunaś no śe (de) deve 'entriśteser muğo por la propyya kabza ke kon la prośpera no śe deve muğo de alegrar komo tenemoś aberiguado 'i 'eśtaś śinko propyedadeś pośtreraś śignifikaron byen nu'eśtroś śaby'oś 'i noś dyeron 'enelyyaś 'ekśelente dotrina por modo de konparasy'on do diğeron ke loś 'inğuryadoś 'i ke non 'inğuryan 'oyen śu repudy'o 'i no reśponden hazen por 'amor 'i alegranśe kon laś tribulasy'oneś[139] śobre '[e]lyyoś dize la 'eśkritura 'i śuś amigoś komo śalir 'el śol kon śu fu'ersa 'i set-[140] ke 'en la primera partida ke dize loś 'inğuryadoś 'i set- śignifikaron la propyedad 'oğaba la kual 'eś ke no resibe 'el magnyanimo pasy'on de laś deś'onraś 'i 'inğuryaś ke pyensan algunoś hazerle pu'eś śon śin ğuśtisy'a komo 'eś diğo

'I 'enla śegunda partida ke dize ke 'oyen śu repudy'o 'i set- kyeren śignifikar ke no śe alteran konla prośperidad ke a'un ke śean tan prośperoś ke ninguno 'oze vituperaloś ni repreh[e]nderloś 'ensu prezensyya śalbo 'ensu a'uzensyya 'i vyene 'el tal vitupery'o 'i reprehensy'on aśu notisyya por 'o'idaś de 'otroś no śe altera ni śe 'enśoberveśe konśuś prośperidadeś para r[e]śponder 'i por 'eśto diğo 'oyen śu repudy'o 'i no diğo śon repudyadoś al modo ke diğo 'enloś 'inğuryadoś 'i set- śikni-

---

[139] Shabbat 88b, Yoma 23b; Maimonides, *Character Traits,* ed. Weiss and Butterworth, 32–33 (*Hilkot Deᶜot,* chap. 2, halakah 3).

[140] Judges 5.31; Shabbat 88b, Yoma 23b.

Book of the Regimen of Living ‹fol. 76b–77a›

fikando lo ke avemoś diğo ke kuando fu'eren tan p(v)rośperoś ke no śon 'inǧuryadoś 'en prezensyya śalbo ke 'oyen śu repudy'o por 'entersisy'on de medyaneroś non reśponden porke no tyenen akelyya tal prośperidad fortu'ita 'i transitory'a por byen prinsipal ni śe alegran ni śe alteran muǧo konelya[141] 'eśtoś taleś śon loś perfektoś konforme ala nobena propyedad la tersera partida ke dize ke śon loś ke hazen por 'amor 'i śe alegran konlaś tribulasy'oneś 'i set-[142] 'eś manifyeśto śer konforme ala desima propyedad ke konla advers[id]ad no śolo no śe 'entriśtesen maś anteś śe alegran konsidrando śer todo produzido de la primera kabza afin de byen 'i truǧeron para loś perfektoś 'en todaś treś devinisima konparasy'on dizyendo ke 'eś 'enǧenplifikado kyen tal hiz[y]ere al śol kuando śe pu'ede 'enel dezir ke śale kon toda śu fortaleza[143] ke forsado 'a de śer kuando akaeśe śer 'iklipsado al medyo di'a ke 'entonśeś śe dize śalir 'el śol de la konǧunsy'on kon la luna 'i pareser 'a noś kon toda śu fortaleza ke 'eś al medyo di'a por ke a'un ke por la manyana śe diga śalir 'el śol no śe dize śalir kon todo śu vigor 'i fortaleza maś anteś kuanto maś va śe va maś 'eśforsando faśta 'el medyo di'a 'i kuando śe aparta del miridyano no śe dize śalir śalbo akośtar 'o apartar 'i set- komo 'eś magnifyeśto akyen śolo loś prinsipyoś de 'eśtroloǧi'a 'a le'ido de manera ke no śe pu'ede kumplida mente dezir 'enel śalir 'i ke śe'a kon śu fortaleza śalbo kuando [CW. akaesyere]}

‹fol. 77a›
{ᶜZ ḤELEK B PEREK Y' [PART TWO CHAPTER ELEVEN]
akaesyere 'iklipse del śol 'a medyyo di'a komo avemoś diǧo 'eśtonseś śale konla meśma fu'ersa ke teni'a 'enel meśmo tyenpo deśu 'iklipse ke nunka la luna fizo 'enel falta alguna śalbo ke kito śu klaridad de nu'eśtra viśta 'i por 'eśto diǧo konśu fortaleza śiknifikando ke la fu'ersa 'i fortaleza konke śale kuando śale del 'iklipse no śele 'enoba al tyenpo de śalir de la meśma manera akaese al magnyanimo ke kuando śele hazen 'inǧuryaś no śon a'el feǧaś aśi komo 'el śol 'enel tyenpo del 'iklipśe a'un ke dezimoś 'iklipśarśe no reśibe 'el 'enśi tremudasy'on alguna ni falta de śu klaridad ni śe 'eśkureśe ni la adverśidad al magnyanimo 'eś moleśta ni la prośperidad le altera porke 'el 'enel grado de śu grandeza no menǧu'a ni kreśe por 'eśo aśi komo 'enel śol no haze mudansa ninguna 'el śalir amedyo di'a ke 'eśta 'a noś kon toda la fu'ersa de śu klaridad maś ke kuando śale por la manyana por śer 'enel todo de 'un meśmo modo 'i baśta lo diǧo para loke aki konbyene :

---

[141] "He [the great-souled man] will not rejoice overmuch in prosperity, nor grieve overmuch at adversity" (Aristotle, *NE* IV.iii.18 [1124a 15–16], trans. Rackham, 219).

[142] Shabbat 88b, Yoma 23b.

[143] Judges 5.31; Shabbat 88b, Yoma 23b.

BOOK OF THE REGIMEN OF LIVING ⟨FOL. 77A–77B⟩

'EŚTAŚ śinko propyedadeś prośteraś delaś dyeś diğaś kiğeron nu'eśtroś śaby'oś mośtrar komo śe falyyaban 'en toda perfeksy'on 'en nu'eśtro devinisimo porfeta ke fu'e 'enlevado 'en 'eśta virtud komo tenemoś diğo donde dišeron ke akel grande diğo de nu'eśtro śapy'entisimo rey Š^elomoh ke dišo 'i bağo de 'eśprito aśufrira 'onra 'i set-¹⁴⁴ fu'e diğo por Mošeh Rabbenu porke halyyaron 'en 'eśte diğo śignifikasy'on de todaś śinko kozaś ke de dezir bağo de 'eśprito notaron la śeśta 'i de dezir aśufrira 'onra notaron la śetena keryendo dezir ke no aśufre śalbo lo ke 'onra śe deve lyyamar dela śe(b)[n]tensyya delaś doś ke kyere dezir ke 'el ke 'eś 'umilde 'i bağo de 'eśprito akel tal aśufre la 'onra notaron la 'oğo 'i nu'ebe 'i dyeś ke śe 'entyende por lo diğo ke ni śe alegra konla prośperidad ni śe abate ni 'entrišteśe konlaś 'inğuryaś ke le śon feğaś por [ke] śu prinśipal 'intensy'on no 'eś 'otro ke 'a śufrir 'i 'eśforsar la 'onra verdader'a ke 'eś śenyal de virtud 'i kon akelyo śe glorifika 'i no kon loś byeneś 'i maleś 'eśtrinśikoś :

K[A]PITULO 'ONZENO

'EŚ la y'- [11] propyedad ke loś byeneś de fortuna 'eleban 'el magnyanimo 'en 'ekśelensy'a syendo 'el ya perfekto konlaś vertudeś komo śe'a perśupu'eśto la razon 'enešto 'eś višta ke komo kyera ke todo 'el trato del magnyanimo 'eś aserka de laś grandeś 'obraś 'i 'el bu'eno kuanto maś prośpero 'eś tanto 'eś maś 'onrado de laś ğenteś por tanto 'eś maś 'ekśelente 'en la virtud de la magnyanimidad pu'eś 'eś maś 'enšalśado 'en akelyo ke konśište la magnyanimidad ke 'eś la 'obra [CW. ke la]}

⟨fol. 77b⟩
{ke la rikeza loś 'eśtadoś 'i 'otroś śemeğanteś byeneś tanto kuanto mal hazen aloś maloś ke tyene konelyyoś maś poder para hazer mal tanto maś byen hazen aloś bu'enoś ke tenyendo kon 'elyyoś maś poder para 'efektuar 'el byen śon maś 'ekśel[e]nteś 'i śon 'enešto loś byeneś de fortuna konparadoś al planeta Merkuryo por kuyo medyo 'el Dyo bendiğo noś da 'eśtoś byeneś śegun kyeren loś 'eśtrologoś ke 'el por śi no 'enklina 'a byen 'o mal śalbo śegun 'el aśpekto [ke] tyene kon 'otro planeta fortunado 'o 'infortunado aśi ayuda para byen 'o para mal por lo kual diğeron Merkuryo kon loś maloś malo kon loś bu'enoś bu'eno¹⁴⁵ 'i 'ešto parese śer la 'entiliğensy'a

---

¹⁴⁴ Prov. 29.23.

¹⁴⁵ The precise source of this statement is unknown to me. Pedro Mexía's *Silva de varia lección* (1550–1551) reproduces the judgment in inverted form: "el planeta llamado Mercurio, que está en el cielo segundo, planeta convertible, bueno con los buenos y malo con los malos" (ed. A. Castro [Madrid, 1989], 1:521).

de lo ke nu'eśtro sapyentisimo rey Šᵉlomoh diğo longura de diaś 'en śu dereğa 'en śu 'eśkyerda rikeza 'i 'onra 'i set-¹⁴⁶ keryendo dezir ke kuando 'el 'ombre akośtare ala parte dereğa ke 'eś śignifikadura del byen del alma la kual śe 'entitula ala parte dereğa eśtonśeś loś byeneś de fortuna ke śon śignifikadoś por la parte śinyeśtra śeran ğuntoś kon 'onra lo kual no akośtando al byen verdadero la rikeza de la śinyeśtra no śera kon 'onra 'i set- 'i 'eneśtoś byeneś fu'e tan loado nu'eśtro śanto porfeta ke diğeron nu'eśtroś śaby'oś ke 'una de laś kozaś ke konbyene a[']el porfeta para ke poze 'enel la porfesi'a 'eś śer riko 'i probanlo por 'el de adonde notaron śer rikisimo¹⁴⁷ :

'EŚ la dozena ke a'un ke 'otroś alkansen 'eśtadoś grandeś 'i hagan 'obraś 'eśtiry'oreś śemeğanteś alaś dela magnyanimidad aserka de grandeś 'onraś por grande poder ke tengan para 'elyyo no syendo perfektoś 'enloś abitoś virtu'ozoś no loś lyyamara magnyanimoś ni loś terna por taleś de manera ke 'eś 'eśta propyedad kunplida 'i konprehendida kazi por la primera 'i śegunda 'i 'eś la konkuluzy'on delyya ke syendo 'el magnyanimo virtu'ozo no değara de loar aloś virtu'ozoś ni loara aloś ke karesen de virtud a'un ke tengan muğo poder 'i 'eśta no 'eś menéster dezir kuan perfekta śe halyyaba 'en nu'eśtro śanto porfeta pu'eś tenemoś probado 'i 'eś magnifyeśto kuan perfektisimo 'era 'en todaś laś vertudeś 'en śumo grado de 'ekselensyya 'i pu'ede śer ke śignifikando 'eśta propyedad dišo nu'eśtro rey Šᵉlomoh 'en śuś deviniśimoś probyerby'oś 'eśm[e]radero para la plata 'i krizol para 'el 'oro 'i varon śegun śu lo'or¹⁴⁸ keryendo dezir ke aśi komo śe afina la plata 'i śe manifyeśta śu bondad 'en perfeksy'on 'eśmerandola 'ilo mesmo haze 'el 'oro 'enel krizol anśi śe konośe 'el 'ombre 'i śe 'eśpirmenta loke 'el 'eś 'enel lo'or ke 'el lo'a 'a 'otroś ke śi aloś bu'enoś 'i akozaś bu'enaś lo'a 'eś bu'eno 'i śi lo'a al kontrary'o 'eś malo 'i set-

'EŚ la treze ke 'el magnyanimo no śe deve 'oponer aloś peligroś por poka koza śalbo por kabza 'i 'onra grande komo por śalvar 'una tyera 'o 'otra koza śemeğante porke no 'eś 'eśta virtud śalbo aserka de kozaś}

⟨fol. 78a⟩
{ᶜH
grandeś komo tenemoś diğo :

---

¹⁴⁶ Prov. 3.16.
¹⁴⁷ Shabbat 92a.
¹⁴⁸ Prov. 27.21.

BOOK OF THE REGIMEN OF LIVING ‹FOL. 78A›

'I 'eś la katorze ke kuando śe 'entrega aloś peligroś no 'eliğe 'el peligro por 'el p[e]ligro 'enśi śalbo por 'el fin del byen ke de alyi 'eśpera ke 'eś 'el byen dela virtud porke 'eśta 'eś la 'onra verdader'a aserka de kozaś grandeś kuando por tal fin śe 'obra :

'EŚ la kinze 'el 'entregarśe aloś peligroś 'en kozaś grandeś 'i de grande 'onor kuando konbyene 'en lugar ke konbyene reğido por la dereğa razon ke 'eśto 'eś muy propyyo del magnyanimo :

'EŚ la diziśeyś ke kuando kyera ke śe 'entrega 'el magnyanimo aloś peligroś komo konbyene no resela muğo śu vida ni fya(d)[r]a muğo śobre 'elyya ke le parese no śer razon de bivir śin venser 'i 'obrar śegun virtud 'enel 'ultimo grado de perfeksy'on 'i tyene 'el morir por 'eśta vi'a por pura filisidad 'i śon 'eśtaś kuatro propyedadeś prośteraś śegun la virtud de la fortaleza komo avemoś 'enelyya deklarado 'en lo kual fu'e tan loado nu'eśtro beatisimo porfeta 'i ponyendo nu'eśtroś śaby'oś 'en laś kondisy'oneś del porfeta ke śe'a fu'erte lo preban del ke 'enel tyenpo ke desendi'a kon laś primeraś tablaś de la ley keryendolaś ronper[149] śegun dereğa razon śyendo defendido 'enelyyo de loś śetenta vyeğoś ke no kerian konśentir ke laś ronpyeśe baśto kontra todoś alaś ronper vyendo ke konveni'a ronperlaś por la mala 'enklinasy'on de loś ğudyos ke 'entonśeś tenian ke śi leś dyera akelyyaś tablaś no pudyeran mantener akelyyoś mandamyentoś ke 'enelyyaś mandaba 'el Dyyo glory'ozo ke guardaśen 'i kebrantandoloś 'i pasandoloś śyendo mandado del Dyyo meresian maś pena por tanto 'uzo de akelyya virtud de fortaleza 'en ronperlaś afin de byen komo fu'e deśpu'eś loado del Dyyo śegun nu'eśtroś śaby'oś diğeron śobre lo ke diśo 'el Dyyo 'a Mośeh Rabbenu mandandole kavakar laś śegundaś tablaś do dize 'i 'eśkrivire śobre laś tablaś laś palabraś ke 'eśtaban śobre laś tablaś primeraś ke kebraśte 'i set-[150] do dizen ke lo ke kiğo dezir 'en dezir ke kebraśte 'i set- śe lo diğo 'en śu lo'or komo ke diğeśe byen hiziśte ke laś kebraśte[151] de adonde śe nota śer perfektiśimo 'enla virtud dela fortaleza dela kual 'eś manifyeśto śer kunplido 'en 'eśtaś kuatro 'ultimaś propyedadeś ke śon aserka dela fortaleza komo tenemoś diğo :

'EŚ la diziśyete ğunto kon 'otraś 'oğo ke 'eś faśta numero de vente 'i śinko śegun la virtud dela liberalidad 'i 'eśta primera 'eś ke 'el magnyanimo deve perkurar de hazer byen 'a 'otroś kon toda śu posibilidad ke śyendo bu'eno śegun la primera propyedad 'eś razon ke haga byen 'a 'otroś ke del bu'eno 'eś muy propyyo hazer 'a 'otroś byen

---

[149] Exod. 32.19.
[150] Exod. 34.1, Deut. 10.2.
[151] Bava Batra 14b, Menaḥot 99b.

235

BOOK OF THE REGIMEN OF LIVING ‹FOL. 78A–78B›

'EŚ la dizi 'oğo ke śe avergu'ensa del byen ke resibe de 'otroś porke del magnyanimo 'eś propyyo hazer 'i no padeser ke tanto kuanto}

‹fol. 78b›
{'el hazer 'i dar 'eś delektable tanto 'el re(t)[s]ebir 'i padeser 'eś mizerable porke 'el ke resibe 'eś śubdito 'a 'el ke leda 'i 'el magnyanimo no 'a deśer śubdito 'a ninguno maś anteś 'a deśer muy libre por tanto śe avergu'ensa 'i adigeśta 'ile peza del byen ke de 'otro resibe :

'EŚ la dizi nu'ebe ke kuando resibe de alguna preśona por kual kyer vi'a 'o reśpekto ke śe'a konvyene kele torne maś deloke 'el resibyyo tanto ke ağuśta razon kede obligado 'el ke le dyyo a'un ke fu'e primero 'enel dar ke 'eś grande vantağe porke 'el magnyanimo deve de perkurar por todaś laś viaś posibleś ake aninguno śe'a debdor ni obligado porke no śe'a śubdito komo tenemoś diğo :

'I 'eśta propyedad 'eś byen manifyeśta 'enlaś 'eśpiaś ke mando Yᵉhošua͑ kuando vinyeron 'en kaza de Raḥab la zona do ku'enta la 'eśkritura ke avyendoleś 'elyya feğo tanta mersed komo 'eś manifyeśto ke leś śalbo la vida leś dišo 'i agora ğurar 'ora ami ke hize kon voś'otroś mersed 'i hareyś tambyen voś'otroś kon la kaza de mi padre mersed 'i dareyś ami śenyyal de verdad 'i set-¹⁵² 'i 'elyyoś reśpondyeron konforme 'a 'eśta yt- [19] propyedad 'i 'en fin de śuś palabraś diğeron 'i śera 'en dar anoś H‹a-Šem› la tyera 'i haremoś kontigo mersed 'i verdad 'i set-¹⁵³ 'i deveśe de notar 'enloke 'elyya leś avizo averleś heğo mersed porke diğo 'i hareyś tambyen voś konla kaza de mi padre mersed¹⁵⁴ pu'eś 'elyya meśma fu'e la ke hizo la mersed konelyyoś 'i śi por ventura 'elyya keri'a ke hizyeśen la diğa mersed kon la kaza deśu padre por darle a'el la 'onra 'oke keri'a maś 'el byen para śu padre ke para 'elyya propyya konke razon 'o korteźi'a no konsedyeron 'elyyoś hazerla konla kaza deśu padre pu'eś reśpondyeron 'i haremoś kontigo mersed 'i verdad 'i set-¹⁵⁵ ke parese no kerer konseder kuanto 'elyya demando pu'eś demando ke hizyeśen la mersed konla kaza deśu padre 'i la verdad konelyya 'i 'elyyoś parese ke no kiğeron maś ke hazer konelyya śola laś doś la mersed 'i la verdad koza 'inmerita para kyen tanto benefisy'o resiby'o por lo kual pyenśo ke śe'a la 'intensy'on konforme aloke tenemoś diğo aserka deśta propyedad ke a[']elyya viśto ke avi'a 'enpesado 'a hazer konelyyoś mersed ke toda koza ke no 'eś devida śe deve lyyamar mersed le paresyyo kuanto 'elyyoś podrian hazer konelyya de a'i por delante no podi'a śer mersed maś anteś verdad pu'eś todo lo

---

¹⁵² Josh. 2.12.
¹⁵³ Josh. 2.14.
¹⁵⁴ Josh. 2.12.
¹⁵⁵ Josh. 2.14.

Book of the Regimen of Living ⟨fol. 78b–79a⟩

devian hazer por ğuśta verdad por la 'obligasy'on 'enke le[ ]'eran por loke 'elyya por 'elyyoś avi'a heğo por lo kual leś dezi'a ke pu'eś konelyya no podian hazer mersed ke alo menoś la hizyeśen 'o 'uzaśen kon 'elyya śenyal de verdad ke 'eś pagar 'el debito para ke kedaśe loke kon śu padre hizyeśen mersed porke śi 'a 'elyya no pagaban kedaba loke konśu padre hazian verdad 'i no mersed pu'eś lo debian aśu hiğa 'i por tal reśpekto lo hazian 'enpero pagando 'a 'elyya 'i hazyendo kon 'elyya verdad kedaba loke hazian konśu padre}

⟨fol. 79a⟩
{ᶜT
mersed 'i por 'eśto demando laś doś kozaś 'i 'elyyoś reśpondyeron komo magnyanimoś 'i perfektoś 'eneśta propyedad 'i dišeron ke harian tanto ke no kale dezir konla kaza deśu padre ke harian mersed pero ke a'un konelyya la harian keryendo dezir ke śeri'a tanto loke konelyya meśma harian ke śeri'a pagado todo lo pasado 'i ke 'elyya leś kedari'a debdora de tal manera ke konelyya hizyeśen mersed 'i verdad ke 'eś pagar todo lo pasado 'i 'enpesar de nu'ebo 'a fazer mersed konelyya 'i kon la kaza deśu padre komo ku'enta deśpu'eś la devina 'eśtory'a kelo hizyeron do dize 'i 'a Raḥab la zona 'i 'a kaza de śu padre 'i 'a todo loke 'a 'elyya abivigu'o Yᵉhošuaᶜ 'i set-[156] ke syerto kunplyeron perfekta mente 'eśta propyedad

'EŚ la vente ke 'el magnyanimo deve tener kontino 'en memory'a loś benefisy'oś ke 'el haze 'a 'otroś por ke la tal memory'a le da delektasy'on por śer 'obra de virtud śegun śu magnyanimidad 'i maś ke la memory'a de lo pasado śera kabza de 'eśforsarlo 'en la 'obra de la virtud

'EŚ la vente 'i 'una ke loś byeneś 'i benefisy'oś ke 'el magnyanimo resibe de 'otroś no loś debe traer ala memory'a por ke la memory'a delyyoś le kabza moleśty'a 'i 'enoğo por ke 'el resebir 'eś pokedad 'i mizery'a komo tenemoś diğo pero deve perkurar de benefisyar 'i gualardonar al ke le dyyo 'en tanta manera ke kede 'el 'otro obligado a'el komo tenemoś deklarado 'en la propyedad dizinu'ebe 'i śi por ventura 'eneśto dubdareś ke te paresera 'ingratitud perkurar de 'olvidar 'el byen ke resibe ke maś razon parese ke śeri'a 'olvidarśe del ke 'el haze 'i tubyeśe śyenpre 'a memory'a 'el ke resibe aś de śaber ke loke śe dize ke 'el magnyanimo no 'a de traer ala memory'a loś byeneś ke resibyo no kyere dezir ke no trayyga ala memory'a 'a kyen le hizo akel byen 'o le dyyo akelyya dadiba ke 'eśto tal śeri'a pura 'ingratitud maś anteś konbyene ke 'el magnyanimo tenga kontino 'enla memory'a 'a kyen lo dyo 'o benefisy'o para hazerle byen pero 'a de perkurar de 'olvidar loke le dyyo porke 'eś pokedad śuya averlo resebido 'i 'eś le 'enoğoza la memory'a del kuanto delektable le

---

[156] Josh. 6.25.

Book of the Regimen of Living ‹fol. 79a–79b›

'eś la prezensyya de loke 'el dyyo 'i 'eśto fara kon pagar tan byen loke resiby'o ke no ayya nesesidad de akordarśe delyo yamaś de manera ke no por 'olbidar loke resiby'o śe pu'ede dezir 'ingrato pu'eś tyene 'en memory'a 'a kyen le dyo 'i set- :
'EŚ la vente 'i doś ke 'el magnyanimo resibe alegri'a 'i delektasy'on de 'o'ir 'el benefisy'o ke 'el 'a heğo 'a 'otro por śer 'obra bu'ena 'i porke la memory'a delyyo le kabza hazer maś byen komo avemoś diğo :
'EŚ la vente 'i (kuatro)[tres] ke syente pasy'on 'en 'o'ir 'el benefisy'o ke 'el 'a resebido de 'otro 'i por 'eśta kabza trae 'el filosofo 'enel kuarto dela 'etika[157] kela reyna Tetiś demando de Ğupitero mersed avyendole 'elyya feğo muğoś śervisy'oś}

‹fol. 79b›
{'i no le mento nada de kuanto 'elyya avi'a feğo maś anteś le truğo ala memory'a muğoś benefisy'oś ke 'elyya del abi'a resebido :
DE la meśma manera keryendo demandar loś Lasedemonyyoś syertaś mersedeś de loś Atiny'enśiś[158] avyendoleś heğo muğoś śervisy'oś por kuyya kabza 'eran meresedoreś de laś diğaś mersedeś nunka leś truğeron ala memory'a śu merito anteś 'otraś muğaś mersedeś ke loś meśmoś Lasedemonyyoś avian delyyoś resebido de donde śe deve ğuśgar por grande yero 'en loś ke piden 'a 'otroś mersedeś traerleś ala memory'a loke 'elyyoś an heğo 'o śervido 'o benefisyado 'a akelyyoś de loś kualeś demandan laś taleś mersedeś ke lo meğor 'eś ke 'el ke pide la mersed trayyga ala memory'a de akel akyen la pide 'otraś (ś)[k]e del 'a resebido ke 'eśto le śera alegre 'i delektable de 'o'ir kuanto le 'eś moleśto 'o'ir 'el benefisy'o resebido ke alyende de 'eśto ğuśga al ke le vyene pedir la mersed por agradeśido pu'eś tyene memory'a del byen resebido ke 'eś todo 'eśto konforme 'a 'eśtaś doś propyedadeś diğaś :
'EŚ la vente 'i kuatro ke 'el m(g)a[g]nyanimo no tyene nesesidad de ninguno porke komo kyera ke 'el 'eś aserka delaś kozaś grandeś 'i 'eśtaś akaesen pokaś veześ por tanto tyene muy pokaś veześ nesesidad de 'otro 'i al tyenpo ke tyene tal nesesidad de 'otroś śe pu'ede dezir ke 'entonseś tyenen 'elyyoś maś nesesidad del ke 'el delyyoś porke a'el no le falta moneda ni virtud śolo terna alguna veś nesesidad de ğente para 'oponerśe 'a kozaś grandeś ke śin ğente no lo pu'ede hazer komo akaese aloś prinsipeś 'i grandeś śenyyoreś ke an meneśter ğente para śuśtentar śuś 'eśtadoś 'i 'entonseś loś ke 'a 'elyyoś śe alyegan śon loś ke maś ganan :

---

[157] Aristotle, *NE* IV.iii.25 (1124b 17–18), alluding to Homer, *Iliad* 1.504–510.
[158] Aristotle, *NE* IV.iii.25 (1124b 18–19), alluding to an anecdote told by Callisthenes (cf. CAG 20.189.12–18).

BOOK OF THE REGIMEN OF LIVING ‹FOL. 79B–80A›

LA vente 'i śinko 'eś ke 'el magnyanimo 'a deśtar de kontino diśpu'eśto 'a dar 'i hazer mersedeś aloś ke del tubyeren nesesidad para ke 'en kual kyer tyenpo ke fu'ere rekerido no kede por 'el 'en ninguna manera 'eśtaś nu'ebe prośteraś propyedadeś śon aserka dela virtud dela liberalidad 'i mu'eśtran la poka nesesidad ke 'el magnyanimo tyene de ninguno 'i 'eśtaś todaś teni'a 'en śumo grado de perfeksy'on 'el śumo delaś profetaś ke no śolo śe kontentaba konel śer perfektisimo 'enelyyaś śi no ke 'a 'un 'enel tyenpo ke 'ubo nesesidad de 'eleğir 'ombreś ke ğuśga( )śen 'el pu'eblo por 'el śano konśeğo de śu śu'egro dizen nu'eśtroś śaby'oś ke loke leś 'entitulo la ley 'en titulo de varoneś de fonsado 'i set-[159] : ke propyya mente śon magnyanimoś fu'e porke no tenian nesesidad de katar faseś 'a nadi ni guardar reśpekto por la poka nesesidad ke de ninguno tenian[160] pu'eś kyen 'eśta śu'erte buśkaba para ke śuplyeśen parte deloke 'el avi'a de hazer kuan śin konpr'[e]nsy'on śeri'a 'el 'en todo 'eśto perfeksy'onado 'enel kabo dela 'ekśelensyya :}

‹fol. 80a›
{P ḤELEK B PEREK YB [PART TWO CHAPTER TWELVE]

KAPITULO DOZENO

'EŚ la vente 'i śeyś aśerka de laś konversasy'oneś del magnyanimo 'i 'eś ke 'a deśer grande 'i tenerśe por tal 'entre loś grandeś 'i prośperoś 'en 'eśtado 'i bu'ena fortuna komo śe nota 'eśto de nu'eśtra śanta 'eśkritura do dize tanbyen 'el varon Mošeh g(+)rande muğo 'en 'oğoś de 'eśklaboś de Par°oh 'i 'en 'oğoś de 'el pu'eblo 'i set-[161] donde śignifika śu grandeza kon loś grandeś ke śon loś 'eśklaboś del rey por ke 'el 'eśklabo del rey 'eś rey[162] :

'I tambyen kon la republika toda ke konelyyoś tambyen deve 'uzar 'el magnyanimo de śu grandeza

'EŚ la vente 'i syete ke 'el magnyanimo konverśe kon loś medyanoś medyana mente 'i no śe haga grande kon loś ke no śon grandeś por ke la virtud 'a de śer aserka del difisil 'i no aserka lo fasil 'i komo kyera ke para śer grande 'entre loś grandeś 'eś muy difisil alyi konśiśte la virtud 'enpero komo kon loś medyanoś śe'a fasil hazerśe no śe dev[e] hazer śalbo medyana mente 'i final mente kon loś grandeś śe deve hazer grande 'i śi kon loś medyanoś 'en alguna manera śe deve hazer kon loś bağoś 'en ninguna manera konbyene 'i 'eśta tambyen 'eś viśta 'enel nu'eśtro mayoral de loś

---

[159] Exod. 18.25.
[160] Rashi Exod. 18.21.
[161] Exod. 11.3.
[162] Shevuot 47b.

porfetaś por la de anteś deśta ke pu'eś dize la ley ke kon loś 'eśklaboś del rey 'era grande śe pu'ede notar ke kon 'otroś bağoś no śe konparaba :

'EŚ la vente 'i 'oğo ke no śe'a muy negosyado 'en kozaś bağaś 'i negosy'os de poka 'inportansa 'i ke śe'a vagarozo 'en śuś mobimyentoś kuando śe mobyere 'a kozaś de poka kalidad porke no 'eś razon ke ponga muğa diliğensyya śino fu'ere 'en kozaś grandeś 'i de muğa 'inportansa ke 'en taleś kozaś konvyene śer preśto 'i diliğentisimo komo śe 'eśkribyyo 'en nu'eśtra śantisima ley śobre nu'eśtro maeśtro do dize 'i apreśuro Mošeh 'i 'umilyyośe 'a tyera 'i 'enkorbośe 'i dišo śi halye grasy'a 'i set-¹⁶³ :

'EŚ la vente 'i nu'ebe ke no śe deve 'oponer 'a muğaś kozaś por ke komo kyera ke no 'a de 'obrar śalvo aserka de kozaś grandeś pokaś veześ akaesen por tanto akaese pokaś veześ ponerśe 'en algunoś negosy'oś 'i akelyyoś 'enke śe pone śon grandeś 'i muy kalefikadoś komo fu'eron todaś laś 'obraś 'enke nu'eśtro devinisimo porfeta śe 'opuzo deśde pekenyyo komo 'eś noto :

'EŚ la trentena ke 'el magnyanimo kuando fu'ere 'enemigo de kual kyera no 'a de śer 'enemigo 'enkubyerto ke 'eśto 'eś muğo de pośilanimo 'i timido 'i 'el magnyanimo ke de ninguna koza 'a de reselar deve śer 'enemigo deśkubyerto de kyen 'eś byen ke lo śe'a 'i 'eśta propyedad loaron nu'eśtroś śaby'oś 'en loś ermanoś de Yosef do dize nu'eśtra śantisima ley ke no le podian hablar 'a paś 'i set-¹⁶⁴}

‹fol. 80b›
{do dizen ke del vitupery'o delyyoś notamoś śu lo'or 'i set-¹⁶⁵ ke 'eś //śigni[f]ikasyyon// deśta propyedad lo meśmo ku'enta nu'eśtra śakra 'eśkritura aserka de Abšalom kon Amnon do dize 'i no hablo Abšalom kon Amnon de mal haśta byen 'i set-¹⁶⁶

'EŚ la trenta 'i 'una ke śe'a amigo deśkubyerto de kyen kyera ke lo fu'ere por ke śer amigo 'enkubyerto no kareśe de temor 'infamyya 'o de alguna perdida lo kual 'eś ağeno del magnyanimo por śu 'entera perfeksy'on :

'EŚ la trenta 'i doś ke 'el magnyanimo 'a de hablar kontinu'a mente verdad ke no akośte ya maś ala //'opiny(r)on// del vulgo 'o de algun partikular por konplazerle 'i dezir śu 'intensy'on konforme aśu dereğo ğu'izy'o komo maś śe deklarara aserka

---

¹⁶³ Exod. 34.8–9.
¹⁶⁴ Gen. 37.4.
¹⁶⁵ Rashi Gen. 37.4.
¹⁶⁶ 2 Sam. 13.22.

Book of the Regimen of Living ‹fol. 80b–81a›

de la virtud de la verdad ke an de śer konformeś la veluntad 'i boka del ke la dize[167] :
'EŚ la trenta 'i treś ke kual kyera koza ke diğere 'o determinare la diga 'i haga śin reselo publika mente por ke 'el ke dize 'o haze koza alguna //(absuluta) ['okulta]// mente teme śer reprehendido lo ke 'el ma(l)[g]n[y]animo no deve reselar śalvando algunaś 'obraś ke rekyeren śer 'okultaś :
'EŚ la trenta 'i kuatro ke 'el magnyanimo 'a de loar akyen loare 'en publiko 'i aśi vituperyar akyen vituperyare 'en publiko śin guardar reśpekto alguno aśi //(aśi) [kon]// 'el 'uno komo kon 'el 'otro :
'EŚ la trenta 'i śinko ke kuando al magnyanimo le konvyene kontar algunaś grandezaś ke 'a heğo 'eś razon ke diminuya algo de lo ke 'eś por ke no pareśka ke śe kyere loar aśi meśmo ke 'eś koza muy vituperable 'en toda preśona kuanta maś 'enel magnyanimo :
'EŚ la trenta 'i śeyś ke kuando 'el no śe'a de loar 'i 'a de kontar menoś de lo ke pasa 'eś kuando akontese kontarlo 'en publiko delante muğa ğente bağa ante loś kualeś no deve 'el magnyanimo hazerśe grande komo tenemoś diğo 'en la propyedad dizisyete pero kuando fu'ere 'en prezensya de grandeś no deve değar de dezir la verdad puntual mente komo pasa :
'EŚ la trenta 'i syete ke 'el magn[y]an[i]mo no śe deve ağuntar para konversar kon 'ombreś bašoś 'en ningun modo śalbo kon śuś amigoś por ke 'el ke śe haze konverśable atodoś no pu'ede değar de śer liğunğero 'i śyendo tal śe haze 'infiry'or a'elyyoś koza ağena del magnyanimo 'i 'eśtaś nu'ebe prośteraś propyedadeś 'eśtan todaś relatadaś por 'eśtenśo 'enel śalmo ke dize David śenyyor kyen pelegrinava 'en tu tyenda kyen morara 'en monte detu śantidad andan 'en preniśmidad 'i 'obran ğuśtisy'a 'i hablan verdad 'en śu korason 'i set-[168] 'onde kyen byen atentare laś halyy[a]ra fasil mente todaś nu'ebe 'i a'un algunaś maś ke dizen nu'eśtroś śaby'oś ke David dišo 'eśte śalmo por Mośeh Rabbenu 'i śakandolo del berbo 'i titulo ke le atribuye 'i deśpresyyado 'en śuś 'oğoś 'i set-[169] dizen ke}

‹fol. 81a›
{//(S')[P']// {RMK: Folios 81a–88a are misnumbered 91a through 98a. Fol. 91a number is struck, and a superscript correction, 81a, is printed, 95a is corrected in the same way; other folios through 88a are uncorrected.}

---

[167] Meṣudat David Ps. 145.18.
[168] Ps. 15.1–2.
[169] Ps. 15.4.

menośpresy'o la preza de 'Eğito por 'okuparśe 'en loś gü'eśoś de Yosef[170] donde kiğeron śignifikar ke todo kuanto 'enel diğo śalmo 'eś diğo śe aplika a'el ke 'en śolo dezir hablan verdad 'eśtan konprehendidaś todaś laś nu'ebe propyedadeś

'EŚ la trenta 'i 'oğo ke no śe'a de admirar 'el magnyanimo dezir kozaś grandeś por ke de razon no 'a de aver koza tan grande ke le śe'a a'el admirable 'i no kale dezir ke de kozaś bağaś no śe deve admirar por ke konvyene ke atente 'en todaś laś kozaś kon prudenśya śuś kabzaś 'i prinsipy'oś ke deśta manera de nada śe admirara śegun dereğa razon :

'EŚ la trenta 'i nu'ebe ke no trayga ala memory'a laś 'inğuryaś kontra 'el kometidaś por ke 'el ke pretendyyo 'inğuryarlo aśi meśmo haze 'el mal komo ya tenemoś diğo aserka de la propyedad 'oğo 'i dyeś ke[ ]komo kyera ke kuando le hazen laś 'inğuryaś no laś deve 'eśtimar komo alyi deklaramoś de la meśma manera deve menośpreśyyar la memory'a delyyaś 'i[ ]de lo ke alyi śe diğo de kuan kunplida mente śe falyyaben 'en nu'eśtro beatisimo porfeta 'eś magnifyeśto falyy[a]rśe 'enel 'eśtaś doś prośteraś 'en śumo grado de perfeksy'on

'EŚ la kuarenta kon 'otraś kuatro komo śe deve aver 'el magnyanimo aserka de la ğuśtisyya 'i 'eśta 'eś ke 'el magnyanimo no śe deve de 'entremeter 'en negosy'oś ağenoś ni hablar 'en[e]lyyoś ke śegun ğuśta razon ningun perfekto deve hablar 'en heğoś ağenoś śin śer pu'eśto 'o 'eliğido para 'elyyoś ni a'un 'en śuś propy'oś negosy'oś deve muğo 'entremeterśe ni hablar 'enelyyoś por ke la bondad delyyoś loś ğuśtefikara śin nesesidad de maś palabraś ni negosy'oś

'EŚ la kuarenta 'i 'una ke no 'a de holgarśe de ke le lo'en 'otroś por ke śuś 'obraś lo an de loar

'EŚ la kuarenta 'i doś ke no śe 'entristeśe kuando algunoś lo vituperyan pu'eś 'eś libre de kulpa ke 'el lo'or 'i vitupery'o 'a de śer de śuś meśmaś 'obraś 'i no de palabraś ağenaś

'EŚ la kuarenta 'i treś ke 'el magnyanimo no śe deve de loar 'a śi meśmo por ningun reśpekto ke 'eś muğo digno de vitupery'o komo diğo nu'eśtro śapyentisimo rey Š^{e}lomoh 'en śuś devinoś probyerboś lo'ete 'eśtranyyo 'i no tu boka 'i set-[171]

'EŚ la kuarenta 'i kuatro ke 'el magnyanimo no deve hablar mal de ninguno por ke non śu[e]na byen 'en boka del magnyanimo 'el mal śalvo kuando konbyene para amoneśtar 'o kaśtigar 'a loś maloś afin de byen ke por mal tratarloś pu'eden venir 'a śer muy bu'enoś

KOMO halyyamoś 'en nu'eśo śanto profeta 'uzando deśta devinisima virtud de la ğuśtisy'a ke konprende 'eśtaś 'ultimaś śinko propyedadeś kuando halyyo loś doś

---

[170] Makkot 24a, Rashi Prov. 10.8, Song of Sol. R. 1.3.
[171] Prov. 27.2.

Book of the Regimen of Living ‹fol. 81A–81B›

ğudy'oś peleando diğo a'el malo 'i kondenado porke fyereś atu konpanyero 'i set-[172] ke le lyyamo malo 'o kondenado por 'uzar de la amoneśtasy'on konvenible para resebir la 'enmyenda 'i set-[173]}

‹fol. 81b›
{ 'EŚ la kuarenta 'i śinko ğunto kon la ke śe śige aserka del reğimyento ke konbyene dyentro de śu kaza 'i 'eś 'eśta primera ke 'el magnyanimo no śe'a de keğar 'en ningun tyenpo de kośa alguna ni menoś śe'a de abağar 'a pedir lo ke le 'eś nesesary'o por ke a'el magnyanimo no suseden kozaś por 'onde śe pu'eda keğar ni le 'a de faltar lo nesesary'o :

'EŚ la kuarenta 'i śeyś ke kuando 'el magnyanimo konprare para śu kaza kual kyer koza no 'a de śer 'a fin de ganar 'enelyya komo śi 'en śu kaza hizyere 'una gu'erta por śu pasa tyenpo no plante 'enelyya arboleś 'a fin de ganar 'el fruto de 'elyyoś 'o śi merkare abeś 'o kual kyer 'otro animal no śe'a 'a fin de multiplikar 'en la meśma 'eśpesyya por ganansy'a ke todo 'eśto 'eś ağeno del magnyanimo por ke todo 'elyyo 'eś bağeza 'i mizery'a maś anteś śi haze gu'erta deve de plantar 'enelyya kozaś 'odoriferaś 'i deleytableś ala viśta maś ke 'utileś 'i 'eśtaś doś non kale dezir komo śe halyyaban 'en nu'eśo śanto profeta ke pu'eś 'era paśtor 'i reğidor 'onibersal 'i tan gran śenyyor non kale dezir ke non śe 'okupaba 'en kozaś tan bağaś 'i tan mizerableś maś a'un 'eś syerto ke la mayor parte de śu 'okupasy'on 'era 'en la devina kontenplasy'on

'EŚ la kuarenta 'i syete ğunto kon laś 'otraś treś 'ultimaś hata kunplimyento de laś śinku'enta aserka loś mobimyentoś korporaleś de 'el magnyanimo 'i 'eś 'eśta primera ke śe deve de mober pezada mente 'i de vagar por ke 'el magnyanimo 'eś aserka de la 'onra 'i la 'onra konśiśte 'en la grabedad de laś kozaś de adonde diğeron nu'eśoś gramatikoś[174] kon razon ke 'el termino de 'onra śegun nu'eśa śanta lengu'a 'eś deribado [de] grabedad de manera ke śer 'el 'ombre tal 'en śuś mobimyentoś 'eśpesyal 'en śu 'andar 'eś la propyya 'onra ke 'eś propyyo de 'el magnyanimo :

---

[172] Exod. 2.13.

[173] Sanhedrin 58b, Exod. R. 1.29, Num. R. 18.12; an alternate source is possible.

[174] The mentioned etymological derivation is well-known; see Rashi's commentary on the Bible. The "gramatikoś" M.A. may have had in mind would include: Saadya ben Joseph (882 Fayyum–942), Samuel the Nagid (Ismail ibn Nagrelᶜa) (993 Córdoba–1055/56 Granada), Judah ben David Hayyuj (Fez c. 945–Córdoba c. 1000), Jonah Ibn Janah (c. 985 Córdoba–c. 1040 Zaragoza); and, finally, Abraham Ibn Ezra (1089 Tudela–1164).

BOOK OF THE REGIMEN OF LIVING ‹FOL. 81B–82A›

'Eś la kuarenta 'i 'oǧo ke śe'a tambyen gra(nd)[v]e 'en śu hablar ke non śe'a la boz muy alta ke 'el ke alsa muǧo la boz parese kerer śer 'o'ido por fu'ersa ke 'eś koza muy vituperable por lo kual konbyene moderarśe tanbyen 'enel hablar kon gravedad konvenible :
 'Eś la kuarenta 'i nu'ebe ke alyende de non śer la boz alta perkure 'el magnyanimo ke non śe'a preśuroza la habla maś anteś algo tardi'a 'i kon repozo por ke komo 'el magnyanimo śe ayya de 'oponer 'a pokaś kozaś komo avemoś (r)[d]eklarado 'en la propyedad vente 'i nu'ebe 'eś razon ke 'en lo ke śe 'entremetyere ke śe'a grabe 'i vagarozo kuando 'el tyenpo lo padese 'i 'el negosy'o 'enśi lo śufre 'i rekyere :
 'Eś la śinku'enta 'i 'ultima de todaś ke 'el magnyanimo non śe'a de poner 'en pleytoś ningunoś śuyoś ni aǧenoś por ke loś pleytoś brigaś 'i baraǧaś śon por alkansar kozaś grandeś 'o kozaś neses(y)aryaś 'i pu'eś 'el magnyanimo}

‹fol. 82a›
{Ṣ {RMK: 90 count 82a.}
no 'eś falto de nada ni ninguna koza 'eś para 'el grande no deve 'en ninguna manera ponerśe 'en pleyto ninguno por ke alyende de lo diǧo 'eś grande deśa'utorizamyento de śu preśona 'i demośtrasy'on de mala 'enklinasyyon de 'apetito danyyado apareǧado para pelear kośa muy aǧena 'i 'eśtranyya de 'el magnyanimo :
 'I 'eśtaś kuatro prośteraś manko 'eś meneśter dezir ni prebar kuan perfektisima mente śe halyyaban 'en nu'eśtro śantisimo profeta ke śuś kozaś 'i 'obraś 'eran 'eroykaś 'en kontinu'a kontenplasy'on 'elebado 'enla 'ekselensy'a dela verdader'a glory'a :
 'I kiǧe aplikar todaś 'eśtaś propyedadeś 'a nu'eśtro devinisimo porfeta Mošeh Rabbenu pu'eśto ke tanbyen 'en nu'eśoś śantoś patryarkaś 'i re'eyś śe halyyaron por śer 'enel maś manifeśtoś 'i 'en śumo grado de 'ekselensyya 'i maś para tenerlaś maś konǧuntaś ala memory'a por la konformidad del nombre mi'o 'i tuyo konel śuyo śanto 'i glory'ozo para imitar a'el śi 'el Dyyo kiǧere por śu śanta mizerikordy'a ke aśi śe'a :
 'I kon lo ke tenemoś diǧo aserka de 'eśta virtud me parese ke abaśta para venir aśu verdadero konosimyento
 'I 'eś byen tenerla de kontino 'enla memory'a por śuś propyedadeś porke 'eś syerto śublime virtud 'en 'ultimo grado de 'ekselensyya śobre todaś laś vertudeś por ke prośupone laś 'otraś 'enel meśmo grado komo tenemoś diǧo
 'I de la deśkrisy'on de la meśma virtud śe 'entendera 'i śe konprendera la verdader'a deśkrisy'on de śuś 'eśtremoś ke 'el ke puǧare 'en 'oponerśe 'a maś de lo ke konbyene 'en tyenpo 'i lugar 'i kozaś deśkonvenibleś 'eś 'el visy'ozo 'en la puǧa 'i 'el ke mankare de 'oponerśe 'en lo ke konbyene kuando konbyene 'i set- 'eśte tal 'eś pozilanimo ke 'esede 'en la falta
 KONTRA 'el kual diǧo nu'eśtro śapyentisimo rey Š^elomoh 'en śuś probyerby'oś de

BOOK OF THE REGIMEN OF LIVING ‹FOL. 82A–82B›

śuś kaminoś śe farta 'el pozilanimo 'i de śobre 'el 'ombre bu'eno[175] ke kyere dezir ke 'el pozilanimo śe harta preśto de todo lo ke anda por śu kamino de la vida 'i non k[y]ere 'oponerśe 'a kozaś grandeś kuando konbyene ke lu'ego śe harta 'i le parese ke le baśta lo ke pose'e pero 'el ke 'eś bu'eno no śe harta kon lo ke 'el pozilanimo śe harta śalbo kon lo ke 'eś śobre 'el de 'otro mayor grado hata venir a'el medy'o komo konbyene 'i set- 'i 'eśto kiǧo dezir dizyendo 'i 'ombre bu'eno de śobre 'el 'i set- ke 'el 'ombre bu'eno ke 'uza śegun dereǧa razon śe harta de lo ke 'eś śobre 'el pozilanimo ke 'eś 'el medy'o de manera ke non kyere kedar 'en la falta ni kyere tanto śubir ke 'eseda 'en la puǧa por ke 'enel medy'o konsiśte 'el byen 'i kon 'eśto ke tenemoś diǧo kual kyera konprendera muǧaś 'infinitaś partikularidadeś}

‹fol. 82b›
{ḤELEK B PEREK YG [PART TWO CHAPTER THIRTEEN]
ke ayy aserka de 'eśta virtud ke por hu'ir de la proliǧidad deǧamoś de 'eśpasifikar :

KAPITULO TREZENO

LA deśkrisy'on de la seśta virtud ke 'eś la modeśty'a lyyamada filot(o)[i]mi'a 'en grego 'eśta viśta 'i deklarada dela suzo diǧa virtud porke no difyeren śalvo 'en śer aserka laś 'onraś grandeś 'i medyanaś dela meśma manera ke difyeren la liberalidad dela maknifiśensy'a komo ya tenemoś diǧo ke anśi komo la liberalidad difyere dela maknifiśensy'a 'en śer aserka de kośaś grandeś 'o maś baǧaś 'enla diśtribu'isy'on dela moneda dela meśma manera śon 'eśtaś doś 'enlaś kośaś dela 'onra ke 'eśta 'eś aserka de 'onraś 'infiry'oreś alaś 'onraś ake śe 'opone 'el magnyanimo ke 'el ke śe 'opuzy'ere 'a kośaś medyanaś komo konbyene kuando 'i kuanto konbyene 'i set- 'eśte tal śera perfekto 'en 'eśta virtud :

'I 'el ke 'esedyere de 'eśtaś śerkonśtansyaś 'i faltare enelyaś śera visy'ozo 'en 'uno deloś doś 'estremoś 'i śi fu'ere 'enla puǧa śera anbisy'ozo 'i śi 'enla falta remiśo :

'I 'eneśta virtud no 'eś meneśter alargar pu'eś por la virtud dela magnyanimidad 'eśta byen viśta 'eśta kon śuś 'eśtremoś ke todaś doś śon de 'un meśmo tenor 'i non difyeren śegun faze 'a nu'eśtro perpozito śalvo de maś 'a menoś komo tenemoś diǧo :

ŚOLO 'eś razon ke deklaremoś por ke no śe tome 'eneśto 'eror śi alguno kiǧere argu'ir dizyendo ke 'eneśta virtud non deve aver visy'o 'enla puǧa ke parese 'a prima

---

[175] Prov. 14.14.

BOOK OF THE REGIMEN OF LIVING ‹FOL. 82B–83A›

višta ke śi 'uno śe kiğere 'oponer ala 'onra maś de medyana mente 'eś kerer imitar 'a 'el magnyanimo de manera ke la puğa 'enla modeśty'a pu'ede śer 'el medy'o dela magnyanimidad 'o alyegarśe 'a 'elyya 'i tener kon 'elyya maś partisipasy'on 'i śimilitud pu'eś komo lyyamaremoś visy'o lo ke 'a maś 'eselente virtud aśemeğa 'i śe alyega ke parese muy fu'era de razon 'i verdad

PARA lo kual diremoś ke aśi komo śe konsidra aserka de la liberalidad ke 'el ke gaśta maś de loke konbyene no śe lyyamara maknifiko śalvo prodigo del meśmo modo 'eś aserka dela modeśty'a porke non todoś loś 'ombreś śon para laś kozaś grandeś komo tenemoś diğo śalvo 'el ke fu'ere perfekto 'en todaś laś propyedadeś del magnyanimo diğaś ni menoś todoś loś tyenpoś ni todoś loś lugareś śon konvenyenteś maś 'a de śer todo komo 'i kuando 'i kuanto konbyene 'a kyen konbyene 'i set- :

'ı Śı por ventura a[']el ke le falta algunaś de laś propyedadeś de}

‹fol. 83a›

{ṢG {RMK: 93 count 83a.} HELEK B PEREK YD [PART TWO CHAPTER FOURTEEN] 'el magnyanimo śe kiğere 'oponer 'a 'onraś grandeś 'oke 'en kozaś medyanaś kiğere 'uzar de grandeś 'eśte tal śe lyyama anbisy'ośo 'i non magnyanimo ni śemeğante 'a 'el porke loke haze śer virtud 'o visy'o 'eś la 'orden 'i deś'orden de la 'obra 'o varyasy'on delaś śerkonśtansyaś :

DE modo ke keryendo ponerśe 'el 'ombre 'en kozaś mayoreś de loke 'a 'el konbyene śera visy'ozo 'enla puğa aśi komo 'el keda kuando dyere maś de loke 'a 'el konbyene śe lyyamara prodigo a'un ke de menoś kantidad dela ke konelyya 'el maknifiko śera falto porke 'eśto todo śe'a de ğuśgar śegun laś śerkonśtansyaś komo muğaś veześ tenemoś 'eśkrito 'i de 'eśte modo 'eś viśto ke kyen değare de 'oponerśe ala 'onra medyana kele konbyene 'eś del todo remiśo 'i 'eśto baśtara 'a 'el preśente konlo diğo para loke konbyene ala deśkrisy'on deśta virtud 'i deśuś 'eśtremoś por hu'ir de la proliğidad ke lo demaś śe vera fasil mente por loke tenemoś 'eśkrito aserka de la virtud de la magnyanimidad :

KAPITULO KATORZENO

'I para loke konbyene śaber 'enla mansedumbre śingulariśima virtud 'i śebtima 'enel numero de laś vertudeś moraleś a'un ke śeri'a byen 'i muy 'util alargar 'enelyya por śer tan 'eselente virtud 'i de tanta suśtansy'a por non 'eseder del 'eśtilo ke 'en laś 'otraś avemoś lyevado diremoś 'enelyya konforme 'a lo ke 'en laś 'otraś tenemoś diğo 'i algo maś por śer loś 'ombreś maś 'enklinadoś ala 'ira ke ala pasensy'a 'i 'eś meneśter muğo perkurar de moderar 'el 'apetito 'enelyya para 'eśtar 'enel medy'o 'i non 'eseder ke kaśi 'eś 'inposible poder ninguno 'eśtar 'enel medy'o de adonde nasy'o akelyya deviniśima dotrina de nu'eśoś śaby'oś ke noś amośtraron ke aserka de 'eśta

Book of the Regimen of Living ‹fol. 83a–83b›

virtud śe deve de poner 'el 'ombre 'enel 'eśtremo de la falta ke a'un ke 'en todaś laś vertudeś 'eś la falta vituperable 'eneśta 'eś loable non por 'elyya 'en śi ke 'eś gran yero de kyen tal penśare śalvo por non kaer 'en 'otro visy'o pe'or ke 'eś la puǧa por ke śi 'eśtubyere 'enel medy'o 'eś 'inpośible non 'eseder 'en la puǧa 'i śi 'eśtubyere 'en la falta 'el de śuyo verna muy śerka del medy'o

'I 'eśto 'eś lo ke kiǧo śentir 'el śenyyor Rabbenu Mošeh 'en la glośa de akel diǧo de nu'eśoś śaby'oś ke dize muǧo muǧo śe'ey baǧo de 'eśprito ke 'eśperansa del 'ombre verme 'i set-[176] do dize konbyene aloś bu'enoś akośtar 'eneśta virtud a'el 'eśtremo de la falta por ke non venga 'a pasar a'el 'eśtremo de la puǧa 'i set-[177] 'i maś lo deklara 'enel kuarto kapitulo de loś 'oǧo kapituloś ke 'en śu prologo haze alyi[178] :}

‹fol. 83b›
{ 'I 'eś byen viśta la 'intensy'on de śuś palabraś konforme 'a lo ke tenemoś diǧo 'i non komo algunoś pensaron śer 'el 'eśtremo de la falta aserka de 'eśta virtud bu'eno 'i loable ke 'eśo 'era dezir ke fu'eśe 'el medy'o visy'o 'i non virtud kontra toda razon 'i filosofi'a moral :

'I para venir 'en verdadero konosimyento de 'eśta virtud 'eś meneśter śaber lo primero ke aserka dela 'ira śe konsidran doś 'eśtremoś loś kualeś śon muǧa 'ira 'i pribasy'on de 'ira 'i 'un medyyo 'entre 'eśtoś doś 'enel kual medy'o konsiśte 'eśta virtud ke 'eś la mansedumbre 'i komo tenga maś śimilitud 'i komunikasy'on 'el medy'o kon la falta lyyamamoś komun mente tanbyen ala falta mansedumbre :

'I 'eś meneśter maś śaber ke la 'ira la kual aserka de 'elyya śe konsidran loś treś terminoś diǧoś śe 'enǧendra 'enel 'ombre p(+)or muǧaś kauśaś 'i diversas para laś kualeś 'entender 'eś meneśter la deśkrisy'on 'o difinsy'on de 'ira śegun la difine 'el filosofo 'enel śegundo de la retorika[179] do dize śer 'un 'apetito 'o deśe'o kon triśteza para punir 'i kaśtigar 'a kyen de 'el śe le śige 'o alguna deś'onra 'o 'inǧury'a 'o kual kyer koza 'otra kontra śu veluntad :

'I kon 'eśto 'eś viśto ke la 'inǧury'a 'o deś'onra por la kual śe kauśa la 'ira pu'ede śer por diversaś kauśaś 'o por ke tokan 'en la preśona 'o 'onor del ke śe a'yra 'o 'en śuś byeneś tenporaleś 'eśtrinsikoś 'i laś maś de laś veześ por pareserle ke resibe 'inǧury'a 'en śer kontraśtada śu veluntad kon 'apetito 'i deśe'o de la vengansa :

---

[176] Avot 4.4.
[177] Rambam *Hilkot De ͨot,* Perek 2, Halakah 3.
[178] Maimonides, "*Eight Chapters,*" ed. Gorfinkle.
[179] Aristotle, *Rhetoric* II.ii.1 (1378a 30–33), trans. J. H. Freese (Cambridge, MA, 1926), 173.

BOOK OF THE REGIMEN OF LIVING ⟨FOL. 83B–84A⟩

'I kon 'eśto 'eś byen viśto ke kuando 'el 'ombre śe a'yra śobre kośaś ke konbyene a'yrarśe 'i kontra 'ombreś ke konbyene 'i fu'ere la 'ira 'enel modo ke konbyene kuando 'i kuanto konbyene 'i set- 'eśtonseś śera la tal 'ira konforme ala dereğa razon 'i prosedyendo de abito śera virtu'oza :
   'I para ke meğor śe pu'eda konservar 'eśta devinisima virtud 'i manko 'erar 'enelyya diremoś algunaś propyedadeś 'en ke 'eś meneśter muğo atentar por ke 'eś 'el yero muy fasil 'eśpesyal 'en loś ke por śuś konplisy'oneś liğera mente toman 'ira 'i muy dura mente śe pu'eden refrenar tenyendo delyyo harta nesesidad
   'I 'eś la primera ke 'el manso kuando śe a'yra 'enel tyenpo ke konbyene komo konbyene 'i set- deve de akabidarśe 'en gran manera ke la pasy'on de la 'ira no lo turbe ni lo mude de lo ke anteś 'era maś anteś konbyene ke tenga 'el ğ(z)uizy'o 'inkoruto 'i 'el 'eśprito repozado 'i la voluntad pronta 'i konforme ala dereğa razon para ke tenga laś r[y]endaś a'eśte deśfrenado 'apetito ke no le perverta 'el ğu'izy'o para 'ordenar kon la 'ira laś kozaś ke konbyene komo konbyene 'i set- ke śi 'el 'en alguna manera śe 'enflama 'enel kalor de la 'ira śin [CW. ğu'izy'o]}

⟨fol. 84a⟩
{ṢB {RMK: 92 count 84a.}
ğu'izy'o prudensyal no podra hazer koza bu'ena :
   'I 'EŚTO 'eś ami ver lo ke kiğo dezir nu'eśtro śapyentiśimo rey Šᵉlomoh dizyendo maś vale 'ira ke rizo ke kon malisy'a de faseś śe abonigu'a 'el korason 'i set-[180] ke 'en nu'eśtra śantisima lengu'a śe pu'ede tomar 'el termino de ke por kuando 'i śera komo ke diğeśe maś vale 'ira ke rizo kuando kon malisy'a de faseś 'i set- 'i tanbyen śe podri'a 'entender no tirando 'el termino de śu propy'a śignifikasy'on komo ke diğeśe maś vale la 'ira ke kon malisy'a de faseś śe abonigu'a 'el korason ke non 'el ğu'ego 'o rizo ke a'un ke 'eśte 'el termino de ğu'ego 'en medy'o śe 'entyenda komo śi 'eśtubyeśe al kabo 'i la 'intensy'on de kual kyer modo ke śe'a konforme 'a loke tenemoś diğo 'eś ke la 'ira 'eś meğor ke 'el ğu'ego 'o rizo ke 'eś aserka de laś deleytasy'oneś de la konverśasy'on komo deklararemoś maś adelante 'i kyero dezir ke syendo todoś doś reğidoś por la dereğa razon komo konvyene 'i set- komo śe nota por 'el termino de maś vale 'i set- ke parese diferir 'enla bondad 'i 'enel valor de maś 'a menoś dize ke vale maś la 'ira ke la burla 'o ğu'ego p(+)ero dize ke 'a de śer kon tal kondisy'on ke la tal 'ira a'un ke śe amu'eśtre 'enla kara ke no pu'ede ser menoś por hazerśe por 'enflamasyon de loś 'eśpritoś no śe'a tanto ke perverta 'el ğu'izy'o śalvo ke 'eśte 'el

---

[180] Eccles. 7.3.

BOOK OF THE REGIMEN OF LIVING ‹FOL. 84A–84B›

korason repozado 'i 'ešto kiğo dezir dizyendo kuando konla malisy'a de la kara še abonigu'a 'el korason 'i set-[181] :
TYENE 'otra šegunda prop[y]edad 'el manso la kual 'eš perdonar 'el yero 'a todoš 'i non punir ni apenar 'a alguno kyero dezir ke kon toda prešona ke le ayya 'erado 'uza mizerikordy'a 'i pyadad mirando 'el merito de kada kual anteš ke 'eraše teni'a 'i todaš laš kaušaš ke 'a 'erar lo mobyeron 'i por 'ešto še 'enklina 'a perdonar maš ke 'a punir :
POR la kual propyedad fu'e loado nu'eštro devinisimo profeta 'entitulado 'enešta šingularisima virtud ke diğo 'el Dyyo por 'el 'i 'el varon Mošeh manso muğo 'i set-[182] ke para šiknifikar komo 'eštaba apartado de 'el 'eštremo de la puğa 'en'el kual maš ke 'en la falta pekan loš 'ombreš diğo muğo 'i set-
'I '[e]š(y) de notar konforme a'ešta propyedad ke non fu'e 'entitulado 'en tal titulo šalbo kuando maš šu pasensy'a tra(n)se[n]dy'o 'en šufrir ašu 'ermano 'i 'ermana ke tan šin razon hablaron kontra 'el šobre 'el kašo de la muğer 'ety'opi'a ke tomo komo ku'enta la šakra 'eškritura 'i hablo Miriyam 'i 'Aharon 'en Mošeh šobre kaušaš de la muğer 'ety'opi'a 'i set-[183] donde kiğo 'el Dyyo glory'ozo moštrar kuanta razon teni'a Mošeh Rabbenu 'en kuanto hazi'a komo tengo byen deklarado šobre 'el tešto 'en šu lugar[184] ke traerlo 'a( )ki šeri'a proliğidad 'i šalir muğo de nu'eštro prepozito šolo fu'e aki la 'inte[n]sy'on prebar de 'elyo la 'ekselensy'a de 'ešta virtud ke tan [CW. loado]}

‹fol. 84b›
{loado fu'e por 'elyya nu'ešo porfeta 'enel tyenpo ke 'el 'ušo dešta šegunda propyedad komo tenemoš diğo :
'I de 'eštaš doš propyedadeš de 'ešta virtud 'eš byen višto 'el vitupery'o de šuš 'eštremoš
KE 'el değar de a'yraršé 'el 'ombre 'onde konbyene kuando 'i kontra kyen konbyene 'eš syerto falta 'enel virtu'ozo ke parese šer //'inse[n]sible// 'i pareše ke non še atrišta de laš kozaš 'indevidaš por laš kualeš deve šegun dereğa razon de a'yraršé :
'I šigeše 'otro 'inkonbenyente ke non perkura vengarše donde konbyene tomar vengansa konbyene šaber de šuš 'enemigoš 'i maš propy'a mente deloš 'enemigoš del

---

[181] Eccles. 7.3.
[182] Num. 12.3.
[183] Num. 12.1.
[184] He refers to *Tefilah le-Mošé* or *Piruš al Piruš ha-Torah le-Rashi*.

BOOK OF THE REGIMEN OF LIVING ‹FOL. 84B›

Dyyo pu'eś no tyene 'ira kelo deśpyerte 'a vengarśe ni prudensy'a para reğirla adonde konbyene 'i 'eśto 'eś di(k)[g]no de grande vitupery'o porke no 'eś lisito 'en todo apyadar śobre 'el 'enemigo ni 'en todo tyenpo ni por todaś kośaś a'un ke 'el perdonar 'enśi śe'a bu'eno ke 'eś diminu'ir la pena komo konvyene no 'eś lisito kitarla de todo punto de 'el 'enemigo 'i kuando de todo śe kitare 'a de śer konforme ala dereğa razon loke pokaś veześ akonteśe :

'I apyadar 'a 'el 'enemigo 'onde non konbyene no śe pu'ede nyegar śer yero 'i vitupery'o manifyeśto :

DEL kual fu'e //rep[r]endido// nu'eśtro famoziśimo rey Šaul de Šᵉmu'el 'el porfeta 'en gran manera por aver apyadado śobre 'Agag rey de ᶜAmalek kuando lo prendy'o bivo syendo 'enkomendado de 'el Dyyo ke non apyadaśe śobre 'el por lo kual meresy'o 'o'ir de boka de[ ]'el porfeta ke le diğo 'i porke non 'o'iśte 'en boz de 'el Dyyo 'i set-[185] :

KE toda akelyya 'eśtory'a noś 'ensenyya kuanto deve 'el virtu'ozo vengar laś 'inğuryaś del 'enemigo 'eśpesyal de loś 'enemigoś del Dyyo 'i de śu ley 'onde konbyene komo konbyene 'i set- de manera ke 'eś byen viśto ke 'el ke faltare 'enla 'ira 'onde konbyene śera visy'ozo 'i vituperado

'I porke 'e viśto ke Šeneka famoziśimo 'eśtoyko kiğo prebar kon muy śutil argu'ir kela 'ira 'en ninguna manera fu'e bu'ena ni 'util para la virtud[186] poko ni muğo kontra dela 'opiny'on del filosofo 'enel komento dizi('i)śyete del libro kuarto dela 'etika[187]

'EŚ razon ke digamoś śuś razoneś 'o alo menoś la rezolusy'on de 'elyyaś 'i reśponder por 'el meğor modo ke posible śera 'en muy brebe 'a 'un ke 'el alarga byen 'enelyyaś laś kualeś śon 'eneśta forma :

LA primera ke Šeneka da 'eś ke komo śe'a la 'ira 'apetito dela vengansa[188] śegun la difinyeron loś antigoś 'i śe'a la vengansa vituperable kuando no 'eś 'a fin de kaśtigar 'a kyen merese 'el tal kaśtigo parese śegun 'eśtaś doś porpozisy'oneś śer la 'ira śuperflu'a śin ninguna 'utilidad pu'eś 'el kaśtigo 'a 'el tal pu'ede śer [CW. śin]}

---

[185] 1 Sam. 15.20.
[186] Seneca, *De Ira* I.ix.1, xxi.1, trans. Basore, 1:129, 165.
[187] Aristotle, *NE* IV.v.3–11 (1125b 32–1126a 29).
[188] Let one example from *On Anger* (I.xii.6) stand for many: "Now no passion is more eager for revenge than anger" (Seneca, *De Ira* I.xii.6, trans. Basore, 1:139).

BOOK OF THE REGIMEN OF LIVING ‹FOL. 85A›

‹fol. 85a›
{//(ṢG)[PG] {RMK: Printed ṢG [93] struck, superscript correction PH; count 85a.}
ḤELEK B PEREK YD
śin 'ira ni deśe'o de vengansa 'ordenado por ğu'izy'o prudensyal śegun dereğa razon 'i set-[189] :
'I la śegunda 'eś ke la dereğa razon 'eś la ke deve de reğir 'i 'enkaminar alaś 'obraś konvenibleś śegun 'el tyenpo 'i 'el lugar 'i la kantidad kon todaś laś 'otraś śerkonśtansyaś de la virtud 'i śi la 'ira partisipare 'eneśte tal reğimyento no pu'ede mankar de 'una de doś 'oke la tal 'ira a'umente la 'obra maś delo 'ordenado por la dereğa razon 'o no 'i śi anyade 'eś manifyeśto 'el danyyo porke todo loke śe a'umenta śobre loke la dereğa razon 'ordena 'eś maś de loke konbyene 'i śi la 'ira no a'umenta la 'obra maś de lo 'ordenado śegun dereğa razon lu'ego la 'ira 'eś śuperflu'a 'i śin ninguna 'utilidad[190] :
LA tersera razon ke deklara para prebar komo la 'ira śe'a vituperable de kual kyer modo ke śe'a 'eś ke toda kośa ke no 'eś 'ordenada de parte del 'entendimyento no śe pu'ede 'entitular 'en titulo de byen komo 'eś manifyeśto pu'eś komo kyera ke la 'ira no 'eś 'ordenada de parte del 'entendimyento komo 'el filośofo deklaro 'enel śebtimo dela 'etika do diğo ke la 'ira 'eś komo la borağeś 'i set-[191] lu'ego la 'ira no śe pu'ede dezir śer byen pu'eś no 'eś 'ordenada por parte del 'entendimyento 'i dereğa razon[192] :
'EŚTAŚ śon laś maś prinsipaleś razoneś por laś kualeś determino 'el gran śaby'o Śeneka ke non konbyene partisipar la 'ira 'en ninguna manera konla virtud dizyendo ke 'onde 'entra la 'ira śe 'enśenyyore'a de tal manera ke no śe değa refrenar[193] :

---

[189] Seneca's lengthy discussion of this point in *De Ira* (I.xv.1–xix.8) may be epitomized by the statement: "For the one who administers punishment nothing is so unfitting as anger, since punishment is all the better able to work reform if it is bestowed with judgement" (I.xvi.2, trans. Basore, 1:145).

[190] Similar statements are found in *De Ira:* "And anger is altogether unbalanced" (I.xvii.7, trans. Basore, 1:153); "It is not profitable that anger should be increased; therefore, that anger should exist either. That is not a good which by increase becomes an evil" (I.xiii.2, trans. Basore, 1:141).

[191] Aristotle, *NE* VII.iii.7–8 (1147a 10–24); See also VII.iii.12–13 (1147b 7–13) and VII.vi.1–5 (1149a 25–1149b 27).

[192] He refers to the contrary relationship between reason and anger: "These two do not dwell separate and distinct, but passion and reason are only the transformation of the mind toward the better or the worse" (Seneca, *De Ira* I.viii.3, trans. Basore, 1:127).

[193] Representative statements of this idea are found in *De Ira:* "Once we admit the emotion

Book of the Regimen of Living ‹fol. 85a–85b›

PERO byen atentando parese śer la 'opiny'on del filosofo verdader'a konforme ala 'opiny'on de nu'eśoś śaby'oś 'en diversaś parteś ke laś razoneś de Śeneka fasil mente śe pu'ede 'a 'elyaś reśponder ke no konśta por 'elyyaś averśe de deśeǧar la 'ira del todo komo 'el penso

KE 'en kuanto la primera śe pu'ede dezir ke 'a 'un ke para kaśtigar 'a 'uno baśta la dereǧa razon para 'ordenar la pena komo konbyene kuando 'i kuanto konbyene 'i set- kon todo 'eśto ayy grandisima nesesidad de la 'ira para perfeksy'on de laś 'obraś 'eśtiry'oreś laś kualeś non śe pu'eden byen 'efektuar śin la 'ira ke ayuda 'i da fu'ersa 'i a'umenta 'el poder kon 'el deśe'o de la vengansa kontra loś 'enemigoś kede 'elyya śe rezulta śegun śu difinsy'on komo tenemoś deklarado 'i śegun 'el meśmo Śeneka dize ke 'ira 'eś kobdisy'a de tirar 'el dolor 'i set-[194] :

'I kon 'eśto meśmo 'eśta deśbaratada śu śegunda razon porke a'un ke la 'ıra no a'umente 'enla 'orden de la dereǧa razon toda vi'a 'eś meneśter para 'efektuar lo 'ordenado por la diǧa dereǧa razon ke 'el perfekto 'i virtu'ozo deve a'yrarśe kuando konbyene vengarśe del 'enemigo ke fu'ere kontra śu familyya 'o śu republika[195] [CW. 'o]}

‹fol. 85b›
{'o śu ley komo 'eśkriby'o 'el filosofo 'enel śegundo de la re(y)torika do dize ke 'eś meǧor vengarśe del 'enemigo ke perdonarle 'i set-[196] 'i aśi 'eśkriby'o Tuly'o ke la vengansa 'eś śegun dereǧo natural 'i set-[197]

'I lo ke kiǧo prebar por la tersera razon 'eś byen viśto kuan poko konśta ke lo ke diǧo 'el filosofo ke la 'ira 'eś komo boraǧeś[198] 'eś śyendo deś'ordenada 'i śin medida ke akelyya tal 'eś la ke diǧeron por 'elyya nu'eśoś śaby'oś ke 'el ke alyega 'a grado de

---

and by our own free will grant it any authority, reason becomes of no avail; after that it will do, not whatever you let it, but whatever it chooses" (I.viii.1, trans. Basore, 1:125); and: "It suffers no limitation, it is a baneful thing and is not to be counted as a helpful agent. Thus either anger is not anger or it is useless" (I.ix.4, trans. Basore, 1:131).

[194] Seneca (*De Ira* I.iii.1 as preserved by Lactantius) defines anger as the desire to avenge injury: "ira est cupiditas ulciscendae iniuriae" (ed./trans. Basore, 1:112 n. a); he declares that it differs little from Aristotle's definition: "anger is the desire to repay suffering" (*De Ira* I.iii.3, trans. Basore, 1:115).

[195] Aristotle, *Rhetoric* II.ii.1–3 (1378a 30–1378b 10) (trans. Freese, 173).

[196] Apparently he restates *Rhetoric* I.ix.24 (1367a 20–21): "To take vengeance on one's enemies is nobler than to comes to terms with them" (trans. Freese, 97).

[197] Cicero, *De Inventione* II.161.

[198] Aristotle, *NE* VII.iii.7–8 (1147a 10–24).

BOOK OF THE REGIMEN OF LIVING ‹FOL. 85B›

'ira alyega 'a grado 'o konkluzy'on de yero 'i set-[199] ke 'eś la ke haze perve[r]ter 'el ğu'izy'o 'i konturbar la razon

'ENPERO la 'ira śegun virtud ke lyyamamoś mansedumbre la kual 'eś 'el medy'o aserka de la pasy'on de la 'ira komo tenemoś diğo 'eśta tal non konturba 'el ğu'iz[y]'o maś anteś 'eś 'ordenada por la dereğa razon komo konbyene kuando 'i kuanto konbyene 'i set-

DE manera ke la vengansa ke fu'ere por parte de la tal 'ira 'ordenada por la probidensy'a śegun laś śerkonśtansyaś de la virtud 'eś la vengansa loable 'i konvenible komo la ke 'el Dyyo glory'ozo mando tener de kontino 'en la memoryya kontra ᶜAmalek por lo kual 'eśkriby'o 'en la ley aku'erdate de loke hizo ati ᶜAmalek 'i set-[200] ke mandarnoś ke noś akordasemoś del mal ke noś hizo 'eś para ke tenyendo 'en memory'a la 'ofensa ke noś tyene heğa noś a'yremoś para 'efektuar la vengansa la kual ğunto kon 'elyya 'eśkriby'o do dize ke deśfazer deśfaraś la memransa de ᶜAmalek[201] ke 'eś la vengansa komo konbyene 'i set-

'I kon lo diğo 'eśta byen viśto kuanto la falta de la 'ira 'onde konbyene a'yrarśe 'eś vituperable a'el virtu'ozo kontra la 'opiny'on de Śeneka 'i set-

'I non 'eś meneśter muğo alargar para prebar kuan vituperable 'eś la puğa 'en la 'ira maś de lo ke konbyene 'i 'en tyenpo ke non konbyene 'i ke tura maś de lo ke konbyene 'i por kozaś ke non konbyene por 'elyaś a'yrarśe 'o a'yrarśe muy liğera mente maś de lo ke konbyene ke 'el vitupery'o de todo 'eśto 'eś viśto de lo ke tenemoś diğo ke todoś śon konformeś 'en la malisy'a de la puğa 'i la kondenan maś de lo ke Śeneka 'eśkriby'o

'I śi la deśdiğa de algun 'ombre lyegare ake ğunta mente todaś laś deśkonvenensyaś de la 'ira tubyere konbyene 'a śaber ke śe'a muy preśurozo 'enel a'yrarśe 'i ke śe a'yre maś de lo ke konbyene ke ture la 'ira muğo maś de lo ke konbyene 'i ke śe a'yre por kośaś ke no konbyene a'yrarśe 'i set- 'eśte tal no pu'ede muğo turar ni bivir ke 'el mal koronpe aśi meśmo komo diğo Aristotel 'enel kapitulo kinto del kuarto de la 'etika[202] 'el kual diğo 'eś verisimo 'i difikulto('o)zisimo 'i 'en śu deklarasy'on muğoś śaby'oś 'eraron 'i yo tengo muğo 'eśkrito 'i alargado śobre 'el 'i deklarado la verdad del 'entento de śuś palabraś :}

---

[199] Rashi Num. 31.21.
[200] Deut. 25.17.
[201] Deut. 25.19.
[202] Aristotle, *NE* IV.v.7 (1126a 12–13).

BOOK OF THE REGIMEN OF LIVING ‹FOL. 86A›

‹fol. 86a›
{SD {RMK: 94 count 86a.} ḤELEK B PEREK TV [PART TWO CHAPTER FIFTEEN]

KAPITULO KINZE

POR ke loś 'ombreś śon divididoś 'en todaś śuś paśy'oneś 'en kuatro partidaś diferenteś por la diferensy'a de laś konplisy'oneś ke śon kuatro 'eśpesyaś śangino 'i koleriko malenkoliko 'i flematiko dividyeron nu'eśtroś śaby'oś la puğa 'i falta de la 'ira 'en kuatro 'eśpesyaś diferenteś konformeś alaś diğaś kuatro konplisy'ones :

DO diğeron ke la primera 'eś la kondisy'on del ke 'eś liğero de a'yrarśe 'i liğero de afalagarśe 'el kual dizen ke śale śu śalary'o por śu danyyo 'i set-[203]

LA kual 'eś kondisy'on de 'el śanginyyo komo deklara Abiscna 'enel Kanon libro tersero 'ofan 'onze disy'on primera kapitulo terśero do dize ke 'el kalyente 'i 'omido 'eś la 'ira 'enel preśta 'i flaka 'i set-[204] 'i 'eśta tubyeron por manko mala por la kual diğeron ke śalyyo 'el śalary'o del afalago 'en la fin para 'enmendar 'el danyyo de la priśa 'enel prinsipy'o :

'I kontaron por śegunda kondisy'on la de 'el malenkoliko ke 'eś 'el ke 'eś tardi'o 'enel a'yrarśe por śer fri'o 'i śeko 'i por la meśma kabza 'eś tanbyen tardi'o 'enel afalagarśe loś kualeś 'eseden 'enla puğa komo loś primeroś pero difyeren 'enke loś primeroś śe a'yran por kośaś ke no konbyene a'yrarśe por 'elyyaś maś preśto deloke konbyene 'i 'eśtoś śe a'yran maś deloke konbyene 'i tura la 'ira maś tyenpo deloke konbyene 'i set- 'i syendo 'eśtoś pe'oreś ke loś primeroś diğeron por 'elyyoś ke śalyo 'el danyyo dela tardansa[205] del afalago 'a kontraśtar 'el śalary'o dela tardansa dela 'ira 'enel prinsipy'o :

'I la tersera kondisy'on ke kontaron 'eś del koleriko la kual 'eś la maś 'eśtremada 'enla maldad 'o vitupery'o la kual 'eś del preśurozo 'enel a'yrarśe 'i duro 'i tardi'o 'enel afalagarśe 'a 'el kual 'entitularon 'en titulo de malo[206] ke 'eśte tal por parte dela kalor śe 'enflama de liğero śobre kozaś ke non konbyene a'yrarśe 'i 'en tyenpo ke non konbyene 'i set- 'i por parte dela śekedad śon muy duroś de afalagar 'i por parte de la kalyentura 'i śekedad ğunta mente 'eś la 'ira 'enelyyoś agudisima 'i muy preśuroza

---

[203] Avot 5.14.
[204] Ibn Sina, *Canon,* Bk. 3, Pt. 11, thesis 1, chap. 3. Cf. *Avicenne Liber Canonis Medicine,* Latin translation by Gerard of Cremona (Venice, 1523; repr. Brussels, 1971).
[205] Avot 5.14.
[206] Avot 5.14.

Book of the Regimen of Living ‹fol. 86a–86b›

'I tyenen 'un grandisimo mal loś kolerikoś demazyado de lo ke konvyene ke kuando śe 'ensanyan śi non 'efektuan la vengansa śe a'umenta la 'ira 'i la triśteza 'en tanta manera ke 'eś 'enpesible 'i 'inorme :
'I 'eśto por doś kauśaś la 'una por ke loś kol(o)[e]rikoś no deśkubren la kabza deśu 'ira 'i karkomeśense 'entre śi meśmoś kontrary'o del śangino ke komo 'eś de śu kondisy'on deśkubrir lu'ego la kabza de śu 'ira le pasa lu'ego :
'EŚ la śegunda kauśa por ke no deśkubryendo la}

‹fol. 86b›
{kauśa deśu 'ira no ayy kyen loś afalage por non śaber la kauśa delyya :
'I komo 'elyoś deśu natural śon duroś de afalagar por śu konplisy'on an meneśter muğo tyenpo para śalir dela 'ira 'i triśteza 'enke 'eśtan pu'eśtoś 'i apasyonadoś 'i muğaś veześ abaśta natural mente 'una pasy'on de 'ira 'a 'un koleriko 'a kauśarle 'una grabe dolensy'a 'o alo menoś 'una 'efimera por parte dela triśteza ke laś maś delaś veześ akaeśe muy fasil mente :
'I 'eś la kuar[t]'a kondisy'on la de 'el flematiko ke anteś 'esede por śu konplisy'on 'enla falta ke 'enla puğa komo konbyene aserka de 'eśta virtud komo tenemoś deklarado por la deśkrisy'on delyya por lo kual 'entitularon 'a 'el ke 'eś duro de a'yrarśe 'i liğero de afalagarśe 'en titulo de bu'eno 'i virtu'oziśimo[207]
'I 'eśta 'eś la kondisy'on ke todoś deven śegir 'i todaś laś 'otraś śon dignaś de vitupery'o 'i difyeren 'enel visy'o de maś 'a menoś syendo todaś 'en 'onibersal puro visy'o 'i 'eśta śola virtud :
'I por 'eseder nu'eśtro deviniśimo porfeta algo 'en la puğa de la 'ira a'un ke muy poko por śer 'onde non konveni'a ke fu'e 'enel tyenpo del śakar 'el agu'a de la penyya[208] śe le fu'e kontado por muy grabe pekado por ke a'un ke fu'eśe komo fu'e muy poko reśpektuado 'enel śublime grado de śu 'ekśelensy'a fu'e kontado por muğo 'en lo kual tengo yo muğo alargado 'enel kuarto libro de la 'etika komento[209] diziśyete deklarando byen kuan liğero fu'e 'el pekado 'i por kuan grabe fu'e tenido :
POR laś razoneś diğaś śe deve kual kyera akavidar de non kaer 'enel yero de la puğa de 'eśta virtud 'i poner toda la diliğensy'a posible para moderar 'eśta pasy'on de la 'ira ke danyya 'el ku'erpo 'i 'el alma śegun tenemoś diğo 'i 'eś manifyeśto :

---

[207] Almosnino inverts the third and fourth character types presented by Avot, where the third is the saint and the fourth the wicked man.
[208] Num. 20.6–13.
[209] The reference is to *Pne Mośe*. The Aristotle passage would be *NE* IV.v (1125b 27–1126b 11).

Book of the Regimen of Living ⟨fol. 86b–87a⟩

'I śiknifikase byen 'enel 'Eklisyastes donde akavida nu'eśo śapyentisimo rey Šᵉlomoh dizyendo non turbeś tu 'eśprito para a'yrarte 'i set-[210] 'i '[e]ś(y) de notar ke no digo no te a'yreś 'i set- por ke syendo la 'ira komo konbyene śegun derega razon 'eś loable komo tenemoś digo pero akavido ke fu'eśe 'ordenada śegun la derega razon de tal manera ke de kontino kedaśe 'el 'eśprito ky'eto 'i repozado 'i non turbado 'i set-
'I 'eś 'el medy'o 'eneśta pasy'on muy difisil porke 'eś mene(t)[ś]ter mugo atentar komo śe'a de a'yrar 'i 'enke 'i porke 'i kontra kyen 'i kuando 'i kuanto 'i set- ke para todo 'eśto 'eś meneśter grandisima 'eśtimatiba ke alaś veześ śusedera kauzo ke konvyene a'yrarśe mugo kuando 'eś kontra 'enemigoś del Dyo 'o deśu ley por lo kual mugaś veześ lyyamamoś aloś a'yradoś fu'erteś por śer la 'ira konvenible para la virtud dela fortaleza 'onde konvyene 'i alaś veześ loamoś loś mugo pasyenteś 'onde konvyene 'i set- de manera ke todo keda ala 'eśtimatiba del virtu'ozo [CW. porke]}

⟨fol. 87a⟩
{Ṣ H {RMK: 95 count 87a.} ḤELEK B PEREK YD [PART TWO CHAPTER FOURTEEN] {RMK: A vertical bar scratched between PEREK and YD is the only sign of a correction} porke 'el medy'o no konśiśte 'enla 'obra 'eśtiry'or komo 'otraś veześ tenemoś deklarado śalbo 'enla konvenensy'a de 'elya 'i śer 'ordenada por la derega razon komo todaś laś 'otraś vertudeś :
'I aś de śaber ke śe konsidran 'enla 'ira kuatro kozaś la primera 'eś por la kual śi śe a'yra 'el a'yrado ke 'eś la 'ingury'a ke śe le 'eś hega 'o 'otra koza kual kyera ke le kauśa la 'ira 'i 'eśta primera konsidrasy'on la da triśteza ke śegun 'el grado dela tal triśteza 'eś 'el grado dela 'ira :
'I de 'eśta primera vyene 'a konsidrar 'i kontenplar 'en kyen le kauśa la tal 'ira ke 'eś la preśona kontra 'el kual śe a'yra ke 'eś śegunda konsidrasy'on la kual le kauza 'un 'ody'o 'i aboresimyento kontra kyen lo 'ofendy'o 'i kauzo la tal 'ira :
'I gunto kon 'eśto konsidra 'el modo de la vengansa ke 'a de tomar de kyen le 'ofendy'o kontra 'el kual śe a'yra ke 'eś tersera konsidrasy'on la kual le da alguna deleytasy'on afigurando la vengansa porke toda koza ke śyendo 'en puro a'uto 'eś deleytable la 'eśperansa de 'elyya anteś ke śe haga kauśa tanbyen deleytasy'on 'i komo kyera kela vengansa de pu'eś de 'efektuada kauśa alegri'a komo dišo nu'eśo rey David alegrarśe'a guśto ke vido vengansa 'i set-[211] por tanto la 'eśperansa tanbyen delyya kauśa alegri'a

---

[210] Eccles. 7.9.
[211] Ps. 58.11.

Book of the Regimen of Living ‹fol. 87a–87b›

'I depu'eś ke 'el a'yrado konsidra 'eśtaś treś konsidrasy'oneś śe mu'ebe 'a poner la vengansa 'en a'uto ke 'eś la kuarta konsidrasy'on la kual deśpu'eś de 'efektuada kauśa grandisima deleytasy'on

'I alaś veześ 'eśta pośtrera konsidrasy'on falta 'en loś a'yradoś komo akaese 'a loś maś deloś śanginoś ke śupito śe leś pasa la 'ira 'i non śe mu'eben ala vengansa ke de 'eśta 'eśpesy'a fu'e la 'ira de nu'eśo śanto porfeta :

'I 'el ke śe a'yrare 'eś meneśter ke pare byen myenteś 'eneśtaś kuatro konsidrasy'oneś ke śean byen konsidradaś śegun dereğa razon 'i non śupito ke fasil mente vyene yero 'enelyyaś komo akaesy'o 'a 'Iyob 'enel prinsipy'o de śuś tribulasy'oneś ke dizen nu'eśoś śaby'oś ke kuando le fu'e diğo ke loś kalde'oś puzyeron treś kabeseraś 'i set-[212] 'enpeso 'a 'ordenar śu 'eğersito para pelear kontra 'elyyoś 'i diğo ke 'era bağa nasy'on deśpresyyada 'i ke non teni'a temor de 'elyyoś 'i set-[213] 'i dizen ke komo le diğeron fu'ego de 'el Dyyo kayo de 'el syelo 'i set-[214] diğo ke 'eś lo ke hago masada del syelo 'a kaido debo kalyyar 'i set-[215] :

'I 'eś syerto de ver 'i śentir 'eneśtaś palabraś ke parese tener nu'eśtroś śaby'oś ke primero le fu'e diğo kalde'oś puzyeron treś kabeseraś 'i set- 'i de pu'eś le diğeron fu'ego del Dyyo kayo de loś syeloś 'i set- 'i por la 'eśkritura parese al kontrary'o ke primero ku'enta ke le fu'e diğo fu'ego del Dyyo kayo de loś syeloś 'i set- 'i de pu'eś dize ke lo fu'e diğo kalde'oś puzyeron 'i set- [CW.por]}

‹fol. 87b›
{ḤELEK B PEREK TV [PART TWO CHAPTER FIFTEEN]

POR lo kual pyenśo ke la 'intensy'on śe'a de 'entender 'eneśta forma ke komo kyera ke śupito ke le diğeron la nu'eba del fu'ego lu'ego traś delyya le fu'e diğo la de loś kalde'oś śin ninguna diśtansy'a de tyenpo komo ku'enta la 'eśkritura ke 'eśtando 'el 'uno a'un hablando lyegaba 'el 'otro[216] 'el komo 'oyo la nu'eba de 'el fu'ego atriśtośe por la primera konsidrasy'on pero kontenplando 'en laś 'otraś treś konsidrasy'oneś vyendo śer 'inposible la vengansa kalyaba 'eśtando 'eneśta kontenplasy'on komo śupito ğunto kon 'eśto le fu'e diğo lo ke loś kalde'oś avian heğo a'yrośe kontra

---

[212] Job 1.17.
[213] Akin to Ruth R. 2.10.
[214] Job 1.16.
[215] Ruth R. 2.10.
[216] Job 1.17.

Book of the Regimen of Living ‹fol. 87b–88a›

'elyyoś 'i konsidro todaś laś kuatro konsidrasy'oneś śupito ke śe a'yro laś kualeś 'eśtan konklu'idaś 'i śiknifikadaś 'en laś palabraś diğaś ke 'en dezir komo le fu'e diğo kalde'oś puzyeron treś kabeseraś 'i set-[217] śiknifikaron la primera konsidrasy'on ke 'eś la 'ofensa 'i 'inğury'a ke śe le fu'e feğa 'i 'en dezir ke diğo ke loś kalde'oś 'eran ğente 'i nasy'on deśpresyada[218] śiknifikaron la śegunda ke 'eś la preśona kontra kyen 'eś la 'ira komo tenemoś diğo 'i 'en dezir ke diğo non tengo de 'elyyoś temor 'i set-[219] śiknifikaron la tersera konsidrasy'on ke 'eś 'el modo de la vengansa la kual dezi'a ke pu'eś no reselaba de 'elyyoś de kual kyer modo ke kiğeśe la podi'a fazer 'i dizen ke konsidrando laś treś śe moby'o 'a 'enpesar 'a 'ordenar śu 'eğersito para 'efektuar la vengansa[220] ke 'eś la kuarta

'I 'eś la regla 'i 'orden de laś palabraś 'eneśta forma ke kuando konsidro la primera konsidrasy'on śe moby'o lu'ego ala vengansa ke 'eś la pośtrera por ke śupito ğunto kon la primera konsidro laś 'otraś doś ke śon la śegunda 'i tersera 'i kyeren dezir ke 'enel 'inpetu de la 'ira 'i la poka diśtansy'a de tyenpo de la 'una nu'eba ala 'otra no tubo tyenpo de konsidrar ke la 'ofensa ke loś kalde'oś le avian heğo 'era tanbyen por parte de la probidensy'a por lo kual dizen ke komo kyera ke anteś de 'eśta nu'eba avi'a 'o'ido la de 'el fu'ego komo repozo algo del 'inpetu de la 'ira parando myenteś 'en la nu'eba del fu'ego ke anteś de 'eśta avi'a 'o'ido konsidro ke 'eśta de loś kalde'oś tanbyen 'era del syelo por parte de la probidensy'a 'o kośtelasy'on 'i değośe de 'efektuar la vengansa 'i 'eśto 'eś lo ke kiğeron dezir 'en dezir 'i komo 'oyo ke le diğeron fu'ego de 'el Dyyo kayo 'i set-[221] 'i no dizen kuando 'oyo śalvo komo 'oyo ke kyere dezir ke komo kyera ke ya avi'a 'o'ido anteś de 'eśto ke fu'ego del Dyyo avi'a kaido del syelo 'i kon la pasy'on de la 'ira no konsidraba śer 'eśto por la meśma kauśa komo vağo algo la pasy'on de la 'ira konsidro śer 'eśto meśmo de parte del syelo pu'eś lo de anteś fu'e del syelo

DE adonde śe nota kuanto deve perkurar 'el ke śe a'yra de non perve[r]ter 'el ğu'izy'o komo tenemoś diğo 'eśpesyal loś kolerikoś ke śon muy duroś de moderar la pasy'on de la 'ira ke 'el yero de la}

‹fol. 88a›
{ṢV {RMK: 96 count 88a.}
puğa 'enelyyoś śera grandisima 'i kazi 'inkurable śin remedy'o ninguno :

---

[217] Job 1.17.
[218] Ruth R. 2.10.
[219] Ruth R. 2.10.
[220] Ruth R. 2.10.
[221] Job 1.16.

Book of the Regimen of Living ‹fol. 88a›

'I alargo algo 'enesto maś de lo ke aki pense 'eśkribir por ke ve'o tu konplisy'on muy kol(o)[e]rika 'i reselo muğo no śeaś lyebado ala 'ira maś delo ke konbyene 'i no śe haga 'enti abito por 'el kośtumbre a'un ke hata aki no te 'e viśto hazer por 'elyya koza 'indevida ni pyenso ke la haraś pero 'eś byen ke 'eśteś de kontino avezado ke no śeaś vensido del 'apetito 'irasible no kuidando 'i te perberta 'el ğu'izy'o ke deśpu'eś de reynado no 'ira 'en tu mano reğiśtir ala 'ira 'i śera 'el arep[e]ntimyento de pu'eś kauśa de darte maś dolor 'i pasy'on no pudyendo 'enmendar lo pasado por ke 'eś la 'ira deś'ordenada komo diğo Śeneka[222] komo 'el dardo ke depu'eś ke śale de la mano no va 'en poder del 'ombre tornarlo atraś[223] por lo kual deve de perkurar kual kyera virtu'ozo apartarśe delyya 'en gran manera maś de 'en 'el tyenpo ke konbyene komo tenemoś diğo hata ke śe haga abito 'el śufrir 'en tanta manera ke no syenta ke śufre 'el ke padese la 'inğury'a śalvo ke śe alegre kon 'elyya komo ya tenemoś notado de mente de nu'eśoś śaby'oś aserka de la virtud de la magnyanimidad :

KONFORME alo kual śe ku'enta de 'un filosofo ke avyendole 'un 'ombre muy mal 'inğuryado 'i muy deś'ordenada mente de boka 'i manoś 'i kuanto kiğo śin responderlo ni dezirle 'el diğo filosofo palabra ninguna deśpu'eś de harto 'el tal 'ombre de aver 'inğuryado a'el filosofo paresyendole ke avi'a konosido 'el maś 'eśtremado 'en la pasensy'a ke śer podi'a le diğo 'el filos(y)[o]fo alo menoś abraś konosido ke śoy pasyente alo kual reśpondy'o akel tal 'ombre 'i diğo śe lo konosyera śi no lo diğeraś[224] :

KERYENDOLE dezir ke ya no 'era pasyente pu'eś le paresi'a a'el śer pasensy'a ke śi fu'era feğa 'enel la pasensy'a abito no le paresyera a'el aver śufrido maś anteś le paresyera aver 'uzado lo ke konbyene por ke no śolo no le 'a de pareser a'el manso ke śufre maś a'un śe'a de alegrar kon laś 'inğuryaś por ke alegrandośe kon 'elyyaś konosera averśe heğo ya abito firme :

KOMO ku'enta 'el śenyyor Rabbenu Mośeh de 'un filosofo tan pasyentisimo ke vinyendo 'en 'una nabe 'en k[o]npanyi'a de muğoś śe paro 'uno 'a verter śuś aguaś 'en riba de 'el śin ninguna kauśa maś ke kererlo 'inğuryar 'i viśto 'eśto 'el diğo filosofo śe alegro 'i amośtro śu alegri'a kon 'un muy tenplado rizo por 'el kual amośtraba śer le deleytable 'i syendo demandado de 'el la kauśa de śu plazer 'i alegri'a reśpondy'o 'i diğo ke śe alegraba 'en grandisima manera por aver kon(y)[o]śido śi meśmo

---

[222] Cf. Seneca, *De Ira* II.vii.2, trans. Basore, 1:273; cf. I.xvi.6, 1:149.
[223] For a congener, see Knust, *Mittheilungen aus dem Eskurial,* 194 n. a.
[224] The source of this anecdote is unknown to me.

Book of the Regimen of Living ⟨fol. 88a–88b⟩

aver alyegado 'a akel grado de la virtud de la mansedumbre śin resebir ningun modo de alterasy'on de kuanto le avi'a 'ofendido[225] :
LAŚ kualeś fu'eron palabraś dignaś [CW. de]}

⟨fol. 88b⟩
{ḤELEK B PEREK YV [PART TWO CHAPTER SIXTEEN]
de gran lo'or 'i perpetu'a memory'a ke śe deve kual kyer virtu'ozo alegrar 'en gran manera kuando le susede kaśo 'onde śe manifyeśta 'el abito de la virtud śer firme 'i feğo 'enel 'i ke non 'eś lyebado a'el 'apetito lo kual lo'a 'el śenyyor Rabbenu Mośeh 'en gran manera a'un ke 'el lo ku'enta 'en 'otra forma ke dize ke le demandaron a'el tal filosofo kual fu'e 'el di'a ke maś śe avi'a alegrado 'en śu vida 'i ke 'el reśpondy'o ke nunka tanta alegri'a tomo komo 'el di'a ke le fu'e heğo akelyya 'inğury'a 'en la nabe 'i set-[226] 'i aśi 'eś muğo meğor diğo a'un ke la 'intensy'on 'eś toda 'una :

DE adonde śe nota la 'eselensy'a de la pasensy'a 'i ke ningun 'ombre deve de a'yrarśe por ningun ku'ento śi no fu'ere por kauśa muy liśita 'ordenada por la dereğa razon komo tenemoś diğo por ke 'el ğu'izy'o kon la 'ira non pu'ede śer rekto :

KONFORME alo kual ku'enta Śeneka de Sokr[a]t[eś] ke a'yrandośe kontra 'un kryado śuyo lyegando a'el para ferirlo kon 'el 'inpetu de la 'ira le diğo śi non 'eśtubyera a'yrado te firyera[227] śiknifikando 'el pasyentisimo śaby'o ke firyendole kon 'ira non podi'a hazer kon ğu'izy'o rekto lo ke ke(y)r[i]a ke hizyeśe por ke 'eś komo la borağeśkomo diğo 'el filosofo[228] por lo kual 'enkliminaron nu'eśoś śaby'oś 'en grandisima manera 'el ke haze kual kyer a'uto kon 'ira 'a tanto ke diğ[e]ron ke 'el ke ronpe śuś atu'endoś kon 'ira 'eś tanto komo śi 'idolatraśe[229]

'I diğeron 'otroś muğoś vitupery'oś de loś a'yradoś 'i altiboś de 'eśprito 'i muğaś lo'oreś de loś mansoś donde diğeron ke 'el ke peka 'en la preśunsy'on 'i altibidad ke kauśa la 'ira 'eś digno de śer kortado 'i matado[230] 'i dizen maś ke 'eśtoś taleś non śe alevantaran 'enel tyenp(+)o de la resure'eysy'on kon loś m[u]'ertoś de Yiśra'el[231] :

---

[225] The story appears in Maimonides' *Commentary on Avot* 4. 4, and is quoted in A. J. Heschel, *Maimonides,* 2nd ed. (New York, 1982), 50.
[226] Heschel, *Maimonides,* 50.
[227] Seneca, *De Ira* I.xv.3. (trans. Basore, 1:145).
[228] Aristotle, *NE* VII.iii.7–8 (1147a 10–24).
[229] Shabbat 105b.
[230] Sotah 5a.
[231] Sotah 5a.

BOOK OF THE REGIMEN OF LIVING ‹FOL. 88B–89A›

'I diğeron 'en lo'or deloś perfektoś 'eneśta beatisima virtud ke 'en todo lugar 'onde halyyamoś ke śe nombra la grandeza del Dyyo alyi mismo śe nombra śu mansedumbre 'i set-[232] dizen ke 'eśto 'eś diğo 'i berifikado 'en la le'ey śegundado 'en loś porfetaś atersyado 'en todaś laś 'otraś 'eśkrituraś 'eśkritaś por 'eśprito devino 'i set-[233] donde kiğeron śignifikar 'el śublime grado de śu 'ekselensy'a :

KAPITULO DIZIŚE[Y]Ś

AŚ de śaber maś aserka de 'eśta materyya ke algunoś pensaron śer la kru'eldad 'i pyada(r)[d] aserka de 'eśta virtud reğidoś por 'el diğo del vulgo ke komun mente lyyaman kru'el a'el muy a'yrado 'el kual kaśtigando akual kyera kon la 'ira a'un ke śe'a kon ğuśtis[y]'a 'i razon dizen 'uzar kru'el mente 'i nasy'o 'eśta 'eror por [CW. parte]}

‹fol. 89a›
{PT {RMK: 89 count 89a.}
parte dela kru'eldad ke 'eś apenar śin kauśa 'a kyen no śe deve a'yrar kontra 'el śin kauśa :
'I ala verdad la pyadad 'i mansedumbre śon vertudeś deśtintaś 'i la 'irakundy'a 'i kru'eldad visy'oś diferenteś ke 'un 'ombre podra śer byen kru'el kaśtigando 'a 'otro śin a'yrarśe 'i lo meśmo pu'ede śer a'yrarśe 'uno kontra 'otro lisita mente kon kauśa ğuśta 'i razon manifyeśta 'i a'un ke śe'a la 'ira muy 'ensendida maś de loke konbyene no śe lyyamara kru'eldad pu'eś fu'e kon kauśa maś lyyamarśe'a 'irakundy'a pu'eś fu'e maś de loke konbyene :
'I 'eś byen viśto ke la kru'eldad 'i pyadad śon konklu'idaś aserka de la gran virtud dela ğuśtisy'a porke punir 'o kaśtigar śin razon ni śin kauśa 'eś śin ğuśtisy'a 'i no 'irakundy'a komo pensaron :
'I değo de diśkutir byen 'eśta matery'a a'un ke śe pudyera byen meter 'enelyya la mano porke 'eś algo diśforme 'a nu'eśo tratado 'i 'intensy'on ke byen baśta ke konprendaś de aki ke 'a( )'yrarśe 'el 'ombre maś de loke konbyene a'un ke śe'a mobido de kauśa lisita 'eś visy'o vituperable lyyamado 'irakundy'a 'i kaśtigar 'a 'uno śin kauśa a'un ke śe'a śin 'ira 'eś śin ğuśtisy'a 'i lyyamaśe kru'eldad 'i kuando śe ağuntaren loś doś visy'oś komo laś maś de laś veześ śu'ele śer ke reynando 'el 'uno śe akonpanyya kon 'el 'el 'otro śera 'eśtonseś 'un visy'o k[o]npu'eśto de 'irakundy'a 'i

---

[232] Megillah 31a.
[233] Megillah 31a.

kru'eldad ke 'eś muy vituperable 'i 'eśto te baśta śaber al preśente aserka deśta materyya

POR la meśma kauśa değo de deklarar aki loke 'en 'otra parte[234] tengo muy larga mente aberiguado 'eś 'a śaber kual 'eś maś digno de lo'or 'o kual śe dira maś virtu'ozo aserka de 'eśta virtud de mansedumbre śi 'el koleriko 'o 'el flematiko syendo loś doś 'en 'un meśmo grado de virtud 'i 'obrando 'igual mente śuś 'obraś porke parese aver razon para anbaś laś parteś 'i kual kyera vera 'ividentisima mente aver konsidrasy'oneś diferenteś por kual kyera de laś doś ke por 'una konsidrasy'on parese śer 'el koleriko maś virtu'ozo śobre śer 'igual 'enla virtud kon 'el flematiko porke adkiry'o la tal virtud kon maś trabağo kontraśtando śu natural konplisy'on kon muğa difikultad lo kual no tyene 'el fl'[e]matiko komo śe'a de śu natural 'enklinado ala mansedumbre no syendo maś virtu'ozo ni tan loado komo 'el pu'eś 'eśte lo tyene de śu natural 'i 'el 'otro por śu travağo 'i diliğensy'a :

POR 'otra parte ay[y] śegunda konsidrasy'on parese śer 'el flematiko maś virtu'ozo por śer maś firme 'enla virtud por parte de śu natural konplisy'on ke konfirma maś 'el 'obrar śegun virtud heğo por końtumbre ke tanto maś 'eś 'e(n)[k]selente la virtud kuanto maś firme 'eś 'enel virtu'ozo :

'OTRAŚ muğaś konsidrasy'oneś ayy para anbaś laś parteś laś kualeś komo no śean tan 'utileś ni tan 'a nu'eśo perpozito laś değo para maś 'oportunidad [CW. 'eśto]}

⟨fol. 89b⟩
{'eśto śolo deveś de konprehender de lo diğo 'i 'eś ke 'el koleriko 'i flematiko syendo todoś doś 'en 'un meśmo grado de bondad śolo difyeren 'en śer 'el 'uno maś digno de lo'or ke 'el 'otro ke kon maś razon śera loado 'el koleriko kuando fu'ere manso pu'eś alkansa la tal virtud kon muğo trabağo 'i gran difikultad kontra śu natural 'enklinasy'on :

'I 'eśta propy'a diferensy'a 'eś 'en todaś laś 'otraś vertudeś ke a'un ke śean 'igualeś de la virtud śera maś loable 'el ke deśu konplisy'on fu'ere maś 'enklinado aloś visy'oś 'i moderar laś pasy'oneś :

'I la meśma deśtinsy'on 'i diferensy'a 'eś la ke ponen nu'eśoś śaby'oś 'entre 'el ke de kontino fu'e ğuśto 'a 'el ke fu'e malo 'i torno 'a śer bu'eno por ke ayy 'enelyyoś konsidrasy'oneś diferenteś por laś kualeś parese śer kada kual de loś doś meğor ke 'el 'otro por śu konsidrasy'on a'un ke 'el ke torna 'eś maś loable por ke 'eś bu'eno kon maś difikultad komo tengo diğo

---

[234] Probably this reference is to *Pne Mośe*, his commentary on Aristotle's *Ethics* (the Aristotle passage is *NE* IV.v [1125v 27–1126b 11]).

Book of the Regimen of Living ‹fol. 89b–90a›

'I aś de notar ke 'eśto todo śe'a de 'entender syendo 'el ǧuśto 'i 'el ke torna 'igualeś 'enel grado de la bondad 'i virtud 'i no ke śe'a 'el ke torna kontinente ke loś 'interpeteś lyamaron 'en nu'eśtra lengu'a śanta kobeś komo algunoś a'utoreś modernoś de loś nu'eśoś pensaron śer 'eśta la 'intensy'on de nu'eśoś śaby'oś donde diǧeron ke 'en lugar donde 'eśtan loś ke tornan 'a śer bu'enoś no pu'eden 'eśtar loś ǧuśtoś[235] kon lo kual śe admiraron del śenyyor Rabbenu Mośeh komo diǧo 'enel kapitulo śeśto de loś 'oǧo famoziśimoś kapituloś ke hizo 'enel prologo de śu komento 'a Masseket 'Abot ke 'el ǧuśto 'i bu'eno 'era meǧor ke 'el kontinente[236] paresyendoleś śer kontra la 'opiny'on verdader'a del diǧo de nu'eśoś śaby'oś ke diǧo avemoś 'i fundaron śu admirasy'on por no poderlo śalvar kon dezir ke 'el no kre'i'a 'el tal diǧo maś anteś kre'i'a 'el kontrary'o pu'eś 'eś kontradisy'on 'en nu'eśoś meśmoś śaby'oś arguyendo ke 'el meśmo śenyyor Rabbenu Mośeh amośtra kre'erlo pu'eś haze del fundamyento 'en śu famozisimo libro kapitulo śebtimo de Hilkot Tˉśubah 'i kon 'eśto śe admiraron del paresyendoleś kontradezirśe deśi aśi 'en loś diǧoś lugareś 'i de razon por parte del meśmo argumento debyeran berifikar ke 'el kontinente ke 'en śuś 'oǧo kapituloś 'enmenta no se'a 'el ke 'enmenta 'en śu libro 'en titulo del ke torna 'a śer bu'eno porke śin dubda ami ver todo 'el 'engany'o nasy'o de pensar ke 'el ke torna ke diǧeron nu'eśoś śaby'oś śe'a 'el kontinente :

LO kual yo no kre'o ni ninguno kon ǧuśta razon deve kre'er porke śi 'eś kontinente a'un no śe pu'[e]de dezir aver tornado 'a śer bu'eno ke 'el kontinente no 'eś bu'eno 'i pu'eś lo lyamaron tornado no k[i]ǧeron dezir ke kedaśe kontinente ni nunka 'el Dyyo kyera ke ninguno de nu'eśoś śaby'oś diǧeśen ke 'el kontinente [CW. valga]}

‹fol. 90a›
{Ṣ
valga maś ke 'el ǧuśto ni 'ubyeśe 'enelyyo kontradisy'on por lo kual determino determinada mente 'el śenyyor Rabbenu Mośeh 'enel seśto kapitulo diǧo de śuś 'oǧo kapituloś śer 'el ǧuśto meǧor ke 'el kontinente[237] 'i aprobo 'i afirmo 'en śu famoziśimo libro 'enel śebtimo kapitulo[238] diǧo 'el gran diǧo del śaby'o ke diǧo ke 'enel lugar 'i grado donde 'eśtan loś ke tornan 'a śer bu'enoś ke śon 'enel meśmo grado de

---

[235] Berakot 34b.
[236] Maimonides, "*Eight Chapters,*" chap. 6, para. 1, ed. Gorfinkle, 75. The passage addresses the question of the difference between the "man of self-restraint" (*ha-mośal be-nafśo*) and the "saintly man" (*ha-ḥassid*).
[237] Maimonides, "*Eight Chapters,*" ed. Gorfinkle, 75.
[238] *Hilkot Teśubah,* chap. 7.

Book of the Regimen of Living ‹fol. 90a›

bondad ke śon loś ǧustoś no pu'eden 'estar loś ǧustoś[239] pu'eś adkiryeron la diǧa virtud kon maś difikultad komo diǧo avemoś a'un ke 'en 'otra konsidrasy'on parese śer loś ǧustoś meǧoreś ke 'eś por parte dela multitud delaś 'obraś ke an heǧo loś ǧustoś ke nunka fu'eron maloś :

'I a'un 'ozari'a dezir ke 'el mesmo śaby'o ke diǧo ke 'onde 'estan loś ke tornan no pu'eden 'estar loś ǧustoś[240] no kiǧo dezir ke determinada mente śean de mayor grado śalvo ke 'en konsidrasy'on del trabaǧo 'i difikultad konke śe alkansan laś 'obraś deloś 'unoś 'i de loś 'otroś śe'a mayor 'el grado de loś ke tornan ke deloś ǧustoś 'i kre'e ke por 'esta parte śe'a mayor 'el merito 'i premy'o de loś ke śe konvyerten 'i 'enesto kontradize konel ke le antesedy'o pero no deǧa de konoser 'el mesmo ke por parte de laś 'obraś 'i multitud de 'elyyaś śe'a meǧor 'el ǧusto :

'I kon 'esto pyenśo śer śastifeǧo de 'un admirabilisimo diǧo deste mesmo śaby'o nombrado por nombre Rabbi Abahu ke dizen 'en Bᵉre'šiṭ Rabbah[241] 'enesta forma 'enel prinsipy'o dela kreasy'on del mundo vido 'el Dyyo loś heǧoś de loś bu'enoś 'i loś heǧoś deloś maloś 'esto 'eś loke 'esta 'eskrito ke śabe 'el Dyyo karera de ǧustoś 'i set-[242] 'i la tyera 'era vana 'i vazi'a 'i set-[243] 'estoś śon loś heǧoś de loś maloś 'i diǧo 'el Dyyo śe'a luz 'i set-[244] 'estoś śon loś heǧoś delos ǧustoś 'enpero no śe 'en kual delyyoś 'envolunta śi 'enla 'obra destoś śi 'en la 'obra destoś pu'eś ke 'esta 'eskrito 'i vido 'el Dyyo ala luz ke bu'ena[245] 'eś visto ke 'enlaś 'obraś delos ǧustoś 'envolunta 'i no 'en laś 'obraś de loś maloś[246] 'estaś śon laś palabraś deste famozisimo śaby'o del kual no śe deve kre'er ke śe'a 'el 'entento delyyaś lo ke aprima vista parese ke nunka 'el Dyyo kyera ke tan śingularisimo śenyyor 'ubyera de dubdar ni aber menester prevar ke 'el Dyyo 'envelunta 'en laś 'obraś de loś bu'enoś 'i no 'en laś de loś maloś ǧunto kon 'esto 'eś de dubdar porke pone la veluntad devina 'en laś 'obraś de loś ǧustoś 'i no 'en loś mesmoś ǧustoś alyende de 'otraś muǧaś dubdaś partikulareś ke śe pu'eden lisita mente dubdar laś kualeś por ke śeran aśolvidaś kon lo ke kyere dezir laś deǧo de 'espasifikar 'i diǧo ke komo 'este śapyentisimo śenyyor fu'eśe de 'opiny'on ke por parte del tr[a]baǧo 'i fatiga ke padese 'el ke torna hata tornar 'a śer bu'eno

---

[239] Berakot 34b.
[240] Berakot 34b.
[241] Gen. R. 2.5.
[242] Ps. 1.6.
[243] Gen. 1.2.
[244] Gen. 1.3.
[245] Gen. 1.4.
[246] Gen. R. 2.5.

Book of the Regimen of Living ‹fol. 90a–90b›

tenga mayor merito ke 'el ğ[u]śto //(r)[d]ubd[o]// 'eneśtotro śu d[i]ğo śi por parte de la 'obra 'era meğor 'el ğuśto ke 'e[l] ke //(ḥ)[t]orna// 'i determinaśe}

‹fol. 90b›
{ḤELEK B PEREK YZ [PART TWO CHAPTER SEVENTEEN]
ke por parte de la 'obra śe'a de mayor grado 'el ğuśto ke 'el ke torna komo diğo avemoś 'i haze śu 'eśpikulasy'on 'eneśta forma prosuponyendo ke a[']el Dyyo bendito 'eśta todo lo ke anoś 'eś futuro reprezentado 'en śu prezensy'a por lo kual śe deve kre'er ke 'enel prinsipy'o de la kreasy'on del mundo vido laś 'obraś de loś ğuśtoś 'i vido laś 'obraś de loś ke tornan de kuando 'eran maloś 'i no ke lyyame aloś ke tornan maloś śalbo 'eś komo ke diğeśe ke konsidrando laś 'obraś de loś ğuśtoś ke de kontino fu'eron 'obraś de ğuśtoś 'i konsidrando laś 'obraś de loś ke tornan 'enel tyenpo ke 'eran maloś ke 'a 'opiny'on de nu'eśoś śaby'oś laś meśmaś 'obraś del tyenpo ke 'eran maloś deśpu'eś de tornado laś pone 'el Dyyo 'en numero de laś 'obraś bu'enaś[247] dubdaba śi 'el Dyyo 'envoluntaba maś 'en laś 'obraś de loś ğuśtoś ke de kontino fu'eron ğuśtoś 'o 'en laś 'obraś deloś maloś deśpu'eś ke tornaban 'i komo halyyo 'en la śakra 'eśkritura ke la nada 'o vanidad 'eś 'enğenplo ala 'obra de loś maloś[248] a'un ke deśpu'eś tornen 'i la luz 'eś 'enğenplo ala de loś ğuśtoś 'i dize la 'eśkritura ke vido 'el Dyyo ala luz ke 'era bu'ena[249] determinada mente determino 'eśte śenyyor ke 'el Dyyo 'envelunta maś propy'a mente 'en laś 'obraś de loś ğuśtoś ke 'en laś 'obraś de loś maloś deśpu'eś ke bolbyeron 'i por 'eśo no diğo ke 'envelunta 'el Dyyo maś 'en loś ğuśtoś śalbo 'en la 'obra de 'elyyoś śiknifikando ke la dubda no naśe śalvo por parte de laś 'obraś ke por parte delyyoś ya śe det[e]rmino mereser maś 'el ke torna 'i por 'eśo 'entitulo aloś ke tornan 'en termino de maloś por śer la dubda por parte de laś 'obraś ke hizyeron syendo maloś anteś ke tornasen komo diğo tengo[250]

KAPITULO DIZIŚYETE

'EŚ la 'oktaba virtud la afabilidad la kual kon 'otraś doś ke śe śigen śon aserka de la konversasy'on 'umana komo por 'elyyaś śe deklarara 'i 'eśta primera ke 'eś 'oktaba

---

[247] This is stated in the Soncino Talmud: "According to R. Jose b. Hanina: The Lord forgiving, wipes the sins off completely, or, in the case of the man's repentance, changes his very sins into virtues" (Arakin 8b n9); the editors refer to Rosh HaShanah 17a.

[248] 2 Kings 17.15, Jer. 2.5, and Jer. 23.16.

[249] Gen. 1.4.

[250] Cf. Ezek. 33.11–12.

Book of the Regimen of Living ‹fol. 90b–91a›

'enel numero de laś vertudeś moraleś 'eś aserka del fablar 'i platikar komun 'enla konversasy'on la kual 'eś śer afabil agradable 'ensu habla 'a todoś loś ke le 'oyen 'i ke resiban deleytasy'on 'en 'o'irle hablar :

'I porke śe konprehende meğor la deśkrisy'on de 'eśta virtud konosyendo śuś 'eśtremoś deklarare 'en breve la kalidad de 'elyyoś :

LOŚ ke aserka de 'eśta virtud 'eseden 'en puğa śon loś 'ombreś ke śon alegreś kon todoś 'i loan kon plazer kuanto dizen todoś bu'eno śe'a 'o malo 'i no 'eś la 'intensy'on de 'elyyoś 'eneśto mentir ke 'eśto 'eś śegun 'otro visy'o śola 'eś śu 'intensy'on no 'enoğar ni atriśtar 'a nadi 'i śer 'a todoś deleytable aplazible 'i agradable 'i 'a 'eśa 'intensy'on loan todaś kuantaś kozaś 'oyen aśuś konpanyeroś por ke śaben śer leś 'enoğo 'o'ir vituperar lo ke dizen 'i ke śe deleytan 'en śer loado 'i 'eśto śe lyama komun mente liğonğa 'i adulasy'on visy'o muy vituperable por nu'eśoś śantoś profetaś 'i śaby'oś 'i de todaś laś nasy'oneś tenido por muy abominable visy'o 'i 'eś la falta aserka 'eśta virtud 'una pura konśidraśy'on ke}

‹fol. 91a›

{Ś'
tyene algunoś 'en laś konversasy'oneś por visy'o kontradezir 'a kuanto dizen śuś proğimoś 'i vituperar śuś diğoś ke śean bu'enoś 'o maloś no por maś ke por 'inğuryarloś śin ningun reśpekto ni konsidrasy'on mala ni bu'ena :

'EŚ 'eśta falta aserka de 'eśta virtud visy'o muy vituperable 'el kual lyamaron loś antigoś kontensy'on[251] 'i loś ke 'eśte visy'o reyna 'i florese 'enelyyoś śon muy deśagradableś ala ğente 'i mal 'enklinadoś 'a todo de visyyo

'EŚ 'el medy'o 'entre 'eśtoś doś 'eśtremoś loke lyyamamoś afabilidad ke 'eś loar loke konbyene 'i vituperar loke konbyene por bu'en modo prudentisima mente 'en tal manera ke no resiba moleśty'a kyen fu'ere reprehendido kuanto posible fu'ere por loś meğoreś terminoś 'i 'oneśtoś ke konbyene :

'I para ke meğor śe pu'eda konprehender la deśkrisy'on de 'eśta virtud te deklarare kuatro propyedadeś ke ayy 'enelyya ke 'eśtaś viśtaś 'i konosidaś śe konosera śu 'ekselensy'a :

'EŚ la primera ke 'el afabil śe'a de ağuntar kon kual kyer 'ombre ke śe ağuntare afin de byen para platikar konel 'i 'enla tal platika aprobeğarle 'i alegrarle 'i no atriśtarle kyero dezir ke kuando platikare kon 'otro 'i konvinyere vituperyar kośa digna de vitupery'o lo deve reprehender porel meğor 'eśtilo ke posible fu'ere 'o ke menoś pasy'on resiba ke 'eneśto śe manifeśtara śer 'a bu'en fin virtu'ozo :

---

[251] Cf. Seneca, *De Ira* III.viii.4, trans. Basore, 1:275.

BOOK OF THE REGIMEN OF LIVING ‹FOL. 91A–91B›

'EŚ la śegunda ke 'el afabil kuando vyere 'a 'otr(i)[o] h[a]blar 'enlaś konversasy'oneś kozaś 'indevidaś ke no konvyene deleytarśe konelyyaś 'el bu'eno 'i virtu'ozo laś vitupere 'en gran manera 'i no laś konsyenta 'en kuanto pudyere ke 'eneśto haze probeǧo aloś meśmoś ke tal platikan 'i develo de hazer por la meǧor vi'a 'i maś konvenible ke posible 'eś para ke manko atriśte 'a 'el ke fu'ere reprehendido :

'EŚ la tersera propyedad deśta virtud ke 'el ke la pose'e 'a de tener 'una bu'ena 'eśtimatiba para platikar kon kada kual śegun śu dignidad ke a'un ke śe'a śu fin alegrar 'a todoś 'i aprobeǧarle 'a fin de byen komo tenemoś diǧo 'eś razon ke atente 'i śe'a byen advertido de alegrar 'a kada 'uno 'i hablar konel śegun śu grado de 'eśtado 'i de virtud 'i śegun fu'eren a'el maś konosidoś 'o paryenteś konforme a'el tyenpo a'el lugar 'i set- ke todaś 'eśtaś 'i 'otraś maś śon aremetidaś ala bu'ena 'eśtimatiba del virtu'ozo śegun dereǧa razon :

'EŚ la kuarta ke 'el afabil 'en todaś śuś kozaś 'i platikaś 'ilaś konversasy'oneś deve de tener 'el 'oǧo dereǧo mirando kontino 'i akatando 'el byen futuro maś ke 'el byen prezente 'i dekontino deve de 'eskoǧer 'el poko danyyo 'i triśteza por 'ebit[a]r 'el mayor ke akelyo tal śe pu'ede dezir alegrar pu'eś 'eś kauśa de privar 'otra triśteza mayor por lo kual no deve de perkurar de alegrar 'enel pre(n)śente al ke konel konversare loandolo 'i aprobando loke dize syendo digno de vitupery'o porke 'el alegrarlo 'en akel 'iśtante 'eś kauśa de atriśtarle 'en gran manera 'enlo futuro deśpu'eś ke venga 'en konosimyento de śu yero}

‹fol. 91b›
{ḤELEK B PEREK YḤ [PART TWO CHAPTER EIGHTEEN]
DE 'eśta propyedad prośtera parese 'uzar byen loś konpanyeroś de 'Iyob 'en kontradezir kon 'el 'i no deǧarle de reprehender lo ke 'era razon de śer reprehendido tenyendo 'eneśto akatamyento a'el 'util ke śele śegi'a al kabo 'en śer reprendido 'i śer konputadaś śuś razoneś por ke a'un ke 'enel preśente lo atriśtasen 'en kontradezirlo 'i reprehenderlo 'uzaban 'eneśto komo virtu'ozisimo aserka deśta virtud pu'eś 'era afin de tirarlo de 'eronyaś 'opiny'oneś para alegrarlo por pośtre deśpu'eś de konosida la verdad :

'I 'eśto parese ke kiǧeśe śignifikar śu fidelisimo konpanyero Bildad kuando le diǧo 'i śera tu prinsipy'o poko 'i tu prośtemeri'a a'umentara muǧo 'i set-[252] keryendo śignifikar ke la triśteza 'enel prinsipyyo śeri'a poka 'i la alegri'a 'i deleytasy'on 'enel fin muǧa kon śer alumbrado de la verdad komo maś klaro por śu proseder śe nota ke no 'eś tanto 'a nu'eśtro porpozito :

---

[252] Job 8.7.

BOOK OF THE REGIMEN OF LIVING ‹FOL. 91B–92A›

ŚOLO fu'e mi 'ente[n]sy'on por 'eśtaś propyedadeś darte byen 'a '(v)[e]ntender 'eśta virtud por laś kualeś 'eśta ami ver byen konosida 'i no ayy nesesidad de maś alargar 'en śu deklarasy'on :
    'I de lo ke de 'elyya śe konprende śe vera la deklarasy'on de śuś 'eśtremoś 'i śera ke 'el ke alegrare 'a todoś śin mirar ni tener ningun reśpekto al fin de śer bu'eno 'o 'util 'eśte tal 'eś 'el ke 'esede 'en la puǧa ke 'es 'uno de loś 'eśtremoś deśta virtud 'el kual lyyamamoś adulasy'on 'i 'el ke atriśtare atodoś kon 'eśprito de kontradisy'on no syendo 'a fin de byen ni 'util 'eśte tal 'eś 'el ke 'esede 'en la falta ke 'eś 'el 'otro 'eśtremo 'el kual lyyamamoś kontensy'on 'i a'un ke aserka de 'eśtoś meśmoś doś 'eśtremoś ayy muǧaś 'eśpeśyaś de visy'oś diferenteś por lo ke tenemoś diǧo me parese ke śe konprehende(da) fasil mente todo por lo kual me paresy'o ke para lo ke konbyene śaber aserka de 'eśta virtud 'i de śuś 'eśtremoś baśta byen lo diǧo 'ofresyendo miś fu'ersaś 'en lo de maś para tyenpo 'i lugar maś 'oportuno

KAPITULO DIZI'OǦO

'I lo ke konbyene śaber aserka la verdad ke 'eś nona 'enel numero de laś vertudeś moraleś ke konsiśte tanbyen 'en la konversasy'on 'umana diremoś 'en breve a'un ke 'eś tanbyen de muǧa 'utilidad 'i muy nesesary'a 'i agradable 'en laś konversasy'oneś
    'I lo primero ke 'eneśto 'eś meneśter śaber para la deśkrisy'on deśta virtud 'eś ke anśi komo la pasada virtud 'eś aserka laś deleytasy'oneś 'i triśtezaś de laś konversasy'oneś aśi 'eś [CW. 'eśta]}

‹fol. 92a›
{SB
'eśta aserka del pensar 'o h[a]blar 'o 'uzar verdad 'o mentira 'o[ ]falsi'a 'en laś meśmaś konversasy'oneś la kual konsi(t)[ś]te 'en treś ǧeneroś 'enel penśamyento 'i 'enla habla 'i 'enla 'obra ke 'en todaś treś śe konsidra verdad 'i mentira 'o falsi'a komo maś al delante deklararemoś :
    'I 'eś syerto ke por 'eśtoś treś ǧeneroś diǧo nu'eśtro devinisimo rey David 'enel prinsipy'o de śu p[e]śaltery'o byen aventurado 'el varon ke non andubo 'en konśeǧo de maloś 'i set-[253] keryendo śiknifikar ke la byen aventur[a]nsa konsiśte 'en akabidarśe 'i guardarśe de non 'inkurir 'eneśtoś treś ǧeneroś de mentira ke śon madreś de todoś loś maleś 'i 'enel konśeǧo de maloś śik(y)nifiko 'el ǧenero del mentir 'enel penśamyento ke 'el konśeǧo malo de nota venir de penśamyento malo 'i falso 'i 'en

---

[253] Ps. 1.1.

BOOK OF THE REGIMEN OF LIVING ‹FOL. 92A–92B›

dezir 'i 'en karera de pekadoreś non andubo[254] śiknifiko la falsi'a 'enla 'obra ke no 'eś 'otro 'el kamino de loś 'enkontinenteś 'i pekadoreś śino pura falsi'a 'enśuś a'utoś 'eśtiry'oreś 'i 'en dezir 'i 'en asyento de 'eśkarnidoreś no śe asento[255] śiknifiko la habla ke 'el 'eśkarneser no 'eś śino hablar mentira 'i falsi'a 'i kiğo dezir ke 'el ke 'eneśtoś treś visy'oś flor[e]syere 'i a'un 'en śolo 'uno delyyoś śe pu'ede lyyamar mal aventurado 'i 'el ke fu'ere aredrado de todoś deveśe de tener por feliśe 'i ('i) beatiśimo 'i la razon 'eś lo meśmo ke adelante dize ke śe śegira de aki pose'er la pura verdad ke 'eś nu'eśa śakra ley ke verdad 'eś lyyamada 'en boka de todoś nu'eśoś profetaś 'i śaby'oś por ke değando de śegir 'eśtoś treś ğeneroś de falsi'a lu'ego śe 'enklina la veluntad 'a śegir la verdad kontinu'a mente 'i 'enklinada la veluntad ala ley 'eś de tal propyedad ke haze kontinuar 'enelyya 'i 'eśto kiğo manifyeśtar dizyendo ke śalbo 'en ley de H‹a-Šem› śu voluntad 'i 'en śu ley hablara de di'a 'i de noğe[256] komo ke diğeśe ke 'eś byen aventurado 'el ke 'eś apartado de 'eśtaś treś falsiaś porke ayy 'otra porpozisy'on manifyeśta 'i 'eś ke kon śolo tener la voluntad ala ley del Dyyo śe śige lu'ego ke hable 'enelyya de di'a 'i de noğe porśu 'ekśelensy'a 'i tirada la voluntad del mal abito de laś treś diğaś 'eś śabido 'enklinarśe forsado ala verdad ke 'eś la menor del śeloğiśmo la kual no tubo neseśidad de dezir ke 'elyya de śuyo 'eśta diğa 'i manifyeśta 'i 'enklinada la voluntad ala ley ke 'eś la pura verdad śe śige hablar 'i kontinuar 'enelyya de di'a 'i de noğe ke 'eś la mayor la kual 'ubo neseśidad de manifyeśtar ke 'eś propyedad śola 'a nu'eśa śantiśima ley ke 'eś pura verdad :

'I 'eś meneśter śaber maś aserka 'eśta virtud ke todoś loś doś 'eśtremoś tanto de puğa komo de falta 'eś todo 'eśpesy'a de mentir porke todo loke 'eśede de la verdad tanto de maś komo de menoś no pu'ede değar de}

‹fol. 92b›
{H̱ELEK B PEREK YZ [PART TWO CHAPTER SEVENTEEN] {RMK: Misplaced chapter number}
śer mentira ke la verdad 'eś komo 'el sentro 'enla śirkunf[e]rensy'a 'i komo 'el polo 'enel syelo ke 'eś 'inmov(+)il 'i todo lo ke 'eśede de akel punto 'eś mobil 'i varyabil[257] :

---

[254] Ps. 1.1.
[255] Ps. 1.1.
[256] Ps. 1.2.
[257] Cf. Aristotle, *De Caelo* II.2 (285b 8–25), II.4 (286b 10–287a 5), also II.8 (289b 1–290a 30).

BOOK OF THE REGIMEN OF LIVING ⟨FOL. 92B⟩

PERO 'eś la diferensy'a 'entre la puǧa 'i la falta 'eneśta forma ke 'el ke 'esede 'enla puǧa ke 'eś 'el ke śe lyyama arogante peka 'en doś kozaś la 'una ke 'imaǧina aver 'enel muǧo maś de loke ayy 'i la 'otra ke la koza ke ayy 'enel syendo poka 'i de baǧa kalidad la tyene por muǧa ke lo primero 'eś yero 'enel kon(y)[o]simyento de śi meśmo ke pyensa aver 'enel maś de loke ayy 'i lo śegundo 'eś yero 'enel konosimyento dela meśma kośa ke la kośa de poka kalidad le parese śer muǧa :

'I komo yera 'en konoser aśi meśmo 'i 'en konoser la kośa ke 'enel ayy por tanto śe lo'a de grande porel yero primero 'i śe lo'a de aver 'enel kośaś grandeś por 'el yero śegundo 'i 'el ke 'esede 'enla falta 'eś 'el kontrary'o 'enlaś meśmaś doś ke dize de kontino manko de loke 'enel ayy 'i syendo de muǧa kalidad dize śer de poka kalidad de manera ke falta 'enlaś meśmaś doś ke śobro 'el aroǧante komo tenemoś diǧo 'i lyyamaśe 'eśta falta desimulasy'on :

'EŚ 'el medy'o 'entre 'eśtoś doś 'eśtremoś 'el ke manifyeśta la verdad de todo loke 'enel ayy tanto 'enla habla komo 'en todoś śuś mobimyentoś 'i 'obraś 'i pensamyentoś porke 'eś 'en todo verdadero 'i 'uśa 'en todo verdad 'i habla 'i pyensa verdad komo konbyene 'i kuando konbyene 'i set- :

KOMO manifeśto 'eśto Yosef 'el ǧuśto kuando fu'e demandado del rey Par^{c}oh dizyendole ke avi'a 'o'ido dezir por 'el śer gran śoltador de śu'enyyoś diǧo 'uzando de 'eśta virtud afu'eraś demi 'el Dyyo reśpondera la paś de Par^{c}oh 'i set-[258] : ke non nego śu perfeksy'on 'i abili(de)dad ni śe amośtro 'en manko de loke kre'i'a verdader'a mente aver 'enel ke 'en śemeǧante lugar 'i śemeǧante preśona 'i tyenpo konveni'a śegun dereǧa razon

'I '[e]ś(y) aśi de notar maś aserka 'eśta virtud ke dezimoś 'eśte medyyo śer loable kuando no 'eś 'a 'otro ningun fin maś ke dezir 'i 'uzar verdad por la meśma verdad 'enśi 'i dezimoś loś 'eśtremoś śer visy'oś vituperableś kuando no śon 'a 'otro fin ke mentir dizyendo maś 'i menoś deloke 'eś kon 'intensy'on de mentir por śolo mentir :

PORKE alaś veześ podra śer ke alguno diga verdad 'i no por fin de dezir verdad śalvo penśando ke myente 'o por ventura a'un ke śepa ke dize verdad dezirl'a 'a fin ke śe'a kre'ido 'en 'otra mentira ke kera formar 'i alaś veześ por temor ke no śe'a tomado 'enla mentira 'o por 'otro reśpekto śemeǧante ke 'eśte tal no śera virtu'ozo aśerka de 'eśta virtud ni deve de śer loado por tal :

AŚI meśmo alaś veześ konbyene 'a algun virtu'ozo 'i bu'eno hazerśe menor de loke 'eś [CW. 'i]}

---

[258] Gen. 41.16.

Book of the Regimen of Living ‹fol. 93a›

‹fol. 93a›
{SG ḤELEK B PEREK YT [PART TWO CHAPTER NINETEEN] {RMK: Misplaced chapter number}
'i alaś veześ maś de loke 'eś por algunoś reśpektoś konvenibleś konformeś 'a 'el tyenpo 'i lugar ke śe halyya 'onde śe rekyere śegun dereğa razon 'uzar de la puğa 'o falta deśta virtud 'a fin de byen 'i pura virtud 'i 'eśte tal no śera vitupery'o de lo kual 'uzo nu'eśo devinisimo re'ey David komo śe denota por 'el śalmo ke kom[y]ensa 'a David 'en śu mudar śu razon delante 'Abimelek 'i set-[259]

DE manera ke śe dira śer la difinsy'on deśta virtud pensar 'i hablar 'i 'uzar verdad 'en todaś laś kośaś komo konbyene 'i 'onde konbyene 'i kuando 'i kuanto konbyene 'i set- 'i śera la de loś 'eśtremoś 'el mentir 'en diminu'ir 'o a'umentar de la verdad de laś kośaś 'onde no konbyene 'i kuando no konbyene 'i komo no konbyene 'i set-

'I de 'eśtoś doś 'eśtremoś 'eś byen manifyeśto 'i viśto śer pe'or 'el de la puğa por ke 'eś maś kontrary'o ala verdad ke dize loke no 'eś 'i dize aver 'enel lo ke no ayy lo kual 'el ke diminuye no 'eś maś ke değar de dezir kuanto ayy 'enel 'i menoś de lo ke 'eś por lo kual kual kyera śe deve de akabidar 'en gran manera de no kaer 'enel visy'o de la puğa ke 'eś muy vituperable maś ke 'el de la falta komo avemoś diğo :

'I para ke meğor śe konprenda la deśkrisy'on deśta virtud deklararemoś algunaś divizy'oneś ke ayy 'en loś diğoś 'eśtremoś ke śe rekyeren śaber para śaber apartarśe kual kyer virtu'ozo delyyoś ke śon muy abominableś

'I para 'eśto aś de śaber ke loś 'eśtremoś 'en la puğa śon divididoś 'en treś 'eśpesyaś diferenteś

'EŚ la primera de loś ke śe loan maś de lo ke ayy 'en[e]llyyoś komo tenemoś diğo 'i hazen 'eśto śolo por śer akośtumbradoś 'a no dezir 'en ninguna manera la verdad por ke śe deleytan kon 'apetito danyado 'i korupto kon la mentira 'i falsi'a 'i 'eśtoś taleś tyenen muğa komunikasy'on kon loś maloś 'o por meğor dezir no pu'eden değar de śer lo komo diğo nu'eśo devinisimo re'ey Šᵉlomoh 'en śuś proberbyoś malo haze 'obra de falsi'a 'i set[-][260] keryendo śiknifikar ke deleytarśe kon la falsi'a 'i 'uzar de 'elyya mana de 'un 'oriğin de pura malisy'a 'i tanbyen kiğo notar ke toda malisy'a 'eś pura falsi'a por ke komo tenemoś diğo śon komunikanteś 'i partisipanteś la malisy'a 'i falsi'a 'en gran manera

'EŚ la śegunda 'eśpeśy'a de loś ke myenten loś ke śe loan tanbyen maś de lo ke 'en[e]llyyoś ayy pero no 'eś por reśpekto ni fin del meśmo mentir 'enśi śalvo por

---

[259] Ps. 34.1.
[260] Prov. 11.18.

BOOK OF THE REGIMEN OF LIVING ‹FOL. 93A–93B›

adkerir por 'entresisy'on de akelyya mentira algun probeǧo ke śi mankaśe 'el fin del probeǧo no la dirian komo akaeśe 'en algunoś medikoś 'o 'en loś maś ke por ke śean lyamadoś de loś 'enfermoś śe loan aver heǧo grandeś kuraś 'o aver librado de mu'erte 'a muǧoś 'i kuando 'eś manifyeśto aver mu'erto alguno por śuś yeroś perkuran de buśkar razoneś 'i prevan sofiśtika mente la kauśa por 'onde 'era forsado morir śin remedy'o por vi'a de medisina 'i [CW. śobre]}

‹fol. 93b›
{ḤELEK B PEREK YḤ [PART TWO CHAPTER EIGHTEEN]
śobre ver byen 'elyoś meśmoś śer todo mentira no dešan de dezirlo por ganar kon 'elyo loke śin 'elyyo perderian 'i de 'eśta 'eśpesya śon loś keśe hazen adevinoś 'i heǧizeroś 'i loś maś de loś 'ofisyaleś artifiseś ke śe loan 'en śuś 'ofisy'oś maś de loke śon śobre konoser 'enśi śer mentira por fin de 'el 'util ke delyyoś śeleś śige 'i'a 'opiny'on de algunoś 'eś 'eśta śegunda 'eśpesy'a pe'or ke la primera pero a'un ke no śe'a pe'or alo menoś 'eś 'eśta tanbyen muy mala 'i vituperable :

'EŚ la tersera de loś ke tanbyen myenten 'en loarśe maś de loke ayy 'enelyyoś por reśpekto 'i fin de adkerir 'onor komo algunoś śabyyoś hazen ke no syendo perfektoś 'enel śaber śe syerben de diǧoś de 'otroś śaby'oś 'i dizen śer śuyoś por ganar 'onor kośa muy vituperable 'entre loś ke verdader'a mente śon śaby'oś²⁶¹ 'i algunoś 'inkuren 'eneśte visy'o por śolo tener de śu natural de deleytarśe kon 'el lo'or de śi meśmoś 'i 'eśta tersera 'eśpesy'a 'eś syerto la menoś mala de todaś treś a'un ke todaś 'en ǧeneral śon malaś 'i vituperableś ke al fin todaś śon 'eśpesyaś de puǧa aserka de la verdad komo tenemoś diǧo :

'I tanbyen 'enel 'eśtremo śegundo ke 'eś la falta aserka de 'eśta virtud śe konsidran diferenteś 'eśpesyaś :

'I 'eś la primera 'i manko mala de loś ke śe diminuyen 'enśuś lo'oreś de loke ayy 'enelyyoś por hu'ir de hazerśe altiboś ni prezumiśy'oś 'i 'eneśtoś no 'eś 'el yero śi no 'en śolo hazer 'eśto kontinu'a mente tanto 'onde konbyene komo 'onde no konbyene komo tenemoś śiknifikado :

'EŚ la śegunda 'eśpesy'a lo ke komun mente lyamamoś 'ipokritaś ke mu'eśtran śer muy baǧoś para ke loś tengan por taleś 'i śean loadoś delyyo ke 'eś 'otro 'eśtremo de alteza kauteloza 'i de aki nase ke loś 'ipokritaś 'enkubren laś kozaś pekenyaś ke ayy 'enelyoś ke śon pekenyaś de verdad 'i śi algunaś kozaś grandeś ayy 'enelyyoś ke atodoś śon man[i]fyeśtaś akelyyaś taleś diminuyen porke komo no śe'a la 'intensy'on

---

²⁶¹ Compare Hacker's appraisal of this problem's effect on intellectual affairs in Salonika ("Intellectual Activity," 98).

'el abağarśe maš anteś 'el alsarse 'enkubren laś kozaś bağaś ke 'enelyoś ayy 'i abağanśe 'enlaś grandeś
'I 'eśtoś taleś algunaś veześ kuando śe loan nunka śe loan 'en lo ke 'eś manifyeśto 'enelyyoś śalvo 'en lo ke por ventura no ayy 'enelyyoś de manera ke[ ]śon visy'ozoś 'en loś doś 'eśtremoś ğunta mente : 'i vyenen 'a mentir 'en doś maneraś 'en dezir 'en algunaś kośaś menoś de lo ke ayy 'enelyyoś 'i 'eśto hazen 'en laś kośaś manifyeśtaś komo tenemoś diğo ke śaben ke a'un ke lo digan no an de śer tenidoś por taleś maś anteś an de śer de 'elyyo loadoś 'i 'en algunaś dizen maś de lo ke ayy 'enelyyoś pensando de śer kre'idoś pu'eś 'en lo manifyeśto ve'en todoś ke dizen manko de lo ke 'enelyyoś ayy
'EŚTA 'eśpesy'a de visy'o ke}

⟨fol. 94a⟩
{SD
lyyamamoś 'ipokrezi'a 'uzan de 'elyya loś 'ipokritaś 'en diferenteś maneraś ke algunoś śe mośtraran bağoś 'en loś veśtidoś 'i trağeś de bağa manera maś de lo ke 'a 'elyyoś konbyene konforme aśu fakultad : 'i algunoś 'en buśkar lugareś maś bağoś de loś ke aśu grado konbyene de bağo de 'otroś ke fu'era razon presederloś 'i algunoś 'en laś platikaś 'i korteziaś demazyadaś de lo ke a'elyyoś konvyenen hazer 'a 'otroś maś bağoś ke 'elyyoś
KOMUN mente śon 'eśtoś de la 'eśpesy'a ke diğo por 'elyyoś 'el profeta Y^{e}ša^{c}yahu de mente del Dyyo glory'ozo kon śu boka 'i kon śuś laby'oś me 'on(')raron 'i śu korason śe aparto de mi 'i set-[262] ke kiğo dezir 'el vitupery'o de loś ke komun mente no konforman laś pal[a]braś kon la 'intrinsika voluntad :

KAPITULO DIZINU'EBE

PARA maś aklarar 'eśta virtud 'i śaśtifazer 'a doś dubdaś ke parese razon de dubdar alargare algo maś 'eneśto 'eśpasifikando kuantaś 'eśpesyaś de verdad 'i de śuś 'eśtremoś śe pu'eden konsidrar konlo kual kedaran laś dubdaś śaśtifeğaś :
'EŚ la primera dubda ke parese śer la verdad virtud 'intelektual maś ke moral porke verdad 'i mentira komun mente śe dize aserka del 'entendimyento te'oriko konforme aloke 'el śenyor Rabbenu Mošeh dize 'enel śegundo kapitulo deśu famoziśimo libro 'enla avśolusy'on de akel gran argumento ke le fu'e argu'ido de 'Adam Ha-Ri'šon ke paresi'a aver ganado 'en aver pekado pu'eś de a'i adelante śupo byen 'i

---

[262] Isa. 29.13.

Book of the Regimen of Living ‹fol. 94a–94b›

mal loke anteś no avi'a śavido adonde para asolver 'el diǧo argumento pone 'una verisima deśtinsyyon de byen 'i mal 'a verdad 'i falsi'a de donde śe nota ke byen 'i mal śe konsidra aserka del 'apetito k[o]rporal 'i verdad 'i falsi'a aserka de 'el 'entendimyento te'oriko²⁶³ 'i kon 'eśto śaśtifaze ala dubda prevando 'ividente mente ke śabyendo anteś verdad 'i falsi'a 'era 'en mayor grado de perfeksy'on ke de pu'eś 'en śaber byen 'i mal tanto kuanta diferensy'a ayy de lo 'eśpritual alo korporal de adonde kual kyera parese ke dubdara kon razon porke śe pone 'eśta virtud 'en numero delaś vertudeś moraleś :

'EŚ la śegunda dubda ke parese śer lisito mentir algunaś veześ por 'ebitar 'otro mayor 'inkonbenyente 'i aśi 'eś konfirmado de nu'eśoś śaby'oś²⁶⁴ de manera ke kual kyera tanbyen dubdara komo determinamoś absuluta mente śer toda mentira vituperable :

KEDARA la primera dubda śaśtifeǧa deklarando 'espasifikada mente 'en kuantaś maneraś śe konsidra la verdad

'I kedara śaśtifeǧa la śegunda dubda deklarando 'en kuantoś modoś śe konsidra}

‹fol. 94b›
{ḤELEK B PEREK YT [PART TWO CHAPTER NINETEEN]
la mentira 'i falsi'a :

PARA lo kual aś de śaber ke la verdad śe reparte 'en sinko parteś 'i konsidrasy'oneś diferenteś :

'EŚ la primera la ke pura mente śe dize verdad ke 'eś 'el śer dela kośa 'enśi ke kuanto maś tyene la kośa del śer tanto maś tyene deśta 'eśpesy'a de verdad porke 'el śer 'i la pura verdad 'eś 'una meśma kośa de adonde 'eś viśto ke komo śe'a 'el Dyyo glory'ozo 'el puro śer 'en toda la perfeksy'on 'infinita anśi 'eś 'el la pura verdad ke 'eś 'eśta primera 'eśpesy'a por lo kual śe 'entitula 'en nu'eśa śantiśima ley 'i 'en boka de loś porfetaś 'i śaby'oś 'en titulo de verdad bendito śe'a 'el ke 'el 'eś la meśma verdad 'en 'eterno anśi komo 'el 'eś 'el puro śer 'i da 'a todoś śer 'i por 'eśta 'eśpesy'a de verdad lo nombra 'el profeta Yirmᶜyahu do diǧo 'i H‹a-Šem› Dyyo de verdad 'i set-²⁶⁵ :

'EŚ la śegunda 'eśpesy'a loke śe lyyama komun mente verdad 'enla dotrina 'i 'enla sensy'a ke 'eś lo ke afirma 'el 'entendimyento te'oriko 'i deśta 'uzan loś śaby'oś 'enla sensy'a 'enel platikar do dizen 'uno 'a 'otro dezir verdad 'o mentira ke 'eś la

---

²⁶³ Maimonides, *Guide*, trans. Pines, 24–25 *(MN,* Pt. 1, chap. 2).
²⁶⁴ Yevamot 65b.
²⁶⁵ Jer. 10.10.

Book of the Regimen of Living ⟨fol. 94b–95a⟩

konformidad del 'entendimento 'i diśformidad konla sertenidad de la kośa[266] ke śe 'eśtudy'a 'o śe trata :

'EŚ la tersera 'eśpesy'a lo ke tanbyen lyyaman komun mente verdad aserka la konformidad del 'entendimyento 'enel reğimyento de la vida śegun dereğa razon komo śon laś vertudeś moraleś 'i laś 'enkomendansaś ke ⟨H⟨a-Šem⟩ 'el Dyyo 'en nu'eśa śakra 'eśkritura noś 'enkomendo ke por 'eśta 'eśpesy'a diğo nu'eśo devinisimo re'ey David 'ensu peśaltery'o 'enkaminame 'entu verdad 'i dotriname 'i set-[267] ke komun mente loke 'eś 'ordenado 'enel reğimyento de la vida śegun 'el 'entendimyento pratiko konforme 'a ley 'i razon lyamamoś verdad 'i aśi śe deve lyamar :

'EŚ la kuarta lo ke ğuśga 'el 'entendimyento rekta 'i ğuśta mente 'enlaś kozaś ke śon śegun ğuśtiśy'a ke 'eś konformidad del 'entendimyento kon 'el verdadero kamino de la ğuśtisy'a la kual komun mente lyyamamoś tanbyen verdad ke kuando 'uno ğuśga lo syerto 'i ğuśto dezimoś dezir 'i ğuśgar verdad 'i kuando 'esede dela ğuśtisy'a dezimoś dezir 'i ğuśgar mentira 'i falsi'a 'i por 'eśta 'eśpesy'a diğo nu'eśo devinisimo rey Šᵉlomoh rey ğuśgan kon verdad pobreś śu silyya para śyenpre śera konpu'eśta 'i set-[268]

'EŚ la kinta 'eśpesy'a 'eśta deke noś'otroś tratamoś ke 'eś konformidad de loke habla 'el 'ombre por la boka konlo ke tyene 'ensu konsebto 'i voluntad 'i ke la 'obra 'i śer de la kośa śe'a konforme konlo ke por la boka śaka 'i lo meśmo 'a de 'uzar 'enloś mobimyentoś korporaleś ke śean konformeś 'a loke ayy 'enel komo konbyene 'i 'eśta tal verdad de 'eśta kinta 'eśpesya 'eś 'eśa virtud de ke (de ke) tratamoś ke 'eś viśto śer moral 'i no 'intelektual la kual 'eś 'un abito 'enel anima del virtu'ozo ke śegun akel abito dize verdad 'ensu voluntad}

⟨fol. 95a⟩
{ŚH
'i 'ensu boka 'i 'en śuś a'utoś 'eśtiry'oreś komo konbyene 'i kuando konvyene 'i set-
'i kon 'eśto 'eś viśto kedar śaśtifeğa la primera dubda

'I para śaśtifasy'o[n] dela śegunda dubda diremoś ke la mentira 'o falsi'a śe konsidra 'en doze modoś 'i 'eśpesyaś diferenteś porke byen atentando śe değa de dezir la verdad 'en kuatro modoś 'o ğeneroś 'onibersaleś 'eś 'el primero por 'inoransy'a de no śaber kual 'eś la verdad 'i tomanlo kontrary'o por lo syerto 'i afirman śer akelyyo verdad paresyendoleś śer aśi :

---

[266] Cf. Aquinas: *adaequatio mentis ad rem* (*Summa Theol.*, I Pars. 9.16, aa. 1–2, taken from Isaac Israel, *Liber definitionis*).
[267] Ps. 25.5.
[268] Prov. 29.14.

BOOK OF THE REGIMEN OF LIVING ‹FOL. 95A–95B›

ŚEGUNDO 'eś 'el modo de loś ke 'enkubren la verdad 'i la değan de dezir śabyendola loś kualeś śe dize ke myenten 'en śolo kalyar 'i 'enkubrir la verdad :
ŚON del terser modo loś ke myenten negando la verdad ke śabyendola al tyenpo ke śon demandadoś nyegan lo ke śaben 'i dizen no śaberlo :
ŚON del kuarto modo loś ke pura mente kontraryan la verdad kon 'intensy'on de dezir 'el kontrary'o de loke 'eś la koza '[e]nśi ke 'eśta 'eś la ke maś propy'a mente lyamamoś mentira :
'EŚTOŚ kuatro ğeneroś 'o modoś śe reparten 'en 'eśpesyaś diferenteś ke 'el primer ğenero ke 'eś por parte de 'inoransy'a 'eś 'en 'una śola manera 'i 'el manko vituperado (k)[d]e todoś 'i 'eś komo kuando demandaśen 'a 'uno śi 'el rey 'eśta 'ensu p[a]lasy'o 'i 'el pensando ke no 'eśta 'eśtando 'enel dize ke no 'eśta pensando dezir verdad 'eśta tal śe dize falsi'a a'un ke no myente 'enla 'intensy'on 'i 'eśta 'eś la primera :
'I 'eś la śegunda 'i la tersera laś doś 'eśpesyaś ke konprende 'el śegundo ğenero porke 'el 'enkubrir la verdad pu'ede śer 'en doś maneraś 'i modoś diferenteś 'o kalyyando ke 'eś la śegunda 'eśpesy'a 'enel numero de laś doze 'o hablando palabraś 'ikibokaś ke śe 'enkubra enelyaś la verdad dela kośa lyevando laś palabraś doś 'ententoś de manera ke 'el ke lo 'oye 'entyenda por 'elyaś lo kontrary'o de la verdad a'un ke 'el no lo dize 'i 'eśta 'eś la tersera 'eśpesy'a del numero de laś doze :
'EŚ la kuarta 'i kinta 'i śeśta 'i śebtima laś kuatro 'eśpesyaś ke konprende 'el ğenero tersero porke 'el nyegar la verdad pu'ede śer 'en kuatro maneraś ke alaś veześ śe nyega la verdad burlando la kual śe lyama mentira ğokośa alaś veześ śe nyega por probeğo de akel akyen śe nyega komo akaese muğaś veześ dezir al dolyente 'i darle 'a 'entender ke 'eś lo amargo dulśe[269] porke lo tome porśu probeğo 'i śalud 'i alaś veześ nyegan la verdad por hazer danyo 'a akel akyen la nyegan 'i alaś veześ nyegan la verdad por śolo mentir śin ningun 'otro reśpekto śino śolo por apetit(y)[o] de kerer mentir la kual śe lyyama mentira mendoza
'EŚ la 'oktaba 'i nona laś doś 'eśpesyaś del kuarto ğenero por ke 'el kontraryar la verdad śu'ele śer[ ] 'en doś maneraś 'o aśegurando 'i afirmando kon ğuramento no śer la koza aśi maś anteś śer 'el kontrary'o lo kual śe lyyama perğuro ke 'eś 'oktabo 'enel numero}

‹fol. 95b›
{'i kontraryar la verdad kon boześ 'i fu'ersaś lo kual śe lyyama kontensy'on ke 'eś la nona 'enel numero diğo śon la dezena 'i 'onzena 'i dozena laś ke ya 'emoś deklarado aserka de loś 'eśtremoś deśta virtud la primera 'eś kuando 'el 'ombre amu'eśtra śer

---

[269] Cf. Isa. 5.20.

Book of the Regimen of Living ‹fol. 95b›

maś de lo ke 'eś ke 'eś 'el 'eśtremo 'en la puǧa ke lyamamoś arogansy'a 'i lyamaśe ǧaktansa la kual 'eś desima 'enel numero de laś doze la 'otra 'eś 'el 'eśtremo 'en la falta ke amu'eśtra manko de lo ke 'eś la kual lyamamoś desimulasy'on 'i lyyamaśe 'ironi'a ke 'eś 'onzena 'enel numero de laś doze 'i 'eś la dozena la de loś 'ipokritaś ke śe halyan 'en 'elyyoś laś doś diǧaś ǧunta mente komo tenemoś deklarado :

'EŚTOŚ śon loś doze modoś 'i 'eśpesyaś diferenteś de mentiraś ke śu'elen loś 'ombreś visy'ozoś 'uzar de 'elyyaś 'i trae muǧa 'utilidad a'el 'ombre śaverlaś para śaverśe śalvar 'i apartar de kual kyera de 'elyyaś ke śon muy vituperableś 'i tirada la primera 'eśpesy'a ke śe lyama falsi'a todaś laś 'otraś śe lyyaman mentira por ke śon kontra lo ke śabe śer verdad :

'I kon lo ke tenemoś diǧo 'eś viśta la śaśtifazy'on 'o asulusy'on de la śegunda dubda ke byen 'eśpekulando tirando la primera 'eśpesy'a ke akelyo no va 'en mano del 'ombre guardarśe delyya pu'eś vyene por 'inoransy'a la kual 'eś la ke komun mente 'uzan loś ke platikan 'en la sensy'a ke kada 'uno pyensa dezir verdad por lo kual diǧeron nu'eśoś śaby'oś por laś 'opinyyoneś diferenteś ke halyyaron 'en nu'eśo Talmud ke 'unoś kontradizen kon 'otroś[270] todaś śuś palabraś de 'unoś 'i de 'otroś śon pal[a]braś del Dyyo bibo 'i set-[271]

TODAŚ laś 'otraś 'onze paresen śer vituperableś ke no deve ninguno 'en ninguna manera 'uzar de 'elyyaś 'i śi 'en algun tyenpo 'eś lisito 'uzar de alguna delyyaś 'eś de la kinta 'eśpesy'a ke 'eś por probeǧo de akel akyen śe nyega la kual lyyamamoś 'ofisy'ośa komo śi akaesy'eśe korer 'uno kon 'inpetu de 'ira kon 'una 'espada 'en la mano para matar 'a 'otro śin kulpa 'i akel 'otro akyen kyere matar śe 'eśkondyese 'en 'un lugar 'okulto 'i 'uno ke lo vyeśe alyi 'entrar fu'eśe demandado del ke lo vyene 'a matar śi 'entro alyi 'eś lisito ke diga ke no 'entro alyi 'i ke nyege la verdad 'en tal kaśo por ke śi no la nyegaśe hazi'a grande danyyo aloś doś 'i aśi 'otroś kazoś śimileś donde konbyene 'uzar deśta śola 'eśpesy'a de mentira ke de 'eśta 'eśpesy'a 'eś la ke diǧeron nu'eśoś śaby'oś ke 'eś lisito 'i śe konsyente 'uzar de 'elyya por adkerir la paś[272] 'onde konbyene ke 'eś śuprema 'utilidad :

'I de ninguna de laś 'otraś no 'eś lisito 'uzar delyaś 'en ninguna manera ni 'en ningun tyenpo kon lo kual me parese 'eśtar śaśtifeǧa 'en alguna manera la śegunda dubda deśtingendo 'eneśtaś doze maneraś 'i 'eśpesyaś de mentiraś komo tenemoś deśtingido :}

---

[270] Hagigah 3b.
[271] Eruvin 13b, Gittin 6b.
[272] Yevamot 65b.

Book of the Regimen of Living ‹fol. 96a›

‹fol. 96a›
{SV
PERO porke 'eśta 'eś matery'a de muğa 'utilidad 'i alguno's kiğeron dezir ke a'un de 'eśta kinta 'eśpesy'a no śe avi'a de 'uzar 'en ningun tyenpo por ninguna manera viśto śer 'opiny'on kontra diğa por 'el filosofo 'i por nu'eśoś śaby'oś komo tenemoś diğo te dire 'en brebe treś razoneś ke 'elyoś diğeron para afirmar śu 'opiny'on 'i reśpondyendo a'elyyaś kedara la dubda byen asolvida 'i śaśtifeğa

'EŚ la primera razon ke 'el ke myente deśbarata 'el fin de la habla 'umana porke 'el fin verdadero de la habla 'eś amośtrar 'i manifeśtar la verdad komo diğo 'el filosofo 'enel primero de śu politika[273] konforme 'a akel gran diğo de Zerubbabel 'a 'el rey Daryoś do dišo no ayy komo la verdad fu'erte 'en la tyera 'i set- komo trae nu'eśtro famozišimo 'eśtoryador Yosef ben Goryon 'enel primer kapitulo de śu libro[274] :

'EŚ la śegunda ke parese śer la mentira kontra ğuśtisy'a porke komo śe'a la palabra demośtrasy'on de loke 'eśta 'enel anima 'i 'eśpeğo de 'el 'entendimyento kuando manifyeśte 'el kontrary'o de loke 'eśta 'enel konsebto halyyaśe śer diśformida(r)[d] 'entre 'el 'entendimyento 'i la voluntad 'i 'eśta tal diśformidad 'eś 'inğuśta :

'EŚ la tersera ke parese śer la mentira 'in'umani(')dad porke 'eś kontra la dereğa razon 'i syendo kontra la dereğa razon parese śer kontra la bondad 'i virtud śyendo kontra la bondad ke parese syerto śer 'ilisito 'i vituperable 'en todo tyenpo :

'EŚTAŚ śon śuś razoneś a'un ke 'elyoś alargaron maś 'en koroborarlaś :

PARA reśponder alaś kualeś diremoś tanbyen 'en breve ke a'un ke tubyeron razon 'enlaś dyeś 'eśpesyaś de mentiraś 'enlaś 'otraś doś no konśtan ni 'obligan 'a no mentir 'en ningun tyenpo

KE śi 'eś la primera no 'eś meneśter hablar 'enelyya pu'eś no va 'en mano del 'ombre değar de 'uzar de 'elyya porke 'eś por 'inoransy'a komo tenemoś diğo 'i pu'eś 'elyoś meśmoś 'uzan delyya 'en śuśtentar tal 'opiny'on deśpu'eś de viśto la razon kontra 'elyoś no leś paresera vituperable maś a'un 'enla kinta 'eśpesy'a ke 'eś la 'ofisy'oza no tubyeron ninguna razon porke 'eśto 'eś de doś 'inkonvenyenteś 'eśkoğer 'el menor de manera ke mentir al ke vyene 'a matar aśu konpanyero kon 'ira 'i śin ninguna razon 'eś byen pu'eś 'eś kauśa de 'ebitar 'otro tal mayor ke 'ofende al ku'erpo 'i ala alma :

'I kon 'eśto 'eśta byen viśto kuan poka razon tubyeron 'enśu tersera razon porke no 'eś 'in'umani(')dad mentir 'en tal kaśo maś anteś lo 'eś 'en dezir verdad pu'eś śe

---

[273] Aristotle, *Politics* I.i.10 (1253a 14–16) trans. H. Rackham (New York, 1932), 11.

[274] Josephus, *Antiquities of the Jews,* II.3.6; *Works,* trans. R. Marcus (Cambridge, MA, 1958), 6:339–41.

Book of the Regimen of Living ⟨fol. 96a–96b⟩

śige maś mal dizyendola de manera ke śe pu'ede dezir pura bondad 'el mentir 'en tal kazo 'i 'el dezir verdad pura maldad pu'eś delyo śe śegiri'a śi śe diğeśe tan grande mal komo tenemoś diğo :
'I 'eśta byen viśto komo la śegunda razon 'eś tanbyen}

⟨fol. 96b⟩
{falta por ke la mentira 'en tal kauśo no 'eś kontra ğuśtisy'a maś anteś 'eś 'uzar de la ğuśtisy'a por ke 'eś librar 'a 'uno de 'un mal grande kon 'otro menor ni menoś 'eś 'eśto diśformidad 'entre 'el 'entendimyento 'i la voluntad ni la verdad de la koza por ke 'el meśmo 'entendimyento ğuśga śegun dereğa razon śer lisito mentir 'en akel tyenpo por 'el gran probeğo ke de 'elyo śe śige de manera ke 'el 'entendimento 'eś konforme kon la boka 'i voluntad 'i kon la verdad de la koza ke 'eś traer akel probeğo
'I kon 'eśto 'eś tanbyen viśto 'el deśbarate de la primera razon ke la mal mentira no kontrary'a 'el fin de la habla por ke 'el fin verdadero de la habla 'eś amośtrar 'i manifeśtar la verdad konforme ala virtud 'ordenada śegun dereğa razon 'i la verdad śegun virtud 'i dereğa razon 'eś la ke śe dize śegun konbyene 'i 'enel tyenpo ke konbyene kon todaś laś śerkonstansyaś ke konbyenen 'enel 'obrar śegun virtud :
'I de 'eśta manera 'el ke dize verdad 'enel lugar ke no konbyene dezirśe no dize verdad śegun virtud maś anteś śe dira mentir por ke kontrary'a ala verdad de la virtud ke 'eś la tersera 'eśpesy'a de la verdad :
'I aśi komo śe dize fu'erte valyente 'eśforsado śegun la virtud de la fortaleza 'el ke fuye de loś p[e]ligroś de la gera 'enel tyenpo 'i lugar 'onde konbyene hu'ir aśi śe dira verdadero kuando negara la verdad 'enel tyenpo 'i lugar ke konbyene 'i śet- 'i por 'eśte reśpekto 'i vi'a fu'e lo ke diğeron nu'eśoś śaby'oś ke 'era lisito mudar de la verdad por la paś 'i śet-[275] por ke komo śe'a la paś 'obra de virtud 'el 'obrarla 'i adkerirla 'eś 'uzar verdad śegun dereğa razon
' I 'eśta meśma difenensy'a 'i divizy'on 'ubo 'entre doś śegidoreś de famozisimoś śaby'oś 'en nu'eśo Ṭalmud loś 'unoś 'entituladoś 'en kaza de Šamay loś 'otroś 'entituladoś 'en kaza de Hillel śobre komo śeri'a byen loar la nobyya 'i bayylar delante delyya 'en prezensy'a del nobyyo para ke le fu'eśe a'el agradable lo kual dizen loś de la kaza de Šamay ke digan 'eneśta forma nobyya komo kyera ke 'eś 'i dizen ke la razon por ke śe deve de dezir aśi 'eś por ke la ley diğo de koza de falsi'a te aleğaraś 'i śet-[276] 'i loś de la kaza de Hillel dizen ke dira nobyya hermoza 'i bu'ena[277] kre'yendo

---

[275] Yevamot 65b.
[276] Ketubot 16b–17a, Exod. 23.7.
[277] Ketubot 17a.

por verdad śegun 'eśte famozisimo śenyyor ke 'en loś maś de śuś dig̃oś 'uzamoś komo 'el ke komo śe'a aki 'el fin del mentir por akresentar 'el 'amor 'entre 'el nobyyo 'i la nobyya 'el mentir 'en tal kauśo 'eś dezir pura verdad pu'eś 'eś 'en tyenpo ke konbyene komo konbyene konforme 'a dereg̃a razon 'i set-[278]

'I para ke de kamino śeaś aluminado 'en 'un gran dig̃o de nu'eśoś śaby'oś aserka de loś milagreś[279] te kyero aklarar 'i amośtrar por konparasy'on kuan śimil 'eś 'eśte kazo a'el kazo de loś dig̃oś [CW. milagreś]}

⟨fol. 97a⟩
{SZ
milagreś 'i marabilyyaś ke 'el Dyyo hizo haze 'i hara kontra naturaleza a'un ke ala verdad byen mirando 'i 'eśpekulando todo lo ke 'el Dyyo haze 'eś pura naturaleza para lo kual aś de śaber ke kada koza tyene śu partikular naturaleza 'ordenada por la prima kauśa la kual śe muda por 'otra 'oniversal ke 'eś la 'orden 'i mandamyento devino

DE la meśma manera ke akaese mug̃aś veześ ke por razon de no darśe vaku'o ke 'eś naturaleza 'onibersal ke abyendo 'enel mundo vaku'o no śe podri'a śuśtentar ni śe podri'a 'obrar koza alguna 'enel śube la agu'a para ariba[280] 'i no desyende abag̃o śin aver 'otro ningun 'inpedimyento ke 'eśta 'onibersal natural[e]z(z)a ke la haze subir kontra śu partikular de desender komo 'ividente mente śe ve'e 'en laś bonbaś de loś nabi'oś ke hazen śubir 'el agu'a para ariba por śola razon de vaku'o del meśmo modo ke 'inventaron loś ś(v)[i]rug̃anoś 'en laś g̃iringaś por la meśma kauśa śi tomaren 'un g̃aro de 'una śola boka pekenyya 'i lo 'eng̃iren de agu'a 'i de pu'eś de lyeno lo bolbyeren de boka abag̃o a'un ke la boka 'eśte abyerta no kaera gota de agu'a haśta ke abran 'en riba del g̃aro 'un agug̃ero ke 'entre por 'el 'el ayyre para 'eng̃ir 'el lugar de adonde śale 'el agu'a 'eś byen viśto ke no śe dira ke la agu'a 'en la bonba śube kontra naturaleza ni 'enel g̃aro ke deg̃a de desender maś anteś śe dira ke natural mente śube 'i deg̃a de desender por razon del vaku'o ke 'eś natureza 'onibersal alyende de la 'otra partikular ke 'eś desender para abag̃o :

DE la meśma manera akaese 'en loś milagreś ke haze 'el Dyyo bendito mudando la natureza partikular kuando 'eś 'ordenado por kual kyera 'intensy'on ke aśu probidensy'a plugo 'i depu'eś de 'efektuada śu voluntad torna la kośa ke 'enelyya haze

---

[278] This recalls Yevamot 65b.
[279] Gen. R. 5.5.
[280] Cf. Gen. 1.7 and also Aristotle, *Physics* IV.ix (217a 12–20).

BOOK OF THE REGIMEN OF LIVING ‹FOL. 97A-97B›

'el milagre aśu partikular natureza 'i deśte modo śe pu'ede dezir śer natural 'el kontraśtar la natureza partikular por 'el mandado del Dyyo por ke no 'eś maś la natureza ke 'un mobimyento dado de la primera kauśa a'el fin determinado por śu voluntad śegun 'opiny'on de loś modernoś 'entre loś kualeś fu'e 'el śenyyor Rabbenu Mošeh 'enel kapitulo vente 'i nu'ebe de la śegunda partida de śu famozisimo libro[281] 'i sigyyolo Tomaś 'enel śegundo de loś fizikoś[282]

'I 'eśto śiknifikaron byen nu'eśoś śaby'oś śobre lo ke dize la ley aserka de loś milagroś ke hizo 'el Dyyo bendito kon noś al tyenpo del śalir de Ağibto do dize 'i torno la mar 'a 'ora de tarde aśu fu'ersa 'i set-[283] aśi puz(y)[o] por kondisy'on kon 'el deś(r)[d]e 'el prinsipy'o ke lo avi'a de ronper ke aśi dize 'i torno 'el mar 'a 'oraś de tarde aśu fu'ersa 'i set- aśu kondisy'on ke puz(y)[o] kon 'el deśde 'el prinsipy'o 'i set-[284]

'I 'eś de ver 'eneśte gran diğo para 'entender primero la 'intensy'on del anteś de venir aśu gloza 'i śiknifikasy'on ke parese ke no proba lo ke kyere probar por la śakra 'eśkritura por ke śegun parese nu'eśoś śaby'oś 'ikibokan 'el verbo de [CW. śu]}

‹fol. 97b›
{śu fu'ersa ke kyera dezir de śu kondisy'on 'o pakto ke nu'eśo lašon ha-kodeš śi lo śufre kon traśtokar algo laś meśmaś letraś 'i kyeren dezir ke pu'eś dize la 'eśkritura ke torno 'el mar aśu fu'ersa ke 'eś komo ke diğeśe ke torno aśu pakto 'i kondisy'on lu'ego parese ke teni'a pakto 'i kondisy'on kon 'el Dyyo de averśe de partir kuando 'el kiğeśe 'i syendo aśi 'eś de śentir ke parese no prebar nada de a'i por ke 'eśto 'eś diğo de pu'eś de ya partida la mar 'i kyere dezir ke torno la mar 'a ağuntarśe komo 'eśtaba anteś ke śe partyera pu'eś kuando digamoś ke 'eś komo ke diğeśe 'i tornośe 'el mar a'ora de tarde aśu partido parese ke no preba nada pu'eś 'eś al tyenpo ke śe torno 'a serar

PARA lo kual ami ver śe deve de 'entender deśta manera ke ala verdad no śe lyyama guardar 'el pakto 'enel tyenpo ke śe 'efektu'a maś anteś diri'a yo ke 'efek-

---

[281] Maimonides, *Guide*, trans. Pines, 345–46 (*MN*, Pt. 2, chap. 29).
[282] I initially identified this as Aquinas II Physics Lect. 3, n. 8 (quoted in *Cambridge History of Later Medieval Philosophy* [Cambridge, 1982], 525), but it seems rather to be Aquinas, *In Phys.* II, lect. 14, trans. R. J. Blackwell et al. (New Haven: Yale University Press, 1963), 121–24 esp. 124; the Aristotle passage being *Physics* II 199b 15–33 (the Latin text is ed. M. Maggiolo [Turin, 1954]).
[283] Exod. 14.27. The midrash may be Gen. R. 5.5.
[284] Exodus R. 21.6.

tuar la kondisy'on 'i partido no keda maś partido ni kondisy'on 'i komo 'el Dyyo glory'ozo kuando kre'o loś 'elementoś[285] 'i todaś laś 'otraś kozaś kreadaś loś kre'o kon tal kondisy'on ke 'ordenaśe delyyoś kuanto kiğeśe kontra śu partikular naturaleza hata ke 'el mundo pereśka kuando a'el plazere an de guardar todaś laś kozaś kreadaś 'eśta tal kondisy'on 'i kon 'eśto kuando kyera ke 'el Dyyo 'ordena 'enelyyoś koza kontra natureza partikular a'un ke 'en akelyya sazon no śe pu'ede dezir ke 'eśtan kon akel partido pu'eś lo 'efektuan ke partido no 'eś śalvo 'una potensy'a de kośa ke 'en algun tyenpo śe'a de 'efektuar de pu'eś de 'efektuado 'el partido tornado aśu partikular natureza tornan 'a guardar akelyya meśma kondisy'on ke guardaban anteś para kuando kyera 'el Dyyo 'otra veś 'i 'otra 'a 'infinito 'ordenar 'en 'elyyoś kuanto 'enveluntare 'i de aki tubyeron nu'eśoś śaby'oś lugar de probar byen de nu'eśa ley 'el diğo partido ke pu'eś dize la ley ke de pu'eś de ronpido 'el mar torno aserarśe 'i tornado 'a śerar torno 'a guardar śu partido ke 'en dezir śu partido parese ke 'era partido ke ya de anteś ke śe partyeśe teni'a 'el kual 'era de partirśe 'i komo partyendośe śe 'efektuaba 'i ya no kedaba pakto fu'e nesesary'o dezir ke bolvyendośe 'a śerar bolvi'a 'a guardar śu pakto 'i kondisy'on ke de anteś teni'a de 'obedeser kuando 'el Dyyo maś 'ordenaśe del kontra śu natureza partikular komo diğo avemoś 'i pu'eś dize ke lo ke torno 'a guardar 'el mar fu'e śu partido pasado komo de nota 'el termino de tornar ke no kabe tornar śalvo 'a lo ke de anteś teni'a 'i maś 'en dezir śu kondisy'on ke de nota ke 'era ya śuya de anteś de aki prevaron forsada mente śer verdad ke 'el Dyyo teni'a partido kon 'el mar anteś ke śe ronpyeśe 'el kual 'era ke śe 'ubyeśe de ronper :

'I kiğeron maś śiknifikar 'eneśtaś palabraś lo ke tenemoś diğo ke}

⟨fol. 98a⟩
{ṢH
aśi komo 'enel agu'a kuando śube para ariba por razon del vaku'o[286] no śe dize śer kontra natureza maś anteś ke la meśma natureza ke haze a'el agu'a desender 'eśa meśma 'eś la ke la haze śubir 'en akel tyenpo ke konbyene por razon del vaku'o 'i depu'eś ke sesa la kauśa del vaku'o torna aśu naturaleza partikular kon 'una potensy'a de guardar akelyya 'orden todo tyenpo ke fu'ere nesesary'o del meśmo modo kuando 'el Dyyo haze 'el milagre 'en la kośa kontra śu partikular natureza la meśma natureza 'onibe[r]sal de la kośa ke śe 'influyo 'enelyya 'enel prinsipy'o de śu kreasy'on la 'obliga 'uzar kontra śu partikular 'enel tyenpo ke 'el kreador delyya le plaze

---

[285] In the sixth century John Philoponus explained that all the four elements of Aristotelian physics were covered in the Genesis account: air, earth, water, fire.
[286] Cf. Aristotle, *Physics* IV.ix (217a 12–20).

para mośtrar śu 'infinito poder aśu pu'eblo 'i 'efektuado akelyyo bu'elve aśu natureza partikular kon la potensy'a de guardar la 'onibersal todo tyenpo ke fu'ere 'ordenado de la prima kauśa a'un ke nunka ayya delyya nesesidad por ke 'eśta potensy'a 'eś śerkonśtansy'a de śu natureza propy'a :

DE la meśma manera 'el dezir mentira 'i değar de dezir verdad kuando konbyene komo konbyene 'i set- śera dezir la meśma verdad pu'eś 'eś 'ordenado por la dereğa razon 'i ğu'izy'o del 'entendimyento

'I aśi komo aserka de la natureza tirada la 'onibersal torna la partikular aśu śer de la meśma manera aserka de 'eśta gran virtud tirado 'el tyenpo ke konvyene mentir por la 'orden 'onibersal de la dereğa razon śe'a de bolver ala verdad partikular śin 'eseder delyya kośa ninguna hata 'otro tyenpo ke konbyene 'uzar 'el kontrary'o 'ordenado por la dereğa razon

'I pu'edeśe maś notar deśte devinisimo 'enğenplo ke anśi komo 'el śubir 'el agu'a 'o değar de desender no 'eś śin muğa kauśa komo 'eś por razon del vaku'o ke 'inporta la śuśtentasy'on 'i operasy'oneś del mundo 'i del meśmo modo loś milagreś ke no kyere 'el Dyyo glory'ozo 'uzar delyyoś śin grande nesesidad de la meśma manera deve de śer 'enel nyegar la verdad 'onde konbyene kon fortisima kauśa 'ordenada por la dereğa razon komo 'eś por poner paś 'onde faltando śe śegiri'a muğo mal 'o por śalvar la vida akyen śe deve śalvar por ğuśtisy'a 'o śimil kośa deśtaś

DE manera ke 'el ke 'en lugar 'onde no konvyene diğere verdad 'eśte tal śe dira mentir 'i 'eś 'el ke 'esede 'en la puğa ke 'eś 'uno de loś 'eśtremoś ke śon aserka deśta virtud ke 'eśte tal myente pu'eś 'esede de lo ke la dereğa razon 'ordena komo konbyene 'enel tyenpo ke konbyene 'i set- 'i 'el ke değa de dezir la verdad 'onde konbyene dezirla 'esede 'en la falta ke 'eś 'el 'otro 'eśtremo aserka de 'eśta virtud 'i kon 'eśto 'eśta byen viśto śu deśkrisy'on 'i de śuś 'eśtremoś 'i a'un ke 'era matery'a para maś alargar 'enelyya baśta lo diğo para 'un tan bu'en 'inğeny'o komo 'eśpero ke śera 'el tuyyo śi śigyereś 'el kamino dela dotrina[287] 'i para byen myenteś 'enelyyo [CW. ke 'eś]}

⟨fol. 98b⟩
{ḤELEK B PEREK Ḳ [PART TWO CHAPTER TWENTY]
ke 'eś kośa deśuprema 'utilidad para śaberśe guardar 'el 'ombre de mentir ke 'eś 'un muy vituperable visy'o :

---

[287] Cf. Prov. 4.11.

BOOK OF THE REGIMEN OF LIVING ‹FOL. 98B›

KAPITULO VENTE

'EŚ la desima virtud moral la kortezi'a ke 'eś tanbyen aserka la konversasy'on 'umana la kual 'eś afin de repoz[o] 'i deśkanso tanto por 'el kansansy'o de loś 'eğersisy'oś korporaleś komo por reśpekto de 'el refrizery'o ke de 'elyyo śe śige 'a 'el anima vagando de la 'obra de 'el 'entendimyento porke komo śe'a 'el anima 'en kuanto morare 'eneśta karne rebuśta 'una virtud 'en ku'erpo no pu'ede 'eśtar 'en kontinu'o mobimyento de śemeğante 'eğersisy'o 'i syendo 'el tal repozo konforme 'a dereğa razon komo konbyene 'i kuando 'i kuanto konbyene 'i set- tyene 'i trae śuprema 'utilidad para la 'eśpikulasy'on 'i 'obraś de virtud de la meśma manera ke trae 'el śu'enyo 'utilidad para la perfeksy'on de la viğily'a komo te tengo deklarado 'enla primera partida de 'eśte tratado aserka del reğimyento del dormir :

'I pu'eś 'eś konvenible 'el repozo 'enla vida 'umana 'el kual lo maś konśiśte 'enla konversasy'on deleytable komo konbyene 'i set- 'eś razon kela tal konversasy'on śe'a platikar 'en kozaś konvenibleś 'i 'oneśtaś 'enderesadaś afin de virtud hablando 'en kozaś dignaś de śer habladaś tanto 'en reśpekto del hablador komo de loś 'oyenteś 'i ke śean diğaś kon grabedad 'i kon muğa prudensy'a komo konbyene kuando 'i kuanto konbyene 'i set- 'i de 'eśte modo de konversasy'on 'uzaban nu'eśoś śaby'oś de nu'eśo Ṭalmud kuando śe śentian flakoś del kansansy'o 'i kontinu'o trabağo del 'eśtudy'o[288] 'i 'eran diğaś laś taleś palabraś ke 'elyyoś akośtumbraban dezir por śu deśkanso kon tanta grabedad ke śe śegi'a 'i rezultaba de 'elyyaś muğa dotrina 'i a'un no śe 'entendian śin 'eśtudy'o[289] porke kuando laś platikaś ke śe platikan 'en taleś konversasy'oneś por pasa tyenpo no śon diğaś kon grabedad śon kauśa de hazer 'a loś 'ombreś diśulutoś 'i mal akośtumbradoś 'i 'eśto kiğeron śiknifikar nu'eśoś śaby'oś donde diğeron ke 'el rizo 'i livyandad de kabesa akośtu[m]bran 'a 'el 'ombre 'a deś'oneśtidad 'i set-[290] keryendo dezir ke kuando 'el burlar 'i ğugar kuando konbyene no fu'ere kon grabedad maś anteś fu'ere kon libyandad eśtonśeś 'eś kauśa[ ]de akośtumbrar 'a 'el 'ombre 'a deś'oneśtidad 'i set- lo kual kuando 'eś 'el tal ğu'izy'o 'o burla kon grabedad komo konbyene 'i kuanto konvyene 'i set- 'eś 'oneśto 'i konvenible komo tenemoś diğo :

'I komo kyera ke 'el tal pasa tyenpo 'i repozo śe'a 'enel platikar 'entre amigoś 'i

---

[288] Gorfinkle connects the saying with Shabbat 30b: "Even as Rabbah before he commenced [his discourse] before the scholars used to say something humorous, and the scholars were cheered; after that he sat in awe and began the discourse" (Maimonides, "*Eight Chapters*," ed. Gorfinkle, 72 n. 4).

[289] Avoda Zarah 19b.

[290] Berakot 31a, Shabbat 30b, Pesaḥim 117a.

BOOK OF THE REGIMEN OF LIVING ⟨FOL. 98B–99A⟩

loś modoś de laś platikaś difyeren 'en deśtintaś 'eśpesyaś 'entre laś kualeś ayy muǧaś vituperableś}

⟨fol. 99a⟩
{ST
'i algunaś loableś 'i agradableś por tanto śe deve de konsidrar 'enelyyaś 'un medyo 'eleǧible 'i doś 'eśtremoś vituperableś komo 'en kual kyera de laś 'otraś vertudeś moraleś :
   PARA lo kual aś de konsidrar 'i śaber ke loś 'ombreś ke 'enśuś platikaś hablaren 'i burlaren maś de loke konbyene śi 'enlaś taleś burlaś 'ofendyeren 'a alguno a'uzente 'o preśente 'eśtoś taleś śon loś ke propy'a mente śe lyyaman 'eśkarnidoreś ke por 'elyyoś diǧo nu'eśo devinisimo rey David byen aventurado 'el varon ke 'en asyento de 'eśkarnidoreś no śe asento 'i set-[291] ke syerto śon peśtilensy'a de la republika 'i maldizyenteś de śi meśmoś kuando de 'otroś no halyyan ke dezir :
   'I śi 'enlaś taleś burlaś no fu'ere maś la 'intensy'on ke śolo burlar 'i hablar demaśyado por śerle 'el hablar por śi deleytable śin ningun '(y)[o]tro fin malo ni bu'eno 'eśtoś taleś śe lyyaman ǧokareroś ke 'eś 'el 'eśtremo de la puǧa aserka de 'eśta virtud porke 'el virtu'ozo 'en taleś platikaś no 'a de śer la 'intensy'on kuando burlare 'enlaś konversasy'oneś por laś burlaś 'enśi śalvo śolo por la 'utilidad ke śe[ ]śige delyyaś 'a 'el ku'erpo 'i anima 'i repozo de 'el 'entendimyento komo tenemoś diǧo ke 'eśte 'eś 'el fin verdadero :
   'I loś 'ombreś ke no kyeren śer konversableś ni kyeren 'en ninguna manera platikar 'en platikaś deleytableś 'en ningun tyenpo por ningun modo ni laś kyeren 'o'ir 'eśtoś taleś 'eseden 'enla falta aserka 'eśta virtud ke śon loś ke komun mente lyyamamoś foreśtikoś 'i propy'a mente vilyyanoś komo śon algunoś melankonikoś ke deśean abitar 'en lugareś dezyertoś śolitary'oś por hu'ir de la konversasy'on 'umana kośa asaś deśagradable :
   'EŚ 'el medy'o 'entre 'eśtoś doś 'eśtremoś 'el ke 'uzan del loś virtu'ozoś 'enśuś konversasy'oneś kuando konbyene ke 'eś alegrarśe 'i alegrar 'a 'o(ś)[t]roś ke leś 'oyen kon śuś deleytableś platikaś komo konbyene kuando 'i k[u]anto 'i kon kyen konbyene 'i set- ke todo 'eśto 'a de śer ǧuśgado śegun dereǧa razon kon todaś laś śerkonśtansyaś ke konpeten ala virtud 'i 'eśte tal medy'o śe lyyama propy'a kortezi'a 'i deveśe de atentar muǧo 'eneśta virtud por ke aśi komo laś konpliśy'oneś śe ǧuśgan por loś mobimyentoś korporaleś 'eśtiry'oreś konbyene aśaber ke śi 'eś 'el 'ombre muy preśurozo 'en śu 'andar 'i 'en śuś 'otroś mobimyentoś de nota śer de konpliśy'on kolerika 'i śi 'eś pezado 'i perezozo 'en loś taleś mobimyentoś de nota śer de

---

[291] Ps. 1.1.

BOOK OF THE REGIMEN OF LIVING ‹FOL. 99A–99B›

konplisy'on flematika 'i aśi laś 'otraś konplisy'oneś de la meśma manera laś platikaś 'en laś konversasy'oneś denotan 'i manifyeśtan laś vertudeś 'i kondisy'oneś de kada kual bu'enaś 'i malaś por ke 'el ke muǧo hablare alegrando //(y)aloś// ke le}

‹fol. 99b›
{//'[oy]en// kozaś de burlaś 'i fabulaś de poka suśtansy'a 'eśtoś taleś manifyeśtan 'en śuś platikaś śer maś turhaneś ke korteześ 'i por taleś śon tenidoś :
    POR lo kual 'el ke fu'ere virtu'ozo śegun 'eśta virtud 'a de śer 'ombre byen dotrinado 'i prudente para ke 'en śuś platikaś hable kozaś ke a'un ke śean burlando noten de 'elyyaś loś 'oyenteś muǧa dotrina 'i bondad 'i 'utilidad komo śe śu'ele hazer 'en algunaś farsaś feǧaś por 'ombreś śaby'oś 'i prudenteś ke śe śige de 'o'irlaś muǧo probeǧo 'i dotrina de manera ke deśkansa 'el anima del trabaǧo de śu 'eǧersisy'o 'i resibe refrizery'o 'i glory'a de ke 'en 'o'irlo śe deleyten ke 'eśto todo 'eś loable 'i bu'eno syendo kuando konbyene 'i kuanto 'i komo konbyene 'i set- komo avemoś antisipado 'i komo śiknifiko nu'eśo devinisimo re'ey Šᵉlomoh 'en śu 'Eklizyaśteś do dize 'ora para lyorar 'ora para burlar 'ora para 'o'ynar 'ora para bayylar 'i set-²⁹² donde denoto no 'eśtar la maldad ni bondad de la kośa 'en la 'obra 'eśtiry'or ke ni todaś laś 'obraś bu'enaś por śi śon bu'enaś de kontino ni laś malaś śon por śi malaś ke no 'eśta ni konsiśte la maldad ni la bondad de la 'obra śalvo śegun 'enel tyenpo ke śe 'obra konforme 'o diśforme 'a dereǧa razon komo ya 'otraś veześ tenemoś 'eneśte tratado notado ke la virtud konśiśte 'en laś śerkonśtansyaś de la 'obra por donde 'eś byen viśto ke 'el burlar 'i 'el bayylar 'onde konbyene no śolo no 'eś vituperable maś anteś 'eś loable 'en tal manera komo vemoś ke śe glorifikaba delyyo nu'eśo devinisimo re'ey David kuando bayylaba 'i śaltaba delante la arka del firmamyento 'i set-²⁹³ por śer 'a bu'en fin 'i 'en tyenpo 'i lugar ke konveni'a a'un ke 'el a'uto por śi paresyeśe deśautorizado 'eśpesyal para 'un famozisimo re'ey komo 'el dezi'a tener lo por byen śolo por śer 'en śervisy'o del Dyyo 'i deśu śantisima ley 'eś 'el lugar donde konbyene śegun dereǧa razon
    'I para ke meǧor śe konprenda la deśkrisy'on de 'eśta virtud nombraremoś 'en muy breve laś propyedadeś delyya ke por 'el konosimyento delyyaś podra meǧor 'obrar 'i 'uzar 'el virtu'ozo 'eś la primera ke śe'a 'el ke 'obrare śegun 'eśta virtud libre de visy'oś 'i no śe'a sudito al 'apetito por ke pu'eda libre mente hablar lo ke konbyene 'i no venga 'a hablar lo ke no konbyene por reśpekto de algun 'otro akyen 'el śe'a sudito ke syendo 'el libre hablara konforme 'a dereǧa razon śin ningun reselo :

---

²⁹² Eccles. 3.4.
²⁹³ 2 Sam. 6.14, 16.

Book of the Regimen of Living ‹fol. 99b–100a›

'EŚ la śegunda ke śe'a grasy'ozo por ke śe'a agradable 'i deleytable aloś ke 'oyeren para lo kual 'eś meneśter ke 'ordene śuś platikaś por 'el meǧor 'eśtilo ke posible fu'ere para śer 'a todoś agradable ke ni śe'a tan proliǧo ke lo tengan por 'inportuno ni tan korto ke no śe'a 'entendido 'i diga lo ke kiǧere lo maś //'e(n)[l]okente// mente ke 'el pudyere 'i śupyere para ke maś agradable śe'a aloś ke kon 'el konversaren :}

‹fol. 100a›
{K {RMK: anthropomorphic bird figures, or flowers, bracket the last lines of Part Two and the first lines of Part Three.}

'EŚ la tersera ke śe'a de śuyo 'obedyente 'a guardar 'i konservar todoś loś presebtoś devinoś śin ke ayya nesesidad de śer amoneśtado 'enelyyo ke de 'eśta manera śera aplazible 'a loś bu'enoś 'i śeran śuś palabraś muy 'o'idaś por la a'utoridad de śu preśona śin reselo de śer reprehendido 'i śobre todo deve de ad(y)vertir 'i atentar de no 'ofender 'a nadi ke no '[o]fendyendo 'eś atodoś deleytable 'i trae aśi meśmo grandisima 'utilidad porke 'el repozo 'eś kośa muy nesesary'a para la vida 'umana aśi komo 'el śu'enyo 'i loś 'otroś mobimyentoś nesesary'oś komo ya tenemoś diǧo :

POR lo kual śe konose 'ividente mente śer 'una de laś grandeś mersedeś ke 'el Dyyo 'uzo kon śu pu'eblo Yiśra'el darleś 'el di'a de la folgansa ke śe alegro kon 'el nu'eśtro devinisimo profeta Mośeh ᶜʰh [may he rest in peace] por laś 'inmenśaś 'utilidadeś ke del śe śigen para deśkanso 'i refrizery'o de 'el ku'erpo 'i de la alma por lo kual diǧeron nu'eśoś śaby'oś ke todoś loś diaś de nu'eśaś fyeśtaś śe deven de partir la mitad de 'el di'a para 'el Dyyo ke 'eś 'eśpekular 'enlaś kozaś devinaś 'i medyo para 'el 'ombre por deśkanso de loś 'eśturmentoś korporaleś 'i potensyaś animaleś 'i set-[294] 'i 'eśto lo deve pasar 'en konversasy'on konbenible por la vi'a ke relatado avemoś 'i a'un ke 'eneśta virtud tanbyen śe pudyera maś alargar baśta lo diǧo para venir 'en 'entero konosimyento de 'elyya komo de todaś laś pasadaś

---

[294] Pesahim 68b, Betzah 15b.

PARTIDA TERSERA

KAPITULO PRIMERO

PARA loke konbyene śaber aserka dela ǧuśtisy'a 'undesima 'enel numero delaś vertudeś śeri'a meneśter 'otro tratado porśi ke podri'a byen śer tan largo komo todo lo diǧo porke 'eśta śublimadisima virtud konprende todaś laś vertudeś ke 'eś 'una de laś kuatro kardinaleś komo ya 'otra veś avemoś deklarado 'i alyende de 'eśto 'eś la virtud maś nesesary'a para la suśtentasy'on dela republika 'i pasifikasy'on de 'elyya porke śin 'elyya nośe pu'ede bivir ni ningun prinsipe pu'ede reǧir ni}

‹fol. 100b›
{HELEK G PEREK ' [PART THREE CHAPTER ONE]
suśtentar śu pu'eblo ni śuś suditoś śin 'elyya komo diǧo nu'eśo śapyentisimo re'ey Š^{e}lomoh re'ey kon ǧuśtisy'a suśtentara tyera 'i set-[1] maś komo śean laś propyedadeś 'i partikularidadeś deśta altisima virtud tan 'eśpasifikadaś 'en nu'eśa śantisima le'ey 'i tan aklaradaś por nu'eśoś śaby'oś 'en nu'eśo Ṭalmud no konbyene ke digamoś aki maś ke deklarar śu 'esensy'a komo konbyene 'a virtud moral aśi komo avemoś heǧo 'en laś 'otraś vertudeś 'enel maś breve 'eśtilo ke posible śera para konoser maś 'ividente mente 'el grado de śu 'eselensy'a :

'I lo ke 'eś nesesary'o śaber para 'eśto śon treś kozaś la primera 'eś komo matery'a deśta virtud konvyene aśaber aserka de ke 'obraś śe dize aver ǧuśtisy'a 'o 'inǧuśtisy'a por ke no aserka de todaś laś 'obraś 'umanaś śe dira propy'a mente ǧuśtisy'a 'o 'inǧuśtisy'a ke aserka laś 'obraś de la liberalidad 'i de śuś 'eśtremoś 'o de kual kyer 'otra virtud śemeǧante no śe dira propy'a mente ǧuśtisy'a 'o 'inǧuśtisy'a komo 'eś manifyeśto :

---

[1] Prov. 29.4.

Book of the Regimen of Living ‹fol. 100b–101a›

LA śegunda 'eś komo forma deśta virtud lo kual 'eś śaber komo śe konsidra la ǧuśtisya śer medy'o 'i komo konśiśte 'enel medy'o
'I la tersera 'eś śaber ǧunto kon 'eśto deke 'eśtremoś śe dize la ǧuśtisy'a 'o 'el ǧuśto śer medy'o por ke ala verdad no śe pu'ede dezir aserka de 'eśta virtud ke śe'a medy'o 'entre puǧa 'i falta komo 'en laś 'otraś vertudeś por ke todoś śuś 'eśtremoś 'eś śin ǧuśtisy'a pu'eś no abyendo doś 'eśtremoś diferenteś de puǧa 'i falta parese no poder konsidrarśe ni lyyamarśe la tal virtud medy'o :
'I anteś ke digamoś 'eśto 'eś byen ke śepaś la difinsy'on de ǧuśtisy'a por ke la 'esensy'a de la kośa śe śabe por śu difinsy'on por donde deveś de śaber ke śegun la difine 'el filosofo 'enel primer kapitulo del kinto de la 'etika la ǧuśtisy'a 'eś 'un abito por 'el kual 'el ǧuśto haze 'obraś de ǧuśtisy'a 'i kon 'el 'obra ǧuśtisy'a 'i kyere ǧuśtisy'a[2] ke śon treś kozaś deśtintaś ke ś[e śi]gen de 'eśta virtud 'enel ǧuśto 'i no te 'enganyeś 'eneśta difinisy'on ke śe'a aśi 'en la ǧuśtisy'a devina a'un ke veaś 'en nu'eśa śantisima le'ey 'i śakra 'eśkritura ke 'entitula al Dyyo glory'ośo 'en titulo de ǧuśto ke 'enel no śe 'entyende la ǧuśtisy'a deśta manera por ke 'enel no 'eś produzido 'el abito por laś 'obraś de ǧuśtisy'a por ke 'el 'i la ǧuśtisy'a todo 'eś 'una meśma kośa ke no 'eś a'umentada śobre śu 'esensy'a ni 'eś aśidente komo 'en noś 'el Dyyo noś guarde de tal 'eror por lo kual diǧo nu'eśo devinisimo re'ey David ke ǧuśto H‹a-Šem› ǧuśtedadeś ama der[e]ǧo veran śuś faseś 'i set-[3] 'i atenta byen 'i pondera 'el diǧo ke no diǧo ǧuśto H‹a-Šem› ke ǧuśtedadeś ama śalvo ke ǧuśto H‹a-Šem› ǧuśtedadeś ama 'i set- keryendo śiknifikar ke por śer 'el ǧuśto por 'eśo ama la ǧuśtedad 'i no śe pu'ede dezir 'enel komo 'en noś ke por amar la ǧuśtedad}

‹fol. 101a›
{K' śe śige śer ǧuśto 'i no diǧo dereǧedad veran śuś faseś śalvo dereǧo veran 'i set- keryendo śiknifikar ke kon śolo ver śuś faseś la kośa keda la tal koza dereǧa 'i 'eś komo ke diǧeśe dereǧo 'eś vyendolo śuś faseś por ke kon śolo ver 'el Dyyo śantisimo la kośa keda dereǧa komo avemoś diǧo
PERO la ǧuśtisy'a 'umana komo śe'a kalidad asidental ke śe 'enoba 'i śe haze 'enel 'ombre abito por 'el kośtumbre de laś 'obraś de ǧuśtisy'a konsidranśe 'enel diǧo abito laś treś kozaś diǧaś ke 'eś lo primero 'entitularśe 'el ǧuśto 'enel tal abito para 'eśtar diśpu'eśto 'a 'obrar por 'el toda 'obra de ǧuśtisy'a kuando le vinyere 'a kaśo lo śe- gundo 'eś ke kon 'el tal abito 'efektuan loś ǧuśtoś laś 'obraś de ǧuśtisy'a ke 'eś la 'obra 'estiry'or lo //(ǧ)[t]ersero// 'eś ke kon 'el diǧo abito deśean 'i 'enveluntan

---

[2] Aristotle, *NE* V.i.3 (1129a 8–10).
[3] Ps. 11.7.

Book of the Regimen of Living ‹fol. 101a–101b›

kontinuar 'a hazer laś 'obraś de ǵuśtisy'a 'i loś meśmoś treś śe konsidran 'en la 'inǵuśtisy'a ke 'el 'inǵuśto śera 'el ke tubyere 'el abito del visy'o 'eneśta virtud ke por 'el tal abito śe lyyamara 'inǵuśto 'en potensy'a 'i fara 'inǵuśtisy'a 'en puro a'uto ke 'eś la śegunda 'i deśeara 'i apetesera la śinǵuśtisy'a ke 'eś la tersera :

'I śiknifikando 'eśtaś treś diǵo nu'eśtro prinsipe David andan preniśmo 'i 'obran ǵuśtisy'a 'i hablan verdad 'en śu korason 'i set-[4] ke śiknifikando la primera dize andan preniśmo keryendo dezir ke a'un 'enel tyenpo ke no 'obra 'el a'uto 'eśtiry'or anda preniśma 'i 'entera mente diśpu'eśto para 'obrar todo tyenpo ke śe 'ofresyere 'i por 'eśo diǵo andan preniśmo keryendo dezir ke anda 'enel kamino de la vida śin parar kontinu'a mente preniśmo 'i perfekto kon 'el abito deśta sublimadisima virtud 'i śiknifikando la śegunda ke 'eś la 'obra 'eśt[i]ry'or diǵo 'i 'obran ǵuśtiśy'a ke 'eś la 'obra 'eśtiry'or 'i śiknifikando la tersera ke 'eś la perfekta voluntad diǵo 'i hablan verdad 'en śu korason 'i śiknifikando laś meśmaś treś 'en la śinǵuśtisy'a diǵo no meśklo kon śu lengu'a no fizo aśu konpanyero mal 'i repudyo no lyebo por śu śerkano 'i set-[5] śiknifikando la primera diǵo no meśklo kon śu lengu'a ke 'eś la habla 'inǵuśta 'i śiknifikando la śegunda diǵo no fizo mal aśu konpanyero ke 'eś 'en la 'obra 'eśt[i]ry'or komo tenemoś diǵo 'i śiknifikando la privasy'on de la tersera partida ke 'eś 'en la korupsy'on de la voluntad diǵo repudy'o no lyebo por śu śerkano ke 'eśte termino de śerkano śegun la diribasy'on 'en ke lo toman nu'eśoś śaby'oś śe dize por 'el 'entendimyento 'o por la voluntad komo lo toman algunoś de nu'eśoś glozadoreś donde de kual kyer modo de loś doś 'eśta manifyeśta la 'intensy'on konforme 'a lo ke tenemoś diǵo :

'I depu'eś de 'eśto śabido para 'entender la primera kośa de laś treś ke diǵimoś ke 'eś nesesary'o śaber aserka deśta devinisima [CW. virtud]}

‹fol. 101b›

{virtud ke 'eś komo matery'a delyya komo diǵimoś aś de śaber ke 'un varon śapyentisimo[6] reparty'o laś 'obraś aserka de laś kualeś 'eś la ǵuśtisy'a śegun la repartisy'on de loś presebtoś ke loś 'ombreś deven guardar para alkansar 'el śumo grado de la byen aventuransa loś kualeś presebtoś dize dividirśe 'en treś 'eśpesyaś diferenteś :

LA primera 'eś loś presebtoś ke la naturaleza 'obliga a'el 'ombre 'a averloś de guardar 'i por 'eśta kauśa loś lyyama presebtoś naturaleś la kual 'eśpesy'a divide 'el 'en seyś parteś

---

[4] Ps. 15.2.
[5] Ps. 15.3.
[6] Cicero, *De Finibus* V.12.36; cf. *De Officiis* II.xi.38, *De Inventione* II.160.

Book of the Regimen of Living ‹fol. 101b–102a›

'EŚ la primera 'el 'onor ke śe deve al Dyyo glory'ozo ke la naturaleza 'obliga dar 'onor akyen noś kre'o 'i noś suśtenta kontinu'a mente kon śu partikular probidensy'a por lo kual nu'eśa śantisima ley 'i todoś nu'eśoś profetaś noś akavidan ke demoś 'onor al Dyyo alto la kual partida lyyama 'el religy'on

'EŚ la śegunda la 'onor 'i revenensy'a ke natural mente śe deve aloś padreś 'i alaś madreś donde noś akabida nu'eśa śantisima ley 'onra atu padre 'i atu madre 'i set-[7] 'i 'enelyya śe konprende 'el 'amor natural del padre aloś hiğoś la kual 'en 'onibersal lyyama 'el pyadad :

'EŚ la tersera la 'onor ke natural mente śe deve de dar aloś prinsipeś 'i grandeś śenyyoreś por 'el meresimyento de śuś 'eśtadoś la kual partida lyyama 'el 'obśervans[y']a 'o revenensy'a :

'EŚ la kuarta 'el 'onor ke natural mente deve de dar kual kyera aśu proğimo konforme aśu meresimyento la kual lyyama 'el agrad'[e]simyento :

'EŚ la kinta la verdad ke śe deve de 'uzar kon todoś loś 'ombreś 'en todaś laś kośaś ke 'el 'ombre śegun ley de naturaleza deve de 'uzar verdad 'en śuś negosy'oś por ke la falsi'a 'eś kontra naturaleza de adonde śe ve'e loś ninyoś hablar verdad natural mente 'i no śaber mentir hata ke kon la 'edad deprenden akel mal kośtumbre kontra śu naturaleza ke śe kryaron kon 'elyya :

'EŚ la se[ś]ta defender laś 'inğuryaś heğaś kontra razon por 'entresisy'on de la vengansa komo konbyene ke la naturaleza 'ensita a'el 'ombre a'elyya 'i atodaś 'eśtaś seyś partidaś de 'obraś lyyama ğuśtisy'a natural por ke śon kośaś ke la ley de naturaleza laś 'obliga :

LA śegunda 'eśpeśy'a dize ke 'eś loś preśebtoś ke śe deven hazer por 'el bu'en kośtumbre 'i 'eśta śe divide 'en treś partidaś :

'EŚ la primera la ğuśtisy'a ke śe 'uza aserka del trato :

'EŚ la ś[e]gunda la ğuśtisy'a ke śe 'uza śegun 'igualdad 'enlaś repartisy'oneś ke śe hazen śegun porporsy'on 'EŚ la tersera la ğuśtisy'a ke śe haze por 'entresisy'on del ğu'ez ke 'eliğen loś ke tyene diferensy'a 'entreśi 'el kual śe lyyama ğu'ez arbito ke todaś}

‹fol. 102a›
{KB
'eśtaś treś śon pura ğuśtisy'a :

LA tersera 'eśpesy'a dize śer la ğuśtisy'a legal la kual 'eś guardar 'i konservar la ley 'en kuanto manda 'i 'ordena 'i laś partidaś deśta no reparty'o por ke no ayy nesesidad delyyo ke śegun fu'ere la ley aśi śe deve guardar aśu ver :

---

[7] Exod. 20.12.

Book of the Regimen of Living ⟨fol. 102a⟩

DE adonde 'eś muy manifyeśta la 'ekselensy'a de nu'eśt[r]a śantisima ley devina ke 'enelyya 'eśtan todaś 'eśtaś 'eśpesyaś kon todaś śuś departisy'oneś 'i 'infinitaś maś 'en śumo grado de perfeksy'on :

ARISTOTEL 'en[e]l kinto de la 'etika[8] reparte laś 'obraś 'en laś kualeś konsiśte 'eśta virtud de la ğuśtisy'a 'en 'otro modo ke dize repartirśe 'en treś 'eśpesyaś diferenteś algo de 'eśtaś 'i maś 'onibersaleś

LA primera de laś kualeś lyyama ğuśtisy'a legal ke 'eś la ğuśtisy'a tomada 'en 'onibersal 'en todo lo ke laś le'eyś 'ordenan la kual konprende todaś laś vertudeś

LA śegunda 'eś maś partikular ke 'eś ğuśtisy'a śegun 'igualdad la kual 'eś aserka loś byeneś tenporaleś 'en repartir 'a kada 'uno lo ke le konbyene aserka de laś 'onraś 'i de la hazyenda 'i de la śanidad[9] 'i diześe tanbyen aserka de la deleytasy'on 'en la ganansy'a ke 'eś razon de moderarśe 'enelyya komo konbyene de bağo de la kual 'eśta no kobdisyar 'el 'ombre lo ke no 'eś śuyo komo noś akabido nu'eśa śantisima ley no kobdisyeś kaza de tu konpanyero 'i set-[10] ke 'en todaś 'eśtaś kozaś diğaś deve de dar 'el ke tal repartyere 'a kada 'uno lo ke le konbyene śegun ğuśtisy'a 'i lyamaśe ğuśtisy'a diśtribu'itiba 'i 'eś śu kontrary'o 'el deś'igual konbyene aśaber ke no reparte śegun 'igualdad komo konbyene 'i set-

'EŚ la tersera aserka de laś repartisy'oneś 'i kontratoś ke konpeten de śi 'a 'otro partikular 'i lyyamaśe ğuśtisy'a kumutatiba la kual konprende doś parteś por ke loś kontratoś śe dividen 'en doś partidaś diferenteś ke ayy 'unoś veluntory'ozoś ke 'el prinsipy'o delyoś 'eś por voluntad 'i konkordy'a 'i ayy algunoś śin voluntad 'i 'en todoś doś konsiśte 'eśta 'eśpeśy'a tersera de ğuśtisy'a ke 'eś 'uzar 'en 'elyoś komo konbyene 'eś la primera partida komo 'el merkar 'i vender 'i 'el baratar 'i 'el śalir fyansa 'i 'el depozito 'i 'el 'enpreśtimo 'i 'otroś śimileś ke śe lyyaman voluntory'ozoś por ke 'el prinsipy'o delyoś fu'e por voluntad[11] 'i depu'eś al fin nasen divizy'oneś 'i diferensyaś 'en 'elyyoś

'I la śegunda partida 'eś algunaś partikularidadeś ke śe dizen śin voluntad por śer 'el prinsipy'o delyyaś '[o]k[u]lta mente komo 'eś 'el robo 'i 'el adultery'o heğo śin tener notisy'a delyyo 'el patron 'o 'el 'ofendido 'i 'el śonbair 'el 'eśklabo śin lisensy'a de śu patron 'i 'el dar teśtimony'o falso 'en a'uzensy'a 'o maldezir 'o 'otraś muğaś śemeğanteś [CW. 'i]}

---

[8] Aristotle, *NE* V.1.15 (1129b 30), V.3.4–10 (1131a 15–1131b 10), V.4.1–8 (1131b 25–1132a 30).

[9] Aristotle, *NE* V.ii.12 (1130b 30–31).

[10] Exod. 20.17.

[11] Aristotle, *NE* V.ii.13 (1131a 4–6).

BOOK OF THE REGIMEN OF LIVING ‹FOL. 102B›

‹fol. 102b›
{'i algunaś śe dizen śer śin voluntad por śer 'el prinsipy'o delyyaś kontra voluntad 'i por fu'ersa komo 'el ke 'eś ferido 'o preśo de śu 'enemigo 'i śufre por fu'ersa 'o 'el ke 'eś robado aśuś 'oǧoś 'o 'el ke 'eś 'infamado 'en śu meśma preśensy'a śin poder reǧiśtir[12] 'i de 'eśta manera 'eś todo ǧenero de 'obra ke le hazen hazer 'o atorgar por fu'ersa 'i vy'olensy'a ke todaś 'eśtaś śe lyyaman śin voluntad a'un ke konsyenta 'el 'ombre enelyaś pu'eś konsye(y)nte kontra śu voluntad

'I por ke 'eśtoś ǧeneroś todoś de ǧuśtisy'a 'eśtan maś 'eśpasifikada mente deklaradoś 'en nu'eśo Talmud muy por 'eśtenso 'i todo śiknifikado 'en nu'eśa śantisima l[e]'ey de la kual 'eś todo śakado por tanto no alargo 'eneśta partida maś ke darte 'a 'entender ke todaś kuantaś 'eśpesyaś de ǧuśtisy'a puzyeron todoś loś śaby'oś antigoś 'en todaś śuś repartisy'oneś 'eśtan konklu'idaś 'en nu'eśa śantisima le'ey de manera ke todoś loś presebtoś ke nu'eśa śantisima le'ey manda hazer 'i todaś laś 'obraś ke noś manda 'obrar śon laś ke 'enelyyaś konśiśte 'el nombre de ǧuśtisy'a komo diǧo nu'eśo devinisimo rey David boka de ǧuśto habla śensy'a 'i śu lengu'a hablara ǧuśtisy'a ley de śu Dyyo 'en śu korason no reśvalara śuś pasadaś[13] śiknifikando kuanto 'eśta śublimadisima virtud konprende todaś laś vertudeś komo virtud kardinal komo tenemoś diǧo por lo kual 'eśta konǧunta kon la prudensy'a ke 'en muǧaś parteś śe denota kon termino de sensy'a komo tengo byen deklarado 'enel seśto de la 'etika[14] por tanto diǧo ke la boka del ǧuśto habla śensy'a keryendo dezir ke kuando 'el ǧuśto habla ǧuśtisy'a 'eś hablar śensy'a pu'eś 'eś todo hablado por prudensy'a 'i 'eśo 'eś lo ke deklara maś dizyendo 'i śu lengu'a habla ǧuśtisy'a no ke kyera dezir ke hable doś kośaś diferenteś śalvo komo ke diǧeśe ke hablando śu lengu'a ǧuśtisy'a 'en akelyya meśma habla repreśenta śu boka sensy'a 'i mirando byen la diribasy'on deśtoś doś terminoś de hablar diferenteś śegun nu'eśa ley śanta 'el primero denota la habla 'intiry'or 'i 'el śegundo la 'eśtiry'or de adonde 'eśta byen //viś(ǧ)[t]o// lo ke tenemoś(v) diǧo ke kiǧo dezir ke a'un kelaś palabraś ke reprezenta la lengu'a 'eśtiry'oreś śean ǧuśtisy'a vyenen 'enderesadaś del 'entendimyento de manera ke 'en akelyyaś meśmaś palabraś śe reprezenta la sensy'a 'intiry'or 'i 'en konkluzy'on dize lo ke tenemoś diǧo ke toda la perfeksy'on de laś 'obraś deśta virtud nase 'enel ǧuśto por tener la nu'eśa devinisima le'ey 'ensu korason ke 'eśto 'eś lo ke le haze reǧir todaś laś 'obraś śegun dereǧa razon śin reśbalar śuś pasadaś 'en kuanto andubyere de manera ke por 'el kośtumbre del trabaǧar 'enelyya 'eśte araygada 'enel korason ke kon 'eśto nunka pu'ede śer menoś

---

[12] Aristotle, *NE* V.ii.13 (1131a 6–10).
[13] Ps. 37.30–31.
[14] Cf. Aristotle, *NE* VI.3.2–4 (1139b 19–36).

BOOK OF THE REGIMEN OF LIVING ‹FOL. 102B–103A›

śalbo ke hable ǧuśtisy'a 'i sensy'a pu'eś tyene 'enel korason la le'ey ke no le deǧa treśbaryar ni reśbalar komo tenemoś diǧo [CW. 'i komo]}

‹fol. 103a›
{KG ḤELEK G PEREK B [PART THREE CHAPTER TWO]
'i komo śe'a 'eśto verdad 'i noś 'otroś tenemoś nu'eśa śantisima ley 'i nu'eśo Ṭalmud lyeno de laś 'obraś 'i partikularidadeś deśta virtud no konbyene ke deklaremoś maś 'en lo ke 'eś tomado por matery'a delyya ke śon laś 'obraś aserka de laś kualeś śe konsidra komo tenemoś diǧo :

KAPITULO ŚEGUNDO

'I para loke konbyene śaber aserka deloke śe toma komo forma de 'eśta virtud ke 'eś (y)[ ]śaber komo śe konsidra 'eśta virtud śer medy'o 'o komo konsiśte 'enel medyyo konforme alaś 'otraś vertudeś diremoś 'en breve lo ke abaśtara por konprender śu de(y)śkrisy'on konforme ala repartisy'on de Aristoteleś ke reparty'o la ǧuśtisy'a 'enlaś treś partidaś diǧaś ke śon legal 'eśtribu'itiba 'i ('i)kumutatiba komo avemoś deklarado[15] :
'I 'enla diśtribu'itiba 'eś byen viśto ke pu'eś 'eś 'una 'igualdad 'enlaś repartisy'oneś 'i toda 'igualdad 'eś medyo 'entre doś 'eśtremoś deś'igualeś[16] 'eś viśto śer 'eśta medy'o 'i 'eśto byen konsidrado aś de śaber ke komo 'eśtaś taleś repartisy'oneś śean aserka del premy'o ke śeda 'a kada 'uno de loś 'endividoś 'enla republika śegun śu kalidad 'i meresimyento repartidoś śegun porporsy'on ǧe'ometrika ke 'eś tener porporsy'on la kośa ke śeda 'a 'uno kon la ke śeda 'a 'otro komo la porporsy'on ke ayy de 'uno 'a 'otro de loś resebidoreś[17] 'i no śegun porporsy'on aridmetika komo tengo byen deklarado 'enel komento 'oktabo del kinto de la 'etika[18] 'eś viśto ke 'el dar 'a 'uno 'en laś taleś repartisy'oneś maś de loke konbyene por la tal porporsy'on konforme aśu meresimyento 'eś puǧa 'i darle manko de lo ke le konbyene konforme 'a śu meresimyento 'eś falta de manera ke repartyendo 'a kada 'uno loke le konvyene konforme 'a śu meresimyento śegun la porporsy'on diǧa 'eś 'el medy'o 'i 'eśta śe

---

[15] For these three classes of Justice in Aristotle's *NE*, see: Legal, V.vii (1134b 19–1135a 15); Distributive, V.ii.12 (1130b 30–1131a 2) and V.iii (1131a 10–1131b 24); and Corrective, V.ii.13 (1131a 3–9) and V.iv and v (1131b 25–1134a 16). Cf. Aristotle, *NE* V.1.15 (1129b 30), V.3.4–10 (1131a 15–1131b 10), V.4.1–8 (1131b 25–1132a 30).

[16] Aristotle, *NE* V.iii.3 (1131a 1–15).

[17] Aristotle, *NE* V.iii.6 (1131a 20–25), 8–13 (1131a 30–1131b 15).

[18] The reference is to *Pne Mośe*.

Book of the Regimen of Living ‹fol. 103a–103b›

lyyama ǧuśtisy'a 'eśtribu'itiba 'i de 'eśta manera śe konsidra śer virtud ke 'eś śer medy'o 'entre puǧa 'i falta dando 'a kada 'uno lo ke konbyene konforme aśu 'obra 'i meresimyento de adonde diǧo nu'eśo devinisimo rey David ke 'eśte modo de repartisy'on repartido por nu'eśo Dyyo glory'ozo 'eś mersed 'i no ǧuśtisy'a pu'eśto ke śe'a repa[r]tisy'on komo la repartisy'on śegun ǧuśtisy'a por śer ke laś repartisy'oneś ke aki śe hazen por la vi'a diǧa śon por 'obligasy'on de dar 'el premyyo por 'el trabaǧo ke no śe haze de balde 'i la ke 'el Dyyo haze no ayy 'enelyyoś 'obligasy'on ninguna por lo kual dize 'i ati H‹a-Šem› mersed kuando pagaś akada 'uno por śu 'obra 'i set-[19] 'eśta man[i]fyeśto śin maś glośa kerer dezir ke 'el pagar 'a kada 'uno śegun śu 'obra 'i tr[a]baǧo [CW. por la]}

‹fol. 103b›
{por la porporsy'on ke konbyene ke aka 'entre noś 'eś ǧuśtisy'a 'en śu reśpekto 'eś pura mersed 'i set- :

'I 'enla ǧuśtisy'a kumutatiba ke 'eś maś partikular ke la diśtribu'itiba 'eśta tanbyen viśto por la meśma 'orden 'i la diferensy'a 'entre laś doś 'eś ke la repartisy'on 'en la diśtribu'itiba 'eś śegun porporsy'on ǧe'ometrika ke 'eś mirar la diferensy'a del m[e]resimyento de kyen resibe aśi komo la diferensy'a de la kośa ke śe leś[ ]da komo tenemoś diǧo

'I la repartisy'on śegun la ǧuśtisy'a kumutatiba 'eś porporsy'on aridmetika ke no śe konśidra la diferensy'a de loś ke resiben la tal ǧuśtisy'a ke todoś śon 'igualeś 'enelyya 'el riko komo 'el pobre 'i 'el malo komo 'el bu'eno 'i no śe 'entyende 'eśta tal ǧuśtisy'a śalvo 'en lo ke śe da ke śe'a 'igual la perdida kon la gansansy'a tanto laś kozaś ke śuś prinsipy'oś śon heǧoś por voluntad komo 'eś 'enel trato 'i 'en laś tru'ekaś 'i 'en śuś 'enganyyoś 'i 'otroś śimileś komo laś kośaś ke 'el prinsipy'o de 'elyyaś fu'eśen śin voluntad 'i kontra voluntad komo loś roboś 'i 'otraś śemeǧanteś de manera ke la ǧuśtisy'a kumutatiba 'eś 'un medy'o 'entre 'el danyyo 'i 'el probeǧo ke śe śige 'entre taleś kontratoś 'i diferensyaś 'entre 'uno 'a 'otro 'i 'eś la puǧa aserka 'eśto dar a'uno maś del probeǧo ke le konbyene 'o maś del danyyo ke le konbyene 'i la falta dar a'uno menoś del probeǧo ke le konbyene 'o menoś del danyyo ke le konbyene dar 'i por ke 'el 'ombre p(+)or la kobdisy'a ke le haze kerer perkurar de puǧar 'en la gansansy'a 'i diminu'ir 'enel danyyo 'i perdida por lo kual no śe ǧuśtefika 'el aśi meśmo mando 'el Dyyo 'en nu'eśa śantisima ley ke śe fizyeśen ǧu'eześ para ke ǧuśgaśen la verdad 'i 'igualasen 'eśtaś diferensyaś ke no śe 'uze ninguno deśtoś doś 'eśtremoś 'i akabida aloś taleś ǧu'eześ ke no katen kara de 'ombre 'i no hagan diferensy'a de pekeny'o 'a grande ni de riko 'a pobre por ke aserka de 'eśta parte de

---

[19] Ps. 62.13.

Book of the Regimen of Living ⟨fol. 103b–104a⟩

ǧuśtisy'a no śe konsidra la kalidad de kyen resibe la tal ǧuśtisy'a komo tenemoś diǧo por lo kual dize no konosadeś faseś 'enel ǧu'izy'o komo 'el pekeny'o komo 'el grande 'o'yredeś 'i set-[20] ke 'en dezir ke no konośkan faseś de nota ke śe deven de deśkonoser de todoś 'i deśnudarśe de todo modo de 'ody'o 'o amiśtad 'i afiksy'on komo ke nunka loś 'ubyeśe viśto ni śupyeśe 'entre 'elyyoś ninguna diferensy'a 'en śuś kalidadeś de śer 'uno paryente 'o leǧano amigo 'o 'enemigo 'i 'en dezir komo 'el pekeny'o komo 'el grande 'oigan kyeren dezir ke tanto al riko ke śe lyyama grande komo al pobre 'oigan ke todoś śon para 'eśto 'igualeś 'i 'en dezir non temadeś de varon[21] śiknifikaron ke no miren reśpekto 'a śer 'uno fu'erte 'i poderozo para hazerle danyyo al ǧu'ez śi no ǧuśgare por śu parte 'i 'otro flako 'i da la}

⟨fol. 104a⟩
{KD
razon 'en todo la kual 'eś por śer la ǧuśtisy'a devina produzida del Dyyo glory'ozo ke no guarda reśpekto ninguno kon 'el de manera ke 'en śu reśpekto todoś śon 'igualeś 'i 'a 'eśta kauśa śe lyyaman loś ǧu'eześ 'en nu'eśa lengu'a śantisima 'enel meśmo nombre de 'Elodim[22] ke 'entitulamoś al Dyyo alto por ke kuando ǧuśgan la tal ǧuśtisy'a komo 'eś razon de ǧuśgar śe pu'ede dezir ke śon 'en akelyya tal ǧuśtisy'a komo 'el Dyyo por lo kual diǧeron nu'eśtroś śaby'oś śiknifikando 'eśto ke todo 'el ke ǧuśga ǧu'izy'o de verdad aśu verdad śe haze konpanyero al Dyyo bendito 'i set-[23] keryendo dezir ke pu'eś 'el Dyyo glory'ozo no mira reśpekto 'en la 'igualdad diśtribu'itiba maś ke la pura verdad por la verdad 'enśi lu'ego 'el ke de 'el meśmo modo ǧuśgare ke 'eś ǧuśgar la verdad por la verdad 'enśi 'i no por 'otro ningun reśpekto 'eśte tal 'eś 'el ke śe pu'ede dezir ke 'imita 'eneśto 'a 'el Dyyo porke no baśta para imitar al Dyyo ǧuśgar la verdad śi la ǧuśga por reśpekto de temer 'o 'otra kauśa kual kyera śi no la ǧuśga por la verdad 'enśi 'i por 'eśto diǧeron 'el ke ǧuśga ǧu'izy'o de verdad aśu verdad ke 'eś komo ke diǧeśe ke ǧuśga la verdad por la meśma verdad 'i no por 'otro ningun reśpekto :
'I laś partikularidadeś 'enke konsiśte 'eśta parte de ǧuśtisy'a 'i 'el modo de la 'igualdad 'enelyyaś 'eśta byen diǧo 'en nu'eśa śantisima le'ey 'i muy 'eśpasifikada mente deklarado 'en nu'eśo Talmud :

---

[20] Deut. 1.17, Sanhedrin 7b.

[21] Deut. 1.17.

[22] Cf. Maimonides, *Guide*, II.6, trans. Pines, 261; cf. I.2, trans. Pines, 23–25. Note the euphemistic spelling of the Name.

[23] Shabbat 10a, Rashi Exodus 18.13.

Book of the Regimen of Living ‹fol. 104a–104b›

'I 'el śenyyor Rabbenu Mošeh 'ensu famozišimo libro 'enla tersera partida del deklara byen laś razoneś 'en 'onibersal aserka de loś danyyoś ke hazen loś 'endividoś 'unoś 'a 'otroś 'i 'enel modo de laś penaś 'i reśtitu'isy'oneś ke manda nu'eśtra śantisima ley hazer[24] lo kual podraś por alyi byen 'entender ke no kiğe ke śupyeraś por lo diğo śalvo komo śe konsidra 'eśta śegunda 'eśpesy'a de ğuśtisy'a śer virtud 'i medyyo 'entre puğa 'i falta ke 'eś komo forma para konoser 'i konprender byen śu deśkrisy'on :

'I śolo 'eśto 'eś byen ke śepaś porke no kedeś //'eśkrupulo[zo]// 'enelyyo porke kon razon dubdaraś ke syendo verdad ke aserka de 'eśta parte de ğuśtisy'a ke 'eś la ğuśtisy'a kumutatiba no śe konsidra la kalidad ni meresimyento ni sofisensy'a de laś preśonaś śalvo la kalidad de loke śeda 'i toma porke dizen nu'eśoś śaby'oś ke lo ke diğo nu'eśa ley ke śi 'uno firyere 'a 'otro 'i le śakare 'un 'oğo ke le saken 'otro 'i set-[25] kyere dezir ke page la vali'a de 'el 'oğo[26] de adonde pareśe ke no śeda la pena 'igual 'a 'el danyyo ke śegun 'eśta 'eśpesy'a de ğuśtisy'a debri'a śer 'igual por lo kual śe afirmaron loś pitagorikoś antigoś[27] ke avi'a de śer aśi ke le śakaśen 'el propy'o 'oğo 'el ke lo śakaśe aśu konpanyero maś komo la tal 'opiny'on fu'e [CW. derokada]}

‹fol. 104b›
{derokada de todoś por muğoś 'inkonbenyenteś ke tan 'eśpasifikada mente deklararon nu'eśoś śaby'oś 'en nu'eśo Ṭalmud 'i 'el śenyyor Rabbi 'Abraham Ibn ʿEzra' 'en śu glośa ke hizo 'en nu'eśa śantisima ley[28] muğoś maś por donde 'obliga śer la moneda la ke 'iguala laś penaś ke śi śe dyeśe myembro por myembro śerian muy deś'igualeś por laś meśmaś razoneś keda muy aśolvida la dubda por ke ala verdad śi 'a 'uno ke śako 'el 'oğo 'a 'otro 'i kedo bibo le śakaśen 'el śuyo 'i vinyeśe 'a morir por la diferensy'a del tyenpo 'o diferensy'a de la diśpozisy'on del śuğebto śe halyy[a]ri'a śer maś la pena ke le dyeron ke 'el danyyo ke fizo 'i 'eśto 'eś śin ğuśtisy'a komo tenemoś diğo 'i no 'eś 'oğo por 'oğo komo parese por la śuprefisy'a de la letra de lo ke dize nu'eśtra ley por lo kual no śe pu'eden 'igualar 'eśtaś penaś śi no 'eś kon 'el dinero ke śe śaśtifaga kon 'el danyyo por 'igual 'i lo ke nu'eśa ley dize 'oğo por 'oğo

---

[24] Maimonides, *Guide,* trans. Pines, 558–68 (*MN,* Pt. 3, chap. 41).
[25] Exod. 21.24, Lev. 24.20.
[26] Bava Kamma 83b–84a.
[27] Aristotle, *NE* V.v.1 (1132b 21–24).
[28] Abraham Ibn Ezra (1092–1167). C. Sirat characterizes Ibn Ezra's method and significance, providing examples of his commentary (*History of Jewish Philosophy in the Middle Ages* [Paris–Cambridge, 1985], 104–12) and fundamental bibliography (425–26).

Book of the Regimen of Living ⟨fol. 104b–105a⟩

mano por mano 'i set-²⁹ ke parese ke śe śake 'el meśmo 'oğo al ke lo śakare aśu konpanyero kiğo dezir la deśkrisy'on de la 'igualdad por la maś 'eselente medida 'i maś verdader'a por loś meğoreś terminoś ke posible 'eś ke 'en dezir 'oğo por 'oğo 'eś komo ke diğeśe ke 'el 'oğo śe'a de komensurar kon 'otro 'oğo lo kual 'eś 'inposible śer śalvo kon la vali'a del ke de 'otro modo no śeda 'oğo por 'oğo śalvo 'oğo 'i alma por 'oğo komo dizen nu'eśoś śaby'oś 'oğo por 'oğo 'i no 'oğo 'i alma por 'oğo 'i set-³⁰ lo kual śeri'a śinğuśtisy'a :

'I nota 'eśto ke[ ]'eś de muğa suśtansy'a ke kon 'eśto 'entenderaś 'un diğo muy 'eśkuro de 'entender ke 'el śenyyor Rabbenu Mośeh diğo aserka deśto 'en 'el kapitulo kuarenta 'i 'uno de la tersera partida de śu famozisimo libro do dize ke a'un ke parese śer diferente lo ke nu'eśoś śaby'oś dizen 'en nu'eśo Ṭalmud de lo ke parese por la letra de nu'eśtra śakra 'eśkritura 'el tyene 'en lo ke nu'eśoś śaby'oś dizen syerta razon 'i 'opiny'on la kual no kiğo poner por 'eśkrito 'i değola para dezir la kara 'a kara³¹ 'i 'eś la 'intensy'on ami ver ke lo ke la ley diğo 'oğo por 'oğo 'eś komo ke diğeśe ke lo ğuśto śeri'a 'oğo por 'oğo propy'a mente śi posible fu'eśe hazer tal 'igualdad 'i ke loke dizen nu'eśoś śaby'oś ke śe'a vali'a de 'oğo por 'oğo kyere dezir ke 'eś razon ke śe 'iguale kon kośa ke śe pu'eda dezir ke 'eś 'oğo por 'oğo pu'eś no śe pu'ede manko hazer 'i de la meśma manera śe deve de konsidrar ke lo ke dizen nu'eśoś śaby'oś ke todaś laś penaś śon śegun 'el ke 'ofende 'i 'el 'ofendido³² de adonde diğeron ke śi 'el mayoral de Yiśra'el 'ofendyere a'un hedyota no le 'ofenderan a'el la meśma 'ofenśa³³ no dizen 'eśto por ke śe mire la diferensy'a de la kalidad de śuś preśonaś por 'elyyoś 'en śi śalvo para lo ke konbyene por la diferensy'a de la meśma pena por ke no 'eś 'igual asotar 'a 'un vilyyano kon asotar 'a 'un śenyyor a'un ke todo śe'a asotar ke mayor pena resibe 'el [CW. śenyyor]}

⟨fol. 105a⟩
{KH
śenyyor 'en śer asotado ke 'el vilyyano 'en ferir le 'i atormentarle kon grabeś tormentoś ke la diferensy'a del śuğebto haze la diferensy'a de la pena de manera ke no keda dubda ninguna ke 'en todaś 'eśtaś kozaś 'i 'otraś taleś ke konśiśte 'enelyyaś la ğuśtisy'a no śe konsidra la kalidad del śuğebto por 'el śuğebto 'enśi śalvo por lo ke

---

²⁹ Exod. 21.24.
³⁰ Ketubot 38a, Bava Kamma 84a.
³¹ Maimonides, *Guide,* trans. Pines, 558–68 (*MN,* Bk 3, chap. 41).
³² Ketubot 40a, Bava Kamma 83b, Bava Kamma 86a.
³³ Bava Kamma 86a? The Hebrew term *hedyot* means an "ordinary man" (Rashi Lev. 1.1).

konpete ala diferensy'a dela kośa ke śe da por la 'otra komo tenemoś diğo 'i 'en reśpekto delyya śe dize la ğuśtisyya śer medyyo 'entre puğa 'i falta de maś 'a menoś 'i 'eneśte medyyo 'eś nesesary'o ke śepaś maś ke 'el filosofo 'enel kinto dela 'etika dize śer 'eśta 'eśpesy'a de ğuśtisy'a medyyo 'entre 'obrar śin ğuśtisy'a 'i 'entre padeser śinğu(t)[ś]tisy'a konvyene 'a śaber ke tomar 'el 'ombre para śi la mayor parte del probeğo 'i dar 'a śu konpanyero la menor parte[34] 'eśto 'eś puğa 'i falta kela puğa 'eś 'el tomar 'el maś delo ke konvyene 'i la falta 'eś dar aśu prośimo menoś de lo ke le konvyene 'i 'el medyyo 'eś tomar para śi meśmo loke le konvyene tomar śegun dereğa razon 'i 'igualdad 'i non maś 'i dar aśu konpanyero loke le konbyene 'i no menoś :

'I a'eśto ayy muğaś dubdaś

LA 'una 'eś ke 'el medy'o śegun virtud deve de śer 'entre doś 'eśtremoś ke kada 'uno delyyoś śe'a visy'o 'i abito malo 'i 'enel padeser no śe konsidra visy'o ni abito malo :

ŚEGUNDA ke 'el hazer 'i padeser 'eś 'una meśma kośa komo deklaramoś 'enel tersero deloś fizikoś[35] pu'eś komo śe dira śer la ğuśtisy'a medyyo 'entre doś kozaś ke śon 'u[n]a meśma kośa

TERSERA 'i maś prinsipal dubda ke pu'eś halyyamoś 'otroś doś 'eśtremoś apartadoś 'igual mente dela ğuśtisy'a no śe deve dezir aver 'otroś 'eśtremoś ke śe'a la ğuśtisy'a medyyo 'entre 'elyyoś berbi grasy'a ke śi diğeremoś ke And(d)[r]inopla[36] 'eś medyyo 'entre Brusa[37] 'i Śaloniki 'enla diśtansy'a del kamino no śe dira ke śera medyo 'entre Kośtantina[38] 'i Śaloniki pu'eś Brusa 'eś maś diśtante de Andrinopla ke Kośtantina 'i 'eś 'igual ala diferensy'a de Śaloniki a'elya 'i aserka laś vertudeś no falyamoś aver 'un medyo 'en maś de doś 'eśtremoś 'i pu'eś halyyamoś doś 'eśtremoś diśtanteś del medyo 'igual mente 'i todoś doś visy'oś no śe deve de dezir ke śean 'otroś 'i śon viśtoś 'eśtoś 'otroś doś 'eśtremoś śer verdaderoś por ke 'el ke haze śin ğuśtisy'a 'en śimileś repartisy'oneś 'eś 'el ke toma para śi la mayor parte 'i da aśu

---

[34] Aristotle, *NE* V.v.17 (1133b 30–33).

[35] He makes reference to his commentary on Aristotle's *Physics, Piruš al Sefer ha-Ś*^{e}*maa ha-Tabai;* see Ben-Menahem, "Bibliography," 283–84. Cf. Aristotle, *Physics* III.iii (202a 15–21).

[36] Modern Edirne, it lies 313 miles northeast of Salonica. Until the conquest of Constantinople in 1453, it was the European capital of the Ottoman Empire (Epstein, *Ottoman Jewish Community*, 21).

[37] Modern Bursa, in Anatolia, is located 54 miles south of Istanbul.

[38] Istanbul.

Book of the Regimen of Living ‹fol. 105a–105b›

konpanyero la menor[39] 'i 'el kontrary'o deśto 'eś 'el ke toma para śi menoś de lo ke le konbyene 'i da aśu konpanyero maś de lo ke le konbyene 'i deśte modo 'eś 'el medyo 'entre 'eśtoś doś 'eśtremoś 'el tomar para śi lo ke le konbyene 'i dar aśu konpanyero loke le konbyene 'i aśi 'eś la ğuśtisy'a medyyo 'entre doś 'obraś 'i no 'entre 'obrar 'i padeser 'i todaś malaś ke 'el tomar 'el 'ombre menoś de [CW. loke]}

‹fol. 105b›
{HELEK G PEREK G- [PART THREE CHAPTER THREE]
loke le konbyene 'eś hazer mal 'en alguna manera ke verna por 'elyyo 'a nesesidad 'i śegirśean de 'elyyo muğoś 'inkonbenyenteś śalvo //śi (no)// lo[ ]da por liberalidad ke 'eśto 'eś śegun 'otra virtud 'i no śegun ğuśtisy'a ke śegun ğuśtisy'a 'eś visy'o vituperable tomar manko de loke le konbyene 'i dar maś de loke konbyene 'a kyen no 'eś obligado por ğuśtisy'a de darśelo aśi komo la prodegalidad 'eś visy'o vituperable aserka de la liberalidad 'i 'eśto 'eś byen viśto 'i no 'eś nesesary'o alargar 'enelyyo por donde parese no tener 'otroś 'eśtremoś ke 'un medyyo no pu'ede śer medyyo de maś ke de doś 'eśtremoś komo tenemoś diğo :

PARA saśtifazy'on de lo kual diremoś konforme 'a la verdad 'i 'opiny'on del filosofo ke 'el medyyo tomado 'en diferenteś konsidrasy'oneś pu'ede śer medy'o 'entre muğoś 'eśtremoś[40] ke byen śe dira Andrinopla śer medyyo 'entre Brusa 'i Śaloniki 'en konsidrasy'on de la diśtansy'a de 'el lugar 'i dezirśe'a tanbyen śer medyyo 'entre Kośtantina 'i Śaloniki 'en konsidrasy'on de la śanidad 'o de 'otra kośa tal

DE MANERA ke la ğuśtisy'a śe dira śer medyyo 'entre hazer śin ğuśtisy'a 'i 'entre padeser śinğuśtisy'a 'en konsidrasy'on de la 'igualdad de la kośa ke śeda ke 'uno toma maś 'i 'otro menoś 'i 'eś 'el medyyo tomar kada 'uno loke le konbyene ke lo ğuśto 'eś medy'o 'entre maś 'a menoś[41] 'i śe dira tanbyen 'entre 'el tomar maś 'i dar menoś a'el tomar menoś 'i dar maś ke 'el medy'o 'eś 'el meśmo de ariba 'el kual 'eś manifeśto śer tomar lo ke konbyene 'i dar lo ke konbyene komo tenemoś diğo 'i de 'eśtoś doś 'eśtremoś 'eś la ğuśtisy'a medyyo komo kual kyera de laś 'otraś vertudeś ke śon todoś śuś doś 'eśtremoś maloś komo tenemoś diğo :

'ENPERO porke 'eśte 'eśtremo de falta śe falyya muy pokaś veześ ke por marabilyya śe falyyara kyen toma manko para śi 'i de maś para śu konpanyero por tanto no kiğo 'el filosofo nombrar 'eśtoś doś 'eśtremoś 'i diğo ke 'eś 'entre a'usy'on

---

[39] Aristotle, *NE* V.v.17 (1133b 30–33).
[40] Aristotle, *NE* V.v.17 (1134a 1–2).
[41] Aristotle, *NE* V.v.17 1133b 30–35).

BOOK OF THE REGIMEN OF LIVING ‹FOL. 105B–106A›

'i pasy'on a'un ke 'en değar de śer loś doś 'eśtremoś visy'oś 'i maleś no śon tomadoś komo 'en laś 'otraś vertudeś komo 'el meśmo filosofo 'enel meśmo de la 'etika dize :

KAPITULO TERSERO

'I 'en la ǧuśtisy'a legal 'eśta tanbyen viśto komo śe'a virtud 'i medyyo 'entre śuś 'eśtremoś por ke syendo la ǧuśtisy'a legal ǧuśtisy'a 'onib[e]rsal komo tenemoś diǧo la kual konprende todaś laś 'otraś parteś de ǧuśtisy'a 'i a'un todaś laś 'otraś vertudeś ke todaś 'eśtan konprendidaś 'en la ley 'i kuanta maś 'en nu'eśa ley devina lu'ego loś 'eśtremoś de todaś laś vertudeś 'i de laś 'otraś parteś deśta virtud śe}

‹fol. 106a›
{KV
podra dezir śer śuś 'eśtremoś delyya ke la ley 'eś medyyo 'i 'igualdad de todoś loś 'eśtremoś 'en todaś laś vertudeś komo tenemoś diǧo
'I 'en 'otra ś[e]gunda manera śe pu'eden maś propinka mente konsidrar śuś 'eśtremoś hazyendote śaber la 'esensy'a de la 'epike'a[42] la kual no difyere 'en ǧenero de la ǧuśtisy'a maś anteś śe dize kon razon śer la mayor 'i maś 'eselente parte de la ǧuśtisy'a por ke 'eś la ǧuśtisy'a konsidrada 'i tomada kon todaś śuś śerkonśtansyaś :
'I para ke la 'entyendaś aś de śaber ke komo kyera ke laś partikularidadeś ke 'eśtan de bağo de razon de ǧuśtisy'a ke śe 'enoban kontinu'a mente śon 'infinitaś ke no abaśta 'inǧeny'o 'umano 'a konprenderlaś por tanto ninguna ley no pone kośaś partikulareś ke śeri'a nunka poder akabar śalvo reglaś 'onibersaleś 'i depu'eś loś ǧu'eześ kon śu bu'en 'inǧeny'o 'i verdader'a 'eśtimatiba deven de ǧuśgar laś kośaś partikulareś konforme 'a akelyyaś reglaś 'onibersaleś por lo kual noś 'enkomendo nu'eśa śantisima ley 'i diǧo kuando śe 'enkubryere de ti koza a'el ǧu'izy'o 'i set- 'i vernaś aloś sasardoteś 'i a'el ǧu'ez ke fu'ere 'en akelyyoś diaś 'i set-[43] vyendo ke no abaśtan laś reglaś 'onibersaleś para ǧuśgar por 'elyyaś abśuluta mente laś kozaś partikulareś 'i no śolo 'eśto śi no ke kuando 'eśkribyeren partikular mente todoś loś ǧu'eześ ke susedyeren depu'eś de dada nu'eśa śantiśima ley a'un ke proseden 'a 'infinito no baśtan para kual kyera kaśo partikular ke śe 'enoba śi 'el ǧu'ez de 'el meśmo tyenpo ke śe 'enoba no la komensura byen 'i la ǧuśga konforme 'a 'el tyenpo 'i śuǧebto kon todaś laś 'otraś śerkośtansyaś ke śe rekyeren komensurar por tanto 'enkomendo ke fu'eśen al ǧu'ez ke fu'ere 'en akelyyoś diaś ke śe 'enoba la tal kośa ke por śer laś par(k)ti[k]ularidadeś 'infinitaś laś değo ala 'eśtimatiba del ǧu'ez :

---

[42] Cf. Aristotle, *NE* V.x.1 (1137a 32–1137b 6).
[43] Deut. 17.8–9.

Book of the Regimen of Living ‹fol. 106a–106b›

'I ALAŚ veześ akaesera ke paresera ke ǧuśga 'el ǧu'ez kontra de laś reglaś 'oniberśaleś ke 'eśtan pu'eśtaś 'enla ley ke byen mirando no śe dira akelyyo śer kontra la ley maś anteś 'el değarlo de hazer 'eś kontra ley komo 'uno ke vyere 'a 'otro ke 'eśbibla 'el nombre de 'el Dyyo 'eś byen de matarlo 'i kual kyera ke lo mata tyene premy'o por 'elyyo a'un ke noś manda nu'eśa le'ey no mateś 'i set-[44] konsidrando 'el kauśo del a'uto ke akel haze 'eś byen de matarlo de la meśma manera noś di[z]en nu'eśoś śaby'oś ke konbyene hazer algunaś kozaś 'en algunoś tyenpoś ke la ley no da lugar a'elyaś 'en 'onibersal pero śegun 'el tyenpo 'i 'el lugar ke konbyene hazerlo[45] no śe 'entendyyo 'en akelyyo akelyya regla 'onibersal komo vemoś ke la ley noś manda ke guardemoś 'el Šabbaṭ kon p[le]na krimen[46] 'i nu'eśoś śaby'oś noś mandan ke konbyene no guardarlo para lo ke konbyene hazer para śokorer 'a 'un dolyente [CW. ke 'eśta]}

‹fol. 106b›
{ke 'eśta 'en peligro de mu'erte[47] maś anteś noś mandan ke śe le haga todo lo ke 'eś nesesary'o por mano de loś mayoreś de Yiśra'el[48] ke 'en todo śe deve de hazer śegun 'el tyenpo 'i 'el lugar komo konbyene perkurando de konformar konlaś reglaś 'onibersaleś de manera ke a'un ke 'a 'el 'ombre pareśka ke va kontra laś reglaś 'onibersaleś no deve de değar de śegir lo ke 'el ǧu'ez ǧuśgare konforme a'el tyenpo ke por todo 'eśto diǧo nu'eśa ley por la ley ke te amośtraran 'i por 'el ǧu'izy'o ke diran ati no te t[i]reś de la kośa ke (r)[d]enunsyaran ati dereǧa 'o 'eśkyerda 'i set-[49] 'i deklaran nu'eśoś śaby'oś ke kyere dezir a'un ke te digan śobre la dereǧa ke 'eś 'eśkyerda 'i śobre la 'eśkyerda ke 'eś dereǧa 'i set-[50] 'i 'eś syerto de śentir 'i śaber por 'onde śakaron 'eśta gloza ke por 'el niteral de la letra parese dezir ke nośe tiren del kamino 'a 'una parte ni 'a 'otra pero komo vyeron nu'eśoś śaby'oś ke para kerer dezir 'eśto ke śe 'entyende por la śuprefisy'a de la letra no 'era menester dezir lo porke ya 'eśta diǧo 'en dezir por la ley ke te amośtraren 'i set- 'i maś ke 'en dezir no te tireś dela kośa ke te diǧeren abaśtaba ke śi no śe tirare de 'elyya 'eś viśto ke no akośtara 'a ninguna parte fu'era de 'elyya por tanto ǧuśgaron kon razon ke loke dize dereǧa 'o 'eśkyerda kyere dezir a'un ke te digan śobre loke te parese ati 'eśkyerda dereǧa 'i lo ke te parese

---

[44] Exod. 20.13.
[45] Yevamot 90b, Sanhedrin 46a.
[46] Exod. 31.14.
[47] Yoma 82b.
[48] Yoma 84b.
[49] Deut. 17.11.
[50] Song of Sol. R. 1.2.2.

BOOK OF THE REGIMEN OF LIVING ‹FOL. 106B–107A›

dereğa 'eśkyerda 'i set-[51] ke lo ke kyera ke diğere 'el verdadero ğu'ez ğuśgando konforme 'a 'el tyenpo 'i la partikularidad de la kośa kon todaś śuś śerkośtansyaś komo konbyene akelyo 'eś la verdad 'i akel tal ğu'ez 'eś 'el 'ep(+)ike tomado śegun filosofi'a moral[52] a'un ke loś 'interpeteś lo 'interpetan 'en 'un termino ke tyene 'otra śiknifikasy'on 'en nu'eśa lengu'a śanta :

'I 'eśte śe pu'ede dezir ke śe'a 'el ke diğeron nu'eśoś śaby'oś por 'el ke śe haze parsero 'a 'el Dyyo alto ğuśgando la verdad aśu verdad[53] ke 'en śegunda 'intensy'on de la ke tenemoś diğa podra śer ke 'eś 'el konformar 'el ğu'izy'o partikular ke 'eś la verdad konforme a'el tyenpo kon la regla 'onibersal ke 'eś śu verdad 'onibersal :

'I por 'eśta kauśa 'inkriminan nu'eśoś śaby'oś 'el pekado de 'el ğu'ez ke śe pone 'a ğuśgar śimileś ğu'izy'oś śin aver alyegado 'a alkansar la sofisensy'a ke śe rekyere para 'elyyo 'a tanto ke dizen ke 'el ke pone 'en 'una republika 'un ğu'ez ke no 'eś śofisyente 'eś komo ke plantaśe 'un arbol de 'idolatri'a[54] 'i dizen maś 'en 'otra parte muğoś matadoś 'eğo 'i set-[55] 'eśte 'eś 'el aprendiś ke no 'a lyegado 'a ğuśgar 'i ğuśga 'i set-[56] porke komo kyera ke 'eś nesesary'o tener grandisima prudensy'a para śaber konsidrar la verdad partikular de la kośa kon todaś laś śerkośtansyaś ke śe rekyeren para 'el tal ğu'izy'o 'el ke no fu'ere}

‹fol. 107a›
{KZ
muy śaby'o 'i prudente 'i kiğere ğuśg(+)ar por śolaś laś reglaś 'onibersaleś 'eśtru'ira 'el mundo no śabyendo ğuśgar lo ke śe rekyere ğuśgar partikular mente lo ke konbyene 'enel tyenpo ke śe halyya 'i 'eśte tal lyyaman nu'eśoś śaby'oś 'epike loko 'i ponen 'enğenplo muy konforme 'a loke tenemoś diğo do dizen ke 'eś komo 'el ke ve'e hundir 'una muğer 'enla mar 'i dandole la mano la pu'ede śalvar 'i no lo kyere hazer porke tyene por regla 'onibersal ke 'eś pekado de tokar ni mirar 'enla kara 'una muğer 'i set-[57] lo kual 'eś yero manifyeśto ke 'el verdadero 'epike deve byen konsidrar ke akelyya regla 'onibersal no śe deve de 'entender 'en akel tyenpo 'i ğuśgara kon

---

[51] Song of Sol. R. 1.2.2.
[52] Cf. Aristotle, NE V.x.1 (1137a 32–1137b 6).
[53] Shabbat 10a, Megilla 15b, Sanhedrin 7a, Tanḥuma Shoftim chap. 8.
[54] Avodah Zarah 52a.
[55] Prov. 7.26.
[56] Avodah Zarah 19b.
[57] Sotah 21b.

BOOK OF THE REGIMEN OF LIVING ‹FOL. 107A›

prudensy'a ke de loś doś 'inkonvenyenteś śe deve de 'eskoğer 'el me(ğ)[n]or por donde vera ke mayor pekado 'era değar de śalvar akelyya muğer pu'eś 'eśtaba 'en śu mano de śalvarla ke mirarla 'enla kara ni tokarla pu'eś 'era 'a fin de śalvarla konprendyendo todo 'eśto diğo nu'eśo devinisimo rey David 'en muy breveś palabraś 'ora por fazer 'a H‹a-Šem› baldaron tu ley 'i set-[58] ke kyere dezir kuando baldan śu ley del Dyyo ke śon akelyyaś reglaś 'onibersaleś ke 'en 'elyya 'eśtan pu'eśtaś no śe dira ala verdad ke śe baldan maś anteś ke 'eś fazer por 'el Dyyo pu'eś la 'ora lo rekyere 'i komo ke diğeśe kuando baldan tu ley 'ora 'eś de hazer por Adonay :

'I kon 'eśto ke tenemoś diğo aserka de la 'epike'a[59] a'un ke muy breve mente maś de lo ke śe rekyere 'eśta byen viśto ke konforme a'elyya 'en śegunda konsidrasy'on śe dira śer medyyo la ğuśtisy'a legal 'entre doś 'eśtremoś de puğa 'i falta 'el kual medyyo 'eś ğuśgar konforme a'el tyenpo partikular 'i śeran loś 'eśtremoś śegun 'eśto puğa 'i falta kela puğa śera dar laś penaś a'el ke pekare maś de lo ke konbyene konforme a'el tyenpo 'i 'el pekado kon todaś laś 'otraś śerkośtansyaś 'i śera la falta darle menoś pena de lo ke konbyene śegun la regla partikular diğa 'i de la meśma manera loś premy'oś 'i de la meśma manera todaś laś 'otraś reglaś 'onibersaleś 'el 'uzar delyyaś konforme a'el tyenpo kon todaś laś 'otraś śerkośtansyaś ni maś ni menoś komo śe konsidra 'en laś 'otraś vertudeś

'I kon 'eśto me parese ke baśta para lo ke konbyene śaber para 'el konosimyento deśta virtud konforme 'a lo ke tenemoś diğo aserka de laś 'otraś vertudeś ke kon 'elyyo podraś byen konprender todo lo ke maś aserka delyya śe pu'ede dezir baśta byen ke kon lo diğo 'eśta viśto śer 'eśta virtud tan śublimada ke 'el mundo no śe podri'a śuśtentar śin 'elyya ni pu'eden doś 'ombreś bivir 'uno 'en konpanyi'a de 'otro a'un ke śean loś maś maloś del mundo śin 'elyya kuando todaś laś 'otraś mankasen ke a'un loś ke śon konformeś 'a hazer kon 'otroś śinğuśtisy'a no śe pu'eden konformar ni śuśtentar śin 'elya 'i 'eś tanto nesesary'a 'enel mundo ke dizen nu'eśoś śaby'oś ke Mošeh Rabbenu 'entrego śu vida por la ğuśtisy'a 'i set-[60]}

---

[58] Ps. 119.126.
[59] Cf. Aristotle, *NE* V.x.6 (1137b 25–28).
[60] Exod. R. 30.4, Tanhuma Parshat Bishlah, chap. 10.

‹fol. 107b›
{HELEK G PEREK D [PART FOUR CHAPTER FOUR]
'i 'otraś kozaś 'infinitaś 'eśkribyeron 'i pudyeran muğo maś 'eśkribir 'en laś 'utilidadeś ke de 'elyya śe śigen 'en la republika por lo kual no 'eś nesesary'o dezir aki maś delyya ke kon lo ke 'eśta manifyeśto de la grandeza de nu'eśa śantisima ley ke 'eś la meśma ğuśtisy'a 'onibersal kon todaś śuś partikularidadeś 'eśta byen manifyeśta śu 'ekselensy'a :

KAPITULO KUARTO

'I para lo ke konbyene śaber aserka de la amiśtad tube de kontino 'intensy'on de hazer 'un tratado aparte por ke me parese śer 'el konosimyento delyya muy 'util 'i a'un nesesary'o para la suśtentasy'on de la vida 'umana 'i değelo de hazer por aver viśto muy famozisimoś a'utoreś ke an 'eśkrito por 'el maś alto 'eśtilo ke posible 'eś por lo kual me paresi'a kaśi 'inoransy'a meter pluma 'enelyyo por ke pensar de dezir maś 'o meğor de lo ke 'elyyoś diğeron 'eś 'inposible 'i dezir menoś 'eś falta pu'eś dezir lo meśmo 'eś śuperflu'o pero pu'eś ya aki 'en 'eśte tratado 'onibersal no me pu'edo 'eśkuzar de 'eśkribir konforme a'el 'eśtilo ke 'e lyebado 'en laś 'otraś vertudeś no hare maś ke deklarar por loś maś breveś terminoś ke pudyere la deśkrisy'on dela amiśtad kon algunaś propyedadeś śuyyaś ke konbyene śaber para 'el verdadero konosimyento delyya ke te śera maś agradable ke kuanto tenemoś diğo

'I a'un ke 'en śaber śi 'eś virtud komo laś 'otraś vertudeś ayy muğa difikultad de adonde śe śige tanbyen 'otra diferensy'a 'en śaber śi 'eś a'usy'on 'o pasy'on no kyero ponerme aki 'a diśkutir 'eśta matery'a ke baśta byen lo ke tengo alargado 'eneśto 'enel prinsipy'o del 'oktabo de la 'etika[61] śolo 'eś meneśter śaber para lo ke aki konbyene ke 'o 'eś virtud grandisima 'o 'eś kon virtud 'i de kual kyer modo ke śe'a konbyene al filosofo moral h[a]blar 'enelyya 'i 'a kual kyera ke kyere śer virtu'ozo 'i śegir 'el kamino de loś byen aventuradoś por muğaś razoneś

LA primera 'eś por śer komo tenemoś diğo 'o virtud 'o kon virtud por lo kual a[']el virtu'ozo 'eś nesesary'o tener konosimyento delyya 'i śaber komo śe deve reğir 'enelyya

LA śegunda por śer kośa muy nesesary'a para la suśtentasy'on de la vida 'umana porke no ayy kyen kyera bivir śin amigoś por la konversasy'on ke śe tyene konelyy[o]ś por donde diğeron nu'eśoś śaby'oś śobre 'uno ke 'eśtubo muğo tyenpo apartado de śuś amigoś 'i kuando vino 'a buśkarloś falyyo ke 'eran falyesidoś 'i hizo

---

[61] Aristotle, NE VIII.i.i (1155a 4–5).

Book of the Regimen of Living ⟨fol. 107b–108a⟩

'orasy'on al Dyyo ke lo hizyeśe morir 'i fu'e 'o'ida śu 'orasy'on por lo kual det[e]-r(y)minaron por 'elyyo nu'eśoś śaby'oś 'i diğeron 'o konpanyi'a 'o mu'erte 'i set-[62] konforme alo k[u]al ku'enta Tuly'o [de] Demente de Arkitaś Tarentino[63] ke diğo ke śi alguno [CW. śubyeśe]}

⟨fol. 108a⟩
{K Ḥ
śubyeśe al syelo 'i vyeśe la 'eselensy'a de loś syeloś 'i śu armoni'a 'i no le dyeśen lugar para tornar ala tyera para kontar aśuś amigoś akelyya śuma deleytasy'on 'i alegri'a ke alyya alkanso no śe alegrari'a kon kuanto vyeśe 'i alkanśase komo 'eś viśto 'eśto meśmo 'en la grandeza ke 'el rey 'Ahaśveroś dyyo 'a Haman ke no śe le kunplyyo śu alegri'a hata ke vino 'a śu kaśa 'i mando traer todoś śuś amigoś 'i leś konto toda śu grandeza[64] para ke 'elyoś partisipasen 'i komunikasen 'enelyya por ke 'el byen ke no 'eś komunikado no 'eś byen

'EŚ manifyeśta la nesesidad de loś amigoś para la vida 'umana 'en todoś loś 'ombreś 'i 'en todoś loś tyenpoś 'i 'en toda la vida ke śi śon rikoś 'o pu'eśtoś 'en grandeś 'eśtadoś maś nesesidad tyene delyyoś ke ninguno 'otro por ke 'eś manifyeśto ke 'el byen de loś rikoś 'o de la rikeza 'eś hazer byen kon 'elyya a'otroś 'i 'el hazer byen deve de śer aloś amigoś por ke śe deve hazer 'a bu'enoś 'i loś bu'enoś deven de śer amigoś 'i 'el ke 'eś riko 'i no haze byen kon śu rikeza 'eś por śu mal komo la konkluyyo nu'eśo śapyentisimo rey Šᵉlomoh do diğo rikeza guardada para śu du'enyyo por śu mal 'i set-[65] ke kyere dezir ami ver ke syendo la rikeza guardada para śolo śu du'enyyo no syendo diśtribu'ida 'onde konbyene 'eś por śu mal de śu du'enyyo aśi por kauśa natural komo por parte dela probidensy'a 'i de 'eśo ayy 'en nu'eśo Talmud 'enğenploś 'infinitoś de hazyendaś grosisimaś ke śe perdyeron por no averśe diśtribu'ido komo konvyene :

PU'EŚ loś ke 'eśtan 'en altoś 'eśtadoś tyenen muğa maś nesesidad deloś amigoś para śuśtentarśe 'enelyyoś reselando la kaida ke 'eś maś de temer 'en 'elyyoś ke 'en loś bağoś komo 'emoś viśto kaer 'a muğoś por falta de amigoś 'i 'otroś śubir por kauśa delyyoś ke 'eneśto no 'eś meneśter alargar porke 'eś todo śabido :

PU'EŚ śi loś rikoś 'i grandeś śenyyoreś tyenen nesesidad de amigoś komo

---

[62] Ta'anit 23a.
[63] Cicero, *De Amicitia,* chap. 23. Diogenes Laertius identifies the Archytas in question as Archytas of Tarentum, a fourth-century B.C.E. correspondent of Plato (*Philosophers,* trans, Hicks, 2:393).
[64] Esth. 5.10–11.
[65] Eccles. 5.12.

Book of the Regimen of Living ‹fol. 108a–108b›

tenemoś diǧo muǧo maś tyenen nesesidad de 'elyyo loś pobreś 'i de baǧoś 'estadoś para śokorerśe 'a 'elyyoś 'enśuś nesesidadeś 'o alo menoś para ke komuniken kon 'elyyoś śuś tribulasy'oneś ke 'esto 'eś medyyo alivy'o de śuś pasy'oneś komo diǧo Tuly'o 'ensu famozísimo libro de amistad[66] śon nesesary'oś loś amigoś 'a loś rikoś para komunikar konelyyoś śuś deleyteś 'i aloś pobreś para relyebar konelyyoś śuś pasy'oneś komunikando konelyyoś śuś 'enoǧoś komo 'uzaban akelyyoś treś famozisimoś 'i verdaderoś amigoś de 'Iyob ke śe konformaron de venir kada 'uno de śu lugar 'a partisipar 'ensu tribulasy'on ke 'eś grande alivy'o 'i konsolasy'on porke śe diminuye la pasy'on kuando komunikan muǧoś 'enelyya al modo del proberby'o antigo komun 'en todaś laś nasy'oneś ke dize mal de muǧoś 'eś k(n)[o]nsu'elo[67] por donde 'eś byen visto śer loś amigoś muy nesesary'oś 'a pobreś [CW. 'i 'a]}

‹fol. 108b›
{'i 'a rikoś 'eś verdad ke 'el riko loś pu'ede hazer fasil mente 'i 'el pobre kon trabaǧo konforme 'a 'el diǧo de nu'eśo śapyentisimo rey Šᵉlomoh ke diǧo todoś loś ermanoś del pobre lo aboresyeron 'i loś amigoś del riko muǧoś 'i set-[68] delo kual 'eś byen visto śer neseśary'oś loś amigoś 'a toda śu'erte de 'ombreś 'i 'en todoś loś tyenpoś tanto 'enla prosperidad komo 'eś por la mayor parte 'enloś rikoś komo 'enla adversidad ke 'eś por la mayor parte 'enloś pobreś

PU'EŚ śer neseśary'oś 'en todoś loś tyenpoś dela vida 'umana 'eś tanbyen manifyesto ke loś manseboś tyenen neses[i]dad de loś bu'enoś amigoś para ke loś aparten de loś visy'oś 'i para deleytarśe konelyyoś 'en śuś konversasy'oneś 'en lo ke 'eś lisito de deleytarśe

PU'EŚ loś vyeǧos no 'eś nesesary'o dezirśe ke por śu flakeza 'i falta de virtud tyenen nesesidad de kyen leś ayude 'i leś śyerba 'i leś śokora 'a śuś faltaś porke śi 'el vyeǧo no tyene paryente 'o amigo verdadero 'ensu veǧeś maś le vale 'enterarśe 'en vida 'espesyal śi akaese śer la tal veǧeś kon pobreza ke 'eś mal 'inkurable por donde 'eś visto śer nesesary'oś loś amigoś 'en todoś loś tyenpoś 'a todoś loś 'ombreś por lo kual konbyene 'a kual kyer virtu'ozo 'espekular 'enla amistad para śaber del modo ke śe deve reǧir 'el bu'eno 'en[e]lyya pu'eś tan neśesary'a 'eś para la vida 'umana komo tenemoś diǧo konforme alo kual śe śertifika aver akaesido 'en tyenpoś antigoś ke doś amigoś muy 'intimoś abyendo śe'ido 'uno delyoś kondenado amu'erte śin

---

[66] Cicero, *De Amicitia,* chap. 6.

[67] Cf. the Judeo-Spanish *refrán:* "Mal de muchos, consuelo de locos" (R. Foulché-Delbosc, "Proverbes judéo-espagnols," *RHi* 2 [1895]: 320; for congeners, see D. Levy, "Refranes Judeo-Españoles de Esmirna," *NRFH* 12 [1958]: 17).

[68] Prov. 14.20.

Book of the Regimen of Living ⟨fol. 108b–109a⟩

ǧuśtisy'a dizyendo ke avi'a heǧo 'un malefisy'o śabyendo śu amigo kuan libre 'era śu amigo de akelyya kulpa 'i kuan śin razon 'era kondenado 'i ǧuśtisyado śe reprezento delante la ǧuśtisy'a 'i leś dišo ke 'el 'era 'el ke avi'a heǧo akel malefisy'o 'i ke śu amigo 'era libre del alo kual 'el amigo no konsintyendo tal fu'e la diferensy'a tan grande 'entre 'elyyoś ke kada 'uno delyyoś doś keri'a śer 'el kondenado 'i ke śu konpanyero kedaśe por libre ke sintyendolo 'el prinsipe 'o 'el rey loś libro aloś doś por śolo aver konprehendido de loś doś śer tan verdaderoś amigoś ke kuando 'otra virtud ke akelyya no śe halyyaśe 'enelyoś pu'e[ś] tan 'eśtremadoś 'i perfektoś 'eran 'enla amiśtad no 'eran para perder taleś doś[69] :

'I de 'otroś doś śe ku'enta 'una amiśtad maś śublimada ke 'eśta ke syendo 'el 'uno kondenado para mu'[e]rte śin razon 'eśtando preśente śu amigo verdadero al tyenpo del ǧuśtisyarle le demando de grasya 'i mersed al kondenado ke le deǧaśe a'el morir 'i padeser 'en śu lugar 'i ke diri'a ala ǧuśtisy'a ke 'el 'era 'el delinkente 'i ke a'un ke byen ve'[i]'a ke 'el hazi'a 'en 'eśto agraby'o 'en deǧar aśu amigo bivir śolo śin konpanyi'a ke 'era morir kada 'ora 'i 'el 'una veś śola ke śelo [CW. demandaba]}

⟨fol. 109a⟩
{KT
demandaba por mersed por la 'eśtremada amiśtad ke hata 'entonseś le avi'a tubido porke 'era tan flako ke no podi'a śufrir la vida śin śu (k) konpanyi'a[70] komo akaese 'en algunoś ke śe matan por no śufrir algunaś pasy'oneś 'i tribulasy'oneś 'i ku'entan por grande manyyanimidad al kondenado 'en hazer mersed 'a śu amigo ke muryeśe 'ensu lugar 'i 'el kerer bivir 'i padeser tan 'eśtremada pasy'on de śoledad 'i apartamyento de śu amigo pudyendolo padeser de 'una śola vez 'i a'un ke byen śe ke 'enel tyenpo prezente por la grande falta ke ayy de tan 'eśtreǧa amiśtad burlaran 'i re'iran del ke kiǧo morir 'en lugar deśu amigo pensando ke resibi'a 'enelyyo mersed byen mirando śegun virtud 'i verdader'a amiśtad konsidrando kuan difisil 'eś de halyyar 'un verdadero amigo 'i kuanto tyenpo 'i kuanta 'eśperensy'a 'eś meneśter para averlo de konfirmar 'i kuanto nesesary'o 'eś para la vida 'umana 'i kuan atribulada vida pasa 'el ke lo pyerde kual kyera vera ke 'era maś de burlar del amigo ke konsinty'o bivir

---

[69] Thompson, *Motif-Index*, P319.3, *Friend's intercession saves man from execution.* Italian Novella: Rotunda; *Disciplina Clericalis* 2 (from Thompson, *Motif-Index*); H. Schwarzbaum, "International Folkore Motifs in Petrus Alphonsi's *Disciplina Clericalis*," *Sefarad* 21 (1961): 289–94; M. Gaster, *The Exempla of the Rabbis* (New York, 1924, repr. 1968), 249, no. 362 and 263, no. 419; Cicero, *De Officiis*, Bk. 3.10.

[70] Thompson, *Motif-Index*, P316, *Friend sacrifices his life for the other.* Buddhist myth: Malalasekera II 1369 (from Thompson, *Motif-Index*).

Book of the Regimen of Living ‹fol. 109a–109b›

'el muryendo śu amigo pudyendo śer 'el kontrary'o 'i padeser 'una śola vez 'i no muğaś 'i a'un ke 'eś difisil de afigurar 'eśto por no poder afigurar ke ayya 'entre amigoś tan 'eśtreğa amiśtad poderśe'i'a byen berifikar 'en la amiśtad natural ke kuando 'un padre vyeğo tubyeśe 'uniko hiğo 'en kyen puzo śu 'amor 'i fu'eśe 'el hiğo kondenado 'a mu'erte kual kyera ğuśgara ke mayor mersed resebira 'el triśte vyeğo 'en morir 'el 'en lugar deśu hiğo ke morir 'el hiğo[71] 'i kedar 'el muryendo kada 'ora pu'eś kyen afigurare ke abra amigoś ke śe kyeran 'en akel 'eśtremo grado de amiśtad porke no figurada lo meśmo ke syerto śyendo la amiśtad tan nesesary'a para paśar la vida la vida śin 'el verdadero amigo no 'eś vida por lo kual 'eś razon de hablar 'enelyya komo tenemoś diğo :

LA tersera kauśa 'eś por śer la amiśtad natural 'en loś 'ombreś alyende de śer 'eliğible 'i veluntary'oza ke natural mente 'a 'el 'om[b]re ama 'el 'omb(b)re ke 'eś śimil 'a 'el maś ke 'a ninguna 'obra kośa delaś kozaś kreadaś komo diš[o] 'el filosofo 'enla desima partikula de śuś problemaś[72] ke 'el 'ombre śe(v) atriśta maś 'en ver la korupsy'on del animal ke la dela pla[n]ta 'i del animal rasy'onal muğo maś ke del bruto 'i del ke fu'ere deśu nasy'on maś ke del ke no fu'ere tal 'i aśi por 'el konśigyente kuanto maś alyegado fu'er[e] 'a 'el tanto śe atriśtara maś deśu korupsy'on 'i śe ale- grara maś konśu suśtentasy'on natural mente 'i 'eśto 'eś viśto 'ividente mente por la(v)[ś] amiśtadeś ke natural mente vemoś ke tyenen [CW. loś]}

‹fol. 109b›
{loś padreś 'i madreś 'a śuś hiğoś a'un ke no ayyan resebido delyyoś kośa por 'onde lo mereśkan ni ayyan konosido a'un de 'elyyoś śer dignoś de śer amadoś śolo por akelyya 'amor natural ke la naturaleza leś 'ordeno ke loś amaśen[73] komo 'eś viśto 'enloś animaleś brutoś ke aman 'a śuś hiğoś natural mente 'i śe ponen 'a muğoś peligroś por śalvarloś 'i no śolo kon śuś hiğoś maś a'un kon loś ke śon de śu rele'a kada animal ama 'i śe ağunta kon 'el ke 'eś de śu //('ofisy'o) ['eśpesy'a]// komo dizen todo ku'erbo 'a śu 'eśpesy'a[74] 'i śegun parese resiben 'enelyya deleytasy'on 'i pu'eś 'eśto śe halyya 'i śe ve'e por 'eśperensy'a 'enloś animaleś brutoś muğo maś śe[ ]deve falyyar 'enloś 'ombreś ke tyenen konosimyento verdadero para deleytarśe 'en laś

---

[71] Cf. 2 Sam. 19.1.

[72] I do not find the statement in Aristotle's *Problems* X. An analogous question, however, is raised at VII.7: "Why is it that when we see anyone cut or burned or tortured or suffering pain from any other cause, we also suffer in mind?" (Aristotle, *Problems,* trans. Hett, 1:175).

[73] Aristotle, *NE* VIII.xii.2–3 (1161b 17–34).

[74] Lev. 11.15.

Book of the Regimen of Living ⟨fol. 109b–110a⟩

konversasy'oneś por la kual kauśa deven de śer loadoś loś amigoś kuando deś'enganyyada mente śe aman 'unoś 'a 'otroś porke no pu'ede śer la amiśtad śalvo puro byen pu'eś 'imita 'i śemeǧa ala 'obra de la naturaleza ke todaś śuś 'obraś śon bu'enaś 'i perfektaś śin falta 'ordenadaś por 'una 'entiliǧensy'a aśeparada ke nunka yera komo 'eś śabido :

'I 'a 'eśta kauśa noś amoneśta 'el Dyyo 'en nu'eśa śantisima ley ke amemoś 'a nu'eśo proǧimo komo 'a noś meśmoś do dize 'i amaraś atu konpanyero komo ati 'i set-[75] ke kyere dezir ke aśi komo tu keriaś ke te amaśe tu konpanyero 'en toda la perfeksy'on de amiśtad verdader'a aśi 'eś razon ke tu lo ameś 'a 'el 'i 'eś 'un gran diǧo ke śe konkluye 'enel toda la ǧuśtisy'a 'i pasifikasy'on 'i suśtentasy'on de la republika 'i 'a 'eśta kauśa diǧeron nu'eśoś śaby'oś ke 'eśte diǧo konprende toda nu'eśa ley 'i set-[76] porke la medida de loke deve hazer 'un amigo por 'otro 'o kua(n)[l] kyera por śu proǧimo para no aver 'entre 'elyyoś ninguna diferensy'a 'i bivir 'en 'entera 'i verdader'a pasifikasy'on 'eś hazer kon 'el 'otro loke 'el keri'a ke 'el 'otro hizyeśe porel 'i loke no k[e]ri'a 'el kele hizyeśen no hazer lo 'el 'a 'otro

'I pu'edeśe maś notar deśte diǧo 'a nu'eśo perpozito ke no noś 'ubo de meneśter akabidar ke amaśemoś 'a nu'eśo proǧimo por śer yya de śuyo natural kośa amarlo śolo noś akabido ke fu'eśe la 'amor ke le amamoś komo amamoś 'a noś meśmoś ke 'eśto 'eś nesesary'o akabidar para ke śe'a la amiśtad perfekta 'i por ǧuśta medida de 'igualdad de adonde śe nota delo diǧo śer la 'esensy'a dela amiśtad natural :

'I 'eśto śe ve'e maś 'ividente mente 'enloś kaminanteś ke kuando algun kaminante yera 'el kamino 'i śe halyya alyi prezente algun 'ombre ke lo śepa 'i konośka vyendole 'andar fu'era de kamino a'un ke śe'a fu'era de śu nasy'on śe mu'ebe natural mente 'a 'enkaminarle por akel 'amor natural ke reyna 'enel kon 'el ke 'eś de śu 'eśpesy'a komo avemoś diǧo :

KONFORME alo kual kuando Yosef andaba abuśkar śuś ermanoś abyendo}

⟨fol. 110a⟩

{KE

'erado 'el kamino dize nu'eśtra śakra 'eśkritura 'i halyolo varon 'i hek traśyeranśe 'enel kanpo 'i demandole 'el varon ke buśkaś 'i set-[77] ke 'eś byen de dubdar śegun lo ke parese por la śuprefisy'a dela letra komo le demando ke buśkaś ke de razon le[ ]debyera de demandar adonde vaś por donde 'a 'opiny'on de algunoś ǧuśgan

---

[75] Lev. 19.18.
[76] Gen. R. 24.7.
[77] Gen. 37.15.

BOOK OF THE REGIMEN OF LIVING ‹FOL. 110A›

nu'eśoś śaby'oś ke 'era 'el anğel Gabri'el[78] 'en figura de 'ombre ke śabi'a byen ke buśkaba aśuś ermanoś 'i por tanto le diğo ke buśkaś 'i set- 'i ami ver no pyenso ke por aki lo śaken por ke śi fablaba komo anğel no teni'a nesesidad de demandarle nada pu'eś ya śabi'a lo ke buśkaba śalvo dezirle lu[e]go la verdad de lo ke 'era nesesary'o dezir 'i śi keri'a finğir de hablar komo 'ombre 'ubyerale de demandar komo 'ombre adonde vaś komo 'e diğo por donde loke yo para mi kre'o ke nu'eśoś śaby'oś ğuśgaron śer anğel por dezir la 'eśkritura 'i halyyolo 'ombre 'i set- ke de razon avi'a de dezir 'i halyyo 'ombre 'i demandole 'el 'ombre ke buśkaś ke de razon 'el ke kamina 'i falyya 'un 'ombre 'eśtante 'en 'un lugar no śe[ ]dira ke akel tal 'ombre falyya a'el ke kamina śalvo 'el ke kamina falyya a'el ke 'eśta kuanta maś ke alyende de 'eśto no śe dira ğuśta mente ke 'uno falyya a'otro śi no lo va 'a buśkar ke śin buśkar 'uno 'a 'otro kon porpozito no śe dira ke lo falyyo śalvo ke topa kon 'el por lo kual pyenśo ke ğuśgaron verdader'a mente 'i kon muğa razon ke pu'eś ke dize ke lo halyyo 'eś śenyal ke lo 'iba buśkando para apartarlo del kamino 'erado 'i 'enderesarle 'enel kamino verdadero 'i aśi no podi'a śer śalvo anğel 'i por śer ke 'eśte nombre de varon lo falyyamoś 'en Gabri'el ke aśi dize la 'eśkritura 'i 'el varon Gabri'el 'i set-[79] por 'eśta kauśa ğuśgaron ke 'era 'el anğel Gabri'el 'i aśi halyyaraś ke de loś doś byerboś primeroś śakan 'eśto nu'eśtroś śaby'oś do dizen 'i falyyolo varon 'eśte 'eś Gabri'el 'i set-[80] de manera ke ami ver por dezirle ke buśkaś no śakaron por aki śer anğel de donde parese śer la demanda liśita deśta manera 'i deveśe de 'entender aśi değando la glośa de nu'eśoś śaby'oś aparte 'i prosuponyendo ke fu'eśe 'ombre ke komo akel 'ombre vido 'a Yosef ke 'i(')[b]a fu'era de kamino ğuśgo ke podi'a śer 'una de[ ]doś 'o ke avi'a perdido algo 'i lo 'iba por alyi buśkando 'o ke avi'a 'erado 'el kamino 'i por no śaber 'el kamino real andaba por alyi 'i 'el tal 'ombre kon 'el deśe'o natural de kererlo 'enderesar a'el kamino paresyendole ke 'era posible ke 'ubyeśe algo perdido pu'eś no demandaba por donde 'era 'el kamino real le demando primero ke buśkaba 'i set- kon 'intensy'on ke śi le diğera aver 'erado 'el kamino ke 'el le 'enderesari'a 'enel 'i komo le diğo ke buśkaba aśuś ermanoś 'eśtonseś le dyyo nu'eba de 'elyyoś komo ku'enta la 'eśkritura :

POR donde parese syerto śer la amiśtad de 'uno 'a 'otro de śu 'eśpesy'a natural por lo [CW. kual]}

---

[78] Rashi Gen. 37.15.
[79] Rashi Gen. 37.15.
[80] Rashi Gen. 37.15.

BOOK OF THE REGIMEN OF LIVING ‹FOL. 110B›

‹fol. 110b›
{HELEK G PEREK H [PART THREE CHAPTER FIVE]
kual 'eś muğa razon de hablar 'enelyya komo tenemoś diğo 'i por tanto le 'entitulo 'en titulo de varon śiknifikando ke por lo ke deve 'un varon kual kyera 'a 'otro lo devi'a hazer

LA kuarta kauśa por la kual 'eś razon ke 'el filosofo moral hable 'en la amiśtad 'eś por śer ke la suśtentasy'on de la republika depende de la amiśtad[81] ke syendo loś 'endividoś amigoś 'unoś kon 'otroś 'eśta la republika pasifika ky'eta 'i repozada por ke kon la amiśtad śe 'ebitan laś brigaś 'i diferensyaś de manera ke maś nesesidad ayy 'en la republika de amiśtad ke de ğuśtisy'a[82] por ke 'onde 'ubyere amiśtad komo konbyene no ayy nesesidad de ğuśtisy'a partikular 'i abyendo ğuśtisy'a śi kon 'elyya 'ubyere 'ody'o no śe podra byen konśervar la republika lo ke abyendo amiśtad 'eśtreğa komo konbyene ayy todo byen por ke por 'enteresisy'on de la amiśtad śuplen 'unoś 'a 'otroś laś nesesidadeś 'i partisipan 'unoś 'en laś adversidadeś de loś 'otroś ke 'eś 'un grande alivy'o 'i śokoren 'a 'ebitarlaś kuanto pu'eden lo ke no deve hazer por ğuśtisy'a konforme alo kual diğo nu'eśo śapyentisimo rey Šᶜlomoh 'en toda 'ora ama 'el konpanyero 'i 'ermano para anguśty'a 'eś nasido 'i set-[83] ke 'eś la 'intensy'on ami ver ke 'el verdadero amigo ke śe pu'ede 'entitular 'en titulo de konpanyero ama 'en toda 'ora ke śyenpre 'eśta apareğado para amar śin ninguna falta 'i al tyenpo de la nesesidad 'i anguśty'a 'el diğo konpanyero śe torna 'ermano para partisipar 'en[e]lyya komo 'ermano 'i 'eś komo ke diğeśe ke 'el diğo konpanyero al tyenpo de la anguśty'a śe haze komo 'eśtonseś nasy'eśe 'ermano śuyo ke 'eśte termino de naser śe toma 'en nu'eśa lengu'a śanta por kual kyera kośa ke akaese komo ke diğeśe ke 'el konpanyero diğo śe haze 'ermano al tyenpo de la anguśty'a 'i set-

POR todaś 'eśtaś razoneś 'i 'otraś muğaś maś ke 'eśtan konklu'idaś 'en laś diğaś 'eś byen manifyeśto kuanto konbyene hablar 'en la amiśtad pu'eś tanto byen śe śige delyya para la suśtentasy'on de la vida byen aventurada :

KAPITULO KINTO

AŚ de śaber ke la amiśtad śe toma 'en muğaś maneraś ke śe dize amiśtad la konformidad de todaś laś kozaś kreadaś 'i komo dependen 'unaś de 'otraś 'en komo partisipan 'en śuś mobimyentoś la kual lyyamo Tol(y)[o]me'o 'en śu muzika amiśtad

---

[81] Cf. Aristotle, *NE* VIII.i.4 (1155a 24–25).
[82] Cf. Aristotle, *NE* VIII.i.4 (1155a 24–25).
[83] Prov. 17.17.

BOOK OF THE REGIMEN OF LIVING ‹FOL. 110B–111A›

muzika⁸⁴ de la kual trata 'el metafiziko⁸⁵ ke a'el konbyene hablar 'enelyya 'i ayy 'otra 'eśpesy'a de amiśtad maś partikular ke 'eś la amiśtad de laś 'eśpesyaś 'entre śi 'eśpesyal la de loś animaleś 'endividoś kada 'uno 'ensu 'eśpesy'a ke 'eś amiśtad natural komo tenemoś diğo de la kual trata 'el fiziko⁸⁶ ke a'el}

‹fol. 111a›
{KY'
konbyene maś ke a'el filosofo moral ayy 'otraś doś maś partikulareś 'una de laś kualeś 'eś la amiśtad 'umana 'entre loś amigoś 'en 'onibersal śin konsidrasy'on del 'endivido partikula(l)r 'i 'eśta a'un ke konvyene a'el f[i]losofo moral no hablaremoś aki muğo 'enelyya śolo 'enla amiśtad maś partikular ke ayy[ ]'entre 'un partikular a'otro śegun la diferensy'a de loś 'endividoś

PARA lo kual 'eś meneśter ke śepaś primero la 'esensy'a dela amiśt(t)ad porke ayy 'una dubda muy grande 'entre loś filosofos a(g)[n]ti(n)[g]oś 'en śaber ke 'eś amiśtad ke algunoś diğeron ke 'eś śimilitud por ke loś amigoś śon śimileś 'i kuanto maś śimileś maś amigoś por donde ve'emoś por la 'eśperensyya ke 'un śimil kyere 'a śu śimil 'i 'eśta 'eś la 'opiny'on maś aprobada de todoś 'i afirmada porel filosofo 'enel prinsipy'o del 'oktabo dela 'etika⁸⁷ :

'I algunoś kiğeron afirmar por algunaś razoneś falsaś ke kuanto maś śimileś tanto maś 'enemigoś porke śe ve'e śer verdadero 'el prober[b]y'o antigo ke dize kyen 'eś tu 'enemigo 'el ke 'eś de tu 'ofisy'o 'i set-⁸⁸ 'i por loke śe ve'e natural mente ke la tyera śeka deśe'a ala agu'a 'omida ke 'eś śu kontrary'o 'i la agu'a deśe'a desender ala tyera⁸⁹ komo dizen nu'eśoś śaby'oś ke no tyene la lyyubyya 'otro deśe'o śalvo ala tyera 'i set-⁹⁰ 'i por lo ke śe ve'e 'en todaś laś kośaś ke 'obran 'i padesen ke no 'eś śalvo por parte de kontralyeda(r)[d] ke 'el śimil no 'obra 'enel śimil ke 'el fu'ego no 'obra 'enel fu'ego 'i aśi por 'otraś razoneś śimileś determinaron 'i diğeron ke la amiśtad śe hazi'a 'en loś kontrary'oś 'obrando 'uno 'en 'otro 'i set-⁹¹ :

---

⁸⁴ Perhaps he refers to *Peri Rhopon*, a treatise on the balancings and tunings of the scale attributed to Ptolemy.
⁸⁵ Cf. Aristotle, *Metaphysics* III.ii.24 (997b 20–24).
⁸⁶ Cf. Aristotle, *Physics* II.1 (192b 8–193a 2).
⁸⁷ Aristotle, *NE* VIII.i.6 (1155a 34–35).
⁸⁸ Aristotle, *NE* VIII.i.6 (1155a 35–36).
⁸⁹ Aristotle, *NE* VIII.i.6 (1155b 2–4).
⁹⁰ Gen. R. 20.7 on Ps. 65.10.
⁹¹ Cf. Aristotle, *NE* VIII.viii.7 (1159b 20–21).

BOOK OF THE REGIMEN OF LIVING ⟨FOL. 111A–111B⟩

'I a'un ke diskutir byen 'esta materyya no 'es tanto de nu'eso perpozito 'es byen visto ser la primera 'opiny'on la verdader'a ke kuanto mas son los amigos similes tanto mas se konfirma la amistad 'i por tanto 'el 'ombre kyere mas al animal ke al veǧitatibo 'i al rasy'onal ke al animal komo tenemos diǧo 'i si 'un 'ofisyal kyere mal 'a 'otro no lo kyere mal propy'a mente por ke 'es de su 'ofisy'o ke por 'esta parte lo kyere muǧo mas salvo por 'el danyyo ke se le sige de aver muǧos de su 'ofisy'o ke si no se le sigyese akel danyyo de 'el kedari'a la amistad 'entre 'elyyos muǧa mas ke si fu'ese de 'otro 'ofisy'o :

'I si 'el agu'a kyere ala tyera seka 'i la tyera ala agu'a no se lyyama akelyyo amistad salvo dese'o 'i ayy diferensy'a grande de 'uno 'a 'otro komo 'es sabido por tanto se pu'ede byen afirmar ke la amistad no se'a salvo 'en los similes por ke 'elyya no 'es si no 'una 'igualdad 'i similtud 'entre 'uno 'a 'otro komo tenemos diǧo [CW. 'i toda]}

⟨fol. 111b⟩
{'i toda a'usy'on 'i pasy'on 'enlas kozas naturales no pu'ede ser salvo por parte de alguna semeǧansa 'i 'igualdad komo lo prebo 'el filosofo 'enel libro de ǧenerasy'on 'i korupsy'on[92] ke por ser la materyya prima 'una 'en todas las kozas ke 'obran 'i padesen por tanto 'obran 'unas 'en 'otras por lo kual las kosas basas no 'obran 'enlas kozas altas 'i set-[93] de adonde 'es visto ke todas sus demostrasy'ones se pu'eden fasil mente desbaratar 'i ser la verdader'a 'opiny'on la ke tenemos diǧo ke la amistad no se falyya salbo 'enlos similes :

'ES menester mas saber kela amistad se konsidra 'en tres kozas diferentes komo 'es manifesto ke 'es 'en 'el 'onesto 'el kual 'es 'el byen ke 'es porsi byen 'i 'enel 'util 'i 'enel deleyte 'enlas kuales tres se konkluyen todas las amistades delos 'ombres 'uno kon 'otro 'i non 'en mas[94] 'i la kausa de 'esto 'esta manifesta 'i 'es ke komo kyera ke lo malo no solo no lo ama 'el 'ombre mas antes kual kyera huye de loke le parese ser malo 'i lo aborese por tanto 'es visto ke lo ke se ama se ama de baǧo de razon de bu'eno 'i syendo 'esto ansi komo kyera ke de loke huyen los 'ombres 'es 'o de lo malo ke verdader'a mente 'es malo 'o de lo ke 'es danyyozo 'o de loke 'es 'enoǧozo 'i le da tristeza ke todo lo ke aborese 'el 'ombre no pu'ede deǧar de ser por 'una de 'estas tres por tanto loke ama 'es de baǧo de razon de 'una de las 'opozitas 'a 'estas tres ke 'es de baǧo de razon de bu'eno 'i 'onesto ke por si se'a bu'eno 'o de baǧo de razon de 'util

---

[92] Aristotle, *De Gen. et Corr.* I.vii–viii (323b 1–324b 35).
[93] This seems to be Aristotle, *De Gen. et Corr.* I.v (320a 8–320b 25), cf. II.iv (331a 7–332a 2).
[94] Aristotle, *NE* VIII.iii.1 (1156a 7–13).

Book of the Regimen of Living ⟨fol. 111b–112a⟩

ke 'el lo tyene por bu'eno 'o de bağo de razon de deleytable ke 'el lo tyene tanbyen por byen :
DE manera ke śe dize komun mente laś amiśtadeś śer treś laś kualeś śon amiśtad por 'el 'onesto amiśtad porel deleyte amiśtad porel 'util 'i la verdad byen 'eśpekulando no śon maś de doś ke amiśtad por 'el 'util por 'el 'enśi no la ayy ke kyen ama 'el 'util no lo ama por śi śalvo 'o por 'el deleyte ke śe le śige de 'elyyo 'o para 'el 'onesto ke kyere 'obrar konel de manera ke la amiśtad por 'el 'onesto 'i por 'el deleytable śon amiśtadeś komo fineś ke laś ama 'el 'ombre por 'elyyaś meśmaś :

'I la amiśtad śe toma de bağo de razon de byen kyero dezir ke le parese al ke la ama ke 'eś byen por ke 'a la verdad no śe 'a de amar todo 'el byen ke 'eś byen por śi śalvo 'el ke 'eś byen para 'el ke lo ama ke no todo loke 'eś byen por śi 'eś byen para todoś porke vemoś muğoś byeneś ke śon byeneś 'enśi 'i no śon todoś loś 'ombreś abileś para 'elyyoś komo 'el reğimyento de la republika ke 'eś puro byen 'i no para todoś ke 'ombre abra ke a'un ke śe'a muy bu'eno por no śer 'eśprimentado no śera byen ke lo haga 'i aśi 'otraś kozaś śimileś de manera ke śe'a de tomar 'el byen partikular konforme 'a 'el ke lo 'obra 'i 'a 'el lugar 'i tyenpo komo konbyene kon todaś [CW. laś]}

⟨fol. 112a⟩
{KY(')[B]
laś śerkonśtansyaś ke śe rekyeren 'i set- 'i de la meśma manera 'el deleytable 'i 'util :
'I aś de śaber maś ke 'el ke tyene amiśtad por 'el 'onesto tyene todaś treś por ke 'el ke ama 'a 'otro por ke 'eś bu'eno 'i 'onesto śe deleyta kon la tal amiśtad ke pu'eś lo ama por śu bondad deleytaśe 'en la tal amiśtad 'i resibe muğo 'util de 'elyya 'en laś kośaś ke verdader'a mente śe pu'ede dezir 'util ke 'eś 'enel byen de la anima ke śe le śige de śer amigo de bu'eno ke 'eś kauśa de perfeksy'onar 'a śu amigo 'en todaś laś kośaś bu'enaś 'i 'onestaś ke todo 'eśto 'eś aśaś 'util :

'I anteś ke deklaremoś partikular mente kada 'una de 'eśtaś treś 'eśpeśyaś 'i partidaś diferenteś de amiśtad te deklarare 'en breve la deśkrisy'on de la amiśtad 'en 'onibersal por śu difinsy'on para lo kual 'eś meneśter ke śepaś ke para ke śe'a amiśtad 'eś meneśter ke tenga treś kondisy'oneś :

LA primera[95] 'eś ke 'el ke ama śe'a amado de śu amigo por ke śi 'uno ama 'a 'otro 'i akel 'otro no lo ama a'el akelyyo tal nośe lyyama amiśtad 'i pu'ede śe dezir ke śe'a 'eśta la 'intensy'on de loke dize nu'eśa śantisima ley 'i amaraś atu proğimo komo ati 'i set-[96] ke kyera dezir amaraś atu konpanyero kuando akel tal konpanyero śe'a komo

---

[95] Aristotle, *NE* VIII.iii.1 (1156a 9–10).
[96] Lev. 19.18.

BOOK OF THE REGIMEN OF LIVING ‹FOL. 112A–112B›

tu meśmo kyero dezir ke te ame komo tu ameś 'a 'el ke deśte modo 'eś 'el ko(t)[m]o tu 'i tu komo 'el 'i de 'otra manera no 'eś amiśtad komo tenemoś diğo :
'I LA śegunda 'eś kela amiśtad no śe dize halyyarśe śalvo kon kośa animada ke no śe dira tener amiśtad 'el 'ombre konel dinero 'o 'otra kośa śimil porke komo no ayya amiśtad śalvo 'onde ayy 'o 'onde pu'ede aver gualardon dela amiśtad 'i 'enla kośa 'inanimada no ayy gualardon lu'ego no ayy amiśtad[97] :
'I maś porke no ayy amiśtad śalbo kon kyen śe deve de kerer śu byen ke la amiśtad 'eś kerer 'el byen del amigo 'i konla kośa 'inanimada no śe dira ke kyere 'el 'ombre śu byen śalvo kela kyere por 'el byen ke śele śige delyya ke śi kyere 'el 'ombre 'el dinero no kyere ke 'el tal dinero tenga byen ke 'eśto 'eś diğo de burla 'i de 'eśkarneser śalvo ke kyere para śi 'el byen ke śele śige del dinero 'i aśi 'otra kośa śemeğante 'i a'un por la primera no pu'ede śer la śegunda ke komo śe'a ke 'el ke ama 'a 'otro para ke śe diga amiśtad 'a de śer 'el amado dela kośa amada 'i la koza 'inanimada no pu'ede amar lu'ego no pu'ede śer amada 'i a'un ke 'ubo alguno deloś antigoś ke kreyo aver amiśtad de 'uno a'otro ke no fu'eśe amado del 'otro 'el filosofo berifiko byen dezirśe 'eśto kerer byen maś no amiśtad ke amiśtad nośe dira śino 'eś doblada de 'uno 'a 'otro 'i 'el 'otro 'a 'el komo tenemoś diğo :
'I 'eś la 'otra tersera kondisy'on ke śe'a la amiśtad deśkubyerta 'i 'ezenta ke śi 'eś 'okulta a'un ke śe'a de 'el 'a 'otro 'i del 'otro 'a 'el no śe lyyamara verdader'a amiśtad śalvo byen kerensy'a komo akaese 'en alğunoś [CW. ke śe]}

‹fol. 112b›
{HELEK G PEREK V PART THREE CHAPTER SIX
ke śe kyeren byen śin averśe viśto ğamaś ke 'eśta tal no śe lyyamara amiśtad komo tenemoś diğo porke para la ğenerasy'on dela amiśtad śean de halyyar todaś laś 'obraś de amiśtad 'una delaś kualeś 'eś konversasy'on komo śe deklarara maś adelante la kual falta 'enla amiśtad 'okulta :
KON 'eśtaś treś kondisy'oneś diğaś 'eśta byen deklarada la difinsy'on de la amiśtad 'i 'eś viśto ke śe'a kon kyen śe'a gualardonada 'igual mente 'i śe'a kośa animada 'i manifyeśta[98] ke no śe'a 'okulta komo avemoś diğo ke 'el amigo no deve de 'enkubrir nada de śu amigo komo diğo 'el Dyyo alto por 'Abraham 'entitulado 'en titulo de śu amigo śi 'enkubryen yo de 'Abraham lo ke yo fazyen 'i set-[99] 'i deklaro 'eśto maś nu'eśo śapyentisimo re'ey Šᵉlomoh dizyendo maś vale kaśtigo publiko ke

---

[97] Aristotle, *NE* VIII.ii.3 (1155b 27–30).
[98] Aristotle, *NE* VIII.ii.2 (1155b 22–25).
[99] Gen. 18.17.

BOOK OF THE REGIMEN OF LIVING ‹FOL. 112B–113A›

amiśtad 'enkubyerta 'i set-[100] keryendo dezir ke a'un ke 'el amigo no[ ]'a de kaśtigar aśu amigo 'en publiko śalvo de śi a'el 'i śi tal haze no 'eś 'entera amiśtad kon todo 'eśto 'eś 'eśta meǧor amiśtad ke la amiśtad 'enkubyerta a'un ke śe'a 'el kaśtigo deśi a'el ke meǧor no śe dize śalvo 'enel ke śolo difyere de maś 'a menoś komo 'eś śabido :

KAPITULO SEŚTO

ǦUNTO kon aver śabido la difinsy'on dela amiśtad 'en 'onibersal komo aś viśto la kual difinsy'on 'eś verdader'a 'en kada 'una delaś treś 'eś byen ke te haga śaber maś 'eśpasifikada mente kada 'una delaś treś partidaś diǧaś por 'eśtenso 'i la diferensy'a ke ayy de 'una 'a 'otra porke aśi komo 'el byen 'i 'el 'util 'i 'el deleyte śon treś kozaś ke difyeren śegun 'eśpesy'a aśi 'el amar kada 'una delyyaś 'a de diferir 'en 'eśpesy'a de laś 'otraś tomadaś 'eśtaś amiśtadeś komo laś toma 'el vulgo porke tomadaś śegun dereǧa razon no difyeren 'una de 'otra ni 'eśtan 'una śin 'otra komo deklararemoś maś al delante 'i komo avemoś algun tanto deklarado :

'I aś de śaber ke la amiśtad por 'util 'i por deleytable difyeren de la amiśtad por 'el 'oneśto 'en muǧaś kozaś la primera 'eś ke 'el ke ama aśu amigo por 'el 'util ke de 'el śe le śige śe halyya ke no ama al propy'o amigo por 'el amigo śalvo por 'el 'util ke delyyo śele śige[101] 'i aśi śu amigo a'el 'i de la meśma manera śera kuando ama por 'el deleyte ke no ama la kośa kon ke śe deleyta por śi śalvo por 'el deleyte ke delyyo śe le śige[102] de manera ke 'eneśtaś doś 'eśpesyaś de amiśtad no śe dira 'el ke ama ke ama aśu amigo śalvo ke ama aśi meśmo pu'eś lo ama por 'el 'util 'o deleyte ke a'el śele śige de 'elyyo komo śe manifyeśta 'eśto 'en laś amiśtadeś ke śe tyenen kon loś 'ofisyaleś por śuś laboreś de śuś 'ofisy'oś [CW. ke no]}

‹fol. 113a›
{KYG
ke no los aman por śi meśmoś śalvo por la 'obra ke de 'elyoś resiben por lo kual vemoś ke muǧaś veześ tyenen algunoś 'a algun bu'en 'ofisyal por 'enemigo 'i le kyeren mal 'i aman la 'obra ke haze 'i kerian ke no muryeśe a'un ke 'eś śu 'enemigo por no aver kyen le haga akelyyo tan byen komo 'el :
LA śegunda[103] 'eś ke 'eśtaś doś amiśtadeś śon asidentaleś por lo kual no turan

---

[100] Prov. 27.5.
[101] Aristotle, *NE* VIII.iii.1 (1156a 10–11).
[102] Aristotle, *NE* VIII.iii.2 (1156a 15–17).
[103] Aristotle, *NE* VIII.iii.2–3 (1156a 18–24).

BOOK OF THE REGIMEN OF LIVING ‹FOL. 113A–113B›

maś ke kuanto tura la kauśa asidental ke 'eś 'el 'util 'o la deleytasy'on ke śon kauśa de la amiśtad 'i tirada la kauśa śe tira 'el 'efekto ke 'eś la amiśtad :
    LA tersera 'eś ke la kauśa por lo ke ama 'el 'uno 'a 'el 'otro no ama 'el 'otro 'a 'el ke śi 'el ke konpra la 'obra de 'el artifise ama al diğo artifise por śu 'obra 'el artifise lo ama 'a 'el por śu dinero 'i muğaś veześ akaese ke 'uno ama 'a 'otro por 'el deleyte 'i 'el 'otro le ama 'a 'el por 'el 'util de manera ke 'eś 'el gualardon deś'igual śegun 'eśpesy'a 'i por todaś 'eśtaś kauśaś laś taleś amiśtadeś no śon turableś ni śon 'en todoś loś tyenpoś ke la amiśtad por 'el 'util śe halyya maś 'en loś vyeğos[104] komun mente ke 'en loś de 'otra 'edad por ke leś parese ke tyenen nesesidad de la hazyenda para śuplir la flakeza de la karne 'i fu'ersaś 'i porke śe syenten 'inabileś para ganar la 'i temen de perder lo ke tyenen por tanto śon maś 'eśkasoś ke 'en la mosedad por lo kual huyen de 'el deleyte porke śe adk[y]ere kon dinero 'i 'en loś ninyyoś śe halyya tanbyen la amiśtad por 'el 'util a'un ke no tanto komo 'enloś vyeğos pero śon 'en alguna manera śemeğanteś 'a loś vyeğos ke 'a la veğeś re'iteran 'i 'enloś ninyyoś akaese muğaś veześ ke no śe kyeren ağuntar 'en konpanyi'a ke no 'eśperen de 'elyya probeğo 'i de pu'eś ke kresen maś 'i śon manseboś śe traśponen 'enla 'otra 'eśpesy'a 'i perkuran la amiśtad por 'el deleytable por śer vensidoś maś del apetit(y)[o] konkupisible 'i virtud śensitiba śegun loś apetit(y)[o]ś korporaleś[105] 'i fu'elgan kon laś konversasy'oneś de 'otroś manseboś para deleytarśe konelyyoś komunikando konelyyoś śuś plazereś 'i 'eśto no tura maś ke kuanto tura la flor de la mosedad ke fasil mente śe konronpe 'eś verdad ke akaese 'en loś manseboś la tal amiśtad śer muy rezy'a 'i fu'erte 'i 'eśtremada 'i alaś veześ kon toda akelyya fu'ersa 'i vigor 'eś 'en śupito mudable mudandośe 'el 'apetito 'o la kauśa kon ke śe deleytan 'i por la deś'igualdad ke 'eneśtaś doś 'eśpesyaś ayy nasen laś diferensyaś 'enelyyaś porke 'eś difisil 'igualar laś kośaś ke śon diferenteś 'enśi :
    KU'ENTAŚE aserka de 'eśto de 'un rey tirano ke śe lyyamaba Dy'onizy'o 'i śe deleytaba muğo de muzika 'i fu'ian loś muzikoś de venir 'a 'el porke no leś pagaba konforme 'a śu trabağo [CW. akaesy'o]}

‹fol. 113b›
{akaesy'o de venir aśu tyera 'un famozisimo muziko 'i gran tanyedor ala fama de ke 'eśte re'ey śe deleytaba muğo dela muzika 'i deśke śupo ke 'era tan tirano śele hizo de mal de 'ir 'a tanyer delante del 'i sintyendo 'eśto 'el re'ey lo mando lyyamar 'i le 'ofresy'o de pagarle tanbyen ke 'a ğu'izy'o de todo 'ombre kedaśe byen śaśtifeğo śin tener razon de poderśe keğar 'i kon 'eśte 'ofresimyento śe alegro 'el muziko 'i tanyyo

---

[104] Aristotle, *NE* VIII.iii.3 (1156a 25–26).
[105] Cf. Aristotle, *NE* VIII.iii.5 (1156a 32–35).

Book of the Regimen of Living ‹fol. 113b›

delante 'el re'ey 'un grande 'eśpasy'o de tyenpo muy alegre kon la 'eśperansa de la bu'ena paga ke 'el rey le avi'a 'ofresido de ke akabo de tanyer keryendośe deśpedir 'eśperando la paga le diğo 'el diğo re'ey byen te pu'edeś 'ir ke yo te 'e pagado paga 'igual 'a ğuśta razon komo te 'ofreśi porke tu me deleytaśte kon tu muzika 'i yo te deleyte kon la 'eśperansa ke te di dela bu'ena paga 'i tanto kuanto duro mi deleytasy'on kon tu muzika duro la tuyya kon la tal 'eśperansa de manera ke fu'eron pagaś 'igualeś śin ninguna diferensy'a ke śi te 'ubyera de pagar kon dinero fu'era muy difisil de 'igualar la paga por la diversidad del 'util al deleyte 'i kedar[i]aś s[y]enpre keğozo loke agora no keda lugar para poderte keğar kon razon syendo la paga de la meśma[106] 'eśpesy'a fu'e repu'eśta komo de tirano 'i de 'elyya śe nota loke tenemoś diğo ke nasen laś diferensyaś 'eneśtaś amiśtadeś por śer 'elyyaś diśformeś 'enśi :

KONTRARY'O de todo 'eśto śe halyya 'en la verdader'a amiśtad ke 'eś por 'el 'oneśto komo śe ve'e por sinko 'o śeyś propyedadeś ke śe halyyan 'enelyya por laś kualeś śe manifyeśta la 'ekselensy'a de 'eśta 'eśpesy'a de amiśtad maś ke laś 'otraś :

'EŚ la primera[107] la kontrary'a de lo ke tenemoś diğo 'en laś 'otraś doś la kual 'eś ke 'eśta 'eśpesy'a de amiśtad 'eś 'entre loś doś amigoś suśtansyal mente 'o no asidental por ke no ama 'el 'uno al 'otro por kośa asidental ke ayya 'enel probeğo 'o deleytasy'on śalvo por śu bondad 'i de 'eśta manera ama a'el por śi meśmo 'i no por 'otra kośa por ke la bondad vyene por parte de la virtud 'i la virtud 'eś abito 'enel anima de manera ke la bondad 'eś suśtansy'a 'enel 'ombre 'i 'el amigo verdadero komo 'a de kerer la pura bondad para śu amigo komo para śi meśmo 'i 'el byen para śi meśmo 'eś suśtansyal aśi 'el ke kyere para śu amigo 'eś suśtansyal lo ke nada deśto ayy 'en laś 'otraś doś komo tenemoś diğo :

'EŚ la śegunda produzida de la primera ke syendo la amiśtad por 'el 'oneśto suśtansyal por la bondad 'en śi 'i toda bondad 'eś śustansy'a 'i abito fiğe 'i firme 'i permanente toda la vida del bu'eno aśi la amiśtad por l(s)[a] bondad 'es fiğa 'i firme toda la vida del amigo śin ninguna mudansa por ke komo la kauśa ke 'eś la bondad 'i virtud 'eśta firme aśi 'eś tanbyen la amiśtad firme pu'eś no 'eś amiśtad por kośa}

---

[106] Thompson, *Motif-Index*, J1551.3, *Singer repaid with promise of reward: words for words*. Aristotle, *NE* IX.i.4 (1164a 16–19) (trans. Rackham, 518 n. b) quotes Plutarch (*De Alexandri fortuna*, ii.1): "the story of the tyrant Dionysius, who promised the musician a talent [. . .] but next day told him he had already been sufficiently paid by the pleasure of anticipation" (*Moralia*, trans. F. C. Babbitt [Cambridge, MA, 1957], 4:425).

[107] Aristotle, *NE* VIII.iii.6 (1156b 7–19).

‹fol. 114a›
{KYD
'eśtiry'or mudable[108] ke 'eś lo meśmo ke nu'eśoś śaby'oś diğeron toda amiśtad ke depende de alguna kośa baldandośe la kośa śe balda la amiśtad 'i la ke no depende de kośa no śe balda nunka ğamaś 'i set-[109] 'i aś de śaber ke kośa śe toma por kośa 'eśtiry'or asidental ke la suśtansy'a no śe 'entitula 'en termino de kośa pu'eś 'eś 'eśtabile 'i traen konparasy'on de notoryaś amiśtadeś para laś doś 'eśpesyaś do dizen kual 'eś la amiśtad ke depende de kośa 'eśta 'eś la amiśtad de Amnon 'i Ṭamar 'i la ke no depende de kośa 'eś la amiśtad de David 'i(y) Y^ehonaṭan 'i set-[110] ke truğeron 'enğe[n]plo para 'una de laś doś mudableś ke 'eś por 'el deleytable de Amnon 'i Ṭamar komo 'eś manifyeśto 'i para 'el 'oneśto de la maś fiğe 'i firme ke śe śabe la kual fu'e de David 'i Y^ehonaṭan ke dize por 'elyyoś la 'eśkritura ke 'en śu vida ni 'en śu mu'erte no śe '[e]śpartyeron 'i set-[111]

'EŚ la tersera lo ke ya tenemoś diğo ke 'en la amiśtad por 'el 'oneśto 'eśtan todaś laś treś ğuntaś por ke la amiśtad de loś bu'enoś 'i perfektoś ke 'eś por śuś bondadeś 'i non por ningun 'otro reśpekto kyeren 'el byen suśtansyal para śuś amigoś

'EŚ la kuarta produzida deśta 'i deklarada ya ariba la kual 'eś la amiśtad śegun 'oneśto no 'eś śino 'en laś 'igualeś śemeğanteś pu'eś śe haze por 'igualdad 'i śemeğansa ke ayy 'entre 'elyyoś de bondad 'i virtud komo 'emoś diğo :

'EŚ la kinta konklu'ida de todo lo diğo ke komo 'eneśta 'eśpesy'a śe halyyan todaś laś 'otraś kon todaś laś propyedadeś diğaś śe pu'ede byen konkulu'ir ke 'eśta 'eśpesy'a de amiśtad śe'a la maś grande 'i maś bu'ena ke todaś laś 'eśpesyaś de amiśtadeś ke 'eś maś grande por ke todaś 'eśtan konklu'idaś 'enelyya 'i 'eś meğor por ke 'eś por la bondad 'i virtud 'enśi komo tenemoś diğo :

'EŚ la seśta ke 'eneśta 'eśpesy'a de amiśtad por 'el 'oneśto 'enśi no akaese halyyarśe muğoś amigoś komo śe halyyan 'enlaś 'otraś doś 'eśpesyaś diğaś 'i la kauśa deśto 'eśta viśta por ke komo 'eśta amiśtad no 'eś śino 'enloś bu'enoś 'i virtu'ozoś loś kualeś śe halyyan muy pokoś por nu'eśtroś pekadoś por tanto laś taleś amiśtadeś śon muy raraś ke loś taleś amigoś śon muy pokoś 'i ayy śegunda razon para 'elyyo 'i 'eś ke 'eśta 'eśpesy'a de amiśtad no śe konfirma 'enloś amigoś śalvo depu'eś de verdadero konosimyento de 'uno 'a 'otro 'el kual no pu'ede śer śalvo kon diśkurso de tyenpo konforme alo kual dize 'el prober[b]y'o antigo 'i lo trae 'el filosofo 'enel 'oktabo dela

---

[108] Aristotle, NE VIII.iii.7.
[109] Avot 5.19.
[110] Avot 5.19.
[111] 2 Sam. 1.23.

BOOK OF THE REGIMEN OF LIVING ‹FOL. 114A–114B›

'etika¹¹² ke anteś ke konośka byen 'un 'ombre 'a 'otro śe kome 'una kila de śal 'i 'eś muğa razon ke anteś ke śe konfirme la amiśtad 'entre loś bu'enoś śe konośka byen 'uno 'a 'otro porke komo kyera ke la amiśtad 'entre loś bu'enoś 'a de śer firme 'i fiğa de manera ke śe konfi'e 'el 'uno}

‹fol. 114b›
{del 'otro komo de śi meśmo 'eś meneśter ke anteś śepa byen 'i konośka la bondad del 'otro śer verdader'a lo kual 'eś d[i]fisil de konoser śin diśkurso de tyenpo por lo k[u]al no śe deve de konfirmar la amiśtad 'entre 'elyyoś śin 'el tal konosimyento porke no 'a de konfyar de śu amigo koza ke 'en ningun tyenpo śe pu'eda arepentir ke 'el ke konfi'a śuś śekretoś akyen pyensa ke 'en algun tyenpo le pu'ede śer 'enemigo 'o pu'ede konronperśe la amiśtad 'eś muy 'inorante porke śe haze 'eśklabo śuyyo¹¹³ :

KONFORME alo kual diğo Byaś 'el filosofo ama atu amigo de manera ke lo pu'edaś aboreser¹¹⁴ ke fu'e syerto muy gran diğo 'i[ ]de muğa 'eśtima digno de[ ]perpetu'a memory'a ke kiğo dezir ami ver ke komo kyera ke para konfirmar la amiśtad 'eś meneśter verdadero konosimyento 'i 'el verdadero konosimyento śe'a de hazer kon diśkurso de tyenpo ke pu'ede śer ke loke no śe konose al[ ]prinsipy'o śe konose al fin por tanto 'el ke peśkiryere 'eśte tal konosimyento para konfirmar la amiśtad no deve de konfyar tanto del amigo śuś śekretoś ake depu'eś śi vyere ke no 'eś digno de śer amado no le pu'eda aboreser por aver ya kedado śu katibo por lo kual 'eś 'una devinisima dotrina a'el amigo 'enla konfyansa konśu amigo hata venir 'a verdadero konosimyento 'i komo 'eśto śe'a de hazer kon gran diśkurso de tyenpo komo tenemoś diğo śon muy raraś laś taleś amiśtadeś maś akelyaś ke śon kuando ya śon konfirmadaś śon muy 'elevadaś 'i dignaś de śer muy loadaś 'i 'eśtimadaś porke 'enelyyaś 'eśta 'el byen verdadero komo tenemoś diğo por la amiśtad verdader'a hizo nu'eśo śapyentisimo rey Šᵉlomoh 'el libro de kantar deloś kantareś todo fundado śobre la 'eselensy'a deśta 'eśpesy'a de amiśtad komo parese por 'el prinsipy'o do dize

---

¹¹² His discussion of the sixth species follows Aristotle, *NE* VIII.iii.8 (1156b 25–28) where the same proverb is cited.

¹¹³ Compare Menander's dictum: "Don't tell your secret to your friend and you'll not fear him when he turns into an enemy" (*Fragments,* trans. Allinson, 523).

¹¹⁴ Diogenes Laertius reports that Bias of Priene advised men to exercise great caution regarding friendship: "to love their friends as if they would some day hate them, the majority of mankind being bad" (*Philosophers,* trans. Hicks, 1:91). He was one of the "Seven Wise Men" who dine and converse in Plutarch's *Dinner of the Seven Wise Men* (*Moralia,* trans. Babbitt, 2:429); See also W. K. Guthrie, *A History of Greek Philosophy* (Cambridge, 1962), 1:412 n. 2.

BOOK OF THE REGIMEN OF LIVING ⟨FOL. 114B–115A⟩

kantar deloś kantareś 'i set-[115] ke todo kantar denota 'amor ke vyene de 'entero kontentamyento 'i komo 'eśta 'eśpesy'a de amiśtad konprende todaś laś 'otraś doś 'eśpesyaś komo tenemoś diğo por 'eśo diğo ke 'eś kantar deloś kantareś ke 'eś komo śi diğeśe amiśtad delaś amiśtadeś 'i set- 'i pu'ede śer ke śe'a 'eśta la 'intensy'on de nu'eśoś śaby'oś 'enloke diśeron ke todoś loś kantareś śon śantidad 'i 'el kantar deloś kantareś 'eś śantidad delaś śantidadeś 'i set-[116] keryendo dezir ke todaś laś amiśtadeś por 'el 'util 'o por 'el deleyte pu'eden śer śantaś śi śon 'enderesadaś 'a bu'en fin a'un ke śean por 'el 'util 'o por 'el deleytable pero kuando 'eś por 'el 'oneśto komo 'eś la amiśtad ke śe 'eśpisifika 'en akel śantiśimo libro ke 'eśtan todaś laś 'otraś 'en śumo grado de perfeksy'on komo tenemoś diğo śe deve lyyamar śantidad de (ś) śantidadeś 'i set-

AYY 'otra 'eśpesy'a de amiśtad ke 'el vulgo la lyyama amiśtad por śer algo maś turable ke laś doś 'eśpesyaś del 'util 'i del deleytable la kual 'eś la amiśtad ke tyene 'uno [CW. kon]}

⟨fol. 115a⟩
{KTV ḤELEK G PEREK Z [PART THREE CHAPTER SEVEN]
kon 'otro ke 'eś de śuś kondiśy'oneś ke por la śemeğansa delaś kondiśy'oneś śon amigoś 'i konversan ğuntoś tanto kuanto tura la 'igualdad 'i śemeğansa delaś kondisy'oneś[117] :

'I al fin alfin 'eśta 'i todaś laś 'otraś śon muy fasileś de koronper 'en reśpekto dela amiśtad verdader'a por ke kual kyera deśtaś 'otraś amiśtadeś abaśtara 'un mal metedor 'o mal hablador 'a koronperla fasil mente 'i la amiśtad śegun 'oneśto kuando 'eś konfirmada 'entre doś amigoś virtu'ozoś no abaśtan todoś loś mal dizyenteś del 'oniberso 'a koronperla 'ila razon 'eśta viśta deloke tenemoś diğo[118] 'i 'eś ke komo la tal amiśtad no śe konfirma śalvo depu'eś de verdadero konosimyento kon diskurso de tyenpo kuando vinyere 'un mal dizyente 'a poner mal 'entre 'uno 'a 'otro komo 'enbidy'ozo de tal amiśtad komo 'a 'el prezente floreśen muğoś 'en la republika 'el ke 'eś verdadero amigo dela manera diğa no le pu'ede dar kredito 'a ningun mal ke diğere porke ninguno lo pu'ede aver konosido komo 'el pu'eś śe konfirmo 'ensu amiśtad 'i pu'eś 'el 'en tanto tyenpo no konosy'o akelyyo 'ensu amigo ke tanto 'eśpekulo 'en śaber śuś kondisy'oneś komo lo pu'ede konoser 'un mal dizyente ke no

---

[115] Song of Sol. 1.1.
[116] Rashi Song of Sol. 1.1, Tanḥuma, Parashat Teṣaveh, Siman 5.
[117] Aristotle, *NE* VIII.iv.4 (1157a 31–34).
[118] Aristotle, *NE* VIII.iv.3 (1157a 21–25).

BOOK OF THE REGIMEN OF LIVING ‹FOL. 115A–115B›

lo peśkizo tanto komo 'el por lo kual no le da kredito porke ya lo myente aśu amigo konosido por bu'eno 'i del bu'eno tyene konsebido ke no pu'ede śalir del koza mala :
 DE manera ke la amiśtad verdader'a 'eśta de kontino fiğa 'i firme komo tenemoś diğo :

KAPITULO SEBTIMO

'I a'un ke alguno dubdara kon alguna razon ke parese poderśe mudar la amiśtad por algunaś razoneś 'una delaś kualeś 'eś porke pu'ede śer ke la bondad del amigo śe korompa komo vemoś algunoś bu'enoś danyyarśe 'i hazerśe maloś 'i pu'ede śer tanbyen ke śe korompa por śegunda kauśa 'i 'eś ke a'un ke śe'a firme 'enla bondad śera mudable por la mudansa de loś 'eśtadoś ke śi 'uno de loś amigoś śubyere 'a śer prinsipe 'o gran śenyyor perderśe'a akelyya amiśtad por loke tenemoś diğo ke la amiśtad 'a de śer 'enloś 'igualeś 'i śemeğanteś konforme alo kual parese ke 'era la 'intensy'on de loke dezi'a Y^ehonaṭan 'a David no temaś ke no te alkansara la mano de Šaul mi padre 'i tu 'enreynaraś śobre Yiśra'el 'i yo sere ati śegundo 'i set-[119] ke parese syerto fe'o 'un tan virtu'ozo komo Y^ehonaṭan adkerir loś 'eśtadoś śemeğanteś śin śer rekerido kuanto maś dezirlo por la boka ke 'eś koza aśaś vituperable para tan manyanimo komo 'el por donde parese syerto śer la 'intensy'on ke keri'a ke no śe perdyeśe la [CW. amiśtad]}

‹fol. 115b›
{amiśtad 'entre taleś doś 'enreynando David por la diśtansy'a de loś 'eśtadoś por lo kual amośtraba kerer ke fu'eśe de modo ke 'ubyeśe 'en śuś 'eśtadoś algun modo de śimilitud 'i 'igualdad para ke no śe perdyeśe de 'entre 'elyyoś la amiśtad :
 AYY 'otra kauśa tanbyen para koromperśe 'i maś konğunta 'i posible 'en todo tyenpo ke 'eś 'el falyeser 'uno de loś amigoś por 'onde parese ke no śe pu'eda lyyamar 'eterna ke śi 'eś por ke dura 'en kuanto tura la vida de loś doś ğunta mente muğoś amigoś de laś 'otraś 'eśpesyaś de amiśtad ke 'el vulgo lyyama amigoś ternan 'eśto 'i turaran 'en la amiśtad 'en kuanto leś turare la vida :
 ALO kual śe pu'ede fasil mente reśp(+)onder konforme ala verdad suśtentando lo ke tenemoś diğo ke la amiśtad verdader'a nunka śe korompe 'el abito ni śe muda 'i keda firma(n)[m]ente 'en 'eterno
 'I 'en kuanto 'a la primera razon 'eś manifyeśto śer falsa por ke 'el bu'eno 'i virtu'ozo verdader'a mente nunka śe korompe 'el abito de śu virtud ke de śu natural

---

[119] 1 Sam. 23.17.

Book of the Regimen of Living ⟨fol. 115b–116a⟩

'eś śer muy fiğe 'i firme śin ninguna korupsy'on 'i śi algun bu'eno ve'emoś ke śe korompe 'i śe torna malo ğuśgaremoś kon verdadero ğu'izy'o ke nunka fu'e bu'eno ni lo konosimoś byen lo ke 'el ke 'eś amigo verdader'a mente porel 'onesto komo tenemoś diğo no 'a de śer śalvo de pu'eś de verdadero konosimyento de śu bondad 'i virtud śer 'enel fiğe 'i firme komo avemoś diğo

'I 'en kuanto la śegunda razon me parese syerto yero manifyeśto pensar ke la amiśtad verdader'a de pu'eś de konfirmada śe pyerda por la dibersidad de loś 'eśtadoś por ke komo kyera ke la amiśtad śe'a heğa abito 'enel anima komo laś 'otraś vertudeś a'un ke por la diferensy'a de loś 'eśtadoś śe pyerda la konversasy'on komo la śolian tener no śe perdera por 'eśo la amiśtad de pu'eś de konfirmada maś anteś kedara muy firme 'i fiğa 'enel anima de kada 'uno de loś doś 'i no değan de śer śimileś 'i 'igualeś 'en la kośa ke por 'elyya śon amigoś ke 'eś la virtud 'i bondad suśtansyal ke loś 'e[ś]tadoś śon asidenteś 'i no śe'a de perder 'i koromper la suśtansy'a por loś asidenteś 'i śi Y^ehonaṭan dezi'a 'a David ke 'el le śeri'a śegundo no 'era por ke śin 'eśo śe perdi'a la amiśtad komo algunoś glośaron śalvo ke no keri'a perder la konversasy'on ke 'entre 'elyyoś avi'a ke 'eś 'una de laś 'obraś de amiśtad komo maś adelante śe aklarara 'i por 'eśo diğo 'i yo śere ati por śegundo 'i set-[120] ke baśtara byen ke diğera tu 'enreynaraś śobre Yiśra'el 'i yo śere śegundo[121] ke ya 'eś śabido ke no śe dize 'eśte termino de śegundo śalvo porel ke 'eś śegundo a'el rey pero kiğo śiknifikar 'en[e]śte byerbo demazyado ke todo śu fin 'era ke no śe perdyeśe 'el ağuntamyento 'i konversasy'on kon la diśtansy'a 'i diferensy'a}

⟨fol. 116a⟩
{KYV
de loś 'eśtadoś ke 'eśto 'eśta byen śiknifikado 'en dezir 'i yo śere 'a ti por śegundo komo śi diğeśe 'i yo śyendo śegundo śere alyegado 'a ti ke 'eśta 'eś mi 'intensy'on :

'I 'enla tersera kauśa podemoś afirmar 'i dezir ke a'un kon la mu'erte del amigo no śe pyerde la amiśtad porke komo kyera ke tenemoś berifikado ke śe'a la amiśtad 'un abito komo virtud 'enla anima del amigo a'un ke śe mu'era 'el amigo keda la amiśtad 'enel anima del bibo komo keda la virtud dela liberalidad fiğa 'i firme 'enel anima de 'el virtu'ozo a'un ke śe pyerda la moneda kon ke śe 'obra la liberalidad 'i a'un ke 'eśte śolo 'en 'una montany'a śin aver 'en kyen 'obre 'i 'eğersite la tal virtud kuanta maś ke śe pu'ede 'eğersitar la amiśtad ke tyene kon 'el amigo di( )funto 'en śuś hiğoś komo akaese 'en muğoś amigoś ke de pu'eś de mu'ertoś śuś amigoś 'uzan de akelyya amiśtad kon loś hiğoś ke kedan de akel śu amigo ke mury'o por ke 'el ke

---

[120] 1 Sam. 23.17.
[121] 1 Sam. 23.17.

Book of the Regimen of Living ‹fol. 116a–116b›

'eś amigo por la bondad de śu amigo aśi komo la bondad no pereśe ni mu'ere 'en morir 'el amigo maś anteś keda la bondad 'eterna aśi keda la amiśtad 'eterna konforme 'a lo kual diğo Tuly'o[122] por Sipy'on śu amigo deśpu'eś de mu'erto 'en 'eśta forma Sipy'on mi amigo a'un ke mury'o śupito 'eśta bibo aserka de mi 'i bivira para śyenpre porke śu bondad 'i perfeksy'on no mury'o 'i set[-] ke fu'eron palabraś de śemeğante śaby'o komo 'el donde śiknifiko todo loke tenemoś diğo

'I Seneka kiğo sentir lo meśmo dizyendo 'en muğoś 'i diversoś lugareś ke la kośtelasy'on no pu'ede tirar śalvo lo ke da 'i set-[123] śiknifikando ke la virtud 'i bondad ke no da la kośtelasy'on no la pu'ede tirar a'un ke kite la vida al virtu'ozo de adonde 'eś byen viśto ke la amiśtad verdader'a a'un deśpu'eś de mu'erto 'el amigo permaneśe a'un ala 'opiny'on deśtoś filosofos kuanto maś ala verdad berifikada por nu'eśa śantisima ley ke kre'emoś syerto permaneśer 'el anima 'i śentir laś kozaś de aka depu'eś de partir deśta vida preśente 'i tener konśigo konğunta toda la bondad ke aka tubo 'en muğo maś 'ekselente grado de perfeksy'on ke 'eś byen viśto ke a'un deśpu'eś de mu'ertoś todoś loś doś amigoś ke( )da 'eterna akelyya virtud de la verdader'a amiśtad 'en laś animaś de loś amigoś difuntoś de manera ke no śe dira 'eśpartirśe 'uno de 'otro śalvo 'enel śolo punto de la mu'erte ke anteś 'i depu'eś śyenpre śe pu'eden lyyamar amigoś 'i ğuntoś 'i no 'eśpartidoś komo śe diğo por la amiśtad de David 'i Y^eḥonaṭan 'en śu vida ni 'en śu mu'erte no śe 'eśp(+)artyeron 'i set-[124] ke śiknifikaron śer la amiśtad 'enelyyoś 'eterna komo tenemoś diğo lo kual pyenśo ke kiğo śiknifikar akelyya śenyyora Ruṭ aśu śu'egra ke tantaś veześ le avi'a diğo ke śe tornaśe aśu Dyyo 'i aśu pu'eblo la kual por 'ultimo reśpondy'o 'i diğo no ru'egeś 'en mi para değarte para tornar de 'enpu'eś ti ke 'a lo ke [CW. andubyereś]}

‹fol. 116b›
{andubyereś andare 'i 'onde manyereś manere tu pu'eblo mi pu'eblo 'i tu Dyyo mi Dyyo 'i set- 'en lo ke muryereś morire 'i a'i śere 'enterada aśi faga 'el Dyyo ami 'i aśi 'enyyada ke la mu'erte 'eśpartira 'entre mi 'i 'entre ti 'i set-[125] ke la 'intensy'on 'en todaś 'eśtaś palabraś 'eś viśta kon lo ke tenemoś diğo 'i 'eś ke komo Ruṭ 'ubyeśe konosido 'en todo akel diśkurso de tyenpo ke kon 'elyya avi'a konversado muğa bondad 'i virtud determinaba de konfirmar kon 'elyya la verdader'a amiśtad kon

---

[122] Cicero, *De Amicitia*, 27.
[123] Seneca, *De Constantia Sapientis*, v.4: "Nihil eripit fortuna nisi quod dedit; uirtutem autem non dat" (ed./trans. Basore, 1:60). Cf. *Ep. Mor.* 88.14–15, trans. Gummere, 2:357–59.
[124] 2 Sam. 1.23.
[125] Ruth 1.16–17.

BOOK OF THE REGIMEN OF LIVING ‹FOL. 116B›

'eśtar 'en kontinu'a konversasy'on komo konvyene aloś verdaderoś amigoś 'i komo vido ke tanto porfyaba konelyya ke śe bolbyeśe atanto ke ya le paresi'a deśkortezi'a kerer porfyar de 'ir kon 'elyya por ke kisa le daba pasy'on śu konpanyi'a 'i no 'eś kortezi'a kerer 'ir 'uno 'en konpanyi'a de 'otro kontra śu voluntad 'eśpesyal 'en loś kaminanteś 'i por śer ke 'elyya no le dezi'a ke no keri'a śu konpanyi'a śalvo ke śe bolvyeśe donde denotaba ke no śelo dezi'a por ke le dyeśe pasy'on śu konpanyi'a śalvo por lo ke tokaba a'elyya ke no śe 'eśpartyeśe de loś śuyoś por tanto le diğo no me ru'egeś ke te değe para tornar atraś ke 'eś komo ke diğeśe ke śi 'eś tu 'inte[n]sy'on para ke te değe ke no me akonpanye kon ti 'eśto hare yo a'un ke me pezara delyyo hazer lo por ke no[ ]'e de 'ir konti[go] kontra tu voluntad pero değarte para tornarme ke śon doś kozaś no me ru'egeś por ke adonde tu vaś vo yo ke kyere dezir 'el fin tuyo 'eś 'el mi'o 'i set- 'i kon 'eśto 'eśtan byen aśentadaś 'eśtaś palabraś ke paresen dobladaś ke baśtara ke diğera no me ru'egeś ke te değe //('i)['o]// no me ru'egeś ke torne atraś śalvo ke kiğo śiknifikar lo diğo 'en loś maś breveś terminoś ke posible 'eś 'i 'eś darle 'a 'entender komo teni'a konfirmada la amiśtad kon 'elyya 'i por śu bondad 'i virtud le diğo 'i le ğuro ke śolo 'el punto de la mu'erte śeri'a 'el ke 'eśpartiri'a 'entre laś doś ke anteś 'i de pu'eś ś[y]enpre śerian ğuntaś 'i 'eśto kiğo dezir 'en dezir ke la mu'erte 'eśpartira 'entre mi 'i 'entre ti 'i set-[126] ke la mu'erte verdader'a mente śe toma por 'el punto del 'eśpartir 'el alma del ku'erpo 'i no por lo de anteś ni depu'eś deśte punto[127]

'I syendo śuś 'intensy'on(v)[e]ś tan konformeś 'i 'el fin 'i akatamyento a'el Dyyo todo 'uno no podi'a değar de śer aśi kon lo kual fu'e śaśtifeğa Naᶜami 'i no k[u]ro de hablarle maś

DE adonde parese byen lo ke tenemoś diğo śer verdad ke la amiśtad śegun 'oneśto 'eś permanente 'i perdurable 'en 'eterno 'en vida 'i mu'erte por lo kual 'eśta byen viśta la diferensy'a delyya alaś 'otraś 'eśpesyaś

TYENE maś 'eśta verdader'a amiśtad 'otra propyedad ke no tyene laś 'otraś 'i 'eś ke śegun 'eśta amiśtad verdader'a no pu'ede tener 'un 'ombre muğoś amigoś ni pu'ede śer muy verdader'a ni 'eśtremada amiśtad komo konbyene śer śalvo kon 'uno no maś[128] 'i 'eśto śe pu'ede berifikar por treś razoneś 'ividenteś

LA primera 'eś por ke 'eśta amiśtad para śer komo konbyene 'a de śer 'enel 'eśtremo [CW. por lo]}

---

[126] Ruth 1.17.
[127] Cf. Aristotle, *De Anima* I (411b8–9).
[128] Aristotle, *NE* VIII.vi.2 (1158a 11–13), cf. also IX.x.5–6 (1171a 9–20).

‹fol. 117a›
{KYZ
por lo kual no pu'ede śer maś ke kon 'uno ke 'el 'eśtremo 'i kabo pośtrero no pu'ede śer maś de 'uno 'i śi tyene maś de 'un amigo no śera 'en 'eśtremo kon ninguno pu'eś śe reparty'o la amiśtad 'enloś doś 'i śi fu'eren maś śera manko kon kada 'uno porke para śer 'en 'eśtremo la amiśtad 'a de śer ke 'eśten kontinu'a mente ğuntoś loś amigoś 'i konversen ğuntoś 'i komuniken ğuntoś todaś śuś kośaś 'i 'eśto 'eś viśto ke kon doś no śe pu'ede hazer 'eśtremada mente porke śi 'uno 'i 'otro tubyeren 'una alegri'a 'en 'un meśmo tyenpo 'i 'el 'a de komunikar 'el plazer kon kada 'uno de 'elyyoś 'eśpesyal śyendo de 'elyyoś lyyamado 'a kyen de 'elyyoś 'era ke 'a kual kyera de 'elyyoś ke vayya ya keda 'el 'otro śumenoś 'i agrabyyado pu'eś śi no va 'a ninguna no 'uza kon ninguno de 'elyyoś komo amigo verdadero 'eśtremado 'en la amiśtad 'i kuanto maś śi loś doś 'eśtan apasy'onadoś 'en 'un meśmo tyenpo ke deve 'el de śuyo apreśurarśe 'a komunikar konśu amigo la pasy'on anteś ke śe'a de 'elyyo rekerido pu'eś 'a kual de 'elyyoś akudira syendo loś doś verdaderoś amigoś ke no kede 'el 'uno agrabyado 'i a'un 'eśkandalizado pu'eś kuando 'el 'uno tubyere alegri'a 'i 'el 'otro pasy'on 'i triśtura ke śon doś kontrary'oś 'en 'un meśmo tyenpo komo podra komunikar kon loś doś komo konbyene por donde parese keno pu'ede tener 'un 'ombre maś de 'un amigo :

LA śegunda razon 'eś ke komo kyera ke por la difinsy'on ke deklaramoś de la amiśtad 'a de śer ke śe'a 'igual de 'uno 'a 'otro komo del 'otro 'a 'el de manera ke ayya gualardon de laś 'obraś 'igual mente 'eś viśto ke śi tubyere muğoś amigoś no podra 'el gualardonar 'a todoś 'igual mente komo kada 'uno hara kon 'el no te( )nyendo kada 'uno de 'elyyoś maś ke 'a 'el 'i 'el tenyendo 'a todoś :

LA tersera razon 'eś maś manifyeśta ke todaś por lo ke tenemoś antisipado ke 'eśta tal 'eśpesy'a de amiśtad no śe'a de konfirmar śalvo depu'eś de verdadero konosimyento del amigo 'el kual konosimyento no pu'ede śer śalvo kon muğo diśkurso de tyenpo komo tenemoś diğo[129] por tanto no pu'ede tener muğoś amigoś deśta 'eśpesy'a porke la vida 'umana 'eś korta para poder loś konoser ke no abaśta para poder konoser byen 'en toda la vida maś de doś 'o treś amigoś śegun 'eśta 'eśpesy'a de amiśtad kuando muğo pu'eś depu'eś ke 'el 'ombre bu'eno 'i virtu'ozo ke konose kuanta perdida 'eś perder 'el tyenpo śin probeğo del alma ayya gaśtado tanto tyenpo hata halyyar 'uno bu'eno de kyen śe pu'ede konfyar depu'eś de tan largo 'i verdadero konosimyento komo keda gaśtar maś 'otro tyenpo tan largo 'en buśkar 'otro kon dubda ke al fin del tyenpo konośera no śer tal kual penso 'enel prinsipy'o 'i halyyarśe'a aver gaśtado tanto tyenpo 'en baldeś ke no 'eś poka perdida :

---

[129] Aristotle, *NE* VIII.vi.3 (1158a 14–16).

BOOK OF THE REGIMEN OF LIVING ‹FOL. 117A–117B›

POR lo kual diğo Menandro 'el grego ke 'el 'ombre ke le akaese tener śolombra de 'un amigo no maś 'eś razon de tenerlo 'en posisy'on de 'ombre muğo de byen 'i set-[130] keryendo dezir ke kyen tyene muğoś amigoś no pu'ede śer perfekto amigo [CW. de]}

‹fol. 117b›
{de ninguno de manera ke kyen tyene tan śola mente 'una śolombra de amigo 'eś demośtrasy'on aver heğo muğa diliğensy'a por alkansarlo 'i kon todo kuanto trabağo no alkanso 'un śolo amigo 'entero 'i denota śer 'ombre de byen ke vido 'i konosy'o 'un 'ombre komo 'eś razon de konoser śegun 'eśta virtud alyegando al kabo de la peśkiza ke konbyene hazerśe para konformar 'un amigo 'en alguna manera a'un no por 'entero śalvo 'en grado de śolombra kuanto maś konfirmar muğoś ke 'eś kośa 'inposible 'en 'eśta 'eśpesy'a de amiśtad komo tenemoś diğo

POR todaś 'eśtaś treś razoneś 'eś viśto ke 'en laś 'otraś doś 'eśpesyaś de amiśtad no śe halyya 'eśta propyedad 'en 'elyyaś por ke laś 'otraś doś amiśtadeś no śon 'en 'eśtremo komo 'eśta verdader'a para ke śe diga ke śe diminuye syendo kon muğoś ni śon tan konversableś ke no pu'ede 'el amigo kunplir 'oneśta mente kon muğoś amigoś 'i gualardonar 'a kada 'uno konforme 'a lo ke de 'el tyene resebido ni 'eś meneśter ke śe antisipe konosimyento anteś ke śe konfirme porke śin ningun konosimyento śe hazen 'eśtaś taleś amiśtadeś abyendo la kauśa ke 'eś 'el 'util 'o 'el deleyte

'I 'eśta kon 'eśto byen viśto la diferensy'a de la amiśtad por 'el 'oneśto alaś 'otraś doś ke śon por deleyte 'i por 'util a'un ke laś doś 'entreśi śean diferenteś kela ke 'eś porel deleyte tyene alguna maś śimilitud konla ke 'eś porel 'oneśto[131] kela 'otra ke 'eś por 'el 'util porke la ke 'eś deleytable 'eś maś durable 'i maś alyegada al 'eśtremo kela ke 'eś porel 'util komo avemoś ya tokado ariba 'i maś ke 'eś alaś veześ 'eliğida por śi ke 'eś komo fin prośtero loke no tyene 'el 'util ke nunka 'eś 'eliğido porśi komo tenemoś tanbyen 'eśto diğo 'i 'eś maś śin fatiga kela ke 'eś porel 'util por lo kual śe halyya 'en loś mosoś 'i manseboś ke huyen de śu natural del tr[a]bağo

AYY 'otra 'eśpesy'a de amiśtad diferente de laś treś 'eśpesyaś diğaś la kual 'eś komo la amiśtad de 'el padre al hiğo 'i del hiğo al padre del vyeğo al moso 'i del moso al vyeğo del 'ombre aśu muğer 'i de la muğer al 'ombre del śenyyor al śudito 'i del

---

[130] Among Menander's unidentified minor fragments is a similar statement: "Does not each man think that he has discovered some unusual blessing if he gains even the semblance of a friend?" (*Fragments*, trans. Allinson, 493).
[131] Aristotle, *NE* VIII.vi.4 (1158a 18–20).

Book of the Regimen of Living ‹fol. 117b–118a›

śudito al śenyyor ke 'eśtaś amiśtadeś todaś a'un ke śon de 'una meśma 'eśpesy'a śon laś diğaś partidaś diferenteś 'una de la 'otra ke no 'eś la amiśtad del padre al hiğo komo la del vyeğo al moso ni a'un komo la del marido ala muğer ke śon muy diferenteś 'una de 'otra komo 'eś manifyeśto 'i no śolo 'eśto śi no ke a'un 'en 'una meśma partida no 'eś 'igual la amiśtad del 'uno al 'otro konla del 'otro a'el ke no 'eś 'igual 'el 'amor 'i amiśtad del padre al hiğo konla del hiğo al padre ni la del śenyyor al śudito konla del śudito al śenyyor 'i aśi kada 'una de laś 'otraś partidaś porke de śer loś amigoś 'i laś kauzaś de laś amiśtadeś dif[e]renteś śon laś meśmaś [CW. amiśtadeś]}

‹fol. 118a›
{KYḤ ḤELEK G PEREK [Z]
amiśtadeś diferenteś komo 'eś śabido ke de kauśaś diferenteś śe śigen 'efektoś diferenteś[132] 'i komo 'el padre no 'eś 'igual 'a 'el hiğo ni 'el śenyyor al śudito aśi 'el 'amor ke 'el 'uno tyene al 'otro no pu'ede śer 'igual de la meśma manera la kauśa porke 'el padre ama al hiğo no 'eś la meśma kauśa por la kual ama 'el hiğo 'a 'el padre ke 'el padre ama al hiğo bu'eno porke le 'onra 'i haze śu mandado 'i le 'eś 'obedyente 'i 'el hiğo ama al padre porke lo mantyene 'i lo dotrina 'i lo 'inpone 'en todo ğenero de[ ]perfeksy'on[133] 'i de la meśma manera 'el marido ama ala muğer bu'ena porke le sirve 'i le miniśtra 'i le 'eś 'obedyente 'i śudita 'i śobğekta a'el komo śe deve 'i 'elyya lo ama porke la mantyene 'i la viśte 'i kalsa 'i set-[134] de la meśma manera 'el prinsipe 'o śenyor ama al śudito bu'eno porke haze śu mandado 'i le 'eś fy'el 'ensu śervisy'o 'i 'el śudito ama al prinsipe 'o al śenyor bu'eno porke suśtenta 'el reyno 'o 'el śenyyori'o kon ğuśtisy'a 'i değa bivir 'a kada 'uno 'en śu le'ey 'i loś konserva 'i loś śalva de śuś 'enemigoś de la meśma manera 'el vyeğo ama al moso porke le 'eś 'obedyente 'i ayuda para loke 'eś nesesary'o 'a la flaka veğeś 'i 'el moso ama al vyeğo por 'el konśeğo ke del resibe kuando tyene a'un konśeğo 'o 'otra kośa tal de manera ke komo laś kauzaś de śuś amiśtadeś śon diferenteś por 'eśta vi'a diğa por tanto laś amiśtadeś 'enśi de 'uno 'a 'otro śon diferenteś komo tenemoś diğo :

---

[132] Aristotle, *NE* VIII.vii.1 (1158b 12–20).

[133] Aristotle, *NE* VIII.xii.5 (1162a 5–7).

[134] This is reminiscent of one of Aristotle's statements on husbands and wives: "they supply each other's wants, putting their special capacities into the common stock" (*NE* VIII.xii.7 [1162A 23–24]).

BOOK OF THE REGIMEN OF LIVING ‹FOL. 118A–118B›

KAPITULO 'OǦO

'I depu'eś ke ya aś byen viśto algunaś propyedadeś(+) de la verdader'a amiśtad por laś kualeś abraś konosido 'oneśta mente la diferensy'a de 'elyya 'a laś 'otraś 'eśpesyaś kon lo ke tenemoś diǧo ke todo 'el ke ama 'a de śer amado 'eś byen de śaber kual 'eś meǧor 'en grado de bondad 'i perfeksy'on śi 'el amar 'o 'el śer amado 'i porke todo 'el ke ama 'eś amado kyero dezir ke porke parte 'eś meǧor 'i maś loable 'el amigo śi por la parte ke 'el ama aśu amigo 'o por la parte ke 'eś del amado :
    PARA lo kual aś de śaber ke 'el vulgo tyene por meǧor śer amadoś ke amar :
    'I la kauśa deśto 'eś porke tyene para śi ke lo ke 'elyyoś lyyaman 'onra la kual lyyamo yo vaniglory'a komunika 'i partisipa muǧo kon la amiśtad 'o alo menoś p[y]ensan śer muy alyegadoś 'i komo tengan por 'opiny'on śer meǧor śer 'onradoś ke 'onrar tyene tanbyen por 'opiny'on ke lo meśmo 'eś śer amadoś ke amar por lo kual determinan śer meǧor śer amadoś ke amar 'i komo akaese laś maś de laś veześ 'a loś ke 'eśta 'opiny'on tyenen ke śon loś maś 'o todoś de nu'eśo śiglo ke 'onran 'a 'otroś por ke 'elyyoś leś 'onren 'a 'elyyoś aśi aman 'i mu'eśtran amar por ke śean amadoś[135] 'i liǧungean kon palabraś [CW. 'i kon]}

‹fol. 118b›
{ḤELEK G PEREK Ḥ [PART THREE CHAPTER EIGHT
'i kon heǧoś por mośtrar ke leś aman para ke 'elyyoś loś amen por ke 'el ke li(n)ǧunǧe'a 'a 'otro śe haze maś baǧo 'i a'un ke ala verdad śe'a maś alto alomenoś 'en la 'obra del liǧunǧear śe haze 'el 'infiry'or 'i 'eneśte hazerśe 'infiry'or todo śu fin 'eś por śer del 'onrado 'o amado por 'el 'util 'i deleytable 'i ala verdad ni 'eśta amiśtad 'eś amiśtad ni 'eśta 'onra 'eś 'onra ke todo 'eś por 'otroś reśpektoś ke kuando 'onran 'a 'otroś 'o liǧunǧean 'a 'otroś 'o mu'eśtran amarleś por ke leś amen 'i loś 'onren no lo hazen por ke leś amen por la amiśtad 'enśi ni por ke leś 'onren por la 'onra 'enśi śalvo por algun 'util 'o reśpekto ke śe le śige al tal delyyo ke digan la ǧente ke 'eś amado 'o ke 'eś 'onrado delyyoś ke 'eś 'un modo de deleytasy'on de akelyya vaniglory'a 'o por kelo tengan 'en posisy'on de bu'eno 'o de grande pu'eś ke 'eś 'onrado 'i amado de bu'enoś 'i grandeś de manera ke ninguno deśtoś lo haze por la amiśtad 'enśi śalvo por algunoś asidenteś ke śe śigen delya komo tenemoś diǧo[136] :
    POR lo kual 'en la verdader'a amiśtad ke no 'eś por ningun reśpekto śalvo por la bondad 'enśi ke 'eś amar 'el byen porel byen 'enśi 'eś viśto śer 'el kontrary'o ke

---

[135] Aristotle, *NE* VIII.viii.1 (1159a 15–18).
[136] Aristotle, *NE* VIII.viii.2 (1159a 19–27).

BOOK OF THE REGIMEN OF LIVING ‹FOL. 118B-119A›

muğo meğor 'i maś loable 'eś amar ke śer amado por muğaś razoneś 'i muy 'ivideriteś :
LA primera 'i maś viśta 'eś ke komo la amiśtad verdader'a 'eś 'un abito 'enel alma para 'obrar laś 'obraś dela amiśtad kon śu amigo por la bondad 'enśi 'i non por 'otro ningun reśpekto tanto kuanto śe avantağa 'el 'obrar śegun virtud al padeser tanto śe avantağa 'el amar 'a śer amado pu'eś 'el amar 'eś virtud 'o kon virtud komo tenemoś diğo 'i 'eś viśto śer deleytable 'a 'el 'ombre amar 'a 'otro śin śer amado por loke ve'emoś 'enel 'amor natural delaś madreś aśuś hiğoś kuando loś krian ke a'un ke śaben ke ala sazon no śon delyoś amadaś no değan de alegrarśe kon amarloś 'i kryarloś[137] de adonde parese śer 'el amar 'a 'otro virtud deleytable a'un ke no ayya gualardon de amiśtad pu'eś ve'emoś ke la alegri'a deloś padreś 'i madreś kon śuś hiğoś 'eś konla perfeksy'on de śuś hiğoś 'i tanto kuanto maś byen 'i perfeksy'on leś ve'en tanto maś leś aman :
KONFORME alo kual diğo nu'eśo śapyentisimo rey Šᵉlomoh mi fiğo śi śe aśabentara tu korason alegrarśe'a mi korason tanbyen yo 'i set-[138] keryendo dezir ke śi la śensy'a de 'el hiğo fu'ere de korason heğa abito 'intiry'or 'i no asidental aśi tanbyen la alegri'a ke tomara 'el padre śera de korason 'i 'eśto śignifiko konel termino de tanbyen ke 'eś komo ke diğeśe śi śe aśabentara tu korason konvyene 'a śaber ke śe'a tu sensy'a sustansyal 'i de korason tanbyen yo mi alegri'a śera de korason i 'eśto kiğo dezir 'en dezir alegrarśe'a mi korason tanbyen yo 'i set-[139] donde denota 'el 'eśtremado 'amor deloś padreś konla bondad 'i perfeksy'on deloś hiğoś porke '[e]l 'amor deloś padreś [CW. aloś]}

‹fol. 119a›
{KYT
aloś hiğoś 'eś natural por lo kual śe konfirma anteś de konosimyento de byen ni mal komo 'eś viśto por akel devinisimo ğu'izy'o ke ğuśgo nu'eśo śapyentisimo re'ey Šᵉlomoh 'entre akelyyaś malaś muğereś ke por śaber 'el śapyentisimo ğu'ez kela muğer por mala ke śe'a kyere byen aśu hiğo ğuśgo kela madre verdader'a no keri'a konsentir de matar aśu hiğo a'un ke lo apartaśen delyya ke 'era para 'elyya asaś pasy'on por donde para hazer la 'eśperensy'a mando traer 'una 'espada para partirlo por medyo 'i diğo alyi la 'eśkritura 'i diğo la muğer ke śu hiğo 'era 'el bibo 'i set-[140]

---

[137] Aristotle, *NE* VIII.viii.3 (1159a 28-34).
[138] Prov. 23.15.
[139] Prov. 23.15.
[140] 1 Kings 3.26.

Book of the Regimen of Living ‹fol. 119a–119b›

ru'ego mi śenyyor dar 'a 'elyya 'el ninyo bibo 'i no lo matedeś 'i set-[141] ke vye(y)ndo la pyadoza madre la mu'erte del hiğo kiğo anteś śufrir la pasy'on del ponerlo 'en mano ağena ke śufrir śu mu'erte por la 'amor natural kele teni'a komo tenemoś diğo

LA śegunda razon 'eś ke la kauśa por la kual 'eś 'el 'ombre maś loado 'eś la meğor 'i pu'eś ve'emoś ke śi 'el 'ombre 'eś loado no 'eś por śer amado de 'otroś ke 'eneśto no haze 'el nada 'i 'enloke 'el 'ombre no haze nada no ayy razon ke śe'a por 'elyyo loado 'i śi 'a de śer loado no 'a de śer śalvo por amar 'el a'otroś lu'ego parese ke 'el amar 'eś meğor ke śer amado 'i por 'eśta kauza para śer verdader'a la amiśtad 'i fiğa 'i firme 'entre doś amigoś 'eś meneśter ke kada 'uno deloś doś ame al 'otro para ke todoś doś 'obren śegun 'eśta virtud ke kon 'el 'obrar śe haze 'el abito dela virtud 'i no kon 'el padeśer komo 'eś śabido 'i syendo aśi nunka śe korompe la tal amiśtad ni dezi'a 'el 'uno al 'otro mal 'en ninguna manera maś anteś śi 'el 'uno 'eliğe alguna kośa mala 'o deś'oneśta 'el 'otro perkura de 'ebitarla porke lo meśmo ke kyere para śi kyere para śu amigo ke an de śer komo 'una meśma alma 'en doś ku'erpoś 'i set-[142] :

POR todaś 'eśtaś kauśaś 'eśta viśto śer la amiśtad de loś maloś de kual kyera de laś doś 'eśpesyaś al kontrary'o de la amiśtad verdader'a ke nunka tyene amiśtad fiğa ni firme komo kyera ke 'eś por kauza de algunoś asidenteś ke no śon durableś komo tenemoś diğo ni kyere 'el 'uno al 'otro loke 'el 'otro kyere a'el ke śon deś'igualeś aśi komo laś kauśaś asidentaleś por laś kualeś śe aman śon deś'igualeś[143] ke tal 'eś 'el 'efekto komo la kauśa komo tenemoś diğo 'i kuando 'el 'uno śige 'el mal 'el 'otro lo 'eśfu'ersa 'i lo 'inpone maś 'enelyyo komo kyera ke śu ağuntamyento no 'eś śalvo por 'eśte fin por donde determinaron nu'eśoś śaby'oś 'i diśeron ke 'el 'eśpartimyento aloś maloś 'eś byen para 'elyyoś 'i para 'el mundo 'i 'el ağuntamyento delyyoś 'eś mal para 'elyyoś 'i para 'el mundo 'i set-[144] 'i por 'el kontrary'o dizen ke 'eś 'en loś bu'enoś ke 'el ağuntamyento delyyoś 'eś byen para 'elyyoś 'i para 'el mundo 'i set-[145] 'i la kauśa 'eś viśta por kauśa de laś [CW. 'intensy'oneś]}

‹fol. 119b›
{'intensy'oneś de loś 'unoś 'i de loś 'otroś ke komo kyera ke 'el ağuntamyento de loś maloś 'eś afin de 'obrar 'el mal 'eśpartyendoloś no ternan tanta fu'ersa 'i poder para

---

[141] 1 Kings 3.26.
[142] Diogenes Laertius, *Philosophers,* trans. Hicks, 1:463. The saying is widespread in classical literature and is often attributed to Aristotle.
[143] Cf. Aristotle, *NE* IX.iii.1 (1165b 1–8).
[144] Sanhedrin 71b.
[145] Sanhedrin 71b.

BOOK OF THE REGIMEN OF LIVING ‹FOL. 119B›

'obrarlo 'i 'eśto 'eś byen para 'elyyoś ke değaran de 'obrar 'el mal 'i 'eś byen para 'el mundo konbyene 'a śaber para loś ke padesen loś maleś ke loś maloś hazen 'i por 'eśta meśma kauśa 'el ağuntamyento aloś bu'enoś 'eś kauśa de a'umentar 'i 'eśforsar la virtud para 'obrar 'el byen por lo kual 'eś byen para 'elyyoś 'i para 'el mundo 'i set-[146] 'i tyene maś loś maloś 'en śuś ağuntamyentoś 'i 'obraś ke śon lyenoś de arepentimyentoś 'en kuanto hazen komo dizen nu'eśoś śaby'oś loś maloś śon lyenoś de arepentimyentoś 'i set-[147] 'i nunka śe alegran kon loke hazen ni kon śuś amiśtadeś komo dize nu'eśo devinisimo rey David muğaś doloreś 'a 'el malo 'i 'el ke śe 'enfy'uzy'a 'en 'el Dyyo merseḋ lo arodeara 'i set-[148] keryendo dezir ke aśi komo a'el malo arodean muğaś doloreś 'en laś 'obraś ke haze ke 'el meśmo mal lo kaśtiga komo diğo 'el profeta Y^{e}ša^{c}yahu kaśtigarte'a tu mal 'i set-[149] k[e]ryendo dezir ke 'el meśmo mal kon 'el dolor ke kauśa al malo lo kaśtiga kon darle manzilyya 'i amargura del mal meśmo ke haze 'i del derokamyento de śu ku'erpo 'i alma ke trae kon śigo del meśmo modo 'el byen ke 'el bu'eno 'obra 'el meśmo byen le da śu premy'o 'i le haze mersedeś 'en darle alegri'a 'i kontentamyento del byen ke 'obra komo deklaro maś todo 'eśto 'el diğo profeta 'en dezir dezid ğuśto ke bu'eno ke fruto de śuś manoś komeran 'i set-[150] guayy a'el malo mal ke gualardon de śuś manoś śera feğo a'el 'i set-[151] ke la 'intensy'on 'eśta manifyeśta konforme alo ke tenemoś diğo ke dize 'el profeta ke todoś deven dezir 'i 'otorgar ke śer ğuśto 'eś bu'eno por ke 'eśta viśta la bondad 'i 'eś tan manifyeśta ke komen aki 'el fruto delyya 'i 'el kabdal 'eś guardado para gozar del 'en la vida advenidera 'i 'eśpekulando maś 'en śuś palabraś dize lo propy'o ke tenemoś diğo ke 'en 'obrar 'el byen komen 'el fruto 'i la glory'a de la meśma bondad ke 'eśto śe lyyama fruto de laś propyaś 'obraś 'i por 'el kontra[ry]y'o dize ke 'eś 'en 'el malo ke 'el guayy del 'eś 'el meśmo mal por ke 'el meśmo śe da aśi meśmo 'el gualardon ke 'el mereśe 'i 'eśto kiğo dezir 'en dezir ke 'el gualardon de śuś manoś śera feğo a'el 'i set-[152] komo ke diğeśe ke 'el gualardon de śuś propyaś manoś akel śera feğo a'el kon

---

[146] Sanhedrin 71b.
[147] Akin to what is said of the wicked at Jer. 5.27: "So are their houses full of deceit." Radak Jer. 5.27 reproduces the first two words of the Hebrew marginalia, " 'the evil are full' ", but "regrets" is replaced by "deceit".
[148] Ps. 32.10.
[149] I believe this is in fact Jer. 2.19, which closely resembles Isa. 3.11.
[150] Isa. 3.10.
[151] Isa. 3.11.
[152] Isa. 3.11.

Book of the Regimen of Living ‹fol. 119b–120a›

laś doloreś 'i pasy'oneś ke śele śigen de 'obrar 'el mal śin ke 'otro de fu'era le de la pena :
 POR donde parese śer 'el 'ombre maś 'eselente 'i virtu'ozo por amar ke por śer amado komo tenemoś probado konforme alo kual Tuly'o hablando aserka de 'eśto śi 'eś meǧor 'el ke ama ke 'el ke 'eś amado dize ke 'el amigo no ama al bu'eno śalvo por parte de amarśe aśi meśmo 'i por parte de śu virtud lo ama por ke 'eś natural de la virtud 'el 'obrar laś 'obraś de la virtud 'i set- 'i Śeneka 'en śuś 'epiśtolaś[153] dize ke 'el śaby'o perkura de amar 'a 'otroś por śer kela amiśtad 'eś virtud 'i por tanto 'el prudente 'i śaby'o}

‹fol. 120a›
{KK
perkura de halyyar 'obǧekto para 'obrar 'enel śegun virtud aśi komo 'el liberal perkura de halyyar 'en kyen 'obrar śu liberalidad 'i śe alegra kuando lo halyya por ke 'eś kauśa de 'obrar śegun virtud 'i set-[154] ke 'eneśtaś breveś palabraś konprendy'o byen todo kuanto tenemoś diǧo de adonde 'eśta byen viśto śer la 'eselensy'a deśta virtud por parte de amar maś ke por parte de śer amado
 DE pu'eś de 'eśto śabido 'eś byen ke śepaś maś ke la amiśtad 'eś konforme ala ǧuśtisy'a ke aśi komo la ǧuśtisy'a 'eś 'entre doś ke komunikan 'en alguna kośa aśi la amiśtad 'eś 'entre loś ke komunikan 'i konversan 'i śe aǧuntan 'uno kon 'otro de tal manera ke tanto kuanto maś 'eś la konversasy'on 'i aǧuntamyento tanto maś 'eś la amiśtad 'eśtremada 'i 'eśtreǧa 'en todaś laś 'eśpesyaś de la amiśtad de adonde sumary'a mente 'a todoś loś ke vemoś ke konversan ǧunta mente lyyamamoś amigoś kon razon por ke la amiśtad śe haze medyante la konversasy'on komo tenemoś diǧo porlo kual noś akabido nu'eśa śantisima ley 'i nu'eśoś profetaś 'i śaby'oś ke noś devemoś de apartar del aǧuntamyento de loś maloś por ke no śe venga 'a hazer amiśtad kon 'elyyoś por loś 'inkonvenyenteś ke tenemoś diǧo 'i por 'eśto konkluyyo nu'eśo devinisimo rey David 'en prinsipy'o de śu libro ke la byen aventuransa konsiśte 'en hu'ir de la konversasy'on 'i aǧuntamyento de loś maloś 'i por ke laś taleś konversasy'oneś pu'eden śer 'en loś konśeǧoś maloś ke 'eś por parte de laś 'intensy'oneś danyyadaś 'o 'en la habla 'i platikaś 'o 'en la 'obra 'eśtiry'or tiro todaś treś

---

[153] Cicero, *De Amicitia*, 10.

[154] Seneca addresses the point in Epistle 9: "The wise man, I say, self-sufficient though he be, nevertheless desires friends if only for the purpose of practising friendship, in order that his noble qualities may not lie dormant" (*Ep. Mor.*, trans. Gummere, 1:47); and similarly in Epistle 109: "Good men are mutually helpful; for each gives practice to the other's virtues and thus maintains wisdom at its proper level" (3:255).

Book of the Regimen of Living ‹fol. 120a–120b›

'i diğo byen aventurado 'el varon ke non andubo 'en konśeğo de maloś[155] ke 'eś la konformasy'on de loś pensamyentoś 'i 'en kamino de pekadoreś no 'eśtubo[156] 'eś por la konversasy'on 'en laś 'obraś ke śe śigen ğunta mente de la mala 'intensy'on 'i 'en asyento de 'eśkarnidoreś no śe asento[157] por la konversasy'on 'en laś platikaś 'i hablaś danyadaś 'i dize ke tirandośe de todo 'eśto śele śegira de śuyo 'el byen verdadero de tal manera ke no terna 'en 'otro la voluntad śalvo 'en la ley del Dyyo tr[a]bağara de[ ]di'a 'i de noğe[158] por ke komo śe'a natural del 'ombre 'obrar porke toda vida 'eś 'obra komo 'eś śabido

POR tanto 'eś viśto ke 'el keśe tira de 'obrar 'el mal lu'ego 'obra 'el byen 'i 'eśto kiğo dezir 'en dezir ke śolo 'en ley de H‹a-Šem› śu voluntad 'i 'en śu ley hablara de di'a 'i de noğe 'i set-[159] komo ke diğeśe ke tirandośe de todo lo diğo ariba //(ke no) [salvo]// 'en la //le['e]y// del Dyyo śera śu voluntad //ke no// pu'ede 'eśtar baldi'a por lo kual tirada del mal lu'ego śe traśpone de śuyo 'enel byen 'i syendo bu'ena la 'obra śe śige konforme a'elyya 'i 'eśto meśmo kiğo śentir 'en 'otro lugar do dize tanbyen no 'obraron tortura 'en śuś kaminoś andubyeron 'i set-[160] ke 'eś komo ke diğeśe ke no kale dezir kuando 'en puro a'uto 'obran 'el byen ke andan 'en śuś kaminoś maś a'un 'en değar de 'obrar 'el mal 'o la tortura lu'ego śe śige 'el 'andar 'en śuś kaminoś de adonde 'eś byen viśto lo ke [CW. tenemoś]}

‹fol. 120b›
{tenemoś diğo ke de la konversasy'on śe fazen laś amiśtadeś 'i tantaś śon laś 'eśpesyaś de la amiśtad komo śon laś diferensyaś de laś konver(b)[ś]asy'oneś 'i ağuntamyentoś 'i loś fineś por ke śe fazen loś taleś ağuntamyentoś

LOŚ kualeś śon treś 'eśpesyaś diferenteś konforme 'a treś 'eśpesyaś diferenteś de ağuntamyentoś ke śe konsidran 'en la politika ke 'eś 'el reğimyento de la sibdad

'EL primero de loś kualeś 'eś 'el ke śe lyyama reyno ke 'eś kuando la republika 'eś reğida por 'un śolo prinsipe 'o rey[161] 'i 'eśte 'eś 'el meğor ağuntamyento 'i kongregasy'on[162] ke śe rekyere para la suśtentasy'on 'i pasifikasy'on de la republika ke

---

[155] Ps. 1.1.
[156] Ps. 1.1.
[157] Ps. 1.1.
[158] Ps. 1.2.
[159] Ps. 1.2.
[160] Ps. 119.3.
[161] Aristotle, *NE* VIII.x.1 (1160a 33), cf. *Politics* III.14 (1284b 35–1285b 33).
[162] Aristotle, *NE* VIII.x.2 (1160a 35).

Book of the Regimen of Living ⟨fol. 120b–121a⟩

syendo reǧida por 'uno śolo akyen tyene todoś akatamyento 'i temor tura maś 'el reǧimyento ke 'eneśto 'imita maś a'el Dyyo glory'ozo lo kual syendo muǧoś śyenpre nase 'entre 'elyyoś alguna divizy'on 'o diśkordy'a la kual vyene(n) al fin 'a padeśer la republika komo śe ve'e muǧaś veześ 'en laś kozaś ke śon 'ordenadaś 'i reǧidaś por muǧoś

'I 'el śegundo 'eś kuando la republika 'eś reǧida por śenyyori'a 'o śenado de vyeǧos 'i virtu'ozoś ke śon '[e]leǧidoś por meǧoreś 'i mayoreś de la republika[163] komo konbyene 'a 'onor 'i gobernasy'on de toda la republika śegun śuś kalidadeś de virtud 'i 'edad konbenible para 'el reǧimyento komo 'era 'el reǧimyento de loś Sanhedrin 'en Yiśra'el 'en tyenpo antigo 'i komo fu'eron antiga mente reǧidoś loś romanoś 'i 'eś al tyenpo preśente la śenyyori'a de Veneṣy'a 'i 'otraś taleś ke śon śuś 'eśtadoś reǧidoś 'i 'ordenadoś por konśeǧo de loś maś prudenteś 'i antigoś 'i virtu'ozoś 'i de laś mayoreś kaśa(da)ś de la republika 'i 'eśte tal reǧimyento a'un ke śe'a muy prudente mente 'ordenado no pu'ede śer tan bu'eno ni tan firme komo 'el primero por laś kauśaś ke tenemoś diǧo de loś probeǧoś ke śe śigen de śer 'un śolo reǧidor :

'I 'eś la tersera 'espesy'a de reǧimyento 'el aǧuntamyento ke 'eś reǧido por 'ombreś '[e]leǧidoś por laś komunidadeś ke 'eliǧen loś prinsipaleś delyyoś meśmoś la kual 'eś viśto śer maś fasil de koromperśe ke todaś laś 'otraś

'I 'eśtoś treś modoś de aǧuntamyentoś ke śu'ele la republika śer byen reǧida 'i 'ordenada por 'elyyoś algunoś tyenpoś tyene kada 'espesy'a de 'elyyoś śu kontrary'o malo 'i danyyozo

KE 'el kontrary'o del primero 'eś kuando 'el rey 'eś malo 'i tirano 'i 'eśte 'eś 'el pe'or ke todoś[164] por ke aśi komo 'eś meǧor por ke no tyene kyen le vayya ala mano kuando haze la ǧuśtisy'a aśi 'eś 'el 'el pe'or kuando 'eś malo por ke tyene maś poder 'i no ayy kyen le vayya ala mano kuando haze śinǧuśtisy'a ni mira 'el byen de la republika śalvo 'el śuyo propy'o 'i 'eśto akaeśe laś maś de laś veześ kuando no 'eś de kaśta de re'eyś śalvo alevantado por śu'erte 'o ventura ke 'el ke 'eś de śangre real 'i vyene de linaǧe de reyś śyenpre 'uza ǧuśtisy'a kon śu pu'eblo : [CW. 'i 'el]}

⟨fol. 121a⟩
{KK'
'I 'el kontrary'o del śegundo modo de aǧuntamyento 'eś kuando loś śensoreś śon maloś 'o guarda kada 'uno reśpekto aśi 'i no a'el byen komun 'enel konseǧo 'i reǧimyento de la republika ke deśte modo nunka vyenen 'a konformar ala verdad por ke

---

[163] Aristotle, *Politics* II.9 (1270b 24–25).
[164] Aristotle, *NE* VIII.x.3 (1160b 10), cf. *Politics* IV.10 (1295a 1–24).

Book of the Regimen of Living ⟨fol. 121a⟩

kada 'uno śige śu kamino diferente del 'otro ke 'el fin verdadero no 'eś maś ke 'uno komo 'el śentro de la śirkunferensy'a 'i loś fineś falsoś 'i 'eradoś śon 'infinitoś por ke a'un ke śon konformeś todoś 'en 'erar śon muy diśformeś 'en laś 'eśpesyaś de loś yeroś ke loś 'ombreś 'enel 'erar 'en 'onib[e]rsal śon komo laś 'obeğaś ke yerando 'una yeran todaś pero śon diśformeś 'enel modo de 'erar ke laś 'obeğaś por donde va la primera van todaś pero loś 'ombreś deśpu'eś ke śon konformeś 'enel 'erar kada 'uno va aśu kamino ke 'eś lo meśmo ke diğo 'el profeta Y^{e}ša^{c}yahu todoś noś komo 'obeğaś 'eramoś kada 'uno aśu kamino akatamoś 'i set-[165] ke kyere dezir ke 'el 'erar yeramoś todoś 'en 'onibersal komo laś 'obeğaś ke 'en la 'onibersalidad del yero 'en śer komun 'a todoś śomoś śemeğanteś a'elyyaś 'enpero 'en la partikularidad del yero no śemeğamoś a'elyyaś maś anteś śomoś muy diferenteś ke 'elyyaś todaś śigen 'un kamino a'un ke 'erado 'i noś 'otroś śegimoś kada 'uno 'el śuyo diferente 'uno de 'otro komo tenemoś diğo :

'I 'el kontrary'o del tersero modo de ağuntamyento 'eś kuando śe alevantan laś meśmaś komunidadeś 'a kerer 'elyyoś meśmoś śin śup[e]ry'or mandar 'i 'ordenar 'i reğir 'el pu'eblo ke 'eśtruyen la republika por ke no miran śalvo 'el 'util ke de akelyyo śeleś śige komo śean loś maś delyoś nesesitadoś 'i kon 'eśto no miran de hazer lo ke 'eś ğuśto 'i 'oneśto śalvo lo ke leś 'eś probeğozo 'i ponen por kabeseraś 'a kyen da maś dineroś 'i 'otraś kozaś muğaś 'inormeś śin regla hazen ke no śe pu'eden śufrir por lo kual śe vyenen 'a koromper de śuyo por la deśkonformidad de 'elyyoś 'entre śi meśmoś

'I del meśmo modo ke śe konsidran 'eśtoś treś reğimyentoś 'i ağuntamyentoś 'en la republika aśi śe konsidran tanbyen 'en la 'ekonomika ke 'eś 'el reğimyento de la kaśa ke lo ke 'eś śimil al reğimyento del rey kon śu ğente[166] 'eś 'el ağuntamyento 'i reğimyento del padre kon śuś hiğoś kuando 'eś komo konbyene ke 'el padre 'en la kaśa 'eś 'el mayor de toda la kaśa 'i 'eś 'uno 'i manda 'en śu kaśa komo 'el rey 'en śu reyno konforme alo ke dizen 'un proberby'o antigo nu'eśoś śaby'oś 'en nu'eśo Talmud 'el pelado 'en śu kaśa 'eś prinsipe 'i set-[167]

'I lo ke 'eś śemeğante al reğimyento de śenyyori'a 'o śenado ke 'eś 'el śegundo modo de reğimyento ke śe haze por loś meğoreś 'i mayoreś de la republika ke śon pokoś 'i bu'enoś 'i byen avenidoś 'eś 'el reğimyento de la kaśa del marido 'i la muğer kuando kada 'uno riğe 'i 'ordena 'i manda komo konbyene 'en loś hiğoś 'i hiğaś 'i kryadoś 'i kryadaś de la kaśa ke śon loś meğoreś 'i [CW. mayoreś]}

---

[165] Isa. 53.6.
[166] Aristotle, *NE* VIII.x.4 (1160b 24–26).
[167] Megillah 12b.

BOOK OF THE REGIMEN OF LIVING ‹FOL. 121B›

‹fol. 121b›
{mayoreś dela kaśa 'i todo 'el reśto de la kaśa leś deven katar muǧa 'onra 'i venerasy'on 'i kada 'uno tyene kargo de lo ke konbyene para la suśtentasy'on 'i paś de la kaśa aśi komo 'enel reǧimyento de la śenyyori'a kada 'uno tyene kargo de lo ke śele 'ordena tener kargo para suśtentasy'on 'i pasifikasy'on de la republika :
'I lo ke 'eś śemeǧante ala tersera partida de aǧuntamyento 'i reǧimyento diǧo 'eś kuando akaeśe 'en la kaśa aver muǧoś ermanoś ke algunoś delyyoś riǧen aloś 'otroś ke 'eś śimil a'el reǧimyento diǧo 'en ke loś ke riǧen 'i loś reǧidoś śon de 'un meśmo grado ke todoś śon ermanoś komo alyya todoś śon dela meśma komunidad¹⁶⁸ 'en 'eśtaś komparasy'oneś a'un ke muǧo maś śe podri'a alargar para demośtrar komo śon muy konformeś 'en 'otraś muǧaś partikularidadeś komo no śe'a tanto 'a nu'eśo porpozito akorto 'enelyyo kuanto posible 'eś :
ŚOLO 'eś byen dezirte a'un ke 'eś de śuyo viśto ke tanbyen 'enel reǧimyento dela kaśa śe konsidran śuś kontraryaś deśtaś treś 'eśpesyaś de reǧimyento ke 'el kontrary'o del bu'en reǧimyento del padre kon śuś hiǧoś 'eś kuando 'el padre no kyere maś aśuś hiǧoś ke para śervirśe delyyoś aśu probeǧo 'i no para probeǧo 'i prośperidad de loś meśmoś hiǧoś komo konbyene 'a kual kyer padre bu'eno aśi komo 'el rey tirano ke śu fin 'eś a'el probeǧo śuyo 'i no de la republika¹⁶⁹
'I 'el kontrary'o del śegundo reǧimyento de la kaśa 'eś kuando 'el 'ombre kyere mandar 'i reǧir 'en laś kośaś ke no le konbyene¹⁷⁰ 'i 'elyya 'en kośaś ke no le konbyene 'entender 'en 'elyyaś por lo kual śe vyene 'a koromper 'el reǧimyento 'i aǧuntamyento dela kaśa 'eśpesyal kuando la muǧer kyere mandar maś ke 'el marido 'en laś kośaś ke konbyene mandar maś 'el ke 'elyya por ke no 'obedesyendo la muǧer 'el mandado de śu marido śe vyene 'a perder la kongregasy'on 'i aǧuntamyento de loś doś komo śe manifyeśta por 'el heǧo de 'Aḥaśveroś kuando mando venir delante del 'a Vaṧti śu muǧer 'i no vino por lo kual fu'e kondenada 'a mu'erte komo ku'enta la 'eśkritura 'i set-¹⁷¹ :
'I 'el kontrary'o ala tersera 'eśpesy'a de aǧuntamyento 'eś kuando loś ermanoś no kyeren 'obedeser 'unoś 'a 'otroś 'i kada 'uno śe haze 'el mayor 'i kyere mandar maś ke todoś ke 'eś komo 'el alevantamyento de komunidadeś ke kada 'uno kyere śer kabesa komo tenemoś diǧo
'I aśi komo ayy 'eśtoś treś modoś de aǧuntamyentoś 'enel reǧimyento de la republika 'i 'enel reǧimyento de la kaśa de la meśma manera śe konsidran laś treś

---

¹⁶⁸ Aristotle, *NE* VIII.x.6 (1161a 5–8).
¹⁶⁹ Aristotle, *NE* VIII.x.4 (1160b 29–33).
¹⁷⁰ Aristotle, *NE* VIII.v.5 (1160b 35–1161a 1).
¹⁷¹ Esther 1.1.

BOOK OF THE REGIMEN OF LIVING ‹FOL. 121B–122A›

'eśpesyaś de amiśtad ke tenemoś diǧo ke śon śegun loś meśmoś treś modoś de aǧuntamyento ke 'enel aǧuntamyento de 'el rey bu'eno 'i ǧuśto kon śu republika śe halyya 'una 'eśpesy'a de amiśtad del 'a 'elyyoś para konservarloś 'i guardarloś komo 'el paśtor aśu ganado[172] 'i tenerloś pasifikoś kon la ǧuśtisy'a 'i delyyoś 'a 'el para servirle 'i 'onrarle 'i akatarle 'i rogar por śu vida porke ve'en ke [CW. batalyya]}

‹fol. 122a›
{KKB
batalyya kontra loś 'enemigoś para ke la republika 'eśte ky'eta 'i repozada 'i de la meśma manera 'eś 'el 'amor ke tyene 'el padre aloś hiǧoś ke trabaǧa por mantenerloś 'i konservarloś 'i perfeksy'onarloś a'un ke 'eś maś 'eśtreǧa 'i kon maś benefisy'o partikular la del padre aloś hiǧoś ke la del rey al pu'eblo[173] 'i a'eśte modo rogamoś 'a nu'eśo altiśimo Dyyo glory'ozo ke noś ame 'i por tanto lo 'entitulamoś 'en titulo de rey 'i 'en titulo de padre 'i 'en titul[o] de paśtor ke todo 'eś 'una meśma 'eśpesy'a de 'amor komo tenemoś diǧo 'i de la meśma manera 'enel aǧuntamyento de loś ke śon del konśeǧo 'enel śenado kon la republika 'i de la republika kon 'elyyoś ayy 'otra 'eśpesy'a de amiśtad ke loś pekenyyoś 'i suditoś katan 'un modo de 'onra aloś ke śon śenyyoreś 'i reǧidoreś a'un ke no 'eś tanto komo la de la republika a'el rey 'i del meśmo modo leś tyene 'amor por 'el bu'en reǧimyento ke hazen 'en la republika 'i del meśmo modo 'elyyoś kyeren byen ala republika por ke śon delyyoś śervidoś 'i 'onradoś 'i set- 'i del meśmo modo de amiśtad ayy 'enel aǧuntamyento 'i reǧimyento de marido 'i muǧer kon la reśta de la kaśa ke śe aman 'unoś 'a 'otroś kuando 'eś reǧida komo konbyene[174] :

DEL meśmo modo 'enel terser modo de aǧuntamyento de komunidadeś kuando 'eliǧen 'ombreś ke loś riǧan komo konbyene ayy 'una 'eśtreǧa amiśtad 'entre loś reǧidoś 'i reǧidoreś aśi komo 'enla kaza ayy 'eśtreǧa amiśtad 'entre loś ermanoś kuando kada 'uno delyyoś śe deǧa reǧir de 'otro de lo ke 'eś razon ke śe'a reǧido[175] ke 'eśto 'eś lo ke kiǧo dezir nu'eśo devinisimo rey David donde diǧo hek kuan bu'eno 'i kuan śuabe 'eśtar ermanoś tanbyen a'una 'i set-[176] komo ke diǧeśe ke bu'eno 'eś 'eśtar ermanoś ǧuntoś pero 'eś meneśter tanbyen 'una kondisy'on la kual 'eś ke 'eśten a'unadoś 'i konformeś ke 'eśto 'eś 'eśtar a'una 'i set- 'i de la meśma manera ke śe

---

[172] Aristotle, *NE* VIII.xi.1 (1161a 10–14).
[173] Aristotle, *NE* VIII.xi.2 (1161a 16–19).
[174] Aristotle, *NE* VIII.xi.4 (1161a 24–25).
[175] Aristotle, *NE* VIII.xi.5 (1161a 27–30).
[176] Ps. 133.1.

Book of the Regimen of Living ‹fol. 122a–122b›

konsidran śuś kontrary'oś 'i korupsy'oneś de laś treś 'eśpesyaś de reǧimyento diǧaś śe konsidra la korupsy'on de laś amiśtadeś diǧaś :
'I a'un ke 'en todaś 'eśtaś 'eśpesyaś de amiśtad avi'a muǧo ke 'eśpekular 'en śaber la diferensy'a de 'una 'a 'otra 'i 'en śaber 'en kada 'una por śi la diferensy'a de la amiśtad del mayor al menor ala del menor al mayor 'i śuś porporsy'oneś ke 'en todo te pudyera traer 'enǧenploś antigoś por loś kualeś tubyeraś deśtaś 'eśpesyaś de amiśtad 'entero konosimyento por ke 'el tyenpo 'i miś 'inmenśaś 'okupasy'oneś no me dan lugar para maś no hago maś ke dezirte laś konkluzy'oneś de todo 'i śi algun tyenpo tubyere maś 'oportunidad śeraś maś alumbrado 'en todo 'eśto a'un ke 'eśpero 'enel Dyyo ke tu lo alkansaraś byen de tuyo śolo 'eś byen ke śepaś ke halyy[a]raś 'en algunaś bandaś ke dize 'el filosofo ke 'el padre ama maś al hiǧo ke 'el hiǧo al padre[177] 'i 'en 'otra parte dize ke 'eś razon ke ame maś 'el hiǧo al padre ke 'el padre al hiǧo[178] 'i 'eś meneśter 'eś(ś)tin(ǧ)[g]ir [CW. ke]}

‹fol. 122b›
{ke ala verdad 'en grado de 'amor natural maś ama 'el padre al hiǧo ke 'el hiǧo al padre komo śe ve'e por loś animaleś brutoś por 'eśperensy'a 'i byen mirando 'eś viśta la razon 'enloś 'ombreś natural mente ke 'eś porke konośen primero loś padreś 'i madreś aloś hiǧoś ke loś hiǧoś a'elyyoś 'i kuanto maś 'eś 'el tyenpo del konosimyento de la kośa amada tanto maś 'eś la amiśtad[179] 'enpero 'en 'obligasy'on deve maś 'el hiǧo de amar al padre ke le dyyo 'el śer ke 'el padre al hiǧo a'un ke 'el 'amor natural no 'eś tanto 'i por 'eśo noś akabida tanto nu'eśa śantisima ley ke 'onremoś 'a nu'eśoś padreś 'i set-[180]
'I kon 'eśto baśta por 'el preśente para lo ke konbyene śaber 'enel konosimyento 'i deśkrisy'on de la amiśtad la kual śe perfeksy'ona kon treś kośaś ke śon 'obraś de la amiśtad laś kualeś śon benibolensy'a benefisensy'a 'i konversasy'on ke 'eś la primera kerer 'el amigo aśu amigo byen 'i deśearle 'el byen verdadero por todaś laś viaś posibleś
ŚEGUNDA hazerle byen 'en todaś laś kozaś ke śe 'ofresyeren kon toda śu posiblidad śin ninguna falta :
TERSERA 'eś la konversasy'on ke 'a de tener kon śu amigo verdadero 'i komunikar 'ensu byen 'i 'ensu mal 'en śu prośperidad 'i 'en śu adverśidad[181] śola 'una

---

[177] Aristotle, *NE* VIII.xii.2 (1161b 25–27).
[178] Aristotle, *NE* VIII.vii.2 (1158a 20–29) and VIII.xiii.1 (1162b 3–4).
[179] Aristotle, *NE* VIII.xii.2 (1161b 25–27).
[180] Exod. 20.12, Deut. 5.16.
[181] Aristotle, *NE* IX.xi.1–2 (1171a 22–34).

BOOK OF THE REGIMEN OF LIVING ⟨FOL. 122B–123A⟩

diferensy'a 'a de aver 'en 'eśtoś tyenpoś diferenteś 'i 'eś ke 'enel tyenpo de la prośperidad 'i alegri'a de śu amigo 'a de 'eśperar 'a śer lyyamado[182] 'i 'enel tyenpo de la adversidad 'i pasy'on 'a de apreśurarśe 'a 'ir 'a komunikar śu pasy'on kon 'el anteś ke śe'a lyamado komo hizyeron loś konpanyeroś de 'Iyob kon 'Iyob 'enel tyenpo de śu tribulasy'on[183] 'i 'el kontrary'o an de 'uzar loś ke padesen ke al tyenpo de śuś prośperidadeś 'i alegriaś śe an de apreśurar 'a lyyamar aśuś amigoś para komunikar kon 'elyyoś śuś alegriaś 'i plazereś 'i 'enel tyenpo deśuś pasy'oneś 'i tr[a]bağoś no an de dar parte aśuś amigoś hata ke 'elyyoś de śuyo vengan 'a śokorerloś śi no fu'ere kośa de dandoleś parte 'o notisy'a lo pu'eden remedyar ke 'en tal kaśo no serian verdaderoś amigoś śi no śe śokoryeśen a'elyyoś

'I a'un ke para 'eśkribir 'en la amiśtad śegun yo teni'a penśado 'ubyera de alargar byen 'en muğaś propyedadeś ke ayy 'en kada 'eśpesy'a de la amiśtad 'i 'en muğaś deśtinsy'oneś ke 'en kada 'una delyyaś 'eś meneśter deśtingir 'i 'en laś kauśaś por donde śe vyenen algunaś delyyaś 'a koromper maś por 'eśtenso deloke tenemoś diğo 'i 'en komo 'en kada 'eśpesy'a delyaś ayy 'igual amiśtad 'i deś'igual 'i 'en komo la deś'igual por la deś'igualdad de loś amigoś śe deve 'igualar śegun la porporsy'on deśuś kalidadeś 'i 'en komo 'o porke nasen laś keśaś 'i barağaś 'entre loś amigoś 'i 'en katorze dubdaś ke dubdo 'el filosofo 'enel nono dela 'etika[184] afu'era de 'otraś muğaś ke 'otroś filosofoś moraleś dubdaron 'enla amiśtad :

TODO lo değo para maś 'oportunidad aremityendome aloke larga mente}

⟨fol. 123a⟩
{ḲḲG ḤELEK G PEREK T [PART THREE CHAPTER NINE]
tengo 'eśkrito 'enel libro 'oktabo 'i nono dela diğa 'etika ke podraś byen ve'er porke alyi tengo todo 'eśkrito muy por 'eśtenso 'i 'eśto baśta para aki para śolo śaber la deśkrisy'on deśta virtud śumary'a mente :

ŚOLO 'eś byen de advertir ke ninguno pu'ede śer bu'en amigo verdadero por 'el 'oneśto śino 'eś śaby'o porke no śyendo tal no pu'ede śer ninguno mayor 'enemigo de 'el ke 'el propy'o 'en no perkurar para śi la śensy'a 'i la virtud ke 'eś la 'ultima filisidad 'i 'eśto pu'ede śer ke śe'a la verdader'a 'intensy'on del profeta do dize kaśtigarte'a tu mal 'i set-[185] k[e]ryendo dezir ke 'a 'el malo 'i 'inorante la pribasy'on del byen ke 'el meśmo śe kauśa kon śer malo 'eś 'el mayor kaśtigo ke 'enel śe pu'ede afigurar de adonde 'eś viśto ke kyen tan 'enemigo 'eś de śi meśmo ke priba de śi 'el

---

[182] Aristotle, *NE* IX.xi.6 (1171b 22–25).
[183] Job 2.11.
[184] Aristotle, *NE* IX.i.4 (1164a 14–23), cf. VIII.xiv (1163a 25–1163b 30).
[185] Jer. 2.19.

BOOK OF THE REGIMEN OF LIVING ‹FOL. 123A›

byen pudyendolo adkerir mal pu'ede śer amigo de 'otro lo kual deveś tener kontino 'enla memory'a para guardarte 'i apartarte de amigo 'inorante :

KAPITULO NU'EBE

'I PARA loke konbyene a'el 'ombre 'enel 'e(r)ğe[r]sitar 'eśta virtud para ke śepaś reğirte 'enelyya te hago śaber ke 'en toda 'eśpesyya de amiśtad delaś ke tenemoś diğo 'i de 'otraś muğaś ke śe pu'eden dezir maś partikulareś śe deve de tener por mağima śabida ke kyen kyere śer amado 'a de amar 'i kyen no ama nunka 'eśpere de śer amado porke la amiśtad tyene 'eśta propyedad muy konğunta konelyya 'i 'eś ke del meśmo modo 'i 'enel meśmo grado ke 'el 'uno ama al 'otro de akel meśmo grado 'el 'otro lo amara a'el śin ninguna dubda de manera ke 'el ke verdader'a mente kera ğuśgar loke tyene 'ensu amigo de amiśtad 'o de fidelidad ke śe śige de la amiśtad mire lo ke ayy 'enel meśmo para akel tal amigo 'i śepa śin dubda ke lo meśmo halyyara 'enel 'otro para 'el komo diğeron loś antigoś ke loś korasoneś deloś amigoś śon komo loś 'eśpeğoś ke śe traśponen laś figuraś 'i 'imağeneś del 'uno 'enel 'otro 'i del 'otro al 'otro 'igual mente de manera ke loke śe ve'e 'enel 'uno śe ve'e 'enel 'otro śin ninguna diferensy'a[186] 'i deśte modo 'el ke vyere 'el 'uno śabra loke ayy 'enel 'otro 'el kual fu'e 'enğenplo muy konforme ala 'intensy'on verdader'a porke śe pu'ede sertifikar kual kyera ke 'eś 'o kyere 'o pyensa śer amigo de 'otro ke śi 'enla voluntad le 'eś amigo lo meśmo le śera 'el 'otro a'el 'i no le śera śino komo 'el le fu'ere de manera ke 'el 'amor śe paga kon 'amor la voluntad kon voluntad 'i por palabraś śe dan palabraś 'i laś 'obraś śe pagan kon 'obraś la aparensy'a kon aparensy'a la 'eğiśtensy'a kon 'eğiśtens(v)[y']a 'i kyen kyere 'obraś del amigo alaś de 'obrar 'el konel kyen va perkurando 'eśta virtud tan 'elevada

KONFORME alo kual diğo nu'eśo śapyentisimo rey Š^elomoh kon verisima 'eśpikulasy'on 'en śuś tan 'elevadisimoś}

---

[186] An exact source for this ancient mirror/friend metaphor eludes me, though it is abundant in philosophical and literary texts, as well as in *romances* and proverbs. A good analogue to Almosnino's citation is the Judeo-Spanish proverb: "No hay mižor espežo que un amigo viežo" (Besso, "Judeo-Spanish Proverbs," 381, no. 147). Multiple examples of the mirror/beloved metaphor in Peninsular, European, and Arabic literatures are collated and studied by S. G. Armistead and J. H. Silverman, *Folk Literature of the Sephardic Jews* (Berkeley, 1986), 254–56. A thorough survey of the *speculum* title in medieval philosophy is made by Bradley, "The Title *Speculum*"; see also Grabes, *Mutable Glass.*

BOOK OF THE REGIMEN OF LIVING ‹FOL. 123B›

‹fol. 123b›
{ḤELEK G PEREK (H)[T]
probyerby'oś komo aguaś de laś faseś 'a faseś aśi korason de 'ombre 'a 'ombre 'i set-[187] ke śegun lo ke todoś syenten del 'a prima viśta 'eś lo ke tenemoś diğo konforme al proberby'o antigo de loś 'eśpeğoś ke 'eś komo ke diğeśe ke aśi komo 'enel agu'a śe traśpone la figura de la kara 'en 'elyya komo 'en 'eśpeğo 'i no ayy diferensy'a ninguna de la kara ke śe represénta 'enel agu'a ala kara verdader'a por ke 'eś traśpu'eśta 'una por 'otra aśi 'eś 'el korason del 'ombre 'a 'otro 'ombre ke no ayy diferensy'a del 'uno al 'otro ke lo ke syente 'el 'un amigo 'en śi ke fari'a por śu amigo kre'a ke akelyyo meśmo fara śin dubda śu amigo por 'el 'i 'eśto a'un ke 'eś verdad konforme alo ke tenemoś diğo no me parese śentir 'eśto la letra por ke avi'a de dezir komo 'en laś aguaś laś faseś 'a laś faseś 'o komo laś faseś alaś faseś 'en laś aguaś aśi 'el koraśon del 'ombre 'i set- ke 'en dezir komo aguaś laś faseś 'i set- parese ke de la meśma agu'a haze konparasy'on 'i no de lo ke śe represénta 'en 'elyya por donde me pareśe ke dira 'en śegunda 'intensy'on maś konforme ala letra 'i 'a lo ke tenemoś diğo 'i digo ke kyere konparar alaś meśmaś aguaś laś karaś kon laś karaś de loś amigoś ke 'eś la aparensy'a kon la aparensy'a ke śe 'entitula 'en toda lengu'a 'en termino de kara 'i muğo maś 'en nu'eśa lengu'a śanta 'i la 'eğiśtensy'a kon la 'eğiśtensy'a ke śe 'entitula 'en termino de korason por śer verdader'a de korason konpara tanbyen 'a laś meśmaś aguaś 'i kon 'eśto 'eśtan todaś laś palabraś byen asentadaś ke dize ke aśi komo laś aguaś todaś śuś parteś śon 'igualeś komo 'eś viśto por la difinsy'on de loś 'elementoś ke difiny'o Abisena 'enel prinsipy'o del Kanon do dize loś 'elementoś śon ku'erpoś śinpleś 'i śon parteś primeraś a'el ku'erpo 'umano[188] 'i 'otro tal ke 'eś 'inposible ke śe repartan 'en ku'erpoś diferenteś 'en formaś 'i set- ke kyere dezir ke 'el 'elemento komo 'eś ku'erpo śinple 'i no konpu'eśto a'un ke śe reparta 'en parteś 'infinitaś la forma de todaś laś parteś 'eś 'una śin ninguna diferensy'a lo ke no akaese 'en laś kośaś konpu'eśtaś ke śi śe parten laś parteś de loś kualeś śe hizo la konpozisy'on ke śin loś 'elementoś kada p(+)arte tyene śu forma diferente komo śe ve'e 'en laś 'eśtilasy'oneś de laś yerbaś kuando śe 'eśtilan ke laś parteś (triśteś) [tere'aś] kedan abağo 'en laś bosaś 'i laś del fu'ego śe traśponen 'en fu'ego 'i laś de ayyre 'en ayyre 'i laś de la agu'a śon laś aguaś 'eśtiladaś ke kaen por 'el alanbike lo ke non tyenen loś 'elementoś syendo śinplisimoś śin ninguna miśty'on ke śi śe konronpen no śe konronperan 'en parteś diferenteś komo 'eś śabido 'i aśi tanbyen śi śe parten laś kośaś konpu'eśtaś de śuś kantidadeś śon laś parteś diferenteś 'en śuś figuraś komo 'eś

---

[187] Prov. 27.19.
[188] *Canon,* Bk. 1, Pt. 1, Thesis 2, 19 (trans. Gruner, 34).

Book of the Regimen of Living ‹fol. 123b–124a›

śabido lo ke no śc dira 'enloś 'elementoś ke todaś laś parteś śe diran agu'a a[']un ke 'eneśta konsidrasy'on tanbyen konforman kon 'elyyoś loś myembroś śinpleś 'i todo}

‹fol. 124a›
{KKD ḤELEK G PEREK (H)[T]
konpu'eśto ke no tyene parteś diferenteś de figura komo palo 'i pyedra 'i 'otroś taleś komo 'eś śabido pero komo 'en la primera konsidrasy'on śon diferenteś no śe dira abśuluta mente ke laś parteś todaś śon de 'una forma śalvo 'enloś 'elementoś 'i komo śe'a la agu'a 'el 'elemento 'en kyen maś śe pu'ede 'eśto ve'er por tanto puzo la konparasy'on 'enel agu'a porke la tyera komo ay(')[y] 'enelyya miśty'on muğa de yerbaś 'i aguaś 'i 'otraś kośaś taleś no parese śer laś parteś muy konformeś komo 'enel agu'a ke todaś laś parteś paresen 'unaś meśmaś 'i a'un ke 'enel ayyre 'i 'enel fu'ego śe'a lo meśmo porke nośe konprenden al śentido vizible tanto komo 'el agu'a por tanto no hizo la konparasy'on śalvo 'enlaś aguaś 'i kiğo śentir ke aśi komo todaś laś parteś paresen 'unaś 'a 'otraś 'i śon 'unaś 'i no śon diferenteś 'en śuś formaś ni 'en śuś figuraś dela meśma manera śon laś karaś alaś karaś ke 'eś la aparensy'a ala aparensy'a 'i aśi meśmo 'el korason del 'uno al korason del 'otro ke 'eś la voluntad ala voluntad komo tenemoś diğo :

'I 'en konkluzy'on de todo lo diğo digo ke todaś laś amiśtadeś śon niğil 'i vanidad śino 'eś la amiśtad deloś bu'enoś konloś bu'enoś porel byen ke 'eśta 'eś la amiśtad ke nunka śe korompe komo tenemoś prevado 'eś verdad ke de 'eśta śu'erte de amiśtad ayy muy pokoś porke 'eś muy difisil ke la virtud 'eś aserka del difisil 'i 'uno no pu'ede tener 'en toda śu vida maś de 'un amigo 'i kuando muğo doś hata treś[189] :

'I śobre todaś 'eś la amiśtad 'i 'amor ke devemoś tener al Dyyo glory'ozo ke 'enelya konsiśte la beatitud 'i byen aventuransa porke 'enel 'amor 'eśta la deleytasy'on komo 'eś śabido 'i 'enel 'amor del Dyyo 'eśta la śuma deleytasy'on 'i 'eśte 'eś 'el fin 'ultimo 'i verdadero de pu'eś dela 'eśpikulasy'on porke aśi komo laś bu'enaś 'obraś 'enkaminan 'a la 'eśpikulasy'on 'en laś kośaś devinaś aśi la 'eśpikulasy'on 'enkamina a'el 'amor del Dyyo porke tanto 'eś maś grande 'i 'eśtremado 'el 'amor kuanto 'eś 'el konosimyento dela kośa amada[190] porke porel konosimyento ama la voluntad 'i tanto maś śe alegra 'el ke ama konla kośa ke ama kuanto 'eś maś 'el konosimyento de manera ke 'el 'eśpekular 'enlaś kośaś devinaś 'eś 'el fin pośtrero ke depende de 'el 'ent[en]dimyento te'oriko 'i 'el fin maś 'ultimo ke la 'eśpikulasy'on 'eś 'el 'amor del

---

[189] Aristotle, *NE* IX.x.5 (1171a 6–13).

[190] This Neoplatonic truism is found in Augustine. Cf. G. Vajda, "Le néoplatonisme dans la pensée juive du moyen âge," in *Mélanges Georges Vajda,* ed. G. E. Weil (Hildesheim: Gerstenberg, 1982), 407–22.

BOOK OF THE REGIMEN OF LIVING ‹FOL. 124A—124B›

Dyyo ke konsiśte 'enel 'entendimyento pratiko 'i 'enla voluntad ke 'eśto śe lyyama 'obra a'un ke 'eś 'intiry'or por śer del 'entendimyento pratiko 'i 'eśto pyenso ke śe'a 'a 'opiny'on de todoś nu'eśoś śaby'oś antigoś 'i modernoś porke ninguno pu'ede nyegar ke 'enel byen 'onde śe halyya la śuma deleytasy'on 'i la alegri'a konsiśte la byen aventuransa 'i akel 'eś 'el b[y]en verdade(')ro 'i 'eś śabido ke 'enel 'eśpekular śinple mente no ayy alegri'a ni deleytasy'on porke no śe konsidra alegri'a ni deleytasy'on 'enlaś kośaś ke śe toman de baǧo de razon de verdad}

‹fol. 124b›
{HELEK G PEREK T
śinpleś mente śal(')vo 'enlaś kozaś ke śe toman de baǧo de razon de byen 'i de baǧo de 'eśta razon śe dize 'enelyyaś amiśtad 'o 'ody'o lu'ego 'enel 'amor del Dyyo kon(t)-[ś]iśte la byen av(v)[e]nturansa 'i śuma deleytasy'on komo avemoś diǧo :
'I KYEN byen parare myenteś 'enlaś palabraś del śenyyor Rabbenu Mośeh 'en todo śu famozisimo libro halyyara kre'er 'el tanbyen a'un ke algunoś no śelo kyeren aplikar ke 'el 'amor de 'el Dyyo 'eś 'el fin pośtrero por ke a'un ke dize 'enel 'ultimo kapitulo del diǧo libro ke 'el fin pośtrero 'eś la 'eśpikulasy'on[191] kyere dezir ke laś 'obraś 'eśt[i]ry'oreś bu'enaś traen ala 'eśpikulasy'on ke 'eś fin del byen 'obrar 'i komo 'el 'amor del Dyyo 'eś kośa ke śe śige dela verdader'a 'eśpikulasy'on no la nombro por fin pośtrero porke 'en dezir ke la 'eśpikulasy'on 'eś 'el fin pośtrero 'eś diǧo komo 'el 'amor ke śige a'el 'eś maś pośtrero :
'I 'eśto 'eś loke noś akabido nu'eśa śantisima ley do dize 'oye Yiśra'el H‹a-Šem› nu'eśo Dyyo Adonay 'uno 'i amaraś 'a Adonay tu Dyyo kon todo tu korason 'i set-[192] ke kyere dezir para myenteś Yiśra'el 'i 'eśpekula byen komo 'el Dyyo 'eś nu'eśo Dyyo ke aki śe konkluye śer poderozo 'i ke probe'e partikular mente 'i 'otroś muǧoś artikuloś de nu'eśa ley 'i 'eśpekula komo 'eś 'uno abśuluta mente 'i kon 'eśte konosimyento śe śegira ke lo amaraś kon todo tu korason 'i set-[193] ke del 'entero 'i verdadero konosimyento śe śige 'el 'entero 'i verdadero 'amor komo tenemoś diǧo por donde parese śer 'el 'ultimo fin 'el amar al Dyyo komo parese por akel gran diǧo del śenyyor Rabbi ᶜAkiba' 'en nu'eśo Talmud kuando lo śakaron ala hogera 'i le peynaban śu karne kon peyneś de fyero 'eśtando kontenplando kon toda śu debosy'on śin

---

[191] Maimonides, *Guide*, trans. Pines, 632–38 (*MN*, Pt. 3, chap. 54).
[192] Deut. 6.4–5.
[193] Deut. 6.5.

Book of the Regimen of Living ‹fol. 124b–125a›

ninguna konturbasy'on diğeronle śuś diśiploś maeśtro nu'eśtro hata aki 'i set-[194] admirandośe komo 'era posible alyegando al 'eśtremo de la pasy'on del tormento pudyeśe tener ky'eto 'el 'eśprito para poder kontenplar alo kual reśpondyyo ke toda śu vida 'eśtubo triśte kuando podri'a afirmar akel pasuk[195] ke tenemoś diğo ke 'eś 'i amaraś atu Dyyo kon todo tu korason 'i tu alma 'i set-[196] ke glozan nu'eśoś śaby'oś ke kyere dezir a'un ke te kiten tu alma 'i ke agora pu'eś le vino ala mano poderlo afirmar komo lo avi'a de değar de afirmar por lo kual parese ke 'eśtubo rezy'o 'ensu kontenplasy'on hata 'el meśmo punto kele śaly'o 'el alma dizyendo 'el primer pasuk dela Š'ma' 'i kon 'el pośtrer byerbo 'enla boka le śalyo la alma 'i dizen nu'eśoś śaby'oś ke śalyyo 'una selik[e]h boz ke dezi'a byenaventurado 'ereś tu Rabbi ᶜAkiba' ke śalyo tu alma kon 'eḥad[197] de adonde śe nota śer la verdader'a 'opiny'on de nu'eśoś śaby'oś ke por 'eśte 'eśtremadisimo 'amor ke tubo 'eśte śingularisimo śenyyor 'i 'otroś taleś ke śimileś mu'erteś padesen por amar 'i śervir al Dyyo śon lyyamadoś abśuluta mente byen aventuradoś 'i pose'en la vida 'eterna ke 'eśto todo no vyene por parte del 'entendimyento te'oriko a'un}

‹fol. 125a›
{KKH
ke 'el 'eś kauśa de 'elyyo porke trae 'a amarle śalvo de 'el 'entendimyento pratiko 'i la voluntad ke kyere śufrir porel 'amor del Dyyo akelyyaś pasy'oneś 'i tormentoś :
  'I kon 'eśto ke tenemoś diğo 'entenderaś 'un diğo de nu'eśoś śaby'oś de muğa śuśtansy'a 'i ami ver kaśi 'in'entiliğible a'un ke muğoś pensaron aver lo byen 'entendido 'el kual 'eś 'una diśputa ke 'ubo 'en nu'eśo Talmud 'entre doś grandisimoś śenyyoreś ke śon Rabbi Tarfon 'i Rabbi ᶜAkiba' śobre 'una demanda ke fu'e demandada 'en prezensy'a de muğoś vyeğoś śi la 'obra 'era mayor kela 'eśpikulasy'on 'o la 'eśpikulasy'on mayor ke la 'obra donde dize ke diğo Rabbi Tarfon ke la 'obra 'era mayor reśpondy'o Rabbi ᶜAkiba' 'i diğo la 'eśpikulasy'on 'eś mayor konformaron todoś 'i diğeron la 'eśpikulasy'on 'eś mayor porke trae 'a 'obra 'i set-[198] ke ala verdad 'eśta konkluzy'on keda maś konfuza kela divizy'on de loś doś porke 'eś śabido ke todo lo ke trae 'a 'otra kośa 'eś akelyya 'otra kośa mayor porke 'eś komo fin alo ke śe antisipa 'a 'elya 'i todo fin 'eś mayor 'i meğor ke todo loke śe antisipa a'el komo 'eś śabido por donde parese ke por la meśma kauśa ke la 'eśpikulasy'on 'eś mayor ke 'eś porke

---

[194] Berakot 61b.
[195] That is a "biblical verse" or "sentence".
[196] Deut. 6.5.
[197] Berakot 61b.
[198] Kiddushin 40b, Song of Sol. R. 2.5.

Book of the Regimen of Living ‹fol. 125a–125b›

trae ala 'obra por 'elyya parese śer la 'obra mayor 'i por śer 'eśto aśi verdad halyyamoś 'en 'otra parte 'en nu'eśo Ṭalmud ke keryendo dezir 'un śingularisimo śenyor ke 'eś Rabbi Yoḥanan ke śobre mu'erte de 'un gran śenyyor 'era lisito dezir ke afirmo todo lo ke[ ]avi'a 'en la ley 'i no 'era lisito dezir deprendy'o todo lo ke 'eśta 'eśkrito 'en la le'ey[199] ke paresyendo por 'eśtaś palabraś ke kyere konklu'ir ke valga maś la 'eśpikulasy'on kela 'obra le arguyyo 'el Ṭalmud pareser 'el kontraryyo deśta konkluzy'on de aki ke tenemoś diğo ke dize ke 'eś mayor la 'eśpikulasy'on porke trae 'a 'obra 'i set-[200] 'i dize akel śingularisimo glozador denu'eśo Ṭalmud Rabbenu Š^elomoh ke trae 'a 'obra 'i set-[201] lu'ego parese ke la 'obra 'eś mayor 'i set- ke 'eś lo meśmo ke tenemoś diğo ke lyeba akel śenyor por maśima 'eneśta konkluzy'on ke śe'a la 'obra mayor pu'eś 'eś fin dela 'eśpikulasy'on a'un ke 'otroś kre'en ke arguye por 'otra vi'a de kual kyer modo ke śe'a paresen 'eśtaś palabraś 'inplikar 'enśi kontradisy'on 'i palabraś śin 'entento ke śi 'eś meğor la 'eśpikulasy'on porke trae ala 'obra lu'ego la 'obra 'eś meğor pu'eś śi aśi 'eś komo śe dira kela 'eśpikulasy'on 'eś mayor

'I maś 'eś de marabilyar deśte diğo por śer noto 'i manifyeśto ke tanto 'o maś trae la 'obra bu'ena ala 'eśpikulasy'on komo la 'eśpikulasy'on ala 'obra bu'ena komo 'eś viśto por palabraś de nu'eśoś śaby'oś 'en diverśoś lugareś 'eś lu'ego marabilyyar komo śe konformaron 'eśtoś śenyoreś 'i śe determinaron 'enke la 'eśpikulasy'on 'eś mayor 'i no dizen por 'otra kauza ninguna śalvo por ke trae ala 'obra śyendo ke por la meśma kauza 'i razon śe pu'ede dezir ke śe'a mayor la 'obra porke trae ala}

‹fol. 125b›
{'eśpikulasy'on 'i 'eś maś de ver 'i śentir 'enlaś palabraś porke dizen ke trae 'a 'obra 'i non dizen ke trae ala 'obra śi 'eś la 'obra 'enke tubyeron diferensy'a śi 'era mayor kela 'eśpikulasy'on de adonde parese syerto kerer śentir la letra ke loke diğeron kela 'eśpikulasy'on 'eś mayor porke trae 'a 'obra[202] no 'eś la 'obra 'enke tubyeron 'el debate por donde pyenso ke śe'a la 'intensy'on verdader'a konforme aloke tenemoś diğo ke komo ayy doś modoś de 'obraś ke śon laś 'obraś 'eśtiry'oreś 'i laś 'intiry'oreś ke 'eśtan 'en śola la voluntad 'i 'en 'el 'entendimyento komo 'el amor 'i la deleytasy'on 'i alegri'a kon la kośa amada ke todo 'eś por parte del 'entendimyento pratiko komo tenemoś diğo la 'obra 'i 'eśpikulasy'on 'en ke fu'e la diśputa 'entre 'eśtoś doś śenyyoreś kual delyyoś 'era mayor śe'a de 'entender por la 'obra 'intiry'or ke 'uno dezi'a

---

[199] Bava Kamma 17a.
[200] Tosafot Bava Kamma 17a.
[201] Rashi Bava Kamma 17a.
[202] Kiddushin 40b.

Book of the Regimen of Living ⟨fol. 125b–126a⟩

ke vali'a maś la 'obra ke la 'eśpikulasy'on por ke toda 'obra 'eś śervir al Dyyo ke depende de la voluntad 'i 'el ke syerbe al Dyyo hazelo por 'amor del 'i pyensa śer 'eśte 'el fin pośtrero del byen 'umano 'i a'un ke byen ve'e ke la 'obra 'eśtiry'or trae ala 'eśpikulasy'on komo tenemoś diğo ke parese śer la 'eśpikulasy'on fin maś 'ultimo pyensa ke no la trae komo fin śalvo ke śe śige delyyo śekundary'a mente de la bu'ena diśpozisy'on para 'eśpekular ke śe haze medyante la 'obra 'i 'el 'otro dezi'a ke la 'eśpikulasy'on vale maś ke la 'obra 'eśtiry'or pu'eś la 'eśpikulasy'on 'eś fin delyya komo tenemoś diğo 'i 'eś śabido ke 'el fin vale maś ke loke śe antisipa a'el 'i de todoś 'otorgado 'i 'eś de mayor 'ekselensy'a pu'eś 'eś del 'entendimyento te'oriko ke 'eś de mayor grado ke 'el pratiko viśtaś todaś 'eśtaś razoneś de pro 'i kontra de kada 'uno deśtoś śenyyoreś ke ninguna de 'elyyaś konvenśe para 'una parte maś ke para 'otra śe konformaron por 'otra razon 'ıvıdente ke 'eś meğor la 'eśpikulasy'on ke la 'obra 'eśtiry'or 'i kela kauśa delyyo 'eś porke la 'eśpikulasy'on trae 'otra 'obra maś 'elebada ke la primera ke 'eś 'el 'amor del Dyyo ke śe śige depu'eś de 'eśpekular 'i konoser laś kozaś devinaś del Dyyo glory'ozo 'i tan grande 'eś 'el grado del 'amor al Dyyo kuanto maś 'eś 'el śaber 'i alkanśar 'el verdadero konosimyento de laś kozaś śuyyaś 'i 'eśto kiğeron śentir 'en dezir por ke la 'eśpikulasy'on trae 'a 'obra ke 'eś 'otra 'obra ke la nombrada śobre la kual fu'e la diśputa 'i 'eś 'el kaśo ke a'un ke la 'obra 'eśtiry'or trayyga tanbyen 'en alguna manera a'el 'amor del Dyyo ke ninguno lo sirve śalvo porke le ama no lo trae tan rekta 'i tan perfekta mente komo la 'eśpikulasy'on porke todo 'amor 'i amiśtad vyene de konosimyento de la kośa amada komo tenemoś diğo[203] 'i komo śe'a manifeśto ke 'el verdadero konosimyento prosede de la 'eśpikulasy'on 'enla kośa ke śe kyere por tanto 'eś viśto ke 'el 'amor ke prosede de la 'eśpikulasy'on 'eś 'el 'amor verdadero ke vyene por vi'a [CW. dereğa]}

⟨fol. 126a⟩
{KKV
dereğa 'i linyya rek(ś)[t]a 'i 'eśto pu'ede śer ke kiğo śentir nu'eśo famozisimo glozador Rabbenu Šᵉlomoh do dize ke la 'eśpikulasy'on trae 'obra 'i set-[204] halyyanśe todoś doś 'ensu mano 'i set-[205] ke kiğo śiknifikar loke tenemoś diğo ke komo la 'eśpikulasy'on trae rekta mente 'el 'amor halyyanśe todoś doś 'en puro a'uto 'en mano del 'ombre ke todaś doś 'eśtan 'enel 'entendimyento 'uno 'enel te'oriko 'otro 'enel

---

[203] Cf. Vajda, "Le néoplatonisme."
[204] Rashi Bava Kamma 17a.
[205] Rashi Kiddushin 40b.

Book of the Regimen of Living ‹fol. 126a–126b›

pratiko lo kual la 'obra 'eśtiry'or a'un ke trayyga ala 'inter[y]'or no keda la 'eśtiry'or 'enel 'entendimyento śalvo la 'intiry'or komo 'eś śabido por donde śe afirma ke la 'obra 'eśtiry'or śe'a manko ke la 'eśpikulasy'on 'i la 'eśpikulasy'on manko ke la 'obra 'intiry'or pu'eś trae a'elyya 'i 'elyya 'eś fin de la 'eśpikulasy'on por lo kual śe determino tanbyen alyya 'onde arguye deśte diğo ke parese śer maś la 'obra ke la 'eśpikulasy'on ke alyya śe'a de 'entender por la 'obra 'intiry'or ke afirmar lo ke la ley dize 'eś afirmar 'el 'amor del Dyyo verdader'a mente ke 'aki śe konkluye afirmar todo 'i atyenta byen 'en 'eśto ke 'eś byen advertido a'un ke śi me dyera 'el tyenpo lugar alarga(d)[r]a maś 'enelyyo ke 'era byen meneśter

ŚOLO kiğe dezir 'en todo lo diğo ke 'el verdadero 'i pośtrero fin 'umano 'i byen verdadero 'eś 'el amar al Dyyo 'i kontenplar 'enel 'i glorifikarśe konla tal kontenplasy'on ke 'eśto todo śe śige de la verdader'a 'eśpikulasy'on komo tenemoś diğo 'i 'el śenyyor Rabbenu Mošeh 'eśto k[r]e[']e(re) a'un ke 'a 'opiny'on de alguno's pyensan kre'er ke śe'a la 'eśpikulasy'on mayor ke la 'obra a'un ke śe'a 'intiry'or ke por śolo 'o'ir nombrar 'el nombre de 'obra pyensan śer maś bağa ke la 'eśpikulasy'on 'enlo kual yeran syerto ami ver por non śaber ke kośa śe'a la 'obra 'intiry'or ke śi śupyeśen ke 'eś 'el amar al Dyyo 'el kual śe śige de la 'eśpikulasy'on no dirian ni penśarian tal 'enel śenyyor Rabbenu Mošeh komo 'el meśmo deklaro 'enel kapitulo śinku'enta 'i 'uno dela tersera partida de śu famoziśimo libro depu'eś de konklu'ido akel 'enğenplo tan famado ke alyi pone donde dize 'enpero 'eś razon de 'enpesar 'eneśta 'eśpesy'a de śervisy'o de pu'eś de alkansado a'el Dyyo 'i aśuś 'obraś śegun lo 'eśpekulare 'el 'entendimyento 'i set-[206] 'i dize maś 'i la ley noś aklaro ke 'eśte śervisy'o 'ultimo ke avemoś mobido 'eneśte kapitulo no 'eś śalvo depu'eś de averlo alkansado do dize por amar 'a Adonay vu'eśo Dyyo 'i set-[207] 'i ya avemoś deklarado muğaś veześ ke 'el 'amor 'eś śegun loke śe alkansa 'i set-[208] 'eśtaś todaś śon śuś palabraś 'enel diğo kapitulo de adonde 'eś byen viśto kre'er 'el ke loke śe śige depu'eś del konosimyento del Dyyo 'eś 'el 'amor 'i ke 'eśto lyyama śervisy'o ke 'eś 'obra 'intiry'or komo tenemoś diğo 'i ke deśte śerviśy'o ke 'eś 'el 'amor vyene 'el ağuntamyento konel Dyyo alto 'i 'el kontenplar 'enel kontinu'a mente 'i la alegri'a 'inmenśa 'enla tal kontenplasy'on 'i ağuntamyento de manera [CW. ke]}

‹fol. 126b›
{ḤELEK G PEREK Y [PART THREE CHAPTER TEN]
ke 'el 'amor 'eś 'el fin pośtrero ke 'eśta konğunto 'i koliğido konla kośa amada ke 'eś

---

[206] Maimonides, *Guide,* trans. Pines, 619–28 (*MN*, Pt. 3, chap. 51).
[207] Deut. 11.13.
[208] Maimonides, *Guide,* trans. Pines, 618–28 (*MN*, Pt. 3, chap. 51).

Book of the Regimen of Living ‹fol. 126b–127a›

'el fin dela glory'a 'i śuma deleytasy'on 'i refrizery'o 'el kual śi lo śigyereś komo konbyene te hara bivir 'en kontinu'a deleytasy'on 'eneśta vida 'i 'enla advenidera porke 'eśte 'eś 'el 'ultimo fin 'umano komo tenemoś diğo 'i kon 'eśto baśta al preśente para loke konbyene śaber aserka deśta devinisima virtud ğunto kon todaś laś 'otraś vertudeś moraleś 'a 'el prezente

KAPITULO DYEŚ

'I para loke konbyene para 'el verdadero konosimyento de laś vertudeś 'intelektualeś a'un ke śeri'a nesesary'o alargar byen 'en 'elyo te lo hare 'entender 'en muy breveś palabraś porke no ayy delyyo muğa nesesidad para loke toka 'a nu'eśa śantisima le'ey ke 'eś 'el verdadero fin nu'eśo porke 'eśtaś vertudeś śe toman 'en nu'eśa śakra 'eśkritura 'en 'otraś śiknifikasy'oneś diferenteś de loke śe toma 'en la filosofi'a por tanto baśtara byen deklararte muy breve mente komo śe 'entyende 'enel moral 'o 'en 'otra kual kyera sensy'a kada 'una de laś śinko vertudeś 'intelektualeś porke ala verdad 'eś nesesary'o 'en alguna manera śaberlo para 'entender perfekta mente lo ke tenemoś diğo 'en laś vertudeś moraleś ke an de śer reğidaś por la dereğa razon ke 'eś la prudensy'a la kual 'eś 'una de laś vertudeś 'intelektualeś

PARA lo kual aś de śaber ke laś vertudeś repartidaś 'en moraleś 'i 'intelektualeś 'eś komo dezimoś repartirśe 'el anima del 'ombre 'en parte ke propy'a mente 'eś 'intelektual ke 'eś lo ke lyyamamoś 'entendimyento 'i 'en parte ke propy'a mente lyamamoś voluntad 'i aśi dezimoś ke todaś laś vertudeś moraleś ke avemoś diğo śon 'i konsiśten 'en la voluntad 'i laś vertudeś 'intelektualeś śon 'i konsiśten 'enel 'entendimyento

'I porke 'el 'entendimyento śe reparte 'en doś partidaś 'otraś ke 'eś 'el 'entendimyento te'oriko 'i 'el 'entendimyento pratiko por tanto dezimoś aver doś modoś de vertudeś algunaś del 'entendimyento te'oriko 'i algunaś del 'entendimyento pratiko[209]

'I para ke 'entyendaś 'eśto byen 'i no kaygaś 'en algun yero a'un ke ya 'en 'otro lugar pyenso avertelo deklarado 'eś byen tornarlo 'a}

‹fol. 127a›
{KKZ
deklarar por ke 'el yero a'un ke śe'a poko 'enlaś kośaś altaś 'eś muy grande komo kyen reśvala 'en lugar alto ke por poko ke śe'a 'eś la kaida muy peligroza 'i 'eś ke

---

[209] Aristotle, *NE* VI.i.4–5 (1138b 35–1139a 12), *NE* VI.ii.3 (1139a 25–30).

BOOK OF THE REGIMEN OF LIVING ‹FOL. 127A›

a'un ke dezimoś ke śe reparte 'el anima 'en doś parteś 'i ke śe reparte 'el 'entendimyento 'en 'otraś doś parteś komo tenemoś diğo no śe'a de 'entender ke śean parteś deśtintaś 'o deśeparadaś ke toda 'eś 'una alma 'i todo 'eś 'un meśmo 'entendimyento śalvo ke 'eś komo ke diğeśemoś ke la alma 'en kuanto 'envelunta śe dize śer 'una parte 'en reśpekto deśta konsidrasy'on dela voluntad 'i 'en kuanto 'entyende 'i 'eśpekula śe dize śer 'otra parte :

'I dela meśma manera 'el 'entendimyento 'en kuanto 'eśpekula laś kozaś 'onibersaleś 'i forsozaś tomadaś de baśo de razon de verdad 'o falsi'a śe dize 'entendimyento te'oriko 'i 'en kuanto 'eśpekula 'enlaś kośaś posibleś ke pu'ede śer ke śean 'o dešen de śer 'i kabe 'en[e]lyyaś konśeğo tomadaś de bağo de razon de byen 'o mal śe dize 'entendimyento pratiko ke 'eś la deśtinsy'on ke 'el śenyyor Rabbenu Mošeh haze 'enel śegundo kapitulo dela primera partida deśu famoziśimo libro[210] :

'I 'eś komo dezimoś ke 'el Dyyo glory'ozo 'eś 'uno abśuluta mente 'i 'eś lyyamado 'en nombreś diferenteś śegun la diferensy'a delaś 'obraś ke alkansamoś ke 'obra aka baśo komo dišeron nu'eśoś śaby'oś 'i dišo 'el Dyo 'a Mošeh mi nombre buśkaś por śaber śegun miś 'obraś aśi śoy lyyamado veześ ayy ke śo lyyamado Dyyo veześ Abaśtado 'i set- kuando ğuśğo laś kryaturaś śo l(')yyamado Dyyo 'i set-[211] ke 'eneśto śiknifikaron ke a'un ke loś nombreś śean diferenteś por la diferensy'a delaś 'obraś no difyere la śuśtansy'a dela kośa lyyamada 'i śiknifikaron maś kela diferensy'a deloś nombreś del Dyyo no 'eś śalvo 'en nu'eśo reśpekto śegun la diferensy'a delaś 'obraś ke 'obra 'en nośotroś :

DE la meśma manera śe'a de 'entender 'enel 'entendimyento te'oriko 'i pratiko ke difyeren śegun laś 'obraś

'I śegun 'eśta manera de repartisy'on por la diferensy'a del 'obğekto 'enke 'obra 'el 'entendimyento śon repartidaś laś śinko vertudeś 'intelektibaś ke treś de 'elyyaś śon 'enel 'entendimyento te'oriko laś kualeś śon 'entendimyento sensy'a sapyensy'a 'i doś śon del 'entendimyento pratiko laś kualeś śon prudensy'a 'i arte[212] 'i 'eś 'eśta repartisy'on forsada śegun la diferensy'a de loś modoś de 'eśpekular ke eśpekula 'el 'entendimyento 'umano laś kośaś porke alaś veześ śera la 'eśpikulasy'on del 'entendimyento 'umano 'en kośaś forsadaś por śuś kauśaś ke no pu'eden değar de śer aśi komo śon laś ke 'eśpekula de bağo de razon de verdad 'o falsi'a komo tenemoś diğo [CW. aśi]}

---

[210] Maimonides, *Guide,* trans. Pines, 23–26 (*MN,* Pt. 1, chap. 2).
[211] Exodus R. 3.6.
[212] Aristotle, *NE* VI.iii.1 (1139b 15–18).

BOOK OF THE REGIMEN OF LIVING ‹FOL. 127B›

‹fol. 127b›
{aśi komo kuando 'eśpekula 'el 'ombre ke loś treś anguloś del tryangulo śon 'igualeś 'a doś deregoś[213] 'o 'otra kośa tal ke 'eśte modo de śaber 'eś 'en kośaś ke 'eś forsado śer komo śon 'i no 'eśtan de bago de razon de byen ni mal śalvo de bago de razon de verdad 'o mentira

'I alaś veześ 'eśpekulara 'el 'ombre 'en kośaś posibleś ke pu'eden śer 'i degar de śer por lo kual konsiśte 'en 'elyyaś 'el konśego laś kualeś laś 'eśpekula de bago de razon de byen 'o mal komo tenemoś digo

'I lo ke 'eśpekula debago de razon de verdad 'o mentira ke 'eś 'enlaś kośaś forsadaś komo tenemoś digo pu'ede śer 'en 'uno de treś modoś diferenteś

'EL primero 'eś la 'eśpikulasy'on 'en kośaś ke 'el 'e(t)n[t]endimyento laś alkansa de śuyo de prima viśta śin ningun 'otro medyyo komo 'eś la eśpikulasy'on 'i 'el śaber de loś primeroś prinsipy'oś ke loś alkansa 'el 'entendimyento natural mente śin ke ayya nesesidad de antisiparśe ningun modo de śaber 'i 'eśte modo de 'eśpikulasy'on prosede de 'un abito 'enel anima kon ke 'el tal śaber śe alkansa 'i lyyamaśe 'el tal abito 'entendimyento 'o 'entiligensy'a

'EL śegundo modo 'eś la 'eśpikulasy'on 'en laś kozaś ke 'el 'entendimyento alkansa por medyyo de loś primeroś prinsipy'oś ke tomando loś primeroś prinsipy'oś por primiśaś haze śelogiśmoś 'i 'el abito 'enel alma del kual prosede śaber akelyya porpozisy'on por 'enteresisy'on de akelyyoś primeroś prinsipy'oś śe lyyama sensy'a

'I 'el tersero 'eś 'el abito kon ke alkansa la alma la verdad de la koza por 'enteresisy'on de porpozisy'oneś alkansadaś por śelogiśmoś 'i peśkizaś komo śon todaś laś sensyaś ke 'eśkribyeron todoś loś śaby'oś 'el kual śe lyyama sapyensy'a 'o śabiduri'a

'I dela meśma manera 'el 'eśpekular 'enlaś kośaś posibleś ke no śon posibleś asidental mente 'o por p(r)a[r]te de la kośtelasy'on ke 'eśtaś taleś a'un ke śon posibleś no 'eśtan 'en mano del 'ombre por lo k[u]al no kabe 'enelyyaś 'eśpikulasy'on ni konśego śalvo laś ke śon posibleś por parte del 'ombre 'i śu libre alvedri'o tomadaś de bago de[ ]razon de byen 'o mal pu'ede śer 'en modoś diferenteś de la kual difer[e]nsy'a nase śer loś abitoś kon ke śe 'eśpekulan difer[e]nteś :

'EL primer abito 'eś kon 'el kual 'eśpekula 'el 'ombre 'en ke la 'obra ke 'obrare śe'a 'enderesada 'a fin de lo ke konbyene para 'el byen de la vida 'umana 'i fin pośtrero 'el kual śe lyyama prudensy'a

'I 'el abito kon ke 'eśpekula 'el 'ombre 'en la 'obra ke haze 'a fin de la perfeksy'on de la meśma 'obra śin ningun 'otro reśpekto ni akatamyento śe lyyama arte

DE manera ke śon todaś laś vertudeś 'intelektualeś śinko treś de 'el 'entendi-

---

[213] Cf. Aristotle, *De Anima* I.i (402b 20–21).

Book of the Regimen of Living ‹fol. 127b–128a›

myento te'oriko ke 'eś 'en laś kośaś forsadaś de bağo de razon de verdad 'i mentira [CW. komo]}

‹fol. 128a›
{KKH HELEK G PEREK Y' [PART THREE CHAPTER ELEVEN]
komo tenemoś diğo 'i doś 'en laś kośaś posibleś de bağo de razon de byen 'o mal
    'I aś de śaber ke lo ke lyyamamoś 'opiny'on 'o pensamyento 'en kual kyer kośa no śe 'entyende ni śe konkluye ni konprende 'en ninguna deśtaś śinko porke la 'opiny'on no 'eś fiğa ni firme 'enel 'entendimyento ke pu'ede śer ke śe'a falsa ke por 'eśo śe lyyama 'opiny'on 'i dela meśma manera 'el pensamyento lo kual la sensy'a 'i la śabiduri'a no ayy 'enelyyaś falsi'a 'en ningun modo porke kuando 'el śaby'o 'eśpekula 'en kual kyer kośa 'i alkansa la verdad śe pu'ede dezir verdader'a mente ke la alkansa por parte del abito ke tyene 'ensu alma ke śe lyyama śabiduri'a por lo kual lyyamamoś lo propy'o ke 'a alkansado 'i 'el alkansarlo śabiduri'a porke 'el 'entendimyento 'i la kośa 'entendida 'i 'el 'entender śe tornan 'una meśma kośa komo 'eś śabido lo kual kuando 'el 'entendimyento no alkansa la verdad dela kośa 'i konkuluye algun yero lyyamarśe'a 'opiny'on porke akelyyo no le vino por parte de śabiduri'a maś anteś por falta 'i privasy'on delyya porke la śabiduri'a 'i la sensy'a no śon śalvo aserka dela verdad pura forsada 'onibersal komo tenemoś diğo :

KAPITULO 'ONZENO

'I para ke meğor pu'edaś konprender la verdader'a deśkrisy'on deśtaś śinko vertudeś 'i la diferensy'a de 'una 'a 'otra ke 'eś algo difisil konoserlo laś deklarare algo maś por 'eśtenso 'enel maś breve modo ke posible śera por ke byen ve'eś ke miś 'infinitaś 'okupasy'oneś no me dan 'a maś lugar 'i deklarartelaś'e por la regla ke laś deklaro 'el filosofo 'enel seśto de la 'etika[214] 'onde yo tengo byen alargado
    'I primero deklararemoś la sensy'a por ke 'eś maś fasil de deklarar por lo ke tenemoś diğo 'i 'eś ke la sensy'a no 'eś śalvo śaber laś kośaś por śuś kauśaś ke deśta manera śon forsadaś 'i no posibleś 'i 'a de śer ke śe'a śabido por laś kauśaś ke le antisipan 'i ke śepa verdader'a mente ke akelyyaś śon śuś kauśaś 'i no 'otraś ke deśta manera śe podra dezir śer forsado ke śe'a aśi la kośa śabida komo la śupo 'el 'entendimyento 'i no de 'otra 'i deśta manera śe dize śer la koza śabida 'eterna porke la kośa ke 'eś forsado de śer śenpre 'eś 'i śera 'a 'infinito 'enğenplo delo kual śe pu'ede tomar de kual kyera porpozisy'on matematika komo loke 'emoś diğo del śaber

---

[214] The discussion follows Aristotle, *NE* VI.iii.2–4 (1139b 19–36), except that the mathematical example is closer to *De Anima* I.i (402b 20–21).

Book of the Regimen of Living ⟨fol. 128a–128b⟩

ke loś treś anguloś del tryangulo śon 'igualeś 'a doś deregoś 'i set- ke 'eśto 'eś sensy'a porke 'eś pura verdad 'i 'eś forsado de śer aśi 'i nunka değara de śer aśi 'en 'eterno śin ninguna mudansa por śer forsado śer aśi por śuś kauśaś antesedenteś komo tenemoś diğo de manera ke a'un ke śe korompa la kośa ke śe śupo la verdad delyya nunka śe korompera ğamaś [CW. lo]}

⟨fol. 128b⟩
{loke śe śupo delyya 'i 'eśto 'eś viśto ke 'el śaber (k)[d]e 'un 'endivido rasy'onal partikular 'eś śensible ke 'eś śabido por 'otra kośa śabida ke todo animal 'eś śensible kedara śabido 'en 'e(n)terno ke akel tal 'endivido partikular śe'a śensible 'i a'un ke śe korompa 'i mu'era akel tal partikular śyenpre kedara 'eśta porpozisy'on 'en 'eterno porke no vino 'eśte tal śaber por la parte ke śe korompe ke no śe ğuśgo śer 'el śensible por śer 'el maś ke 'otro 'endivido de śu 'eśpesy'a śalvo por śer 'endivido de akelyya 'eśpesy'a 'en 'onibersal ke 'eś por parte de śer 'ombre ke 'eś animal rasy'onal 'i 'eśta parte de 'umanidad 'o rasy'onalidad nunka śe korompe por lo kual 'eśta porpozisy'on keda permanente 'i aśi del meśmo modo loke śe śabe 'en todaś laś 'otraś kośaś ğenerableś 'i korutibleś no 'eś por parte de śer partikulareś por la kual parte śon ğenerableś 'i korutibleś śalvo por parte de śu 'esensy'a 'onibersal ke 'eś forsada por śuś kauśaś ke 'eśto 'eś permanente komo tenemoś diğo por donde 'eś viśto ke 'el[ ]śaber 'eśto por śuś kauśaś antesedenteś 'eś sensy'a 'el kual 'eś 'un abito 'enel anima 'intelektiba ke 'eś loke lyyamamoś 'entendimyento te'oriko konel kual alkansa la verdad de tal forma ke no pu'ede śer 'el kontrary'o de akelyyo ke alkansa 'en ninguna manera :

POR lo kual 'eś viśto ke an de śer al śaby'o maś notaś laś kauśaś de la kośa por donde vyene 'a śaber la verdad de śu 'esensy'a ke la verdad de la kośa 'en śi por ke śi 'eś maś śabida la kośa ke śuś kauśaś śera akel śaber asidental ke 'el śaber la suśtansy'a de la kośa 'eś por śuś kauśaś komo 'el ke śabe kuando 'a de śer 'iklipśe de śol 'o de luna 'i no lo śabe por laś kauśaś verdaderaś de śuś mobimyentoś kon todaś laś 'otraś kauśaś ke śe rekyere śaber para akel 'efekto śe dira śaber lo asidental mente por ke śabyendolo por śuś kauśaś 'eś pura mente śaber forsado komo tenemoś diğo

'I 'eśte modo de śaber forsado 'eterno 'eś 'en konsidrasy'oneś diferenteś 'i syendo todo por parte de demośtrasy'on śe lyyama sensy'a komo laś porpozisy'oneś de matematika 'o de[ ]fizika 'o metafizika śakaraś por demośtrasy'on komo kuando dezimoś todo 'ombre 'eś animal 'i todo animal syente lu'ego todo 'ombre syente 'i set-[215] ke 'eś seloğiś(y)mo de la primera figura de doś 'onibersaleś afirmatibaś de manera

---

[215] Aristotle, *Prior Analytics* I.iv (25b 27–26b 33), trans. H. Tredennick (Cambridge, MA, 1938), 209.

BOOK OF THE REGIMEN OF LIVING ‹FOL. 128B–129A›

ke śaber ke todo 'ombre syente 'eś sensy'a śakada por demośtrasy'on ke no pu'ede değar de śer aśi por ninguna manera 'i del meśmo modo śe konsidra tanbyen sensy'a 'en kośa ke ayya ya pasado komo kyen diğeśe todo tyenpo ke śe ağuntaron loś luminary'oś mayoreś 'en la kabesa 'o kola del dragon[216] fu'e 'iklipśe ke 'eśto 'eś forsado por laś kauśaś de śuś mobimyentoś komo 'eś śabido [CW. 'i dela]}

‹fol. 129a›
{KKT
'i de la meśma manera śe podra konsidrar 'en lo futuro ke verdader'a mente śe dira ke todo tyenpo ke śe ağuntaren loś diğoś luminary'oś 'en alguno de loś doś lugareś diğoś śera 'iklipśe 'i set- 'i del meśmo modo śe konsidra la sensy'a 'en laś kośaś ke 'eś 'inposible halyyarśe nunka 'en a'uto komo kuando diğeśemoś 'el vaku'o 'eś lugar śin ku'erpo ke a'un ke śe'a 'inposible halyyarśe vaku'o śegun verdader'a 'opiny'on aprobada por 'el filosofo 'en loś fizikoś[217] kon todo 'eśto 'eś 'eśta porpozisy'on verdader'a ke a'un ke nunka ayya vaku'o 'eś verdad ke la difinsy'on del vaku'o 'eś lugar śin ku'erpo ke śon laś treś dimensy'oneś śi fu'era posible halyyarśe 'i 'eś verdad forsada por śuś kauśaś 'i porpozisy'on 'eterna komo tenemoś diğo a'un ke 'eśta 'eternidad no 'eś 'eternidad abśuluta komo la 'eternidad del Dyyo alto 'i glory'ozo 'i kon todo 'eśto la 'eternidad de la sensy'a tyene alguna maś śimilitud kon la 'eternidad del Dyyo ke kual kyer 'otra kośa ke lyamaron loś śaby'oś 'eterna por parte de no tener prinsipy'o ni fin :
'I por 'eśte modo de śimilitud fu'e diğo 'en la kreasy'on del 'ombre fagamoś 'ombre 'en nu'eśtra figura komo nu'eśtra śemeğansa 'i set-[218] ke 'en dezir 'en nu'eśtra figura śiknifika la forma suśtansyal rasy'onal ke 'eś la forma 'eśpisifika komo dize 'el śenyyor Rabbenu Mośeh 'enel primer kapitulo deśu famozisimo libro 'i 'en dezir komo nu'eśtra śemeğansa śiknifiko 'el modo de 'entender[219] 'i por śer ke 'el modo de alkansar 'el 'entendimyento 'umano la verdad no 'eś ni 'entra 'en ğenero konel modo de 'el 'entendimyento devino dize komo nu'eśtra śemeğansa 'i no dize 'en nu'eśtra

---

[216] An astronomical reckoning: "the Dragon's Tail, [. . .] the point where a planet (esp. the moon) passed from the northern to the southern side of the ecliptic" (W. W. Skeat, glossary to *The Complete Works of Geoffrey Chaucer* [Oxford, 1894], 34). See also F. Cantera Burgos, "Notas para la historia de la astronomía en la España medieval: el judío salmantino Abraham Zacut," *Revista de la Academia de Ciencias,* 2 ser. 27 (1931): 360–62.

[217] Aristotle examines this question at length in the *Physics* IV.vi–ix (213a 12–217b 28), trans. P. Wicksteed and F. M. Cornford (Cambridge, MA, 1929–1934), 1:239–71.

[218] Gen. 1.26.

[219] Maimonides, *Guide,* trans. Pines, 17–23 (*MN,* Pt. 1, chap. 1).

BOOK OF THE REGIMEN OF LIVING ‹FOL. 129A–129B›

ś[e]meğansa por ke no 'eś śalvo 'un modo de[ ]śimilitud 'en alguna manera 'en la verdad de la kośa śabida 'i 'en la 'eternidad delyya a'un ke śon muy diferenteś 'enel modo 'i 'eternidad komo del syelo ala tyera 'i 'en konkluzy'on 'eśta viśto de todo lo diğo la verdader'a deśkrisy'on deśta virtud 'intelektual ke 'eś la sensy'a la kual 'eś viśto śer 'un abito 'enel anima rasy'onal kon 'el kual 'entyende 'el 'entendimyento te'oriko la kośa śabida por 'entersisy'on de loś primeroś prinsipy'oś komo avemoś diğo :
'I para lo ke konbyene śaber para la verdader'a deśkriśy'on de la arte ke 'eś del 'entendimyento pratiko komo avemoś diğo sigyendo por la regla ke laś deklaro 'el filosofo por ke tyene 'en alguna manera maś śimilitud kon la sensy'a 'en ke todoś ğuśgan por primeroś prinsipy'oś aś de śaber ke la arte 'eś 'un abito 'enel anima rasy'onal kon 'el kual 'el artifise 'enderesa la 'obra 'a fin de la perfeksy'on 'i la bondad de la 'obra 'en śi 'i no a'otro ningun fin[220]
'I a'un ke la prudensy'a 'enderesa tanbyen 'a la perfeksy'on 'i bondad de la 'obra ayy grandisima diferensy'a de la arte ala prudensy'a por parte de la 'intensy'on 'en la kauśa final ke la prudensy'a 'enderesa ala perfeksy'on de la 'obra 'a fin del byen ke śe le rezulta al 'ombre delyya[221] [CW. 'i la]}

‹fol. 129b›
{'i la arte 'enderesa 'a fin del byen 'i la perfeksy'on dela meśma 'obra 'enśi komo konbyene ala perfeksy'on de la arte por lo kual śi 'un artifise bu'en maeśtro fraguador fu'eśe 'enkomendado de hazer 'una kaśa heğa de tal modo ke akabo de dyeś diaś 'o vente kayyga la kaśa śobre loś ke śe halyyaran dyentro delyya 'eś viśto ke hazyendola 'en toda la perfeksy'on ke konbyene para tal fin 'i kayendo la kaśa al tal tyenpo śe dira ke 'el tal fraguador 'eś perfekto maeśtro 'i ke 'obro perfekta mente śegun la virtud dela arte porke 'obro konforme aśu 'intensy'on 'i fin adkerido pero no śe[ ]dira ke 'obro śegun la virtud de la prudensy'a porke no 'obro 'en akelyyo 'a fin de loke konbyene al byen 'umano śalvo ala perfeksy'on dela arte komo tenemoś diğo 'i aśi komo loś abitoś 'i vertudeś śon diferenteś aśi tanbyen śon diferenteś śuś 'obğektoś ke 'uno depende del 'otro de manera ke śe'a de 'entender ke 'el 'obğekto dela prudensy'a śe lyyama akto 'i 'el de la arte śe lyyama fakto 'i del meśmo modo la 'obra dela prudensy'a śe lyyama //ak(')sy'on// 'i la dela arte faksy'on 'i para maś 'entender la verdader'a deśkrisy'on deśta virtud dela arte aś de śaber ke 'eśta virtud 'eś 'un abito 'enel alma konel kual 'el 'entendimyento pratiko 'enderesa ala perfeksy'on dela 'obra 'en treś kośaś ke konbyene ke śe konsidren 'en toda arte :

---

[220] Aristotle, NE VI.iv.4–6 (1140a 12–15, 21–24).
[221] Aristotle, NE VI.v.4 and VI.v.6 (1140b 5–8, 13–20).

BOOK OF THE REGIMEN OF LIVING ‹FOL. 129B–130A›

LA primera 'eś la perfeksy'on dela 'obra :
LA śegunda la perfeksy'on de la matery'a 'enke śe 'obra :
LA tersera la perfeksy'on del 'obrar 'enǧenplo 'el śapatero para kerer hazer 'unoś bu'enoś 'i perfektoś śapatoś 'a de konsidrar 'o afigurar primero 'el fin ke le ko[n]byene ke 'eś la perfeksy'on dela 'obra 'i 'eś ke depu'eś de akabadoś śean komo konbyene ala perfeksy'on de la arte konforme ala 'intensy'on :
DEPU'EŚ 'a de konsidrar 'el ku'ero del kual loś haze ke śe'a konvenible para la perfeksy'on dela 'obra konforme ala 'intensy'on 'i deśpu'eś 'a de konsidrar 'el modo ke loś 'a de hazer kela 'eśpikulasy'on de todaś 'eśtaś treś kozaś 'eś por parte del 'entendimyento pratiko [kon] lo kual śe perfeksy'ona todo lo diǧo por 'eśte abito 'i virtud ke lyyamamoś arte :
'I kon 'eśto 'eś viśto ke 'eśta virtud no 'eś aserka de laś kośaś forsadaś śalvo aserka de laś kośaś posibleś ke 'el śapatero posible 'eś ke haga loś śapatoś 'i posible 'eś ke loś deǧe de hazer la kual posiblidad vyene por parte del artifise 'i no por parte dela 'obra ke por parte de la 'obra tanbyen laś kośaś ke vyenen 'a kaśo śon posibleś 'i tanbyen laś kośaś naturaleś śe dizen posibleś por parte dela 'obra aśi komo dezimoś ke la lyyubyya 'eś natural averla 'en 'invyerno ke tanbyen śera posible ke no la ayya 'i 'eśte modo de posiblidad a'un ke 'eś posible porśi 'eś forsado por śuś kauśaś de śer 'o deǧar de śer [CW. 'i maś]}

‹fol. 130a›
{KL
'i maś ke 'el prinsipy'o de śer 'o de deǧar de śer 'eśta 'en la propy'a kośa lo ke no 'eś 'en la arte ke 'el prinsipy'o de śer 'o de deǧar de śer 'eśta 'enel artifise komo tenemoś diǧo
'I para la perfeksy'on deśta virtud 'en laś 'obraś ke hazen loś perfektoś deven buśkar artifiseś ke śean tanbyen virtu'ozoś 'en todaś laś 'otraś vertudeś 'intelektualeś para śaber 'i 'eśpekular 'i 'enderesar la 'obra 'a fin del byen 'umano ke 'una virtud 'eś kauśa de a'umentarśe 'i perfeksy'onarśe la 'otra por lo kual mando 'el Dyo glory'ozo 'en la 'obra del tabernaklo ke fu'eśe feǧa por akel famozisimo 'i sapyentisimo artifise Bᶜsal'el ke 'era perfekto 'en todaś laś vertudeś 'intelektualeś komo teśtifika porel nu'eśa śantisima ley do dize 'i hinǧo a'el de 'eśprito del Dyyo 'en śabiduri'a 'en prudensy'a 'i 'en sensy'a 'i 'en toda arte 'i set-[222] ke śon laś kuatro vertudeś 'intelektualeś 'i manko 'el 'entendimyento por ke no 'eś meneśter dezirlo ke halyy[a]ndośe la sensy'a 'o la śabiduri'a no pu'ede śer śin 'el 'entendimyento komo 'eś viśto de lo ke tenemoś diǧo 'i deklarando 'el probeǧo ke śe śige 'en śe'er 'obrada la 'obra por 'un

---

[222] Exod. 35.31.

BOOK OF THE REGIMEN OF LIVING ‹FOL. 130A–130B›

tan 'elevado artifise dize maś 'i por pensar pensamyentoś para fazer 'enel 'oro 'i 'en la plata 'i set-[223] keryendo dezir ke 'eśtaba 'enel la perfeksy'on del 'entendimyento 'en todaś laś vertudeś para loke konbyene penśar anteś ke śalga la 'obra 'en 'efekto ke 'eśto vyene por parte de śer śaby'o 'i 'eśto kiğo dezir 'en dezir por pensar pensamyentoś 'i set-[224] 'i śiknifiko la perfeksy'on de la arte para poner la 'en puro a'uto 'en dezir por fazer 'enel 'oro 'i 'en la plata 'i set-[225] ke 'eś para śalir la 'obra 'en 'efekto komo tenemoś diğo

'I ğunto kon 'eśto diremoś lo ke konbyene śaber para la verdader'a deśkrisy'on de la prudensy'a[226] por śer maś alyegada ala arte ke todaś doś śon del 'entendimyento pratiko komo tenemoś diğo 'i a'un ke śe podri'a 'i śe deveri'a byen alargar 'en 'elyya ke 'el k[o]noserla byen 'eś muy 'util dire delyya muy poko 'i muy breve komo 'enlaś 'otraś hata aver maś 'oportunidad la kual śe'a de śaber por la deśkrisy'on deloś virtu'ozoś 'en 'elyya ke śon loś prudenteś loś kualeś 'eś śabido śer loś ke pu'eden dar konśeğo para 'enderesar laś kośaś bu'enaś 'i 'utileś 'a 'el 'ombre por parte ke 'eś 'ombre 'i 'el abito ke tyenen loś taleś prudenteś 'enel alma konel kual dan 'el konśeğo 'i regla perfekta śegun dereğa razon para alkansar laś kozaś bu'enaś 'i probeğozaś para la perfeksy'on dela vida 'umana śe lyyama prudensy'a 'i de aki 'eś viśto komo la prudensy'a no 'eś aserka laś kośaś forsadaś śalvo aserka de laś posibleś komo tenemoś diğo porke aserka delaś kozaś forsadaś ke no pu'eden değar de śer no kabe 'enelyyaś konśeğo ke 'eś la 'obra dela prudensy'a por tanto 'onde no kabe konśeğo no ayy prudensy'a komo diğo Mošeh Rabbenu por loś 'enemigoś de Yiśra'el}

‹fol. 130b›
{ke ğente perdida de konśeğo 'elyyoś 'i non 'enelyyoś prudensy'a 'i set-[227] keryendo dezir loke tenemoś diğo ke mankando 'el konśeğo manka la prudensy'a por donde 'eś viśto śer diferente la prudensy'a dela sensy'a kela sensy'a 'eś aserka delaś kozaś forsozaś ke no pu'eden değar de śer 'i la prudensy'a 'eś aserka de laś kozaś posibleś por lo kual kabe 'enelyyaś 'el konśeğo 'i 'eś viśto tanbyen komo 'eś diferente dela arte por parte del fin komo tenemoś diğo porke la arte 'enderesa ala perfeksy'on de la 'obra tan śola mente por la 'obra 'enśi komo konbyene para artifise 'i no komo konbyene para 'ombre 'i la prudensy'a 'enderesa a'el byen 'i 'util ke śe śige de la 'obra para la vida 'umana komo konbyene para 'ombre por śer 'ombre komo tenemoś diğo :

---

[223] Exod. 35.32.
[224] Exod. 35.32.
[225] Exod. 35.32.
[226] The discussion follows Aristotle, *NE* VI.v.1–3 (1140a 25–1140b 63).
[227] Deut. 32.28.

BOOK OF THE REGIMEN OF LIVING ‹FOL. 130B–131A›

'I aś maś de śaber ke la tenplansa[228] ke avemoś ya deklarado 'en laś vertudeś moraleś 'eś muy participante konla prudensy'a ke 'eś la ke konserva la prudensy'a por ke komo kyera ke la prudensy'a 'eś 'una dereğa razon ke ğuśga ke śe deve de apartar 'el 'ombre de laś kośaś malaś 'i 'eśto ğuśga śeloğizandolo por 'unoś prinsipy'oś resebidoś 'i śabidoś tomadoś 'i konsidradoś por loś fineś 'i 'el ke 'eś deśtenplado paresyendole byen la deleytasy'on korporal tanbyen le paresera ke 'obrar 'a fin de la deleytasy'on korporal 'eś byen de manera ke śe pyerde total mente la prudensy'a por ke 'inorando la bondad 'i 'el fin 'inora loś primeroś prinsipy'oś por donde ğuśga la prudensy'a por ke loś primeroś prinsipy'oś 'enel moral śon tomadoś śegun loś fineś komo tenemoś diğo 'eś viśto lu'ego ke la templansa ke 'eś la moderasy'on del 'apetito konkupisible 'eś konśervasy'on de la prudensy'a 'i konronpyendośe 'el abito dela templansa śe konronpe 'el abito dela prudensy'a por tanto 'el malo ke 'eś tan malo ke le parese byen 'el mal ke haze pyerde loś prinsipy'oś 'i perdidoś loś prinsipy'oś 'i reglaś 'onibersaleś para 'obrar 'el byen 'eś 'inkurable śi 'otro de fu'era no lo 'enkamina por lo kual vyendo 'el Dyyo altisimo 'enel siglo del dilubyyo aver todoś perdido loś prinsipy'oś ke śon kamino para 'el byen verdadero ğuśgo śer todoś korompidoś śin remedy'o ninguno por lo kual leś trušo 'el dilubyyo do dize 'i vido 'el Dyyo ala tyera 'i hek danyyada ke danyyo toda kryatura śu karera śobre la tyera 'i set-[229] ke kyere dezir ke vido 'el Dyyo loś moradoreś de la tyera ke 'eran danyyadoś 'a tanto ke śe podi'a dezir sumary'a mente ke la tyera śe avia danyado 'i deklara la kauśa 'i dize ke 'eś por averśe korompido 'el kamino ke trae al byen ke 'eś la prudensy'a 'i 'eśto kiğo dezir ke danyy(y)o toda kryatura śu karera 'i set- ke la karera apropyyada a'el 'ombre ke śe pu'eda dezir propy'a mente śu karera 'eś 'el kamino por 'el kual śe alkansa la byen aventuransa 'i a'un ke nu'eśoś śaby'oś lo glozan por 'otra vi'a no diśkrepante deśta 'intensy'on no śe'a de değar de dezir lo ke śe syente por la letra :
'I la diferensy'a ke ayy de la prudensy'a [CW. alaś]}

‹fol. 131a›
{KL'
alaś 'otraś vertudeś 'eś kela prudensy'a 'eś aserka del ğu'izy'o dela koza ke ğuśga śegun dereğa razon ke 'eś byen de śer 'obrado 'i a'un ke la tal 'obra nunka śalga 'en 'efekto konkluyyo ya la prudensy'a śu 'obra

---

[228] The discussion follows Aristotle, *NE* VI.v.6 (1140b 18–22).
[229] Gen. 6.12.

BOOK OF THE REGIMEN OF LIVING ⟨FOL. 131A⟩

'I para loke konbyene śaber para 'el verdadero konosimyento dela virtud ke lyamamoś 'entendimyento no 'eś menester muğo alargar ke de loke tenemoś diğo aserka de las 'otraś śe podra byen konprender ke 'el 'entendimyento[230] 'eś 'un abito 'enel alma de 'el 'ombre konel kual konose 'i śabe todoś loś primeroś prinsipy'oś śin hazer ningun śeloğiśmo ke del depende todo 'el śaber 'i 'eś 'el 'oriğin de adonde mana toda la sensy'a konforme alo kual diğo nu'eśo śapyentisimo rey Š^{e}lomoh 'enśuś probyerby'oś manadero de vida 'entendimyento de śu du'enyyo 'i set-[231] ke kyere dezir ke komo loś primeroś prinsipy'oś śon 'el 'oriğin de adonde mana toda la sensy'a 'i la sensy'a verdader'a 'eś la vida verdader'a del 'ombre porke toda vida 'eś 'obrar 'i la 'obra del 'entendimyento 'eś la meğor 'obra lu'ego la śensy'a 'eś la meğor vida falyyaśe ke 'el 'entendimyento konel kual śe alkanśan 'eśtoś primeroś prinśipy'oś 'eś 'el manadero dela vida 'i de aki naśe ke la dotrina de loś 'inoranteś 'eś 'inoranśy'a porke 'inorando loś primeroś prinśipy'oś śe 'inora la dotrina ke 'eś la śensy'a ke śe śige delyyoś de manera ke la difinśy'on deśta virtud 'eś 'un abito verdadero de afirmasy'on 'i negaśy'on aśerka deloś primeroś prinśipy'oś alkanśadoś 'i śabidoś por śi meśmoś śin 'entereśiśy'on de 'otro ningun medyyo para lo kual 'eś menester śaber ke ayy muğaś 'eśpeśyaś de primeroś prinśipy'oś ke ayy algunoś 'oniberśaleś ke śe śaben porel partikular komo dezir ke todo todo 'eś maś ke la parte 'o komo dezir ke kual kyer kośa 'eś 'o değa de śer 'o ke śi 'un animal 'eś mu'erto no 'eś bibo '(y)[o] ke 'eś 'inpośible ke 'una meśma kośa śe'a 'i değe de śer 'en 'un meśmo tyenpo 'o ke śe'a biba 'i mu'erta[232] 'o 'otroś taleś primeroś prinśipy'oś śabidoś 'infinitoś 'i ayy algunoś ke śon tanbyen 'oniberśaleś ke śon tanbyen śabidoś por laś kozaś partikulareś viśtaś porel śentido korporal komo śaber ke 'el fu'ego 'en 'oniberśal 'eśkalyenta ke 'eś śabido porke ve'emoś 'i śentimoś 'eśkalyentar 'el fu'ego partikular 'i ayy algunoś 'otroś primeroś prinśipy'oś partikulareś ke todoś śe alkanśan por parte de 'el śentido 'enlaś kośaś pośibleś 'i ayy algunoś 'oniberśaleś total mente komo śon loś prinśipy'oś ke śe dizen 'en la arte de la loğika 'i 'en la metafizika 'i ayy algunoś 'oniberśaleś 'en 'una konśidraśy'on 'i partikulareś 'en 'otra komo loś prinśipy'oś de alguna śenśy'a partikular 'i ayy algunoś 'otroś prinśipy'oś ke śon śabidoś 'a algunoś śaby'oś i aloś ke no śon śaby'oś no śon śabidoś komo śon loś maś de loś prinsipy'oś de la matematika 'i por 'eśto 'eś 'eśta virtud 'un abito 'enel alma para konoser por 'elyya 'i

---

[230] The discussion follows Aristotle, *NE* VI.vi.1–2 (1140b 30–1141a 9).

[231] Prov. 16.22.

[232] Aristotelian law of the excluded middle: *Metaphysics* IV.vi.10 (1011b 17–18); which is quoted in Avicenna's *Compendium on the Soul*, Lat. tr. A. Alpago, Venice, 1546. D. Gutas, *Avicenna and the Aristotelian Tradition* (Leiden: Brill, 1988), 17 with n. 2.

BOOK OF THE REGIMEN OF LIVING ‹FOL. 131A–131B›

alkansar kual 'eś primero prinsipy'o ke 'eś śabido por śi 'i no por 'entreśiśy'on de 'otra kośa [CW. ke la]}

‹fol. 131b›
{ke la virtud kon ke śe alkansa 'eśto śe lyyama 'entendimyento komo tenemoś diǧo 'I para lo ke konbyene śaber para 'el verdadero konosimyento de la śabiduri'a[233] ke 'eś la pośtrera de laś śinko vertudeś 'intelektualeś 'en la regla ke aki śe'a prosedido aś de śaber ke sumary'a mente śe dize śaby'o 'el ke 'eś śaby'o 'en kual kyer modo de śabiduri'a 'i maś verdader'a mente śe dize śaby'o 'el ke 'eś śaby'o 'en todaś konforme alo kual pyenso ke lo difinyeron nu'eśoś śaby'oś do diǧeron kual 'eś śaby'o 'el ke deprende de todo 'ombre 'i set-[234] ke kyeren dezir ke 'el ke śe pu'ede lyyamar verdader'a mente śaby'o 'eś 'el ke śe pu'ede dezir por 'el ke deprende de kual kyer śu'erte de śaby'o 'en kual kyer sensy'a ke 'eśto 'eś śenyal ke 'eś 'el 'onibersal 'en todaś pu'eś 'eś abil para deprender de todoś 'i traen nu'eśoś śaby'oś para 'eśto preba de 'un devinisimo diǧo de nu'eśo rey David ke diǧo de todoś miś abezanteś 'entendi 'i set-[235] ke 'eś lo meśmo ke tenemoś diǧo ke śe loaba David śer 'onibersal 'en todaś laś sensyaś de tal manera ke 'entendi'a de kual kyera śaby'o ke le abezaba 'i da la razon para 'elyyo la kual 'eś por śer ke de kontino hablaba 'en nu'eśa ley ke konprende toda śu'erte de sensy'a de manera ke verdader'a mente no śe lyyamara śaby'o śalvo 'el ke 'eś śaby'o 'en nu'eśa śantisima ley ni śe lyyamara verdader'a mente śabiduri'a śalvo nu'eśa śantisima ley por ke konprende todaś laś śabiduriaś komo 'eś manifyeśto
'I partikular mente śe dize śaby'o porel ke 'eś śaby'o 'enla metafizika ke 'eś la śabiduri'a prinsipal de todaś laś śabiduriaś porke para śaber 'eśta 'eś meneśter ke śe śepan anteś todaś laś 'otraś sensyaś 'i diześe 'eśta śer maś verdader'a ke laś 'otraś porke 'eśpekula 'en kośaś maś verdaderaś ke śu śuǧebto 'eś 'el 'ente por parte ke 'eś 'ente 'inmudable la kual propy'a mente śe dize por nu'eśtra te'oloǧi'a śakra 'eśkritura devinisima ke 'eś toda pura verdad śin falsi'a ninguna :
'I 'eś diferente la śabiduri'a dela sensy'a ke la sensy'a 'eś loke śe alkansa por 'enteresisy'on deloś primeroś prinsipy'oś tan śola mente lo kual la śabiduri'a 'eś loke depu'eś śe śabe delaś porpozisy'oneś śakadaś 'i alkansadaś de loś primeroś prinsipy'oś de manera ke 'enel meśmo grado de antisipasy'on ke 'eś 'el 'entendimyento 'en reśpekto dela sensy'a 'eś la sensy'a 'en reśpekto de la śabiduri'a ke //k(on)[e]lo// ke śe alkansa por loś primeroś prinsipy'oś ke 'eś loke śe lyyama sensy'a 'eś 'el medy'o

---

[233] The discussion follows Aristotle, *NE* VI.vii.1–3 (1141a 10–22).
[234] Avot 4.1.
[235] Ps. 119.99.

BOOK OF THE REGIMEN OF LIVING ‹FOL. 131B–132A›

para la perfeksy'on de la śabiduri'a 'a 'infinito ke no tyene fin 'eśpesyal 'el śaber de nu'eśa śantisima ley :
'I 'eś viśto śer la śabiduri'a diferente tanbyen dela prudensy'a ke la prudensy'a 'eś ǧuśgar la verdad aserka loke konbyene para 'el byen dela vida 'umana [CW. ke 'eś]}

‹fol. 132a›
{KLB HELEK G PQ YB [PART THREE CHAPTER TWELVE]
ke 'eś perfeksy'on del 'entendimyento pratiko 'enlaś kośaś posibleś 'i la śabiduri'a 'eś aserka dela verdad ke 'eś perfeksy'on del 'entendimyento te'oriko 'enlaś kośaś forsozaś 'onibersaleś komo tenemoś diǧo :

KAPITULO DOZE

NO kyero aki dezir maś ke la repartisy'on delaś śensyaś 'i no 'en śaber kualeś śon laś ke lyyaman sensy'a 'i kual arte porke ayy 'en algunaś delyaś diferensyya komo 'enla medisina ke Abisena la lyyama sensy'a[236] 'i 'otroś maś antigoś la lyamaron arte[237] dela meśma manera la loǧika pyenso kre'er Platon ke 'eś arte 'i 'otroś muǧoś 'uno deloś kualeś fu'e 'el śenyyor Rabbenu Mośeh ke de kontino la nombra por arte[238] 'i tomando la arte śegun la tomo Tuly'o[239] śe lyyaman laś syete sensyaś liberaleś syete arteś liberaleś ke 'eś la primera la gramatika 'i la śegunda la loǧika 'i la tersera la retorika ke todaś 'eśtaś treś lyyaman loś gregoś loǧika porke śon aserka dela perfeksy'on dela habla 'i logoś 'en grego kyere dezir habla 'eś la kuarta la aridmetika 'i la kinta la ǧe'ometri'a 'i la śeśta la muzika 'i la śeptima 'eś la preśpektiba[240] 'i 'eśtaś kuatro pośtreraś lyyaman loś latinoś matematikaś 'i lyyamanśe todaś syete liberaleś por ke no konbyenen śalbo 'a 'ombreś libreś 'i no śuǧebtoś 'a 'otroś todaś laś 'otraś sensyaś komo fizika 'i metafizika 'i 'otraś partikulareś no 'ubo ninguno ke no konformaśe 'enke śe lyyamen śabiduri'a kuanta maś nu'esa devinisima le'ey ke komo tenemoś

---

[236] Ibn Sina does define medicine as a science: "Medicine is the science by which we learn [...]" ("*Canon of Medicine,*" trans. Gruner, 25).

[237] Chadwick and Mann prefer "The Science" over "The Art of Medicine" as their title for Hippocrates' apology because: "it is the writer's main contention that Medicine is an exact science not an undefinable art" (*Medical Works,* 81).

[238] The *Treatise on Logic* exemplifies that usage: see Maimonides, "*Treatise on Logic,*" trans. I. Efros (New York, 1938), 34.

[239] Cf. Cicero, *De finibus* V.18.

[240] That is, "optics".

BOOK OF THE REGIMEN OF LIVING ‹FOL. 132A–132B›

diğo konprende todaś laś sensyaś 'i arteś 'i prudensy'a 'i śabiduri'a 'i 'en konkluzy'on śe pu'ede dezir verdader'a mente ke 'eśtan konklu'idaś 'enelyya todaś laś vertudeś moraleś 'i 'intelektualeś por lo kual halyamoś nu'eśo devinisimo rey David 'i śu hiğo Šᵉlomoh ke 'entitulan nu'eśa le'ey 'en tituloś diferenteś ke 'a veześ la lyyaman ğuśtisy'a alaś veześ preseptoś alaś veześ temor del Dyyo alaś veześ prudensy'a alaś veześ śensy'a alaś veześ śabiduri'a 'i set- por ke konprende todo komo tenemoś diğo :
    ŚOLO 'eś mi 'intensy'on dezirte aki 'en breve 'el 'eśtilo ke deveś lyevar 'en deprender la sensy'a por śuś prinsipy'oś śola mente lo ke te baśtara para 'entender laś palabraś de nu'eśoś śaby'oś 'en nu'eśo Ṭalmud 'i 'en 'otroś lugareś ke no değaron sensy'a ni śabiduri'a ke no 'eśpekularon 'i komo vengan śuś palabraś muy seradaś ke no kiğeron dezir maś ke laś śiknifikasy'oneś de laś kozaś porke para loś śaby'oś akelyyo abaśta por tanto 'eś meneśter le'er 'en alguna manera por loś libroś deloś f[i]losofoś ke alargaron 'enla sensy'a para poder byen konprender la 'intensy'on de nu'eśoś śaby'oś :
    'I porke la vida 'eś muy [CW. breve]}

‹fol. 132b›
{breve 'i la śabiduri'a muy larga 'i laś 'okupasy'oneś muğaś²⁴¹ 'eś razon de buśkar 'el maś breve kamino ke konbyene 'enel le'er 'eśtaś sensyaś para diśtribu'ir 'el maś del tyenpo 'i 'el meğor 'en nu'eśa śantisima ley :
    POR lo kual mi pareser 'eś ke delaś arteś liberaleś delaś treś primeraś ke śon aserka dela habla no kureś de śaber maś kela loğika porke 'eś muy nesesary'a komo 'eśturmento para kual kyera 'otra sensy'a ke porelyya śe konose la verdad 'en todo śaber 'i de la gramatika 'i retorika no tyeneś nesesidad ninguna para 'entender nu'eśa śantisima ley ke 'eś 'el fin de todo śaber ke baśta byen nu'eśa gramatika 'i retorika ke 'eśkriben nu'eśoś śaby'oś porke la gramatika no 'eś śalvo 'enlaś śiknifikasy'oneś deloś byerboś 'i letraś la kual tenemoś nośotroś muy maś perfekta mente komo konbyene para 'entender loś byerboś de nu'eśa śantisima le'ey 'i la retorika no 'eś śalvo aserka dela hermozura dela habla 'i 'enel modo delaś kautelaś ke konbyene 'uzar para preśuadir ke 'eś 'el fin del retoriko 'enlo kual 'eśkribyeron muğoś de nu'eśoś śaby'oś antigoś 'i modernoś por muy 'eselentisimo 'eśtilo retoriko 'i 'enlaś 'otraś kuatro ke

---

[241] The first three clauses of Hippocrates' First Aphorism. For an English translation and general discussion, see D. W. Richards, "The First Aphorism of Hippocrates," *Perspectives in Biology and Medicine* 5 (1961): 61–64. F. Rosenthal discusses the Arabic commentators' treatment of its importance in medieval medicine and philosophy: " 'Life is Short, the Art is Long': Arabic Commentaries on the First Hippocratic Aphorism," *Bulletin of the History of Medicine* 40 (1966): 226–45.

śe konprende la matematika no tyeneś nesesidad de deprender maś ke la aridmetika ke 'eś aserka dela kantidad deśkreta 'i la ğe'ometri'a ke 'eś 'enla kantidad kontinu'a porke 'eśtaś doś śerviran muğo para 'entender muğoś diğoś de nu'eśoś śaby'oś 'en nu'eśo Ṭalmud 'i maś ke śon muy nesesary'oś para la 'eśtroloği'a ke 'eś muy 'eśtimada sensy'a aserka de nu'eśoś śaby'oś 'i muy deleytable 'i muy presyada 'enśi 'i de muğa 'utilidad :

'I laś 'otraś doś ke śon la muzika 'i la preśpektiba no ayy nesesidad delyyaś maś ke por 'elyyaś 'enśi porke la muzika trata dela kantidad deśkreta aserka del 'o'ir 'ila preśpektiba trata dela kantidad kontinu'a aserka del ver 'i 'eśtaś doś no śon abśuluta mente matematikaś ke maś konbyenen 'enel natural komo deklara 'el filosofo 'enel śegundo de loś fizikoś[242] 'i del meśmo modo la 'eśtroloği'a ağuntaron 'en alguna manera ala sensy'a natural porke trata del 'ente mobile ke 'eś 'el ku'erpo śeleśtre 'i set- por lo kual lyamaron la 'eśtroloği'a śabiduri'a 'i no arte :

'I 'enel modo ke aś de tener para le'er 'eśtaś treś arteś liberaleś ke tenemoś diğo aś de advertir ke 'en la loğika no tyeneś nesesidad de le'er 'enloś libroś de loś antigoś komo Profiry'oś[243] 'i 'otroś taleś komo akonśeğa 'el śenyor Rabbenu Mošeh 'a śu kerido hiğo[244] ke no gaśte 'el tyenpo 'enelyyo ke 'eś 'in( )'util ke baśta byen ke leaś la loğika ke 'eśkribyeron loś moroś maś modernoś komo Abubakar[245] 'i Abisena[246] 'i 'Abuḥamid[247] ke todoś 'eśkribyeron byen 'i korto 'i lo maś kursado 'entre nośotroś 'eś

---

[242] Almosnino refers to Aristotle's statement in *Physics* II.ii: "those sciences which are rather physical than mathematical, though combining both disciplines, such as optics, harmonics and astronomy" (trans. Wicksteed and Cornford, 1:121).

[243] That is, Porphyry's *Isagoge*.

[244] Maimonides, "Letter of Moral Instructions to his Son Abraham," trans. L. D. Stitskin, in *Letters of Maimonides* (New York: Yeshiva Press, 1971), 137–58.

[245] Abu Bakr Muhammad B. Zakariyya' Al-Razi (Razes). See *Encyclopaedia of Islam,* viii, 474a–478b.

[246] See Ibn Sina, *Remarks and Admonitions, Part One: Logic,* trans. S. C. Inati (Toronto, 1984). For a brief overview of Ibn Sina's writings, see *Encyclopaedia of Islam,* iii, 941a–947b. For detailed analysis and bibliography, see S. Afnan, *Avicenna* (London, 1958); H. A. Davidson, *Alfarabi, Avicenna, and Averroes on Intellect* (Oxford, 1992); L. E. Goodman, *Avicenna* (London, 1992); and N. Siraisi, *Avicenna in Renaissance Italy* (Princeton, 1987).

[247] Abu Ḥamid Muḥammad B. Muhammad Al-Tusi Al-Ghazzali. M. Alonso Alonso published a Spanish translation of the *Maqasid* (*Intenciones de los filósofos* [Barcelona, 1963]), and C. H. Lohr edited a medieval Latin translation ("*Logica Algazelis,*" *Traditio* 21 [1965]: 223–90). For general information about the author's writings, see M. Fakhry, *History of Islamic Philosophy* (New York, 1970), 244–61, and *Encyclopaedia of Islam,* ii, 1038b–1041b.

BOOK OF THE REGIMEN OF LIVING ‹FOL. 132B–133A›

la loǧika de 'Abuḥamid 'Algazel 'ensu libro ke lyyamo laś 'inte(t)[n]sy'oneś deloś [CW. filosofoś]}

‹fol. 133a›
{KLG
filosofoś ke śi mirareś laś notasy'oneś ke yo tengo 'eśkrito śobre 'el[248] baśtara byen para loke 'eś nesesary'o śaber aserka de la loǧika 'i para 'entender kual kyer 'otro libro de loǧika ke ala mano te vinyere 'i para la aridmetika 'i ǧe'ometri'a no me parese ke te pu'edeś 'eśkuzar de le'er 'el 'Euklides ke byen le'ido kon bu'en maeśtro baśta para 'entender kual kyer 'otro libro de kual kyera de 'eśtaś doś arteś ke konelyyo 'entaraś 'enla 'eśtroloǧi'a alo menoś 'enloś doś libroś ke hize yo la 'entrepetasy'on de 'elyyoś ke 'eś la 'Eśpera de Ǧuan de Śakrobośko[249] ke yo lyame Kaśa de 'el Dyyo 'i la reparti 'en kaśaś 'i kamaraś por śuś repartisy'oneś konvenibleś 'i la Te'orika deloś planetaś[250] de Ǧorǧe Probaǧy'o ke yo lyyame Pu'erta del syelo 'el kual reparti 'en pu'ertaś porke le'ido ke ayyaś 'eśtoś doś libroś kon lo ke yo 'enelyyoś tengo byen alargado 'enśuś glozaś me parese ke baśtara para 'entender 'otro kual kyera libro komo 'Alfargani[251] 'i Ṣuraṭ Ha-'Areṣ[252] 'i la 'Eśfera Solida[253] 'i todoś loś libroś de kuantoś modernoś 'eśkribyeron 'en 'eśtroloǧi'a tirado ke śi kiǧereś deprender 'el 'Almaǧeśto de Tolome'o[254] ke aś meneśter muǧo trabaǧar 'enel lo kual me parese ke lo deveś 'eśkuzar le'ido byen 'eśtoś 'otroś :

---

[248] He refers to *Migdal Oz*. See Ben-Menahem, "R. M. Almosnino," 281.
[249] Thorndike, *Sphere*.
[250] Pedersen, "*Theoricum planetarum* Literature."
[251] Al-Farghani (ca. 800–ca. 870) [Alfraganus]. Likely this is a reference to *Kitāb al-fusūl al-thalathīn* (*De scientia astrorum*), which F. J. Carmody describes as a well-known introduction to astronomy (*Arabic Astronomical and Astrological Sciences in Latin Translation* [Berkeley, 1956], 113–16); see also *Encyclopaedia of Islam* ii: 793. Pedersen mentions the popularity among astronomers of Johannes Hispalensis' Latin translation *Liber 30 differentiarum* (*A Survey of the Almagest* [Odense, 1974], 15 n. 2).
[252] The first part of a larger work by Abraham bar Hiyya (d. c. 1136), *Hokmat ha-Hizzayon*. For a Spanish translation and edition see J. M. Millás Vallicrosa, *Forma de la Tierra* (Barcelona, 1956). Sirat briefly summarizes bar Hiyya's philosophy (*History of Jewish Philosophy*, 97–104).
[253] The reference seems to be Averroes' *De substantia orbis:* see ed. and trans. Arthur Hyman (Cambridge–Jerusalem, 1986).
[254] For a recent English translation and edition of the *Almagest*, see *Ptolemy's Almagest*, trans. G. J. Toomer (London, 1984). Pedersen offers a clear description of the work and its historical importance (*Survey of the Almagest*).

BOOK OF THE REGIMEN OF LIVING ‹FOL. 133A›

'I para le'er 'enla sensy'a natural komo 'eś (la) razon no me parese ke te deveś 'eśkuzar de le'er loś fizikoś[255] 'i śi loś leereś no gaśteś 'el tyenpo 'enloś kortoś ni medyanoś de 'Ibn Rušd śalvo 'enloś largoś[256] ke le'ido loś largoś byen le'idoś no tyeneś nesesidad de le'er 'otro ningun libro para 'entender kual kyer kośa dela senśy'a natural 'i śi 'el Dyyo me dyere la vida no me 'eśkuzare de atemar de 'interpetar loś fizikoś al modo ke tengo heğo loś doś libroś primeroś 'i 'el pri(r)[n]sipy'o del tersero kon śu gloza tan larga kuanto 'eś meneśter adonde trayygo todo loke loś glozadoreś antigoś komo Aleğandro 'i 'Ibn Rušd 'i Arğiropolo 'i 'otroś muğoś glozaron[257] :

'I para loke konbyene para la 'ultima sensy'a ke 'eś la metafizika loke 'entre noś'otroś 'eś kursado le'er 'eś la de 'Abuḥamid 'Algazel[258] la kual śi tu kiğereś le'er halyyaraś ke kon laś notasy'oneś ke yo tengo 'eśkrito al deredor del libro baśtara byen para 'entender loke konbyene 'entender de palabraś de nu'eśoś śaby'oś travağando de pu'eś de todo 'eśto 'enel famoziśimo libro ke hizo 'el śenyor Rabbenu Mošeh ke lyyamo 'el Moreh[259] kon perkurar de 'entender byen 'el śenyyor Rabbi 'Ab[r]aham ‹Ib›n ᶜEzra'[260] 'en todoś śuś libroś ke a'un ke akorto muğo 'enla habla alarga muğo 'enla 'intensy'on śiknifikando 'en breveś terminoś loke 'otroś 'en muy largoś no lo abaśtan 'a deklarar atanto ke śoy de 'opiny'on ke le'idoś byen 'i byen 'entendidoś loś tratadoś deśtoś doś śenyyoreś 'en kuanto 'eśkribyeron no 'eś meneśter maś le'er para loke toka 'a nu'eśa te'oloği'a fin de todo śaber para 'entender laś kozaś devinaś ke vyenen 'en nu'eśa śantisima ley ke 'eś 'el fin 'ultimo de nu'eśa 'eśpikulasy'on para la perfeksy'on de la anima 'i 'entendimyento te'oriko : [CW. 'i para]}

---

[255] The reference is to Aristotle's *Physics*.

[256] The distinction among Averroes' short, middle, and long commentaries on Aristotle is explained in *Cambridge History of Later Medieval Philosophy* (48); for a chronology of their composition, see *Encylopaedia of Islam*, iii: 910.

[257] Apparently he refers to *Piruš al Sefer ha-Šᵉmaa ha-Tabai*, his now lost commentary on Aristotle's *Physics*. See Ben-Menahem, "M. A. Almosnino," 283–84. "Alexander" is Alexander of Aphrodisias; "Argyropoulos" is John Argyropoulos who translated Aristotle's *Nicomachean Ethics* into Latin (see *Oxford Dictionary of Byzantium* [New York, 1991], 1:164).

[258] For a modern Spanish translation, see *Intenciones,* trans. Alonso Alonso. For a medieval Latin translation, see *Algazel's Metaphysics: A Medieval Translation,* ed. J. T. Muckle (Toronto, 1933).

[259] A reference to Maimonides' *Guide*.

[260] Sirat gives an overview of Ibn Ezra's life and importance (*History of Jewish Philosophy*, 104–12) with bibliography (425–26). Etan Levine's introduction to a facsimile edition of Ibn Ezra's *Commentary to the Pentateuch* (cod. Vat. Eb. 38) includes useful summaries of Ibn Ezra's thought (*Abraham Ibn Ezra's Commentary to the Pentateuch* [Jerusalem, 1974]).

BOOK OF THE REGIMEN OF LIVING ‹FOL. 133B›

‹fol. 133b›

{ 'I para lo ke konbyene para la perfekśy'on del 'entendimyento pratik[o] 'i moderaśy'on del 'apetito ke 'en 'eśto konśiśte la famoziśima śensy'a de la filosofi'a moral baśta ke leaś 'el libro de la 'etika ke hizo Aristotel kon lo ke aś viśto ke 'e alargado 'enel konforme 'a mug̃oś dig̃oś de nu'eśtroś śaby'oś ke syerto 'eś libro de muga suśtansy'a para ayudar 'a śegir 'el kamino de la byen aventuransa komo 'enel tengo muy larga mente prebado 'i śi kig̃ereś le'er algo 'en la medisina alo menoś la te'orika delyya por Abisena 'eś byen ke leaś por ke 'eś todo sensy'a kon la glośa de Baruk 'ibn Ya°iš²⁶¹ ke fu'e 'el meg̃or glozador ke 'ubo de loś glozadoreś g̃udy'oś 'i 'el trae al Konsilyyador²⁶² 'i al G̃entil²⁶³ 'i 'a 'otroś mug̃oś glozadoreś 'i 'en lo de maś de la platika tanto de la medisina komo de la 'eśtrolog̃i'a no hablo por ke 'eneśto no konśiśte 'el byen ni perfeksy'on del 'entendimyento

'I kon lo ke tengo 'eśkrito me parese ke baśta para lo ke konbyene śaber 'enel reg̃imyento de la vida 'umana 'enel kual konśiśte la byen aventuransa por ke kon lo ke tenemoś dig̃o de laś vertudeś moraleś 'i 'intelektualeś 'eśta konklu'ido todo kuanto 'el 'ombre pu'ede 'obrar 'en la vida komo konbyene por ke komo ya tenemoś algo tokado ariba ke toda vida 'eś 'obrar 'i la ke propy'a mente śe lyyama 'obra 'eś la 'obra bu'ena ke la mala 'inpropy'a mente śe lyyama 'obra ke 'eś propy'a mente pribasy'on de la 'obra bu'ena por lo kual dig̃eron nu'eśoś śaby'oś ke loś maloś śon mu'ertoś 'en śuś vidaś²⁶⁴ ke 'eś por la dig̃a kauśa ke komo toda vida śe'a 'obrar 'i 'obrar mal no 'eś 'obrar lu'ego no 'eś vida 'i komo laś 'obraś no pu'eden deg̃ar de śer 'en 'una de doś modoś 'o 'obra ke reśta 'enel 'entendimyento te'oriko 'o pratiko laś kualeś śe perfeksy'onan por laś śinko vertudeś 'intelektualeś 'o 'obra 'eśtiry'or ke śe mu'ebe 'el 'ombre 'a hazerlaś por parte dela voluntad laś kualeś śe perfeksy'onan por laś doze vertudeś moraleś ke tenemoś deklarado 'eś viśto ke 'eg̃ersitando laś 'obraś 'umanaś

---

²⁶¹ Baruk ben Isaac Ibn Ya°ish (fifteenth century) wrote a Hebrew commentary on Avicenna's *Medicamenta cordialia* entitled *Be'ur la-Sammim ha-Libbiyyim:* see *EJ* 16:703.

²⁶² The *Conciliator differentiarum philosophorum et precipue medicorum* of Peter of Abano (ca. 1250–1316), a Paduan Averroist (Grant, *Source Book in Medieval Science,* 807 n. 15), records two hundred and ten disputations on the subject of the equality of medicine and philosophy (Lindberg, *Science in the Middle Ages,* 404) and attempts to reconcile differences between philosophers and physicians (144 n. 43).

²⁶³ An appeal to Gentilis as an authority on proper scientific method is made by Jacopo da Forlì in a commentary on Galen's *Tegni:* "This exposition is approved by the Conciliator, Diff. 8, and by Gentilis, and by other moderns since them. [Jacopo]" (quoted in Grant, *Source Book in Medieval Science,* 722).

²⁶⁴ Berakot 18b.

BOOK OF THE REGIMEN OF LIVING ‹FOL. 133B–134A›

śegun 'eśtaś vertudeś por la 'orden ke tenemoś diğo kontinuando konelyyo 'a trabağar 'en nu'eśa śantisima ley ke konprende todo lyegara 'el 'ombre al kabo dela byen aventuransa 'i filisidad 'umana adonde 'eśta konğunta la deleytasy'on verdader'a 'i śi algo 'esede deśte kamino verdadero nunka lyegara ala pozada adkerida 'o fin dela vida verdader'a 'i deveśe de atentar lu'ego 'enel prinsipy'o de la ğornada ke no ayya yero ke 'eś 'enla mosedad porke 'el 'erar 'el kamino kuanto maś 'enel prinsipy'o 'eś tanto maś fasil 'eś de tornar 'a 'enkaminarśe 'enel :

'I 'eś de notar kel prinsipy'o del kamino de nu'eśa vida śe reparte 'en doś modoś muy diferenteś 'el 'uno del 'otro ke kuando laś 'obraś 'umanaś śe mu'ebe 'el 'ombre a'elyyaś por parte del 'entendimyento śeran laś 'obraś perfektaś 'i 'enkaminaran [CW. al fin]}

‹fol. 134a›
{KLD
al fin verdadero 'i śi śe mu'ebe 'a 'elyyaś por parte de la 'imağinasy'on no pu'ede aribar 'a pu'erto śeguro ni 'a fin verdadero ke 'el 'entendimyento del 'ombre 'enel prinsipy'o 'eśta diśpu'eśto para śegir kual kyera deloś doś 'o śer 'el 'entendimyento śudito ala 'imağinasy'on 'i śegir loś apetitoś korporaleś ke śon kauśa de perderśe 'i koromperśe 'el ku'erpo 'i 'el alma 'o tener la 'imağinasy'on sudita al 'entendimyento lo kual śe alkansa konel kośtu[m]bre deśtaś vertudeś ke a'un ke 'en[e]l prinsipy'o śe'a algo difisil depu'eś śe hazen tan fasileś 'i tan deleytableś ke no śe afigura 'enla tal deleytasy'on ninguna miśty'on de triśteza :

DE manera ke a'un ke 'el kamino 'erado 'eś fasil 'enel prinsipy'o 'i deleytable śegun la deleytasy'on korporal por la mala 'enklinasy'on dela matery'a 'eś muy triśte ala fin loke akaese al kontrary'o 'enel verdadero kamino ke tanto kuanto 'eś trabağozo 'i 'enoğozo 'enel prinsipy'o tanto 'eś fasilimo 'i deleytable 'a 'el fin depu'eś de kośtumbre :

ŚIKNIFIKANDO 'eśtoś doś kaminoś diğeron nu'eśoś śaby'oś 'un kauzo ke akaesy'o 'en akel famoziśimo śaby'o Rabbi Yᵉhošuaᶜ ben Levi 'en modo metaforiko 'en 'eśta forma Rabbi Yᵉhošuaᶜ ben Levi andaba por 'un kamino 'i falyyo 'un ninyyo ke 'eśtaba 'en 'eśpartimyento de kamino diğole hiğo mi'o kual 'eś 'el kamino para la sibdad diğole 'eśte 'eś korto 'i lu'engo 'i 'eśte 'eś lu'engo 'i korto andubo Rabbi Yᵉhošuaᶜ 'en akel kamino ke 'era korto 'i lu'engo kuando alyego ala sibdad halyyo gu'ertaś 'i verğeleś ke arodeaban la sibdad torno 'a 'el ninyyo 'i diğole kual 'eś 'el kamino para la sibdad diğole tu 'ereś 'el śaby'o ke ayy 'en Yiśra'el no te diğe ke 'eśte 'era korto 'i lu'engo 'i 'eśte 'era lu'engo 'i korto 'eśtonśeś diğo Rabbi Yᵉhošuaᶜ ben Levi byen aventuradoś voś Yiśra'el ke todoś śoyyś śaby'oś del pekenyyo hata 'el grande 'i set-[265]

---

[265] Eruvin 53b identifies the protagonist as R. Yehoshua Ben Hananiah. Cf. Thompson, *Motif-*

BOOK OF THE REGIMEN OF LIVING ‹FOL. 134A–134B›

KE ala verdad 'eś de ver 'en 'eśtaś palabraś 'i śentir muğaś dubdaś lo primero 'eś de ver ke 'en dezirle 'el ninyyo 'eśta 'eś korta 'i lu'enga 'i 'eśta lu'enga 'i korta paresen 'unaś palabraś ke no śe 'entyenden ke parese no aver diferensy'a de lu'enga 'i korta 'a korta 'i lu'enga 'i 'eś de ver maś komo śe kontento Rabbi Y°hošua° kon 'eśtaś palabraś śin maś demandar 'i śi 'entendy'o la 'intensy'on delyyaś komo yero 'i 'ubo menesńter tornar 'a demandar 'i ya ke torno 'a demandar komo śe kontento kon ke le diğo 'el ninyo laś meśmaś palabraś ke le avi'a diğo anteś 'i kedo muy śaśtifeğo
POR lo kual pyenśo ke kiğeron śiknifikar 'en 'eśtaś palabraś 'el modo ke śe'a de tener para śegir 'el kamino verdadero de la vida 'umana para alyegar al kabo de bu'ena 'eśperansa ke 'entitularon 'en termino de vilyya ke 'eś 'el fin 'i akatamyento ke 'a de tener 'el byen aventurado 'i dizen ke Rabbi Y°hošua° 'eśtaba 'enel prinsipy'o de śu kaminar por 'eśte kamino de la vida ke 'era bivir śin averśe heğo [CW. 'enel]}

‹fol. 134b›
{HELEK G PEREK YG [PART THREE CHAPTER THIRTEEN]
'enel abito 'el byen ni 'el mal total mente ke 'era pribado del mal 'i no 'inpu'eśto a'un 'en 'el byen 'i 'enpeso 'a 'eśpekular 'en śaber kual 'era 'el kamino verdadero para la vilyya de la morada perpetu'a 'en la vida 'eterna lo kual kontenplando halyyo 'el 'entendimyen(d)[t]o ke 'eś 'entitulado 'en titulo de ninyo por ke śe perfeksy'ona poko 'a poko 'el komo ninyo 'i dize ke lo vi'o pu'eśto 'onde śe 'eśpartian doś kaminoś ke 'eś śiknif[ik]asy'on aloś doś kaminoś ke tenemoś diğo ke 'el 'entendimyento 'eśta 'enel medyyo para ğuśgar 'el kamino verdadero śegun dereğa razon 'i kontenplando 'i demandando aśu 'entendimyento kual 'era 'el kamino de la vida para alkansar 'el fin dize ke le reśpondy'o ke 'un kamino de akelyyoś 'era korto ke lu'ego alyegari'a al kabo del pero ke 'era muy largo ke no śe alkansa por alyi 'el fin verdadero ke 'eś 'el kamino deloś visy'oś ke 'eś muy faśil 'ir al kabo pero depu'eś de kaminado no śe halyya loke śe buśka 'i 'eś menester tornar 'a traś pero ke 'el 'otro a'un ke 'era lu'engo 'i trabağozo 'enel prinsipy'o 'era korto para alyegar al fin verdadero 'i Rabbi Y°hošua° ben Levi mośtrando śer poko 'eśprimentado 'en ninguno de loś doś komo tenemoś diğo vyendo ke 'el korto 'enel alkansar 'era maś faśil 'enel pr[i]nsipy'o andubo porel śin maś 'eśpekular 'i kuando alyego al kabo a'un ke fu'e preśto vido ke no avi'a 'otro fin ke loś meśmoś visy'oś ke śe 'entitulan 'en gu'ertoś 'i verğeleś 'i ke

---

Index, J21, *Counsel proved wise by experience* and J21.5.3, *A way short yet long;* see also D. Noy (Neuman), "Motif-Index of Talmudi-Midrashic Literature" (Diss., Indiana University, 1954), 2:510. For a medieval congener, see Gaster, *Exempla of the Rabbis,* 103.

BOOK OF THE REGIMEN OF LIVING ‹FOL. 134B-135A›

'elyoś 'eran loś ke 'inpedian de alyegar 'i de 'entrar ala vilyya ke 'eś 'el fin verdadero 'i ke 'era meneśter tornar 'a traś 'i tornar 'a 'eśpekular kual 'era 'el kamino verdadero lo kual depu'eś de yya 'eśprimentado 'el kamino 'erado kuando 'el 'entendimyento le torno 'a traer ala memory'a loke anteś le avi'a diğo lo 'entendyyo byen 'i vido ke 'en baldeś avi'a kaminado 'i konosy'o la 'ekśelensy'a del 'entendimyento 'eśpesyal 'el ke 'eś 'influ'ido dela 'influ'ensy'a devina komo śon todo Yiśra'el grandeś 'i pekenyoś por lo kual diğo 'i determino ke 'eran todoś byen aventuradoś pu'eś 'eran tan alumbradoś del 'entendimyento para śegir 'el kamino dela verdad 'i ke śi veni'a 'el yero no veni'a śalvo por parte dela matery'a ke kyere śegir loke 'eś fasil 'i hu'ir del difisil 'i kon 'eśto 'eśtan śaśtifeğaś todaś laś dubdaś fasil mente 'i 'eśta byen viśto ke 'el kamino verdadero para alyegar al fin 'ultimo 'i śumo grado dela byen aventuransa 'eś la perfeksy'on del 'entendimyento te'oriko 'i pratiko ke del depende 'el 'amor del Dyyo ke 'eś 'el 'ultimo fin verdadero komo tenemoś diğo :

KAPITULO TREZE

'I porke atentando 'enlaś 'intensy'oneś deloś 'ombreś 'enśuś 'obraś 'eneśta vida preśente halyyamoś no śalir de 'una de treś 'eśpesyaś diferenteś konformeś alaś treś 'eśpesyaś de amiśtad ke tenemoś deklarado ke 'unoś trabağan 'en toda śu vida de adkerir hazyenda 'i perkurar por a'umentarla [CW. hata]}

‹fol. 135a›
{KLH
hata ke mu'eren ke 'eś konforme ala amiśtad por 'el 'util 'i 'otroś ke no tyene 'otro akatamyento ke 'el deleyte komo komer 'i bever 'i holgar 'i 'en konkluzy'on 'enplean todoś śuś diaś 'en deleytasy'oneś korporaleś ke 'eś konforme ala amiśtad por 'el deleytable 'i 'otroś ke tyene akatamyento 'a 'el fin verdadero ke 'eś konforme ala amiśtad por 'el 'oneśto te kyero traer aki 'un 'enğenplo de la vida de loś 'ombreś deśde ke vyenen 'en 'eśte mundo hata ke śalen del ke halye 'en 'uno de nu'eśoś śaby'oś muy moderno a'un ke pyenso śer 'el 'enğenplo muy antigo konforme 'a nu'eśa ley adobando 'enel lo ke konbyene 'i 'en algunaś parteś faltando 'i 'en 'otraś akreśentando para śer konforme alo ke tenemoś diğo ke 'eś digno de perpetu'a memory'a por ke por 'el śe manifeśtara kuanto van 'eradoś loś ke kual kyera de loś doś kaminoś primeroś śigen 'i kuan faltoś 'i arepentidoś śe halyyan 'enel fin 'i por 'el kontrary'o 'el ke 'el kamino verdadero śigyere kuanta alegri'a 'i deleytasy'on verdader'a terna 'a 'infinito

DIZEN ke 'un grandisimo rey prudentisimo 'i śaby'o 'i ğuśto teni'a pu'eśta 'en todo śu reyno 'una ley 'i kośtumbre ke no śe dyeśe premy'o ni 'eśtado ni 'onor śi no

Book of the Regimen of Living ‹fol. 135a–135b›

śolo 'a kyen lo 'ubyeśe meresido 'en śervisy'o del rey 'o de la republika konforme aśu merito kon diśkurso del tyenpo nasyeron 'en la korte treś ninyyoś de śangre real ke vinyendo 'en kunplido kresimyento fu'eron perfektisimoś 'en todo ğenero de perfeksy'on 'i dotrina 'i ley hermozoś 'i ğentileś de śuś preśonaś 'i muy byen kondisy'onadoś 'en śuś kośtumbreś dignoś de śer keridoś 'i amadoś de kuantoś loś vyeśen 'i keryendoleś 'el rey muğo 'i amandoloś 'en 'eśtremo deśeando de ponerloś 'en 'eśtado konforme aśuś meresimyentoś 'i aśu voluntad leś diğo 'eśtaś palabraś hiğoś mi'oś mi voluntad 'eś hazer'oś toda la 'onor 'i probeğo ke śe pu'ede 'a śemeğanteś ke voś 'otroś hazer 'i mi deśe'o 'eś poner'oś 'en alto 'eśtado maś ke 'a kuantoś 'eśtan 'en mi korte por ke ave'eyś halyyado grasy'a 'en miś 'oğoś 'i yo 'oś 'e viśto abileś para todo ğenero de virtud 'i bondad pero todo 'el pu'eblo śaben 'i voś 'otroś tanbyen lo śabe'eyś ke tengo pu'eśta tal ley 'en mi reyno de la kual no me pu'edo tornar ni la pu'edo 'en ninguna manera kebrantar ke no pu'eda dar 'onor ni grandeza ni 'eśtado 'a nadi śi no fu'ere 'en pago del śervisy'o ke abra heğo 'en 'obraś bu'enaś 'i virtu'ozaś por lo kual para yo dar'oś 'el 'eśtado 'i 'onor ke yo deśe'o dar'oś no lo podeyś g(n)anar ni alkansar 'eśtando aki 'en mi korte por 'onde mi konśeğo 'eś ke śalgayyś de la korte 'i voś 'eśpand'eyś por 'el reyno 'onde meğor 'oś paresra 'i perkura[yś] de hazer alyya 'obraś por laś kualeś śe'eyś meresedoreś de hazer'oś la 'onor ke deśe'o hazer'oś konforme ala ley ke tengo pu'eśta 'en mi reyno 'i 'eśtar'eś por alyya hata 'el tyenpo ke yo mande por voś 'otroś 'i 'eśtonśeś traere'eyś la memory'a de vu'eśtraś 'obraś 'i konforme '(')[a] 'elyyaś resebire'eyś de mi 'el premy'o}

‹fol. 135b›
{'i a'un ke loś diğoś mosoś resibyeron moleśty'a 'i pasy'on de partirśe de la korte real vyendo ke 'el mandado del rey 'era tan 'eśpreśo no pudyeron 'eśtar 'i deśpidyeronśe del rey 'i 'enbarkaronśe 'en 'un navi'o 'i kon bu'en tyenpo śe partyeron a'onde la ventura loś 'eğaśe depu'eś de muğo apartadoś de la korte 'en 'otraś probinsyaś leğoś de la korte asomaron 'a 'una 'iśla ke de leğoś vyeron śer muy frutifera 'i de( )leytable 'en medyyo de la kual 'eśtaba 'un muy grandisimo 'i deleytable verğel fornido de todoś modoś de arboleś frutiferoś 'i 'odoriferoś al kual determinaron 'enderesar 'i gozar del deś'enbarkando 'en la diğa 'iśla fu'eronśe hazy'a 'el verğel 'i alyegando ala pu'erta del halyyaron treś portaleroś 'en regla 'i a'un ke ninguno delyyoś leś deteni'a la 'entrada kada 'uno delyyoś leś akabido de 'una kośa

'EL primero leś diğo ke tubyeśen 'en memoryya ke no pensasen de kedarśe alyya dentro ke śupyeśen ke 'era forsado aver de tornar 'a śalir ke ninguno alyi 'entro ke śe kedaśe alyya ke aśi 'era alyi la regla ke 'unoś 'entraban 'i 'otroś śalian

'EL śegundo leś diğo ke alyende lo ke 'el primero leś avi'a diğo tubyeśen maś 'en memory'a ke del meśmo modo ke 'entraban de akel meśmo modo avian de śalir ke no pensaśen de śakar konśigo ninguna kośa de kuanto pose'yeśen dentro del verğel ke

Book of the Regimen of Living ‹fol. 135b–136a›

alyya dentro gozaśen de kuanto kiğeśen aśu plazer ke ninguno leś 'inpediri'a śu deleyte pero ke śe akabidaśen de no lyebar konśigo nada de kuanto alyi vyeśen :
'EL tersero leś diğo 'i leś dyyo 'una muy bu'ena dotrina para lo ke leś konveni'a 'enel bu'en reğimyento de loś ke alyi 'entraban alyende de lo ke loś 'otroś doś diğeron 'i fu'e ke parasen myenteś 'i fu'esen akabidadoś de no[ ]śer d[e]ś(y)tenpladoś 'en śuś śolas(v)[e]ś 'i pasatyenpoś 'en 'el diğo verğ[e]l śalvo ke 'eśkoğeśen lo bu'eno 'i 'onesto 'i no kurasen de hazer kozaś deś'oneśtaś ke 'esto leś aprobeğari'a muğo para suśtentasy'on de śuś vidaś
'O'IDAŚ por akelyyoś manseboś akelyyaś tan konsertadaś palabraś 'entraron 'enel verğel 'enel kual halyyaron maś de lo ke por defu'era paresi'a 'i vyeron muğoś arboleś frutiferoś 'i muğaś floreś 'odoriferaś de diversaś koloreś 'i 'oloreś konfortatibaś de rozaś 'i ğaśmineś 'i asusenaś 'i de 'otraś śu'erteś 'infinitaś kon muğoś arboleś altisimoś komo asipreześ 'i 'otroś taleś 'i 'otroś muğoś de śombra abundoza komo platanoś 'i alamoś 'i 'otroś taleś 'en riba de loś kualeś kantaban rosinoleś 'i 'otraś 'infinitaś 'eśpesyaś de aveś kon tanta melodi'a ke adormesian loś śentidoś 'i vyeron muğaś alberkaś de aguaś śuabisimaś 'i ri'oś 'ordenadoś de tal manera ke śe regaba todo 'el verğel por la meğor 'orden ke posible 'era loś kualeś gozaron del diğo verğel aśu plazer 'i śe deleytaron 'enel kon muğa alegri'a 'i komyeron [d]e akelyya tan śuabe 'i 'odorifera fruta 'i bevyeron [CW. de śuś]}

‹fol. 136a›
{KLV
de śuś dulśisimaś aguaś delo kual resibyeron gran deleytasy'on de bağo dela śombra deloś maś 'odoriferoś arboleś al śon dela dulse armoni'a ke laś aveś hazian kon 'un muy tenpladito ayyre ke mobi'a laś ramaś de loś arboleś para ke trasendyeśe maś 'el śuabe 'olor de śuś floreś 'i komo 'eśtubyeron a'i algun tyenpo vinyeronśe 'a 'eśpartir 'uno de 'otro 'i deramarśe por 'el verğel 'i śegir kada 'uno la 'orden de śu vida 'i deleytasy'on śegun le paresy'o
POR lo kual 'el 'uno delyyoś vyendo la abundansa de laś frutaś 'i aguaś del verğel 'i śer tan deleytableś de termino de 'eğarśe traś de akelyyaś deleytasy'oneś por kuantaś viaś pudo alkansar de komer 'i bever 'i dormir 'i pasar bu'ena vida deleytable aśu 'apetito kuanto podi'a 'a ryenda śu'elta 'a tu'erto 'i 'a dereğo 'onesto 'i deś'onesto śin ningun 'otro akatamyento 'olvidandośe 'el konśeğo 'i dotrina ke 'el terser portalero leś akabido ke 'eśkoğeśen lo 'onesto 'i set-
'EL 'otro vyendo 'enel verğel muğa abundansa de 'oro 'i plata 'i p(+)yedraś presy'ozaś puzo todo śu akatamyento 'en fornirśe delyyaś kuanto pudyeśe 'i de śuś veśtidoś hizo śakoś para 'enğirloś delyyo 'i tenyendo 'esta 'intensy'on no komi'a ni bevi'a ni dormi'a por śolo 'entender 'en fornirśe byen de akelyyoś byeneś 'eśtiry'oreś tomando 'unoś 'i değando 'otroś paresyendole 'unoś meğoreś ke 'otroś 'el kual 'eśtilo

Book of the Regimen of Living ‹fol. 136a–136b›

śigy'o 'en kuanto a'i 'eśtubo 'i değo de gozar de loś deleyteś del verğel 'olvidandośele lo ke 'el śegundo portalero le avi'a diğo ke gozaśe alyi de kuanto kiğeśe 'i no guardaśe nada por ke no podi'a śakar de alyi maś de lo ke truğo

'EL tersero tenyendo byen 'a memory'a todaś laś palabraś de akelyyoś portaleroś no le paresy'o byen ningun kamino de akelyyoś ke 'eliğeron śuś konpanyeroś por ke vido śer kaminoś 'in'utileś 'i 'eradoś 'i danyyozoś diśkrepanteś de akelyya dotrina ke 'el prośter portalero leś dyyo ke fu'eron palabraś dignaś de perpetu'a memory'a por laś kualeś le paresy'o ke 'era byen gozar de akel deleytozisimo verğel de śolo lo ke 'era nesesary'o para la suśtentasy'on dela vida 'oneśta mente 'i 'enlo de maś gaśto śu tyenpo 'en konte[n]plar 'en akel verğel por todaś laś parteś del 'enlaś plantaś diferenteś 'i 'enloś animaleś ke alyi 'eśtaban admirandośe 'i marabilyyandośe de loś milagroś dela naturaleza 'en tanta diversidad de frutaś 'i floreś 'i yerbaś 'i tanta diversidad de animaleś 'i kada kośa śer diferente 'en konplisy'on 'i figura dela 'otra 'i aśi meśmo laś propyedadeś de kada planta diferente dela 'otra 'i mirando maś partikular mente 'enlaś frutaś vido śer muy konservadaś laś simyenteś para permaneśer 'i perpetuar la 'eśpesy'a :

'I parando myenteś 'enlaś alberkaś 'i ri'oś kuan 'ordenadaś 'eśtaban ke de loś ri'oś śubian laś aguaś alaś alberkaś 'i śalian 'a [CW. regar]}

‹fol. 136b›

{regar 'el verğel aśuś 'oraś por śuś kaminoś de tal manera ke no kedaba ninguna yerba ni planta 'en todo 'el verğel ke no fu'eśe probe'ida dela agu'a 'ensu tyenpo 'i deloke delaś alberkaś reverti'a kai'a 'en 'unaś pilaś ke de kontino 'eśtaban lyenaś de akelyya muy klarisima agu'a para bever loś animaleś muy abundoza mente kedaba de ver toda 'eśta regla tan 'ordenada de kada koza 'ensu lugar paśmado 'i marabilyyado 'i mirando por todaś 'eśtaś partikularidadeś kon tan marabilyyoza 'orden no vyendo alyi ningun 'ortelano ke akelyyo 'ordenaśe śe poni'a 'a kontenplar kyen podi'a śer 'el 'ordenador de todaś akelyyaś kozaś de adonde śe determino ke no podi'a śer akelyyo asidental mente 'en ninguna manera śalvo ke avi'a de aver algun 'ortelano 'o patron de akel gu'erto sapyentisimo 'en 'eśtremo ke todo akelyyo 'ordenaba a'un ke 'era 'invizible 'i andando kon 'eśta determinasy'on 'eśpekul(n)a[n]do 'i kontenplando kada di'a maś 'enla 'orden tan reglada ke kada di'a ve'i'a maś partikular mente śele a'umentaba 'el deze'o de konoser 'i śaber 'i ve'er kyen 'era 'el patron del verğel de adonde a'un ke 'era a'uzente por laś 'obraś ke ve'i'(y)a del tan byen 'ordenadaś le teni'a 'eśtremadisimo 'amor por la deleytasy'on ke 'el śe deleytaba 'en 'eśpekular 'enśuś kośaś 'i kaminaba kontinu'a mente por todaś laś parteś del verğel perkurando śi pudyeśe halyyar 'el patron del 'o alguno ke le dyeśe del nu'ebaś 'oneśtandośe 'enśuś 'obraś ke no 'ofendyeśe 'en kośa ninguna de akelyya 'orden komo ke 'eśtubyeśe prezente 'el patron del verğel :

Book of the Regimen of Living ‹fol. 136b–137a›

'EŚTANDO todoś treś 'en 'eśta 'orden de vida kada 'uno por śu parte śegun la diversidad delaś 'intensy'on(v)[e]ś 'i fin ke kada 'uno 'eliǧy'o alyego 'un 'eśklabo del rey ke loś avi'a mandado kon 'eśpresa śentensy'a ke śupito ke akel me[n]śaǧero śuyyo lyegaśe no pudyeśen tardar 'un punto ke śe vinyeśen ala korte 'a dar ku'enta kada 'uno de śu vida

LOŚ 'ombreś vyendo 'el mandado del rey no pudyendolo rebelar 'enkaminaron lu'ego hazy'a la pu'erta para śalir 'i 'ir a'el lugar de adonde vinyeron 'i 'eran lyyamadoś

'I 'el primero ke śe avi'a 'eǧado 'a komer 'i bever 'i deleytarśe del verǧel 'en todaś laś deleytasy'oneś korporaleś de akelyyaś frutaś 'i aguaś 'i ayyre deleytozo komo śalyyo dela pu'erta del verǧel śintyendo la mudansa del ayyre 'i falta delaś deleytasy'oneś ke 'era akośtumbrado a'elyyaś lu'ego śe le hinǧo 'el vyentre 'i kayo deśu 'eśtado 'en tyera śin poderśe sośtener 'enśi 'i mury'o :

VINYENDO traś del 'el śegundo kargado komo 'un animal bruto de plata 'i 'oro 'i muǧaś pyedraś presy'ozaś ke konla deleytasy'on ke resibi'a 'en penśar ke avi'a de pose'erlaś 'a 'infinito no śenti'a 'el trabaǧo dela karga tan pezada alyegando ala pu'erta del verǧel loś portaleroś śe 'eśpantaron [CW. de]}

‹fol. 137a›
{KLZ
de verlo tan kargado 'i hizyeronlo deśkargar alyi de kuanto lyevava komo 'era la 'orden 'i no le deǧaron śi no śolo lo ke 'el podi'a lyebar 'eśkondido 'ensu peǧo ǧunto konla karne 'i śalyendo dela pu'erta 'a fu'era 'otroś guardyaneś ke arodeaban la serka del verǧel le 'eśkuadronyyaron 'i lo maltrataron kon muǧoś golpeś 'i heridaś ke le dyeron 'i le tiraron kuanto levaba 'eśkondido 'i lo hizyeron tornar komo vino de lo kual kedo 'el deśdiǧado pobre 'i adoloryado 'i atormentado lyyorando 'i ǧimyendo muy atribulado 'i kansado del tr[a]baǧo pasado

'EL tersero 'en 'oyendo la boz del menśaǧero ke leś vino 'a lyyamar por mandado del rey śe alegro kon 'el deśe'o ke teni'a de śaber kyen 'era 'el 'ordenador 'i reǧidor de akel verǧel paresyendole ke pu'eś alyi dentro no lo avi'a podido alkansar ke por ventura śalyendo de alyi lo alkansari'a 'i śe deleytari'a kon 'el por 'el 'amor ke alyi le avi'a tomado paresyendole no aver 'ofendido todo 'el tyenpo ke dyentro 'el verǧel 'eśtubo 'en kośa ke le paresyeśe śer kontra la 'orden del patron maś anteś 'en kuanto avi'a 'obrado avi'a śe'ido konforme alo ke a'el le paresy'o ke śeri'a śu voluntad 'i kontentamyento 'el kual śe moby'o 'a śalir śin ninguna tardansa 'i akordandośe de todo lo ke akelyyoś portaleroś le avian diǧo no lyebo konśig(+)o kośa ke 'ofendyeśe ni 'esedyeśe de lo ke le avian akabidado por lo kual fu'e muy byen resebido de 'elyyoś 'i de 'otroś muǧoś śervidoreś del patron del verǧel ke por alyi arodeaban ke le śalyeron 'a resebir vyendo kuan alegre 'i kontente 'iba al mandado del rey

Book of the Regimen of Living ⟨fol. 137a–137b⟩

'I ya kuando lyegaron loś doś serka la korte del rey ke leś mando 'a lyyamar 'el primero 'iba tan kansado 'i flako 'i deśkonosido ke no śe podi'a tener 'en śuś pyeś 'i a'un ke 'iba br[a]mando 'i dizyendo ke 'era de śangre real ke fu'eśe byen resebido no daba ninguno kredito aśuś palabraś de kuantoś 'eśtaban 'en la korte por verlo tan diferensyado de lo ke fu'e 'i tan deśkonosido 'i deśpresyado por lo kual resibyendo por 'ofensa ke tan deśpresy[a]bil 'ombre diğeśe ke 'era alyegado al re'ey fu'e tan mal tratado de kuantoś 'eśklaboś del rey 'eśtaban 'en la korte ke lo 'enpuğaron 'i 'eğaron fu'era de alyi muğo aśu deś'onra por donde fu'e 'eğado 'en la karsel donde loś priśy'oneroś del rey 'eśtaban preśoś donde 'eśtubo purgando śuś pekadoś

'I tanto kuanto 'eśte fu'e mal tratado tanto fu'e byen resebido 'el tersero kon todo 'el 'onor ke posible fu'e ke todoś loś ke 'en la korte 'eśtaban śalian aśu 'enku'entro vyendo śu ğentileza 'i perfeksy'on ke śu kara leś demośtraba śer de kaśta real 'i digno de muğa 'onor por lo kual todoś lo abrasaban 'i lo akonpanyaban 'i lo 'inponian maś adentro hata ponerlo 'enla kamara donde 'el rey 'eśtaba vyendo ke 'era digno de ver la kara del rey 'i de resebir del merseded 'el kual repre[ś]e[n]tado ke fu'e delante de 'el rey śe 'enkorbo a'el 'i 'el rey śe alegro de verlo venir tan byen diśpu'eśto}

⟨fol. 137b⟩
{'i tan byen 'ensenyado tenyendo del verdader'a notisy'a del modo ke śe avi'a reğido 'i kon todo le demando del lugar de adonde veni'a 'i ke avi'a heğo 'enel 'el kual le reśpondy'o ke 'el lugar 'era muy perfekto 'en śumo grado de perfeksy'on śin ninguna falta 'i depu'eś ke le 'ubo kontado toda la 'eselensy'a del deleytable verğel por todaś śuś partikularidadeś 'i 'ordeneś tan byen regladaś le diğo ke de todo akelyyo avi'a konsebido aver 'en akel verğel 'un patron muy śapyentisimo ke no podi'a śer śino ke 'eśtubyeśe por alyi muy konğunto a'un ke 'era 'okulto 'i 'invizible lo kual le avi'a kedado 'un 'eśtremadisimo deśe'o de konoser akel tal patron para deleytarśe konel por 'el 'amor ke por ver śuś 'obraś le teni'a :

ALO kual reśpondy'o 'el rey pu'eś ke tanbyen aś 'enpleado tu vida yo te kyero kunplir tu deśe'o 'i amośtrarte 'el patron de akel verğel ke lo konośkaś de tal manera ke veaś muy 'ividente mente komo śe śige de 'el akelyya tan konsertada 'orden 'en todaś laś kośaś ke viśte kon lo kual śe te a'umentara 'el 'amor ke le tyeneś 'i la deleytasy'on kon śu verdadero konosimyento lo kual le diğo por 'ultimo ke 'el meśmo 'era 'el patron de akel verğel 'i ke deśde alyi probe'i'a 'en todaś laś kozaś ke alyya vido por 'entresisy'on de śuś (m) minis̆tro(t)[ś] 'i ke no avi'a animal ni yerba ni planta muy pekenyya ke fu'eśe 'en todo 'el verğel ke no tubyeśe 'un śyerbo śuyo ke probyeśe 'enelyya 'i la hizyeśe kreser lo kual viśto por akel beatisimo 'ombre la 'orden ke akel rey teni'a 'en probe'er tan partikular mente 'en akel verğel por 'entresisy'on de śuś miniśtroś śin ninguna falta śe le a'umento 'el 'amor ke anteś le teni'a śin tener del 'entero konosimyento 'i fu'e alegre 'en śumo grado de alegri'a 'i deleytasy'on 'infinita

BOOK OF THE REGIMEN OF LIVING ‹FOL. 137B–138A›

śin ninguna miśty'on de triśtesi'a ni pasy'on 'enla kual śe deleyto 'en 'infinito glorifikandośe kon ver la kara del rey 'i 'eśtar 'ensu korte konla 'onor ['en] ke kada 'uno de loś muy alyegadoś 'a 'el 'eśtaban ke 'eś 'el mayor premy'o ke śe le podi'a dar[266] :

'EŚTE 'eś 'el 'enğenplo 'i konloke tenemoś antisipado 'eśta viśta la 'intensy'on de loke 'enel śe pu'ede fasil mente 'enğenplifikar ke 'el rey 'eś nu'eśo altisimo 'i glory'ozo Dyyo probe'edor 'i fazedor de todaś laś kośaś kreadaś 'i 'el verğel 'eś 'eśte mundo ke 'enel śe kontyenen tanta diverśidad de animaleś 'i plantaś komo ve'emoś 'i loś treś 'ombreś śon laś treś 'eśpesyaś de 'ombreś ke tenemoś diğo ke śe reparten 'en 'elyyoś todoś loś 'ombreś ke 'eneśte mundo naśen śegun la diversidad de śuś 'intensy'oneś 'i akelyyoś treś diğoś de loś treś portaleroś śon loś treś diğoś ke śabemoś śer verdad por nu'eśtra śakra 'eśkritura 'el primero de 'elyyoś 'eś 'el ke fu'e diğo por nu'eśo altisimo Dyyo 'a nu'eśo padre antigo ke polvo tu 'i 'a polvo tornaraś 'i set-[267] 'i 'el śegundo fu'e akel diğo ke diğo 'Iyob deśnudo śali de [CW. ventre]}

‹fol. 138a›
{KLḤ
vyentre de mi madre 'i deśnudo tornare alyya 'i set-[268] 'el tersero fu'e akel gran diğo de Mośeh Rabbenu ke diğo demente del Dyyo glory'ozo ve'e di delante deti 'oy ala vida 'i a'el byen ala mu'erte 'i a'el mal[269] 'i 'eskoğeraś 'enla vida 'i set-[270] ke kiğo dezir ke la vida konsiśte 'en 'obrar 'el byen 'i la mu'erte 'enel mal porke tenemoś diğo ke toda vida 'eś 'obrar 'i 'obrar mal no 'eś 'obrar lu'ego toda vida 'eś 'obrar byen por lo kual kyen atentare byen 'eneśtoś treś diğoś 'i loś tubyere kontino 'enla memory'a no podra 'erar 'el kamino verdadero dela vida para alyegar 'a akel deśkanso 'i repozo ke śe alkansa kuando deśta vida śe parte(n) :

---

[266] Unidentified source. P. Pascual Recuero reproduces a slightly different version of this tale he copied from a collection there titled *Aqidat Niṣṣabim* (*Antología de cuentos sefardíes* [Barcelona, 1979], 21–24). Cf. Thompson, *Motif-Index,* L10, *Victorious youngest son,* and AT 550, *The Three Sons,* 577; D789.4, *Disenchantment by breaking tabu;* F129.4.2, *Voyage to otherworld island;* H1242, *Youngest brother alone succeeds on quest;* H1289, *Quest to other realms.*

[267] Gen. 3.19.
[268] Job 1.21.
[269] Deut. 30.15.
[270] Deut. 30.19.

Book of the Regimen of Living ‹fol. 138a-138b›

'I notaśe maś de 'eśte devinisimo 'enǧenplo ke laś animaś 'eśpesyal laś de Yiśra'el ke 'eśtoś śon de śangre real alyegadoś al rey śon 'influ'idaś 'i mandadaś de la korte śeleśtre para darleś 'el premy'o por śuś meres[i]myentoś 'i ke depu'eś ke de aki parten loś ke tyene[n] tanta ventura ke no yeran 'el kamino del byen 'i verdader'a 'eśpikulasy'on 'i alyegan 'a akel grado del fin pośtrero ke 'eś 'el amar al śenyyor 'i probe'edor de todo 'el mundo 'eśtoś śon loś ke śe tornan 'a reprezentar 'en lo maś alto 'i 'intrinsiko dela korte śeleśtre donde śe glorifikan laś animaś kon śuma deleytasy'on 'en ver śin ningun 'obśtakulo ni 'inpedimyento 'en puro a'uto lo ke aki no pudyeron alkansar tan perfekta mente ke 'eś komo la diferensy'a de 'un syego ke nunka vido 'el tyenpo ke 'eśta syego 'i kamina todaś laś kalyeś 'i 'entra 'en todaś laś kaśaś tentando 'i akośtumbrandośe a'elyyaś a'el tyenpo ke vyene de pu'eś 'a ver por grasy'a devina ke //śe// glorifika kon ver 'en a'uto lo ke anteś afiguraba kon śu 'inǧeny'o tentando 'i palpando

DE adonde podraś byen notar kuanto probeǧo 'i deleytasy'on śe śige de śegir 'el kamino de la byen aventuransa 'enderesando kontinu'a mente a'el Dyyo alto 'i glory'ozo ke tenyendo 'eśto por hito nunka śe pu'ede 'erar komo diǧo nu'eśo śapyentisimo rey Šᵉlomoh 'en todoś tuś kaminoś konośelo 'i 'el 'enderesara tuś kareraś[271] keryendo dezir ke kuando 'el 'ombre 'en todaś śuś 'obraś partikulareś tubyere akatamyento ke śean todaś 'enderesadaś 'a śervisy'o del Dyyo alto 'eśte śolo akatamyento kauśa de 'enderesarle loś kaminoś para alyegar al fin verdadero 'i 'andar 'eśta ǧornada de la vida śin 'erar

LO kual te digo 'en konkluzy'on ke todo depende de kontinuar 'enel tr[a]baǧo de nu'eśa śantisima ley por ke 'en 'elyya śe konkluyen todoś loś byeneś 'i perfeksy'on de la anima 'i 'entendimyento te'oriko 'i pratiko de adonde depende todo 'el byen 'umano por la kual 'en konkluzy'on nu'eśo śapyentisimo rey demente del Dyyo alto 'i glory'ozo diǧo ke le'ey bu'ena di 'a voś mi l[e]'ey non deǧedeś 'i set-[272] ke kiǧo śiknifikar laś doś partidaś ke ayy 'en nu'eśa śantisima ley ke la parte ke konsiśte 'en 'elyya la perfeksy'on de laś 'obraś śe deve lyyamar}

‹fol. 138b›

{{RMK: The type on this page is set in the shape of a goblet}propy'a mente le'ey del 'ombre 'i la parte ke konsiśte 'en 'elyya la perfeksy'on del 'entendimyento te'oriko 'en śaber laś kośaś devinaś śe deve lyyamar propy'a mente ley del Dyyo por lo kual diǧo śiknifikando la primera partida ke ley bu'ena di avoś komo ke diǧeśe voś di 'una partida de ley ke 'el 'obǧekto de 'elyya 'eś 'en vośotroś 'i pu'ede śer ke śe'a komo ke

---

[271] Prov. 3.6.
[272] Prov. 4.2.

BOOK OF THE REGIMEN OF LIVING ‹FOL. 138B›

diğeśe ke ley del byen di 'a voś 'i 'eś la primera partida ke tenemoś diğo ke 'eś aserka de lo ke śe toma de bağo de razon de byen 'i śiknifikando la śegunda partida ke 'eś debağo de razon de verdad diğo mi ley no değe'eyś 'i se-'l pu'ede śer ke nu'eśo devinisimo rey David śu padre kiğeśe śiknifikar lo meśmo 'en dezir ke śalvo 'en ley de H‹a-Šem› śu voluntad 'i 'en śu le'ey fablara de di'a 'i de noğe 'i set-[273] ke kyere dezir ke 'enla partida ke 'eś śu ley de 'el 'ombre byen aventurado ke ariba diğo 'a meneśter fablar 'enelyya de di'a 'i de noğe para akośtumbrar 'a hazer 'el byen 'en puro a'uto : konlo kual konkluyyo rogando 'a nu'eśo altisimo śenyyor te ponga de kontino 'en voluntad de no 'eseder de 'el kamino de la byen aventuransa para alkansar 'a gozar de la śuprema deleytasy'on ke 'en 'el śegir tal kamino konsiśte tenyendo byen ala memory'a 'eśte devinisimo 'enğenplo ke te 'e prośupu'eśto 'el kual te śera muy 'util para śegir 'el beatisimo kamino de 'eśta vida tenyendo por 'eśpeğo lo ke 'en 'eśte tratado tengo 'eśkrito 'el por śu pyadad 'i mizerikordy'a 'infinita te de deśkanso 'i kontentamyento para poderlo byen 'efektuar amen :

FIN DEL REĞIMYENTO DE LA VIDA

ṬAM}

---

[273] Ps. 1.2.

‹fol. 139a›
{KLT {RMK: anthropomorphic bird figures, or flowers, bracket each of lines one through three.}

AKI KOMYENSA 'EL TRATADO DE LOŚ ŚU'ENYOŚ

HAKᶜDEMAH [INTRODUCTION]

PROLOGO DEL A'UTOR

MI 'ILUŚTRE ŚENYOR diśkuryendo muğaś veześ por la memory'a muğoś tratadoś ke 'en preśensy'a de vu'eśa merṣed śe pratikaron 'enel tyenpo ke yo goze deśu devina konversasy'on 'entre 'elyyoś śe me akordo al preśente aver me diğo 'un Šabbaṭ 'eśtando 'en Bel Veder[1] ke deśeaba 'en grande manera 'o'ir kośa bu'ena 'enel kaśo de loś śu'enyyoś anśi 'enla 'esensy'a delyyoś komo 'enśuś kauśaś 'i śer śatiśfeğo de treś dubdaś ke aserka delyyoś śyenpre tubo :

LA primera śaber komo śe avi'a de 'entender loke algunoś śaby'oś dizen ke śegun śon laś konplisy'oneś de loś 'ombreś aśi śon śuś śu'enyoś diferenteś ke pu'eś la konplisy'on 'eś śegun la konpozisy'on materyal por śer kalidad ke śe rezulta de kalidadeś kontraryaś śegun śu difinsy'on 'i la 'im[a]ğinasy'on por 'entresisy'on de la kual parese śer loś śu'enyyoś 'eś virtud 'enel anima 'i no matery'a komo haze śuś formaś diferenteś śegun la diferensy'a dela tal konpozisy'on materyal :

LA śegunda 'i ke maś deśeaba śaber 'era śi avi'a alguna razon natural ke śatiśfizyeśe para byen 'entender komo śiknifikan laś formaś ke parese konponer la 'imağinasy'on kozaś ke an de venir 'i ke śe'a syerto aśi komo 'enel śu'enyyo śe

---

[1] The sumptuous palace Joseph Nasi built on the western shore of the Bosphorus (Grunebaum-Ballin, *Joseph Naci*, 151). Roth is uncertain if it was located in Ortaköy, on the outskirts of Galata, or in Galata itself where Doña Gracia had her residence (*House of Nasi*, 2:11).

THE TREATISE ON DREAMS ‹FOL. 139A–139B›

śiknifika śegun nu'eśoś śaby'oś kyeren LA tersera ke śe'a la kauza ke śu'enyya 'el
'ombre kozaś de muğo tyenpo 'olvidadaś ke 'eśtando deśpyerto no le vyenen ala
memory'a 'i ğunto koneśto ke deśeaba 'en 'eśtremo 'o'ir byen 'eśponer 'el teśto śobre
loś śu'enyyoś ke Yosef śoltaba 'i śonyyava 'i śaber śi śe podi'a dar 'enelyyoś alguna
razon natural alyende de śer komo parese por 'influ'ensy'a devina
 YO śenyyor deśeando muğo de śaśtifazer 'a vu'eśa mersed a'un ke 'en akel
'iśtante me paresy'o aver diğo 'en 'onibersal algunaś razoneś sofisyenteś por pare-
serme no kedar vu'eśa mersed del todo śatiśfeğo halyyandome al preśente 'enel tyenpo
ke le'emoś loś śu'enyyoś ke Yosef śonyyava 'i śoltava² 'i ğunto koneśto abyendo yo
śonyyado 'enel meśmo tyenpo 'un śu'enyyo muğo ami kontentamyento kon todaś laś
śerkonśtansyaś ke śe rekyeren para śer śu śiknifikasy'on verdader'a aserka 'el
kresimyento 'i a'umento del prośpero 'i felise 'eśtado de vu'eśa mersed 'el kual rela-
tare al fin de todo por 'eśtenso ğunto kon śu śiknifikasy'on ke 'enel meśmo śu'enyyo
śoltava buśkando razon natural para śer 'el 'efekto de lo śiknifikado syerto me paresy'o diśkutir byen 'eśta matery'a}

‹fol. 139b›
{HAKᶜDEMAH [INTRODUCTION]
'enel maś breve 'eśtilo ke śer podra ke śe ke aśi lo kyere 'i vu'eśtra mersed tomara
delyo loke meğor le paresera :
 'I para poder byen 'entender loke aserka deśto śe'a de dezir 'eś meneśter śaber
loke 'enel reğimyento dela vida aserka del dormir tengo 'eśkrito³ ke al prezente tengo
repasado 'i abrevyado algo maś por mandado de vu'eśa mersed 'i repartido 'en treś
parteś 'i kada parte 'en kapituloś 'enla parte primera kapitulo śebtimo diğe ke toda
kośa korporal tyene kuatro modoś de śer 'uno meğor ke 'otro 'el 'uno 'eś 'el śer dela
kośa 'enśi anteś de śer reprezentada 'a 'el śentido konprendida por śuś treś dimensy'oneś śegundo 'eś depu'eś de reprezentada al śentido 'eśtiry'or syendo śu 'oğekto ke
śu figura śe 'inprime 'enla viśta por lo kual śe dize 'eśtar 'el śer dela meśma kośa
'enel propy'o 'oğo pu'eś 'eśta 'enel śu figura tersero 'eś depu'eś de a'uzentada la kośa
dela viśta ke keda la diğa forma 'i figura 'inprimida 'i guardada no deśtinta dela matery'a 'en la 'imağinasy'on alkansada por 'enteresisy'on del śentido komun kela
resiby'o deloś śentidoś 'eśtiry'oreś ke 'eś virtud deśtinta dela 'imağinasy'on śegun loś
filosofoś 'i 'eś 'una śola śegun loś medikoś :

---

² This reference to the Torah reading cycle indicates the autumn as the general time *TS*, or at least the introduction, was composed.

³ See *RV*, Bk. One, chaps. six through eight, fols 23a–33a above.

The Treatise on Dreams ‹fol. 139b–140a›

'Eś la kuarta la forma sustansyal dela koza ke resibe 'el 'entendimyento por 'entresisy'on dela 'imağinasy'on śeparando la forma dela matery'a adonde śe torna 'el 'entendimyento 'i 'entender 'i 'entendido 'una meśma kośa 'i 'eśto 'eś loke lyyamamoś forma 'intelektual 'en puro a'uto komo alyya maś largo śe deklaro 'i komo 'el śenyor Rabbenu Mošeh byen deklaro 'enel kapitulo s'ḥ [68] dela primera parte deśu famoziśimo libro[4] :

'Eś menester maś śaber ke la anima 'eś la ke haze todaś laś operasy'oneś 'enel 'entendimento por 'entersisy'on de loś śentidoś 'o 'imağinasy'on 'o 'entendimyento ke śi dezimoś ke 'el 'oğo ve'e 'eś 'inpropy'a mente diğo 'i aśi śi dezimoś ke la 'imağinasy'on 'imağina por ke 'el anima 'eś la ke ve'e 'i 'oye 'i set- kyero dezir ke 'eś la kauśa fazedora del ver 'o del 'o'ir 'i de todaś laś operasy'oneś ke 'enel anima śe fazen laś kualeś śon propyaś del animal komo dize Aristotel 'enel primero de anima[5] ke dezir 'el alma śe 'ensanya ke 'eś komo dezir la alma teğe 'o fila ke meğor 'eś dezir 'el 'ombre śe 'ensanya por kauśa de la alma por śer 'efisyente 'i formal 'i loś myembroś 'eśturmentoś komo diğo Alberto Manyo ke 'eś 'oğo 'el 'eśpeğo animado[6] por 'entersisy'on de loś 'eśpritoś ke manda aloś diğoś śentidoś ke śon komo 'eśturmentoś para konprender 'el 'oğekto 'i del meśmo modo śe dize ke la anima 'imağina 'i 'entyende por 'entersisy'on de la 'imağinasy'on komo 'eś noto 'i komo deklaro 'el diğo śenyor Rabbenu Mošeh 'enel kapitulo primero de loś 'oğo kapituloś ke 'eśkriby'o 'enel prinsipy'o del komento de loś Pᶜrakim[7]}

‹fol. 140a›
{KM
'I 'eśto śabido ğunto konlo ke 'enel meśmo kapitulo larga mente deklaramoś 'enla kauśa del dormir konforme aloke 'el filosofo deklaro 'enel libro de śu'enyyo 'i viğilyya[8] 'i 'el 'Algazel algo maś largo 'ensu fizika komo 'enmiś notasy'oneś śobre 'el

---

[4] Maimonides, *Guide,* trans. Pines, 163–66.
[5] Aristotle, *De Anima* I.i (403a 17–403b 19), trans. Hett, 13–15.
[6] Unidentified source. For a summary of Albert the Great's theory of sense, intellect, and imagination, see *Cambridge History of Later Medieval Philosophy* (602–5).
[7] The *Eight Chapters* precede Maimonides' commentary on *Avot*. In Chapter One he writes: "The *imagination* is that faculty which retains impressions of things perceptible to the mind, after they have ceased to affect directly the senses which conceived them" (*"Eight Chapters,"* ed. Gorfinkle, 41).
[8] Aristotle, *On Sleep and Waking* II (455a14–455b27), trans. Hett, 321–31.

The Treatise on Dreams ‹fol. 140a›

tengo razonable mente alargado[9] śe podra fasil mente konprehender la kauśa del śu'enyyo 'i śu 'esensy'a 'i la diferensy'a ke 'enelyoś śe mu'eśtra 'i la verdader'a kauśa de 'unoś śer syertoś 'i 'otroś varyableś porke śegun alyi deklaramoś 'el dormir akaese por kauśa de rekonsent[r]arśe loś 'eśpritoś ala parte 'intiry'or por kual kyera delaś kauśaś ke loś antigoś 'eśkribyeron 'o por buśkar 'el repozo 'i ky'etud del kansansy'o 'enla 'obra de loś śentidoś 'eśtiry'oreś ke śe haze por 'enteresisy'on delyyoś mandadoś del korason śegun 'opiny'on deloś filosofos 'o del śelebro śegun loś medikoś[10] 'o por ayudar ala diğeśty'on kuando 'el 'eśtomago 'eśta reple(k)to lo kual śe mu'eśtra 'en loś maś deloś 'ombreś ke abyendo komido demazyado leś susede gana de dormir de kual kyer modo ke śe'a 'eśta byen viśto ke la kauśa del dormir 'eś śer rekoğidoś loś 'eśpritoś delaś parteś 'eśtiry'oreś porke retirandośe alaś parteś 'intiry'oreś sesa la 'obra deloś śentidoś 'i keda la anima deś'okupada dela 'operasy'on de 'elyyoś 'i 'eśto 'eś loke lyyamamoś dormir por lo kual diğeron nu'eśtroś śaby'oś ke 'eś 'una de sesenta parteś dela mu'erte[11] porke syendo la mu'erte la pribasy'on de todaś laś 'obraś del animal aśi 'eśtiry'oreś komo 'intiry'oreś sesando parte delaś 'obraś komo sesan 'en 'el tyenpo del dormir komo tenemoś diğo 'i berifikado śe dira kon razon śer parte dela mu'erte 'i 'el dezir ke 'eś 'una parte de sesenta no 'eś por śer aśi puntual mente ke 'enlaś maś delaś kośaś para denotar 'una parte del todo lo śu'elen poner 'eneśte numero 'i pyenso ke guardaron 'eneśto 'el reśpekto ke guardaron loś 'eśtrologoś 'en partir 'el grado 'en //se(n)se(')[nt]a// minutoś 'i set- komo deklare byen 'enel komento dela te'orika dela luna[12] aserka la deklarasy'on deloś minutoś porporsy'onaleś konforme alo ke 'el Tolome'o 'eśkriby'o 'enel primero del 'Alm[a]ğeśto[13] ke no ayy numero manko ke 'el ke śe reparte 'en tantaś parteś //ś(o)[i]n// kebradoś komo 'el numero sesenta ke śe halyya poderśe partir 'en dyeś modoś por ke śe reparte 'en medyyo 'i 'en tersy'o 'i 'en kuarto 'i 'en kinto 'i 'en seśto 'i 'en desimo 'i 'en dozabo 'i 'en kinzabo 'i 'en ventabo 'i 'en trentabo afu'era del numero 'entero ke 'eś 'el meśmo sesenta de kual kyer manera ke śe'a tubyeron razon de lyyamar al dormir parte dela mu'erte pu'eś 'eś sesar 'el anima dela 'obra ke haze por 'enteresisy'on deloś śentidoś

---

[9] Probably M.A. refers to his own commentary on al-Ghazzali's *Maqasid al-falasif, Migdal Oz*.

[10] Note the contrast between the location of the seat of perception: Aristotle places it in the heart, Hippocrates situates it in the brain.

[11] Berakot 57b.

[12] This refers to *Bet Elohim ve-Šaʿar ha-Šamayyim*.

[13] Ptolemy, *Almagest*, I.10–11, trans. Toomer, 48–60. Also ed. E. Glowatzki and H. Gottsche, *Die Sehentafel des Klaudios Ptolemaios* (Munich, 1976).

The Treatise on Dreams ‹fol. 140a–140b›

'eśtiry'oreś por lo kual 'eś viśto ke 'entonseś 'eśta 'el anima maś deś'okupada para 'obrar por 'enteresisy'on dela 'imağinasy'on 'o fantazi'a ke 'eś apartar 'o ağuntar 'o konponer laś formaś ke resiby'o deloś śentidoś por}

‹fol. 140b›
{'entresisy'on del śentido komun ke 'eś 'el tersero modo de śer dela kośa komo tenemoś diğo 'i 'eśto 'eś śu'enyyo ke 'eś laś formaś ['i]mağinatibaś 'enel anima del ke śu'enyya loke 'eśtando deśpyerto 'el 'ombre no pu'ede tan larga mente hazer por 'eśtar 'el anima 'okupada 'enla 'obra deloś diğoś śentidoś 'eśtiry'oreś :

'I 'eśto podra byen ver 'i śentir kual kyera śer aśi por loke muğaś veześ akaese 'a muğoś 'eśpesyal 'a loś ke tyene rezy'a 'imağinasy'on ke a'un 'eśtando deśpyertoś diśtraidoś dela 'obra de diğoś śentidoś atrayendo ala memoryya laś formaś 'i 'eśpesyaś ke 'enla 'imağinasy'on 'eśtan 'inprimidaś 'eśtando algun 'eśpasy'o de tyenpo 'eneśta kontenplasy'on deś'okupada 'el anima algun tanto dela 'obra deloś śentidoś tyene maś lugar para la 'obra dela diğa 'imağinasy'on 'i para reprezentarśele muğaś formaś imağinatibaś ke kuando torna 'enśi le parese ke 'eśtaba śonyando

'I 'a veześ akaese pareser le ke konprendyeron loś meśmoś śentidoś akelyya forma de la 'imağinasy'on aśi komo 'enel meśmo śu'enyo 'imağina ke loś śentidoś konprenden todaś akelyaś formaś ke śele reprezentan komo 'eś manifyeśto 'i a'eśte modo śon laś fantaśmaś ke algunoś pyensan ke śeleś aparesen de di'a 'o de noğe ke lyyaman 'el vulgo demony'oś ke 'el pensar śer aśi 'en puro a'uto komo de 'elyyoś śe ku'enta kauśa 'enloś ke tal pyensan temor 'i 'el temor haze 'eśforsar la 'imağinasy'on 'i no 'okuparśe 'el anima 'en maś ke 'en kontenplar 'enla tal 'imağinasy'on komo 'eś natural de kual kyera ke teme de 'una kośa ke todo tyenpo ke akel temor tura no kontenpla 'el anima 'en 'otra kośa maś ke 'en akelyyo ke resela 'i 'okupada la anima 'en śolo 'eśta 'imağinasy'on diśtraida de todaś laś 'otraś operasy'oneś śele reprezentan akelyyaś formaś ke fantazean temyendo delyyaś 'enla figura ke śe laś pintaron 'i 'el 'imağina śer aśi 'i ğurara 'i afirmara ke laś vido 'en puro a'uto 'eśtiry'or porke 'el śentido del vizo fu'e pribado 'en akel 'iśtante por averśe 'ok[u]pado 'el anima 'enla 'obra dela 'imağinasy'on muy 'efikaś mente komo dize Aristotel 'enel śegundo de anima[14] ke 'eśtando atyentoś 'a 'una fu'erte 'imağinasy'on no vemoś laś kozaś ke ante loś 'oğoś śe noś reprezentan por 'okuparśe 'el anima tan rezy'a mente śolo 'en

---

[14] Cf. Aristotle, *De Anima* II.ii (413b 22–23), trans. Hett, 77. Aristotle later observes that "visions are seen by men even with their eyes shut" (*De Anima* III.iii [428a 15–16], trans. Hett, 159).

The Treatise on Dreams ‹fol. 140b–141a›

akelyya 'imağinasy'on komo avemoś diğo komo parese 'enel meśmo śu'enyyo ke ve'e 'el ke śu'enyya laś figuraś ke fantaze'a 'o 'imağina porke 'el śentido del ver vaga 'en akel 'iśtante ğunto kon loś 'otroś śentidoś 'eśtiry'oreś komo 'e diğo 'i 'eśto akaese laś maś delaś veześ 'en loś ninyyoś 'i muğereś 'o 'otroś śemeğanteś de flako 'inğeny(z)o ke fasil mente 'eś lyebada la anima por la flakeza del 'entendimyento 'a taleś 'imağinasy'oneś :

'I '(')[a] veześ a'un ke muy raraś akaese 'eśto tanbyen 'en 'ombreś de bu'en 'inğeny'o ke kontenplando rezy'a mente 'en 'una kośa [CW. śin]}

‹fol. 141a›
{KM' HA-SUG HA-' HA-MIN HA-' [THE FIRST CLASS FIRST SPECIES]
śin tener ala sazon kośa ke le 'okupa ni 'inpida para porelyya śer diśtraido delyya śe 'eśfu'ersa la 'imağinasy'on 'i haze 'okupar 'el anima 'en śola la kontenplasy'on de akelyaś formaś ke 'imağina hata diśtraerla 'i pribarla de la 'obra de loś śentidoś kaśi komo 'enel meśmo śu'enyo ke le parese ke ve'e 'i 'oye la kośa ke 'imağina 'i kuando buśkamoś 'una preśona kon 'efikasy'a kual kyera ke vemoś noś pareśe śer 'el ke buśkamoś 'eśto kedara para 'otro lugar ke aki no fu'e maś ke tokar 'en 'elyyo por ke tanbyen śe pratiko delante vu'eśtra mersed muğaś veześ

ŚOLO al prezente fu'e la 'intensy'on 'enlo diğo para ke 'ividente mente śe pudyeśe konprender la 'esensy'a 'i kauśa de loke lyyamamoś śu'enyyo durmyendo no śabido por lo śabido 'i viśto kuando 'eśtamoś deśpyertoś para śatiśfazer ala primera kośa ke vu'eśa mersed keri'a śaber de adonde śe ve'e ke no 'eś maś la diferensy'a ke śer 'el anima maś deś'okupada durmyendo de la 'obra de loś śentidoś 'eśtiry'oreś komo 'eś diğo :

'I para verdader'a mente śaber la kauśa dela diferensy'a ke 'enelyyoś śe falyya 'i śaśtifazer por 'entero alaś dubdaś ke vu'eśa mersed moby'o ke śon grande ayuda para 'inponer 'a kual kyera 'enla verdad dela repu'eśta diğo śenyor ke loś śu'enyoś śe dividen 'en treś parteś 'o ğeneroś diferenteś[15] :

'EL primer ğenero 'eś loś śu'enyoś śinpleś 'insyertoś :
'EL śegundo'eś loś śu'enyoś śinpleś syertoś 'i verdaderoś 'enśuś śiknifikasy'oneś :
'EL tersero 'eś loś śu'enyyoś ke ayy 'enelyyoś alguna 'eśpirasy'on 'o modo de 'influ'ensy'a devina :

---

[15] Berakot 55b discusses three species of dreams. This is partly based on the classic formulation as found in Macrobius, *Commentary on the Dream of Scipio* I.3.1–20. Cf. Oberhelman, *Oneirocriticon*, 41–43, 49–55.

The Treatise on Dreams ‹fol. 141a–141b›

'EL ǧenero p(+)rimero śe divide 'en treś 'eśpesyaś diferenteś 'una dela 'otra 'i todaś 'insyertaś

LA primera 'eś loś śu'enyoś 'insyertoś ke akaesen śer taleś por parte dela komplisy'on 'o konpośisy'on 'o diśpośisy'on del 'endivido komo vu'eśtra mersed preśupuśo 'o por alguna kalidad 'eśtrany'a a'utiba 'o p(+)asiba ke altera 'el ku'erpo 'umano

'I 'eśto no śe pu'ede negar ke vemoś muǧaś veześ śobre puǧando 'enel 'ombre algun kalor demaśyado natural 'o 'eśtranyo śu'enya loś śu'enyoś konforme 'a akelya kalidad komo ke 'eśta 'enel banyyo 'o serka de 'un gran fu'ego ke śe kalyenta 'enel 'o 'otra kośa śemeǧante 'i śi śobre puǧa 'enel fryaldad śu['e]nya śobre nyebe 'o yelada 'o 'otra kośa tal 'i del meśmo modo śegun 'el 'umor ke śobre puǧa 'enel aśi śon śuś śu'enyoś ke śi 'eś melankoliko śeran śuś śu'enyoś temerozoś 'i 'eśpantozoś 'o ke śe syente pezado 'o tulyido ke śe va araśtando por 'el śu'elo ke no pu'ede kaminar ni dar paso

'I śi koleriko śonyyara ke abola 'o 'otra kośa tal ke vyene por parte de la kolera 'i śi flematiko śonyara ke 'eśta śobre aguaś 'en mar 'o 'en ri'o 'o 'otra kośa tal de manera ke konforme a'el 'umor ke puǧa 'enel śeran śuś śu'enyoś}

‹fol. 141b›
{'i 'el Razi 'enel śegundo del Almanṣor[16] maś alargo ke 'otro tomando loś śu'enyoś por śenyal de laś 'enfermedadeś 'en loś pasyenteś 'i śaber por 'elyyaś kual 'eś 'el 'umor pekante

'I la kauśa 'i modo komo śe haze 'eśto ke 'eś la primera dubda ke vu'eśtra mersed moby'o 'eśta manifyeśta kon lo ke tenemoś antisipado 'i 'eś ke komo kyera ke la meśma anima ke syente ve'e 'i 'oye gu'ele 'i guśta 'i apalpa por 'entreśisy'on de loś 'eśturmentoś ke para 'eśto śon apropyadoś por medy'o de loś 'eśpritoś komo tenemoś diǧo 'eś la meśma ke 'imaǧina por 'enteresisy'on de la 'imaǧinasy'on ke śu lugar 'eś 'el 'intiry'or ventrikulo del s[e]lebro ke 'eś komo 'eśturmento para por medy'o del kontenplar 'el anima 'en laś formaś imaǧinatibaś aśi komo 'el 'oǧo para 'el ver śigeśe de aki ke aśi komo danyyado 'el 'eśturmento porel medyo del kual ve'e 'el anima 'el 'obǧekto antepu'eśto no lo podra perfekta mente konprehender maś anteś śi 'el 'oǧo 'eśtubyere kolorado 'o de kual kyera 'otra kolor kuanto vyere le paresera dela meśma kolor ke 'eśta 'el 'oǧo ke śi 'eśtubyere 'enśa[n]grentado komo muǧaś veześ akaese todo le paresera de kolor dela meśma śangre porke para ǧuśgar de todaś laś koloreś

---

[16] Abu Bakr Muḥammad b. Zakariyya al-Razi's *Manṣuri*: see *Encyclopaedia of Islam* viii, 474a–478b.

The Treatise on Dreams ⟨fol. 141b–142a⟩

'eś nesesary'o ke 'el 'eśturmento por 'entresisy'on del kual śe ğuśgan śe'a pribado de todaś laś koloreś komo śe demośtro 'enel śegundo de anima[17] 'i del meśmo modo vemoś por 'eśperensy'a muğaś veześ tanbyen 'enel śentido del guśto ke 'eś ğuśgar de loś śaboreś ke śi tubyere la boka amarga todo kuanto guśtare le paresera amargo 'i set- anśi 'enloś 'otroś 'eśturmentoś apropyadoś[18] para loś 'otroś śentidoś konbyene śer vaku'oś 'i pribadoś delaś kośaś ke por 'elyyoś śe ğuśga del meśmo modo kuando la kalor 'o fryaldad śobre puğare 'enel ku'erpo 'umano 'i 'eśkalyentare 'o 'eśfryare 'en tanta kantidad ke alyege hata 'el krany'o ke arode'a al senebro 'i por śu 'entresisy'on śe 'eśkalyentare 'o 'eśfryare la suśtansy'a del selebro ke 'eś 'eśturmento para la 'imağinasy'on komo avemoś diğo la anima ke syente la tal kalor alyegando 'enel 'eśturmento porel kual 'imağina akelyyaś formaś fantaśtikaś kalefikadaś konla kalidad ke tyene 'el 'eśturmento por medyo del kual laś 'imağina toda la 'imağinasy'on śe a-plika 'a akelyya kalidad

'I komo de śu natural 'eś konponer 'una kośa kon 'otra komo maś adelante de-klararemoś 'imağina ke 'eśta 'enel banyyo porke tubo la 'eśpesyya del banyyo ke tomo de loś sentidoś 'eśtiry'oreś guardada 'enśi ke todaś laś 'eśpesyaś resebidaś por medyo de loś śentidoś 'eśtiry'oreś 'eśtan guardadaś 'enla fantazi'a komo tenemoś antisipado :

'I śi śe 'eśfri'a la parte diğa del śelebro afigura ke 'eśta śobre nyebe 'o 'otra kośa tal 'i aśi 'en kual kyera delaś kalidadeś pasibaś 'i set- : [CW. komo]}

⟨fol. 142a⟩
{[KMB]{RMK: no pagination assume KMB.}
KOMO śe ve'e 'eśto kuando 'eśpyertoś 'eśpesyal śi 'eśtan dolyenteś ke tan byen 'imağinan laś kośaś aplikadaś al 'umor ke paresen ke śi 'eśta fri'o 'el pasyente 'imağina ke 'eśta 'en 'una montany'a yelada 'i alaś veześ 'imağina 'el kontrary'o de loke parese dezeandolo por remedy'o dela kalidad ke le da pasy'on por lo kual 'imağinara ke 'eśta al fu'ego por śer lo ke deśe'a 'el fu'ego para remedyar 'el fri'o 'i aśi kuando 'eś 'el 'umor pekante kolera ke 'eś kalyente 'i śeka la kual kauśa sed por parte dela śekedad deśeando 'el remedy'o 'imağina 'en kuantaś fu'enteś tyene viśtaś 'i guardadaś 'en la fantazi'a ke 'eś komo 'en 'el śu'enyyo 'en 'el tyenpo del dormir 'i todo prosede por śer la anima la meśma ke syente 'i 'imağina 'i 'entyende komo tenemoś antisipado por 'entreśisy'on 'i medyo deśtoś 'eśturmentoś diferenteś por loś kualeś hazen diferenteś operasy'oneś 'i padesyendo kual kyera deloś 'eśturmentoś padese 'el anima ke śige laś meśmaś pasy'oneś :

---

[17] Aristotle, *De Anima* II.vii (418b 28–419a 22), trans. Hett, 106–7.
[18] Aristotle, *De Anima* II.vii (418b 28–419a 22), trans. Hett, 106–7.

THE TREATISE ON DREAMS ‹FOL. 142A–142B›

DE adonde śe śige ke de kual kyer danyyo ke ayya 'enel selebro komo apośtema 'o 'otr'a kośa tal śe konronpe la virtud animada ke 'eśta 'en akelyya parte del selebro ke śi fu'ere 'enel ventrikulo delantero śera korupsy'on de la 'imağinasy'on 'o fantazi'a 'i śi 'enel ventrikulo del medyo śera korup(y)sy'on del pensamyento 'i śi fu'ere 'enel ventrikulo pośtiry'or śera korupsy'on dela memory'a komo śe mu'eśtra por loke loś medikoś 'eśkribyeron aserka deśtaś 'enfermedadeś 'i śuś remedy'oś[19] :

POR lo kual 'eśta viśto ke laś pasy'oneś ke padese 'el selebro mudan la 'imağinasy'on 'i la hazen diferente 'i durmyendo haze 'imağinar formaś konvenibleś ala tal kalor komo fu'egoś 'o banyyo 'o 'otro tal ke 'eś lo ke lyyamamoś śu'enyyo komo avemoś diğo 'i aśi meśmo de kual kyera 'otra kalidad ke 'el selebro padesyere śeran laś formaś de la diğa 'imağinasy'on konformeś 'a 'elyya :

AYY 'otra kauśa maś 'onibersal 'i maś 'ividente kon lo ke 'eśta ya diğo 'i 'eś ke komo śe'a la meśma anima la ke syente 'i la ke 'im[a]ğina komo 'eś diğo sintyendo kual kyera pasy'on ke vyene por parte dela matery'a 'enel tyenpo ke sesa la 'obra de loś śentidoś 'imağina la meśma anima ke syente la tal pasy'on 'i 'el śentir la pasy'on 'eśtando durmyendo 'eś por 'entresisy'on del takto ke loś śentidoś 'eśtiry'oreś no śon totalisima mente pribadoś al tyenpo del dormir ke loś 'eśpritoś ke van aloś 'o'idoś para 'o'ir a'un ke śe rekonsentran al tyenpo del dormir śyenpre keda alguna partezita delyyoś alyi 'eśpesyal śi no 'eś muy porfundo komo 'eś al t[y]e[n]po del śonyar 'i 'eśta 'eś la kauśa ke muğaś veześ 'eśtando durmyendo 'o'imoś loke śe habla a'un ke no muy perfekta mente 'i del meśmo modo 'eś 'enloś 'otroś śentidoś ke por no śer tan perfekta mente śu [CW. 'obra]}

‹fol. 142b›
{'obra komo kuando deśpyertoś tyene poder la 'imağinasy'on de traśponerlo 'en 'otra fig[u]ra konforme 'a akelyya 'obra del śentido 'i noś parese ke śonyyamoś 'i set-

'I muğaś veześ no 'eśtando 'el 'ombre 'entera mente durmyendo medy'o durmyendo 'i medy'o deśpyer(p)[t]o śi 'eśta 'en lugar donde le lyyu'ebe 'enriba 'o le vente'a rezyyo vyento 'o le dan de paloś 'o kual kyer 'otra koza tal ke la alma padese delyya 'imağina komo śonyyando ke lyyu'ebe 'o haze vyento 'o ke le dan de paloś 'o kual kyer 'otro tal 'i kuando del todo deśpyerta pensando ke 'eś śu'enyyo halyya śer aśi 'en puro a'uto 'i fu'e ke la alma 'imağina la forma de loke padese śintyendo lo ke śenti'a deśpyerto algo maś perfekta mente ke 'en 'el śu'enyyo komo avemoś diğo :

KONFORME alo kual 'eśkribyeron loś medikoś todoś 'i Abisena 'en 'el libro

---

[19] Cf. Pseudo-Hippocrates, *De Regimine* IV: see Oberhelman, *Oneirocriticon*, 32–36.

THE TREATISE ON DREAMS ‹FOL. 142B–143A›

tersero 'en la fin primera disy'on kinta kapitulo tersero[20] śobre 'una 'enfermedad keśe lyyama 'en latin 'inkubuś 'i 'el vulgo lyyaman pezadilyya ke 'imağina śonyyando 'el ke la tal 'enfermedad tyene ke śe le pone alguna koza 'enriba ke le peza muğo
'I LA kauza de śonyyar 'eśto 'eś porke komo śe'a laś maś de laś veześ 'eśta 'enfermedad por kauśa 'intiry'or de 'un fumo 'o vapor gru'eśo flematiko 'o śangino 'o melankoliko ke śube de laś taleś 'umoreś 'i syera 'i 'opila 'el selebro 'i 'el korason de manera ke loś 'eśpritoś no śe 'eśpanden perfekta mente por 'el ku'erpo 'i mankando loś 'eśpritoś keda la karne pezada komo śi śele puzyeśe 'una karga 'ensima 'i komensando 'a mankar de loś 'eśtremoś 'i vinyendo mankando hazy'a ariba śintyendo 'eśto 'el anima 'imağina ke 'una figura de 'ombre 'o de kual kyera 'otro animal 'o 'otra kośa tal ke śe le pone 'ensima 'i ke kom[y]ensa 'a śubirle por loś pyeś hata ke vyene 'a ahogarlo śi loś fumoś 'o vaporeś śon tantoś 'i tan gru'eśoś abyendo muğo demazyado komido 'o bevido ke kavzen śerar tanto loś pasoś por donde pasan loś 'eśpritoś ke parese a[']el alma pasy'on grande hata rezolverśe loś diğoś fumoś 'o vaporeś :

POR lo kual kuando 'eśto akaese 'en kryaturaś pekenyyaś de teta lo kual akaese muğaś veześ por śer muy 'omidoś no pudyendo rezolver 'i deśfazer loś taleś vaporeś por la flakeza de la virtud śe afogan 'i 'eś loke laś muğereś komun mente lyyaman bruğaś :

DE manera ke por lo diğo 'eśta byen viśto loke keremoś dezir ke porel anima padeser kual kyera pasy'on por parte dela matery'a śu'enyya 'el 'ombre śu'enyoś por figuraś konformeś 'a akelyya pasy'on por śer ke la meśma alma ke syente la tal pasy'on 'eś la meśma ke 'imağina akelyyaś aparensyaś 'i fantaśmaś konformeś ala diğa pasy'on komo avemoś diğo :

'I 'eśtoś taleś śu'enyyoś śon 'insyertoś 'i varyableś porke śon kavzadoś por laś kalidadeś ke alteran 'el ku'erpo 'umano 'o de 'umor pekante demazyada ke śobre puğa maś de loke konvyene [CW. 'o]}

‹fol. 143a›
{KMG HA-SUG HA-'- HA-MIN HA-B- [THE FIRST CLASS SPECIES TWO]
'o de vapor fri'a 'o kalyente asidental por parte del komer 'o del bever ke śube al selebro de kual kyer modo ke śe'a komo śean 'eśtoś taleś śu'enyoś kauśadoś por kauśaś 'eśtiry'oreś ke depende delyyaś la tal 'imağinasy'on 'eś byen viśto no śe poder ğuśgar por loś taleś śu'enyoś kośa s[y]erta ni verdader'a
LA śegunda 'eśpesy'a 'eś loś śu'enyoś ke śe kauśan por 'eśtar la alma abituada

---

[20] *Canon*, Bk. 3, Pt. 1, thesis 5, chap. 3; cf. trans. Gruner, 273, 277.

The Treatise on Dreams ‹fol. 143a–143b›

'i 'okupada 'en muğoś pensamyentoś perfundoś 'en 'el tyenpo de la viğilyya ke śe treśpasan fasil mente 'en la 'imağinasy'on 'i la kauśa 'eś ke komo 'el di'a anda la anima kontinuando 'en akelyyoś pensamyentoś 'enramadoś kon la 'imağinasy'on sesando de la 'obra de loś sentidoś 'eśtiry'oreś ke 'eś 'el dormir komo avemoś diğo va śigyendo 'en akelyyoś pensamyentoś kon maś fu'[e]rsa 'i vigor por ke tyene maś lugar para fantazear 'en 'elyyoś por no 'eśtar tanto 'okupada komo kuando 'eśta 'el 'ombre deśpyerto por la razon diğa 'i la fantazi'a resebidaś 'en śi akelyaś formaś 'o 'eśpesyaś laś traśpone 'en 'otraś figuraś konponyendo 'una kośa kon 'otra komo 'eś śu natural de hazer depu'eś de sesar laś 'obraś de loś śentidoś

'I de aki vyene ke loś 'ombreś muy pensatiboś 'i ke andan kuando deśpyertoś kon 'imağinasy'oneś perfundaś 'i kontinuaś śon loś ke maś kontinu'a mente śu'enyyan ke śe treśpasan laś taleś 'imağinasy'oneś 'enel tyenpo del dormir śigyendo la fantazi'a śuś formaś 'o figuraś kon maś fu'ersa :

'I laś maś de laś veześ akaesen śer loś taleś śu'enyyoś 'insyertoś por śegir la 'imağinasy'on 'en 'elyyoś lo ke resibe de loś diğoś śentidoś 'eśtiry'oreś 'eśpesyal śi loke syente 'eśtando deśpyerto por loś śentidoś le kauśa admirasy'on 'o temor ke 'eś kauśa de 'inprimirśe akelyya 'eśpesy'a resebida del śentido 'en la 'imağinasy'on 'i de aki vyene ke 'el 'ombre ke maś śe admira de 'una kośa maś śu'enyya 'en 'elyya por ke admirandośe muğo pyensa muğo 'en 'elyya 'i 'el pensamyento 'enramado kon la 'imağinasy'on 'imağina rezy'a mente 'en akelyya kośa ke de 'elyya śe admira 'i śi le kauśa temor śera 'eśto muğo maś ke aśi ve'emoś ke 'el 'ombre ke anda muy temerozo de 'una kośa śu'enyya kontinu'a mente 'en[e]lyyo por ke no va 'imağinando kontenplando 'i fantazeando śalvo komo śe'a de śalvar dela tal kośa 'o komo śele pu'ede śegir 'el danyo 'o la 'ofensa 'i 'eśtoś pensamyentoś kontinu'oś del di'a 'eśtando deśpyerto śe treśpasan al tyenpo del dormir 'i faze la 'imağinasy'on figuraś konformeś 'a akelya kośa 'i 'a loś danyoś 'o 'inkonbenyenteś ke de 'elya 'imağino poderśe śegir por lo kual śu'enyya śu'enyoś temerozoś 'i set- :

'I akaese tanbyen 'en algunoś 'inoranteś 'i śinpleś ke no śe 'okupa śu anima por śinpleś 'en 'eśpekular śino śolo 'en kontinuar 'a hablar 'i dezir por la boka loke 'oyen de 'otroś ke 'eś tan flako śu 'entendimyento ke no p[y]ensan 'enlo ke an viśto 'o 'o'ido de 'otroś śino ke śolo tornan 'a dezir lo por la boka}

‹fol. 143b›
{admirandośe delyyo śin maś 'eśpikulasy'on ke 'eneśto śemeğan algo tant[o] alaś aveś ke 'enśenyan 'a h[a]blar komo la pega 'o papagalyyo ke tornan 'a dezir laś meśmaś palabraś ke 'oyen

'I loś 'ombreś taleś ke hablan 'eśtaś palabraś admirandośe delyyaś śe 'inprimen 'en la 'imağinasy'on por ke tanto kuanto 'eś la admirasy'on de la kośa ke śe ve'e 'o śe

The Treatise on Dreams ‹fol. 143b–144a›

'oye tanto maś śe 'inprime komo tenemoś diğo 'i 'inprimyendośe 'en la 'imağinasy'on vyene al tyenpo del dormir 'a śonyar 'en 'elyyo por ke 'eśtonseś la 'imağinasy'on śige śu 'obra kon maś fu'ersa 'i traśpone la kośa 'en formaś aparenteś 'i afigura kimeraś konforme alo ke 'el tal śonyador hablo 'i śe le 'inprimy'o 'en la 'imağinasy'on 'eśtando deśpyerto

'I 'eśto kiğo śentir nu'eśo śapyentisimo rey Š^{c}lomoh 'en śu 'Ekliśyaśteś do dize no te turbeś śobre tu boka 'i tu korason no śe apreśure para śakar kośa delante 'el Dyo por ke 'el Dyyo 'en loś syeloś 'i tu śobre la tyera por tanto śean tuś palabraś pokaś ke vyene 'el śu'enyo kon muğedumbre de kaśo 'i boz de 'inorante kon muğedumbre de palabraś[21] 'eśta 'eś la verdader'a 'entrepetasy'on de śuś palabraś 'i kon lo ke tenemoś diğo 'eśta byen 'entendida la 'intensy'on delyaś 'i 'eś ke 'el śapyentisimo rey depu'eś de byen 'eśpekulado akabida a'el 'ombre 'en doś kozaś la 'una ke la habla de la boka no śe'a apreśurada kon turba ni admirasy'on 'i 'eśto kiğo dezir 'en dezir no te turbeś śobre tu boka 'i set- konbyene śaber ke no śe'a la palabra turbada presuroza por ke 'eśto 'eś kauśa de hazer grandisima 'inp(y)resy'on 'en la 'imağinasy'on komo 'eś diğo 'i tanbyen akabida al korason no śe'a apreśurado 'a śakar la rezolusy'on 'o konsekensya de lo ke kontenplare 'en laś kozaś devinaś por ke akaese laś maś de laś veześ 'en 'elyaś 'el yero 'i 'inoransy'a 'i 'eśto kiğo śiknifikar 'en dezir 'i tu korason no śe apreśure para śakar kośa delante 'el Dyyo 'i set- ke kyere dezir ke 'el pensamyento 'o fantazi'a no śe apreśure 'a śakar la rezolusy'on de la kośa ke 'eś lo ke propy'a mente śe lyyama kośa abśuluta mente 'i dize ke 'eśto akabida śola mente 'en laś kozaś devinaś ke kontenplando 'en 'elyaś śe dize 'eśtar 'el 'ombre 'en la tal kontenplasy'on delante 'el Dyyo ke śe proś[u]pone por 'obğekto de la 'ima(y)ğinasy'on 'i dyyo la kauśa 'en 'elyyo la kual 'eś la ke tenemoś diğo ke laś kośaś devinaś śon muy difisileś de alkansar por ke 'el Dyyo 'eśta 'en loś syeloś muy alto 'i muy 'elebado 'i 'el 'ombre 'eśta 'en 'otro 'eśtremo muy bağo para poder 'en 'elyyo algo alkansar por tanto 'eś razon ke tanto la palabra del korason komo la de la boka śean pokaś por ke śe'a manko 'el yero 'i 'eśto kiğo śiknifikar dizyendo por ke 'el Dyyo 'en loś syeloś 'i tu śobre la tyera por tanto śean tuś palabraś pokaś 'i set-

'I dize maś preśuponyendo 'el 'inkonbenye[n]te grande ke del preśto konklu'ir 'i muğo hablar [CW. de]}

‹fol. 144a›
{[KMD] {RMK: no pagination assume KMD.}
de priśa 'enlaś kośaś devinaś śe śige 'el kual 'eś 'en kuanto la habla del korason ke

---

[21] Eccles. 5.1–2.

The Treatise on Dreams ‹fol. 144a›

'eś la pośtrera ke vyene 'el śu'enyyo por muğo penśar 'i muğo 'imağinar 'en muğoś kaśoś 'i 'eśto kiğo śentir 'en dezir ke vyene 'el śu'enyyo kon muğedumbre de kazo 'i set-[22] konbyene śaber ke por muğedumbre de kazoś ke 'imağina 'el 'ombre 'i fantazi'a 'el di'a 'eśtando deśpyerto śe treśpasan la noğe 'enel tyenpo del dormir 'enla 'imağinasy'on lo kual 'eś lo ke lyyamamoś śu'enyyo komo avemoś diğo 'i penśara 'el ke tal śonyyare ke śiknifika verdad syendo kauśado porel pensamyento por laś maś de laś veześ falso por śer 'en kośaś ke śe alkansa 'enelyyaś muy poko dela verdad komo 'eś diğo por tanto 'eś razon ke 'el korason no śe apreśure śin muğo 'eśtudyar 'a sakar la rezolusy'on dela kośa porke no śe 'inprima lo ke de 'inprobizo alka[n]sa 'enla 'imağinasy'on 'i venga 'a śonyyar 'en 'elyyo :

'I 'en kuanto la primera ke 'eś la habla dela boka dize ke la boz del 'inorante 'enel śu'enyyo ke avemoś diğo ke no 'eś maś ke boz vyene por muğedumbre de palabraś 'i la konkluzy'on de śu 'intensy'on 'eś ke śean pokaś laś palabraś 'i pensamyentoś apreśuradoś 'enlaś kośaś devinaś porke fasil mente śe treśpasan 'enel śu'enyyo 'i la 'imağinasy'on haze formaś 'i kimeraś formadaś śobre loś taleś pensamyentoś ke depu'eś pensando aver 'en akel śu'enyyo alguna koza śyerta nasera grandisimo 'eśkandalo afirmandośe akelyya 'opiny'on 'eronyya 'enel konsebto konsebida por 'el śu'enyyo :

DE todo lo diğo kiğimoś śola mente notar śer loś pensamyentoś 'i hablaś del tyenpo dela viğilyya kauśa de loś śu'enyyoś konformeś aloś taleś pensamyentoś :

'I 'eśto pyenso ke kiğeron śiknifikar loś ermanoś de Yosef 'en lyyamarlo du'enyyo deloś śu'enyyoś 'i set-[23] keryendo dezir ke 'el 'era kauśa de 'elyyoś andando kon loś pensamyentoś 'i fantazi'a fantazeando kontinu'a mente de śobre puğar 'i 'enśenyyorear śobre 'elyyoś śintyendo 'enśi 'el amor ke śu padre lo amaba a'el maś ke atodoś loś 'otroś 'i akelyyaś 'imağinasy'oneś 'inprimyendośe rezy'a mente 'enel anima śe treśpasaban 'enel tyenpo de 'el dormir 'i kavzaba śonyyarlaś de manera ke 'el por śuś pensamyentoś 'en 'el tyenpo de la viğilyya kavzaba loś taleś śu'enyyoś durmyendo por lo kual lo 'entitulaban patron deloś śu'enyyoś[24] 'i loś atribu'ian 'a 'el por lo kual dezian tanbyen 'i veremoś ke śeran śuś śu'enyyoś 'i set-[25] ke 'en dezir śuś śu'enyyoś kiğeron śiknifikar tanbyen loke tenemoś diğo ke loś śu'enyyoś 'eran śuyoś kavzadoś porel 'i set- ke paresyendoleś aloś ermanoś śer śuś śu'enyyoś 'insyertoś por śer kavzadoś de śuś pensamyentoś diğeron 'i agora 'andad 'i matemoślo 'i 'eğemoślo 'en

---

[22] Eccles. 5.2.
[23] Gen. 37.19.
[24] Gen. 37.19.
[25] Gen. 37.20.

The Treatise on Dreams ‹fol. 144a–144b›

'uno de loś pozoś 'i set-²⁶ burlando deloś 'efektoś ke 'el pensaba ke śiknifikaban śuś śu'enyyoś 'inorando 'elyyoś la verdad dela śertenidad de śu śiknifikasy'on por ke la 'enbidy'a [CW. ke]}

‹fol. 144b›
{ke kauśaba 'enelyoś tenerle 'ody'o seraba laś pu'ertaś del 'entendimyento para konoser kuan syertoś devian de śer por razon natural komo deklararemoś 'enel fin de todo konel ayuda del Dyyo glory'ozo ke 'elyyoś yeraron 'en pensar ke prosedi'a 'el śu'enyyo śuyo porel pensamyento vano 'i no por ǧu'izy'o verdadero
  'I a'eśta kauśa 'el profeta Yᵉšaᶜyahu aloś ke apanyaban para konkiśtar 'i deśtru'ir 'a Yᵉrušalayim determinado 'entre śi poderla deśtru'ir konel grande deśe'o ke 'enelyyoś reynaba de ponerlo 'en 'efekto konparaba aloś ke śu'enyan ke komen 'eśtando fambryentoś ke la fambre ke kauśaba 'eśtando deśpyertoś 'el deśe'o de komer leś haze śonyar ke komen 'i dela meśma manera la demazyada sed del sedyondo le haze śonyar ke beve del[ ]meśmo modo 'el deśe'o ke tenian laś ǧenteś komo Sanḥerib 'i 'Ašur de konkiśtar 'a Yᵉrušalayim 'i 'a Ṣiyon leś hazi'a pensar de ponerlo 'en 'efekto²⁷ 'i por 'eśto diǧo 'i śera komo śu'enya 'el fambryento 'i hek komyen 'i 'eśpyerta 'i 'eś vazi'a śu alma 'i aśi komo śu'enyya 'el śeke'ozo 'i hek bevyen 'i deśpyerta 'i hek laso 'i śu alma deśeante aśi śera muǧedumbre de todaś laś ǧenteś śobre monte de Ṣiyon 'i set-²⁸ keryendo dezir ke laś maś delaś veześ ke śu'enya 'el 'ombre ke kome 'eś kuando śe 'eǧa fambryento ke sintyendo 'i padesyendo 'el anima la hambre 'eś kauśa de śonyar ke kome 'i poreśo no diǧo 'i śera komo śu'enyya 'el 'ombre 'i hek komyen 'i set- ke no 'eś la konparasy'on 'igual śalvo kuando 'eś fambryento 'el ke tal śu'enya 'i set-²⁹ de manera ke 'eś śu'enyyo 'insyerto pu'eś 'eś kauśado por la hambre 'i aśi tanbyen 'el ke tyene sed 'i śu'enya ke beve '(o)[i]ke śe harta de śuabisima agu'a ke la 'imaǧinasy'on terna 'en algun tyenpo konprendido por 'entresisy'on de loś sentidoś 'eśtiry'oreś del meśmo modo dize ke śeran laś ǧenteś ke 'imaǧinan konkiśtar 'i poner fonsado kontra Ṣiyon ke śe halyaran tan faltoś de loke 'imaǧinan komo akel hambryento kuando śe 'eśpyerta ke śe halyya falto de la 'imaǧinasy'on ke durmyendo 'imaǧinaba de adonde 'eś byen viśto lo ke tenemoś diǧo ke loś śu'enyyoś śon kavzadoś por parte de 'el pensamyento ke pyensa 'el ke tal śu'enyya kuando 'eśta deśpyerto 'i kontinu'a 'enel tal pensamyento hata treśpasarlo 'enel tyenpo del dormir

---

²⁶ Gen. 37.20.
²⁷ Cf. 2 Kings 18–19, Isa. 36–37, and 2 Chron. 32.
²⁸ Isa. 29.8.
²⁹ Isa. 29.8.

The Treatise on Dreams ‹fol. 144b–145a›

ke 'eśta 'eś la maś komun 'eśpesy'a 'enloś maś de loś 'ombreś ke kavza(n) śer loś śu'enyyoś 'insyertoś 'i varyableś :
  LA tersera 'eśpesy'a 'eś loś śu'enyyoś ke śu'enyyan 'ombreś śinpleś de flako 'i de vil 'inǧeny'o poko 'eǧersitado 'en 'eśpikulasy'on ke a'un ke śean 'ombreś śanoś alyegadoś 'en śuś kompliśy'oneś ala 'igualdad ke śe rekyere para la perfeksy'on de laś 'obraś 'umanaś śin alterasy'on de 'umor ni kalidad 'eśtrany'a ke lo kauze 'i śin śer 'ombreś de muǧoś pensamyentoś ni muǧaś palabraś ke śin laś doś kauzaś ke avemoś diǧo ke loś haze śer varyableś 'i 'insyertoś śegun laś doś primeraś 'eśpesyaś śolo por la pokedad de śu [CW. 'entendimyento]}

‹fol. 145a›
{KMH
'entendimyento 'i flakeza de śu 'inǧeny'o para kontraś(+)tar 'i deśbaratar laś formaś 'i figuraś kela 'imaǧinasy'on 'inventa 'eśta viśto śer laś taleś 'imaǧinasy'oneś 'insyertaś por ke śyendo 'el diǧo 'entendimyento tan flako keda lugar ala 'imaǧinasy'on 'a śegir śuś formaś 'o figuraś 'a ryenda śu'elta śin śer deśbaratadaś halyyandośe la alma deś'okupada dela 'obra de loś śentidoś 'okupandośe 'en śola la 'obra dela 'imaǧinasy'on no tenyendo 'el abito del freno de la razon para 'irle ala mano da lugar 'a konponer diǧa 'imaǧinasy'on 'una kośa kon 'otra de adonde śe hazen formaś 'i figuraś varyableś 'i syendo śola mente por parte dela 'imaǧinasy'on śin partisipar la razon ni 'el 'entendimyento 'eś viśto no tener ninguna śiknifikasy'on verdader'a pu'eś no 'eś maś ke śolo śegir la 'imaǧinasy'on śu kurso komo 'eś de śu natural de 'inventar śimileś figuraś a'un 'enel tyenpo dela viǧily'a kuanta maś 'enel tyenpo del dormir ke tyene maś lugar para 'elyyo komo 'eś diǧo konlo kual kedara byen konprendida la razon del primer ǧenero de loś śu'enyyoś śer 'insyertoś 'i aśolvida la dubda primera ke vu'eśa mersed dubdo :
  'EL ŚEGUNDO GENERO 'eś loś śu'enyoś ke demośtran la verdad dela kośa ke 'eśta por venir 'i la sertenidad de lo ke śera 'enelya ke 'eś la śegunda dubda ke vu'eśa mersed moby'o loś kualeś śu'enyoś no śe hazen por ninguna delaś kauśaś diǧas ke kauśan śer 'insyertoś 'i varyableś 'i 'eśtoś śon divididoś 'en doś 'eśpesyaś diferenteś a'un ke laś kauśaś śean laś meśmaś 'en anbaś laś 'eśpesyaś
  LA primera 'eśpesy'a donde la razon natural śe mu'eśtra maś 'ividente mente komo maś śe deklarara 'eś loś śu'enyoś ke śu[ʼe]nyan 'ombreś no penśatiboś ke 'eś 'una delaś kauśaś de śer 'insyertoś komo 'eś diǧo 'i ke śean de rezy'o 'inǧeny'o para kontraśtar 'i deśbaratar 'i deśtru'ir kon razon verdader'a 'i prebaś śofisyenteś laś falsaś 'imaǧinasy'oneś kela fantazi'a śu'ele konponer no andandole ala mano : LA śegunda 'eśpesy'a 'eś loś śu'enyoś ke śu'enyan loś maś de loś 'ombreś ke no śon śaby'oś ni le'idoś syendo repozadoś 'i de razonable 'inǧenyyo ke 'eneśtoś taleś śeran

The Treatise on Dreams ‹fol. 145a–145b›

syertoś śuś śu'enyoś porel ğu'izyyo ke śu 'entendimyento faze 'enlo por venir por śola la 'eśperensy'a ke tyene 'enlo pasado ke kon razonable 'inğeny'o ke tenga atentando b[y]en 'enelyyo lo hara syerto śin faltar 'enel 'efekto
'I 'en todaś 'eśtaś doś 'eśpesyaś 'a de śer de tal manera ke no keden laś formaś de la 'imağinasy'on kuando 'eseden del ğu'izy'o del 'entendimyento 'inprimidaś 'enel a(ṣ)[n]ima del ke śu'enya ke 'eś 'una kauśa de laś ke diğimoś ke kauśan śer 'insyertaś 'i ke śe'a 'eśtando śanoś 'i[ ]byen akonpl[i]śy'onadoś [CW. 'i ke]}

‹fol. 145b›
{HA-SUG HA-B- HA-MIN HA-'-VEHA-B- [THE SECOND CLASS SPECIES ONE AND TWO]
'i ke no śe'a 'el śu'enyo del prinsipy'o del dormir lu'ego deśpu'eś de la komida ke todo 'eśto 'eś śegun la primera kauśa ke diğimoś ke haze śer 'insyertoś śalvo 'el śu'enyo de hazy['a] la manyana por lo kual determinaron verdader'a mente nu'eśoś śabyoś ke 'el śu'enyo de hazy'a la manyana 'eś 'el verdadero[30] porke 'eśtonseś śon rezolvidoś loś vaporeś dela komida ke kauśan śer varyableś 'i maś apartada la anima del 'eğersisy'o dela viğilya 'en vary'oś penś[a]myentoś kon maś ky'etud 'i repośo śin ningun 'ośtakulo para kontemplar 'enla verdad de laś kośaś 'i por 'eśtaś 'eśpesyaś de śu'enyoś syertoś diğeron nu'eśoś śaby'oś śer 'una de sesenta parteś de profesi'a[31] pu'eś tanto partisipan 'en la verdad tomando la parte de 'el numero sesenta por lo diğo ariba
'I śer loś śu'enyoś syertoś 'en taleś 'ombreś 'i 'en tal tyenpo loke kyera ke demośtran 'i śiknifikan 'enlo futuro śegun laś reglaś verdaderaś ke para 'entender la verdad de śu śiknifikasy'on śe rekyer(o)[e]n ke 'eś la śegunda dubda ke vu'eśa mersed dubdo 'eś byen viśto atentando 'enlaś kauśaś ke kauśan loś taleś śu'enyoś ke por laś kauśaś verdaderaś śe śigen loś 'efektoś syertoś :
   LA kauśa primera 'i maś natural 'eś ke komo śe'a porpozisy'on manifyeśta 'i berifikada de todoś loś śaby'oś ke la kośa ke 'eś posible porśi śe śige laś maś delaś veześ por śuś kauśaś komo śe 'entyende 'enśu lugar ke para aki aklararlo byen śeri'a meneśter muğo alargar 'eś viśto ke aśi komo akaese 'eśtando 'el 'ombre deśpyerto ke kontenplando 'i 'eśpekulando byen konśu bu'en 'inğeny'o 'i ğu'izy'o prudensyal śegun dereğa razon 'enlaś kauśaś delaś kośaś ke enelyaś kontenplare śean laś digaś kauśaś śegun naturaleza 'o 'orden komun 'o śegun la kośtelasy'on 'obliga śi 'en 'el tal

---

[30] "R. Johanan said: Every dream just before morning is fulfilled immediately" (Gen. R. 89.5). The formulation appears in Achmet's *Oneirocriticon* §301: see Oberhelman, *Oneirocriticon*, 66, 245.
[31] Berakot 57b.

THE TREATISE ON DREAMS ‹FOL. 145B–146A›

kauśo fu'ere pratiko ǧuśgara por 'elyaś la verdad del 'efekto 'i aśi śera śin falta por la porpozisy'on diǧa śi kaere 'i asertare byen 'i verdader'a mente 'enlaś kauśaś :
DEL meśmo modo 'i a'un maś perfekta mente śera 'eśtando durmyendo porke 'eśtando la alma deś'okupada del trabaǧo 'i 'okupasy'on dela 'obra de loś śentidoś 'eśtiry'oreś komo avemoś diǧo śige śu kontenplasy'on maś ky'eta mente peśkiryendo laś kauśaś delaś kośaś ke le pu'eden suseder 'i determinando 'el 'efekto porel 'entendimyento la 'imaǧinasy'on ke 'eś virtud 'enla meśma alma lo reduze 'i aplika 'i traśpone 'en formaś partikulareś 'en śuǧebtoś materyaleś śegun laś 'eśpesyaś ke 'enśi tyene la fantazi'a guardadaś 'i resebidaś por 'entresisy'on de loś śentidoś komo 'eśta ya diǧo porke 'elyya 'eś la ke 'inpide de no poder 'el 'ombre ni a'un deśpyerto kontenplar 'enla forma 'intelektual total mente komo 'elya 'eś 'enśi śalvo 'en alguna figura partikular kela traśpone la 'imaǧinasy'on komo 'eś śabido 'i kual kyera lo vera 'enśi ke a'un kuando kontenplamoś 'enlaś 'entiliǧensyaś deśeparadaś}

‹fol. 146a›
{KMV
'en puro a'uto no laś podemoś 'imaǧinar śalvo 'en alguna figura materyal komo 'eś śabido ke para averlo byen de deklarar śeri'a meneśter tanbyen 'en 'eśto byen alargar[32] :
PU'EŚ śi tyene poder la 'imaǧinasy'on para hazer 'eśto 'eśtando 'el 'ombre deśpyerto kuanto maś 'eśtando durmyendo ke tyene maś vigor 'i fu'ersa śin 'inpedimyento ni 'okupasy'on komo tenemoś diǧo 'i aberiguado por lo kual 'eś byen viśto ke ningun śu'enyo demośtra lo meśmo ke 'a de suseder 'en 'efekto śalvo traśpu'eśto 'en 'otraś figuraś ke traśpone la 'imaǧinasy'on konforme aloke ǧuśgo 'i determino 'el 'entendimyento 'i la razon ke 'a de śuseder por śuś kauśaś śi no fu'ere 'en algunoś ke tyene tan rezy'o 'i fu'erte 'el 'entendimyento 'i tan flaka la 'imaǧinasy'on ke no baśta 'a kontraśtar a'el 'entendimyento para deǧarśe venser ake traśponga laś formaś

---

[32] Almosnino's understanding of *intelligences en acte* is noted by S. Munk: "Moïse Almosnino, savant rabbin espagnol à Salonique, que vivait aux XVIᵉ siècle, parle de l'ouvrage d'Ibn-Gebirol d'une manière très vague que montre qu'il n'avait pas lu cet ouvrage. Il ne le connaissait notamment par la traduction hébraïque que ce dernier (selon le témoignage du même Almosnino) avait faite de la *Quaestio de spiritualibus creaturis* de Saint Thomas. Almosnino dit que l'opinion d'Ibn-Gebirol, qui attribue une matière subtile aux substances simples ou aux anges, avai trouvé de nombreux adversaires, mais, ajoute-t-il, j'ai entendu dire qu'il est revenu de cette opinion, et qu'il a confessé la vérité, savoir, que ce sont des *intelligences en acte*, d'une simplicité absolue. Voy. Le recueil des discours d'Almosnino intitulé: *Meammes Koah* (Venise, 1588), in-4°, fol. 117"
S. A. Munk, in *Mélanges de philosophie juive et arabe* [Paris: Franck, 1857–1859], 304).

THE TREATISE ON DREAMS ‹FOL. 146A–146B›

'intelektualeś 'en imağinatibaś 'i a'un 'eneśtoś a'un ke śeran muy pokisimoś no podra śer totalisima mente lo meśmo śino fu'ere kon miśty'on de fantaśma alguna por 'eśtar 'el 'entendimyento 'enramado konla 'imağinasy'on komo tenemoś antisipado por lo kual determinaron nu'eśoś śaby'oś kon ğuśta razon por loke tenemoś diğo ke no ayy śu'enyo śin kośaś baldiaś 'i set-[33] śiknifikando ke por muy verisimo ke śe'a 'el śu'enyo 'i 'en 'ombreś de muy 'eśforsado 'inğeny'o no pu'ede değar de partisipar 'en algo la 'imağinasy'on :

POR loke tenemoś diğo 'eśta viśta la neses[i]dad ke 'ubo de śoltar loś śu'enyoś ke 'eś buśkar laś śiknifikasy'oneś 'i venir porel 'efekto ala kauśa ke 'eś por laś formaś imağinatibaś ke śe ve'en 'enel śu'enyo śaber laś 'intelektibaś ke konforme a'elyaś śe traśpuzyeron 'enla 'imağinasy'on pu'eś no śon laś meśmaś komo avemoś diğo :

PARA lo kual 'el śoltador 'en todaś laś doś 'eśpesyaś diğaś de śu'enyoś syertoś 'eś meneśter ke śe'a śaby'o prudente 'i tenga bu'ena 'eśtimatiba 'i 'eśperensy'a para venir del 'efekto ala kauśa 'i ğuśgar por razon natural por laś figuraś 'i formaś dela 'imağinasy'on ke podi'a śer loke 'el 'entendimyento ğuśgo 'o por 'eśpikulasy'on 'o por 'eśperensy'a śegun la kalidad del śonyador para kela 'imağinasy'on lo traśpuzyese 'en akelyyaś formaś maś ke 'en 'otraś ke a'eśta vi'a 'eran todoś loś śoltadoreś de śu'enyyoś ke ku'entan 'en nu'eśo Ṭalmud ke por grande kośa dizen ke avi'a 'en Y^eruśal[ayi]m vente 'i kuatro śoltadoreś de śu'enyoś[34] loke 'en 'otro ningun lugar śe halyaba porke avi'a meneśter ke fu'eśen muy śaby'oś 'i prudentisimoś 'i muy 'eśprimentadoś de bu'ena 'eśtimatiba para konsidrar la kalidad dela kośa konforme ala kalidad del śonyador ke 'un meśmo śu'enyo 'en doś 'ombreś diferenteś haze diferenteś śiknifikasy'oneś del meśmo modo ke 'eś aserka loś ğu'izy'oś ke śe ğuśgan por la 'eśtroloği'a de tal manera ke kayygan verdader'a mente 'enla razon konsidrando byen laś konsidrasy'oneś ke 'el ke}

‹fol. 146b›
{śu'enya 'a de tener para śer śuś śu'enyoś syertoś por laś reglaś antisipadaś ke byen atentando 'en algunoś 'i a'un 'en todoś kuantoś 'en nu'eśo Ṭalmud śe ku'enta delyyoś ke śoltaban śu'enyoś śe ve'e klara mente śer por bu'ena 'eśtimatiba buśkando 'i 'eśpekulando śegun razon natural la forma 'intelektual por la 'imağinatiba :

KOMO śe trae de 'un 'ombre ke śonyaba ke laś vigaś de śu kaza śe kebraban 'i vinyendo 'a kontar 'el kazo a'un śingularisimo śenyyor de akel tyenpo le diğo ke śik-

---

[33] Berakot 55a, Rashi Gen. 37.10, Ramban Gen. 37.10.
[34] Berakot 55b.

The Treatise on Dreams ⟨fol. 146b–147a⟩

nifikaba ke śu muğer avi'a de parir 'un hiğo 'i aśi fu'e 'en 'efekto[35] 'I 'eneśte kaśo yeran muğoś 'en tomar 'eśtaś reglaś 'en 'onibersal pensando ke kual kyera ke 'eśto śonyare parira śu muğer hiğo porke 'eśtaś reglaś no śon verdaderaś 'en todoś ni 'en todo tyenpo ke podri'a śer ke 'el ke tal śonyyaśe no tubyeśe muğer ni 'eśperaśe tenerla ğamaś 'i podri'a śer akel meśmo śenyor ke akelyo śolto śi 'otro lo śonyyara no lo śoltara aśi komo śe halyya 'en nu'eśo propy'o Talmud 'en doś famoziśimoś śaby'oś śoltadoreś de śu'enyoś ke 'en 'un meśmo śu'enyo 'en preśonaś diferenteś 'uno loś śoltaba de 'un modo 'i 'otro de 'otro 'i todoś doś śe afirmaban 'i śalian 'en 'efekto del meśmo modo ke 'elyyoś lo śoltaban[36] 'i del meśmo modo śe halyya śoltar 'un meśmo śu'enyo 'en tyenpoś diferenteś 'enel meśmo śonyador 'i śer śoltado 'en modoś diferenteś 'i todoś doś afirmarśe del meśmo modo ke fu'eron śu'eltoś[37] ke todo 'eśto 'eś demośtrasy'on verdader'a kelo śoltaban akelyyoś śenyoreś por razon natural atentando 'i mirando 'en todaś laś konsidrasy'oneś ke śe rekyere atentar 'i 'eśpekular byen 'i mirar 'el tyenpo 'i la komplisy'on del śonyador 'i la kalidad de śu 'eśtado kon todaś laś 'otraś śerkonśtansyaś ke śe rekyere atentar 'en tal kaśo por lo kual 'eś śabido ke akel ke śolto 'a akel ke śonyaba ke laś vigaś de śu kaśa śe ronpian ke śu muğer avi'a de parir 'un hiğo no manko de 'eśpekular 'i peśkerir muy byen anteś ke lo śoltaśe śi la muğer del ke tal śonyaba 'eśtaba prenyada 'i ke 'op(v)[i]ny'on teni'a 'el 'en loke avi'a de parir 'i porke kauśa 'i vyendo ke por laś kauśaś ke 'el tal śonyador teni'a konsebidaś 'enśi konosyendo '[e]nel tener bu'en 'inğeny'o ky'eto 'i (r) repozado para ğuśgar la verdad por 'elyyaś 'o por 'eśpikulasy'on śegun la 'eśpesy'a primera 'o por 'eśperensy'a śegun la śegunda ğuśgo 'el tal śaby'o ke śiknifikaba ke śu muğer avi'a de parir hiğo ğuśgando kon dereğa razon ke akel 'ombre 'enel tyenpo del dormir ke śu 'entendimyento 'eśtaba ky'eto 'i deś'okupado dela 'obra 'eśtiry'or deloś śentidoś śe determino 'o por 'eśpikulasy'on 'o por 'eśperensy'a 'i śenyaleś de 'otraś veześ ke lo hizo śer pratiko ke śu muğer avi'a de parir hiğo 'i la 'imağinasy'on traśponyendo laś kośaś ke 'el 'entendimyento determina 'en figuraś imağinatibaś komo avemoś diğo tenyendo la 'imağinasy'on 'o fantazi'a}

⟨fol. 147a⟩
{KMZ
guardado 'enśi por 'entresisy'on de loś śentidoś ke la konpozisy'on de loś myembroś de 'el 'ombre 'eś komo 'una fabrika 'envigada 'i 'enkadenada 'una parte kon 'otra 'i

---

[35] Gen. R. 89.8 and Lam. R. I.1.18.
[36] This seems to be in reference to Berakot 56a.
[37] Berakot 55b.

THE TREATISE ON DREAMS ⟨FOL. 147A–147B⟩

tener śabido ke loś doloreś dela ke pare hiǧo śon maś 'i maś agudoś ke loś de la ke pare hiǧa śabyendo del ke aśi lo teni'a 'entendido 'o por 'o'ida 'o por razon natural śi 'era śaby'o la 'im[a]ǧinasy'on konponyendo 'una fabrika kon 'otra 'imaǧinando ke kon 'el muǧo dolor de la ke pare hiǧo todoś śuś myembroś śe le kebrantan determinando 'el 'entendimyento ke avi'a de parir hiǧo heǧa 'eśta konparasy'on 'o konpozisy'on por la 'imaǧinasy'on ke tyene 'enśi laś 'eśpesyaś de laś doś kozaś guardad[a]ś 'en la fantazi'a komo 'eś diǧo traśpuzo 'unaś 'en 'otraś komo śu'ele hazer 'i śonyo ke laś vigaś de la kaśa śe ronpian 'i 'el śapyentisimo śoltador byen 'eśpekulando laś //k[a]uśaś// por donde 'un bu'en 'inǧeny'o komo 'el //(ke)// tal śony'o syendo deś'okupado 'i ky'eto komo 'eś al tyenpo del dormir por laś figuraś ke traśpuzo la 'imaǧinasy'on ǧuśgo laś verdaderaś figuraś ke determino 'el 'entendimyento 'i pudyera śer ke 'en 'otro tyenpo no 'eśtando la muǧer del ke tal śonyaśe prenyada 'i 'eśtando 'el mal diśpu'eśto kon kebrantamyento del ku'erpo 'o de alguna kaida ke a'el le padesyeśe 'o śintye( )śe averśele roto alguna końtilya delo kual 'el 'entendimyento ǧuśgaśe ke avi'a de padeser 'o p(y)[a]deser de akel mal komo kyen meǧor lo syente la 'imaǧinasy'on traśponyendolo 'en 'otra forma konforme a'el tal ǧu'izy'o afiguraśe ke laś vigaś de la kaza śe kebran 'i 'el śoltador prudente byen 'eśpekulando 'en todoś loś asidenteś pasadoś ǧuśgaśe ke avi'a de morir ǧuśgari'a verdad

'I por 'eśta vi'a 'i 'orden śon todoś 'o loś maś de loś śu'enyoś ke śe ku['e]nta 'en nu'eśo Ṭalmud ke śoltaban loś śaby'oś ke 'en akel tyenpo śe falyaban por lo kual 'otro kual kyera yerara 'en gran manera śi por akelyaś reglaś śoltare tomadaś 'en 'onibersal 'en kual kyer tyenpo 'i 'en kual kyera 'ombre śin maś 'eśpekular 'en laś śer konstansyaś ke partikular mente konbyene 'eśpekular komo 'eś diǧo

'I 'eśta śu'erte de śu'enyoś ǧuśgando porel 'entendimyento 'el 'efekto ke 'a de suseder 'i traśponerloś la 'imaǧinasy'on 'en figuraś konformeś alaś 'eśpesyaś ke 'enśi tyene guardadaś komo 'eś diǧo pu'ede śer 'en doś modoś diferenteś por laś kualeś dividimoś laś doś 'eśpesyaś diferenteś śegun la diferensy'a deloś 'ombreś keloś taleś śu'enyoś śu'enyan :

'EL primero 'i ke manko śe halyya 'eś loś dela primera 'eśpesy'a ke śon kuando 'el śonyador 'eś 'ombre śaby'o ke 'eśpekulando 'en laś kauśaś delaś kośaś śe determina 'enel 'efekto ke 'a de suseder //'eśpesyal śi fu'ere 'eśtrologo// 'i determinado por 'el 'entendimyento 'el tal 'efekto 'enel tyenpo del dormir traśpu'eśto por la 'imaǧinasy'on 'en figuraś konformeś 'a 'el tal ǧu'izyo 'o determinasy'on 'el śaby'o ke 'eśte tal śu'enyo śoltare peśkiryendo 'en laś kauśaś konsebidaś 'enel 'entendimyento del tal śonyyador [CW. 'i]}

⟨fol. 147b⟩
{'i 'el tanbyen fu'ere 'eśtrologo komo 'el śonyador kaera fasil mente 'enla verdad deśu śiknifikasy'on alo kual śe pu'ede tomar 'enǧenplo kazi del meśmo śu'enyyo por-

The Treatise on Dreams ‹fol. 147b›

śupu'eśto ke śonyyaśe kelaś vigaś dela kaza śele ronpian 'en tal tyenpo 'o 'en tal meś śabyendo 'el śonyyador la regla del animodar ke 'el Tolome'o 'eśkribyyo 'ensu Śento Loky'o[38] ke 'el ke śupyere 'el punto dela konsebsy'on śabra 'el punto del nasimyento dela kryatura porel 'i del meśmo modo 'el ke śupyere 'el punto del naśimyento śabra por 'el 'el punto dela konsebsy'on 'i 'eś la regla 'eneśto ke 'el grado del śenyo ke fu'ere //as(n)e[n]dente// 'enla 'ora 'i punto dela konsebsy'on śera lugar dela luna al punto del nasimyento 'i 'el verdadero lugar dela luna ala 'ora dela //ko(y)[n]sebsy'on// śera asendente ala 'ora del nasimyento syendo 'el śonyador 'eśtrologo 'i 'el śoltador tanbyen śabyendo ke 'el tal śonyador śabi'a 'el verdadero punto dela konsebsy'on 'i lo ke 'era asendente al tal punto 'i 'enke lugar 'eśtaba la luna śin ke 'el tal śoltador lo śepa kon śolo śaber ke 'el ke śonyo lo śabi'a 'i ke śony'o ke śele ronpian laś vigaś dela kaza 'en akel tal tyenpo śoltara ke 'a de parir 'en akel tyenpo por la regla antisipada ke ǧuśgando śabyya mente por laś reglaś diǧaś śabidaś ke por 'elyyaś 'el 'entendimyento pu'ede ǧuśgar 'el punto ke 'a de śer 'el nasimyento 'i la 'imaǧinasy'on la traśpuzo 'en akelyya forma ke 'eś konforme 'onibersal mente al parir por śuś doloreś komo tenemoś diǧo :

'O śi śonyaśe ke ve'i'a 'una fruta nu'eba 'en tal tyenpo ke 'eś traśponerlo 'en 'otra figura śiknifikando lo meśmo 'i para konsidrar perfekta mente la sensy'a 'o śapyensy'a del śonyador por la kual vino 'a determinar 'el 'efekto 'eś meneśter ke 'el śoltador śe'a śapyentisimo para ke śi 'el śonyador fu'ere 'eśtrologo śepa ke vino 'a akely'a determinasy'on por la regla diǧa 'o śemeǧante de laś reglaś de la 'eśtroloǧi'a 'en ǧuśgar delo futuro :

---

[38] The "Rule of Animodar" is defined immediately in the text and again in the *Be'ur,* item no. 190. The pseudo-Ptolemaic *Centiloquium* (Greek *Karpos*) is found in manuscripts of the *Almagest* and singly; Hugh of Santalla translated it as a single title (Lindberg, *Science in the Middle Ages,* 63). Pedersen notes its popularity in the Middle Ages, and characterizes it as "a disorderly compilation of one hundred astrological aphorisms" (*Survey of the Almagest,* 406). The Center for Research Libraries' online catalogue cites the *Centiloquium:* "Quadripartitum. — Centiloquium. — Hermes Trismegistus, Centiloquium. — De stellis beibeniis. — Bethem, Centiloquium et de horis planetarum. — De signifiactione triplicitatum ortus. — Almansor [. . .]. Venezia, Bonetus Locatellus for Octavianus Scotus, 1493." It also figures in the 1405 statutes of the Bolognese student university of arts and medicine as a textbook in astrology for medical students (Lindberg, *Science in the Middle Ages,* 135). Abraham Ibn Ezra wrote a commentary on it (see R. Levy, "The Astrological Works of Abraham Ibn Ezra," Ph.D. Diss., Johns Hopkins University, 1927; Baltimore: Johns Hopkins University Press, 1927) and Gerard of Cremona made a Latin translation of Ibn Ezra's commentary (Venice, 1507).

The Treatise on Dreams ⟨fol. 147b–148a⟩

'I śi fu'ere filosofo natural 'i vyere 'enel ke abra ǧuśgado por la konplisy'on śuya 'i de śu muǧer ǧunto konlaś 'otraś śerkonśtansyaś ke śe rekyeren para ǧuśgar porelyaś loke 'a de parir la tal muǧer 'o 'enel tyenpo ke 'a de parir 'i vyere figuraś ke kon śu śaber 'i prudensy'a kon bu'ena 'eśtimatiba ǧuśgara ke la 'imaǧinasy'on traśpuzo la f(z)[o]rma verdader'a 'intelektual 'en 'elyyaś verna 'a śoltar la verdad por laś taleś figuraś 'i set- ke 'eśto todo 'eś byen visto 'en 'oǧoś de kual kyera śaby'o śer aśi :

'EL śegundo modo 'eś loś śu'enyoś ke śu'enyan loś 'ombreś ke no śon śaby'oś komo śon komun mente loś maś deloś 'ombreś ke śon de la śegunda 'eśpesy'a ke tenyendo razonable 'inǧeny'o 'o syendo algo prudenteś 'o porla 'eśperensy'a ke tyenen delo pasado ǧuśgaran muǧaś veześ lo futuro komo vemoś muǧoś ruśtikoś ke pornośtikan muǧaś vez(v)[e]ś loś tenporaleś ke an de}

⟨fol. 148a⟩
{KMḤ
suseder no por maś dela 'eśperensy'a ke tyenen por laś śenyyaleś anteśedenteś 'eśtoś taleś komensurando 'el ke śuś śu'enyoś śoltare loke śu 'inǧeny'o pu'ede ǧuśgar por la 'eśperensy'a ǧuśgara fasil mente por laś formaś ke la 'imaǧinasy'on traśpuzo 'enel śu'enyo lo ke kyera ke śu 'entendimyento determinaba 'i deśta 'eśpesy'a 'eran loś maś ke śe śoltaban 'enel tyenpo de nu'eśo Talmud

DEL kual modo ami ver fu'eron loś śu'enyoś ke Yosef śolto al 'eśkansyano 'i panadero de Par^coh[39] ke abyendo kontado la 'eśkritura ke 'eśtubo Yosef kon 'elyyoś ǧunta mente 'en guardy'a algunoś diaś 'enel kual tyenpo averi'a byen 'entendido de 'elyyoś la kauśa partikular deśu prizy'on 'eśpasifikando kada 'uno delyyoś śu delito vyendo 'i konsiderando 'el 'ofisy'o 'i grado de kada 'uno 'i 'el delito kuando 'el 'eśkansyano le konto la forma del śu'eny'o ǧuśgo prudentisima mente śegun dereǧa razon ke 'el 'eśkansyano deberi'a por razon ǧuśgar ke por śer śu 'ofisy'o 'en prezensy'a del rey ke le 'eśkansyaba 'i poni'a 'el vazo 'en la mano 'i śegun nu'eśoś śaby'oś kyeren ke fu'e 'el pekado averśe halyado 'una mośka 'enel vazo[40] 'i śer 'eśto kośa ke muǧaś veześ akaese de 'inprobizo 'i no 'eś viśto por tanto dezi'a śer de razon perdonado śu pekado ke no fu'e tanto śu deśkuido 'i 'eśto ǧuśgari'a por la 'eśpery'ensy'a de 'otroś 'eśkansyanoś ke muǧaś veześ abrian kaido 'en semeǧanteś yeroś 'i fu'eron perdonadoś de pu'eś de aver algun tyenpo padesido 'enla karsel 'i ǧuśgo kon razon keśi tanto avi'a 'eśtado 'en la karsel śin śer perdonado 'era por no averśe akordado 'el rey del por śuś 'okupasy'oneś ni aver kyen lo akordaśe pero śi 'en algun tyenpo avi'a

---

[39] Gen. 40.9–22.
[40] Gen. R. 88.2.

The Treatise on Dreams ⟨fol. 148a–148b⟩

de śer perdonado 'era 'enel di'a śabido 'a todoś del nasimyento del rey ke kada anyo 'en akel di'a śoli'a hazer konbite 'i remirar todoś śuś miniśtroś por lo kual verni'a 'a memory'a śu negosy'o 'i andando 'el di'a kontinuando 'a hazer 'eśtoś 'i śimileś śeloǧiśmoś śegun natural paresyendole ke 'el tyenpo ke 'el ǧuśgaba śer maś 'oportuno para 'efektuar śu pens[a]myento śe 'iba maś alyegando 'i ke no avi'a maś hata 'el de treś diaś 'eśtando durmyendo 'eśforsandośe 'el 'ente[n]dimyento 'enla tal kontenplasy'on śe determino ke śeri'a aśi komo avemoś diǧo

'I la 'imaǧinasy'on śigyendo 'el diǧo ǧu'izy'o konforme a'el komo 'eś śu kośtumbre komo 'eś diǧo lo traśpuzo 'enla forma ke ku['e]nta la 'eśkritura ke ve'i'a 'una vid ke 'i'a floresyendo aśi komo 'el byen kuando 'a de śer syerto va floresyendo 'i por śer ke heǧa la fruta śale fasil mente 'el vino de 'elyya 'en 'efekto śonyyo ke la 'eśprimi'a 'enel vazo de Par^coh 'i komo 'el ǧu'izy'o de 'el diǧo 'entendimyento 'era ke avi'a de śer de a'i 'a treś diaś porla 'eśperensy'a ke deloś anyyoś pasadoś teni'a puzo la forma 'en treś sarmyentoś 'i set- :

LO kual Yosef vyendo 'el laś meśmaś kauzaś ke 'el 'eśkansyano por 'elyyaś avi'a de razon ǧuśgado 'el 'efekto [CW. 'i ke]}

⟨fol. 148b⟩
{'i ke de razon avi'a de śer 'enel tyenpo maś 'oportuno para 'elyyo vyendo la figura ke 'en 'el śu'enyo śe mośtraba de la 'imaǧinasy'on śer konforme a'elyyo śolto 'el śu'enyo komo śe mu'eśtra por la 'eśkritura konforme alo ke tenemoś diǧo

'I 'el panadero a'un ke śegun kyeren nu'eśoś śaby'oś fu'e tanbyen śu delito por averśe halyado 'otra mośka 'o 'un turon de tyera dentro de 'una rośka ke 'el avi'a heǧo[41] 'era muǧo mayor śin konparasy'on 'el yero 'enel ke 'enel 'eśkansyano por muǧaś kauśaś la 'una por no śer 'en prezensy'a del rey ke 'el ke 'eśta 'en śu prezensy'a 'eśta turbado 'i no 'eś muǧo 'en no atentar 'i maś ke 'enel vazo pu'ede śer aver kaido 'enel momento 'o muy poko anteś ke fu'eśe viśta lo kual 'el pan(')adero ke śe halya 'en śu pan 'el turon 'eś digno de muǧa kulpa por no atentar 'en śu masa todo tyenpo ke la 'eśta amaśando 'i maś ke 'el 'eśkansyano 'eś maś kalefikado 'i de maś valor aśerka de 'el rey ke 'el panadero 'i maś kiśto del rey por śer maś reprezentado delante del por lo kual deve śer maś relyebada śu kulpa 'i 'el rey de razon 'a de tener maś voluntad de perdonarle a'un ke 'el pekado fu'eśe 'en loś doś 'igual

POR todaś 'eśtaś kauśaś temi'a 'el panadero ke fu'eśe 'eśekutada śu pena 'i le paresi'a ke śi hata 'eśtonseś no la avian 'eśekutado 'era por deśkuido pero ke de a'i 'a treś diaś ke 'era 'el tyenpo ke śe rekonosian todoś loś miniśtroś komo avemoś diǧo

---

[41] Gen. R. 88.2.

The Treatise on Dreams ⟨fol. 148b–149a⟩

akordandośe de 'el śeri'a kondenado 'a mu'erte śegun la 'eśpery'ensy'a teni'a 'en 'otroś averśe heğo 'en śimil tyenpo lo kual 'eśtando tanbyen 'el kon 'eśte temor alyegandośe 'el tyenpo 'en la meśma noğe ke 'el 'otro śonyyo ğuśgo tanbyen śu 'entendimyento lo diğo por la vi'a 'i kauśa antisipada //'en// la 'imağinasy'on traśpuzo 'el ğu'izy'o prudensyal 'en figuraś konformeś a'el 'i a'el tyenpo komo śe mośtra por la 'eśkritura ke 'en hazer ke la abe komyeśe la komida 'enriba de śu kabesa denoto la mu'erte 'en la forma ke fu'e 'i aśi lo śolto Yosef konforme ala razon ke 'el lo devi'a ğuśgar 'i 'a 'eśta kauśa vera vu'eśtra mersed ke 'el 'eśkansyano komo konfyado 'ensu ğu'izy'o a'un ke algo triśte por la konfuzy'on dela vizy'on 'enla forma kela 'imağinasy'on la avi'a traśpu'eśto śupito ke fu'e demandado de Yosef komo kyen teni'a grandisima 'eśperansa de bu'ena śiknifikasy'on śe adelanto śin maś dilasy'on 'a kontarle śu śu'enyo 'i 'enel panadero komo temerozo por loke la razon le 'obligaba ke śeri'a mala la śiknifikasy'on de pu'eś de asolvido 'el śu'enyo del 'eśkansyano dize ke por aver viśto ke avi'a śoltado byen 'a 'el 'eśkansyano konto 'el śuyo śiknifikando ke śino fu'era porke vido ke avi'a śoltado 'el primero byen pareśyendole muy śimil 'a 'el śuyo nunka lo kontara por pareserle ke no podi'a śiknifikar byen pu'eś la razon le mośtraba 'el kontrary'o por lo kual parese syerto śoltarloś Yosef [CW. por]}

⟨fol. 149a⟩
{KMT
por razon natural 'i syendo todoś doś kazi 'igualeś 'enla pena 'i 'en 'un meśmo lugar preśoś kela diferensy'a dela prizy'on de nota la diferensy'a del pekado 'o delito 'i śer 'el diğo pekado 'en 'un meśmo tyenpo 'i aśi 'el śu'enyo 'i pudyendośe aplikar la śinifikasy'on del 'uno 'enel 'otroś mośtro śu prudensy'a para mirar 'i konsidrar kada 'uno partikular mente por śuś kauśaś de lo kual fu'e loado depu'eś por 'el 'eśkansyano do diğo Par^{c}oh śe 'ensanyo śobre śuś syerboś 'i set-[42] śiknifikando la kondenasy'on 'i pena 'igual por la propy'a 'ira del rey ke 'eś la mu'erte aneğa a'elya 'i diğo maś 'i puzo ami 'en guarda de kaśa de mayoral de loś degolyadoreś ami 'i 'a mayoral de loś panaderoś 'i set-[43] denotando śer 'el delito 'igual pu'eś la karsel 'era 'una 'a loś doś 'i diğo maś 'i śonyamoś śu'enyo 'en 'una noğe 'i set-[44] śiknifikando śer todo 'en 'un tyenpo ke pudyera śer ke la diferensy'a de loś tyenpoś hizyera loś śu'enyoś diferenteś 'i diğo maś kada 'uno komo śoltura de śu śu'enyo śonyamoś 'i set-[45] śiknifikando ke vyeron la śoltura 'enel meśmo śu'enyo lo ke no śu'ele śer aśi ke

---

[42] Gen. 41.10.
[43] Gen. 41.10.
[44] Gen. 41.11.
[45] Gen. 41.11.

THE TREATISE ON DREAMS ‹FOL. 149A–149B›

'una kośa śu'ele śer 'el śu'enyo 'i 'otra la śoltura por śer ke la 'imağinasy'on traśpone la kośa 'en 'otra forma komo avemoś diğo komo maś largo śe deklarara maś al delante todoś 'eśtoś diğoś del 'eśkansyano 'a Parᶜoh por lo kual kual kyera śoltador śaka por 'una kośa 'otra 'i nunka dize ke 'el meśmo śu'enyo 'eś la ś[o]ltura komo 'eś aki ke 'el 'eśkansyano śonyaba ke teni'a 'el vazo de Parᶜoh 'en śu mano 'i aśi śe lo śolto 'i 'el 'otro ke śony'o ke la ave komi'a 'el manğar del seśto ke 'eśtaba 'enriba de śu kabesa le śolto ke aśi komeri'a la ave de la karne de śu kabesa 'i Yosef tubo 'eneśto la verdader'a konsidrasy'on 'en ğuśgar ke la 'imağinasy'on no tubyeśe tanta fu'ersa para traśponer 'el ğu'izy'o delyyoś 'en 'otra forma totalisima mente por 'eśtar 'en fu'erte kontenplasy'on 'en lo ke kada 'uno deśtoś ğuśgaba ke podi'a śer aserka de śuś negosy'oś komo kyen 'eśta preśo por kośa krimen komo 'elyoś 'eśtaban ke no 'entyende(n) 'en 'otro ke 'en śu śalvasy'on 'o kondenasy'on por laś viaś ke pu'ede suseder 'o 'uno 'o 'otro

LA śegunda kauśa 'i maś filosofika para śer loś śu'enyoś diğoś syertoś 'eś loke algunoś śaby'oś 'eśkrivyeron prinsipal mente Abisena[46] 'i depu'eś 'el 'Algazel 'en śu fizika[47] disy'on kinta śobre lo kual 'en miś notasy'oneś tengo byen alargado 'enśu lugar 'i la konkluzy'on delyyoś 'eś ke 'eśtando 'el anima deś'okupada del trabağo dela 'obra deloś śentidoś 'eśtiry'oreś rekonsentrandośe loś 'eśpritoś alaś parteś 'intiry'oreś komo avemoś diğo no sesando de 'entender 'enlaś 'eśpesyaś 'i formaś resebidaś por 'enteresisy'on deloś śentidoś tiradoś loś 'inpedimyentoś ke por parte delyoś le śon 'ośtakulo 'eś kauza de 'eśtar diśpu'eśta 'i a'uta para konligarśe 'i konğuntarśe konlaś 'entiliğensyaś śeparadaś[48] 'eśpesyal kon akelya 'entiliğensy'a [CW. ke]}

‹fol. 149b›
{ke 'elyoś dizen 'eśtar de bağo del konkabo dela 'eśfera dela luna[49] 'enla kual dizen 'eśtar laś formaś de todoś loś 'enteś ke 'eśtan deśde 'el diğo lugar hata 'el śentro de la

---

[46] Cf. Ibn Sina, "*Canon of Medicine*," trans. Gruner, 273–74 (no. 492). Cf. *Avicenna Latinus: Liber de Anima*, ed. G. Verbeke and S. van Riet (Leiden: Brill, 1972; repr. Louvain: Peeters); cf. also F. Rahmon, *Avicenna's Psychology* (Oxford, 1952), 68–68, 115–18.

[47] A reference to *Aṭ-Tabī'yyāt* (*Physic*) a section of one of Ibn Sina's major works, the *Shifā*. See Jules L. Janssens, *An Annotated Bibliography on Ibn Sina (1970–1989)* (Leuven: Leuven University Press, 1991), 3: 275–78; For the original text, see *Mu'allafāt Ibn Sina* (*Mahrajān Ibn Sina*), ed. G. C. Anawati (Cairo: Dār al-Ma'ārif, 1950).

[48] This may be a reference to Avicenna's *De Anima*. Cf. Thomas Aquinas, *Summa Theologiae*, I Pars, 9.89. On dreams, see also 9.iiia.3 with Aristotle references, and II.II, 9.95a.6.

[49] Almosnino's discussion illustrates the importance given to the lunary/sublunary boundary in medieval cosmology.

tyera 'i ke 'eśtan 'enla tal 'entiliğensy'a diğaś formaś 'en śumo grado de perfeksy'on 'i de 'elyya śon 'influ'idaś 'i 'eśte 'entendimyento dizen śer 'el ke 'obra 'enel nu'eśtro para śakarlo de potensy'a 'en a'uto komo maś larga mente 'elyyoś aklararon de manera ke determinaron 'i diğeron ke 'eśtando 'el anima konligada 'i konğunta konla diğa 'entiliğensy'a hazyendośe kon 'elyya 'una meśma kośa 'enel tyenpo de 'el dormir por 'el repozo 'i ky'etud del anima 'enel tal tyenpo por la pribasy'on deloś śentidoś ke 'eś kauśa de 'inpedirle 'enel tyenpo dela viğilyya todaś akelyaś formaś 'intelektualeś ke 'eśtan konklu'idaś 'en śumo grado de perfeksy'on 'en akelyya 'entiliğensy'a śeparada śe traśponen 'i treśpasan 'enel anima por 'eśforsarśe 'enel tal tyenpo la 'obra de 'el 'entendimyento śegun 'el grado de perfeksy'on del anima del śonyyador de maś 'a menoś

'I 'eś 'eśto 'enel anima 'enel tyenpo del dormir komo 'un 'eśpeğo ke ponyendolo 'enfrente de 'otro 'eśpeğo śe traśp(+)onen 'enel todaś laś figuraś ke 'enel 'otro śe mośtran komo 'eśkriby'o 'el a'utor dela preśpektiba[50] 'i śe mu'eśtra porla 'eśperensy'a ke muğaś veześ akaese kuando 'un 'ombre tyene 'una lyyaga 'enla kabesa 'o 'enla parte pośtiry'or del peśku'eso 'o 'en kual kyera 'otro lugar ke no pu'ede verlo 'en dereğo tomando doś 'eśpeğoś 'i ponyendo 'uno 'enfrente la tal lyyaga 'i 'el 'otro śegundo 'enfrente del primero 'en lugar ke 'el pu'eda ver laś figuraś ke 'enel śe mośtran vera 'enel diğo śegundo 'eśpeğo la figura del primero konla lyyaga dentro de 'el :

DEL meśmo modo akaese 'enlaś animaś de loś śaby'oś 'i virtu'ozoś dignoś por śu 'eśpikulasy'on verdader'a 'o bondad perfekta de śer konğuntoś 'i (k) konligadoś 'en śuś kontenplasy'oneś kon kual kyera de laś 'entiliğensyaś deśeparadaś mağima 'enel tyenpo del dormir kuando maś vigor tyene 'el 'entendimyento komo 'eś diğo hazyendośe 'una meśma kośa konel por parte de śu kontenplasy'on 'i 'eśpikulasy'on 'enel de manera ke todaś akelyyaś formaś 'intelektualeś verdaderaś ke 'eśtan 'enla tal 'entiliğensy'a komo 'en 'eśpeğo muy luśito 'i muy klaro śe traśponen 'enel anima de akel tal śonyyador ke 'eś 'eśtonseś tanbyen 'elyya 'en reśpekto de la diğa (') 'entiliğensy'a komo 'otro 'eśpeğo śegundo a[n]tepu'eśto 'a 'el primero komo avemoś diğo por 'eśtar 'eśtonseś deś'okupada del trabağo dela 'obra deloś śentidoś 'i set- a'un ke no komo klaro 'eśpeğo por laś konturbasy'oneś de la 'imağinasy'on ke no laś değa traśponer del meśmo modo ke laś alkansa 'i 'elyyaś 'eśtan 'enla 'entiliğensy'a 'onibersaleś deśeparadaś de matery'a śalvo komo la 'imağinasy'on laś traśpone deśpu'eś [CW. de]}

---

[50] Piero della Francesca, author of *De Prospectiva pingendi*? More likely it refers to a work by Al-Kindi, Ibn Hazm, or Roger Bacon. David Lindberg provides an exhaustive study of the *Perspectiva* tradition in his *Roger Bacon and the Origins of "Perspectiva" in the Middle Ages* (Oxford, 1996); cf. also his *Theories of Vision from Al-Kindi to Kepler* (Chicago, 1976).

The Treatise on Dreams ‹fol. 150a›

‹fol. 150a›
{KN
de alkansadaś 'en kośa partikular materyal konforme 'a loke 'el 'entendimyento determina por laś kauzaś 'i formaś 'intelektualeś 'oniberśaleś porke la partikularidad dela kośa vyene por parte dela materyya 'i la 'onibersalidad por la forma deśeparada komo 'eś śabido 'ensu lugar de manera ke komo la 'imağinasy'on no konprende la 'eśpesy'a dela kośa śalvo por la 'entresisy'on de loś śentidoś 'eśtiry'oreś ke la konprehenden por śuś dimensy'oneś komo avemoś diğo tyene la 'imağinasy'on 'enśi guardadaś laś 'eśpesyaś de laś kośaś konprendidaś aśi materyaleś komo laś konprendy'o aloś kualeś aplika laś formaś 'intelektualeś ke 'enel 'entendimyento 'eśtan traśpu'eśtaś 'enel dela 'entiliğensy'a śeparada komo de 'un 'eśpeğo 'en 'otro komo 'eś diğo 'i por 'eśto śe mu'eśtran 'enel śu'enyo 'en figuraś partikulareś materyaleś konformeś ala verdad del 'efekto ke 'entendy'o 'el 'entendimyento por laś formaś 'i kauśaś 'oniberśaleś ke śe 'inprimyeron 'enel anima dela 'entiliğensy'a ke 'el śaby'o 'i prudent[i]simo śoltador por laś diğaś figuraś kon razonable 'eśtimatiba śakara por 'elyyaś 'el 'efekto ke konforme a'el śe formaron 'enel anima :

'I deśte modo śe pu'ede śalvar kuanto tenemoś diğo 'enla primera kauśa 'i maś natural tanto 'enloś śu'enyoś de loś śaby'oś komo deloś h[e]dyotaś 'i 'ombreś legoś ke kon dereğa razon kauśada por la 'eśpery'ensy'a kontenplando rekta mente 'enlaś kauśaś de laś kośaś ke aka suseden śe konğuntan kon akel dador delaś formaś ke 'eśtoś śaby'oś kre'en 'eśtar de bağo del konkabo dela 'eśfera dela luna komo avemoś diğo 'i determinan 'el 'efekto ke no ayy deśta kauśa ala 'otra ninguna diferensy'a śalvo śer la 'eśpikulasy'on del 'entendimyento śolo porśi ğuśgando por laś kauśaś ke maś verdaderaś 'i klaraś ve'e 'i kontenpla 'enel tyenpo del dormir por laś kauśaś diğaś 'o śer por parte dela 'entiliğens[y]'a ke 'eś de fu'era de śi kontenplando 'enlaś kauśaś 'oniberśaleś ke śon por parte de laś formaś suśtansyaleś 'intelektualeś ke śe haze nu'eśtra anima 'enla tal kontenplasy'on 'una konla meśma 'entiliğensy'a 'enla kual 'eśtan laś diğaś formaś 'en śumo grado de perfeksy'on

DE manera ke kual kyera delaś doś kauśaś ke śe'a verdader'a 'eśta por 'elyya byen viśto por razon natural śer la śiknifikasy'on deloś śu'enyoś syertoś 'enlo futuro verdader'a konlo kual 'eśta ami ver śatiśfeğa la śegunda dubda ke vu'eśa mers[e]d dubdo

'I syendo la kauśa verdader'a la primera komo ami ver 'eś 'o 'eśta śegunda śegun 'opiny'on de algunoś śingularisimoś śenyoreś modernoś deśpozitoreś de nu'eśtra ley 'eśta byen viśta 'i anboś 'en doś ğeneroś de śu'enyoś śinpleś kon śuś 'eśpesyaś laś kauśaś de śer 'unoś syertoś 'i 'otroś 'insyertoś 'i la śiknifikasy'on de loś syertoś śer verdader'a [CW. 'i ğunto]}

THE TREATISE ON DREAMS ‹FOL. 150B›

‹fol. 150b›
{ 'I ǧunto konelyo 'eśta tanbyen viśta la kauśa de repreśentarśe 'enel śu'enyyo(v) formaś de muǧo tyenpo 'olvidadaś ke 'eś la tersera dubda ke vu'eśa mersed moby'o ke parese śer komo kuando 'el 'ombre 'eśta ansy'ozo 'i rebolve 'eśkrituraś antigaś ke tyene guardadaś 'ensu arka ke rep[a]sandolaś halya enelyaś kośaś de muǧo tyenpo 'olvidadaś

'I 'eś ke komo la fantazi'a ke 'a 'opiny'on de loś filosofoś 'eś d[i]śtinta dela 'imaǧinasy'on[51] ke la 'imaǧinasy'on 'eś komo aǧente 'i 'elya komo paśyente ke tyene diǧa fantazi'a guardadaś 'enśi 'i konservadaś todaś laś 'eśpesyaś resebidaś de loś śentidoś 'eśtiry'oreś por tanto 'a 'eśtaś 'eśpesyaś aplika de kontino la 'imaǧinasy'on laś formaś ' 'intelektualeś konponyendo 'una kon 'otra komo śu'clc :

KOMO 'enel śu'enyo 'eśta 'el anima maś deś'okupada de laś 'obraś 'eśtiry'oreś komo 'eś diǧo tyene maś lugar para 'entender 'i 'imaǧinar 'i 'entendyendo kozaś ke 'el di'a 'eśtando deśpyerto por śu 'okupasy'on n[o] śe pudo determinar determinaśe 'enel tyenpo del dormir por laś kauśaś śabidaś 'i preśupu'eśtaś del tyenpo dela viǧily'a 'i la 'imaǧinasy'on hazyendo śu 'obra de aplikar todaś laś kośaś 'en figuraś imaǧinatibaś va rebolbyendo 'i buśkando formaś konbenibleś alo ke 'el 'entendimyento determina d[e] todaś laś 'eśpesyaś ke 'eśtan guardadaś 'en la fantazi'a a'un ke śean de muǧo tyenpo 'olvidadaś ke la 'imaǧinasy'on 'obrando maś rezy'a mente 'enel tyenpo del śu'enyo ke 'enel dela viǧily'a 'i 'eśtando laś 'eśpesyaś todaś guardadaś 'enla fantazi'a toda 'eśpesyya ke alyi 'eśta guardada a'un ke śe'a de muǧo tyenpo 'olvidada śe reprezentara 'enla 'imaǧinasy'on para aplikar a'elyya loke 'el 'entendimyento determino 'i śi no 'ubyere determinasy'on del 'entendimyento por śu flakeza 'o por kual kyer 'otro 'inpedimyento tambyen śera lo meśmo ke la 'imaǧinasy'on komo aǧente 'i la fantazi'a komo paśyente 'eśtando 'enelyya guardadaś todaś 'eśpesyaś resebidaś de loś śentidoś 'obrando 'en 'elyyaś la 'imaǧinasy'on tan rezy'a mente komo 'eś 'enel śu'enyo komo 'eś diǧo śe repreśentan todoś 'en todo tyenpo faśil mente 'i la 'imaǧinasy'on konpone 'unaś kon 'otraś 'i heǧa la konpozisy'on 'imagi(m)- [n]a śer aśi 'en puro a'uto 'i 'eśto 'eś 'el śu'enyo ke 'eś la 'obra dela 'imaǧinasy'on komo avemoś diǧo 'i de 'eśto se podra byen tomar 'eśperensy'a de la viǧily'a ke muy muǧaś veześ deś'okupandośe 'el 'ombre 'i diśtrayendośe de la 'obra de loś śentidoś 'eśtiry'oreś 'okupandośe maś 'en akel 'iśtante 'en la 'obra de la 'imaǧinasy'on byen metido 'en 'elyya kon 'efikaś kontenplasy'on 'imaǧinara 'en kośaś 'olvidadaś de muǧo tyenpo 'i śe le repreśentaran 'en figuraś konpu'eśtaś 'i traśpu'eśtaś dela diǧa 'imaǧinasy'on 'en algun modo [CW. diferente]}

---

[51] Cf. Aristotle, *De Anima* I.i (403a 8–10), and III.iii (427b 14–17). Cf. also *Avicenna's Psychology*, trans. Rahman, 68–69 (on active and passive).

The Treatise on Dreams ‹fol. 151a›

‹fol. 151a›
{KN' HA-SUG HA-G HA-MIN HA-' [THE THIRD CLASS SPECIES ONE]
diferente deloke 'elyaś 'eran porke nunka la 'imağin(y)[a]sy'on 'imağina 'enla koza śinpleś mente komo 'elya 'eś śino 'eś kuando 'el 'ombre 'eśta deśpyerto 'i muy advertido 'enloke 'elya 'imağina 'i a'un 'eśtonseś no totalisima (m) mente porke śyenpre 'obra 'en akelyaś 'eśpesyaś konservadaś 'enla diğa fantazi'a konponyendo 'i '[e]ngiryendo 'una kośa 'en 'otra del meśmo modo 'eś 'enel tyenpo del dormir ke no difyeren śalvo de maś 'a menoś 'i 'eś ke 'enel tyenpo del dormir 'eśtando la alma deś'okupada totalisima mente dela 'obra 'eśtiry'or 'obra maś rezy'a mente la 'imağinasy'on komo 'eś diğo por lo kual ami ver 'eśta byen viśta la razon 'i aśolvida la tersera dubda ke vu'eśa mersed dubdo

'I p[y]enso konlo diğo śaśtifazer byen śegun razon natural 'en todaś laś śolturaś ke traen 'en nu'eśo Ṭalmud ke 'en akel tyenpo śe śoltaban ke parese no poder śer śalvo por 'influ'ensy'a devina ke todaś tyenen śu razon natural por laś reglaś pro-śupu'eśtaś ke por hu'ir la proliğidad değe de 'eśpisifikar ke konlo diğo 'en 'onibersal kual kyera dara fasil mente la razon 'en todo 'i al prezente baśta byen lo diğo para nu'eśtra 'intensy'on 'eneśte ğenero de (ś) śu'enyoś śinpleś syertoś 'i verdaderoś 'en-śuś śiknifikasy'oneś 'enlo futuro komo avemoś diğo 'i argu'ido 'en todaś śuś 'eśpesyaś :

'EL TERSERO GENERO 'eś loś śu'enyoś ke no śon śola mente śu'enyoś śinpleś śalvo kon 'eśpirasy'on 'o 'influ'ensy'a devina 'entre loś kualeś śe konkluyen tambyen loś śu'enyoś deloś profetaś ke 'el Dyyo mośtraba 'enelyyoś aloś taleś loke 'enel mundo avi'a de 'obrar por 'ebitar loś maleś de śu pu'eblo 'i śalvarloś de loś 'inkonvenyenteś :

'EL kual ğenero 'eś dividido 'en doś 'eśpesyaś diferenteś 'onibersaleś ke laś partikularidadeś de kada 'una de 'elyyaś śon muğaś pero porke no 'eś tanto de nu'eśo perpozito ke 'eśto 'eś 'otro tratado de porśi dire śola mente 'en 'onibersal lo ke śe rekyere para byen konprehender 'el grado de kada 'eśpesy'a delyyaś 'i tanbyen porke kon 'elyyo śe 'entendera muğa parte de loś śu'enyyoś ke Yosef śoltaba pu'eś śenti kerer 'enelyyoś 'o'ir vu'eśa mersed alguna bu'ena deklarasy'on :

LA primera 'eśpesy'a 'eś 'el śu'enyo ke ayy 'enel ke tal śu'enyya alguna 'eśpirasy'on devina 'influ'ida dela kauśa prima 'en akel 'endivido partikular śonyador a'un ke porśi no śe'a diśpu'eśto ni meresedor de resebir śimil 'influ'ensy'a 'o 'eśpirasy'on komo parese por laś palabraś del śenyor Rabbenu Mośeh 'en śu famozisimo libro 'enla parte śegunda del kapitulo kuarenta 'i 'uno[52] la kual 'eśpirasy'on 'eś mobida del Dyyo kon alguna 'intensy'on 'okulta anoś ke pu'ede śer ke 'el kyere traer 'en 'efekto por 'entresisy'on del tal śonyador algun kauśo partikular}

---

[52] Maimonides, *Guide,* trans. Pines, 385–88 (*MN,* Pt. 2, chap. 41).

THE TREATISE ON DREAMS ⟨FOL. 151B⟩

⟨fol. 151b⟩
{'a veześ śobre la 'onibersalidad de śu pu'eblo apropyado 'a 'el 'a veześ śobre algun perfekto śanto muy alyegado a'el ke tanbyen śe pu'ede dezir 'onibersal pu'eś 'eś konǧunto 'i konligado konel por parte deśu (') 'entendimyento 'i devina kontenplasy'on 'i 'eśta tal 'eśpesy'a de śu'enyo no 'eś śu'enyo de profesi'a ni tyene konel śimilitud ni konparasy'on ninguna ke 'eśte de kontino vyene meśklado kon 'otroś śu'enyoś śinpleś partikulareś ke śu'ele 'el tal śonyador śonyar por parte dela 'imaǧinasy'on pribado de la tal 'eśpirasy'on totaliśima mente 'i vyene akel śu'enyo devino 'influ'ido del Dyyo komo avemoś diǧo meśklado 'en akel śonyador kon śu'enyoś partikulareś apropyadoś ala 'imaǧinasy'on komo 'el śenpre śu'ele śonyar para ke śe'a 'ividente 'a todoś ke akel tal śonyador no 'era diśpu'eśto para 'el por śi śer meresedor de tal 'influ'ensy'a śi no śolo por śer aśi la voluntad del Dyyo por alguna kauśa 'okulta anoś ke venimoś 'a śaber depu'eś porel 'efekto ke laś maś de laś veześ vemoś śer por 'efektuar algun byen 'o tirar algun danyo 'o 'inkonvenyente de la 'onibersalidad de śu pu'eblo 'o de algun 'endivido alyegado a'el komo avemoś diǧo ke 'en alyegarśe a'el śe torna 'onibersal komo 'eś śabido 'i komo 'el śenyor Rabbenu Mośeh aklaro largo 'enel diǧo libro 'enla parte tersera kapitulo dizy'oǧo aserka dela probidensy'a devina 'en loś 'endividoś partikulareś śegun 'el grado de śu perfeksy'on 'i set-[53]

'I de 'eśta 'eśpesy'a fu'e 'el śu'enyo de 'Abimelek por 'onor de 'Abraham śu kerido del Dyyo 'i śanto patrya[r]ka nu'eśtro 'enel kual le fu'e narado por 'eśpirasy'on devina ke le tornaśe la muǧer do dize la 'eśkritura 'i diǧo a'el 'el Dyyo 'enel śu'enyo ta[n]byen yo śupe ke kon śinpleza de tu korason fiziśte 'eśto 'i vede tanbyen yo ati de pekar ami 'i set-[54] 'i agora torna la muǧer del varon 'i set-[55]

'I del meśmo modo fu'e 'el śu'enyo de Laban por 'onor 'i 'utilidad de Ya^cakob nu'eśo padre śanto do dize 'i vino 'el Dyyo 'a Laban 'el 'Arami 'en śu'enyo dela noǧe 'i diǧole guardate no hableś kon Ya^cakob 'i set-[56] ke anboś śon a'un meśmo modo

'I deśta meśma 'eśpesy'a fu'e 'el śu'enyo de Par^coh ke 'eś lo ke maś al prezente keremoś śaber 'el kual keryendo la probidensy'a devina 'efektuar medy'oś loś maś alyegadoś 'a razon natural ke posible 'eś 'i modoś 'i maneraś laś maś konvenibleś keśe rekyeren para arodear ke loś hiǧoś de Yiśra'el (d) desendyeśen 'a Aǧibto viśto por la meśma probidensy'a devina ke akel 'era 'el meǧor medy'o 'i maś konvenible para 'elyyoś alkansar 'el śumo grado de perfeksy'on para ke 'ividente mente

---

[53] Maimonides, *Guide,* trans. Pines, 474–77 (*MN,* Pt. 3, chap. 18).
[54] Gen. 20.6.
[55] Gen. 20.7.
[56] Gen. 31.24.

The Treatise on Dreams ⟨fol. 151b–152a⟩

konosyeśen śu 'infinito poder 'enloś milagreś ke alyi avi'a de hazer por loś kualeś fu'eśen diśpu'eśtoś 'i a'utoś para resebir la ley 'i konoser śu poder 'infinito komo 'eśto todo maś larga mente 'ensu lugar t(y)engo byen aklarado [CW. tenyendo]}

⟨fol. 152a⟩
{KNB
TENYENDO por mağima verdader'a aberiguada 'i koroborada por 'el śenyor Rabbenu Mošeh 'en muğaś 'i diversaś parteś de śuś tratadoś ke loś milagreś noloś haze 'el Dyyo ni kyere hazerloś śino 'eś kuando por 'otra ninguna vi'a śe pu'ede 'efektuar la 'intensy'on ke 'en fazerloś tyene 'el Dyyo glory'ozo ke no kyere agrabyar la naturaleza śi no fu'ere kuando por 'otra vi'a natural no śe pu'ede śegir 'el tal 'efekto komo 'enel reğimyento de la vida aserka deśto alargamoś

KON 'eśto 'eś viśto byen ke syendo viśto porśu sensy'a 'infinita ke para 'eśto 'efektuar natural mente śin nesesidad de milagre 'era meneśter śer 'eśta 'eśpirasy'on 'en Par'oh a'un ke 'el porśi no lo meresyeśe ni fu'eśe diśpu'eśto para 'elyo ke śi 'a 'otro 'eśte śu'enyo śe mośtrara no dyera 'el kredito para moberśe por 'el 'o poner la 'orden ke puzo i 'enlaś kozaś ke śe rekerian para 'elyo kiğo ke 'el propy'o lo śon[y]aśe a'un ke no fu'eśe meresedor porśi delyo śolo para ke 'el meśmo lo śintyeśe 'i le fu'eśe berifikado todo para poner la 'orden 'enloś medy'oś ke śe rekerian para 'efektuar la 'intensy'on del Dyyo glory'ozo a'un ke 'el porśi no fu'eśe de tal 'eśpirasy'on meresedor komo avemoś diğo

POR lo kual 'eneśtoś taleś śu'enyoś śe halyyan doś kośaś ke por la primera delyaś śe mu'eśtra no śer 'eśtoś taleś śu'enyoś śinpleś komo loś deloś ğeneroś pasadoś 'i por la śegunda śe mu'eśtra no śer komo loś śu'enyoś de profesi'a ke śon loś dela śegunda 'eśpesy'a deśte ğenero ke adelante deklararemoś

LA primera 'eś ke 'eśte śu'enyo ke avemoś diğo ke vyene por 'eśpirasy'on devina no śe reprezenta ni śe aparese 'a 'el ke tal śu'enya 'el 'efekto traśpu'eśto 'en figuraś (') imağinatibaś komo śu'ele śer 'o komo avemoś diğo ke 'eś 'en todaś laś 'eśpesyaś 'eśpiśifikadaś 'enloś doś ğeneroś pasadoś śalvo la propy'a kośa ke 'el Dyo kyere 'efektuar 'eś reprezentada al tal śonyador para amośtrar 'i berifikar ke no vyene por parte del śonyador komo śu'elen śer loś śu'enyoś śinpleś naturaleś ke avemoś diğo śalvo por parte del Dyyo ke le 'influye akelyya 'eśpirasy'on ke no ayy 'enelya miśtura ninguna de figura 'imağinatiba śalvo todo puro 'entendimyento 'en puro a'uto

POR tanto halyyamoś 'en 'Abimelek ke dize la 'eśkritura ke le diğo 'el Dyyo klaro 'enel śu'enyo bu'elve la muğer del varon 'i set-[57] ke 'eś la meśma kośa ke 'el Dyyo keri'a ke h[i]zyeśe 'en 'efekto 'i del meśmo modo 'enel śu'enyo de Laban diğo guar-

---

[57] Gen. 20.7.

The Treatise on Dreams ‹fol. 152a–152b›

date no fableś kon Ya^cakob 'i set-[58]
'I del meśmo modo 'eś 'en Par^coh ke le moś́tro la hartura 'i la hambre 'en mośtrarle laś vakaś 'i laś 'eśpigaś lyenaś 'i flakaś[59] ke 'era dezirlo klaro ke 'el arar ke 'eś 'el tyenpo del śenbrar 'el kual śe haze kon la fu'ersa de laś vakaś 'i loś bu'eyś 'i 'el koǧer ke 'eś kuando 'eśta [CW. 'el]}

‹fol. 152b›
{'el trigo 'en 'eśpiga śeri'a 'el 'uno prośpero 'i 'el 'otro adverśo komo fu'[e]
'I kon 'eśto śera avśolvida 'una gran dubda 'i 'eś komo pu'ede śer ke tantoś śaby'oś 'i śoltadoreś de śu'enyoś ke teni'a Par^coh śegun kyeren nu'eśoś śaby'oś no kaian 'enla śiknifikasy'on verdader'a[60] syendo tan klara komo 'eśtaba śu demośtrasy'on[61] 'i andaban buśkando 'otraś śolturaś muy leǧoś de la 'intensy'on ke śiknifikaban ke śegun kyeren nu'eśoś śaby'oś le dezian ke śiknifikaban ke avi'a de 'enǧendrar syete hiǧaś 'i 'otraś tantaś 'enterar 'i venser syete probinsyaś 'i set-[62] ke tenyendo 'enla mano la śiknifikasy'on verdader'a propinka 'ivan buśkando kośaś muy leǧoś 'i 'eśtranyaś dela śiknifikasy'on verdader'a 'i figura del śu'enyo :

PERO konloke tenemoś diǧo 'eśta byen viśta la razon ke komo akelyoś śoltadoreś śoltaban śegun razon natural pareśyendoleś śer śu'eny'o śinple komo śoli'a śenpre śer 'enel 'i 'enelyoś śabyendo ke la 'imaǧinasy'on traśpone la determinasy'on del 'entendimyento 'en figuraś ' imaǧinatibaś 'i ke nunka śe mu'eśtra la meśma kośa ke 'a de śer 'en 'efekto del meśmo modo ke 'a de śer śalvo traśpu'eśta 'en 'otra forma por 'entresisy'on dela 'imaǧinasy'on komo 'eś diǧo a'eśta kauśa 'iban buśkando 'otraś 'entrepetasy'oneś 'i śiknifikasy'oneś de loke 'era la propy'a figura ke śe repreśentaba 'enel śu'enyo por lo kual no kedaba Par^coh śatiśfeǧo kon śuś śolturaś pareśyendole a'el 'eseder 'eśte śu śu'enyo de todoś loś 'otroś ke 'el śoli'a śonyar 'enla 'orden del 'i 'ensu modo 'i ver ke 'elyyoś no śintyendo 'eśta diferensy'a lo śoltaban porla vi'a (') akośtumbrada a'elyoś 'enloś śu'enyoś śinpleś por lo kual andaba vasilando deśeando śaber kyen le śoltaśe diferente mente de loke loś śu'enyoś śinpleś śe śu'elen śoltar :

'I kon 'eśto 'eśta byen viśto ke 'eś la kauśa ke 'el mayoral deloś 'eśkansyanoś śe le akordo de Yosef al kabo de tantaś śolturaś 'i no al prinsipy'o deśde ke 'enpeso Par^coh 'a kontar śu śu'enyo ke de razon la primera veś ke ve'e 'el 'ombre la kośa ke

---

[58] Gen. 31.24.
[59] Gen. 41.17–23.
[60] Gen. 41.24.
[61] Cf. *infra* 153a.
[62] Gen. R. 89.6, Rashi Gen. 41.8.

THE TREATISE ON DREAMS ‹FOL. 152B–153A›

'eś kauśa de akordarśe de 'otra śimil a'elyya śe aku'erda de 'elyya maś ke depu'eś de algun tyenpo ke la ayya viśto por ke la primera veś ke la 'oye 'o ve'e komo maś śe 'okupa 'i śe diśpone 'a atentar 'enelyya 'eś kauśa demaś traer ala memory'a la 'otra śimil a'elyya ke 'el muǧo atentar 'i 'eśpekular 'en la kośa kauśa traer ala memory'a 'otra śimil a'elyya :

'I MAŚ 'eś de dubdar ke ya ke śe le akordo 'en kual kyera tyenpo ke fu'era komo la 'enmento delante Par^coh syendo 'en perǧu'izy'o śuyo ke 'era kauśa de traer ala memory'a śuś delitoś komo 'el diǧo pudyendośe 'eśkuzar de 'elyyo pu'eś nadi lo śabi'a 'i śin perǧudikar 'enel śervisy'o 'i fidelidad ke devi'a 'a 'el rey pu'eś teni'a tantoś soltadoreś tan śaby'oś ke le śoltaban muǧaś śolturaś ke śegun regla de śoltar śu'enyoś [CW. paresian]}

‹fol. 153a›
{KNG
paresi[a]n śer verdaderaś 'i konformeś 'a razon natural komo avemoś diǧo pu'eś 'el no śabi'a ke akelyaś śolturaś no 'eran verdaderaś pu'eś 'eran 'enlo futuro por donde parese syerto ke de razon no lo 'ubyera de 'enmentar por śolo aver dado la palabra pu'eś 'era tanto 'en perǧu'i[z]y'o śuyo 'eśpesyal no tenyendo 'el por syerto ke 'ubyeśe de śer verdadero 'enla śoltura ke śoltaśe 'a Par^coh komo fu'e 'enla śuya 'i de mayoral deloś panaderoś ke ya pudyera śer ke 'el śu'enyo ke 'elyoś śonyaron lo śoltaran tanbyen komo 'el kual kyera de loś śoltadoreś de Par^coh ke 'eśtaban śuś śiknifikasy'oneś muy klaraś lo kual 'el śu'enyo de Par^coh por śer śu śiknifikasy'on muy 'eśkura⁶³ no śe alkansaba aśi fasil mente ni Yosef la pudyera alkansar pu'eś 'elyoś todoś kon toda śu śensy'a no la alkansaban por lo kual podi'a śer ke no śolo perǧudikaśe aśi śi no a'un tanbyen 'a Yosef ke no dizyendo kośa ke śaśtifizyeśe 'a Par^coh kedaba deśgrasyado para ke nunka maś śalyeśe dela karsel ke Yosef no le rogo śalvo ke lo memoryaśe 'a Par^coh komo rey ǧuśtisy'ero kon dezirle komo 'era pu'eśto alyi śin razon 'i śin ǧuśtisy'a pero no ke le diǧeśe ke 'era śoltador de śu'enyoś :

PERO kon loke 'eśta diǧo me parese śaśtifazer todaś laś dubdaś 'i 'eś ke konosyendo 'el diǧo mayoral de loś 'eśkansyanoś ke de kontino 'eśtaba repreśentado delante Par^coh ke ninguna de kuantaś śolturaś śoltaban le śaśtifazian komo dize la 'eśkritura 'i non śoltan a'elyoś 'a Par^coh 'i set-⁶⁴ 'i deklaran [nu'eśoś] śaby'oś ke kyere dezir ke śoltadoreś 'i śolturaś muǧaś avi'a pero ninguna śaśtifazi'a 'a Par^coh 'i set-⁶⁵

---

⁶³ Cf. *supra* 152b.
⁶⁴ Gen. 41.8.
⁶⁵ Gen. R. 89.6.

The Treatise on Dreams ‹fol. 153a–153b›

'I konosy'o 'i śinty'o 'en Par^coh komo maś familyar śuyo ke la kauśa porke no le kuadraban ni śastifazian akelyaś śolturaś 'era porke akel śu'enyo śuyo ve'i'a śer diferente de todoś loś ke 'el śoli'a śonyar 'i ke śenti'a 'enśi śer kośa 'influ'ida de fu'era pu'eś 'otro komo akel tan reglado 'i 'ordenado nunka śonyo 'eśpesyal syendo aśegundado 'enla meśma noğe ke śon todaś śenyaleś de śer verdadero komo avemoś diğo 'i komo śuś śu'enyoś todoś 'eran varyableś por lo kual nunka venian regladoś ni konlaś śenyaleś ke por 'elyaś śe mu'eśtran śer verdaderoś paresyendole 'eśte tan diferente 'en todo deloś 'otroś ğuśgaba ke no śe debi'a śoltar al modo deloś 'otroś ke la diferensy'a de loś śu'enyoś 'obliga a[v]er 'eśpesyaś diferenteś de śolturaś por lo kual no kre'i'a ke 'eśte śu śu'eny'o śe avi'a de śoltar por la regla ke loś 'otroś śinpleś komun mente śe śu'elen śoltar preśuponyendo śer figuraś traśpu'eśtaś por la 'imağinasy'on :

'I śintyendo 'el 'eśkansyano todo 'eśto 'en Par^coh paresyendole ke lok[e] 'el 'i 'el mayoral deloś panaderoś śonyyaron 'i Yosef leś śolto no 'era śegun la regla natural ke śe tyene 'en komun por tanto śe akordo 'eśtonśeś de Yosef ke 'era loke śinty'o por pośtre ke Par^coh keri'a [CW. 'i]}

‹fol. 153b›
{'i a'un ke 'era algo 'ensu perğu'izy'o paresyendole ke maś perğudikaba 'enel serv[i]sy'o del re'ey śilo değaba de dezir pu'eś ve'i'a kuanto k(y)[o]nforme 'era a( )loke 'el buśkaba lo diğo 'i maś porke ve'i'a tanbyen kuanto kon 'eśto śe śegiri'a byen 'a Yosef avyendo dado tan 'eśtreğa mente la palabra de akordarśe del 'ensu probeğo tenyendo por s[y]erto śaśtifazerle 'el maś ke 'otro ninguno por loke śenti'a 'enla 'intensy'on de Par^coh :

'I por 'eśta kauśa relato delante del todo lo paśado para darle 'a 'entender komo la śoltura ke Yosef leś avi'a śoltado no 'era por ra[z]on ni regla natural komo śe śu'elen śoltar todoś loś śu'enyoś śinpleś komo avemoś diğo por lo kual teni'a 'i kre'i'a syerto ke 'el śatiśfari'a a'el re'ey maś ke ninguno de kuantoś le avi'a śoltado pu'eś śenti'a del ke ninguno delyoś le śatiśfazi'a por śoltarloś por laś reglaś komuneś 'en loś śu'enyoś śinpleś komo diğimoś :

POR lo kual konfesando śu yero komenso 'a dar muğaś razoneś 'i muy śofiśyenteś por laś kualeś paresi'a śer la śoltura ke Yosef śoltaba kontra toda regla komo ke 'en todoś śoltadoreś 'en 'onibersal śe halyya

'I śiknifikando la primera diğo Par^coh śe 'ensany'o śobre śuś 'eśklaboś 'i set-[66] ke ami ver kiğo dezir ke n[o] śe 'ensany'o śobre 'elyoś doś tan śola mente para ke pudyeśe ğuśgar fasil mente por 'el yero 'o delito de kada 'uno delyoś 'o por la

---

[66] Gen. 41.10.

The Treatise on Dreams ⟨fol. 153b–154a⟩

diferensy'a de śuś kalidadeś lo ke podi'a de razon suseder 'a kada 'uno śalvo ke fu'e 'un di'a de furya 'onibersal de 'el rey ke śe 'ensanyo śobre todoś śuś 'eśklaboś komo ke diğeśe ke a'un ke fu'e la śanya 'onibersal mente śobre todoś no mando prender ni poner 'en guarda 'a maś ke a'el 'i a'el mayoral de loś panaderoś ke kual kyera ğuśgari'a por dereğa razon śegun 'eśto ke no śe mandaron poner 'elyoś 'en la karsel maś ke todoś loś 'otroś syendo la fury'a kontra todoś śino fu'eśe kon muğa razon byen 'eśaminada 'i kondenadoś anboś 'a doś 'a grabe pena 'igual mente pu'eś 'elyoś śoloś 'entre todoś fu'eron 'igual mente preśoś 'i 'eśto kiğo dezir 'en dezir Par^coh śe 'ensany'o śobre śuś 'eśklaboś 'i puzo ami 'en guardy'a 'i set-[67] ami 'i 'a mayoral de loś panaderoś 'i set-[68] komo ke diğera ke akelyyo mośtraba śer 'el pekado 'igual por lo kual kual kyera ğuśgara por razon natural ke la pena avi'a de śer tambyen 'igual

'I apunto maś śegunda razon 'en dezir ke la karsel 'era 'en kaza de mayoral de loś degolyadoreś 'i set-[69] śiknifikando maś la 'igualdad del pekado 'i de la kondenasy'on 'en loś doś de 'un meśmo modo pu'eś fu'eron preśoś 'en 'un meśmo lugar donde śe pone por kośa krimen ke la diferensy'a de la karsel denota la diferensy'a del delito 'i la kondenasy'on ke no todaś laś karseleś śon 'igualeś komo śe ve'e al preś[e]nte 'en todoś lo[ś] reynoś 'i lugareś : [CW. 'i diğo]}

⟨fol. 154a⟩
{KND
'I diğo maś tersera razon 'en dezir ke fu'e 'el śu'enyo ke śonyaron 'en 'una meśma noğe ke por la diferensy'a del tyenpo en ke śe śu'enya 'el śu'enyo pu'ede śer ke kauśe diferensy'a grande 'en la śoltura komo tenemoś diğo ke a'un 'en 'un meśmo 'ombre śonyando 'una meśma kośa 'en tyenpoś diferenteś terna diferenteś śiknifikasy'oneś

'I diğo 'otra kuarta razon 'i maś prinsipal por la kual maś le paresi'a konvenible para śoltar 'el śu'enyo de Par^coh por lo ke de 'el śenti'a komo avemoś diğo la kual 'eś ke Yosef no avi'a śoltado 'el śu'enyo porla regla komun ke śe śu'elen śoltar komo ke 'ubyeśe śoltura alyende del meśmo śu'enyo maś anteś determino 'i ğuśgo ke 'el propy'o śu'enyo 'era la meśma śoltura kontra lo ke akaese 'en todoś loś ś(')oltadoreś ke ğuśgan śiknifikar 'otra kośa de lo ke 'eś 'el meśmo śu'enyo 'i 'eśto diğo por aver viśto ke por 'eśto no śaśtifazian 'a Par^coh śuś śoltadoreś por śoltarśelo 'en 'otra kośa de lo ke 'era 'el meśmo śu'enyo por lo kual le paresi'a ke Yosef 'era 'el ke maś le

---

[67] Gen. 41.10.
[68] Gen. 41.10.
[69] Gen. 41.10.

The Treatise on Dreams ‹fol. 154a–154b›

podi'a śaśtifazer por 'eśta parte ke 'enel avi'a viśto 'en śuś śu'enyoś lo kual kiğo śentir 'en dezir kada 'uno komo śoltura de śu śu'enyo śonyamoś 'i se[t]-[70] 'i depu'eś kontando la śoltura ke Yosef leś śolto torna 'a dezir kada 'uno komo śu śu'enyo śolto 'i set-[71] keno debyera mudar 'i 'ubyera de dezir kada 'uno komo śoltura de śu śu'enyo śolto 'i set-[72] komo diğo al kontar 'el propy'o śu'enyo pero kiğo śiknifikar lo ke tenemoś diğo ke 'eś komo ke diğeśe ke śobre aver śonyado śu'enyoś ke 'a viśta 'i ğu'izy'o de kual kyer śoltador demośtraba śiknifikar 'otra kośa de lo ke 'era 'el meśmo śu'enyo komo śon komun mente todoś loś śu'enyoś 'i kon todo 'eśto no lo śolto śalvo komo 'el propy'o śu'enyo 'i no komo śoltura ke 'eś alyende del śu'enyo 'i por 'eśto diğeron al kontar 'el śu'enyo ke śegun śe vido depu'eś por la śoltura ke Yosef śolto kada 'uno śonyo la śoltura 'enel meśmo śu'enyo i no 'otra kośa ke śiknifikaśe la śoltura śalvo komo 'era la śoltura aśi śonyaron propy'a mente 'i 'eśto kiğo śentir 'en dezir kada 'uno komo śoltura deśu śu'enyo śonyamoś[73] konbyene śaber kada 'uno fu'e śu śu'enyo la meśma śoltura 'i al kontar la śoltura diğeron ke akada 'uno komo 'el propy'o śu'enyo śolto 'i set- porke ya teni'a prośupu'eśto ke 'el propy'o śu'enyo fu'e la meśma śoltura 'i por 'eśto diğo kada 'uno komo śu śu'enyo śolto 'i set-[74] 'i kiğo dezir 'en todo 'eśto ke syendo aśi kual kyera śoltador yerari'a fasil mente 'en la śoltura 'i śiknifikasy'on de lo ke 'eś 'el meśmo śu'enyo por śer ke la 'imağinasy'on traśpone la śiknifikasy'on de la verdad 'en 'otraś figuraś de lo ke 'a de śer 'el meśmo 'efekto 'i Yosef kon todo 'eśto leś śolto komo 'el meśmo śu'enyo 'i no komo śoltar śolturaś śalvo komo śoltar 'el meśmo śu'enyo konbyene śaber ke ğuśgo śer la śoltura 'el meśmo śu'enyo 'ino 'otra kośa śiknifikada 'enel komo 'eś śolito por lo [CW. kual]}

‹fol. 154b›
{kual le paresi'a ke 'eśte por 'eśta razon maś ke por todaś laś 'otraś konveni'a para śoltar 'el śu'eny'o de Parᶜoh maś ke todoś loś 'otroś śoltadoreś

'I kon 'eśto ku'enta la 'eśkritura ke śupito ke 'oyo 'el rey 'eśtaś palabraś syendo laś razoneś tan sofisyenteś 'i tanto konformeś aśu 'intensy'on 'i voluntad mando śin maś dilasy'on lyamar 'a Yosef

'EL kual traido ke fu'e tenyendo konosido de Parᶜoh no śer meresedor por śi 'a

---

[70] Gen. 41.11.
[71] Gen. 41.12.
[72] This seems to be a conflation of Gen. 41.11 and 41.12.
[73] Gen. 41.11.
[74] Gen. 41.12.

THE TREATISE ON DREAMS ‹FOL. 154B›

ke 'en 'el śe 'influyeśe tal 'eśpirasy'on devina 'i śabyendo por muy perfekta 'eśpikulasy'on 'en laś partikularidadeś del śu'enyo śer por 'eśpirasy'on devina 'i no śer śu'enyo śinple pu'eś tantaś śerkonśtansyaś ke para śer verdadero śe rekyeren teni'a śe determino śer 'influ'ido de la kauśa prima por algun 'efekto 'onibersal por lo kual 'era forsado śer la śiknifikasy'on 'el meśmo śu'enyo komo avemoś diğo 'i por 'eśto diğo kon ğu'izy'o devino lo ke 'el Dyyo kyere hazer denusy'o 'a Par^coh 'i set-[75] donde śiknifiko toda la suśtansy'a de kuanto tenemoś diğo kon loke adelante deklaro maś do diğo 'elya la kośa ke hable 'a Par^coh todo lo ke 'el Dyyo haze mośtro 'a Par^coh 'i set-[76] śiknifikando ke lo meśmo ke 'el Dyyo keri'a hazer 'i 'efektuar mośtro 'a Par^coh 'i no por 'enteresisy'on de figuraś traśpu'eśtaś de 'una kośa 'en 'otra komo 'eś śolito de hazer la 'imağinasy'on 'enel śu'enyo

'I d[i]ğo primero 'en 'onibersal denusy'o 'i depu'eś mośtro śiknifikando ke no śolo fu'e la 'intensy'on del Dyyo mośtrarle 'eśto ke avi'a de śer śalvo dezirśelo 'i denusyarselo para ke 'el puzyeśe la 'orden ke śe rekeri'a para 'el remedy'o de la hambre ke avi'a de suseder

'I kiğo maś śiknifikar ke lo ke 'enel prinsipy'o le avi'a diğo ke lo ke 'el Dyyo hazi'a denusy'o 'a Par^coh[77] 'eśtaba 'enelyo konklu'ido ke lo ke hazi'a mośtro 'i no por figuraś por ke laś kośaś ke 'el Dyyo dize 'a śimileś ke 'el no laś mu'eśtra por figuraś komo avemoś diğo 'i por 'eśto diğo 'eśta la kośa ke hable 'a Par^coh 'i set-[78] ke 'en 'onibersal kiğo śiknifikar nu'eśa porpozisy'on śer verdader'a ke no le vino la tal 'eśpiraśy'on por śu diśpozisy'on ke no 'era digno ni diśpu'eśto porśi para 'elya śino śolo porla voluntad del Dyyo glory'ozo porel 'efekto ke de 'elyo śe avi'a de śegir komo 'eśta diğo :

'I 'eśto pu'ede śer ke kiğo tanbyen śiknifikar 'en dezir lo ke 'el Dyyo haze mośtro 'i set-[79] śiknifikando ke por voluntad del Dyyo tan śola men(m)[t]e le fu'e a'el narado 'i mośtrado komo ke diğeśe śolo por śu kerer śin 'el śer meresedor delyyo śelo denusy'o 'i set-

'I kon 'eśto śe śaśtifaze tanbyen 'una gran dubda antiga ke dubdaron muğoś buśkando razon komo śe aparese 'el Dyyo aloś maloś śemeğanteś 'a Par^coh śin tener diśpozisy'on ni meresimyento para śer 'influ'idoś de śemeğante 'eśpirasy'on lo kual

---

[75] Gen. 41.25.

[76] It is noteworthy that Gen. 41.28 does not mention the qualifier "all", the fulcrum for Almosnino's subsequent interpretation (nor does 41.25).

[77] Gen. 41.25.

[78] Gen. 41.28.

[79] Gen. 41.28.

The Treatise on Dreams ‹fol. 154b–155a›

'eśta byen viśto ke por aver nesesidad de śalvar 'un pu'eblo 'o 'un 'endivido tan perfekto ke śe'a meresedor delyo lo konsyente 'i aśi lo 'ordena [CW. la]}

‹fol. 155a›
{KNH
la probidensy'a devina por śer 'el tal śonyador 'el medy'o maś konvenible para ke por śu 'enteresisy'on venga la 'intensy'on śuya 'en 'efekto komo avemoś diǧo

LA śegunda kośa ke śe halyya 'eneśta 'eśpesy'a de śu'enyoś ke ayy 'en 'elyyoś 'eśpirasy'on devina 'eś ke vyenen śenpre meśkladoś kon 'otroś śu'enyoś partikulareś varyableś 'i 'insyertoś del primer ǧenero antepu'eśtoś kauśadoś de la 'imaǧinasy'on śinpleś mente 'en [l]o kual śe mu'eśtra śer muy diferente de loś ś[u]'[e]nyoś de profesi'a ke śon loś de la 'eśpesy'a ke deśpu'eś deśta śe śegira 'en 'eśte meśmo ǧenero ke 'en taleś śu'enyoś de profesi'a no śe meśkla 'en 'elyyoś ningun 'otro śu'en[y]o partikular fu'era de lo ke 'eś 'influ'ido del Dyyo 'en akel kazo ke 'el le kyere mośtrar 'enel 'i śiknifikando 'eśto fu'e diǧo 'enel śu'enyo de 'Abimelek 'i diǧo 'el Dyyo a'el 'enel śu'enyo 'i set-[80] ke no 'era meneśter dezir ke lo ke 'el Dyyo le diǧo 'era 'enel śu'enyo ke ya 'eś śabido no śer de 'otro modo kuando 'el Dyyo habla aloś taleś ke no śeleś aparese vizible mente ke 'en 'otroś lugareś muǧoś 'eśta diǧo loke 'el Dyyo dize śin kontar ke fu'e 'en śu'enyo syendo aśi komo 'eś śabido pero fu'e aki la 'intensy'on 'en dezir 'en śu'enyo komo ke diǧeśe ke lo ke 'el Dyyo le diǧo fu'e meśklado a'el 'entre śuś śu'enyoś partikulareś :

'I MAŚ deklarado 'eśta 'enel śu'enyo de Laban ke dize 'i vino 'el Dyyo 'a Laban 'el 'Arami 'en śu'enyo dela noǧe 'i set-[81] ke 'el berbo de la noǧe parese 'eśtar totalisima mente śuperflu'o śino ke 'eś syerto komo ke diǧeśe ke 'entre 'el śu'enyo śolito dela noǧe vino 'el Dyyo a'el 'i set- :

'I muǧ[o] maś viśto 'eśta 'eśto 'en 'el śu'enyo de Par^coh ke 'en todoś loś 'otroś 'en dezir 'i Par^coh śonyan 'i hek 'eśtan śobre 'el ri'o 'i set-[82] ke parese syerto demazyado 'i śin nesesidad de averśe de dezir ke baśtara byen dezir 'i fu'e de fin de doś anyoś Par^coh śonyaba[83] ke de 'el ri'o śubian syete vakaś 'i set-[84] 'i no 'eran meneśter maś preanbuloś por lo kual pyenso ke śe'a la 'intensy'on lo ke tenemoś diǧo ke noś da la ley 'a 'entender ke Par^coh 'eśtando śonyando ś[u] śu'enyo akośtumbrado ke 'era

---

[80] Gen. 20.6.
[81] Gen. 31.24.
[82] Gen. 41.17.
[83] Gen. 41.1.
[84] Gen. 41.2.

The Treatise on Dreams ‹fol. 155a–155b›

śonyar ke 'eśtaba śobre 'el ri'o 'el kual 'era de la śegunda 'eśpesy'a del primer ǧenero antepu'eśto ke veni'a por parte de 'el kontinu'o pensamyento ke pensaba śer 'el ri'o śu Dyyo śegun kyeren nu'eśoś śaby'oś ke 'enel adoraba[85] 'i pyenśo 'eśtar 'eśto śiknifikado 'en dezir 'i Par^c oh śonyan 'i no dezir 'i Par^c oh śonyaba śiknifikando ke 'era śonyan śu śu'enyo śegun a'el 'era śolito ke śi diǧera '[i] Par^c oh śonyaba no śe 'entendyera maś ke dezirnoś ke 'en akelyya sazon śonyaba 'el śu'[e]nyo śigyente :
  'I depu'eś ke prośupone śu śu'enyo akośtumbrado ke 'era śonyar ke 'eśtaba śobre 'el ri'o ku'enta 'el śu'enyo ke konel śuyo śinple śe meśklaba kon akelyya 'eśpirasy'on devina ke avemoś diǧo do dize 'i hek de 'el ri'o śubian syete vakaś 'i set-[86] ke fu'e mośtrarle lo m[i]śmo ke avi'a de suseder 'i lo ke ve'i'a ke laś vakaś magraś 'englutian alaś gru'esaś 'i}

‹fol. 155b›
{no śe konosi'a ke 'entraba 'enśuś 'entranyaś 'i set-[87] 'era ke la hambre ke avi'a de suseder la kual śiknifikaban laś magraś avian de śer kauśa ke no śe śintyeśe la hartura la kual śiknifikaban laś gru'esaś 'i 'era ke guardando la sibera 'enel tyenpo de la hartura para 'el tyenpo dela hambre 'eś 'englutir la hambre 'a la hartura 'i no śentirse la diǧa hartura por 'eśkuzar la probizy'on para 'el mal tyenpo ke 'eś lo propy'o del śu'enyo komo avemoś diǧo 'i '[e]śto deklaro maś 'en dezir 'i no śera konosida la hartura 'enla tyera delante la hambre 'i set-[88] :
  'I kon 'eśto śe śaśtifaze 'otra dubda grande ami ver 'en la śoltura ke Yosef śolto ke parese deśmandarśe maś de la razon 'i 'eseder 'el limite de la kortezi'a 'en dezir 'i agora ve'a Par^c oh varon 'entendido 'i śaby'o 'i pongalo śobre tyera de Aǧibto 'i set-[89] 'i dize maś adelante haga Par^c oh 'i 'enkomende 'enkomendadoreś 'i set- 'i akinte'en 'i set-[90] ke todo 'eśto parese maś kerer dar konśeǧo ke 'otra kośa lo kual parese ke le fu'era byen 'eśkuzado pu'eś a'el no lo avian lyamado para tomar kon 'el konśeǧo śi no śolo para śoltar 'el śu'enyo por lo kual debyera hazer lo ke le tokaba hazer komo śoltador 'i no maś
  PERO kon lo ke tenemoś diǧo 'eśta byen viśto ke todo 'eśto ke dezi'a no 'era konśeǧo deśtinto de la śoltura śalvo de la meśma śoltura ke 'en mośtrarle 'enel

---

[85] Gen. R. 89.4.
[86] Gen. 41.2.
[87] Gen. 41.20–21.
[88] Gen. 41.31.
[89] Gen. 41.33.
[90] Gen. 41.34.

THE TREATISE ON DREAMS ‹FOL. 155B–156A›

śu'enyo ke laś flakaś tragaban 'i 'englutian alaś gru'eśaś 'i no śe konosi'a ni śe śabi'a kelaś avian 'englutido 'era dezirle ke no śe śentiri'a la fartura por kauśa de la hambre ke depu'eś avi'a de suseder komo diğo Yosef 'i 'eneśto le śiknifikaban ke avi'a de poner 'el la 'orden ke śe rekeri'a para ke 'eśto fu'eśe aśi ke 'era kintear la tyera 'i poner 'enkomendadoreś 'i set-[91] 'i guardar la sibera para ke śe afirmaśe no śentirśe la hartura ke śi no śe mośtrara 'enel śu'enyo maś ke laś vakaś 'i 'eśpigaś magraś 'i gru'esaś 'i set- nunka 'el diğera maś ke śu śiknifikasy'on verdader'a konbyene śaber ke laś 'unaś śiknifikan hartura 'i laś 'otraś hambre pero 'en ver ke śe le represento 'otra kośa maś lo kual fu'e ke laś 'unaś 'englutian alaś 'otraś 'i ke laś gru'eśaś no 'eran śentidaś no śabidaś 'i set-[92] fu'e forsado deklararle la śiknifikasy'on deśto 'i komo śe avi'a de konfirmar ke 'era deśu 'ofisy'o dezir komo śoltador todo 'el 'efekto ke 'en 'el śu'enyo 'eśtaba śiknifikado :

'I tornar adezir haga Par^coh 'i set-[93] parese syerto demazyado 'i śuperflu'o ke depu'eś ke diğo ke buśkaśe 'i vyeśe 'un 'ombre śaby'o 'i 'entendido 'i lo puzyeśe śobre la tyera[94] para poner toda la 'orden ke 'era meneśter poner akel 'ombre terni'a 'el kargo de hazer todo lo neses(y)ary'o de poner 'enkomendadoreś 'i kintear la tyera 'i set-[95] por lo kual parese syerto demazyado dezir haga Par^coh 'i 'enkomende 'i set-[96] [CW. 'i ya]}

‹fol. 156a›
{KNV
'I YA ke keri'a 'o le paresi'a ke Par^coh lo hizyeśe baśtara ke diğera 'enkomende Par^coh 'enkomendadoreś 'i set- para ke 'era meneśter dezir haga Par^coh ke parese 'una proliğidad śin nesesidad ninguna 'i śin śentensy'a

PERO kiğo śiknifikar ami ver ke pu'eś 'a 'el le amośtraban 'en śu'enyo todaś akelyaś partikularidadeś ayya śiknifikasy'on ke keri'a 'el Dyyo ke fu'eśe heğo todo por śu mano ke 'el 'era 'el maś konvenible medy'o ke podi'a śer para 'efektuar la 'intensy'on del Dyyo 'enel tal 'efekto 'i 'era komo śi le diğera ke śi 'el Dyyo no kiğera ke fu'era 'eśto heğo por śu propy'a mano no teni'a nesesidad de mośtrarle maś ke la śiknifikasy'on deloś anyoś dela fartura 'i dela hambre 'i kon akelyo 'el puzyera la

---

[91] Gen 41.33–34.
[92] Gen. 41.20–21.
[93] Gen. 41.34.
[94] Gen. 41.33.
[95] Gen. 41.34.
[96] Gen. 41.34.

The Treatise on Dreams ‹fol. 156a–156b›

'orden de śuyo para 'el remedy'o ke le konveni'a 'i la reśta mośtrara depu'eś akyen tubyera 'el kargo dela tal 'orden : POR lo kual 'en mośtrarlo todo 'a 'el paresi'a ke keri'a 'el Dyo ke 'el lo hizyeśe todo 'i 'eśto śiknifiko 'enel prin(y)sipy'o 'en dezir todo loke 'el Dyyo haze 'i set-[97] ke 'enel termino de todo śiknifiko lo diğo ke baśtara byen ke diğera loke 'el Dyyo haze 'i set-[98] 'en dezir todo lo ke 'el Dyyo haze kiğo dezir ke todo śin mankar nada mośtro 'a 'el para ke porśu mano śe hizyeśe todo ke aśi konveni'a para perfekta mente 'efektuarśe 'i por 'eśto diğo haga Par^c oh ke 'eś śente[n]sy'a por śi śiknifikada 'enel meśmo śu'eny'o ke aśi śe determinaba por 'el ke 'el meśmo hizyeśe todo 'i mandaśe 'i 'ordenaśe kada partikularidad ke 'eś komo ke le diğeśe ke 'el Dyyo mośtra ke haga Par^c oh 'eśto 'i set[99]

'I deśkub(y)ry'o Yosef loś yeroś ke yeraban loś śaby'oś 'i śoltadoreś de Par^c oh por lo kual nunka podrian kaer 'en la śiknifikasy'on verdader'a 'el primero 'el ke tenemoś diğo ke pensaron śer śu'enyo śinple komo 'eś śolito śer 'en loś maś de loś 'ombreś komun mente por lo kual no avi'a de śer 'el meśmo 'efekto 'el propy'o śu'en[y]o śalvo traśpu'eśto 'en 'otra figura komo avemoś diğo por 'el kual yero diğo loke 'el Dyyo haze mośtro[100] komo tenemoś ya aklarado 'el śegundo fu'e pensar ke laś vakaś 'i laś 'eśpigaś śiknifikaban diferenteś śiknifikasy'oneś 'i no 'una śola kośa komo śu'ele śer 'en loś śu'enyoś śinpleś kelaś figuraś diferenteś śiknifikan kośaś diferenteś konprendidaś por 'el 'entendimyento

POR lo kual diğo lu'ego Yosef 'o'ido ke 'ubo 'el śu'enyo śu'enyo de Par^c oh 'uno 'eś 'i set-[101] śiknif[ik]ando 'el yero śegundo ke avemoś diğo keryendo dezir ke no 'era maś de 'una śiknifikasy'on laś vakaś 'i 'eśpigaś ke laś vakaś śiknifikaban 'el tyenpo del arar 'i laś 'eśpigaś 'el tyenpo del koğer komo avemoś diğo

POR lo kual 'o'idaś por Par^c oh laś śofisyentiśimaś razoneś ke 'el mayoral deloś 'eśkansyanoś le avi'a diğo : viśta la prudentisima repu'eśta de Yosef deśkubryendo loś [CW. yeroś]}

‹fol. 156b›
{HA-SUG HA-G HA-MIN HA-B [THE THIRD CLASS SPECIES TWO]
yeroś 'enke loś 'otroś śoltadoreś avian kaido 'en pensar ke 'eran śiknifikasy'oneś diferenteś 'i ke 'era 'otra la śiknifikasy'on de lo ke 'era 'el meśmo śu'enyo ke fu'e todo

---

[97] Gen. 41.28 does not include "todo" (cf. *supra*, n. 76).
[98] Gen. 41.28.
[99] Gen. 41.34.
[100] Gen. 41.28.
[101] Gen. 41.25.

The Treatise on Dreams ‹fol. 156b›

'eśto darle 'i asertarle 'enel punto de la kauśa ke a'el no śaśtifazian ni kuadraban śuś śolturaś śe determino lu'ego 'a hazer kuanto Yosef dezi'a

KON lo kual 'eśta aśolvida 'otra dubda grandisima ke 'eś komo Par^coh le dyyo 'a Yosef tanto kredito śin ver ninguna 'eśperensy'a de kuanto avi'a diğo ni śin tener del ninguna 'otra notisy'a maś delo ke akel mayoral śuyo le avi'a 'informado por 'un śolo kazo ke konel avi'a pasado ke pudyera śer ke kual kyera 'otra preśona hizyera akel ğu'izy'o 'i parese no baśtar akelyo śolo para darle tanto kredito 'i mandar lu'ego poner 'en 'efekto kuanto 'el 'ordenaba śin maś konśeğo ke kon lo diğo 'eśta la razon byen 'ividente ke v[y]endo kelaś razoneś de Yosef 'eran muy verdaderaś 'i a'el maś śatiśfazian ke kuantoś le avian śoltado abyendo 'o'ido kuanto 'en 'elyo śe podi'a 'o'ir no le kedando lugar por donde pudyeśe dubdar śe determino 'a poner la 'orden ke para tal 'efekto 'era meneśter 'i konprendyendo por laś razoneś de Yosef śu 'eśtremadisima prudensy'a 'i muy marabilyoza 'eśtimatiba por aver kaido de 'inprobizo 'en la verdader'a śiknifikasy'on 'i konośimyento de loś yeroś 'en ke loś 'otroś 'eśtaban śe determino śupito ke no śe podi'a halyar para 'el propy'o kargo 'otro maś śofisyente ke 'el por lo kual diğo depu'eś de averte heğo śaber 'el Dyyo 'eśto no ayy prudente ni śabido komo tu 'i set-[102]

LA ŚEGUNDA 'EŚPESY'A

'eś loś śu'enyoś de profesi'a ke śegun 'opiny'on de loś ke ponen 'el 'entendimyento ağente fu'era de nu'eśo 'entendimyento de bağo 'el konkabo de la 'eśpera de la luna komo avemoś diğo kre'en ağuntarśe 'el alma del profeta kuando 'el Dyyo kyere kon diğo 'entiliğensy'a 'i kon la tal konğunsy'on alkansar śin ningun 'inpedimyento la verdad de laś kośaś ke kyere 'el Dyyo ke le śean al profeta deśkubyertaś 'i śabidaś para byen de śu pu'eblo 'o de śuś muy alyegadoś 'i amadoś komo maś por 'eśtenso deklaro 'el diğo śenyor Rabbenu Mośeh 'en la śegunda parte de śu famozisimo libro kapitulo trenta 'i śeys[103] 'i muğo maś 'otroś muğoś modernoś ke le śigyeron

'I śegun loś ke kre'en no aver fu'era de nu'eśaś almaś 'entendimyento ağente 'en noś maś kela 'influ'ensy'a devina dela propy'a kauśa prima k(e)re'en śer diğa profesi'a 'inf(v)lu'ida del Dyyo no por 'enteresisy'on de 'otra kośa alguna 'enla kual le mośtra al profeta la kośa ke 'a de suseder laś maś delaś veześ 'en śu'enyo 'enla kual vizy'on no śe 'entrepo[n]en kośaś baldiaś komo 'enloś śu'enyoś ke no tyene[n] maś de śu'enyo ke śerle mośtrada la verdad por figuraś [CW. muy alyegadaś]}

---

[102] Gen. 41.39.
[103] Maimonides, *Guide*, trans. Pines, 369–73 (*MN*, Pt. 2, chap. 36).

The Treatise on Dreams ‹fol. 157a›

‹fol. 157a›
{KNZ
muy alyegadaś ala śiknifikasy'on verdader'a tirando la profesi'a de Mošeh Rabbenu ke 'era diferente de la de todoś loś 'otroś por ke 'era komo kyen ve'i'a 'en 'un 'eśpeǧo muy klaro 'i relumbrante śin śer traśpu'eśta la verdad de la kośa 'en forma 'imaǧinatiba al modo de loś 'otroś a'un ke no śe mośtraban ni a'un a'el totalisima mente laś formaś 'intelektualeś komo diremoś pero 'era muy diferente de loś 'otroś 'i 'enel reśto de loś profetaś avi'a muǧoś gradoś diferenteś de profesi'a śegun la diferensy'a de loś meśmoś profetaś loś kualeś śegun 'opiny'on del diǧo śenyor Rabbenu Mošeh 'en diǧa partida de śu libro kapitulo kuarenta 'i śinko[104] śe reparten 'en 'onze gradoś diferenteś delyaś deśpyertoś delyaś durmyendo ke todo 'era lo meśmo por ke no podian alkansar akelya vizy'on śi no 'era baldandośe todoś loś śentidoś korporaleś 'eśtiry'oreś 'i deś'okupada 'el anima totalisima mente de la 'obra de todoś 'elyoś

'I 'EN todoś 'eśtoś gradoś ke 'el śenyor Rabbenu Mošeh prośupone 'o '[e]n maś śi maś śon ningun profeta ve'i'a laś formaś śuśtansyaleś 'intelektualeś 'onibersaleś totalisima mente komo 'elyaś 'en śi śon śin ninguna meśkla de 'imaǧinasy'on komo avemoś diǧo ke 'en todaś 'o poko 'o muǧo 'era 'enramado 'el 'entendimyento kon la 'imaǧinasy'on 'i diferian de poko 'a muǧo komo diǧo 'el diǧo śenyor Rabbenu Mošeh 'enel prologo del diǧo libro do diǧo ke a'un la profesi'a de Mošeh Rabbenu ke fu'e tan alta 'i tan 'elevada 'i diferente de la de loś 'otroś profetaś komo 'el Dyyo propy'o diǧo por 'el 'a 'Aharon 'i 'a Miriyam no 'era maś śi no komo 'uno ke śe halyyaśe 'en 'una noǧe muy 'eśkura 'i relanpagaśe tanto 'i tan amenudo 'i tan ǧunto 'un relanpago kon 'otro ke le paresyeśe 'eśtar 'en kontinu'a luz ke no śintyeśe la 'eśkuridad de la noǧe 'i set-[105] 'el kual 'enǧenplo 'eś de muǧa śuśtansy'a 'i tyene muǧaś śiknifikasy'oneś 'i

---

[104] *MN*, Pt. 2, chap. 45 describes eleven degrees of prophecy: (1) Divine assistance induces and encourages a person to do something good and grand; (2) A person who is awake and in possession of his senses feels a new power and speaks by the Holy Spirit; (3) A prophet, who begins his speech with a phrase akin to "the word of the Lord came unto me," sees an allegory in a dream; (4) A prophet hears something in a prophetic dream but does not see the speaker; (5) A person addresses the prophet in a dream; (6) An angel speaks to the prophet in a dream; (7) In a prophetic dream it appears to the prophet as if God spoke to him; (8) The prophet sees allegorical figures in a prophetic vision; (9) A prophet hears words in a prophetic vision; (10) A prophet sees a man who speaks to him in a prophetic vision; and (11) A prophet sees an angel that speaks to him in a vision (Maimonides, *Guide,* trans. Pines, 396–403).

[105] *MN*, Introduction: "Among us there is one for whom the lightning flashes time and time again, so that he is always, as it were, in unceasing light. Thus night appears to him as day. That is the degree of the great one among the prophets [Moses], . . . of whom it was said: *that the skin*

The Treatise on Dreams ‹fol. 157a–157b›

muy fondaś laś kualeś por no śer tanto de nu'eśo tratado no kurare de dezir al preśente 'i maś por śer kośa 'en ke todoś nu'eśoś śaby'oś modernoś hablan 'i alargan ke no tenemoś aki nesesidad maś ke deklarar 'en konkluzy'on la 'esensy'a deśta 'eśpesy'a 'ultima ke 'eś diferente de la primera 'en doś kośaś

LA 'una 'en non aver 'en 'eśta 'eśpesy'a de śu'enyoś meśkla de 'otroś śu'enyoś śinpleś al tyenpo ke 'el śu'enyo de profesi'a 'era influ'ido 'en 'el profeta komo avemoś diğo

'I la 'otra 'eś ke 'eśta 'eśpesy'a de śu'enyoś no 'eran 'influ'idoś 'enel profeta śin tener 'el la diśpozisy'on ke śe rekyere para śer meresedor delya ke 'a 'opiny'on de nu'eśoś śaby'oś 'era meneśter ke fu'eśe śaby'o 'i fu'erte 'i riko 'i set-[106] kon 'otraś muğaś śerkonśtansyaś ke śon meneśter para śer perfekto 'i śobre tener toda 'eśta diśpozisy'on ke śe rekyeren keryendo 'el Dyyo profetizaba de manera ke 'eran meneśter doś kośaś ke śon la diśpozisy'on 'i perfeksy'on de 'el profeta por śi [CW. 'i]}

‹fol. 157b›
{'i la voluntad del Dyyo ke 'enveluntaśe ke lo fu'eśe lo ke 'en la 'eśpesy'a antisipada no śe rekeri'a diśpozisy'on komo diğimoś

'I porke no tenga ninguno ningun lugar de dubdar śi vyere 'o 'oyere diğoś de nu'eśoś śaby'oś 'o palabraś de nu'eśa ley ke pareśe[n] dezir ke algunoś ke no fu'eron del pu'eblo de Yiśra'el profetizaron ke 'a prima viśta parese śer profesi'a deśta śegunda 'eśpesy'a 'i no de la antisipada por lo kual kedari'a algun 'eśkrupulo 'en lo diğo ke pu'eś 'el profeta 'a de śer tanto 'en śumo grado de perfeksy'on komo 'eś posible ke profetizo Bilᶜam[107] 'o algunoś 'otroś śimileś a'el

POR tanto me parese byen manifeśtar la verdad 'en 'elyyo 'en breve deklarando 'un diğo de nu'eśoś śaby'oś de adonde depende la verdad de lo ke 'en 'eśto śe deve kre'er do dizen 'en 'eśta forma

DIĞO Rabbi Yiṣḥak[108] 'en kuanto no śe alevanto 'el tabernakulo 'era falyyada profesi'a 'en loś 'otroś ğenti'oś del mundo 'i depu'eś ke śe alevanto 'el tabernakulo

---

of his face sent forth beams, and so on [Exod. 34.29]" (Maimonides, *Guide*, trans. Pines, 7).

[106] Maimonides, "*Eight Chapters*," ed. Gorfinkle, 80; Nedarim 38a and Shabbat 92a contain the same phrase except *Nevuah* is replaced by *Shekinah*.

[107] Num. 22–24.

[108] R. Yiṣḥak ben Eleazar, one of two Palestinian Amoraim of that name; he lived in the second half of the fourth century C.E. His sayings are quoted by the leading halakhists and aggadists of the following generation: see *EJ* 9:17–18.

The Treatise on Dreams ⟨fol. 157b–158a⟩

śe tiro de 'entre 'elyyoś ke aśi 'eś diǧo trabelo 'i no lo afloǧare 'i set-[109] diǧeronle veś aki 'a Bilᶜam ke profetizo diǧoleś 'i śi para byen de loś ǧudy'oś profetizo ke aśi diǧo kyen konto polvo de Yaᶜakob 'i set-[110] 'i trae 'otraś muǧaś prevaś de śuś palabraś dizen maś ke diferensy'a ayy 'entre loś profetaś de Yiśra'el aloś profetaś de la reśta de la[s] ǧenteś 'i set-[111] 'uno dize ke la difer[e]nsy'a 'eś ke aloś ǧenti'oś no śe mu'eś(ś)[t]ra 'el Dyyo śalvo kon medy'a palabra 'i aloś profetaś de Yiśra'el kon palabra 'entera 'i prebalo todo por pᵉsukim[112] de nu'eśtra ley 'otro dize ke la diferensy'a 'eś ke aloś ǧenti'oś śe deśkubre kon terminoś brutoś 'i 'a Yiśra'el kon terminoś linpy'oś śantoś 'i klaroś kon loś kualeś loś anǧeleś loan al Dyyo 'i set-[113] 'eśta 'eś la mera letra del diǧo de nu'eśoś śaby'oś

'I para byen 'entender śu 'intensy'on 'eś meneśter 'entender laś dubdaś ke parese aver 'en śuś palabraś para por 'elyyaś '[e]ntender byen la 'intensy'on

'I digo śenyor ke lo primero 'eś de dubdar ke kauśa 'eś 'el alevantarśe 'el tabernakulo 'o deǧarlo de alevantar para no aver profesi'a 'o averla 'en loś ǧenti'oś ke śi loś ǧenti'oś no 'eran diśpu'eśtoś ni a'utoś para śer profetaś por no śer aluminadoś de la luz de nu'eśtra ley śakra lu'ego śigeśe ke ni anteś ke 'el tabernaklo śe levantaśe no avian de profetizar pu'eś śe rekyere para 'elyo śimil diśpozisy'on 'i śi podian 'i 'eran diśpu'eśtoś 'i a'utoś para 'elyo syendo bu'enoś 'i meresedoreś de tal byen por ke depu'eś de lebantado 'el tabernaglo śe avi'a de pro'ibir de 'elyoś pu'eś tenemoś por maǧima verdader'a ke 'el Dyyo glory'ozo no veda 'el byen de kyen lo merese 'i abyendo ya kiśto de anteś ke 'el tal byen tubyeśe no śe afigura mudansa 'en śu voluntad syendo la diśpozisy'on la meśma komo 'eś śabido

ŚEGUNDO ke de pu'eś ke próśupuzo Rabbi Yiṣḥak ke depu'eś de levantado 'el tabernaklo śe tiro de 'elyoś ke śe 'entyende ke no 'ubo maś [CW. 'en]}

⟨fol. 158a⟩
{KNḤ
'en 'elyoś profetaś 'en ninguna manera kuando le arguyeron de Bilᶜam ke parese ke profetizo depu'eś de lebantado 'el tabernakulo komo śaśtifaze 'el diǧo argumento kon dezir ke por byen de Yiśra'el profetizo[114] ke toda vi'a no reśponde la dubda ke 'eś

---

[109] Song of Sol. 3.4.
[110] Lev. R. 1.12.
[111] Gen. R. 52.5.
[112] "Biblical verses" or "sentences".
[113] Gen. R. 74.7.
[114] Lev. R. 1.12.

The Treatise on Dreams ‹fol. 158a›

kontra la sentensy'a ke primero diğo ke no śe halyyaban profetaś 'i se[t]-[115] keśe 'entyende ke no loś avi'a de ninguna manera depu'eś de levantado 'el tabernakulo 'i maś ke no parese aver razon para ke 'ubyeśe profetaś 'a medyaś ke śi 'era para byen avi'a de śer por la meśma razon para mal pu'eś no 'eś 'otro ke alkansar la verdad deloke 'a de suseder 'i a'un kon maś ğuśta razon avian de śer 'elyyoś apropyadoś para profetizar 'el mal pu'eś no śon tan bu'enoś ke para 'el byen

'I 'eś de ver maś ke parese no traer preba del diğo de Š^elomoh para loke kyere del prevar 'en dezir trabelo 'i non lo afloğare 'i set-[116] ke no śe preba por a'i ke loś ğenti'oś no profetizaśen ke kuando śe'a prebar ke Yiśra'el profetizaśen śin falta baśta pero ke 'otroś no profetizaśen no śe rezulta del tal diğo

'I maś 'eś de ver 'enloś diğoś de loś 'otroś doś śenyoreś ke ponen la diferensy'a de 'unoś profetaś 'a 'otroś por śer 'en 'unoś kon medy'a palabra 'i a'otroś 'entera ke para la suśtansy'a dela profesi'a no parese 'inportar śer medyya 'o 'entera ke 'eśto no śe'a de 'entender aśi komo ala [a]parente parese

'I 'en loke 'el 'otro śenyor pośtrero dize ke la diferensy'a 'eś fablar 'en lengu'a linpya 'i set-[117] 'eś de ver ke kiğo 'eneśto śiknifikar

'I para byen deklarar todo 'eśto 'i 'entender laś palabraś diğaś 'eś meneśter śaber treś porpozisy'oneś muy verdaderaś

LA primera 'eś śaber ke 'el termino de profesi'a śe toma 'en 'onibersal por nu'eśtroś śaby'oś por toda demośtrasy'on ke 'eś amośtrada a'el 'ombre syerta 'i verdader'a śin falta anteś ke suseda por kual kyera vi'a ke la śepa por lo kual śi śe dize 'enloś ğenti'oś ke profetizan 'eś komo ke diğeśen ke śaben loke 'a de [s]useder eś 'enel mundo por parte dela kośtelasy'on 'i lo pornośtikan anteś ke s[a]lga 'en 'efekto komo hazen loś bu'enoś 'eśtrologoś

LA śegunda 'eś ke anteś ke śe alevantaśe 'el t(r)abernakulo no tenian loś hiğoś de Yiśra'el todoś ğuntoś 'en 'onibersal kauśa propinka por la kual 'eśtubyeśen konğuntoś 'i konligadoś konel Dyyo tanto ke porelyyo fu'eśen dignoś ke 'el Dyyo kontraśtaśe la kośtelasy'on 'ila 'inpidyeśe deśu kurso natural por privar delyoś 'el mal ke śobre 'elyoś 'obligaśe śino fu'eśe por algun 'endivido tan alyegado a'el komo nu'eśoś śantoś patryarkaś

LO kual depu'eś ke śe levanto 'el tabernakulo por '[e]ntresisy'on del kual śe konğuntaron 'i konligaron loś hiğoś de Yiśra'el 'en 'onibersal konel Dyyo 'i 'el Dyyo 'influyyo 'en 'elyoś śu devina 'influ'ensy'a de a'i por delante 'en todo loke la koś-

---

[115] Lev. R. 1.12.
[116] Song of Sol. 3.4.
[117] Gen. R. 74.7.

The Treatise on Dreams ‹fol. 158a–158b›

telasy'on 'obligaba algun mal 'o danyo kontra 'elyyoś 'en 'onibersal 'el Dyyo lo vedaba 'i kontraśtaba la diğa kośtelasy'on
DEŚTA śegunda śe śige 'otra tersera ke 'eś ke kual kyera ke fu'ere pratiko 'en lo ke [CW. 'obliga]}

‹fol. 158b›
{'obliga la kośtelasy'on aka abağo kual kyer śu'erte de 'ombre ke śe'a de pu'eś ke śe levanto 'el tabernakulo śi pornośtikare por lo ke 'ubyere alkansado 'o viśto ke denota la diğa kośtelasy'on byen 'a Yiśra'el śera śin falta śu pronośtika verdader'a porke 'el byen ke 'obliga la kośtelasy'on śobre 'elyoś 'el Dyyo nunka lo veda maś anteś lo refirma lo kual śi pornośtikare ke 'a de suseder mal 'a 'elyyoś mośtrandolo la diğa kośtelasy'on no śera śu pornośtika syerta porke a'un ke aśi śe'a ke la kośtelasy'on lo mu'eśtre 'el Dyyo la kontraśta 'i haze ke 'el tal mal no śe 'efektu'e :
KON 'eśtaś treś kozaś verdaderaś pro śupu'eśtaś 'eśtan byen 'entendidaś todaś 'eśtaś palabraś de nu'eśoś śaby'oś ke nunka 'el Dyyo kyera ke 'en 'otra ğente ninguna fu'era de Yiśra'el 'ubyeśe profesi'a verdader'a komo 'era 'en Yiśra'el
'I loke 'enlaś 'otraś ğenteś śe dize profetizar 'eś śenpre por loke alkansan 'i pornośtikan por parte dela kośtelasy'on śegun la primera porpozisy'on 'i por 'eśto diğo Rabbi Yiṣḥak ke anteś ke śe alevantaśe 'el tabernakulo avi'a la tal profesi'a 'enelyoś 'i 'era ke pornośtikaban la verdad de loke 'obligaba la kośtelasy'on 'en todo 'el mundo por la kauśa diğa 'enla śegunda porpozisy'on por lo kual de pu'eś de alevantado 'el tabernakulo ke 'el Dyyo kontraśtaba diğa kośtelasy'on kuando 'obligaba mal 'a Yiśra'el no śali'a 'en 'efekto śu pronośtika 'i poreśto depu'eś ke 'el tabernakulo śe alevanto śe tiro la tal profesi'a de 'elyyoś por la razon diğa 'enla diğa porpozisy'on śegunda de lo kual 'eśta byen viśto ke kuando le arguyeron de Bil ͨam ke 'eran śuś pornośtikaś verdaderaś reśpondy'o sofiśyentisima mente 'en dezir ke porel byen de Yiśra'el profetizo keryendo dezir ke śi fu'era pornośtikar mal a'un ke aśi lo 'obligara la kośtelasy'on no śalyera 'en 'efekto por śer depu'eś de levantado 'el tabernakulo ke 'el Dyyo partikular mente probe'i'a 'enelyoś komo diğimoś 'i trae syete p ͨsukim para prevar 'eśto loś kualeś ami ver kiğo demośtrar 'enelyoś syete razoneś ke ayy para ke loś syete planetaś 'obren 'eneśte mundo 'infiry'or loś kualeś todoś syete 'obligaban 'el byen ke 'a loś hiğoś de Yiśra'el avi'a de suseder ke para aklararlo 'eśpasifikada mente 'era meneśter byen alargar kedara para 'otro lugar ke lo diğo aki abaśta para 'entender laś palabraś de Rabbi Yiṣḥak
'I porke 'el no deklaro la verdader'a difinsy'on de la profesi'a verdader'a vinyeron loś doś śenyyoreś postreroś 'a deklarar la diferensy'a ke 'eś lo meśmo ke avemoś diğo por muy breveś 'i fakundisimoś terminoś
'EL 'uno diğo kela diferensy'a 'eś ke alaś ğenteś komo fu'e 'a Bil ͨam komo kyera

The Treatise on Dreams ‹fol. 158b–159a›

keno 'eś maś ke alkansar loke la kośtelasy'on 'obliga aka abağo por la 'orden ke 'el Dyyo leś puzo aloś planetaś 'i śenyoś no amu'eśtra 'el Dyyo aloś taleś por 'entresisy'on delyyoś demośtrasy'on syerta maś kela meatad de loke [CW. 'a]}

‹fol. 159a›
{KNT
'a de suseder ke 'eś 'el byen ke śiknifika 'a Yiśra'el lo kual 'el mal ke 'eś la 'otra meatad pu'eś todo śe konprende de bağo de razon de byen 'i mal no lo mu'eśtra konbyene śaber ke no śaben 'enelyo lo syerto a'un ke la kośtelasy'on lo 'oblige komo avemoś diğo

LO kual loke loś profetaś de Yiśra'el alkansan komo no 'eś loke 'el Dyyo leś mu'eśtra por parte de la kośtelasy'on śalvo la pura verdad de loke 'a de suseder 'eś palabra 'entera ke tanto 'el byen komo 'el mal 'en todo alkansan lo syerto 'i la verdad de loke 'a de suseder

'I pu'ede śer ke śe 'entyenda 'en śegunda 'intensy'on 'i 'eś ke loś ke ğuśgan por loke siknifika la kośtelasy'on 'eś 'en kośaś posibleś porke la kośtelasy'on 'enklina maś 'a 'una parte ke 'a 'otra pero no 'obliga forsado por lo kual keda śenpre la kośa ke śiknifika posible tanto 'a 'una parte komo 'a otra 'i 'eśto śe lyyama medy'a habla pu'eś no 'eś syerta 'entera mente la tal demośtrasy'on 'i loke 'el verdadero profeta alkansa 'eś palabra 'entera kunplida mente śin aver posiblidad ala parte kontrary'a

'I 'el pośtrero deklaro maś breve mente la diferensy'a de lo kual keda deklarada la verdader'a difinsy'on por 'entero 'i 'eś ke laś kośaś ke śe alkansan por la kośtelasy'on no śe ve'en klara mente komo an de suseder por lo kual akaese 'el yero enelyaś laś maś de laś veześ

LO kual loś ke alkansan loke 'a de suseder por 'influ'ensy'a devina 'i 'eśprito verdadero de profesi'a ke 'el Dyyo loś amośtra la sertenidad de la kośa ke 'a de śer 'eśtoś śon loś ke śe pu'ede por 'elyyoś dezir ke alkansan laś kozaś 'en palabraś klaraś linpyaś 'i śantaś ke 'eś alkansar la verdad pura de la kauśa aśi komo laś 'entiliğensyaś śeparad[a]ś konla kual loan al Dyyo konvyene śaber ke kon 'elyya 'entyenden laś kośaś del Dyyo ke 'eśta 'eś la verdader'a lo'or al Dyyo śanto glory'ozo 'i por 'eśto diğo 'el pośtrero ke la diferensy'a 'eś ke aloś ğenti'oś śe deśkubre 'el Dyyo kon terminoś brutoś 'i 'a loś profetaś de Yiśra'el kon terminoś linpy'oś klaroś 'i śantoś 'i set-[118] de kual kyer modo ke śe'a 'eśta byen viśta 'i konprendida la difinsy'on verdader'a deśta 'ultima 'eśpesy'a 'i kual kyera vera ke śe pu'ede byen konprender por loke tenemoś diğo aserka loś śu'enyoś śinpleś antisipadoś 'el śumo grado dela verdad ke 'enloś

---

[118] Gen. R. 74.7.

The Treatise on Dreams ⟨fol. 159a–159b⟩

deśta 'ultima 'eśpesy'a śe mośtraba 'i por 'el kontrary'o tambyen 'el ke byen śupyere 'o 'entendyere la verdad de loke aserka deśta 'ultima 'eśpesy'a śe pu'ede konprender konosera 'i vera śer verdad loke aserka loś śu'enyoś śinpleś diğimoś de śer śuś śiknifikasy'oneś 'enlo futuro verdaderaś [lo] kual baśtara byen para śaśtifazer 'en 'onibersal alaś dubdaś de vu'eśa mersed 'i śi 'enlo diğo śintyere algun yero me lo relyebe ke la brevedad del tyenpo i mi kontinu'a 'okupasy'on 'en mi 'eśtudy'o no me dyeron maś lugar 'i śupla mi linpy'a voluntad la falta de la 'obra :}

⟨fol. 159b⟩
{ḤATIMAT HA-'IGGERET [END OF THE TREATISE]

HEĞO todo 'el diśkurso pasado de loś śu'enyoś syertoś i 'insyertoś komo 'eś diğo dire 'a vu'eśa mersed 'el śu'enyo ke śonyaba 'el kual me moby'o prinsipal mente 'a toda 'eśta 'eśpikulasy'on pasada 'i śertifiko 'a vu'eśa mersed ke akabando ke 'ube de śonyar me 'eśperte 'i a'un ke 'era hazy'a la manyana vyendo ke a'un no 'era de di'a me torne 'a dormir 'i śupito fu'e traśpu'eśto 'enel propy'o śu'enyo 'i por pośtre me paresi'a śonyar ke 'era śu'enyo 'i ke yo propy'o lo śoltaba

'EL kual 'eś 'eśte paresiame 'eśtar 'enel Midraś ke vu'eśa mersed frago 'en Bel Veder 'eśtando 'el diğo Midraś muy śuntu'oza mente paramentado de muy rikisima tapiseri'a aśi laś paredeś del komo todoś loś asyentoś al deredor 'i ve'i'a 'a vu'eśa mersed aśentado 'en 'una śilya muy rika

'I de la 'otra parte 'eśtaba 'el śenyor don Šᵉmu'el śu 'ermano 'en 'otra

'I paresiame śer di'a de grandisima fyeśta 'i alegri'a komun 'i ke para selebrar maś la fyeśta śe śakaban loś Sᵉfarim del Hekel[119] 'i śe ponian de manera ke veni'a 'a 'eśtar vu'eśa mersed ğunto pegado kon 'elyoś ala parte dereğa 'i 'el śenyor don Šᵉmu'el śu 'ermano ala 'otra

'I me paresi'a ke laś pu'ertaś de red[or] de anbaś laś parteś 'eran abyertaś de par 'en par 'onde 'eśtaban la beatisima śenyora 'i śenyoraś śu hiğa 'i śobrina śentadaś

'I la reśta de la ğente de kaśa kon muğoś 'otroś de fu'era muy kalefikadoś 'en deredor muy byen akomodadoś 'i todoś loś ḥakamim[120] 'eśtaban aśentadoś 'en 'un banko muy 'elevado ke vu'eśa mersed mandaba poner de bağo del asyento de loś Sᵉfarim 'entre śu śilya 'i la del śenyor don Šᵉmu'el 'entre loś kualeś por me hazer fabor komo śenpre hazi'a me mandaba aśentar

'I asentado ke 'era alsaba loś 'oğoś para vu'eśaś mersedeś alegrandome kon śu prośpero 'eśtado 'i ve'ialeś tener 'a kada 'uno 'en la mano dyeśtra 'una palma muy

---

[119] That is, brought out the "Torah Scrolls" from the "Ark".
[120] That is, the "wise" or "pious" men.

The Treatise on Dreams ‹fol. 159b–160a›

verde 'i muy dereğa 'i 'en la śinyeśtra 'una sedra muy freśka 'i muy linpy'a[121] komo śe rekyeren para hazer kon 'elyoś la m[i]ṣvah ke 'el Dyyo noś mando hazer śegun nu'eśoś śaby'oś 'eśkribyeron

'I 'eśtando aśi 'en 'eśta vizy'on tan 'elevado me paresi'a ke vu'eśa mersed mobi'a diğa palma ğunto kon la sedra 'a todaś parteś dizyendo 'a alta boz dira agora Yiśra'el ke para śenpre śu mersed[122] 'i reśpondiamoś todoś kuantoś alyi noś halyyabamoś 'i deziamoś load 'a Adonay ke bu'eno ke para śenpre śu mersed[123]

'I 'eśtando kon 'eśtaś palabraś 'en la boka me deśperte

'I keryendome alevantar para byen kontenplar 'enel śu'enyo paresyendome a'un algo tenprano me torne śupito 'a dormir 'i de 'inprobizo me paresy'o traśponerme 'enel meśmo lugar 'en la meśma vizy'on donde śenti'a tornar 'a dezir vu'eśa mersed diran agora temyenteś de Adonay ke para śyenpre śu mersed[124] 'i todoś reśpondiamoś al meśmo modo ke anteś aviamoś reśpondido [CW. lo kual]}

‹fol. 160a›
{KS

LO kual ğuśgaba yo 'enel meśmo śu'enyo ke todo akelyo ke avi'a viśto 'era śonyando 'i ke 'era śu'enyo de muğa suśtansy'a 'i śonyaba 'enel meśmo śu'enyo kela śoltura del śu'enyo 'era

KE la palma śiknifikaba 'una rekta 'i prośpera vitory'a komo todoś loś antigoś 'eśkribyeron muy konforme 'a loke nu'eśoś śaby'oś dizen aserka dela razon de tomar la palma 'enel tyenpo ke maś apropyado kiğo 'el Dyyo ke fu'eśe para selebrar nu'eśtra fyeśta 'i alegrarnoś delante del

'I tenerla vu'eśa mersed 'enla mano muy verde 'i muy rekta meneandola 'a todaś laś parteś del mundo 'era verdader'a demośtrasy'on de śer śu vitory'a rekta 'i florida 'ordenada por la probidensy'a devina de tal manera ke trasendyeśe śu fama 'i fu'eśe byen notory'a 'en todaś laś parteś del mundo 'en kontinu'o a'umento de prośperidad de modo ke 'enel śe afirmaśe 'el diğo de nu'eśo devinisimo rey śalmiśta do diğo ğuśto komo la palma floreśida 'i set-[125] :

'I la sedra ke 'eś fruto tan śuabisimo 'en śabor 'i 'olor maś ke 'otro alguno komo nu'eśoś śaby'oś kyeren 'era śiknifikasy'on 'a loś beatisimoś hiğoś ke vu'eśa mersed

---

[121] Cf. Ps. 92.12.
[122] Ps. 118.2.
[123] Ps. 118.1.
[124] Ps. 118.4.
[125] Ps. 92.13.

The Treatise on Dreams ⟨fol. 160a–160b⟩

'i 'el śenyor don Šᵉmu'el ternan perfektisimoś 'en 'eśpikulasy'on ke śiknifika 'el 'olor 'i byen 'obrar ke śiknifika 'el śabor ke 'eś la propy'a konparasy'on ke nu'eśoś śaby'oś hizyeron

'I todoś ǧuntoś padreś 'i hiǧoś ke delyyoś śalran śera la fama de śuś 'obraś 'i devina 'eśpikulasy'on 'eśpandida ǧunto konśu vitory'a por todaś laś parteś del mundo

'I 'eśtar vu'eśaś mersedeś ǧunto konloś sᵉfarim 'era śiknifikasy'on ke śeran todaś śuś 'obraś kon todaś śuś prośperidadeś konformeś 'a nu'esa śakra ley 'i por śuś kauśaś 'i 'entresisy'on śera diǧa ley śublimada 'i 'enǧalsada 'en publiko 'i no amagada por lo kual 'eśtaban loś sᵉfarim defu'era 'i 'en alto maś ke 'el 'andar del asyento de vu'eśa mersed śiknifikando ke ta[n]to kuanto vu'eśa mersed fu'eśe 'enǧalsado tanto maś 'enǧalsari'a la ley ǧuśgando la kauśa porel 'efekto konforme 'a 'el diǧo de nu'eśo śapyentisimo re'ey Šᵉlomoh 'enśuś probyerby'oś do dize 'enǧalsala 'i 'enalteserte'a 'i set-[126] :

'I tener nu'eśa beatisima śenyora 'i la śenyora śu hiǧa 'i śobrina ke 'el Dyyo guarde laś pu'ertaś abyertaś mirando todo lo diǧo 'era śiknifikasy'on ke śe glorifikaran 'i alegraran kon la prośperidad manifyeśta 'a todo 'el mundo 'i 'enǧalsamyento de la ley ke 'elya śenpre tubo 'i tyene por kośtumbre de hazer ke tan purifikada 'i śakra 'intensy'on 'el Dyyo nunka manka de poner en 'efekto komo nu'eśoś śaby'oś dizen ke la 'intensy'on bu'ena 'el Dyyo la trae 'a 'efekto 'i set-[127] konforme 'a lo ke nu'eśo devino rey David diǧo voluntad de śuś temyenteś fara 'i set-[128]

'I por ke de śu fabor 'i prośperidad 'i deloś ke de 'elyoś susederan śe rez[u]ltara byen 'a todo Yiśra'el dezi'a vu'eśa mersed dira agora Yiśra'el ke para śyenpre śu mersed 'i set-[129] lo kual por ke śera de todoś [CW. konsedido]}

⟨fol. 160b⟩
{konsedido ǧunta mente 'i 'a altaś boześ reśpondiamoś 'i deziamoś kon ǧuśta razon loar todoś al Dyyo 'i dezir śu mersed śer 'infinita 'en darnoś tan bu'en medy'o para nu'eśtro byen

'I 'el asyento ke vu'eśa mersed mandaba meter para loś ḥakamim de baǧo del asyento de loś Sᵉfarim 'entre 'el 'i 'el śenyor don Šᵉmu'el 'era śiknifikasy'on ke loś śaby'oś ke de kontino tyenen la ley śobre śuś kabesaś[130] trabaǧando 'en 'elya komo

---

[126] Prov. 4.8.
[127] Kiddushin 40a.
[128] Ps. 145.19.
[129] Ps. 118.2.
[130] Cf. Deut. 6.8, 11.18.

The Treatise on Dreams ‹fol. 160b›

deven śeran śublimadoś 'i abrasadoś de todaś laś parteś del fabor 'i 'onor 'i prośpero 'eśtado de vu'eśaś mersedeś para ke por śuś manoś śe afirme 'el diğo de nu'eśo profeta Y^eša^cyahu do diğo H‹a-Šem› 'envoluntan por śu ğuśtedad ke śe 'engrandeśa la ley 'i set-[131]

POR lo kual tornando 'a dormir traśponyendome 'en la meśma vizy'on 'o'i'a dezir śegunda veś 'a vu'eśa mersed diran agora temyenteś de H‹a-Šem› ke para śenpre śu mersed 'i set-[132] ke 'era śiknifikar śèr partikular mente manifyeśta 'i konosida la mizerikordy'a devina 'en todo 'eśte byen aloś temyenteś a'el Dyyo alyende del konosimyento ke la 'onibersalidad de Yiśra'el ternan 'el kual śiknifiko 'el primero diğo

'EŚPERO 'en nu'eśo klementisimo śenyor ke aśi śera komo lo śoltaba 'i ke todoś loś d[i]ğoś ke tan alegre mente deziamoś śe afirmaran por ke alyende de śer la razon 'ividente de no poder mankar de śer aśi 'ordenado por la probidensy'a devina abyendo tanto meresimyento 'i razon para 'elyo

TENGO 'eśperansa por la śiknifikasy'on deśte mi śu'enyo ke aśi śe'a por śuś kauśaś naturaleś 'o filosofaleś konforme 'a kuanto tenemoś diğo avyendo byen atentado 'i viśto ke no mankaron 'enel ninguna de laś śerkonśtansyaś ke nu'eśoś śaby'oś por ( ) śuponen ke śe rekyeren para śer śu śiknifikasy'on verdader'a konforme 'a razon natural

LO primero 'eśtar yo al preśente bendito 'el Dyyo śano śin alterasy'on de ninguna kalidad 'eśtranya 'i śer 'el śu'enyo hazy'a la manyana ke dizen nu'eśoś śaby'oś ke syendo aśi no manka 'el 'efekto[133] 'i 'eś por śer depu'eś de akabada la 'ultima diğeśty'on de la komida ke kauśa la 'ezelasy'on de fumoś 'o vaporeś al selebro lo kual 'eś todo demostrasy'on de no aver ninguna kauśa de laś ke tenemoś diğo aserka dela primera 'eśpesy'a del primer ğenero antepu'eśto ke kauśan śer loś śu'enyoś 'insyertoś

LO śegundo śer 'el diğo śu'enyo śobre 'otra preśona fu'era del ke śu'enya ke dizen nu'eśoś śaby'oś ke 'el śu'en[y]o ke śu'enya 'uno 'en kaśoś de 'otroś 'eś 'el ke maś syerto śe afirma 'i set-[134] 'i la 'intensy'on deśto pyenso ke śe'a por śalvar la śegunda 'eśpesy'a del primer ğenero de śu'enyoś 'insyertoś 'i la kauśa śera ke kuando 'el meśmo śonyador śu'enya kaśoś ke śiknifikan algun 'efekto 'enel meśmo pu'ede śer laś maś de laś veześ por 'andar fantazeando 'en 'elyo ke d(+)eśeandolo muğo 'i pensando rezy'a mente 'enel [CW. 'eś]}

---

[131] Isa. 42.21.
[132] Ps. 118.4.
[133] Berakot 55b, Gen. R. 89.5.
[134] Berakot 55b.

The Treatise on Dreams ‹fol. 161a›

‹fol. 161a›
{KS'
'eś kauza de treśpaśarśe 'enla 'imağinasy'on al tyenpo del dormir komo diğimoś lo k[u]al syendo ke 'otro afu'era de 'el lo śu'enya a'un ke muğo lo deze'e 'en 'eśtremo ğuśga maś deśapasy'onada mente la razon del 'efekto por lo kual 'eś byen viśto no śer 'eśte mi śu'enyo dela śegunda 'eśpesy'a del primer ğenero antepu'eśto :
PU'EŚ no śer dela terśera 'eśpesy'a no dubdo porke a'un ke mi 'inğeny'o śe'a muy flako 'i 'ikli(k)psado alo menoś por la pratika 'i 'eśperensy'a tengo por syerto nunka aver konsebido 'enmi konsebto 'imağinasy'oneś vanaś ni varyableś ke no lebaśen alguna razon natural :
LO kual tengo por fortisima kauśa para no śer mi śu'enyo de ninguna 'eśpesy'a del ğenero primero 'en ninguna manera :
Maś anteś syento muğaś razoneś 'ividenteś 'i śenyaleś verdaderaś śer diğa śoltura verdader'a :
LA primera śer 'el śu'enyo śonyyado doś veześ ke 'eś g(+)randisima demośtrasy'on de śer verdadero 'i ke śera preśto 'el 'efekto konel ayuda del Dyyo :
'I la razon 'eneśto 'eśta viśta ke 'eś demośtrasy'on de no śer figura 'inventada dela 'imağinasy'on śola mente śin aver 'enelyo ğu'izy'o prudensyal por parte del 'entendimyento ke śi aśi fu'era nunka konformaran 'enlaś doś veześ laś 'unaś konlaś 'otraś maś fu'eran muy diśformeś komo 'eś śolito de hazer la 'imağinasy'on kontino figuraś diferenteś pu'eś no śon regladaś ni 'ordenadaś śegun dereğa razon por lo kual konpone 'unaś kon 'otraś laś maś delaś veześ no syendo refrenada dela razon por parte del 'entendimyento
'I 'eśto kiğo śentir Yosef 'en la śiknifikasy'on tan verdader'a ke śolto 'enel śu'enyo de Par^coh 'en dezir 'i śobre śer aśegundado 'el śu'enyo 'a Par^coh doś veześ ke apareğada la kośa de kon 'el Dyyo 'i apreśuranśe 'el Dyyo para fazerla 'i set-[135] ke 'eśta byen viśta la 'intensy'on ke por śer 'el śu'enyo aśegundado komo ku'enta la 'eśkritura ke fu'e 'eś demośtrasy'on de śer 'el ğu'izy'o devino verdadero 'i śer 'el 'efekto preśto[136]
LA śegunda 'eś la ke nu'eśoś śaby'oś muğo afirman do kyeren 'i dizen ke 'el śu'enyo ke śe śu'elta 'enel meśmo śu'enyo akelya śoltura 'eś la ke verdader'a mente 'i śin falta śe afirma 'i s[e]t-[137] 'i tubyeron 'en 'eśto grandisimo fundamyento de razon

---

[135] Gen. 41.32.
[136] Berakot 55b.
[137] Berakot 55b.

The Treatise on Dreams ‹fol. 161a–161b›

natural por ke s[y]endo verdad lo ke 'el filosofo diğo 'enel libro de śu'enyo 'i viğilya[138] ke kuando 'el 'ombre śu'enya ke śu'enya 'el śonyar ke śu'enya no pu'ede śer śu'enyo kavzado por la 'imağinasy'on komo 'eś lo ke lyamamoś śu'enyo komo avemoś diğo śalvo verdader'a determinasy'on 'i śentensy'a del 'entendimyento ke determina ke 'eś 'obra de la 'imağinasy'on por ke la meśma 'imağinasy'on nunka pu'ede 'elya 'imağinar ke 'imağina komo akaese muğaś veześ 'eśtando deśpyertoś pu'eśtoś 'en a[l]guna rezy'a 'imağinasyyon ke depu'eś determinamoś kon dereğa razon del 'entendimyento(ś) kontenplando 'enlo pasado śer 'imağinasy'on ke}

‹fol. 161b›
{'a de śer fu'era dela meśma 'imağinasy'on 'i 'eśto 'eś śabido 'i aberiguado 'i podri'a śer ke fu'eśe 'eśta la 'intensy'on 'enloś śu'enyoś de Yosef ke dize 'i śonyo Yosef śu'enyo[139] ke 'eś komo ke diğeśe śonyo ke śonyaba 'i por 'eśto śe afirmaba 'en śer verdadero 'i porla meśma kauśa śentensyo śer verdaderoś loś śu'enyoś del 'eśkansyano 'i 'el panadero porke diğeron 'i śonyamoś śu'enyo syendo 'eśta la 'intensy'on ke 'eś komo ke diğeśen śonyamoś ke śonyavamoś 'i set-[140] :
POR todaś 'eśtaś razoneś 'eśta byen viśto śer la śiknifikasy'on de 'eśte mi śu'enyo verdader'a
'I śi 'eś dela primera 'eśpesy'a del śegundo ğenero determinado 'el 'efekto por 'eśpikulasy'on 'o dela śegunda konsidrando por 'eśperensy'a no me afirmo śer maś por 'una ke por 'otra ke podri'a śer aver laś doś ğunta mente :
'I ke śe'a por 'una 'o por 'otra ke kauśan la śiknifikasy'on śer verdader'a 'enlo futuro komo avemoś diğo :
'EN 'eśte mi śu'enyo me determino śer śimil 'a loś śu'enyoś ke Yosef śonyaba 'i kontaba aśuś ermanoś deloś kualeś a'un ke 'elyoś śe burlaban no manko 'el 'efekto śiknifikado śin falta por lo kual Yaͨakob śu padre 'i nu'eśo śanto patryarka sintyendo la razon 'i fundamyento ke loś taleś śu'enyoś mośtraban tener śegun razon natural guardo la kośa 'ensu korason 'o'ido ke 'ubo 'el śu'enyo 'eśperando 'el 'efekto śiknifikado 'enel por lo kual dize la 'eśkritura 'i 'enbidyaron 'enel śuś ermanoś 'i śu padre 'eśpero la kośa[141] 'o guardo la koza ke 'el byerbo 'eś 'ikiboko ke pu'ede śufrir

---

[138] Aristotle, *Parva Naturalia* 3 (*On Sleep and Waking*) iii (456b 9–15); also cf. *PN* 4 (*On Dreams*) i (458b 29–459a 8, 19–23), iii (462a 2–8), and 5 (*On Prophecy in Sleep*) i (463a 22–25).
[139] Gen. 37.5.
[140] Gen. 40.8.
[141] Gen. 37.11.

The Treatise on Dreams ⟨fol. 161b–162a⟩

loś doś 'ententoś 'i todoś śon konformeś ala 'intensy'on ke vyendo Ya'akob śer 'el śu'enyo tan reglado 'i aver para 'efektuarśe loke 'enel śe śiknifikaba tantaś razoneś komo diremoś guardo la kośa 'entreśi porke śuś ermanoś no lo śintyeśen 'i fu'eśe kauśa de aboreserlo maś por lo kual ku'enta la 'eśkritura ke 'eśtulto 'enel 'i le niğilo diğo śu'enyo 'i no değ(e)[o] por 'eśo de 'eśperar diğo 'efekto :

'I la razon natural ke syento aver 'en diğoś śu'enyoś no negando ke pudyeśe śer por 'influ'ensy'a devina ke 'eś lo 'ultimo ke vu'eśa mersed mośtro deśear de śaber pyenso ke śe'a ke syendo Yosef 'el maś śaby'o ke todoś śuś ermanoś śegun kyeren nu'eśoś śaby'oś ke 'en lyyamarlo la 'eśkritura hiğo de veğeześ[142] kyere dezir hiğo śaby'o[143] lo kual tubyeron lugar ami ver 'a 'eśta glośa por ver ke Benyam[i]n 'era maś pekenyo ke 'el 'i la regla komun 'eś lyyamar al maś pekenyo hiğo de beğeś pu'eś śe hizo 'en tyenpo de maś veğeś ke 'el de anteś del por tanto diğeron ke kyere dezir hiğo śaby'o porke la sensy'a śe halya 'enloś vyeğos komo diğo nu'eśo re'ey śapyentisimo 'enśuś probyerby'oś 'enloś vyeğos sensy'a 'i set-[144] 'i dizen maś nu'eśoś śaby'oś śobre 'eśte meśmo diğo ke kuanto avi'a deprendido Ya'akob de Šem 'i de 'Eber abezo 'a Yosef 'i set-[145] :

'I syendo aśi ğunto kon śer 'el 'el maś familyar 'enla kaza deśu padre 'i ke śabi'a byen todaś śuś partikularidadeś maś ke}

⟨fol. 162a⟩

{KSB
'otro kual kyera delyyoś teni'a byen konosido 'el śumo grado de 'eselensy'a 'i śupremo meresimyento deśu padre porel kual konosimyento ğunto konśu śaber 'i prudensy'a le kavzaba 'entender 'i determinar śegun dereğa razon 'i rekto ğu'izy'o ke no podi'a mankar de śer probe'ido por la pr[o]bidensy'a de[v]ina de tal manera ke 'el 'i todoś śuś susesoreś fu'eśen 'en 'un muy próspero 'eśtado de todoś loś byeneś 'en śupera( )- bundansy'a aśi tenporaleś komo byeneś verdaderoś del anima 'i kontenplando 'i ğuśgando śegun dereğa razon ke 'el meğor medy'o 'i maś konvenible ke 'el Dyyo podi'a apareğar para traer śimil 'efekto 'era 'el por laś razoneś diğaś śe determinaba aver de śer por śu 'entresisy'on 'i andando kontenplando 'i peśkiryendo 'el medy'o ke para tal 'efekto la probidensy'a devina 'ordenari'a maś alyegado 'a razon natural ke fu'eśe

---

[142] Gen. 37.3.
[143] Onkelos, Rashi, Rambam Gen. 37.3.
[144] This seems rather to be Job 12.12.
[145] Unidentified source. For references to the tradition that Shem and Eber founded a college for the study of Torah, see Gen. R. 618, 624, and Exod. R. 5.

The Treatise on Dreams ⟨fol. 162a–162b⟩

pośible komo 'eś śolito de hazerśe konsidrando deśpyerto algunoś medy'oś 'en 'onibersal pyenso ke lo primero ke śe determino fu'e ke 'eśto avi'a de śer heğo por mano de algun prinsipe poderozo ke de 'el fu'eśen muy faboridoś 'i ke kuando aśuś śusesoreś fu'eśe kontrary'o pudyeśe maś mośtrar la probidensy'a devina śu poder 'infinito 'o śimil kośa ke 'eśta ke 'eśpyerto kon śu kontinu'a 'eśpikulasy'on perfektisima mente kaeri'a 'en la verdad 'i śi algo mankaśe 'en la partikularidad delyyo atemari'a de alkansar durmyendo por 'eśtar 'el anima 'eśtonseś maś deś'okupada (k)[']i a'uta para alkansar 'i determinar maś la verdad śegun deklaramoś 'en la primera kauśa de loś śu'enyoś śer syertoś de śegundo ğenero laś kualeś determinasy'oneś la 'imağinasy'on traśponi'a 'en figuraś śiknifikanteś 'el 'efekto ke śu 'entendimyento determinaba lo kual parese por 'el 'efekto ke ğuśgado 'i determinado por Yosef ke de razon avi'a de śer 'eśto por śu 'entresisy'on 'i ke devi'a de śer por mano de algun prinsipe poderozo komo avemoś diğo 'i ke no podi'a śer śalir śu padre de akel lugar śi no fu'eśe kon muğa nesesidad '[i] syendo la mayor nesesidad la hambre ke no śe pu'ede 'en ninguna manera śuśtentar la vida śin mantenimyento komo 'eś manifyeśto śe determino 'enel tyenpo del dormir ke partikular mente avi'a de śer por kauśa del diğo mantenimyento por śu mano por lo kual la 'imağinasy'on lo traśpuzo 'en ke gabilyyaban gabilyyaś 'entre 'el kanpo 'i set-[146] por lo kual referi'a ke śe avian de 'ir todoś a'el 'a 'enkorbar 'i set-[147] lo kual syendo fundada la tal determinasy'on śobre tan sofisentisimaś razoneś no manko '[en] 'efekto

'I śegun la śegunda kauśa ke alya deklaramoś 'eśta muğo ma[ś] viśta la razon de śer verdadero ke konligandośe 'i konğuntandośe kon la 'entiliğensy'a ke ponen 'obrar 'en nu'eśo 'entendimyento no śe deve dubdar ke alkansaśe la pura verdad del 'efekto por la śertenidad de laś kauśaś 'i formaś de laś kośaś ke tan verdader'a mente śe traśpasarian 'enel anima beatisima de tan ğunto śapyentisimo śonyador komo 'el 'era komo śe mośtro por 'el 'efekto : [CW. por]}

⟨fol. 162b⟩
{ POR LA MEŚMA kauśa me afirmo 'enla śiknifikasy'on deśte mi śu'enyo por todaś śuś parteś śer aśi komo yo tengo śoltado konfyando 'enel Dyyo ke aśi śera porke abyendo yo konośido tan 'eśpaśifikada mente 'i 'eśpekulado byen por 'eśtenso 'el śumo grado de 'eselensy'a dela beatisima kaśa de vu'eśaś merśedeś

NON podi'a mi 'inğeny'o por flako ke fu'eśe değar de ğuśgar ke pudyeśe por

---

[146] Gen. 37.7.
[147] Gen. 37.7.

ninguna manera mankar de śer śimil kaśa śublimada 'i pu'eśta 'enla kumbre de felise 'i próśpero 'eśtado 'ordenado porla probidensy'a devina :

'I ǧuśgando 'eśto mi 'entendimyento śegun dereǧa razon komo avemoś diǧo traśpasandośe 'el tal ǧu'izy'o 'enel tyenpo del dormir syendo 'el anima maś deś'okupada para maś verdader'a mente alkansar la verdad śe determino 'i afirmo śer aśi 'ila 'imaǧinasy'on la traśpuzo 'enla forma ke relatado tengo konforme 'a 'el ǧu'izy'o verdadero ke fu'e la śoltura :

DE manera ke lo ke Yosef alkanso por puro śaber 'i verdader'a 'eśpikulasy'on pyenso aver yo alkansado alo menoś por 'eśpery'ensy'a syerta 'i dereǧa razon ke syendo tan manifyeśtaś laś kauśaś kual kyera ǧuśgara no poder mankar tal 'efekto 'i śer aśegundado 'el śu'enyo 'i 'enel tyenpo ke fu'e 'i śer śoltado 'enel meśmo śu'enyo[148] 'eś śenyal de lo ke Yosef diǧo ke 'eś la kośa 'ordenada 'i apareǧada 'i konpu'eśta de kon 'el Dyyo 'i ke śe apreśurara 'a hazerlo[149] 'i aśi śe'a 'i 'el lo konfirme amen : 'a śervisy'o de vu'eśa mersed Mošeh Almośnino

TAM [THE END]

{RMK: handwritten note in Hebrew :
l. 1 unclear

l. 2 I bought it [the book] for the work of Him Who Will Be Blessed, I am the young man David crown [honor?] of Samuel ben Yakar Z"L

l. 3 For [or abbreviation of *le-Elui Nišamat,* that is, for the spiritual exaltation of his soul or my son] the young man the student Joseph Yakar Z"L may his memory be for a blessing.[150]}

---

[148] Berakot 55b.

[149] Gen. 41.32.

[150] Regarding line 3: if the child is dead, one understands (and this is common) that the book is purchased and donated in the belief that using and studying it influences the child's soul so that it gets into an upper level of heaven; if not, and Z"L is not written, then we are to understand that it was purchased "for my son."

SPANISH–HEBREW GLOSSARY

⟨fol. 163a⟩
ביאור המלות

{col. 1}

אות האלף
1. 'amônêsta'syôn   התראה
2. 'êśpikûla'syôn   חקירה ועיון
3. 'in'iśtima'blê   בלתי נערך
4. 'infᵉlû'îdô   מושפע
5. 'êfika'ś   דבר בקיום וחוזק
6. 'imîta'r   לדמות זה לזה
7. 'inprôbîzô   מואשל אל הפתאומיות
8. 'êśôrta'sî'ôn   התעוררו' להני' רצון אחר
9. 'antêsêdêntêś   קודמות
10. 'orîğîn   מקור והתחלה
11. 'a'ûtā   ראויה ומוכנת ונאותה
12. 'êğêrsîsî'ô   תנע' בכל דב' וביחו' הטיו

{col. 2}
13. 'îra'sîblê   כעסני והוא מלשון כעס
14. 'advêrtênsî'ā   השקפה בדבר
15. 'îgnôtô   בלתי ידו' וביחו' על הש"י
16. 'êlîksî'ôn   בחירה
17. 'îvîdêntê   נר' לעין ומפורסם לכל
18. 'asêndêntê   צומח באופק
19. 'întᵉrînsîka'ś   פנימיות
20. 'întîrî'ôrêś   ג"כ פנימיות
21. 'êśpᵉrîtû'al   רוחני

436

Spanish–Hebrew Glossary

22. 'êndîvîdôś — אישים או יחידים
23. 'êśpîsîfîka'ś — הוא שם נגזר ממין
24. 'anêǧa'ś — נלוות וקרובות זו לזו
25. 'êśtᵉrînsîkôś — חצוניים

{col. 3}
26. 'înêptā — בלתי נאותה
27. 'întᵉrôdûtô — בקי ויודע בדבר מה
28. 'înfôrtûnî'ô [second vav unpointed] — רוע המזל
29. 'îpîtêtô — ר"ל תואר נאות למתואר
30. 'êśtûrmêntôś — כלים
31. 'adkêrîr — השגת הדבר המבוקש
32. 'îlûśtᵉrê — בהיר
33. 'advêrsā fôrtûnā — מערכה הפכיית
34. 'êsênsî'ā — מהות
35. 'îklîpsê — לקות
36. 'aprôba'r — ראיה לקיים דבר מה
37. 'ûtîlî(r)[d]a'd — תועלת
38. 'anpᵉlā mêntê — באופן רחב

{col. 4}
39. 'asôlûsî'ôn — התרת חספק
40. 'abîlîda'd 'abîl — כדאי וראוי
41. 'artîkûlôś — עקרים
42. 'ênvîśtîga'r — השגת הדבר מצד חקירה
43. 'êdônî'ô — נאה ומתקבל
44. 'adô'êśtô — גנות וכעור
45. 'înmôbîlêś — בלתי מתנועעים
46. 'êpîlênsî'ā — כפיה והוא חולי הנופל
47. 'êfîsyêntê — פועלת
48. 'êndîǧîśtā — בלתי מעוכלת
49. 'ûmôreyś — לחות והם הד' ליחות
50. 'ênsîta'sî'ôn — התעוררו' לעשו' דבר מה
51. 'êśpîlîdā — דחויה

‹163b›
{col. 1}
52. 'ôpôrtûnîda'd — שעת הכושר וזמן נאות
53. 'alyєyntôś — אידים

Spanish–Hebrew Glossary

54. 'ɛynpīna'dô   נצב ביושר
55. 'antīpa'rīśta'zeyś   הנחת המנגד קרו' להפכו
56. 'īğênî'ô [ד](ש)אשיי נגזר מא
57. 'ɛynpᵉrīnsî'ônɛyś   חקיקות
58. 'ɛyśtî'ô   קיץ
59. '[a]'ûtônô [second vav unpointed]   חורף
60. 'ɛynfᵉl'ama'sî'ôn   התלהבות
61. 'ɛyś'ala'sî'ôn   היות הדבר עולה בהתכה
62. 'akî'ā   מימיות
63. 'aśpêktôś   מובטים
64. 'ôpîô   אפיאון

{col. 2}
65. 'învyêrnô   הוא זמן הסתו
66. 'ôbğêktô   מובט
67. 'ɛyśtīrî'ôrɛyś   חצוניים
68. 'aśîśtêntɛyś   עומדים שם
69. 'ôrîzôntê   אופק והוא עגול ומצוייר
70. 'aśtrôlûğîkô   תכוניי
71. 'ôpūzîsî'ônêś   דברים נגדיים ונכוחיים
72. 'ôbśᵉta'kûlô   מעיק או מוקש
73. 'ôdôrîf+ɛyra'ś   ריחניים
74. 'ôsî'ôzî[y]da(y)'d   בטלה
75. 'ênkôntînêntê   חוטא והוא בלתי כובש
76. 'īkğa'rsî'aś   הו' שם חלקי בנין הספיני
77. 'abômîna'blê   מגונה מאד

{col. 3}
78. 'ɛyśtîma'tîbā   השערה
79. 'ɛyśpīsîf+īka'r   היות מפרט הענין
80. 'înpôrtûnô [third vav unpointed]   נאמ' על המדנר' יות' מדאי
81. 'ênkᵉlîna'dô   נכנע אל דבר מה
82. 'êntîlîğênsî'ā   שכל וביחוד השכל הנבדל
83. 'înôrmê   בלתי ישר יוצא מהנאות
84. 'êśka'brôzô   דרך רבת המכשולות
85. 'în'iśpôna'blê   מקו' שהו' במצור ובמצוק
86. 'ûna'nîmɛyś   נפש אחד בשני גופים
87. 'ɛyleyga'ntɛyś   מסולסלי' והועתק חרוצי'
88. 'af+a'bîlîda'd   תאר אל המשמח בדבורו

Spanish–Hebrew Glossary

89.	'ôrba'nîda'd	הו' שם נאמ' על מציא' חן
90.	'ê'ôtra'pêli'ā	הוא התחברות טוב

{col. 4}

91.	'ɛylôkêntê	צח הלשון ומליץ טוב
92.	'aśtûtôś	פקחים והוא ביחוד להרע
93.	'însa'sia'blê	בלתי שבע
94.	'însêsa'ntê	בלתי עומד במנוחה
95.	'ôra'dôr	הו' נאמ' על המדבר בהלצה
96.	'însûlûblê	בלתי מתורץ הספק
97.	'atînênsîś	אנשי אתינאש
98.	'in'êntîliğîblê	בלתי מוכן ובלתי מושכל
99.	'adûlt^{e}rî'ô	הוא הניאוף
100.	'învizîblê	בלתי נראה לעין
101.	'a'ûmêntô	תוספת ועליה
102.	'abśûrdôś	שאין ראוי לשומעו
103.	'ɛyklîzî'aśteyś	קהלה וביחוד ספר קהלת

‹164a›

{col. 1}

104.	'însêpa'ra'blê	בלתי נבדל
105.	'îndîvîdā	בלתי ראויה
106.	'ômîdô ra'dîka'l	לחות שרשי
107.	'înkônpûsîblê	אשר לא יוקש עם אחר
108.	'a'ûśt^e(y)[ê]rā vîdā	חיים קשים חיי צער
109.	'armôni'ā	התיחסות קולות נאות
110.	'ɛynt^e(y)rêsîsi'ôn	אמצעות
111.	'êrônya'h	מוטעית
112.	'îndîsîzā	בלתי נגזר ובלתי מבואר
113.	'êntêroga'sî'on	שאלה לידע האמת
114.	'ɛyteyrnô	נצחי
115.	'abêteyrnô	בלתי התחלה וראשית
116.	'abśûlûtā	מתורצת הקושיא

{col. 2}

117.	'înśta'ntê	העתה והוא נקודת ההוה
118.	'ağeynteyś	פועלים פעולה מה
119.	'înmûta'bley	בלתי משתנה
120.	'îndɛypeyndêntê	בלתי נתלה באחר

Spanish–Hebrew Glossary

121.	'înma'kûla'dā	תמימה אשר אין בה מום
122.	'înisya'tîbô	המוגבל ראשין
123.	'af+înîda'd	קורבה שאינה אשר בשר
124.	'ômîsîdî'ô	שפיכות דמים' באדם
125.	'însênsîbilîda'd	העדר ההרגשה
126.	'ê'ûśt^era'sî'ô	הוא שם פילוסוף אחד
127.	'ana'lêś	דברי הימים והשנים
128.	'artê mîlît'ar	תלאכת הנהגת המלחמה
129.	'êśpônta'nyô	בא מאליו

{col. 3}

130.	'êrôykô [shewa under yod]	מעולה מאד
131.	'amôr pa'têrnô	אהבת האב לבן
132.	'atlêta'ś	שם המתעמלים זה בזה
133.	'întênsô	חזק האיכות
134.	'eyśtûpêndā	דבר מתמיה
135.	'ênmîta'blê	בלתי נדמה לאחר
136.	'înkômeynsûra'bley	בלתי משוער אש' לא ימד
137.	'eykseyrsîtô	מחנה המלחמה
138.	'êśtîptîkô	קובץ
139.	'aktô vêneyrî'ô	פועל משגליי
140.	'în'êf+a'bîlê	דב' טוב שאי' ראוי לדב' בו
141.	'a'ûśtînênsî'ā	מניעה וסגוף מהתאות
142.	'eyśp^elîka'r	פירוש וביאור

{col. 4}

143.	'amôr pêkûna'rî'ô	אהבת הממון
144.	'înveynsîblê	בלתי מנוצח
145.	'îkî vôkô	שם משותף
146.	'ôpôzîtôś	נכוכיים ומתנגדים
147.	'ôzûrā 'ôzûrêrôś	רבית ומלוים ברבית
148.	'înf+a'mêś	שיש להם שם רע
149.	'êśteynśô	בפרטות
150.	'eyśtrôlôgî'ā	תכונה והיא מלה יונית
151.	'înf+îrî'ôreyś	פחותי' מאשר למעל' מהם
152.	'ôpônê	תאר הנכנס בעסק מה
153.	'anbîsî'ôzô	רודף מאד אחר הכבוד
154.	'îrā kûndî'ā	הוא שם הכעס הגדול
155.	'în(ye)t[ê]rpêtêś	מעתיקים

Spanish–Hebrew Glossary

‹164b›

{col. 1}

156.	'adūla'sî'ôn	חנופה
157.	'arôga'ntê	מחשיב עצמו הרבה
158.	'artif+îsêś	בעלי מלאכה
159.	'īpôkrîta'ś	הו' שם נאמ' על הצבועים
160.	'īn'êtêrnûm	נצח סלה ועד
161.	'êntêntôś	הבנות או כונות
162.	'ôf+îsî'ôzā	מלאכותיית
163.	'īlîsîtô	בלתי ראיו
164.	'īnmênsa'ś	לא ימדו ולא יספרו מרוב
165.	'ôbsêrva'nsî'ā	שמירת הנאות להעשות
166.	'arbîtrô	השופט הנבחר ברצון
167.	'êśteynsô	נאמר בארכות ומופשט
168.	'êśtᵉrîbû'îtîbā	הוא שם הצדק המחלק

{col. 2}

169.	'êśkᵉrūpūlôzô	מסופק ונבוך בדבר מה
170.	'a'ūsî'ôn	פועל והוא הפך הפעלות
171.	'êpîkê'ā	החסידו' בחכמה המדיני'
172.	'êśtîlô	סדר והוא נאמ' בכל דבר
173.	'êbîta'n	מונעים
174.	'êśta'bîlê	עומד קיים
175.	'īngra'tô	כפוי טובה
176.	'ênteyndîmîyentô	שכל
177.	'artê	מלאכה
178.	'angūlôś	זויות
179.	'ôpînî'ôn	סברא
180.	'êndîvîdô ra'syôna'[l]	איש מדבר
181.	'ônîbêrsa'lɛyś	כוללות או כוללים

{col. 3}

182.	'êgiśteynsî'ā	מה שהוא נמצא בפועל
183.	'ɛyterna	נצחית
184.	'aktô	הו' ג"כ פועל הפך הפעלו'
185.	'ɛyntê	נמצא
186.	'arîdmeytîkā	היא חכמת המספר
187.	'abyêśô	בלתי ישר
188.	'īma'ǧīna'sî'ôn	דמיון

Spanish–Hebrew Glossary

189.	'admira'sî'ôn	תמיהה
190.	'anîmôd'ar	הוצא רגע המולד מצד רגע ההריון וכן להפך
191.	'ênğîrî'ɛyndô	הרכבת דבר אחד באחר
192.	'êśpîra'sîyôn dêvî[-nā]	התעוררות אלהי
193.	'ağêntê	פועל והוא הפך המתפעל

{col. 4}

194.	'ardû'ā	קשה ועמוקה
		אות הבית
195.	bêheymeynsî'ā	זריזות וחריזות בחוזק
197.	bêneyra'bleyś	ראויים לכבוד
198.	byêneyś tênpôra'ley‹ś›	טובות חצוניות
199.	beynîbôleynsî'ā	אהבת טוב או רצון טוב
200.	beyneyf+îsênsî'ā	עשיית טוב
201.	brîga'ś	קטטות ומריבות
202.	ba'zîś	תושבת ויסוד הדברים
		אות הגימל
203.	ğeyneyrîka'ś	סוגיות מלשון סוג
204.	ga'lyya'rdô	חזק ובריא אולם
205.	ğûreyś kônśûltôś	יודעי דת ודין

‹165a›
{col. 1}

206.	ğôsā dê ga'na'dô	סוכה לב"ח
207.	ğôkôzā	דבר בדרך שחוק והתול
208.	ğênêra'blêś	הוות מלשון ההויה
209.	ğê'ômêtrî'ā	הנדסה
		אות הדלת
210.	dîf+îsîl	קשה ההשגה או העשיה
211.	dêf+ra'ûda'r	הו' נאמ' ביחו' על האונא'
212.	dôt'ar	לתת בנדוניא
213.	dêlêkta'sî'ôn	תענוג
214.	dêśtîntā	מחולקת ונפרדת
215.	dêf+êktû'ôzô	בעל מום
216.	dîśpônê	מכין מלשון הכנה

{col. 2}

217.	dêpût'ad'aś	מיוחדות

Spanish–Hebrew Glossary

218. dêś'a'ût(i)ôrîza'mên-tô   פחיתות ובזיון
219. dîğîśtîbā   נאמר על הכח המעכל
220. dêstênpᵉla'nsā   בלתי הסתפקות
221. dībîlîtā   מחליש
222. dîmînsî'ônêś   מרחקי' וביחו' הג' מרחקים
223. dîsîrnîr   ברירה דבר מתוך דבר
224. dî'ûrnô   יומיי
225. dêkôrô   שמירת כל דבר הנאות לו
226. da'rdô   רומח או כיוצא לזה
227. dîklîna'sî'ôn   ירידה
228. dîf+însî'ôn   גדר
229. dêdîkô dêdîka'sîyôn   הוא חנוך

{col. 3}

230. dî'amêtrô   קוטר ונקרא אלכסון
231. dɛylînkêntê   חוטא
232. dênômînā   משים שם
233. dîśta'nsî'ā   מ(ד)[ר]חק
234. dɛyśkᵉrîpsî'ôn   רושם
235. dînûmîna'dô   נזכר ונכר בשם
236. dêsîmûla'sî'ôn   עושה דבר א' ומרא' אחר
237. dêśtînğêndô   הוא מלשון הבדל ופרוד
238. dîśûlûtôś   חצופים ומשולחים
239. dîrîba'sî'ôn   דבר נגזר מדבר אחר
240. dîvîzî'ôn   חלוק ופרוד
241. dîf+ûntô   מת ונפטר מן העולם
242. dîśkûtîr   לברר הדבר בכל חלוקיו

{col. 4}

243. dîśtᵉra'îdā   מתקבצת לעצמה אות ההא
244. hɛdyôta'ś   הדיוטו' לקוח מלשו' הקדש אות הוו
245. vîgôr   כח וחוזק
246. virtûd 'atra'ktî-b[a]h   כח המושך
247. vɛyhɛymɛynsî'ā   זריזות בחוזק
248. vêra'nô   הוא האביב
249. vîša'sî'ôn   תנועה ממקו' למקו' בצער
250. va'rî'ablêś   בלתי עומדים במצב אחד

Spanish–Hebrew Glossary

251. vênênô הוא סם ממית
252. viǧila'nsi'ā תעורה

‹165b›
{col. 1}
253. vêrîsîmîl דבר נדמה שהוא אמת
254. velôsîd'ad מהירות ותכיפה
255. vi'ôleynsi'ā הכרח ואונס
256. vîtûpêrî'ô גנות וחרפה וקלון
257. va'kû'ô ריקות
258. vɛyrbô תיבה ומלה
259. veyrtûdeyś מעלות
260. va'pôreyś אידים
261. va'rî'ableyś בלתי מסודרי' ומתחלפים
262. va'gā הוא בטל
263. vênt‎ᵉrîkûlô חדר המוח או הלב
264. va'sîla'ndô בלתי עומד בדבר אחד

{col. 2}
אות הטית
265. tôlêra'nsi'ā סבלנות בהכרח
266. tê'ôlôǧî'ā דבור אלהי והי' לשון יוני
267. tr'ankîlîd'ad מנוחה והשקט
268. têrê'ā ארציית
269. têtûbey'andô בלתי עמידה על דבר אחד
270. tra'nsîtôrî'ā עוברת
271. tra'sā רקב ועש
272. tra'śpa'rêntê ספיריי
273. tîmîdô ירא ורך הלבב
274. ta'ktô משוש
275. teynpᵉla'nsā הסתפקות
276. tê'ôrîkô עיוני

{col. 3}
277. trîbûla'sî'ôneyś מאורעות רעות
278. trî'angûlô משלש הזויות
אות הלמד
279. lûsîdîsîmô מאיר מאד
280. la'brôtêra'ś טפות גסו' שנתבו' מהשלג

Spanish–Hebrew Glossary

281. līnya'ś   קוים
282. la'sêdêmônî'ôś   אנשי מקום לאסידימוניא
283. līkôr   משקה שהוא נתך
284. la'meynta'sî'ôneyś   קינות
285. lêğêśla'tôr   נותן התורה
286. lûğûrî'ā   רבוי המשגל
287. līğûnğêrô   חנף

{col. 4}
288. lêga'l   דתיי
289. lûmîna'rî'ôś   מאורות
290. lôğīkā   הגיון
291. lêgôś   הם עמי הארץ אות המם
292. môdeyrnôś   אחרונים
293. ma'gnᵉya'nîmôś   גדולי הלב
294. mêta'fīzīkôś   חכמים באלהיות
295. mînîśtᵉrôś   משרתים
296. metê'ôrô lôğīka'ś   הפעליות מאותו' עליונו'
297. miśtôś   מעורבים ומורכבים
298. mêta'ûrôś   אותות עליונות

‹166a›
{col. 1}
299. mīkrô kôśmô   עולם קטן ביון
300. ma'ndᵉra'gôrā   דודאים
301. mônśᵉtrû   הדבר היוצ' מדרך הטבע
302. ma'rtîrî'ôś   יסורין
303. môleyśtî'ā   נאמר על הצער והדאגה
304. môra'lɛyś   מדותיו(ם)[ת]
305. môna'rkā   מולך בכיפה
306. mɛyntê   שכל
307. ma'rtîrɛyś   נמסרי' למיח' לקדוש' הש"י
308. mêlôdî'[a]h   ערבות קולות מתיחסות
309. môdeyra'sî'ôn   תקון והשואה
310. merîtrîśî   הוא שם זונה
311. ma'knîfīsɛynsî'ā   הוא שם מעלת השוע

Spanish–Hebrew Glossary

{col. 2}
312. môdêśtî'ā   אהבת הכבוד כפי הראוי
313. mîrîdî'anô   קו חצי היום
314. môbîlê   מתנועע
315. mêndôzā   שקרנית או מלאה שקרי'
316. ma'têma'tika'ś   למודיות
317. mînûtôś   דקים
318. mêla'nkôlikô   שחוריי
319. mêrā   פשוטה בלתי עירוב כלל
    אות הנון
320. nûnsî'ô   שליח
321. nûdā   פשוטה וערומה
322. nîtera'l   שטחיות העניין

{col. 3}
323. na'ra'dô   דבר נאמר או מסופר
324. nêf+a'ndā   דבר מגונה מאד
    אות הסמך
325. sîlênsî'ô   שתיקה והעדר הדבור
326. sêlikeh   שמיימית
327. sînsêrā   נקיה ומזוקקת
328. sêvêrêda'd   כובד והעדר קלות
329. sêlêbr'ar   רבוי השמח' וביחו' לכב' ה'
330. sêrkônsᵉta'nsî'aś   תנאים
331. sêntᵉrô   מרכז
332. sôf+iśtīkā   מזוייפת
333. sôf+îsêyentyeś   מספיקות

{col. 4}
    אות הפא
334. pêrpêktû'ā   נצחית
335. f+îlîsîda'd   אושר
336. prôdûzîdā   נמשכת
337. f+a'kûndîsîmā   מספקת מאד
338. f+a'mîlia'r   בין בית
339. f+ûtûrô   עתיד
340. f+a'nta'śmā   צורה דמיונית בדויה
341. f+îśa'sî'ôn   עמידה בקיום וחוזק
342. pô'êtā   משורר

Spanish–Hebrew Glossary

343.	f+ōrtū'ītôŝ	דברי' נמשכי' מפאת המזל
344.	prôbîdênsî'ā	השגחה
345.	prîba'sî'ôn	העדר

‹166b›
{col. 1}

346.	prêplêǧô	פוסח על שתי הסעיפים
347.	pa'trî'arkā	אב הראשון והי' מלה יוני
348.	prêsêbtô	מצוה
349.	prêmî'ô	שכר
350.	prôśpêrô	מוצלח
351.	pa'rtisîpa'ntê	משתתף עם אחר
352.	prîva'r	מניעת דבר מדבר
353.	f+îǧôś	קיימים
354.	prôlôgô	הקדמה
355.	prôpînka'ś	קרובות
356.	pôzîtîbā	מונחת
357.	prôbleyma'ś	שאלי' בהיו' הטעם להפך
358.	pla'nêta'ś	הוא שם ככבי לכת

{col. 2}

359.	pênêtra'sî'ôn dê d[i]ymeynsî'ôneyś	הכנס' המרחקי' אלו באלו
360.	f+a'nta'zî'ā	הכח המחשב או המדמה
361.	pōlô	קוטב והי' נקודה בשמים
362.	preytôr	שופט
363.	prô'îbîdô	דבר שנאסר להעשות
364.	prôlîǧîda'd	אריכות בדברים
365.	pêsîmô	רשע ורע מאד
366.	pôrpôrsî'ôn	התייחסות
367.	preysêbtôr	נגיד ומצוה לאומים
368.	f+ra'ǧîl	מוכנת להשבר מהר ה
369.	peyrma'nêntê	נצחית
370.	pêrveyrsôŝ	מעוותים

{col. 3}

371.	pôzîla'nîmô	קטן הלב
372.	f+ra'zeyś	המשך הדבור
373.	peyrsêbêra'nsā	ההתמדה ברע
374.	pôrpûzîsî'ôn	הנחה

SPANISH–HEBREW GLOSSARY

375.	pôtênsî'ā	כחניות
376.	f+a'la'sî'ā	טעות
377.	f+adô	נאמ' על המזל והמערכת
378.	pûnyêndô	בהיותו מעניש
379.	pêrî'êrmîna'ś	הוא שם ספר המליצה
380.	plûra'r	לשון רבים
381.	f+ilôtîmî'ā	אהבת הכבוד
382.	prûdênsî'ā	תבונה
383.	prôdêga'lîda'd	פזור והוא הפך הכליות

{col. 4}

384.	prêkla'rā	בהירה ושלמה
385.	prôpîsîmā	מיוחדת מאד
386.	pa'ûpêrîmôś	עניים ודלים מאד
387.	p(+)êsîmô	הוא שם לרע בהפלגה
388.	pêrpêtû'ā	נצחית
389.	prîva'tîbā mêntê	דרך שלילה ולא דרך חיוב
390.	pêrveyrteyr	מלשון עוות ושנוי
391.	pêśa'ltêrî'ô	הוא שם ספר תהלים
392.	f+êlîsê	מאושר
393.	pêrnêsî'ôzā	ממיתה
394.	pêrğûrô	הוא הנשבע לשוא ולשקר
395.	pôlîtîkā	הנהגת המדינה
396.	f+ôrêśtikôś	הצוניים בלתי מדיניים

⟨167a⟩
{col. 1}

397.	f+lêma'tîkā	לבניית
398.	pôndêra'r	לדקדק בענין
399.	pîta'gôrîkôś	כת פיטאגוראש החכם
400.	f+îzîkôś	טבעיים
401.	peydrîka'meyntô	מאמר
402.	f+a'ksî'ôn	הפעלות
403.	prôpinkā	מיוחדת
404.	peyrma'nêntê	נשאר
405.	prîmîsa'ś	שם ההנחות הראשונות
406.	prôpôzîsî'ôneyś	הנחות
407.	f+a'ktô	פעולה
408.	p(+)rêśpêktîbā	חלוף המבטים
409.	pôśtîrî'ôr	אחרון

Spanish–Hebrew Glossary

{col. 2}
410.	pôrnôśtîkā	הקדמת הידיעה	
411.	prê'anbûlôś	הקדמות החצעות אות הקוף	
412.	kômūnîka'dô	משותף	
413.	kôrûpsî'ôn	הפסד	
414.	kônpêteyn	יאותו	
415.	kôśtêla'sî'ôn	מערכת	
416.	kônpᵉlîsî'ôn	מזג	
417.	kûmbᵉrê	רום וגובה גדול	
418.	kûbā	חבית או גיגית	
419.	ka'pa's	מכיל	
420.	kônf+êrîr	הקש דבר אל דבר אחר	

{col. 3}
421.	kîlô	המאכל כשיתעכל	
422.	kônśᵉtā	מכריח או מנצח	
423.	kôlîğîdôś	מקובצים	
424.	kônğûnsî'ônêś	חבורים משני דברי'	
425.	kônka'bô	קערירות	
426.	kûmûta'tîbā	נאמר על הצדק המישיר	
427.	kômôdôś	מועילים	
428.	klîmā	אקלים	
429.	ka'nsêr	סרטן	
430.	ka'prîkôrnô	גדי	
431.	krîpûśkûlôś	נשפים נשף יום ונש' לילה	
432.	kông(+)ᵉrêga'sî'ôn	קבוץ דברים וחבורם יחד	
433.	kônkôrdî'ā	התאחדו' הסברו' והדעות	

{col. 4}
434.	kônta'ğî'ôzā	מתדבקת	
435.	ka'pita'l	מחוייב בראשו	
436.	kônsôrsî'ô	חברת אהובים	
437.	kônf+îsî'ôn	הוא הודאה וודוי	
438.	kônsêbtô	קבלת דבר מה בשכל	
439.	ka'dûkā	נופלת	
440.	kôntᵉra'śta'r	היות מנגד לאחר וחולק	
441.	kra'sā	עבה ועכורה	
442.	kôrôbôra'r	חוזק הענין בראיות	
443.	kônpûta'ndô	בחושבן	

Spanish–Hebrew Glossary

444. ka'rdîna'lêś   מעלו' הכוללו' שא' המעלו'
445. kôntênênsî'ā   כשרות וכבישת היצר
446. krônika'ś   ספרי דברי הימים

⟨167b⟩
{col. 1}
447. kômênta'dôr   מפרש
448. kôytô   משגל
449. klêmêntêś   הם העושים חסד
450. ka'lêf+îka'dôś   גדולי האיכות
451. ka'ûta'r bênîbôlên-sî'ā   מציאת חן
452. kî'êtûd   מנוחה והשקט
453. kôntênsî'ôn   כשרו' וכבישת הי(נ)[ע]ר הרע
454. kônkûpîsîblê   תאוני
455. kômênsûra'r   לשער ענין מה
456. kôrûtîblêś   נפסדות
457. ka'ntîda'd dêśkᵉrê-tā   כמה מתפרד
458. ka'ntîda'd kôntînû-ā   כמה מתדבק
459. ka'lkûla'dô   משוער בחשבון ברור

{col. 2}
460. kônsêbidô   הוא מלשון הריון
461. kra'nî'ô   הוא גולגלת הראש
462. kîmêra'ś   צורות בדויות דמיוניות
463. kôśtêla'sî'ôn   מערכה אות הריש
464. rêzîśtîr   התקוממות נגד המנגד
465. rêf+rîzêrî'ô   תענוג
466. rêtîntîbā   כח המחזיק באדם
467. rôbûśtā   עכורה
468. rêf+lêksî'ôn   התהפכות הנצוצות
469. rêpêrkûtîbôś   מרתעים
470. rêbêrbêra'sî'ôn   הוא התהפכות הניצוצות
471. rêkônsêntra'dôś   מקובצות אל המרכז

{col. 3}
472. reśtîtû'îsî'ônêś   תשלומין
473. rêkûpîlā   כולל בדברים מועטים
474. reybôlûsî'ôneyś   סבובים והקפים

Spanish–Hebrew Glossary

475.	rûdô	גס השכל
476.	ra'sî'ôna'l	מדבר
477.	rêdêmsi'ôn	פדיון
478.	rêzêrva'dô	שמור
479.	rêmîsô	רפה ורך
480.	rêlîğî'ôz(ê)ôś	נזירים ואדוקים בדת
481.	rêsûrê'îsî'ôn	תחיית המתים
482.	rê'îtêra'n	חוזרי' למה שהיו בתחלה
483.	//rêp(+)lêtkô//	מלא
		אות השין

{col. 4}

484.	śôbğêktô	נושא
485.	śeynsû'alîda'd	הרגשה והו' הכח המרגיש
486.	śôlîdā	מקשיית
487.	śêndêrîzîś	ההתחלות הידועות לכל
488.	śîrkûnf+ɛyrensî'ā	הקף
489.	śeylêbêrimô	אדם מוחזק לאדם שלם
490.	śûblima'dā	דבר מעולה
491.	śîrkûnśᵉpêktô	משער ומשקיף בדברים
492.	śûpref+lû'ô	מותר
493.	śûpref[î]ysî'ā	שטח
494.	śî'ɛyntif+îkā	בחכמה גדולה
495.	śûpînā	בטלה
496.	śeylêśtê 'ênflûğû	השפעה שמיימית

‹168a›
{col. 1}

497.	śûplîsî'ô	[ייסו]רין
498.	[śûpûzîsi]y'ôn	[הנחה]
499.	[śeyvêrîd]a'd	[כבדי' והו'] משותף לאכזריו
500.	śingûl'ar	[יחיד]
501.	[śûsîntā mêntê]	[בקצור דברים כוללי'] הכל

{col. 2}

502.	śînôkā	הוא שם מין קדחת
503.	śeyf+a'lya' śa'f+ênā	שמו' ורידים שמקיזי' בהם
504.	śôrdîdô	מטונף
505.	śû('ô)ntû'ôza'ś	רבותה ההוצאה

SPANISH–HEBREW GLOSSARY

506. śêlôğíśmô   הקש

{col. 3}
507. śêka'zɛyś   ההולכי' בשטה מה
508. śîgnôś 'ô ś[e]ynyôś   מזלות
509. śênsî'ā   דעת
510. śa'pênsî'ā   חכמה
511. śêleyśtᵉrê   שמימיי

{col. 4}
512. śêlêbrô   מוח
513. śêntô lôkî'ô   מאה דבורי' והו' שם ספר
514. śôlîtô   נהוג ומורגל
515. śôba'ltêrna'dô   נכנע תחת אחר
516. śa'gra'dā śa'kra   דבר קדוש

ERRATA

{CB 1}
A record of the printing errors in these books that change the understanding of the intention of the [author's] meaning, save the spelling errors [which are] easily amended when reading the books. Page 16a the end of line four, for *'ensi segun* read *'ensi salvo segun*. Page 21a line two in the new chapter, for *'a 'oras devidadas,* read *devidas;* and some lines before the end of the same page at the beginning of the line, for *repistir* read *rexistir*. Page 30a line eight, for *komunyamos* read *komunikamos;* and at the beginning of line ten, for *vidad* read *vida*. Page 3(5)[8]a the beginning of the last line, for *memory(z)a 'eselente* read *'un 'eselente*. Page 3(7)[9]b in the next to the last line, for *kuarto modo todo saby'o* read *'uza todo savy'o*. Page 4(5)[3]b the beginning of line seven, for *alkansando* read *alkansado*. Page 48b the beginning of line six, for *Yesaᶜyahu* read *Yermiyahu*. Page 59b fourth line from the end of the page at the beginning of the line, for *'inmitable* read *'inmutable*. Page 65a at the end of the page the last line is missing: *kontenplasy'on lo fazen destenplado 'y son tantos los males 'enesto*. Page 67a line 19, for *'enel dar 'enel tomar,* read *'enel dar mas ke 'enel tomar*. Page 75a line 14, for *desu minimo,* read *desu animo*. Page 75b line 18, for *'i kual kyera,* read *ke kual kyera*. Page 80b at the end of line one, for *signiykasyyon,* read *signif+ikasyyon:* line nine, for *'opiniron,* read *'opinyon;* six lines below, for *absuluta* read *'okulta;* and the end of line 18, for *asi asi* read *asi kon*. Page 8(2)4[b]

Spanish–Hebrew Glossary

the beginning of line six, for *'insesible* read *'insensible;* line 18, for *rependido,* read *reprendido.* Page 90 the last line but one, for *robd* read *dubdo* the last line, for *horna* read *torna.* Page 99 the end of the page is incomplete, *'oyen* where it should read *yaloś ke le 'oyen.* Page 99b the last line but one, for *'ekokente* read *'elokoente.* Page 101 line eleven, for *ğersero* read *tersero.*}

‹C 168a›
{Page 102b line 29, for *vis̆ğo* read *vis̆to.* Page 104 the end of line 28, for *'es̆krupulo* read *'es̆krupulozo.* Page 105b line two, for *śino loda* read *śilo da.* 109b line seven, for *'ofisy'o* read *'es̆pesy'a.* Page 116, for *no me ru'eges̆* read *'o no me ru'eges̆* : Page 120 the end of line 34, for *ke no 'enla ley* read *śalvo 'enla le'ey* and for *pu'ede* read *ke no pu'ede.* Page 129[b] the end of line 15, for *akasy'on* read *aksy'on* : Page 131b line 34 for *ke konloke* read *kelo ke* : Page 138 line 22, for *ke glorif+ika* read *ke śe glorif+ika* : Page 140 end of line 26, for *sensy'a* read *sesenta* : line 30, for *śon* read *śin.* Page 147 line twelve, for *kos̆as̆* read *kaus̆as̆* : *'el ke tal* should read *'el tal* : line 36 after *'a* [*de suseder*] is missing *'es̆pesyal śi fu'ere 'es̆trologo* : Page 147b line nine, for *asnedente* read *asendente* : line ten, *koysebsy'on* should read *konsebsy'on* : Page 148 line 24, for *'en la* read *'i la 'imağinasy'on.* In the glossary, for *ref+letko* read *ref+lekto*
It is complete and finished.}

Biblical, Talmudic, and Midrashic Passages

BIBLICAL PASSAGES

Genesis

1.1, 14a
1.2, 90a
1.3, 90a
1.4, 75b, 90a, 90b
1.14, 1b
1.16, 45a
1.26, 129a
1.27, 8b
2.18, 8a, 32b
3.5, 7b
3.16, 32b
3.19, 8b, 137b
6.12, 8b, 130b
18.15, 73b
18.17, 8b, 112b
20.6, 151b, 155a
20.7, 151b, 152a
21.8, 73b
31.24, 151b, 152a, 155a
32.25, 4b
37.1, 12a a

37.3, 161b
37.4, 5a, 80a
37.5, 161b
37.7 162a
37.11, 161b
37.15, 8b, 110a
37.19, 10b, 144a
37.20, 10b, 144a
40.8, 161b
41.1, 11b, 155a
41.2, 155a
41.8, 153a
41.10, 149a, 153b
41.11, 149a, 154a
41.12, 154a
41.16, 8a, 92b
41.17, 155a
41.20, 155b
41.21, 155b
41.23, 155b
41.24, 152b

455

Biblical, Talmudic, and Midrashic Passages

41.25, 154b, 156a
41.28, 154b, 156a
41.31, 155b
41.32, 12a, 161a, 162a, 155b

41.34, 11b, 155b, 156a
41.39, 156b
43.23, 1b
48.16, 1b

Exodus

2.2, 8a, 75b
2.11, 8a, 76a
2.13, 8a, 76a, 81b
3.6, 7b
11.3, 8a, 80a
14.27, 6a, 97a
18.19, 8a
18.25, 8a, 79b
20.5, 8a, 18a
20.8, 4a
20.12, 8a, 8b, 101b, 122b
20.13, 106a
20.14, 8a

20.17, 102a
21.15, 49b
21.24, 6b, 104a, 104b
23.7, 96b
31.14, 106a
32.19, 78a
33.13, 8a, 18b
34.1, 5a, 78a
34.7, 8a, 18a
34.8, 8a, 80a
34.9, 8a, 80a
35.31, 8b, 130a
35.32, 8b, 130a

Leviticus

11.15, 8a, 109b
19.18, 6b, 8a, 109b, 112a

19.32, 8a, 20b
24.20, 6b, 104a

Numbers

2.2, 1b
11.4, 8a, 22a
12.1, 8a, 84a
12.3, 8a, 55b, 84a
12.7, 11b

12.8, 11b
22.2, 11b
29.18, 4a, 7b
31.10, 1b

Deuteronomy

1.17, 8a, 103b
5.16, 122b
6.4, 8b, 124b

6.5, 8b, 58a, 124b
6.8, 160b
6.24, 41a

BIBLICAL, TALMUDIC, AND MIDRASHIC PASSAGES

10.2, 78a
11.13, 126a
11.18, 160b
15.10, 8a, 67b
16.17, 8a, 67a
17.8, 8a, 106a
17.9, 8a, 106a
17.11, 6b, 8a, 106b
20.8, 9b, 57a
25.17, 85b

25.19, 8a, 85b
26.16, 8a, 41a
28.9, 4b, 67a
30.15, 8b, 138a
30.19, 138a
32.2, 1a, 1b
32.28, 130b
33.4, 1b
33.16, 10a
34.28, 8b

Joshua

2.12, 9b, 78b
2.14, 78b, 9b

6.25, 9b, 79a

Judges

5.31, 5a, 76b

1 Samuel

4.11, 18a
15.19, 9b

15.20, 84b
23.17, 9b, 115a, 115b

2 Samuel

1.23, 9b, 114a, 116a
6.14, 99b
13. 22, 9b, 80b

18.23, 1b
19.1, 9b, 57b

1 Kings

3.26, 9b, 119a

2 Kings

17.15, 90b

Biblical, Talmudic, and Midrashic Passages

Isaiah

    3.10, 9a, 119b
    3.11, 9a, 119b
    5.18, 2b, 9a
    5.18, 9a, 32b
    5.20, 95a
    15.9, 1b
    26.9, 1b
    29.8, 10b, 144b
    29.13, 94a

    38.7, 1b
    40.4, 1b
    40.27, 9a, 49b
    40.28, 9a, 49b
    42.21, 160b
    51.8, 44b
    53.6, 9a, 121a
    54.17, 3b
    55.9, 51a

Jeremiah

    2.2, 1b
    2.19, 9a, 9a, 48b, 119b, 123a
    4.19, 1b
    5.27, 7a, 119b

    10.10, 9a, 94b
    10.23, 9a, 52a
    17.1, 1b
    18.4–6, 2a

Ezekiel

    18.32, 18b

    20.40, 53a

Hosea

    6.2, 9a, 41b, 42a

Joel

    3.4, 9a

Malachi

    3.23, 9a, 41b

Psalms

    1.1, 8b, 92a, 99a, 120a
    1.2, 8b, 92a, 120a, 138b

    1.6, 90a
    1.7, 8b

BIBLICAL, TALMUDIC, AND MIDRASHIC PASSAGES

11.5, 2a
11.7, 100b
15.1, 5a, 8b, 80b
15.2, 8b, 80b, 101a
15.3, 8b, 101a
15.5, 80b
16.11, 8b, 12b
17.13, 8b, 18b
18.2, 1b
20.5, 8b, 8b, 62a
23.5, 1a
25.5, 94b
32.10, 7a, 8b, 48b, 119b
34.1, 93a
36.1, 48a
37.18, 3a, 42b
37.30, 8b, 102b
37.31, 8b, 102b
56.14, 1b
58.7, 9b, 9b
58.11, 8b, 87a

62.13, 8b, 103a
63.7, 8b, 31a
66.9, 1b
73.26, 1b
85.14, 1b
87.1, 1a
92.8, 8b, 18
92.13, 160a b
101.7, 8b, 36a
112.7, 60b
118.1, 159b
118.2, 159b, 160a
118.4, 159b, 160b
119.3, 120a
119.62, 8b, 31a
119.99, 131b
119.112, 1b
119.126, 8b, 107a
133.1, 122a
144.2, 1b
145.19, 160a

Proverbs

1.6, 1b
3.3, 23b
3.5, 60b
3.6, 8b, 9a
3.6, 43b, 138a
3.16, 8b, 77b
3.18, 8a
4.2, 9a, 138a
4.8, 160a
4.11, 98a
4.22, 1b
5.1, 20b
6.4, 8b, 30a
6.9, 8b, 30b
6.10, 8b, 30a

6.25, 63b
7.3, 23b
7.26, 6b, 106b
8.22, 2a
10.24, 7a
11.18, 8b, 93a
13.25, 8b, 22a
14.14, 8b, 82a
14.20, 108b
14.30, 3b
15.20, 1b
15.23, 8b, 38b
16.22, 131a
17.3, 8b
17.17, 8b, 110b

BIBLICAL, TALMUDIC, AND MIDRASHIC PASSAGES

19.7, 8b
20.13, 30a
21.30, 7b
22.6, 1a
23.15, 9a, 118b, 119a
27.2, 8b, 81a
27.5, 9a, 112b
27.19, 7b, 9a, 123b

27.21, 8b, 77b
29.4, 100b
29.14, 8b, 94b
29.23, 77a
30.21, 8b, 32a
30.22, 8b, 32b
30.23, 8b, 32b

Job

1.1, 9a
1.8, 17b
1.16, 87a, 87b
1.17, 87a, 87b
1.21, 9a, 138a
2.11, 9a, 108a, 122b
4.18, 9a, 41b, 43a

8.7, 9a, 91b
11.6, 1b
12.12, 161b
15.15, 2b
15.20, 7a
31.34, 5b
33.18, 1b

Song of Solomon

1.1, 9a, 114b
3.4, 157b, 158a

6.4, 5b
8.6, 1b

Ruth

1.16, 9a, 116b
1.17, 9a, 116b

Lamentations

3:33, 1b, 9b
3.38, 52a, 52b
3.39, 9b, 52a, 53a

4.7, 1a
5.15, 9b, 45a
5.16, 9b

Ecclesiastes

3.4, 9a, 99b
5.1, 10b, 143b

5.2, 10b, 143b, 144a
5.12, 9a, 69a, 108a

BIBLICAL, TALMUDIC, AND MIDRASHIC PASSAGES

5.13, 69a
5.14, 69a, 69b
5.15, 9a, 71a
7.1, 9a, 41a, 45a
7.3, 9a, 84a
7.9, 9a, 86b

7.10, 9a, 45b, 47a
7.17, 9a, 42b
8.15, 3b, 9a
8.15, 45a
11.9, 9a, 44b, 47b
12.14, 47b

Esther

1.1, 121b
1.3, 9b
1.4, 9b

1.17, 9b
2.18, 9b
5.10, 9b

Daniel

1.4, 2b, 9a, 29b

Wisdom of Solomon

4.2, 41b

Ben Sira

41.1, 41b
45.14, 41b

RABBINIC PASSAGES

Miṣudat David

Ps. 145.18, 80b
Prov. 13.13, 4a, 57a

Ralbag

Job 4.26, 2a

BIBLICAL, TALMUDIC, AND MIDRASHIC PASSAGES

Ramban

Deut. 11.1, 4b, 67a

Rashi

Gen. 1.1, 2a
Gen. 37.3, 161b
Gen. 37.4, 5a, 80b
Gen. 37.15, 6b, 110a
Exod. 6.23, 2a
Exod. 18.21, 79b

Lev. 19.18, 6b
Lev. 19.32, 35b
Num. 31.21, 5a, 85b
Song of Sol. 1.1, 7a, 114b
Eccles. 8.15, 3b, 45a

Tanḥuma

Shemot 12, 5a, 75b

Targum

Job 10.17, 5b

TALMUD

Berakot 7a, 18a
Berakot 14a, 4b, 64b
Berakot 17a, 3a, 41b
Berakot 18b, 8a, 44b, 133b
Berakot 19b, 7b
Berakot 21a, 28b
Berakot 31a, 6a, 98b
Berakot 34b, 5b, 89b, 90a
Berakot 48b, 4a, 60b, 61a

Shabbat 10a, 6b, 106b, 104a
Shabbat 10b, 5a, 76a
Shabbat 30b, 3b, 6a
Shabbat 61a, 6b
Shabbat 88b, 3b, 5a, 76b

Berakot 55a, 146a
Berakot 55b, 10b, 12a, 146a, 160b, 161a, 162a
Berakot 57b, 2b, 10a, 10b, 30a, 140a, 145b
Berakot 60a, 4a, 60b
Berakot 61b, 4a, 4b, 7b, 58a, 59a, 59b, 71b, 124b

Shabbat 92a, 5a, 11b, 77b, 157a
Shabbat 105b, 5b, 88b
Shabbat 152a, 33b
Eruvin 13b, 6a, 95b
Eruvin 53b, 8a, 134a

BIBLICAL, TALMUDIC, AND MIDRASHIC PASSAGES

Pesahim 49ab, 14a
Pesahim 50a, 19b
Pesahim 68b, 100a
Yoma 82b, 106b
Yoma 83a, 6b
Yoma 84b, 6b, 106b
Sukkah 52a, 2b, 32b
Rosh HaShanah 17a, 90b

Yevamot 65b, 6a, 94a, 95b, 96b
Yevamot 90b, 6b, 106a
Ketubot 16b–17a, 6a, 96b
Ketubot 38a, 104b
Ketubot 40a, 6b, 104b
Ketubot 59b, 3a
Ketubot 66b, 4b, 6b, 72a
Ketubot 66b–67a, 72b

Bava Kamma 17a, 125a
Bava Kamma 83b–84a, 104a
Bava Kamma 84a, 6b
Bava Kamma 86a, 104b
Bava Batra 14b, 5a, 78a
Bava Batra 110a, 2a, 13b
Sanhedrin 7b, 103b
Sanhedrin 58b, 81b
Sanhedrin 71b, 7a, 119a, 119b
Sanhedrin 93b, 2b, 29b
Sanhedrin 94b, 3a, 36b
Sanhedrin 104a, 65a
Sanhedrin 107a, 4b
Makkot 24a, 5a, 81a
Shevuot 47b, 80a

Ta'anit 23a, 6b, 107b
Megillah 12b, 7a, 121a
Megillah 31a, 89a
Megillah 41a, 5b
Moed Katan 28a, 2a, 18a, 33a
Hagigah 3b, 6a, 95b
Hagigah 5a, 3a, 3b, 43a

Ketubot 67a, 4b
Ketubot 111b, 4a, 53a
Sotah 5a, 5b, 89a
Sotah 12a, 5a
Sotah 21b, 6b, 107a
Sotah 44a, 57a
Kiddushin 40b, 7b, 125a, 125b, 160a

Avodah Zarah 19b, 6a, 6b, 98b, 106b
Avodah Zarah 52a, 6b, 106b
Avodah Zarah 55a, 4a, 51b
Avot 2.20, 7b
Avot 3.3, 22b
Avot 3.4, 2b
Avot 3.11, 7b
Avot 4.1, 2a, 4a, 5b, 15b, 56a, 131b
Avot 4.4, 5a, 83a
Avot 5.14, 86a
Avot 5.19, 7a, 114a
Hullin 25a, 4b, 66b
Hullin 60a, 66b
Hullin 91a, 4b, 68b
Kinim 25a, 3a

BIBLICAL, TALMUDIC, AND MIDRASHIC PASSAGES

COMMENTARY

Rashi

Talmud Berakot 41b, 3a
Moed Katan 6b, 2b, 24a

Kiddushin 40b, 7b, 126a
Bava Kamma 17a, 125a, 126a

MIDRASHIM

Genesis Rabbah

2.5, 5b, 90a
5.5, 96b, 97a
17.2, 33a
20.7, 7a, 111a
24.7, 109b
52.5, 11b, 157b
58.1, 3a, 42b, 43a

74.7, 157b, 158a, 159a
88.2, 148a, 148b
89.4, 155a, 11b
89.5, 12a, 145b
89.6, 11a, 152b, 153a
89.8, 10b, 146b

Exodus Rabbah

1.20, 75b
3.6, 7b, 127a
5, 161b

7.5, 2a, 13a
21.6, 6a, 97b
30.4, 6b, 107a

Leviticus Rabbah

1.12, 11b, 157b, 158a

Numbers Rabbah

10.2, 3b, 47b

Song of Solomon Rabbah

I.2.2, 6b, 106b

BIBLICAL, TALMUDIC, AND MIDRASHIC PASSAGES

Ruth Rabbah

2.10, 87a, 87b

OTHER

Tosafot Bava Kamma 17a, 125a
Otsar Hamidrashim Amud 27 p. 56?, 2b
Otsar Hamidrashim Amud 27 p. 56?, 23b

Glossary

The glossary offers a point of reference for unusual forms or terms and the location of their first occurrence in the text. For terms whose apparent sense is different in two places, the first location for each sense is given. The words are glossed from Amigo, *El léxico del Pentateuco de Constantinopla y la Biblia Medieval Romanceada Judeo-española*; idem, *El Pentateuco de Constantinopla y la Biblia Medieval Romanceada Judeoespañola*; Corominas and Pascual, *Diccionario crítico etimológico castellano hispánico*; Crews, "Extracts from *Meam Loez*"; and Pascual Recuero, *Diccionario básico Ladino-Español*. Latin alphabetical order is followed except that the sequence of special characters is g, ğ, h, ḥ, s, ś, and š; aleph is excluded from consideration.

abariza 'avaricia' 55a
abaśtan *see* abaśtar
*abaśtar 'bastar, suffice': abaśtan 14b
abezar 'avezar' 19a
*abiviguar 'give life, save': abiviguarnoś 41a
*abolar 'volar': abola 140b
*abonar 'hacer bien, mejorar': abonar 45a
*abonigu'arśe 'hacer bien, mejorar': aboniguarte'a 44b
abto 'acto' 17b
abundansa 'abundancia' 68b
ado'eśto 'censure' (?) 21a
afabil 'afable' 91a
*afermoziguarar 'embellecer': afermoziguaraś 20b
afinkada 'ahincada' 65a
*afogar 'ahogar': afoge 27a
*aforarśe 'consume, exhaust': aforarśe'a 68a
agazağar 'agasajar' 73b
*aguzear 'aguzar': aguzean 71a

Glossary

Ağibto 'Egipto' 97a
ağipsy'o 'egipcio' 76a
*akabidar 'precaver, warn' akabida 13b
akabidarśe 'apercibirse, precaverse, take care' 29a
akavidarśe *see* akabidarśe
akazo 'acaso' 15a
*akośtar 'inclinar': akośta 20b
*alevantarśe 'levantarse': te alevantaraś 20b
alhinde 'acero' 41b
alkitara 'alambique' 25a
*alyegar 'llegar': alyegare 13b
aneğaś 'anejas' 15a
*aniğilar 'anihilar': aniğilando 49b
anśi 'así' 25a
antigoś 'antiguos' 17a; antigu'o 14b
apanyyadizo 'mixed multitude' 22a
apreśuranśe *see* apreśurarśe
apreśurarśe 'apresurarse': apreśuranśe 'apresurándose' 161a
*araśtar 'arrastrar': araśtan 34a
*asebtar 'aceptar': asebta 13a
asipreześ 'cipreses' 135b
*aśabentarse 'make oneself wise' śe aśabentara 13b
*aśenyalar 'señalar': aśenyala 13a
ata 'hasta' 37b
atemar 'destruir' 18b
atemarśe 'acabarse' 14b
*atentar 'observe, perceive, try': atente 22b
atorgar 'otorgar, consent, agree' 102b
atriśtar 'entristecer' 90b
*atriśtarśe 'entristecerse': śe atriśta 84b
a'usy'on 'acción' 105b
a'uta 'apta' 51b
a'utiba 'activa' 141a
*aver 'haber': averi'a 'habría' 148a
averi'a *see* aver 'habría' 148a

bafo 'vaho' 26a
*baldar 'impedir, hacer inútil, abolish, suspend': baldośe 46a, baldan 107a

GLOSSARY

bandaś 'lugares' (?) 122a
barağozo 'barajoso' 26b
bašeğa 'bajeza' 32b
baziś 'base' 45a
benifikar 'verificar' 25b
berbo *see* byerbo
*bever 'beber': bevyen 'bebiendo' 144b
bevyen *see* bever
bosaś 'residues after distillation' (?) 123b
*bośeśar 'bostezar': bośeśen 35b
bu'eyś 'bueyes' 151a
byerbo 'palabra' 115b

dar 'dando' 67b
*deber 'deber': debri'a 'debería' 104a
debri'a *see* deber
defezo 'defendido, prohibido' 34b
dekolgadoś *see* dekolgar
*dekolgar 'depend': dekolgadoś 18a
delekteś 'deleites' 47a
*delgazar 'adelgazar': delgazando 24b
demanda 'pregunta' 45b
dende 'desde' 14b
*deperder 'destrozar, perder': depyerde 36b
deśkaymyento 'decaimiento' 2a
deśkreto 'discreto' 41a
deśle'erśe 'acobardarse, desmayarse': śe deśle'e 58b
*deśparzir 'esparcir': deśparze 25a
deśpedidoś 'unimpeded' 17a
deśpender 'gastar, malbaratar' 27b
deśtingendo *see* deśtingir
*deśtingir 'distinguir': deśtingendo 'distinguiendo' 95b
deśtintoś 'distintos' 20a
*dešar 'dexar': dešando 18a
*dezir 'decir': dišo 'dijo' 16b; dirlo'e 'lo diré' 17a; dišeśe 'dijese' 18b
dibilita 'debilita' 27b
difenensy'a 'diferencia' 96b
difinsy'on 'definición' 24b

GLOSSARY

dirlo'e *see* dezir
*diśponer 'disponer': diśporna 'dispondra' 38b
diśporna *see* diśponer
diśulutoś 'disolutos' 98b
dišeśe *see* dezir
dišo *see* dezir
do 'donde' 13b
dubda 'duda' 14b
dyentro 'dentro' 19b

'edony'o 'idoneo' 21a
'eğersitar 'ejercitar' 17a
'eḥad (H.) 'one' 124b
'eliksy'on 'elección' 59b
'Elodim (H.) 'euphemistic spelling for Elohim' 104a
'enbezar 'acostumbrar' 40b; 'enbezo 'acostumbrado' 43b
'endibidu'oś 'individuos' 15a
'endiğiśta 'indigesta' 22b
'endividoś 'individuos' 103a
'enflušu 'influjo' 49a
*'enfy'uzy'arśe 'tener fe, creer': śe 'enfy'uzy'a 119b
'enğalsado *see* enšalśar
'enğir 'henchir' 97a
*'enkliminar 'praise, denounce': 'enkliminaron 36b, 88b
*'enkubrir 'encubrir': 'enkubryen 'encubriendo' 112b
'enkubryen *see* 'enkubrir
*'enmaleser 'hacer mal, maleficiar': no 'enmaleśkaś 42b
*'enmentar 'mentar, recordar': 'enmenta 89b
*'enobarśe 'innovarse': śe 'enoba 77a
*'enpesar 'empezar': 'enpese 'empiece' 21a
'enpese *see* enpesar
'enpesible 'dañable' 86a
'enprinsy'oneś 'engravings, inscriptions, articulations' (?) 24b
'enpueś 'despues' 116a
*'ensitar 'incitar': 'ensita 101b
'enśarśyaś 'jarcias' 34a
*'enšalśar 'ensalzar': 'enšalśado 77a; 'enğalsado 160a
'enšenplo 'ejemplo' 19b

470

GLOSSARY

'entento 'intención' 85b
'enteresisyon 'intercesión' 18b
'entiliğensyya 'inteligencia' 51a
'entiliğible 'inteligible' 39b
'enveluntar 'wish, desire' 61a
'enviśtigar 'investigar' 20b
'enyade see 'enyadir
*'enyadir 'añadir': 'enyade 13a
'epilensy'a 'epilepsia' 22b
'erada see 'erar
*'erar 'errar': 'erada 17a
'eselente 'excelente' 106a
'esortasy'on 'exhortación' 13b
*'eśbiblar 'envilecer, profanar': 'eśbibla 106a
'eś'elasy'on 'exhalation' 24b
'eśekuto 'ejecutó' 18a
*'eśkapar 'terminar', deliver': 'eśkapen 'terminen' 17b, 'eśkapa 'deliver' 18b
*'eśkarar 'escarbar': 'eśkaren 35b
'eśkarsoś 'escasos' 70b
'eśkoğendo see 'eśkoğer
*'eśkoğer 'escoger': 'eśkoğendo 'escogiendo' 56b
*'eśkuadronyyar 'buscar, search, examine': 'eśkuadronyyaron 137a
'eśku'entra 'contra' 71a
'eśkyerdo 'izquierdo' 31b
'eśpandir 'extender': 'eśpanden 142b
'eśpartirśe 'separarse, apartarse' 116a
'eśpasifikando see 'eśpasifikar
'eśpasifikar 'especificar' 89b; 'eśpasifikando 12a
'eśperensy'a see 'eśprensy'a
'eśpertamyento 'wakefulness' 24a
'eśpikulasy'on 'especulación' 19b
'eśpilida 'postponed, repelled' 23b
'eśpisifikar see 'eśpasifikar 116a
'eśprensy'a 'experiencia' 26b; 'experiencia' 119a
'eśprimentadoś 'experimentados' 17a
'eśpritoś 'spirits, souls' 21a
'eśtan see eśtar
*eśtar 'estar': 'eśtan 'estando' 155a

GLOSSARY

'eśtiry'or 'exterior' 56b
'eśtonseś 'entonces' 24a
'eśtory'a 'historia' 84b
'eśtribu'itiba 'distribuitiva' 103a
*'eśtru'ir 'destruir': 'eśtru'ira 107a
'eśtudyya 'study' 37b
'eśturmentoś 'instrumentos' 16a
'ezenta 'exenta' 112a

fablaś 'hablas' 39b
fado 'hado' 19a
fambryento 'hambriento' 21b
fartura 'hartura' 12b
faseś 'rostro' 79b
*fazer 'hacer': fazyen 'haciendo' 112b
fazyen *see* fazer
feğo 'hecho' 22a
*ferir 'herir' : firyen 'hiriendo' 49b
firyen *see* ferir
fišo 'fijo': firme 'i fišo 14b
*folgar 'holgar': fu'elga 39a
fonsado 'hueste, ejército' 144b
fraguar 'construct, erect, build' 73a
fu'elga *see* folgar
fy'uzyya 'fiucia, fe, confianza' 34a

*gabilyyar 'to make sheave': gabilyyaban 162a
gabilyyaś 'sheaves' 162a
gera 'guerra' 96b
gu'erta 'huerta' 81b
gu'eśpedeś 'huespedes' 73b
*ğazer 'yacer': ğazeraś 30b
ğoyyaś 'joyas' 16a
ğu'ego 'burla, broma' 84a
ğu'ez 'juez' 18a
ğuśgar 'juzgar' 20b

Ha-Šem (H.) 'the Name, euphemism for God' 160b
hata 'hasta' 14b

GLOSSARY

hedyotaś (Greek) 'ignorant men' 150a
hek 'hic' 155a
Heḳel (H.) 'the holy ark' 159b
ḥaḳamim (H.) 'wise men, scholars' 159b

'ikibokaś 'equívocas' 95a
'indibido 'indebido' 48b
'inkonpusible 'incomponible' 46a
'inorante 'ignorante' 47a
'inportansa 'importancia' 80a
'intiry'oreś 'interiores' 27b
'iny'ota 'ignota' 47a
'iśtante 'instante' 58b
'ividenteś 'evidentes' 31b

*kabturezar 'cauterizar': kabturezando 58b
kabza 'causa' 13b
kale + infinitivo 'ser necesario': no kale dezir 29b
kalefikado 'calificado' 66b
*karkomerśe 'carcomerse': karkomeśense 86a
*ka'er 'caer': kayaś 'caigas' 49a
kauzos 'causas' 15b
kavakar 'grabar' 78a
kaver 'caber' 49b
kayaś *see* ka'er 'caigas' 49a
*kebrarse 'quebrarse': śe kebre 14a
*kerer 'querer': kiǧo 'quiso' 13a; kiśto 'querido' 23b
keśty'on 'cuestión' 15b
kiǧo *see* kerer
kiśto *see* kerer
kᵉṭubbah (H.) 'marriage contract' 72a
ḳobeš (H.) 'conqueror' 89b
*koǧer 'coger': koǧi'a 43a
*komer 'comer': komyen 'comiendo' 144b
komyen *see* komer
konkuluzy'on 'conclusión' 40a
konplisy'on 'complexión' 13a
konsidrar 'considerar' 19a
konśekensya 'consecuencia' 38b

473

kontente 'contento' 21a
kontino 'continuo' 12b
kontra 'para' 32b
kontralyedad 'contrariedad' 111a
korer 'correr' 34a
kośtelasy'on 'constelación' 18b
kryasy'on 'creación' 13b
kuando 'cuanto' 20a

lanber 'lamer' 19a
lašon ha-kodeš (H.) 'the holy tongue, Hebrew' 97b
*lebar 'llevar': lebados 33a
leendo *see* le'er
*le'er 'leer': leendo 'leyendo' 30
le'esy'oneś 'lecciones' 13a
lemuny'o 'tristeza, aflición' 46a
*levar *see* *lebar
leyś 'leyes' 35b
liğonğa 'lisonja' 39a
luğury'a 'luxuria' 23a

magnifyeśto 'manifiesto' 64a
*malenkonizar 'melanconizar, entristicerse': malenkonizando 46a
malino 'maligno' 66a
malśin 'calumniador' 39b
*maner 'morar': manere 116b
manko 'menos' 21b
meatad 'mitad' 158b
meldar 'leer' 58a
memorozo 'memoroso' 38b
memransa 'memoria' 85b
meneśteroś 'dependents' 68a
meśmo 'mismo' 17a
Midraš (H.) 'Midrash, house of study' 159b
milagre 'milagro' 44b
miṣvah (H.) 'commandment' 159b
mośtran *see* mośtrar
*mośtrar 'mostrar': mośtran 15b

GLOSSARY

nadi 'nadie' 24a
natureza 'naturaleza' 23a
nebla 'niebla' 25a
niğil 'nihil, nada' 124a
niteral 'literal' 106b
noś 'nosotros' 26b
nu'eśo 'nuestro' 19b
nyegar 'negar': nyegando 27a, nyegar 38a

'oğoś 'ojos' 16b
*'o'ir 'oír': 'oyamoś 'oigamos' 26b
'omido 'humedad' 46a
'oniversal 'universal' 17a
'opilar 'narcotizar' 27a
'oponerśe 'ponerse' 79a
'ordenar 'ordenando' 97b
'oyamoś *see* 'o'ir
'o'ynar 'llantear, plañir' 99b
'ozureroś 'usereros' 71b

*pagar 'pagar': page 'pague' 104a
page *see* pagar
palabra 'oración, sentencia' 65a
*paresera 'parecer': paresra 'parecerá' 135a
paresra *see* parecer
pasuk (H.) 'verse, sentence' 124b; pl. p^{e}sukim 157a
*pelegrinar 'peregrinar': pelegrinava 80b
perfundo 'profundo' 18a
perkurar 'procurar' 13b
perpleśo 'perplejo' 17a
perpozito 'propósito' 24a
perverter 'pervertir' 87b
platika 'práctica' 133b
pobreğo 'provecho' 31a
*poder 'poder': poderloaś 'lo podrás' 18a
poderloaś *see* poder
porfeta 'profeta' 32b
pozilanimo 'pusilánime' 82a

GLOSSARY

*pratikar 'platicar': śe pratiko 141a
preba *see* prebar
*prebar 'probar': preba 18a
precebto 'precepto' 17b
preniśmidad 'perfección' 80b
preniśmoś 'perfectos, enteros' 42b
preśona 'persona, human being' 16b
prima 'primera' 90a
probeza 'pobreza' 16a
prodegalidad 'prodigalidad' 105b
prolar 'plural' 52b
propinkas 'propincuas' 21b
prośtero 'postrero' 117b
puğa 'surfeit' 54b
p^{e}sukim *see* pasuk
pyadad 'piedad' 49a

refriğery'o 'relief' 55b
refrizery'o *see* refriğery'o
regmisy'on 'remission' 55a
*reğiśtir 'resist': reğiśte 24b
rele'a 'ralea' 109b
relyebar 'relevar' 108a
*reponyar 'repugnar': reponya 59a
*reproğar 'reproach': reproğe 39b
repu'eśta 'respuesta' 18a
reśta 'resto, demás' 159b
reśtabrasy'on 'restauración' 31a
revenensy'a 'reverencia' 101b
riśko 'riesgo' 43b

sedyondo 'sediento' 144a
Sefer (H.) 'Torah scroll': pl. S^{e}farim 159b
selikeh 'celeste' 59b
senebro 'cerebro' 141b
S^{e}farim *see* Sefer
sibdadanoś 'ciudadanos' 17b
solombra 'sombra' 36a

GLOSSARY

soto 'bajo' 43b
*śaber 'saber': śabyen 'sabiente' 42b
śabyen *see* śaber
*śalir 'salir': śalran 'saldrán' 160a
śalran *see* śalir
śaśtifazer 'satisfacer' 17a
śe'ey *see* śer
śegedad 'brevedad' (?) 33b
śegirśean 'se seguirán' 28a
śegundo 'según' 37b
śenpre 'siempre' 13a
śensy'a 'ciencia' 16b
*śer 'ser': śo 'soy' 37a; śe'ey 'sed' 83a
śiknifikasyon 'significación' 20a
śimpleś 'simple' 63b
śinoka 'synochus' 62b
śo *see* śer
śonbair 'seduce, deceive' 102a
śonyan *see* śonyar
*śonyar 'soñar: śonyan 'soñando' 155a
śudito 'subdito' 17b
śuğebto 'sujeto' 14b
śumenoś 'abismado' (?) 117a
śuprefisy'a 'superficie' 44b
Š^{e}ma^c (H.) 'Shema' 124b

ṣ^{e}dakah (H.) 'charity, justice' 72a

*tener 'tener': ternan 'tendrá' 40b; terni'a 'tendría' 155b
ternan *see* tener
terni'a *see* tener
teśtoś 'textos' 14b
tornar 'tornando' 155b
*traer 'traer': trušo 'trajo' 20b; trušere 'trajere' 47b
trasa 'polilla' 44b
tremudasy'on 'alteration' 77a
treśbaryar 'to stumble' (?) 102b
*treśtornarśe 'trastornarse': treśtornośe 46a

GLOSSARY

triśteś 'terreas' (?) 123b
trušere *see* traer
trušo *see* traer
turar 'durar' 58a

vaniglory'a 'vanagloria' 118b
varyabil 'variable' 92b
veluntad 'voluntad' 13a
*venir 'venir': verna 'vendrá' 45a
verna *see* venir
vidro 'vidrio' 41a
viğitar 'visitar' 16b
višasy'on 'vexación' 34a
vizo 'vista' 140b

yelada 'helada' 141a

zona (H.) 'harlot' 78b

Bibliography

Moše ben Baruk Almosnino. *Ha-K^edemah le-Sefer Neve Šalom*. Constantinople: Eleazar Soncino, 1538 (5298).

———. *Pirke Moše*. Salonika: Yosef Yaabes, 1563 (5323), repr. Jerusalem: Makhon Torah Shelemah, 1969; Farnborough: Gregg, 1971; New York: Charles Reich, 1992.

———. *Tefillah le-Moše*. Salonika: Yosef Yaabes, 1563 (5323), repr. Krakow: s.n, 1820; Podgorze: S. H. Daytsher, 1900; Tarnow: s.n., 1903; with introduction by Herbert Davidson, Farnborough: Gregg, 1971; Tel Aviv: Ha-Makhon le-Heker Yahadut Saloniki, 1987. (Carmoly, *Famille Almosnino*, 18, cites a Krakow 1586 edition.)

———. *Ha-N^ehagat ha-Ḥayyim. Regimiento de la vida. Tratado de los sueños*. Salonika: Yosef Yaabes, 1564 (5324), repr. Farnborough: Gregg, 1971; New York: Charles Reich, 1992. (Carmoly, *Famille Almosnino*, 19, cites a phantom Venice 1604 edition.)

———. *Yede Moše*. Salonika: Yosef Yaabes, 1572 (5332), repr. Venice: Daniel Zaneti, 1597; Tel Aviv: Ha-Makhon le-Heker Yahadut Saloniki, 1980–1985; Farnborough: Gregg, 1969; New York: Charles Reich, 1992.

———. *Meammes Koah*. Constantinople: Yosef Yaabes, 1588 (5342), repr. Farnborough: Gregg, 1969; Tel Aviv: Ha-Makhon le-Heker Yahadut Saloniki, 1980–1985; New York, Charles Reich, 1992.

———. *Extremos y grandezas de Constantinopla*. Madrid: Francisco Martínez, 1638.

———. *Sefer ha-N^ehagat ha-Ḥayyim. Regimiento de la vida*. Transcription by Semuel Mendes de Sola, Joseph Siprut Gabay, and Jeudah Piza. Amsterdam: Semuel Mendes de Sola, Joseph Siprut Gabay, and Jeudah Piza, 1729 (5489).

———. *Transformaciones de Morpheo*. Transcription by Semuel Mendes de Sola and Abraham Mendez Chumazero. Amsterdam: Semuel Mendes de Sola and Abraham Mendez Chumazero, 1734 (5494).

———. n.d. *Rešit Da^cat*. Salonika: s.n., n.d.

BIBLIOGRAPHY

———. n.d. *Tikkun soferim*. Livorno: Yaakov Nunes Weis, n.d., repr. Livorno: Nella Stamp. Di Gio. Vinc. Falorni, 1789.
———. *Tešuvot*. s.n., n.d.
———. *Tosafot Beur al Divrei ha-Raba* (Abraham Ibn Ezra). s.n., n.d.

MANUSCRIPTS

The list of manuscripts is alphabetically ordered by title. Witnesses to each title are listed earliest to latest, and more specific to less specific date. Those entries in which the last element is the letter "F" plus five digits, e.g. F 42591, the catalogue code of the manuscript in the Institute of Microfilmed Hebrew Manuscripts, Jerusalem, are derived from that catalogue.

———. *Beth Elohim*. 1546. 1a–50a. New York, Columbia University X 893 AL 6, acephalous. See I. Mendelsohn, "Descriptive Catalogue of Semitic Manuscripts (mostly Hebrew) in the Libraries of Columbia University" (typewritten), F 41564; *Ibid*. 1551. Rišon Leṣiyon, Israel. Nahum Kuzi 1/[1] acephalous, F 42591; *Ibid*. 1552. 34a–35b. Oxford, Bodleian Library MS Mich. *Neubauer-Catalogue*, 2013, Supplement of Addenda and Corrigenda to Vol. I *Neubauer-Catalogue* (Oxford, 1994), F 19298; *Ibid*. Date 15th cent. 1a–113b. St. Petersburg, Russian National Library Evr. II A 25 (Part of Firkovitch collection) F 63947; *Ibid*. Date 15th cent. 1a–50b. Oxford, Bodleian Library *Neubauer-Catalogue*, 2036/1, old no. OX Mich 109. OX Mich. 389, *Neubauer-Catalogue*, 2046, F 19321; *Ibid*. Date 15th cent.–16th cent. 62b–73a. Mantova, Comunità Israelitica MS ebr. 116, F 02242; *Ibid*. Venice, 1605, 1a–72a. Biblioteca Palatina Cod. Parm., 3037/1. *Hebräischen Übersetzungen*, p. 693. Also J. B. De Rossi, *Mss. Codices Hebraici Bibliothecae Parmae* (1803), Parma 3037, Parma De Rossi 0109, F 34164; *Ibid*. Venice, 1638. 1a–51a. Oxford, Bodleian Library MS Mich. 423. Owner Jacob Abram Nunes. *Neubauer-Catalogue*, 2037, F 19322; *Ibid*. Venice, 1656. 140 fols. Berlin, Staatsbibliothek (Preussischer Kulturbesitz) Or. Fol. 2193. M. Steinschneider, *Verzeichniss der hebraïschen Handschriften* (Berlin, 1878–1897), no. 229, F 02060; *Ibid*. Date 16th cent. 2a–41b. Biblioteca Palatina Cod. Parm. 22278. De Rossi, *Mss. Codices Hebraici Bibliothecae Parmae*, De Rossi 1285, F 13186; *Ibid*. Date 16th cent. 13a–167b. St. Petersburg, Institute of Oriental Studies of the Russian Academy A 218. *Hebräischen Übersetzungen*, p. 645, F 52902.

———. 1546. *Beth Elohim ve-Šaʿar ha-Šamayyim*. 100 fols. Oxford, Bodleian Library MS Hunt. 98. *Neubauer-Catalogue*, 2038. *Neubauer-Catalogue*, II (1906), 2038,

F 19323; *Ibid.* Date 15–. 61a–157b folios. Oxford, Bodleian Library, *Neubauer-Catalogue,* 2036/2, combines both texts on facing pages, F 19321; *Ibid.* Venice, 1656. 140 fols. Berlin, Staatsbibliothek (Preussischer Kulturbesitz) Or. Fol. 2193. Steinschneider, *Verzeichniss der hebraïschen Handschriften,* no. 229. *Beth Elohim* and *Šaʿar ha-Šamayyim* on facing pages, F 02060; There is also a codex of *Beth Elohim ve-Šaʿar ha-Šamayyim* (Salonika, mid-16th cent.) in the collection of Lawrence J. Schoenberg, University of Pennsylvania, Philadelphia.

———. 1551. *Šaʿar ha-Šamayyim.* Rišon Leṣiyon, Israel, Nahum Kuzi 1/2, F 42591; *Ibid.* Date 15th cent. 113b–156a. St. Petersburg, Russian National Library Evr. II A 25, F 63947; *Ibid.* Date 15th cent.–16th cent. 57 fols. New York, Jewish Theological Seminary MS 5514, F 37278; *Peruš Sefer ʿIyun ha-Ḳokavim ha-Mišartim m'et Georg Probaḳ.* Date 15th cent.–16th cent. 83 fols. New York, Jewish Theological Seminary MS 5515, F 37279; *Šaʿar ha-Šamayyim.* Date 16th cent. 50a–128a. New York, Columbia University X 893 AL 6, F 41564; *Ibid.* Venice, 1605. 131 fols. Parma, Biblioteca Palatina Cod. Parm. 3037. *Hebräischen Übersetzungen,* P. 645. De Rossi, *Mss. Codices Hebraici Bibliothecae Parmae,* De Rossi 0109, F 34164; *Ibid.* Venice, 1639. 52a–132b. Oxford, Bodleian Library MS Mich. 423. *Neubauer-Catalogue,* 2037/2. Owner Jacob Abram Nunes, F 19322.

———. 1558. *Piruš sefer hamidot šel aristo.* 1558. 200 fols. Oxford, Bodleian Library *Neubauer-Catalogue,* 1435. Oxford, Bodleian Library MS Mich. 409. Owner Abraham Karion, F 22515. This is *Pne Moše.* Steinschneider (*Hebräischen Übersetzungen,* 215) indicates it was printed by Simon Almosnino in 1584; Graetz indicates it is cited in a 1552 sermon ("Moses Almosnino," 31 n. 14); Carmoly mentions it (*Famille Almosnino,* 19); and Tirosh-Samuelson confirms it is Oxford, Bodleian Library 1435 (= Michael 409) ("Jewish Philosophy," 563).

———. 1567. *Crónica de los reyes otomanos* (Milan, Biblioteca Ambrosiana, x-126-sup. ant. ms. III, 32); ed. P. Romeu Ferré, Barcelona: Tirocinio, 1998.

———. 1569. *Migdal Oz.* 142 fols. Parma, Biblioteca Palatina Cod. Parm. 2625. It appears to be an autograph. De Rossi, *Mss. Codices Hebraici Bibliothecae Parmae,* no. 1218. *Hebräischen Übersetzungen,* P. 322, F 13541; *Ibid.* Date 16th cent. Madrid, Biblioteca de la Real Academia de la Historia Hebr. 6. *Hebräischen Übersetzungen,* P. 322. F. Cantera, "Nueva serie de manuscritos hebreos en Madrid," *Sefarad* 28 (1958): 229–240; 29 (1959): 3–35, F 31653.

———. 1574. *Tefillah le-Moše.* 124 fol. New York, Jewish Theological Seminary MS 2079, 1574. At the head: "With the consent of Joseph Ben Solomon Tsaitsak as printed in Salonika, 1563." Owner Hermann Lotze, F 11177; *Ibid.* 1598. 5 fols. Jerusalem, Mosad Rav Kook MS 209, F 21482.

———. 1582. *Piruš al-Piruš ha-Torah le-Rashi.* 25b–129b. Oxford, Bodleian Library

BIBLIOGRAPHY

MS Mich. Add. 69.24. *Neubauer-Catalogue,* 234. The colophon notes it was copied in the house of don Yosef Nasi, F 16370.

———. 1582. *Tosafot le-Piruš ha-Rabbi Abraham Ibn ᶜEzra le-Torah* (Genesis). 1b–24b. Oxford, Bodleian Library MS Mich. Add. 69. *Neubauer-Catalogue,* 234/1 (cf. *Neubauer-Catalogue,* 1886). See Naftali Ben-Menahem, "Additional Explanation," *Sinai* 19 (1946): 138–71. The colophon notes it was copied in the house of don Yosef Nasi, F 16370.

———. 1630. *Mebo' be-Astrologiah be-Sefaradit.* 48 fols. St. Petersburg, Russian National Library Evr. II A 161/7a, F 6174.

———. 15th cent. *Derašot.* 204a–261a. Moscow, Russian State Library, MS Günzburg, 1053, F 28013; *Ibid.* Date 15th cent. 132 fols. Moscow, Russian State Library, MS Günzburg 60, F 06741; *Ibid.* 1a–70b. Moscow, Russian State Library, MS Günzburg 158, F 06838.

———. 16th cent.–17th cent. *Kibuṣ Šaᶜalot ve-Tešuvot ve-Pesuqim me-Ḥokme ha-Mizraḥit.* 405 fols. New York, Jewish Theological Seminary Rab. 1385; New York, Jewish Theological Seminary MS 7131. Salonika (composed before 1588), F 43406. This would appear to be *Šaᶜalot ve-Tešuvot* (cited in *Meameṣ Koaḥ,* fol. 234b).

———. 17th cent. *Tikkun soferim.* 59 fols. Jerusalem, Benayahu O 162. Owners: The youth Abraham ben Rabbi Yosef Amarilyo, Isaac ben Michal Bedahav, F 72070.

———. 17th cent.–18th cent. *Yede Moše.* Amsterdam, Library M. H. Gans Film 5173/20, F 41293.

———. n.d. *Ḥibbur betakonah.* 110 fols. St. Petersburg, Russian National Library, Evr. II A 15 (Second Firkovitch collection), F 64174.

LOST WORKS

———. (before 1563). *Iggeret ha-Nefeš* (cited in *Pirke Moše,* fol. 37b).

———. (before 1563). *Iggeret Teḥiyat ha-Metim* (cited in *Pirke Moše,* fol. 37a).

———. (before 1588). *Deruše ha-Našim* (cited in *Meameṣ Koaḥ,* fol. 134a) (given to Doña Gracia in Adrianople).

———. (c. 1568). *Al Binyan ha-Halirut ("Muslimlik") le-Yehudei Saloniki* (cited in *Meameṣ Koaḥ,* fol. 5b) (narrative of the embassy to Constantinople 1565–1568).

———. (before 1564). *Piruš al-Sefer ha-Šᶜmaa ha-Tabᶜi* (cited in *Ha-Nᶜhagat ha-Ḥayyim,* fol. 133a).

———. (before 1572). *Piruš al Tehilim* (cited in *Yede Moše,* fol. 92a).

———. (before 1563). *Piruš al Mišle* (cited in *Tefillah le-Moše,* fol. 17a).

BIBLIOGRAPHY

———. (before 1563). *Piruš al Iyob* (cited in *Tefillah le-Moše*, fol. 28a).
———. (before 1563). *Torat Moše* (cited in *Pirke Moše*, introduction, and *Tefillah le-Moše*, fol. 11b).

PRIMARY SOURCES

Abraham Ibn Ezra. *Abrahe Auenaris Judei Astrologi peritissimi in re judiciali opera: ab excellentissimo philosopho Petro de Abano post accurata[m] castigationem in latinum traducta*. Venice: Ex officina Petrus Liechtenstein, 1507.
———. *Abraham Ibn Ezra's Commentary to the Pentateuch, Vat. Ebr. 38*, with an introduction by Etan Levine. Jerusalem: Makor Publishing, 1974.
———. *Piruše ha-Torah le-Rabbi Ibn ᶜEzra*, ed. Asher Weiser. 3 vols. Jerusalem: Mahbarot le-sifrut, 1977.
Abraham bar Ḥayya. *The Meditation of the Sad Soul*, trans. Geoffrey Wigoder. New York: Schocken Books, 1969.
Aegidius Romanus. *Commentaria in octo libros phisicorum* [sic] *Aristotelis*. Venice, 1502; repr. Frankfurt, 1968.
Aelian. *Historical Miscellany*, trans. N. E. Wilson. Loeb Classical Library. Cambridge, MA: Harvard University Press, 1997.
Albertus Magnus. *Opera omnia*, ed. Bernhard Geyer. 15 vols. Münster: Aschendorff, 1951–1999.
Al-Ghazzali. *Algazel's Metaphysics: A Medieval Translation*, ed. J. T. Muckle. Toronto: St. Michael's College, 1933.
———. *Maqasid al-Falasifa o Intenciones de los filósofos*, trans. P. Manuel Alonso Alonso. Libros 'Pensamiento', Serie difusión, 3. Barcelona: Juan Flors, 1963.
———. "*Logica Algazelis*," ed. Charles H. Lohr. *Traditio* 21 (1965): 223–90.
Aquinas, Thomas. *D. Thomae Aquinatis Summae theologiae partis I, Quaestiones 75–77 de essentia et potentiis animae in generali, una cum Guilelmi de La Mare Correctorii articulo 28 edidit, adnotavit, praefatus est Bernardus Geyer*. Bonn: P. Hanstein, 1920.
———. *In Physics* II, trans. R. J. Blackwell et al. New Haven: Yale University Press, 1963.
Aristotle. *The "Art" of Rhetoric*, trans. John Henry Freese. Loeb Classical Library. London: William Heinemann; New York: G. P. Putnam's Sons, 1926.
———. *Physics*, trans. P. Wicksteed and F. M. Cornford. 2 vols. Loeb Classical Library. Cambridge, MA: Harvard University Press; London: William Heinemann, 1929–1934.

———. *Politics,* trans. H. Rackham. Loeb Classical Library. London: William Heinemann; New York: G. P. Putnam's Sons, 1932.

———. *The Metaphysics,* trans. Hugh Tredennick. 2 vols. Loeb Classical Library. Cambridge, MA: Harvard University Press; London: W. Heinemann, 1933–1935.

———. *The Nicomachean Ethics,* trans. H. Rackham. Loeb Classical Library. London: William Heinemann; New York: G. P. Putnam's Sons, 1934.

———. *Minor Works,* trans. W. S. Hett. Loeb Classical Library. Cambridge, MA: Harvard University Press, 1936.

———. *Problems,* trans. W. S. Hett. 2 vols. Loeb Classical Library. Cambridge, MA: Harvard University Press; London: William Heinemann, 1936.

———. *Organon.* Vol. I. *The Categories; On Interpretation,* trans. H. P. Cooke; *Prior Analytics,* trans. H. Tredennick. Loeb Classical Library. Cambridge, MA: Harvard University Press; London: William Heinemann, 1938.

———. *On The Heavens,* trans. W. K. C. Guthrie. Loeb Classical Library. Cambridge, MA: Harvard University Press; London: William Heinemann, 1939.

———. *Meteorologica,* trans. H. D. P. Lee. 2d ed. Loeb Classical Library. Cambridge, MA: Harvard University Press, 1952.

———. *On The Soul. Parva Naturalia. On Breath,* trans. W. S. Hett. Loeb Classical Library. Cambridge, MA: Harvard University Press; London: William Heinemann, 1957.

———. *Physica: Translatio Vetus,* ed. F. Bossier and J. Brams. Aristoteles Latinus VII.1.2. Leiden–New York: Brill, 1990.

Aulus Gellius. *The Attic Nights of Aulus Gellius,* trans. John C. Rolfe. 3 vols. Loeb Classical Library. London: William Heinemann; New York: G. P. Putnam's Sons, 1927–1928.

Averroes. *De Substantia Orbis,* ed. and trans. Arthur Hyman. Cambridge, MA: The Medieval Academy of America; Jerusalem: The Israel Academy of Sciences and Humanities, 1986.

Bar-Ilan University. *Judaic Library.* Bible-Talmud-Commentaries & Halachic Responsa. Version 5 [CD-ROM].

Biblia Hebraica Stuttgartensia, ed. K. Elliger and W. Rudolph. 2d ed. Stuttgart: Deutsche Bibelgesellschaft, 1983.

Boethius. *De Consolatione Philosophiae,* trans. W. V. Cooper. 3d ed. London: J. M. Dent, 1933.

———. *The Consolation of Philosophy,* trans. Patrick G. Walsh. Oxford–New York: Oxford University Press, 1999.

Cicero. *Cicero's Three Books of Offices,* trans. Cyrus R. Edmonds. New York: Harper & Bros., 1855.

Diogenes Laertius. *Lives of Eminent Philosophers,* trans. R. D. Hicks. 2 vols. Loeb

Bibliography

Classical Library. Cambridge, MA: Harvard University Press; London: William Heinemann, 1925, repr. 1966.

Ecclesiasticus. *The Wisdom of Ben Sira,* trans. Patrick W. Skehan, ed. Alexander A. Di Lella. The Anchor Bible 39. New York: Doubleday, 1987.

Epictetus. *Epictetus. The Discourses as Reported by Arrian, The Manual, and Fragments,* trans. W. A. Oldfather. 2 vols. Loeb Classical Library. London: William Heinemann; New York: G. P. Putnam's Sons, 1926.

Erasmus. *The Colloquies of Erasmus,* trans. Craig R. Thompson. Chicago: University of Chicago Press, 1965.

Escorial Bible I.J.4. Vol. 1: *The Pentateuch,* ed. O. H. Hauptmann. Philadelphia: University of Pennsylvania Press, 1953; *Escorial Bible I.J.4.* Vol. 2, ed. O. H. Hauptmann and Mark G. Littlefield. Madison, WI: The Hispanic Seminary of Medieval Studies, 1987.

Euclid. *Elementa,* ed. Isaac Todhunter, intro. T. L. Heath. London: J. M. Dent, 1948.

———. *Elements,* trans. T. L. Heath. New York: Dover, 1956.

———. *The Latin Translation of the Arabic Version of Euclid's "Elements" commonly ascribed to Gerard of Cremona,* ed. H. L. L. Busard. Leiden: E. J. Brill, 1984.

Flavius Josephus. *The Works of Flavius Josephus,* trans. H. St. John Thackeray, Ralph Marcus, Allen Wikgren, and Louis H. Feldman. 9 vols. Loeb Classical Library. London: William Heinemann; Cambridge, MA: Harvard University Press, 1926–1965.

Hippocrates. *The Medical Works of Hippocrates,* trans. John Chadwick and W. N. Mann. Oxford: Blackwell Scientific Publications, 1950.

The Holy Scriptures. Philadelphia: JPSA, 1917, repr. 1955.

Ibn Sina. *A Treatise on "The Canon of Medicine" of Avicenna Incorporating a Translation of the First Book,* trans. O. Cameron Gruner. London: Luzac & Co., 1930.

———. *Avicennae Arabum medicorum principis liber canonis medicinae,* trans. Gerardus Cremonensis. Venice, [1523], 1608; repr. Brussels: Culture et civilisation, 1971.

———. *Mu'allafāt Ibn Sina (Mahrajān Ibn Sina),* ed. G. C. Anawati. Cairo: Dār al-Ma'ārif, 1950.

———. *Remarks and Admonitions, Part One: Logic,* trans. Shams Constantine Inati. Toronto: Pontifical Institute of Mediaeval Studies, 1984.

Josephus. *Antiquities of the Jews.* In *Works,* trans. R. Marcus. Cambridge, MA: Harvard University Press, 1958.

Menander. *The Principal Fragments,* trans. Francis G. Allinson. Loeb Classical Library. London: William Heinemann; New York: G. P. Putnam's Sons, 1921.

Midrash Rabbah. The Soncino Midrash Rabbah, ed. H. Freeman and Maurice Simon. 3d ed. 10 vols. London: The Soncino Press, 1983.

BIBLIOGRAPHY

Moses Maimonides. *The Guide for the Perplexed,* trans. M. Friedlander. 2d rev. ed. London: Routledge & Kegan Paul, 1904.

———. *The "Eight Chapters" of Maimonides on Ethics (Shemonah Perakim),* ed. Joseph I. Gorfinkle. Columbia University Oriental Studies 7. New York: AMS Press, 1912, repr. 1966.

———. *Maimonides' "Treatise on Logic,"* trans. Israel Efros. New York: American Academy for Jewish Research, 1938.

———. *Dalalat al-hairin: The Guide of the Perplexed,* trans. Shlomo Pines, introduction by Leo Strauss. Chicago: University of Chicago Press, 1963.

———. "Moses Maimonides' 'Two Treatises on the Regimen of Health,' " trans. Ariel Bar-Sela, Hebbel S. Hoff, and Elias Faris. *Transactions of the American Philosophical Society* 54.4 (1964): 3–50.

———. *The "Medical Aphorisms" of Moses Maimonides,* ed. and trans. Fred Rosner and Suessman Munter. 2 vols. Studies in Judaica 3. New York: Yeshiva University Press, 1970–1971.

———. *Laws Concerning Character Traits.* In *Ethical Writings of Maimonides,* ed. Raymond Weiss and Charles Butterworth, 27–58. New York: New York University Press, 1975.

———. *Letters of Maimonides,* trans. L. D. Stitskin. New York: Yeshiva University Press, 1977.

Physiologus. *Der Physiologus nach den Handschriften G und M,* ed. Dieter Offerman. Meisenheim am Glan: Hain, 1966.

Plotinus. *The Enneads,* trans. Stephen MacKenna. 4th ed. London: Faber and Faber, 1917–1930, repr. 1969.

Plutarch. *Plutarch's Lives,* trans. Bernadotte Perrin. 11 vols. Loeb Classical Library. London: William Heinemann; New York: G. P. Putnam's Sons, 1914–1926.

———. *Plutarch's Moralia,* trans. Frank Cole Babbitt et al. 15 vols. Loeb Classical Library. Cambridge, MA: Harvard University Press; London: William Heinemann, 1927–1969.

Porphyry. *Isagoge,* trans. Edward W. Warren. Toronto: Pontifical Institute of Medieval Studies, 1975.

———. *Porphyrii Philosophi Fragmenta,* ed. A. Smith. Stuttgart–Leipzig: Teubner, 1993.

Ptolemy. *Ptolemy's Almagest,* trans. G. J. Toomer. London: Gerald Duckworth & Co., 1984.

Saadia Ben Joseph Gaon. *The Book of Beliefs and Opinions,* trans. Samuel Rosenblatt. Yale Judaica Series 1. New Haven: Yale University Press, 1948.

Seneca. *Ad Lucilium epistulae morales,* trans. Richard M. Gummere. 3 vols. Loeb

BIBLIOGRAPHY

Classical Library. London: William Heinemann; New York: G. P. Putnam's Sons, 1917–1925.

———. *Moral Essays,* trans. John W. Basore. 3 vols. Loeb Classical Library. London: William Heinemann; New York: G. P. Putnam's Sons, 1928.

———. *Natural Questions,* trans. Thomas H. Corcoran. 2 vols. Loeb Classical Library. Cambridge, MA: Harvard University Press; London: William Heinemann, 1972.

Talmud. The Soncino Talmud, ed. Isidore Epstein. London: The Soncino Press, 1976–1989.

Themistius. *In Aristotelis Physica,* ed. H. Schenkl. CAG 5.2. Berlin: Reimer, 1900.

———. *Thémistius: Commentaire sur le traité de l'âme d'Aristote, traduction de Guillaume de Moerbeke,* ed. Gerard Verbeke. Corpus Latinum Commentariorum in Aristotelem Graecorum 1. Louvain: Publications Universitaires de Louvain, 1957.

———. *Themistius: On Aristotle's "On the Soul",* trans. Robert B. Todd. Ithaca, NY: Cornell University Press, 1996.

Theobaldus, Episcopus. *Theobaldi "Physiologus",* ed. and trans. P. T. Eden. Leiden: Brill, 1972.

Usque, Samuel. *Consolaçam as tribulaçoens de Israel. Edição de Ferrara, 1553.* 2 vols. Lisbon: Fundação Calouste Gulbenkian, 1989.

Wisdom of Solomon, trans. David Winston. The Anchor Bible 43. Garden City, NY: Doubleday, 1979.

SECONDARY SOURCES

Aarne, Antti, and Stith Thompson. *The Types of the Folktale.* 2d rev. ed. Folklore Fellows Communications 184. Helsinki: Academia Scientiarum Fennica, 1961.

Abeles, Charles J. "Moses Almosnino, His Ethical and Other Writings." Ph.D. Diss., The Dropsie College for Hebrew and Cognate Learning, 1957.

Abraham, Richard D. "The Vocabulary of the Old Judeo-Spanish Translation of the 'Canticles' and their Chaldean Paraphrase." *HR* 41 (1973): 1–5.

Afnan, Soheil M. *Avicenna.* London: George Allen & Unwin, 1958.

Altmann, Alexander. "The Delphic Maxim in Medieval Islam and Judaism." In *Biblical and Other Studies,* ed. Alexander Altmann, 196–232. Cambridge, MA: Harvard University Press, 1963.

Amarillo, Abraham Shaul. "The Great Talmud Torah of Salonika" (Hebrew). *Sefunot* 13 (1971–1978): 273–308.

Amigo Espada, Lorenzo. *El léxico del Pentateuco de Constantinopla y la Biblia Medieval Romanceada Judeoespañola. Fundación Juan March, Serie Universitaria, 159. Madrid: Fundación Juan March, 1981.

———. *El Pentateuco de Constantinopla y la Biblia Medieval Romanceada Judeoespañola*. Salamanca: Biblioteca Salmanticensis, 1983.

Armistead, Samuel G., and Joseph H. Silverman, with musical transcriptions by Israel J. Katz. *Folk Literature of the Sephardic Jews*, II. *Judeo-Spanish Ballads from Oral Tradition 1: Epic Ballads*. Berkeley: University of California Press, 1986.

Baron, Salo Wittmayer. *A Social and Religious History of the Jews*. 2d ed. 18 vols. New York: Columbia University Press and Philadelphia: JPSA, 1952–1983.

Bartlett, John, and Justin Kaplan, gen. ed. *Bartlett's Familiar Quotations*. Boston: Little, Brown and Company, 1855, repr. 1992.

Benardete, Mair Jose. *Hispanic Culture and Character of the Sephardic Jews*. New York: Hispanic Institute in the United States, 1952.

Benbassa, Esther, and Aron Rodrigue. *Juifs des balkans*. Paris: Éditions La Découverte, 1993.

———. *The Jews of the Balkans: The Judeo-Spanish Community, 15th to 20th Centuries*. London: Blackwell, 1995.

Ben-Menahem, Naftali. "Additional Explanation to R. Abraham Ibn Ezra's Statement by R. M. Almosnino" (Hebrew). *Sinai* 19 (1946): 138–71.

———. "Writings of R. M. Almosnino" (Hebrew). *Sinai* 19 (1946): 268–85.

———. "The Bibliography of R. M. Almosnino" (Hebrew). *Otsar Yehude Sefarad* 5 (1962): 126–28.

Ben-Sasson, H[aim] H[illel]. "Exile and Redemption through the Eyes of the Spanish Exiles" (Hebrew). In *Yitzhak F. Baer Jubilee Volume*. ed. S. W. Baron, B. Dinur, S. Ettinger, and I. Halpern, 216–27. Jerusalem: The Historical Society of Israel, 1961.

Berenblut, Max. "Some Trends in Judaeo-Spanish Romance Translations of the Bible." *RPh* 3 (1949–1950): 258–61.

Besso, Henry V. "Judeo-Spanish Proverbs, Their Philosophy and Their Teaching." *BHi* 50 (1948): 370–87.

———. "Judaeo-Spanish — Its Growth and Decline." In *The Sephardi Heritage*, ed. R. D. Barnett, 2 vols., 1:603–35. London: The World Sephardi Federation, 1971.

Blondheim, D. S. *Les Parlers Judéo-Romans et la Vetus Latina*. Paris: Librairie Ancienne Édouard Champion, 1925.

Bnaya, Meir Zvi. "Moses Almosnino and the Influx of Portuguese Jewish Immigrants to Salonika" (Hebrew). In *From Lisbon to Salonika and Constantinople*, ed. Zvi Ankori, 95–120. Tel Aviv: Tel Aviv University Press, 1988.

———. *Mošeh Almosnino of Salonika. His Life and Work*. Publications of the Diaspora Research Institute 14 (Publications of the Chair for the History and Culture of the

BIBLIOGRAPHY

Jews of Salonika and Greece 3 [new series], ed. Minna Rozen). Tel Aviv: Tel Aviv University Press, 1996.
Bodenham, C. H. L. "The Nature of the Dream in Late Mediaeval French Literature." *Medium Ævum* 54 (1985): 74–85.
Bradley, Ritamary. "Backgrounds of the Title *Speculum* in Medieval Literature." *Speculum* 29 (1954): 100–15.
Bundy, Murray Wright. *The Theory of Imagination in Classical and Medieval Thought.* University of Illinois Studies in Language and Literature 12. Urbana: University of Illinois Press, 1927.
Bunis, David M. *A Lexicon of Hebrew and Aramaic Elements in Modern Judezmo.* Jerusalem: Magnes Press/Misgav Yerushalayim, 1993.
Cambridge History of Later Medieval Philosophy, ed. Norman Kretzmann, Anthony Kenny, and Jan Pinborg. Cambridge: Cambridge University Press, 1982.
Cambridge Translations of Medieval Philosophical Texts. Vol. 1. *Logic and the Philosophy of Language,* ed. Norman Kretzmann and Eleonore Stump. Cambridge: Cambridge University Press, 1988.
Camhy, O. "Le Judeo Espagnol–facteur de conservation pendant quatre siècles." In *The Sephardi Heritage,* ed. Barnett, 2 vols., 1:560–603.
Cantera Burgos, Francisco. "Notas para la Historia de la Astronomía en la España Medieval. El judío salmantino Abraham Zacut." *Revista de la Academia de Ciencias* 2a ser. 27.2 (1931): 63–398.
———. "Nueva serie de manuscritos hebreos de Madrid." *Sefarad* 19 (1959): 3–47.
———. "A Hebrew Manuscript Rediscovered" (Hebrew). In *Yitzhak F. Baer Jubilee Volume,* ed. Baron et al., 287–90. Jerusalem: The Historical Society of Israel, 1961.
Caravaggi, Giovanni, ed. *Jorge Manrique. Poesía.* Madrid: Taurus, 1984.
Cardoner Planas, A. "La interpretación de los sueños en la antigüedad y en la Edad Media." *Revista de Dialectología y Tradiciones Populares* 15 (1959): 70–88.
Carmody, Francis J. *Arabic Astronomical and Astrological Sciences in Latin Translation.* Berkeley: University of California Press, 1956.
Carmoly, Eliakim. *La famille Almosnino.* Paris, 1850.
Castro, Antonio, ed. *Pedro Mexía. Silva de varia lección.* 2 vols. Madrid: Catedra, 1989–1990.
Cohen, Martin A., trans. *Samuel Usque's "Consolation for the Tribulations of Israel."* New York: JPSA, 1964, repr. 1977.
Corominas, Joan, and José A. Pascual. *Diccionario crítico etimológico castellano hispánico.* 6 vols. Biblioteca Románica Hispánica 5. Diccionarios 7. Madrid: Gredos, 1980.
Crews, Cynthia. *Recherches sur le judéo-espagnol dans les pays balkaniques,* ed.

Mario Roques. Société de publications romanes et français 16. Paris: Droz, 1935.
———. "Notes on Judaeo-Spanish." *PLPLS* 7 (1955): 192–99.
———. "Notes on Judaeo-Spanish II." *PLPLS* 7 (1955): 217–30.
———. "Some Arabic and Hebrew Words in Oriental Judaeo-Spanish." *Vox Romanica* 14 (1955): 296–309.
———. "Notes on Judaeo-Spanish III." *PLPLS* 8 (1956): 1–18.
———. "Miscelanea Hispano-Judaica." *Vox Romanica* 16 (1957): 224–45.
———. "Extracts from the *Meam Loez* (Genesis) with a Translation and a Glossary." *PLPLS* 9 (1960): 13–106.
———. "Miscelanea Hispano-Judaica II." *Vox Romanica* 20 (1961): 13–38.
———. "A Judeo-Spanish Medical MS (ca. 1400–1450)." *Vox Romanica* 22 (1963): 192–218.
———. "One Hundred Medical Recipes in Judeo-Spanish of ca. 1600." *REJ* 126 (1967): 205–63.
———. "Some Linguistic Comments on Oriental and Moroccan Judeo-Spanish." *Estudios Sefardíes, anejo 2* (*Miscelanea Crews*) (1979): 3–20.
Cronan, Urban. "Refranes que dizen las viejas tras el fuego." *Revue Hispanique* 25 (1911): 134–219.
Cull, John, and Brian Dutton, eds. *Un manual básico de medicina medieval. Bernardo de Gordonio, "Libro de medecina."* Edición crítica de la versión española, Sevilla 1495. Madison, WI: The Hispanic Seminary of Medieval Studies, 1991.
Cuomo, Lisa. *Una traduzione giudeo-romanesca del libro di Giona.* Beihefte zur *Zeitschrift für romanische Philologie* 215. Tübingen: Max Niemeyer Verlag, 1988.
Dan, Joseph. *Jewish Mysticism and Jewish Ethics.* Northvale, NJ: Jason Aronson, 1986, repr. 1996.
Danon, Abraham. "La communauté juive de Salonique au XVIe siècle." *REJ* 40 (1900): 206–30; 41 (1901): 98–117, 250–65.
Davidson, Herbert A. *The Philosophy of Abraham Shalom.* University of California Publications in Near Eastern Studies 5. Berkeley: University of California Press, 1964.
———. *Alfarabi, Avicenna, and Averroes on Intellect.* Oxford: Oxford University Press, 1992.
De Rossi, J. B. *Mss. Codices Hebraici Bibliothecae Parmae.* Parma: Publico typographeo, 1803.
Demaitre, Luke E. *Doctor Bernard de Gordon: Professor and Practitioner.* Studies and Texts 51. Toronto: Pontifical Institute of Mediaeval Studies, 1980.
Efros, Israel. *Philosophical Terms in the "Moreh Nebukim."* Columbia University Oriental Studies 22. New York: Columbia University Press, 1924.

BIBLIOGRAPHY

———. *Studies in Medieval Jewish Philosophy.* New York: Columbia University Press, 1974.
Emmanuel, Isaac Samuel. *Histoire de l'industrie des tissus des Israélites de Salonique.* Paris: Librarie Lipschutz, 1935.
———. *Histoire des Israélites de Salonique.* Paris: Librarie Lipschutz, 1936.
Encyclopaedia Judaica. Jerusalem: Encyclopaedia Judaica; New York: Macmillan, 1972.
Encyclopaedia of Islam, new ed., ed. B. Lewis, V. L. Ménage, Ch. Pellat, and T. J. Schacht. 8 vols. Leiden: E.J. Brill; London: Luzac & Co., 1960–1995.
Epstein, Mark Alan. *The Ottoman Jewish Communities and their Role in the Fifteenth and Sixteenth Centuries.* Islamkundliche Untersuchungen 56. Freiburg: Klaus Schwarz Verlag, 1980.
Eshkenazy, Elly H., and S. D. Ghichev. *Opis na evreiskite staropechatni knigi v Bulgariya* (Descriptive Catalogue of the Old Printed Hebrew Books in Bulgaria), Vol. 1, 16. v. Sofia: Bulgarian Academy of Sciences, 1966.
Fakhry, Majid. *A History of Islamic Philosophy.* Studies in Oriental Culture 5. New York: Columbia University Press, 1970.
Fotinis, Athanasios P., ed. and trans. *The "De Anima" of Alexander of Aphrodisias: A Translation and Commentary.* Washington, DC: University Press of America, 1979.
Foulché-Delbosc, R. "Proverbes judéo-espagnols." *RHi* 2 (1895): 312–52.
Franco, Moise. *Essai sur l'histoire des Israélites de l'Empire Ottoman depuis les origines jusqu'à nos jours.* Paris: Librairie A. Durlacher, 1897.
Funkenstein, Amos. *Theology and the Scientific Imagination from the Middle Ages to the Seventeenth Century.* Princeton: Princeton University Press, 1986.
Fürst, Julius. *Bibliotheca Judaica. Bibliographisches Handbuch der gesammten jüdischen Literatur, mit Einschluss der Schriften über Juden und Judenthum und einer Geschichte der jüdischen Bibliographie.* 3 vols. in 2. Hildesheim: G. Olms, 1849–1863, repr. 1960.
Gaster, Moses. *The Exempla of the Rabbis.* Prolegomenon by William G. Braude. New York: Ktav Publishing House, 1924, repr. 1968.
Gerber, Jane. *The Jews of Spain.* New York: The Free Press, 1992.
Gnuse, Robert. "Dream Reports in the Writings of Flavius Josephus." *Revue Biblique* 96 (1989): 358–90.
———. *Dreams and Dream Reports in the Writings of Josephus: A Traditio-Historical Analysis.* Arbeiten zur Geschichte des antiken Judentums und des Urchristentums 36. Leiden: E. J. Brill, 1996.
Goldberg, Harriet. "The Dream Report as a Literary Device in Medieval Hispanic Literature." *Hispania* 66 (1983): 21–31.

BIBLIOGRAPHY

González Llubera, Ignacio. Review of Hauptmann, ed. *Escorial Bible I.J.4* (Philadelphia, 1953). *RPh* 12 (1958): 94–100.

Gonzalo Maeso, David. *Šelomó ibn Gabirol. Selección de Perlas (Mibhar ha-Peninim)*. Biblioteca Nueva Sefarad 1. Barcelona: Ameller Ediciones, 1977.

———, and Pascual Pascual Recuero. *Me‘am Lo‘ez. El gran comentario bíblico sefardí. Tomo preliminar: Prolegómenos*. Madrid: Gredos, 1964.

Goodblatt, Morris D. *Jewish Life in Turkey in the XVIth Century as Reflected in the Legal Writings of Samuel de Medina*. New York: JPSA, 1952.

Goodman, L. E. *Avicenna*. London: Routledge, 1992.

Grabes, Herbert. *The Mutable Glass. Mirror Imagery in Titles and Texts of the Middle Ages and English Renaissance*, trans. Gordon Collier. Cambridge: Cambridge University Press, 1973, repr. 1982.

Graetz, Heinrch Hirsch. "Moses Almosnino." *Monatsschrift für Geschichte und Wissenschaft des Judentums* 13 (1864): 22–36, 57–67.

Grant, Edward, ed. *A Source Book in Medieval Science*. Cambridge, MA: Harvard University Press, 1974.

Greene, William Chase. "The Paradoxes of the *Republic*." *Harvard Studies in Classical Philology* 63 (1958): 199–216.

Grunebaum-Ballin, P. *Joseph Naci, duc de Naxos*. École Pratique des Hautes Études–Sorbonne, Études Juives 13. Paris: Mouton, 1968.

Guthrie, W. K. C. *A History of Greek Philosophy*, Vol. 1. *The Earlier Presocratics and the Pythagoreans*. Cambridge: Cambridge University Press, 1962.

Guttmann, Julius. *Philosophies of Judaism,* trans. David W. Silverman. New York: Schocken Books, 1973.

Haboucha, Reginetta. *Types and Motifs of the Judeo-Spanish Folktales*. Garland Folklore Library 6. New York: Garland Publishing, 1992.

Hacker, Joseph. "The Intellectual Activity of the Jews of the Ottoman Empire during the Sixteenth and Seventeenth Centuries." In *Jewish Thought in the Seventeenth Century,* ed. Isidore Twersky and Bernard Septimus, 95–135. Cambridge, MA: Harvard University Press, 1987.

———. "Superbe et désespoir: l'existence sociale et spirituelle des Juifs ibériques dans l'Empire ottoman." *Revue Historique* 277 (1991): 261–94.

Halkin, A.S. "The Medieval Jewish Attitude Toward Hebrew." In *Biblical and Other Studies,* ed. Alexander Altmann, 233–48. Cambridge, MA: Harvard University Press, 1963.

Hassan, Iacob M. "Transcripción normalizada de textos judeoespañoles." *Estudios sefardíes* 1 (1978): 147–50.

———, and Pilar Romeu. "Apuntes sobre la lengua de la *Crónica de los reyes otomanos* de Moisés Almosnino según la edición del manuscrito aljamiado del siglo

XVI." In *Actas del II Congreso Internacional de Historia de la Lengua Española (Sevilla, 1990)*, ed. M. Ariza et al., 2 vols., 2:161–69. Madrid: Pabellón de España, 1992.

Hauptmann, O. H. "A Glossary of the *Pentateuch* of Escorial Biblical Manuscript I.J.4." *HR* 10 (1942): 34–46.

———. "Notes on the Lexicon of Old Judaeo-Spanish Bible Translations." *RPh* 3 (1949–1950): 157–59.

———. "Bible Translations." *RPh* 5 (1951–1952): 163–65.

Herberger, Maximilian. *Dogmatik. Zur Geschichte von Begriff und Methode in Medizin und Jurisprudenz.* Ius commune Sonderheft 12. Frankfurt am Main: Vittorio Klostermann, 1981.

Herrera, María Teresa, et al. *Diccionario de términos médicos del español medieval.* Madrid: Arcos Libros, 1996.

Heschel, Abraham Joshua. *Maimonides.* New York: Farrar, Strauss, Giroux, 1935, repr. 1982.

———. *A Dictionary of Medieval Hebrew Philosophical Terms.* Cincinnati, 1941.

Hill, Brad Sabin. "The Bulgarian State Collection of Hebraica." *Newsletter* (Oriental Department of the British Library) 48–49 (1993): 12–13.

Husik, Isaac. *Philosophies of Judaism.* New York: JPSA, 1916, repr. 1940.

Ivars, José Francisco, trans. *Arnau de Vilanova de la Interpretación de los sueños (De Somniorum Interpretatione).* Madrid: Labor, 1975.

Janssens, Jules L. *An Annotated Bibliography on Ibn Sina (1970–1989).* Leuven: Leuven University Press, 1991.

Jastrow, Marcus. *Dictionary of the Targumim, Talmud Babli, Yerushalmi and Midrashic Literature.* New York: The Judaica Press, 1903, repr. 1991.

Jewish Encyclopedia. 12 vols. New York: Funk and Wagnalls, 1906.

Jopson, N. B. "Literary Style in Judaeo-Spanish." In *Gaster Anniversary Volume. In Honor of Haham Dr. M. Gaster's 80th Birthday,* ed. Bruno Schindler and A. Marmorstein, 272–82. London: Taylor's Foreign Press, 1936.

Kahane, Henry and Renée, and Andreas Tietze. *The Lingua Franca in the Levant.* Urbana: University of Illinois Press, 1958.

Kayserling, Meyer. *Biblioteca española-portugueza-judaica; dictionnaire bibliographique des auteurs juifs, de leurs ouvrages espagnols et portugais et des oeuvres sur et contre les Juifs et le judaïsme avec un aperçu sur la littérature des Juifs espagnols et une collection des proverbes espagnoles.* Nieuwkoop: B. De Graaf, 1890, repr. 1961.

Kessels, A. H. M. "Ancient Systems of Dream-Classification." *Mnemosyne,* ser. 4, 22.4 (1969): 389–424.

Kirk, G. S., J. E. Raven, and M. Schofield. *The Presocratic Philosophers*. 2d ed. Cambridge: Cambridge University Press, 1983.

Klmaleh, Leon, trans. *Dreams, Their Origin and True Nature by Rabbi Moses ben Baruch Almosnino*. Philadelphia, 1934.

Knust, Hermann. *Mittheilungen aus dem Eskurial*. Bibliothek des Litterarischen Vereins in Stuttgart 141. Tübingen: Litterarischer Verein, 1879.

Krappe, Alexandre Haggerty. "Les sources du *Libro de exemplos*." *BHi* 39 (1937): 5–54.

Kuyt, Annelies. "A 'Traumdeutung' before the *Traumdeutung:* Shlomoh Almoli's *Pitron Ḥalomot*." *Frankfurter Judaistische Beiträge* 23 (1996): 55–73.

Landau, J. M., ed. *The Jews in Ottoman Egypt (1517–1914)*. Jerusalem: Misgav Yerushalayım, 1988.

Lattes, Moses. *Notizie e documenti di letteratura e storia giudaica*. Padova: Tipografia Crescini, 1879.

Leroy, Béatrice. Review of Nehama, *Histoire des Israélites de Salonique,* vols. 6 and 7. *BHi* 81 (1979): 341–57.

Levy, Avigdor. *The Sephardim in the Ottoman Empire*. Princeton: The Darwin Press, 1979.

Levy, Dena. "Refranes Judeo-Españoles de Esmirna." *NRFH* 12 (1958): 1–35.

Levy, Raphael. "The Astrological Works of Abraham Ibn Ezra." Ph.D. Diss., The Johns Hopkins University, 1927; Johns Hopkins Studies in Romance Literatures and Languages 8. Baltimore: The Johns Hopkins University Press, 1927; repr. New York: Johnson Reprint, 1973.

———. "A Note on the Judaeo-Spanish Bible E_3." *RPh* 3 (1949–1950): 261–62.

———, and Francisco Cantera. *"The Beginning of Wisdom." An Astrological Treatise by Abraham Ibn Ezra*. Johns Hopkins Studies in Literatures and Languages Extra Volume 14. Baltimore: The Johns Hopkins University Press, 1939.

Lindberg, David C. "Alhazen's Theory of Vision and Its Reception in the West." *Isis* 58 (1967): 321–41.

———. *Theories of Vision from Al-Kindi to Kepler*. Chicago: University of Chicago Press, 1976.

———, ed. *Science in the Middle Ages*. Chicago: University of Chicago Press, 1978.

———. *Roger Bacon and the Origins of "Perspectiva" in the Middle Ages*. Oxford: Clarendon Press, 1996.

Lowry, Heath W. "Portrait of a City: The Population and Topography of Ottoman Selanik (Thessaloniki) in the Year 1478." *Diptycha* 2 (1980–1981): 254–93.

———. "From Lesser Wars to the Mightiest War: The Ottoman Conquest and Transformation of Byzantine Urban Centers in the Fifteenth Century." In *Continuity and Change in Late Byzantine and Early Ottoman Society,* ed. A. Bryer and idem, 323–38. Washington, DC: Dumbarton Oaks, 1986.

Luria, Max A. "A Study of the Monastir Dialect of Judeo-Spanish Based on Oral Material Collected in Monastir, Yugo-Slavia." *RHi* 79 (1930): 232–583.

Lyons, M. C. *An Arabic Translation of Themistius' Commentary on Aristotle's "de Anima."* Columbia, SC: University of South Carolina Press, 1973.

MacDonald, D. B. "*The Meaning of the Philosophers* by al-Gazzali." *Isis* 25 (1936): 9–15.

———. "Note on *The Meaning of the Philosophers* by al-Gazzali." *Isis* 27 (1937): 9–10.

Mansion, Augustin. "L'immortalité de l'âme d'après Aristote." *Revue Philosophique de Louvain* 53 (1953): 444–72.

Márcova, Ala. "El *Tratado del Astrolabio* de Mosé Almosnino en un manuscrito de Leningrado." *Sefarad* 51 (1991): 437–46.

Martínez Kleiser, Luis. *Refranero general, ideológico español.* Madrid: Real Academia Española, 1953.

McKeon, Richard. "Aristotle and the Origins of Science in the West." In *Science and Civilization,* ed. Robert C. Stauffer, 3–29. Madison, WI: University of Wisconsin Press, 1949.

Mehlman, Israel. "Chapters in the History of Printing in Salonika" (Hebrew). *Sefunot* 13 (1971–1978): 215–72.

Millás Vallicrosa, José María, ed. and trans. *La obra Forma de la Tierra.* Traducción del hebreo, con prólogo y notas. Instituto Arias Montano ser. D, 5. Barcelona: CSIC, 1956.

Minervini, Laura. *Testi giudeospagnoli medievali (Castiglia e Aragona).* 2 vols. Naples: Liguori, 1992.

———. Review of Moshe Lazar, ed., *Siddur Tefillot. A Woman's Ladino Prayer Book* (The Sephardic Classical Library 10; Lancaster, CA: Labyrinthos, 1995). *RPh* 51 (1998): 404–19.

Molho, Isaac. "Rabbi Moshe Almosnino, Procurer of Independence for the Salonika Community in the Sixteenth Century" (Hebrew). *Sinai* 8 (1941): 245–56.

———. "Rabbi Moses Almosnino, The Author and Scholar" (Hebrew). *Sinai* 10 (1942): 198–209.

———. "La littérature judéo-espagnole en Turquie au premier siècle après les expulsions d'Espagne et du Portugal." *Otsar Yehude Sefarad* 1 (1959): 15–25.

———. "Manuscripts of Moshe Almosnino" (Hebrew). *Otsar Yehude Sefarad* 4 (1961): 148–49.

———. "Concerning Recent Discoveries in the Manuscripts of Moshe Almosnino" (Hebrew). *Otsar Yehude Sefarad* 5 (1962): 161–64.

BIBLIOGRAPHY

———. "Un humaniste sefardí de Salonique: M. Almosnino (1518–1581)." *Otsar Yehude Sefarad* 7 (1964): 49–58.

———. "Rabbi Moshe Almosnino" (Hebrew). In *Saloniki, Ir va-Em be-Yisrael* (*Salonique Ville-Mère en Israël*), 41–52. Jerusalem–Tel Aviv: Daf-Hen, 1967.

———. and A. S. Amarillo. "A Collection of Communal Regulations in Ladino from Salonika" (Hebrew). *Sefunot* 2 (1958): 26–60.

Molho, Michael. *Usos y Costumbres de los Sefardíes de Salónica*. Biblioteca Hebraicoespañola 3. Madrid: CSIC, 1950.

———. "Dos obras maestras en ladino de Moisés Almosnino." In idem, *Estudios y ensayos sobre tópicos judíos*, 95–102. Yivo Institute for Jewish Research. Buenos Aires: Instituto Científico Judío IWO, 1958.

———. *Literatura Sefardita de Oriente*. Biblioteca Hebraicoespañola 7. Madrid: CSIC, 1960.

Morreale, Margherita. "Los catálogos de virtudes y vicios en las Biblias romanceadas de la Edad Media." *Nueva Revista de Filología Hispánica* 12 (1958): 149–59.

———. "La Biblia de Ferrara y el Pentateuco de Constantinopla." *Otsar Yehude Sefarad* 5 (1962): 85–91.

Moscona, Isaac. "The Books in the Library of the Central Synagogue in Sofia." *Annual of the Social, Cultural, and Educational Association of the Jews in the People's Republic of Bulgaria* 9 (1974): 167–200.

Munk, Salomon. *Mélanges de philosophie juive et arabe*. Paris: Franck, 1857–1859.

Nehama, Joseph. *Histoire des Israélites de Salonique*. 7 vols. Paris–Salonique: Durlacher-Molho; Salonique: Libraire Molho, 1935–1977.

Neubauer, Adolf, and Arthur E. Cowley. *Catalogue of the Hebrew Manuscripts in the Bodleian Library*. 2 vols. Oxford: Clarendon Press, 1886–1906; rev. ed. Oxford–New York: Oxford University Press, 1994.

Neuman (Noy), Dov. "Motif-Index of Talmudic-Midrashic Literature." Ph.D. Diss., Indiana University, 1954.

Oberhelman, Steven M. "The Interpretation of Prescriptive Dreams in Ancient Greek Medicine." *Bulletin of the History of Medicine* 36 (1981): 416–24.

———. "Galen, on Diagnosis from Dreams." *Bulletin of the History of Medicine* 38 (1983): 36–47.

———. "The Diagnostic Dream in Ancient Medical Theory and Practice." *Bulletin of the History of Medicine* 42 (1987): 47–60.

———, ed. *The Oneirocriticon of Achmet: A Medieval Greek and Arabic Treatise on the Interpretation of Dreams*. Lubbock, TX: Texas Tech University Press, 1991.

———. "Dreams in Graeco-Roman Medicine." In *Aufstieg und Niedergang der Römischen Welt*, ed. W. Haase, II.37.1: 121–56. Berlin–New York: W. De Gruyter, 1993.

BIBLIOGRAPHY

Oelschläger, Victor R[udolph] B[ernhard]. *A Medieval Spanish Word-List*. Madison, WI: University of Wisconsin Press, 1940.
Olson, Glending. *Literature as Recreation in the Later Middle Ages*. Ithaca, NY: Cornell University Press, 1982.
Palley, Julian. *The Ambiguous Mirror: Dreams in Spanish Literature*. Valencia–Chapel Hill, NC: Albatros, 1983.
Pascual Recuero, Pascual. *Diccionario básico Ladino-Español*. Barcelona: Ameller Ediciones, 1977.
———. *Antología de cuentos sefardíes*. Barcelona: Ameller Ediciones, 1979.
———. "Aproximación a las *Crónicas Otomanas* de Moisés Almosnino." *La Rassegna Mensile di Israel* 49 (1983): 668–96.
———. *Ortografía del Ladino: Soluciones y Evolución*. Granada: Universidad de Granada, 1988.
Peden, Alison M. "Macrobius and Dream Literature." *Medium Ævum* 54 (1985): 59–71.
Pedersen, O. "Theorica. A Study in Language and Civilization." *Classica et Mediaevalia* 22 (1961): 151–66.
———. "The *Theoricum planetarum* Literature in the Middle Ages." *Classica et Mediaevalia* 23 (1962): 225–32.
———. *A Survey of the Almagest*. Acta Historica Scientiarum Naturalium et Medicinalium Universitatis Hauniensis 30. Odense and Copenhagen: Copenhagen University Press, 1974.
Penny, Ralph. "Dialect Contact and Social Networks in Judeo-Spanish." *RPh* 46 (1992): 125–40.
Rahman, F. *Avicenna's Psychology*. Oxford: Oxford University Press, 1952.
Rather, L. J. "Systematic Medical Treatises from the Ninth to the Nineteenth Century: The Unchanging Scope and Structure of Academic Medicine in the West." *Clio Medica* 11 (1976): 289–305.
Regev, Shaul. "R. Moses Almosnino's Charter of Liberty (*Musellimik*) Sermon: Philosophical or Historical Source." In *Ladinar: Studies in the Literature, Music and History of the Ladino Speaking Sephardic Jews*, ed. Judith Dishon and Shmuel Refael, 2 vols, 1:139–55. Tel Aviv: The Institute for Study of the Jews of Salonika, 1998–2001.
Richards, Dickinson W. "The First Aphorism of Hippocrates." *Perspectives in Biology and Medicine* 5 (1961): 61–64.
Rodríguez de Castro, José. *Biblioteca de Escritores Rabinos Españoles*. 2 vols. Madrid: Imprenta Real de la Gazeta, 1781–1786.
Romeu Ferré, Pilar. "Diferencias y paralelismos entre *La Crónica de los reyes otomanos* de Rabi Mosé Ben Baruj Almosnino y *Los Extremos y grandezas de*

BIBLIOGRAPHY

Constaninopla de Iacob Cansino." In *History and Creativity in the Sephardi and Oriental Jewish Communities* (*The Third International Congress for Research on the Sephardi and Oriental Heritage*), ed. Tamar Alexander et al., 1:189–200. Jerusalem: Misgav Yerushalayim, 1994.

———, ed. *Moisés Almosnino. Crónica de los Reyes Otomanos.* Barcelona: Tirocinio, 1998.

———. "Ejemplificar con el ejemplo: *Mešalim* y *maᶜsiyot* en el *Regimiento de la vida* de Moisés Almosnino." In *Arbor Scientiae: Estudios del Próximo Oriente Antiguo dedicados a Gregorio del Olmo Lete,* ed. M. Molina et al., 2 vols., 2: n.a. Barcelona: Ausa, 2000.

Rosanes, Solomon Abraham. *Divre Yeme Yisrael be-Torgama.* 6 vols. Jerusalem: Mossad ha-Rav Kuk, 1937–1945, repr. 1945.

Rosenthal, Franz. "Al-Farghani." In *Encyclopaedia of Islam,* 2:793.

———. " 'Life is Short, The Art is Long': Arabic Commentaries on the First Hippocratic Aphorism." *Bulletin of the History of Medicine* 40 (1966): 226–45.

Rosner, Fred. "The Introduction of Maimonides to his *Commentary on the Aphorisms of Hippocrates.*" *Clio Medica* 11 (1976): 59–64.

Roth, Cecil. *The House of Nasi: Doña Gracia.* New York: JPSA, 1948.

———. *The House of Nasi: The Duke of Naxos.* New York: JPSA, 1948.

———. "Jewish Society in the Renaissance Environment." *Journal of World History* 11 (1968): 239–50.

Sachs, George E. "Fragmento de un estudio sobre la *Biblia medieval romanceada.*" *RPh* 3 (1948–1949): 217–28.

Sala, Marius. *Le Judéo-Espagnol.* Trends in Linguistics, State-of-the-Art Reports 7. The Hague: Mouton, 1976.

Salman, D. "Algazel et les Latines." *Archives d'Histoire Doctrinale et Littéraire du Moyen Age* 10 (1935–1936): 103–27.

Saperstein, Marc. *Jewish Preaching, 1200–1800.* New Haven: Yale University Press, 1989.

Saporta y Beja, Enrique. *Refranero Sefardí.* Biblioteca Hebraicoespañola 6. Madrid: CSIC, 1957.

Schwarzbaum, Haim. "International Folklore Motifs in Petrus Alphonso's *Disciplina Clericalis.*" *Sefarad* 21 (1961): 267–99; 22 (1962): 17–59, 321–44; 23 (1963): 54–73.

Schwartzman, Julia. "Where is the Heaven? The Story of an Aristotelian Problem and its Presentation in Jewish Medieval Sources." *REJ* 153 (1994): 67–85.

Schwarzwald, Ora Rodrigue. *The Ladino Translations of Pirke Aboth.* Hebrew University Language Traditions Project 13. Jerusalem: The Hebrew University, 1989.

Bibliography

Sephiha, Haim Vidal. *Le Ladino, Judéo-Espagnol Calque. Deutéronome, versions de Constantinople, 1547 et de Ferrare, 1553: édition, étude linguistique et lexique.* Collection Thèses, mémoires et travaux 24. Paris: Institut d'etudes hispaniques, 1973.

―――. *L'Agonie des Judéo-Espagnols.* Paris: Entente, 1977.

―――. "Créations lexicales en ladino (judéo-espagnol calque)." In *Estudios ofrecidos a Emilio Alarcos Llorach,* 3 vols., 2:241–55. Oviedo: Universidad de Oviedo, 1977.

Septimus, Bernard. *Hispano-Jewish Culture in Transition.* Cambridge, MA: Harvard University Press, 1982.

Shaw, Stanford J. *The Jews of the Ottoman Empire and the Turkish Republic.* New York: New York University Press, 1991.

Shmuelevitz, Aryeh. *The Jews of the Ottoman Empire in the Late Fifteenth and the Sixteenth Centuries.* Leiden: E. J. Brill, 1984.

Sipahigil, Teoman. "Ovid and the Tempest in *Othello.*" *Shakespeare Quarterly* 44 (1983): 468–71.

Siraisi, Nancy G. *Avicenna in Renaissance Italy.* Princeton: Princeton University Press, 1987.

Sirat, Colette. *A History of Jewish Philosophy in the Middle Ages.* Paris: Editions du Centre National de la Recherche Scientifique; Cambridge: Cambridge University Press, 1985.

Skeat, Walter W. *The Complete Works of Geoffrey Chaucer.* Oxford: Oxford University Press, 1894.

Sorabji, R. "Body and Soul in Aristotle." *Philosophy* 49 (1974): 63–89.

Starr, Joshua. *Romania. The Jewries of the Levant after the Fourth Crusade.* Paris: Office des éditions universitaires, 1949.

Steinschneider, Moritz. *Verzeichniss der Hebraïschen Handschriften.* Die Handschriften-Verzeichniss der Koeniglichen Bibliothek zu Berlin, Bd. 2, Abt. 1–2. 2 vols. Berlin: Königlichen Bibliothek zu Berlin; A. Asher, 1878–1897; repr. Hildesheim, New York: G. Olms, 1980.

―――. *Die hebräischen Übersetzungen des Mittelalters.* Graz: Nachdruck der Akademischen Druck, 1893, repr. 1956.

Taylor, Barry. "Wisdom Forms in the *Disciplina Clericalis* of Petrus Alfonsi." In *Circa 1492 (Proceedings of the Jerusalem Colloquium: Litterae Judaeorum in Terra Hispanica),* ed. Isaac Benaubu, 175–88. Jerusalem: Misgav Yerushalayim, 1992.

Thompson, Stith. *Motif-Index of Folk Literature,* rev. ed. 6 vols. Bloomington: Indiana University Press, 1955–1958.

Thorndike, Lynn. "Some Unfamiliar Aspects of Medieval Science." In *Science and Civilization,* ed. Robert C. Stauffer, 33–64. Madison, WI: University of Wisconsin Press, 1949.

BIBLIOGRAPHY

———. *The Sphere of Sacrobosco and its Commentators*. Chicago: University of Chicago Press, 1949.

Tirosh-Rothschild (Tirosh-Samuelson), Hava. "Jewish Philosophy on the Eve of Modernity." In *History of Jewish Philosophy*, ed. Daniel H. Frank and Oliver Leaman, 499–573. Routledge History of World Philosophies 2. London: Routledge, 1997.

———. "The Ultimate End of Human Life in Post-Expulsion Philosophic Literature." In *Crisis and Creativity in the Sephardic World 1391–1648*, ed. Y. H. Yerushalmi and B. Gampel, 223–54. New York: Columbia University Press, 1997.

———. Review of Bnaya, *Mos̆e Almosnino*. *JQR* 89 (1998): 250–52.

Tracey, Theodore. "The Soul/Boatman Analogy in Aristotle's *De anima*." *Classical Philology* 77 (1982): 97–112.

Twersky, Isadore. *Introduction to the "Code of Maimonides."* New Haven: Yale University Press, 1980.

Urvory, Dominique. *Ibn Rushd (Averroes)*, trans. Olivia Stewart. London: Routledge, 1991.

Vajda, Georges. *Isaac Albalag, Averroïste Juif, Traducteur et Annotateur d'al-Ghazâlî*. Études de Philosophie Médiévale 40. Paris: J. Vrin, 1960.

———. "Le néoplatonisme dans la pensée juive du moyen âge." In *Mélanges Georges Vajda*, ed. Gérard E. Weil, 407–22. Hildesheim: Gerstenberg, 1982.

Vakalopoulos, Apostolos E. *A History of Thessaloniki*, trans. T. F. Carney. Hidryma Meletou Chersonesou tou Haimou 63. Thessaloniki: Institute for Balkan Studies, 1972.

Valle, Carlos del. "El manuscrito hebreo del *Tratado del astrolabio* de R. Mosé Almosnino." *Sefarad* 51 (1991): 455–57.

Verbeke, Gerard, and S. Van Riet. *Avicenna Latinus: Liber de Anima*. Leiden: Brill, 1972; repr. Louvain: Peeters, 1972.

Von Grunebaum, G. E., and Roger Caillois. *The Dream and Human Societies*. Berkeley: University of California Press, 1966.

Wagner, David L., ed. *The Seven Liberal Arts in the Middle Ages*. Bloomington: Indiana University Press, 1983.

Wagner, Max Leopold. *Beiträge zur Kenntnis des Judenspanischen von Konstantinopel*. Vienna: Höfler, 1914.

———. *Caracteres generales del judeo-español de oriente*. *RFE* Añejo 12. Madrid: Hernando, 1930.

Wainmann, A. W. "An Analysis of the Judeo-Spanish Glossary in *El regimiento de la vida* by M. Almosnino (Salonika, 1564)." In *Actes du premier Congrès international des études balkaniques et sud-est européennes*, 6:175–79. Sofia: Editions de l'Academie Bulgare des Sciences, 1967–1977.

Bibliography

Watt, W. Montgomery. "The Study of Al-Ghazzālī." *Oriens* 13–14 (1961): 121–31.
———. *Islamic Philosophy and Theology*. Islamic Surveys 1. Edinburgh: Edinburgh University Press, 1962.
Weiker, Walter F. *Ottomans, Turks and the Jewish Polity: A History of the Jews of Turkey*. Lanham, MD: University Press of America, 1992.
Weiner, Leo. "The Ferrara Bible." *Modern Language Notes* 10 (1895): 81–85; 11 (1896): 24–42, 84–105.
Weisner, Christa. *Jüdisch-Spanisches Glossar zum "Me ͨam Lo ͨez" des Iacob Kulli: Genesis und Exodus bis Teruma*. Hamburg: Helmut Buske Verlag, 1981.
Weiss, Raymond, and Charles Butterworth, eds. *Ethical Writings of Maimonides*. New York: New York University Press, 1975.
Williams, Kathleen. "Spenser: Some Uses of the Sea and the Storm-tossed Ship." *Research Opportunities in Renaissance Drama* 13–14 (1970–1971): 135–42.
Wimsatt, James I. *Allegory and Mirror. Tradition and Structure in Middle English Literature*. New York: Pegasus, 1970.
Wolf, Johan Christoph. *Biblioteca Hebrea*. 4 vols. Hamburg: Christiani Liebezeit, 1715–1733.
Wolfson, Elliot R. *Through a Speculum that Shines*. Princeton: Princeton University Press, 1994.
Wolfson, Harry A. *Crescas' Critique of Aristotle*. Harvard Semitic Series 6. Cambridge, MA: Harvard University Press, 1929.
———. *Philo. Foundations of Religious Philosophy in Judaism, Christianity, and Islam*. 2 vols. Cambridge, MA: Harvard University Press, 1948.
———. "The Plurality of Movers in Aristotle and Averroës." *Harvard Studies in Classical Philology* 63 (1958): 233–53.
Yaary, Abraham. *Hebrew Printing at Constantinople. Its History and Bibliography*. Supplement to *Kirjath Sepher* 12. Jerusalem: The Magnes Press–The Hebrew University, 1967.
Zemke, John. "El alma : el cuerpo :: el piloto : la nave (*De anima* 413a8). El regimiento de la vida de Moše ben Baruk Almosnino." In *Proceedings of the European Association for Jewish Studies Congress (July 20, 1998, Toledo, Spain)*, 2 vols., 2: 694–701. Leiden: Brill, 1999.
Zobel, M. N. "On the History of R. Moses Almosnino" (Hebrew). *Sinai* 11 (1942): 133–39.

Index

Aaron, 248, 420
Abariza. See meanness
Abbahu, R., 63, 264–65
Abeles, Charles, 2, 3 n. 5, 4 n. 12, 6 n. 17, 7, 21 n. 56, 22 n. 57
Abimelech, 78, 82, 271
    dream of, 408, 409–10, 416
Abito. See habit
Abraham (biblical), 225, 316, 376, 408
    Isaac, sacrifice of, 100
Abraham bar Ḥiyya, 365 n. 252
    Ṣuraṭ Ha-'Areṣ, 365
Abraham Ibn Ezra, 10, 28, 43, 82
    Bible, commentary on, 297
    metaphysics, 366
Abraham Mendez Chumazero, 11 n. 38, 41
Abraham Shalom, 10, 22 n. 58
    prophecy, 32
Abraham Shaul Amarillo, 3 n. 4
Absalom (biblical), 188–89
    Amnon, 240
Absalom Almosnino, 4 n. 10
Abšalom. See Absalom
Abu Bakr al-Razi, 79, 364, 385
Abukrat. See Hippocrates
Action, human, 20 n. 54
    circumstance, judgment and, 286
    external, 208, 223, 228, 234, 252, 256, 286, 289, 290, 334, 347, 348, 349, 367, 382, 397, 407
    good, 154, 367
    —, origin in Divine Light, 177–78
    —, omission, analogy with despising God, 170
    —, crown, analogy with, 155
    imagination, 368
    intellect, 368
    intentions of, three, 370
    interior, 347, 349, 382
    justice, 288–305
    life, 367
    modes of, two, 347, 367–68
    perfection of, analogy with law, 377–78
    purpose of, good and virtuousness, 210
    repose, 284
    speculation, 344–50
    subject and object, equivalence of, 298–99
    virtuous, definition of, 182
    wickedness of, 177–78
    See also art; good; human beings; prudence; speculation, divine
Action, pure, 348

INDEX

action, good, 335, 377
art, 358
forms, dream, 387, 406
—, intellectual, 380
God, His comprehension, 124, 174
injustice, 290
intelligences, separate, 395
liberality, 213
love, 348
pleasure, 256
prophecy, 409
soul, 377
speculation, 348
thought, 383
See also intelligences, conjunction of the
Adam (biblical), 273
Adrianople. *See* Edirne
Adulasyon. See flattery
Advice. *See* counsel
Afabilidad. See affability; friendliness
Affability, 50, 63, 64, 65, 181. *See also* boorishness; buffoonery
Agag, 250
Age, old, 54, 106
friendship, 307
man, 137–38
poverty, 307
Ağibto. *See* Egypt
Aharon. *See* Aaron
Aharon Afia, R., 4, 10 n. 34
Aḥašveroś, 306, 38
Air, 116
element, 343-44
regions of, three, 116-17, 121
vision, as medium of, 176. *See also res non naturales*
al-Farghani, 365
al-Ghazzali, 81

commentaries on, 9, 18, 29, 53
Maqasid al-falasifa, 10, 123, 364, 366
perception, theory of, 403
ᶜAkiba, R., martyrdom of, 69, 190, 193, 195, 345-46. *See also* Tarfon, R.
Alanbike. See distillation; still
Albert the Great, 381
Aleğandro. *See* Alexander of Aphrodisias
Alexander of Aphrodisias, 366, 366 n. 257
Alexander the Macedonian, 51, 97
Alkitara. See distillation; still
Allegory. *See* example
Almosnino, family, 3-4
Alyento. See smoke; vapor
Amalek, 250, 253
Amarillo, Abraham Shaul, 3 n. 4, 5 n. 15, 5 n. 16
Ambition. *See* irascibility (vice of magnanimity)
America, continent of, 10 n. 34
Amistad. See friendship
Amnon, 240
Tamar, 320
Amsterdam, Jews in, 11 n. 38
Anbisyon. See irascibility (ambition)
Anbisyośo. See vanity
Angels, 172
Anger. *See* irascibility
Anima (animo). See soul
Animal, definition of, 115
pleasure, 203
Apetito. See appetite
Appetite, 92, 372
doctrine, 169
reason, 113, 186

INDEX

reason, control of, 113
spiderweb, analogy with, 134–35
virtues, moral, 180, 367
wicked, judgment of, 110
wind, analogy with, 93
Appetite, concupiscient (*apetito konkupisible*), 90, 134, 180
    pleasure, 181
    —, individual (*tenplansa*), 181
    —, reciprocal (*afabilidad, kortezia. verdad*), 181
    utility, 181
    —, correct (*ğustisya*), 181
    —, great (*maknifisensya*), 181
    —, median (*liberalidad*) 181
    youth, corruption of, 90
    See also pleasure; utility
Appetite, corporeal (*apetito korporal*), good and evil, 274
Appetite, irascible (*apetito irasible*), 134, 180
    evil, 180–81
    —, past (*mansedumbre* and *pasiensya*), 181
    —, present or future (*fortaleza*), 180–81
    goodness, 180–81
    —, great (*manyanimidad*), 181
    —, median (*modestya*), 181
Arabic language, 4
    Hebrew language, and, 152
    Turkish speakers of, 152
Archytas of Tarentum, 306
Arğiropolo. *See* John Argyropoulos
Arising. *See* regimen
Aristotle, 96, 97
    anecdote about, 151
    De Caelo, 120
    De Generatione et Corruptione, 314

dreams, 30, 32, 85
friendship, 316
happiness, definition of true, 23
—, theory of true, 22 n. 57, 22 n. 59
humility, 61–62
justice, 65, 291, 294, 299, 301
love, 68
median, 25–26
—, definition of, 57
Metaphysica, 201, 313
Meteorologica, 33, 52, 117, 119, 120, 121
middle, law of the excluded, 360
Nicomachean Ethics, 3, 18, 21, 22 n. 57, 23, 33, 57, 59, 60, 87, 94, 103, 104, 106, 125, 127, 135, 170, 180, 182, 183, 187, 191, 194, 207, 211, 217, 218, 227, 238, 250, 251, 253, 289, 291, 299, 301, 313, 320, 340, 353, 367
On Interpretation, 173
On Sense and Sensible Objects, 52, 59, 120, 123, 201
On Sleep and Waking, 85, 118, 121, 381, 432
On the Soul, 52, 59, 138 n. 130, 178, 381, 383, 386
Parva Naturalia, 30, 52
philosophy of, Jewish reception of, 4 n. 12, 9
Physics, 52, 111, 313, 355, 364, 366
Problems, 9, 33, 120, 309
—, translation of, Hebrew, 118
Rhetoric, 33, 247, 252
sight, 385–86
sophrosyne, 27

505

INDEX

Arithmetic, 362
    definition of, 364
    Euclid, 365
    See also mathematics
Arogansya. See boastfulness
Art ("*arte,*" location in the practical intellect), 21, 27, 50, 352, 356–58
    definition of, 356
    object of, action is, 356
    purpose of, 356
    See also virtues, intellectual
Arte. See art
Arts, Seven Liberal, 362. *See also* arithmetic; geometry; grammar; logic; music; perspective; rhetoric
Astrology, 51, 56, 94, 96, 101, 102, 103, 177, 215, 258
    goods, extrinsic, 233
    See also astronomy; prophecy
Astronomy, 10 n. 34, 129, 232, 367, 399
    definition of, 364
    degree, sixty minutes and one, 382
    dreams, 399
    future, rules for judgment of the, 399
    mathematics, 364
    See also astrology; dreams, interpretation of
Atinyensís. See Athenians
Athenians, 151, 238
Averroes, commentaries of, 366
    De substantia orbis, 365 n. 253
Avicenna. *See* Ibn Sina
Azariah, 127

Baḥya Ibn Paquda, *Hovot ha-Levavot,* 1, 23, 23 n. 60

Baron, Salo Wittmayer, 8 n. 24
Baruḵ, *kahya. See* Salonika
Baruḵ Almosnino (father), 4, 4 n. 9, 38, 48
    death of, 5
Baruḵ Almosnino (son), 5
Baruḵ ben Isaac Ibn Yaʿish, 367
Bathing, 54, 140
Bath Kol, 69, 346
Battle, 186–88
Beatitude. *See* happiness, true
Bed, 133
Benbassa, Esther, and Aron Rodrigue, 3 n. 4
Beneficence, 340
Benevolence, 340
Benjamin (biblical), 433
Ben-Menahem, Naftali, 2, 43
Bernard of Gordon, 111
Bʿṣalʾel, 357
Betalmius. *See* Ptolemy
Bias of Priene, 321
Bible, *romanceamiento,* 12
    verses, 25 n. 66, 49, 71–76, 455–62
Bilʿam, 423, 424, 425
Bildad. *See* Job, companions
Birds, 372, 389, 403
Birth pangs, 398
Bnaya, Meir Zvi, 2, 2 n. 3, 3 n. 4, 3 n. 5, 4, 5 n. 14, 6 n. 17, 43
Boastfulness, 185
    definition of, 270
Bodies, corporeal, 123
    modes of being, 123–24, 380
    —, first (form is three-dimensional), 123, 380
    —, second (form is represented to the senses), 124, 380

INDEX

—, third (form is represented to the imagination), 124, 380
—, fourth (form is represented to the intellect), 124, 381
See also body; imagination; substance; things
Body, destruction of, vices and, 114
health of, 17
members of, 397
partition from God, 28
perfection of, 19 n. 51, 53, 109, 129–36
potency of, 137
purification of, 16 n. 46
ship, analogy with, 137–38
soul, instrument of the, 110, 112
See also bodies, corporeal; food; *res contra naturales; res naturales; res non naturales*
Boethius, 22
Bondad. See goodness
Boorishness, 185, 285
Brevity, 54, 147–52
Hebrew, 152
Turks, 152
Brugaś. See witches
Bryson, 90, 108
Bueno. See good; goodness
Buffoonery, 185, 285
Bursa, 299, 300
Byen. See good; goodness
Byen aventuransa. See happiness, true
Byen verdadero. See good, true

Cantera Burgos, Francisco, 10 n. 33
Carmoly, Eliakim, 2, 3 n. 5, 7 n. 21, 8 n. 24, 43
Causes, absence of, 318
dreams, 396–407

effects, 329, 332
—, and knowledge of, 115, 164, 174, 394–95
—, —, accidental, 354
efficient, 112, 116
necessary, 70
See also dream
Centerpoint of circle, 144, 269, 337
Cerebrum, anterior ventricle of, location of imagination in, 385, 387
imagination, instrument of the, 386–87
injury to the, 79, 387
medial ventricle, location of thought in, 387
posterior ventricle, location of memory in, 387
sensation and motion, location of, 121–22
Charity, 61
Children, 94
perfection of, 107, 331
Chimera, 389, 391
Chronicles, 187
Chyle, 111, 121
Cicero, 22
art, 362
courage, 187
friendship, 306, 307, 325
justice, definition of, 65, 290–91
love, 334
vengeance, 252
Cipion (Scipio), 325
Citizen, 114
Cloud. *See* meteorology
Coitus, 112, 202–6
pleasure, 206
species, conservation of the, 206–7

507

INDEX

Color. *See* light
Comets. *See* meteorology
Common people, 208, 240, 261, 317, 322, 323, 330, 383, 387
Conimbriel, family. *See* Mośe ben Baruk Almosnino, mother of
Conscience, 147, 161. *See also* soul
Consciousness, 31. *See also* soul
Constantinople, 40, 41, 198, 299, 300
    Jewish population, 3 n. 6
    printing press, 9 n. 26
    Turkish conquest of, 3 n. 6
Constellation, children, 101
    events, God counters, 103, 424–25
    —, obligatory, 94, 96, 102, 215, 325, 394, 424–26
    —, possible, 103, 352, 426
    prophecy, 425–26
    virtuousness, 103, 162, 426
Constitution, 112, 177, 254
    choleric (irascible), 112, 123, 254–58, 285
    definition of, 379
    melancholic, 123, 164, 254
    movements, judgment and external, 285
    phlegmatic, 62, 112, 123, 255, 285
    sanguine, 123, 254
    See also dreams; human beings
Contingents, future, 173–74
Conversation, 140–41
    definition of, 340
    friendship, 305, 307, 309, 335
    liberality, 209
    soul, restoration of the, 185
Cosmography, 10 n. 34
Counsel, 58, 70
    good, first species of, 94
    magnanimity, 229–30

    properties of, eleven, 197–98
    virtue, second property of, 197
    taking, 199
    See also prudence
Counselor, 20
    prudence of, 358
Courage, 21, 22 n. 57, 50, 57–58, 186–95, 207
    class of, 186, 195
    —, first (self-control), 186
    —, —, definition of, 186–87
    —, second (endurance, forbearance), 187
    —, third (physical), definition of, 181
    virtues, comprises all, 186
    See also cowardice; rashness
Court, celestial, 105, 377
Courtesy, 63–64, 114, 181. *See also* friendliness
Courtesy in speech, 50, 184, 284–87
    definition of, 185
    eutrapelia, 147
    gravity, 284
    properties of, 286–87
    soul, repose for the, 284
    See also speech
Courtier, 182
Coward, 181
Cowardice, 54, 181, 195
Creation, 21
    true purpose of, 91
Crónicas Otomanas, 9
Cruelty, 261
    definition of, 261
Cupidity. *See* greed
Customs, 112
    good, 92
    bad, 92, 108

INDEX

Daʿat. See science
Dan, Joseph, 22, 23 n. 60, 34
Daniel (biblical), 127
Daniel ben Peraḥiah Hacohen, R., 4
Danon, Abraham, 2, 3 n. 4
David (biblical), 88, 102, 131, 142, 188–89, 199, 241, 256, 268, 271, 286, 289, 290, 293, 295, 304, 333, 339, 361, 429
    Jonathan, and, 320, 323, 325
    Law, name of Jewish, 363, 378
David Israel Athias, 11 n. 38
David Yakar, 12
Davidson, Herbert, 18, 22 n. 58, 32, 43
Death. See friendship; human beings
Delektasyon. See pleasure
Demons, 78, 383
Demosthenes, 205
Desonra. See honor
Deśtenplansa. See profligacy
Deśverguensamyento. See shamelessness
Determinism. See predestination
Dew, 118–19
Dialectics. See logic
Digestion, 109, 122
Diǧo. See example; proverb
Diogenes Laertius, 60, 97, 133, 145 n. 140, 146 n. 142, 151 n. 151, 332 n. 142
Diogenes the Cynic, 97, 133, 212, 219
Dionysius, 319
Disease. See res contra naturales
Distillation, 117, 343
Doorkeepers, 370–77
    warnings of, 376–77
Dragon's Tail, 355
Dream diviners, 80, 81, 82, 402
    astronomy, 398
    cause and effect, 396

    characteristics of, 396
    dreamer, constitution and circumstances of, 397
    interpretation, universal rules, 397–98
    Jerusalem, twenty-four in, 396
    —, forms of the imagination and the intellect, 396, 397
    Pharaoh, 410
    philosopher, natural, 400
    prudence of, 396, 397, 398, 405
    reason, natural, 396, 397, 398
    rule for, universal, 412
    Talmud, 396, 397–98, 407
    —, class two dreams and, 398, 400
    wisdom of, 397–98, 399–400, 405
    See also Joseph; Pharaoh
Dreamer, astronomer, 398
    circumstances of, 396–98
    constitution of, 379, 396–98
    dreams, dreaming, 432
    unworthiness of, 407–20
    See also dream diviners; dreams; Joseph; Mošé ben Baruk Almosnino
Dreams, 13, 30–32, 47, 79
    astronomy, 398
    beams of house, 397
    causes, 379
    circumstances, 81, 396–98
    classes of, 32, 77–78, 384. See also dreams, classes one, two, and three
    disease, symptom of, 385
    dreamer, constitution of, 379
    —, different interpretations for, 413. See also constitution
    definition of, 382–83, 406
    essence of, 379

events, foretelling of, 30, 80, 394
false, 31, 77
figures, transposition of effects into, 395
forms in, 30
humors, 387–88
imagination, 77, 79–80, 379–92, 393–99, 414, 434. *See also* dream diviner; dreamer; soul
intellect, 79
—, soul of dreamer attached to active, 82. *See also* intelligences, conjunction of the
interpretation of, 47, 48, 80–81, 396–99
—, Divine Influence on, 380, 384, 407
—, dream is its own, 80, 85, 403, 413–15
—, dream is different from, 403
—, natural reason for, 379, 396, 400, 407, 430, 434
—, time of dream and, 413, 430
memories in, forgotten, 82, 380, 406–7
nightmare, 79, 387–88
perception in, 32
prophecy in, 30 n. 76, 80, 84
reasons for, natural, 77, 379–80
senses, external, 380–87
sleep, 32, 79
subjects of, 430
theory of, 32
true, 31, 77–78
—, doubling of, 84, 412
waking, 31, 79, 380–84, 386
See also Joseph; Moše ben Baruk Almosnino; *TS*
Dreams, class one (simple, untrue), 77, 384–93, 430–31
cause of, external, 385–88
—, humor, 77, 385–88
—, imagination, 77, 79–80, 388–92
species of, 385
— (first) cause, external stimulus or dreamer's consititution, 385–88
— (second) cause, transfer of image or word perceived in waking, 388–92, 416
— (third) cause, weak intellect, 77, 80, 389–93
Dreams, class two (simple, true), 31, 77–78, 393–407
dreamer, experienced or intelligent or prudent, 77, 80, 400–7
—, strong intellect of, 77, 80, 393–99
events, foretelling of, 30, 80, 394–95
intellect, forms of the imagination and the, 393–99
intelligences, conjunction of the, 403–4
interpretation, natural reasons for, 396
—, experience or speculation, 393–400
—, storm, analogy with foretelling of, 400
prophecy, one-sixtieth of, 394
species, 393
— (first), strong intellect, 393–99
— (second), reasonable intellect, 393–94, 399–407
time of, 394
truth of, natural reasons for, 403–4

INDEX

See also dream diviners; Pharaoh; Joseph; —, chief butler; —, chief baker
Dreams, class three (Divine Inspiration, true), 78, 82–83, 407–26, 431
    dream, doubling of the, 84, 412, 430
    dreamer, prophet, 78, 407, 420–26
    —, unworthiness of, 78, 82, 407–20
    —, worthiness of, 422
    figures, transposition of effects into, 414, 434
    images, not from imagination, 409
    species, 407
    — (first), admixture of other dream class elements, 408, 409, 416
    —, —, definition of, 425–26
    —, —, God does not reveal Self in, 416
    — (second), no admixture of other dream class elements, 416, 422
    —, Divine Will, 408, 422
    —, intelligences, conjunction of the, 420
Drink, spiritual, 162. *See also res non naturales*
Duke of Naxos. *See* Joseph Nasi, Don

Earth, 116
    element, 343–44
Earthquake, 120
Eating. *See* regimen
Eclipse. *See* sun
Economy, 17 n. 48
    definition of, 337
Edirne, 299, 300

Effects. *See* causes
Eğalasyon. See exhalation
Eğemplo. See example
Egypt, 281, 408, 417
Elders, Seventy, 235
Election. *See* will
Elements, 281
    definition of, 343.
    See also air; earth; fire; water
Eli, sons of, 101
Emmanuel, Isaac, 2, 3 n. 4, 3 n. 5, 4 n. 11, 5 n. 15, 6 n. 17, 7 n. 19, 43
Enbidya. See envy
Enemistad. See enmity
Enemy, 153. *See also* enmity
Engimyento. See vulgarity
Enmity, 185, 317. *See also* enemy
Enšenplo. See example
Ente, 361, 403
Entendimyento. See intellect; reason
Envy, 152, 186
    understanding, 392
Eotrapelya. See courtesy in speech
Epaminondas, 213
Epictetus, 95
Epicureanism, 201
Epikea. See justice, equity
Epilepsy. *See res contra naturales*
Epistemology, 23
Epstein, Mark Alan, 3 n. 4, 5 n. 15, 6 n. 17, 7 n. 19, 8 n. 24
Error, 336
    infinite, 337
Esau (biblical), 213
Esfera Solida, 129, 365
Eskarnidoreś. See scorn
Eskaseza. See paltriness
Espeğo. See mirror

INDEX

Eśperansa, buena. See hope
Eśpritoś, 108, 111, 122, 165, 248, 382, 385, 386, 387, 388, 403
Ethics, 17 n. 48
    Jewish, 22, 23 n. 60, 34
Euclid, 22 n. 57, 197, 365
Evil, 57, 93, 96–97
    falsehood, 268
    multiplicity of, 178
    self-destruction, 253, 333–34
    See also theodicy; human beings, wicked
Examples, 21, 54, 62, 66, 67, 70, 71
    ᶜAkiba, R., 345–46
    arrow, 259
    beams of house, 397, 399
    blind man, 377
    bloodletting, 200
    celestial court, 104–5
    coitus, 205–6
    courage, 182, 186
    dog and hare, 203
    dogs, Lycurgus', 103
    eye, 385
    figs, unripe, 158
    friendship, true, 307–8
    garden, world is a, 370–77
    gentleness, 195
    house, collapsed, 356
    irascibility, Socrates', 260
    knowledge, example gives full, 340
    lightning, vision of prophet and, 421
    lion and ox, 203
    lion and stag, 203
    love, maternal, 331
    lust, 203, 205
    metaphysics, 175
    mirrors, different substances and, 153
    —, images in opposing, 404
    musician, 318–19
    philosopher, patience of, 259–60
    physician, 200
    piety, foolish, 303
    profligacy, 221–22
    road short yet long, 70, 368–70
    road, wrong, 160–61
    sheep, 337
    shipwreck, 137–38, 259–60, 374
    shoemaker, 357
    sons of king, three, 370–77
    soul, 385
    traveler, 310–11
    troubadours, 215
    truthfulness, 145–46
    vacuum, 280–83
    voyage to other-world island, 370–77
    wealth and poverty, 101, 306
    will, free, 173
    woman, drowning, 303–4
Exercise. *See res contra naturales*
Exhalation, 116
    definition of, 119
Exodus, 77, 280–82, 408–9, 433–34
Experience, 120
Eyes, 167, 168, 178
    cataracts, 137
    mirror of the soul, 381

Faculties (appetitive, irascible, sensible), 57, 110, 273
Face, appearance of, 343
Falsehood, 54, 64, 142–43
    action, 269
    classes of, 147
    definition of, 271, 273
    evil, source of, 268
    fortune-teller, 271

INDEX

injustice, 278
justice, 275
—, corruption of, 143–44
lie, 277
mendacious, 276
officious, 276, 278
—, miracle, analogy with, 282
—, peace, permitted to safeguard, 277
origin of, 143
plagiarism, 272
prohibition on, 143, 277
reason, right, 278
republic, destruction of, 143
self-destruction, 144
sorcery, 271
soul, damage to, 142
species of, 178
—, twelve, 275–77
speech, 269, 278
thought, 269
truth, circumstances and, 282–83
unpleasantness, 144
utility, 272
wickedness, analogy with 144
—, supreme, 146
See also liar
Fame, oil, analogy with, 154–55, 164
prince, 223
Fantasma. See fantasy; ghost
Fantasy, 124, 137, 140, 199, 383, 384, 386, 387, 389, 390, 391, 393, 395, 397, 398, 407, 430
imagination, 396, 406
—, patient of, 406
species received from external senses, conservation of, 406
Fantazia. See fantasy
Farces, utility of, 286
Fate, 177. See also predestination

Favor, definition of, 236
Fear, imagination, 383
sin, 188
Fire, 116–17, 343–44
definition of, 119
Flattery, 153, 184, 330
definition of, 266
Flood, generation of the, 359
Flosedad. See spiritlessness
Flowers, 372
Food, spiritual, 162. See also regimen; *res non naturales*
Forgetfulness, 164, 239, 373, 380, 405–7
Jacob, 213
Form, elements and, 343
matter and, 134
husband and wife, analogy with, 135
Forms, dream, events, forgotten, 380
imaginative, intellectual and, 396
meaning of, 379–80
sages, 380, 396
See also dreams
Forms, intellectual, action, pure, 381
soul, transfer to, 403–5
substantial universal, 421
truth, emanate from, 144
universality of, 404–5
See also action, pure; imagination; intelligence; realm, sublunar
Fortaleza. See courage
Fortitude. See courage
Fortuna. See fortune
Fortune, 93, 94, 95–97, 145–46, 196, 371
Fortune-teller, 272
Franco, Moise, 3 n. 4, 3 n. 5
Frank, D. H., 3 n. 4
Free will. See will

513

Friendliness, 326
    definition of, 184, 265–68
    good, future, 267
    properties of, 266–67
    See also affability; courtesy; flattery; gravity; quarrelsomeness; speech
Friends, condition, similitude of, 314, 322
    false, 153
    —, ignorance and, 328, 342
    heart of, 342–43
    —, mirror, 342–43
    true, 319–28
    —, conversation, 326–27
    —, death of, 307–8, 323, 324–26
    —, children of, 324
    —, knowledge of, 321, 325, 327
    —, one (few) only, 326–27, 344
    —, one soul in two bodies, 332
    —, sage and, 341
    See also friendship
Friendship, 21, 50, 181
    action, nature, 310
    actions, 108, 316, 340, 342
    adversity, 341
    age, old, 307
    causes of, 66, 67, 305–12, 329
    classes of, 66–67, 70, 312–17, 335, 339–40, 370
    —, conjugal, 328–29
    —, maternal and filial, 331–32
    —, paternal and filial, 309, 328–29, 340
    —, pleasure, 314, 317–18, 320, 328, 330
    —, prince and subject, 329
    —, *senex* and *puer,* 328–29
    —, utility, 313–14, 317–18, 328, 330
    —, virtue, 314, 317, 319–28, 341
    conversation, 334, 340
    —, species of, 335
    definition of, 67, 185, 315
    essence of, 313–14
    —, similitude is, 314, 322
    existence of, 342
    flattery, 330
    God, 344–45
    good, pure, 310
    human beings, classes of, 70–71, 370–78
    justice, 334
    life, 306
    loss of, 67, 323–29
    love, 310, 330
    mutability of, 323
    natural, 309–11
    perfection of, 146, 340
    poverty, 307
    prosperity, 341
    purposes of, 67, 317–23
    reciprocity, 317–18, 327
    republic, 312
    true, 330
    —, definition of, 331
    —, eternal, 323–26
    —, life without, 309
    —, reciprocity of, 332
    truthfulness, perfection of, 146
    virtue of, 305
    wealth, 306
    wickedness, 332
    will, 342
    words, 342
    youth, 307
    See also beneficence; benevolence; conversation; enmity; friends; human beings, death of; Job; love

INDEX

Fuego. See fire

Gabriel, the archangel, 66, 310–11
Galen, 53
Garçon family, 5
Garden, 370–77
Gems, 96, 372–73
Gentil. See Gentilis
Gentilis, 367, 367 n. 263
Gentleness, definition of, 184, 195, 196, 246–47, 259
    forgiveness, 250
    God, name of, 261
    mercy, 249, 261
    praiseworthiness of, 260
    —, choleric and, 261
    —, phlegmatic and, 262
    properties of, 248–49
    vengeance, 248–53
    See also irascibility
Geometry, 362
    definition of, 364
    Euclid, 365
Ghost, 383
Giles of Rome, 193
God, 17–18, 51
    account before, human being makes final, 168
    action, comprehension in pure, 124
    astrology, 103
    being, infinite, 174
    cause, first, 99, 118, 173, 176, 177, 209, 210, 232, 280, 283, 407, 415, 420
    charity, blesses giver of, 212
    comprehension of, human, 23, 28, 87, 104–6, 374–76
    constellation, counters, 425
    emanation, 56, 78, 89. *See also* dreams, class three
    enemies of, 250, 256
    father, governor, judge, prince, physician, analogy with, 99, 100
    fear of, 159
    figure of, 355
    friendship with, 344
    good, constellation and, 425–26
    —, the worthy and, 422
    goodness, infinite, 171
    Gentiles, speaks in half-terms with, 423–24
    grace of, 155, 177, 377
    human beings, 370–77
    love for, 23 n. 61, 27–30, 99, 125, 170–71, 344–45, 370, 377
    —, definition of, 344–45
    —, true good, 170
    influence on human beings, 56–57, 99–100, 171, 176–80, 196, 370, 377, 380–84, 408–26
    —, definition of, 176
    instant, eternal, 168, 173
    Israel, speaks in full terms with, 423–24
    justice, 289
    king, 375–76
    knower of good and evil, 93
    knowledge, 56, 175
    —, *ab eterno,* 172–74, 265
    —, angels, 172
    —, determinism, 171
    —, eternal, 174
    —, human beings, 172, 390
    —, omniscient, 171–74
    Love, Divine, 170
    mercifulness of, 102
    miracles, 280–83, 408
    name of, profanation of, 190, 302
    names of, 339, 351

INDEX

nature, 201
obedience to, 159
omnipotence of, 173, 409
perfection of, 201
principle of philosophers (God is *intellectus, ens intelligens,* and *ens intelligibile*), 78
saints, no reliance on, 158
service to, 370–76
—, interior action, 349
truth, 144, 274
unity of, 69, 78, 351
virtuous, tests the, 100
Will, Divine, 264, 408, 414–16, 422–23
will, free, 56, 169–75
See also dreams; Grace, Divine; *intellectus;* intelligence, separate; light; miracle; prime mover; princes; Providence, Divine; wisdom
Gokareria. *See* buffoonery
Gold, 96
Good, 50
actions, 92–93, 177
communication of, 306
crown of, just and virtuous wear, 155
estimation of, 96
father, and, 101
final ultimate, 154
physical, 88
species of, 50, 51, 92–98
—, first (spiritual), 94, 96, 165–66
—, second (corporeal, temporal), 94, 96, 98, 166
—, third (astrological, extrinsic, fortuitous [of Fortune]), 94–95, 97, 98, 99
—, —, good, help for the, 233
—, —, wicked, hindrance for the, 233
—, —, happiness, help or hindrance for true, 101
—, —, honor is greatest, 229
—, —, hand, analogy with left, 234
—, —, magnanimity, 231, 233
—, Mercury, 233
—, wealth, 215
virtuousness, 98, 101
uniqueness, 178
wicked, 51, 96, 97–104
See also counsel; good, true; goodness; virtuousness
Good, True, 90, 93, 114, 131, 162, 170
God, love of, 170
knowledge of, 94
life and, terrestrial, 150
means, external, 199
possession of, 156
principles of, 359
sign of, 153
soul and, celestial world of the, 160
training, 160
virtuous implore God for, 155
See also counsel; good; goodness; virtuousness
Goodblatt, Morris D., 3 n. 4, 4 n. 9, 5 n. 15, 5 n. 16, 6 n. 17, 8 n. 22
Goodness, 95
eternal, 325
substance in human beings, 319
virtue, 319
See also good
Gorfinkle, Joseph, 22 n. 58, 28
Grace, Divine. *See* God
Gracia Mendes, Doña, 6, 31, 41, 427, 429

INDEX

—, daughter and nieces of, 427, 429
Graetz, Heinrich, 2
Grammar, 362, 363
    definition of, 363
    Hebrew, 363
    See also Hebrew language
Greed, 88, 183, 218, 221, 252, 292, 295
Greek language, 362
Grunebaum-Ballin, P., 3 n. 4, 8 n. 24
Ǧupiter. See Jupiter
Ǧustisya. See justice

Habit, 92–93
    action, virtuous, 182
    tree, analogy with, 93
Hacker, Joseph, 3 n. 4, 8, 10 n. 33
Hado. See fate
Hail, 119
Ha-malakah. See art
Haman, 306
Hananiah, 127
Hand, left, analogy with extrinsic goods, 234
    right, analogy with spiritual goods, 234
Hanhagot, 16 n. 45
Happiness, transitory, 162
Happiness, True, 16, 87, 89, 96, 162
    achievement of, 21, 22, 23, 26, 27, 93, 101, 359, 376
    definition of, 23–24, 26, 29–30, 153, 268
    falsehood, 268
    friendship, 185, 305, 344–45
    goal, constant, 159, 377
    God, 344–45
    —, love of, 344–45, 370–77
    hindrance, 127, 162

    intellect, practical, 346
    justice, 291
    Law, Divine, 104, 368
    Nicomachean Ethics, 367
    possession of, 153, 190, 345–50
    rule for, general, 163
    science, 341
    truth, 146
    virtue, 341
    virtuousness, 96
    watchwords, three, 377
    See also God; happiness
Hassan, Iacob N., and Romeu Ferré, Pilar, 5 n. 16
Heart, 168
    existence, name for, 343
Hebrew language, 9, 89, 152, 172, 243, 263, 281, 290, 293, 296, 303, 312, 324, 343, 432
Hedonism, 58, 110
Heroism, 54, 58
Higado. See liver
Hillel the Elder, 58, 195
    school of, 64, 279–80
Hippocrates, 53
    aphorisms of, 70, 125, 363
Hokmah. See logic
Honor, 61, 94–95, 195, 233, 246
    definition of, 95
    etymology, Hebrew, 243
    good, extrinsic, 229
    intemperance, 207
    liberality, 222
    love, mistaken for, 330
Hope, 368
Hosiah (biblical), 155
Horse. *See* music
Hovot ha-Levavot. See Bahya Ibn Paquda
Huesca, 3
Human beings, anger, 246

appetites, 87, 92, 113
birth, 81, 92, 103, 154–55, 397–99
character of, 32
—, training, 103
choleric, 385
classes of, 70–71, 70–78. *See also* human beings, good, just, virtuous, wicked
conception, time of, 81. *See also* Rule of Animodar
death of, 55, 138, 154–55, 158–64, 188, 377
—, atonement for sin, 138
—, better than day of birth, 155, 164
—, cause of, cold, dry humors, 164
—, definition of, 193, 326, 382
—, infants, 388
defects in, 28
eyes, cause for good and bad, 167
God, service to, 91, 100, 110, 134, 159, 168, 187, 188, 190, 195, 286, 370–77
—, action and, 344–50
—, love of God and, 169, 349
—, speculation and, 345–50
happiness of, 56, 96, 146
—, diurnal, 165
—, invernal, 165
—, nocturnal, 165
—, vernal, 165
heart, cause for good and bad, 167
ignorant, abandon study, 164
—, lack theoretical intellect, 157
judgment from God, 170
king, service to, 371, 411
knowledge, 175
—, of good and evil, 273

life, false, 88
—, true, 89, 180
—, work, 335
Love, Divine, 170
melancholic, 165, 385
merit, individual, 171
movements, 136, 240, 242
phlegmatic, 385
perfection of, 18–19, 23, 27, 32, 54, 57, 88–90, 106
pleasure, 183, 200
praiseworthiness, 262–65, 332
Precepts, obedience to Divine, 100
procreation, 91
purpose of, ultimate true, 19, 19 n. 51, 21, 29–30, 68, 69, 90–91, 125, 137, 157
receiving, 219
repentance, 62–63, 262–65
—, good actions, 335
righteousness, 55, 62–63, 68
self-control, 27, 32, 262–65
sins, fearful owing to, 188
time, experience of, 173–74
wise, 91
See also God; happiness, true; love; Law, Divine; time
Human beings, Good, 94
actions of, 236, 333
adversity, eternal life, 103
conversation, 140
corruption, 323
death of, and day of birth, 154–55
—, eternal glory, 158
—, full in days, 156–57
—, pure goodness, 100
—, redemption of others, 100
evil into good, transformation of, 97–98

518

INDEX

friendship, 306, 327, 332–33, 344
herbs, analogy with odiferous, 99
Moses, name for, 229
praiseworthiness of, 234
prosperity, not source of own, 99
reward, just, 179
sin, 102
species of, three, 99, 376
Human beings, Just, good and, 333
    Law in heart, Divine, 293
    praiseworthiness of, 262–65
    reward, terrestrial and celestial, 333
    wealth, expenditure of, 213
Human beings, Virtuous, 26, 26 n. 70, 106
    adversity, 58, 99–100, 196
    danger, 188
    death of, youthful, 158–59
    evil, father and, 100–1
    happiness, 98, 103
    —, adversity and, 260
    injuries, avenging of, 250
    intellect, judgment of, 110, 256
    phlegmatic, 255
    prosperity, 99–100, 196
    soul of, 404
    See also intelligences, conjunction of the
Human beings, Wicked, 68, 70, 90, 94, 96–98, 102, 359
    appetite, judgment of, 110
    birth, death and, 155
    classes of, 178–79
    company of, 334
    falsehood, 269
    friendship of, 332–33
    God, instrument of, 102
    intellect, blindness of, 170
    intellect, lack practical, 157
    life, death in, 367
    punishment of, just, 165, 179, 333
    redemption of, no, 102
    regrets, full of, 333
    self-destruction of, 333–34
Humility (modesty), 50, 61–62, 181, 233, 245–46
Hunain Ibn Isḥaq, 19
Hypocrisy. *See* self-depreciation

Ibn Rushd. *See* Averroes
Ibn Sina, *Canon,* 18, 19, 33, 52, 53, 68, 81, 109, 111–12, 125, 128, 131, 132, 254, 343, 367
    incubus, 388
    intelligence, sublunar, 176, 403
    medicine, 361
    perception, 403
    Remarks and Admonitions, Part One, Logic, 364
Ideas, 53, 78, 80. *See also* imagination; intelligible; perception, theory of; soul
Idleness, 136, 138–39
Idolatry, 62
    irascibility, 260
    judge, incompetent, 303
Ignorance, definition of, 217
Imagination, 32, 52, 99, 140
    absorption in, 193, 406
    deterioration of, 79
    fantasy, species of, 394–98, 406
    fear, 383
    figures of, invention of, 393
    forms of, transformation of effects from the external senses and, 379, 394–98
    —, passions and, 387
    —, representation of, 383–84

—, retention of perceived forms, 124
—, transformation of intellectual forms received in the soul and, 404–6
human beings, defeat of, 140, 368
imagining, does not imagine, 432
intellect, 368, 395–96
—, agent of, 406
location of, anterior ventricle of the cerebrum, 385, 387
—, soul is, 78
senses, external, 395
—, perception of dimension, 405
sleeping, 395, 405–7
soul, 78
—, instrument of the, 381, 385
—, occupation with the, 383–84
—, strength of, 383–84
—, virtue in the, 379, 394
waking, 395, 407
See also dreams; fantasy; perception, theory of; soul
Incest, 205
Incubus, 79, 388
cause, 388
Infants, death of, 388
Injustice, 185
definition of, 278, 290
See also justice
Inquisition, Portuguese, 38
Insensibilidad. See insensibility
Insensibility, 183
Instant, eternal. *See* God
Intellect ("*entendimyento*"), 20 n. 54, 24, 89
action, pure, 124
circumference of a circle, analogy with, 144
child, name for, 370
delight, definition of, 164
effects, judgment from, 394–95
falsehood. *See* truthfulness
food, damage from, 109–10
heart, mover of the, 168
imagination, 368, 395–96, 421
Influence, and Divine, 370
neighbor, name for, 290
perfection of, 109, 369
res intelligibiles, 164, 167
soul, 383
—, mirrors, analogy with opposing, 404–5
soul, cause of the, 78
speech, ambassador of, 151
truth, 168
truthfulness, 273–74, 283
virtue, 161
virtues, location of intellectual, 350
See also Light, Divine; virtues, intellectual; speculation, divine
Intellect, Active. *See sekel nivdal*
Intellect, Practical, 94, 125, 199, 275, 345–46, 350
action, 67
intellect, theoretical, 351
perfection of, 366, 370
virtues of, 351
wickedness, 156
See also will
Intellect, Pure, 409
Intellect, Separate. *See sekel nivdal;* intellect, theoretical
Intellect, Theoretical (Speculative), 23 n. 61, 94, 125, 344–46, 350
action, pure, 367, 395
ignorance of, 157

INDEX

incomparability of, 355
intellect, practical, 348, 351
Law, name for Divine, 378
perfection of, 201, 310, 366, 370
speculation, 348
unity of, 52–53
virtues of, 351
Intellectual (*"Maskil"* [*"ens intelligens"*]), 53, 78
Intellectus (*"Sekel"*), 50, 53, 78. See *also* intellect; intelligence
Intelligence (intellectual virtue), 21, 27, 50
    abstract, 80
    human, 24, 32
    —, Divine Law and, 104
Intelligence, Separate sublunar, 176, 403–4
    action, potential and, 403
    agent, 420
    conjunction with, prophetic dreamer and, 420, 426
    entes, 403
    soul, 403–5
    See also soul
Intelligences, Conjunction of the, 124, 192, 349, 390, 403–5, 407–8, 434
    Israel and God, 424, 426. *See also* prophecy; prophets; soul; speculation, Divine; wisdom
Intelligences, Separate, 192, 395
Intelligibles, 52, 78
Intemperance. *See* profligacy
Ipokrezia. See self-depreciation
Ira. See irascibility (anger, vice of gentleness)
Irakundya. See irascibility (anger, vice of gentleness)

Irascibility (anger, vice of gentleness), 62, 112, 246–53, 254–61
    action, perfection of, 252
    body and soul, damage to, 255
    causes of, 247–48
    cruelty, 261
    definition of, 247, 250, 252
    drunkenness, analogy with, 251
    idolatry, 260
    injury, consideration of, 256–57, 259
    judgment, 248
    laughter, 248
    pleasure, 256
    resurrection, 260
    Seneca, 250–52, 253, 259
    sin, 252
    vengeance, 149, 150, 247, 249, 250, 251, 252–53, 255, 256–57, 258, 291
    —, natural reason for, 252
    virtue, 248–253, 256
    vituperability, 260
    will, 248
    See also appetite, irascible
Irascibility (ambition, vice of magnanimity), 184
Isaac (biblical), 100
Isaac (*converso*), 38, 41, 43, 156
Isaac Almosnino, 3, 4 n. 10
Isaac Garçon, 41
Isaac Ḥayyim Abendana de Brito, 11 n. 38
Isagoge. See Hunain Ibn Isḥaq
Isaiah, the prophet, 134, 172, 273, 333, 337, 392, 430
Israel, 18, 222, 345, 429–30
    dead, resurrection of, 156, 260
    Egypt, 281, 408, 417
    elders of, 299, 302

enemies of, 358
Exodus, generation of, 408–9
Favor, Divine, 407, 429
Influence, Divine, 369–70
kings of, Divine Influence and, 187–88, 323–24, 377
Law, Divine, 91
—, reception of, 408–9
planets, seven, 425
prophecy, 422–26
Sabbath, 287
Sanhedrin, 336
tabernacle, 422–25
See also prophecy

Jacob (biblical), 213, 391, 408, 410
hunger, 434
Joseph, 433
teachers of, 433
Jacob Asher, 4
Jacob ben Meir Kulli, 1–2, 2 n. 2
Jacob Ibn Nehmias, 43
Japhet Almosnino, 4, 4 n. 10
death of, 5
Jean de Gara, 41
Jedadiah ben Abraham Bedersi, 33 n. 80, 115, 174, 175
Jeremiah, the prophet, 106, 178, 274
Jerusalem, 60, 62, 66, 396
children of, wise, 70
destruction of, 392
dream diviners in, twenty-four, 80
Jethro (biblical), 229, 239
Jeudah Piza, 11 n. 38, 41
Job, 62, 99, 154, 158, 257, 376
companions of, 267, 307, 341
John Argyropoulos, 366, 366 n. 257
Jonathan, magnanimity of, 323. See also David

Jorge Manrique, 128
Joseph (biblical), 30
baker, chief, 31, 400, 410–13, 420
—, dream of, 401, 411, 432
bones of, 242
brothers of, 85, 240, 391, 433
—, envy, 391–92
butler, chief, 30, 83, 410–13
—, dream of, 400–2, 411
counselor, 83, 417
dream diviner, 270, 380, 391, 392, 411
dream interpretations of, 81, 400–2, 407, 410–15, 434
—, divine cause for, 412
—, natural reasons for, 81, 380, 400–2, 414–15
dreams of, 85, 380, 391–92, 432–33
Jacob, 433
love, natural, 310–11
Pharaoh, 419–20
—, dream diviners of, 82, 419
—, dreams of, 31, 380, 411–12
—, overseer for, 418–19
prudence of, 402, 420, 433
test of, 83
truthfulness of, 270
See also dreams, interpretation
Joseph Hamon, 8 n. 24
Joseph Karo, 1,
Joseph Nasi, Don, 6, 40, 84, 384
Belveder, 31, 379
Beth Midraš, 427
death of, 41
dreams, doubts about, 379–80, 385–407, 427
Law, Divine, 429
marriage, 39

Moše Almosnino, patron of, 8, 8 n. 24, 11 n. 36, 13
printing press, 9 n. 26
prosperity, 429–30, 434–35
RV, abbreviation of, 380
TS, destinatory of, 30, 47, 48, 78, 379–80, 385, 405, 423, 427–28
—, request for, 379–80, 407
Joseph Taitazak, R., 5
Joseph Wakar. *See* Joseph Yakar
Joseph Yakar, 12, 435
Josephus, 278
Joshua (biblical), 236–37
Joshua Safarti, R., 5
Judd, Richard, 11 n. 37
Judeo-Spanish, 11, 11 n. 38. *See also* Jacob ben Meir Kulli; Joseph Karo; Moše ben Baruk Almosnino
Judges, 65, 295–96
    particulars, universals and, 301
    prudence, 303
    republic, 303
    truth, 296
Judgment, intellect, and practical, 170
    prudential, 208, 213, 223, 226, 230, 248, 251, 394, 401, 431
    See also reason, right
Jupiter, 61, 238
Justice, 21, 50, 62, 181, 288–305
    actions, 290–91
    —, Divine Law and Talmud, 293–94
    classes of, 65–66
    corrective. *See* justice, commutative
    cruelty, 261
    definition of, 275, 289–91, 300

    equity, 301, 303–4
    extremes, 289
    form, 289, 294
    friendship, 310, 334
    happiness, true, 291
    Law, Divine, 293
    liberality, 211
    matter, 288
    median, 65, 294–301
    mercy, 261
    nobility, 336
    precepts of, 291
    —, good customs, 291
    —, legal, 291
    —, natural, 291
    particulars, infinite, 301
    proportionality of, 65
    republic, 288, 303, 305
    science, 293
    virtues, comprises all, 288, 293
    world, sustains the, 304
    See also God; law, natural; injustice; judges
Justice, Commutative, 65, 292, 294
    definition of, 295
    —, Aristotle, 299
    —, involuntary, 292
    —, voluntary, 292
    Law, Talmud and Divine, 296
    proportion, arithmetic, 295
    punishment, 297–98
Justice, Distributive, 65
    Aristotle, 292, 294–95
    definition of, 295
    obligation, 295
    proportion, geometric, 295
Justice, Divine, 289
    obligation, no, 295
Justice, Legal, 65–66, 291, 294, 301–5

INDEX

Aristotle, 292
   median, 304
   precepts of, 291
   universal justice, 185, 301
   virtues of, 301
Justice, Natural, 291
   princes honor, 291
   truthfulness, 291
Justice, Particular, definition of, 185. See also justice, commutative; justice, distributive
Justice, Religious. See Justice, Legal

Kabbalists, 189
Kamino. See road
Karsel. See prison
Kavalyero. See knight
Kayserling, Meyer, 3 n. 5
Kilo. See chyle
Kimera. See chimera
King. See prince
Klmaleh, Leon, 30 n. 76
Knight, 99, 103, 146, 181
Knowledge, human, 2
   —, causes, effects and, 164
   —, eternal, 354
   pure, 163
   speculation, 348. See also speculation
Kobarde. See coward
Kobdisya. See greed
Konplisyon. See constitution
Konsilyyador. See Peter of Abano
Kontensyon. See quarrelsomeness
Kontento. See happiness
Korimyento. See shyness
Kortezano. See courtier
Kortezia. See courtesy
Kostelasyon. See constellation

Kostumbres. See customs
Koza korporal. See things, corporeal
Kozas del entendimyento. See res intelligibiles
Krueldad. See cruelty
Kueba en la mar. See whirlpool

Laban the Arami, 78, 82, 408, 409, 416
Lacedemonians, 151, 238
Landau, J. M., 3 n. 4
Langaza, 40
Lasedmonyyos. See Lacedemonians
Laughter, 208, 248
   inappropriate, 284
Law, definition of, 301
   ethical, 65
   —, Jews and, 91
   human, 143, 377–78
   justice, 290–91
   natural, 65, 143, 205
   See also justice; Law, Divine; law, Jewish; light
Law, Divine, 23, 23 n. 62, 24–25, 71–77, 104, 110, 139, 143, 152, 170, 171
   adherence to, 56
   comprehension of, 27, 104
   good, true, 180
   honor of, 189
   justice, comprises all forms of, 292–93, 301
   life, eternal, 180
   —, true, 180
   light, 423
   mercifulness of, 261
   names of, 70, 144
   obedience to, 100
   soul, sustains the, 162
   truth, 144, 269, 377–78

INDEX

See also Law, Jewish
Law, Jewish, 18, 33, 95, 104–6, 141, 171, 282
   arts, 362–63
   festivals, 129, 210, 287
   —, Passover, 210, 225
   —, Sukkot, 428. See also Sabbath
   gift, divine, 180
   God's love for humans, affirmation of, 349
   Imitatio Dei, 210, 296
   judges, 295, 301–3
   justice, 288, 301–3, 305
   knowledge, final ultimate purpose of, 366
   marriage, 209
   names of, 363
   prayer, 54, 125, 133
   —, benediction after meal, 110–11
   —, daily, 125
   —, Sabbath, 230, 287, 302
   —, S^ema^ca, 345
   precepts, 154, 160, 162, 180, 187, 246–47, 287, 310, 340, 363
   —, justice, 293–94, 297–98
   Temple, sacrifices in the, 224
   —, Ten Commandments, Tablets of the, 235
   —, truth, 275
   —, violation merits death, 189
   prudence, 363
   rabbis, authority of, 301–3
   science, comprises all, 361–63
   soul, comprises all good for, 377
   —, eternal, 325
   study, 363
   —, continuous, 88, 180
   —, morning, 130
   —, nighttime, 110
   wisdom, 361, 363
   See also justice; Law, Divine; prayer
Leaman, D., 3 n. 4
Legal justice. See justice
Lev Avot. See Solomon Le-Bet Ha-Levi
Levitas of Yavneh, R., 62
Levy, Avigdor, 3 n. 4
Liar, arrogance of, 277
   dissemblance, 277
   God, despised of, 142
   human purpose, true, 143–44
   hypocrisy, 272, 277
   pleasure, 271–73
   republic, 142
   semblance of, 143
   soul, 146
   truth, 276
   See also falsehood
Liberal Arts. See arts, seven liberal
Liberalidad. See liberality
Liberality, 50, 59–60, 181, 208–17, 300, 324, 334
   charity, 212, 222
   conversation, 209
   definition of, 183, 208, 209
   extremes, 59–60, 208–22
   giving and receiving, 209
   honor, 222
   justice, 210
   magnificence, 228
   properties of, sixteen, 209–16, 239
   wealth, 213
   —, inherited, 214
   See also meanness; profligacy; wealth
Liberty, 165, 180

man, name for, 179
Lie. *See* falsehood
Life, eternal, 180
—, palace of, 369
periods of, 159–61
—, first (childhood), 160, 161
—, modes, 368
—, second (youth), 160, 161, 168, 169
—, third (old age), 160
work, 335
Light, color, 177
creation story, 229, 264–65
Law, Divine, 423
See also Moses; sun
Lightning. *See* meteorology; prophecy
Ligonga. See flattery
Liver, 133
Logic, 50, 360, 363
Porphyry, 364
science or art, 361
See also RV; syllogism; wisdom
Lowry, Heath, 3 n. 4, 3 n. 6
Love, animal, irrational, 309
beloved and lover, 67–68, 330–42
classes of, 67–68
Divine, 170–71
honor, 330
how to, 68–69, 342–50
maternal and filial, 331–32
maxim, 342
paternal and filial, 67, 68, 189, 309, 310, 331
—, which greater, 340
reason, 314
true, complete knowledge and, 345
ultimate human purpose, 68
See also friendship; God; honor; human beings
Lumbre. See light
Lust, 203, 205
Lutheranism, 56, 171
Lycurgus, 103
Lying. *See* falsehood
Lying down. *See* regimen

Macrobius, 22
Macrocosmos (*"el mundo grande"*), 118–19
Magnanimity, 50, 60–61, 81, 96, 181, 210, 227–44
adversity, 231
circumstances, 241
counsel, 229
danger, 234–35
definition of, 184, 227–28
dishonor, 231
economy, domestic, 243
enmity, 240
flattery, 241, 242
friendship, 240
honor, 228, 229
independence, 238
justice, 230, 242
lawsuits, 244
magnificence, 228
malignity, 242
median, 231, 244
modesty, 228, 244
Moses, 229–35, 239–44
movements, 243
pleasure, 237–38
properties of, fifty, 61, 227–44
prosperity, 232
speech, 240, 240, 244
truthfulness, 236, 240
virtues, comprises all, 60

virtuousness, 228–29
See also pusillanimity; vanity
Magnificence, 50, 60–61, 181, 223–27
  action, 224–25
  definition of, 183, 223, 226
  liberality, 223, 226, 227, 228, 245
  magnanimity, 228
  nobility, 225
  properties of, 223–24
  wisdom, 226
  See also paltriness; vulgarity
Maimonides, 62, 65
  Abraham, letter to his son, 364
  allegory, 51–52, 104–5. *See also* example
  Aphorisms, 132
  controversy, 105–6, 262
  dreams, 30
  Eight Chapters, 18, 23 n. 60, 33, 63, 65, 78, 247, 262–64, 381
  Guide of the Perplexed, 16, 29, 30, 33, 51, 53, 56, 59, 69, 70, 78, 82, 84, 104–5, 124, 172, 273, 281, 297, 345, 351, 366, 381
  God, human comprehension of, 104–5
  —, Divine Influence on human beings, 22 n. 58
  —, His Knowledge and human knowledge, 175
  —, service to, 349
  —, speculation on, 104–5, 344–50
  Hilkot Shabbat, 66
  intellect, 351
  justice, 297
  Laws Concerning Character Traits, 18, 26, 27, 33, 126, 128, 130, 131, 132, 133
  logic, 362
  Mishneh Torah, 52, 53
  patience, 259
  philosophy of, 22, 26
  physician, 132
  prophecy, 28, 32, 407–8, 420–21
  prophets, 84
  purpose, final ultimate human, 344–50
  Regimen of Health, 19, 21, 109
  repentance, 63
  soul, perfection of the, 21, 104–5
Maknifisensya. See magnificence
Mal. See evil
Maldizyente. See talebearer
Malebolensya. See malevolence
Malevolence, 186
Malsin. See talebearer
Mandragora, 122
Mansedumbre. See gentleness
Manṣuri. See Abu Bakr al-Razi
Manyanimidad. See magnanimity
Marriage, 89–90
Martyrdom, 58, 69, 146, 187, 189–90. *See also* ʿAkiba, R.
Mašal. See example; mirror, analogy
Maskil ("ens intelligens"). See intellectual
Master. *See* slave
Materia. See matter
Mathematics, 353–54, 360
Matter, 134
  intellect, instrument of the, 166
  —, perfection of the, 137
  primary, 314
  soul, 134
  See also substance

INDEX

Me*ᶜam Loᶜez. See* Jacob ben Meir Kulli
Meanness, 60, 183, 218, 220, 227
   classes, 220
   endemic, 221
Medicine, 109, 367
   excess, 109
   science or art, 361
Medicine, Practical, 19
   drugs, 19
   regimen, 19, 21, 130
   ethical implications of, 20
   surgery, 19
Medicine, Theoretical, 19, 367. *See also res naturales; res contra naturales; res non naturales*
Mehlman, Israel, 8 n. 26
Memory, 88, 103, 109, 114, 128, 131, 133, 147, 150, 152, 157, 160, 161, 163, 180, 185, 221, 222, 237, 242, 244, 259, 321, 342, 369–78, 411
   forms and species, soul attracts, 383
   good, past, 166–67
   happiness, true, 377
   location of, posterior ventricle of the cerebrum, 387
   Moše Almosnino, 379
   res intelligibiles, delight of the intellect in, 164
   See also dreams; forgetfulness
Menander, 328
Mercenaries, 183
Mercy, 261
Mersed. See favor
Metaphysics, 23 n. 62, 28, 175, 177, 354, 360, 362, 366
   sage, 361
   subject, 361
Meteorology, 20, 52, 115–21

clouds, 98
comets, 116, 119
fog, 117
lightning, 116, 119
—, classes of, 120
—, and thunder, 116, 119–20
rain, 120–21, 356
—, generation of, 115–21
snow, 118
vapor, 116–18
winds, 120–21
Microcosmos ("*el mundo ǧiko*"), 118
Midrash, 12, 24, 464–654. *See also* sages
Miracle, Exodus, 280–82, 409
   nature, 409
Miriam. *See* Moses
Mirror ("*espeǧo*," "*specularia*," "*speculum*"), 28, 31
   analogy, 81–82, 404
   substances, different, 153
   title, 31 n. 79
   See also RV, mirror
Mišael, 127
Mistos. See mixture
Mixture, 116
Modesty, definition of, 184
   magnificence, 228, 246
   See also humility; irascibility; spiritlessness
Molho, Isaac, 2, 3 n. 4. *See also* Amarillo, Abraham Shaul
Moon, 129, 176, 232, 399
   eclipse, 232, 354
   realm, sublunar, 176, 403, 405, 420
   Rule of Animodar, 399
Moreh. See Maimonides, *Guide of the Perplexed*

INDEX

Moše ben Baruk Almosnino, R., author,
    9–10, 47, 48, 89, 109, 155
  Beth Elohim, 10, 39, 129, 191,
    365
  biography, 2–8, 38–41
  birth, date of, 3, 38
  brothers. *See* Absalom Almosnino;
    Isaac Almosnino; Japhet Al-
    mosnino
  children. *See* Baruk Almosnino
    (son); Šimon Almosnino
  commentary, al-Ghazzali, 123
  —, biblical, 9, 33
  —, Five Scrolls, 40, 41
  —, Jedadiah ben Abraham Ber-
    dersi, 115
  daughter, 5
  death of, 3, 41
  dreams of, 8 n. 25, 31, 84, 380,
    427–35
  —, analogy with dreams of Jo-
    seph, 432–33
  —, interpretation of, 430–35
  —, —, analogy with interpreta-
    tions of Joseph, 435
  —, —, reasons for, natural, 432–
    33
  —, truth of, natural reason for, 382
  education, 4–5, 38
  elegy, 7 n. 21
  embassy to Sultan, 5 n. 16, 8, 9,
    39, 40
  —, dream foretelling success of, 8
    n. 25
  —, report of, 5 n. 16, 41
  *Extremos y grandezas de Constan-
    tinopla,* 5 n. 16, 40, 41
  father. *See* Baruk Almosnino
  Exodus, analogy with generation

  of the, 31 n. 77, 433–34
  health, 430
  Hebrew, preference for, 9, 89
  —, translation, 9, 118
  Iggeret Tehiyat ha-Metim, 43,
    156
  Joseph Nasi, service to, 435
  Judeo-Spanish, attitude toward,
    49, 89
  Kaza del Dyyo. See Beth Elohim
  Meammes Koah, 4 n. 10, 8 n. 23,
    10, 41, 43
  Migdal ᶜOz, 10, 41, 365, 366
  Moše Garçon, affinity with, 89–
    90
  mother, 4
  —, death of, 5, 41
  namesake, 244
  Neve Šalom, preface to, 10, 38
  orator, 7, 7 n. 21
  philosophy, 3, 7, 20 n. 54, 23, 32
  Pirke Moše, 10, 38, 39
  Piruš al Iyob, 99
  Piruš al Sefer ha-Šᶜmaa ha-Tabai,
    299, 366
  Pne Moše, 10, 24, 33 n. 81, 39,
    48, 101, 102, 104, 106, 125,
    135, 140, 170, 172, 175,
    192, 194, 200, 217, 255,
    293, 295, 305, 341, 353, 367
  —, sources of, 18 n. 50
  Problems, Hebrew translation of
    Aristotle's, 9, 118
  *Puerta del syelo. See Šaᶜar ha-
    Šamayyim*
  rabbi, 7–8, 32, 33, 48
  —, *Leviath Hen,* 8, 39
  —, —, contract terms, 8 n. 23
  —, posts, 6–7, 39

responsa, 9, 43, 365
Šaʿar ha-Šamayyim, 10, 39, 130, 365
sister, 4–5, 91
Tefillah le-Moše, 10, 38, 39
Teorika de la luna, 382
Tikkun Soferim, 10
time, press of, 89, 227, 340, 353, 427
Torat Moše, 42
Tosafot Beur ʿal Divrei ha-Raba, 10
Treatise on Friendship, 41, 305
uncle. *See* Samuel Almosnino
writings, complete, 43–44
wife. *See* Simḥa (née Safarti) Almosnino
Yede Moše, 10
See also Joseph Nasi
Moše de Boton, R., 4
Moše Garçon, 5, 16, 31, 33, 41, 47, 48–49, 87, 88, 175, 358
Hebrew, knowledge of, 128
intelligence, 283
mother and father, 91, 160
namesake, 244
RV, request for, 160
sleep habits, 128
See also RV, destinatory, specific
Moše Rabbenu. See Moses
Moses, the prophet, 28, 61, 66, 69, 102, 184, 351
Aaron, 249, 420
birth, 229
courage, 235
death of, 230, 304
gentleness, 249
good, name for, 229
hero, 229
honor, 230
irascibility, 255, 257
Joseph, bones of, 242
justice, 230, 242, 304
lawgiver, 230
magnanimity, 229–35, 239–44
mercy, 249
Miriam, 249, 420
repose, 287
Moses ben Maimon. *See* Maimonides
Music, 165, 362
definition of, 364
friendship, 322
horse, 203
lust, 202
See also example, sound
Musician. *See* example
Muskal. See idea

Naʿami. *See* Naomi
Nakdimon ben Gurion, 60, 221
Naomi, 325–26
Nature, definition of, 281
God orders, 201
miracles, 409
See also intelligence, separate
Nave. *See* ship
Nebuchadnezzar, 127
Nehama, Joseph, 3 n. 4, 6 n. 17, 7 n. 19, 10, 34
Neve Šalom (Maimonidean apology). *See* Abraham Shalom
Neve Šalom (synagogue). *See* Salonika
Nightmare. *See* dreams
Nobility, 225
Nobleza. See nobility

Old age. *See* Age
Olson, Glending, 20

Onra. See honor
Opinion, 353
Opium, 122
Ottoman Empire, commerce in, Jewish, 5 n. 15
  life in, Jewish, 1, 7 n. 19
  Selim II, 5 n. 16, 8
  Süleiman I, 5, 40
Ovid, 96
Ozadia. See rashness
Ozyosos. See idleness

Palabra. See speech
Palm fronds, 427–28
Paltriness, 184, 223, 226, 227, 228
Parables. *See* examples
Paradoxes, 19
Partido ("condition," "state," "pact"), 282
Pascual Recuero, Pascual, 5 n. 16, 15
Passion. *See* appetite; *res non naturales*
Pasyensya. See patience
Patience, 50, 61–63, 181, 246–54, 259–60, 261–65
Patriarchs (biblical), 103, 424
  See also Abraham; Isaac; Jacob
Pelestria, 39, 40
Pena infernal. See punishment, infernal
Pentateuco de Constantinopla, 12
Perception, theory of, 31, 52, 89, 380–403
  —, al-Ghazzali, 403
  —, Ibn Sina, 403
  See also fantasy; imagination; soul
Pereza. See spiritlessness
Perspectiva. See perspective
Perspective, 362, 364
  soul, 404
  See also mirror

Peter de Abano, 367, 367 n. 262
Pezadilyya. See dreams, nightmare
Pharaoh, 78, 82, 85
  birthday, 401
  dream diviners of, 82–83, 410–11, 419
  —, natural reason, 410
  dreams of, 380, 409–19
  —, Divine Influence and, 415–16
  God of, river, 417
  irascibility of, 402, 412–13
  slaves of, 239
  unworthiness of, 414
  See also Joseph, chief butler, chief baker; dream; dreamer, unworthiness of; dream diviners
Philosophers, 52
  books of, 363
  fantasy, imagination and, 406
  principle of, God is *intellectus, ens intelligens,* and *ens intelligibile,* 78
  See also philosophy
Philosophy, Greek and Jewish, 22 n. 58, 28, 171
  human beings, perfection of, 23, 27, 52, 104–7
  medicine, 20
  moral, 6, 16 n. 45, 22 n. 59, 48, 97, 169, 305, 312–13, 341, 366
  —, definition of, 367
  natural, 97, 105
  —, dream diviners and, 396, 397, 398, 400, 432–33
  utility of, practical, 24–25
  See also Maimonides; science
Phlegmatic, 62, 112, 255. *See also* constitution

INDEX

Physicians, 99, 113, 128, 147, 200, 380
   cerebrum, 382
   —, damage to, 387
   death, 164
   digestion, 122
   dissembling, 272
   heart, 121
   incubus, 388
   See also regimen
Physics, 23 n. 62, 354, 362
   Averroes, 366
   See also Aristotle; science
Piety, foolish, 303–4
Pilot, 137. *See also* example; ship
Plagiarism, 272
Plague, 38, 39, 40, 41
Planets, seven, 425. *See also* astrology; astronomy; dreams; predestination
Plato, 22, 22 n. 59, 100 n. 23, 106, 108, n. 45, 144
   logic, 361
Pleasantness. *See* courtesy in speech
Pleasure, actions, 96, 166, 193
   —, good, 190
   coitus, 202–5
   corporeal, 167, 201–3
   food, 109
   honesty, 169
   intellectual, 167, 191
   irascibility, 256
   memory of, 166
   rational, 203
   res intelligibiles, 192
   speculation, Divine, 191, 201
   speech, 148, 268
   truthfulness, 145–46
   See also appetite, concupiscient; utility

Plutarch, 99
Pobreza. See poverty
Politics, 17 n. 48
   definition of, 335
   See also regimes, political; republic
Porphyry, 193, 364
Poverty, 96, 101
   Fortune, evil of, 97
   friendship, 307
   home, prince in own, 337
   See also goods; human beings
Pozilanimidad. See pusillanimity
Prayer. *See* Law, Jewish
Predestination, 26, 56–57, 171, 176–80, 352, 425–26
   God, omniscience of, 171, 172
   See also dreams, class three, type one; God; human beings; will, free
Preśpektiba. See perspective
Press, printing. *See* Constantinople; Joseph Nasi; Salonika; Yosef Yaabes
Prezunsyon. See boastfulnesss
Prime Mover, 57, 415, 416. *See also* God
Prince, 165, 187
   advisors, 113
   anger, analogy with death, 402
   danger, 58, 188–89
   friendship, 306
   God, instrument of, 433–34
   justice, 336
   magnanimity, 238
   magnificence, 223
   nakedness, 140
   republic, necessary for the, 188–89

INDEX

tyrants, 220
   See also Pharaoh
Principles, First, 50, 352, 356, 361, 362
   ignorance of, 359
   senses, five external, 360
   species, 360
   —, universal, 360
Prison, 165, 375, 400, 402, 411, 414
Probagio. *See* Puerbach, Georg von
Prodegalidad. See profligacy
Profligacy, 183, 200–4, 215–16, 218, 227, 300
   definition of, 207, 246
   flattery, 219
   impoverishment, 218–19
   prudence, 359
Prolixity, 54, 147–52
Prophecy, 16, 61
   definition of, 424
   degrees of, 421
   dreams, 30–31, 47, 78, 84, 394. *See also* dreams, class three
   Gentiles, 422–26
   —, astrology, 424–25
   Influence, Divine, 420
   Israel, 423–25
   knowledge, 32
   Moses, 421
   philosophy, 28, 28 n. 73, 30 n. 76, 32
   tabernacle, 422–25
   wealth, 234
   See also Abimelech; Bil^{c}am; dreams; God; Joseph; Moses; Pharaoh; prophets
Prophets, 84
   forms unseen, substantial intellectual universal, 421
   Gentiles, 84
   —, half word of God, 425
   Israel, 84, 170
   —, full word of God, 426
   See also Bil^{c}am; dreams; Moses; prophecy
Proverb, 50, 92, 98, 136, 140, 146, 156, 221, 222, 223, 307, 313, 321, 342, 343
Proverbs. *See* Solomon
Providence, Divine, 96, 258, 430
   adversity, definition of, 102
   —, prosperity and, 98–99, 101–2, 220, 221–22
   good, eternal, 158
   —, source of, 99
   individual, 100, 408
   infinite, 171
   Joseph, 433
   nature, 408
   son, judgment against father, 101
   virtuous, test of the, 99
   See also dream, class three; God; theodicy
Prudence (location in practical intellect), 17 n. 48, 21, 27, 50, 70, 181, 200, 352, 358–59
   circumference of a circle, analogy with, 144
   counsel, 199, 358
   definition of, 358
   Flood, generation of the, 359
   intellect, practical, 362
   judgment, 359
   justice, 293
   location, 362
   object of, faction is, 356
   purpose of, 356
   reason, right, 211, 350

temperance, 358–59
truth, judgment of, 361
virtues, source of, 183
wisdom, 362
See also reason, right; virtues, intellectual
Prudensya. See prudence
Psyche. *See* soul
Ptolemy, 81, 312
   Almagest, 365, 382
   Centiloquium, 399
Puerbach, Georg von, *Theorica Nova Planetarum,* 10, 39, 130, 365
Punishment, infernal, 161
Purification, 16 n. 46
Pusillanimity, 184, 228, 229, 244
Pyadad. See mercy
Pythagoreans, 297

Quarrelsomeness, 184
   definition of, 266

Rabbenu Mošeh. *See* Maimonides
Raḥab, 236–37
Rain. *See* meteorology
Rashi. *See* Solomon bar Isaac
Rashness, 182
Rational, 203
Rav Ibn Ḥasdai, 69
Rayo. See lightning
Razal. See sages
Razes. *See* Abu Bakr al-Razi
Razon. See reason
Realm, sublunar, 81, 162, 176, 405, 420
   entes, 403
   See also Ibn Sina; intelligences, conjunction of the; intelligences, separate sublunar; moon; soul
Reason ("*entendimyento,*" intelligence, apprehends first principles, location in theoretical intellect), 352, 360–61
   definition of, 360
   natural, 93, 105, 171
   science, origin of, 360
   See also intelligence; philosophy; reason, right; science; virtues, intellectual
Reason, right ("*dereğa razon*"), 90, 113, 115, 128, 134, 155, 161, 164, 177, 184, 187, 188, 200, 210, 211, 216, 286, 432, 435
   actions, governs and directs, 251, 282
   definition of, action in the soul, 209
   —, prudence, 350, 358–59
   falsehood, 278
   judgment of, 180, 199, 208, 213, 217, 221, 223, 226, 228, 229, 235, 248, 257, 274, 317, 395, 400
   virtue, 256
   See also prudence
Redemption, 177
Regev, Shaul, 5 n. 16
Regimen, arising, 50, 53, 129–36
   drinking, 50, 52, 111–14
   —, public, 112–14
   eating, 16, 50, 52, 107–11
   —, intemperance, 207
   —, preservation of health, 109
   —, public, 113
   —, sleep, 121
   lying down, 50, 53, 129–36
   —, damage to the soul, 131
   sleep, 16, 50, 121–22, 125–26

—, amount of, 130
—, causes of, 52, 115–22, 380
—, danger of, 128–29
—, death, one sixtieth of, 53, 78, 128, 382
—, definition of, 115, 121, 382
—, disorderly, 128
—, essence of, 53, 115–22, 380
—, excess, 125
—, half-sleep, 132, 387
—, how to, 131–33, 135
—, metaphor, 20
—, purpose of, 123, 284
—, smoke, 116
—, vapors, 121
waking, 20, 52–53, 121–29, 406
—, definition of, 115
See also medicine
Regimes, political, 68, 335–40
See also republic; tyranny
Regimiento de la vida, 1, 16–30, 31, 39, 409
abbreviation of, 380
contemporary scene, reference to, 209, 215, 217, 220, 221, 272, 306, 308, 322, 323, 413
contents of, 17 n. 48
—, moral summa, 31
—, terrestrial world of the soul, 155–56
—, universal rule, 87, 88
curriculum, 23, 23 n. 62, 24–25, 29, 33–34, 88
destinatary, general reader, 88, 90, 218, 221
—, specific reader, 5, 13, 31, 47, 88–89, 98, 103, 107, 124, 133, 135, 136, 138, 142, 152–53, 160, 169, 178, 227, 237, 259, 262, 266, 278, 280, 284, 289, 301, 305, 315, 317, 340, 342, 350, 362, 365, 366, 370, 378
—, age of, 106, 153
—, judgment of, 208. *See also* Moše Garçon
edition of, 1, 11
—, facsimile, 1 n. 1
—, Latin character, 1, 11, 11 n. 38
—, Rashi character, 1, 11
—, —, punctuation, 14
—, —, transliteration, 13–15
glossary, Hebrew and Judeo-Spanish, 11 n. 37, 12, 15, 47, 49, 436–52
—, Judeo-Spanish and Spanish, 468–78
introduction, Hebrew, 1, 19
Judeo-Spanish, 11 n. 37, 12, 15, 47, 49, 436–52, 468–78
marginalia, Hebrew, 12
meliṣa, 12
mirror, analogy with, 16, 48, 107, 152, 153, 378
organization of, 17–21, 50, 87
prooftext, 25
purpose of, 16–19, 33, 34, 131, 341
—, *Nicomachean Ethics,* propaedeutic, 104
—, moderation of appetites, 169
—, rule for true and proper life, 88–90
—, rule for True Happiness, 161, 367
—, rule for virtuous action, 185
—, Talmud, propaedeutic, 363

INDEX

rhetoric 18, 25, 33. *See also meliṣa*
sources, 18, 18 n. 50, 21, 32–33
—, Maimonides, 22 n. 58
—, *Nicomachean Ethics,* 22 n. 57
syllogism, 25, 269, 352, 353–54, 358, 400
translation, biblical verses into Judeo-Spanish, 11, 11 n. 38, 12
—, Hebrew into English, 14
virtues, moral, 107
youth, parents and instruction of, 90
—, analogy with tree, 90
—, lessons of, 106
—, virtuous habits, 90, 103, 106
Regalo, 185
Regmisyon. See spiritlessness
Repose, conversation, 284
necessary, 287
speculation, virtuousness and, 284
Republic, 100, 142, 146, 187, 239, 377
aristocracy, 336
—, analogy with household, 337
—, Rome, 336
—, Venice, 336
constitutional, 336
democracy, 337
—, analogy with household, 338
friendship, 310, 339–40
— and justice, 312
governance of, pure good, 315
judges, 303
justice, 288, 305
—, distributive, 294–95
magnificence, 224, 227
monarchy, 335–36, 339
—, analogy with household, 337
oligarchy, 336

scorn, 285
tyranny, 336
—, analogy with household, 338
Res contra naturales, 19
epilepsy, 111
Res intelligibiles, 166
Res naturales, 19
Res non naturales, 19–20, 52
contraries, definition of, 192
doctrine of, ethical, 20
food, damage to the intellect, 109–10
framework, narrative, 21
passions, imagination and, 386
—, simultaneous contrary, 190–92
Rhetoric, 362
definition of, 363
River, 372, 417
Road, Happiness, True, 87, 88, 89
short yet long, 368–70
wrong, 160–61
Rodrigue, Aron. *See* Benbassa, Esther
Rome. *See* republic
Romeu Ferré, Pilar, 5 n. 16
Rooster, 205
Rosanes, Solomon Abraham, 3 n. 5
Roth, Cecil, 6 n. 17, 8 n. 24, 8 n. 25
Rufus (physician), 131
Rule of Animodar, 81, 399. *See also* astronomy, rule for judging future
Rustiko. See rustic
Rustic, 114, 137, 165
storm, foretelling of, 400
Ruth, 325–26

Saadia Gaon, 23
Saadia Longo, 7 n. 20
Sabbath. *See* Law, Jewish

INDEX

Śabyo. See sage
Sacrobosco, John, 10, 129, 365
Sadness, 93, 165, 193
   irascibility, 255
   melancholy, 165
   wickedness, 96
Sages, 12, 21, 24–26, 49, 51, 54, 95, 100, 101, 103, 104, 110, 113, 114, 125, 134, 135, 139, 155, 158, 162, 175, 368, 410, 411, 428
   definition of, 361
   dreams, 396, 400
   liars, contemporary, 272
   metaphysics, 361
   Pharaoh, God of, 417
   prophecy, 423
   —, definition of, 424
   speculation, 353
   See also wisdom
Sailors, 121, 137. See also example; ship; pilot
Salonika, 3, 198, 299, 300
   conversos, Portuguese, 6, 33
   demography, 3 n. 6
   earthquake, 41
   fires, 4, 38
   Jews in, 3 n. 4, 6 n. 17
   —, exemptions and privileges of, 5 n. 16, 38, 40
   —, intellectual life of, 8–9
   —, Jewish quarter, 3 n. 6
   —, kahya Baruk and, 7 n. 19
   —, müssellimlik, 40
   —, rabbinic reforms, 5, 5 n. 15
   —, ram tribute, 39, 40
   —, relations, intra- and intercommunal, 7 n. 19, 8 n. 22
   —, taxation of, 5 n. 16, 41
   location of, 129, 191
   printing press, Hebrew, 9
   synagogue, 7 n. 21
   —, Calabrese. See Neve Šalom
   —, Catalan, 4, 6, 38
   —, Catalan, Old and New, 4
   —, founding of, 225
   —, Kahal Kadosh Yahya. See Leviath Ḥen
   —, Leviath Ḥen, 6, 39
   —, Neve Šalom, 6, 39
   —, prohibition on new, 6 n.17
   Talmud Torah, 5 n. 16, 40
Salt, 60, 321
Šamay, school of, 279
Samuel, 250
Samuel Almosnino, 4
Samuel ben Yakar, 435
Samuel de Medina, 4 n. 9, 5 n. 15, 8 n. 22, 43
Samuel Kelai, 43
Samuel Nasi, 31, 41, 427–29
   children of, 429
Sanhedrin, 336
Santippe. See Xanthippe
Saperstein, Marc, 4 n. 12
Sapyensyya. See Wisdom
Satan, 99
Satiety, 109–10
Saul, 250, 323
Šaul. See Saul
Scales, 182
Science ("sensya," apprehension by means of first principles, location in theoretical intellect), 21, 24, 27, 50, 70, 104, 352, 353–56, 361–70
   action, 355
   definition of, 353, 356, 361

537

interpretation, dream, 31, 32, 302, 394–427
life, true, 360
moral, 111, 350
natural, 111, 115–21, 164, 366
truth, eternal, 353–54
See also grammar; imagination; logic; mathematics; philosophy; rhetoric; theology; virtues, intellectual
Scipio. *See* Cipion
Scorn, 285
Seasons, 118, 122, 166
S*e*farim. *See* Torah scrolls
Sekel. *See intellectus*
Sekel Nivdal, 58, 81
    action, pure, 395
    form, human being imagines material, 395
    nature, 143–44, 201, 310
    See also Intellect, Theoretical
Self-depreciation, 185, 270
    classes of, 271–73
Selim II. *See* Ottoman Empire
Selo. *See* zeal
Šemuel. *See* Samuel
Semuel Mendes de Sola, 11 n. 38, 41
Senderizis ("the absence of basic human principles"), 143
Seneca, 21, 51, 59, 62, 95, 96, 97, 156, 208, 211, 213
    irascibility (anger), 250–52, 253, 259, 323
    love, 334
Sense, common, 124, 380
    imagination, 380
Senses, five external, 55, 57–59, 113, 123–25, 137, 204, 380, 382–88
    body, attribute of, 115

heart, location in, 121, 381
object, apprehension of, 381
objects of the, 201–2
pain and pleasure, 201
soul, 382
—, attribute of, 78, 115
temperance, 183, 200–5
See also color; dreams; eyes; pleasure; sight; soul; sound; things
Shame, 108, 113, 186
Shammai, school of, 64
Shaw, Stanford J., 3 n. 4, 3 n. 5, 4 n. 9, 4 n. 10, 7 n. 19, 8 n. 25
Ship, 137–38, 259–60, 371
Shmuelevitz, Aryeh, 3 n. 4, 3 n. 6, 7 n. 19, 8 n. 22
Shyness, 186
Sight, 120, 167, 177, 381, 385–86
    action in the soul, pure, 377
    images, dream, 383–84
    intellect, minister of, 168
    intellectual, 176
    See also eyes; sound; speculation
Silence, 20, 50, 54, 142–46
    speech, 148–49
    See also speech
Simḥa (née Safarti) Almosnino, children of, 5
    death of, 5, 39
    epitaph, 39, 43
Šimon Almosnino, 5, 39, 41
Sin, 56, 101, 102, 114, 134, 187, 189, 195, 375
    Adam, 273
    baker, chief, 400, 402, 413
    butler, chief, 401, 402, 413
    death, atonement for, 138
    eyes, 168
    heart, 168

INDEX

irascibility, 252
judge, 303
lust, 205
Moses, 255
piety, foolish, 303
public, 189
sinners, 57, 269, 335
will, free, 177, 178, 179
Sin ğustisyya. *See* injustice
Sitting, 16, 50, 53–54, 136–42
Slave, master and, 113
Sleep. *See* dream; regimen
Smoke, 116
Snow. *See* meteorology
Śoberbyya. *See* vanity
Socrates, 54
    condemnation of, 144–45, 146
    irascibility, 260
    poverty, 213
Solomon (biblical), Ecclesiastes, 154, 157, 164, 219, 248, 256, 286, 306, 390
    Law, name of Jewish, 363
    Proverbs, 107, 110, 128, 134, 148, 154, 157, 159, 234, 242, 244, 271, 275, 288, 308, 312, 316, 331, 343, 360, 376, 429, 433
    Song of Solomon, 321, 424
    wealth of, 234
Solomon Avigdor, 39
Solomon bar Isaac, 69, 139, 347, 349
Solomon Ibn Gabirol, 23, 149 n. 146, 149 n. 148, 151 n. 150
    Tikkun Midot ha-Nefesh, 23
Solomon Le-Bet Ha-Levi, 10 n. 34
    Lev Avot, 23 n. 62
Śolturaś. *See* dreams, interpretation
Song. *See* music

Sorcery, 272
Soul, 78
    accidents of, 21, 88
    achievements of, Divine Grace and, 155
    body, mistress of the, 134
    —, virtue in the, 284
    causes, knowing, 81
    constitution, 112. *See also* constitution; *res non naturales*
    destruction of, 96, 114
    division of, bipartite, 350
    forms, imagination of, 386–87
    God, speculation on, 377
    goods of, analogy with right hand, 234
    imagination, occupation with the, 381–84, 394, 433
    Influence, Divine, 377
    intellect, governor of the, 381
    life, eternal, 55, 71, 87–88, 189, 325
    matter, subordination to, 134
    nature of, 386
    perception, 386
    perfection of, 16 n. 45, 19 n. 51, 23, 26, 55, 87–88, 366
    senses, external, 382, 385–90, 394–95, 405–7
    sensible, 385–87
    sleep, conjunction with sublunar intelligence in, 403–6
    times (worlds) of, three, 18, 19, 55, 152–58
    —, celestial, 19, 102, 155, 377
    —, —, definition of, 160
    —, resurrection, 19, 62, 154, 156
    —, terrestrial, 19, 102, 154, 156, 377

—, —, length of, 156
—, —, subject of *RV,* 155
unity of, 78, 351
virtues of, 137
wise, study makes, 111
See also conscience; consciousness; human beings; intellect; intelligences, conjunction of; perception, theory of; senses, external
Sound, 120
Spanish. See Judeo-Spanish
Speaking, 50, 53–54, 136–42. See also brevity; prolixity; speech
Specularia. See mirror
Speculation, 16, 19, 23–24, 27–29, 69, 88, 103, 104, 150
   action, 348
   good and evil, 353
   knowledge, true, 348
   Love, Divine, 344–45
   modes of, 353
   pleasure, 201
   repose, 284
   true, 137, 377
   truth and falsehood, 353
   See also human beings; virtues, intellectual
Speculation, Divine, action, 344–50
   crown, 155
   drink, 162
   intellect, theoretical, 348
   Moses, 230
   purpose, true human, 125, 344–50
   See also action, human; intellect; intelligences, conjunction of; Maimonides
Speculum. See mirror

Speech, 20, 142, 265–68
   anecdote, 147
   brevity, 151
   class of, 149
   —, first (flattery), 149
   —, second (offensive), 149–50
   —, third (fiction), 150
   —, fourth (theology), 150–51
   dreams, 389–91
   intellect, mirror of, 151, 278
   medicine, analogy with, 147, 148
   opportune, 148–49, 152
   pleasure, 273
   purpose of, truth is, 278
   sages, 26, 148, 284
   silence, 148–49
   soul, mirror of the, 151
   See also courtesy in speech; falsehood; friendliness; prolixity; truth; truthfulness; vices; virtues
Sphere. See Sacrobosco, John
Spies, Twelve, 236
   magnanimity, 237
Spirit, perfection of. See soul
Spiritlessness, 184
Starr, Joshua, 3 n. 4
Steinschneider, Moritz, 2
Still, 117, 343. See also distillation
Stoicism, 22 n. 59
Storms. See meteorology
Study, continuous, 88, 190
   morning, 130
   nighttime, 110
Sublunar realm. See realm, sublunar
Substance, 320
   animate and inanimate, 115
   See also matter
Süleiman I. See Ottoman Empire

Šulḥan Aruk. *See* Joseph Karo
Sun, 98
    eclipse of, 98, 232, 354–55
    light of, 97–98
    magnanimity, 232
    rays of, 116–17
    stars and planets, analogy with, 118
Ṣuraṭ Ha-'Areṣ. *See* Abraham bar Ḥiyya
Synagogue. *See* Salonika

Tabernacle, 357, 422–25
Tale. *See* example
Talebearer, 149–50, 322
Talmud, 4, 22, 24–25, 48, 104, 105, 139, 157, 158, 263, 277, 279, 284, 288, 293, 294, 296, 297, 298, 302, 303, 305, 306, 337, 345, 346, 347, 363, 364, 396, 397
    index of citations, 462–63
    See also dream diviners
Talmudists, 105
Tamar. *See* Amnon
Tarfon, R., 69, 346
Teacher, 113
Tebunah. *See* prudence
Teleology, of creation, 18
Temor. *See* cowardice
Temperance, 50, 58–59, 70, 108–9, 181, 200–8
    definition of, 183, 200
    prudence, 358–59
    See also insensibility; profligacy
Tenplansa. *See* temperance
Testigo. *See* Satan
Tetiś. See Thetis
Themistius, 192
Theodicy, 57, 58, 93, 102. *See also* God

Theorica Nova Planetarum. *See* Puerbach, Georg von
Thetis, Queen, 61, 238
Things, corporeal, classes of, four, 123–24
    external accidental, 320
    nature, first cause and, 280
    particularity, determination of, 404–5
    possible, from causes, 395
    See also bodies; good, corporeal
Thirst. *See* regimen, drinking
Thomas Aquinas, 281
Tikkun Midot ha-Nefe. *See* Solomon Ibn Gabirol
Time, experience of, 173
    —, past and present, 55, 163–68
    —, melancholy, 164, 165
    See also God
Tirosh-Rothschild, Hava. *See* Tirosh-Samuelson, Hava
Tirosh-Samuelson, Hava, 2, 2 n. 3, 4 n. 12, 7 n. 20, 9 n. 27, 10, 10 n. 34, 19 n. 51, 21 n.55, 22 n. 57, 22 n. 58, 26 n. 70, 28, 29 n. 74
Tolomeo. *See* Ptolemy
Torah. *See* Law, Divine
Torah scrolls, 427, 429
Transformaciones de Morpheo. *See Tratado de los suenyos*
Tratado de los suenyos, 1, 9
    composition, date of, 380
    destinatary, 13, 30–32, 47, 48, 78, 379–80, 384–85, 402, 405, 406, 423, 427–28. *See also* Joseph Nasi
    editions of, 1, 11, 41
    introduction, 77–85

Moše Almosnino, dream of, 379–435
   RV, 13, 31–32, 380, 409
   subjects of, 30
   See also dreams; *RV*
Trees, 371
Tristeza. See sadness
Troubadour, 214–15
Truth, 54
   being, analogy with, 144
   centerpoint of a circle, analogy with, 144, 337
   children, 143
   forms, intellectual, 144
   Fortune, 145–46
   friendship, perfection of, 146
   God, 274
   —, seal of, 54, 144
   good, analogy with, 144
   happiness, 146
   intellect, 167
   justice, 275
   parts of, five, 274–75
   pleasure, 345
   pure, being is, 274
   science, 274, 277
   speech, 142, 275
   strength, 278
   unique, 178
   universe, sustains, 144
   virtue, 279
   virtues, moral, 147, 275
   —, emanation of, 144
   wisdom, 353
   See also reason; science; speech; truthfulness; wisdom
Truthfulness, 50, 61, 63–64, 181, 268–73
   action, 268, 270
   centerpoint of a circle, analogy with, 269
   circumstances, 279
   deficiency, 269
   definition of, 185, 271
   example of, 145–46
   excess, 269
   extremes of, 63–64, 269
   movement, 270
   pleasure, 144, 268
   species of, 63–64, 273–83
   speech, 268, 270
   thought, 268, 270
   virtue, intellectual, 273
   virtuousness, 270
   —, cause for, 146–47
   See also boastfulness; falsehood; self-depreciation; speech; truth
Tulyo. See Cicero
Turim. *See* Jacob Asher
Turkish language, 4
Turks, brevity, 152
   literacy, 152
Tyera. See earth
Tyranny, 182, 220. *See also* regimen, political

Ultimate Human Purpose, Final. *See* human beings; speculation
Unconsciousness. *See* consciousness
Understanding. *See* intellect; reason
Universidad. See university
University, 224
Utility, 96, 181

Vacuum, 280, 282
   definition of, 355
Vanity, 184, 208, 244–45

INDEX

insanity, 228
Vapor, 116–18, 388
Varon. See liberty
Vašti, 338
Veluntad. See will
Vengeance. *See* irascibility
Venice. *See* republic
Ventura. See fortune
Verdad. See truthfulness
Verguensa. See shame
Vice, 28
    age, old, 90, 136–38, 368–70
    definition of, 182, 246
    destructive, 114, 136
    extremes of, 114
    garden, analogy with, 370
    garments, analogy with, 114
    partition from God, 28
    virtues, 90
Viego. See age, old
Vigilya. See regimen, waking
Villainous, 143, 182, 285, 298
Vilyyania. See boorishness; buffoonery
Vilyyano. See villainous
Virtue, 88
    action, 182
    childhood, 161
    conditions, 93, 182, 190, 194, 201, 209
    definition of, 139, 223, 246, 286
    —, concerns the difficult, 239, 344
    —, habit in the soul, 209, 211, 228, 275, 319, 324, 325, 360, 379
    —, median, 182
    —, mode of action, 209, 228, 256
    extremes, 182, 247
    goodness, 182
    name, 210
    pleasure, 211
    properties of, five, 194
    See also Aristotle, median
Virtues, Ethical, 17, 26, 27, 50, 160
    garments, analogy with, 114
    number, 57
Virtues, Intellectual, 17, 27, 51, 87, 160
    classes of, 350–62, 367
    —, location in practical and theoretical intellect, 350–62, 367
    essence, 69–70, 350–62
    intellect, 350
    Law, Divine, 350
    necessity, 353, 357
    possibility, 353, 357
    soul, habit in the, 252–53
    See also art; intelligence; prudence; science; wisdom
Virtues, Moral, 20–21, 57, 87, 169, 180–86
    constitution, bias to vice, 262
    good, foundation of human, 207
    happiness, true, 113
    number of, 180–81
    possession of, 27
    properties of, 58, 93, 194–200
    RV, 107
    truth, 275
    will, location in the, 350
    See also affability; courage; courtesy in speech; friendship; gentleness; humility (modesty); justice; liberality; magnanimity; magnificence; pleasantness; temperance; truthfulness
Voluntad. See will

Vulgarity, 184, 223, 225, 227
Vulgo. *See* common people

Waking. *See* regimen
Walking, 16, 50, 53–54, 139–42
Water, 52
   digestion, 112
   element, 113–14, 343–44
   See also regimen
Wealth, 60, 94, 97, 101, 102
   action, good, 306
   —, instrument of virtuousness, 220
   friendship, 306
   inheritance of, 214–16
   See also good, third species
Weiker, Walter F., 3 n. 4, 5 n. 16, 7 n. 19, 8 n. 24, 8 n. 26
Whirlpool, 121
Will, 16 n. 46, 20 n. 54, 345–46
   election, 93, 94, 171, 194, 197, 199, 200
   free, 20, 26, 56, 169–75, 177
   —, proof of, 179
   —, speculation, 352
   intrinsic, delight of, 164
   neighbor, name for, 290
   perfection of, 23 n. 61
   virtues, location of moral, 350
Wind. *See* meteorology
Wine, 52, 111. *See also* regimen, drinking
Wisdom ("*sapyensya*," dialectics, location in theoretical intellect), 21, 27, 50, 169, 352, 353–55, 361–64
   astronomy, 364
   causes, 354
   celestial world, location in, 169
   God, analogy with eternity of, 355
   intellect, theoretical 362
   intelligences, conjunction of, 353
   law, Jewish, 361
   prudence, 362
   sciences, necessary for, 363
   truth, 353
   See also virtues, intellectual
Witches, 79, 388
Woman, 135
   virtuous, 91
   See also mirror
Wool industry, 5, 5 n. 15
Work. *See* human beings, life
Worlds, three. *See* soul
Wrestling, 191

Xanthippe, 144–45

Yaary, Abraham, 8 n. 26
Yehuda Gedalia, 8 n. 26
Yeudah Piza, 11 n. 38, 42
Y^{e}hošua^c. *See* Joshua
Y^{e}hošua^c ben Levi, 70, 368–70
Yiṣḥak ben Eleazar, 422–25
Yiṣḥak Yaabeṣ, 48
Yitro. *See* Jethro
Yoḥanan, R., 83, 347
Yoḥanan ben Zakay, 60, 221
Yosef. *See* Joseph
Yosef ben Goryon. *See* Josephus
Yosseph Sipruth de Gabay, 11 n. 38, 42
Yosef Yaabeṣ, printing press, Constantinople, 8 n. 26
—, Salonika, 8 n. 26, 11, 40, 48
Youth, 50
   appetites of, 135
   boy forbidden feminine things, 133–34
   conduct, proper, 53–54

INDEX

father and teacher, 54, 112–13, 139, 140, 141, 142
friendship, 307
parents, 133, 135
Proverbs, destinatory of, 107
silence, 149
sleep, proper, 126
—, awakening from first, 136
speech, 148
temperatures, extreme, 133
vices, bias to, 136
work, avoidance of, 329
Yᵉšaᶜyahu. *See* Isaiah

Zeal, 185. *See also* malevolence
Zion, 392
Zobel, M. N., 2, 3 n. 4

MRTS

MEDIEVAL AND RENAISSANCE TEXTS AND STUDIES
is the major publishing program of the
Arizona Center for Medieval and Renaissance Studies
at Arizona State University, Tempe, Arizona.

MRTS emphasizes books that are needed —
editions, translations, and major research tools —
but also welcomes monographs and
collections of essays on focused themes.

MRTS aims to publish the highest quality scholarship
in attractive and durable format at modest cost.